REFERENCE

D1336810

The SAGE
Handbook *of* the
Sociology of Religion

The SAGE
Handbook *of* the
Sociology of Religion

Edited by
James A. Beckford
and N. J. Demerath III

Los Angeles | London | New Delhi
Singapore | Washington DC

First published 2007
Reprinted 2009

SAGE Publications Ltd
1 Oliver's Yard
55 City Road
London EC1Y 1SP

SAGE Publications Inc.
2455 Teller Road
Thousand Oaks, California 91320

SAGE Publications India Pvt Ltd
B 1/I 1 Mohan Cooperative Industrial Area
Mathura Road
New Delhi 110 044

SAGE Publications Asia-Pacific Pte Ltd
33 Pekin Street #02-01
Far East Square
Singapore 048763

Library of Congress Control Number: 2007921005

British Library Cataloguing in Publication data

A catalogue record for this book is available from the
British Library

ISBN 978-1-4129-1195-5

Typeset by CEPHA Imaging Pvt. Ltd., Bangalore, India
Printed in Great Britain by the MPG Books Group
Printed on paper from sustainable resources

Contents

List of Figures and Tables

About the Contributors

William S. Bainbridge earned his doctorate in sociology from Harvard University, with a dissertation based on research about the space program. He is the author of 13 books, four textbook-software packages, and about 200 shorter publications in information science, social science of technology, and the sociology of religion. He has published extensively on new religious movements, including the general textbook, *The Sociology of Religious Movements* (1997), and sociological case studies of two movements: *Satan's Power* (1978) and *The Endtime Family* (2002). His most recent works in this area are *God from the Machine* (2006), a study using artificial intelligence techniques to understand religious belief, and the forthcoming book, *Across The Secular Abyss*, a study of tension between science, religion, and human well being. With Rodney Stark, he wrote three books outlining a general social-scientific approach to religion: *The Future of Religion* (1985), *A Theory of Religion* (1987), and *Religion, Deviance and Social Control* (1996).

John P. Bartkowski is Professor of Sociology at Mississippi State University. Much of his work examines the connections between religion, gender, family, and social welfare. He is the author of *Charitable Choices: Religion, Race, and Poverty in the Post-Welfare Era* (New York University Press, 2003), *The Promise Keepers: Servants, Soldiers, and Godly Men* (Rutgers University Press, 2004), and *Remaking the Godly Marriage: Gender Negotiation in Evangelical Families* (Rutgers University Press, 2001). Bartkowski is currently working on two books – one on Latter-day Saint teen religiosity and another on faith-based social service provision in different regions of the U.S. His work has appeared in such journals as *Sociology of Religion, Journal for the Scientific Study of Religion, Social Forces, Sociological Quarterly, Social Science Quarterly, Social Science Research, Criminology, Journal of Marriage and Family, Gender & Society*, and *Qualitative Sociology*.

James A. Beckford, Fellow of the British Academy, is Professor of Sociology at the University of Warwick. He was President of the Association for the Sociology of Religion in 1988 and President of the International Society for the Sociology of Religion from 1999 to 2003. His main publications include *Religious Organization* (1974), *The Trumpet of Prophecy. A Sociological Analysis of Jehovah's Witnesses* (1975), *Cult Controversies. The Societal Response to New Religious Movements* (1985), *Religion and Advanced Industrial Society* (1989), (with Sophie Gilliat) *Religion in Prison. Equal Rites in a Multi-Faith Society* (1998), *Social Theory and Religion* (2003), and (with D. Joly and F. Khosrokhavar) *Muslims in Prison: Challenge and Change in Britain and France* (2005). He is the editor of *New Religious Movements and Rapid Social Change* (1986), and co-editor of *The Changing Face of Religion* (1989), *Secularization, Rationalism and Sectarianism* (1999), *Challenging Religion* (2003), and *Theorising Religion: Classical and Contemporary Debates* (2006).

Peter Beyer is Professor of Religious Studies in the Department of Classics and Religious Studies at the University of Ottawa, Canada. His publications include *Religions in Global Society* (Routledge, 2006), *Religion and Globalization* (Sage, 1994), *Religion in the Process of Globalization* (ed., Ergon, 2001), and numerous articles in diverse journals and collected volumes. His research specializations include religion and globalization, social theory of religion, religion and transnational migration, and religion in Canada. He is currently conducting research into the religious lives and attitudes of second generation Hindu, Muslim, and Buddhist youth in Canada.

Roberto Blancarte is Director of the Centro de Estudios Sociológicos (Centre of Sociological Studies) at El Colegio de México. He obtained his Ph.D. at the École des Hautes Études en Sciences Sociales in Paris, France (1988). He is the author of *Salinismo e Iglesia católica; ¿una nueva convivencia?* (1991); *Historia de la Iglesia católica en México* (1992); *Afganistán; La revolución islámica frente al mundo occidental* (2001); *El sucesor de Juan Pablo II; Escenarios y candidatos del próximo cónclave* (2002) *Entre la fe y el poder; Religión y política en México* (2004). He has also edited *Cultura e identidad nacional* (1994); *Religiones, Iglesias y democracia* (1995); *El pensamiento social de los católicos mexicanos* (1996); and *Laicidad y valores en un Estado democrático* (2000). His major area of research is church–state relations, laicity, and secularization.

Irena Borowik, Professor at Jagiellonian University, Poland, is a sociologist of religion in the Institute for the Scientific Study of Religion and has been President of Nomos Publishing House since 1991. She is interested in theoretical and methodological problems of the sociology of religion, religious change in post-communist countries, and the religiosity of European societies. Her recent publications include (in Polish) *Rebuilding of Memory. Religious Change in Central and Eastern Europe after the Collapse of Communism* (2000), *Religious and Moral Pluralism in Poland* (with T. Doktór, 2001) and a number of books in English, edited and co-edited, concerning religions and churches in Central and Eastern Europe, among others *New Religious Phenomena in Central and Eastern Europe* (1997, with G. Babinski), *Church-State Relations in Central and Eastern Europe* (1999), *Religion and Social Change in Post-Communist Europe* (2001, with M. Tomka), *Religions and Patterns of Social Transformation* (2004, with D. Marinović-Jerolimov and S. Zrinščak).

Pierre Bréchon is a Professor of Political Science at the Institute of Political Science in Grenoble (France). He works on the analysis of political and religious values, electoral sociology and international sociological surveys. He has written several books, including *Comportements et attitudes politiques*, 2006; and *La France aux urnes*, 4e édition, 2004. He has also edited *Les partis politiques français*, 2e édition, 2005 and *Les valeurs des Français*, 2nd edition, 2003. His recent publications in English include 'Integration into Catholicism and Protestantism in Europe: the impact on moral and political values', in Loek Halman and Ole Riis (eds), *Religion in Secularizing Society. The European's Religion at the end of the 20th century*, 2003, pp. 114–161; 'Religious voting in a secular France', in David Broughton and Hans-Martien ten Napel (eds), *Religion and Mass Electoral Behaviour in Europe*, 2000, pp. 97–117; and 'Influence of religious integration on attitudes: a comparative analysis of European countries', *Revue française de sociologie*, 2004/45, Supplement, pp. 27–49.

Kevin J. Christiano is an Associate Professor of Sociology at the University of Notre Dame in Indiana. He received his B.A. degree from the College of William and Mary in Virginia, and the M.A. and Ph.D. in sociology from Princeton University. In addition to numerous articles in scholarly journals, Christiano is the author of two books: *Religious Diversity and Social Change* (Cambridge University Press, 1987) and *Pierre Elliott Trudeau: Reason Before Passion* (ECW Press, 1994 and 1995). He is also co-author (with William H. Swatos, Jr, and Peter Kivisto) of *Sociology of Religion: Contemporary Developments* (AltaMira Press, 2002). A second edition of this text is scheduled to appear in 2007. Christiano is a past president of both the Association for the Sociology of Religion and the American Council for Québec Studies.

Randall Collins is Dorothy Swaine Thomas Professor of Sociology at the University of Pennsylvania. His books include *Weberian Sociological Theory* (1986); *The Sociology of Philosophies* (1998); *Macro-History* (1999); and *Interaction Ritual Chains* (2004). His recent work applies the study of rituals to violence, in a forthcoming book, *Violence: A Micro-Sociological Theory of Antagonistic Situations* (Princeton University Press).

Douglas E. Cowan is Associate Professor of Religious Studies and Social Development Studies at Renison University College, the University of Waterloo. The author of numerous works, he has written or edited three books on religion and the Internet, including *Cyberhenge: Modern Pagans on the Internet* (Routledge, 2005). Most recently, he has written *Cults and New Religions: A Brief History* (with David G. Bromley) and *Sacred Terror: Religion and Horror on the Silver Screen*. In addition to a number of projects dealing with religion and popular culture, his work on cinema horror has led him to a wider interest in the socio-historical relationships between religion and fear.

Marcela Cristi, originally from Chile, emigrated to Canada in 1976. She started graduate studies in her late 40s and completed her Ph.D. in sociology at the University of Waterloo in 1998. She currently teaches in the Department of Sociology at Wilfrid Laurier University. She is the author of *From Civil to Political Religion* (2001) and has published several book chapters dealing with religion, culture and politics. She is particularly interested in totalitarian types of civil religion. Her article 'Civil Religion in Comparative Perspective: Chile under Pinochet (1973–1989),' *Social Compass* (1996), co-authored with Lorne Dawson, focuses on the political manipulation of civil religion. Her current research is on civil religion in the context of nationalism and globalization. A chapter on this topic is forthcoming in *Civil Religion, Nationalism and Globalization* (2008).

Lynn Davidman is Professor of Judaic Studies, American Civilization and Gender Studies at Brown University. She is the author of the award-winning *Tradition in a Rootless World* (1990) and *Motherloss* (2000), both published by the University of California Press. She is also co-editor, with Shelly Tenenbaum, of *Feminist Perspectives on Jewish Studies* (Yale, 1994). She has received several grants and awards for her research on religion and gender, including a fellowship at the Institute for the Study of Religion at Princeton and at the Bunting Institute at Radcliffe. She is currently working on a book on individuals in Israel and the United States who leave Orthodox Judaism as adults. She has recently published essays on unsynagogued Jews in the *Journal for the Scientific Study of Religion*, with Wendy Cadge, and in the *Handbook of the Sociology of Religion*. Two additional papers on this topic are scheduled to be published soon.

Lorne L. Dawson is Professor of Sociology and Religious Studies at the University of Waterloo in Canada, and Director of the Laurier-Waterloo Ph.D. program in religious diversity in North America. He is the author of *Comprehending Cults*, 2nd edn. (Oxford University Press, 2006), the editor of *Cults and New Religious Movements: A Reader* (Blackwell, 2003), and co-editor (with Douglas Cowan) of *Religion Online* (Routledge, 2004). He has published over 60 articles and book chapters on questions of theory and method in the study of religion, new religions, and religion and the Internet. His current research is on the nature and operation of charismatic authority (e.g., 'Psychopathologies and the Attribution of Charisma,' *Nova Religio*, 2006), the cultural significance of new religions (e.g., 'Privatization, Globalization, and Religious Innovation' in *Theorizing Religion*, edited by James Beckford and John Wallis, 2006), and the social processes conditioning how religious groups respond to the failure of prophecy (e.g., 'Prophetic Failure in Millennialist Movements' in *The Oxford Handbook of Millennialism* edited by Catherine Wessinger, 2007).

Jay Demerath is the Emile Durkheim Distinguished Professor of Sociology at the University of Massachusetts, Amherst. Before arriving at UMass as Chair in 1972, he received his A.B. from

Harvard and his Ph.D. from the University of California at Berkeley, and spent ten years at the University of Wisconsin, Madison, the last two of which on leave as Executive Officer of the American Sociological Association. Past-President of the Society for the Scientific Study of Religion, the Association for the Sociology of Religion, and the Eastern Sociological Society, his recent books include *A Bridging of Faiths: Religion and Politics in a New England City* (with Rhys Williams), *Crossing the Gods: World Religions and Worldly Politics*, and *Sacred Circles and Public Squares: The Multicentering of American Religion* (with Arthur Farnsley II *et al.*).

Michele Dillon, is Professor of Sociology at the University of New Hampshire and past Chair of the American Sociological Association section on the Sociology of Religion. Her most recent book, *In the Course of a Lifetime: Tracing Religious Belief, Practice, and Change* (co-authored with Paul Wink, University of California Press, 2007), uses longitudinal data gathered over 60 years, to explore questions of religious autonomy in American culture, and the dynamic role of religious and spiritual engagement in anchoring individuals' everyday lives from adolescence through early, middle, and late adulthood. She is also the author of *Catholic Identity: Balancing Reason, Faith, and Power* (Cambridge University Press, 1999), *Debating Divorce: Moral Conflict in Ireland* (University Press of Kentucky, 1993), and several research articles. Dillon edited the *Handbook of the Sociology of Religion* published in 2003 by Cambridge University Press.

Arthur E. Farnsley II is a Fellow of the Center for the Study of Religion and American Culture at Indiana University Purdue University Indianapolis and Executive Officer of the Society for the Scientific Study of Religion. His work includes *Southern Baptist Politics* (Penn State, 1994), *Rising Expectations: Urban Congregations, Welfare Reform, and Civic Life* (Indiana, 2003), and, with his co-authors, *Sacred Circles, Public Squares: The Multicentering of American Religion* (Indiana, 2005). He also co-edits the Religion and Urban Culture series at Indiana University Press and was research director for the 11-part video series, *Faith and Community: The Public Role of Religion*. His current research considers the religious and political roots of American anti-institutionalism.

Paul Freston is a sociologist. Originally from Britain but resident in Brazil since 1976 and a naturalized Brazilian citizen, he has worked mainly on religion and politics, the growth of Pentecostalism in the global south, and questions of religion and globalization. He currently holds the Byker Chair in sociology at Calvin College, Michigan, and is professor of sociology on the postgraduate program in social science at the Universidade Federal de São Carlos, Brazil. His books include *Nem Anjos Nem Demônios: Interpretações Sociológicas do Pentecostalismo* (co-authored, Vozes, 1994); *Evangelicals and Politics in Asia, Africa and Latin America* (Cambridge University Press, 2001); *Protestant Political Parties: A Global Survey* (Ashgate, 2004); and *Evangelical Christianity and Democracy in Latin America* (Oxford University Press, 2007).

Arthur L. Greil is Professor of Sociology at Alfred University in western New York State. He received his B.A. degree from Syracuse University and his M.A. and Ph.D. degrees from Rutgers University. He is the author of *Georges Sorel and the Sociology of Virtue* and *Not Yet Pregnant: Infertile Couples in Contemporary America*. He is the editor of *Defining Religion: Critical Perspectives on Drawing Boundaries between Sacred and Secular* (with David G. Bromley) and of *Between Sacred and Secular: Research and Theory on Quasi-Religion* (with Thomas Robbins). He has authored over 40 scholarly articles on a wide range of topics, including conversion and identity change, quasi-religion, religion and politics, and infertility. Among the journals in which he has published are *Journal for the Scientific Study of Religion, Sociology of Religion, Review of Religious Research, Journal of Marriage and the Family, Qualitative Sociology,* and *Social Science & Medicine.*

John R. Hall, Professor of Sociology at the University of California – Davis, has served as Director of the UC Davis Center for History, Society, and Culture and Director of the University of California Edinburgh Study Centre. His scholarly research spans the sociology of religion, epistemology, social theory, economy and society, and the sociology of culture. His published books include an edited volume – *Reworking Class* (Cornell University Press, 1997), *Cultures of Inquiry: From Epistemology to Discourse in Sociohistorical Research* (Cambridge University Press, 1999), *Apocalypse Observed: Religious Movements and Violence in North America, Europe, and Japan*, co-authored by Philip D. Schuyler and Sylvaine Trinh (Routledge, 2000), *Sociology on Culture*, co-authored by Mary Jo Neitz and Marshall Battani (Routledge, 2003), and *Visual Worlds*, co-edited by Blake Stimson and Lisa Tamiris Becker (Routledge, 2005). His current research focuses on apocalyptic terrorism and modernity.

Stephen J. Hunt is a Reader in the Sociology of Religion at the University of the West of England, Bristol, UK. He gained his Ph.D. at the University of Reading in 1996 on the subject of the impact of American neo-Pentecostal ministries in the UK. His specialist research interests include the Charismatic movement, the 'New' Black Pentecostal Churches and the 'gay debate' in the Christian Churches. Recent research has focused on religious faith among prison inmates. Dr Hunt's publications include the volumes *Religion in Everyday Life* (Routledge), *Alternative Religion: A Sociological Introduction* (Ashgate), *Religion in the West: A Sociological Perspective* (Palgrave), *The Alpha Initiative: Evangelism in the Post-Christian Era* (Ashgate), *The Life Course: A Sociological Introduction* (Palgrave) and the edited work *Christian Millenarianism* (Hurst Publishing). His forthcoming volume, *The Charismatic Movement in the United States and Britain: A Comparative Reader*, will be published by Edwin Mellen in 2007.

Peter Kivisto is the Richard Swanson Professor of Social Thought and Chair of Sociology at Augustana College. Among his recent books are the following: *Citizenship: Discourse, Theory, and Transnational Prospects* (Blackwell, 2007, with Thomas Faist), *Dual Citizenship: Democracy, Rights, and Identities beyond Borders* (Palgrave Macmillan, 2007, with Thomas Faist), *Intersecting Inequalities* (Pearson Prentice Hall, 2007, with Elizabeth Hartung), *Incorporating Diversity: Rethinking Assimilation in a Multicultural Age* (Paradigm, 2005), and *Multiculturalism in a Global Society* (Blackwell, 2002). Recent articles have appeared in *Acta Sociologica, Ethnic and Racial Studies, Ethnicities,* and the *Journal of the History of the Behavioral Sciences.* He is the editor of *The Sociological Quarterly* and is a member of the board of the International Sociological Association's Research Committee on Migration.

Frank J. Lechner is Associate Professor of Sociology at Emory University. In addition to publishing papers on religion, globalization, and theory, he has written *World Culture: Origins and Consequences* (Blackwell, 2005) and edited *The Globalization Reader* (Blackwell, 2004), both with John Boli. He has papers on 'Religious Rejections of Globalization' in *Religion in Global Civil Society*, edited by Mark Juergensmeyer (Oxford, 2005) and on 'Trajectories of Faith in the Global Age: Classical Theory and Contemporary Evidence' in *Theorising Religion*, edited by James A. Beckford and John Walliss (Ashgate, 2006). A forthcoming book is entitled *The Netherlands: National Identity and Globalization* (Routledge). Future projects include another book on globalization.

Phillip C. Lucas is Professor of Religious Studies at Stetson University. He is founding editor of *Nova Religio*, a scholarly journal dedicated to the study of alternative and new religious movements throughout history. He has written four books: *New Religious Movements in the 21st Century: Legal, Political, and Social Challenges in Global Perspective*, with Thomas Robbins (2004); *Cassadaga: The South's Oldest Spiritualist Community*, with John J. Guthrie, Jr, and Gary Monroe (2000); *Prime Time Religion: An Encyclopedic Guide to Religious Broadcasting*, with J. Gordon Melton and

Jon R. Stone (1997); and *The Odyssey of a New Religion: The Holy Order of MANS from New Age to Orthodoxy* (1995).

Philip A. Mellor is Professor of Religion and Social Theory and Director of the Institute for Religion and Public Life in the Department of Theology and Religious Studies at the University of Leeds. He is the author of *Religion, Realism and Social Theory: Making Sense of Society* (Sage, 2004) and, with Chris Shilling, of *The Sociological Ambition: Elementary Forms of Social and Moral Life* (Sage, 2001) and *Re-forming the Body: Religion, Community and Modernity* (Sage, 1997), as well as many articles in a range of academic journals in sociology and religious studies. His research interests are in the areas of contemporary religion, embodiment and cultural change.

Sharon E. Nepstad is Associate Professor of Sociology at the University of Southern Maine. Her research focuses on the role of religion in social movements. She is the author of *Convictions of the Soul: Religion, Culture, and Agency in the Central America Solidarity Movement* (Oxford University Press, 2004). Her forthcoming book, *Religion and War Resistance in the Plowshares Movement* (Cambridge University Press, 2008), examines how radical Catholics have used controversial tactics of property destruction to obstruct the production and use of nuclear weapons.

Paula Nesbitt is Visiting Associate Professor in Sociology at the University of California, Berkeley. Having researched clergy careers for 20 years, her publications include *Feminization of the Clergy in America: Occupational and Organizational Perspectives* (Oxford University Press, 1997) an edited volume, *Religion and Social Policy* (AltaMira Press, 2001), and various articles in the *Journal for the Scientific Study of Religion, Sociology of Religion,* the Review of Religious Research and other journals. Her current research involves a longitudinal analysis of religious leadership and multiculturalism in the worldwide Anglican Communion. She holds a Ph.D. and M.Div. from Harvard University.

Laura R. Olson is Professor of Political Science at Clemson University. Recent books include (as co-author) *Women with a Mission: Religion, Gender, and the Politics of Women Clergy* (University of Alabama Press, 2005) and *Religion and Politics in America: Faith, Culture, and Strategic Choices* (Westview, 2004); and (as co-editor) *The Encyclopedia of American Religion and Politics* (Facts on File, 2003) and *Christian Clergy in American Politics* (Johns Hopkins University Press, 2001).

James T. Richardson, J.D., Ph.D., is Foundation Professor of Sociology and Judicial Studies at the University of Nevada, Reno, where he directs the Grant Sawyer Center for Justice Studies and the Judicial Studies graduate degree program for trial judges. He combines an interest in the law and its operation in society with an interest in the Sociology of Religion, particularly new religious movements. His recent work has focused on social control of new religions, exemplified by a recent edited volume *Regulating Religion: Case Studies from Around the Globe* (Kluwer, 2004). He has published numerous articles in journals, including *Sociology of Religion, The Journal for the Scientific Study of Religion*, and *Social Compass*, as well as in law reviews.

Thomas Robbins is a semi-retired sociologist of religion. He received a Ph.D. from the University of North Carolina at Chapel Hill in 1973. He has held teaching or research positions at Queens College (CUNY), Yale University, and Central Michigan University. He is the author of *Cults, Converts and Charisma* (Sage, 1988) and has co-edited six collections of original papers, including *In Gods We Trust* (Transaction, 1981, 1990), *Millennium, Messiahs and Mayhem* (Routledge, 1997), and *Misunderstanding Cults* (University of Toronto, 2002). He has published numerous articles, essay and reviews in edited collections and in social science and religious studies journals. He lives in Rochester, Minnesota.

Stephen Sharot is Professor of Sociology, Ben-Gurion University of the Negev, Beer-Sheva, Israel. His major publications are: *A Comparative Sociology of World Religions; Virtuosos, Priests and Popular Religion* (New York University Press, 2001); *Ethnicity, Religion, and Class in Israeli Society* (co-authored with E. Ben-Rafael, Cambridge University Press, 1991); *Messianism, Mysticism, and Magic; A Sociological Analysis of Jewish Religious Movements* (University of North Carolina Press, 1982). His articles have appeared in *Sociology of Religion, Journal for the Scientific Study of Religion, Review of Religious Research, Comparative Studies in Society and History, British Journal of Sociology, Religion,* and *Ethnic and Racial Studies.* He is currently working on representations of class in American cinema.

Susumu Shimazono is Professor in the Department of Religious Studies of the University of Tokyo, and has published widely on modern and contemporary religious movements as well as on modern Japanese religions in general. He has published eight Japanese books, one in Korean, and an English book titled *From Salvation to Spirituality: Popular Religious Movements in Modern Japan* (Trans Pacific Press, 2004). He edited with Mark Mullins and Paul Swanson *Religion and Society in Modern Japan* (Asian Humanities Press, 1993). Although his works are based mainly on empirical and historical research on religions in Japan, he has always been interested in comparative perspectives between Japan on the one hand and the West and various parts of Asia on the other. He was invited to teach at the University of Chicago, at the Ecole des Hautes Etudes en Sciences Sociales, and at Eberhardt Karls Universität Tübingen. Recently he is working on the area between religion and medicine including bioethics and a new interdisciplinary area of death and life studies.

James V. Spickard is Professor of Sociology at the University of Redlands and Research Consulting Professor at the Fielding Graduate Institute. He has published widely on various aspects of the sociology of religion, on human rights, on religious social activism, on social theory, and on the social foundations of ethics. His interest in reflexive ethnography resulted in his recent edited collection *Personal Knowledge and Beyond* (NYU Press, 2002). He is currently writing a book on non-Western social theories, tentatively titled *After Colonialism.* He is also preparing a book on the future of religion in the late modern world.

David Voas is a demographer whose recent research has concerned religion and religious change. Following degrees at the London School of Economics and Cambridge he spent many years outside academic life prior to taking up a university post in 1998. He currently works at the University of Manchester, where he is Senior Research Fellow at the Cathie Marsh Centre for Census and Survey Research. His work has been published in *Sociology,* the *British Journal of Sociology, American Sociological Review, Population and Development Review,* and elsewhere. He is particularly interested in cross-national comparisons, the intergenerational transmission of religious involvement, the social mechanisms of secularization, and related topics.

Rhys H. Williams is Professor of Sociology at the University of Cincinnati (USA). His publications generally focus on the intersection of religion, politics, and social movements in the US. He is currently editor of the *Journal for the Scientific Study of Religion,* and in the 2006–2007 academic year was Chair of the American Sociological Association's Section on Collective Behavior and Social Movements.

Patricia Wittberg is Professor of Sociology at Indiana University Purdue University Indianapolis. Her most recent book is *From Piety to Professionalism – And Back? Transformations in Organized Religious Virtuosity.* She has written widely on religious organizations, especially Catholic religious orders.

Currently, she is working with the Center for Applied Study in the Apostolate, a research group affiliated with Georgetown University, on a study of newly founded Catholic religious orders and lay movements.

Linda Woodhead is Head of the Department of Religious Studies and Professor of Sociology of Religion at Lancaster University. From January 2007 she will be Director of the AHRC/ESRC Research Programme on Religion and Society. Much of her research is focused on religion in contemporary Britain, with a particular interest in the decline of the churches and the rise of alternative forms of spirituality. She is currently involved in an EU funded research project on the Muslim veil in the UK, and is writing on religion and emotions, and religion and gender. Recent publications include: *The Spiritual Revolution: Why Religion is Giving Way to Spirituality* (with Paul Heelas, Blackwell, 2005), *Christianity: A Very Short Introduction* (Oxford University Press, 2004), *An Introduction to Christianity* (Cambridge University Press, 2004), and *Congregational Studies in the UK* (co-edited with Mathew Guest and Karin Tusting, Ashgate, 2004).

Fenggang Yang is Associate Professor of Sociology at Purdue University. He received his B.A. from Hebei Normal University in 1982, his M.A. from Nankai University in 1987, and his Ph.D. from The Catholic University of America in 1997. His sociological research has focused on immigrant religions in the United States and religions in China. He is the author of *Chinese Christians in America: Conversion, Assimilation, and Adhesive Identities* (Penn State University Press, 1999), the co-editor of *Asian American Religions: The Making and Remaking of Borders and Boundaries* (New York University Press, 2004), *State, Market, and Religions in Chinese Societies* (Brill Academic Publishers, 2005), and *Conversion to Christianity among the Chinese* (a special issue of the *Sociology of Religion: A Quarterly Review*, 2006). His current research focuses on the political economy of religion in China, Christian ethics and market transition in China, and Chinese Christian churches in the United States.

Introduction

JAMES A. BECKFORD AND N. J. DEMERATH III

Discussion of religion seems to be everywhere in the first decade of the twenty-first century. Television documentaries, newspaper stories, magazine articles, online user groups, blogs, cartoons and websites all compete to offer the latest story about religion. Sensationalist accounts of violence and exploitation associated with religion tend to dominate. It has become a cliché to claim that religion must be taken seriously because of its association with extremism, terrorism, violence and doomsday scenarios. This is how many journalists and programme makers see it. They also have a tendency to focus on the growing popularity of various forms of conservative religiosity around the world. This is fine – as far as it goes – and fully understandable. But the narrow focus on these sensational, headline-touted and eye-catching phenomena fails to do justice to the richness and diversity of other facets and developments of religion. It also conceals the trajectory of intellectual development in the sociological study of religion. A more inclusive and even-handed approach to the sociology of religion is, therefore, our aim. Without overlooking religious violence and the spread of conservatism, this Handbook will also delve into religion's relationship with such things as politics, community development, healthcare, education and personal experiences through the life cycle.

Long-standing expectations that religion would merely wither away as modernisation progressed have proven simplistic. Religion has become more complicated, newsworthy, contentious and problematic. And if there is any consensus to be had on religion, it is that there is a lot of religion around. Indeed, many pundits are surprised that religion has such high visibility in the twenty-first century. Many sociologists have come to realise that it makes no sense now to omit religion from the repertoire of social scientific explanations of social life. On the contrary, it has become increasingly essential to have a clear sociological understanding of the ways in which religion operates as one of the many forces shaping – and being shaped by – our increasingly globalised – and globally conflicted – world.

The reasons for wanting to study the sociological aspects of religion are diverse in the extreme. Interest may arise from curiosity about the workings of religious organisations or religious movements. Equally, interest may centre on questions about religious motivation, experiences or emotions. There may be concern with the economic, political or moral implications of religious beliefs and values. And the conflicts and intertwining of religions, cultures and civilisations lend themselves well to sociological investigation. In other words, the reasons for wanting to understand the sociology of religion know no limits. They cover the entire range from personal curiosity to a concern for national security or peace and justice in the world.

SOCIOLOGICAL APPROACHES TO RELIGION

If the need for a sociological understanding of religion has rarely been greater, just what is distinctive about such an understanding? Five characteristics loom large. First, a sociological approach is partly distinguished by what it is not. Of course, some people consider religion to be eternal truth, divinely inspired law or unquestionable values as ordained by gods or spirits. But sociology does not provide ultimate answers to ultimate questions. The sociological agenda does not involve evaluations of particular faiths and convictions, nor does it assess the transcendental postulates on which they are based. Given the vicissitudes of religious dynamics, sociology offers more paradoxology than doxology.

Second, as this Handbook will amply demonstrate, there are many different sociological approaches. Nevertheless, they all focus on the social dimensions of religion and the religious dimensions of the social. The sociology of religion is not restricted to understanding churches, sects, cults, temples and mosques – though this is one part of its challenge. It also has a mandate to seek out the myriad ways in which religion at various levels affects the seemingly non-religious aspects of social life. Religion is social because it finds expression in and shapes social relationships and processes that range from the micro-world of the individual to the macro-world of whole societies. Religion is also social in that it both involves and influences the communication of meanings through ideas, images, rituals, emotions, texts, styles of self-presentation, gestures, music, song, dance and so on. From a sociological perspective, there are few more misleading conceptions of religion than George Santayana's remark that 'Religion is what man does in his own solitariness'. Even when practised alone, religion is rooted in the social.

Third, sociological perspectives on religion embrace the widely differing meanings attributed to the term 'religion'. Dictionaries typically define religion as 'beliefs and practices relative to deities, spirits or other superhuman powers'. This type of definition is certainly close to the commonsense meaning of the term, but it is too narrow for sociological purposes. For example, it does not refer to aspects of religion such as emotions, experiences, groups or organisations. Nor does it include beliefs and practices that can be considered religious in spite of the fact that they have no place for deities, spirits or other superhuman powers. What is needed, then, is an approach that recognises that the meaning of 'religion' is itself varied, changing and subject to social influences. Instead of relying on a definition that more or less arbitrarily includes only some defining characteristics of religion and excludes others, a better approach is to regard the definition of religion as an open-ended, often contested and on-going social process. There is argument and disagreement about what counts as religion in everyday life, and this is a topic for sociological investigation in its own right. It goes almost without saying that public opinion about the value of religion also ranges widely between utter condemnation and enthusiastic embrace.

Fourth, sociological approaches to religion utilise research methods that are as diverse as religion itself. Religion can have social, cultural, historical, political, economic, moral, psychological, aesthetic, philosophical, linguistic and legal dimensions – and some would add genetic and neurophysiological to the list. Consequently, research techniques and strategies need to be properly attuned to the particular dimension at issue. There is certainly no single 'sociological method' for the study of religion. It is more a question of being sensitive to the complex interweaving of religion with other aspects of social or cultural life and of selecting appropriate methods for studying it. Sociological approaches are also frequently involved in interdisciplinary and cross-disciplinary investigations required by religion's multi-faceted phenomena.

Fifth, the sociology of religion both borrows from and contributes to other fields of sociology. Many of its insights come from scholars who were not personally religious – for example, the great triumvirate of Marx, Weber and Durkheim. Much of its conceptual and methodological core reflects broader inquiries into non-religious cultures, organisations, patterns of inequality, and questions of self and identity. At the same time, sociology as a whole has benefited considerably from scholarship on religion. Again the aforementioned triumvirate offers a case in point, as we shall see. Sociology's understandings of social change, of power and authority, of social movements and of institutional commitment have all been influenced by research on religion. In some sense, religion is only one part of the wider sphere of what can be sacred to individuals and society.

THE INTELLECTUAL TRAJECTORY OF THE SOCIOLOGY OF RELIGION

The development of sociological thinking about religion has undergone many changes since the late nineteenth century. Some ideas have run into the sand; others have declined in popularity but revived at a later date; and there has been a continuing percolation of new ideas. There is both continuity and creativity. And, with the passing of time, the diversity of approaches has increased both within and between the various linguistic communities in which sociologists of religion publish their writings, the largest of which being English by far. The sociology of religion began in close proximity to the work of other social scientists, especially social anthropologists and political economists. It subsequently drifted away from the central concerns of social science before starting to align itself with them once more. The closing decades of the twentieth century witnessed an increasingly creative and mutual engagement between sociologists of religion and intellectual developments in other fields of sociology as well as with other social sciences. As a result, sociological interest in religion has

now returned to a position close to the centre of intellectual curiosity about the forces shaping socio-cultural life in the early twenty-first century. Elsewhere, one of us has characterised this trajectory in terms of Sir Thomas Beecham's encouragement to orchestras to 'start together and finish together' (Beckford 2000: 481–82).

This is not the place for a detailed history of the sociology of religion (see O'Toole 1984; Beckford 1989, 1990; Willaime 1999; Davie 2003), but shifts in the assumptions underlying sociologists' attempts to make sense of religion are an important part of the context for the chapters that follow. Indeed, numerous contributors pay tribute to the influence that the founding generation of thinkers exercised on sociological ways of understanding religion in the transition from traditional to modern forms of society. And Randall Collins (in this volume) pays particularly careful attention to the pioneering work of Marx, Durkheim and Weber. But it is equally important to realise that their core work was less preoccupied with religion in its own terms than with understanding the broader set of societal dynamics involving modernisation, rationalisation, industrialisation and urbanisation. As a result, the emergence of sociological approaches to religion was inseparable from the consolidation of sociology as a form of methodical investigation of societal continuity and change. And by the middle of the twentieth century, religion had moved even further to the periphery of sociology.

This loss of centrality was associated with three factors. First, many social scientists perceived religion itself as marginal to society, and this was especially the case with modernising society. Second, the dominant school of functionalism tended to relegate religion to the status of a purely conservative or stabilising force in society. Third, sociologists of religion paradoxically de-centred themselves by creating their own problematics and institutions that were poorly articulated with the social science mainstream – for example, their enduring fascination with elaborating the church-sect distinction of Max Weber and Ernst Troeltsch. For all of these reasons, the sociology of religion became relatively isolated from, and insulated against, the issues and ideas that interested most social scientists (Beckford 1985a). Again in Sir Thomas Beecham's terms, it was not playing in time with the majority of the sociological orchestra.

But in the 1960s, a series of developments intimated the eventual re-synchronisation of the sociology of religion. One major factor was the move away from functionalism in the sociology of religion, beginning with the separate and joint writings of Peter Berger and Thomas Luckmann. Their *Social Construction of Reality* (Berger and Luckmann 1966) marked the beginning of an intellectual turn away from questions of systems and functions towards a concern with the social processes that engender experience, knowledge, culture and language. The application of this 'sociology of knowledge' approach to religion had already inspired the German edition of Luckmann's *The Invisible Religion* in 1963 and was to underlie Berger's path-breaking *The Social Canopy* in 1967. In their different ways, Berger and Luckmann represented not only continuity with the themes of the 'classics' but also – and more importantly – a departure from the practice of confining the sociology of religion to the study of formal religious organisations such as churches, denominations and sects as exemplified by Charles Glock and his student, Rodney Stark and by Robert Wuthnow at the University of California, Berkeley. It was there too that Robert Bellah elaborated the Durkheimian notion of a national 'civil religion'.

In general, however, the sociology of religion was relatively slow to follow sociology's 'cultural turn'. In fact, the field's resurgence following the 1960s was due in no small measure to a turning away from religion writ large as a national and societal phenomenon to religion writ small at the level of new movements and new social psychological dynamics. While few were exploring the potential merits of ethnomethodology, the notion of 'framing' or the musical and visual registers of religious activities (but see Morgan 1998), a number started to apply insights from symbolic interactionism to the understanding of the processes whereby meaning and identity could be generated in

settings such as revival meetings, prayer groups, faith healing activities, and particularly the rapidly growing visibility of controversial new religious movements in the 1980s. The melding of insights from the sociology of knowledge and symbolic interactionism (Neitz 1990) transformed our understanding of, for example, 'active' conversion (Richardson 1985), healing in religious settings (McGuire 1988), 'implicit religion' (Bailey 1990) and religious experience (Neitz and Spickard 1990).

Meanwhile, Marxist ideas continued to influence only a few sociologists of religion in advanced industrial societies. They studied the capacity of religion to comfort the oppressed, to stimulate rebellion against exploitation or to provide ideological justification for the most powerful social classes in society. In spite of extensive theoretical discussion, empirical investigation and historical inquiry, however, few Marxists showed interest in religion as a sociological phenomenon. And even fewer mainstream sociologists of religion integrated Marxist perspectives into their research (but see Maduro 1982). Not even the quasi-Marxist Critical Theory – with its mixture of humanistic Marxism, psychoanalysis and cultural theory – made much of an impact on the sociology of religion. Nor did the fashion for Liberation Theology or theologies of struggle lead to many fresh initiatives in the sociology of religion except in some specialised studies of countries in Latin America and South East Asia (but see Smith 1991). Again, the sociology of religion's marginality to currents of Marxism demonstrated its remove from ideas that were, at least temporarily, dominant among other sociologists.

Although most sociologists of religion resisted Marxist notions of religion as opiate and false consciousness, many were interested in religion's intersection with social class and other forms of inequality. This makes it all the more surprising, then, that one of the major factors shaping the intellectual trajectory of the sociology of religion in the final three decades of the twentieth century was the unexpected outburst of so-called new religious movements (NRMs). The movements that attracted most sociological interest at the time included the Unification Church, the Church of Scientology, the International Society for Krishna Consciousness, and the Children of God. Unlike predecessors such as the Salvation Army or the first wave of Pentecostalism, members of the NRMs that achieved high visibility and notoriety, especially in the 1970s and 1980s, did not come from disadvantaged backgrounds. This is one of the reasons why Marxist perspectives appeared to offer very little purchase on NRMs. In fact, the movements tended to recruit relatively young, well educated people from middle class families. In this respect, NRMs were similar to 'new' social movements in the fields of feminism, peace, environmentalism and human rights (Hannigan 1993). Sociologists were therefore obliged to look for new explanations of the capacity of NRMs to mobilise followers and resources on a scale that alarmed their critics and provoked numerous controversies (Robbins and Lucas in this volume). Debate centred on a wide range of would-be explanations involving 'brainwashing', charismatic leaders, civil religion, identity theories, anomie, alienation and so on. More importantly, the rise of NRMs in the late twentieth century led sociologists of religion to examine the role of the mass media in framing controversies – and the response of police and politicians to 'cult controversies' (Beckford 1985b). And, in view of the transnational operations of the most controversial NRMs, it became important to understand how the response to them varied from country to country.

Studies of NRMs also brought new methodological techniques and issues to the sociology of religion. Because these small groups were generally only accessible to field research – and sometimes actual 'participant observation' – they prompted a surge of qualitative ethnography. But this led in turn to ethical issues about the social relations between sociologists and the movements they were studying, especially as some of the movements were reluctant to be closely observed (Robbins *et al.* 1973; Barker 1983; Ayella 1993). Questions were raised about the challenge of studying religion in some of its controversial forms (Robbins 1983; Richardson 1991). The importance of accounting for the gendered aspects of NRMs was also strongly emphasised (Jacobs 1991). And sociologists of religion found themselves facing the dilemma of whether to appear as expert witnesses in courts of law considering NRM-related cases (Wilson 1998; Hervieu-Léger 1999). Moreover, research on NRMs was a powerful vector for the introduction of broader concerns with religious liberty, the regulation of religion and the relation between human rights and religions (Shepherd 1982; Richardson 2004). The reverberations of all these methodological challenges continue to rattle through the sociology of religion, although the topic of NRMs is no longer so controversial in itself. In fact, by the beginning of the twenty-first century religion was more often controversial for reasons to do with violence, fraud and sexual abuse. But it was the confrontation between sociologists and NRMs that first placed religious controversies on the sociological agenda.

New developments in qualitative research methods have lent themselves well to the sociology of religion overall (Spickard *et al.* 2002) notably in relation to ethnographic, narrative, visual, discourse analytic, biographical and autobiographical forms of investigation (Spickard in this volume). And recent sociohistorical studies of religion have demonstrated both the centrality of religion to a well-balanced understanding of historical change and the variety of increasingly self-reflexive methods that sociologists of religion are deploying in their analyses of religious change (Hall in this volume) and narratives of religion's place in the life-course (Hunt in this volume).

Studies of mainstream religious traditions and organisations have also become more ambitious and sophisticated in their use of research methods, often combining qualitative and quantitative techniques. This is certainly the case with large-scale investigations of parishes (Hornsby-Smith 1989), congregations (Roof and McKinney 1987; Ammerman 1997; Ammerman *et al.* 1998; Harris 1998; Becker 1999; Demerath and Farnsley in this volume), 'immigrant congregations' (Warner and Wittner 1997; Ebaugh and Chafetz 2000), generations of believers (Roof 1993, 1999; Dillon in this volume), denominations (Ammerman 1990;

Chaves 1997) and religious organisations (Demerath *et al.* 1998). Growing methodological sophistication is also a hallmark of innovative studies of religion and charitable activities (Wuthnow 1991), the expanding scope of 'spirituality' (Wuthnow 2001), the changing character of clergy training and careers (Carroll *et al.* 1997; Nesbitt 1997, and in this volume) and the rising salience of 'special purpose groups' (Wuthnow 1988).

Very different methodological developments in the sociology of religion have been associated with increasingly sophisticated manipulation of quantitative data generated by large-scale surveys of beliefs, attitudes and opinion (Voas in this volume). In particular, the continuing expansion of the European Social Survey, Eurobarometer, the European Values Survey, the World Values Survey, the International Social Survey Programme and the Pew Global Attitudes Project has enabled sociologists of religion to chart continuity and change in quantitative indicators of religious belief over time and across a growing number of countries (for example, Norris and Inglehart 2004; Bréchon in this volume).

All of these methodological advances helped in re-synchronising the sociology of religion with sociology as a whole. But similar theoretical advances also helped in the re-centring. Mainstream sociological theorising had responded to the various claims that modernity had advanced to a stage of 'late modernity', if not 'post-modernity' (Christiano in this volume). While relatively few sociologists of religion saw good reason to restructure their research in accordance with these claims, David Lyon (2000) made the most plausible case for arguing that religion in the early twenty-first century displayed some post-modern characteristics – albeit against a background in which the forces of modernity were still at work. Other theorists saw evidence of post-modernity in theological and philosophical concerns with the re-enchantment of the everyday world, with the resurgent interest in liturgies and with the apparent belief that New Age spiritualities were capitalising on the failure of modern rationality to go on enhancing the quality of human life in the absence of supernatural ideals. Partly in connection with these developments, other sociologists have turned their attention to the embodied character of human experience – including religion – and to the neglected realm of embodied emotions (Mellor in this volume).

If the majority of sociologists of religion were less than enthusiastic about the usefulness of orienting their research towards the idea of a post-modern turn, it is nevertheless true that many theorists of the post-modern condition have seen fit to regard recent changes in religion as evidence in support of their general claims. Anthony Giddens (1991), for example, associates the growing popularity of conservative religious practices in late modernity with 'the return of the repressed'. Zygmunt Bauman (1992) also regards the search for moral and spiritual certainty as a sign that post-modern sensibilities have burst out of their modernist constraints. Elsewhere, the tendency is to highlight the exotic, playful or pastiche-like characteristics of aspects of religion in, for example, some New Age spiritualities or some hybridised forms of liturgy without taking proper account of their relative insignificance in the broader picture of religion. The closely related argument that New Age spiritualities epitomise consumerism, the logic of late capitalism and even the colonisation of the life-world is also a highly selective interpretation of complex and varied phenomena that defy simplistic categorisation (Bainbridge in this volume). Moreover, the focus on post-modern baubles or post-modern 'metatwaddle' (Gellner 1992: 41) runs the risk of obscuring our view of much more important phenomena such as the growing power of conservative evangelicalism, Pentecostalism, fundamentalism and religious nationalism – as well as the changing but persistent intertwining of religion with ethnicity and 'race' (Kivisto in this volume). It is questionable whether these phenomena can be most usefully understood as post-modern.

An emerging alternative – with special relevance to the study of religion – is to characterise the contemporary era as 'ultramodernity' (Willaime 2006). This term means that the forces of modernity not only continue to operate but also become more radical. The modernising dynamic of secularisation, for example, has allegedly entered a new phase in which its implications are themselves radicalised. As a result, so the argument goes, politicians and policy makers increasingly turn to religion as a cultural resource to replace the out-moded modernist notion that social or political problems can simply be 'managed' by secular, rational methods. Another way to put this is to call it the re-ethicisation of aspects of social life that were supposed – in the modernist model – to have become the preserve of rational calculation alone. Religion is therefore believed to have retained or regained a role as a powerful source of moral values and visions (Bartkowski in this volume) as well as of personal and collective identities (Greil and Davidman in this volume) especially in relation to political power (Demerath and Williams 1992; Demerath 2001), faith-based initiatives (Farnsley in this volume), political attitudes and actions (Olson in this volume), civil religion (Cristi and Dawson in this volume) and political protest (Nepstad and Williams in this volume). Religion is also achieving recognition as an integral part of the nexus of relations between states, violence and human rights (Demerath in this volume).

Some currents of feminist thought have also helped to rescue religion from the irrelevance to which many notions of modernity had consigned it (Woodhead in this volume). On the one hand, feminist scholars have clearly documented the gendered distribution of authority and power in religious traditions and organisations (Wallace 1996). Others have investigated the contribution made by religions towards the identification and self-identification of women as dependent on, or subservient to, men. Evidence is plentiful of the exclusion, marginalisation, oppression and abuse of women in some religious settings. Sociological studies of religion have therefore been an integral part of the wider study of discrimination against women – crisscrossed in places by discrimination based on ethnicity, 'race' and social class.

On the other hand, sociological studies have also explored the capacity of women to transform religious ideas, rituals, roles, groups and organisations into tools of sociability, empowerment and liberation. Whether it be women in religious orders (Wittberg 2006), new religious movements (Jacobs 1991), Catholic parishes (Wallace 1992) or goddess groupings (Griffin 2000), research has brought to light their actual or potential capacity to produce the changes in personal, social and cultural life for which they strive in the name of their different religious commitments.

At the same time, religious phenomena have presented feminist scholars with some formidable challenges. For example, the clear-sighted decision of some women to commit themselves to religiously inspired ways of living that necessarily subject them to the authority of men requires special consideration (Davidman 1991). Another challenge is to understand the controversies that surround Muslim women in the West who adopt forms of self-presentation and dress in public that clearly separate them from the majority. Still one more conundrum involves the difficulties facing women who do – or do not – take action against the abuse that they receive in religious groups from male leaders (Nason-Clark 2001). In short, religion is a 'site' on which some of the most hotly contested debates about gender in theory and practice are located.

Since the mid-1980s, it has also become clear that religion presents major challenges and opportunities to social scientific explorations of globalisation and, especially, of 'glocalisation' – or the tendency for global imports to take on local forms and functions (Robertson 1992; Beckford 2003: 103–49; Beyer in this volume). Starting from the perception that the world is increasingly experienced as a smaller place as a result of changes in the volume, intensity and speed of communications and movement across national boundaries, sociological analysis has thrown light on religion's contributions to global forces as well as on their impact on religion. The main challenge has been to explain how systems of belief and practice – such as 'world religions' – that claim universal truth and validity can be successfully adapted to, and melded with, diverse local circumstances. At the same time, 'local' faith traditions increasingly foster claims to universal applicability. The dynamic mutual implication between the local and the global is as clearly evident in the realm of religion as in any other sphere of culture or society. Syncretistic and hybrid forms of religion have therefore proliferated in many parts of the world with the aid of global communications media such as the Internet and satellite broadcasting (Bunt 2003; Cowan in this volume). The missionary outreach of mainstream forms of religion has also benefited from the new information technologies, thereby aiding the spread of, for example, Christianity, Hinduism and Islam into relatively new mission territories (Coward *et al.* 2000). Fundamentalisms and conservative evangelical Christian churches (Freston in this volume) are undoubtedly benefiting from glocalisation, but it is a mistake to underestimate the extent to which some liberal, sectarian, pagan and New Age expressions of religion or spirituality can now take advantage of the new global opportunities.

But for all the loose talk and tight scholarship concerning globalisation today, there is an opposite topic to which the sociology of religion has been slower to respond. If the spread of globalisation mistakenly implies the spread of a syncretic consensus, the rise of nationalism more realistically entails conflict and potential violence both within and between the great faith traditions (Demerath 2001, and in this volume). We noted above the sociology of religion's resurgence some twenty-five years ago when it moved from the macro to the micro. Perhaps now is the time for yet another leap forward with a return to the macro and specifically the world of national and cross-national politics.

Meanwhile, another recent development in the sociology of religion is more epistemological and involves the arrival on the scholarly scene of the economics of religion. From this perspective, religious behaviour is best understood in terms of rational choice or 'subjective rationality' (Stark and Finke 2000). As Frank Lechner (in this volume) and others have shown, this is not a new perspective, but, in parallel with thinking about the rational foundations of economic and political conduct, a growing number of sociologists have argued

that explanations of religion should assume that its practitioners act rationally in the sense of basing their actions on calculated choices. This assumption rests largely on an instrumental notion of rationality, which 'assumes the presence of subjective efforts to weigh the anticipated rewards against the anticipated costs, although these efforts usually are inexact and somewhat casual' (Stark and Finke 2000: 37).

Rational choice perspectives have given a new twist to some venerable topics in the sociology of religion. They have, for example, helped to call in question some long-standing ideas about the inevitability of secularisation as one of the master trends of modernity (Warner 1993). They have also provided theoretical underpinning for explanations of the relative popularity of conservative churches (Iannaccone 1994), for the expansion of sectarian organisations (Stark and Iannacconne 1997), for the diversity of sectarian and cultic phenomena (Bainbridge in this volume) and for revival and reform in the Catholic Church (Finke and Wittberg 2000; Wittberg in this volume). Rational choice perspectives have also led to new lines of research on topics as diverse as the historical demography of US churches (Finke and Stark 1992) and the reasons for the successful expansion of early Christianity in the Roman Empire (Stark 1996).

Nevertheless, the critical response to these theoretical perspectives has been mixed. Some critics have applauded the attempt to place the sociology of religion on a firm basis in propositional theory and thereby to challenge some taken-for-granted views. Others have welcomed the methodical efforts to 'translate' existing knowledge into theoretical terms that can be clearly specified and – in some cases – quantified. And there has been a general welcome for a style of research that brings the sociology of religion into line with research in other branches of the social sciences. By contrast, the psychological assumptions underlying the rational choice discourse of compensators and rewards have attracted strong criticism (Bruce 1999). The perspective's failure to take account of differential perceptions of costs and benefits at the level of actors and entire cultures is another accusation (Spickard 1998).

In addition, the logical distinction between ideal-type theorising and real-life situations is often blurred in rational choice perspectives (Beckford 2001).

The influence exercised by rational choice perspectives on some – primarily American – sociologists of religion is certainly evidence that they are once more increasingly talking the same language as many other social scientists. At the same time, it has become difficult to hold the middle ground between the zealous advocates of rational choice and its equally determined despisers. Rational choice perspectives are not only challenging but are also contentious – perhaps more so than in other fields where they have been deployed. This is another case in which the sociology of religion has become a zone of scholarship hosting some of the most timely and heated debates in the social sciences.

To round off this assessment of the intellectual trajectory described by the sociology of religion, we return to questions about the conceptualisation of religion and secularisation. This is because – for all the developments in sociological ways of thinking about the complex intersections between religion and other spheres of social and cultural life – it remains impossible to avoid or to resolve once and for all the questions about the meaning of the central terms in the sociology of religion. While this may appear to be frustrating, we want to suggest that it is actually a source of considerable inspiration and innovation. Studies of religion as a social phenomenon can never take anything for granted because their principal object of study can be understood in so many different ways. This amounts to a continuous challenge not only for sociologists of religion but also for other scholars who may be seeking to understand religion from other points of view.

The opening chapter by Randall Collins traces the origins of the most influential sets of theoretical ideas about the nature of religion as an object for sociological investigation. Marx, Engels, Nietzsche and Freud each reduced religion to an illusory artefact of ideological interests or psychological projection. Durkheim portrayed religion as a functional mechanism for generating the ritual, symbolic and moral basis of social solidarity. And Max Weber's approach gave priority to religions as sources and vehicles of meanings and motivations that have shaped societal developments in crucial ways. Each of these theoretical perspectives makes assumptions about the meaning of the term 'religion': explicit in the case of Durkheim, but largely implicit in the other cases. Entire chains of sociological research on religion have descended from these assumptions but without ever settling their differences or resolving the question of definition once and for all. This high degree of variation in definitions is both a reflection of the 'real world's' widely differing understandings of religion and a sign of the sociology of religion's openness towards competing approaches.

As editors, we have chosen to showcase variations in the understanding of what religion means in sociological terms. Indeed, two of our own contributions emphasise the importance of understanding religion – as well as secularity – as the product of social and intellectual struggles to construct it in certain ways. Thus, Demerath's chapter on secularisation and sacralisation shows how the sociology of religion could benefit from framing its subject matter, first, in terms of an irregular oscillation between sacralisation and secularisation and, second, as a sub-set of culture. The effect is both to shift the focus away from the unproductive question of whether religion is in decline or not and, at the same time, to situate sacralisation and religion in the broader context of cultural change. Moreover, the chapter by Beckford and Richardson shows how the categorisation and definition of religion are subject to cultural, political and legal processes of regulation. The meanings attributed to religion in the 'real world' are therefore a matter of struggle, conflict and compromise (Beckford 1999) as well as intellectual genealogy (Asad 2003).

PLANNING AND PRODUCING THE HANDBOOK

This Handbook represents an effort to meet several key objectives. First, it began with our attempt to lay out an unusually encompassing sense of the field conceptually and methodologically. Based on our knowledge of the developing literature in the field over the past half-century and more, we produced a template that covered the field as a whole while suggesting its major component parts and the subtopics within those parts that deserved chapter treatment.

We had to be selective. We had to decide which topics were important enough to be included – and which ones could be reluctantly omitted. We were determined to provide a balanced set that fairly represented the core of the sociology of religion. At the same time, we resisted the temptation to favour quirky or sensational topics that were tangential to religion's overall social and cultural significance in the early twenty-first century. We had no illusions of providing a 360° coverage of the sociology of religion, or of confusing a Handbook with a wikipedia.

Of course, our most general aim was to guide readers through the most important issues in the sociology of religion. But how did we assess 'importance'? One criterion was whether we thought that a topic was a prerequisite for grasping the sociological meaning of religion at virtually any place or time. This is the 'can-you-really-call-yourself-a-sociologist-of-religion-without-knowing-about-this-topic' consideration. Another criterion was whether a topic was central to generating interesting research on religion. In other words, the topic had to be fruitful as well as interesting. Yet another was whether a new topic – or a new angle on an old topic – presented a worthwhile challenge to the prevailing wisdom. Would it make experienced sociologists sit up and pay attention? Certainly it was important for us to include chapters on a range of methodological approaches to the sociology of religion, including the historical dimension of the discipline. Finally, we deliberately included chapters by non-Anglo-American authors and that dealt with religion outside North America and Western Europe; and we encouraged all authors to make cross-national comparisons, where appropriate. This makes our Handbook virtually unique.

We then embarked upon the critical process of seeking experts for each of the chapter topics and asking them to take on the responsibility of reviewing and assessing classic as well as recent work in the area with a list of references that would orient any student – indeed any professor – to the topic. Rather than invite scholars to contribute papers of their own choosing that we would try to stitch together at the last moment, we assigned specific chapters to specific scholars with our fingers crossed.

Happily, our response rate would make survey researchers blush with envy; we were able to secure the overwhelming majority of our first-choices. And as if to test our writers' thresholds of annoyance, we asked them first for detailed outlines of their prospective chapters, and then for first drafts. We then had the temerity to provide feedback on both. All of the authors were patient to the point of long-suffering. Alas, a few had to bow out later owing to various personal contingencies. But we were able to back and fill so that only three chapters of the original thirty-seven have come up blank – albeit important chapters on social class, sexualities, and India. Otherwise we were gratified that contributors brought their own good ideas for how to treat their topics and approaches. After all, we wanted original contributions, not merely annotated bibliographies. In addition to analysing the central arguments and empirical findings in an area, all chapters reflect their authors' original sense of what is most important in where the field has been and where it is heading. We were especially pleased with those that draw on intellectual resources rarely accessible to readers unfamiliar with languages other than English.

Finally, it may seem puzzling that a printed Handbook is being published at a time when so much information about religion is now available online or in other media. So, why go to the lengths of putting together a large edited collection? Paradoxically, the ready availability of so much information makes a wide-ranging Handbook all the more useful as a series of charts that will help readers to navigate the rapidly rising sea of materials about religion. Put another way, a Handbook can provide a variety of devices for 'decoding' signals that might otherwise make no sense – or fail to be detected. Equally important, this Handbook offers *critical* assessments of the concepts, methods and theories that are embedded in various accounts of religion in its social and cultural contexts. In other words, a Handbook is a distillation of up-to-date scholarly knowledge and expertise. As such, it enables readers to pause and reflect critically on the flood of digitised information that can sometimes seem engulfing.

Still another function of this Handbook is to connect the past, the present and the future of the sociology of religion in terms of ideas, challenges and prospects. Again, this is a way of channelling the flux of information into frameworks of meaning which can help to make sense of it. Sociological questions about religion have evolved in various ways over more than one hundred years. Not only have the questions changed, but the reasons for asking them have also changed. Assessing the value of current ways of understanding religion necessarily involves knowing about their historical development. Similarly, an informed sense of how sociological approaches to religion may develop in the future depends in large part on understanding their emergence from the past into the present.

CONSTELLATIONS OF TOPICS

Now that we have specified the distinctive characteristics of sociological approaches to religion, provided a brief history of the field that highlights developments, and recounted the process behind the Handbook, we want to conclude by describing its organisation. The chapters are grouped in a relatively small number of constellations or 'parts'. These are clusters of closely related topics that often occur in the research conducted by sociologists of religion. In view of the wide variety of topics in the sociology of religion – and of the reasons for studying them – we have arranged the contents in a way that caters to as many interests as possible. All of the Handbook's eight main Parts begin with an introductory note

about the significance of the material covered in each chapter. Here we shall simply indicate the general scope of each Part.

I   Theories and Concepts

Without wishing to privilege any particular approaches, we begin with a cluster of high-level theoretical paradigms and the issues that they are both provoked by and provoke. They all provide influential arguments about and distinctive vantage points on the sociological significance of religion. Conversely, they illustrate how religion's social and cultural importance varies with the perspective from which it is assessed. These chapters take up respectively religion in the classical tradition of Marx, Weber, and Durkheim; in modernity and post-modernity; in the midst of secularisation and sacralisation; in the perspective of rationality and rational choice; and in a globalising world. They are rife with ideas about the direction of long-term religious change and the engines that drive them. On the one hand, theories in the sociology of religion serve as convenient summaries or frameworks of general ideas that have emerged from empirical investigations. On the other hand, theories can also stimulate research by pointing either to puzzling tensions within existing knowledge or to intriguing questions that have never been asked before. Debates about theories provide both continuity and transformation in the history of the sociology of religion.

II   Methods of Studying Religion

The focus of the second constellation is on the methods of doing research in the sociology of religion. Its chapter topics range from qualitative field work to large-scale quantitative surveys and then historical research. The aim is to discuss ways of collecting or generating the kind of information that is required to answer sociological questions about religion. A cluster of methodological issues has developed around attempts to make sense of religion in sociological terms. The fundamental challenge is to find ways to make the social aspects of religion available for systematic examination. How can one measure differences in sanctity, faith or reverence? What are the trade-offs between intensive depth and extensive scope? The debate about appropriate indicators, variables, scales, classifications and typologies of religious phenomena – to say nothing about measurement and comparison – is the 'ground bass'. To describe research methods as the 'tools' of the sociology of religion is to underestimate their importance in helping to determine what can count as evidence of religion in a socio-cultural phenomenon. The choice of methods has a crucial impact on what can be discovered – or, at least, claimed – about religion in different forms and different settings.

III   Social Forms and Experiences of Religion

The third constellation deals with some of the primary social forms for producing, reproducing and experiencing religion. They include mainstream congregations, new religious movements, New Age spiritualities and civil religion. It is useful to think of them all as social 'vehicles' or 'vessels' that transport religion from place to place and across generations. They also give rise to collective identity and solidarity – as well as tension and conflict – among their practitioners. And they convey values, beliefs and practices that are expressed in distinctive forms of language, gesture, ritual, emotion and experience. Moreover, they reflect social and cultural influences filtered by gender, age, family upbringing, sexual orientation, ethnicity, nationality and other factors.

IV   Issues of Power and Control in Religious Organisations

Here the central question involves issues of power – both internal and external – facing religious organisations. Chapters focus on religious professionals, religious orders and schismatic sects, the influence of the Internet, and faith-based initiatives within the US. The changing distribution of authority in religious organisation has long been of particular interest to

sociologists and dates from the classic distinction between church-type and sect-type organisations. But the issues involved radiate beyond Christian groups to affect power and administration in synagogues, mosques, temples and gurdwaras. Analysis of authority and leadership is also inseparable from an understanding of the resources on which religious organisations depend. These topics have been central to the sociology of religion since the late nineteenth century, but their significance has recently been transformed by new technologies of communication. In particular, the Internet has made it possible for religious organisations to develop new forms of authority, leadership and resourcing.

V   Religion and Politics

Relations between religion and politics have invariably been close and complex in all regions of the world. The frequently heard claim that Islam is somehow different from other religions because it supposedly does not keep religion and politics separate flies in the face of the facts. In fact, one of the major reasons for studying the sociology of religion is precisely to understand how the spheres of religion and politics influence each other. Chapters here concern religion, the state and violence; America's distinctive controversy over 'faith-based initiatives'; religion as regulated and regulator; religious, social and political movements; and religion's relationship to individuals' political and ideological preferences. Faith often intervenes in politics to promote its agendas; politics often seeks the legitimacy and influence afforded by faith. Religion has a broader political significance in so far as it contributes towards the regulation of social life and it is, itself, an object of social regulation.

VI   Individual Religious Behaviour in Social Context

Religion can evoke intensely subjective and private experiences and emotions as well as strongly held convictions. Nobody seriously doubts that the significance of religion can also be crucial for personal identity, states of mind and self-worth. Nevertheless, sociological research shows that *social factors* help to shape these subjective phenomena. For example, surveys of reported religious beliefs and experiences generate cross-national patterns of similarity and difference, which – in turn – point to the influence of social factors at the national level. Such findings do not call in question the reality of individual beliefs or experiences; they merely emphasise the need to situate subjective phenomena in broader social and cultural contexts. The list of these contexts is potentially lengthy, but we have selected three of them for especially careful consideration here: ethnicity, age and generation. In each case, sociological research has documented clear – albeit complex – patterns of association between these factors and religion. But this is also an area of research where the testing of existing knowledge and the investigation of new ideas are constantly challenging received wisdom.

VII   Religion, Self-identity and the Life-course

In addition to the broad social factors that shape religion at the individual level, sociological research has increasingly turned to examination of identities and the lived experience of religion. This involves looking at the patterned ways of being religious and expressing religious identities. The gendering of the lived experience of religion, for example, has emerged as a highly significant dimension of the sociology of religion. Less attention has been given to the embodied character of religious practice, but researchers are beginning to take more seriously the challenge of understanding the implications of the human body – including the embodied nature of emotion – for the practice of religion. This also involves consideration of the life-course and of the changing links between religion and different stages of life.

VIII   Case Studies from Around the World

The final part of the Handbook contains five case studies that illustrate some of the cross-national variations observed in the nexus between religion, society and culture. These chapters also show that many of the generalisations discussed by other contributors need to be placed in national contexts as well as in a global setting. In fact, each of them calls in question concepts that are routinely used by sociologists of religion in North America and Western Europe. They 'problematise' these concepts by showing how they have to be adapted to the particular circumstances that affect religion in other regions of the world. For example, Yang's chapter shows that the regulation of religion takes very distinctive forms in China, despite evidence of marketisation; the relation between religion and identity is particularly complex in Central and Eastern Europe, according to Borowik's chapter, following the collapse of communist regimes; the intersection between religion and ethnicity in Israel is overlaid by messianism and neo-traditionalism, as is clear in Sharot's chapter; Shimazono argues in his chapter that the subtleties of State Shinto in Japan do not fit into a neat category of religious nationalism; and, according to Blancarte's chapter, Mexico defies many aspects of the 'Western' understanding of popular religion and secularisation.

So much for the Handbook's eight main topic areas. But it is essential to grasp that they constitute only a device for scanning the extent and variety of the territory. In reality, sociological research on religion often cuts across the divisions between constellations. For example, the study of individual emotions or experiences usually situates them in the context of particular forms of religious organisation. Similarly, questions about the intersection between religion and politics often take account of differences in ethnicity, gender or age. These Parts and chapters indicate the various ways in which religion – however it is defined – can be understood in its social and cultural contexts. Taken together, they also make the case that sociological approaches to religion are different from theological, philosophical or psychological approaches. All these approaches can complement and assist each other, but they have different starting points; ask different questions, and seek different answers. There is no implication here that sociology is superior to the other approaches to religion (*pace* Milbank 1990), although tensions can arise between them (Radcliffe 1980).

REFERENCES

Ammerman, Nancy T. 1990. *Baptist Battles: Social Change and Religious Conflict in the Southern Baptist Convention*. New Brunswick, NJ: Rutgers University Press.

Ammerman, Nancy T. 1997. *Congregations and Community*. New Brunswick, NJ: Rutgers University Press.

Ammerman, Nancy T., Jackson W. Carroll, Carl S. Dudley and William McKinney (eds) 1998. *Studying Congregations: A New Handbook*. Nashville, TN: Abingdon.

Asad, T. 2003. *Formations of the Secular. Christianity, Islam, Modernity*. Stanford, CA: Stanford University Press.

Ayella, Marybeth 1993. '"They must be crazy": some of the difficulties in researching "cults"'. In C. Renzetti and R. M. Lee (eds), *Researching Sensitive Topics*. London: Sage, pp. 108–24.

Bailey, Edward 1990. 'The implicit religion of contemporary society: some studies and reflections'. *Social Compass* 37 (4): 483–97.

Barker, Eileen V. 1983. 'Supping with the devil: how long a spoon does the sociologist need?' *Sociological Analysis* 44 (3): 197–206.

Bauman, Z. 1992. *Intimations of Postmodernity*, London: Routledge.

Becker, Penny Edgell 1999. *Congregations in Conflict: Cultural Models of Local Religious Life*. New York: Cambridge University Press.

Beckford, James A. 1985a. 'The insulation and isolation of the sociology of religion'. *Sociological Analysis* 46 (4): 347–54.

Beckford, James A. 1985b. *Cult Controversies. The Societal Response to New Religious Movements*. London: Tavistock.

Beckford, James A. 1989. *Religion and Advanced Industrial Society*, London: Unwin-Hyman.

Beckford, James A. 1990. 'The sociology of religion 1945–1989'. *Social Compass* 37 (1): 45–64.

Beckford, J. A. 1999. 'The politics of defining religion in secular society: from a taken-for-granted institution to a contested resource'. *The Pragmatics of Defining Religion: Contexts, Concepts and Conflicts*. J. G. Platvoet and A. L. Molendijk (eds). Leiden: E.J. Brill, pp. 23–40.

Beckford, James A. 2000. '"Start together and finish together": shifts in the premises and paradigms underlying the scientific study of religion'. *Journal for the Scientific Study of Religion* 39 (4): 481–95.

Beckford, James A. 2001. 'Choosing rationality'. *Research in the Social Scientific Study of Religion* 12: 1–22.

Beckford, James A. 2003. *Social Theory and Religion*. Cambridge: Cambridge University Press.

Berger, Peter L. 1967. *The Social Canopy*. Garden City, NJ: Doubleday [published in the UK in 1969 as *The Social Reality of Religion*, London: Faber & Faber].

Berger, Peter L. and Thomas Luckmann 1966. *The Social Construction of Reality*. Garden City, NJ: Doubleday.

Bruce, S. (1999). *Choice and Religion. A Critique of Rational Choice*. Oxford, Oxford University Press.

Bunt, G. 2003. *Islam in the Digital Age – E-Jihad, Online Fatwas and Cyber Islamic Environments*. London, Pluto Press.

Carroll, Jackson W. Barbara G. Wheeler, Daniel O. Aleshire and Penny Long Marler 1997. *Being There: Culture and Formation in Two Theological Schools*. New York: Oxford University Press.

Chaves, Mark 1997. *Ordaining Women: Culture and Conflict in Religious Organizations*. Cambridge, MA: Harvard University Press.

Coward, H., J. Hinnells and R. B. Williams (eds) 2000. *The South Asian Religious Diaspora in Britain, Canada, and the United States*. Albany, NY: State University of New York Press.

Davidman, Lynn 1991. *Tradition in a Rootless World*. Berkeley, CA: University of California Press.

Davie, Grace 2003. 'The evolution of the sociology of religion: theme and variations'. In M. Dillon (ed.) *Handbook of the Sociology of Religion*. New York: Cambridge University Press, pp. 61–75.

Demerath, N. J., III 2001. *Crossing the Gods. World Religions and Worldly Politics*. New Brunswick, NJ: Rutgers University Press.

Demerath, N. J., III and Rhys H. Williams 1992. *A Bridging of Faith. Religion and Politics in a New England City*. Princeton: University of Princeton Press.

Demerath, N. J., III, P. D. Hall, T. Schmitt and Rhys H. Williams (eds) 1998. *Sacred Companies. Organizational Aspects of Religion and Religious Aspects of Organizations*. New York: Oxford University Press.

Ebaugh, Helen Rose and Janet S. Chafetz (ed.) 2000. *Religion and the New Immigrants: Continuities and Adaptations in Immigrant Congregations*. Walnut Creek, CA: Alta Mira Press.

Finke, Roger and Rodney Stark 1992. *The Churching of America 1776–1990: Winners and Losers in our Religious Economy*. New Brunswick, NJ: Rutgers University Press.

Finke, Roger and Patricia Wittberg 2000. 'Organizational revival from within: explaining revivalism and reform in the Roman Catholic Church'. *Journal for the Scientific Study of Religion* 39 (2): 154–70.

Gellner, E. 1992. *Postmodernism, Reason and Religion*. London: Routledge.

Giddens, A. (1991). *Modernity and Self-Identity. Self and Society in the Late Modern Age*. Cambridge, Polity Press.

Griffin, Wendy (ed.) 2000. *Daughters of the Goddess. Studies in Healing, Identity and Empowerment*. Walnut Creek, CA: Alta Mira.

Hannigan, John A. 1993. 'New social movement theory and the sociology of religion'. In W. H. J. Swatos (ed.) *A Future for Religion?* Newbury Park: Sage, pp. 1–18.

Harris, Margaret 1998. *Organizing God's Work. Challenges for Churches and Synagogues*. Basingstoke: Macmillan.

Hervieu-Léger, Danièle 1999. 'The sociologist of religions in courts: neither witness nor expert?' *Swiss Journal of Sociology* 25 (3): 421–26.

Hornsby-Smith, M. P. 1989. *The Changing Parish. A Study of Parishes, Priests and Parishioners after Vatican II*. London: Routledge.

Iannaccone, L. R. (1994). 'Why strict churches are strong'. *American Journal of Sociology* 99 (5): 1180–1211.

Jacobs, Janet L. 1991. 'Gender and power in new religious movements. A feminist discourse on the scientific study of religion'. *Religion* 21 (4): 345–56.

Luckmann, Thomas 1963. *Das Problem der Religion in der modernen Gesellschaft*. Freiburg im Breisgau: Verlag Rombach [published in English translation in 1967 as *The Invisible Religion*, New York: Macmillan].

Lyon, David 2000. *Jesus in Disneyland. Religion in Postmodern Times*. Cambridge: Polity.

Maduro, Otto 1982. *Religion and Social Conflicts*. Maryknoll, NY: Orbis.

McGuire, Meredith with D. Kantor 1988. *Ritual Healing in Suburban America*. New Brunswick, NJ: Rutgers University Press.

Milbank, John 1990. *Theology and Social Theory. Beyond Secular Reason*. Oxford: Blackwell.

Morgan, David 1998. *Visual Piety: A History and Theory of Popular Religious Images*. Berkeley, CA: University of California Press.

Nason-Clark, Nancy 2001. 'Woman abuse and faith communities: religion, violence, and the provision of social welfare'. In Paula D. Nesbitt (ed.) *Religion and Social Policy*. Walnut Creek, CA: Alta Mira Press, pp. 128–45.

Neitz, Mary Jo 1990. 'Studying religion in the eighties'. In H. S. Becker and M. M. McCall (eds). *Symbolic Interaction and Cultural Studies*. Chicago: University of Chicago Press, pp. 90–118.

Neitz, Mary Jo and James V. Spickard 1990. 'Steps toward a Sociology of religious experience: the theories of Mihaly Czikszentmihalyi and Alfred Schutz'. *Sociological Analysis* 51 (1): 15–33.

Nesbitt, Paula D. 1997. *The Feminization of the Clergy in America*. New York: Oxford University Press.

Norris, Pippa and Ronald Inglehart (2004). *Sacred and Secular. Religion and Politics Worldwide*. Cambridge: Cambridge University Press.

O'Toole, Roger 1984. *Religion: Classic Sociological Approaches*. Toronto: McGraw-Hill Ryerson.

Radcliffe, Timothy 1980. 'Relativizing the relativizers: a theologian's assessment of the role of sociological explanation of religious phenomena and theology today'. In D. Martin *et al.* (eds) *Sociology and Theology. Alliance or Conflict?* Brighton: Harvester, pp. 151–62.

Richardson, James T. 1985. 'The active vs. passive convert: paradigm conflict in conversion/recruitment research'. *Journal for the Scientific Study of Religion* 24 (2): 163–79.

Richardson, James T. 1991. 'Reflexivity and objectivity in the study of controversial new religions'. *Religion* 21 (3): 305–18.

Richardson, James T. (ed.) 2004. *Regulating Religion. Case Studies from around the Globe*. New York: Kluwer.

Robbins, Thomas 1983. 'The beach is washing away: controversial religion and the sociology of religion'. *Sociological Analysis* 44 (3): 207–14.

Robbins, Thomas, Dick Anthony and Thomas E. Curtis 1973. 'The limits of symbolic realism: problems of emphatic field observation in a sectarian context'. *Journal for the Scientific Study of Religion* 12 (3): 259–71.

Robertson, Roland 1992. *Globalization: Social Theory and Global Culture*, London: Sage.

Roof, Wade Clark 1993. *A Generation of Seekers: The Spiritual Journeys of the Babyboom Generation*. San Francisco: Harper & Row.

Roof, Wade Clark 1999. *Spiritual Marketplace: Baby Boomers and the Remaking of American Religion*. Princeton, NJ: Princeton University Press.

Roof, Wade Clark and William McKinney 1987. *American Mainline Religion*. New Brunswick, NJ: Rutgers University Press.

Shepherd, William C. 1982. 'The prosecutor's reach: legal issues stemming from the new religious movements'. *Journal of the American Academy of Religion* 50 (2): 187–214.

Smith, Christian 1991. *The Emergence of Liberation Theology: Radical Religion and Social-Movement Activism*, Chicago: University of Chicago Press.

Spickard, James V. 1998. 'Rethinking religious social action: what is "rational" about rational choice theory?' *Sociology of Religion* 59 (2): 99–115.

Spickard, James V., J. Shawn Landres and Meredith McGuire (2002). *Personal Knowledge and Beyond: Reshaping the Ethnography of Religion*. New York: New York University Press.

Stark, Rodney 1996. *The Rise of Christianity. A Sociologist Reconsiders History*. Princeton, NJ: Princeton University Press.

Stark, Rodney and Roger Finke 2000. *Acts of Faith: Explaining the Human Side of Religion*. Berkeley, CA: University of California Press.

Stark, R. and L. Iannaccone 1997. 'Why the Jehovah's Witnesses grow so rapidly: a theoretical application'. *Journal of Contemporary Religion* 12 (2): 133–57.

Wallace, Ruth A. 1992. *They Call Her Pastor: a New Role for Catholic Women*. Albany, NY: SUNY Press.

Wallace, Ruth A. 1996. 'Feminist theory in North America: new insights into the sociology of religion'. *Social Compass* 43 (4): 467–79.

Warner, R. Stephen 1993. 'Work in progress toward a new paradigm for the sociological study of religion in the United States'. *American Journal of Sociology* 98 (March): 1044–93.

Warner, R. Stephen and Judith Wittner (eds) 1997. *Gatherings in Diaspora. Religious Communities and the New Immigration*. Philadelphia: Temple University Press.

Willaime, Jean-Paul 1999. 'French-language sociology of religion in Europe since the Second World War'. *Swiss Journal of Sociology* 25 (2): 343–71.

Willaime, Jean-Paul 2006. 'Religion in ultramodernity'. In James A. Beckford and John Walliss (eds) *Theorising Religion. Classical and Contemporary Debates*. Aldershot: Ashgate, pp. 77–89.

Wilson, Bryan R. 1998. 'The sociologist of religion as expert witness'. *Swiss Journal of Sociology* 24 (1): 17–27.

Wittberg, Patricia 2006. *From Piety to Professionalism – and Back Again? Transformations in Organized Religious Virtuosity*. Lanham, MD: Lexington Books.

Wuthnow, Robert 1988. *The Restructuring of American Religion*. Princeton, NJ: University of Princeton Press.

Wuthnow, Robert 1991. *Acts of Compassion: Caring for Others and Helping Ourselves*. Princeton, NJ: Princeton University Press.

Wuthnow, Robert 2001. 'Spirituality and spiritual practice'. In R. K. Fenn (ed.) *The Blackwell Companion to Sociology of Religion*. Oxford: Blackwell, pp. 306–20.

Theories and Concepts

Part I presents six primary theoretical traditions concerning the social and cultural significance of religion. In their different ways these traditions represent the conceptual foundations – the basic building blocks – for the sociology of religion. They also catalyse a wide range of new research questions that promise to throw fresh light on the meaning of religion in its various contexts.

Randall Collins argues in Chapter 1 that the very idea of sociology originated in a controversy about religion in revolutionary France and that religion was at the heart of some of the earliest attempts to establish sociology as an intellectual discipline. He adds that even the founding generation of sociologists displayed a variety of theoretical approaches to the understanding of religion. Some, such as Karl Marx, Friedrich Nietzsche and Sigmund Freud, tried to reduce religion to a matter of harmful illusions, whereas others followed Emile Durkheim's example in regarding religion as the basis of ritual order and morality in societies. A third perspective developed in the wake of Max Weber's studies of religion as a form of social organisation and a source of ideas driving social and cultural change. These three theoretical approaches to the study of religion remain influential among sociologists today and are still evolving in new directions. Their divergent and subtle interpretations of secularisation are particularly germane to the debates

that flared up at the end of the twentieth century about the future of religion. This is surely a major reason why the so-called classics persist as both an anchor to the past and an engine into the future.

In support of the notion that classical sociology remains powerful despite and because it is amenable to fresh interpretations, **Kevin Christiano** contends in Chapter 2 that religion's sociological significance varies with the terms and conditions of 'modernity', 'post-modernity' and 'ultra-modernity'. Whereas the classical contributions sought to explain religious change as part of the emergence of new ideas, structures and processes in post-medieval Europe, many current sociologists see religion as a reflection of either the super-session or the intensification of modernity. The post-modern gaze brings into focus such things as the declining force of claims to absolute truth, the loss of respect for tradition and authority, the creation of hybrid mixtures of symbols and rituals, and a fondness for irony, pastiche and playfulness. It would also highlight the individualisation, subjectivisation and privatisation of religion as just three among many competing forces in a post-modern world lacking authoritative structures. By contrast, the advocates of the notions of 'ultra-modernity' and 'supermodernity' (*surmodernité*) believe that religion is now well placed to take advantage of post-modern disruptions in order to reassert a new sense of order and spiritual purpose in areas of life previously corroded and demoralised by aggressive secularity. Studies of phenomena as different as New Age spiritualities and Pentecostalism have confirmed that their practitioners place a high value on a form of religion that is personal, practical and emotionally experiential.

Implicit in many attempts to track down the expressions of religion that have survived modernity is the assumption that secularisation has largely eroded or marginalised the societal significance of religion – at least, in the advanced industrial democracies. But in Chapter 3 **Jay Demerath's** radically new approach to secularisation charts a new course between the idea that religion is doomed to disappear and the idea that secularisation is merely a European cultural conceit. His review of the often heated polemics surrounding secularisation aims at a better balanced portrayal of secularisation and its contrary force – sacralisation – as continually intertwined processes that occur in culture more broadly as well as in religion more narrowly. By means of a four-fold typology, he outlines the variety of scenarios in which the process of secularisation can be either internal or external to a society and can also be directed or non-directed. Examples from various regions of the world illustrate the explanatory power of simultaneously recognising the possibility of secularisation *and* sacralisation. Study of the fluctuations between these two processes could therefore help to bounce the sociology of religion out of a rut and move it closer to mainstream concerns with broader cultural change.

Another recent attempt to re-orient the sociology of religion towards the theoretical mainstream concerns the idea of 'rational choice'. This more economistic perspective envisions a religious marketplace that depends upon the individual's self-conscious assessments of costs and benefits. Its proponents see it as offering the sociology of religion a sound new footing. However, **Frank Lechner's** Chapter 4 combines a straightforward presentation of such claims with scepticism about this

particular attempt to re-orient the sociology of religion away from the 'old' paradigm. Lechner notes that people do not necessarily abandon their rationality when they practise religion, but he questions the assumption that religious actors seek to maximise their interests in pursuit of fixed preferences and that it is in the interest of religious organisations to increase their market share without permitting 'free riders'. He also challenges the rational choice view that religious pluralism fosters religious vitality and that secularisation is a self-defeating process. Noting Adam Smith's warning about the danger of adopting a single 'system' in the social sciences, Lechner casts doubt on the usefulness of a unified theory of rational choice and other economic metaphors. Nevertheless, his conclusion does not simply reject rational choice theory; it recommends exploring a productive combination of the best of the 'old' and 'new' paradigms.

Finally one more theoretical initiative that advances the sociology of religion to a new set of issues with broad ramifications is **Peter Beyer's** argument in Chapter 5 for placing religion simultaneously in the context of global *and* local forces. Moving beyond the expansive bromides of globalisation, Beyer endorses the notion of 'glocalisation' by which one may be led to think globally but adapt locally. He identifies four axes on which glocalisation varies; namely, the degrees to which religion is (a) institutionalised or non-institutionalised, (b) publicly influential or privatised, (c) traditional/conservative or modern/liberal, and (d) enacted specifically as religion or conveyed by non-religious forms with religious functions. Using copious examples from many regions of the world, Beyer demonstrates the close association between forms of glocalisation and 'pluralisation', especially in the wake of extensive migration from the global South to the North and the collapse of communist regimes in Eastern Europe. In effect, he argues for reframing ideas about religion in conditions of modernisation and secularisation with new ideas about glocalisation and pluralisation.

The Classical Tradition in Sociology of Religion

RANDALL COLLINS

The sociology of religion is entwined with sociological theory from its very beginnings. Sociology even began in a controversy over religion. During the 1789 French Revolution, Christianity was abolished, and replaced by a civic cult celebrating Reason. This new cult lasted only from 1794 to 1801, and Christianity was restored by Napoleon; but the anti-religious extremism of the revolution was one of its most shocking features to contemporaries, along with the execution of aristocrats and priests on the guillotine. Controversy began almost immediately over the significance of religion for society. Conservative exiles such as Comte Joseph de Maistre argued that Papal theocracy was the only protection from anarchy; and the Vicomte de Bonald held in his *Théorie du pouvoir politique et religieux* (1796) that religious orthodoxy is necessary for a well-regulated state. The French Revolution was like a huge experiment in contriving a secular society, and the experiment failed. These conservative thinkers are regarded as early forerunners of sociology by raising its biggest questions: what is the basis of social order, and the processes of change.

The first explicit sociologists emerged after the restoration of the monarchy in 1815. These were progressives, believing that change was inevitable, but attempting to formulate a religion appropriate for modern society. The Comte de Saint-Simon, in *Catéchisme des industriels* (1823) *and Nouveau christianisme* (1825), saw the new industrial era as progressing under an elite of inventers and engineers, who would work for the good of society. Saint-Simon is often regarded as the founder of technocracy, but it should be remembered that what he called industrialism was a form of religion. Another modern substitute for Christianity was put forward by Auguste Comte in *Philosophie positive* (1830–42), in which he also created the term 'sociology' for his new science. Comte proposed that history goes through three stages: (a) theological, in which religion provides the system of belief, the military aristocracy is dominant, and the basic social unit is the family; (b) metaphysical, in which law provides the belief system and the state is the social unit; and finally (c) positive stage, in which industry is dominant and all humanity becomes the social unit. In 1852, Comte published his *Catéchisme positiviste, ou sommaire exposition de la religion universelle*, which was to provide the modern belief system, Positivism, and established himself as the high priest of Humanity.

Comte had not yet disentangled the founding of a new religion from the scientific or academic field which studies society. His most notable successors, Emile Durkheim and Max Weber, were not only the great systematizers and theorists of sociology at the turn of the 20th century; they also were the first great classic sociologists of religion. For both, religion was a key to their sociology. For Durkheim, religion is the prototype of solidarity, what holds society together. Moreover, religion reveals the social processes which generate the entire range of human symbolism and belief, and the morality by which human groups in their varying ways distinguish good and bad. Durkheim traces social change in the collective consciousness produced by rituals; even secular life without traditional religious practices is upheld by rituals of its own. Weber is most famous for arguing that Protestantism produced modern capitalism; later in his comparative studies he attempted to demonstrate that each of the great world religions laid down the tracks along which Europe, the Islamic world, India, and China moved in their distinctive directions. Weber is also the systematic sociologist of stratification, bureaucracy and other non-religious social institutions; but he worked out his entire sociology in the process of tracing the patterns of historical change connected to religion.

The classic tradition comprises these early founders and especially those who crystallized the scholarly discipline. In what follows I will take up three strands: the social thinkers who regard religion as an illusion to be exposed or an evil to be overthrown – like the most militant of the French Revolutionists; sociologists who analyze religion as the basis of ritual order and morality; and those who analyze religion as a form of social organization and a carrier group for social change.

THE REDUCTIONIST OR ILLUSIONIST TRADITION

There have been skeptics, atheists and detractors of religion through the centuries. They were especially frequent in the 18th century, including most famously Voltaire. The most important of these for the sociological tradition are not merely those who declared religion an illusion, but the reductionists who went on to propose what religion was really about beneath the surface. We will consider Marx, Nietzsche, and Freud.

For Marx, religion was the opium of the masses. It is the primary form of false consciousness, keeping the laboring classes of each historical era from recognizing their own interest in revolt against the property-owning class. 'There'll be pie in the sky, when you die' mocked the IWW (International Workers of the World) song at the turn of the 20th century. Religion is a chief part of the dominant ideology, the set of beliefs which permeate society's consciousness and uphold the interests of the ruling class, making the social order seem natural and inevitable. In *The German Ideology* (1846), Marx and Engels stated that the ruling ideas are those of the property-owning class, because they control the material means of mental production. Ideas are produced and propagated only where there are writing implements, scribes, printing presses and other media, along with material means of support for intellectuals and artists to do their work. In ancient and medieval societies, churches and monasteries were virtually the only places where thinkers could have careers; even the universities were church institutions. Rulers and aristocrats endowed and supported these institutions and received in return a religious covering for their rule.

There are two difficulties with the dominant ideology theory. One is that religion at times provided the vehicle for revolt by the masses. Until the 18th century, virtually the only occasions when peasants or urban workers took part in large-scale revolts was in the form of religious movements, especially millennial movements propagating a new revelation. In 16th century Germany during the Peasants' Wars, radical Anabaptists burned and seized their landlords' property; in China there were a series of revolts against the government, ranging from popular Taoists in the Han Dynasty (*c.* AD 200), to the Taiping (Great Heavenly Peace) Rebellion in the Qing dynasty (1851–64). The key feature is that the religion provides an organizing device, a technique for mobilizing large numbers of persons across a considerable territory, providing leadership, discipline as well as inspiration. Religious missionaries and proselityzation were the chief model for organizational change and growth before the modern era, and these could be adapted from below as much as from on high. Indeed it can be argued that Marxism itself was a species of secularized religious movement, spreading with millennial fervor to transcend the merely utilitarian trade-union consciousness of the labor movement.

The second difficulty is that historically the dominant ideology has had a stronger effect on the dominant classes than on their subordinates. In medieval Europe, Christianity was largely the faith of the aristocracy; it was they who were foremost in devotions in church and castle, and who staffed the priesthood (or at least its higher ranks), the monasteries and nunneries with their superfluous sons and daughters. Where possible, aristocrats required their servants and retainers to worship along with themselves. But the latter were largely going through the forms, while their own beliefs ranged from cynicism to magical beliefs reminiscent of paganism. And outside the immediate range of aristocratic influence, the bulk of the rural and poor population was irreligious or near-pagan. It was only with the Reformation and the ensuing Catholic Counter-Reformation that churches began to incorporate the masses into their devotions and beliefs as a systematic form of discipline (Wuthnow 1989; Gorski 2000). The spread of religion into the lives of ordinary people was part of the penetration of the state into society, a top-down process of unification around a national culture that was a chief dynamic of modernization. Ironically, more people were religious in the 19th and 20th centuries, as modernization and secularization proceeded, than in the so-called age of faith of medieval society.

What this implies is that the dominant ideology was primarily a device for unifying the ruling class, giving them coherence and consciousness of their own superiority. It did not keep the lower classes in their place so much by indoctrinating them as by keeping aristocrats and prosperous bourgeois better mobilized than those below them. Religion aided a small minority in ruling over masses that greatly outnumbered them. But religion also was an organizational weapon that could be used by the lower classes themselves, at least at those moments when movements of resistance were propagated. The chief difference was that religion was an instrument of revolt only for comparatively brief, volatile periods; once settled down to peaceful routine, religious practices were again dominated by elites and contributed to social order and upholding the status quo.

Marx was deeply influenced by the French Revolution, which exemplified for him not only the transition from the feudal mode of economic production to capitalism, but the accompanying transition in the realm of ideology. Religion, as the ideology appropriate to an unemancipated stage of historical development, was therefore doomed by the march of history. This was the position as well of the Young Hegelians in Germany, the circle in which Marx and Engels were initiated in the 1830s; Hegel too had been impressed by the French Revolution which he saw as the historical dialectic nearing its completion.

It is useful to compare the analysis by Alexis de Tocqueville of the same event. In *The Old Régime and the French Revolution* (1856), Tocqueville noted that the Revolution was especially ferocious because it combined two revolutions, political and religious; both kinds of revolutions had happened before (e.g. the Reformation was a religious revolution), but never at the same time. The Revolution was prepared, in Tocqueville's analysis, by the growth of state bureaucracy, which displaced the aristocrats and made them superfluous; they remained a privileged class in outward forms, while bureaucrats wielded real power and bourgeois outpaced them in wealth. The regime prohibited any real political opposition but tolerated and even fostered general and abstract criticism and proposals for reform; intellectuals – *philosophes* like Voltaire – criticized religion as superstition contrary to the advance of reason.

Tocqueville notes that religion was an easy target since it too was part of the medieval establishment now being replaced by royal bureaucrats, while religious authority was irksome in its remaining powers of occasional censorship of intellectual life. The aristocrats were in the lead in anti-religious cynicism; the Marquis de Sade, whose writings published in the 1790s depict sexual depravity as proof of the impotence of God to rule the world, was only the most spectacularly outrageous of many witty lords and ladies of fashion. But after the Revolution abolished the privileges of the aristocracy, this former ruling class made an about-face; Tocqueville notes that this most anti-religious class before the Revolution became the most piously traditionalistic afterwards. When they no longer had any claim to status but their antiquity of descent, religion too became part of their honorific self-presentation.

Tocqueville held that religion was not necessarily outmoded, provided that it was structured in keeping with contemporary social institutions. In America, which he visited during the 1830s, he found that religion was prospering, not as a state-supported Establishment, but as a plethora of local congregations. He found this an analogy in the religious sphere to his argument in the political sphere that government prospers best when there are intermediate groups between the individual and the state authority. Here we have a third alternative to Marx's dominant ideology: not just that religion can support upper class rule or lower class rebellion, but middle class intermediary groups which temper the power of the state and provide participation and self-rule in the torso of the social body.

Nietzsche, writing in the 1870s and 80s, turned the critique of religion in an anthropological and psychological direction. As a classical philologist, expert in the language and culture of ancient Greece, Nietzsche discerned a difference between two kinds of religion. In the classic period the focus was upon what he called the Apollonian gods, idealized nature spirits representing reason, proportion, and control. Behind these were the Dionysian gods, representing emotion, intoxication, and orgiastic ritual practices; these gods were historically older, and had been displaced by the

Apollonians, but they retained their power among the peasantry and made periodic returns in the form of 'Saturnalia' and other popular festivals. Christianity was a development of the Apollonian religion of self-control, which resolutely repressed Dionysian practices. Along with this came a transition in morality. For the classic Greeks, good and bad were not categories of inner spiritual status, but overt descriptions of social standing: aristocrats were good and beautiful, the poor were bad and ugly; good and bad was straightforwardly a matter of winners *vs*. losers, those who were favored by the gods and those who were not. Nietzsche called this the hero-morality of the Greeks. It was displaced by the slave-morality of Christianity. Resentment by the lower classes – especially the slaves – brought a revolution in religion and morality; good no longer meant worldly success but repressing one's sensual desires; self-denial in this life would be compensated by rewards after death, while the worldly dominators would be punished for their sins in Hell.

The Christian morality of self-repression held sway across the Middle Ages, but in the secularizing societies of the late 19th century Nietzsche discerned a prediction of the future: 'God is dead', he declared, looking at the empty formality of contemporary religions; churches are merely tombs and monuments for dead belief. But even the modern secularist, he felt, was still trammeled by Christian morality, with its self-restraint and its emphasis upon sacrificing the individual to the ethical claims of the larger group. Altruistic, do-gooding movements ranging from alcohol prohibitionism to international socialism were all extensions of Christian repression of self in the name of larger ideals. Nietzsche preached instead for a return to Greek morality, a 're-evaluation of all values'. Speculating about the future of biological evolution in a Darwinian vein, Nietzsche foresaw the coming of the *Übermensch* – 'Superman' (literally 'over-man') – who would be completely unrepressed, joyously creative as well as destructive, as Nietzsche envisioned the ancient Dionysian cults.

Nietzsche's construal of the historical path of religions has been criticized as inaccurate by Weber; and Nietzsche's theory of the social sources of morality was replaced by a more adequate theory, applicable to all historical epochs, by Durkheim. We shall meet these below. Nietzsche's chief contribution has been as a pioneer, one of the first to theorize the differences among religions based on ancient and anthropological evidence; and above all, to see there is a genuine sociological question in explaining standards of right and wrong.

Nietzsche's most important successor in the theory of religion was Sigmund Freud. For Freud, religion is a projection of basic psychological components of the human self, the trinity of Ego, Id, and Superego. Ego is the rational consciousness (like Nietzsche's Apollonian gods); Id is the unconscious self, revealed in dreams and neurotic symptoms, a reservoir of primal energies, chiefly composed of sexual lust and violent aggression (in effect, the Dionysian gods). The Superego is also an unconscious part of the self, but it is the opponent and repressor of Id; it contains the ideals of restraint, morality, and punishment for violations. When Superego is in command, the human individual feels guilty not only for sinful actions, but even for illicit thoughts and unconscious wishes. Freud made a rather fanciful historical interpretation of how the earliest humans first established a Superego (by killing the father-ruler of the primal hoard and then feeling guilty about it); but his more important argument is that the Superego is internalized into each child in the process of growing up. The Superego is the father, who represents authority and punishment within the family; the infant begins with Id impulses of seeking erotic pleasure and venting aggression, but is gradually forced to learn self-control; the crucial stage, within the first five years, is when the little boy identifies with his father, internalizing him as one's own Superego. The little girl's pathway is more complex, and neo-Freudians (especially feminists) have theorized about its peculiarities; but in general both sexes end up with a Superego which internalizes parental authority. For Freud, the Superego is the source of religion; the worldly father, internalized, becomes the Heavenly Father.

Freud's chief writing about religion is entitled *The Future of an Illusion*, (1927), the title leaving no doubts as to where he stood. The religious illusion could be cured the same way that neuroses and other psychological problems could be cured, by psychoanalysis. The aim is to expand the scope of the Ego, of conscious self-reflection and deliberate decision, replacing the infantile willfulness of the Id, and the harsh punitiveness of Superego. Through the benefit of psychotherapy, humans will be freed from illusion and repression, while still maintaining a healthy medium of pleasurable impulse and realistic deliberation and control. Has this come about? To some extent, both Nietzsche and Freud are correct in discerning a trend towards lessening repressiveness, in the 20th century and beyond, in both erotic life and violent aggression. But this has not followed strictly from adopting a Dionysian religion or from the spread of psychoanalysis. Freud's own version of psychotherapy, after a vogue of half a century, has been criticized on technical grounds and largely replaced in practice by a variety of non-Freudian therapies. Even so, the trend towards non-repression and permissiveness has occurred among vast numbers of persons who have never had psychotherapy. The source of the trend must be found more widely in other social patterns. And Freud's prediction of the disappearance of religion is only partially accurate; it describes the attitudes and practices of many intellectuals and highly educated liberal professionals, but altogether these make up less than 10% of the population in America (though atheism and irreligion are wider in Europe, Russia and China). Ultimately, the flaw is that religion cannot be explained merely on the level of the psychology of individuals; although psychology provides a component of religious behavior (like all behavior), religion is an eminently social phenomenon which varies by group and historical period. This is true of irreligion as well; the emancipated followers of Marx, Nietzsche, and Freud occur in distinct groups and historical circumstances. Thus we turn to the great comparative sociologists to explain when and where religion (as well as irreligion) exists.

RELIGION AS SOCIAL ORDER
AND MORALITY

Durkheim, writing at the turn of the 20th century, systematized and generalized from work done by his predecessors and contemporaries in the new scholarly fields of comparative religion and anthropology. Much of this work was directed towards the discovery of ancient cult practices. James Frazer, in *The Golden Bough* (1890), noted that besides Olympian gods of ancient Greece and Italy were numerous minor deities and spirits, each connected with local cult practices. These included oracles, agricultural fertility rites, sacrifices, harvest festivals and re-enactments, which leave their remnants even today in Halloween, May Day, and other celebrations. The biblical scholar William Robertson Smith, in *The Religion of the Semites* (1889), argued that the religion of the ancient Hebrews could still be found among the Bedouin tribes of Arabia and Palestine, with their communal meals and animal sacrifices. This work crystallized in what became known as the 'Cambridge School' (Jane Ellen Harrison, F.M. Cornford, and Gilbert Murray) who held that myths should be interpreted not in terms of belief but as justifications of cult practices of the original believers. As R. R. Marrett, one of the members of the Cambridge School, commented, 'primitive religion was not thought out, but danced out'. The same year the Cambridge scholars published their major works, 1912, was also the date of Durkheim's crowning work, *Elementary Forms of Religious Life*. Here Durkheim sets forth a theory of religion as based on rituals, which he generalizes and applies to the social construction of solidarity, symbolism and morality in all types of societies.

Durkheim concentrated on recently published reports on the Aborigines of the central Australian desert; his rationale was to seek the simplest existing society, with no stratification among social classes, no state, and no intellectuals, in order to study the elementary forms of religion in their purest form – and therefore their most theoretically generalizable form. Durkheim first disposes of alternative explanations of the nature of religion, which previous scholars had largely cast in the form of answers to the question of the historical or evolutionary origins of religion. Durkheim shifts the emphasis: the search for origins is historical, whereas Durkheim is analytical; he seeks the principles of the functioning of religion in social life whenever it is found. Previous theories had suggested that religion arises from dreams, which seem to reveal an alternative to the waking world; or from death, which produced dread of what comes after; or again, from awe of nature and its powerful forces like thunder and lightning; or from the experience of miracles or magic which cannot be naturally explained. The problem with all these explanations, Durkheim argues, is that they assume religion is based on a mistake in thinking by primitive people, which modern rational people would not make. But religion cannot be merely a hallucination or a mistake; or else how did it survive so long, and become such a powerful force in human societies? Religion must correspond to something real in human experience, and that experience is at the core of social life.

Durkheim proposes another approach, via comparisons. What do all religions have in common? Not the specific contents of beliefs, nor particular kinds of god or spirit. Religions are too various along these lines, ranging among beliefs in animistic spirits, polytheism, monotheism, Nirvana or other spiritual worlds, etc. The only thing these all have in common is a belief dividing the world into two parts, the sacred and the secular (ordinary, utilitarian, banal). Durkheim now offers a definition of religion: religion is action towards sacred objects; indeed rites or ritual can be considered rules of conduct in the presence of the sacred. The sacred can take many forms: images and ikons; sacred places, buildings, and costumes; holy books, words, songs, dances, and gestures. Sacred objects are both positive and negative, good and evil, god and devil. Both kinds of sacred objects are treated with respect, as powerful and dangerous.

Durkheim now concentrates on the rites and sacred objects of the Australian aborigine clans. The central feature is the totem specific to each clan (for instance a clan may regard the red kangaroo as its totem). This means both the animal itself, as one sees it in the wild, but even more importantly, the totem is an emblem, painted on a rock, or sometimes on a portable device such as a wooden placard or shield. The symbolic nature of the totem is shown by the fact that respect is given to the painted representation, even more than to the animal itself. For it is this emblem, rather than the living animal in the desert, that is at the center of the ceremonies in which the clan gathers and worships.

Durkheim now shows that the tribal totem provides virtually all of the structure and the rules of conduct which make up the social order of the clan. The totem provides, first of all, the name of the clan. We are the red kangaroo people, it is what we call ourselves. It gives us our identity. It becomes an emblem of membership; we know who we are – and who other people are – by seeing what totem they carry or give respect to. Durkheim notes that tribal members may stamp the totem on their goods, to mark them as items of property; or even paint or tattoo it upon their bodies. It is similar to the use of a coat-of-arms among the nobility of the Middle Ages, which also was stamped on the wall of one's home, embroidered on one's flags, shields, and clothes.

The totem also sets forth the basic principles of moral behavior. It is prohibited to kill or eat the totem animal of one's clan. Why? Because it is kin with us; it is our ancestor, our brother. Beneath this belief is a wider prohibition on killing, or harming other members of the clan. We are all red kangaroos, we do not kill or harm each other. The moral prohibition is not universal. Outside us are other clans, the clan of the white cockateel, for example; they can kill the red kangaroo, and indeed they might kill us too. (And we can kill them.) There is no moral prohibition against harming outsiders; it might not be prudent to do so, and it may lead to an act of revenge; but morality extends only up to the boundary of the group. Further widening of the scope of moral injunctions depends upon widening social membership.

Humans have bonds with their totem, and thus with each other. Principles of justice, in a simple society without specialized police agents or judiciary, are essentially religious prescriptions. Punishments for violations are carried out by the community out of their feeling that a spiritual force with which they are usually attuned has gone wrong, and that ritual atonement must be made to set things right. Punishment might occur for acts of utilitarian consequence, such as killing or stealing; but the most serious violations are purely ritual ones, in which the sacred object is not treated with proper respect. To fail to carry out a ritual properly, or to intrude into a ritual where one is not a proper member, is to incite the emotional boundary of the group; it leads to rituals of punishment filled with moral dread.

What is the source of this belief in the sacred realm standing apart from society, and ruling over it? Durkheim's most famous argument is that god represents society. That is to say, whatever the type of sacred object in that particular religion, it represents in symbolic form the group's consciousness of social membership. Durkheim offers a series of parallels between god and society, showing that the latter has all the qualities that people attribute to the former. Society is prior to and outlasts the individual; it was here before we were born, and will be here after we are dead. Society is more powerful than the individual, and is the exemplar of power itself as it affects one's life. Society indeed creates each individual person; quite literally one is born from other people, and they from others in an endless chain. Society establishes moral force over the individual, telling it right from wrong. And society, at its peak moments of interaction, raises the individual out of oneself, endowing one with feelings of inspiration and of contact with something greater than oneself. All the characteristics attributed to god or spiritual beings – eternity, transcendence, omnipotence, creation, moral law, consolation, inspiration and aid – are characteristics of society, projected into a symbolic realm. Thus it is society that awakens the sense of the sacred.

Durkheim goes on to give several kinds of evidence for his argument.

First, the strength of religious sentiments are variable, rising and falling with the presence of group rituals. Religious feeling is a variable which correlates with the strength of consciousness of society. Drawing on the aborigines, Durkheim points out that the tribe goes through phases in time, alternating between dispersion and concentration. Much of the time the clan is split into little groups, wandering in the desert looking for food. During certain times of the year, when food and water are abundant at particular places (the site at which these observations were made is now the town of Alice Springs, in central Australia), the clan begins to gather. As people get closer and the social density goes up, they become more excited. This excitement finally culminates in a grand ceremony carried out together, full of dancing, animated movements and noise-making; Durkheim refers to it as collective effervescence. It is during these gatherings that the group focuses upon its religious emblems; it is simultaneously conscious of its religion and of its social presence.

Since the tribe cannot spend all its time in these gatherings and at a peak of collective effervescence, the sense of society and of religion would fade away if there were no way to remember them. An emblem is necessary to externalize the feeling in a collective representation, and thus to make it enduring. Symbols are devices by which society reminds its members of itself during the time when the group is not assembled, or when the emotional intensity is low. Hence there is need to repeat rituals periodically or else symbols lose their meaning. If people do not take part in its gatherings over a period of time, their belief fades away. Moderately strong commitments are renewed by meeting about once a week, as in the standard weekly religious service. Very intense commitments, as in cults, are kept up by holding ceremonies every day, or more than once a day. Persons who attend once or so per year have only nominal commitment; those who stop attending for a couple of years attenuate their faith to the point where it disappears. The argument is not that frequency of attendance is an indicator of strength of religious commitment, but the other way around: attending is what generates the faith, and lack of participation lets the meanings fade. Martin Luther responded in a similar vein when he was asked by a monk what to do when he felt doubts about his faith; Luther's reply was, 'pray all the more, the faith will come.' Ritual participation creates belief.

Religion thus leads to the social construction of time. Ceremonies become time-markers; it is the repetitive schedule of reassembling the group for particular kinds of rituals that produces a calendar. The only aspects of time which are naturally given are the alternation of day and night, and the seasonal cycle of the year; all the other divisions – hours, days of the week, months, yearly holidays and commemorations, birthdays – are human constructions. All of these initially were markers of times when the group gathered for particular kinds of religious rituals; even the emphasis on hours of the day was given prominence by monks who carried out a daily round of prayers. Durkheim is the great social constructivist; all the basic categories of human experience are laid down by the organization of social gatherings and events. It is because the emotional memory of the strongest of all experiences – the focused arousal of the group – is transient unless it is periodically renewed, that humans have constructed a symbolic scheme of time, as a guide to reassembling in order to repeat their experiences.

Durkheim's second line of argument that god represents society is macro-comparative (whereas his first argument is micro-comparative). The type of god or religious symbol corresponds to the type of social structure. Durkheim launched this analysis already in an earlier work, *The Division of Labor in Society* (1893). Schematically, all societies in human history can be laid out on a continuum in which their division of labor ranges from low to high – to use Talcott Parsons' (1964) terminology, their degree of differentiation. Each pole of the continuum corresponds to its own type of collective conscience, which Durkheim labels respectively, mechanical solidarity and organic solidarity. Where the group structure consists in a small community, tightly bounded to outsiders, and containing few distinctive roles among its members, its law or moral code is punitive and repressive. Virtually all of its law is what we would call criminal law, calling for violent punishments or infliction of bodily pain; these sanctions are strongest and most frequent for violations of ritual prohibitions or taboos, or as sacrifices to rectify the improper carrying out of a ritual. Symbolic violations take priority over merely practical, utilitarian violations. In contrast, where the social structure is complex and differentiated, law swings preponderantly towards restitution and rehabilitation; civil law becomes much larger than criminal law (for evidence, check a law library); symbolic violations are downplayed in favor of restoring the injured party's property or awarding damages. Even criminal law swings toward a sentiment of rehabilitation over punishment; morality shifts towards forgiveness and altruistic hopefulness. All this can be stated in terms of modern social network theory: where the group's network is dense, with many redundant overlapping social ties, the group has a very strong consciousness of itself, as its beliefs and sentiments reverberate throughout the network. This is what Durkheim called mechanical solidarity, an intense state of the collective consciousness; hence symbolic violations are felt with great intensity, and the group responds with a strong repressive emotion. In contrast, where the network structure is diffuse and wide-ranging, individuals have a variety of social ties and remote connections, and the sense of group consciousness is weaker. The chief social sentiment is that of exchange with persons different than oneself (the division of labor); it is this solidarity-with-difference that Durkheim calls organic solidarity. (For an analysis, see Rawls 2003).

Differences in collective consciousness are expressed in religious symbolism. At the mechanical solidarity end of the continuum, the gods or spirits are arbitrary and peremptory; obedience to ritual injunctions is always in full force and punishment for violations is automatic. At the organic solidarity end, god becomes more forgiving, more benevolent; in the complex differentiated networks of modern times, religious injunctions turn into a call for spiritual sympathy and altruism to all people. A parallel development occurs in the realm of religious symbols. In densely connected, isolated communities, religious symbols are particularistic; each little tribe or clan has its own spirit or totem, which is regarded as different from the sacred being of neighboring tribes. It is only one's own group's symbol that is efficacious and binding upon oneself; the landscape may be populated by spirits because there are a variety of peoples out there, but this animism is radically pluralistic. Such symbols are reified, treated literally as if they were things. As social complexity grows and networks become larger and more differentiated, religious symbols change as well; the scope of a god's power expands, and eventually the gods become regarded as not quite literally the way they are depicted. Zeus becomes regarded not so much as the king of the gods ruling on Mt. Olympus, but as the spirit of law and justice. Christianity and other world religions (although they also have particularistic elements) come to treat their god or spiritual principle (such as Buddhist Nirvana or Hindu Atman) as invisible, incorporeal; they occupy a metaphysical plane which is recognized as not to be confused with worldly categories of representation. In short, with the growing differentiation of social structures, religious symbols change from particularistic to abstract, and from reified and literal to reflexive. As Bellah (1964) has argued, religion changes from local and particularistic to universalistic. Durkheim's explanation is that the collective consciousness becomes more generalized and abstract to encompass many differences among social roles.

A caveat is in order here. The reader might have noted above, in the discussion of moral codes shifting from punitive to rehabilitation, that not everyone in modern society goes along with this; there are strong advocates of the death penalty and other punitive law, as well as liberal altruists who go in the other direction. Contemporary sociology (Collins 2004) recognizes that the Durkheimian model applies to the kinds of network structures that persons actually experience, rather than to the overall structure of society. Not everyone in a complex society is necessarily involved in cosmopolitan and long-distance networks; there exist pockets of high social density, little communities of strong believers in their own faith, and here a greater degree of mechanical solidarity prevails.

There is no simple evolution from small isolated dense communities to large interconnected ones; long-term historical change can incorporate many small dense communities within a larger differentiated structure. Hence there can be conflicts within contemporary society between the two kinds of symbolism and their contending moral codes.

Durkheim's model has been tested systematically by Guy Swanson in *The Birth of the Gods* (1962). Using comparisons from the Human Relations Area Files, Swanson shows that the number of levels of social hierarchy correlates with the power and unity of the god. In stateless tribes or clans, in which everyone is of the same social rank, the religion is generally a form of animism; the people are relatively egalitarian and so are the spirits, none taking precedence over another. In societies where an aristocracy exists above the common people, religion takes the form of a high god or gods, literally reigning from their abodes in the sky (or a holy mountain like Olympus). Geopolitics creates polytheism; where there are coalitions among aristocratic states, or shifting conquests of one state by another, the gods of one's enemies and allies become incorporated into a pantheon. Finally, in centralized empires monotheism is favored. Thus Christianity arose within the Roman empire, Buddhism in the Maurya empire in ancient India, Islam in the process of developing a conquest state taking advantage of the stalemate between the Byzantine and Persian empires which weakened both. Max Weber makes a similar analysis: the great world religions arise with the development of regularized long-distance trade, diplomacy and conquest; the seeds of the world religions may precede the actual formation of empires, and their universalism may cause them to proselytize outside their state boundaries; but it is the shift to a world-scale of social connectedness that produces the ecumenical outlook. As Durkheim would put it: as social connections spread out to encompass a sense of a community of human interaction encompassing the entire world, religious symbolism develops into a conception of a god or spiritual entity which encompasses all.

We might add: in the era of global contacts, especially with the increasing frequency of long-distance trade, travel and war in the 19th and 20th centuries, the various world religions have come to confront each other. This produces a paradox of rival monotheisms; each has its geographical sphere of origin and popularity, but each claims by its very nature to be the one true god. Along the lines of Durkheim's theory of collective consciousness, a new meta-level of religious consciousness has arisen. Sometimes referred to as multi-culturalism, it is actually a meta-ethic which enjoins respect for the particularisms of each of the world cultures. The paradox is that this meta-culture is itself a culture with its own network of social adherents, competing with the more particularistic networks and their visions. In Durkheimian terms, history is always a conflict between parts of the world with more universalistic consciousness and those with more particularistic consciousness.

A third line of argument for Durkheim's proposition that god reflects society is the formulation of a general theory of ritual. Durkheim developed his theory of ritual with respect to Australian aborigines, although he was clear that the general principles applied to rituals of other religions, and even of secular life. He pointed, for instance, to the flag of the regiment that soldiers in combat would die to protect. The general applicability of a theory of rituals provides a means to test Durkheim's propositions with new levels of evidence, showing how the ingredients of social rituals, when put together in requisite combinations and intensities, lead to the kinds of outcomes Durkheim specified. I have formalized Durkheim's model in *Interaction Ritual Chains* (Collins 2004).

There are four main ingredients for a successful ritual: 1. bodily co-presence: persons assemble in the same place. Religious rituals require assembling the congregation; although rituals can be broadcast through the media, this is never as satisfactory as actually attending, and there must always be at least some group present. ('For when two or three are gathered together in my name, there am I in the midst of them.' Matthew 18:20). Bodily co-presence is crucial because this is what makes possible the feedback of emotion and signs of bodily micro-attention (detailed in another context by Goffman 1963) which produce a heightened sense of the social.

2. Barrier to outsiders: the walls of the church or chapel mark a sacred space which differentiates what goes on inside from the mundane activities outside. The barrier facilitates group focus and gives a clear marking of its boundaries and hence of its identity.

3. A mutual focus of attention: individuals focus upon the same thing or action, and become mutually aware that each other is so focusing. This is the crucial step which creates a strong sense of shared consciousness or intersubjectivity; the nouns here are misleading, since these are not things but processes, contingent ongoing accomplishments enacted over a period of time to just the extent that the mutual awareness of common focus is sustained. The kinds of things that can be focused upon vary enormously; and although particular religious groups have their habitual ways of focusing, the key is not their distinctive objects, but rather the process. The common terms 'ritual' or 'ritualistic' sometimes have a pejorative sense of mindless, stereotyped actions; this comes from the sense that particular rituals generally have fixed formulas, traditional actions that are always repeated. But the stereotyping is merely an aid; the crucial thing is that everyone performs the same thing at the same time, focuses their attention in the same direction, and is aware that others are so focusing.

4. A shared emotional mood: a ritual takes place with an emotional tone held throughout the congregation. This may be reverence or awe in the presence of the sacred objects, or the seriousness and silence which falls over the group. But the content of the emotion can vary widely; it can be sorrow at a funeral, righteous anger at a violator or enemy, joy at a triumph. In every case, the ritual works if the emotion is shared widely.

It should be noted that rituals vary also in their success or failure. The ingredients can be stronger or weaker; some of them may be totally absent. Such conditions can make rituals fail, or at best give a pallid sense of group consciousness. The variability of rituals and their outcomes thus provides evidence of the workings of Durkheim's model. The most crucial ingredients are numbers 3 and 4; a successful ritual is one in which there is a strong mutual focus of attention and a strong collective mood; thus I have suggested an alternative name for ritual theory would be 'the mutual focus / emotional entrainment model.'

Once the ingredients are present, the ritual builds up intensity. There is feedback through rhythmic entrainment: micro-sociological observations show that in successful rituals bodies become aligned and coordinated in great detail; people feel unity because they are caught up in the same rhythm. Mutual focus and emotional intensity feed back into each other; the stronger the emotions the greater the magnetic pull of collective focus, and vice versa. These are the details of what Durkheim referred to as collective effervescence.

If the ritual is successful, four kinds of outcomes follow:

(a) group solidarity: participants feel themselves members of a group and committed to its identity;

(b) symbols representing membership. These are the sacred objects. Whatever the group focuses upon becomes an emblem of the group. Symbols which already exist (the cross, the Bible, the Koran, etc.) are resuscitated and filled again with meaning;

(c) emotional energy. The individual who takes part in a successful ritual feels uplifted, more confident in oneself, stronger. This is one of the great attractions of religion for individuals; it is why persons in periods of stress (such as wartime) or in moments of concentration and struggle (such as an athlete entering a game) often use religious rituals like praying or crossing oneself. Durkheim notes that this feeling of emotional energy is an apportionment of the heightened energy of the group in its ritual assembly. He uses the Polynesian term *mana* for this collective emotion. We might note that rituals throughout are emotional transformers: starting with a shared emotion as a necessary ingredient; ramping up the emotion through collective effervescence; and ending with feelings of solidarity in the group and a portion of that in individuals as their own inner strength;

(d) moral standards of right and wrong: rituals create the basic standards of morality. Foremost is respect for the symbols of the group; the worst possible sin is an offense against the god or its representations. And since symbols represent group membership, morality also enjoins solidarity with one's fellow members.

Since ritual effects dissipate over time, people who are already attached to a group feel the need to repeat its rituals periodically. This is not merely a functionalist argument; groups may benefit from having rituals, but they do not always carry them out, and some groups lose solidarity or even fade away. The feedback link that keeps the rituals continuing is that individuals who experience the emotional energy and the respect for its symbols carry a device for motivating themselves to reassemble to repeat the ritual. Symbols are also reminders of group solidarity when the individual is back in ordinary life or alone. Hence one can use a religious symbol (a cross, a Bible, rosary beads) to carry out private rituals. Rituals are not always public, but they are always social, in the sense that private rituals derive from collective rituals. Even a religion of lonely inward meditators, such as certain branches of Hinduism and Buddhism, has a group organization in which individuals are initiated into how to mediate, and in the sacred meanings of meditation. Zen monks, for instance, may meditate in a state of inwardness, but they generally do this together in a meditation hall; they may turn their faces to the wall and away from the others, but there is an atmosphere of group consciousness; it is a great aid to individual concentration when others are concentrating around you.

It is appropriate to end this section on Durkheimian theory with a quotation from Durkheim himself; although his group of scholars contributed mightily to his work, and they themselves were well aware that it was a collective enterprise, they referred to Durkheim as the great 'tabou-totem' of their group (Collins 2005):

> … the real function of the cult is to awaken within the worshippers a certain state of soul, composed of moral force and confidence … The essential thing is that men are assembled, that sentiments are felt in common and expressed in common acts; but the particular nature of these sentiments and acts is something relatively secondary and contingent. To become conscious of itself… the necessary thing is that (the group) partakes of the same thought and the same action… Before all, rites are the means by which the social group reaffirms itself periodically… (Tribal rituals) translate and maintain a sentiment of pride, confidence, and veneration wholly comparable to that expressed by the worshippers in the most idealistic religions when, being assembled, they proclaim themselves the children of the almighty God… This sentiment is made up of the same impressions of security and respect which are awakened in the individual consciousness by this great moral force which dominates and sustains them, and which is the collective force (*Elementary Forms*, book 4, chapter 4) (1912/1964: 431–2).

RELIGION AS ORGANIZATION AND CARRIER GROUP

The third major approach to sociology of religion is exemplified by Max Weber. Weber is known above all for the 'Weber thesis', but his work is wider than this; and his importance for the theory of religion comes largely from the latter part. We may in fact discern two Weber theses discussed in reverse order:

Weber Thesis I. (1904–1905) *The Protestant Ethic and the Spirit of Capitalism.* Weber Thesis II. (1915–1920): a comparative sociology of world religions as determining the trajectory of each major part of world.

The latter thesis encompasses three works published in German and translated into English under the titles *The Religion of China*; (originally *The Economic Ethics of the World Religions: Confucianism and Taoism*, 1916); *The Religion of India*; (originally *Hinduism and Buddhism*, 1916–1917); and *Ancient Judaism*; (1917–1919). Weber also planned but died before he could write the remainder of the sequence, comprising books on Islam, early Christianity, and medieval Catholicism. We might note that the *Protestant Ethic*, the first written, would thus come at the end of Weber's comparative sequence; had he lived that long, doubtless he would have considerably modified some of its arguments.

In addition to these comparative studies of the world religions, Weber set forth his systematic theory in the work translated as *The Sociology of Religion* (a long chapter in *Economy and Society*, posthumously published in 1922); and in a chapter which he wrote to introduce his collection of comparative studies, which in English was titled 'Social Psychology of the World Religions' (in the famous Gerth and Mills reader *From Max Weber,* 1946). Its original title was 'Economic Ethics of World Religions', and this gives us a clue to Weber's guiding interest. He was concerned above all with the origins of modern capitalism; and his Protestant Ethic study had given him the idea that religions provided the key, both in the direction of capitalism, and against it. Weber defines an economic ethic as 'the practical impulses for action which are founded in the psychological and pragmatic contexts of religion' (Gerth and Mills 1946: 267). Specifically, he means the impulses for economic action; but in fact his studies commented widely on the political, military, artistic and other kinds of action which also flow from religion.

We should note that Weber's primary concern is with the world religions: those of large size and geographical spread. These are also world religions in the sense that in principle they are open to everybody, as religions of universal recruitment. This is one meaning of universalistic religion, in Parsons' sense; they are universal not only in their symbolism, but in their organization; they are all missionary or proselytizing religions, since they motivate their followers to bring their salvation to all the world. Hence they are monotheisms or equivalent (such as Buddhism, which is atheistic at the highest level of some of its ontologies). World religions stand in contrast to tribal religions and to polytheisms on just these points. Weber is a comparative medievalist; it is in the medieval period of each part of the world, after its breakthrough into a world religion and a cosmopolitan large-scale political and economic structure, that the pathways into the future are laid down.

Each religion has a primary carrier group, 'the strata whose styles of life have been at least predominantly decisive for certain religions' (Gerth and Mills 1946: 268). This means that these are *status groups*, in Weber's terminology, with a distinctive lifestyle and social prestige. In contrast to economic classes, they are not mere statistical categories of persons with a particular relationship to property, but an associational community – people who actually associate together, and tend to exclude others who lack the same status. At the most intimate level, status groups are held together by *commercium* – commensality among sets of persons who visit each others homes and eat together at the same table, and *connubium* – intermarriage. Weber comments that these are markers of status in everydaylife: 'their absence signifies status differences' (Gerth and Mills 1946: 300–1). The most extreme of such status groups are Brahmins in the Indian caste system; their demand for absolute ritual purity has the effect that they will not eat with anyone other than those who carry out the same rituals, members of their own caste. Jewish kosher practices, similarly, were another extreme example of religiously based *commercium*; in this case these were practices instituted during the disaspora, which ensured that the Jewish community would remain together after it had lost its state temple in Jerusalem.

Weber's analysis hinges on the status group whose lifestyle is most strongly representative of the religion; or to put it another way, the status group is often formed out of persons who become committed to the religious practices to a degree that they become standards for the conduct of their entire lives. This gives them a culture and a lifestyle, and also sets of level of prestige in the surrounding society. Weber comments that honor can be positive or negative. The former makes others look up to that status group, and thus through the emulation they receive they can be widely influential in setting the tone of the entire society. The prestige of the Brahmins in India became so great that other groups imitated them by establishing their own prohibitions on social intercourse with others lower than themselves; in this way the caste system spread downwards through society, formulating barriers not only among the four main castes but elaborating numerous sub-castes, each making its own claim for status against those near them. Negative status honor defines a group which is shunned by all, or segregated into a ghetto; Weber calls them 'pariah groups', examples of which have been the Jews in medieval Europe, Parsees in India, gypsies and others. Such pariah groups nevertheless on occasion have played important roles in economic life, since standing outside of normal social rules they may carry out tasks ordinary persons are prohibited from; e.g. in medieval Europe Jews were moneylenders and in that capacity were often protected by kings.

Following, then, is an epitome of each of the world religions, in terms of the status group or carrier that is its most distinctive representative:

Confucianism is 'the status ethic of the prebendaries', i.e. the scholar-officials who staffed the bureaucracy of the Chinese empire. More exactly, Confucians were the status group of men educated in the ancient texts and their commentaries, especially in the orthodox lineage going back to Confucius. They were not always in office; in part because sometimes the empire was too fragmented to have a bureaucracy, or was controlled by alien ethnic conquerors who sometimes favored their own aristocrats, or appointed Taoists or even Buddhists. But the Confucian *ju* (to give them their Chinese name) were keepers of the texts and upholders of a distinctive way of life; whether they were in or out of office, they were always prepared to take office, or studying for the imperial examinations which grew up in the later dynasties. Their prime doctrine is that good social order depends upon correctly carrying out of rituals; in this respect they were like Durkheimians, and even put ritual ahead of belief. Confucius is reputed to have said, 'respect the gods and keep them at a distance,' meaning that one should perform the rituals for traditional gods, but merely a social good form; the gentleman does not become carried away with spiritual belief, which Confucians deemed characteristic of the lower classes. The Confucian lifestyle emphasized the formal side of religion almost to the exclusion of all else; Confucians often had an almost secular outlook,

in which religion was regarded as good for the well-regulated state, but not a matter of belief for the literary elite themselves.

Early Hinduism was organized around the Brahmins educated in the Vedas, the techniques of carrying out rituals. Initially they are an occupational group of priests, 'ritualistic and spiritual advisors' to communities. It was this monopoly over ritual practice that the Brahmins elaborated into dominance within the caste system.

Later, in the period around 400 BCE – AD 200, non-Brahmin ascetics competed with them over religious primacy. The most successful of these ascetics were the Buddhists, but there were other orders such as the Jainas (known for their extreme doctrine of non-harming any form of life), as well as freelance *shramanas* who performed feats of self-abnegation and meditation, demonstrating their apartness from the material concerns of everyday life. These ascetics formed their own status groups, and acquired so much social prestige that the traditional Brahmins eventually began to emulate them, establishing their own ascetic practices while nevertheless holding on to their practice of ritual.

In late medieval India came another innovation, popular religious movements which incorporated those who had been excluded by the elite purity of the Brahmins and the ascetic world-renunciation of the monks. Weber calls these movements the 'ardent sacramental religiosity of the savior, borne by lower strata with their plebian mystagogues'.

Buddhism centered on contemplative, mendicant monks who rejected the world; 'only these were full members of the religious community; all others remained religious laymen of inferior value'. Buddhism thus is a religion concentrated in monasteries, and it was this form of organization, even more than its doctrine and ritual practice, that had its strongest effects upon societies. Buddhism was one of the early movements to challenge the Brahmins in India; it dominated many of the major states of India until around the seventh century, when it eventually began to be displaced; meanwhile it spread to south-east Asia, as well as northward to Tibet, China, Korea, and Japan. In some of these places it allied with native aristocrats to establish theocracy (Tibet);

or fought over precedence with Confucians (China, Korea); its greatest influence was perhaps in Japan, where the Buddhist monasteries dominated the late Middle Ages as the strongest military units, as well as the centers of economic growth. One can argue, extending Weber, that the status ethic of the Buddhists, together with their organizational form, was so important in Japan that it prepared the way for the most successful takeoff into Asian capitalism independently of Europe (Bellah 1957; Collins 1997).

Early Islam was carried by world-conquering warriors who launched the religion by 100 years of conquest around the Mediterranean and the Middle East. Medieval Islam brought a new status group within settled urban life: mystical Sufism 'under leadership of plebian technicians of orgiastics'; these created brotherhoods of petty bourgeois craftsmen, which made religious faith a marker for the ordinary middle-class person. In both these forms, it should be noted, Islamic religiosity is carried by ordinary laymen (the gender here is deliberate), not by specialized priests or withdrawn monks. Islam is thus a practice for everyday life, with a popularistic orientation rather than respect for hierarchy. This is one of the features that has kept Islamic states from enjoying a high level of legitimacy in their own right; and it also helps explain the moral and political fervor of Islamic activists down to our times.

Diaspora Judaism is the 'religion of civic pariah people' in the sense explained above; 'civic' here means the preference for living in cities, even at a time when most societies were overwhelmingly agricultural. In medieval times came the dominance of rabbi intellectuals; somewhat like Islam, the leaders of the religion were not priests, but simply learned men who acquired respect in their community by their knowledge of the scriptures; 'rabbi' simply means 'teacher'. Again like Islam, these learned men acted as judges as well as advisors; they constituted the courts of law in their communities, even though they had no state power and would rely on others to enforce their verdicts. Rabbis were the carrier group of Judaism during the long centuries when it no longer had a homeland nor a temple with its high priests. One long-term consequence has been the high respect for learning in the Jewish community;

this carried over into the secular era of the 19th and 20th centuries, where Jews became prominent both in ideologically oriented social and political movements (such as Marxism), and in the educated professions and intellectual life.

Christianity began as a religion of itinerant artisan journeymen. Weber finds it characteristic that Jesus was a carpenter, a skilled tradesman in his day who recruited his followers from others of the same quasi-commercial social class. During the Middle Ages, Christianity became dominated by monks; their monastic organization, operating outside the bounds of family and kinship, had a special advantage in settling land and setting up pockets of literate administration in northern Europe, and hence monasteries were favored by kings extending their rule. In the later Middle Ages (a point that Weber did not live to elaborate; see Southern 1970; 'The Weberian Revolution of the High Middle Ages' in Collins 1986), the church built up a large bureaucracy of priests and bishops, with a legal and administrative system centered on the Pope. This displaced the monks from being the central carrier group (and opened the way for them to be eliminated by the Reformation). One might argue, in Weber's way, that the chief carrier group of late medieval Catholicism became its Papal bureaucrats.

The Protestant Reformation, in one aspect, was the downsizing of the Papal bureaucracy to the various national kingdoms; for instance the Church of England, or the various Lutheran churches in Germany and Scandinavia, maintained much of the centralized administrative structure and the rituals of the Catholics, but transferred authority to the local prince. The more radical, and in Weber's view more socially consequential churches of the Protestant Reformation, were the sects of pietism and methodism. These split radically from priest-centered and ritualistic religion, to emphasize the priesthood of all believers and the necessity of strict guidance by religious principles in one's work. Here we come full circle, to Weber Thesis I. Having made the journey around the world on the vehicle of comparative religions, we can see that Weber regarded radical Protestants as having a chief carrier group too: the pious businessman.

We may sum up Weber's emphasis upon the social effects of religion by his famous statement of importance of world images for action: 'Not ideas, but material and ideal interests, directly govern men's conduct. Yet very frequently the world images that have been created by ideas have, like switchmen, determined the tracks along which action has been pushed by the dynamics of interests. From what, and for what, one wanted to be redeemed (i.e. salvation)… depended upon one's image of the world' (Gerth and Mills 1946: 280).

Weber provides a wealth of analytical devices for understanding the many facets of religions and the way in which they mesh with the larger system of stratification, economy, politics and everything else. He remains our great classic sociologist of religion (and indeed of everything else) because he knew more about world history than almost anyone, and at the same time managed to structure it through insightful theoretical categories. Since Weber wrote almost 100 years ago scholars have learned a great deal more about world history, and the deficiencies of some of Weber's works have been exposed (I would say, especially in regard to the social and economic histories of China, Korea and Japan). Nevertheless, we still lack a more recent scholar with Weber's synthesizing accomplishments, and the theoretical tools he developed remain basic to our work as comparative sociologists, even as we apply them to new materials. In this spirit, I will close by offering a sketch of one of Weber's most significant pieces of intellectual chart-making. This is his typology of paths to salvation, which nicely lays out the main forms of religious action and organization. (It is found in *The Sociology of Religion*, Chapters 10–12.) It should be noted that these are ideal types: that is to say, they are pure forms, oversimplifications of what is usually found in historical reality. Nevertheless ideal types are important for theory; like chemical elements, they are the basic processes which may be combined to produce more elaborate mixtures.

There are four main paths to salvation: magic; ceremony; asceticism; and mysticism. The last two in turn subdivide into inner-worldly and other-worldly branches.

Magic may be regarded as a zero-order concern for salvation. Magic is the use of religious forces for worldly ends: to cure an illness, save a life, ease a childbirth, make crops grow, win a battle, kill an enemy. Magic is not ethical; it is merely a technical means to an end. The ends are worldly, not transcendent. Magic lacks organization, but consists of individual practitioners. Magic is embedded in everyday life; its effects on conduct are to reinforce a worldly orientation. Magic is characteristic of tribal and ancient religions; it survives at the margins of the world religions, viewed with varying degrees of sympathy or suspicion by the devout. Magical religion lacks leverage to change the world; neither in motivation, nor in goals, nor in forms of organization does it do anything to promote social change or restructure society. Weber considers it significant that one of the historically transformative world religions, Judaism, developed a strong antagonism to magic. This is one of the things that made it a seedbed for social developments.

Ceremonial religion places emphasis upon ritual; salvation is accomplished by partaking of the proper sacraments. Thus it is the Durkheimian religion par excellence. Its chief form of organization is the priest and his followers, in a downward direction, and in an upward direction the hierarchy of the church going up to its supreme pontiff (in Catholicism, the Pope, who is the channel of sacramental salvation). The main social effect of ceremonial religion is to maintain the group (as Durkheim would say), and (a more Weberian note) the stratification within the church. There is a double layer of stratification: the priest is above the ordinary congregation; some are religiously more worthy than others. And among the laity, there is stratification in terms of piety: those who are assiduous in their attendance and participation in ceremonies; some may even build up additional merit by pilgrimages, contact with holy objects, fasts and other practices of correct ritual attitude. The pious are stratified above those of lesser piety. Weber holds that the main social effect of ceremonial religion is to maintain the status quo; this is the type of religion favored by conservatives. Confucianism, whose main doctrine is the necessity for correct ceremonies, is the leading example. In modern society as well, Weber predicts that the most ceremonial religions are those favored by the upper classes (such as Episcopalianism in the US), and are least oriented to social change. In contrast, magic-oriented religions are most common in the lower class, where they practice faith-healing and hold out provisions for material success. The difference in social class is one reason that upper-class ceremonial religions may look down on magical religion.

Asceticism comes in two varieties, other-worldly and inner-worldly. Other-worldly means oriented towards the other world, towards transcendence of ordinary reality. Ascetics mortify the body in search of salvation; they give up sex, family life, good food, clothes (sometimes to the extent of living naked, as among some Indian sects), all property and possessions; they may go further and practice austerities such as kneeling or standing in uncomfortable positions for long periods of time, or even self-torture such as flagellation, crowns of thorns or beds of nails. Not all ascetics go to these extremes; Buddhism called itself the middle path, because it was between the extremes of self-torture and worldly life; it practiced a moderate asceticism of withdrawal from the world, while concentrating on meditation as the path to salvation. (More on this below, under Mysticism.)

Organizationally, asceticism can take the form of living in monasteries, practicing asceticism together in a group; this is especially characteristic of Christian (and after the Reformation, Catholic) monasteries. Or ascetics could live alone as holy beggars, receiving alms from pious folk who believe there is religious merit in their offerings. Weber regards asceticism as a pathway which harnesses enormous energy for the religious life. It creates tremendous tension with the ordinary world, by the negative path (a term also used by Durkheim to describe asceticism) of rejecting worldly concerns and pleasures, and indeed putting as much distance between oneself and them as possible. But as long as ascetics remain apart from the world, sequestered in monasteries or making social contact only through begging, this tension has no larger effects. Indeed, Weber regarded it as siphoning religious motivation into a channel where the most religious persons are withdrawn from ordinary life, leaving the normal world to persons who have little or no religious orientation.

Inner-worldly asceticism, on the other hand, harnesses this energy. By 'inner-worldly' Weber means in-the-world (the term is ambiguous because in English it might also be taken to mean an inner world, inside the self, but this is the opposite of Weber's meaning). The inner-worldly ascetic is the person who maintains self-control from religious motives, but who nevertheless keeps up their usual work and family. Asceticism is like a bowstring being drawn back; the greater the tension of the pull, the more power in the trajectory of the arrow when it is released. Weber sees the ascetic religions, above all medieval Catholic monasticism as pulling the bow to a high tension point. The Reformation is the releasing of the bow. Luther's most significant act, Weber held, was abolishing the monasteries. Henceforward persons who wanted to be especially holy would have to do it in ordinary life; everyone would have to become a monk. It was this inner-worldly asceticism that was expressed in the most radical Protestant sects, and which became the motivation for the development of modern capitalism.

We should add that inner-worldly ascetics have transformed not only the economic world, but to a considerable extent the political. Although Weber did not develop this point very far, ascetics in politics are quite common in radical movements; they are puritanical about themselves and often impose their puritanical controls on others if they are successful. The militant political reformers are like monk-soldiers of the Middle Ages; in more recent centuries they appear shorn of their overtly religious motivations. In the English Revolution of the 1640s, though, the Puritan cause was more visible in politics than in economics, in the short-lived effort to establish a Commonwealth of the religiously righteous (Walzer 1970). Gorski (2001) describes how similar revolutions of ascetic Protestantism transformed politics into disciplinary states in the Netherlands and Prussia.

To avoid misunderstanding, a further note is needed about Weber's types of capitalism.

Weber was well aware that merchants, trade, and money-making were activities found in many societies from ancient Mesopotamia onwards. But this is not the kind of capitalism which transformed the modern world. The key is not merely profit-making, an orientation towards making money in the market. This motivation has existed since ancient times throughout the world, in several varieties of non-modern capitalism which Weber refers to as traditional capitalism (in which habitual methods are used over again without innovation); or as robber-booty capitalism (a mixture of piracy, trading, and sharp-dealing); or political capitalism (using state franchises, grants and contracts as protected ways of making money). In contrast, what Weber calls modern capitalism or rationalized capitalism is characterized by the systematic application of calculation to business enterprise, and by the ascetic orientation. The rational modern capitalist does not merely make profits; he plans for the future, plows back his earnings into further expansion. He has a drive to transform the world – similar to the quest for salvation but aimed at the material sphere; hence he constantly experiments with new forms of organization, new technologies of production and distribution. The modern capitalist entrepreneur thus sets up the drive towards constantly renewed innovation that distinguishes modern capitalist markets from traditional markets. Modern capitalism does not merely engage in the quantitative expansion of trade (hence arguments that China had a higher volume of trade than the West are beside the point), but in self-sustaining capitalist growth. It is this that is the inheritance of religion in launching modern capitalism; more specifically, the transformative effect of inner-worldly capitalism.

As is true with everything in Weber, there is even more to it than these elements; the modern rational capitalist is an entrepreneur in the Schumpeterian sense, who comes into existence only where there is a social structure which allows all the factors of production – land, labor, capital – to move freely in a competitive market, and where property rights are guaranteed by favorable political institutions. Many of the pathways to these prerequisites to modern

capitalist enterprise are only distantly related to religious causes, if at all; so I will say no more about them here (for elaboration, see 'Weber's Last Theory of Capitalism' in Collins 1986).

This is the culmination of Weber's argument, and of his lifework, where Weber Thesis II meets Weber Thesis I. To go on after this may seem anticlimactic, but we still have one more path to salvation to consider: mysticism. *Mysticism* is the most direct pathway to salvation. The mystic uses techniques such as meditation or concentrated prayer so as to achieve immediate experience of the Divine. One does not have to die to go to Heaven; mystics reach the experience in their own lives. At least such is the aim; by all accounts, it is not an easy path to achieve. Mysticism is often confused with asceticism; and in actual instances the two may overlap. Mystics are usually ascetics of some degree (though often mild ones), and ascetics sometimes attempt to achieve mystical experience by ascetic means. The organizational forms are also similar; ascetics generally live either as isolated hermits or as residents of monasteries. In Weber's typology, most mystics are other-worldly mystics; they attempt to transcend the ordinary world, and may regard as it merely a veil of illusion, which will be pulled aside when one comes to experience Nirvana, Atman, or the great Wordless conceptual reality. Mystics, like ascetics are in tension with the world, and also siphon off religious motivation from economic and political activities. They bend the bow, but they never release it into social change. And Weber would say they do not bend the bow as tight as the ascetics do; it is the releasing of the ascetic tension that is the pathway to modernity.

But there is an inner-worldly version of mysticism: mysticism as practice-in-the-world rather than withdrawing to a monastery or hermitage. Weber does not elaborate much on this variant of mysticism, noting the tendency to quietism in western mystics who live in the world. Nevertheless, Weber noted (*The Sociology of Religion*, p. 176) that 'the core of the mystical concept of the oriental Christian church was a firm conviction that Christian brotherly love ... must necessarily lead to unity in all things.' Thus authority could be dispensed with, since everyone is filled with the same spirit. The mystical element in Quakerism made them resistant to all authority, both within the church and in the state. Extending this analysis further than Weber's own remarks, we may note that in the political realm, inner-worldly mystics have a tendency towards promoting altruistic movements; because they see the divine everywhere, they can see it in all other human beings. Thus may arise a kind of gentle reformism, an altruistic sympathy for the poor and downtrodden of the world. St. Francis was an early example of a mystic who took the path to worldly activism, setting off a movement of religious men and women living among the poor; the Franciscans in this respect are the forerunners of modern leftist social movements. (At any rate movements of a particular kind of inner-worldly ascetic leftism, to be distinguished from the harsher, more tension-driven kind of political radicals who aim to transform the world by seizing state power.) We may remind ourselves that the reformist movements of 19th century America such as the anti-slavery movement based in New England came out of the same circles as the Transcendentalists, who were a branch of liberal Protestantism advocating a kind of gentle pantheistic nature-mysticism. (A good exemplar of this mysticism as applied to human beings is the poetry of Walt Whitman.) And in the 20th century as well, periodic eruptions of mystical movements, like the 'flower children' of the 1960s, revived the outlook and social practices of inner-worldly mystics.

One other influence of inner-worldly mysticism that Weber mentions is aesthetics. Mystics in everyday life are prone to see the spiritual aspect of their surroundings, and to put it into poetry or painting. These were favorite practices of Taoists during the middle dynasties of China; at least among the gentry (there were also lower-class Taoists purveying magical amulets to the peasantry) aesthetics was regarded as spiritual action, gently and quietly getting into the Tao, the unspoken Way which lies behind all things and which is best expressed outside of expository language. In other societies as well, there have been inner-worldly mystics devoted to the aesthetic lifestyle.

Among the lessons of Weber's typology is that these orientations can exist among various groups even in modern secular times. We still find practitioners and customers of magic; there are still religious ceremonialists (although their prestige has fallen relative to more fervent or activist churches). It is chiefly the other-worldly forms of religion that have faded away; it is hard to find ascetics or cloistered mystics today. But the inner-worldly versions of asceticism and mysticism still exist: in business, in politics (where indeed they tend to dominate the political landscape, especially among the more dedicated or extremist movements), and in the aesthetics of private life.

I will end on a note about Weber personally. He is most famous for his analysis of ascetic Protestants; but he himself was not one of them. He was impressed by their historical achievements, but he did not like them. He saw them as hard, cold, calculating people, with their eyes on a distant horizon and running over all obstacles including the human beings before them. Weber rarely expresses his personal preferences in his writings, but one can see his style brighten up when he comes to the mystical worldview (see *Religion of India*, pp. 133, 177, 190–1). He himself had no calling for mysticism; indeed he said that in all things he was 'religiously unmusical'. But where religion touches a chord in him it is in the form of the political altruism and everyday sensitivity of the inner-worldly mystics. These are indeed the antidotes to the toughness of the inner-worldly ascetics. One can conjecture that in Weber's view, modern life would be unbearable unless one were balanced by the other.

CONCLUSION

The movements of scholarship emanating from Durkheim and Weber have made up a considerable portion of the sociology of the religion from their days until ours. In that sense the classical traditions are still very much alive, although developed in significant new directions. In this chapter I have not treated all the scholars who have had major influence, and many of them could also be honored with the epithet 'classic'. The Durkheimian school was particularly rich in innovative developers, such as the work of Marcel Mauss and Henri Hubert on magic, and on sacrifice. Talcott Parsons and his student Robert Bellah made influential syntheses and applications of both Durkheimian and Weberian traditions. Going further back, we could add Ernst Troeltsch and his writings on the social teachings of the Christian churches; but Troeltsch was closely allied with Weber, and even lived for a while in his house in Heidelberg. Even some of the radical new departures in the sociology of religion in the late 20th century, such as the religious market theory of Rodney Stark and colleagues, have an element of Weber, insofar as they consider religion as providing supernatural compensators for the ills of the social world. And although the classic sociologists were all inclined to the view that modern society was secularizing away from religion, the renewed debate over secularization in recent decades is foreshadowed in some respects by classic themes; Durkheimians in particular see religion-like processes at the core of social life, and thus unlikely to disappear.

Sociological research of course moves onward, and new discoveries are always to be admired. Yet the classic traditions have established a solid base from which to grow.

REFERENCES

Bellah, Robert N. 1957. *Tokugawa Religion*. NY: Free Press.

Bellah, Robert N. 1964. 'Religious Evolution.' *American Sociological Review* 29: 358–74.

Collins, Randall 1986. *Weberian Sociological Theory*. Cambridge and New York: Cambridge University Press.

Collins, Randall 1997. 'An Asian route to capitalism: Religious economy and the origins of self-transforming growth in Japan.' *American Sociological Review* 62 (Dec.): 843–65.

Collins, Randall 1998. *The Sociology of Philosophies*. Cambridge: Harvard University Press.

Collins, Randall 2004. *Interaction Ritual Chains*. Princeton University Press.

Collins, Randall 2005. 'The Durkheimian Movement in France and in world sociology.' In Jeffrey Alexander and Phil Smith (eds). *The Cambridge Companion to Durkheim*. Cambridge: Cambridge Univ. Press.

Durkheim, Emile 1893/1964. *The Division of Labor in Society*. New York: Free Press.

Durkheim, Emile 1912/1964. *The Elementary Forms of Religious Life*. New York: Free Press.

Frazer, Sir James 1890/1936. *The Golden Bough*. New York: St. Martin's Press.

Freud, Sigmund 1927/1975. *The Future of an Illusion*. New York: W. W. Norton.

Gerth, H. H. and C. Wright Mills (eds) 1946. *From Max Weber: Essays in Sociology*. NY: Oxford Univ. Press.

Goffman, Erving 1963. *Behavior in Public Places. Notes on the Social Organization of Gatherings*. New York: Free Press.

Gorski, Philip S. 2000. 'Historicizing the secularization debate: church, state and society in late medieval and early modern Europe.' *American Sociological Review* 65: 138–68.

Gorski, Philip S. 2001. *The Disciplinary Revolution. Calvinism and the Rise of the State in Early Modern Europe*. Berkeley: Univ. of California Press.

Marx, Karl and Friedrich Engels 1846/1970. *The German Ideology*. New York: International Publishers.

Parsons, Talcott 1964. 'Evolutionary universals in society.' In Parsons, *Sociological Theory and Modern Society*. New York: Free Press.

Rawls, Ann Warfield 2003. 'Orders of interaction and intelligibility: interaction between Goffman and Garfinkel by way of Durkheim.' In A. Javier Trevino (ed.), *Goffman's Legacy*. Boulder, CO: Rowman and Littlefield.

Southern, R. W. 1970. *Western Society and the Church in the Middle Ages*. Harmonsworth: Penguin.

Swanson, Guy E. 1962. *The Birth of the Gods*. University of Michigan Press.

Tocqueville, Alexis de 1856/1983. *The Old Régime and the French Revolution*. NY: Random House.

Walzer, Michael. 1970. *The Revolution of the Saints*. NY: Athenaeum.

Weber, Max. 1904–5/1998. *The Protestant Ethic and the Spirit of Capitalism*. Los Angeles: Roxbury.

Weber, Max. 1906. 'The Protestant Sects and the Spirit of Capitalism.' In Gerth and Mills 1946.

Weber, Max. 1917/1958. *The Religion of India*. New York: Free Press.

Weber, Max. 1922/1991. *The Sociology of Religion*. Boston: Beacon Press.

Wuthnow, Robert. 1989. *Communities of Discourse: Ideology and Social Structure in the Reformation, the Enlightenment, and European Socialism*. Cambridge: Harvard University Press.

2

Assessing Modernities:
From 'Pre-' to 'Post-' to 'Ultra-'

KEVIN J. CHRISTIANO

For more than a century, or for as long as sociology has existed as a defined discipline, its theorists and practitioners have concerned themselves with discovering the origins and documenting the effects of modernity. The first generations of scholars to identify themselves as sociologists (the 'classical' contributors to the field) lived, after all, in a time when awareness of the enormous changes of the eighteenth and nineteenth centuries, and of their impact throughout society, was building to a climax (Giddens 1971: xi–xii and 201; Nisbet 1966/1993: 21–44).

The displacement of huge populations from the countryside to the city created concentrations of people – and their problems – to a degree that no one had seen before. The transition from back-breaking cultivation of the land to mechanized production in factories forced these masses of people into new settings for work. There they encountered new technologies of the machine age that shaped and applied their labor differently. In the process, people came to new understandings about how society as a unit was to be regulated: the powers of old élites crumbled and slipped into memory as new masters arose. To match these changes, people adopted new ways of thinking and of expressing that thought, so that their common cultural energies spawned new styles for collective life.

In response, institutions that had become brittle and petrified over long expanses of slow-moving history, when the repetition of traditional patterns normally sufficed to meet any challenge, practically groaned and buckled under the pressures of adaptation to accelerated change and the novelty that it introduced. Society was entering a wholly unprecedented stage; it was becoming, in a familiar word, *modern*. The persons who would both analyze and advance this new period of modernity were sociologists. Declares the British commentator James A. Beckford (1992: 12), 'It is virtually a truism to say that all the formative contributions towards classical sociology were preoccupied with trying to understand modernity' (compare Beyer 2001: 419; Giddens, with Pierson 1998: 66–7; Hunter 1994: 14; and Willaime 2006: 77–8).

Moreover, those who sought to develop this understanding, the sociologists of the classical era (Karl Marx, Émile Durkheim, Max Weber, Georg Simmel, and others), reserved in their analyses, as we shall see, a privileged place for the action of religion. Their theories would not regard religious belief and behavior, even under the strains that modernity imposes, as if they were minor and marginal human habits. Although these thinkers differed in their predictions for the future trajectory of religious ideas and institutions, each believed that no sociology that is worthy of the name henceforth could overlook the primacy of religion as a model and a motivation for human action. Quite the contrary: as the French sociologist Jean-Paul Willaime (2006: 77–8) has noted, 'It is precisely because sociological thinking made a strong connection between the analysis of modernity and the analysis of religion that the present-day sociological study of the religious must take serious account of analyses of the changes in modernity itself.'

From such perceptive comments about sociology's past comes the mandate for this chapter about the past, present, and future of religion. The section that immediately follows offers an assessment of the dimensions of theories that chart religious change as a process of evolution. In succeeding sections, the reader is presented with accounts of religion in the transition to modernity, as viewed first through the eyes of classical sociologists and then through those of more recent critics who write of a self-aware and self-oriented 'reflexive' modernity. Finally, this essay explores whether there is underway at present a movement to a new stage of social development ('post-,' 'ultra-,' or 'supermodernity'), and, if so, what changes this trend and others portend for a 'new age' of religion, institutional and personal.

CONCEPTIONS OF RELIGIOUS EVOLUTION

In Europe, evolutionary theories of religious development and change date back at least to the eighteenth century, while in North America, such thinking flourished especially toward the end of the nineteenth century and at the beginning of the twentieth (see Verkamp 1991: 538–9). During the latter phase, theological scholars and social scientists joined in a common search for the roots of religion, and shared their speculations and discoveries in the pages of their own and each other's academic reviews (e.g., Mathews 1895, 1896).

Although the matter is axiomatic to the contemporary student of religion, sociologists like Charles A. Ellwood (1873–1946) were treading on relatively new turf when they held '...that the religious consciousness is a form of social consciousness, and that a religious vision necessarily includes a social vision. The patterns for the religious life always come from the social life and always have a social significance' (Ellwood 1923: 130 [emphasis in the original]).

'Religion is a growing, evolving thing,' proclaimed Ellwood, a president of the American Sociological Society, in the journal titled *The Biblical World* (Ellwood 1920: 456). For the religious side, Shailer Mathews, for twenty-five years (1908–1933) dean of the Divinity School at the University of Chicago, concurred. His general *credo* was neatly summed in a single sentence: 'All religions,' he declared, 'are phases of religion.' To one who would insist that 'religion is the gift of God and therefore has no historical development,' he could reply merely that 'the facts are against him' (Mathews 1911: 57). If religion were constantly moving and changing, it was only natural that analysts of religion would want to track that growth and development: 'The tracing of some sort of an evolution in religious belief and practice,' wrote the pioneering philosopher and psychologist of religion Irving King (1909a: 38), 'has long been a favorite task with those engaged in the scientific study of religion.'

King (1874–1937), who was also a founding influence in the field of religious education, made his own contribution to this pursuit in a series of articles leading to the publication of his 1910 book, *The Development of Religion*. Remarked King in a publication for philosophers (1909a: 44–5):

> The problem of the evolution of religion is then the problem of tracing the connection between various religions and the cultural matrix out of which they have sprung, of noting how, in certain environments, and in the face of certain life-problems, the religious type of attitude tends to develop in particular ways, and how, in like manner, its content and form vary with these external conditions.

He was to state the case for a social and evolutionary approach to religious change only slightly differently for the readers of an early volume of the *American Journal of Sociology* (1909b: 434):

> …the religious consciousness has been built up, or differentiated, from a back-ground [*sic*] of overt activity and relatively objective phases of consciousness. The assumption underlying the problem is that the religious attitude of mind has had a natural history, that there was a time in the history of the race when a definite religious attitude did not exist, and that, in its genesis and in its development, it has been conditioned by the same laws according to which other mental attitudes may be described.

Likewise, Dean Mathews (1863–1941), who would go on to figure prominently in the popularization of the Social Gospel in America through works like *The Social Teaching of Jesus* (1917), asserted both the inherently historical and social natures of religion. There is no such thing as 'generic religion,' he taught; 'religions never existed except as interests and institutions of people.' For that reason, he called upon his fellow theologians to abandon what he condemned as their 'scholastic abstractions,' for 'religion is not a thing in itself, possessed of independent, abstract, or metaphysical existence.' Rather, to Mathews, religion was 'a name for one phase of concrete human activity.' He concluded, moreover, that it was 'only from a strictly social point of view that either religion or religions will in any measure be properly understood. We know only people who worship in various ways and with various conceptions of what or whom they worship' (Mathews 1911: 58 and 59). In other words, Mathews explained, 'when we speak about religion we are speaking about the activities of real people acting and reacting in very real social situations from which institutions, customs, and programs evolve' (Mathews 1911: 74).[1]

Despite this initial burst of scholarly activity around the turn of the twentieth century, within several decades evolutionary theory in sociology broadly – and particularly in the sociology of religion – had largely vanished from the view of research. The perspective on social change that evolution provided, along with its main defenders in academic circles, had come under criticism when enthusiasm for the liberating insights of Charles Darwin

began to wane. Not until much later, in the 1960s, did there appear what was to be the most significant and lasting of many sociological studies on the evolution of religion: the elegant essay by Robert N. Bellah with the simple title, 'Religious evolution' (Bellah 1964; see also Beckford 1989: 68–9).

Religious change, to Bellah, is neither linear nor unidirectional, nor does one stage of development obliterate all examples of its precursors. Nevertheless, Bellah begins his overview by dividing the religious history of humanity into five ideal-typical periods: *primitive, archaic, historic, early modern,* and *modern* (pp. 360–1). Movement from the oldest to the latest stages, assumes Bellah, means gravitation to 'more differentiated, comprehensive, and in Weber's sense, more rationalized formulations' (p. 360). In each instance of religion over time, Bellah (p. 362) outlines four dimensions of distinction: 'the kind of symbol system involved, the kind of religious action it stimulates, the kind of social organization in which this religious action occurs and the implications for social action in general that the religious action contains.'

In the case of *primitive religion*, the symbol system is a 'mythical world' full of imagery that is detailed and particular at the same time as it is fluid and 'free-associational' (pp. 362 and 363). Religious action is anchored in rituals from which the group derives its very identity. No hierarchy separates religious practitioners from the simply pious; they 'have become one with the myth.' In addition, there is no religious organization, strictly speaking: 'Church and society are one. Religious roles tend to be fused with other roles, and differentiations along lines of age, sex and kin group are important' (p. 363). The effect of primitive religious action, according to Bellah (p. 364), is to reinforce the solidarity of the social group (compare Casanova 1992: 52; and Durkheim 1912/1965).

The most salient feature of Bellah's second period, *archaic religion*, is a symbol system in which, for the first time, mythical actors are 'more definitely characterized' (p. 364); that is to say, they take on the properties of gods. Archaic religions, Bellah contends, 'elaborate a vast cosmology in which all things divine and natural have a place' (p. 364).

In contrast to archaic religions, what Bellah terms *historic religions*, which arise in literate societies, conceive of a world in which human experience is radically split, with religion residing in a supernatural space 'above' everyday reality. Historic religions are thus dualistic, in that they 'are all in some sense transcendental' (p. 366). Religious action is motivated to seeking salvation, or entry into the life that is beyond earthly existence. The organization of historic religions 'is associated with the emergence of differentiated religious collectivities' (p. 367); a new religious élite joins the political class in competition for popular support.

The paradigmatic case of *early modern religion* is the Protestant Christianity of the Reformation era (Freitag 1999: 201). In its democratic religious impulse, notes Bellah, we witness an open challenge to the legitimacy of hierarchy in both spiritual and political settings. Salvation is distinguished through inner-worldly activity. The outcome of these beliefs, in terms of religious organization, is the separation of individuals into two sharply opposed camps: the saved (or 'elect') and the unredeemed sinners. Finally, the social implications of Protestantism are well known to students of sociology: the so-called 'Protestant ethic' and its effects on economics, science, and the law (see Weber 1904–1905/2001).

Bellah's last phase of evolution, *modern religion*, 'represents,' he says, 'a stage of religious development in many ways profoundly different' from what went before it (p. 371). Modernity, according to Bellah's famous description, ushers in 'an infinitely multiplex' world; with the collapse of many elaborate orthodoxies, 'it is not that life has become again a "one possibility thing,"' he remarks, 'but that it has become an infinite possibility thing' (p. 371; compare Wilson 1976: 1). Unlike previous stages of religious evolution, the modern period establishes unmistakably that 'man in the last analysis is responsible for the choice of his symbolism' (p. 373).

As long ago as the 1950s, Bellah could ascertain that 'for many churchgoers the obligation of doctrinal orthodoxy sits lightly indeed, and the idea that all creedal statements must receive a personal reinterpretation is widely accepted' (p. 372). The signal attribute of the modern stage of religious evolution, according to Bellah, is cultural and personal freedom. Although such freedom carries with it the danger of 'pathological distortion,' Bellah elects to close on an essentially optimistic note, one that could have been sounded perhaps only in the dewy dawn of the 1960s counterculture. The erosion of old structures and practices with the onset of modernity should be seen, he urges, as 'offering unprecedented opportunities for creative innovation to every sphere of human action' (pp. 373–4). Forty years later, after persistent poverty, racial unrest, regressive revolutions, grinding wars – and intolerance, genocide, and despotism around the world – not everyone would regard the modern age in quite the same manner. What is more, the 'postmodernists' among them are in our day poised to take full advantage of their disillusionment.

SOCIOLOGICAL CLASSICISM AND THE ROAD TO MODERN RELIGION

Most summaries of religious change in sociology are not as historically ambitious as Robert Bellah's. In fact, they have concentrated in the main on the passage between premodern and modern structures of society. As others have observed, these types of sweeping changes – whether welcome or not – are exactly what classical sociology developed in the first instance to address. Examples of this mission include the thought of Germans Karl Marx (1818–1883) and Max Weber (1864–1918), and of the French theorist Émile Durkheim (1858–1917). As Randall Collins argues in the preceding chapter of this Handbook, both Marx and Weber attributed the majority of the social changes of the eighteenth and the nineteenth centuries to the onset of capitalism in the West, a change that, in their view, produced the individualization of social structures and the rationalization of social relations (Beck 1986/1992: 95–9; Giddens 1971: 178–84; and

1990: 7–9 and 11–16; Lemieux 1992: 217; Lyon 1994/1999: 29–30 and 37–8; and 2000: 24–7; Spohn 2003: 265–70).

Karl Marx

Marx, working with his faithful friend and collaborator Friedrich Engels (1820–1895), envisioned capitalism in its industrial maturity darkly, for it engendered 'uninterrupted disturbance of all social conditions, everlasting uncertainty and agitation' (Marx and Engels 1848/1987: 25–6). Together they foresaw the dissolution of the mostly static societies (with their traditional lifestyles) to which premodern peoples had grown accustomed. 'All fixed, fast-frozen relations, with their train of ancient and venerable prejudices and opinions, are swept away,' they wrote, in one of the more lyrical passages from *The Communist Manifesto*; 'all new-formed ones become antiquated before they can ossify. All that is solid melts into air,[2] all that is holy is profaned, and man is at last compelled to face, with sober senses, his real conditions of life and his relations with his kind' (Marx and Engels 1848/1987: 26).

For Marx, the 'real conditions of life' were ones that excluded religion, because belief in an Almighty and an afterlife over which He presided quelled exactly the discontent that would be necessary to spark a revolution to deliver humanity while on earth.

Max Weber

For Weber, it was religion itself, embodied in the ascetic Protestantism of the Reformation, that helped to eradicate magical notions from social life and to usher in a radical 'disenchantment' of the modern world (Giddens 1971: 214–16; Luckmann 1991: 168–9). The Reformation conceived human actors, in the corrupt and degraded condition of their creation, as completely separated from God. The severe precepts and self-denying practices of Calvinism, with its doctrine of predestination, served in particular to exacerbate the 'unprecedented inner loneliness'

(Weber 1904–1905/2001: 60) that people endured as a necessary aspect of existence. Neither ritual formulae nor acts of devotion were deemed sufficient to win grace for those whom God had already condemned to perdition.

However, successful activity in the world could potentially convince the believer (if not the Maker) of his or her election for sainthood – and the more organized and efficient such activity the better. Vigorous and methodical work could not be bartered for salvation, yet the fledgling Protestant nevertheless might interpret an enterprise that prospered as a sign of divine favor. Capitalism, propelled at first by religious fervor, later jettisoned its moral strictures only to retain its adherence to an unstinting rationality.

The long-term effects of this change were, to Weber, even more dispiriting than they were for Marx. 'The modern man,' he wrote, 'is in general, even with the best will, unable to give religious ideas a significance for culture and national character which they deserve' (Weber 1904–1905/2001: 125). The results are stark at best:

> Where the fulfillment of the calling cannot directly be related to the highest spiritual and cultural values, or when, on the other hand, it need not be felt simply as economic compulsion, the individual generally abandons the attempt to justify it at all. In the field of its highest development, in the United States, the pursuit of wealth, stripped of its religious and ethical meaning, tends to become associated with purely mundane passions, which often actually give it the character of sport (Weber 1904–1905/2001: 124).

So do modern individuals progress from a religious ideology that places them at an unbridgeable distance from God to a concrete setting in which their own efforts at work are estranged from any higher meaning whatsoever.

Émile Durkheim

Durkheim premised his theory of social change on the expectation, in general, of an increasing differentiation among the units of society, and, in particular, of an increasing division of labor (Durkheim 1893/1984; see also Bellah 1959; Merton 1934, 1994; and Schnore 1958). Less modern ('primitive') societies were characterized, Durkheim held, by a pattern of organization that he dubbed the *mechanical division of labor* (Freitag 1999: 191 and 193; Schnore 1958: 621–2). Under this arrangement, segments of society achieved cohesion by virtue of their sheer identity. With mechanical solidarity, as the American demographer Leo F. Schnore (1958: 621) put it, 'The basis of social unity is likeness or similarity … The "social segments" of the community (families and kinship units) are held together by what they have in common, and they derive mutual support from their very likeness.'

To account for more modern societies, in contrast, Durkheim laid out 'another and fundamentally different mode of organization,' which he called the *organic division of labor*. Like the integrated systems of organs in the human body, this pattern relies not on the similarity of its units (as had mechanical solidarity), but on arrays of complementary differences. Here people and groups are connected by the obligations of contracts. 'According to Durkheim, a complex and heterogeneous society, like all but the most rudimentary organisms,' noted Schnore (1958: 621–2), 'is based on an intricate interdependence of specialized parts. Labor is divided; all men do not engage in the same activities, but they produce and exchange different goods and services.'

In Durkheim's theory, the direction of history's motion is away from any solidarity that is mechanical and toward, albeit incompletely, its organic form (Giddens 1971: 76–9 and 101; Merton 1934: 321). More specifically, organic solidarity arises and expands from the modern 'condensation' of greater numbers of social units in a fixed space (*physical density*). This concentration then generates a heightened rate of interaction among the units (*moral or dynamic density*), which causes them to compete and ultimately to specialize (Bellah 1959: 452; Christiano 1987: 68–9; Giddens 1971: 216–19; Merton 1934: 320–1 and 325–6).

The effects of this process of transformation on religion can be witnessed in its changed circumstances under modernity.[3] The very similarity of social units in the premodern stage permitted a common belief system – or a small number of them – to dominate society. Indeed, in the extreme case of the simplest groups, religious belief and a consciousness of society were, for Durkheim, largely the same thing: 'everything social was religious – the two words were synonymous.' Yet, with increasing social complexity, he asserted, 'religion extends over an ever diminishing area of social life.' The deity is 'at first present in every human relationship,' but over time He 'has progressively withdrawn. He leaves the world to men and their quarrels' (Durkheim 1893/1984: 119; see also Giddens 1971: 111–12).

The 'common consciousness' that, for Durkheim (1893/1984: 120, 230, and 238–241), bound social actors into a single, self-aware unit was dissipating in intensity and gravitating toward a loose and indistinct abstraction. It followed, too, that in this state 'personal ties are few and weak,' suffering as they did from 'mutual indifference' (Durkheim 1893/1984: 240). Contradictions would amass while common feeling would break down. Thus religion, in so far as it persisted as a social phenomenon, fell victim to institutional isolation in its specialized forms, and to vague vacuity in its more general manifestations. More and more, people became free to adapt rules, customs, and traditions to their own purposes. In the latter-day literature, Robert Bellah (1959: 454) summarized this point: 'Implicit throughout the *Division of Labor* is the notion that the performance of complex differentiated functions in a society with an advanced division of labor both requires and creates individual variation, initiative, and innovation, whereas undifferentiated segmental societies do not.'

Durkheim himself (see also Christiano 1987: 93; Hervieu-Léger 1993/2000: 92–7; Hill 1992: 217–21; Luckmann 1991: 175–6; Nielsen 2001: esp. 122–4; and Westley 1978, 1983) follows the causal connections in, and draws out the implications of, his theory as clearly as any commentator:

> As societies become more voluminous and spread over vaster territories, their traditions and practices, in order to adapt to the diversity of situations and constantly changing circumstances, are compelled to maintain a state of plasticity and instability which no longer offers

adequate resistance to individual variations. These latter, being less well contained, develop more freely and multiply in number; that is, everyone increasingly follows his own path. At the same time, as a consequence of a more advanced division of labour, each mind finds itself directed towards a different point on the horizon, reflects a different aspect of the world and, as a result, the contents of men's minds differ from one subject to another. One is thus gradually proceeding towards a state of affairs, now almost attained, in which the members of a single social group will no longer have anything in common other than their humanity, that is, characteristics which constitute the human person in general (Durkheim 1898/1969: 26; compare Bellah 1959: esp. 452–4).

In their most extreme impact, the 'plasticity and instability' to which Durkheim alludes above produce an essentially religious sentiment that envelops the person but can extend no farther than to the traits that the individual shares with all of humanity. Out of this development is heralded what Durkheim described as a 'Cult of Man' (Durkheim 1912/1965, 1898/1969; see also Giddens 1971: 72–4, 79–80, 105–7, 199, 218; Hill 1992: 218–20; Isambert 1992; Prades 1990; and Westley 1983: 5–9), wherein the sacred is so radically diversified that it comes finally to reside not in cultic expressions of community but within each human individual (Westley 1978: 137, 139).

MODERNITY AND THE SOCIAL SCIENTIFIC EYE

As Durkheim understood, with the spread of modernity, a process arrived through which core meanings of religious belief and devotion were herded into the private sphere (Beyer 1990: 373–6; Casanova 1992: 17–20, 34–7, 55; Luckmann 1991).[4] Nevertheless, 'there are certainly grounds for suggesting,' writes Beckford (1992: 16), 'that the anticipated privatization of religion is at least being paralleled by a process whereby religion is also becoming more publicly visible and controversial.' Thus, in its latter stages, modernity has fostered an attraction of popular attention to religion's remaining public presence in institutions like denominational organizations and especially

with respect to the state (Lyon 1996: 20–1). This outcome has been labelled by one theorist (Casanova 1992: 19) 'the deprivatization of religion' (see also Casanova 1994). How might this happen?

The German theorist Ulrich Beck (1986/1992: 10–11) envisions three distinct stages to social development: the tradition of 'pre-modernity,' the 'classical modernity' of industrial society, and a newer stage: 'reflexive modernity' (see also Giddens 1990; Mellor 1993; and Willaime 2005). In this last period, the action of modernity becomes *about* modernity itself, and especially about coping with novel threats to the environmental and social arrangements that are necessary to sustain common life. Notes Beck tartly: '…the engineering sciences' claim to a monopoly on rationality in risk perception is equivalent to the claim of infallibility of a Pope who has converted to Lutheranism' (Beck 1986/1992: 59).

Nevertheless, much of Beck's focus is on science and technology; he does not explain at any great length the implications of reflexive modernity for change in the institutional location of religion. Indeed, for Beck the 'countermodern' belief in progress effectively replaces religion (compare Giddens 1990: 46; and Wuthnow 1988: 268–96). 'It is a type of *secular religion of modernity,*' he claims (emphasis in the original):

All the features of a religious faith apply to it, such as trust in the unknown and the intangible [,] or trust against one's own better judgment, without knowing the way or the 'how.' Faith in progress is the self-confidence of modernity in its own technology that has become creativity. The productive forces, along with those who develop and administer them, science and business, have taken the place of God and the Church (Beck 1986/1992: 214).

A comparable neglect of the religious implications of reflexive modernity is evident in the work of the theorist whose name is most closely associated with that expression, Anthony Giddens (Beckford 2003: 121–4; Lyon 1994/1999: 34; Mellor 1993). To Giddens, modernity consists in the distinctive 'modes of social life' that 'emerged in Europe from about the seventeenth century onwards' and that spread from there throughout almost the entire world (Giddens 1990: 1). With modernity, he explains, the new institutions of society are characterized by the *pace* of social change that they undergo (extremely rapid), the *scope* of this change (wide: 'waves of social transformation crash across virtually the whole of the earth's surface'), and the *nature* of its results (change introduces truly novel social forms) (Giddens 1990: [emphases in the original]).

In turn, Giddens is adamant in his belief that the modernity that was born in the transition to the industrial age has not yet given way to a period that is defined by an aimless, amorphous, and subversive postmodernity (Giddens 1990: 45–7; Giddens, with Pierson 1998: 116–17; Mellor 1993). Instead, he insists, 'we are moving into one in which the consequences of modernity are becoming more radicalized and universalized than before' (Giddens 1990: 3). What is 'post-modern,' then – in the literal sense that it follows the familiar form of modernity – is not a fashionable 'postmodernism' but rather an intensified and reflexive version of modernity's former self.

This version of modernity, according to Giddens (1990: 53 [emphasis in the original]; compare Lyon 1994/1999: 25–6), underlines '*the separation of time and space*'; the reorganization of social relations, in order to join impersonally the large gaps that are so created; and the generation of objective knowledge about these processes, which knowledge can alter or substitute for an earlier reliance upon different traditions. The overall outcome is that, more than ever before, humans today live in conditions that they themselves have had a hand in devising (compare O'Neill 1988: 495). Like Bellah and Casanova, Giddens stresses the possibilities for cognitive re-invention and personal liberation that are embedded in the structures of modern circumstance. In the situation of modern people, the world and their experience of it are open to them; they live, says Giddens (Giddens, with Pierson 1998: 94), 'in the future rather than in the past.' Yet, about the place of religion in this future, Giddens ventures merely that in an era of reflexive modernity, fundamentalist forms of faith will cause deep conflict (Giddens, with Pierson 1998: 130–2; compare Beckford 2003: 123–4).

Michael Hill, a sociologist of religion, is more helpful in elaborating the effects of modernity on religion. Hill identifies six characteristics that he regards 'as typifying the religion of modern, complex societies.' About a modern religion, according to Hill, it may be said that:

(1) It is *individualistic*.... (2) It emphasizes an *idealized human personality*.... (3) It maintains a degree of *tolerance*.... (4) It is *syncretistic*.... (5) It is *monistic*.... [and] (6) It emphasizes a process whereby individuals are '*morally remade*' or *empowered* (Hill 1992: 224–5 [emphases appear in the original]).

The paramount truth that shows through all of these various conceptualizations of the modern is that modernity constitutes the most notably problematic stage in the development of societies. That is to say, many of what sociologists today take to be their fundamental problems were bequeathed to the discipline by the transition to modernity. If during the modern age simple social practices and small-scale patterns of human behavior succumb to differentiation and institutional complexity, if broadly based social functions are incorporated into multipurpose arrangements with specialized parts, if cultural diversity abounds and fragmentation of identities ensues, if vast systems of social action render us ever more interdependent, and if old traditions are blurred but not obliterated under modernity, then every social scientist is now a modernist – or better, a commentator on modern matters. And in the course of these changes, he or she may monitor religion both backpedaling into the realm of the intimate and charging headlong into the political give-and-take of modern times.

POSTMODERNISM AND ALL THAT: ANTI-FORMS OF POSTMODERN FAITH

'Postmodernism' is at the same time a much-used yet still a badly understood concept. One cause of this problem is its manifold, and seemingly multiplying, meanings (Lemieux 1992: 187). They are as numerous, it sometimes appears, as the legions of the idea's enthusiasts and detractors combined. Indeed, some (see, e.g., Beckford 1996: 34; Bruce 1998: esp. 28–9 and 34; Featherstone 1988: 202; and Freitag 1999: 212–13) would insist that postmodernity is not at all distinct from the developmental stage that is considered to precede it, but rather that it really inheres in the continuation and extension of trends long recognized as modern. 'The argument, in this regard,' writes Paul Heelas (1998: 9), 'is that virtually everything discussed in the present context under the heading "postmodernity" can be found within the setting of modernity.'

If intellectual historians (e.g., Macquarrie 1963/2001: 447) and other commentators (e.g., Featherstone 1988: 203, 208) are correct, artists and architects – and not philosophers or social scientists – probably introduced the word 'postmodern' to the twentieth-century vocabulary. In the 1960s, denizens of the art scene in New York City glommed onto the term, while critics of the built environment appropriated it consistently in the 1970s when reaching for a means to describe the more joyfully ornamental habits of design that grew up in opposition to the austere and sterile modernist structures of twentieth-century greats like Le Corbusier (1887–1965) and Mies van der Rohe (1886–1969). But in relatively little time, the term assumed a variety of often competing and confusing usages.

Postmodernism is, for example, both a thing, and a broad style of describing and accounting for that thing. It is a direction of social change leading beyond (or in addition to) the modern, to the state of having achieved postmodernity. Thus it is a characteristic tendency of late-industrial societies, a trajectory of their development as well as an attribute of their cultures. Yet it is also a philosophical concept, a mode of literary and artistic creation, and a theory of criticism for the evaluation of those creations. In truth, there are almost as many definitions of postmodernism as the number of persons who have invoked it, whether in praise or in dismissal.

Probably the best known definition of postmodernity comes from the work of Jean François Lyotard, the French philosopher.

'I define *postmodern* as incredulity toward metanarratives . . .,'[5] he wrote – especially unbelief in the Enlightenment claim that positive science will deliver human liberation. Indeed, skeptical reaction against Enlightenment reason as the intellectual underpinning of modernity is a basic attribute of most things that are properly considered postmodern (see Featherstone 1988: 204–5; Lyon 1993: 118, 120–1; and 2000: xi; Macquarrie 1963/2001: 448–9; and Woller 1997: 9).

Also associated with the concept, reports Jeffrey C. Alexander (1994/2003: 209), are 'frank revelations of theoretical perplexity, testimonies to dramatic shifts in reality, and expressions of existential despair.' Mike Featherstone (1988: 203) further spies 'a stylistic promiscuity favouring eclecticism and the mixing of codes; parody, pastiche, irony, playfulness and the celebration of the surface "depthlessness" of culture.' To these descriptions the historical anthropologist Ernest Gellner (1992: 30) adds a 'jerky fragmentariness' of style.

A harsh opponent of postmodernism, Gellner is himself skeptical of the skepticism that postmodernism exhibits so unapologetically. In one passage from his short book on *Postmodernism, Reason and Religion*, he professes a mock-ignorance of his first-named topic:

> Postmodernism is a contemporary movement. It is strong and fashionable. Over and above this, it is not altogether clear what the devil it is. In fact, clarity is not conspicuous amongst its marked attributes. It not only generally fails to practise it, but on occasion actually repudiates it (Gellner 1992: 22–3).

In another segment, he melds a British style of wry description with both negative definition and negative affect or attitude:

> Postmodernism would seem to be rather clearly in favour of relativism, in as far as it is capable of clarity, and hostile to the idea of unique, exclusive, objective, external or transcendent truth. Truth is elusive, polymorphous, inward, subjective . . . and perhaps a few further things as well. Straightforward it is not (Gellner 1992: 24).

However amusing Gellner's reactions may be, they fail finally as reliable formulations. A more frontal reconnaissance is the route of

James Beckford. As he has noted (Beckford 1992: 19; see also Lyon 1996: 19; and 1994/1999), a rejection of received rigidities, a tendency to combine elements that had heretofore been held in isolation, and a concession that grand perspectives may not supply the answers to persistent questions, are all hallmarks of a postmodern sensibility.[6]

Last, a more literary inventory of the cultural characteristics of postmodernity springs from the architectural criticism of Charles Jencks:

> The Post-Modern Age is a time of incessant choosing. It's an era when no orthodoxy can be adopted without self-consciousness and irony, because all traditions seem to have some validity…. Pluralism, the 'ism' of our time, is both the great problem and the great opportunity: where Everyman becomes a Cosmopolite and Everywoman a Liberated Individual, confusion and anxiety become ruling states of mind and ersatz a common form of mass-culture…. Between inventive combination and confused parody the Post-Modernist sails, often getting lost and coming to grief, but occasionally realising the great promise of a plural culture with its many freedoms. Post-Modernism is fundamentally the eclectic mixture of any tradition with that of the immediate past; it is both the continuation of Modernism and its transcendence. Its best works are characteristically doubly-coded and ironic, making a feature of the wide choice, conflict and discontinuity of traditions, because this heterogeneity most clearly captures our pluralism (Jencks 1987: 7).

Assuming that a usable minimum of this record – stronger as description than as definition – is accurate, what then would a truly postmodern religion resemble? To initiate an answer to this question, we could stipulate with confidence that a postmodern religion would not be captured within a church – or not a highly conventional such organization, anyway. More likely, a postmodern faith would lock the lone adherent in its gaze, yet ask her or him actually to adhere to very little. The religious truths of ages would have given way to the presumed validity of personal experimentation and experience. Postmodern religion would vacate the seat of authority to entertain difference and dissidence; it would violate sharp boundaries and indulge in ironic contradictions. It would invite transgression as a means of transcendence. Religion in postmodernity would be a-historical and anti-traditional.

Most of all, it would not hesitate to implode on the individual, and it would not regret the mess: Paris would be worth it.

OTHER PHASES? ULTRA-MODERNITY AND SUPERMODERNITY

Ultra-modernité

Ultra-modernité, as the name suggests, is a concept that originated in France, a country that not only has undergone the same process of secularization that has affected the rest of the industrialized West, but that also has sustained a unique relationship to the secular via its civic doctrine of *laïcité*. Although *laïcité* is difficult to define outside its formative context, in French history it has come to represent the active legal residue of the Enlightenment and the Revolution, the events that introduced modern notions of citizenship and republicanism to France, and that correspondingly moved the potentially fractious institutions of religion to the periphery of collective life. The combined effect of these phases on the national polity has been to establish in French society today an officially – and some would say vigorously – secular environment, especially in the civil and educational spheres.

The sociologist Jean-Paul Willaime first coined the term *ultra-modernité* to lay out the most salient attributes of religion under the legally secular (*laïc*), post-Revolutionary régime in his home country, although it has come to bear implications for the functions of faith in modernized nations around the world. The meaning of the concept is best revealed in what Willaime describes (in French) as the '*laïcisation de la laïcité*,' or 'the secularization of *laïcité*' – put differently, the cancellation through evacuation of the characteristically French expectation that, in properly modern circumstances, religion should be expunged from the public realm, from the state and from state-supported schools (Willaime 2000: 392–3; 2004: 374 [and Note 3], 375, and 377; and 2006: 83).

Ironically, however, the identical force of modern criticism that pushes religion from public prominence, under ultra-modernity reacts back upon itself, undermining the acceptance of an officially secular condition for society. In ultra-modernity, the corrosive actions of modern styles in thought and culture are so severe that they weaken the power even of individual outlooks that previously were stridently modern – that is, *secular*. Explains Willaime:

A strikingly important development has been the demystification of modernity itself. Modernity becomes disillusioned with itself when it exercises its faculties of self-reflection and self-criticism. In other words, modernity has become critical of modernism and of its own utopian absolutism…. Ultra-modernity is still modernity, but radicalized – a modernity disenchanted and problematized. This is to say a modernity undergoing the set-back of systematic reflexivity which it brought upon itself (Willaime 2004: 383–4 and 375; compare Lambert 1999: 311; and Willaime 1998: 28–31; and 2005: 3).

Thus are scientific rationality, political authority, and a triumphant secularity all drawn into question, and no more than a moment after what is perceived as their instant of success. 'The great demythologizing ideologies find themselves demythologized' and society enters 'a stage where modernity has itself demythologized its own enchantments' (Willaime 2000: 393 and 394 [Note 3]; compare Willaime 2005: 3; and 2006: 79).[7] Or, stated more colorfully, ultra-modernity 'is a modernity which is hit by a counter-punch from the systematic reflexivity that it had unleashed' (Willaime 2006: 79). According to Willaime (1998: 31):

A modernity that has been successfully accomplished (what I call 'ultra-modernity'), that has learned to demythologize itself, feels the full force of the very disenchantment of modernity…. Protestantism finds itself shaken in an ultra-modernity characterized by the movement toward uncertainty, including uncertainty with respect to modern ideals (the fallout from progress, misgivings about accelerating change, and about individualism itself), … Now, ultra-modernity, which no longer has to win its autonomy from religion, tends to reinvent religion as religion: it is no longer a matter of a secularized religion seeking to rejoin society, but a religion all the more inclined to assert itself in a spiritual tone because it is trying to express itself in a society that it inhabits in its heart.[8]

The impact on religion of this change is to create an opening in the culture that allows religious faith to re-enter public discourse and display – not as an overarching unity of belief, but instead as 'a possible symbolic resource' out of which new (if more limited) 'subcultural' identities may be formed and new (though more modest and less sweeping) values may arise (Willaime 2005: 3–5). Together, these new creations can humanize modern societies, Willaime argues; they 'could help to prevent politics from being transformed into the mere management of individual aspirations and to prevent modernity from dissolving into widespread relativism' (Willaime 2006: 85; see also 2006: 87–8).[9]

A new socio-religious configuration is emerging in which the religious, far from appearing in the form of a tradition resisting modernity, appears instead in the hyper-modern form of a tradition that prevents ultra-modernity from dissolving into a self-destructive critique. Increasingly, religion provides identities and offers to individuals the possibility of social integration and direction within individualistic and pluralistic societies (Willaime 2004: 375).

Surmodernité

Of all the widely differing permutations on the concept of modernity, 'supermodernity' ('*la surmodernité*') may qualify as the most intriguing successor. The idea derives from the work of the French anthropological theorist Marc Augé (1992/1995; see also Augé 1998), who consciously sought to avoid invoking the conflicted term 'postmodernity' as the setting for his thought (see Augé 1998: 97).

Supermodernity, in Augé's (1992/1995: 29–31) conceptualization, stems from the human need to impart meaning to the present world, a place that seemingly drains meaning away from itself faster than it can be replenished. It is marked most by its 'essential quality,' an inclination to sheer excess: 'overabundance of events, spatial overabundance, the individualization of references' (pp. 29 and 40). The first surplus is evidenced in a proliferation of 'occasions on which an individual can feel his own history intersecting with History, can imagine that the two are somehow connected' (pp. 29–30).

An excess of space is apparent in the distances that social actors in supermodernity are prone to placing around themselves. As the scale of human experience expands to a historically unparalleled degree, we do more to insulate ourselves from the others who enter our field of cognition. To employ Augé's example, we may watch images of faraway locales beamed to us by satellites in outer space, but we do so in the increasing isolation of private homes. Though highly realistic, these images present a 'false familiarity' in which distant figures take on the aura of media celebrities or sports stars. 'We may not know them personally,' Augé (1992/1995: 32) concedes, 'but we recognize them.'

With supermodern change, the places that we once occupied by virtue of personal attachments and local identities are supplanted by 'non-places' (pp. 111–12) that are populated by those who share the statuses of 'passengers, customers or Sunday drivers' (p. 101). More and more, we do not 'live there,' in the sense that our presence will be socially registered and uniquely acknowledged. On the contrary, in a non-place a person 'is relieved of his usual determinants' (p. 103). In more and more contexts we are anonymous travellers, men or women who are merely *passing through*. We are 'people who, for a time, have only to keep in line, go where they are told, check their appearance…. The space of non-place creates neither singular identity nor relations; only solitude, and similitude' (pp. 101 and 103).

The third form of supermodern overabundance is the most relevant to religion today:[10] the individualization of references to persons. In the instance of persons as religious believers, there is the record of ever-mounting rejection of coercive authority over the group:

> Sociologists of religion have revealed the singular character even of Catholic practice: practising Catholics intend to practise in their own fashion …. never before have individual histories been so explicitly affected by collective history, but never before, either, have reference points for collective identification been so unstable. The individual production of meaning is thus more necessary than ever (Augé 1992/1995: 37).

If Augé's diagnosis of supermodern society is correct, we should expect confirmation of it in the most pronounced traits of contemporary religion. Does it lay a track for the individual seeker leading *away from* the traditional verities, which are backed by conventional piety, and *toward* delving much more deeply into solitary explorations of the self? Should we anticipate religion that is, in the words of one critic (Wolfson 2002: 124; compare Hervieu-Léger 2001), 'a radically individualized affair, shorn of all shared theological beliefs and ecclesiastical and public bonds'?

WHAT NEXT? RELIGIONS *OF* AND *FOR* THE FUTURE

Émile Durkheim (see also Giddens 1971: 116; and Hervieu-Léger 1993/2000: 26–7) forecasted nearly one hundred years ago that modern persons might be embarking on a period (some would refer to it as a 'New Age') in which they and their groups attach themselves with increasing frequency to new gods: deities designed for, and so made suitable to, their own time. However, he regarded this trend as – in at least one respect – as encouraging as it may have seemed inevitable. Ruminating in 1914 on 'The Future of Religion,' Durkheim posited that:

> The old ideals and the divine figures that embodied them are in the process of dying, because they do not adequately respond anymore to the new aspirations that are emerging, and the new ideals that will be necessary for us to guide our life are not born. We thus find ourselves in an intermediary period, a period of moral chill that explains the various symptoms of which we are, at each moment, the anxious or saddened, depressed witnesses….
>
> …there is one idea that it is necessary for us to get used to: it is that humanity is deserted on this earth, left to its capacities alone and able to rely only upon itself to direct its fate. As one moves forward through history, this idea only gains ground; I doubt, therefore, that it will lose any in the future. At first glance, the idea can upset the man who is accustomed to depicting as extra-human the powers that he leans on. But if he comes to accept that humanity by itself can provide him with the support that he needs, is there not in this perspective something highly reassuring, since the resources that he is calling for are found thus placed on his doorstep and, as it were, right at hand? (Durkheim 1914/2002: 7–8).[11]

Nor was this French founder alone in thinking that a New Age was aborning. Just two years later, in the middle of the First World War, the often allusive (if occasionally elusive) Georg Simmel (1858–1918) proffered an opinion that was remarkably similar to Durkheim's:

> In our present context the essential fact is the existence of large social groups who, in pursuit of their religious needs, are turning away from Christianity … the widespread rejection of any fixed form of religious life is in keeping with our general cultural situation. Thus supra-denominational mysticism has by far the strongest appeal to these groups. For the religious soul hopes to find here direct spontaneous fulfillment, whether in standing naked and alone, as it were, before its God, without the mediation of dogma in any shape or form, or in rejecting the very idea of God as a petrefaction and an obstacle, and in feeling that the true religion of the soul can only be its own inmost metaphysical life not moulded by any forms of faith whatever (Simmel 1916/1997: 95).

About the last part of this passage, David Lyon (1993: 119) has commented that 'One could be forgiven for hearing premonitions of New Age in this quotation.'

So precisely what do sociologists of religion mean when they invoke the phrase 'New Age'? Danièle Hervieu-Léger describes 'New Age' religion in the following fashion. It is, she says:

> …a religious belief entirely centered upon individuals and their personal accomplishment, and characterized by the primacy accorded to personal experience which guides everyone according to their own way. It is not a matter of discovering and committing oneself to a truth outside the self; it is a matter of experimentation – everyone finding their own truth for themselves. In spiritual matters, no authority defines and imposes an external norm upon the individual. The objective pursued is the perfection of the self, perfection which is not concerned with the moral accomplishments of the individual, but with access to a higher state of being (Hervieu-Léger 2001: 164).

Empirical research on the religious faith of the currently rising rank-and-file of religious adherents supports many of these insights, yet it also disputes others (see, in the case of the external authority of 'holism,' Beckford 1984). For example, among the earliest such studies was the project on groups promoting a 'New Religious Consciousness' in the San Francisco Bay area (1972–1975), which was centered at the University of California in Berkeley (Glock and Bellah [eds] 1976;

Wuthnow 1976). One of the contributors to this research, Donald Stone (1978: 127–30), detected a finite series of four features running through the plural belief systems of these new groups: (1) they acknowledged the authority of scientific knowledge; (2) they displayed a 'pragmatic attitude,' privileging practices that yielded tangible results ('If it works, do it.'); (3) they operated as 'open' organizations, allowing syncretism and tolerating differences in perspectives; and (4) they rejected 'dualistic theology' for a 'holistic' approach, because in them 'God becomes immanent and man transcendent.'

Two decades later, such patterns as these, if anything, had widened geographically from hotbeds of cultural ferment to the mainstream of modern societies. The research studies that Wade Clark Roof and his colleagues (Roof et al. 1995) compiled from an international team of scholars who focused on the post-Second-World-War birth cohorts in their countries featured several common themes: the new generation of believers favored formulations of faith that submitted to individual choice, allowed a mixture of group and personal beliefs (even if such a combination seemed contradictory on its face), promised unusual religious experiences, and tilted against the institutional character of the churches (see also Dobbelaere 2000: 445).

North of the U.S.-Canadian border, the sociologist Raymond Lemieux (1992) found that his fellow Quebeckers routinely ascribed three traits to those elements of contemporary religion and spirituality to which they were most committed. 'Why do you believe in what you believe?,' he asked them.[12] Their answers had a trio of ravelled threads. According to Lemieux (1992: 206–17), these favored beliefs and practices: (1) possessed a practical utility – they 'worked' for the individual follower; (2) held a worth that could be directly experienced, not merely accepted or understood; and (3) appealed to the 'common sense' of the individual.

CONCLUSION

The names that sociologists attach to varieties of religion today, and the traits that are associated with them, are many and sometimes confusing. Nevertheless, one can cut through a great deal of the complexity in the present picture by disregarding for an instant the issue of what labels these constellations of conditions wear, and retaining in mind the conditions that themselves appear and re-appear in their respective descriptions. Whatever else may be debatable, as Clark Roof has concluded, '…it's hard to dismiss the fact that the religious stance today is more internal than external, more individual than institutional, more experiential than cerebral, more private than public' (Roof 1996: 153; see also Roof *et al.* 1995; Roof 1999; and Wolfson 2002).

Thus, contemporary religion – whether it is classified as modern, late-modern, or postmodern – holds at its center the spirit and soul of the individual. 'If a century ago Durkheim offered us the "*conscience collective*" as the supposedly real basis of religion – the notion that in a sense society is religion – today,' notes David Lyon (1993: 123; see also Campiche 2003: 298–9; and Hervieu-Léger 2001), 'we are offered little more than an inner quest, the search for self-identity and the realization of human potential.' José Casanova (1992: 28) concurs: '…the cult of the individual has become, indeed, as foreseen by Durkheim, the religion of modernity.' He explores this image further:

> If the temple of ancient polytheism was the Pantheon, a place where all known and even unknown gods could be worshiped simultaneously, the temple of modern polytheism is the mind of the individual self. Indeed, modern individuals do not believe generally in the existence of various gods. On the contrary, they tend to believe that all religions worship the same god under different names and languages, only they reserve to themselves the right to denominate this god and to worship him/her/it in their own peculiar language. Thomas Paine's 'My mind is my church' or Thomas Jefferson's 'I am a sect to myself' are the paradigmatic 'high culture' expressions of the modern form of individual religiosity (Casanova 1992: 27).

Whether perceived as an obligation or an opportunity, as a chore or a challenge, it may well be the inevitable situation of religious believers in the current cultural setting to have to plot their own courses through the thicket of symbols and meanings – some more recognizably 'religious' than others – that society holds out to them. Although many traditional choices are as available as ever, they exist in the present as precisely that: *choices*, and not fixtures of an identity that is assumed from birth or imparted by an unchanging social environment.

Instead, persons who today seek to explore a religious option will engage necessarily in what Lyon (2000: 43 and 92), in several especially nice turns of phrase, calls 'liturgical smorgasbords, doctrinal potlucks' and 'stained-glass window-shopping.' Beyond that realization, however, it may be less useful for sociologists to ponder how to designate our times: do we, in the end, inhabit 'modern,' 'high-' or 'late-modern,' 'reflexively modern,' 'ultra-modern,' or 'postmodern' circumstances? Or something else altogether? To Lorne L. Dawson (1998: 132), it would be worthwhile alternatively for sociology 'to stop identifying religion intrinsically with one side of various essentially invidious dichotomies.' For the urgent question for sociologists of religion in the twenty-first century might be less *why* people find themselves in the position of choosing than *what* they make of their opportunities once they get there.

NOTES

1. Religion is 'never absolutely static,' Mathews observed. Mirroring the *genetic method* that is found in some classical sociology of religion, he maintained that an evolutionary perspective on religious conditions hence was valuable because 'we must study comparatively both the highly developed religious systems and the simplest type of religion as it exists among primitive people.' Why do this? Answered Mathews: 'we must study the simplest religious organisms in order to understand the more complicated' (Mathews 1911: 59; compare Durkheim 1912/1965; see also Bellah 1959: esp. 456–8).

2. David Lyon (1993: 118 and 124 [Note 9]; and 1994/1999: 12 and 112 [Note 15]) assesses this language and tracks its literary echoes back to their source in William Shakespeare's play, *The Tempest* (Act 4, Scene 1, Line 150).

3. James A. Beckford (1989: 26) captures compactly the essence of Durkheim's theoretical prediction.

4. This section follows my earlier explanation in Christiano (2000: 86–8).

5. In Lyotard's original French phrasing, '*l'incrédulité à l'égard des métarécits*' marks '*la condition postmoderne*.' Whether too radically simplified or not, this is the most oft-cited description of postmodernism in the literature on the concept. (See, among other examples: Jeffrey 1994: 94; Jencks 1987: 36; and Lyon 1993: 118; 1994/1999: 16; and 2000: 42.)

6. Somewhat sympathetically, Beckford (1992: 19) enumerates in fuller and more formal language four attributes that surface repeatedly in discussions of the matter:

(a) A refusal to regard positivistic, rationalistic, instrumental criteria as the sole or exclusive standard of worthwhile knowledge.

(b) A willingness to combine symbols from disparate codes or frameworks of meaning, even at the cost of disjunctions and eclecticism.

(c) A celebration of spontaneity, fragmentation, superficiality, irony and playfulness.

(d) A willingness to abandon the search for overarching or triumphalist myths, narratives or frameworks of knowledge.

7. These are my tr anslations from the original French phrases: '*Les grandes idéologies démythologisatrices se trouvent elle-mêmes démythologisées … un stade où la modernité a elle-même démythologisé ses propres enchantements*.'

8. Although this translation is my own, I am grateful to James A. Beckford for his assistance with rendering accurately some of the conversational phrasing.

9. Interestingly, a rather similar type of assertion appears in the argument of the American historian of religion George M. Marsden for what he submits is *The Outrageous Idea of Christian Scholarship* (1997). The modern focus on 'race, class, and gender' – and the biases that each injects into scholarly research – has opened the door, he contends, to taking seriously again the role of religion in intellectual life. So, too, has the reign of postmodernism in universities across the United States crippled the truth claims of even modern, rational, and 'objective' forms of study that there ought to be no objection henceforth to entertaining within ivied walls, on the same basis, the historical contents of Christianity. Its claims are natural ammunition, he thinks, with which to combat reductionism and relativism. It may be no accident to the shape of their thought that both Willaime and Marsden work as committed Protestants in what is a highly secularized *milieu*.

10. Nevertheless, Augé confesses elsewhere (Augé 1998: 96) that, when he first conceived of *la surmodernité*, he did not intend thereby to extend his thinking to religious matters ('*…je ne songeais pas à la question religieuse*').

11. This, again, is my translation. A somewhat stricter though more stilted translation from the French appears as Durkheim (1919/1994: 186 and 187). A cognate passage, translated by Anthony Giddens, appears in his *Capitalism and Modern Social Theory* (Giddens 1971: 116).

12. In French, '*Pourquoi croyez-vous en ce en quoi vous croyez?*' (Lemieux 1992: 207).

REFERENCES

Alexander, J. C. 2003. 'Modern, anti, post, and neo: How intellectuals explain "our time".' In J. C. Alexander (ed.), *The Meanings of Social Life: A cultural sociology*, pp. 193–228. New York: Oxford University Press. Originally published in 1994.

Augé, M. 1995. *Non-places: Introduction to an anthropology of supermodernity*. J. Howe, trans. London: Verso. Originally published in 1992.

Augé, M. 1998. La surmodernité: Héritage chrétien ou récurrence polythéiste? Entretien avec Marc Augé.' In P.-O. Monteil (ed.), *La grâce et le désordre: Entretiens sur la modernité et le protestantisme*, pp. 95–110. Collection: '*Autres temps*,' No. 7. Genève: Labor et Fides.

Beck, U. 1992. *Risk Society: Towards a new modernity*. M. Ritter, trans. London: Sage. Originally published in 1986.

Beckford, J. A. 1984. 'Holistic imagery and ethics in new religious and healing movements.' *Social Compass* 31: 259–72.

Beckford, J. A. 1989. *Religion and Advanced Industrial Society*. London: Unwin Hyman.

Beckford, J. A. 1992. 'Religion, modernity, and postmodernity.' In B. Wilson (ed.), *Religion: Contemporary Issues. The All Souls seminars in the sociology of religion*, pp. 11–23. London: Bellew.

Beckford, J. A. 1996. 'Postmodernity, high modernity, and new modernity: Three concepts in search of religion.' In K. Flanagan and P. C. Jupp (eds), *Postmodernity, Sociology and Religion*, pp. 30–47. London: Macmillan; New York: St. Martin's Press.

Beckford, J. A. 2003. *Social Theory and Religion*. Cambridge: Cambridge University Press.

Bellah, R. N. 1959. 'Durkheim and history.' *American Sociological Review* 24: 447–61.

Bellah, R. N. 1964. 'Religious evolution.' *American Sociological Review* 29: 358–74.

Beyer, P. F. 1990. 'Privatization and the public influence of religion in global society.' *Theory, Culture & Society* 7: 373–95.

Beyer, P. F. 2001. 'Contemporary social theory as it applies to the understanding of religion in cross-cultural perspective.' In R. K. Fenn (ed.), *The Blackwell Companion to Sociology of Religion*, pp. 418–31. Oxford: Blackwell.

Bruce, S. 1998. 'Cathedrals to cults: The evolving forms of the religious life.' In P. Heelas, with D. Martin and P. M. Morris (eds), *Religion, Modernity and Postmodernity*, pp. 19–35. Oxford: Blackwell.

Campiche, R. J. 2003. 'L'individualisation constitue-t-elle encore le paradigme de la religion en modernité tardive?' *Social Compass* 50: 297–309.

Casanova, J. 1992. 'Private and public religions.' *Social Research* 59: 17–57.

Casanova, J. 1994. *Public Religions in the Modern World*. Chicago: University of Chicago Press.

Christiano, K. J. 1987. *Religious Diversity and Social Change: American cities, 1890–1906*. Cambridge: Cambridge University Press.

Christiano, K. J. 2000. 'Church and state in institutional flux: Canada and the United States.' In D. Lyon and M. Van Die (eds), *Rethinking Church, State, and Modernity: Canada between Europe and America*, pp. 69–89. Toronto: University of Toronto Press.

Dawson, L. L. 1998. 'Anti-modernism, modernism, and postmodernism: Struggling with the cultural significance of new religious movements.' *Sociology of Religion* 59: 131–56.

Dobbelaere, K. 2000. 'From religious sociology to sociology of religion: Towards globalisation?' *Journal for the Scientific Study of Religion* 39: 433–47.

Durkheim, É. 1965. *The Elementary Forms of the Religious Life*. J. W. Swain, trans. New York: Free Press. Originally published in 1912.

Durkheim, É. 1969. 'Individualism and the intellectuals.' S. Lukes and J. Lukes, trans. *Political Studies* 17: 19–30. Originally published in 1898.

Durkheim, É. 1984. *The Division of Labor in Society*. W. D. Halls, trans. New York: Free Press. Originally published in 1893.

Durkheim, É. 1994. 'Contribution to discussion: "Religious sentiment at the present time".' In W. S. F. Pickering (ed.), *Durkheim on Religion* [1975], pp. 181–9. Atlanta, GA: Scholars Press. Originally published in 1919.

Durkheim, É. 2002. 'L'avenir de la religion.' In J.-M. Tremblay (ed.), *Les classiques des sciences sociales*. Chicoutimi, QC: La Bibliothèque Paul-Émile-Boulet, Université du Québec à Chicoutimi. Originally published in 1914.

Ellwood, C. A. 1920. 'A sociological view of Christianity.' *The Biblical World* 54: 451–7.

Ellwood, C. A. 1923. 'Social evolution and Christianity.' *Journal of Religion* 3: 113–31.

Featherstone, M. 1988. 'In pursuit of the postmodern: An introduction.' *Theory, Culture & Society* 5: 195–215.

Freitag, M. 1999. 'La dissolution postmoderne de la référence transcendantale: Perspectives théoriques.' *Cahiers de recherche sociologique* [Montréal] 33: 181–217.

Gellner, E. 1992. *Postmodernism, Reason and Religion*. London and New York: Routledge.

Giddens, A. 1971. *Capitalism and Modern Social Theory: An analysis of the writings of Marx, Durkheim and Max Weber*. Cambridge: Cambridge University Press.

Giddens, A. 1990. *The Consequences of Modernity*. The Raymond Fred West Memorial Lectures at Stanford University. Stanford, CA: Stanford University Press.

Giddens, A., with C. Pierson 1998. *Conversations with Anthony Giddens: Making sense of modernity*. Stanford, CA: Stanford University Press; Cambridge and Oxford: Polity and Blackwell.

Glock, C. Y. and Bellah, R. N. (eds). 1976. *The New Religious Consciousness*. Berkeley, CA: University of California Press.

Heelas, P. 1998. 'Introduction: On differentiation and dedifferentiation.' In P. Heelas, with D. Martin and P. M. Morris (eds), *Religion, Modernity and Postmodernity*, pp. 1–18. Oxford: Blackwell.

Hervieu-Léger, D. 2000. *Religion as a Chain of Memory*. S. Lee, trans. New Brunswick, NJ: Rutgers University Press; Cambridge and Oxford: Polity and Blackwell. Originally published in 1993.

Hervieu-Léger, D. 2001. 'Individualism, the validation of faith, and the social nature of religion in modernity.' M. Davis, trans. In R. K. Fenn (ed.), *The Blackwell Companion to Sociology of Religion*, pp. 161–75. Oxford: Blackwell.

Hill, M. 1992. 'New Zealand's cultic milieu: Individualism and the logic of consumerism.' In B. Wilson (ed.), *Religion: Contemporary Issues. The All Souls seminars in the sociology of religion*, pp. 216–36. London: Bellew.

Hunter, J. D. 1994. 'What is modernity? Historical roots and contemporary features.' In P. Sampson, V. Samuel, and C. Sugden (eds). *Faith and Modernity*, pp. 12–28. Oxford: Regnum.

Isambert, F.-A. 1992. 'NOTE CRITIQUE. Une religion de l'Homme? Sur trois interprétations de la religion dans la pensée de Durkheim.' *Revue française de sociologie* 33: 443–62.

Jeffrey, D. 1994. 'Prolégomènes à une religiologie du quotidien.' *Religiologiques* [Montréal] 9: 93–120.

Jencks, C. 1987. *What is Post-modernism?* (2nd edn). London: Academy Editions; New York: St. Martin's Press. Originally published in 1986.

King, I. 1909a. 'Some notes on the evolution of religion.' *Philosophical Review* 18: 38–47.

King, I. 1909b. 'The evolution of religion from the psychological point of view.' *American Journal of Sociology* 14: 433–50.

King, I. 1910. *The Development of Religion: A study in anthropology and social psychology*. New York: Macmillan.

Lambert, Y. 1999. 'Religion in modernity as a new axial age: Secularization or new religious forms?' A. T. Larson and S. Londquist, trans. *Sociology of Religion* 60: 303–33.

Lemieux, R. 1992. 'Histoires de vie et postmodernité religieuse.' In R. Lemieux and M. Milot (eds), *Les croyances des Québécois: Esquisses pour une approche empirique,* pp. 187–234. Québec: Groupe de recherche en sciences de la religion, Université Laval.

Luckmann, T. 1991. 'The new and the old in religion.' In P. Bourdieu and J. S. Coleman (eds), *Social Theory for a Changing Society,* pp. 167–82. Boulder, CO: Westview; New York: Russell Sage.

Lyon, D. 1993. 'A bit of a circus: Notes on postmodernity and New Age.' *Religion* 23: 117–26.

Lyon, D. 1996. 'Religion and the postmodern: Old problems, new prospects.' In K. Flanagan and P. C. Jupp (eds), *Postmodernity, Sociology and Religion,* pp. 14–29. London: Macmillan; New York: St. Martin's Press.

Lyon, D. 1999. *Postmodernity* (2nd edn). Minneapolis, MN: University of Minnesota Press; Buckingham: Open University Press. Originally published in 1994.

Lyon, D. 2000. *Jesus in Disneyland: Religion in postmodern times*. Cambridge: Polity; Malden, MA: Blackwell.

Macquarrie, J. 2001. *Twentieth-century Religious Thought* (5th edn). London: SCM. Originally published in 1963.

Marsden, G. M. 1997. *The Outrageous Idea of Christian Scholarship*. New York: Oxford University Press.

Marx, K. and Engels, F. 1987. 'Manifesto of the Communist Party.' In *The Communist Manifesto,* pp. 21–58. New York: Pathfinder. Originally published in 1848.

Mathews, S. 1895. 'Christian sociology.' *American Journal of Sociology* 1: 69–78.

Mathews, S. 1896. 'Christian sociology. VII: The forces of human progress.' *American Journal of Sociology* 2: 274–87.

Mathews, S. 1911. 'The evolution of religion.' *American Journal of Theology* 15: 57–82.

Mathews, S. 1917. *The Social Teaching of Jesus: An essay in Christian sociology*. New York: Macmillan.

Mellor, P. A. 1993. 'Reflexive traditions: Anthony Giddens, high modernity, and the contours of contemporary religiosity.' *Religious Studies,* 29: 111–27.

Merton, R. K. 1934. 'Durkheim's *Division of labor in society.*' *American Journal of Sociology* 40: 319–28.

Merton, R. K. 1994. '"Durkheim's *Division of labor in society*": A sexagenarian postscript.' *Sociological Forum* 9: 27–36.

Nielsen, D. A. 2001. 'Transformations of society and the sacred in Durkheim's religious sociology.' In R. K. Fenn (ed.), *The Blackwell Companion to Sociology of Religion,* pp. 120–32. Oxford: Blackwell.

Nisbet, R. A. 1993. *The Sociological Tradition* (Rpt. edn). New Brunswick, NJ: Transaction. Originally published in 1966.

O'Neill, J. 1988. 'Religion and postmodernism: The Durkheimian bond in Bell and Jameson.' *Theory, Culture & Society* 5: 493–508.

Prades, J. A. 1990. 'La religion de l'humanité: Notes sur l'anthropo-centrisme durkheimien.' *Archives de sciences sociales des religions* 69: 55–68.

Roof, W. C. 1996. '"God is in the details": Reflections on religion's public presence in the United States in the mid-1990s.' Plenary address to the Association for the Sociology of Religion, 1995. *Sociology of Religion* 57: 149–62.

Roof, W. C. 1999. *Spiritual Marketplace: Baby boomers and the remaking of American religion*. Princeton, NJ: Princeton University Press.

Roof, W. C., Carroll, J. W. and Roozen, D. A. (eds). 1995. *The Post-war Generation and Establishment Religion: Cross-cultural perspectives*. Boulder, CO: Westview.

Schnore, L. F. 1958. 'Social morphology and human ecology.' *American Journal of Sociology* 63: 620–34.

Simmel, G. 1997. 'The crisis of culture.' In D. Frisby and M. Featherstone (eds), *Simmel on Culture: Selected writings,* pp. 90–101. London: Sage. Originally published in 1916.

Spohn, W. 2003. 'Multiple modernity, nationalism and religion: A global perspective.' *Current Sociology* 51: 265–86.

Stone, D. 1978. 'New religious consciousness and personal religious experience.' *Sociological Analysis* 39: 123–34.

Verkamp, B. J. 1991. 'Concerning the evolution of religion.' *Journal of Religion* 71: 538–57.

Weber, M. 2001. *The Protestant Ethic and the Spirit of Capitalism*. T. Parsons, trans. London and New York: Routledge. Originally published in 1904–1905.

Westley, F. 1978. '"The Cult of Man": Durkheim's predictions and new religious movements.' *Sociological Analysis* 39: 135–45.

Westley, F. 1983. *The Complex Forms of the Religious Life: A Durkheimian view of new religious movements.* Chico, CA: Scholars Press.

Willaime, J.-P. 1998. 'Paradoxes du protestantisme en modernité: Entretien avec Jean-Paul Willaime.' In P.-O. Monteil (ed.), *La grâce et le désordre: Entretiens sur la modernité et le protestantisme,* pp. 21–37. Genève: Labor et Fides.

Willaime, J.-P. 2000. 'L'enseignement religieux à l'école publique dans l'Est de la France: Une tradition entre déliquescence et recomposition.' *Social Compass* 47: 383–95.

Willaime, J.-P. 2004. 'The cultural turn in the sociology of religion in France.' S. Acord and G. Davie, trans. *Sociology of Religion* 65: 373–89.

Willaime, J.-P. 2005. 'Situation sociale et institutionnelle des protestantismes en Europe.' Colloque du centenaire de la Fédération protestante de France, Paris, 22 octobre.

Willaime, J.-P. 2006. 'Religion in ultramodernity.' J. A. Beckford, trans. In J. A. Beckford and J. Walliss (eds), *Theorising Religion: Classical and contemporary debates,* pp. 77–89. Aldershot: Ashgate.

Wilson, B. 1976. *Contemporary Transformations of Religion.* Oxford: Oxford University Press.

Wolfson, A. 2002. 'Review: Postmodern religion.' *The Public Interest* 148, Summer: 123–30.

Woller, G. M. 1997. 'Public administration and postmodernism: Editor's introduction.' *American Behavioral Scientist* 41: 9–11.

Wuthnow, R. 1976. *The Consciousness Reformation.* Berkeley, CA: University of California Press.

Wuthnow, R. 1988. *The Restructuring of American Religion: Society and faith since World War II.* Princeton, NJ: Princeton University Press.

3

Secularization and Sacralization Deconstructed and Reconstructed[1]

N. J. DEMERATH III

Until some thirty years ago, increasing faithlessness was an article of faith among scholars and elites throughout the West, if not worldwide. The notion that religion might give way to non-religion and perhaps irreligion was not only taken for granted by sinners outside the sacred ranks but was actually depended upon by saints within the fold. Philosophers and kings begrudged the influence of organized religion and welcomed the decline of what they perceived to be institutionalized superstition. At the same time, religion everywhere played off the dangers of secularity. Cautionary tales of the slippery slope away from the sacred have long constituted a master religious narrative.

In recent years, much of this has changed. Today anyone who takes 'secularization' seriously and says so runs the risk of being labeled antediluvian, anti-church, or anti-social. At least in some circles, a concept that was once an unquestioned staple of scholarly work has been shunted to the unmucked stables of scholarship past. In the eyes of its critics, secularization is a hypothesis that has been proven false and a term that should be expunged from proper usage. The very fact that religion persists and often thrives is ample rebuttal to the 'secularization thesis' and a signal to abandon

both its explicit assumptions and its implicit agenda.

Secularization has taken on different meanings for different camps. It matters whether the reference is to religion's displacement, decline, or change; to the sacred at the level of the individual, the institution, the community, or the culture; and to a pattern that is long-term, linear and inevitable or short-term, cyclical, and contingent. Clearly, it is possible to construct versions of secularization that are either outrageous or reasonable. It matters greatly how the concept is deployed. For some, it is a prophecy of religious demise – whether a tragic jeremiad or a triumphant anticipation. For others, it is a set of historically and sociologically specified processes that move less linearly and with less certainty through time. For still others, secularization converges with sacralization to form a stream of constantly shifting conceptions and locations of the sacred. Whichever option is at issue, the stakes are far from idle.

Debate here has become deeper and more raucous than is common in the academy, perhaps because the issues concern not just scholarship but all of the potentially personal overtones of religion, not to mention the livelihood of every student of religion. In fact, one of this chapter's objectives is to recapture the argument for social science and rid secularization of connotations that mistakenly threaten both religion and the religious. Six major sections follow. The *first* is historical in reviewing some of the classic treatments of secularization in the sociological literature and their recent detractors. The *second* section is more provocative in describing secularization's detractors and the five principal issues in the debate that has ensued. The *third* section is conceptual in providing a formal definition of secularization, introducing the tandem notion of 'sacralization' and developing a conceptual framework for investigating both. The *fourth* section considers a series of eight paradoxical myths, traps, and misinterpretations lurking for such investigations. The *fifth* section presents a typology of four different scenarios of secularization that can be seen in different settings around the globe. And the *sixth* section extends the importance of secularization beyond religion *per se* to a wider conception of the 'sacred' that is at the core of culture itself.

FROM CLASSICAL TO CONTEMPORARY CONCEPTIONS OF SECULARIZATION

Both the process and the thesis of secularization have precursors in the mist of early history, but it is the Western Enlightenment that provides their first codification – at least for Western consumers. The term itself dates from France in the mid-seventeenth century. The first high priest of this anti-church was the French bourgeois intellectual, Francois-Marie Arouet Voltaire (1694–1778). A professed 'deist' whose belief in impersonal forces stood in sharp contrast to 'theistic' conceptions of a personal God, his writings railed against the Church's sanctimonious superstitions and ecclesiastical trappings (cf. Voltaire, 1756). But Voltaire was not the most materialist figure of his day, and he was distinguished more by the expression of his views than their substance, including his sense that the end of religion was

near – quite possibly in his lifetime. The main thrust of his views was shared by many Europeans and Americans, including Benjamin Franklin and Thomas Jefferson.

And the prophets of secularization multiplied. By the second half of the nineteenth century, they included the sometimes infamous father – or at least namer – of 'sociology,' the French positivist, Auguste Comte (1852). Comte was a prophet of rationalism who conceived of a future controlled more by social science than by religion. His view was shared by contemporaries such as England's Herbert Spencer (1874), whose non-fiction sales rivaled those of Dickens' novels, and by the German, Karl Marx, whose political migrations had by then taken him through France and Belgium to his final residence in England. Marx's conception of religion as an opiate is well-known, though it is often lifted out of its more compassionate – indeed more spiritual – context as follows:

> Religious distress is at the same time the expression of real distress. Religion is the sigh of the oppressed creature, the heart of a heartless world, just as it is the spirit of an unspiritual situation. It is the opium of the people.

Of course, Marx and Engels envisioned a de-narcotized future once the masses learned the real secret of their misery, substituted class consciousness for false consciousness, and exchanged this-worldly action for other-worldly hopes.

Max Weber and Emile Durkheim continued the tradition into the first two decades of the twentieth century. Their positions concerning religion were suffused with irony. Although both came from upstanding religious homes – Lutheran for Weber and Jewish for Durkheim, who came from a long line of rabbis – Weber's self-description as 'religiously unmusical' was apt for Durkheim as well. Still, both provided classic statements concerning the importance of religion – whether Weber's 'Protestant ethic' as a pre-condition of capitalism or Durkheim's conception of religion as the latent worship of society itself. At the same time, each became sensitive to secularization without using the term, though they differed somewhat in their assessments of it.

For Weber (1904), secularization was an implication of the 'rationalization' that was so uniquely characteristic of the West. He was ambivalent about the results. On the one hand, he appreciated its cultural underpinnings of everything from capitalism and bureaucracy to developments in architecture and music. On the other hand, Weber wrote within the legacy of German historiography and a concern for the '*Geist*' or spirit of every age. He lamented a dark side of rationality that would lead to a hollow disenchantment. Towards the very end of his famous *Protestant Ethic and the Spirit of Capitalism*, he summarizes the new capitalists pessimistically as follows:

Today, the spirit of religious asceticism – whether finally, who knows? Has escaped from the cage … and the idea of duty in one's calling prowls about in our lives like the ghost of dead religious belief. No one knows who will live in this cage in the future, or whether at the end of this tremendous development entirely new prophets will arise, or there will be a great rebirth of old ideas and ideals, or, if neither, mechanized petrification, embellished with a kind of convulsive self-importance. For of the last stage of this cultural development, it might well be truly said: 'Specialists without spirit, sensualists without heart; this nullity imagines that it has attained a level of civilization never before achieved' (Weber, 1904 (1995): 182).

Durkheim was more positive about secularization, in part because he was more positivistic, working selectively within the tradition of Comte and French positivism. Durkheim (1961) was optimistic about a secular morality and an autonomous ethic for society. But while he envisioned religious beliefs being displaced by science, he reasoned that the sense of society as a sacred collectivity would remain, and he envisioned a waxing and waning of sacred commitments as part of the natural rhythm of social change. In a passage that might well serve as the text for this sermon, he describes France on the eve of World War I and then looks to the future:

If we find a little difficulty today in imagining what (the) feasts and ceremonies of the future could consist in, it is because we are going through a stage of transition and moral mediocrity. The great things of the past which filled our fathers with enthusiasm do not excite the same ardor in us, either because they have come into common usage to such an extent that we are unconscious of them, or else because they no longer answer to our actual aspirations; but as yet there is nothing to replace them… In a word, the old gods are growing old or already dead, and others are not yet born… It is life itself, and not a dead past which can produce a living cult. But this state of incertitude and confused agitation cannot last forever. A day will come when our societies will know again those hours of creative effervescence, in the course of which new ideas arise and new formulae are found which serve for a while as a guide to humanity…

By the mid-twentieth century, secularization had become one of the master motifs of the social sciences. By then, however, sociology had begun to develop more nuanced versions of secularization. Perhaps not surprisingly, the 1960s produced a bumper crop as a possible response to a decade in which changes of all sorts seemed at hand. In 1960, Talcott Parsons was among the first to develop the notion of societal differentiation as it applied to American religion. As society becomes more complex, all of its institutions become more differentiated from each other and enjoy more autonomy but less overall influence. However, the process does not occur equally, and traditional institutions such as religion are more affected by the changes. And yet Parsons distinguished between religious change and religious decline, arguing that, if anything, religion's new place in the differentiated scheme of things offered it protection against some of the more corrosive secularization:

… a process of differentiation similar to that which has affected the family has been going on in the case of religion and has reached a particularly advanced stage in the United States… Through this process of differentiation religion already has become a more specialized agency than it had been in most other societies. But since the Renaissance and the Reformation (this) process has been going on… (Parsons 1960: 304).

Two works developed this theme in different ways in the late 1960s, though both Peter Berger's *The Sacred Canopy* (1967) and Bryan Wilson's *Religion in Secular Society* (1966) restored the connotation of religious diminishment. Berger dealt with both the rise and decline of religion. Having described religion's importance as a source of meaning for a cosmos that is often inchoate, he went on to note factors involved in religion's erosion. These included privatization, pluralism, and a new religious marketplace, all contributing to a secularization which he defined as '...the process by which sectors of society and culture are removed from the domination of religious institutions and symbols' (1967: 107). The definition has a somewhat backwards quality, as if religion remains and remains unchanged, but society leaves by the backdoor. But clearly religion itself was changing, and Berger assigned some of the blame to influences within the churches rather than laying all the blame on external factors in the secular context. He argued that liberal clergy and theologians were often out ahead of the process in diluting religion to avoid conflicts with a lapsing laity.

If Berger's conception of secularization suggests society pulling away from a still religious core, Bryan Wilson conveyed the opposite scenario by which religion itself recedes to the margins and suffers a diminution of influence. For him, secularization is 'the process whereby religious institutions, actions, and consciousness lose their social significance' (Wilson 1966: xiv). But Wilson was aware of a profound difference between the declining influence of the established churches and the often surging growth of sectarian movements (cf. Wilson, 1990).

Both Berger and Wilson were part of a growing choir singing the anthem of societal differentiation. Often seen as part of a larger process of 'modernization,' differentiation has since been a prominent theme among functionalists such as Parsons in a later work on evolution (1977) and Niklas Luhmann (1982), neo-functionalists like Daniel Bell (1976) and Jürgen Habermas (1988), and religious scholars such as David Martin (1978). But differentiation can take different forms and exact different tolls. The Belgian sociologist, Karel Dobbelaere (1981) draws a parallel between secularization and the French term 'laicization,' which Durkheim and others used to denote a loss of priestly control with a resulting decanonization of religion. While developing the concept for European settings, Dobbelaere draws two important distinctions, one between the processes of differentiation, decline, and change (1981) and the other

between religion's role at the quite different levels of the individual, the organization, and the society (1985). We will return to these distinctions later.

Meanwhile, by this time, secularization had become a major priority on the agenda of social scientists examining religion. Returning to the U.S., Richard Fenn (1979) stressed that secularization involves a blurring rather than a sharpening of the boundaries between the sacred and the secular; still more recently, Fenn refers felicitously to secularization as the 'domestication of charisma' (1993). Certainly secularization is at least a sub-theme of Robert Bellah *et al.* in *Habits of the Heart* (1985), a work that depicts the community's losing struggle with individualism – perhaps the ultimate form of differentiation at the personal level. Wade Clark Roof and William McKinney (1987) describe a similar pattern as a 'new voluntarism' that has displaced old denominational loyalties. And Robert Wuthnow (1988) notes still other forces of differentiation at work to shift religious action away from the denominations and congregations in the direction of 'special purpose groups' whose single-issue agendas are often more a reflection of political morality than religious doctrine or theology. Wuthnow also describes a differentiation between America's liberal and conservative 'civil religions.'

Mark Chaves (1993) distinguishes between declining religion and declining religious authority, noting that the two do not always go hand-in-hand in secularization. Chaves documents the emergence of differentiated 'dual structures' within denominations. He argues that secularization involves a split between declining 'religious' authority, on the one hand, and increasing secular 'agency' authority, on the other. This is consistent with other traditions of organizational analysis within religion, including the classic distinction between 'sects' and 'churches,' and the common process by which the purity of the former's religious authority ultimately gives way to the latter's agency authority.

Still another strand of secularization theory has stressed the shift in location and content of traditional religion. A notion first predicted by

Weber's colleague Ernst Troeltsch in the 1920s under the possibly mis-translated term, 'mysticism,' involves the individuation or 'privatization 'of religion as subsequently developed by Thomas Luckmann along with his sense of a 'shrinking transcendence' (Luckmann, 1967, 1990). Recently Roof has noted similar developments in his survey of 'baby boomer' religiosity and their turn away from traditional religious forms towards spirituality and New Age pursuits (Roof 2001).

Finally, a very recent addition to the reach and contingencies of secularization comes from Pippa Norris and Ronald Inglehart (2004). Their globally comparative study uses a wide variety of data – especially the series of Euro-Barometer and World Values surveys – to test the theories of others and buttress a theory of their own. Essentially they argue that secularization is a function of 'existential security' or confidence in basic life subsistence and life conditions; this explains why it is a clear trend in the West by almost any measure. At the same time, countries experiencing existential *in*-security in Latin America, the Middle East and South Asia show the opposite trend of increasing religious involvement, including extremist religious movements and behavior. In a sense, this returns us to a very old conception of the relationship between social class and religiosity: because the 'poor are always with us' so is religion as a theodicy of needed other-worldly escape and compensation.

So much, then, for a rapid review of some of the high points of the rise of secularization theory in sociology. But even the most ardent supporters of the theory would concede that the review has been one-sided. It is high time to introduce the theory's critics and criticisms.

THE MYTH OF THE MYTH OF SECULARIZATION?

Today it is common to hear that secularization has been categorically 'disproven'. After all – the critics contend – just a quick glance at home or abroad indicates that religion is booming everywhere for weal and for woe.

There is no question that this argument has a certain face validity. But the secularization debate runs deeper and is not so easily decided.

In its most recent incarnation, the late Jeffrey Hadden (1987) was among the first to lay down the gauntlet with a stinging attack on secularization theory and theorists, arguing that the latter had neglected research and analysis in their zeal to convert secularization into a 'taken-for-granted ideology.' Over the next ten years, the rumblings and grumblings grew louder. When Peter Berger partially recanted his earlier secularizationist views in 1997 and later elaborated the point by pointing to a global religious efflorescence (Berger, 1997, 1999), this certainly drew blood. But when the emerging leader of the anti-secular opposition, Rodney Stark, administered secularization's last rites, 'requiescat in pace,' in 1999, he was premature. As so often happens in such debates, the disagreement involves a number of different arguments passing each other in a starless night. In fact, the debate can be dis-aggregated into five debates over five quite different issues.

1. First, there is the question of *degree*; i.e. whether secularization should be considered as a massive all-or-nothing transformation between conditions where religion is all dominant to conditions in which religion has disappeared altogether OR secularization may also be found in smaller, more nuanced shifts well within the former continuum rather than at its poles.

The British anthropologist, Mary Douglas (1982) was among the first to chastise secularization proponents for imagining a mythical past against which the present will inevitably come up short. In her case, the past involved those simple, undifferentiated societies studied by anthropologists but stereotyped by others as convenient foils. Thus, even here religious piety and participation are not always either deep or universal. If these are the beginnings of the neo-evolutionary process of modernization, their religion bears inconvenient similarities with the religion of complex societies toward the end of the process.

Rodney Stark (1999) picked up the point and elaborated it for early Western societies.

To the extent that a secularizing trend depends upon a contrast with a pious ancient and medieval Europe, Stark cites evidence suggesting that this is mythical. Once one looks beyond the public displays of ecclesiastical officialdoms, the masses appear to be at the very least anti-church, if not anti-religious. Attitudes towards organized faith were conspicuous for their alienation, their corruption, and their sheer raucousness. The religion of many 'Christian' nations founded in these early years was only inches deep as a pious surface covering an often impious base.

In its earliest formulations by such foregoing Enlightenment sages as Voltaire (1756), Marx (1844), Comte (1852), and Spencer (1874), there is little question that secularization involved a linear and inexorable decline of religion to the point of its disappearance. Put in this extreme form, it is once again not hard to reject the 'secularization thesis,' as this version of it has come to be known. Both of its extreme poles buckle beneath the weight of evidence. The critics are no doubt correct that the very notion of a totally religious society is a mythical construct unsustained by either historical or anthropological evidence. Whether reaching back to ancient societies or reaching out to isolated tribes, one may find religion as a potent force but never omnipotent. Competing interests, rival claims, status jostling within and without the priesthood – all of these have taken their toll on religious domination. Nor is secularity itself unknown in such settings; people on the margins often become alienated from or indifferent to religion. And at the other extreme, where is the society with no traces of religion? Certainly not the U.S. or anywhere else in the West. Nor for that matter in the several countries around the globe who have mounted official campaigns against religion – the People's Republic of China or the former U.S.S.R. True, religion is sometimes a minority phenomenon in these and other countries, but in no instance can it be described as fully dormant, much less dead.

Surely this should be the death knell of secularization. But once again, not so fast. There is a sense in which the anti-secularization critics have inflated the secularization argument to a point that makes it especially vulnerable to pricking. Using an all-versus-nothing criterion is a very stringent test indeed, and it ignores the important dynamics and variations that may occur in between these extremes. Such prophecy has been virtually non-existent among more measured twentieth-century analyses. Recent critics have preferred to concentrate their fire on the earlier and more extreme versions of the argument and then generalize the results to secularization of any sort and form. Even if secularization is seen as a straight-line, linear process from high to low – and most would argue that this is rarely the case – one can surely imagine a society whose religion is powerful but not all powerful from which there is religious change without decline, and decline that does not reach demise. To deny conceptual standing to lesser changes along the continuum because they do not involve a shift from the extreme maximum to the extreme minimum is akin to denying scientific standing to all sorts of fluctuations from temperature gradients to demographics. The critical dynamics in virtually all matters of change occur within the mid-range of the distributions rather than at the ideal-typical poles.

Virtually all of the major sociological work on behalf of secularization over the past seventy-five years has occurred in this more closely grounded and finely raked terrain. Social scientists have described various aspects of religious decline in the complex societies of the West, but none has made so bold as to claim or predict religion's omnipotent universality or its disappearance especially with the proliferation of sects and cults – or 'new religious movements' as the latter are now called euphemistically. Nowadays religion's mere persistence masks a host of questions concerning religion's changing terms and circumstances. The 'secularization thesis' of mythical proportions with a mythical beginning and a mythical end is indeed in error, but as I have argued elsewhere, it is a largely non-instructive error somewhat akin to disproving Newton, or denying the hypothesis of global warming because we have not yet been burned to a crisp and the nights do, after all, still get cooler (Demerath 1998, 2000c).

2. Meanwhile, even within a less extravagant range of secularization, there are debates. A second major issue concerns *levels*, i.e. does secularization occur at the macro-level of whole societal cultures and structures, the meso-level of religious institutions and organizations, the micro-level of individual forms of religious belief and participation, or all or none of the above?

Surprisingly, once the focus shifts to these less extreme versions of secularization, the disagreement narrows considerably. Consider the following remark regarding the macro- and meso-levels from the arch-critic of secularization, Rodney Stark:

> This refers to a decline in the social power of once-dominant religious institutions whereby other social institutions, especially political and educational institutions have escaped from prior religious domination. If this were all that secularization means, there would be nothing to argue about. Everyone must agree that, in contemporary Europe, for example, Catholic bishops have less political power than they once possessed, and the same is true of Lutheran and Anglican bishops... Nor are primary aspects of public life any longer suffused with religious symbols, rhetoric, or ritual (Stark, 1999: 4–5).

This greatly reduces the gap between secularization's advocates and at least one key antagonist. For many of his opponents, Stark's acceptance of 'macro' as opposed to 'meso' and 'micro' secularization suggests a battlefield conversion – though, in fact, it is not a new position for him (cf. Stark and Bainbridge 1985). Nor is it a trivial concession. Many of the twentieth-century theories of secularization reviewed in the previous section pivot around this point, especially Parsons, Berger and Wilson. But if there is at least some agreement at this one level of secularization, debate continues at the other two levels of institutional and individual religion.

It is here that Stark has concentrated his relentless fire against secularization. His book with Roger Finke, *The Churching of America* (1992), uses actual and reconstructed church membership data to argue that individual religiousness has increased rather than decreased over the last two centuries, and that the real 'winners' have been conservative churches, while the real 'losers' have been the more liberal (and more secular) churches. Critics note that the work is not without problems – for example, spectacular growth rates are less likely among already large denominations and more likely among successful start-ups that have nowhere to go but up, and the thesis refers to rates of growth and decline rather than absolute size where the liberals continue to lead. Moreover, the study assumes that membership is a constantly reliable measure of general religiosity over time when, for example, in the early years it was more a measure of elite community standing than individual piety. Finally, as James Hunter (1987), Philip Jenkins (2002) and others have pointed out, even today's radically conservative churches experience secularization over time and may become tomorrow's modernists.

Many scholars have also noted the continued vitality of religion in America. Stephen Warner's 'new paradigm' (1993) provides a systematic statement of how the American case may differ from the European scene that spawned secularization theory in the first place. But recently Stark has taken his methods and his 'market' model of religion abroad. He and economist Laurence Iannaccone (1994) have argued that even the secularization of European religion was greatly exaggerated – an argument that has had both supporters (Davie 1994; Swatos and Gissurarson 1997) and detractors (cf. Bruce 1995; Dobbelaere 1993; Wilson 1998). Stark and his compatriots use a 'supply-side' interpretation of the religious marketplace, in which they argue that individual demand is less important than the religious organizations' supply. The supply may involve a religious monopoly or religious competition in any given society or region, and their disputed findings indicate that competition is more favorable to religion because it allows the consumer to exercise more 'rational choice' in seeking out the religious benefits.

3. Meanwhile, a third source of contention involves the question of just how should one measure secularization? There are a variety of barometers ranging from the standard counts of church membership, church attendance, and religious media consumption to legislative and judicial decisions, and the uneven compliance

with both. However, all of these indices are suspect in one way or another. Grace Davie (1994) has argued, for example, that a common current syndrome in Britain involves 'believing without belonging.' By contrast, a steady stream of research in the U.S. has long indicated that one can be a church member – even a church attender – without being a believer in the traditional sense. American church membership totals generally exceed church attendance rates by 50%, and recent work by Haddaway *et al.* (1993) has shown that claimed church attendance routinely exaggerates actual church attendance by 50% or more. On the other hand, Robert Woodberry (1998) has shown inflated attendance reports are due largely to religion's continued high standing in the culture and the bias that results from the normative desirability of attendance.

Despite such biases, Hout and Fischer (2002) have analyzed the doubling of those with 'no religious preference' from 7 to 14%, a finding whose significance for secularization has itself been debated (cf. Marwell and Demerath 2003). There are also less obtrusive measures of faith and faithlessness. For instance, increasing sales of religious books and rising ratings of religious media are often cited as evidence against secularization. However, such activity may reflect active minorities swimming against the secularizing current as opposed to a more phlegmatic majorities drifting with a secularizing stream.

Judicial decisions concerning religion may be subject to the reverse misinterpretation. When the U.S. Supreme Court ruled against prayer in the public schools in 1963, this was by no means a reflection of dominant public sentiment. Like most decisions in the area of religion over the past half-century, these reflected the court's protection against the first clause of the Constitution's First Amendment guarding against a religious establishment. In most such cases, the originating plaintiffs were aberrant non-religious types with thick wallets and thicker skins who were resisting local practices. Indeed, many such practices – including school prayer – that have been ruled unconstitutional have been continued below the national radar. It is speculated that even today

some 25% of the nation's public classrooms begin with some form of spoken or silent prayer – the Supreme Court notwithstanding.

Meanwhile, the dispute over secularization is not confined to the West. In fact, the Western version of the debate is comparatively innocuous because it is largely confined to scholars removed from the political ramparts and because the politics of religion has generally been laid to rest save in a few cases such as the tragically contested Northern Ireland and the recent anti-climactic decision of Sweden to sever state ties with the Lutheran Church as of 2000. But once one leaves the West to visit countries elsewhere (cf. Demerath 2000a, 2001), it is hard not to be struck by one area after another where assessments of secularization and secularity have become volatile public issues exacerbated by the ideological conflict between forthright pro- and anti-secularists. From Poland and Eastern Europe through the remains of the U.S.S.R. to Afghanistan; from the Balkans through Turkey and into Iran; from Algeria through Egypt to Israel; from Pakistan through India to Sri Lanka; from Indonesia through China to Japan – these are just a few countries whose national identities now hang in the balance of a prolonged conflict over secularization (cf. Juergensmeyer 1993). I shall have more to say about these non-Western cases later. But the struggles may involve both one religious group versus another and religion generally versus a secular culture.

4. These cases cue still a fourth issue that fuels the larger debate over secularization. Just as we can reject an all-to-nothing temporal trajectory for secularization, it seems clear that we must reject all-or-nothing generalizations that apply to all individuals, all churches, all religions, all social classes, all communities, all regions, or all societies, much less to the world as a whole. Although there has been a persistent tendency towards such overdrawn characterizations, this moves us out of sociology and the world *as it is* into more philosophical and theological treatments of the world *as it ought to be* – as if there were consensuses here.

Since so much of the empirical literature in sociology makes this point, it is hard to know where to begin or end in citing references.

But the aforementioned Norris and Inglehart (2004) volume might suffice for traversing the widest array of such differences in its global survey of secularization. As they make clear, secularization is not a global phenomenon, given major differences between East and West, North and South. Nor are these immune to further macro-, meso-, and micro- variation. World faith traditions differ between themselves (e.g. the more secular Buddhists vs. the less secular Hindus).

But there are also differences within Faith traditions (e.g. within the Abrahamic tree, the more secular wings of Liberal Protestants and Reform Jews versus the generally less secular branches of Islam). Within each of these general groupings, churches, temples and mosques vary, as do the members in or around them. The well-known distinction between churches, sects, and cults reeks of secularization, and certainly some of each are more secular than others. Even among evangelical, fundamentalist or Pentecostal groups, some have moved further down the road to secularization than others, partly as a result of the search for organizational stability and membership growth. Finally, the sociology of religion is replete with demonstrations that individuals within even quite specific religious groups will differ. As sociologists of religion have long demonstrated, individuals differ by parental background, age, gender and ethnicity and social class – to name only a few variables that bear upon the extent of secularization and the degree of secularity.

All of these findings have a self-reflexive impact upon the very scholars researching them. One reason why the secularization paradigm went so long without being challenged is that so many of the scholars supporting it came from cultures, sub-cultures, and organizations that were part of it. In the West, this meant scholars who were themselves largely secular or from the more secular religious backgrounds of Liberal Protestantism and Catholicism or Reform Judaism, as opposed to newer and more conservative movements. As the saying goes, what you see depends upon where you are seated. But to the extent that secularization becomes a more variegated phenomenon as opposed to a single massive

depiction of the world, it is in a better position to draw upon scholars from different backgrounds who will not feel they have personal axes to grind or personal identities at stake.

5. Finally, the fifth and last principal topic for debate concerns the relationship between secularization as religious decline or religious change. Here too Rodney Stark has helped to bring the issue to the fore:

> Of course, religion changes. Of course, there is more religious participation and even greater belief in the supernatural at some times and places than in others, just as religious organizations have more secular power in some times and places than in others. Of course, doctrines change – Aquinas was not Augusteine, and both would find heresy in the work of Avery Dulles. But change does not equate with decline (Stark 1999: 29).

Once again, Stark appears to concede a great deal before snatching it away with his last sentence remark that '… change does not equate with decline.' He is certainly correct that the two are not identical. Moreover, only one equates with secularization, and that is change rather than decline. Of course, there is little question that secularization has come to connote decline, whether in its long-range or short-term form. But as I shall argue momentarily, change may involve secularization without decline; indeed, secularization can be part of a process that is necessary to maintain or even increase religiosity.

DEFINING SECULARIZATION AND INTRODUCING SACRALIZATION

At this point, we are now sufficiently acquainted with the key issues surrounding secularization to consider a definition that is a bit more formal and considerably broader than those mentioned earlier. Of course, there are almost as many definitions as there are broad treatments of the topic, and there is certainly no paucity of the latter, since any serious sociological treatment of religion requires a treatment of secularization (e.g. Beckford 2003). Still, here is my definition:

> *Secularization is a process of change by which the sacred gives way to the secular, whether in matters of personal*

faith, institutional practice, or societal power. It involves a transition in which things once revered become ordinary, the sanctified becomes mundane, and things other-worldly may lose their prefix. Whereas 'secularity' refers to a condition of sacredlessness, and 'secularism' is the ideology devoted to such a state, secularization is a historical dynamic that may occur gradually or suddenly and is sometimes temporary and occasionally reversible.

Several aspects of the definition are worth emphasizing. *First*, it refers to a process of religious change, but not necessarily to religious decline, let alone demise. After all, if religion involves notions of transcendence that are ritually reinforced and collectively supported, this is not immutable; it may take varying forms, and it is not always the oldest or most traditional versions that are the most compelling. Indeed, I will argue momentarily that effective religion often depends upon change – and secularized change at that.

Second, the definition carries no sense of linearity or inevitability. It may – or may not – occur among individuals as an accretion or an epiphany, among institutions such as cults, sects, churches, denominations, and whole faith traditions, and among communities and societies where a particular form of the sacred suffers a diminution of influence.

And *third*, note the emphasis on 'a particular form of the sacred.' Secularization is not a process that sweeps everything sacred before it. As some sacred beliefs, rituals, or influences undergo change, others within the same firmament may remain constant or even experience recrudescence or enhancement.

In fact, this is the cue for the entrance of *sacralization* as the dialectically opposing process which is crucial in understanding the larger context in which secularization often operates. Turning the above definition of secularization on its head, *sacralization is the process by which the secular becomes sacred or other new forms of the sacred emerge, whether in matters of personal faith, institutional practice or political power. And sacralization may also 'occur gradually or suddenly, and may be sometimes temporary and occasionally reversible.'*

Sacralization may take a number of forms. Even established religions generate new sacred commitments over time; witness Catholicism's relatively recent devotion to Mariolatry, beginning in the nineteenth century; Islam's increasingly sacred enmities between Sunnis and Shia where power hangs in the balance, and radical Hinduism's effort to sacralize India as an officially Hindu state. Within American religion, sacralization is apparent in both the tendency of religious 'sects' to revive or revitalize older religious beliefs and practices and the tendency of 'cults' to develop new religious forms, whether through the innovation of a prophetic and virtuosic leader within the society or by importing a religion from outside the society that is effectively new within it. Virtually every Protestant denomination began as either a sectarian effort to recapture a lost religious truth or a theological and organizational innovation. Groups like the Christian Scientists, Mormons, Adventists, the Jehovah's Witnesses, and Waco's Branch Davidians continue to bear strong traces of their original efflorescence. Imported movements such as the Unification Church (South Korea), the Hare Krishna (India) and the Soka Gakkai (Japan) have also had deeply sacralizing effects for their American members.

Sacralization is also apparent at certain points in the history of U.S. 'civil religion,' i.e. *any nation's sense of its shared sacred heritage and commitments.* It is not unusual for a country's civil religious sensibility to wane and wax over time. It would be too simple to argue that its shared Judeo-Christian legacy tends to secularize during relatively uneventful periods of collective complacency, only to sacralize during times of national crisis. But a sense of common religious dedication does tend to surge during and immediately after major external crises, e.g. a true world war or the events of 9/11 when church attendance experienced a temporary spike. However, contrary to the old axioms, there are atheists in both foxholes and deathbeds, and some types of internal societal crises may reduce religion's credibility, as happened in the U.S. during the progressive movements of the 1960s.

The important point is that neither secularization nor sacralization alone is adequate to describe the U.S. or any other nation in holistic and linear terms. While both short- and long-term trends in one direction or another are common, the two tendencies often oscillate and even play off one another as partners in a dialectic. And while these apparent adversaries sometimes respond to each other's pulls in the opposite direction, the next section will point out that they can also be allies. Secularization often serves as a form of adaptation to historical change, and it can prepare the way for a sacralization that is more attuned to contemporary circumstances once the detritus of tradition is cleared away.

Certainly I don't mean to advocate some law-like proposition by which secularization and sacralization are always linked to insure some constant level of sacredness in an individual or social unit. Nor do I mean to suggest a rigid model of religious crop rotation by which secularization always clears the ground for a new sacred planting, since new forms of the sacred may precede and influence the secularization of older forms. The major argument is that tendencies in each direction generally check each other to ward off all-or-nothing extremes of either sort. In fact, this is not a new perspective. As pointed out by Goldstein (2006), virtually every one of the classic and contemporary sociological proponents of secularization – not to mention their critic, Rodney Stark himself (e.g. Stark and Bainbridge, 1985) have made reference to some form of oscillating cycles of more and less religion. Still, exceptions do occur, and there is at least a loose sense in which sacralization without secularization is the equivalent of 'pre-modernity;' secularization without sacralization is not a bad definition of 'post-modernity,' while the two in tandem are central to much of what 'modernity' itself entails. As this suggests, pre-modernity, modernity, and post-modernity are far more defensible as iterative cyclical moments rather than static phases of a single linear trend.

PARADOXES OF SECULARIZATION AND SACRALIZATION

At just the time when one might expect work on secularization to yield a consensually validated paradigm (cf. Tschannen 1991), it is far closer to producing a new set of contentiously divisive paradoxes. Much of this pivots around the very terms at issue. Both 'secular' and 'sacred' are mutually referential in that each makes a statement about the other. To be secular is to be non-sacred; to be sacred is to transcend and transform the secular. Much the same is true when we shift from semantics to social processes. Just as an object must have been sacred for it to be subsequently secularized, so must it have been secular for it to be subsequently 'sacralized.' And just as secularization marks a decline of the sacred, so does sacralization denote an increase in the sacred in one form or another and at one level or another.

But linking the processes of secularization and sacralization can have paradoxical results. Consider the following eight propositions as examples:

(1) *Religious 'awakenings' require previous religious 'naps.'* American religious history has been commonly charted in terms of its eighteenth, nineteenth and possibly twentieth century awakenings (cf. McLoughlin 1978). But later revivals imply earlier slumbers which have equal merit as historical focii (e.g. May 1949; Erikson 1966; Turner 1985). It is the combination of the two that establishes the most basic rhythm of a country's religious history. If this is true at the macro-level, it has a micro-parallel. There is a similar relationship between individuals' religious conversions and their earlier religious indifference. Newspaper headlines and scholarly accounts that stress the former but neglect the latter fail to capture the critical interaction between sacred and secular.

(2) *Modernization may lead to both secularization and sacralization.* The grand narrative of the 'secularization thesis' holds that religion beats a steady and linear retreat in the face of mounting modernization. There is some truth to this, but also some half-truth. In fact, this is what Peter Berger referred to in recently recanting some of his earlier writing on secularization (Berger 1997, 1999). To unpack the mystery,

modernization does often lead to forms of secularization, but these in turn often spark a sacralizing response – one that ironically uses the means of modernity to protest the ends of modernity. Gorski (2000) makes a similar point in discussing the effects of the Protestant reformation in modernizing Europe: it was *both* secularizing and sacralizing. This duality also characterizes the putative 'fundamentalisms' everywhere, whether in the original Christian version in the U.S., or in the Islamic and Hindu variants around the global girdle of religious extremism. As noted earlier, India is one of many countries offering scarred testimony to religion's continuing presence. On the other hand, these countries also bear witness to the incursions of secularity as a perceived threat to religious interests. If either religion or secularity were fully dominant in these settings, the conflicts would be obviated (Beteille 1994).

(3) *The rise of a vital 'religious marketplace' is also evidence of both secularization and sacralization.* As noted earlier, Stark and his colleagues (1999, 2000) and the early Berger (1967) invoke the 'religious marketplace' as a telling metaphor, but each draws out different implications. For Berger, such a marketplace involved an increase in competition that was staged in increasingly secular terms and reflected the crumbling of religion's prior structural monopolies and/or cultural hegemonies. For Stark *et al.*, on the other hand, religious competition led to a rational-choice process by which choosers seek out the most satisfying religious options according to religious criteria. And yet the new consumer's mentality may involve more stained-glass window-shopping than long-term buying, i.e. actually joining a church. The aforementioned debate over changing patterns of religiosity turns on this point, as does a current dispute over the significance of religious 'switching' in the U.S. (cf. Demerath and Yang 1998).

(4) Because movements running against the societal grain often create more friction and more headlines than trends running with it, one must be careful not to mistake the sacred exceptions for the secular rule. It is sometimes tempting to interpret the high heat of a small religious movement as more important than the smoking embers of a larger and more secularized tradition. In the same spirit, one must be wary of confusing growth rates with size. Both have their place, but even those small, conservative religious movements with high growth rates may still be marginal to the larger population and culture. Many of Finke and Stark's (1992) 'winning' conservative denominations with high recent growth rates are still small compared to most of the 'losing' denominations that remain far larger despite recent attrition.

(5) *Sacred manifestations may reflect secular forces, and vice versa.* The relationship between any form of behavior and the motivations behind it is problematic. As we have seen, standard indicators of religiosity such as civil religious loyalty, church membership, church attendance, and religious belief are all subject to myriad interpretations, not all of which are unambiguously sacred (cf. Demerath 1998; Haddaway *et al.* 1993). It may be more that the civil is religious than that the religious is civil; church membership and attendance reflect a variety of sacred and secular meanings that vary across a population and across time; affirming a religious belief may be less a matter of cognitive conviction than of cultural affiliation and continuity. Even the various 'fundamentalist' movements around the world may not be as uniformly or fanatically 'religious' as they are often portrayed. Many of their members have a predominantly secular agenda that is aided by religious legitimation, hence religion may serve in some instances as a means rather than an end in its own right (Demerath 2001). At the same time, a withdrawal from conventional religious frameworks may coexist with a more privatized faith, namely the 'little voice' of the pseudonymous 'Sheila Larson' in Bellah *et al.* (1985: 221). And surely there are any number of

conventionally secular commitments that take on sacred valences for their devotees, as noted earlier.

(6) *Moderate secularization can be a prophylactic against ultimate secularization.* Changing social conditions require changing forms of the sacred if they are to be relevant. Hence, some degree of secularization may serve as a form of sacred adaptation. As one early example, the British historian R. H. Tawney (1962) amended Weber's heavily theological account of the development of Calvinist pre-destinationism, whereby success in this life ultimately became a clue to salvation in the next life. Tawney showed that this was due to a series of takes-and-gives between Geneva's rising middle-class parishioners and a clergy willing to make secularized compromises to keep their pews filled. The same dynamic has been a tactic in the trajectory of Liberal Protestantism over the past century, as pastors and theologians have made comparable concessions to their secularizing adherents (cf. Berger 1967; Demerath 1992). The tactic has been challenged by advocates of strict doctrine and strict churches (Kelley 1972; Iannaccone 1994). But the possibility remains that cleaving to strictness might have cost the churches far more defections than did adapting to the secular.

(7) *Secularization may be more common in conservative than liberal religious communities.* Because secularization involves change, the question is where the greatest change is likely to occur. Since liberal religious organizations have already undergone considerable secularization, many now face a stained glass floor as a constraint against further change. On the other hand, conservative religious groups are closer to the traditional ceiling and have further room to change in a more secular direction. While it is clear that evangelical, fundamentalist and Pentecostal churches are less secular than more mainstream churches, it is by no means clear that they have recently experienced less secularization. The point is well-made by the classic sect-to-church dynamic whereby newer, smaller, and often more precarious religious movements make secular adaptations in the quest for organizational stability. A number of recent studies have described the kind of sacred-secular tensions that often result within conservative religions churches – for example over issues of gender (viz. Bartkowski 2001; Gallagher 2003), and still others have discredited the stereotype of conservative churches as static and homogeneous (e.g. Hunter 1987, and Greeley and Hout 2006).

(8) *Focusing on the fate of old forms of religion may deflect attention from new forms of the sacred.* Obsessing over secularization of the past may preclude analysis of sacralization in the present and future. Just as conventional religion may not necessarily be sacred, so are new sources of the sacred not necessarily religious. Today one hears a good deal of talk – some of it glib – about a growing distinction between religion and spirituality and about profound sacred commitments in everything from socialism to sex. Just because they have attained cliché status does not mean they should be jettisoned as possibilities for deeper investigation (cf. Demerath 2000a).

The eight propositions above lead into a series of issues beyond the scope of this essay: Does every individual need some sense of a sacred commitment and regimen that is self-consciously maintained and ritually reinforced? Does every collectivity and society require something similar that is shared among its members? And if the answers to either or both of these questions are affirmative, what is the relation between the sacredness required and conventional religion, on the one hand, and more secular sources, on the other? To what extent can the sacred reside in high and low culture, moral and ethical convictions, and movements on behalf of political causes, personal identities, and nationalist ambitions? And is it possible to investigate these matters without falling into traps of tautology and teleology? Precisely because these questions are so old, it is time for newly researched and freshly conceptualized answers.

SHIFTING FROM RELIGION
TO CULTURE AT LARGE

To some readers, my earlier definitions of secularization and sacralization may suffer from a glaring omission: they contain no specific mention of religion *per se*. This is not an oversight. I want to stress the broader category of the sacred, noting that religion is only one of many sources of the sacred, and not all of religion qualifies as sacred. In emphasizing the relation between secularity and the 'sacred,' I want to push beyond religion to consider a sociologically richer vein of the sacred; namely, culture.

Of course, secularization is no stranger to cultural analysis. Virtually every major cultural theorist and cultural historian has taken religious secularization into account as either an effect or a cause of historical change, as we have already seen with Marx, Weber, and especially Durkheim who noted the civic

> origin of ceremonies that, by their object, by their results, and by the techniques used, are not different in kind from ceremonies that are specifically religious. What basic difference is there between Christians' celebrating the principal dates of Christ's life... and a citizen's meeting commemorating the advent of a new charter or some other great event of national life? (Durkheim 1912: 429).

This seminal passage was later re-born in Robert Bellah's (1967) famous account of 'civil religion' with specific reference to the U.S. national polity. However, it is worth remarking that Bellah gave the concept a far more narrowly religious thrust than had Durkheim – or for that matter, Durkheim's own predecessor in these matters, the eighteenth-century social philosopher, Jean Jacques Rousseau (1960).

As this suggests, France has been a special source of secularization accounts. The eighteenth-century decline of the French monarchy and the ensuing French Revolution involved a fundamental 'de-sacralization' of the link between church and crown that has been widely analyzed by historians (cf. Merrick 1990; Darnton 1995; Gordon 1998). This in turn is linked to France's role as a seedbed for Enlightenment thought, which provided such critical intellectual second-guessing of religion from Voltaire forward. One strand of this tradition took the form of French positivism. As represented by the mid-nineteenth-century visionary, Auguste Comte, positivism – like Marxism – both sought and prophesied the replacement of religion by social science.

Subsuming religion within a larger category of the sacred has a more extensive pedigree. The great comparativist, Mircea Eliade (1959) was consistently at pains to talk of 'hierophanies' that afforded contact with the 'sacred,' rather than concentrate on religion itself. For him conventional religion by no means exhausted sacred possibilities. If religion was explicitly sacred, other forms qualified implicitly. In fact, Edward Bailey (1998) has made explicit the notion of 'implicit religion' that is itself implicit in the work of Eliade and others. As Rousseau, Durkheim, and Weber would also have agreed, sacred meanings may emanate from the political, the familial, and the quotidian. The quality of sacredness is not inherent in a thing or idea; rather, sacredness is imputed from within a social context.

Meanwhile, if religion is only one form of the sacred, the sacred in turn is one important dimension of something broader still; namely, culture. The relation between religion and culture can be so close as to be confusing. Consider the two definitions below from the anthropologist, Clifford Geertz, and see if it is immediately obvious which refers to religion and which to culture:

> a) _____ is 1) a system of symbols which acts to 2) establish powerful, pervasive, and long-lasting moods and motivations in men by 3) formulating conceptions of a general order of existence and 4) clothing these conceptions with such an aura of factuality that 5) the moods and motivations seem uniquely realistic (Geertz, 1973: 190).

> b) _____ is ... the framework of beliefs, expressive symbols and values in terms of which individuals define their world, express their feelings, and make their judgements. (It) is the fabric of meaning in terms of which human beings interpret their experience and guide their action (Geertz 1973: 144–5).

Both definitions have that perverse element of abstraction that qualifies them as social scientific; both share an emphasis on the kind of 'control system' that Geertz found essential. The first refers to religion and the second to culture, but in the often arbitrary world of conceptual definitions one could do far worse than reverse them.

And yet Geertz' emphasis on cognitive control neglects another element that both phenomena have in common. It is true that both religion and culture are symbol systems that perform powerful directive functions. But one of the reasons for their power is precisely a shared quality of sacredness. The point scarcely needs elaboration for religion. But arguing that culture carries a sacred dimension may be more controversial.

Take the very word 'culture.' In strict etymological terms, it traces back to the notion of 'horticulture' and the spreading of manure – something many critics of culture's conceptual softness will have no difficulty crediting. But if one adds a historically indefensible but conceptually strategic hyphen to produce the term 'cult-ure,' this cues a more instructive story. 'Cult' in its older, non-pejorative, Durkheimian sense refers to that behavioral core of religious beliefs and practices that constitute the center of any religion – and perhaps any cultural system as well (Demerath 2003).

Can a culture operate effectively without having a cultic or sacred component? In responding no, I am using the term sacred in its broader connotation rather than as a synonym for the conventionally religious. Taken in this way, any cultural system of symbols, beliefs, and values is a sacred system in that its components must be accorded a reverential status that allows for the leap of faith required in converting what are often relative and arbitrary judgements into absolute normative standards. Culture's credibility depends less upon the objective, empirical, or rational standing of its tenets than upon a subjective, non-empirical, and a-rational belief in its guidance. This requires a special status that involves the quality of sacredness in at least a latent, if not always manifest, sense. So much for a bridge to our concluding section.

A TYPOLOGY OF SECULARIZATION SCENARIOS

If secularization is alive and well within religion, and if religion is only part of the wider sphere of the sacred which is in turn a crucial component of culture, then it follows that secularization should be an active dynamic within culture itself. The insight is surely not an original revelation. However, it is little acknowledged in the various discussions of cultural change that have occurred in the social science literature. While older theories of history and the more recent but now largely recessed literature on 'modernization' refer to secularization, both refer almost exclusively to the secularization of religion *per se* (e.g. Germani 1981). Secularization of culture as distinct from religion is commonly neglected.

Virtually any form of cultural change both reveals and depends upon the opposite but often symbiotic processes of secularization and sacralization. Take any episode of transition, and it is not hard to find the waning of older 'sacred' beliefs and values, along with the frequent waxing of new ones. This applies to every type of symbol – whether political, economic, scientific, or indeed religious. As indicated above, all cultural components require a sacred quality, and generally this quality must erode before the components may decline and possibly give way to new commitments.

Cultural secularization may involve various syndromes which have rarely been disentangled. As noted previously, even within the narrow sphere of religion, secularization is generally discussed in all or nothing terms. When gradations are admitted, they are gradations of degree not of kind. But in what follows, I want to delineate four basic kinds of secularization that are framed by the intersection of two fundamental distinctions. The two distinctions involve *internal* versus *external* sources and *directed* versus *non-directed* scenarios. The former distinction refers to the difference between secularization that emerges from within the social context of the cultural system at issue versus secularization that is imported or imposed from outside. (See Table 3.1.)

Table 3.1   *A typology of secularization scenarios*

	Internal	External
Non-directed	Emergent	Diffuse
Directed	Coercive	Imperialist

The latter distinction refers to secularization that stems downward from authorities in control versus secularization that seeps upwards from within the cultural system itself. Putting the two distinctions together produces four combinations or types of secularization: 'emergent,' 'coercive,' 'diffused,' and 'imperialist.' In describing each, I shall draw on a wide array of examples, including some drawn from a recently completed fourteen-nation comparative study of religion and politics around the globe (Demerath 2001). This applies the types to whole societies, but they could also be relevant to the secularization of sub-cultures, communities, institutions, or even social movements within a society.

(1) *Emergent Secularization*: This form of internally evolved and non-directed secularization is the classic model for religion. Here secularization is seen as a kind of drift to the left – the unintentional product of increasing education, industrialization, modernization, and differentiation in the social context. This is the secularization described in a stanza of Matthew Arnold's 'Dover Beach:'

> The sea of faith
> Was once, too, at the full, and round earth's shore
> Lay like the folds of a bright girdle furl'd
> But now I only hear
> Its melancholy, long, withdrawing roar,
> Retreating to the breath
> Of the night-wind down the vast edges drear
> And naked shingles of the world.

Arnold wrote in England in the mid-nineteenth century when a number of Western intellectuals had begun to sense that perhaps the Enlightenment had gone too far and produced saddening changes on the part of the many, not just the few. However, the poet who grasped not only secularization but possible sacralization in its wake was W. B. Yeats in his verse, 'The Second Coming:'

> Turning and turning in the widening gyre
> The falcon cannot bear the falconer;
> Things fall apart; the centre cannot hold;
> Mere anarchy is loosed upon the world,
> The blood-dimmed tide is loosed, and everywhere
> The ceremony of innocence is drowned;
> The best lack all conviction, while the worst
> Are full of passionate intensity.
>
> Surely some revelation is at hand;
> Surely the Second Coming is at hand.
> The Second Coming! Hardly are those words out
> When the vast image out of *Spiritus Mundi*
> Troubles my sight; somewhere in sands of desert
> A shape with lion body and the head of man
> A gaze blank and pitiless as the sun,
> Is moving its slow thighs, while all above it
> Reel shadows of the indignant desert birds.
> The darkness drops again; but now I know
> That twenty centuries of stony sleep
> Were vexed to nightmare by a rocking cradle,
> And what rough beast, its hour come round at last,
> Slouches towards Bethlehem to be born?

The historian, James Turner (1985), dates the legitimation of unbelief among American intellectuals at the end of the Civil War. But the Enlightenment altered more than religion; it affected a whole conception of human self-consciousness that included what Arthur Lovejoy (1936) called 'the great chain of being' and what Owen Chadwick (1975) termed 'The Secularization of the European Mind.' Moreover, the Enlightenment was not just an assault upon faith, but a substitution of one faith for another. The notion of progress through thought became a sacred cult in its own right – albeit one that has been subject to secularization since. Meanwhile, there is little question that the rise of Newtonian and Darwinian science as well as the advent of major universities set apart from religious seminaries represented a major cultural change (cf. Koyre 1957; Foucault 1966).

There was no single event, let alone decree, that produced the shift. Certainly this was not the result of any authoritative edict. Rather, it depended on cultural forces that were themselves dependent upon forms of non-religious secularization. Weber was right to point to the rise of the Protestant Ethic as a historical watershed, but most historians now agree that he overestimated the effects of religion and theology themselves. Insofar as Protestantism broke the spell of Catholic dominance over a tightly undifferentiated world, it released a series of developments in the newly differentiated and autonomous spheres of society. Gradually, politics, the economy, and the world of science and education began to march to their own cultural drummers, but not before drumming out some of the older sacred tenets that had conserved the past and inhibited change. In each case, new sacred commitments depended upon the secularization of older cultural faiths.

In politics, democracy took various structural forms, but its cultural core arose only after 'de-sacralization' was well under way for the French monarchy and other absolutist regimes in the West. It is true that part of the legitimating code of the 'ancien regime' involved its ties with the church. But it also involved a conception of top-down civil authority that went far beyond religion.

The rise of capitalism – and most especially its Weberian 'spirit' – depended upon the secularization of a prior economic stage with its attendant economic rituals. Here structural changes influenced the cultural shift, and one might paraphrase Karl Marx to stress the importance of changing modes of economic production in de-sacralizing old social practices. The theme has continued to resonate within twentieth-century 'critical theory' that began in Germany between the two World Wars. Themes of materialistic disenchantment echo deeply within Herbert Marcuse's lament for 'one-dimensional man' (1964); Daniel Bell's concern for the 'end of ideology' (1964) and the loss of meaning within the 'cultural contradictions of capitalism' (1976), and Jürgen Habermas's sense of the 'colonization of the (private) life world by the (public) system (1989).'

But all is not lost, and somehow enchantment has persisted (cf. Schneider 1993). The historian, Daniel Gordon, offers a telling rebuttal to the Weberian despair:

> But when Weber spoke of an 'iron cage,' he meant an absence of meaning, an economy that had no moral ground at all... Yet, had Weber known more about the Enlightenment and its sacralization of capitalism, he would not have created such a radical antithesis between the Reformation and modernity (Gordon, 1998: 151).

Here then is the cultural cycle of secularization and sacralization enacted within the economic sphere itself. The spirit or culture of capitalism had achieved autonomous standing but it had become sacralized in its own terms and for its own sake. While Weber and others might quarrel with the quality of meaning involved, there is little question of its quantity.

The rise of science and education, of democracy and capitalism – these are among the great cultural transformations in Western history. Each depends upon a succession of secularization and sacralization, even though none is conventionally religious. All of this illustrates an internal, non-directed, 'emergent' form of secularization that is more glacial than explosive. It is a cultural dynamic that nevertheless moves mountains.

(2) *Coercive Secularization*: Here is another form of internal secularization but one that is purposely directed by some type of effective authority. There are many types of direction, and the term 'coercion' is meant to suggest a top-down exercise of power – legitimate or not. There are many *loci* and levels of coercion, but for simplicity's sake, I shall focus here mainly on the societal.

Surprisingly, there are those who would place the U.S. in this category. Although no political leader would dare exert public influence on behalf of secularization, this is at least one interpretation of the first part of the First Amendment to the Constitution: 'Congress shall make no laws respecting an establishment of religion ...' Of course, the clause goes on to support the 'free exercise of religion.' But the establishment ban and the judicial decisions in its wake concerning prayer in the public schools, Christmas celebrations on public property, etc. have often been construed as governmental coercion on behalf of 'secular humanism.' This is not the place to debate the greater wisdom of the establishment clause, especially since I have elsewhere defended it as the often neglected but unique mark of genius within the First Amendment (Demerath 2000b and see Chapter 18 in this Handbook). However, it is clear that both clauses of the First Amendment have had both secularizing and sacralizing impacts.

Meanwhile, there are other instances of coercive secularization in the U.S. On the one hand, consider the federal government's role in restricting Native Americans, both territorially and culturally, with secularizing consequences. On the other hand, the federal government has also played a secularizing role in reining in racism and racial segregation. There is little question that racism has long been a part of American culture, especially following the Civil War when emancipation of the slaves required new doctrines of racial inferiority to justify continued discrimination. But how does one change racism? Put more familiarly, how can one secularize the values, norms, and rituals that it entailed? When the government stepped in to produce and implement civil rights legislation that integrated schools, public accommodations, and voting practices, the required changes in behavior ultimately brought about corresponding changes in both social psychology and culture. This is a clearer instance of coerced secularization paving the way to change, though some might argue that the coercion was more external than internal because it came from Washington and the federal government rather than the South.

Insofar as laws and political regimes can influence change, and insofar as virtually every social change requires some secularizing of an older culture to make way for or accommodate the new, virtually every country offers examples of coercive secularization. Turkey, China, and Japan offer three especially instructive cases that combine religious and other cultural changes.

Turkey was once the center of Orthodox Christianity and then later became the center of the once great Islamic 'Ottoman Empire.' Turkey straddles the border between Asia and Europe, and the vicissitudes of its culture reflects its geography. This was especially clear shortly after World War I when the young military officer, Kemal Attaturk, seized control of the state and essentially pivoted the nation 180 degrees to face the West. Influenced by his sympathetic understanding of the European Enlightenment, French positivism, and Emile Durkheim, Attaturk declared that Turkey would henceforth be a secular state rather than

officially Muslim. Over the next several years in the mid-1920s, he was able to pass a series of statutes that amounted to no less than a cultural transformation. These included bans on certain forms of Islamic practice – such as the Sufis' mystical 'whirling dervishes' – and on such items of traditional Islamic dress as the men's 'fez' and the women's veils. Here too the secularization reached beyond religion to other aspects of the traditional culture. It included a Westernization of the written numerical system and mandated alterations in the language itself. More than seventy years later, Attaturk continues to be revered, and his changes endure. Although there is now a resurgence of Islamic identity in life style and politics, this is a minority movement and one held in tight check by an ever-vigilant military. Clearly Attaturk was one of the twentieth-century's most effective statesmen, and his example of directed secularization was not lost on others of his generation, including Lenin and Stalin in Russia, Nasser of Egypt, Ben-Gurion of Israel, Sukarno of Indonesia, and Mao Zedong of China.

Of course, Mao's regime in China offers a particularly infamous example of coercive secularization – especially its hyper-coercive (anti-) 'cultural revolution' during the 1960s and 1970s. One might quarrel with the term 'secularization' here because many Chinese suggest that theirs was never a religious culture to begin with – superstitious and philosophical, yes, but religious, no. But whatever one calls Confucianism, Taoism, and Buddhism, the larger point involves a secularization of sacralized culture embedded in traditional forms. This was most assuredly Mao's objective – again as a way of preparing the nation for a new sacred system; namely, communism. It is ironic that today communism itself has begun to give way: a second-order secularization of a secularization that was once held to be sacred in its own right.

As Susumo Shimazono points out in his chapter in this Handbook, Japan also offers ambiguities with regard to religion. But at least two instances of coercive secularization stand out. First, during the 1860s, a small group of elite figures behind the throne were eager to spark a new sense of Japanese nationalism and industrialization. They fomented the 'Meiji restoration' with the Emperor as the divine head of a new system of 'State Shinto,' which was deliberately grafted on to the traditional and localistic 'folk Shinto.' Buddhism was vigorously suppressed (viz. secularized) throughout the country to create a cultural space for the new national faith so zealously promoted as a way of binding the country together and prodding it forward, both economically and militarily. Some eighty years later, following the ill-fated venture known in Japan as 'the great Pacific war,' the country experienced another form of directed secularization, this time aimed at State Shinto itself. But because here the direction came from the U.S., I shall use it as a segue into a third form of secularization.

(3) *Imperialist secularization*: This is another form of directed secularization, but one that emanates externally, that is, from forces outside the society at issue. It strains no credulity to begin with the U.S. as an imperialist exemplar, though its role in Japan following World War II is not often seen in imperialist terms. The U.S. was understandably eager to uproot State Shinto, downgrade the Emperor's status, and insure that religion would never again serve to mobilize the nation. A new Japanese constitution was the vehicle for these purposes. But just as the earlier secularization under the Meiji restoration was unable to totally eliminate all Buddhist influence, the more recent secularization of State Shinto has not completely expunged all traces. It is one thing to change a political structure with the stroke of a constitutional pen, but quite another to transform a society's culture so quickly.

Meanwhile, there are ample instances of imperialist secularization in other places and other times. India has been a reluctant host to outside powers for almost a millennium. The Muslim Mogul emperors began their succession in the early sixteenth century, only to be followed by the British 'raj.' Both empires exerted secularizing influence over Hinduism, though Hinduism has certainly survived. Both also had secularizing impacts on other aspects of the sub-continent's culture. For weal and for woe, the British altered the area's entire political, economic, and educational infrastructure with wrenching cultural changes. Imposed modernity has had a major secularizing impact on India's traditional culture – including job and educational 'reservations' as a counter to untouchability and the prohibition of practices such as 'sati' when a wife is expected to throw herself on her husband's funeral pyre.

There have been few more imperialistic forces in world history than the converting armies of Christianity. These mobilizations on behalf of new sacred systems have been perhaps more effective in secularizing older ones, sometimes leaving a confused void as a result. In addition to their obvious effects on indigenous religions, they have had important consequences for non-religious cultural elements. For example, Lamin Sanneh (1991) notes that missionary activities in Africa were not all negative from the standpoint of African political development. Because they offered educational programs with a new common language, they tended to break down (secularize) older tribal cultures and divisions, thus clearing the way for new nationalistic bonds.

Nationalism is itself both a secularizing and sacralizing phenomenon, though it is frequently misunderstood. Beginning in the mid-nineteenth century, the spoils of warfare often produced new nation-states. These were assembled out of the remains at war's end through acts of statecraft that frequently had no regard for cultural communities and affinities. The new nations were often cultural hodge-podges in which those exercising power were often strangers to those affected by it. Imperialist secularization was an important means of holding onto power insofar as it diluted competing sources of loyalty – whether ethnic, tribal, regional, or religious. The Soviet Union and its Eastern European satellites were, of course, prime examples. However, as we have seen over the past decade, there are limits to the processes of secularization and re-sacralization. Older cultural identities and enmities have asserted themselves throughout the region with tragic consequences in Bosnia and the former Yugoslavia, including Kosova. Because the new forces of separatism are quite different from the motives behind older nation-states, they might better be termed 'culturalism' than 'nationalism.'

(4) *Diffused Secularization*: The typology's final scenario of secularization involves external forces that spread more by diffusion than direction. These are often the unintended consequences of culture contacts. They result from transmitted cultural innovations that become hegemonic in new locales, and in the process serve to displace old practices, rituals, and beliefs – whether formally or informally sacred.

Imagine the reactions of the New Guinea fishing villagers who, sometime in 1943, awoke to see for the first time a substantial fleet of the U.S. Navy anchored offshore and establishing beach installations with jeeps, guns, and communications equipment, which the villagers were seeing for the first time as the wondrous bounty of a divine providence. It was incidents like these that led to the famous 'cargo cults' of Oceania. These cults worshiped new gods of Western materialism and waited – largely in vain – for their own cargo to materialize. Of course, any new religion comes at the expense of the old. In this instance, sacralization preceded secularization.

Today's 'globalization' offers parallels to the cargo cults, except that here the materialism does materialize. Accounts are legion of television sets aglow in dark slum dwellings in Calcutta, cosmetic sales on the upper Amazon in Brazil, internet communication between stay-at-home families in China and their migrating children, and surgical miracles being performed in African villages. Globalization has some of the qualities of a Western middle class conceit – as if the world were now totally enthralled by our high tech innovations, mass media programming, consumer products, and medical advances, not to mention our environmental depredations and political manipulations in pursuit of our economic interests. But globalization is neither as new nor as totalizing as popular treatments would

have it (cf. Demerath 2006). Cultural exchanges have long followed trade currents, and the spread of Western culture into the far corners of the world began to be reciprocated in the seventeenth century. And wherever one culture diffuses into another, the former is likely to have a diminishing, secularizing effect. Of course, the effect is greatly accentuated when the invading culture enjoys a favorable power differential.

I have used the term 'diffused secularization' for this syndrome in several senses. Obviously it refers to the consequences of the diffuse spread of cultures around the world. But it also needs pointing out that host cultures tend to diffuse and give their own local twists to foreign cultures that reach them, hence the now fashionable but awkward amalgam, 'glocalization.' Finally, local cultures themselves experience some diffusion and dilution as a result. We have certainly witnessed aggressive assertions of traditional faiths and identities as sacralizing responses to this general secularizing trend. 'Fundamentalist' Islamic and Hindu movements as well as more direct political opponents of Western culture have become major players on the world stage.

CONCLUSION

If one secret to scholarly success is writing about a topic where few of one's colleagues are deeply invested and knowledgeable, this chapter has been a ticket to infamy. Among sociologists of religion, secularization is on the tip of the collective tongue, and the concept of secularization may crop up more frequently in this Handbook than any other save 'religion' itself. Nor would this surprise professional religious practitioners, whether in the local congregational trenches or on the Vatican throne. In virtually every generation, the clergy decries and laments a loss of religious literacy and an ebbing of faith compared to generations past. Judging from my own interviews and focus groups over the years, this is as true of their private remarks as their public presentations.

But recently an influential group of sociologists of religion have called for an end to such talk and have provoked heated debate on the topic. While weary combatants sometimes allow such debates to fade away before the issues are resolved, this chapter represents at least one participant's second wind. Indeed, this chapter has sought to extend and elaborate the discourse. After a historical review of classical and contemporary conceptions of secularization, I introduced its critics and showed how the great secularization debate has been poured into five teapots. I shifted discussion away from ultimate prophecies of decline and demise to proximate fluctuations in secularization and its dialectically linked concept of 'sacralization.' More nuanced analysis revealed a series of some eight paradoxes that serve to check simplistic and hyperbolic interpretations either for or against secularization.

But if part of the chapter's objective was to reduce the issue of secularization, another goal was to broaden it. The chapter has sought to alter the emphasis from religion to the sacred, and then go one step further by expanding the reach of secularization from religion and the sacred writ small to culture writ large. Here I presented a typology of secularization scenarios, ranging from the emergent, the coercive, and the diffused to the imperialist. Indeed, I argued that secularization and its companion sacralization are critical to understanding the historical dynamics of all culture, whether at the micro-level or the macro-level.

In one sense, then, I have tried to domesticate secularization by removing its fangs. In another sense, I have tried to enliven and enrich the discussion by widening its scope and raising the stakes. Secularization is by no means a process restricted to religion in its conventional sense. And given our experience with religion as a primary case of the sacred and a major facet of culture, sociologists have an expertise to share. To paraphrase two early prophets of secularization, we have a world to win and nothing to lose but our brain.

NOTES

1. This chapter borrows, draws upon, and extends some of my earlier writings on the topic which are cited in the text and noted in the references.

REFERENCES

Bailey, Edward 1998. *Implicit Religion: An Introduction*. London: Middlesex University Press.

Bartkowski, John P. 2001. *Remaking the Godly Marriage: Gender Negotiations in Evangelical Families*. New Brunswick: Rutgers University Press.

Beckford, James A. 2003. *Social Theory and Religion*. Cambridge: Cambridge University Press.

Bell, Daniel 1964. *The End of Ideology*. Cambridge: Harvard University Press.

Bell, Daniel 1976. *The Cultural Contradictions of Capitalism*. New York: Basic Books.

Bellah, Robert N. 1967. 'Civil Religion in America,' *Daedalus* 96: 1–21.

Bellah, Robert N., Richard Madsen, William M. Sullivan, Ann Swidler, and Steven M. Tipton 1985. *Habits of the Heart*. Berkeley: University of California Press.

Berger, Peter L. 1967. *The Sacred Canopy*. Garden City, NY: Doubleday.

Berger, Peter L. 1997. 'Epistemological Modesty: An Interview with Peter Berger,' *Christian Century* 114: 972–78.

Berger, Peter L. 1999. *The De-Secularization of the World*. Washington, DC: Ethics and Public Policy Center.

Beteille, André 1994. 'Secularism and the Intellectuals,' *Economic and Political Weekly* 29 (10): 559–66.

Bruce, Steve 1995. 'The Truth About Religion in Britain,' *Journal of the Scientific Study of Religion* 34: 417–30.

Bruce, Steve 2002. *God is Dead: Secularization in the West*. Oxford: Blackwell's.

Chadwick, Owen 1975. *The Secularization of the European Mind in the Nineteenth Century*. Cambridge: Cambridge University Press.

Chaves, Mark 1993. 'Denominations as Dual Structures: An Organizational Analysis,' *Sociology of Religion* 54: 147–69.

Comte, Auguste 1852 (1891). *The Catechism of Positive Religion* (3rd edn). London: Routledge.

Davie, Grace 1994. *Religion in Britain Since 1945: Believing Without Behaving.* Oxford: Blackwell's.

Davie, Grace 2002. *Europe: The Exceptional Case.* London: Darton, Longman and Todd, Ltd.

Darnton, Robert 1995. *The Forbidden Best-Sellers of Pre-Revolutionary France.* New York: W.W. Norton.

Demerath, N. J. III 1992. 'Snatching Defeat From Victory in the Decline of Liberal Protestantism: Culture Versus Structure in Institutional Analysis.' In N. J. Demerath, P.D. Hall, T. Schmitt, and R.H.Williams (eds), *Sacred Companies.* New York: Oxford.

Demerath, N. J. III 1998. 'Secularization Disproved or Displaced.' In Rudy Laermans, Bryan Wilson, and Jaak Billiet (eds), *Secularization and Social Integration, Essays Honour of Karel Dobbelaene.* Leuven: Belgium: Leuven University Press, pp. 7–11.

Demerath, N. J. III 2000a. 'The Varieties of Sacred Experience;' Finding the Sacred in a Secular Grove,' *Journal of the Scientific Study of Religion* 39:1–11.

Demerath, N. J. III 2000b. 'Secularization.' In *Encyclopedia of Sociology* (2nd edn). New York: Macmillan, pp. 2482–91.

Demerath, N. J. III 2000c. 'Secularization Extended: From Religious Myth to Cultural Commonplace.' In Richard Fenn (ed.), *Companion to the Sociology of Religion.* Oxford: Blackwell's.

Demerath, N. J. III 2001. *Crossing the Gods: World Religions and Worldly Politics.* New York: Rutgers University Press.

Demerath, N. J. III 2003. 'Cults, Culture and Manure: Why the Root of the Second should be the First rather than the Third.' In J. A. Beckford and J. T. Richardson (eds), *Challenging Religion: Essays in Honor of Eileen Barker.* New York: Taylor and Francis.

Demerath, N. J. III 2006. 'Criss-Crossing the Gods: Globalization and American Religion.' In Bruce Mazlish and Nayan Chanda (eds), *The United States in a Global History Perspective.* Palo Alto: Stanford University Press.

Demerath, N. J. III and Yonghe Yang 1998. 'Switching in American Religion: Denominations, Markets, Paradigms?' In Madeleine Cousineau (ed.), *Religion in a Changing World.* Westport: Praeger.

Dobbelaere, Karel 1981. 'Secularization: A Multi-Dimensional Concept,' *Current Sociology* 20: 1–216.

Dobbelaere, Karel 1985. 'Secularization Theories and Sociological Paradigms.' *Sociological Analysis* 46 (4): 377–87.

Dobbelaere, Karel 1993. 'Church Involvement and Secularization: Making Sense of the European Case.' In Eileen Barker, James A. Beckford, and Karel Dobbelaere (eds), *Secularization, Rationalism, and Sectarianism* Oxford: Clarendon Press.

Douglas, Mary 1982. 'The Effects of Modernization on Religious Change.' In Douglas and Steven M. Tipton (eds), *Religion in America: Spirituality in a Secular Age.* Boston: Beacon.

Durkheim, Emile 1912 (1995). *The Elementary Forms of the Religious Life*, trans. by Karen Fields. New York: Free Press.

Durkheim, Emile 1961. *Moral Education.* New York: Free Press.

Eliade, Mircea 1959. *The Sacred and the Profane.* London: Harcourt, Brace, Jovanovich.

Erikson, Kai 1966. *Wayward Puritans.* New York: John Wiley and Sons.

Fenn, Richard 1979. *Toward a Theory of Secularization.* Society for the Scientific Study of Religion Monograph.

Fenn, Richard 1993. 'Crowds, Time, and the Essence of Society.' In E. Barker, *et al. Secularization, Rationalism and Sectarianism, op. cit.*, pp. 287–304.

Finke, Roger and Rodney Stark 1992. *The Churching of America, 1776–1990: Winners and Losers in Our Religious Economy.* New Brunswick, NJ: Rutgers University Press.

Foucault, Michel 1966. *The Order of Things.* New York: Vintage Books.

Gallagher, Sally K. 2003 *Evangelical Identity and Gendered Family Life.* New Brunswick, NJ: Rutgers University Press.

Geertz, Clifford 1973. *The Interpretation of Culture.* New York: Basic Books.

Germani, Gino 1981. *The Sociology of Modernization* New Brunswick, NJ: Transaction.

Goldstein, Warren S. (ed.) 2006. *Marx, Critical Theory, and Religion: A Critique of Rational Choice.* Leiden: Brill Academic Publishers.

Gordon, Daniel 1998. 'The Great Enlightenment Massacre.' In Haydn T. Mason (ed.), *The Darton Debate.* Oxford: Voltaire Foundation.

Gorski, Philip 2000. 'Historicizing the Secularization Debate: Church, State, and Society in Late Medieval and Early Modern Europe, ca. 1300–1700.' *American Sociological Review* 65: 138–67.

Greeley, Andrew M. and Michael Hout 2006. *The Truth About Conservative Christians.* Chicago: University of Chicago Press.

Habermas, Jürgen 1988. *The Theory of Communicative Action* (2 vols). Cambridge, UK: Polity Press.

Habermas, Jürgen 1989. *On Society and Politics.* Steven Seidman (ed.). Boston: Beacon Press.

Haddaway, C. Kirk, Penny Long Marler, and Mark Chaves. 1993. 'What the Polls Don't Show: A

Closer Look at U.S. Church Attendance.' *American Sociological Review* 58: 741–52.

Hadden, Jeffrey 1987. 'Toward Desacralizing Secularization Theory.' *Social Forces* 65: 3 (March) 587–611.

Hout, Michael and Claude Fischer 2002. 'Why More Americans Have No Religious Preference: Politics and Generation.' *American Sociological Review* 67: 165–90.

Hunter, James Davidson 1987. *Evangelicalism: The Coming Generation*. Chicago: University of Chicago Press.

Iannaccone, Laurence R. 1994. 'Why Strict Churches are Strong.' *American Journal of Sociology* 99: 1180–1211.

Jenkins, Philip 2002. *The Next Generation: The Coming of Global Christianity*. Oxford: Oxford University Press.

Juergensmeyer, Mark 1993. *The New Cold War: Religious Nationalism Confronts the Secular State*. Berkeley: University of California Press.

Kelley, Dean 1972. *Why Conservative Churches Are Growing*. Macon, GA: Mercer University Press.

Koyre, Alexandre 1957. *From the Closed World to the Infinite Universe*. Baltimore: Johns Hopkins University Press.

Lovejoy, Arthur O. 1936. *The Great Chain of Being*. Cambridge: Harvard University Press.

Luckmann, Thomas 1967. *The Invisible Religion*. New York: Macmillan Co.

Luckmann, Thomas 1990. 'Shrinking Transcendence, Expanding Religion.' *Sociology of Religion* 50 (2): 127–38.

Luhmann, Niklas 1982. *The Differentiation of Society*. New York: Columbia University Press.

Madan, T. N. 1998. *Modern Myths, Locked Minds*. Delhi: Oxford University Press.

Marcuse, Herbert 1964. *One-Dimensional Man*. London: Routledge and Kegan Paul.

Martin, David 1969. *The Religious and the Secular*. New York: Schocken Books.

Martin, David 1978. *A General Theory of Secularization*. New York: Harper and Row.

Marwell, Gerald and N. J. Demerath III 2003. '"Secularization" By Any Other Name.' Comment on Hout and Fischer. *American Sociological Review* 68: 314–18.

Marx, Karl 1844 (1963). 'Contribution to the Critique of Hegel's Philosophy of the Right.' In Thomas B. Bottomore (ed.), *Early Writings*. New York: McGraw-Hill.

May, Henry F. 1949. *Protestant Churches in Industrial America*. New York: Harper and Bros.

McLoughlin, W. G. 1978. *Revivals, Awakenings, and Religious Change*. Chicago: University of Chicago Press.

Merrick, Jeffrey W. 1990. *The De-Sacralization of the French Monarchy in the 18th Century*. Baton Rouge: Louisiana State University Press.

Nandy, Ashish 1990. 'The Politics of Secularism and the Recovery of Religious Tolerance.' In Veena Das (ed.), *Mirrors of Violence*. Delhi: Oxford University Press.

Norris, Pippa and Ronald Inglehart 2004. *Sacred and Secular: Religion and Politics Worldwide*. New York: Cambridge University Press.

Parsons, Talcott 1960. *Structure and Process in Modern Societies*. Glencoe, IL: The Free Press.

Parsons, Talcott 1977. *The Evolution of Societies*. Englewood Cliffs, NJ: Prentice Hall.

Roof, Wade Clark 2001. *The Spiritual Marketplace: Baby Boomers and the Remaking of American Religion*. Princeton: Princeton University Press.

Roof, Wade Clark and William McKinney 1987. *American Mainline Religion*. New Brunswick, NJ: Rutgers University Press.

Rousseau, Jean Jacques 1960. 'Of Civil Religion.' In Ernest Barker (ed.), *Social Contract*. London: Oxford University Press.

Sanneh, Lamin 1991. 'The Yogi and the Commissar: Christian Missions and the New World Order in Africa.' In W. C. Roof (ed.), *World Order and Religion*. Albany: SUNY Press.

Schneider, Mark 1993. *Culture and Enchantment*. Chicago: University of Chicago Press.

Spencer, Herbert 1874. *Essays Moral, Political and Aesthetic*. New and Enlarged Edition. New York: D. Appleton and Co.

Spencer, Herbert 1915. *Essays Scientific, Political, Speculative* (3 vols). New York: Appleton.

Stark, Rodney 1992. 'Sociology of Religion.' *Encyclopedia of Sociology*. New York: Macmillan, pp. 2029–37.

Stark, Rodney 1999. 'Secularization R.I.P.' *Sociology of Religion* 60/3 (Fall).

Stark, Rodney and Laurence R. Iannaccone 1994. 'A Supply-side Reinterpretation of the "Secularization" of Europe.' *Journal for the Scientific Study of Religion* 33: 230–52.

Stark, Rodney and Bainbridge, W.S. 1985. *The Future of Religion*. Berkeley, California: University of California Press.

Stark, Rodney and Roger Finke 2000. *Acts of Faith: Explaining the Human Side of Religion*. Berkeley: University of California Press.

Swatos, William H. Jr 1985. *The Future of Religion*. Berkeley: University of California Press.

Swatos, William H. Jr and Loftur Reimar Gissurarson 1997. *Icelandic Spiritualism: Mediumship and Modernity*. New Brunswick, NJ: Transaction Books.

Tawney, R. H. 1962. *Religion and the Rise of Capitalism*. Gloucester, MA.: P. Smith.

Thapar, Romila 1989. 'Imagined and Religious Communities: Ancient History and the Modern Search for a Hindu Identity.' *Modern Asian Studies* 23: 209–31.

Toennies, Ferdinand 1887 (1957). *Community and Society*, trans. and ed. by Charles Loomis. East Lansing: Michigan State University Press.

Tschannen, Oliver 1991. 'The Secularization Paradigm: A Systematization.' *Journal of the Scientific Study of Religion* 30: 395–415.

Turner, James 1985. *Without God, Without Creed*. Baltimore: Johns Hopkins Press.

Voltaire, Francois-Marie Arouet 1756 (1963). *Essai sur les Moers et l'Esprit des Nations* (2 vols). Paris: Garnier.

Warner, Steven 1993. 'Work in Progress Toward a New Paradigm for the Sociological Study of Religion in the U.S.' *American Journal of Sociology* 98: 1044–93.

Weber, Max 1904 (1995). *The Protestant Ethic and the Spirit of Capitalism*. trans. by Talcott Parsons, Intro. by Randall Collins. New York: Roxbury Press.

Wilson, Bryan 1966. *Religion in Secular Society*. London: Penguin.

Wilson, Bryan 1990. *The Social Dimensions of Sectarianism*. Oxford: Oxford University Press.

Wilson, Bryan 1998. 'The Secularization Thesis: Criticisms and Rebuttals.' In R. Laermans, B. Wilson, and J. Billiet (eds), *Secularization and Social Integration, op.cit. Essays Honour of Karel Dobbelaere*.

Woodberry, Robert D. 1998. 'When Surveys Lie and People Tell the Truth: How Surveys Over-Sample Church Attenders.' *American Sociological Review* 63: 119–22.

Wuthnow, Robert 1988. *The Restructuring of American Religion*. Princeton: Princeton U. Press.

Wuthnow, Robert 1998. *After Heaven: Spirituality in America Since the 1950s*. Berkeley: University of California Press.

4

Rational Choice and Religious Economies[1]

FRANK J. LECHNER

Adam Smith may well be the founder of the sociology of religion. His *Wealth of Nations* is a classic text in economics, but Smith ranged beyond the confines of that discipline. In analyzing the institutions of 'commercial society,' he practiced sociology as well. A striking instance is a section on the 'expense of public works and public institutions' in Book V of the *Wealth* (Smith 1976a [1776]). After discussing the proper role of government in commercial society, Smith turns to the role of other institutions, including religion. He points out that clergy who depend on voluntary contributions tend to be more zealous, that sects drawn from the common people are stricter, that without political interference a multitude of sects will flourish, and that over time the authority of clergy is bound to decline. In keeping with the spirit of his book, he implicitly criticizes monopoly religion that is entwined with the state. Established churches may be abused by the powerful and obstruct the 'perfect liberty' Smith envisioned. As important as the specific points Smith makes is the general message he conveys. Religious activity, he implies, is just as reasonable as any other kind. The forces that shape most institutions also affect religion. We can therefore explain religious activity and institutions in the same way as other facets of society. Such explanations sidestep the question of the truth of religion.

Though Smith's analysis of religion had little direct impact, his way of treating religion as an ordinary activity amenable to secular analysis became a hallmark of the sociology of religion as practiced by Weber, Durkheim, and their intellectual descendants. One group of present-day scholars, united under the banner of 'rational choice,' claims a close kinship not just with Smith's approach but also with the substance of his arguments. Drawing on the theoretical arsenal of contemporary economics, itself a mutation of Smith's legacy, they propose that religious activity is inherently rational. In choosing to join a church, take on a religious commitment, or accept a religious belief, people weigh costs and benefits in light of their preferences. Their 'demand' for religion is met by a 'supply' produced by religious organizations. The activities of consumers and producers constitute a market or 'religious economy.' The vitality of a society's religion depends on the way this economy works. Unless the economy suppresses all religious demand, religion is likely to be a viable institution and no society can become wholly secular.

The twin ideas that for individuals religion is a rational choice and that in society religion takes the form of an economy are at the core of a 'new paradigm' for the sociology of religion. According to its advocates, this way of thinking about religion – anchored in Smith's work though different in how it identifies rationality and choice – promises to do two things for the field. Rational choice offers to replace a hotch-potch of ideas with a more coherent theory that accounts for all the important facts of religious life. For the old notion that religion is doomed it substitutes the idea that religion is alive and well in modern societies. This chapter reviews and illustrates the arguments of the paradigm's prolific proponents against the background of relevant points made by Smith. It shows how the paradigm comes in two related versions, each of which has tried to explain religious behavior, religious organization, and religious change.

These explanations are contested. Critics argue that rational choice assumptions are implausible, that the evidence refutes religious economy arguments, and that the new-paradigm picture of religion in modern societies is misleading. For such reasons many sociologists have resisted conversion. In the spirit of Adam Smith, who warned of the risks of applying a single 'system' to human affairs, this chapter suggests that adoption of any one 'paradigm' in the study of religion may be premature in any case. Instead, I propose a more ecumenical approach to explaining religion that draws on many kinds of insights. Constructive competition and collaboration among multiple views should make the sociology of religion more vital.

RELIGIOUS CHOICE

What does it mean to say that religious activity is 'rational'? Advocates of the rational choice approach offer two slightly different answers.

One answer derives straightforwardly from microeconomic theory. As Laurence Iannaccone, an economist trained at the University of Chicago, has explained (1997: 26; also 1990), treating religion as rational activity involves three assumptions:

1. 'Individuals act rationally, weighing the costs and benefits of potential actions, and choosing those actions that maximize their net benefits.'
2. 'The ultimate preferences (or 'needs') that individuals use to assess costs and benefits tend not to vary much from person to person or over time.'
3. 'Social outcomes constitute the equilibria that emerge from the aggregation and interaction of individual actions.'

The first assumption deliberately simplifies human decision-making to help us 'model behavioral changes ... as optimal responses to varying circumstances' (ibid.: 27). In explaining behavior, it is not so much the rational calculation as the varying circumstances that matter: 'Behavioral changes (over time) are the consequence of changed constraints; behavioral differences (across individuals) are the consequence of differing constraints' (ibid.: 28).

This model suggests some new predictions. For example, people who place a relatively high value on their time should be more likely to substitute monetary contributions for time-consuming church attendance – a point Iannaccone finds confirmed in survey evidence. In addition, the model translates well-known sociological insights into new language. For instance, if we think of an individual's religious knowledge as a form of 'human capital,' the fact that people who switch to other denominations tend to pick fairly similar ones makes sense as an effort to preserve the value of their previous religious investments (ibid.: 33). The theory further proposes new explanations of common behavior. A case in point is the idea that religious activity is often collective because collective production reduces the risk associated with religious activities whose supernatural benefits no individual can fully assess (ibid.: 34). In a more speculative vein, the theory suggests that 'portfolio diversification' reduces the perceived risk in religious commodities, leading consumers to patronize multiple firms providing private commodities (ibid.: 37–8). This type of rational choice analysis relies mainly on formal assumptions drawn from economic theory.

Few scholars would dispute that people weigh costs and benefits in deciding on the right course of action. Most also agree that in some ways religion is like other forms of social conduct, so that explanations of that conduct might apply to religion as well. The basic intuition, already implicit in Smith, is that people do not become wholly different creatures by stepping into a church or mosque. But Iannaccone goes several steps beyond this. The question is whether these additional steps pay off. Do individuals in fact maximize their utility? Do their preferences not vary much from person to person or over time? Many scholars reject the maximization assumption, citing psychological evidence on the complexity of actual decision-making. Within short periods and homogeneous groups, preferences may be stable, but as a universal assumption most sociologists find it implausible. Critics therefore argue that since the assumptions are false, the rational choice argument at best serves as a model that makes occasionally useful predictions (Spickard 1998).

These predictions are rarely forecasts about the behavior of specific persons or groups. That is to say, rational choice theorists typically do not diagnose a situation, assess the preferences of actors, and then perform a virtual calculation on their behalf to show how, as rational actors, they are bound to make certain 'optimal' choices. Instead, their predictions are more often 'postdictions,' reconstructions or just-so stories after the fact that purport to show that certain behavior in fact displayed by actors must have been optimal given their preferences under particular constraints, the latter described in ad-hoc fashion. The main reason is that rational choice observers do not have direct access to the actual preference ranking of people prior to their decisions (cf. Bruce 1999). Even if they did have such information, many critics would find the exercise itself implausible. It assumes, after all, that religion is like real commodities, that hard-nosed calculation is at work in religious choices, and that religious participation is a 'standard consumer choice problem' (Iannaccone 1997: 29). Pope Benedict XVI begs to differ, arguing that faith cannot be a 'consumer product' (BBC 2005). Students of religion, with perhaps a slightly smaller stake in the issue, also object that few spiritual seekers approach their decision as a 'standard consumer choice problem,' that many faithful engage in religious actions as a form of expression rather than in search of benefits, and that people's relations to the divine make it difficult for them to think of their faith as simply another commodity (Bryant 2000). The sacred is in some ways also very different from the profane. At least one prominent rational choice theorist, Michael Hechter, recognizes that religious behavior may not be instrumental after all but rather a way of enacting 'immanent' values (Hechter 1997).

A 'thicker' or more sociological version of rational choice theory, proposed by the American sociologists Rodney Stark and Roger Finke, tries to avoid some of the difficulties of the 'thin' economic version by relaxing some of Iannaccone's assumptions while also attributing a wider range of inclinations to individuals (Stark and Finke 2000: 84–5). Stark and Finke start with the proposition that '[w]ithin the limits of their information and understanding, restricted by available options, guided by their preferences and tastes, humans attempt to make rational choices' (ibid.: 85). Realizing that rewards are always scarce, or not directly available at all, 'humans will tend to formulate and accept explanations for obtaining the reward in the distant future or in some other nonverifiable context' (ibid.: 88). Religious explanations are distinctive in that they describe ways of obtaining rewards of immense value while postponing their delivery to an otherworldly context (ibid.). People want religion because it is 'the only plausible source of certain rewards for which there is a general and inexhaustible demand' (ibid.: 85). Religion, then, 'consists of very general explanations of existence, including the terms of exchange with a god or gods' – a form of exchange humans 'will seek' in their pursuit of rewards (ibid.: 91).

These 'micro foundations' of religion have several interesting implications, spelled out in no less than 99 propositions and 36 definitions (Stark and Finke 2000). For example, Stark and

Finke suggest that, as rational actors, people will pay 'higher prices' to gods with more wide-ranging powers (*ibid.*: 98), though they do not actually show that the Christian God with these characteristics in fact commands higher prices than less omnipotent supernatural beings. Similarly, they say that people will seek to postpone or minimize religious costs (*ibid.*: 100), as illustrated, according to Stark and Finke, by the frequency of death-bed conversions. Like Iannaccone, they also translate sociological findings into their language, for example, by arguing that confidence in 'risky' religious explanations increases to the extent that people participate in religious rituals (*ibid.*: 107), or by suggesting that, in trying to conserve social capital, people will tend to convert to the extent that they have or develop stronger attachments to those committed to a different religion (*ibid.*: 119). While Iannaccone makes bold assumptions about rationality and stable preferences, Stark and Finke are equally bold in ascribing to human beings a desire for otherworldly rewards to be obtained via exchanges with gods. The point of their analysis is to show that religion, or choosing to be religious, is not irrational.

This version raises questions as well. The definition of religion seems restrictive in that it focuses only on cognitive 'explanations.' These explanations can make clear how believers might gain certain rewards, or perhaps more commonly, why God bestows certain rewards on the faithful, but it does not follow that explanations themselves are therefore the 'only plausible source' of rewards. Without any apparent caveats, Stark and Finke argue further that 'humans will seek' certain rewards through exchange with the gods, a claim that atheists would dispute. As in the case of Iannaccone, believers might take issue with the point as well, since the worship of or submission to the divine inherent in many religions is not wholly captured in terms of 'exchange.' Few believers actually seem to seek a beneficial exchange, trading in one faith for another if it offers a better deal. One reason is that, once one accepts the values of a faith, what might appear a cost from the outside, becomes inherently meaningful and satisfying conduct. Similarly, religious organizations committed to

a certain faith rarely lower the 'price' of exchange with the gods specified in their doctrine as a way of attracting new customers. From the theory's standpoint, it is understandable that individuals should be attracted to faiths that promise the benefit of eternal salvation. Less clear is why they should choose to accept teachings that expose them to the ultimate cost of eternal damnation. Why should any rational actor striving for rewards wish to be a Calvinist, or a 'sinner in the hands of an angry God'? Once one accepts a certain Calvinist doctrine, the associated cost makes sense. Yet the theory portrays actors as pursuing a most advantageous ratio of rewards to costs. Since not accepting the doctrine in the first place would appear to lower one's potential costs quite substantially, it is puzzling why anyone would want to be a Jonathan Edwards.

Religious skeptics might pursue this line of argument further. Were David Hume to address the issue from the afterlife, an event sure to shake his skepticism, he might say that rational choice arguments do not disprove the skeptical critique of the content of religious belief. The point of that critique is not to argue that people fail to weigh cost and benefits in making religious choices, or that religious organizations do not share any common features with secular ones. For all we know, Hume did not disagree with his good friend Adam Smith on this score. Rather, skeptics typically argue that in accepting and enacting their faith religious actors also think in ways that are very different from those common in secular fields. By dealing with experiences of fear or elation via conceptions of the supernatural, believers accept mysteries not subject to verification, contradictions they would not accept in other contexts, and unreliable reports of miraculous occurrences that happened long ago. Along this skeptical line, Hume would question how believers in the supernatural can properly assess the 'efficiency' of their faith. With regard to the implied earthly benefits, he would doubt that religions in fact do preserve explanations that are 'efficient,' perhaps citing Christians' persistence in praying for peace. Of course, some believers mirror the skeptics' argument by emphasizing that, at bottom, faith and the emotions it embodies are 'irrational' (Chesterton 1905: Ch. 11).

As Hume might stress, skeptics and rational choice theorists simply make different kinds of arguments, with skeptics questioning the reasons for forming certain preferences in the first place, new-paradigm advocates emphasizing rational choices in light of already existing religious preferences. Rational choice therefore cannot dismiss the skeptical critique. For sociology, the point is not to support Hume's own theory of religion or to belabor reasons for skepticism as a kind of intellectual game. It would not be difficult, but less than illuminating, to complicate the skeptics' case by showing that rational calculation in light of arguments, evidence, and sound risk assessment often leaves something to be desired outside the sphere of religion as well. More importantly, the skeptics remind us that religion is stranger, more puzzling than rational choice theorists believe. The challenge for sociology is that if religion is *also* a distinct human activity, it likely requires explanations that take this distinctiveness into account.

RELIGIOUS ORGANIZATION

Adam Smith regarded clergy as rational actors. 'The clergy of every established church,' he said, 'constitute a great incorporation. They can act in concert and pursue their interest upon one plan and with one spirit …. Their great interest is to maintain their authority with the people; and this authority depends on the supposed certainty and importance of the whole doctrine which they inculcate, and upon the supposed necessity of adopting every part of it with the most implicit faith, in order to avoid eternal misery.' Smith's point here is to counsel the 'sovereign' that in this case he can 'never be secure unless he has the means of influencing in a considerable degree the greater part of the teachers of that religion.' Since, in principle, 'the authority of religion is superior to every other authority,' the safer course for the sovereign is to stay out of religious affairs altogether. Smith also has an argument

about the impact of religious demand on the products supplied by organizations. 'Almost all religious sects have begun among the common people, from which they have generally drawn their earliest… proselytes.' Since people of higher rank typically prefer a liberal or 'loose' system of morality, while commoners like their morality more 'strict or austere,' it follows that the 'austere system has… been adopted by those sects almost constantly.' Their strictness, in short, fits customer demand.

Expanding on Smith's idea about the rationality of religious providers, Iannaccone treats churches as 'profit maximizing firms' (1997: 39). Instead of simply trying to maintain their 'authority,' churches, established or not, seek to survive and flourish by attracting committed members. One way to do so, according to economic logic, might be for churches to lower the price of their product. Churches promising eternal salvation in exchange for minimal contributions should be highly popular. Yet in fact, Iannaccone argues, it is 'strict' churches that survive and flourish (*ibid.*: 36). The reason is not the nature of the demand from certain groups, as suggested by Smith. Iannaccone's point is that the strictures are not simply a cost but also provide a benefit: they get rid of religious free riders. In stricter sects, members must participate fully, and exclusively, or not at all. As a result, their members will believe more fervently, attend more frequently, and give more generously, as a comparison of American denominations confirms (Iannacone 1994: 1191–5). Members also benefit from the high commitment of their fellow believers, adding to the attraction of strictness. Strict churches are therefore stronger. In this way, cost-benefit analysis produces a counterintuitive result.

Catholics might object that their church has managed fairly well over two millennia in spite of free riders. Iannacone conveniently defines strength in terms of average member contributions and commitment, which makes Mormons and Jehovah's Witnesses look strong, but measured by size, longevity, or global scope, the Catholic Church would seem just as strong. Academic critics like Marwell (1996) add other objections. For example, since strictness includes costly participation, the argument risks becoming tautological. The statistical finding of high average contributions in strict churches is simply a result of strict organizations forcing backsliders to leave. The quantitative evidence does not cover strict churches that failed, making them seem more successful than they are. The evidence also does not show that solutions to the free riding problem actually induce people to join a particular church. In fact, Marwell concludes, it might be more logical for rational actors to join churches where they can ride free on the efforts of everyone else, but then they would dilute the averages of all churches, leaving no church stronger than any other. As such criticism indicates, this application of rational choice theory to religious organization is still contested (Sherkat and Ellison 1999: 384).

Stark and Finke offer another version of Iannaccone's argument. Sects, they posit, are 'religious bodies in relatively higher tension with their surroundings' (2000: 144). Such tension or deviance will typically raise the cost of membership: 'The higher its level of tension with its surroundings, the more exclusive, extensive and expensive is the level of commitment required by a religious group' from which it follows, say Stark and Finke, that 'to the degree that they manage to attract and to hold members,' if a group's level of tension with its surroundings increases, its members will become more committed (*ibid.*: 145). Or as they say even more emphatically in their book on the 'churching' of America, 'religious organizations are stronger to the degree that they impose significant costs in terms of sacrifice and even stigma upon their members' (Finke and Stark 1992: 238). To explain why rational actors should want to join more costly groups, Stark and Finke suggest that 'despite being expensive they offer greater value' and that they are able to do so 'partly *because* they are expensive' (*ibid.* emphasis in original). This point they support in turn by arguing that groups in tension with their surroundings typically think of god as more dependably providing otherworldly rewards, whereas groups in lower tension conceive of god as more distant, impersonal and unresponsive (*ibid.*: 146). They then suggest that this also explains why

'growth has been concentrated among the higher-tension religious groups, while lower-tension groups have declined.' In their view, the decline of 'mainline' Protestant churches and the growth of conservative ones in the U.S. since World War II confirm the point (Finke and Stark 1992: 249ff.).

The objections to Iannaccone's argument also apply to Stark and Finke, but once again their version raises other questions as well. Even assuming that individuals are attracted to high-cost sects because these offset sacrifices with distinctly valuable otherworldly rewards, one would still expect competing sects to steal customers by offering similar rewards at lower cost. Some American megachurches that accentuate the benefits of Christianity and dispense with the gloomy parts fit this pattern, but religious discounting is still rare. While Stark and Finke attribute the religious beliefs of sects to their tension with the environment, it is at least as plausible to reverse the causality: Jehovah's Witnesses do not believe what they believe due to 'tension' but, rather, what they believe creates the tension in the first place. The meaning of 'tension' remains fuzzy in any case. For example, it is not clear in what sense Southern Baptists are in high tension with their surroundings in the American South. Without such presumed tension, Stark and Finke cannot explain Baptists' conception of the supernatural or their relatively high growth. Some observers of the American South might go a step further and suggest that it is 'liberal' denominations, such as the Unitarian-Universalists, that are in 'tension' with the prevailing culture, which, by the logic of rational choice arguments, should pay off in future growth, though this has yet to materialize.

RELIGIOUS COMPETITION

Smith noted that clergy who depend on voluntary contributions are likely to show greater zeal and industry in their work than those who rely on government support. Secure in their funding, the latter neglect 'to keep up the fervour of faith and devotion in the great body of the people.' Forced to work harder to attract believers, teachers of new religions have an advantage in challenging the establishment and are more likely to keep up the fervor of the faithful. While religious zeal at times has disturbed public order, Smith argues that it is 'innocent' where society is divided into many sects. Surrounded by many others like themselves, members of each sect will treat each other with moderation and respect. This will come about, Smith suggests, if government stays out of religious affairs: 'if politics had never called in the aid of religion ... it would probably have dealt equally and impartially with all the different sects, and have allowed every man to choose his own priest and his own religion as he thought proper. There would in this case, no doubt have been a great multitude of religious sects.' In other words, the separation of church and state promotes pluralism, at least in the sense of actual diversity of options, which in turn fosters religious moderation and civic peace.

Rational choice advocates expand on Smith's diagnosis of government support for religion: 'a state-sponsored religious monopoly will provide only the appearance of piety – an ineffective clergy and an apathetic population lie just below the surface' (Iannaccone 1997: 40). By contrast, pluralistic competition 'will stimulate religious markets just as it does secular markets, forcing suppliers to efficiently produce a wide range of alternative faiths well adapted to the specific needs of consumers' (*ibid.*). This 'supply side' model thus argues that deregulation fosters pluralism, that pluralism creates competition, that competing religious firms will supply more desirable products more effectively, that the wider offerings in a competitive market will more adequately satisfy the latent religious demand of consumers, and that as a result overall religious vitality will increase. Far from harming religion, pluralism helps. Rational theorists argue that this accounts for American religious exceptionalism: because the U.S. has a more open and competitive religious market than overregulated Europe, its people are more religious and its firms more successful (Stark and Finke 2000: 220ff.; Finke and Stark 1992).

Within any society, they argue further, places that have a more competitive market should also be more religious, a point they have supported with studies of American cities (e.g., Finke and Stark 1988). The argument also leads to counterintuitive predictions, such as the audacious one that the more European societies become deregulated, the more competitive their markets will be, the more religious Europeans should become, and the more we can look forward to the 'churching' of Europe (Stark and Iannacone 1994). As a case in point, Introvigne and Stark cite the experience of Italy in the late-twentieth century, where, they suggest, a modest rise in competition for the Catholic Church produced a religious 'revival' of 'guaranteed' durability (Introvigne and Stark 2005: 15).

Each step in the religious economy argument has generated debate. Take the first step first: state regulation of or support for religion in fact need not stifle pluralism, as illustrated by the case of Britain, where the established churches have faced competing independent churches for centuries (Bruce 1995: 426). In the U.S., the presumed second step – disestablishment leading to pluralism – actually occurred in reverse order (Olson 2002: 155–6; Phillips 2004: 148). Contrary to religious economy arguments, pluralism also need not foster actual competition, as in the case of diverse religious communities locked in conflict. Where competition does occur, the religious economy model argues that the market will be stimulated because potential religious customers act like consumers in other markets and respond to better deals. Yet its actual propositions do not support the argument about the way market behavior raises vitality. For example, according to Stark and Finke, people preserve religious capital. Presumably they would agree that car owners do not try to preserve their 'transportation capital' in the same way. It follows, then, that there is something special about religious brand loyalty. Trading in a Ford for a Toyota is easier than switching from Episcopalian to Baptist. But if religious switching is exceptional and potential religious customers do not respond like car buyers to suppliers' incentives, then it is not clear how competition should translate into vitality. In practice, a large portion of church growth does not depend on switching. Successful religious brands, such as conservative churches in the U.S., tend to grow more through effective socialization of members than by gaining new customers through competition. It thus remains an open question to what extent the market analogy really works for religious actors.

The linchpin in the religious economy argument is the link between pluralism and vitality. In one wave of studies, an index of the variety of religious offerings, derived from the market shares of each, measured 'pluralism' while the total participation rate measured 'vitality.' Many such studies report negative findings (cf. Breault 1989). For example, an analysis of U.S. counties finds that pluralism did not increase participation (Land et al. Blau 1991). Another study of the U.S. argues that 'North Americans are religious in spite of, not because of, religious pluralism' (Olson 1999: 171). The most thorough review of relevant research up to 2001 concludes that the evidence 'does not support the claim that religious pluralism is positively associated with religious participation in any general sense' (Chaves and Gorski 2001: 261). Because much early research suffered from technical problems, such negative judgments do not yet settle the issue. To measure pluralism, researchers typically need evidence on how many different churches command at least a small share of the market. But if the measure of pluralism includes information on participation, the independent variable becomes entwined with the one to be explained. The conventionally used Herfindahl index displays this problem, since this measure of 'supply-side' diversity depends mathematically on the 'demand side' (Montgomery 2003: 787). A more serious technical problem is that this index is also very sensitive to variation in the size of large and small congregations and, as a result, produces positive or negative correlations for mathematical reasons (Voas et al. 2002: 215). Instead of treating such correlations as evidence of a causal link between pluralism and the total participation rate, a better model would say that a number of historical and random forces shape denominational

participation rates, from which we can calculate both the level of denominational pluralism and the total participation rate, leaving the link between the latter two variables as an artifact of the calculations (ibid.: 217). In view of this model and the quantitative analysis it inspires, the most plausible reading of previous studies may well be that 'pluralism actually has little or no effect on participation' (ibid.: 227). Until quantitative studies become more refined, the link between pluralism and vitality thus remains in limbo.

Case studies avoid the technical problems just mentioned. They also have the advantage of being able to examine whether increases in pluralism over time lead to greater vitality. A study of Utah shows that, even after the Utah market opened to competitors, the Latter-Day Saints (Mormon) church limited pluralism and maintained its high market share by virtue of its high birth rates, insistence on marrying within the faith, and distinct beliefs and rituals (Phillips 1999). In Aberdeen, as available religious options increased from 15 in 1851 to about 40 in 1991, church attendance fell from about 60 per cent in 1851 to 37 per cent in 1878 to 11 per cent in 1995 (Bruce 1999: 80ff.). In the Netherlands, the more competitive situation that followed the decline of closed and mutually exclusive religious 'pillars' since the 1960s has not yet led to the churching Stark and Iannacone expected (Lechner 1996a). As various Dutch studies have shown, changes in market structure did not significantly affect overall religious attachment and an expanding supply of church options did not lead to greater participation (Becker et al. 1997; Verweij 1998; Sengers 2003). In other words, in an American state, a Scottish city, and a European country the religious market did not produce the expected effects. Other local comparisons, such as the different trajectories of a Boston neighborhood and a Georgia county (Ammerman 1997), reinforce the point. Though it may be too early to say that the qualitative evidence falsifies the theory, the accumulating evidence has put the burden of proof on rational choice advocates.

They have responded to contrary evidence in part by conceding that the effects of competition are contingent. Pluralism may be necessary for competition but it is not always sufficient, since factors other than regulation can constrain choice and 'muffle' competition (Stark *et al.* 1995: 442). Stark and colleagues even turn this point into a formal proposition: 'To the degree that competitive forces are constrained within a religious economy, pluralism will not be related to religious participation' (*ibid.*). The concession is reasonable, but it does not explain in terms of the original theory which factors constrain competition, and to what extent; instead of building general theory, the concession gives way to an ad-hoc account of how numerous mediating factors might promote or restrain the effects of pluralism. Stark and Iannaccone (1996) also attempt to parry the Dutch evidence by arguing that conflict among Dutch religious communities accounts for previously high commitment. The concession correctly recognizes that Dutch religion was quite 'vital' when a competitive market was absent, but, regardless of its historical accuracy, the point that communities in conflict reinforce commitment to norms and raise religious participation does not follow from the argument about religious suppliers seeking adherents in a market, and the rejoinder also leaves unexplained why decades of 'backsliding' failed to produce the expected rechurching (cf. Stark and Finke 2000: 242–3; Lechner 1996b). Though one could view competition and conflict as alternative forms of opposition, as Olson (2002) has suggested, such an argument again departs from the religious economy model. One possible refinement of the religious economy model draws on industrial organization economics to suggest that a market offers a 'richer menu' of options if the denominations present in one include those present in another (Montgomery 2003: 782–3). Unfortunately, evidence on New York towns in 1865 and U.S. counties in 1990 indicates that even with this refinement, the link between competition and participation is negative. As Montgomery concludes from his study of counties, 'U.S. counties with more religious options ... generally have lower religious participation' (*ibid.*: 805).

Such responses to earlier criticism therefore do not bolster the religious economy model's prospects.

RELIGIOUS CHANGE

Looking back at Europe's religious history, Smith argued that '[t]he gradual improvement of arts, manufactures, and commerce, the same causes which destroyed the power of the great barons, destroyed in the same manner, through the greater part of Europe, the whole temporal power of the clergy.' In part, this was the result of self-interested action by the clergy, which 'found something for which they could exchange their rude produce' and who 'wished to get a better rent from their landed estates.' Already by the fifteenth century, the power of the church was limited in much of Europe to its 'spiritual authority,' and even that the clergy sometimes undermined by their lack of 'charity.' Without spelling out all the ways in which it unfolds, Smith paints a picture of secularization, in the sense that with the advancement of competing productive institutions the scope of religious, or more precisely church, authority declines. This line of argument became the hallmark of subsequent work on secularization, which argued that in the process of modernization religion loses its social significance.

Rational choice theorists partly agree with this view of secularization, insofar as they take for granted that secularization, a process that took centuries, greatly changed modern societies, and at times produced intense strife in Europe, is now 'obvious' and 'limited' (Stark and Finke 2000: 60). They say it is evident in the fact that 'primary aspects of public life [are not] any longer suffused with religious symbols, rhetoric or ritual' (*ibid.*). Translating the findings of other scholars, Stark and Finke also describe secularization in their own terms. A monopoly firm, they suggest, will try to 'sacralize' a society by seeking to exert its influence over other institutions (*ibid.*: 60). By contrast, deregulation in a previously regulated economy will lead to desacralization (*ibid.*: 200). Their point, however, is to emphasize that the 'obvious' desacralization of society does not result in the secularization of believers. To think otherwise was the great error of the 'old paradigm' in the study of religion. Its adherents, Stark and Finke assert, believed that only monopoly religions are strong, that pluralism weakens faith, and that in modern societies religion is doomed. By way of example they cite Peter Berger's argument that contention in a pluralistic market calls into question the 'plausibility' of faith (Berger 1969) and the similar claim by Steve Bruce that since 'pluralism universalizes "heresy"', a 'chosen religion is weaker than a religion of faith' (Bruce 1992: 170). To Stark and Finke, America's religious vitality massively refutes such bleak scenarios. The 'new paradigm' based on the religious economy model proposes a sunnier scenario: since competitive pluralism raises religious vitality, there can be no overall trend toward individual secularization. If any secularization does occur, for example in periods of slack competition, it will prove to be temporary, since the market will correct when new providers enter and consumers find religious offerings that suit their needs. Barring artificial constraints on the market, secularization is self-limiting.

The contrast Stark and Finke draw between old and new paradigms overstates the differences among scholars. For example, they chastise Durkheim for suggesting that where multiple groups compete, 'the less [religion] dominates lives' (Stark and Finke 2000: 31), yet Durkheim is hardly predicting the 'demise' of religion but in effect merely states a version of the desacralization argument. That religion becomes 'weaker' under pluralism, in the sense intended by Bruce, need not entail universal decline in faith, though such declines have unmistakably occurred in some large countries. Stark and Finke take another leading secularization scholar, Karel Dobbelaere, to task for evasively suggesting that 'the religiousness of individuals is *not* a valid indicator in evaluating the process of secularization' (*ibid.*: 60), when Dobbelaere simply means to distinguish the issue of individual religiousness from the 'macro' secularization he finds more important, a distinction that is also crucial to the

rational choice argument itself. Similarly, they criticize yet another 'old paradigm' figure for implausibly suggesting that secularization seems hard to reverse (*ibid.*: 259), but fail to add that such irreversibility has to do with the institutional secularization Stark and Finke themselves find 'obvious.' In fact, few sociologists expect the 'demise' or 'extinction' of religion (Beckford 1989). Most agree on the importance of macro secularization *and* on the variability of individual religiosity across time and space. There is much common ground (Demerath 1995: 110).

When rational choice theorists argue that micro secularization cannot happen, they do so partly by assuming that it is impossible. Iannacone assumes that religious preferences are stable, at least across populations, and Stark and Finke similarly assume that humans will keep seeking supernatural rewards exclusively supplied by religion. Of course, if the latent demand for religion is assumed to be constant, no society can become secular without ruthlessly suppressing it. In principle, the theory thus rules out a collapse of the religious market and of individual religious commitment. Yet even in Stark and Finke's terms there is actually good reason to think that people's taste for religion can change over time and that humans vary in the extent to which they seek supernatural rewards. Let us assume, as Stark and Finke rightly do, that human beings devise stories and explanations to make sense of their experience (cf. Stark and Finke 2000: 86–7). Humans want to lead meaningful lives. Religion, by the theory's definition, offers one particular type of explanation. But if religion is one type of meaning supplier, then in principle it faces competition from other stories that offer other answers and rewards. Assuming that the taste for religion remains constant really means that the relative attractiveness of different kinds of explanations cannot vary. But why should that be so? If the key to all the explanatory story-telling is the production of meaning, as Stark and Finke appear to agree, one can well imagine new suppliers of meaning altering the very nature of the demand. In other competitive markets, that happens all the time. Instead of holistic religion giving meaning to all of human experience, upstart providers such as therapists, artists, or even sociologists might claim to shed distinctive light on only a slice of human experience. One question for the sociology of religion is how and to what extent such alternatives might gain favor in the market for meaning. Of course, assuming constant preferences or demand forestalls even raising the question. In a very general sense, to be sure, the demand for meaning may be constant. But just as the introduction of automobiles changed demand for horses, and the advent of personal computers changed demand for mainframes – altering not just the level but also the nature of the previous demand for transportation and communication, respectively – religious demand itself is subject to challenge. If so, then we cannot dismiss micro secularization by assuming it away.

Beyond the assumptions, both versions of the theory argue that the workings of the market moderate any budding tendencies toward individual secularization. The basis for this argument is the crucial link between pluralism and vitality, which, as we have seen, is in doubt. While it is certainly plausible that ineffective churches create opportunities for aggressive challengers, it does not follow that such competition will necessarily stem society-wide declines. In some cases, as recent European experience shows, actual preferences or demand do in fact shift, for reasons not easily captured by the theory. Religion is in fact in decline across Europe, and increasingly 'open' markets did not keep consumption from falling (Voas 2004). This is not to say that Europe is the model for studying religion elsewhere. The point is simply that European evidence refutes one of the religious economy claims. By the logic of falsification à la Popper, one of Stark's heroes (Stark 1997), this is just the kind of critical evidence that should lead to revision of the theory. At least, 'any paradigm that admits an exception as broad as historical Europe has obvious problems of generality' (Demerath 1995: 109).

Taking rational choice propositions at face value, it is not clear that the theory actually should rule out individual secularization. As Iannaccone has rightly suggested, economic

theory 'does not force a particular conclusion' on secularization; for example, if one assumes that at least some of the 'fruits of technology' may substitute for 'religious commodities,' the former may 'crowd out' the latter (Iannaccone 1995: 117). Since Stark and Finke appear strongly committed to their anti-secularization view, the case of the thick version is more complicated. According to one of Stark and Finke's propositions, '[a]n individual's confidence in religious explanations is strengthened to the extent that others express their confidence in them' (Stark and Finke 2000: 107). They also say that participation in rituals strengthens confidence (*ibid.*). It follows that if some people in a group or society lose faith, this should weaken the confidence of others around them, and that if they stop participating in rituals, this also lessens attachment. As we have seen, Stark and Finke argue as well that 'people will attempt to conserve their religious capital' in making religious choices (*ibid.*: 121). If people have invested little in their faith, they have less at stake in changing their allegiance. As Stark and Finke further point out, '[s]ocieties with low levels of religious participation will be lacking in effective religious socialization' (*ibid.*: 202). By the logic of their argument, it follows that if a society begins to tolerate backsliders and to falter in transmitting 'religious capital,' some individuals will lower their religious investments. As they have less reason to stay or become religious, they further affect those around them. The propositions entail that this is more likely to become a self-sustaining than a self-limiting process. Backsliding can easily snowball. A market correction may not occur. The theory does not tell us how to reverse micro secularization once it begins.

In making the case against micro secularization, Stark and Finke ridicule the argument that pluralism in modern societies undermines the plausibility of beliefs. Yet their own theory implies much the same thing. Without stressing the point, Stark and Finke leave open the possibility that the desire for supernatural rewards could actually vary. For example, they say that '[t]o the degree rewards are scarce, or are not directly available at all, humans will tend to formulate and accept explanations for obtaining the reward in the distant future or in some other nonverifiable context' (*ibid.*: 88). They also assume that humans 'will attempt to evaluate explanations on the basis of results, retaining those that seem to work most efficiently' (*ibid.*: 87). Conversely, then, if rewards become less scarce or if new explanations for old problems come to seem 'efficient,' the acceptance or plausibility of older explanations should decline. Now more modern societies, as Smith implied, do offer a much wider range of rewards, though of course no mere mortal enterprise can supply salvation. More pluralistic societies also supply a wider range of 'explanations,' many of which produce 'results' in areas such as health and economic well-being previously covered by religious explanations. The larger the supply of effective secular explanations for life's problems, the more they will call into question the authority, perhaps even the plausibility, of previous religious explanations. At least some humans eager to retain 'those that seem to work most efficiently' may decide to jettison their old beliefs. Change in the 'environment' of religious suppliers can thus trigger change in religious demand (cf. Sengers 2003: 193). Catholics who rejected the Church's teaching on sexuality after the introduction of the contraceptive pill are a case in point. It is to the theory's credit that it can account for such facts, but doing so contradicts the claims some of its authors prefer to make. More clearly than traditional secularization theories, which focused on institutions and the culture at large, the religious economy argument predicts micro secularization in modern societies. While Iannaccone still chases the red herring of the 'death' of religion, he indeed expects that, in the face of competition from other institutions, America's religious institutions are likely to jettison some of their traditional 'supernatural' teachings, shift to support for positive innerworldly experiences, and lose market share to a growing nonreligious segment of the public (Iannaccone 2004). This plausible argument nicely mirrors old-paradigm expectations.

EMBEDDED RATIONALITY AND THE SOCIOLOGY OF RELIGION

In science it is often fruitful to analyze one thing in terms of something else – light waves as particles, genes as information, brains as computers, and so on. In social science it is reasonable to assume that human social behavior is all of a piece and therefore amenable to explanation in terms of one theoretical scheme. The application of rational choice theory to religion combines these strategies. By analyzing religion as a form of rational conduct carried out in a religious economy, it promises to unify the study of religion under one theoretical canopy. Advocates for the new paradigm at times seem to apply their own account of sects as they create tension with their old-paradigm environment, require adherence to strict principles, and promise the transcendent reward of a testable deductive theory. In pursuit of their new truths, they have guarded their core ideas and resisted falsification. Enticed by an approach whose assumptions appeal to modern common sense and derive partly from another high-status discipline, sociologists converting to the new paradigm have not had to sacrifice much intellectual capital. Ritual repetition of its claims and a growing cadre of proponents, at least in the United States, have increased the paradigm's scholarly plausibility.

From a rational choice perspective, the question is whether adoption of rational choice pays off. Does it help students of religion maximize their explanatory utility? Does it reduce costs and add rewards? For individual scholars, much depends on their preferences. Those who prefer to think that human relations to the divine have specific, intrinsic qualities will resist reducing religion to rational exchange in the absence of proof that such reasoning by analogy at least makes descriptive sense (Bryant 2000). From this point of view, the cost of doing violence to the 'real' quality of religion by applying a distorting metaphor is simply too great. Others who are open in principle to a general theory relying on such a metaphor still might question its utility on the grounds that the assumptions of the 'thin' version of rational choice are invalid (Spickard 1998) or that the theory is not as logically unified and deductive as its proponents claim (Chaves 1995) or that the 99 prose propositions of the 'thick' version yield, as we have seen, results at odds with what its authors want to argue.

For most sociologists, neither disagreement about the presumed 'real' nature of religion nor evidence of logical deficiencies in the theory is decisive. Their main concern will be whether the new paradigm accurately answers their questions or fruitfully produces new ones. Certainly, rational choice proponents have raised new questions, translated old ones, and offered provocative explanations of well-known facts. At the same time, their specific accounts of the sources of religious organization, the consequences of religious competition, and the trajectory of secularization are now in doubt (Bruce 1999, 2002). A prime example, as noted, is the religious economy argument about the benefits of pluralism and competition, which appeared to be intuitively promising but has not been confirmed. Of course, social science can learn from productive errors and successful falsification, which in this case point toward significant modification of the new-paradigm thrust. Still, for rational sociologists interested in maximizing returns to their scholarly investments the accumulation of negative results makes it difficult to judge whether the reward of learning outweighs the cost of the research effort expended.

Since sociology as a whole has yet to settle on a single theory and sociologists do not even agree that it is desirable to have one, it may be overly risky to commit a subdiscipline to a paradigm defined in terms of one theory, even one more successful than rational choice has been to date. Adam Smith wisely warned against falling prey to intellectual 'systems,' and perhaps sociologists should take this to heart. Instead of betting on a single horse, or to replace the sociology with the economics of religion, portfolio diversification seems the rational strategy. Collective diversification would still justify concerted efforts by individual scholars to pursue the consequences of a single theory, though in light of shifting

scholarly opinion on the merits of rational choice even in economics this 'pure' play also carries risks. Like sociologists before them, economists are increasingly contextualizing rational choice. In the sociology of religion, the analysis of context has taken many forms. The old 'paradigm' – if we can call family resemblances among wide-ranging views a paradigm – treated religion as a form of social construction embedded in a system of institutions, in processes of interaction, in ecological settings, and in historical conjunctions. Once we understand how they are embedded, especially how religious 'preferences' are themselves shaped by individuals' ties and context (cf. Ellison 1995; Sherkat 1997), the rationality of individuals may help us to explain better, but only a little better, how and why they do what they do – a small portion of the variance, as methodologists might put it.

Notwithstanding the efforts by rational choice theorists to replace a putative old paradigm with a superior new one, friendly competition and even collaboration across a seemingly large theoretical divide might be more rewarding to sociologists who wish to avoid a costly paradigm struggle. On closer inspection, the divide is not so large in any case. After all, Stark and Finke themselves claim that 'stressing the social aspect of religion is a hallmark of the new paradigm' (2000: 35). Since most of their colleagues have been 'stressing' the same thing all along, there is at least a common starting point. To its credit, much of the new paradigm is not so new. In fact, Stark and Finke touch on several ways in which religion is embedded in the wider society. Iannaccone, as well, requires an account of the 'constraints' that do the explanatory work in a theory that holds preferences and calculations constant and itself cannot provide such an account (cf. Lechner 1990; Chaves 1995). In the interest of maximizing explanatory gains, practitioners of the old paradigm might encourage their colleagues to deviate a bit more from rational choice orthodoxy, as a few examples will illustrate.

To introduce the concept of a religious economy, Stark and Finke say that '[r]eligious organizations do not exist in a vacuum' (Stark and Finke 2000: 35). The most important parts of their environment are other religious organizations and 'aspects of the rules and norms governing religious activities' (*ibid.*). Citing Talcott Parsons, they argue that we can analyze religious life, taken *in toto*, as a religious economy, itself a 'subsystem of all social systems' that parallels subsystems 'involved with the secular (or commercial) economy' (*ibid*). Parsons would agree in principle that it is useful to think of religion as an institutional 'subsystem' connected in regular ways to other parts of an overarching social system and that these connections are governed by norms. To explain how religion 'works' in any society we must therefore describe, more clearly than rational choice theorists typically do, the form of the subsystem and its component organizations, show how it depends on and contributes to other such subsystems, and identify the prevailing institutional norms. Parsons' own analysis of America's denominational system, embedded in a differentiated society with a secularized Christian tradition, offers a partial illustration (Parsons 1978). At the same time, Parsons would say that it is a mistake to focus only on religion as an 'economy' and to account for it only by economic reasoning. Such reasoning can only capture some aspects of any institution, he insisted throughout his work. Religious interests guide action within normative constraints, which, with some exceptions, receive little attention in rational choice theory.

Stark and Finke acknowledge that earlier versions of their theory (Stark and Bainbridge 1987) were overly cognitive. To remedy the problem they propose to give more attention to the 'emotional and expressive component of religion' (2000: 83). An example is their proposition that 'prayer builds bonds of affection' between humans and gods (*ibid.*: 109). They 'are entirely willing to give Durkheim and the functionalists their due with respect to the observation that social rituals do generate group solidarity and, in that sense, social integration' (*ibid.*: 108). Similarly, they follow Randall Collins in assigning a greater role to ritual (*ibid.*: 107). From the point of view of Durkheim and Collins – not to mention that of rational choice patron saint Adam Smith in

his theory of 'moral sentiments' (Smith 1976b) – this does not go far enough to incorporate emotional interaction into the theory itself. Collins might urge them to take a few more steps down the old path, to affirm that ideas are not mere instruments of exchange but instead symbols of group membership, that ideas or 'explanations' are themselves created by moral-emotional patterns of interaction, and that religious interaction is but one part of a larger 'market' for interaction rituals (Collins 2004: xi, xiii). Of course, this might lead to further changes in the theory, starting with the overly cognitive definition of religion itself.

As we have seen, religious economy proponents acknowledge that markets have no uniform effects, or in other words, that the possible effects of competition depend on many other factors. They also have been at pains to stress that for individual customers it is the actually available options that matter. The market plus 'other factors' in any one place constitute what Nancy Ammerman (1997) has called the 'social ecology' of religion. Thinking ecologically is necessary to understand 'supply' in relation to 'demand': 'the social ecology of a given community – and the life histories represented by that social ecology – will affect the relationship between institutional supply and religious participation' (*ibid.*: 127). From this point of view, not yet fully incorporated into rational choice explanations, market operations are 'path dependent.' For example, new competition plays out differently in places that have always had it than in former monopolies, especially if older cohorts dominate the community (*ibid.*). Specific cultural contexts 'define desirable religious behavior,' which in one place may mean that many participate in spite of limited choices while elsewhere even ample supply cannot stimulate demand (*ibid.*: 125). Of course, such sensitivity to the impact of time and place complicates attempts to apply general theories to religion.

As a final example of a possible rapprochement between old and new paradigms, recall that Stark and Finke consider macro secularization 'obvious.' As religious providers lose monopoly status, society desacralizes and the public role of religion declines. According to the theory, variations in this process might depend on previous levels of regulation. Supplementing market arguments, Stark and colleagues have also argued that national or communal conflict may prevent desacralization. Here again old-paradigm versions of secularization theory would urge them to go further. Modern societies, David Martin (1978) would insist, display a strong tendency toward differentiation, dividing society into specialized, more systematically organized institutions. This process has special implications for the place of religion in public life, but much depends on when and how its impact is first felt. Differentiation in a former monopoly associated with the 'old regime,' as in France, turns religion into a divisive problem and fosters attempts at radical secularization. Differentiation in a pluralistic society providing norms for voluntary participation, as in America, more modestly reduces its public role and creates conditions in which it can flourish. If we know who the key religious actors are, and how strong and how diverse they are in the 'take-off' period for modernization, we can say much about the subsequent pattern. Martin's work may not be the last word on secularization, but it fruitfully conveys macro secularization as a composite of societal patterns, contingent on the conjunction of near-universal processes and historical conditions.

Without formulating a single overarching theory, generations of sociologists like the ones mentioned have developed systematic ideas for studying religion as a social practice or institution embedded in a larger social structure, produced by processes of interaction, expressed within a community's social ecology, and shaped by the conjunction of large historical forces. To this research tradition rational choice brings a desire for rigor and unity, from which the old paradigm can benefit. In turn, learning from the best the old paradigm has to offer may help new-paradigm advocates address the critical evidence reviewed in this chapter. As their proposed paradigm turns from sectarian upstart into lax denomination, intellectual free riders will borrow from it without becoming true believers. To the extent that this happens, it will not achieve the monopoly status to which its advocates may have aspired. Even for would-be unifiers, this is not all bad. Diverse scholarly markets in which multiple views compete may well produce greater vitality in the sociology of religion and better explanations of its subject. If nothing else, rational choice has given a boost to this ecumenical project. To this project, I trust, Adam Smith would give his blessing.

NOTES

1. I thank the editors and Erik Sengers for their helpful comments.

REFERENCES

Ammerman, Nancy T. 1997. 'Religious Choice and Religious Vitality: The Market and Beyond.' pp. 119–32 in *Rational Choice Theory and Religion: Summary and Assessment*, edited by Lawrence A. Young. New York: Routledge.

BBC 2005. 'Pope Warns against "DIY" Religion.' *news.bbc.co.uk*:August 21.

Becker, Jos, W., Joep de Hart and J. Mens. 1997. *Secularisatie en Alternatieve Zingeving in Nederland.* Rijswijk. Sociaal en Cultureel Planbureau.

Beckford, James A. 1989. *Religion in Advanced Industrial Society*. London: Unwin Hyman.

Berger, Peter L. 1969. *The Sacred Canopy*. New York: Doubleday.

Breault, Kevin D. 1989. 'New Evidence on Religious Pluralism, Urbanism, and Religious Participation.' *American Sociological Review* 54: 1048–53.

Bruce, Steve 1992. 'Pluralism and Religious Vitality.' pp. 170–94 in *Religion and Modernization: Sociologists and Historians Debate the Secularization Thesis*, edited by Steve Bruce. Oxford: Clarendon Press.

Bruce, Steve 1995. 'The Truth about Religion in Britain.' *Journal for the Scientific Study of Religion* 34: 417–30.

Bruce, Steve 1999. Choice and Religion: A Critique of Rational Choice Theory. Oxford: Oxford University Press.

Bruce, Steve 2002. 'The Poverty of Economism or the Social Limits on Maximizing.' pp. 167–85 in

Sacred Markets, Sacred Canopies: Essays on Religious Markets and Religious Pluralism, edited by Ted G. Jelen. Lanham, MD: Rowman and Littlefield.

Bryant, Joseph M. 2000. 'Cost-Benefit Accounting and the Piety Business: Is *Homo Religiosus* at Bottom a *Homo Economicus*?' *Method and Theory in the Study of Religion* 12: 520–48.

Chaves, Mark 1995. 'On the Rational Choice Approach to Religion.' *Journal for the Scientific Study of Religion* 34: 98–104.

Chaves, Mark and Philip S. Gorski 2001. 'Religious Pluralism and Religious Participation.' *Annual Review of Sociology* 27: 261–81.

Chesterton, G. K. 1905. *Heretics*. New York: John Lane.

Collins, Randall 2004. *Interaction Ritual Chains*. Princeton: Princeton University Press.

Demerath, N. J. III 1995. 'Rational Paradigms, A-Rational Religion, and the Debate over Secularization.' *Journal for the Scientific Study of Religion* 34: 105–12.

Ellison, Christopher G. 1995. 'Rational Choice Explanations of Individual Religious Behavior: Notes on the Problem of Social Embeddedness.' *Journal for the Scientific Study of Religion* 34: 89–97.

Finke, Roger and Rodney Stark 1988. 'Religious Economies and Sacred Canopies: Religious Mobilization in American Cities, 1906.' *American Sociological Review* 53: 41–9.

Finke, Roger and Rodney Stark 1992. *The Churching of America: Winners and Losers in Our Religious Economy*. New Brunswick, NJ: Rutgers University Press.

Hechter, Michael 1997. 'Religion and Rational Choice Theory.' pp. 147–59 in *Rational Choice Theory and Religion: Summary and Assessment*, edited by Lawrence A. Young. New York: Routledge.

Iannaccone, Laurence R. 1990. 'Religious Participation: A Human Capital Approach.' *Journal for the Scientific Study of Religion* 29: 297–314.

Iannaccone, Laurence R. 1994. 'Why Strict Churches Are Strong.' *American Journal of Sociology* 99: 1180–1211.

Iannaccone, Laurence R. 1995. 'Second Thoughts: A Response to Chaves, Demerath, and Ellison.' *Journal for the Scientific Study of Religion* 34: 113–20.

Iannaccone, Laurence R. 1997. 'Rational Choice: Framework for the Scientific Study of Religion.' pp. 25–44 in *Rational Choice Theory and Religion: Summary and Assessment*, edited by Lawrence A. Young. New York: Routledge.

Iannaccone, Laurence R. 2004. 'Faith Beyond Time: The Future of Religion in America.' *Futures* 36: 1025–30.

Introvigne, Massimo and Rodney Stark 2005. 'Religious Competition and Revival in Italy: Exploring European Exceptionalism.' *Interdisciplinary Journal of Research on Religion* 1: 1–20.

Land, Kenneth C., Glenn Deane and Judith R. Blau 1991. 'Religious Pluralism and Church Membership: A Spatial Diffusion Model.' *American Sociological Review* 56: 237–49.

Lechner, Frank J. 1990. 'The New Utilitarianism.' pp. 93–111 in *Current Perspectives in Social Theory: A Research Annual*, edited by John Wilson. Greenwich, CT: JAI Press.

Lechner, Frank J. 1996a. 'Secularization in the Netherlands?' *Journal for the Scientific Study of Religion* 35: 252–64.

Lechner, Frank J. 1996b. '"Heads I Win…": On Immunizing a Theory.' *Journal for the Scientific Study of Religion* 35: 272–4.

Martin, David 1978. *A General Theory of Secularization*. New York: Harper and Row.

Marwell, Gerald 1996. 'We Still Don't Know if Strict Churches Are Strong, Much Less Why: Comment on Iannacone.' *American Journal of Sociology* 101: 1097–1103.

Montgomery, James D. 2003. 'A Formalization and Test of the Religious Economies Model.' *American Sociological Review* 68: 782–809.

Olson, Daniel V. A. 1999. 'Religious Pluralism and U.S. Church Membership: A Reassessment.' *Sociology of Religion* 60: 149–73.

Olson, Daniel V. A. 2002. 'Competing Notions of Religious Competition and Conflict in Theories of Religious Economies.' pp. 133–65 in *Sacred Market, Sacred Canopies: Essays on Religious Markets and Religious Pluralism*, edited by Ted G. Jelen. Lanham, MD: Rowman and Littlefield.

Parsons, Talcott 1978. *Action Theory and the Human Condition*. New York: The Free Press.

Phillips, Rick 1999. 'The "Secularization" of Utah and Religious Competition.' *Journal for the Scientific Study of Religion* 38: 72–82.

Phillips, Rick 2004. 'Can *Rising* Rates of Church Participation be a Consequence of Secularization?' *Sociology of Religion* 65: 139–53.

Sengers, Erik 2003. '*Al Zijn Wij Katholiek, Wij Zijn Nederlanders*': *Opkomst en Verval van de Katholieke Kerk in Nederland sinds 1795 vanuit Rational-Choice Perspectief*. Delft: Eburon.

Sherkat, Darren E. 1997. 'Embedding Religious Choices: Integrating Preferences and Social

Constraints into Rational Choice Theories of Religious Behavior.' pp. 65–85 in *Rational Choice Theory and Religion*, edited by Lawrence A. Young. New York: Routledge.

Sherkat, Darren E. and Christopher G. Ellison 1999. 'Recent Developments and Current Controversies in the Sociology of Religion.' *Annual Review of Sociology* 25: 363–94.

Smith, Adam 1976a [1776]. An *Inquiry into the Nature and Causes of the Wealth of Nations*. Oxford: Clarendon Press.

Smith, Adam 1976b [1759]. *The Theory of Moral Sentiments*. Oxford: Clarendon Press.

Spickard, James V. 1998. 'Rethinking Religious Social Action: What is "Rational" about Rational Choice Theory?' *Sociology of Religion* 59: 99–115.

Stark, Rodney 1997. 'Bringing theory back in'. *Rational Choice Theory and Religion*. L. Young (ed.) New York, Routledge: 3–23.

Stark, Rodney and William Sims Bainbridge 1987. *A Theory of Religion*. New York: Peter Lang.

Stark, Rodney and Roger Finke 2000. *Acts of Faith: Explaining the Human Side of Religion*. Berkeley: University of California Press.

Stark, Rodney, Roger Finke and Laurence R. Iannacone 1995. 'Pluralism and Piety: England and Wales, 1851.' *Journal for the Scientific Study of Religion* 34: 431–44.

Stark, Rodney and Laurence R. Iannaccone 1994. 'A Supply-Side Reinterpretation of the "Secularization" of Europe.' *Journal for the Scientific Study of Religion* 33: 230–52.

Stark, Rodney and Laurence R. Iannaccone 1996. 'Recent Religious Declines in Quebec, Poland, and the Netherlands: A Theory Vindicated.' *Journal for the Scientific Study of Religion* 35: 265–71.

Verweij, Johan 1998. *Secularisering tussen Feit en Fictie: Een Internationaal Vergelijkend Onderzoek naar Determinanten van Religieuze Betrokkenheid*. Tilburg: Tilburg University Press.

Voas, David 2004. 'Religion in Europe: One Theme, Many Variations?' Paper presented at conference of the *Association for the Study of Religion, Economics, and Culture*. Kansas City (October).

Voas, David, Daniel V.A. Olson and Alasdair Crockett 2002. 'Religious Pluralism and Participation: Why Previous Research is Wrong.' *American Sociological Review* 67: 212–30.

5

Globalization and Glocalization

PETER BEYER

Globalization is a relatively recent term. It appeared in English-language usage only in the 1960s, albeit without the heavy connotations that it began to carry in the 1990s. Other similar expressions, however, already popularized the core meaning of all people on earth living in a single social space, notably Marshall McLuhan's notion of a 'global village' (McLuhan 1964). Entering social scientific discourse in the early 1980s, globalization itself subsequently became such a widespread term that it has become something close to a general name for the current era in which we all live, for better or worse. And in fact, the evaluation of globalization oscillates uneasily between utopian promise and dystopian menace. Parallel to this ambivalent attitude has been a very consistent tendency to understand globalization in terms of analytic binaries, especially the spatial distinction between the global and the local, or that between universal and particular (see esp. Robertson 1992).

The global in globalization refers both to a geographic limit, the earth as a physical place, and to an encompassing range of influence, namely that all contemporary social reality is supposedly conditioned or even determined by it. This inescapable and inclusive quality contrasts with the notion of modernization, arguably the prime term that globalization has

replaced both in popular and scientific discourse. While modernization excluded various 'others' that were deemed either pre-modern/ traditional or only on the way to modernization, globalization includes us all, even our 'others'. Modernization temporalized its universalism: eventually all would/could become modern. Globalization spatializes it: the local has to come to terms with the global. It (re)constitutes itself in the way that it does this. The reverse side of this mutual relation is that the global cannot be global except as plural versions of the local. Hence globalization is always also *glocalization* (Robertson 1995), the global expressed in the local and the local as the particularization of the global. This difference between modernization and globalization allows us to understand the different attitudes toward religion that prevail under the aegis of each term.

The discussion of this basic thesis in this chapter proceeds as follows: In a first section, I elaborate the idea of the pluralization of religion by isolating and then illustrating four important axes of variation along which this pluralization appears to proceed. On this basis, two further sections then focus on the sociological observation of religion. The first traces the reasons why sociological understanding has shifted away from a modernization emphasis which usually favoured the regional or national society as the default unit of analysis. The second looks at how the subdiscipline has since the 1980s been explicitly or implicitly expanding the basic unit of analysis to include the entire globe, while simultaneously moving away from the assumption of secularization as the dominant trend and toward variations on pluralization instead. These more literature-review oriented sections are then followed by a brief presentation of my own suggestion for how to theorize religion in global/glocal society. Finally, a concluding section considers possible future directions for the sociology of religion in light of the overall analysis.

GLOBALIZATION AND PLURALIZATION OF RELIGION

The dominant sociological thesis about the relation of religion and modernization has been one of incompatibility: a modernizing society was *ipso facto* a secularizing society. Religion, as a comparatively 'irrational' orientation in a modernity defined by rationalization, would lose its broader social influence or become a privatized domain. While not all observers of modernization agreed with this proposition, as globalization has become the regnant universalizing concept, the dissenters have quickly become the majority. In as much as the modern excluded its other side, namely the traditional, modernization could assign religion to that 'other side', allowing only certain restricted religious expression the status of modern religion (cf. Durkheim 1965; Bellah 1970). With globalization, the global includes its defining polar opposite, the local, such that when religion appears as the local, it is thereby also global, or better, glocal. Hence, what stands out with respect to religion in the globalizing as opposed to modernizing world is not secularization but *pluralization*, the inclusion of different *glocalizations* of religion. Theories of religion in the global circumstance correspondingly can be expected to emphasize notions of socially constructed religious plurality from both a global and a local perspective.[1]

Notions of secularization, differentiation, privatization, and the categorization of religion along 'modern/traditional' lines do not cease to make sense in this context. Instead, these ideas become subordinated to the now seeming self-evidence of religious diversity. Rather than an anachronistic presence better suited to bygone eras, religion now appears much more easily as a prime way of being different or particular and therefore as an integral aspect of globalization/glocalization. As such, religion becomes the site of difference, contestation and, not infrequently, conflict. Its previously defining qualities as a provider of *societal* cohesion, integration and solidarity virtually disappear from the screen. Applied to religion, they now make about as much sense as the idea that a globalizing society is also a secularizing society.

AXES OF VARIATION IN GLOCAL RELIGION

On the basis of this observation, the most persistent questions about religion and globalization will concern its plural manifestations, the different ways in which religion glocalizes. Numerous strategies suggest themselves for understanding this variety, but the following four axes of variation seem to stand out:

1. *Religion that is institutionalized as religion vs. religiosity that is non-institutionalized.* Within this continuum would fall new religions and new religious trends or movements, which can enter the continuum and move to the institutionalized pole as they develop; as well as Luckmann's *bricolage* or Bellah *et al.*'s 'Sheilaism' on the non-institutionalized end.

2. *Religion that is publicly influential vs. religion that is privatized.* Unlike under the assumptions of many forms of secularization theory, religion can now be either or both of these in different contexts.

3. *Religion that is traditional/conservative vs. religion that is modern/liberal.* It is difficult to assign precise meanings to the two poles of this axis of variation, but under this

heading fall discussions about so-called 'fundamentalisms', positive or negative orientations to religious plurality itself, and the degree to which religion claims to be determinative for other, non-religious domains.

4. *Religion that is specifically enacted as religion vs. non-religious forms that may nonetheless carry 'religious' functions.* Religion is clearly one of the most evident ways of asserting individual or collective difference in the global context; but there are also other categories which can play central roles in structuring glocality, ones that are neither understood nor performed as religious. Prominent examples are culture, gender, race, and ethnic/nation.

These axes of variation are not necessarily exhaustive; nor will the religious manifestations of today's global society fall neatly onto one side of a continuum or another. Rather, they serve as heuristic distinctions for marking out the field of religious pluralization under the rubric of globalization. Of particular note is that each pole of each axis of variation is itself subject to pluralization. Institutionalized religion, for instance, will manifest as plural religions; while non-institutionalized religiosity is inherently variable. Instances of local 'monopoly' or uniformity, by contrast, will call for special explanation, much like 'strong' religion under the secularization thesis had to be seen as an 'exception'. In addition, although these continua pose the implicit question of what actually counts as religion, defining religion would be misplaced because what is needed is not conceptual uniformity or the isolation of some sort of essence of religion. Instead, what matters is what people in *this global society* actually call and treat as religion. Such orientations can and will be contested and often ambiguous; they will themselves pose the question of pluralization and glocalization.

Some illustrations of how pluralization and glocalization express themselves through these axes of variation will serve to concretize the argument at this point.

Beginning with the institutionalized religions, in practically every country and region, we find a variable set of entities which people there call, treat, and enact as religions (or parallel words in other languages). These generally include Christianity, Hinduism, Islam, Buddhism; and, less consistently, Judaism and Sikhism. Beyond these clearly globalized religions is a varied list of others recognized regionally, for example, Zoroastrianism, Daoism, Jainism, Rastafarianism, Baha'i, Candomblé, or Cao Dai. Two related global continuities are evident here: the specific globally present religions, and the seemingly accepted fact that there are religions which can be named and to which one can belong or not. In either case, the globalized category is already inherently plural. There is no such thing as a single global religion. These overall statements, however, tell us little about concrete situations in various regions. Different religions dominate in different places: Christianity in Europe, Latin America and several African countries; Islam from Northern Africa to Indonesia; Buddhism in eastern Asia; Hinduism in South Asia. Each of these has a significant, if usually minority, presence in most of the other world regions as well. Many of the smaller religions have regional concentrations, like the Punjab for Sikhs, Jamaica for Rastafarians, or Japan for Omotokyo. But like the larger 'world' religions, most of these also have presences in other parts of the world. Large or small, the religions are usually globally spread and locally concentrated. Moreover, the individual religions manifest themselves only as particular variations such as Protestant, Catholic, Orthodox Christianity; Sunni, Twelver Shi'a, or Ismaili Islam; Vaisnava, Saiva, or Advaita Vedanta Hinduism; Mahayana or Theravada Buddhism; and so forth. And within each of these categories there are most often more subvariants such as Anglican or Jehovah's Witnesses (Protestant), Bohra or Nizari (Ismaili), Zen or Shingon (Mahayana), and so forth. Most of these are likewise globally spread with local concentrations. The result is a different local mix of pluralized religions in different regions. In addition, each of the variants receives local colouring: Anglican Protestant Christianity is not the same in Uganda as it is in Canada or even different places in these countries;

Sunni Islam is not quite the same in Indonesia as it is in Turkey, France, or Saudi Arabia; and similarly for all the others. Nonetheless, all this variation, far from vitiating the global single-ness of the religions and their main divisions, actually constitutes them (see Beyer 2003). Both practitioners and external observers understand these religions as unities through variation, in other words, as glocalizations. The universals are real abstractions; concrete, socially effective religions appear only as localized particular-izations of those global universals. Finally, the construction of both global unity and local manifestations occurs with reference to one another: the religions constitute and reproduce themselves in a context of recognized plurality of religions and subdivisions of religions. None of this, of course, excludes disagreement and conflict over and across the various boundaries; rather it explicitly includes such contestation.

As differentiated social entities, the institu-tionalized religions bear variable relations to domains of social life that are not religion. Thus, through their authorities and represen-tatives, particular religions can seek to exert direct influence on these other domains, whether politics and law, economy, science, mass media, education, or a variety of others. They can also focus on their own reproduction through ritual and practice. Of course, most religious groups do both, the latter even being a condition for the former. The alternative of seeking to exert public influence or restricting oneself to privatized religious concerns is rarely that stark. Globally speaking, religion is both a privatized and public concern. The seri-ous variation in this dimension is at the local or particular level, especially as concerns how heavily and effectively institutionalized reli-gion is brought into play in non-religious domains. This variance only overlaps partially with the differences of the religions them-selves. Thus, for instance, Islam is generally more publicly active than many other religions, consistently claiming direct relevance in the operation of all other spheres of life. It is often quite effective in this capacity. Yet even here we see substantial variation, whether over time as movements rise and fade, or geographically,

for example, between relatively 'theocratic' Iran or Saudi Arabia and relatively 'secular' Tunisia or Turkey. In places where Islam is not dominant, usually for very practical reasons this religion tends to be a more privatized con-cern, but that does not exclude public visibility and Muslim attempts to influence what goes on in other domains. By contrast, although per-haps in the majority of areas where Christianity is dominant this religion leans more toward a concentration on its own strictly religious affairs, there are so many exceptions to this pattern that it is little more than a statistical generalization. In countries as varied as the United States, Poland, the Philippines, Zambia, Brazil and Russia, there have over the past few decades been various sometimes quite effective and long-lasting Christian forays into the public arena. Similar statements could be made for virtually every other religion; for Buddhism in Japan or Thailand, for Judaism in the United States or Israel, for Hinduism in India or Great Britain, and so on. All these cases taken together show that, on a global scale alone, religions are both publicly influen-tial and privatized. It is only at the local or par-ticular level that their subvariants may lean more heavily toward one alternative than the other. Although almost all the movements seek-ing to assert public religious influence engage globalized structures such as the system of states, the world economy, cultural flows of various kinds, and indeed other (global) religions, the particular characteristics of such movements, how long they last, and how effective they are, these are a matter of local circumstances and not a global trend in either the direction of increased privatization or general 'resurgence'. An aspect of the glocalized pluralization is unpredictability.

Over the past three decades, the religious developments that have without doubt received the most attention as a global phe-nomenon are so-called 'fundamentalisms'. Chief among these have been the American Christian Right, Religious Zionism in Israel, Islamist movements in a number of countries, as well as Sikh and Hindu nationalist move-ments in India (see Marty and Appleby 1991–95; Kepel 1994). Perhaps the most evi-dent common feature of these movements is that they are religio-political movements, ones that seek public influence for religion. From a slightly different perspective, however, they are also for the most part conservative or neo-traditionalist movements, meaning that their explicit rationale includes a reassertion of values and ways of living warranted by the past, by tradition, and thereby in opposition to orientations conceived as modern, liberal and secular. Among the symbolic issues that most consistently express this opposition are a call for comparatively strict control of (especially female) bodies in contrast to supposed permissiveness or decadence, and a separatist (often nationalist) claim to the exclusive validity of their truth over against a posited global relativism or anomie (Kapur 1986; Lustick 1988; Juergensmeyer 1993; Riesebrodt 1993). It is in fact the traditionalist, 'anti-modern' discourse that most clearly distinguishes those movements labelled as 'fundamentalist', since quite often not particularly militant movements like the Jewish Neturei Karta, the Christian Communion and Liberation, or the Islamic Tablighi Jamaat (see Ahmed 1991; Kepel 1994) are called 'fundamentalist', while publicly and politically engaged, but non-traditionalist, religious movements such as the liberation theology movement in Latin America do not. As movements and as a category, 'fundamentalism' therefore points to the contemporary and global relevance of a kind of religion that, under the aegis of modernization, was deemed to be obsolete and destined to disappear. It represents a clearly possible variant of religious presence in contrast to more liberal and non-exclusive religion, both of which appear to belong in a globalized society.

The recognized religions do not have a monopoly on the religious in contemporary global society. Three other types of phenomena exist alongside and even compete with them. These are new religious movements, especially those that seek to become new, recognized religions; non-institutional, highly individualized, religiosity or 'spirituality'; and broadly speaking religio-cultural expression that is not differentiated as religion. Each of these illustrates the dynamics of glocalization and pluralization in a somewhat different way.

New religions demonstrate the opened-ended possibility for additional institutional religions. From Scientology, The Family, and the Raelians to Won Buddhism, Falun Dafa, and I-Kuan Tao, a bewildering variety of groups often fall under this heading, with their origins in virtually every corner of the world (see Melton and Baumann 2002). Aside from the sheer plurality, what is of relevance here is that the category of a new religion, along with its pejorative version, 'cult' (with strictly parallel terms in other languages), is itself globalized, as is the suspicion with which new religions are treated by others, including recognized religions, mass media, schools and governments. There is in that context significant continuity in the anti-new religions discourse around the world (see Richardson 2004). Moreover, a very large number of these new religions try to establish an international and even worldwide presence, such demonstration of broader appeal clearly forming part of their claim to legitimacy. Thus, even though most new religions are quite small and show even more regional concentration than the larger and older 'world' religions, they participate in the globalized category of an institutionalized and differentiated religion quite as much as do the latter. They thereby further express the pluralization of religion both as a social reality and as a category of observation. Nonetheless, as with the world religions, new religions appear only in particular and local form: pluralization manifests itself as glocalization of these religious movements and that multiple localization is both a condition and a symptom of their globalization.

If the title of new religions refers to those movements that seek recognition as religions, the term 'spirituality' has in recent decades come to designate another important and inherently plural religious phenomenon. Not coincidentally a word that is still in many ways but a synonym for the religious, spirituality now often refers to religion in a highly individualized mode, and in this sense outside or at the margins of the authoritative bounds of institutionalized religions. A variety of trends and manifestations can fall under this heading. From the somewhat amorphous New Age and

Japanese new New Religions to the tendency for a great many people around the world to fashion their own combination of religious beliefs and practices with little reference to specific centres of religious tradition or authority (cf. Roof 1999; Heelas *et al.* 2005), a parallel style of religiosity appears to be gaining attention. Although the global aspect of this development can be subsumed under different headings, for instance Inglehart's notion of post-materialist (Inglehart 1997) religion, the concrete variety of such spirituality can almost by definition only be local. Yet, following Inglehart's analysis, this sort of religiosity seems usually to be pursued by the relatively more privileged segments of the global population, those with a higher probability of having broader global connections and thus being themselves less rootedly local than those large numbers without such power. This sort of highly particular and highly plural religiosity is therefore also in that sense more global and hence glocal.

In some quarters, however, the term spirituality carries a different meaning, shading over into the idea of religio-cultural expression that is not distinguished as religion. Spirituality refers also to the religious ways of aboriginal peoples and thus to a form of religiosity that is glocal in a rather distinct way. The category of 'aboriginal' or 'indigenous' is, from one angle, local by definition: it is what was 'here from the origins' as opposed to that which came here 'from somewhere else' relatively recently. Aboriginal and indigenous people are those who were in a place before its incorporation into globalizing structures. Their 'traditional' cultural expressions can and do thereby claim to be ones that belong to that locality more purely than others. A mark of that belonging is in many cases that the carriers of this indigeneity reject differentiation among various functional modalities, including especially religion, when applied to their cultural traditions, such differentiated structures being seen as that which engenders the homogenization of the local into global patterns. The insistence on aboriginal spiritualities as a non-differentiable dimension of aboriginal culture is thereby a way of constructing the integrity and inviolability of

those cultures or identities vis-à-vis global forces. Ironically, however, the category of aboriginal has itself become globalized, a prime symptom of which is that aboriginal peoples around the world are often in contact and relate to one another *as* aboriginal peoples. Aboriginal spirituality is not so much a way of maintaining the local against the global as it is yet another instance of glocalization, doing the global in local mode. A further indicator of this role is that, in some cases, such as African Traditional Religion in countries like South Africa or Benin (cf. Mndende 1998), or various indigenous religious cultures in Indonesia (see e.g. Schiller 1997), 'aboriginal' people mobilize in the opposite direction: they seek to construct and have their religious ways recognized as distinct religions, with the same goal of cultural recognition and assertion. The situation points to the generally ambiguous but close relation between religion and culture as pluralized and glocalized categories.

Aboriginal people striving for cultural recognition and autonomy are not alone in insisting on an intertwining of religion and culture, thereby melding two categories for asserting glocal difference. The frequency of religious nationalism is another and more powerful manifestation. From State Shinto in pre-World War II Japan and Irish Catholic nationalism to Sinhalese Buddhist nationalism in Sri Lanka and Hindu nationalism in twentieth-century India, this strategy has been a constant of our world throughout the modern era. These and many other religio-nationalist movements have insisted on an intimate link among a particular religio-cultural way of life, a particular territory, and a particular group of people generally attributed with a common ancestry and history in that territory. In each case, a critical warrant for this identification is a rootedness in the past, often the mythic past. As with the aboriginal movements, however, religious nationalisms are not isolated occurrences that just happen to have certain features in common. They are local variations on a globalized theme, even model. The religio-cultural identities structure themselves in deliberate comparison with the rest of the world, almost invariably imagining this outside as homologous 'others', other religio-cultural identities.

THE SOCIOLOGICAL UNDERSTANDING OF RELIGION: FROM MODERN TO GLOBAL CONTEXT

In suggesting pluralization as the prime *leitmotif* for observing religion under conditions of globalization, I do not claim that religious plurality is anything new. Notions of multiplicity in matters religious are as old as the concept itself. What I am proposing is rather that the most significant dimension for understanding religion in the specifically *global society* of today is its pluralization along several axes of variation. The shift to a global perspective is key. Without that change in perspective, the argument loses much of its rationale. It is therefore important to understand how globalization has come to be such a ubiquitous concept and what effect that is having on the sociological observation of religion. Given the influence that the classical thinkers of the nineteenth century still have on this discipline, I begin with Marx, Durkheim and Weber.

Since its nineteenth-century origins, sociology has been informed by the guiding difference between modern and non-modern or traditional societies. Karl Marx focused almost exclusively on the development and fate of capitalism in contrast especially to feudalism; Émile Durkheim built up his theory on the distinction between modern organic and traditional mechanical solidarity societies; Max Weber concentrated on various dimensions of the shift from pre-modern to modern, including themes like rationalization, bureaucracy, political domination and modern capitalism. In one sense, religion occupied a central position for all three of them: as an ideological tool of the dominant classes for Marx, as a foundational aspect of society for Durkheim, and as a key factor in the rise of modern capitalism for Weber. Yet in each case, the prevailing fate of at least institutional religion was decline and even disappearance: to be discarded by proletarians and fade away under communism for Marx, to

be superseded by the 'cult of man' for Durkheim, and to succumb to modern rationality in a disenchanted world for Weber. In one form or another, the reigning historical direction was modernization and the outcome for religion was secularization.

The passage from traditional to modern in classical sociology was in one sense a temporal transition from past to present and future, but it also had spatial reference. First, what we now call the West was modern or at least modernizing, while other regions of the world were at best non-modern. Even though Marx, Weber, Durkheim and other classical sociologists took account of the wider world that they inhabited, their attention to the non-Western regions was limited because from their perspective that is not where their main concern, modernization, was happening. Where they did pay attention, such as in Durkheim's analysis of the religion of Australian Aborigines or Weber's comparative studies of China and India, it was as examples of the pre-modern or traditional. Second, the modernizing West for these thinkers (Marx is a partial exception) came to be seen as divided geographically into 'national societies', which could be compared as to the way modernization occurred in each case. The geopolitical unit of the nation-state, especially during the period from the late nineteenth-century to the early twentieth-century, became more or less synonymous with the idea of a society. From that time, sociological observation became primarily the Western, nation-state based observation of modernization in the West (Albrow 1990; Robertson 1992: 8ff.). Somewhat ironically, however, that same period was one of the most intense in terms of the projection of Western power all over the world. In contemporary conceptual terms, classical sociology took place in a globalizing historical situation, but its understanding was national, perhaps international, but not global. At the beginning of the twenty-first century, the self-evidence of this identity between the (nation) state and society has begun seriously to loosen, but it still informs the discipline to a great extent. This has had corresponding consequences for the understanding of religion.

The secularization assumptions of the classics prevailed in sociology and, to a lesser degree, in the sociology of religion until the latter quarter of the twentieth century. Indeed, they reached a kind of apogee in the 1960s with the influential work of thinkers such as Peter Berger, Thomas Luckmann, Bryan Wilson, Richard Fenn, Talcott Parsons and others. Although there were salient differences in their various perspectives, they shared a threefold assumption: religion was either declining or being pushed to the margins of societal importance; religion's role in society was integrative; and the modern societies of interest were national and Western (now including Japan). Their positions did, however, include a wider 'international' awareness. The national societies could be and were compared in terms of the way religion operated within them. The question of pluralization, usually in terms of pluralism, was also posed at this national level; and the prevailing question in this regard was how it affected the secularization of a society (see esp. Berger 1967; Martin 1978). Pluralization across the nations was hardly even an issue.

What transformed that situation since the 1970s is to some degree a matter of speculation. But one can begin by noting a coincidence not often mentioned. The mid-1980s saw the publication of both Roland Robertson's seminal ideas on globalization and Rodney Stark and William Bainbridge's explicit theoretical rejection of the secularization thesis (Robertson and Chirico 1985; Stark and Bainbridge 1985). Both were the result of work begun in the later 1970s, both suggested a significant reorientation for sociological observation, and both have been highly influential since. They also represent two radically different approaches. What they nonetheless have in common is their shared historical context and here religious developments play a critical role. At the risk of oversimplifying, the year 1979 stands out. Its portentous events include the Iranian revolution, the founding of Jerry Falwell's Moral Majority in the United States, the Nicaraguan revolution, the accession of John Paul II to the papacy, the Soviet invasion of Afghanistan, and the first stirring of the Solidarity movement in Poland. All of these showed that religion could (still) be a public and mainstream force; all of them are to a significant degree incomprehensible without taking into view the wider global context in which they occurred (cf. Beyer 1994). Various ongoing and subsequent religio-political events in places like Israel-Palestine or Sri Lanka only reinforced that impression. What they encouraged is a shift in sociological observation, exemplified in the work of Robertson, Stark and Bainbridge, and a great many others, in which the sociology of religion moves gradually more into the mainstream of the larger discipline at the same time as most sociologists of religion hastily claim to abandon the secularization thesis and pay attention to religious diversity in new ways. Now, in this different context, the variety of ways in which religion and religiousness manifests itself as well as new developments in the religious sphere become that much more obvious and worthy of attention, whether we are speaking, for instance, of the abiding strength of religion in the United States, the continuing efflorescence of new religious movements in every corner of the globe, the growth of already longstanding Pentecostalism or Islamism worldwide, the religious assumptions of seemingly secular Europeans, or the vitality and ever changing face of Christianity in sub-Saharan Africa.

There can be little doubt that the seemingly sudden and precipitous fall of the Soviet empire at the end of the 1980s marked a profound change in world order and, inevitably, a significant shift in how people around the world, including sociologists, understood that world. In a few short years, the self-evident Cold War organizing distinction between East and West disappeared. The world was not just different, it had to be thought anew, and now without the socialist/capitalist divide. These had, in effect, been alternative paths of modernization from which a 'national society' could choose. The signs of transformed observation in the 1990s became quickly apparent. Two tendencies are particularly notable. One has tried to continue with a modified version of the old lines, effacing the socialist alternative and thereby leaving the 'capitalist road' as the only possibility. Francis Fukuyama's early 1990s declaration of the 'end of history' (Fukuyama 1993) and the worldwide anti-globalization movements that emerged toward the end of the decade represent opposing versions of this direction. It touched off the rapid rise in popularity of the term, globalization, understood essentially as global capitalism without the socialist alternative. This understanding of globalization is modernization in a monopolistic guise. It therefore has had little cause to take religion seriously – except as defensive 'fundamentalism' (Barber 1996; cf. Beckford 2003: 103ff.) – and has typically imagined a decline in the power of the national state (see Rudolph and Piscatori 1997; Beck 2000). Both features witness to the difficulty of continuing to observe today's social reality in the normative terms of the 'secular/modern national society'.

The other significant tendency has also adopted a global perspective, accepting that we evidently all now live in the same social world. The result, however, is the observed multiplication of difference rather than (just) progressive homogeneity. This is the direction that I emphasize here. It understands the global in terms of its glocal particularizations. It resonates strongly with the *post*-modern discourse that has paralleled the recognition of globalization (see Lyotard 1984, French original published in 1979). In announcing the end of grand narratives, post-modernism opened the door for the multiplicity of narratives, but also for their contestation. Important in the present context is that these visions no longer *have to assume* the national, territorially delimited, and solidary society as normative. It is also among them that one finds a much stronger place for religion. It is therefore this kind of approach that has more clearly informed very late twentieth and early twenty-first century sociology of religion.

THE SOCIOLOGICAL UNDERSTANDING OF RELIGION IN THE GLOBALIZATION ERA

A closer look at post-Cold War sociological observation of religion can begin by repeating

that neither the national society nor the notion of secularization need be or has been abandoned. As noted, these maintain their importance, only now as aspects of pluralized variation rather than as guiding assumptions. That said, we should not expect the change to take place all at once. Current sociological thinking is in fact in a kind of transitional phase, combining 'modernization' and 'globalization' assumptions. Two of the clearer examples of this are analyses of European 'exceptionalism' and religious market theories, trends well represented in the work of Grace Davie (Davie 2003) and Rodney Stark and his collaborators (Stark and Bainbridge 1987; Finke and Stark 1992; Stark and Iannaccone 1994) respectively. In spite of sharp differences in theoretical perspectives, the two approaches share a continued orientation toward the idea of secularization, the use of the national/regional (Europe and the United States) society as the basic unit of analysis, and *yet also* an explicit contextual awareness of and reference to the rest of the world without, however, giving the notion of globalization an operative place within their theories. Thus Davie's examination of religion in contemporary Europe focuses on this region's exceptionalism in terms of how secularized it is, that by comparison most of the rest of the world is not secularized, and that religion is not thereby simply unimportant in Europe. The exceptionalism only makes sense in global context. And, in spite of their explicit rejection of the secularization thesis, Stark *et al.* analyse religious markets in mostly national/regional terms and with respect to how 'vital', namely *unsecularized*, each of those markets is. They also put great stress on religion's *rationality* (Stark and Finke 2000), a preoccupation that resonates much more with a modernization/secularization orientation. Yet, in seeking to construct a general theory of religion, they expressly claim validity for all religious markets around the world, not just in the West.

This transitional situation also reveals itself in the use of the distinction between religion and spirituality. From Ernst Troeltsch's late nineteenth-century discussion of 'mysticism' (Troeltsch 1931) to Thomas Luckmann's 'invisible religion' of the 1960s (Luckmann 1967), a key element of the secularization thesis has hitherto been privatization, the idea that religion has become more and more the affair of individuals or voluntary associations and less and less a matter of overarching institutional authority. That discussion continues, but there has been a partial shift in emphasis corresponding to a change from privatization as dominant principle to religion/spirituality as axis of variation. On the one hand, a significant literature still operates in the context of the privatization thesis, arguing either positively that privatized spirituality is the (new) dominant trend (e.g. Roof 1999; Heelas *et al.* 2005) or negatively that such non-institutional spirituality is merely 'potential' religion (e.g. Stark and Bainbridge 1985; Bibby 2002). These perspectives generally adopt the national society as their unit of analysis, although sometimes including cross-national comparison. On the other hand, the phenomenon is receiving increasing attention as a globalized trend and alternative. Under this heading would fall Ronald Inglehart's suggestion of a 'post-materialist' religiosity, the growing presence of which he detects on the basis of 'world' values studies (Inglehart 1997). It would also include a varied literature on the New Age movement as a specifically global and not just Western development (Rothstein 2001; Carozzi 2004; Ackerman 2005; Howell 2005). Moving across the continuum, there is the attention that somewhat more institutionalized but still often quite fluid religious developments are receiving. Pentecostal/Charismatic Christianity is a case in point. Although it already began to attract sociological attention in the 1960s and 1970s, many of the more recent contributions focus specifically on its ability to translate itself or glocalize relatively easily around the world, as well as on its global growth (see e.g. Poewe 1994; Cox 1995; Dempster *et al.* 1999; Coleman 2000; Martin 2002; Wilkinson 2006). Somewhat related is the topic of new religious movements. In spite of their small size and often limited geographic range, their global presence, global aspirations, as well as the similarity in the kind of suspicion and opposition that they attract in countries right across the

globe have been topics of growing attention in the sociological literature of the post-Cold War decades (see e.g. Hexham and Poewe 1997; Dawson 1998; Kent 1999; Barchunova 2002; Richardson 2004). This orientation is a notable addition to that which informed the sociological literature on new religious movements that dates from the 1960s to the 1980s, which generally operated mostly in the orbit of secularization assumptions, notably through the dominance of the question of conversion (see, from a great many, Lofland 1966; Judah 1974; Glock and Bellah 1976). That literature was also overwhelmingly oriented to the national or regional society, mostly in the West, but also in Japan (see e.g. McFarland 1967; Brannen 1968; cf. Shimazono 2004).

At the beginning of the twenty-first century, sociological analyses of religion that adopt an overtly global orientation are still not that common. To be sure, ever since the early 1990s, there has been a smattering of such works (e.g. Robertson and Garrett 1991; Ahmed 1994; Beyer 1994; Van der Veer 1996; Rudolph and Piscatori 1997; Haynes 1998; Meyer and Geschiere 1999; Esposito and Watson 2000; Stackhouse and Paris 2000; Beyer 2001; Hopkins *et al.* 2001; Juergensmeyer 2003; Agadjanian and Roudometof 2005; Learman 2005), but their number contrasts markedly with the social scientific literature on globalization itself, which has become unmanageable in volume. There is, however, a very significant literature on religion that is highly relevant to the themes of globalization and glocalization. The bulk of these contributions have centred on two subjects: religio-political mobilization and religion in the context of transnational migration. The literature on the former grew and adopted a global dimension as of 1979 when, in light of the rise of the American New Christian Right, the term began to be transferred from its original context, first to Islam and the Iranian revolution specifically, and then to diverse religio-political movements in Islam, Judaism, Hinduism and Sikhism especially (for early examples, see Haines 1979; von der Mehden 1980). In spite of the dissimilarities among the different so-called 'fundamentalisms' and protests that it was a Western misconception when applied outside the Protestant Christian fold, the term has persisted in social scientific discourse since the early 1980s, arguably because of its ability to name an important global continuity among otherwise highly disparate religious movements. Fundamentalism is in that sense a quintessentially glocal concept.

A somewhat similar analysis applies to the relation between religion and transnational migration. A critical part of the web of communications and flows that has helped to make today's globalized reality so apparent is the movement of people under various guises ranging from tourists to migrants. The importance of the latter category is that it represents the more or less permanent moving of people from one part of the world to another, but in such a way that links between the 'old' country and the 'new' are in most cases maintained, thereby contributing to the density and permanence of global social connections. Religion consistently plays an important role in such migration as resources for immigrant adaptation to new local environments and as one of the social forms that flows from one part of the world to another along the communicative links thus established. Migration is in turn a prime conduit for the globalization of the religions themselves. In light of the intensification of both migration and transnational linkages, it is not surprising that the social scientific literature which focuses on them becomes, in effect, globalization literature with respect to religion. A brief look at some examples will serve to concretize this point.

Beginning in the mid-1990s, American sociologists began to pay concerted attention to the religious expression of that country's post-1960s migrants. Here the work directed by Stephen Warner and Judith Wittner was ground breaking and was notably carried out only in the mid-1990s. Already the title of the major publication emerging from this research, *Gatherings in Diaspora*, pointed explicitly to the linkages of migrant religious forms in the United States with the wider world (Warner and Wittner 1998). What is also characteristic of this volume and of the growing literature that has emerged in its wake is the emphasis on the plurality of these forms in the United States, on their roots in various parts of the world, as well as on the commonalities that they display in response to the particularly American context. In that light, the narrative it tells is no longer overwhelmingly a Christian story with a Jewish minor thread. Other non-Christian religions are the focus along with a new intra-Christian variety. Most importantly in the present context, the transnational dimension is receiving sustained attention, attesting to the explicitly global aspect of this new religious plurality (see e.g. Levitt 1998; Prebish and Tanaka 1998; Lawson 1999; Ebaugh and Chafetz 2002; Haddad and Smith 2002; Guest 2003; Vásquez and Marquardt 2003; Carnes and Yang 2004; Levitt 2004).

Similar but also different developments have occurred among scholars in other regions. These include countries such as Canada and Australia (Coward et al. 2000), but notably and in greater volume, Europe. As with the American literature, recent global migrants to this latter region have raised the double question of how these will challenge the ways that religions take form and importance in European countries, and how their implantation in this region will generate new forms of the recently arrived religions. On both sides, what is at issue is the plural glocalization of religion (see e.g. Burghart 1987; Dessai 1993; Baumann 2000). Somewhat in contrast to the United States, however, the majority of the attention falls on one particular religion, namely Islam. To some extent this is because a majority of migrants in many countries are Muslims, to some degree because Muslims seem to challenge the highly privatized and unobtrusive way that religion has functioned in this region during much of the twentieth century. In consequence, the burgeoning literature on Islam and Muslims in Europe tends very much to operate on the assumption of implicit comparison: Can Islam adapt? Can Europeans maintain their seemingly established ways and demand that Islam conform? (see, from among many, Khosrokhavar 1997; Vertovec and Rogers 1998; Nielsen 1999; Roy 1999; Rath 2001; Jonker 2002). The axes of variation of publicly influential to privatized and of traditional/conservative to modern/liberal are both at play and overlap with the issue of the plurality of religions themselves and of their global presence.

Two other global regions from which highly relevant literature has been emerging are Latin America and the Caribbean and sub-Saharan Africa. Two prime religious vehicles in these cases are Christianity and New World African religions. With respect to the former, although the transnational Roman Catholic Church is certainly still of importance (cf. Lanternari 1998; Casanova 2001), it is Pentecostal and Evangelical Christianity that is receiving the bulk of the attention, arguably because of its transnational presence and recent growth, the ease with which its proponents move around the world from various home bases, and its diverse glocalization in so many regions (e.g. Meyer and Geschiere 1999; Adogame 2000; van Dijk 2001; Alvarsson and Segato 2003). New World African religions like Voudon, Candomblé, or Santería are quite different in their characteristic features, yet they share with Christianity, and with Pentecostalism in particular, a long transnational history in which Africans and their inherited religious expressions play a significant role. The trans-Atlantic connection has been a prime path across which both originally African and European religious impulses travelled eventually to engender new, pluralized, and glocalized religions that are today still in the process of formation (Clarke 1998; Motta 1998). The transnationalism has provided the conditions for reconstructing 'old' world religions in plural fashion; and also, according to some observers, for constructing a new world religion altogether (Frigerio 2004). Therefore, just as the transplantation of other religions along the paths of global migration is resulting in their pluralized and glocalized reconstruction in regions where they had little presence before, so is an older migration spawning new religions that are in turn producing glocalized versions on several continents.

THEORIZING PLURALIZED RELIGION IN A GLOBAL SOCIETY

In light of the increasing sociological attention paid to religion in the context of globalization, the lack of explicit theorizing on the relation between the two terms is perhaps a bit puzzling. As noted, the amount of literature *relevant* to the question is on the rise, but for the most part globalization in these works remains the name for an aspect of the social environment to which religion responds in various ways, not as something that, like capitalism or the sovereign state, is a constitutive dimension of globalization. Partial exceptions are the efforts that emphasize the transnational face of religion and the literature on religio-political movements. But even here, the global context is provided by something other than religion to which religion responds. At best religion thickens global flows. The contributions of Roland Robertson move into the gap to an extent in that he stresses the thematization of globality as an integral facet of the global condition; and that this task is an inherently 'religious' one (Robertson and Chirico 1985; Robertson 2001). Such thematization also allows multiple possibilities, thereby implicitly admitting at least some of the axes of pluralization presented here. In this way, he shows how globalization as a historical development is as religious as it is from other angles economic, political, or broadly speaking socio-cultural. Robertson's efforts are therefore important; but they are at best a beginning. In the following paragraphs, I sketch a theoretical approach that seeks to explain how religion and the pluralization of religion have been a key dimension of the historical process of globalization itself.

It is no accident that the bulk of globalization analyses describe the process primarily in economic, political, and sometimes in technological terms. The justification for this emphasis lies in the fact that the historical construction of today's global society centred on the development and expansion of an initially European-based capitalist economy and of initially European imperial power, both of which have since been appropriated with differential success by virtually every other part of the world. The theoretical key to understanding how religion might fit into this picture and also be constitutive of it is to focus on how the sorts of transformations in the economic and political realms that brought about this expansion and appropriation also happened in the area of religion. This, in turn, requires a conceptualization under which economic, political, religious, and other social modalities can be subsumed and compared. On one level, the sociological notion of institution might serve this purpose. For greater clarity and more detailed comparability, however, I suggest the concept of *societal system* as developed in the work of Niklas Luhmann (Luhmann 1995).

Here cannot be the place for a thorough presentation of the details of this approach (see Beyer 2006, Ch. 1), but the argument about globalization on its basis can be summarized like this: from about the late medieval period in Western Europe, there began to develop roughly simultaneously distinct and yet interdependent social systems, each specializing in different functional areas, including a capitalist economic system, a political system of sovereign states, an empirically based scientific system, and a religious system manifesting itself as a plurality of religions. Each of these systems gradually built up its differentiated structures on the basis of its own rationality; each enhanced its peculiar mode of power. And it was on the combined basis of these institutional systems that the Europeans succeeded in spreading their influence around the world by the beginning of the twentieth century. As an integral part of this process, non-Western regions of the world have appropriated these systemic power modalities, invariably particularizing them to local circumstances and thereby glocalizing them. These systems have thus become the dominant social structures of contemporary global society. Yet they are by no means all that constitutes that society. The societal systems specialize and are therefore selective in what they include. They do not subsume everything that might otherwise appear as economic production/consumption, political regulation, knowledge, or religion. This combination of characteristics opens the way for understanding the pluralization of religion under conditions of globalization, but in such a way as to subsume the older notions of secularization, privatization, and differentiation that dominated

sociological discussion under the rubric of modernization.

A brief historical narrative can outline the development of a religious system in the modern phases of globalization. In Western European society of the high and late Middle Ages, religion already had a well-developed and differentiated presence in the form of the Roman Christian Church. This specialized but also multi-functional institution provided some of the conditions that allowed the rise of other systems, notably the economic, political and scientific. The gradual differentiation of these other systems provided a context for the clearer differentiation of the religious one, a development that manifested itself institutionally through the Protestant and Catholic Reformations and conceptually in the emergence of a new and pluralized understanding of religion itself. Beginning in the sixteenth to seventeenth centuries, Europeans began to conceive religion no longer primarily as a general and singular sort of activity that could express itself through various practices of piety and devotion, but as a differentiated domain of divine/human relations that manifested itself mainly through a set of distinct and systematic religions to which a given person could 'belong' or not. In spite of a continued search for unity in the religious domain, Europeans came to see these religions increasingly as irreducibly distinct. They included initially, under newly minted words, Christianity, Judaism, Mahometanism (i.e. Islam), and Paganism. Given that these semantic and institutional developments happened in the context of European global expansion, however, by the nineteenth century Europeans included an increasing set of additional religions that, armed with their new understanding, they 'discovered' in other parts of the world, including Buddhism, Confucianism, and Hinduism. The response of people in these other regions varied. In the case of Islam, Judaism, Buddhism, and Hinduism, for instance, there was widespread collaboration in the re-imagining and reconstruction of these religio-cultural traditions as one of the religions and thus in the glocalization of this initially Western model of what a religion was. In the case of the

Chinese and Confucianism, there was more or less unanimous refusal. All cases, however, included widespread contestation around the central questions of what belongs to these religions, which religions belong, which variations of these religions are authentic, and in general what are the boundaries of the religious domain itself. Moreover, the development of this religious system is an aspect of the modern process of globalization itself. The religions do not just respond to a globalizing context; they emerge as a part of that process just like the global capitalist economy or the global system of sovereign states. In light of this complex and selective historical development, the pluralized fate of religion along the axes of variation becomes clear.

First, the thesis of a differentiated and globalized religious system along these lines offers an explanation as to why, in spite of significant contestation and ambiguity, there seems to be such widespread global agreement on the existence and legitimacy of a delimited if regionally varied set of religions, and on the fact that these religions are unities in spite of wide-ranging 'internal' variation. Correspondingly, contemporary sociology understands religious 'pluralism' primarily in terms of these religions and their different subdivisions and not, for instance, in terms of individual variation in belief and practice.[2] Religion is not just variable; the religions are plural, both internally and in relation to each other.

Second, in light of the selective and somewhat arbitrary modern (re)construction of religions, the possibility of variation across the boundaries between institutionalized and non-institutionalized religiosity becomes evident. Not everything conceivably religious falls within the authoritative boundaries of the religions; and the elements of these religions could be recombined in a wide variety of ways. Thus, what falls under labels like spirituality or those forms that could be new religions hovers at the boundaries of the recognized religions or outside them altogether. Without the existence of the institutionalized religions, such contrasting variation could gain no observational purchase. We could not recognize them as religions, as spirituality, or as another contrasting

category such as, for instance, culture. In that light, we should expect constant debate and observation concerning how institutionalized religions are faring in a particular region, whether non-institutional religiosity is more prevalent, whether and how new religions are forming and becoming accepted, and so forth. The possibility exists that, in a given region, institutional religions will weaken to the point of irrelevance or, by contrast, will strengthen so as to push non-institutional forms underground. Yet there is nothing in the theory of the religious system that would predict one trend or another, only continued variation along this axis. Since the historical construction of this religious system only makes sense in the context of other analogous systems developing at the same time, the question of the relations between the religious system and these other systems will be an important consideration. This condition points to the salience of the three other axes of variation outlined above.

Third, therefore, the co-existence of these systems introduces the question of whether the social purposes that the religious system serves cannot be fulfilled by one or more of the other systems. For instance, can a sense of the ultimate meaning of life not be provided through the scientific system with its ever-expanding form of knowledge? Can an ultimate sense of belonging and moral rightness not be had through the state as the vehicle of the nation? Can loving acceptance not be found in the intense relationships of the family? Can understanding and socialization not be delivered effectively through academic education? Can cosmic vision not be provided by science or art? Can participation in mass media performances or through sport not supply people with a sense of ritual regularity and incorporation? The idea is not that these alternatives will inevitably replace religion in these functions, but rather that these possibilities are a constant, acting as another source of religious variation over time and in different places.

More critically in this regard, the relation of religion to other systems points to the question of the relative power of these systems. Although the relation of the systems is not hierarchical in any structural sense, they do vary in terms of their prominence. With few exceptions, the global capitalist economy, the system of territorial states and the scientific system are most often far more invasive and unavoidable in the lives of the world's populations than is the authoritative influence of the institutionalized religions. Yet, to the degree that religion constructs itself as one of the dominant systems in global society, that power relation need not be constant and certainly religion should not be expected to disappear. Rather, simply out of that structural relation, one should expect a fluctuation between relative powerlessness of the religious system, manifested for instance in the widespread privatization of religion, and the relative resurgence of religion so as to exert meaningful public influence at least in various regions (cf. Beyer 1994).

Finally, the differentiation of a religious system poses the question of the relation of that system to the society as a whole, including its other dominant societal subsystems and the respective other religions. The axis from 'conservative' to 'liberal' religion enters at this point. The central issue in this regard is the extent to which the religions, through their adherents, will accept the relativization implied in the concentration of religious concern in a particular societal subsystem among others, and one that is moreover internally differentiated into formally equal religions. Given the universal and encompassing visions that what we recognize as religions typically offer, this is an important issue because it concerns the core logic of that system, its claim to render access to the transcendent conditions that make the immanent possible. If religion asserts such a foundational role for all aspects of social and personal life, then how will it respond to limitation and even contradiction of that claim? As noted above, the answers will vary along a continuum from rejection to unproblematic accommodation. On the conservative end one finds responses that claim unique validity for their religion or variant thereof. They reject key features of the modern world deemed representative of the limiting situation, and they valorize of traditions evocative

of past societies which ostensibly allowed true religion its proper role. By contrast, on the liberal side, positive orientations to the differentiated situation tolerate and even celebrate religious and other forms of plurality, laud the 'freedom' and 'inclusion' that it promises (and criticize the failure to live up to these ideals), and accept the relatively autonomous functioning of other institutional societal systems. Such a stance is not, however, identical with the acceptance of religious privatization or the radical secularization of society: a sectarian conservative orientation can also abandon the wider public world to its secularity, and liberal religious positions are often also publicly assertive (cf. Casanova 1994).

CONCLUSIONS: FUTURE DIRECTIONS FOR THE SOCIOLOGICAL OBSERVATION OF RELIGION IN GLOBAL CONTEXT

The theoretical perspective outlined in the last section is but one attempt to gain some greater purchase on the role of religion in the construction of contemporary global society. Its main advantages are that it demonstrates how one can see globalization and religion as intimately linked while at the same time showing that this linkage necessarily implies various forms of glocalized religious pluralization. That said, the field of the sociological understanding of religion in global context is still rather sparsely occupied, probably because we still find ourselves in a transition between a previously dominant secularization/modernization and an as yet only practically recognized pluralization/globalization perspective. So much of the more recent sociological literature on religion operates with an explicit or implicit awareness of the now unavoidably global and religiously plural context, but the often implicit theoretical assumptions that inform this work are frequently still those of the secularization thesis. A main symptom in this regard is that the perceived inadequacy of the latter leads only to the hypothesis that the 'real' situation is just the negation of secularization, for instance, the 'resacralization' of society or that nothing has fundamentally changed since the fifteenth century CE. Just as the post-modern has thus far defined itself primarily as the negation of the core assumptions of the modern, so have post-secularization positions not really gone much beyond observing that the 'king is dead' or that the 'emperor has no clothes'.

Replacing the *leitmotif* of secularization/ modernization positively with that of pluralization/globalization then carries certain implications for the directions that the sociological observation of religion will likely continue to take. The first and most obvious of these directions is that the sheer variety of glocal forms that religion takes will persist as a prime focus of research. Simply documenting that variety is already a significant and ongoing task. Just as important is the issue of the co-existence of these religious forms and variations within the single social space of global society and indeed within a great many localities of that society. The 'problem of religious pluralism' is symptomatic of the basic situation of religion under globalized conditions. Pluralization of religion is not just descriptive, it is also potentially and actually problematic just like secularization was under the assumptions of modernization. Sociological research will therefore have to continue to concern itself with the possible ways that this pluralization is managed, and the consequences of different strategies in this regard. In this regard, although the pluralization thesis concerning religion undermines the possibility of any easy prognosis, the issue of transformations in the religious field and the discerning of religious trends nonetheless remains. If we can no longer convince ourselves that there exists a master trend, then we are still left with the question of the likely outcomes in different regions of global society.

Finally, it must be stressed again that a re-orientation of the sociological observation of religion in the context of globalization and glocalization does not mean the irrelevance of previously dominant concepts, above all secularization, privatization, and differentiation. Pluralization of religion was an important issue under the aegis of the secularization/modernization orientation, but it was subsumed under

those concepts as a symptomatic or contributing factor. Analogously, the older concepts remain important but now subsumed under the dominant motif of pluralization as descriptors along axes of variation. For in the final analysis, the shift from one *leitmotif* to another is more a matter of looking with different eyes at long-standing developments than it is a claim that something radically new has happened only since the new terms rose to prominence. We have lived in an era of globalization and pluralization for quite some time now. The construction and valorization of these partially neologistic ideas only signals a reassessment of what we deem to be most worthy of our attention.

NOTES

1. See e.g. Stark and Bainbridge 1987; Beyer 2006 as two, in their details, radically different examples. Beckford's (2003) much more extensive analysis of secularization, pluralism, globalization and religious movements overlaps in important ways with what I am outlining here. There are, however, also important differences. They are signalled in the choice of the word *pluralization,* a deliberate distancing from *and* echoing of the generally more evaluative *pluralism;* and in the close link I am suggesting between pluralization and globalization, subordinating secularization and movements to these two primary terms. I take Beckford's emphasis on social constructionism as a given.

2. Cf., for example (Bellah *et al.* 1985), who, in seeking to describe just this sort of variation 'across religious boundaries', coin the now well-known term, 'Sheilaism', thereby giving it a name *as if it were another religion,* in effect seeking to model this phenomenon on the taken-for-granted religions.

REFERENCES

Ackerman, Susan E. 2005. 'Falun Dafa and the New Age Movement in Malaysia: Signs of Health, Symbols of Salvation'. *Social Compass* 52: 495–511.

Adogame, Afe 2000. 'The Quest for Space in the Global Spiritual Marketplace: African Religions in Europe'. *International Review of Mission* 89: 409.

Agadjanian, Alexander and Victor Roudometof (eds) 2005. *Eastern Orthodoxy in a Global Age.* Walnut Creek, CA: Altamira.

Ahmed, Akbar S. 1994. *Islam, Globalization and Postmodernity*. London: Routledge.

Ahmed, Mumtaz 1991. 'Islamic Fundamentalism in South Asia: The Jamaat-i-Islami and the Tablighi Jamaat'. pp. 457–530 in *Fundamentalisms Observed*. Edited by Martin E. Marty and R. Scott Appleby. Chicago: University of Chicago Press.

Albrow, Martin 1990. 'Globalization, Knowledge and Society'. pp. 3–18 in *Globalization, Knowledge and Society: Readings from International Sociology*. Edited by M. Albrow and E. King. London: Sage.

Alvarsson, Jan-Åke and Rita Laura Segato (eds) 2003. *Religions in Transition: Mobility, Merging and Globalization in the Emergence of Contemporary Religious Adhesions*. Uppsala: Uppsala University Library.

Barber, Benjamin R. 1996. *Jihad vs. McWorld*. New York: Balantine Books.

Barchunova, Tatyana V. 2002. 'Faith-Based Communities of Practice in Novosibirsk'. In *Conference on Local Forms of Religious Organization as Structural Modernisation: Effects on Community-Building and Globalisation*. Marburg, Germany.

Baumann, Martin 2000. *Migration – Religion – Integration: Buddhistische Vietnamesen und hinduistische Tamilen in Deutschland*. Marburg: Diagonal Verlag.

Beck, Ulrich 2000. *What is Globalization?* Translated by P. Camiller. London: Polity.

Beckford, James A. 2003. *Social Theory and Religion*. Cambridge: Cambridge University Press.

Bellah, Robert N. 1970. 'Religious Evolution'. In *Beyond Belief: Essays on Religion in a Post-Traditional World*. New York: Harper & Row.

Bellah, Robert N., Richard Madsen, William M. Sullivan, Ann Swidler and Stephen M. Tipton 1985. *Habits of the Heart: Individualism and Commitment in American Life*. San Francisco: Harper & Row.

Berger, Peter 1967. *The Sacred Canopy: Elements of a Sociological Theory of Religion*. New York: Doubleday Anchor.

Beyer, Peter 1994. *Religion and Globalization*. London: Sage.

Beyer, Peter (ed.) 2001. *Religion in the Process of Globalization/Religion im Prozeß Globalisierung*. Würzburg: Ergon Verlag.

Beyer, Peter 2003. 'De-Centring Religious Singularity; The Globalization of Christianity as a Case in Point'. *Numen* 50: 357–86.

Beyer, Peter 2006. *Religions in Global Society*. London: Routledge.

Bibby, Reginald W. 2002. *Restless Gods: The Renaissance of Religion in Canada*. Toronto: Stoddart.

Brannen, Noah S. 1968. *Soka Gakkai: Japan's Militant Buddhists*. Richmond, VA: John Knox Press.

Burghart, Richard (ed.) 1987. *Hinduism in Great Britain: The Perpetuation of Religion in an Alien Cultural Milieu*. London: Tavistock.

Carnes, Tony and Fenggang Yang (eds) 2004. *Asian American Religions: The Making and Remaking of Borders and Boundaries*. New York: New York University Press.

Carozzi, Maria Julia 2004. 'Ready to Move Along: The Sacralization of Disembedding in the New Age Movement and the Alternative Circuit in Buenos Aires'. *Civilisations: Revue internationale d'anthropologie et de sciences humaines* 51: 139–54.

Casanova, José 1994. *Public Religions in the Modern World*. Chicago: University of Chicago.

Casanova, José 2001. 'Globalizing Catholicism and the Return to a "Universal Church"'. pp. 201–25 in *Religion in the Process of Globalization*. Edited by P. Beyer. Würzburg: Ergon Verlag.

Clarke, Peter B. (ed.) 1998. *New Trends and Developments in African Religions*. Westport, CT: Greenwood.

Coleman, Simon 2000. *The Globalisation of Charismatic Christianity: Spreading the Gospel of Prosperity*. Cambridge: Cambridge University Press.

Coward, H., J. R. Hinnells and R. B. Williams (eds) 2000. *The South Asian Religious Diaspora in Britain, Canada, and the United States*. Albany, NY: SUNY Press.

Cox, Harvey 1995. *Fire from Heaven: The Rise of Pentecostal Spirituality and the Reshaping of Religion in the Twenty-First Century*. Reading, MA: Perseus Books.

Davie, Grace 2003. *Europe: The Exceptional Case: Parameters of Faith in the Modern World*. London: Darton, Longman & Todd.

Dawson, Lorne L. 1998. 'The Cultural Significance of New Religious Movements and Globalization: A Theoretical Prolegomena'. *Journal for the Scientific Study of Religion* 37: 580–95.

Dempster, Murray W., Byron D. Klaus and Douglas Petersen (eds) 1999. *The Globalization of Pentecostalism: A Religion Made to Travel*. Oxford: Regnum Books International.

Dessai, E. 1993. *Hindus in Deutschland*. Moers: Aragon.

Durkheim, Émile 1965. *The Elementary Forms of the Religious Life*. Translated by J. W. Swain. New York: Free Press.

Ebaugh, Helen Rose and Janet Saltzman Chafetz (eds) 2002. *Religion across Borders: Transnational Migrant Networks*. Walnut Creek, CA: Altamira Press.

Esposito, John L. and Michael Watson (eds) 2000. *Religion and Global Order*. Cardiff: University of Wales Press.

Finke, Roger and Rodney Stark 1992. *The Churching of America, 1776–1990: Winners and Losers in Our Religious Economy*. New Brunswick, NJ: Rutgers University Press.

Frigerio, Alejandro 2004. 'Re-Africanization in Secondary Religious Diasporas: Constructing a World Religion'. *Civilisations: Revue internationale d'anthropologie et de sciences humaines* 51: 39–60.

Fukuyama, Francis 1993. *The End of History and the Last Man*. New York: Avon Books.

Glock, Charles Y. and Robert N. Bellah (eds) 1976. *The New Religious Consciousness*. Berkeley, CA: University of California Press.

Guest, Kenneth J. 2003. *God in Chinatown: Religion and Survival in New York's Evolving Immigrant Community*. New York: New York University Press.

Haddad, Yvonne Yazbeck and Jane I. Smith (eds) 2002. *Muslim Minorities in the West: Visible and Invisible*. Walnut Creek, CA: Altamira Press.

Haines, Byron L. 1979. 'Islamic Fundamentalism and Christian Responsibility'. *Christian Century* 96: 365–66.

Haynes, Jeff. 1998. *Religion in Global Politics*. London and New York: Longman.

Heelas, Paul, Linda Woodhead, Benjamin Seel, Bronislaw Szerszyinski and Karin Tusting 2005. *The Spiritual Revolution: Why Religion is Giving Way to Spirituality*. Oxford: Blackwell.

Hexham, Irving and Karla Poewe 1997. *New Religions as Global Cultures: Making the Human Sacred*. Boulder, CO: Westview.

Hopkins, Dwight N., Lois Ann Lorentzen, Eduardo Mendieta and David Batstone (eds) 2001. *Religions/Globalizations: Theories and Cases*. Durham, NC: Duke University Press.

Howell, Julia Day 2005. 'Muslims, the New Age and Marginal Religions in Indonesia: Changing Meanings of Religious Pluralism'. *Social Compass* 52: 473–92.

Inglehart, Ronald 1997. *Modernization and Postmodernization: Cultural, Economic, and Political Change in 43 Societies*. Princeton, NJ: Princeton University Press.

Jonker, Gerdien 2002. *Eine Wellenlänge zu Gott: Der 'Verband der Islamischen Kulturzentren' in Europa*. Bielefeld, Germany: Transcript.

Judah, J. Stillson 1974. *Hare Krishna and the Counterculture*. New York: Wiley.

Juergensmeyer, Mark 1993. *The New Cold War? Religious Nationalism Confronts the Secular State*. Berkeley, CA: University of California Press.

Juergensmeyer, Mark (ed.) 2003. *Global Religions: An Introduction*. Oxford: Oxford University Press.

Kapur, Rajiv 1986. *Sikh Separatism: The Politics of Faith*. London: Allen & Unwin.

Kent, Stephen A. 1999. 'The Globalization of Scientology: Influence, Control, and Opposition in Transnational Markets'. *Religion* 29: 147–69.

Kepel, Gilles 1994. *The Revenge of God*. Oxford: Blackwell.

Khosrokhavar, Farhad 1997. *L'islam des jeunes*. Paris: Flammarion.

Lanternari, Vittorio 1998. 'From Africa to Italy: The Exorcistic-Therapeutic Cult of Emmanuel Milingo'. pp. 263–83 in *New Trends and Developments in African Religions*. Edited by Peter B. Clarke. Westport, CT: Greenwood.

Lawson, Ronald 1999. 'When Immigrants Take Over: The Impact of Immigrant Growth on American Seventh-day Adventism's Trajectory from Sect to Denomination'. *Journal for the Scientific Study of Religion* 38: 83–102.

Learman, Linda (ed.) 2005. *Buddhist Missionaries in the Era of Globalization*. Honolulu: University of Hawai'i Press.

Levitt, Peggy 1998. 'Local-level Global Religion: The Case of U.S.-Dominican Migration'. *Journal for the Scientific Study of Religion* 37: 74–89.

Levitt, Peggy 2004. 'Redefining the Boundaries of Belonging: The Institutional Character of Transnational Religious Life'. *Sociology of Religion* 65: 1–18.

Lofland, John 1966. *Doomsday Cult: A Study of Conversion, Proselytization, and Maintenance of Faith*. Englewood Cliffs, NJ: Prentice Hall.

Luckmann, Thomas 1967. *The Invisible Religion: The Problem of Religion in Modern Societies*. New York: Macmillan.

Luhmann, Niklas 1995. *Social Systems*. Translated by J. Bednarz, Jr and D. Baecker. Stanford, CA: Stanford University Press.

Lustick, Ian S. 1988. *For the Land and the Lord: Jewish Fundamentalism in Israel*. New York: Council on Foreign Relations.

Lyotard, Jean-François 1984. *The Condition of Postmodernity*. Manchester: Manchester University Press.

Martin, David 1978. *A General Theory of Secularization*. Oxford: Blackwell:

Martin, David 2002. *Pentecostalism: The World Their Parish*. Oxford: Blackwell.

Marty, Martin E. and R. Scott Appleby (eds) 1991–95. *The Fundamentalism Project. 5 vols.* Chicago: University of Chicago Press.

McFarland, H. Neill 1967. *The Rush Hour of the Gods: A Study of New Religious Movements in Japan*. New York: Macmillan.

McLuhan, Marshall 1964. *Understanding Media: The Extensions of Man*. New York: McGraw-Hill.

Melton, J. Gordon and Martin Baumann (eds) 2002. *Religions of the World: A Comprehensive Encyclopedia of Beliefs and Practices*. Santa Barbara, CA: ABC-CLIO.

Meyer, Birgit and Peter Geschiere (eds) 1999. *Globalization and Identity: Dialectics of Flow and Closure*. Oxford: Blackwell.

Mndende, Nokuzola 1998. 'From Underground Praxis to Recognized Religion: Challenges facing African Religions'. *Journal for the Study of Religion* 11: 115–24.

Motta, Roberto 1998. 'The Churchifying of Candomblé: Priests, Anthropologists, and the Canonization of the African Religious Memory in Brazil'. pp. 45–57 in *New Trends and Developments in African Religions*. Edited by Peter B. Clarke. Westport, CT: Greenwood.

Nielsen, J. 1999. *Towards a European Islam*. Basingstoke: Macmillan.

Poewe, Karla (ed.) 1994. *Charismatic Christianity as a Global Culture*. Columbia, SC: University of South Carolina Press.

Prebish, Charles S. and Kenneth K. Tanaka (eds) 1998. *The Faces of Buddhism in America*. Berkeley, CA: University of California Press.

Rath, Jan *et al.* 2001. *Western Europe and its Islam*. Leiden: Brill.

Richardson, James T. (ed.) 2004. *Regulating Religion: Case Studies from Around the Globe*. New York: Kluwer Academic/Penum.

Riesebrodt, Martin 1993. *Pious Passion: The Emergence of Modern Fundamentalism in the United States and Iran*. Translated by Don Reneau. Berkeley: University of California Press.

Robertson, Roland 1992. *Globalization: Social Theory and Global Culture*. London: Sage.

Robertson, Roland 1995. 'Glocalization: Time-Space and Homogeneity-Heterogeneity'. pp. 25–44 in *Global Modernities*. Edited by Mike Featherstone, Scott Lash and Roland Robertson. London: Sage.

Robertson, Roland 2001. 'The Globalization Paradigm: Thinking Globally'. pp. 3–22 in *Religion in the Process of Globalization*. Edited by P. Beyer. Würzburg: Ergon Verlag.

Robertson, Roland and JoAnn Chirico 1985. 'Humanity, Globalization, Worldwide Religious Resurgence: A Theoretical Exploration'. *Sociological Analysis* 46: 219–42.

Robertson, Roland and William R. Garrett (eds) 1991. *Religion and Global Order*. New York: Paragon House.

Roof, Wade Clark 1999. *Spiritual Marketplace: Baby Boomers and the Remaking of American Religion*. Princeton, NJ: Princeton University Press.

Rothstein, Mikael (ed.) 2001. *New Age Religion and Globalization*. Aarhus: Aarhus University Press.

Roy, Olivier 1999. *Vers un islam européen*. Paris: Éditions Esprit.

Rudolph, Susanne Hoeber and James Piscatori (eds) 1997. *Transnational Religion and Fading States*. Boulder, CO: Westview.

Schiller, Anne 1997. *Small Sacrifices: Religious Change and Cultural Identity among the Ngaju of Indonesia*. Oxford: Oxford University Press.

Shimazono, Susumu 2004. *From Salvation to Spirituality: Popular Religious Movements in Japan*. Honolulu: Trans Pacific Press.

Stackhouse, Max L. and Peter J. Paris (eds) 2000. *God and Globalization: Religion and the Powers of the Common Life*. Harrisburg, PA: Trinity International.

Stark, Rodney and William S. Bainbridge 1985. *The Future of Religion: Secularization, Revival, and Cult Formation*. Berkeley, CA: University of California Press.

Stark, Rodney and William S. Bainbridge 1987. *A Theory of Religion*. New York: Peter Lang.

Stark, Rodney and Roger Finke 2000. *Acts of Faith: Explaining the Human Side of Religion*. Berkeley, CA: University of California Press.

Stark, Rodney and Laurence Iannaccone 1994. 'A Supply-Side Reinterpretation of the "Secularization" of Europe'. *Journal for the Scientific Study of Religion* 33: 230–52.

Troeltsch, Ernst 1931. *The Social Teachings of the Christian Churches*. New York: Macmillan.

Van der Veer, Peter (ed.) 1996. *Conversion to Modernities: The Globalization of Christianity*. London: Routledge.

van Dijk, Rijk 2001. 'From Camp to Encompassment: Discourses on Transsubjectivity in the Ghanian Pentecostal Diaspora'. pp. 177–200 in *Religion in the Process of Globalization*. Edited by P. Beyer. Würzburg: Ergon Verlag.

Vásquez, Manuel A. and Marie Friedmann Marquardt 2003. *Globalizing the Sacred: Religion across the Americas*. New Brunswick, NJ: Rutgers University Press.

Vertovec, Steven and Alisdair Rogers (eds) 1998. *Muslim European Youth: Reproducing Ethnicity, Religion, Culture*. Aldershot, UK: Ashgate.

von der Mehden, Fred R. 1980. 'Religion and Development in Southeast Asia: A Comparative Study'. *World Development* 8: 545–53.

Warner, S. and J. G. Wittner (eds) 1998. *Gatherings in Diaspora: Religious Communities and the New Immigration*. Philadelphia: Temple University Press.

Wilkinson, Michael 2006. *The Spirit Said Go: Pentecostal Immigrants in Canada*. New York: Peter Lang.

PART II

Methods of Studying Religion

If concepts and theories are the coins of the realm in any scientific discipline, it is important to avoid inflating the currency beyond what practicality and the facts warrant. This is the role of research methods. Each of the three chapters in this part deals with a different set of techniques for collecting and analysing the kind of information that is best suited to answering the questions at hand. While methodological issues will echo throughout the Handbook, here they receive the front-and-centre treatment they so richly deserve but so seldom receive. The chapters involve qualitative, quantitative and historical-comparative methods respectively. But in actual practice, they are often creatively combined rather than strictly segregated.

In Chapter 6, **James Spickard** stresses the need to select research methods according to their 'fit' with the object of research. Qualitative methods are capable of generating a wide range of information about religion in all its subtlety and complexity. Some methods arise from social phenomenology's concern with human consciousness and experience; others have roots in hermeneutics and people's own interpretations of their life; a third general approach focuses on the analysis of discourse and narrative expressions of religion; and finally ethnography aspires to produce detailed descriptions of groups and collectivities at work and at play. At their best, all of these qualitative

methods are self-reflexive about the special demands and the limits facing researchers trying to understand and explain religion in its manifold social and cultural settings.

Instead of blithely assuming that it is possible to measure every aspect of religion with numerical precision, **David Voas** begins Chapter 7 by acknowledging that the difficulties in doing so are considerable whilst showing how different types of phenomena require different types of measures. However, he goes on to argue that major benefits stem from using quantitative techniques where appropriate, and his examples strengthen his case. He introduces some methodological innovations – such as item response theory, computer simulation, multi-level modelling and social network analysis – that further enhance our capacity to make quantitative sense of patterns in religion. He also presents a very useful practical guide to major data sets for secondary analysis of material on religion.

The methodological net is widened even further in Chapter 8 by **John Hall's** discussion of methods that he labels 'sociohistorical inquiry', i.e., the point where historical sociology serves, and intersects with, the sociology of religion. Three deep-seated antinomies serve to structure his discussion: the fact/value distinction; the history/society division; and the positivism/interpretivism binary. The evolution of sociohistorical inquiry shows just how diverse the styles of historical research on religion have been; and the range of research methods is no less wide today. Hall identifies four particularising and four generalising practices, all of which share forms of discourse relating to value, narrative, social theory and explanation/understanding. A review of the range of historical and comparative studies of religion – including aspects of secularisation, modernity, state formation, apocalyptic movements and fundamentalism – shows just how diverse the application of sociohistorical methods can be. At the same time, scholars are becoming more critically self-reflexive about the philosophical assumptions underlying their choice of methods.

6

Micro Qualitative Approaches to the Sociology of Religion: Phenomenologies, Interviews, Narratives, and Ethnographies

JAMES V. SPICKARD

In the last thirty years, the sociology of religion has undergone a methodological sea change. Where major research was once largely quantitative, built upon large-scale surveys, national and transnational data sets, and the like, most sociologists now accept small-scale qualitative studies as a regular part of the discipline. As I shall show in this chapter, such studies take various forms. Each has its strengths and weaknesses, but all have more cachet than before. Only a few scholars now deride close, qualitative analyses of religious life as 'slow journalism' – a casual reporting that misses the underlying social patterns whose discovery sociologists so esteem.

Despite this change, many methodological writings are stuck in old patterns. Among other things, standard descriptions too often treat qualitative work as exploratory, i.e., as suggesting patterns for later quantitative work to confirm. In reality, the opposite is often the case. For example, Joseph Tamney (2005) used open-ended interviews with participants in two working-class Protestant congregations to cast doubt on the claim that such congregants find strict churches attractive, as some sociologists claim (e.g., Kelley 1972; Iannaccone 1994). Interview respondents reported being drawn to their new congregations by such things as feeling the presence of the Holy Spirit, the family-like nature of congregational life, and the qualities of the pastor. They were specifically not attracted by strict rules of behavior, nor did they find such norms terribly good reasons to stick with the congregation. Moreover, they did not find that their congregations enforced rules strictly, despite being in denominations generally classified at the strict end of the scale.

Similarly, my own interviews with religious social activists (Spickard 2005; McGuire and Spickard 2003) revealed the dominance of rule-based and relational motives, as opposed to means-ends calculations. That is, these activists chose to act based on their sense of 'the right thing to do' or on their relationship with others – two motive-types predicted by religious ethicists (Niebuhr 1963), but not considered important by either rather rational-choice theory or resource-mobilization theory, which consider means-ends calculations the only form of human rationality.

In neither of these cases was qualitative research exploratory. Each project was designed to test a specific sociological theory by figuring out that theory's predictions and then observing to see whether these predictions came to pass.

Nor is it particularly helpful to group all quantitative methods into one pile and all qualitative methods into another – though this, too, is still standard practice. For example, Charles Ragin writes:

> Most quantitative data techniques are data condensers. They condense data in order to see the big picture …. Quantitative methods, by contrast, are best understood as data enhancers. When data are enhanced, it is possible to see key aspects of cases more clearly (Ragin 1994: 92).

On one level, this is right. Most quantitative research does condense data into simpler, more homogenous packages. Much survey research, for example, assigns people to categories such as 'Protestant', 'Catholic', 'Moslem', and 'Hindu'. This is not always a virtue, however. For example, Aisha Khan (2005) shows us that rural south Trinidadian religious discourse contains the terms 'Moslem', 'Hindu', 'Christian', and so on, but these terms do not sort people into separate demographic boxes as they do in Europe and North America. Trinidadian 'Hindus' consult imams and may observe 'a prayers' with their Muslim neighbors. Trinidadian 'Muslims' revere pandits and even sponsor Hindu festivals – making sure to include food that fits both traditions' dietary rules. As Khan repeatedly points out, her informants say 'is all one God, anyhow' – a philosophical-ecclesiastical discourse that emphasizes connection over separation. Khan's ethnography shows us that religious identity can be variable, not just fixed. Survey research based on identity labels would largely miss the point of Trinidadian religious life.

Furthermore, different kinds of qualitative methods are not really similar. To use a language that I find useful, the different methods seek different *research objects*. In my experience, most research errors arise from an investigator's confusion over these objects, so it is worth taking a moment to understand this concept.

We all know that sociological research can investigate many different kinds of things. As sociologists, we can seek patterns in people's behavior, or we can listen to people report that behavior; we can measure their personal characteristics or we can ask them about the identities they claim; we can capture their personal opinions (either casual or deep); we can tap their cultural knowledge and their personal expertise. We can also ask them about their experiences – either as narratives or as that experience presents itself to their consciousness. (This list does not exhaust the possibilities, but it indicates their breadth.)

Metaphysically speaking, each of these things is a different kind of object. Acts, for example, are different sorts of things than reports of acts. The former occur in space and time and are matters of observation. The latter are stories that people tell about what they have done; they unfold in time but not space, and they do so after the fact. They also typically leave out most of what actually happened in order to focus on the meaning of the event from the actor's point of view. That is, narratives focus on those elements of the act that the actor thinks are central, while observation puts the observer in the driver's seat.

Capturing different objects requires different research methods. We can locate the patterns in acts by observing them, but observation cannot capture the thoughts and intentions of those doing the acting. Asking people to report their acts captures such thoughts and intentions, but it fails to capture patterns of which the actors are unaware. If, for example, a teacher unconsciously interrupts women in class while not interrupting men, we cannot discover this by asking her to report her actions; only observation will do. Mere observation will not, however, tell us why she interrupts. We can only discover this by asking her to tell us her version of what is going on.

In general, sociology has adopted different research methods for capturing different kinds of things. Survey research, for example, usefully captures people's surface opinions, because it works best with simple questions that people do not need to struggle to answer. Done well, it can also capture deeper attitudes by combining simple questions into complex wholes.[1] It also captures elements of people's self-identities, especially those that they find unproblematic. Asking people whether they are 'Black' or 'White', for example, produces fewer difficulties in the United States than it does in Brazil, because the former draws a firm color line where the latter does not. Similarly, asking people to identify with a single religion produces fewer problems in the U.S. than in Japan: Japanese participation in multiple religious practices is common, as is a refusal to identify with any particular one of them; in the U.S., this is rare. In short, survey research works better in some places and on some topics than it does in others. Overall, it is not so good at capturing subtlety and nuance. The various qualitative methods do a better job of this, because they are able to tap deeper levels.

Not all qualitative approaches seek the same metaphysical object, however. Each of the methods that I explore in this chapter seeks something different. Phenomenology tries to capture people's subjective experiences as they present themselves to consciousness. Such experiences have social elements, on which social phenomenology concentrates. Narratives collect people's stories on many topics – including their stories about their experiences – and reveal these narratives' patterns. Informants are typically aware of some of these patterns but are unaware of others; narrative analysis works in both realms. Hermeneutic interviewing focuses on the meanings that people make of their lives, experiences, and so on, and is thus limited to people's conscious self-understandings. And ethnography explores the various social patterns, conscious and unconscious, behavioral and mental, that appear in specific settings – as seen from the standpoint of a socially situated ethnographer.

These approaches are not, of course, peculiar to the study of religions. Yet sociologists of religion have put each of them to good use in recent years. I shall devote the rest of this chapter to showing how.

SOCIAL PHENOMENOLOGY

Social phenomenology ultimately traces itself to the work of Edmund Husserl (1913, 1917). He argued for a radical shift in perspective – one that placed human experience at the center of philosophical investigation. By setting aside ('bracketing') our thoughts about things, he argued, we can open ourselves to pure experiencing. This does not allow us to experience the world objectively, but it does allow us to be objective toward our own subjective experience. To use Thomas Luckmann's somewhat convoluted language:

> By using the methods of phenomenological 'reduction' we proceed step by step from the historically, biographically, socially and culturally concrete features of everyday experiences to its elementary structures. ... The goal of phenomenology is to describe the universal structures of subjective orientation in the world (Luckmann 1978: 8–9).

On the face of it, this would seem to sidestep sociology. Sociology, after all, famously locates 'the social' midway between 'the universal' and 'the individual' (Mills 1959). What sense can sociology make of the phrase 'the universal structures of subjective orientation'? How can one claim to describe pure experience when that experience is always shaped and interpreted by cultural factors?[2]

Among other responses, Husserl argued that part of our very experiencing is our experience that our minds generate thoughts about whatever we are contemplating. These may not be completely independent of us, but neither do they completely account for our objects of contemplation. This, in itself, is a universal structure well worth investigating. Humans seem to do this, just as they seem – universally – to need an object to think about. As Husserl noted, consciousness is always consciousness of *something*. The task of the phenomenologist is to chart the subjective shape of various such universal experiences.[3]

I shall describe three different ways in which scholars have used phenomenological analysis in the sociology of religion. The first of these is my own use of phenomenology to deepen the sociological understanding of religious rituals

(Spickard 1991, 2005). The second is David Preston's (1988) social phenomenology of Zen practice. The third is Thomas Csordas's (1993, 1994) cultural phenomenology of illness and healing.

I based my analysis of ritual on Alfred Schutz's (1951) notion of the co-presence of social actors in structured time. Following Husserl's quest for the universal structures of experiencing, Schutz differentiated several experiential 'worlds' within which people subjectively live. These are not external or objective worlds, but rather are experiential attitudes toward the world – what some might today call states of consciousness (though his concept is more subtle than that). In his famous article 'On Multiple Realities' Schutz (1945) explored four of these worlds: 'the world of everyday life', the world of imagination, 'the world of dreams', and 'the world of scientific theory'. Each state exhibits different degrees of attention to external reality, different forms of spontaneity, different experiences of the self, time, sociality, and so on.

In the world of work, for example, social life is based on interpersonal communication about an assumedly shared reality. This reality is vivid: we experience it with our bodies as well as in our thoughts. We do not doubt the world's reality. More precisely, we bracket our doubts in the interests of getting our work done. Sociality is a fact of life, only problematic when we visit a foreign land (see Schutz 1944). The world of dreams, on the other hand, is free from everyday practicality. Dreaming is passive: dreams happen to one, without conscious direction. We express this experience in our retelling: we say 'This happened, then that, then this'. Though sometimes realistic, dreams lack the vivid presence of everyday life. Dreams especially lack full bodily sensation.

Subjectively speaking, people experience religious rituals neither as everyday work nor as dreams – nor, for that matter, as imagination or scientific theorizing. Instead, like music, rituals are experiences that unfold in time. Poly- rather than monothetic, both rituals and music defy translation into other media. The same is true for poetry, which, though it can be summarized, finds its full

nature only in recitation. Unlike ideas, which can be equally well expressed in many forms, poetry, music, and ritual must be enacted. They must be made present to people's experiencing, not just to their minds. Each works by leading people's attention from point 'A' to 'B' to 'C', and so on. As Schutz (1951) points out in his phenomenology of music:

> The flux of tones unrolling in inner time is an arrangement meaningful to both the composer and the beholder, because and in so far as it evokes in the stream of consciousness participating in it an interplay of recollections, retentions, protentions and anticipations which interrelate the successive elements (p. 170).

Experiencing music is a social act, not just because people do so together but because they share the same time-bound experience.

> Although separated by hundreds of years, the [beholder] participates with quasi simultaneity in the [composer's] stream of consciousness by performing with him step by step the ongoing articulation of his musical thought. The beholder, thus, is united with the composer by a time dimension common to both, which is nothing other than a derived form of the vivid present shared by the partners in a genuine face-to-face relation (pp. 171–2).

This time-bound sociality is precisely how people experience religious rituals. Applying this analysis first to Navajo ceremonies (1991), then to Catholic activists' masses (2005), I showed how rituals structure their participants' stream of attention, leading them to experience a changed world. In the Navajo case, I relied on others' fieldwork to validate the experiential force of the Navajo belief that ritual restores the goodness of creation. It may not do so objectively, but it does so subjectively – in the structure of their experiences. In the Catholic case, I used thirteen years of my own fieldwork to chart how the dynamic of a specific activist group's ritual moved the members of that group from discouragement at the difficulty of their task to a sense of renewed experience of community, then to a reconnection with their transcendent purpose. In both cases, my research object was the structure of participants' subjective experience. Both analyses required me to chart the time-bound structure of that experience, recreating it in ideal-typical form.

Preston (1988) took a somewhat different tack. Basing his book on several years of field-work in two California Zen groups, he noted that standard sociological theory fails to account for meditative religions in general and for Zen meditation in particular. Meditation is not just an incidental adjunct to Zen philosophy; it is the core of the Zen experience. Sociology's traditional focus on religious ideas and especially the conversion/commitment paradigms so prominent in the sociological literature when Preston wrote overlooked this in their emphasis on changing worldviews and social allegiances. By focusing on the phenomenon of meditative experience, Preston showed in detail how Zen meditation 'deconditions' the mental processes on which the conversion/commitment views are based. Meditation allows its practitioners to experience a different way of being, which, however, does not escape social patterning. But its patterning is in a different key.

Preston's vehicle was an in-depth look at how the beginner encounters Zen: in *zazen* (sitting meditation) and in *sesshin* (meditation retreats). Building on Becker, Goffman, Schutz and Sudnow, he showed how the beginner first tries to follow the rules of practice: 'sit just so', 'don't look up', 'count breaths', and so on. These rules are socially learned, yet Zen teachers provide little guidance about how to follow them. And the beginner soon discovers that following them does not induce the meditative state. In fact, the harder one works, the farther away that goal seems to recede. Zen offers no alternate ideas, other than to say that ideas are meaningless. So much for theories of reality-construction that emphasize ideas in religious conversions!

If the beginner persists, Preston argued, he or she begins to notice a change. Sitting becomes easier as the body becomes accustomed to it. The 'bodymind' – not the 'self' – becomes more attentive. The body itself becomes 'practiced', and its activities take on a meaning quite distinct from religious ideas. Further practice allows one to improvise spontaneously: one's action becomes the result neither of a consciously directed intention nor of an automatic reproduction of traditional forms.

In Preston's account, the process by which Zen is transmitted is the key to its ability to develop spontaneity in its practitioners. Zen rituals break down the normal sense of self without substituting anything in its place. Zen does not socialize one into a new identity, but forces one to confront the internal processes by which identities are constructed. One must learn to transcend those processes to continue on the path. Bodily experience is the key. Only a close phenomenological attention to the experience of learning to 'sit Zen' can uncover such matters.

Csordas (1990, 1993, 1994, 1995) also starts with the body, but takes a more traditionally philosophical approach. Rather than using Schutz, Becker, or Goffman, he uses the work of Maurice Merleau-Ponty (1962, 1964) to propose a phenomenology of embodiment, 'in which bodily experience is understood to be the existential ground of culture and self, and therefore a valuable starting point for their analysis' (1995). He does not treat bodily experience as generating self and culture; that is not what he means by 'existential ground'. Instead, he sees both self and culture as second-order reflections of a person's experience as an embodied being – but reflections that simultaneously condition that experiencing. His goal is to show how the body/self presents itself to consciousness, shaped by as well as shaping culture. The phenomenologist's task is to describe the ways in which embodied selves take up an existential position in the world – with culture built into the very process.

All this is very abstract; fortunately, Csordas gives examples. His most extensive effort is his study of Catholic charismatic healing (1994), but he provides a briefer, clearer example of his approach in his study of a Navajo man with a cancerous brain lesion (1995). Unable to speak after his injury, this man experienced his struggle to regain speech as a religious quest – one which he understood in traditionally Navajo terms. The Navajo sense of the holiness of exact language (Witherspoon 1977) led him to experience his recovery as something holy – a hard-fought return to a socially valued state of being. Csordas describes how this man's efforts to heal himself into speech grew into a wish to become a medicine man or a minister and thus heal others. Bodily experience and religion are here tied closely together. But, as Csordas puts it:

> The patient's search for words is thematized as religious not because religious experience is reducible to a neurological discharge [in a particular brain region] but because it is a strategy of the self in need of a powerful idiom for orientation in the world.... Our argument goes beyond the pedestrian assertion that culture and biology mutually determine the experience of illness, and toward a description of the phenomenological ground of both biology and culture (p. 287).

Csordas's phenomenology sees religion and culture as resources that selves use to make their embodied way in the world, but sees these resources as bound up with experience rather than separable from it. His effort begins with 'the preobjective and prereflective experience of the body' (1990: 6), showing that the self-conscious self is already engaged in cultural interpretation. It then tracks that engagement, setting aside the concern for causality in the interests of thick description.

These phenomenological approaches have several things in common. Each is built on a close attention to religion's experiential side, as that experience presents itself in the consciousness of the religious participant. Each constructs a standard pattern: of the attention to ritual, of the shift in inner awareness, or of the attempt to come to terms with a body that resists one's bidding. My Navajo study is the most schematic, having been built on others' fieldwork and on an imaginative reconstruction of ritual from the participants' point of view. My depiction of Catholic ritual is more precise because it is based on years of observations and interviews; so is Csordas's phenomenology of healing. Preston's phenomenology of Zen meditation is even more precise, not because his fieldwork was necessarily more acute but because the Zen experience revolves around the same attention to subjective detail that phenomenology requires. Each case produces a typical pattern of experiencing, seen from the subjective point of view.

Analytically, such patterns share traits with Max Weber's 'ideal-types' – though they operate on the level of experience, not of ideas. That is, they are analytic reconstructions of how the experience appears to an idealized observer, not how it exactly appears in any specific person's consciousness. Each analyst expects every empirical experience to have a more-or-less quality to it, without destroying the pattern. The projects are phenomenological precisely because of this typicality. They uncover the structures of subjective experiencing in their respective areas while recognizing that any individual's experience will differ in some details. As with most sociology, it is the pattern that matters; here, the pattern takes place in the subjective experience of religious participants.

Such patterns of subjective experience are different from patterns of individual meaning, from the patterns of narrative, and from the patterns revealed by ethnographers, as we shall see below. Each of these aims for a different research object. Phenomenology works by focusing on the experiential dimension, by bracketing away the ideas accreted to that dimension, and by then reconstructing the typical patterns found in the resulting idea-less experiencing. The process is never perfect: as Luckmann (1978: 8) notes, pure idea-less experience is inexpressible in language, which obviates the phenomenological enterprise. What distinguishes phenomenology from other qualitative methods is the object – experience – toward which it aims. As with all research methods, one does the best one can.

Traditionally, Husserlian phenomenology based itself on the introspective examination of experience. Its validity depended on others' ability to examine their experiences with the same rigor – moving 'step by step from the historically, biographically, socially, and culturally concrete features of everyday experience to its elementary structures' (Luckmann 1978: 8). Alfred Schutz used this introspective approach; the best examples occur in his essays 'Making Music Together' (1951) and 'The Stranger' (1944), though persons wishing more philosophical details should also consult 'On Multiple Realities' (1945). David Sudnow (1978) applied this introspective method to the task of learning to play improvisational piano, with fascinating sociological results.

In recent years, phenomenological psychologists have moved beyond introspection, driven in part by their discipline's devaluing of that approach. In response, Amedeo and Barbro Giorgi (2003) provide a step-by-step method for doing phenomenological interviews. They show how to help their informants separate their experiences from the ideas that accrete to them and how to build these informants' accounts into descriptions of those experiences' elemental structures. David Rehorick and Valerie Bentz (forthcoming) have collected many examples of this technique. Though using interviews rather than introspection, both sets of authors keep the phenomenology's object – raw experience – clearly in mind.

Not all so-called phenomenological writing is so good. Clark Moustakas's (1994) version of the method gets things precisely backwards, by bracketing *the analyst's* prior concepts so as better to hear informants' *ideas about* their experiencing. This is not phenomenology, because it seeks a different research object: it seeks ideas, not experiences. It is more akin to hermeneutics, to which I now turn.

HERMENEUTIC INTERVIEWING

In a very worthwhile piece, David Yamane (2000), criticized my phenomenological approach to Navajo rituals, claiming, first, that the analysis of rituals cannot be built on typological description but requires face-to-face interviews with informants, and, second, that these informants cannot give sociologists access to experience directly. Instead, they provide at best *articulations* of experience – i.e., the transformation of experience into words. Though I obviously question Yamane's claim of the *a priori* inaccessibility of experience, as well as his rejection of observing subjective experience as a sociological tool, I applaud his emphasis on interviewing as a source of knowledge. Talking to people about their religious lives is a fine – and separate – source of sociological data.

Let us start the discussion with the framework that I proposed above. What metaphysical object do interviewers seek – and how does the nature of that object shape their research projects? In principle, we can divide interviews into two types. The first type – hermeneutic interviewing – seeks to capture people's own understandings of their lives. It seeks to portray people's worlds as if from the inside, communicating them to outsiders as accurately as possible. As Jürgen Habermas (1968) notes,[4] this type of research arises from the universal human interest in communication. Among the many things that humans do is to seek to understand one another, and this understanding is grounded in their ability to imagine each other's inner worlds. Hermeneutic interviewing involves the sympathetic apprehension of others' realities as they themselves see them. Its goal is the representation of other people's lives.

Interviews may, of course, do more than this. A second type of interviewing seeks to uncover patterns in the interviewees' answers, including some of which they may not be aware. Though this type does not wish to *mis*understand people, it does not settle for mere understanding. It goes beyond understanding to *explain* why people think the way they do. The focus may be semi-hermeneutic, i.e., having at least some interest in how people understand themselves, or it may be entirely explanatory, not much caring how people view their own lives.

Habermas shows that the truth-test of hermeneutic interviewing is different, in principle, from the truth-test of explanation. One knows whether one's *explanations* are correct when they produce results in the real world: the rocket goes up, the solar array produces power, the voters whom one has tried to manipulate elect one's candidate to office. One knows when one has *understood* someone, on the other hand, only when that interlocutor says so. First, the interviewer listens, and then responds with what she or he has heard: 'This is what I hear you saying: …' The person being interviewed often says, 'No, you have not quite got it right; this is what I meant: …' or 'That's part of it; here's some more: …' The interviewer listens again, again tells what s/he has heard. Finally – ideally – the interviewee says,

'Yes, you understand me!' and the process is done. This is the famous hermeneutic circle, which goes round and round until understanding is confirmed.

Many sociologists of religion have used such hermeneutic strategies. Lynn Davidman (1991) interviewed Jewish women who had converted to Jewish Orthodoxy to understand why they had chosen a religion that counted them as less important than men. One of her two study groups was attracting precisely the educated, independent women whom feminist theory said would reject such situations. After paying close attention to her informants' Davidman discovered that they had not found their independent (and single) lives very satisfying. The interpersonal disconnectedness of contemporary urban middle-class work life left them hungry for companionship and for a sense of tradition. Jewish Orthodoxy provided both. It gave them a firm sense of place and purpose, while simultaneously giving them a family role (and a family!) that met their personal needs. The strength of Davidman's study lies in her ability to listen to her informants' self-descriptions – and then to represent their commonalities and differences to her readers.

Christian Smith and Melissa Denton's (2005) recent study of the religious lives of American teenagers used hermeneutic interviewing as part of its research strategy. After completing an extensive telephone survey of 3370 randomly selected teens and their parents, they conducted 267 in-person follow-up interviews. These provided more details about teens' religious lives, while simultaneously letting them cross-check their survey results. Among other things, they discovered that religion matters a lot to American teenagers. Most are happy with the religious organizations in which they have been raised. Some can be counted as spiritual seekers and some are not religious, but Smith and Denton write that 'most are living out their lives in very conventional and accommodating ways' (p. 171). More significantly, however, Smith and Denton's interviews show that:

Only a minority of U.S. teenagers are naturally absorbing by osmosis the traditional substantive content and character of the religious traditions to which they claim to belong.

For, it appears to us, another popular religious faith, Moralistic Therapeutic Deism, is colonizing many historical religious traditions and, almost without anyone noticing, converting believers in old faiths to its alternative religious vision of divinely underwritten personal happiness and interpersonal niceness. ... The language, and therefore experience, of Trinity, holiness, sin, grace, justification, sanctification, church, Eucharist, and heaven and hell appear, among most Christian teenagers ... to be supplanted by the language of happiness, niceness, and an earned heavenly reward (Smith and Denton 2005: 172).

Smith and Denton's interviews let them paint this picture in great detail.

Much of Robert Wuthnow's voluminous research on American religious life has been similarly designed. For his 1999 study of Americans' religious upbringing, for example, he and his associates interviewed 200 Christians and Jews about their formative religious experiences and about their religious journeys. Not only did he discover the continuing role that religion plays in their lives; his study also reveals the ways that many of them – not all – have moved 'to a more deliberate, intentional approach to faith' (p. 162). Intentional engagement in various personal spiritual practices has shifted their sense of religion's purpose as well as the place of church religion in their personal lives. After giving his readers a great amount of detailed insight into his individual informants' lives, he concludes that:

it is still possible to describe American religion in terms of its congregations and institutions, but increasingly it appears that people are recognizing that participation in these entities may not be the same thing as practicing spirituality. If nothing else, the multiplicity of options available for guiding our spiritual practices now places a heavy responsibility on individuals, alone or in the company of others, to make choices (Wuthnow 1999: 192).

Readers believe him precisely because his hermeneutic interviewing has let him show us his informants' lives so revealingly. Only interviewing designed to provide a full picture of an informant's view of the world allows such detail.

There are, of course, other examples. Stephen Warner's (1988) prize-winning study of a mainline Presbyterian church used the results of hermeneutic interviews to portray the religious attitudes of various church leaders and members in some detail. Julie Ingersoll (2003) used hermeneutic interviews to portray Evangelical women's sense of themselves and the struggles that they encounter belonging to a religion that insists on their second-class status. W. Clark Roof (1993, 1999) interviewed scores of Baby-Boomers to produce his depiction of a generation of religious seekers exploring a vast spiritual marketplace. By focusing on people's own accounts of themselves in religious settings, these and other studies provide views of religion from the inside.

Hermeneutically informed research on religion is not just limited to single-session open-ended interviewing; it extends to any kind of research that seeks to portray people's lives as they, themselves, see them. Some sociologists, for example, have focused on religious life-histories. Their interviews ask people to present their own religious biographies, so that readers can learn something about religion from people's subjective self-presentations.

Karen McCarthy Brown's *Mama Lola* (2001) is probably the most famous example of such a life-history. Brown presents a spiritual biography of Alourdes, a Vodou priestess living in Brooklyn, New York. She weaves her account of Alourdes' life with the stories of her Haitian ancestors, the *lwa* that she serves, and the shifting relationship between her and Brown over the course of their multi-decade association. Like all good hermeneutic work, Brown lets us see Alourdes' life from the inside – at least as much as is possible given the cultural, social, and religious differences between them. That is her goal: to show how Vodou makes religious sense, not just for Alourdes and her fellow Haitians, but for Brown and for her readers.

This task inevitably involves interpretation. As Clifford Geertz (the most famous exponent of hermeneutic anthropology) put it, 'What we call our data are really our own reconstructions of other people's constructions of what they and their compatriots are up to' (1973: 9). The point is to make these reconstructions as accurate as possible. As Geertz also pointed out, hermeneutics is not limited to the retrieval of private meanings (pp. 12–13). Instead, it is a matter of becoming familiar with the imaginative

universe in which our interlocutors live. For all but the mad (and perhaps for them, too), imagination is social. People do not pray to gods and serve the poor idiosyncratically; they do so because these acts have meaning within a shared universe. The point of hermeneutic inquiry is to gain 'access to the conceptual world in which our subjects live so that we can, in some extended sense of the term, converse with them' (p. 24).

Non-hermeneutic research can also use interview methods, but with a different intention. The point here is not just to represent one's informants' subjective views, but to locate patterns in those views of which the informants may not be aware. Jodie Davie (1995), for example, collected spiritual biographies as part of her study of a Presbyterian women's Bible study group. She contrasted their (sometimes rather wild) stories of personal religious experiences with the tamer, less personal accounts that the same women gave in group meetings. This contrast allowed her to draw conclusions about the dynamic between individual and collective spiritual life in that mainline Protestant denomination. Many Presbyterians, including some of her informants, recognized this dynamic once it was pointed out to them. However, few of her interviewees expressed it in their interviews as part of their subjective world.

Brenda Brasher's (1998) interviews with Evangelical Protestant women led her to conclude that Evangelicalism does not disempower women, despite its ideological and institutional insistence that women should not lead men. In this case, some of her informants did reject the outside world's interpretation of their lives, noting that their power was complementary to that of men, not suppressed by it. But for others, the term 'power' did not enter into their subjective worlds at all, and Brasher also reconstructed these informants' accounts using this term – a clear example of the researcher's emphasis on pattern over hermeneutic meaning. Brasher did so to show that Evangelical religion-as-lived supports women's religious agency – a crucial element of 'power' in Brasher's view. Brasher presents her informants as actually powerful, even if they do not realize it, though she does not claim that they are powerful in the same way as Evangelical men.

Julie Ingersoll (2002, 2003) specifically challenges Brasher's interpretation, because her own interviews with Evangelical women show that they recognize male power and often resent it. In what amounts to the classic hermeneutic response to the interpreter who appears to go beyond the informants' self-understandings, Ingersoll wonders how Brasher (and others) can support their claim of female Evangelical empowerment against the testimony of Evangelical women's own subjective sense that they are disempowered. The question dogs nearly all qualitative research. Which gets interpretive priority? The views of the 'natives' – and if so, which ones? – or the views of the outsider?

There are clearly two levels at work here. On the one hand, there is the subjective self-understanding of the informant, which may or may not contain concepts like 'power', 'empowerment', 'subservience', and so on. Some of Brasher's informants used such ideas but others clearly did not. A purely hermeneutic study would portray the latter's religious worlds without using these concepts, and would not draw conclusions about whether or not these informants were 'really' empowered, disempowered, and so on. And it would portray the former's religious worlds by using these concepts in whatever way they themselves did – in Brasher's case by arguing that these women felt empowered by Evangelicalism rather than otherwise. Ingersoll's informants, on the other hand, did use these concepts and they saw themselves as disempowered by their male-dominated religion. Ingersoll reports this in her representation of their views.

On the other hand, the question of what is 'really going on' takes us beyond the mere understanding of one's informants' subjectively viewed worlds. Sociologists who ask this question implicitly pursue a different research object than do pure hermeneuts. Where the latter's intellectual model could easily be 'Stick to the native's viewpoint, please', non-hermeneutic research presumes that the inquirer can know things about her/his informants' views that are hidden to the view-holders.

Social science is no stranger to this phenomenon. Marx's analyses of the origins of class consciousness and Freud's theories of the unconscious both famously contend that asking people what is happening to them is not the best way to discover what is really going on. Such 'hermeneutics of suspicion', to use Paul Ricoeur's (1970) term, propose that an outside analyst can have greater insight into an informant's subjective world than does that informant her/himself. Conceptually speaking, however, this requires that the analyst have a theory of the relationship between the informants' utterances and what is really going on. It requires a theory of interpretation. For Freudians, for example, a dream about a cigar is 'really' a dream about a penis (a conclusion somewhat undercut by Freud's famous statement that this is not always the case: 'A cigar is sometimes just a cigar').

As Habermas (1968) points out, such interpretive theories themselves require justification, because they cannot rely on the classic hermeneutic truth-test: when the informant says, 'You understand me'. To the extent that sociologists engage in science, not fiction, they need to substantiate the grounds on which they interpret their informants' meanings. Hermeneutic interviewing grounds itself in the informants' affirmations that they can see themselves in our writing. Other forms of interviewing must justify themselves in other ways.

In general, sociologists have not been very clear about these distinctions and so have mixed together hermeneutic and non-hermeneutic forms of interpretation. None of this, however, undercuts the importance of interview studies, nor does it undercut the value of the specific studies that I have mentioned. The key point here is the metaphysical distinction between the object of pure hermeneutic interviewing – the portrayal of our informants' subjective views – and the object of other kinds of interview studies. Each time we use our informants' views to make a claim different from one that they subjectively recognize, we must justify our claims.

The question arises of how one should design interview studies; fortunately there are several good models available. I have found guides by Weiss (1995), Wengraff (2001) and Kvale (1996) to be very useful. Wengraff, particularly, provides a clear model for how to develop an interview study that builds on established literature.[5] The appendix to Smith and Denton's (2005) study, mentioned above, provides an exemplary account of how to integrate interview with survey research. Reaching beyond the study of religion, Lynn Davidman's (2000) interview study of sixty men and women whose mothers died young shows not only how to design and carry out deep interviews, but also how to work with one's data so that one does justice to one's informants' understandings while simultaneously revealing underlying cultural patterns.[6]

NARRATIVE AND DISCOURSE ANALYSIS

Interviewers collect their informants' personal narratives. These narratives can appear in other forms as well. Written texts, letters, newspaper articles, even novels and television shows can all take the form of narratives, and all can provide information about religions. Sociologists have lately become adept at mining these narratives for information. As with interview research, one has two choices. One can either focus on the narratives' overt meaning and seek to recreate the world that one's informants describe. Or one can analyze the stories for indications of deeper meanings, including ones of which their tellers are perhaps not aware. These two options seek different research objects, and the second requires the researcher to justify her or his move from the informants' text to a revelation of deeper meanings.

Sociologists of religion have lagged behind their counterparts in anthropology, media studies, and the like in their use of this second option, but an increasing number are finding it attractive. In this section, I shall consider some of these efforts and explore their possibilities for new forms of qualitative discovery.

To start with a recent example, Courtney Bender (2003) paid close attention to the ways

her informants talked about religion at God's Love: We Deliver, a New York City organization that prepares meals for those infected with HIV/AIDS. She tracked the shifting rationales for this charitable work, noting how the organization alternately emphasized and deemphasized the religious aspects of its mission. (At various times and for various audiences it emphasized the spiritual, physical, and/or community-building importance of its work.) She also listened to the ways in which the kitchen volunteers talked about their participation, noting how religion appeared (or didn't appear) in their everyday conversations. By tracking day-to-day talk, she found the various ways in which religion could or couldn't be mentioned. Overtly sectarian language, for example, was virtually taboo, but workers expected that everyone would have a deep, but largely private, spiritual connection with their volunteer activity.

By watching the tentative play of religious language, partly shared, Bender portrays religion-as-lived as a complex balancing act. Individuals use their store of learned religious concepts to explore their own felt sense of purpose without ever quite committing themselves to any one religious vision. Kitchen cooperation broke down either when people felt themselves being forced to conform to a particular religious vision or when they felt that their own vision was undervalued by others. Knowing this, volunteers attempted to share just the right amount of religious talk – enough to maintain the sense of shared purpose but not so much as to make that purpose unsustainable.

In good hermeneutic style, Bender's method depended on understanding her informants, but she moved past mere understanding to reveal the ways in which people use religious language to manage social interactions.

In a similar vein, Aisha Khan (2005) recently explored the shifting discourses of race and religion in southeastern Trinidad. She paid close attention to the ways in which people spoke about religion, about religious differences, and so on, using these ways of speech to draw conclusions about the conceptual worlds in which her informants live – a classic hermeneutic task. At the same time, however, she considered how the taken-for-granted ways of talking about religion shape these conceptual worlds. She notes, for example, that the common phrase 'Is all one God, anyhow' primes people to minimize religious differences. The phrase expresses the Trinidadian perspective that the differences between (for example) Moslems and Hindus are not very important, but it also creates that perspective, by belittling those who seek to accentuate the differences. The established way-of-speaking about religion both expresses and shapes social reality. A close attention to language and language use gives the researcher considerable insight into religion's role in the social world.

Both of these examples focus on 'discourse' – a core concept in Foucauldian and post-modern social theory. 'Discourse' is more than mere language; it is an institutionalized way of thinking, embedded in language, that shapes people's thoughts and behavior. The idea here is relatively simple. It begins with the realization that the fundamental concepts of any human activity are social constructions. People collectively create the ideas with which they grasp the world, and they collectively modify those ideas over time. For example, no one encounters 'poverty' in the raw; we encounter it through a socially constructed discourse about poverty – a collection of public and private talk that encourages us to think that the topic of our conversation is a fixed part of the universe. As Cindy Myers (2005) shows in some detail, 'poverty' means something different to the editorial writers of The New York Times than it does to the editorial writers of the Wall Street Journal. The former see it as powerful and active, as an entity that captures people and mires them, from which they are unable to escape. The latter see people as active, often choosing poverty rather than affluence or (if they are government bureaucrats) making others poor with their misguided policies. Neither vision is 'real', exactly, but both have consequences.

A given discourse presents preformed alternatives that guide thought down particular paths. Someone who blows up buildings, for example, may be seen as a 'terrorist' or a 'freedom fighter' – though this example presents itself more clearly than most, as nearly everyone can see the differences the terms make. The question of whether Scientology is a 'religion' is a more nuanced example, as it draws not only on political posturing but on scholarly differences over religion's nature. Is anything that calls itself a religion really a religion? Are religions allowed to charge set fees for their services? These are live questions that go to the heart of contemporary Western life, given the historic conflicts over religion that shape so many Western institutions.

A good discourse analysis, however, would point out that a distinction embedded in the last paragraph – between 'posturing' and 'scholarship' – is also discursive, as it shapes our attitudes toward various things that people claim to know. Among other things, it privileges 'disinterested' knowledge over advocacy and assumes the latter is more likely to be false. In each of these cases, discourse delivers the vocabulary, expressions and (usually) the style that people use to communicate with one another.

It is worth remembering here that calling religion a discourse does not make it any less real. As Margaret Wetherell and Jonathan Potter (1992: 62) write in another context:

> New Zealand is no less real for being constituted discursively – you still die if your plane crashes into a hill, whether you think that the hill is the product of a volcanic eruption or the solidified form of a mythical whale. However, material reality is no less discursive for being able to get in the way of planes. How those deaths are understood [...] and what caused them is constituted through our systems of discourse.

Few sociologists of religion have applied this concept rigorously to their work, though some are beginning to do so. The most adventurous are beginning to explore 'critical discourse analysis' (CDA) – a style of discourse analysis that seeks to reveal the ways in which people's languages are shaped by systems of social and political power. Critical discourse analysis explores the interactions between discourses and power relationships. First developed by Norman Fairclough (1995), it attempts 'to unpack the ideological underpinnings of discourse that have become so naturalized over time that we begin to treat them as common, acceptable and natural features of discourse' (Teo 2000). Myers' work, already mentioned, explores the political impact of poverty discourse on Americans' lives. Wetherell and Potter (1992) explore racialized discourse in Aotearoa/New Zealand. Fairclough (1995) details the conflicting discourses found in university advertisements.

The only study I know that applies critical discourse analysis to religion is Titus Hjelm's conference paper on religion and newsmaking (Hjelm 2005). Essentially a proposal for sociological activism, Hjelm suggests using CDA as a theoretically informed framework for tackling questions of religion in the news, and shows how expertise in sociology of religion can be used to interpret, influence, or shape the presentation of 'newsworthy' items about religion in ways that undercut existing power relations rather than supporting them. In his reading, CDA allows scholars to free their own intellectual work from ideological servitude – simultaneously promoting more equalitarian social arrangements.

Louise Phillips and Marianne Jørgensen (2002: 60–95) provide a clear outline for how this can be done. In their presentation, critical discourse analysis operates on three simultaneous levels. First, one examines the discursive practices that produce a particular text – perhaps one of the 'Statements' of the U.S. Conference of Catholic Bishops.[7] Such documents do not appear from thin air. They are produced according to specific procedures, and they go through many drafts, consultations, and so on before being approved. They conform to particular genres, use identifiable language, etc. In short, as texts they carry specific embedded social practices. Critical discourse analysis reveals these practices, how these practices shape the texts that result, and whom such practices serve.

Second, one looks at the texts themselves. How does a given text convey its message? To whom is the text directed, and how does it conceptualize its audience? What metaphors does it use and what are their implications? What possibilities does the text offer and what possibilities does it hide? How do wording and even grammar affect the text's message? For example, the bishops' November 2002 'Statement on Iraq' (USCCB 2002a) is written in a highly active voice, which emphasizes the control that American officials have over the choice of whether or not to go to war – a voice that specifically combats any official attempt to avoid responsibility for the consequences. A passive voice statement – 'war was begun today' – would present war as a natural phenomenon that just happened without a responsible agent, as would a nominalization such as 'there was much destruction of the city center'. The active voice suggests that war is a choice and that other choices are possible. Another of the bishops' documents, issued a month later, also uses active-voice language, but differently. The 'Essential Norms' to deal with the sexual abuse of minors by clergy (USCCB 2002b) does not attempt to avoid Church responsibility. It does, however, use a much more bureaucratic tone, giving the impression that procedures are now in place to protect all. This document is meant to reassure – and to underline the fact that the hierarchy previously did not have enough procedures in place to protect parishioners. Now it does, the document tells us, both in words and through the ways it uses language. Critical discourse analysis exposes such textual tricks, surfacing them for all to see.

The third step in a critical discourse analysis is to locate the text in the wider circle of social practices of which it is a part. In the case of the bishops' letters, this would involve describing the ways in which the text is promulgated and used both inside and outside the Catholic Church. Among other things, this would include not just the American church hierarchy's actions but reactions from Catholic laity, the efforts of various Catholic intellectual factions to promote or denigrate the document, the Vatican's private and public rejoinders, responses from other religious groups, government and politicians' efforts to spin the document to support its own positions, etc. Importantly, CDA looks for the pattern of these reactions, especially as they sustain or undercut existing power relations – both within and outside of church organizations. This is its ultimate aim: to show how power shapes the language that we use and how that language in turn reinforces the structures of power.

This logic is admittedly circular. Critical discourse analysis was designed to unmask power, so it looks for power relations. It is no surprise that it finds them; power permeates human affairs, even the most equalitarian. CDA reminds one of the folk saying about hammers and nails: anyone who goes looking for power will find it. This may be why few sociologists of religion have encountered CDA and even fewer have used it. The sociology of religion is one of the least likely of sociology's subdisciplines to explore issues of power (Beckford 1983, 1989), and one of the very least likely to have explored the neo-Marxist tradition in which CDA is based.[8] On the other hand, Hjelm does not 'consider a Marxist perspective the only or even a necessary one for CDA. You can be critical of power relations/hegemony without assuming a fixed view of power in the capitalist system' (Hjelm 2006).

Focusing on the issue of circularity misses the point, however. Though it is not news that power is both shaped and sustained by language, it is still useful to learn exactly how this happens in particular cases. One can use other forms of narrative analysis to investigate other aspects of language. If one wants to see how power operates, however, critical discourse analysis is a constructive (if neglected) tool. The approach is promising enough to recommend it broadly.

Note, again, what research object is being sought. Discourse analysis in general and CDA in particular do not limit themselves to particular texts' overt meanings. Instead, they seek to expose patterns that stand behind these texts – ones of which the writer or speaker is often unaware. Where hermeneutics sticks to that awareness, discourse analysis claims to reveal more.

ETHNOGRAPHY[9]

Despite its simple definition – the scientific description of peoples and cultures – ethnography is anything but simple in practice.

Sociologists have long used this method to describe specific religious locales. Typically, these have been in the form of case studies: studies of congregations (Ammerman 1987; Neitz 1987; Warner 1988), of new religions (Daner 1974; Barker 1984; Zablocki 1980), of networks of Appalachian snake handlers (Birckhead 1976), of Cuban-exile visitors to a Miami shrine (Tweed 1997), or of women who joined the Rajneesh movement (Goldman 1999). Such studies focus on a specific time and place. They do not tell us what people-in-general do; instead they tell us what people do in the particular community they have observed. They produce 'thick descriptions' of these communities, to use Clifford Geertz's (1973) term – ones that bring these communities to life in their readers' minds.

Descriptive ethnography calls for hermeneutic interviewing, as we want to know these locales from the native point of view. But it also calls for more than that. I do not mean just the simple fact that ethnographers observe as often as they interview, or that they conduct censuses, look for hidden patterns, and so on. These are important aspects of the ethnographic project, but they no longer distinguish ethnography from other research methods. Nor does the fact that ethnographers look beneath the surface of things, toward social patterns of which local actors are unaware. The key difference is that contemporary ethnography has become reflexive, by including the ethnographer as well as the community being studied in its field of view. A bit of history tells us why.

Ethnographic anthropology arose at the end of the nineteenth century to serve the needs of Western colonialism. American, British, French, and Russian imperial bureaucrats wanted to avoid the shoals that had sunk their Spanish and Portuguese predecessors. The better they knew their subjects, they reasoned, the easier it would be to control them. So they hired ethnographers, from James Mooney (1896), who investigated the Sioux Ghost Dance, and Frank Cushing (1896), who visited Zuni Pueblo, to E.E. Evans-Pritchard (1940), who explored Nuer politics in the Sudan in the late 1930s – and incidentally led native raids on the Italians in next-door Ethiopia (Geertz 1988: 50ff) – to the less well-regarded 1960s anthropologists who fed the CIA data on the Pathet Lao at the height of the Vietnam War (Horowitz 1974).

Sociological ethnography, on the other hand, was born in the Chicago settlement houses. It sought assimilation, not control. Its guiding question was: How could the 'socially disadvantaged' be helped to join the middle-class world? Sociologists from W. F. Whyte (1943) to Eliot Liebow (1967) and their jour-nalistic successors (e.g., Kozol 1988; Kotlowitz 1991; Lemann 1992) have been guided by the sense that the first step in helping poor people was to know them. Their descriptions of gang members, unemployed African Americans, homeless families, and other social outsiders humanized such people to mainstream readers and who then supported programs to improve their lot.

Clearly, these anthropological and sociolog-ical ethnographies were two-edged. On the one hand, they did help readers understand lives foreign to their own. They 'made the strange familiar', to use the old saw. On the other hand, they amounted to 'poking into the lives of people who are not in a position to poke into yours' (Geertz 1998: 72) – an activity more questioned today than in previous eras.

This is as much a matter of accuracy as it is of ethics. Eliza McFeely (2001) shows how early ethnographers, Cushing included, mis-understood the Zuni because they did not take their own social position into account, and thus failed to understand the ways the Zuni misled them in order to maintain their inde-pendence. Clifford Geertz (1988) documents similar failings in the work of Claude Levi-Strauss, Bronislaw Malinowski, E. E. Evans-Pritchard, and Ruth Benedict. Not that any of these ethnographers did poor work. They did not. But their basic stance amounted to a claim that they understood the natives better than the natives understood themselves. McFeely and Geertz show that their pretense of doing so got in the way of true understanding.

Anthropological ethnographers have lately come to recognize that ethnography's research object is not just the lives of the people that one is studying. The fact is, ethnographers cannot depict their informants' lives without writing about their own relationship with those informants. Only thus can they tell read-ers the full story, including how they know what they claim to know. J. Shawn Landres and I have elsewhere explored the details of this for the social study of religion (Spickard and Landres 2002),[10] so I shall only touch the high-lights here.

Ethnographers typically face three major issues as they design their research. First, the problem of subjectivity, with its correlates, the insider/outsider problem and the question of researcher identity. Second, the problem of social power, of which the above history of ethnography illustrates a part. Third, the prob-lem of representing one's informants to one's readers. All are related, and all are especially important to the ethnographic study of religion.

The problem of subjectivity is relatively easy to grasp, if only because ethnographic work depends so much on the researcher's sensitiv-ity to the patterns that she or he sees. The issue is: What guarantee do we have that any partic-ular presentation of reality is right? Brasher's (1998) previously cited study of evangelical women, for example, portrays them as power-ful despite their churches' formal ideology; Ingersoll's (2003) study shows the opposite. Which picture is more correct? Or are they perhaps both correct, each seeing slightly dif-ferent aspects of the similar social scenes?

To take a different example: Weston LaBarre (1962) presents Appalachian snake-handling as a religion based in extraordinary psycholog-ical needs. Dennis Covington (1995) presents it as a reasonable, yet ultimately unattractive, response to social marginalization. Jim Birckhead (1997) presents it as a not-so-extraordinary part of Southern life, one marked for attention not so much by the natives as by mainstream American culture's fascination with the dangerous and bizarre (see below). Which of these pictures is right? Or are they all partially correct, each contain-ing important insights that depend on the sen-sitivity of their investigators?

Sometimes this problem presents itself as a question of insiders versus outsiders. Who has the best grasp of a given religious reality: an insider, who shares the views of her or his informants; or an outsider, who can (supposedly) see them more objectively? There is no easy answer to this, of course, except to say that no observer ever has a full view. James Chancellor's (2000, 2001) account of being invited to write an oral history of The Family – a much reviled 'cult' group, formerly known as the Children of God – shows the benefits of both positions. The group sought him out to tell their story precisely because he was not a member, and was thus more credible in the eyes of the world. He did not convert, but became enough of an insider that (as of this writing) The Family's website calls his book 'a unique insider's perspective'.[11] At the same time, he reports that his ability to maintain intellectual independence let Family members open up to him in a way that they could not to true insiders. Similarly, Benjamin Zablocki describes the ethnographer being simultaneously a 'serial convert' and a 'serial apostate'. Advocating a policy of 'maximum feasible immersion', he writes:

> When this technique is partly successful, it may result in the important breakthrough of actually being able to enter the sacred time and the sacred space of the religious group at least for short periods.... Such a fleeting experience of sharing this space and time can be as valuable as a zip disk worth of interviews.... Its scientific value resides, I think, in the capacity it gives the researcher to validate and contextualize more conventional observations (Zablocki 2001: 225).

Few researchers – indeed few people – are capable of suspending themselves between inside and outside for very long, in part because the identity struggles are too great. The disciplinary taboo against 'going native' keeps most researchers in line. So does the fact that most ethnographers depend on academic jobs for their livelihood. 'You are really one of us', the academy insists – and financial pressure (along with collegial loyalty) makes most people conform. But getting close to one's informants always raises identity questions. As Mary Jo Neitz (2002) puts it:

> In doing research in religious groups, multiple identities are brought into play: religious identities, sexual identities, gender identities, racial identities, class identities, political and occupational identities. Complex and shifting, each of these is available to be mobilized in constructing and co-constructing the meanings that unfold [in the research setting] (p. 35).

Neitz writes with more honesty than most about the ambiguous identity shifts she encountered during her research with witches. Though she was not a witch herself, she writes:

> I find when I am with the witches I study, and they are engaged in their spiritual pursuits, I sometimes feel earthly, grounded; whereas when I am doing sociology, I sometimes feel rather ghostly.... Woman/feminist/lesbian/witch/ scholar/native/other. There is no easy way to divide up 'them' and 'me'.... A woman I interviewed a number of years ago told me that if you are a woman and you are aware, you are a witch. As I listened to her, I tried out her definition: Am I a woman? Am I aware? Am I a witch? (pp. 33, 35).

Neitz concludes that she can no longer identify as simply the researcher, but she has not become one with her informants. She 'walks between the worlds', struggling to find ways to claim what she knows 'without an authority based on scientific imperialism'.

The problem of power is embedded in ethnography's origins, as I have noted above. It stems from the fact that ethnographers typically have more social power than do the people they study. This partly results from our academic settings: universities give researchers considerably more freedom than do other employers. More important, however, is the relative paucity of ethnographic accounts of society's power centers. Few powerful people wish to have witnesses nosing into their affairs – especially witnesses who will then write about what they find.

There are exceptions, of course. Gideon Kunda (1992) spent a year in the engineering department of a high-tech corporation, unraveling the supposedly 'progressive' nature of this workplace, whose leaders have a good deal more power and prestige than any ethnographer. On the religious front, Simon Coleman (2000, 2002) did his fieldwork in a Swedish evangelical megachurch, which granted him entry so that they could learn from him about how to work cross-culturally. They saw his anthropological expertise as a useful skill for their global evangelism. Televangelist Jerry

Falwell was extremely open with ethnographer Susan Harding (1987, 2000), at least in part, she reports, because he thought that God might be leading her toward conversion. This was not trophy hunting on his part; Harding reports that he genuinely sees God active in individuals' lives and sees himself as an instrument of God's will. Her encounter with this deepened her ethnography – a good example of how examining one's relationships in the field can help one learn more about one's informants than might otherwise be possible.

J. Shawn Landres (2002: 102) reports a similar experience at New Song Church. He argues that 'the field' in which the ethnographer does her or his fieldwork necessarily includes the ethnographer her/himself. As a result, it includes the ways in which one uses one's social position to gain knowledge, consciously or not. And it includes the ways in which one's informants respond, revealing or hiding their knowledge depending (in part) on their relative social power.

This brings us to the problem of representation, about which a great deal of anthropological ink has been spilled. The issue is not just how ethnographers come to know what they know, but also how they convey that knowledge – i.e., how they write about those whom they have studied.[12] Landres (2002) notes that there are eight different levels of representation in every ethnographic encounter. First, ethnographers represent themselves to their informants simply in order to gain access to them. 'I am a scholar trying to understand your religion'; 'I am a non-evangelical Christian trying to understand how evangelical Christians see the world'. These introductions are inevitably partial, revealing only segments of our identity and our program, but they are not necessarily false. Nor are the second representations – the ways in which my prospective informants represent the ethnographer to each other: 'Here is someone who can tell our story'; 'Here is a potential convert, even if he doesn't know it.' These representations inevitably shape the research; ethnographers must account for them if they are to present their research accurately.

The third, fourth, and fifth representations involve ways in which informants present things.

How do my informants represent themselves to each other ('A holy community misunderstood by the world'; 'Hindu immigrants in a strange land')? How do my informants represent themselves to me and to other outsiders ('A caring group of people following Jesus'; 'People just trying to practice their religion')? And – often overlooked, how do my informants represent me to myself? This is a particularly valuable representation, because it often reveals elements of our informants' worldview that we might otherwise miss. For example, Harding's (1987) realization that her informants thought she was a spiritual 'seeker' told her a lot about their outlook. Unfortunately, most ethnography fails to report this – or perhaps to notice it.

Once fieldwork is finished, another set of representations arises: those having to do with ethnographic writing. What choices do ethnographers make as they represent their informants to the public? Do they hide some of their failings, perhaps in the interest of presenting a more balanced truth, as Chancellor (2001) reports doing? Do they reveal them, hoping that they will not be overblown, as Burke Rochford (2001) did with his work on Hare Krishna child abuse? Do they distance themselves from their informants' odd practices, as Winston Davis (1980: vii–x) did with his study of Mahikari spiritual healing? Or do they embrace these practices, as did Karen Brown (2001) becoming a native, at least in a partial way. Each choice has its rationales; each has perils.

Next, what happens when one's informants read one's work? Do they threaten to sue, as Kwame Appiah (2000) reports of the Ugandan Ik after they read Colin Turnbull's *The Mountain People*? Do they say, 'Well, you got us, didn't you?' as the head of The Family told James Chancellor (2001: 51) on reading his manuscript. In either case, one's relationship with one's informants is never the same.

Finally, Landres notes that every piece of ethnographic writing contains not just an image of the people studied but an image of ethnography as a method of research. 'Every new ethnography implicitly presents a prescriptive model of how ethnography ought – or ought not – to be "done"' (p. 110). This may be why current anthropological training begins with reading ethnographies – hundreds of them. Where sociology students take methods courses, often learning cookbook techniques, anthropology students read. They see the skilled and not-so-skilled at work, weigh their representations, and learn.[13]

Let us end this section by taking a leaf from the anthropologists' notebook, to see how the issues of subjectivity, power, and representation play out in a particular case. In a long reflective essay, Jim Birckhead (1997) uses Appalachian snake-handling churches to illustrate various aspects of these issues.

Birckhead begins by noting the vacuity of the traditional view that one's research subjects are 'out there' – as people with a clearly identifiable culture, different from ours, that separates them from us and from others around them. The serpent handlers of his acquaintance are not so isolated. They are just like their neighbors: semi-rural, often poor, victims of an economy that has bled their region of capital and concentrated it in outsiders' hands. They drive pickups, listen to country music, eat Southern foods, travel, and talk just like their neighbors. Yes, they take up serpents and drink poison in church, but not as regularly as popular images would have us believe. Many groups use serpents 'as infrequently as once a month, once a year, or even once in five years (and then only by one or two preachers or elders)' (p. 31). In fact, says Birckhead, 'remove the serpents, poison, and fire, and serpent handling is indistinguishable from the plethora of small, independent, Pentecostal and charismatic groups throughout the South, other parts of the United States, and around the world' (p. 32).

Other Southerners – circus men, animal collectors, zoologists – handle snakes more often, yet they are not seen as bizarre or degenerate. Why, then, does mainstream scholarship let snake-handling define these people and why do we let it define them in such negative terms?

Birckhead suggests that snake-handling is perhaps more significant for mainstream American culture than it is for rural Appalachians. It resonates with our 'dark and abiding cultural obsessions with cults, inbred and degenerate hill people, fanaticism, danger, sex, and death' (p. 33). It taps into non-Southerners' images of 'Appalachian otherness', in fact becoming an icon of that otherness in outsiders' minds (p. 21). To let snake-handling define this religion is to separate oneself from its practitioners, to exoticize them and define them in outsiders' terms. It is to focus on our image of them rather than their image of themselves.

Yet, Birckhead notes that this is too simple. Not only do outsiders treat serpent handling as an icon; insiders do too. Like all humans who must construct a cultural identity – and that means everyone – people from these churches define themselves, at least in part, by the one practice that distinguishes them: their willingness to court death in pursuit of their faith. They construct an identity around snakes, strychnine, and other practices that put their lives on the line.

More complexly, part of this identity is performed. Serpent handlers do not work in private, nor are they and their fellow congregants the only ones to attend their church services. One also finds observers: curious tourists; reporters and camera crews; even the occasional anthropologist. All are drawn by the exotic, to which the participants play. These are not hidden observers, though they may portray themselves as such; like all observers, they influence the scenes they view. Those who take up serpents thus become actors in a dual sense: they take their lives in their hands in a way closed to ordinary people; and they do so before an audience that has come for a show. They thus collude in the identity that the world has given them: they become exotic as part of their process of cultural self-definition.

Serpent handlers are, however, not the only ones constructing identities; so must the other participants in this cultural scene. Film crews, tabloid reporters, and tourists all define themselves by their pursuit of the unusual. The professionals stalk the strange, package it, and sell it – communicating a sense of mystery to the masses. Their stories about snake-handlers and strychnine-drinkers feed a hungry market, for which these reporters have become cultural midwives, serving and reproducing our culture's 'dark and abiding obsession' with the bizarre. The tourists consume such experiences, living their personal obsessions. For both, snake-handling sects are better than 'show biz' because they are 'real'.

Birckhead goes even deeper than this, but the point is made: representations pile on representations. One must sort through such issues in every ethnographic encounter. If the reflexive turn among anthropological ethnographers has accomplished anything, it is to highlight the importance of subjectivity, location, identity, and power in the ethnographic process. Each level of the analysis opens up an aspect of the cultural scene we are attempting to describe. Rather than thinking of them as obstacles to ethnographic understanding, we can profitably think of them as tools to make that understanding more complete.

CONCLUSION

In conclusion, I wish to return us to the framework that I outlined toward the beginning of this chapter. Each of our four qualitative methods seeks a particular object.

- Phenomenology seeks to describe experience as it appears in the subjective consciousness of the experiencer. Csordas, Preston, and I all do this, though in our different ways. Each is worth exploring.
- Hermeneutic interviewing seeks to represent one's informants' conscious views of the world, of themselves, and of their place in it. The test of such research is whether those informants accept one's interpretation – the 'You got us, didn't you' that James Chancellor's depiction elicited.
- Narrative and discourse analysis look beneath these surface views by analyzing one's informants' language for patterns of which they may not be aware. One can do this from various standpoints; the critical analysis of hegemonic discourse is a promising option.
- Ethnographers try to describe their informants' worlds, both from the inside and from the outside. Because no human can escape her or his own social identity and standpoint, however, this requires portraying the ethnographer as part of the picture. Reflexive ethnography uses the multi-leveled, dynamic relationships between ethnographer and 'native' to produce as complete a representation as possible of the chosen social scene.

There are, of course, other qualitative methods to choose from. Each, however, raises issues similar to those detailed here. The fact that there is now so much good qualitative work in the sociology of religion is a sign of the discipline's growing maturity.

NOTES

1. E.g., Andrew Greeley's (1989) use of multiple surveys to capture differences in Protestant and Catholic imaginations.

2. This problem takes many forms. From the theory side, Foucault (1965, 1977), among many others, charts the role that socially informed 'discourses' play in 'naturalizing' one or another socially generated worldview. From the research side, David Yamane (2000) notes that researchers do not collect raw experiences but narratives of experience – narratives that are themselves socially formed.

3. The challenge posed by Foucault, Yamane, and others resembles claims of the late nineteenth-century historicists (e.g., Rickert 1892), who emphasized the historical contingency of human life and the role that particular social contexts play in shaping what people consider 'real'. Though developed as a counter to naive positivism, historicism equally stripped humans of their ability to manage their affairs. In Luckmann's words, 'The modern social sciences developed in continuous danger of either forgetting the barely discovered humanity of their subject matter or of defining it as a trivial epiphenomenon of a truer reality' (Luckmann 1978). Both historicism and positivism are reductionistic: either a reduction of human life to culture and discourse or a vision of life as but a tool of 'objective' forces. The question is: How can we elaborate the structures of experience without losing either their universality or their grounding in subjective experiences? This question is akin to the one facing Max Weber (1922), who similarly sought to mediate historicism and positivism by means of the ideal-typical analysis of social subjectivity.

4. For a concise account of Habermas's argument, see Schroyer (1972).

5. A four-page summary of this method ('How to Construct an Interview Protocol') can be found at *http://www.mcguire-spickard.com/Fielding/ documents.htm.*

6. Davidman includes her interview protocol as an appendix to her book. She provides further insight on her method in Davidman (2002).

7. As I write this, several such statements may be found at *http://www.usccb.org/statements.shtml*.

8. Otto Maduro (2003) is a notable exception.

9. Portions of this section are adapted from Spickard and Landres (2002). Used by permission of the publisher.

10. See also the articles collected in Spickard *et al.* (2002).

11. *http://www.thefamily.org/dossier/books/book9/book9. htm.* Accessed 16 Feb. 2006.

12. Two edited collections were particularly important in articulating the issues for cultural anthropologists: *Writing Culture* by James Clifford and George Marcus (1986), and *After Writing Culture* by Alison James and her associates (1997). The former highlights the question of how ethnographies are written, while the latter focuses on the issue of what such writing really accomplishes.

13. Clever readers will note that I have chosen the anthropologists' option for this essay. I give you not a cookbook for doing qualitative research, but some tasty examples.

REFERENCES

Ammerman, Nancy T. 1987. *Bible Believers: Fundamentalists in the Modern World*. New Brunswick, NJ: Rutgers University Press.

Appiah, Kwame Anthony 2000. 'Dancing with the Moon: A Review of *In the Arms of Africa: The Life of Colin M. Turnbull* by Richard Grinker.' *New York Review of Books* (New York), 16 November.

Barker, Eileen 1984. *The Making of a Moonie: Choice or Brainwashing?* Oxford: Blackwell Publishers.

Beckford, James A. 1983. 'The Restoration of "Power" to the Sociology of Religion.' *Sociological Analysis* 44 (1, Spring): 11–31.

Beckford, James A. 1989. *Religion and Advanced Industrial Society*. London: Unwin Hyman.

Bender, Courtney 2003. *Heaven's Kitchen: Living Religion at God's Love We Deliver*. Chicago: University of Chicago Press.

Birckhead, Jim 1976. 'Toward the Creation of a Community of Saints.' Ph.D. Diss., University of Alberta, Canada.

Birckhead, Jim 1997. 'Reading "Snake Handling": Critical Reflections.' pp. 19–84 in *Anthropology of Religion: A Handbook*, edited by S. D. Glazier. Westport, CT: Greenwood Press.

Brasher, Brenda 1998. *Godly Women: Fundamentalism and Female Power*. New Brunswick, NJ: Rutgers University Press.

Brown, Karen McCarthy 2001. *Mama Lola: A Vodou Priestess in Brooklyn*. Updated and expanded edition. Berkeley: University of California Press.

Chancellor, James D. 2000. *Life In the Family: An Oral History of the Children of God*. Syracuse, NY: Syracuse University Press.

Chancellor, James D. 2001. 'The Family and the Truth?' pp. 37–51 in *Toward Reflexive Ethnography: Participating, Observing, Narrating*, edited by D. G. Bromley and L. F. Carter. Amsterdam: JAI/Elsevier.

Chouliaraki, Lilie and Norman Fairclough 1999. *Discourse in Late Modernity: Rethinking Critical Discourse Analysis*. Edinburgh (Scotland): Edinburgh University Press.

Clifford, James and George E. Marcus (eds) 1986. *Writing Culture: The Poetics and Politics of Ethnography*. Berkeley: University of California Press.

Coleman, Simon 2000. *The Globalisation of Charismatic Christianity: Spreading the Gospel of Prosperity*. Cambridge: Cambridge University Press.

Coleman, Simon 2002. 'But Are They Really Christian?' Contesting Knowledge and Identity in and Out of the Field.' pp. 75–87 in *Personal Knowledge and Beyond: Reshaping the Ethnography of Religion*, edited by J. V. Spickard, J. S. Landres and Meredith B. McGuire. New York: New York University Press.

Covington, Dennis 1995. *Salvation on Sand Mountain: Snake Handling and Redemption in Southern Appalachia*. New York: Penguin Books.

Csordas, Thomas J. 1990. 'Embodiment as a Paradigm for Anthropology.' *Ethos* 18 (1): 5–47.

Csordas, Thomas J. 1993. 'Somatic Modes of Attention.' *Cultural Anthropology* 8: 135–56.

Csordas, Thomas J. 1994. *The Sacred Self: A Cultural Phenomenology of Charismatic Healing*. Berkeley: University of California Press.

Csordas, Thomas J. 1995. 'Words from the Holy People: A Case Study in Cultural Phenomenology.' pp. 269–90 in *Embodiment and Experience: The Existential Ground of Culture and Self*, edited by T. J. Csordas. Cambridge: Cambridge University Press.

Cushing, Frank Hamilton 1896. 'Outlines of Zuñi Creation Myths.' *Annual Report of the Bureau of American Ethnology to the Secretary of the Smithsonian Institution* 13 (6): 321–447.

Daner, Francine Jeanne 1974. *The American Children of Krsna: A Study of the Hare Krsna Movement*. New York: Holt, Rinehart & Winston.

Davidman, Lynn 1991. *Tradition in a Rootless World: Women Turn to Orthodox Judaism*. Berkeley: University of California Press.

Davidman, Lynn 2000. *Motherloss*. Berkeley: University of California Press.

Davidman, Lynn 2002. 'Truth, Subjectivity, and Ethnographic Research.' pp. 17–26 in *Personal Knowledge and Beyond: Reshaping the Ethnography of Religion*, edited by J. V. Spickard, J. S. Landres and Meredith B. McGuire. New York: New York University Press.

Davie, Jodie Shapiro 1995. *Women in the Presence: Constructing Community and Seeking Spirituality in Mainline Protestantism*. Philadelphia: University of Pennsylvania Press.

Davis, Winston 1980. *Dojo: Magic and Exorcism in Modern Japan*. Stanford, CA: Stanford University Press.

Evans-Pritchard, Edward E. 1940. *The Nuer*. 1969. New York: Oxford University Press.

Fairclough, Norman 1995. *Critical Discourse Analysis*. London: Longman.

Foucault, Michel 1965. *Madness and Civilization; a History of Insanity in the Age of Reason*. Translated by R. Howard. New York: Pantheon Books.

Foucault, Michel 1977. *Discipline and Punish: The Birth of the Prison*. Translated by A. Sheridan. New York: Pantheon Books.

Geertz, Clifford 1973. 'Thick Description: Towards an Interpretive Theory of Culture.' pp. 3–30 in *Clifford Geertz: The Interpretation of Cultures: Selected Essays*. New York: Basic Books.

Geertz, Clifford 1988. *Works and Lives: The Anthropologist as Author*. Stanford, CA: Stanford University Press.

Geertz, Clifford 1998. 'Deep Hanging Out.' *New York Review of Books*, October 22, pp. 69–72.

Giorgi, Amedeo P. and Barbro M. Giorgi 2003. 'The Descriptive Phenomenological Psychological Method.' pp. 243–73 in *Qualitative Research in Psychology: Expanding Perspectives in Methodology and Design*, edited by P. M. Camic, J. E. Rhodes and L. Yardley. Washington, D.C.: American Psychological Association.

Goldman, Marion S. 1999. *Passionate Journeys: Why Successful Women Joined a Cult*. Ann Arbor: University of Michigan Press.

Greeley, Andrew 1989. 'Protestant and Catholic: Is the Analogical Imagination Extinct?' *American Sociological Review* 54 (August): 485–502.

Habermas, Jürgen 1968. *Knowledge and Human Interests*. 1971. Translated by J. J. Shapiro. Boston: Beacon Press.

Harding, Susan Friend 1987. 'Convicted by the Holy Spirit: The Rhetoric of Fundamental Baptist Conversion.' *American Ethnologist* 14 (1): 167–81.

Harding, Susan Friend 2000. *The Book of Jerry Falwell: Fundamentalist Language and Politics*. Princeton, NJ: Princeton University Press.

Hjelm, Titus 2005. 'Breaking Out of the Ivory Tower: Toward a Newsmaking Sociology of Religion.' Presented at the Biennial Meeting of the International Society for the Sociology of Religion, 21 July. In *Normative Religion and Its Effect on Sociology: Past and Present*, J. S. Landres, chair, Zagreb, Croatia.

Hjelm, Titus 2006. Letter. Translated by James V. Spickard. In Spickard's possession, 7 February.

Horowitz, Irving Louis (ed.) 1974. *The Rise and Fall of Project Camelot, Studies in the Relationship Between Social Science and Practical Politics*. Rev. edn. Cambridge, MA: MIT Press.

Husserl, Edmund 1913. *Ideas: General Introduction to Pure Phenomenology*. Translated by W. B. Gibson. London: Allen and Unwin, 1954.

Husserl, Edmund 1917. 'Pure Phenomenology, Its Method and Its Field of Investigation' (Inaugural Lecture at the University of Freiburg), trans. R. W. Jordon. In *Husserl: Shorter Works*, edited by P. McCormick and F. A. Elliston. South Bend, IN: University of Notre Dame Press, 1981.

Iannaccone, Laurence R. 1994. 'Why Strict Churches Are Strong.' *American Journal of Sociology* 99 (5): 1180–211.

Ingersoll, Julie 2002. 'Against Univocality: Rereading Ethnographies of Conservative Protestant Women.' pp. 162–74 in *Personal Knowledge and Beyond: Reshaping the Ethnography of Religion*, edited by J. V. Spickard, J. S. Landres and Meredith B. McGuire. New York: NYU Press.

Ingersoll, Julie 2003. *Evangelical Christian Women: War Stories in the Gender Battles*. New York: NYU Press.

James, Allison, Jenny Hockey, and Andrew Dawson (eds) 1997. *After Writing Culture: Epistemology and Praxis in Contemporary Anthropology*. New York: Routledge.

Kelley, Dean 1972. *Why Conservative Churches Are Growing; a Study in Sociology of Religion*. New York: Harper & Row.

Khan, Aisha 2005. *Callaloo Nation*. Durham, NC: Duke University Press.

Kotlowitz, Alex 1991. *There Are No Children Here: The Story of Two Boys Growing Up in the Other America*. New York: Doubleday.

Kozol, Jonathan 1988. *Rachel and Her Children: Homeless Families in America*. New York: Crown Publishers.

Kunda, Gideon 1992. *Engineering Culture: Control and Commitment in a High-Tech Corporation*. Philadelphia: Temple University Press.

Kvale, Steinar 1996. *InterViews: An Introduction to Qualitative Research Interviewing*. Thousand Oaks, CA: Sage.

La Barre, Weston 1962. *'They Shall Take Up Serpents' – Psychology of the Southern Snake-Handling Cult*. Minneapolis: University of Minnesota Press.

Landres, J. Shawn 2002. 'Being (in) the Field: Defining Ethnography in Southern California and Central Slovakia.' pp. 100–12 in *Personal Knowledge and Beyond: Reshaping the Ethnography of Religion*, edited by J. V. Spickard, J. S. Landres and Meredith B. McGuire. New York: NYU Press.

Lemann, Nicholas 1992. *The Promised Land: The Great Black Migration and How it Changed America*. New York: Vintage.

Liebow, Elliot 1967. *Tally's Corner: A Study of Negro Streetcorner Men*. Boston: Little, Brown & Company.

Luckmann, Thomas 1978. 'Preface.' pp. 7–13 in *Phenomenology and Sociology*, edited by T. Luckmann. Harmondsworth, U.K.: Penguin Books.

Maduro, Otto 2003. '"Religion" Under Imperial Duress? Post-Colonial Reflections and Proposals.' *Review of Religious Research* 45 (31): 221–34.

McFeely, Eliza 2001. *Zuni and the American Imagination*. New York: Hill and Wang.

McGuire, Meredith B. and James V. Spickard 2003. 'Narratives of Commitment: Social Activism and Radical Catholic Identity.' *Temenos: Studies in Comparative Religion* 37–8: 131–49.

Merleau-Ponty, Maurice 1962. *Phenomenology of Perception*. Translated by C. Smith. London: Routledge and Kegan Paul.

Merleau-Ponty, Maurice 1964. *The Primacy of Perception*. Translated by J. Edie. Evanston, Illinois: Northwestern University Press.

Mills, C. Wright. 1959. *The Sociological Imagination*. London: Oxford University Press.

Mooney, James 1896. *The Ghost Dance Religion and the Sioux Outbreak of 1890*. Technical Report No. 14th Report, II. Washington: Bureau of American Ethnology.

Moustakas, Clark 1994. *Phenomenological Research Methods*. Thousand Oaks, CA: Sage.

Myers, Cindy 2005. 'Talking Poverty: Power Arrangements in Poverty Discourse.' Ph.D. Diss., Program in Human and Organizational Development, Fielding Graduate Institute.

Neitz, Mary Jo 1987. *Charisma and Community: A Study of Religious Commitment Within the Catholic Charismatic Renewal*. New Brunswick, NJ: Transaction Publishers.

Neitz, Mary Jo 2002. 'Walking Between the Worlds: Permeable Boundaries, Ambiguous Identities.' pp. 33–46 in *Personal Knowledge and Beyond: Reshaping the Ethnography of Religion*, edited by J. V. Spickard, J. S. Landres and M. B. McGuire. New York: NYU Press.

Niebuhr, H. Richard 1963. *The Responsible Self: An Essay in Christian Moral Philosophy*. New York: Harper & Row.

Phillips, Louise and Marianne Jørgensen 2002. *Discourse Analysis as Theory and Method*. Thousand Oaks, CA: Sage.

Preston, David 1988. *The Social Organization of Zen Practice: Constructing Transcultural Reality*. Cambridge: Cambridge University Press.

Ragin, Charles C. 1994. *Constructing Social Research*. Thousand Oaks, CA: Sage Publications.

Rehorick, David A. and Valerie Mahotra Bentz (eds) forthcoming. *Shifting Our Lifeword: Transforming Self and Professional Practice Through Phenomenology*. Lanham, MD: Lexington Books.

Rickert, Heinrich 1892. *The Limits of Concept Formation in Natural Science: A Logical Introduction to the Historical Sciences*. Edited by G. Oakes. Cambridge: Cambridge University Press, 1986.

Ricoeur, Paul 1970. *Freud and Philosophy: An Essay in Interpretation*. Translated by D. Savage. New Haven, CT: Yale University Press.

Rochford, E. Burke, Jr 2001. 'Accounting for Child Abuse in the Hare Krishna: Ethnographic Dilemmas and Reflections.' pp. 157–79 in *Toward Reflexive Ethnography: Participating, Observing, Narrating*, edited by D. G. Bromley and L. F. Carter. Amsterdam: JAI/Elsevier.

Roof, Wade Clark 1993. *A Generation of Seekers: The Spiritual Journeys of the Baby Boom Generation*. San Francisco: Harper.

Roof, Wade Clark 1999. *Spiritual Marketplace: Baby Boomers and the Remaking of American Religion*. Princeton, NJ: Princeton University Press.

Schroyer, Trent 1972. 'The Dialectical Foundations of Critical Theory: Jürgen Habermas' Metatheoretical Investigations.' *Telos* 12 (Summer).

Schutz, Alfred 1944. 'The Stranger: An Essay in Social Psychology.' In *Collected Papers II: Studies in Social Theory*, edited by A. Brodersen. The Hague: Martinus Nijhoff.

Schutz, Alfred 1945. 'On Multiple Realities.' In *Collected Papers I: The Problem of Social Reality*, edited by M. Natanson. The Hague: Martinus Nijhoff.

Schutz, Alfred 1951. 'Making Music Together: A Study in Social Relationship.' pp. 159–78 in

Collected Papers II: Studies in Social Theory, 1964, edited by A. Brodersen. The Hague: Martinus Nijhoff.

Smith, Christian S. and Melissa L. Denton 2005. *Soul Searching: The Religious and Spiritual Lives of American Teenagers*. New York: Oxford University Press.

Spickard, James V. 1991. 'Experiencing Religious Rituals: A Schutzian Analysis of Navajo Ceremonies.' *Sociological Analysis* 52 (2): 191–204.

Spickard, James V. 2005. 'Ritual, Symbol, and Experience: Understanding Catholic Worker House Masses.' *Sociology of Religion* 66 (4 December): 337–58.

Spickard, James V. and J. Shawn Landres 2002. 'Whither Ethnography? Transforming the Social-Scientific Study of Religion.' pp. 1–14 in *Personal Knowledge and Beyond: Reshaping the Ethnography of Religion*, edited by J. V. Spickard, J. S. Landres and Meredith B. McGuire. New York: New York University Press.

Spickard, James V., J. Shawn Landres, and Meredith B. McGuire (eds) 2002. *Personal Knowledge and Beyond: Reshaping the Ethnography of Religion*. New York: New York University Press.

Sudnow, David 1978. *Ways of the Hand: The Organization of Improvised Conduct*. New York: Harper & Row.

Tamney, Joseph B. 2005. 'Does Strictness Explain the Appeal of Working-Class Conservative Protestant Congregations?' *Sociology of Religion* 66 (31, Fall): 283–302.

Teo, Peter 2000. 'Racism in the News: A Critical Discourse Analysis of News Reporting in Two Australian Newspapers.' *Discourse and Society* 10 (4): 7–49.

Tweed, Thomas A. 1997. *Our Lady of the Exile: Diasporic Religion at a Cuban Catholic Shrine in Miami*. Oxford: Oxford University Press.

USCCB 2002a. 'Statement on Iraq.' Retrieved 15 February 2006. USCCB *http://www.usccb.org/bishops/iraq.shtml*.

USCCB 2002b. 'Essential Norms for Diocesan/Eparchial Policies Dealing with Allegations of Sexual Abuse of Minors by Priests or Deacons.' Retrieved 15 February 2006. USCCB *http://www.usccb.org/bishops/norms.shtml*.

Warner, R. Stephen 1988. *New Wine in Old Wineskins: Evangelicals and Liberals in a Small-Town Church*. Berkeley: University of California Press.

Weber, Max 1922. *The Methodology of the Social Sciences*. Edited and translated by E. Shils and H. A. Finch. Glencoe, IL: Free Press, 1949.

Weiss, Robert 1995. *Learning from Strangers: The Art and Method of Qualitative Interview Studies*. New York: Free Press.

Wengraff, Tom 2001. *Qualitative Research Interviewing: Biographic, Narrative, and Semi-Structured Methods*. Thousand Oaks, CA: Sage.

Wetherell, Margaret and Jonathan Potter 1992. *Mapping the Language of Racism: Discourse and the Legitimation of Exploitation*. Hemel Hempstead, UK: Harvester Wheatsheaf.

Whyte, William Foote 1943. *Street Corner Society: The Social Structure of an Italian Slum*. Chicago: University of Chicago Press.

Witherspoon, Gary. 1977. *Language and Art in the Navajo Universe*. Ann Arbor: University of Michigan Press.

Wuthnow, Robert. 1999. *Growing up Religious: Christians and Jews and Their Journeys of Faith*. Berkeley: University of California Press.

Yamane, David 2000. 'Narrative and Religious Experience.' *Sociology of Religion* 61 (2): 171–89.

Zablocki, Benjamin D. 1980. *The Joyful Community: A Communal Movement Now in Its Third Generation*. Chicago: University of Chicago Press.

Zablocki, Benjamin D. 2001. 'Vulnerability and Objectivity in the Participant Observation of the Sacred.' pp. 223–45 in *Toward Reflexive Ethnography: Participating, Observing, Narrating*, edited by D. G. Bromley and L. F. Carter. Amsterdam: JAI/Elsevier.

7

Surveys of Behaviour, Beliefs and Affiliation: Micro-Quantitative

DAVID VOAS

Following a brief defence of the idea that religion can be quantified and a few remarks concerning the scope of the review, this chapter covers:

- Basic issues in the quantitative study of religion, and the types of survey data that are used.
- Difficulties in collecting data and in measuring religious affiliation, behaviour and belief.
- Benefits that none the less derive from quantitative research, both in understanding religious commitment and in assessing its consequences.
- Emerging methods that could be used in the study of religion.
- Key challenges in the field.
- Major datasets that are available for secondary analysis.

SHOULD RELIGION BE QUANTIFIED?

Religion can be studied in the same way as any other social phenomenon, and quantitative sociology offers an important set of tools.

By its nature, description relies on categories. If we describe Fred as a devout Christian, we either treat the qualities of being devout and Christian as irreducible, or we define them in terms of other attributes (Bible reading, orthodoxy, etc.). These characteristics may be binary (present or absent, e.g. having had a church wedding) or variable, in which case we use terms like 'more' and 'less' that rely on implicit quantification. Because any quality can in principle be treated as a quantitative variable, there is no reason to rule out quantitative analysis.

Critics might argue that religion is so complex that in practice one cannot record and classify behaviour and beliefs in a satisfactory way. The need to measure is a strength as well as a weakness, however. While it is certainly true that quantification simplifies what has been observed, these methods force us to be clear about what we are studying. The act of selecting and defining variables imposes a rigour and an openness to criticism that can more easily be escaped in discursive treatments of the same phenomena.

Experience – in the form of qualitative research – shows that we can collect meaningful quantitative data on religious belief and practice.

We need data of this sort in order to discuss big issues, such as the alleged growth in alternative spirituality, the supposed persistence of Christian belief among non-churchgoers, the apparent strength of evangelical and charismatic congregations, the relative religiosity of women, the degree of commitment of young European Muslims, and so on. Unless we are content with guesswork, we have to collect information from representative groups of people through social surveys. Without empirical evidence of this kind we have nothing but case studies, the representativeness of which would be impossible to judge.

Quantification gives us a description of who is religious and how committed they are, by age, sex, ethnicity, marital status, class, and so on. It tells us how far religion and religiosity are associated with values, attitudes, and behaviour of many other kinds: politics and prejudice, morality and delinquency, marriage and family, education and employment, etc. Quantification often provides the best or only way of testing theories about the causes and consequences of religious affiliation and involvement. It is the natural perspective to use in discussing trends, and it facilitates international comparisons.

What Does 'Quantitative' Mean?

Quantitative work often involves using aggregate or group-level data (e.g. on counties or congregations), but for many purposes we want access to the whole set of records from a sample survey. The sociology of religion is characterized by a concern not just for institutional structures but also for individual faith and practice. Sociologists have asked how traditional beliefs and behaviour (as well as the role of the church) have evolved with the coming of modernity. These questions can only be answered by analysing survey microdata, i.e. data on individuals. The analysis should control for other potentially influential variables, which is one advantage of using individual-level rather than aggregated data (and also large samples rather than small ones).

The demarcation between the sociology and the psychology of religion is not always clear, and some surveys might straddle the frontier. Psychologists are typically interested in individual personality, emotional needs and responses, and cognition. They therefore do analyses where not only the things to be explained but also the variables doing the explaining are at individual level. Sociologists accept the relevance of individual differences but are more concerned with how social factors may affect religious attitudes and behaviours.

The line between quantitative and qualitative work can also be slightly fuzzy. Material from unstructured interviews may be coded and analysed using computer software, and conversely surveys may include open-ended questions that invite discursive responses. Some effort at classifying answers is generally necessary if quantitative analysis is to be done. Crucially, too, some form of random (or 'probability') sampling should be used to select respondents in order to generalize findings to an entire group. The samples need to be fairly large: typically a thousand or more, though smaller surveys may be useful.

Religion vs. Religiosity

It would be a mistake to think that religion itself – Catholic, Anglican, Hindu, Buddhist – is necessarily the key variable in this domain. For some people, affiliation is purely nominal; others will have a serious personal commitment, seeing faith as important in their lives. What matters may be not only or even mainly one's notional identity or affiliation, but instead one's degree of religious commitment, or 'religiosity'. (This term is used non-pejoratively to mean the quality of being religious, not – as often in common usage – the display of excessive or affected piety.) Religiosity is bound up with attitudes, behaviour and values, while religion *per se* is arguably more like ethnicity, something that for most people is transmitted to them rather than being chosen by them.

These two concepts lead to quite separate questions. On the one hand there is the issue of the social significance of being Methodist, Mormon or Muslim relative to having some other affiliation, or none; on the other, the issue is how far degree of religiosity matters. Over time there may be aggregate growth or decline in particular denominations or in the commitment shown by those involved.

VARIETIES OF MEASUREMENT

Background

Surveys are now firmly established as a basic tool in the field, but it was not always so:

> Research on religion using quantitative data and methods can be found prior to World War II and even before the turn of the [20th] century. But it has been only since the late 1950s and early 1960s that work of this sort has multiplied to a significant degree. Gerhard Lenski's *The Religious Factor*, which is now regarded as a pioneering work in the quantitative study of religion, was first published in 1961. Thus, when we speak of quantitative religious research, we are speaking of a relatively recent academic development (Wuthnow, 1979: 1).

Early studies of religion tended to focus on the traditional categories of religious identity and attendance at services, though measures of orthodoxy and biblical or doctrinal knowledge were also sometimes included in questionnaires. From the 1970s there have been increasing efforts to capture a more rounded concept of religion and to measure less conventional varieties of belief and spirituality. These efforts have been aided by practical developments: surveys have multiplied, statistical techniques have been developed and refined, and perhaps most importantly, computers have made data analysis far easier than before. Until the beginning of the 1980s, producing even simple cross-tabulations was likely to involve punch cards, complicated instructions, mainframe computers, and a great deal of time. A job that in the past might have taken half a day to prepare – and would perhaps have needed to run overnight – can now be done in seconds.

Quantification requires clarity about what is being measured, but religion does not lend itself to simple description. There is no single marker of having a religion or of being religious. A number of factors may be relevant: belief, practice, membership, affiliation, ritual initiation, doctrinal knowledge, cultural affinity, moral sense, core values, external perception, or something else. It cannot be taken for granted that the concepts of affiliation and religiosity used here are one-dimensional attributes. 'Having a religion' is an ambiguous notion, and 'being religious' is even more difficult to define or observe.

We have various indicators of these attributes, but no real measure, and they may be multi-dimensional qualities. A crucial issue from the outset of rigorous empirical investigation, therefore, has concerned how best to 'operationalize' religion. The challenge, in other words, has been to find variables that capture enough of what we mean by 'religious commitment' (or whatever) that we can justifiably use them in research.

A pioneer in this field was Charles Glock, who from the mid-1950s sought to identify a number of core dimensions in religiosity. He settled on five: belief, knowledge, experience, practice and consequences. The last of these is distinct in being the outcome of involvement rather than a clear component of religiosity; it is probably better seen as an indicator of the significance of religion rather than of personal commitment. Lenski proposed a somewhat different set of four dimensions. Two relate to personal religiosity (doctrinal orthodoxy and devotionalism) and two are types of interpersonal involvement: associational (within the institutional context) and communal (social interaction outside the church setting).

In the years that followed a number of researchers developed survey questions corresponding to these dimensions, the intention being to create scale measures of each. Faulkner and DeJong (1966) were among the first to do so, and they argued that the relatively modest correlations between the different scales they devised showed that religiosity is indeed multi-dimensional. Others disagreed; in particular, Clayton (1971) showed that the items made up a perfectly acceptable unidimensional scale, and in subsequent work offered evidence that belief is the fundamental component of religiosity (Clayton and Gladden 1974). The debate has continued, however, with further results on both sides; the early studies are well reviewed by Roof (1979). While recent evidence supports the view that religiosity can be measured on a unidimensional scale (Voas 2004), it remains true that the construct has multiple facets that one might wish to analyse separately.

Discussions of how to operationalize aspects of religious commitment show no sign of ending. Arguments about evangelicalism in the United States have been marked by disagreement over whom the category should include and how to estimate its size; the issue is expertly reviewed in Hackett and Lindsay (2004).

In recent years it has become conventional to focus on three aspects of religious involvement: belief, practice and affiliation. The first two dimensions seem fundamental, representing the distinction between the internal (belief in creeds, knowledge and acceptance of doctrine, affective connection) and the behavioural (participation in services, private devotion and communal activity). Belief (in God, an afterlife, a transcendent moral order, specific articles of faith, or less directly in the importance of religion) is a basic sign of religious commitment, and profession of faith or agreement with some specific statements of belief may be a good index of personal religiosity. Actual religious behaviour, such as frequent prayer or attendance at services, may be an even stronger sign of religious commitment. Of course some people attend for personal, family or social reasons in the absence of faith or even affiliation, but in general one can reasonably assume (with good evidence) that religious practice in the modern world implies belief.

Although affiliation is simply what Americans label 'religious preference' rather than a measure of commitment, the growth (particularly outside the US) in the number of those who say that they have no religion has ironically turned the simple willingness to accept a denominational label into an indicator of religiosity. Objective measures of religious affiliation (e.g. baptism) now tend to be less important than self-identification. Identity has become a major topic in contemporary sociology, and religion is still capable of being an aspect of personal identity that does not depend on active participation, official membership, or even agreement with basic doctrine.

Types of Survey Data

Most surveys collect data on a cross-section of the population at a single point in time. The resulting data give us a snapshot of the situation, and just as with a picture we can place people and their surroundings in relation to each other. We may find it more difficult, however, to see whether someone has been or will be moving, and in what direction. For many purposes, such as studying social change, we would really like a series of pictures rather than a snapshot – but can surveys provide it?

There are various ways to generate data on change. One is to go back to the same people year after year, decade after decade, to find out what is new and what has stayed the same. These are 'panel' or 'longitudinal' surveys. Such studies require a large investment over a very long period, and there are relatively few of them. Alternatively, a survey may be conducted every year or two with many of the same questions appearing each time. The sample is not the same from one year to the next, and hence there is an additional source of uncertainty: if there are differences, is it because things have changed or simply because new people have been interviewed? Nevertheless these repeated cross-sectional surveys (such as the General Social Surveys in the US and Canada, or the British Social Attitudes survey) often give us the best information we possess about trends.

There are also ways of creating a time series other than through contemporaneous data collection. Respondents can be asked to reconstruct their family, education or work histories. Such retrospective data is also useful with religion; one can ask about religion of upbringing, attendance at certain ages, when churchgoing stopped or started, and so on. Other questions related to childhood concern the religious affiliation or practice of the respondent's mother and father at that time. Indeed, respondents may answer questions about parents, spouses and children, serving in effect as proxies for them in supplying data on entire families.

Mixed Methods

Surveys of representative samples of individuals (or congregations or anything else) are important because they allow us to generalize. Information about a few people, or for that matter about a thousand people not selected at random, only tells us about those individuals. In trying to discover what is happening and (broadly) why, there is no substitute for investigating the population as a whole via sample surveys. Ultimately, however, social processes emerge from the combined and interacting effects of individual action. To understand how things really work at the level of the actors, it is useful to investigate a small number of cases in depth. Such qualitative research may help us to understand the attitudes, motivations and interactions that produce the results we see.

Most scholars are specialists in particular methods as well as certain fields, and most projects involve either quantitative or qualitative research but not both. This specialization is not necessarily a bad thing; others may be better qualified than we are to fill the gaps that we create. Studies using both sample surveys and in-depth interviews tend to demand a great deal of time or money, and the most successful examples typically involve teams of researchers. Such mixed-methods work can be very valuable, though, in producing results that are both broad and deep. Examples include Smith (with Denton 2005) on the religious and spiritual lives of American teenagers and Ammerman (2005) on American congregations.

Mixed-methods research would be of clear value in a number of areas. Identity and ethnicity is one; religion is arguably becoming more rather than less important as a marker of ethnicity in Europe and North America, particularly as an increasing proportion of the ethnic minority population is native-born rather than immigrant. Very good qualitative studies have been weakened by serious errors in quantitative estimation; for example contrast Eck (2001) and STATS (2001) on the issue of how many Muslims there are in the United States.

Religious organizations have long been important providers of education, and religious issues related to schooling are more than ever in need of both quantitative and qualitative exploration. Mixed methods could also be used to good effect in studying a number of other areas in which religion can be relevant, including health and social services, immigration, policing and criminal justice, and employment. Beckford *et al.* (2006) provide a useful review that incorporates some original research, while Chaves (1997) offers a valuable model of what can be achieved by combining evidence from a variety of sources (surveys, a census time series, interviews, archival records, and published reports by participants and observers).

DIFFICULTIES

Data Collection Issues

Many of the difficulties in collecting data on religion for quantitative analysis are those faced by survey researchers in any field. For example, in order for a sample to be drawn, one needs a list of some kind – a 'sampling frame' – of individuals in the relevant population. If the aim is to study members of a minority religious group, there may be no such lists available. Similarly there are common problems of representativeness. Thus while an alternative to conventional sampling is to contact potential respondents on the telephone using random digit dialling, the people who answer may not be representative of the population. In the past many people did not have telephones; now the problem is that some people are only contactable on mobile telephones that may not have numbers generated by the automated system. In any event the growth in telephone marketing has made many people reluctant to respond to surveys.

It is unlikely that merely phoning, knocking on doors or stopping people in the street will produce a representative sample. Those who are at home or out at any given time of the day tend to have special characteristics, which is why the best surveys often involve repeated attempts to interview specific individuals selected for the sample. Surveys conducted via the internet have become common, but again there are many problems of representativeness. Even assuming that everyone has equal access to the questionnaire, those who complete it will be essentially self-selected. A related problem exists even when investigators approach specific individuals selected from a good sampling frame: not all will agree to participate. The issue of non-response bias – the effect on the results of losing those who refuse to do the survey – is a constant concern for quantitative researchers.

Even surveys using the best sampling techniques may not produce representative data if the samples are too small. Size is rarely a problem in looking at simple frequencies for the key variables – most serious surveys have at least a thousand respondents – but it quickly becomes an issue as one attempts to break down the totals by other characteristics. Hence it may be possible to discover (within an acceptable margin of error) what proportion of people believe that our destiny is written in the stars, but it may be impossible to say anything meaningful about how they differ from the general population.

Religion can be a sensitive subject, though it falls a long way short of some others (e.g. sex, drug use) in difficulty. Members of minority groups may be reluctant to identify themselves for fear of persecution (by someone with access to the data, if not by the investigators). Others may be reluctant to answer questions about what they see as personal matters. Social desirability can infect responses, so that people may not want to admit to unusual beliefs or practices and conversely may tend to exaggerate their orthodoxy or frequency of churchgoing.

These effects may be stronger in personal interviews than on more anonymous written questionnaires or even telephone surveys. One technique that can be helpful in face-to-face interviewing is to hand the respondent a card with the answer options identified as A, B, C, etc., so that the 'unpopular' choice is easier to give.

Some questions may not be clear to people. Answers on specific doctrines or religious ideas, e.g. the Trinity or reincarnation, may be difficult to interpret if the concepts are not understood by everyone. The same problem arises when using a word like 'belong'; how formal does the belonging have to be? If the way such questions are understood varies systematically by age, class or culture then the results may be especially misleading. Comparisons over time and cross-nationally are especially hazardous.

Measurement Problems

Notwithstanding the case made at the outset for quantitative studies of religion, there is no denying that many problems exist in practice. The variables that purport to capture religion or religiosity may not be reliable or valid, or may not relate to those dimensions that are relevant to our purpose. Obtaining fully satisfactory data on religion – whether affiliation, attendance or belief – is difficult. Indeed, the following 'law' is at least semi-serious: a quarter of responses to any question on religion are unreliable. Various cases in point follow.

Affiliation

Most people in the West are still able to specify their religious background, just as they can name their birthplace, father's occupation, and secondary school, but whether these things make any difference to how they see themselves or the way they are perceived by others is not at all certain. Different people will see religion in different ways: as a voluntary association (in which membership will lapse unless regularly renewed), as something more like a nationality (which you can have even if you go elsewhere), or simply as an aspect of cultural heritage.

Responses on religious affiliation are heavily influenced by the exact wording and context of the question. At one extreme, for example, the 2001 Census of Population shows 72 percent of people in England and Wales, and 65 percent of those in Scotland, categorized as Christian. On the census form for England and Wales religion follows the questions on country of birth and ethnicity, so that it appears (reflecting the intentions expressed in the government White Paper) to be a supplementary question on the same topic. The positive phraseology ('What is your religion?') combined with tick-box options that simply list world religions (e.g. Christian/Muslim/Hindu) invite the respondent to specify a communal background rather than a current affiliation. Note too that census forms are typically completed by the household head on behalf of all individuals at the address, and to the extent that such persons tend to be older and more religious than average, the numbers may be higher than they would be on confidential individual questionnaires.

The religion question used on the census form in Scotland preceded (rather than followed) those on ethnicity, was worded in a less leading way, and also offered answer categories for specific Christian denominations; perhaps as a result, people were nearly twice as likely as in England to give their affiliation as 'none'. Failure to appreciate the role of questionnaire design has led even astute commentators to interpret these differences in erroneous ways (see for example Dorling and Thomas 2004: 37-8).

In contrast to the census, the question posed in the British Social Attitudes (BSA) survey occurs in the context of a wide-ranging enquiry into opinion and practice, and it is worded in a way that might seem more likely to discourage than to encourage a positive response ('Do you regard yourself as belonging to any particular religion?'). The respondent must interpret for him or herself what 'belonging' might mean, but for most it probably implies some current as opposed to past affiliation. Thus although half the English population could legitimately be counted as Anglican,

having been baptised by the Church of England, fewer than a third identify themselves as such. For all religions combined the BSA 2001 survey gives a total of 58 percent in England and Wales, a very different result than the 79 percent (aged 18+) obtained from the census in the same year.

Research in France has also revealed the substantial impact of exactly how a question is phrased. Use of a filter question ('Do you have a religion?') leading to a follow-up ('Which?') in the event of an affirmative response was found to produce a much higher level of people declaring no affiliation than a single question in which 'none' was merely one option (Lambert 2002: 571).

These problems are not exclusively European or Western. In Japan, the Religions Yearbook published by the Ministry of Education and Bureau of Statistics shows Shinto totals (based on reports from the shrines) amounting to more than three-quarters of the total population. The Agency of Cultural Affairs states that Shinto is followed by half the population, with many of the same people being adherents of Buddhism. Surveys conducted by private groups, though, typically find that only 2 or 3 percent of Japanese identify themselves with Shintoism (Adherents.com 2005; Japan-Guide.com 2005; US Department of State 2000, 2005). The difficulties of deciding what having a religion might mean in Japan are obviously very considerable, with ritual participation (e.g. in 'Christian' weddings) not necessarily being a good index of personal religious identity.

Attendance

People exaggerate their attendance at religious services to a surprising degree. In a celebrated contribution to the scholarly literature on religion in the United States, Hadaway et al. (1993) compared self-reported attendance from polls with actual counts of people in church and found very substantial discrepancies. The latest research suggests that only about 22 percent of Americans attend religious services in any given week, in contrast to the 40 percent commonly found from opinion polls (Hadaway and Marler 2005).

A similar phenomenon can be seen in Britain. A 1999 Gallup poll posing the question 'How often do you go to church?' generated responses that appear somewhat inflated relative to church survey data (as reported in Brierley 2000). Similarly, asking people what they did the previous weekend, offering a list that includes home improvement, visiting friends and other possibilities in addition to churchgoing, results in a figure some 50 percent higher than actual attendance. Even more surprisingly, enquiring whether the individual attended within the last seven days (the question normally used in American Gallup polls) has produced values that are twice as high as observed weekly attendance (Hadaway and Marler 1998).

There are important lessons here for pollsters. A question that seems absolutely precise, to which one can give an unambiguous yes/no response, is being interpreted as something far more complex. As Hadaway and Marler point out, when Gallup asks 'Did you, yourself, happen to attend church or synagogue in the last seven days?', they make the respondent symbolically choose between being churched and unchurched. If being a churchgoer is part of one's personal identity, there may be considerable resistance to answering in a way that places one outside the fold. Subjective feelings of regularity are being translated into unrealistic frequencies; what one might infer about religiosity is an interesting but complicated matter.

Belief

The validity of responses on belief often seems open to doubt. Opinion polls in Britain show high levels of belief, but in all sorts of things, including reincarnation (a quarter of respondents), horoscopes (also a quarter), clairvoyance (almost half), ghosts (nearly a third), and so on (Gill *et al.* 1998). It is far from clear that these beliefs make any difference to the people claiming them. Research suggests that casual believers even in astrology, for example, which is distinguished by its practical orientation, rarely do or avoid doing things because of published advice (Spencer 2003). Studies on

polling show that people are prepared to express opinions about almost anything, whether or not they have any knowledge of or interest in the topic. Views may be uninformed, not deeply held, seldom acted upon, and relatively volatile. People feel that on certain matters they are required to hold and even to express opinions, but that is not the same as finding those issues particularly important.

While 25 percent of respondents may say that they believe in reincarnation, one is not inclined to suppose that they thereby express any basic truths about their own identities. The corollary, though, is that it is difficult to be too impressed by the apparent number of conventional believers. The argument here is not that the large subpopulation acknowledging what has memorably been called the 'ordinary God' (Davie 1994) is shallow or insincere. The point is simply that we cannot conclude from the fact that people tell pollsters they believe in God that they give the matter any thought, find it significant, will feel the same next year, or plan to do anything about it.

A question on the 1991 BSA survey asked about encounters with a powerful spiritual force. Not quite a quarter of people said that they had had such an experience at least once. Interestingly another one in eight responded 'can't say', which seems a wonderfully English answer, rather like being asked 'has the Almighty appeared before you in all His terrifying majesty?' and replying 'I'm not sure'. The English are not alone in being hazy or inarticulate about belief, though; American teenagers are similarly vague about what they believe (Smith with Denton 2005).

Reliability

For all measures of religion and religiosity, test-retest reliability can be surprisingly low. A comparison of waves 1 and 9 (1991 and 1999) of the British Household Panel Survey shows that the frequency distribution of religious affiliation is utterly static, from which it is tempting to conclude that religious identity is a stable attribute. Closer examination at the individual rather than the aggregate level reveals that a remarkable 27 percent of respondents interviewed in both surveys supplied different religious labels for themselves at the two dates. No doubt some of those panel members really did change allegiance (between denominations or between affiliation and no religion), but it is likely that many are simply uncertain or ambivalent. The line between 'C of E' (Church of England) and 'none' can be rather fuzzy.

When faced with questions on religion, many people are prone to be facetious, idiosyncratic or simply non-compliant. An internet campaign that swept through all English-speaking countries conducting censuses around 2000–2001 encouraged people to list their religion as 'Jedi Knight'. (A frequent suggestion was that if numbers reached some threshold governments would be forced to confer official recognition on this 'religion', ignoring that fact that these countries do not maintain lists of accepted faiths.) Some 390,000 people in England and Wales wrote in 'Jedi', exceeding the number of Sikhs, Jews and Buddhists. In Australia there were more than 70,000 Jedi.

For some measures of religion and religiosity, the very small numbers in certain categories make the data sensitive to coding and similar errors. In Scotland, the published total of people writing in 'another religion' on the 2001 census form was about 27,000. A later, more detailed count (commissioned by the Pagan Federation) revealed that most of those respondents described themselves as Jedi Knights and many of the remainder specified a Christian denomination and so belong in a different category. In fact only 5,400 (or 20 percent of the number published) genuinely belong to 'another religion', most of them being Pagans or Spiritualists.

Religion is often viewed as a purely private matter in Western countries. The US census does not broach the topic, and special legislation was required in Britain before the question could be included in 2001. Parliament stipulated that the question should be voluntary, the single exception to the rule that completion of the census form is legally required. The sorrowful precedent of registration in Nazi Germany was mentioned in debate, and there is some evidence that non-response was higher than average in areas with a substantial Jewish population.

BENEFITS

As an editor of this Handbook wrote in the 1960s concerning one of his own early contributions, 'This chapter has been more of a critique and a charting of pitfalls than a celebration of current knowledge concerning individual religiosity' (Demerath and Hammond 1969: 154). *Plus ça change* ... Notwithstanding all of these difficulties, it remains possible to obtain reliable, useful data on religion. Such data are valuable in helping us to understand the nature and sources of religiosity on the one hand, and the consequences of religious affiliation and commitment on the other.

Religion as Dependent Variable

Often we are interested in explaining the relative prevalence of religion or religiosity in different times and places. In statistical terms it is the *dependent variable*, so called because its level is assumed to be dependent on the values of the explanatory (or independent) variables. Many of the main theories of religion (from secularization through supply-side economic approaches) aim to account for the success or failure of the religious enterprise in relation to other factors.

Descriptive statistics give us basic information about the level and distribution of religious characteristics in a population. Common tools such as correlation and regression can reveal associations between these and other variables. Information about changes in beliefs, behaviour or the statistical associations over time provides the basis for studying social change.

From quantitative work we can hope to learn about continuity and change, religious growth and decline, the connection between believing and belonging, non-traditional spirituality, the influence of age, gender and socioeconomic characteristics, inter-generational transmission, cross-national comparisons, and much else besides. The literature is now very large, and it has been many years since it was possible even to attempt an overview

(Wuthnow 1979). A look through the *Journal for the Scientific Study of Religion* – established in 1961 and now publishing more than 30 papers a year, many of which are based on quantitative research – will provide an idea of the range of current work. Survey-based articles on religion can also be found in other specialist journals such as *Sociology of Religion*, the *Review of Religious Research*, and *Social Compass*, and in general journals such as the *American Sociological Review*, *Social Forces*, and the *British Journal of Sociology*.

Religion as Independent Variable

Social scientists are also concerned with the impact of religion on other aspects of life – what are often referred to as 'outcomes'. Religion can affect age at marriage, marital stability, attitudes to family planning and desired family size, health and morbidity, education, economic activity, social equality, crime, alcohol use, social attitudes, and any number of other areas.

Morbidity and mortality

By far the largest literature is in health, where there are journals specifically dedicated to work in this field and a 728-page *Handbook of Religion and Health* summarises 1,600 articles (Koenig *et al.* 2001). The evidence suggests that the positive effects of religion (e.g. on lifestyle, emotional stability and in social support) dominate the potential negative ones (anxiety, fatalism, etc.), but the balance will depend on the particular case.

In one of the best studies done specifically on the effect of religion on mortality, researchers found that in the US the difference in life expectancy at age 20 between non-churchgoers and the most frequent attenders is more than seven years, i.e. roughly as important as the gap between men and women or between black and white (Hummer *et al.* 1999). There is even some evidence that happiness is influenced by religiosity. Data from the US General Social Survey shows that the percentage of people who describe themselves as 'very happy' varies directly with degree of religious participation (Hope 2000). Alternative explanations are possible – happy people may be more inclined to engage in community activities, including religious ones – but it is not implausible that faith provides a sense of meaning and that churchgoing promotes a feeling of security and belonging.

Marriage and fertility

There is a strong association between homogamy of all kinds and marital stability: the more similar spouses are in religion (but also in age, ethnicity, education, social class and so on), the more likely they are to stay married (Waite and Lehrer 2003). A further issue is whether some religions are better for marriage than others (or none). The answer is probably affirmative – the theology and communal structures of some groups strongly discourage separation and divorce – though selection bias may also be relevant (if for example people with no religion tend to be less traditional and more susceptible to partner change than others).

The influence of religion on fertility has been a standard topic in demography, e.g. on its historical role in the European fertility transition (Lesthaeghe and Wilson 1986), the changing importance of 'Catholic' fertility (Westoff and Jones 1979), or its contemporary significance in less developed countries (Iyer 2002). Specifically religious norms may matter little unless the religious institutions supporting them play a significant role in the lives of their members (McQuillan 2004).

Socio-economic position

Religious affiliation may be associated with socio-economic position for many reasons, including not only group values but also historical advantage, social networks and preferential treatment. Education is an important determinant of economic success, and this factor has historically been associated with religion. In the United States 'educational attainment is highest among Jews and lowest among fundamentalist Protestants, with Catholics and mainline Protestants at the centre of the distribution' (Lehrer 1999: 358). An important influence of religion on socio-economic status may be a protective one relating to religiosity rather than affiliation. There is a substantial literature on the inverse association between religious involvement and criminal activity, drug abuse, and a range of risky or anti-social behaviour (Ellis and Peterson 1996; Corwyn and Benda 2000; Johnson *et al.* 2000a; Johnson *et al.* 2000b; Regnerus 2003).

Social and political attitudes

Religious beliefs are likely to influence other social attitudes. In previous decades it was commonplace for political parties on continental Europe to be associated with particular religious groups (or alternatively to appeal to the self-consciously secular), but these links are rapidly disappearing (Norris and Inglehart 2004). Religiosity is now one of the single best predictors of voting intentions in the United States, however; people who go to church voted Republican by a 2-1 margin in the 2004 presidential election, while those who do not attend services voted Democratic in the same proportion.

EMERGING APPROACHES

Methodological innovation has been continuous in quantitative social research. The sections that follow examine four techniques or approaches that could be used in the study of religion: item response theory (as a form of scale measurement), computer simulation, multilevel modelling (to consider context), and social network analysis. None of these approaches is genuinely new, and all have been applied to religion, but each shows a great deal of potential yet to be exploited.

Item Response Theory

We frequently wish to construct scales from a number of variables. The principle is that there is some underlying construct (e.g. religiosity)

that is manifested in various ways, but which is fully captured by no single observation. A very important issue (that can be tested statistically) is whether the concept in question can be measured along a single dimension.

As an example, one might include in the analysis several variables measuring some aspect of religiosity, e.g. religious affiliation, frequency of attendance, frequency of prayer, self-description as religious (or not), and importance of religion in life. The first methodological question to consider is whether these variables can be combined (by adding the values of each) to form a single scale. It is by no means obvious that they do all result from one underlying construct; there might be, for example, a 'private commitment' dimension and a 'public participation' dimension.

The classical approach would be to test the reliability of the scale by examining the intercorrelation of the items composing it. Assuming the value of a standard statistic such as Cronbach's Alpha is sufficiently high, the sum of the variable values would be used as the index of religiosity (which is assumed to be the underlying construct being manifested through the responses).

This method has various problems. In particular, it takes no account of the relative 'difficulty' of the various items. For example, if three variables apply to more than half the population (e.g. being baptised, belief in a higher power, and attendance at least once a year), while a fourth applies to only a small fraction of it (e.g. self-description as highly religious), then the apparently small difference between scores of 3 and 4 would be misleading. At best the scores can be treated as ordinal measures of religiosity. If however we need an index that can be treated as an interval scale (for example because we wish to compare the average religiosity of different groups of people), then the classical approach is unsatisfactory.

Although sociologists have rarely ventured beyond the classical methods, researchers in psychology and education have developed an alternative approach to measurement known as item response theory (IRT). Here the basic idea is that each respondent has more or less of the latent attribute and each item (question) is more or less demanding of that attribute. Depending on their degree of religious commitment, for example, people will exhibit varying levels of belief and practice and religion will be more or less salient in their lives. One or two real sacrifices for the faith may say more about your religiosity than conforming in dozens of conventional ways. By looking at the interaction between items and respondents we can construct a scale that allows us to compare not only one individual with another but also one difference in scores with another.

The requirements that must be satisfied in order to produce this kind of scale are substantially more onerous than under classical measurement theory. For example, the items must form a hierarchy from 'easy' to 'difficult'; the characteristic curves that represent the probability of someone with any given level of the attribute 'passing' each item should not cross. (For further details see Embretson and Reise 2000 and Sijtsma and Molenaar 2002.) Using the World Values Survey, Van Schuur (2003) shows that belief in life after death does not belong on the same scale as the other religious variables; it does not fit comfortably between belief in God ('easy') and belief in hell ('difficult'). Voas (2004) applies IRT to construct a religiosity scale for respondents in the European Social Survey, and is thus able to compare the average religiosity of Swedes and Spaniards, old and young, men and women, etc.

Computer Simulation

In the sociology of religion one often sees conflicts between *generalising* views (that typically emphasise common mechanisms of change) and alternative *particularising* approaches (that emphasise the uniqueness of each period and society). The problem that follows is then to identify which theories or what kinds of facts underpin the best explanations. In assessing whether the most important premises in an argument are the general or the particular statements, we are handicapped by having a rather small set of real episodes to study. It is difficult to evaluate competing explanations

when there are at best a few dozen cases to which they can be applied, rather than hundreds or thousands. Computer modelling can help to solve this problem. Real life provides only a few examples; simulations can be performed for as many circumstances as we can devise, and repeated with random variation a very large number of times. In so doing it is possible to study the relative influence of the 'rules' embodied in the model (the general mechanisms of change) and the 'initial conditions' assigned prior to a run (the social and historical context, here likely to be from hypothetical rather than actual populations). Discovering which has most effect on the outcome, and in what circumstances, may help us to understand the unfolding of events in the real world.

Computer modelling may also be able to assist in identifying the most promising general or particular explanations, though in this situation the approach is somewhat different. In constructing a simulation, after all, one assumes that certain rules are significant. The answers, if they are to be found, emerge in comparing the results derived from different models based on rival assumptions. One may find that the patterns created by some models seem especially 'life-like', or conversely that with others it is difficult to produce output resembling reality. There is no guarantee that such contrasts will be found, but one can reasonably hope to learn something about what evidence may be crucial.

The general area of computer simulation includes a number of distinct approaches. Multi-agent models (in which the behaviour of many discrete 'individuals' determines the outcome) are becoming increasingly popular (see the January 2005 issue of *American Journal of Sociology* introduced by Gilbert and Abbott 2005 for a general overview), though other types of models have also been used (Bainbridge 2006; Hayward 1999, 2002, 2005). Iannaccone and Makowsky (2007) show that if attachment to a religion of origin is in balance with a tendency to adapt to a new environment following a move, regionally distinctive distributions of religion can persist over time. Spickard (2005) uses a similar model to argue that competition and state regulation do not have the effects claimed by proponents of the supply-side theory of religious markets. Chattoe (2006) simulates a population of worshippers and argues that strict churches do not do better than liberal churches in the long run, contrary to earlier claims.

Multilevel Modelling

Much empirical work on religion has suffered from analysing individuals in isolation, often for the good reason that no information on place of residence or the local religious environment was available. It has long been argued, however, that the 'religious ecology' shapes the influence of religion on individual behaviour (Stark et al. 1982; Stark 1996). There is good evidence that national culture and religiosity have a substantial influence on the commitment of churchgoers and the likelihood that children will follow in the parental footsteps (Kelly and de Graaf 1997). A further question is what kinds of context matter and how far. Different levels can be defined, such as country, region, locality, congregation and individual; how much variation in religiosity and in its perceived value is provided by each level?

Multilevel modelling (also called hierarchical modelling) will be useful here. The fundamental feature of the method is its ability to distinguish effects operating at different levels, such as those of the household, the congregation, the town or district, and the region. Data from external sources (e.g. the population census or church attendance surveys) may be integrated with a primary dataset on individuals to provide supplementary independent variables at the area level. Where survey respondents provide their postcode (and this detail is available to researchers, which is often not the case because of confidentiality concerns), there are good opportunities for spatial analysis.

What is the impact of belonging to a conservative church, or of living in an area where your denomination is small, or of being in a particularly religious country? How far is commitment determined by individual choice as opposed to social environment? Statistical regression models in which variables relating to different levels – with coefficients estimated using specialist software such as MLwiN or HLM – may help to provide the answers. (For a basic introduction to multilevel modelling, see Kreft and de Leeuw 1998; more technical treatments are available in Snijders and Bosker 1999, Raudenbush and Bryk 2002 and Goldstein 2003).

Multilevel models have been used to suggest that, at least in respect of adolescent educational attainment in the United States, 'church attendance functions as a protective mechanism in high-risk communities in a way that it does not in low-risk ones' (Regnerus and Elder 2003: 646). To cite another example, it appears that in Iceland (and perhaps more generally) 'The religiosity of individual parents is not significantly related to their children's alcohol use, but female students drink significantly less in schools where religious parents are more prevalent' (Bjarnason et al. 2005: 375). Other studies using the approach are described in Johnson et al. (2000a, b) and Regnerus (2003).

Social Network Analysis

A key task in the sociology of religion is to understand the way that religion – or indifference to it – is transmitted and sustained through family and social networks. One of the underlying ideas relates to the diffusion of innovations. There is now a large literature (with a considerable number of computer programs available) on the transmission of attitudes through social networks. Because of the importance of religious upbringing for participation in later life, it will be especially interesting to study the impact of different patterns of marriage (and marital breakdown) on religious affiliation in the new generation. Religious conversion and revival is a classic diffusion process, but of course indifference can spread in much the same way. There is a considerable amount of inertia in these systems: entrenched religiosity is not quick to change, but likewise people raised without religion tend not to turn to it.

The notion of synergy (treated in more detail later) is also important. There may be feedback between social norms and household choice (e.g. the more it becomes 'normal' not to go to church, the less likely even believers are to attend).

It has long been evident that social relations are important in understanding the spread of a religion or the maintenance of religious commitment. Questions about which of the respondent's five closest friends were members of his or her congregation were used by Glock and Stark in the mid-1960s. Stark and Bainbridge (1980) stressed the importance of network connections in cult recruitment. Olson (1989) showed that strong congregational friendship networks are not an unalloyed good: they can facilitate retention but may hurt recruitment because existing church members are less inclined to incorporate newcomers and may appear to be 'cliquish'. There is still less output on social networks and religion than the importance of the topic would merit, but the pace seems to be quickening; see Ellison and George 1994; Cavendish *et al.* 1998; Mears and Ellison 2000; McIntosh *et al.* 2002; Christerson and Emerson 2003; Smith 2003.

KEY CHALLENGES

What follows is a partial and inevitably personal list of key areas deserving attention in the quantitative study of religion. These include finding mechanisms that explain the associations previous work has identified; distinguishing age, period and cohort effects in religious change; investigating the reciprocal effects of context and commitment; and detecting and measuring manifestations of alternative spirituality.

Mechanisms

Religious life is not static in any society. New religions appear, old ones fade; one kind of practice or belief gives way to another; overall religious involvement goes up or down.

The proximate causes of these cultural shifts must be sought at the individual level, with changes that people make in their own observance and in the raising of their children. In some cases there will be no particular mystery about the mechanisms at work, if for example a new ruler requires religious conformity. Particularly in the modern context, however, it is far from clear why there is conversion or deconversion, revival or apostasy. Carrying the investigation to the level of the particular individual would force us to look to psychology for explanations, but there is an intermediate perspective. The challenge is to understand why people in general change in certain circumstances. Is it because, for example, they are now more likely to choose partners from a different denomination (or none), and such mixed marriages tend not to transmit a clear religious identity? Does religious socialization depend on parents or on peers? Does the existence of options for belief and worship make it more or less likely that people will continue to be religious? We need to understand the mechanisms at work behind aggregate change.

Questions about mechanisms also arise in looking at the alleged effects of religion on other social phenomena. Perhaps religion is simply a proxy for other variables. The existence of an association between religiosity and health, for example, does not necessarily mean that religion *per se* is the proximate determinant or has any causal effect. Religion often acts through lifestyle or other variables, and part of the challenge in this field is to identify such confounding or mediating factors. It may also be the case that religiosity and these various characteristics are influenced by common factors, and to that extent religious status is purely an epiphenomenon. A further problem is that much of the evidence for the significance of religion comes from the United States or from other parts of the world where we know that religion is indeed socially significant.

Selection bias is potentially serious. Does religion cause good outcomes, or do people likely to experience good outcomes tend to be religious? The association between churchgoing and success among inner-city youth in the United States might imply that compulsory church attendance would be beneficial – or alternatively could come about simply because socially dysfunctional people do not go to church while families that favour work and discipline do (Freeman 1986). Recent research suggests that there are genuinely causal connections between religion and various outcomes, but the issue is clearly an important one (Regnerus and Smith 2005).

Distinguishing Age, Period and Cohort Effects

It is hard to explain religious change without first having a good idea of how it operates. In particular, we need to understand what combination of period, cohort and age effects are at work. Are European societies becoming less religious because of forces that have an impact on everyone? Or do those forces have their effect by undermining religious upbringing, so that some generations come to be less religious than their predecessors? And if (as we tend to suppose) people become more religious with age – perhaps on reaching life stages such as childbearing or widowhood – how far does this factor compensate for the other influences?

No analysis can provide unambiguous answers. Each of these variables can be expressed as a combination of the other two (for example, age is simply the difference between the date at any period and an individual's year of birth), and with sufficient ingenuity all purported effects of one kind could be explained in terms of the other two. There remains the possibility, for example, that age and period are both significant but that their net effect is nearly nil (if the tendency is to become more religious with age and concurrently less religious over time). Plausibility and parsimony will generally lead us to favour certain interpretations, however (Harding and Jencks 2003).

Longitudinal datasets are particularly useful in attempting to identify the different effects, and likewise repeated cross-sectional samples provide valuable data for these purposes.

Reciprocal Effects of Context and Commitment

Individual religious commitment will increase or ebb away depending on the investment made to maintain it. At the same time, it will appreciate or depreciate as a function of the valuation placed on religion in the wider society. The individual investment and the social value are linked, however. If there are substantial neighbourhood effects in the erosion or augmentation of religiosity (Voas 2006), then there may be feedback between the micro and macro levels. It is natural to suppose that the local or regional context might affect retention, ability to recruit, etc. If the amount of religious interest shrinks to a certain point, it may become difficult to prevent a shift toward widespread non-participation in religion. Conversely, if religious involvement is sufficiently high (as perhaps in the US), then levels of participation may be self-sustaining.

Changes in religiosity may be as or more important than absolute amounts. Trends at the congregational or national levels may induce positive feedback as people join or leave; likewise individual movements may be reinforced if shifts in attitude towards church become self-fulfilling. English data suggest that the worship experiences of churchgoers who have a strong but declining sense of belonging are even less favourable than among those who do not feel a strong sense of belonging at all (Escott 2006).

Another mechanism for positive or negative feedback is congregational size. The dispiriting impact of having small numbers in large churches has been offered as one explanation for declining religious participation in Britain (Gill 2003).

These conjectures concerning the positive feedback between individual choices and social norms point to a possible mechanism underlying both religious strength and decline. It is natural to take demand for granted in a relatively religious society where church participation and spirituality produce valuable dividends, and with upward momentum producing a virtuous spiral, suppliers may play a key role in determining how much and what kind of religion is produced. Where spiritual entropy has set in, however, demand may diminish and the positive outcomes associated with religion may become progressively diluted. A vicious circle of falling investment and falling return on investment may be created. There are interesting questions about how (and in the long term whether) an equilibrium can be maintained other than at the extremes of general participation or non-participation.

Detecting New Manifestations of Spirituality

Many scholars and pundits argue that spirituality based on personal experience and well-being is growing and even displacing conventional religion (Roof 1999; Heelas and Woodhead 2005). Efforts to assess the scale, nature and significance of alternative spirituality are sorely needed, especially as the size, projected growth, novelty and permanence of this phenomenon are vigorously debated (Voas and Bruce 2007; Heelas 2007).

It is not always easy to say what 'spiritual' means; the label is used to flatter anything from earnest introspection to beauty treatments, martial arts to support groups, complementary medicine to palm reading. Moreover the descriptions of spirituality given by respondents seem to have little to do with the supernatural or even the sacred; it appears to be a code word for good feelings, the emotional rather than the material. Not even a quarter of those from a sample in Kendal, England defined their core beliefs about spirituality in terms that were either vaguely esoteric ('being in touch with subtle energies') or religious ('obeying God's will'). The rest said that it was love, being a decent and caring person, or something similarly terrestrial (Heelas and Woodhead 2005). A proportion even described it as 'living life to the full', on which basis some pop stars might qualify as spiritual masters.

Sociologists need to try to distinguish between the different constituencies currently considered under the holistic banner. Some people are undoubtedly motivated by an attraction to metaphysical spirituality, but others are mainly interested in physical and mental methods of stress relief, or in alternative forms of healing, or in spa-type bodywork, or in opportunities for self-expression and psychological support. How the numbers break down, how much overlap there is between them, whether and when the connections reflect a shared conception of the sacred rather than simply mutual sympathy or common practice – these are the questions to address.

Alternative spirituality may turn out to be even more complex than conventional religiosity. We can use the standard indices: self-identification (e.g. as 'spiritual but not religious'), belief (in characteristic ideas such as past lives or the sacredness of the self) and practice (of activities like astrology or alternative medicine, where they are personally important). The resulting overlap can be quite small (Voas and Crockett 2004). Whereas there is still a reasonably close connection between mainstream religious belief, affiliation and attendance, the realm of spirituality is considerably more diffuse; it is very difficult to predict what people believe, do, or call themselves on the basis of any of the other pieces of information.

APPENDIX: MAJOR DATASETS FOR SECONDARY ANALYSIS

Every investigator dreams of working with data from high quality, purpose-built sample surveys. In practice it is so expensive and time consuming to conduct good surveys that most quantitative work is done on existing data collected for uses not specifically related to religion. Such 'secondary analysis' is often frustrating, principally because questionnaires typically contain far fewer questions on religion than one would like, but the approach does allow a great deal to be done quickly and cheaply.

Regular national surveys are conducted for the purposes of social research in many developed countries. These datasets are typically archived and made available to scholars within a year or two after fieldwork is completed. Most are repeated cross-sectional surveys, and religious affiliation and frequency of attendance at services often feature among the core questions that are asked routinely. Longitudinal studies also exist, though religion is not always included. (In the European Community Household Panel, for example, religion is not one of the variables.)

Table 7.1 provides information on the date of inception and subsequent frequency of the main national surveys in a number of major countries, including their sample size, type (cross-sectional or panel), and a brief indication of which variables on religion are included. In a few instances censuses are listed, although census data are available primarily in the form of standard tables, not individual records. Most census agencies now create samples of anonymized records, however (also known as 'public use microdata samples'). These datasets can be analysed in the same way as any other large survey.

Table 7.1 *Data sources for selected countries*

Country	Data source(s)	Description
Australia	National Social Science Survey	Cross-sectional survey of 2–3,000 adults (aged 18+) with a panel component carried out most years between 1984 and 1996. Data on regularity of attendance, affiliation and beliefs.
	Australian Election Surveys	Surveys of representative sample of c. 2–3,000 adults eligible to vote (aged 18+) carried out in 1987, 1990, 1993, 1996, 1998, 2001 and 2004. Data on affiliation and regularity of attendance.
	Census of Population (5 yearly)	Data on religious affiliation; starting in 1971, respondents were asked to write in 'none' if appropriate.
Canada	Canadian General Social Survey	Annual cross-sectional survey of representative sample of c. 10,000 Canadian adults (aged 15+) carried out since 1985. Data on regularity of attendance and affiliation in all years, data on past attendance in 2001.
	Census of Population (5 yearly)	The Canadian Census provides data on religious affiliation for (almost) the entire Canadian population; tables from 1971 and later available from Statistics Canada.
France	Enquêtes post-électorales françaises	Surveys of voters, typically 4,000+, coinciding with French national elections from 1958 onwards. Data on affiliation and regularity of attendance.
	Baromètre OIP (Observatoire Inter-régional du Politique)	Representative cross-sectional surveys of c. 14,000 adults (c. 700 per region) conducted annually since 1985. Data on affiliation and attendance in most years, and occasionally belief.
Germany	German Socio-Economic Panel	Longitudinal household panel survey started in 1984 with an initial panel size of c. 12,000 adults (aged 17+), extended to the former East Germany in 1990. Data on affiliation (1990, 1991 and 1997) and regularity of attendance (1990, 1992, 1994, 1995, 1996, 1997, 1998, 1999, 2001, 2003).
	German General Social Survey (ALLBUS)	Biennial cross-sectional survey of 3,000–4,500 representative German adults (aged 18+) carried out since 1980 (former East Germany added in 1991). Data on affiliation and regularity of attendance, additional data in 1991 and 1998.
Great Britain	British Household Panel Survey	Longitudinal household survey started in 1991. Constant panel of c. 6,500 adults (aged 16+). Regularity of attendance data in Waves 1, 3, 4, 5, 7, 9, 11 and 14; affiliation in 1, 7, 9, and 14; belief in 1, 7, 9 and 14.

Continued

Table 7.1   *Data sources for selected countries—cont'd*

Country	Data source(s)	Description
	British Social Attitudes Survey	Annual representative cross-sectional survey of c. 3,000 British adults (aged 18+) carried out most years since 1983. Data on regularity of attendance and affiliation in all survey years and religious beliefs in selected years since 1991, and past and past parental attendance in 1991 and 1998.
	Scottish Social Attitudes Survey	Similar to the British Social Attitudes survey, but taking a sample of c. 1,600 exclusively from Scotland. Annual since 1999. A special module on religion was included in 2001.
	Census of Population	A question on religion appeared for the first time in 2001. In England and Wales, the Christian category is not subdivided further. More detail is available for Scotland, where religion of upbringing was also recorded.
Italy	Indagine Longitudinale sulle Famiglie Italiane	Longitudinal survey of a representative sample of 5,000 households. Carried out biennially since 1997. Data on religious affiliation, regularity of attendance and religious beliefs in odd numbered waves.
	Indagine Multiscopo sulle Famiglie	Annual cross-sectional survey carried out since 1987 covering about 20,000 households. Data on regularity of attendance 1993–1996 (not affiliation, but nearly all affiliated people are Catholic).
Japan	Japanese General Social Survey	Annual cross-sectional survey of representative sample of c. 3,000 adults eligible to vote (aged 20–89), annually from 1999 (pilot year) onwards. Data on affiliation, extent of participation, and belief in life after death.
New Zealand	Census of population (5 yearly)	Data on religious affiliation for (almost) the entire population; comparisons are possible from 1986 onwards [1986 was the first year with an explicit 'no religion' option as opposed to an entirely free response].
Poland	Polish General Social Survey	Cross-sectional survey of representative sample of c. 2,000 adults (aged 18+). Carried out annually 1992–1997, thereafter biennially. Data on affiliation, regularity of attendance and beliefs.
United States	General Social Survey	Cross-sectional survey of representative sample of c. 1,500–3,000 US adults (aged 18+) carried out annually most years since 1972 and biennially since 1994. Data on regularity of attendance, affiliation and religious beliefs, with additional data in some years (1988, 1991 and 1998).
	Other	There is no religion question on the census. Many sample surveys on religion are available for secondary analysis, however, often through the American Association of Religion Data Archives (www.thearda.com).

Source: Alasdair Crockett, UK Data Archive, University of Essex

European/World Values Surveys

The European Values Surveys grew out of studies carried out in ten countries in Western Europe. In 1981 the scope was extended to other parts of the world with the aim of investigating changes in beliefs, values and attitudes in relation to political, social and economic circumstances. This larger set of surveys is known collectively as the World Values Survey (WVS). Five waves have been conducted, in 1981–1982, 1990–1991, 1995–1996, 1999–2001, and 2005–2006. More than 80 countries have been included at least once.

Data collection involves stratified, multi-stage random samples of adults (aged 18+). National sample sizes are typically about 1,000, though they have ranged from 300 to 4,000, depending on the country. Since the mid-1990s the European Values Surveys have been effectively a subset of the World Values Surveys.

Questions on the survey forms commonly include:

Current (and past) religious affiliation
Religious upbringing (yes/no)
Frequency of attendance at services
Self-perception as religious person (or not)
Belief in God/soul/hell/reincarnation, etc.
Importance of religion/God in life

Other topics that have been covered at least occasionally include:

Social/moral/spiritual contribution of churches
Importance of religious ceremony to mark birth/marriage/death
God image
Prayer
What is most important for child to learn (one option being religious faith)
Confidence in churches
Belonging to, and voluntary work for, religious organization
Meaning of life (God featuring in some answers)
Lucky charms
Horoscopes
Religion in politics

The great strength of the WVS is its exceptionally broad international coverage; for many countries it provides the only readily accessible data on attitudes and values. The surveys generally include a good set of questions on religion. The dataset has weaknesses, though. Samples are relatively small, the quality of the sampling is variable, and data collection has often been done by different groups in different ways in different years, making comparisons difficult. Even for individual countries, differences between waves (in sampling, data collection and questionnaire design and content) reduce our ability to measure change over time reliably.

International Social Survey Programme

The International Social Survey Programme (ISSP) is a cross-national collaborative effort in which the partner agencies adopt common modules on special topics for incorporation into regular national surveys. The data are then available for international comparative work. The modules have concerned the role of government, social inequality, family and changing gender roles, etc.; religion was the focus in 1991 and 1998. Participating countries in 1998 included 13 countries from Western Europe, 8 from Eastern Europe (including Russia), Cyprus, Israel, Canada, the USA, Australia, New Zealand, Chile, Japan and the Philippines. The next survey on religion is planned for 2008. The questions should provide data in three important areas: the impact of religion on socio-political attitudes and behaviours, religious change, and religious tolerance and extremism.

Opinion Barometers

The Eurobarometer surveys of social and political attitudes are sponsored by the European Commission. The series began in the early 1970s; there are two rounds per year consisting of nationally representative samples of approximately 1,000 from each country in the European Union. Questions typically include religious affiliation, attendance at services, self-described religiosity, and trust in religious institutions. The importance of religion in life featured in early surveys.

Switzerland has a survey following the same model that can be integrated with the standard Eurobarometers. In addition, the Centre for the Study of Public Policy (now based at the University of Aberdeen) runs a number of surveys across Central and Eastern Europe, the Balkans and the former Soviet Union. The New Europe Barometer, taking in most of Eastern Europe (including Belarus, Ukraine and Moldova) started in 1991, the New Russia Barometer a year later, followed by the New Baltic Barometer covering Estonia, Latvia and Lithuania.

Similar surveys on other continents have been launched since the late 1990s. Latinobarómetro (for Latin America) and East Asia (now Asian) Barometer were the first, followed by the Afrobarometer. Even more recent is the Asiabarometer (officially the Japan-ASEAN

Barometer). There is now an organization called Globalbarometer, one of the aims of which is to produce questionnaires that make intercontinental comparisons possible.

European Social Survey (ESS)

The European Social Survey (ESS) is a new programme that currently covers 23 nations. The project is a multinational partnership in which the standards of design, execution and cross-national comparability are exceptionally high. The first round of data collection took place in 2002/2003 and the second in 2004/2005; the intention is to repeat the exercise every two years. Data are collected using personal interviews supplemented by short self-completion questionnaires. A great deal of expert attention has been devoted to sampling strategy, translation, methods, and quality assurance, with the highest possible level of cross-national comparability. In producing representative samples, obtaining a high response rate (the target is 70 percent) is a key objective.

The ESS provides better coverage of religion than most general purpose surveys, notwithstanding the organizers' modest view that with this dataset religion is better used as an explanatory variable than as something to be studied in its own right. The survey questions cover the three main areas of affiliation (current or past identification), practice (attendance at religious services, prayer, organizational participation/support) and belief (self-rated religiosity, importance of religion). While the questions on how religious the respondent is and how important religion is to him/her do not measure beliefs directly, it seems likely that there is a strong association between these variables and strength of religious belief.

Other Surveys

In addition to the datasets described above that are available for secondary analysis by scholars, it is also worth mentioning important surveys conducted by organizations or researchers such as Gallup and Barna in the US, Reginald Bibby in Canada, Opinion Research Business in the UK, etc., that yield important information on religion, though the survey microdata are proprietary and not generally available for use. The Pew Global Attitudes Project is exceptional both in its international scope and in making datasets available once reports have been published. There are in addition many small (and sometimes not so small) surveys touching on religion conducted from time to time by opinion pollsters, churches, academics and public agencies.

Much quantitative information on religion lies outside the scope of this chapter because it concerns aggregates rather than individuals. Such work includes the counts of members or attenders conducted by denominations, congregational studies in which key informants supply data on their churches, periodic surveys that attempt to enumerate adherents or attenders by area and denomination, the published output from population censuses, and other studies in which individual-level analysis is not possible. These figures can none the less serve as important contextual data.

There are ways of collecting quantitative data that do not rely on surveys at all. Many churches maintain and publish statistics on rites of passage (e.g. baptisms, confirmations, marriages and funerals). They may also release financial data on giving. Attendance counts may be conducted non-intrusively. Media attention to religion can be measured by counting items, column inches, or air time, and data may be available on the size of the audience for religious broadcasts or the numbers of hits on religious websites. Book sales, or the space devoted in bookshops to religion and spirituality (e.g. 'mind, body, spirit'), including religious fiction, spiritually based self-help, and so on, are also indicators of religious interest.

REFERENCES

Adherents.com. 2005. 'Major religions of the world ranked by number of adherents'. Retrieved 17 April 2006 from *http://www.adherents.com/Religions_By_Adherents.html#Shinto*.

Ammerman, N. 2005. *Pillars of faith: American congregations and their partners*. Berkeley: University of California Press.

Bainbridge, W. S. 2006. *God from the machine: Artificial intelligence models of religious cognition.* Lanham, MD: Alta Mira.

Beckford, J. A., Gale, R., Owen, D., Peach, C. and Weller, P. 2006. *Review of the evidence base on faith communities.* London: Office of the Deputy Prime Minister.

Bjarnason, T., Thorlindsson, T., Sigfusdottir, I. D. and Welch, M. R. 2005. 'Familial and religious influences on adolescent alcohol use: A multi-level study of students and school communities'. *Social Forces* 84(1), 375–90.

Brierley, P. 2000. *The tide is running out: What the English Church Attendance Survey reveals.* London: Christian Research.

Bruce, S. 2002. *God is dead: Secularization in the West.* Oxford: Blackwell.

Cavendish, J. C., Welch, M. R. and Leege, D. C. 1998. 'Social network theory and predictors of religiosity for black and white Catholics: Evidence of a "black sacred cosmos"?' *Journal for the Scientific Study of Religion* 37(3): 397–410.

Chattoe, E. 2006. 'Using simulation to develop and test functionalist explanations: A case study of dynamic church membership'. *British Journal of Sociology* 57(3):379–97.

Chaves, M. 1997. *Ordaining women: Culture and conflict in religious organizations.* Cambridge, MA: Harvard University Press.

Christerson, B. and Emerson, M. 2003. 'The costs of diversity in religious organizations: An in-depth case study'. *Sociology of Religion* 64(2): 163–81.

Clayton, R. R. 1971. '5-D or 1?', *Journal for the Scientific Study of Religion* 10: 37–40.

Clayton, R. R. and Gladden, J. W. 1974. 'The five dimensions of religiosity: Toward demythologizing a sacred artifact'. *Journal for the Scientific Study of Religion* 13: 135–43.

Corwyn, R. F. and Benda, B. B. 2000. 'Religiosity and church attendance: The effects on use of "hard drugs" controlling for sociodemographic and theoretical factors'. *International Journal for the Psychology of Religion* 10(4): 241–58.

Davie, G. 1994. *Religion in Britain since 1945: Believing without belonging.* Oxford: Blackwell.

Demerath, N. J. III and Hammond, P. E. 1969. *Religion in social context: Tradition and transition.* New York: Random House.

Dorling, D. and Thomas, B. 2004. *People and places: A 2001 Census atlas of the UK.* Bristol: Policy Press.

Eck, D. 2001. *A new religious America.* San Francisco: Harper San Francisco.

Ellis, L. and Peterson, J. 1996. 'Crime and religion: An international comparison among thirteen industrial nations', *Personality and Individual Differences* 20(6): 761–8.

Ellison, C. G. and George, L. K. 1994. 'Religious involvement, social ties, and social support in a southeastern community'. *Journal for the Scientific Study of Religion* 33(1): 46–61.

Embretson, S. E. and Reise, S. 2000. *Item response theory for psychologists.* Mahwah, NJ: Erlbaum.

Escott, P. 2006. 'Keep me praising' til the break of day: An examination of the worship experiences of churchgoers in England'. *Journal of Beliefs and Values* 27(1): 65–80.

Faulkner, J. E. and DeJong, G. F. 1966. 'Religiosity in 5-D: An empirical analysis'. *Social Forces* 45: 246–54.

Freeman, R. B. 1986. 'Who escapes? The relation of churchgoing and other background factors to the socioeconomic performance of black male youths from inner-city tracts'. In R. B. Freeman and H. J. Holzer (eds). *The Black Youth Employment Crisis*, pp. 353–76. Chicago: University of Chicago Press.

Gilbert, N. and Abbott, A. 2005. 'Introduction'. *American Journal of Sociology* 110(4): 859–63.

Gill, R. 2003. *The 'empty' church revisited.* Aldershot: Ashgate.

Gill, R., Hadaway, C. K. and Marler, P. L. 1998. 'Is religious belief declining in Britain?' *Journal for the Scientific Study of Religion* 37(3): 507–16.

Goldstein, H. 2003. *Multilevel statistical models* (3rd edition). London: Edward Arnold.

Hackett, C. and Lindsay, D. M. 2004. 'Measuring evangelicalism: Consequences of different operationalization strategies'. Paper presented at the annual meeting of the Society for the Scientific Study of Religion, Kansas City, October 24.

Hadaway, C. K. and Marler, P. L. 1998. 'Did you really go to church this week?' *The Christian Century*, 6 May: 472–5.

Hadaway, C. K. and Marler, P. L. 2005. 'How many Americans attend worship each week? An alternative approach to measurement' *Journal for the Scientific Study of Religion* 44(3): 307–22.

Hadaway, C. K., Marler, P. L. and Chaves, M. 1993. 'What the polls don't show: A closer look at US church attendance'. *American Sociological Review* 58: 741–52.

Harding, D. J., and Jencks, C. 2003. 'Changing attitudes toward premarital sex: Cohort, period, and aging effects'. *Public Opinion Quarterly* 67(2): 211–26.

Hayward, J. 1999. 'Mathematical modeling of church growth'. *Journal of Mathematical Sociology* 23(4): 255–92.

Hayward, J. 2002. 'A dynamical model of church growth and its application to contemporary revivals'. *Review of Religious Research* 43(3): 218–41.

Hayward, J. 2005. 'A general model of church growth and decline'. *Journal of Mathematical Sociology,* pp. 95–121. 29(3): 177–207.

Heelas, P. 2007. 'The holistic milieu and spirituality: Reflections on Voas and Bruce'. In K. Flanagan and P. Jupp (eds), *A Sociology of Spirituality,* pp. 95–121. Aldershot: Ashgate.

Heelas, P. and Woodhead, L. with B. Seel, B. Szerszynski and K. Tusting 2005. *The Spiritual Revolution: Why religion is giving way to spirituality,* Oxford: Blackwell.

Hope, D. G. 2000. 'The funds, friends, and faith of happy people'. *American Psychologist* 55(1): 56–67.

Hummer, R. A., Rogers, R. G. Nam, C. B. and Ellison, C. G. 1999. 'Religious involvement and US adult mortality'. *Demography* 36(2): 273–85.

Iannaccone, L. R. and Makowsky, M. D. 2007. 'Accidental atheists? Agent-based explanations for the persistence of religious regionalism'. *Journal for the Scientific Study of Religion* 46(1): 1–16.

Iyer, S. 2002. *Demography and religion in India.* Oxford: Oxford University Press.

Japan-Guide.com. 2005. 'Religion in Japan'. Retrieved 17 April 2006 from *http://www.japanguide.com/ topic/0002.html*

Johnson, B. R., De Li, S. Larson, D. B. and McCullough, M. 2000a. 'A systematic review of the religiosity and delinquency literature: A research note'. *Journal of Contemporary Criminal Justice* 16(1): 32–52.

Johnson, B. R., Larson, D. B. and De Li, S. 2000b. 'Escaping from the crime of inner cities: Church attendance and religious salience among disadvantaged youth'. *Justice Quarterly* 17(2): 377–91.

Kelly, J. and de Graaf, N. D. 1997. 'National context, parental socialization, and religious belief: Results from 15 nations'. *American Sociological Review* 62(4): 639–59.

Koenig, H. G., McCullough, M. E. and Larson, D. B. 2001. *Handbook of Religion and Health.* New York: Oxford University Press.

Kreft, I. and de Leeuw, J. 1998. *Introducing Multilevel Modeling.* Thousand Oaks, CA: Sage.

Lambert, Y. 2002. 'La religion en France des années soixante à nos jours'. In *Données sociales—La société française,* pp. 565–79. Paris: INSEE.

Lehrer, E. 1999. 'Religion as a determinant of educational attainment: An economic perspective'. *Social Science Research* 28(4): 358–79.

Lesthaeghe, R. and Wilson, C. 1986. 'Modes of production, secularization, and the pace of the fertility decline in Western Europe, 1870–1930'. In A. J. Coale and S.C. Watkins (eds), *The Decline of Fertility in Europe,* pp. 261–92. Princeton: Princeton University Press.

McIntosh, W. A., Sykes, D. and Kubena, K. S. 2002. 'Religion and community among the elderly: The relationship between the religious and secular characteristics of their social networks'. *Review of Religious Research* 44(2): 109–25.

McQuillan, K. 2004. 'When does religion influence fertility?'. *Population and Development Review* 30(1): 25–56.

Mears, D. P. and Ellison, C. G. 2000. 'Who buys New Age materials? Exploring sociodemographic, religious, network, and contextual correlates of New Age consumption'. *Sociology of Religion* 61(3): 289–313.

Norris, P. and Inglehart, R. 2004. *Sacred and secular: Religion and politics worldwide.* New York: Cambridge University Press.

Olson, D. V. A. 1989. 'Church friendships: Boon or barrier to church growth?'. *Journal for Scientific Study of Religion* 28(4): 432–47.

Raudenbush, S. W. and Bryk, A. S. 2002. *Hierarchical linear models: Applications and data analysis methods* (2nd edition). Newbury Park, CA: Sage.

Regnerus, M. D. 2003. 'Moral communities and adolescent delinquency: Religious contexts and community social control'. *Sociological Quarterly* 44(4): 523–54.

Regnerus, M. D. and Elder, G. H. Jr 2003. 'Staying on track in school: Religious influences in high and low-risk settings'. *Journal for the Scientific Study of Religion* 42(4): 633–49.

Regnerus, M. D. and Smith, C. 2005. 'Selection effects in studies of religious influence'. *Review of Religious Research* 47(1): 23–50.

Roof, W. C. 1979. 'Concepts and indicators of religious commitment: A critical review'. In R. Wuthnow (ed.) *The Religious Dimension: New directions in quantitative research,* pp. 17–45. New York: Academic Press.

Roof, W. C. 1999. *Spiritual marketplace: Baby boomers and the remaking of American religion.* Princeton: Princeton University Press.

Sijtsma, K. and Molenaar, I. W. 2002. *Introduction to nonparametric item response theory.* Thousand Oaks, CA: Sage.

Smith, C. 2003. 'Religious participation and network closure among American adolescents'. *Journal for the Scientific Study of Religion* 42(2): 259–67.

Smith, C., with Denton, M. L. 2005. *Soul searching: The religious and spiritual lives of American teenagers.* New York: Oxford University Press.

Snijders, T. and Bosker, R. 1999. *Multilevel analysis: An introduction to basic and advanced multilevel modelling.* London: Sage.

Spencer, W. 2003. 'Are the stars coming out? Secularization and the future of astrology in the West'. In G. Davie, P. Heelas and L. Woodhead (eds), *Predicting religion: Christian, secular and alternative futures*, pp. 214–28. Aldershot: Ashgate.

Spickard, J. 2005. 'Simulating sects: A computer model of the Stark-Finke-Bainbridge-Iannaccone theory of religious markets'. Retrieved 17 April 2006 from *http://www.coolsociology.net/articles.htm*

Stark, R. 1996. 'Religion as context: Hellfire and delinquency one more time'. *Sociology of Religion* 57(2): 163–73.

Stark, R. and Bainbridge, W. S. 1980. 'Networks of faith: Interpersonal bonds and recruitment to cults'. *American Journal of Sociology* 85(6): 1376–95.

Stark, R., Kent, L. and Doyle, D. P. 1982. 'Religion and delinquency: The ecology of a "lost" relationship'. *Journal of Research in Crime and Delinquency* 19: 4–24.

STATS 2001. 'Counting Muslims in the United States'. Retrieved 17 April 2006 from *http://www.stats.org/record.jsp?type=news ID=116*

US Department of State 2000. '2000 Annual report on international religious freedom: Japan'. Retrieved 17 April 2006 from *http://www.state.gov/www/global/human_rights/irf/irf_rpt/irf_japan.html*

US Department of State 2005. 'International religious freedom report 2005: Japan'. Retrieved 17 April 2006 from *http://www.state.gov/g/drl/rls/irf/2005/51513.htm*

Van Schuur, W. H. 2003. 'Mokken scale analysis: Between the Guttman scale and parametric item response theory'. *Political Analysis* 11(2): 130–63.

Voas, D. 2004. 'Religion in Europe: One theme, many variations?'. Paper presented at the conference on Religion, Economics and Culture, Kansas City, October 2004.

Voas, D. 2006. 'Religious decline in Scotland: New evidence on timing and spatial patterns'. *Journal for the Scientific Study of Religion* 45(1): 107–18.

Voas, D. and Bruce, S. 2007. 'The spiritual revolution: Another false dawn for the sacred'. In K. Flanagan and P. Jupp (eds), *A sociology of spirituality,* pp. 66–94. Aldershot: Ashgate.

Voas, D. and Crockett, A. 2004. 'Spiritual, religious or secular: Evidence from national surveys'. Paper presented at the conference of the British Sociological Association Sociology of Religion Study Group, Bristol, March 2004.

Waite, L. J. and Lehrer, E. 2003. 'The benefits from marriage and religion in the United States: A comparative analysis'. *Population and Development Review* 29(2): 255–76.

Westoff, C. F. and Jones, E. F. 1979. 'The end of "Catholic" fertility'. *Demography* 16(2): 209–17.

Wuthnow, R. (ed.) 1979. *The religious dimension: New directions in quantitative research.* New York: Academic Press.

8

History, Methodologies, and the Study of Religion

JOHN R. HALL

Historical inquiry – arguably the oldest methodology employed in the scholarly study of religion – is today a craft, practiced by the few rather than the many. Nevertheless, at the dawn of the twenty-first century, historical research – and the comparative analysis it inevitably entails – hold signal importance due to their distinctive capacity to get at cultural and institutional issues relevant to religion. Given our resurgent understanding of religion's importance for polities, global structures, and everyday life, it is worth considering how best to use historical and comparative analysis to improve the quality of research on religion, and, potentially, the vitality of public discourse. In this chapter, I explore the genesis and contemporary possibilities of 'methodology' in the broad sense of the term, inextricably linked with epistemological, theoretical, and substantive issues. Because the diversity of approaches to the study of religion is so great as to transcend any narrow characterization of 'historical sociology' or 'the sociology of religion,' I discuss methodological approaches to religion under the rubric of 'sociohistorical inquiry.'

Exploring sociohistorical methodologies in the study of religion, I hope, will help researchers come to terms with three vexsome antinomies. The first, between value-free inquiry and value commitment, springs from the modernist goal that Max Weber pursued, of creating knowledge that is valid in its own right, independent of the value commitments of its producers. In a postmodern era when ideology sometimes demonstrates a powerful capacity to construct reality after its own image, the fact-value distinction has the great merit of cultivating a culture of reason (Bendix 1970). However, the strong modernist division between science and values sometimes has had the unfortunate effect of closing off the kind of moral dialogue that thrived during the Enlightenment. Considering sociohistorical methodologies of studying religion offers an opportunity to explore whether and how such dialogue can be revitalized.

Second, modernist constructions of knowledge tended to warrant a strong distinction between history and society, between past and present as objects of study. Yet social theorists increasingly recognize that historicity – social life, events, and processes unfolding over time – is ontologically central to the character of the social. Whether presentism obtains more strongly in the sociology of religion than in other subdisciplines of sociology is an open question. Certainly, like other sociologists, those interested in religion often focus on their own societies and their own times. Yet separating the present from history is neither possible nor desirable, and thus, exploring sociohistorical methodologies should encourage the analysis of historicity in research on religion more generally.

Third, as a subdiscipline, the sociology of religion is unevenly attached to wider intellectual currents, both interdisciplinary and sociological. Sociologists of religion can easily fall into the modernist trap of accepting a binary of positivist science versus interpretation, and thus fail to connect with postpositivist developments precipitated by the crisis of positivism in the social sciences, and by the cultural, linguistic, and historical turns in the human sciences more generally. Considering sociohistorical methodology thus offers a useful vantage point from which to deepen the epistemological sophistication of the sociology of religion as an enterprise.

This chapter first traces multiple lineages of how religion has been studied historically. I then outline a typology of contemporary sociohistorical methodologies relevant to the study of religion. This typology in turn offers a basis for exploring how scholars have used methodologies to pursue various substantive themes in the study of religion. I conclude by sketching a sociology of knowledge concerned with the role of sociohistorical methodologies in research, and the consequences for contours of knowledge about religion.

HISTORICAL INQUIRY AND RELIGION: A NARRATIVE

The historical sources and styles of sociohistorical inquiry's methodologies are diverse. Already in 1835, in *Democracy in America*, Alexis de Tocqueville demonstrated the power of comparative analysis for explaining societal differences – in part on the basis of religion. Less than a decade later, John Stuart Mill identified formal logics by which inferences can be made through comparison of cases. Others in the nineteenth century, notably scholars of religion, used comparison not for science, but to pursue hermeneutic understanding, and to try to differentiate the historically variable from the phenomenologically essential – that which is enduring in human experience. Under the influence of sociology on the rise, historians began using sociological concepts to broaden the events and processes that they described. No longer was history simply an epic tale of nations and civilizations. It encompassed everyday life, self and identity, labor, technology, economic practices, families, social movements, and popular culture. Historical studies of religion began to connect to all of these topics and more.

For religion, topics of historical inquiry have taken form in relationship to value-based controversies about who should study it, and how. Given these controversies, there is no single 'right' way to recount the development of sociohistorical methodologies in the study of religion. To offer one telescoped narrative: the use of historical and comparative analysis of religion predated the emergence of sociology, and subsequently developed both within sociology and outside it. Both within and outside sociology, the study of religion often mirrored deeper concerns about the character and prospects of contemporary society. It was simultaneously a reflection *of* and a reflection *about* modernity (Kippenberg 2002).

One deep beginning can be found in ancient Judaism's prophetic and sometimes apocalyptic emphasis on the relation of a people's destiny to historical time (Wax 1960; Kumar 2003). Here and in other ways, religion has been fundamentally important to the formation of historical consciousness that is so central to the becoming of modernity.[1] Indeed, in the Europe of the early modern period, religious history amounted to a particularly important version of philosophical or 'universal' history, not only in religious appreciation of history as the great glory of God unfolding (Manuel 1965; Patrides 1972), but in dismissal of it as hypocrisy and superstitious whimsy, for example, at the hands of Scottish philosopher David Hume (1976 [1757]).

By the nineteenth century a particularly rich set of developments converged in the German *Religionswissenschaft*, or analytic science of religions, distinguished from theology and dogmatics by its emphasis on history. Scholars of the eighteenth-century German Enlightenment sometimes puzzled over Augustine's fifth-century formulation of history as the revelation of God's will. At the hands of Immanuel Kant, a moral thread remained, albeit modified. Kant refused to view history as a 'planless conglomeration of human actions.' Religion – and history – could be understood within the bounds of reason, he affirmed. But in place of *telos*, Kant proposed value standards as benchmarks that might chart the 'guiding thread' of history's progress toward enlightenment (1963 [1784]).

Kant was neither theologian nor historian. But for a theologian of the German Enlightenment period – the heterodoxical Friedrich Schleiermacher – religion only becomes something other than a 'dead letter' through its connection to history. Indeed, Schleiermacher held that 'in religion's eyes prophecy is also history, and the two are not to be distinguished from one another – and at all times all true history has first had a religious purpose and proceeded from religious ideas' (1996 [1799], p. 42). Schleiermacher was a romantic who saw in any generation's collective experience the spiritual force of history, thus anticipating Hegel's idealist dialectical model of history. Yet not just theologians embraced such views. Consider Leopold von Ranke, the nineteenth-century German scholar credited with establishing a 'scientific' history concerned with 'what actually happened' (*wie es eigentlich gewesen*). For Ranke, the 'actual' is not reducible to the purely empirical. Rather, exactitude about historical particularities is important, he asserted, because 'every action of the past gives evidence of God, every moment preaches His name' (see Gilbert 1990, pp. 44–5). In Ranke, the study of history consolidated the practice that has become known as 'historicism' – typically understood to suggest that the past needs to be understood in its own self-referential terms. For Ranke, historicism conjoined

scientific with romantic or spiritualist themes (Iggers 1975).

The interplay in Germany between enlightenment, science, and romanticism forged a crucible that shaped later currents of historical scholarship (Reill 1975). In these currents, religion – and more generally culture – brought to the surface all the important neo-kantian controversies of the late-nineteenth-century German *Methodenstreit*, the conflict over methodology that centered on whether science could be objective, what the role of values should be in inquiry, whether cultural sciences focused on hermeneutic understanding require different methods from the natural sciences, and what the status of generalizations is in the cultural sciences, given the uniqueness of history (Köhnke 1991).

For the study of religion, the legacy of German historicism largely traces to the founding philological and comparative work of Max Müller, who consolidated the *Religionswissenschaft* that became known as comparative religion in the U.K., or in the U.S., as the history of religions. Müller both participated in and advanced a broad exploration of prehistory and comparative civilizational analysis made possible by the archeological, ethnographic, and archival developments that resulted from expanding European colonialism. Yet for all the importance of Müller as a founder and a scholar, his work had Hegelian and evolutionary influences that offer little methodological guidance today, and we must look elsewhere.

The significance of religious historicism can be most efficiently detailed via two early twentieth-century scholars who tempered its more romantic and emanationist tendencies – Ernst Troeltsch and Max Weber. Both were historicists in the broad sense: they wanted to respect and capture the particularities of the past. But instead of trying to identify some ephemeral spirit, or *Geist*, of History, each in his own way sought to bring religious history into view by way of social theory, using concepts to analyze the inner meanings of asceticism and mysticism, religious organizational forms, the social roles of religious practitioners, and other aspects of religion.

Of the two, Troeltsch was a student of Wilhelm Dilthey, who worked to link biography and history, and Troeltsch held faster to the central historicist idea that the historical particularity of an era, like the individual person, requires understanding in its own terms. Part theologian, part historian, Troeltsch shared with Ranke the view that history reveals the variegated dispensations of God. But Troeltsch stretched his frame to the world religions, whose believers 'may experience their contact with the Divine Life in quite a different way' from Christians (Troeltsch 1972 [1901], p. 26). He argued that systematic theology and even dogmatics would have to yield to historical understandings of religion, because religious doctrines change over time, and more importantly, religion becomes linked with historical unfolding and destiny. Specifically, he thought, Christianity and especially Protestantism fed into developments of modernity, the contours of which were still emergent. Thus, Troeltsch's understanding of historical processes is inextricably bound up with a distinctive historicized theology. Nevertheless, in good neo-kantian fashion, he sought to distinguish his more value-committed enterprises, such as reconciling Christianity with modern society, from his empirical socio-historical studies, which he sought to pursue with rigorous objectivity (Troeltsch 1912). His critical-historical methodology emphasizes that (1) all historical events are interconnected (in a way that for Troeltsch affirms Divine presence), and (2) the process of interpretation depends upon the use of comparative analogies – both between present experience and the past and between various past events (Troeltsch 1991a [1898], pp. 13–14). This methodology provides a sociological counterbalance to Troeltsch's historicism, for it theorizes parallel developmental processes across different historical cases, and aligns research with sociological concepts such as church, sect, and mysticism. These, Troeltsch used as scaffolding for historical analysis in his famous *Social Teachings of the Christian Churches* (1992 [1912]), which nevertheless must be read as an inquiry structured by its author's distinctive religious commitments.

If Troeltsch was a man of God, Max Weber famously declared himself 'unmusical' in matters of religion. This self-description is belied by: Weber's comprehensive sociological conceptualization of religion, ranging from inner experience, to social roles, and social organization; his seminal works in the comparative historical sociology of the world religions; his classic analysis of the relationship between Protestantism and the spirit of capitalism; and his consolidation of an epistemological and methodological position in relation to the *Methodenstreit* that considerably advanced the possibilities of analyzing religion. Weber developed his methodological position in contention with Heinrich Rickert's analysis of values, for which Troeltsch had great admiration, and this difference signals their methodological divergence in the historical analysis of religion. Of the two, Weber moved much more centrally within modern sociology.

Basically, Rickert sought to establish the possibility of ascertaining objective values, ones that have general cultural validity and the 'unconditional general value' of truth (1986). For Troeltsch (1991b), this approach warrants the project of universal history, which depends upon such a value to create narrative coherence in relation to the chaos of events. Troeltsch recognized the empirical flux of value orientations *in* history, and he certainly did not think that some divine principle could order empirical history. However, his nuanced discussion of Rickert suggests that human destiny underwrites all knowledge, and that a 'metaphysic of history' could itself be a *product* of historical investigations. In these reflections, as in Troeltsch's historical studies, *telos*, religion, and empirical research exist in dialectical tension.

By contrast, Weber recognized Rickert's general warrant for the pursuit of truth, but he maintained a much stronger neo-kantian distinction between an acceptance of the value-laden basis on which the *questions* of inquiry are forged and a 'value-neutral' ethic in the actual *conduct* of inquiry (Oakes 1988; Hall 1999, pp. 39–41). Weber well recognized that he was eurocentric in the questions about modernity that he posed for empirical research, and he asserted that 'all knowledge of cultural reality is knowledge *from particular points of view*' (Weber 1949, p. 81, orig. emph.). Yet despite, or perhaps because of, this resolute ethic of value-neutrality, Weber consolidated a methodology that offered penetrating possibilities for the study of religion comparatively and historically, in ways that get at cultural meanings and their relationships to social action. This methodology centers on (1) *Verstehen*, or the interpretive understanding of meaning, and (2) the use of ideal types – sociohistorical models that bear comparison to empirical cases, identifying social action, organization, and other phenomena and processes in terms that are 'meaningfully adequate,' which is to say, incorporate logics of meaning as analytic components. 'Charisma,' for example, is not a personalistic and psychological characteristic of an individual; rather, it is a phenomenon based on meaningful patterns of action and social relationships, sometimes played out in a community (Weber 1978: 1111–20).

For the study of religion, Weber (1978, chap. 6) coupled *Verstehen* with an analytic framework of ideal types that conceptualize religious social phenomena along four central axes – (1) ideas and meaningful affects (e.g., asceticism, faith, piety, rationality), (2) practitioners (priests, prophets, preachers), (3) organizational structures (church, sect), and (4) the character of congregational participants (who have particular religious needs and interests, often conditioned by their wider social circumstances). Connecting everyday life with history, Weber could open up social phenomena to detailed analysis that linked institutional and organizational arrangements with inner meaningful experience, specific lifeworldly ethics, and typical modes of action associated with one or another social role. Thus, for example, he was able to investigate patterns of life meaning and careers, the institutional structures of power, and social organization in China in relation to both bureaucracy and Confucian and Taoist thought, in a way that allowed comparison to religion, self, and society in the West.

Particularly important for the study of religion, Weber's use of ideal types allowed him to analyze cultural specificities in comparison to general sociological typological concepts, thus neither 'pigeonholing' the specific within a general category, nor treating the subjects of his study as unique phenomena to be discussed only in historicist, idiographic, or individualistic terms. For the analysis of the Protestant ethic, to take one instance, Weber could examine the historically distinctive pathways to 'inner-worldly' (that is, internalized) asceticism of Calvinists, Methodists, Baptists, and Quakers, and contrast these with the 'other-worldly' monastic setting of asceticism that predominated in medieval Catholicism. The controversies over Weber's thesis about Protestantism are legion (Roth *et al.* 1995), but Weber's critics often draw on his methodology, employing *Verstehen* and ideal types to make their points. Weber's methodology thus has a salience even for those who contest his substantive analyses.

Both Troeltsch and Weber tended to be considerably more sociological than many scholars of the *Religionswissenschaft*. Rudolf Otto (1923) and Gerhardus van der Leeuw (1938) were more phenomenological, structuralist, and hermeneutic in their searches for the inner experience of religion, sometimes using comparison and historical analysis specifically to continue to get at the essential core of the sacred (Long 1967), rather than to probe analytic generalizations. Matters were different, but hardly more sociological, in the U.S. where Joachim Wach, and later, Joseph Kitagawa and Mircea Eliade, consolidated a fertile interdisciplinary history of religions at the University of Chicago (Kitagawa 1987, chap. 6). However, its sociology focused on cultural meaning rather than social organizations and institutions (Kitagawa 1959, pp. 19–21). Founders of the history of religions at the University of Chicago abandoned the older idealist historicism that would chart the *telos* of God, but they continued the historicist antipathy toward sociological generalization (Wach 1967 [1935]). Tellingly, Mircea Eliade dismissed Emile Durkheim for treating religion as a 'projection of social experience,' commenting, 'Though Durkheim identified religion with society, *Les formes élémentaires* does not, properly speaking, represent a contribution to the sociology of religion' (1963, p. 99).

Eliade's jibe notwithstanding, Durkheim's place in the sociology of religion remains assured, but for his substantive analysis rather than for any historical methodology. His functionalist approach did not connect well either to the analysis of religious meaning or to the comparative study of religion's social organizational and institutional features. Indeed, Durkheim's analyses in *The Division of Labor* (1947) and *The Elementary Forms of the Religious Life* (1995) in effect set modernity apart from both history and religion, by theorizing that with the complex division of labor in industrial society, 'organic' solidarity would displace 'mechanical' solidarity, undercutting the functional importance of religion for societal integration under modern conditions. This was an historical argument, of course, but one better accommodated to stage theories and functionalism than to a more fine-grained analysis of historical events, institutional structures, and social processes.

Reflecting Durkheim's – and French structuralism's – strong divide between theory and history, and emphasizing the temporal axis of a strong objectivist grid of diachrony versus synchrony, the French historians who founded the famous *Annales* school in the early twentieth century were, like the Chicago history of religions scholars, largely atheoretical in their work, even though it would be hard to miss the sociology implicit in many of their analyses (for example, in Marc Bloch's study) would be hard to miss as framed by Fernand Braudel, were to broaden historicism considerably beyond the political, to encompass multiple scales of time – from the immediate to the institutional, to long-term or 'ecological' time – and to address diverse social and cultural topics of history, from studies of everyday life to technology. Religion was certainly one of these topics. Thus, Lucien Febvre's 1942 study of religious thought artfully turned the question of whether Rabelais was an atheist into a study of *mentalités* concerned with the collective meaning that unbelief would hold in sixteenth-century Europe. Later, Emmanuel Le Roy Ladurie used archives from inquisition

interviews to weave his fascinating cultural inventory of local Pyrenees village life in the late thirteenth and early fourteenth centuries – *Montaillou: The Promised Land of Error* (1979). Much can be learned from Annales school studies, but they innovated more in topic than in method. Like many historians, participants in the Annales school drew on eclectic analytic strategies.

By contrast, the scholars taken to 'found' sociology – Tocqueville, Marx, Durkheim, and Weber among them – often invoked religion historically and comparatively, to explain both the character of modern societal development and its absence. This religious sociological interest in history continued in the early twentieth century, e.g., in the U.S. with H. Richard Niebuhr's (1929) study of American sects and denominations and their organizational developments, and Liston Pope's (1942) detailed study of churches, cotton mills, and the labor movement in a Southern mill town. But by mid-century, U.S.-based sociological positivism and structural-functionalism distanced sociology both from the German interpretive and historical tradition, and from historical research more generally.

Weber's legacy, like Durkheim's and that of the *Religionswissenschaft*, was strongly shaped by his reception in the U.S. – with an unfortunate result. Modernity became the enemy of history. With Europe rebuilding after World War II, Weber's ideas found their central transmission belt into mid-twentieth-century sociology via Talcott Parsons (1937), who read Weber in a decidedly normative and Durkheimian direction, aligning his own work with more conventionally scientific currents in American sociology by substituting a 'more parsimonious' framework of 'analytically real' variables for Weber's historically richer methodology of case comparisons using ideal types (Hall 1999, pp. 107–16).

More widely, many U.S. sociologists during the twentieth century sought to graft Weber's value-neutral approach onto sociology as a supposedly 'value-free' science. In the bargain sociology became divided from both history and any *verstehende* approach to cultural analysis. 'Value-free' social scientists followed the vision of positivism that had been first laid out early in the nineteenth century by Auguste Comte, aiming progressively to obtain knowledge about how society works in order to perfect it. For Comte, the basis of knowledge moves from theological to metaphysical to scientific, and science trumps history through societal control of human destiny. Perhaps connecting to this legacy (and to the strong French structuralist divide between diachrony and synchrony, history and structure), American sociologists of the mid-twentieth century widely embraced a bifurcation between social science and history, and directed their attention to scientifically structured theory and the use of census and survey data to conduct quantitative empirical research on contemporary society. Whence C. Wright Mills's famous critique of establishment sociology and his call in the late 1950s for a 'sociological imagination' that would connect social structure with biography and history.

CONTEMPORARY RESEARCH METHODOLOGIES

After Mills, unhistorical scientism did not last long. In the past fifty years, historicization of the social sciences (and increased social theoretical sophistication of historical inquiry) have created far more auspicious circumstances for sociohistorical research on religion. Already in the 1960s, comparative and historical sociology was emerging as an approach – or more accurately, array of approaches – that offered alternatives to structural-functionalism and quantitative empiricism. In the 1970s, building on pathbreaking research by scholars like E. P. Thompson, Reinhard Bendix, Barrington Moore, Charles Tilly, and Immanuel Wallerstein, historical sociologists began to reflect on the logics of historical and comparative methodologies. These efforts initially centered on exemplars, and on methodological debates over Marxism, the Weberian approach, and the formal logic of John Stuart Mill (see e.g., Roth 1976; contributors to Skocpol 1984a). Notably, both Skocpol and Somers

(1980; Skocpol 1984b) and Charles Tilly (1984) made the point that comparative-historical sociology could not be characterized by a single methodology. Skocpol and Somers identified three different logics of comparative-historical research – theory application, analytic generalization, and contrast-oriented comparison. Tilly sketched four strategies of propositional analysis: the study of individualizing propositions about a unique case, 'encompassing' comparisons dealing with multiple forms of an overall instance (such as a world economy), 'universalizing' analysis that seeks to subsume all instances under a general theoretical model, and 'variation-finding' investigations that identify alternative patterns of a phenomenon in a diverse set of cases.

A third approach, the Qualitative Comparative Analysis (QCA) of Charles Ragin (2000), formalized comparative research by consolidating a methodology to analyze the degree to which cases share patterns of variable attributes measurable across cases. Here, Ragin built on the two famous methods specified by John Stuart Mill in the nineteenth century – (1) the method of agreement, which holds that within a sample of very diverse cases, similarities that occur are likely to be patterned by some shared causal dynamic; and (2) the indirect (because non-experimental) method of difference that is meant to approximate for *in-situ* case studies the logic of experiments with control groups. This logic asserts an identifiable condition to be 'the effect, or the cause, or an indispensable part of the cause' in cases with one outcome, when this outcome is absent in other cases that lack the initial condition. Ragin's innovations, using set theory, are twofold. First, he provides analytically for the possibility that *different* sets of conditions may yield the *same* outcome. Second, he develops a basis for incorporating non-binary variables into comparative case analysis.

These efforts to think through historical and comparative methodologies have precipitated their own internal debates, and completely alternative epistemological developments now challenge them. On the internal front, researchers have explored questions about whether a 'case' could be easily specified as to its boundaries – in relation to other phenomena, and in relation to the question of what it might be a case *of* (see contributors to Ragin and Becker 1992). Related to these puzzles are issues about 'levels' of analysis, namely whether all cases need to be equivalent to each other in 'level' – all nation-states, all social movements, or so forth – or whether (and how) comparative historical analysis might move across 'levels' in studying any given case (such as revolutionary mobilization in the American revolution in cities and towns, colonies, and in the nation as a whole).

On the second front, projects to refine methodology in a formal sense have been countered since the 1970s by critical social epistemologies clustered under what has become known as the cultural (or sometimes, linguistic) turn – the movement associated with postmodern developments more broadly, instigated by historians such as Hayden White (for his critique of 'metanarratives,' such as those driven by the close association of religious meaning with historical narrative), feminists, people of color, and French intellectuals such as Michel Foucault, Jean-François Lyotard, and Jacques Derrida, under which rhetorical and narrative features of social accounts, as well as their relationships to social power and discipline, draw into question any value-neutral claims, and promote a more ironic, self-critical, and reflexive stance toward sociohistorical inquiry. The cultural turn that was unfolding in history and the humanities eventually began to have pronounced effects on methodologies of research. As a consequence, by the end of the twentieth century, sociohistorical inquiry could be understood as a wide interdisciplinary domain marked by 'integrated disparity' – with interrelated but contentiously different methodological practices and agendas of inquiry (Hall 1999).[2]

Methodologically, this domain of sociohistorical inquiry can be mapped by identifying four *particularizing* practices and four *generalizing* practices of research. These eight research practices are connected with one another because they share four methodologically relevant *forms of discourse* that they all employ – (1) value discourse, (2) narrative, (3) social

theory, and (4) explanation/understanding. But the practices differ from one another according to *how* these four forms of discourse articulate with one another in the orchestration of research – narrative in relation to theory, values in relation to explanation/understanding, and so forth. Below, I sketch the four particularizing and four generalizing methodological practices, and briefly mention for each a relevant exemplar in the study of religion. These ideal types in turn provide reference points for understanding, in the sections that follow, how historical scholarship on religion has actually been framed (for more detailed accounts of the methodological practices, see Hall 1999, chapters 8, 9).

Particularizing Practices

To particularize is to be centrally concerned with the study of a single relatively bounded sociohistorical phenomenon. Historians, who along with anthropologists are the scholars most committed to particularizing inquiry, conventionally employ (1) *historicism* as a methodology to analyze unique events in relation to an era or interconnected set of events as an 'historical individual' (e.g., the Reformation, the Cold War). In turn, three other particularizing practices offer alternatives to historicism: (2) *specific history*, centered on a set of events rendered coherent by the mutual orientation of social actors *in* history; (3) *configurational history*, in which a *researcher* frames theoretical or substantive questions that link issues and events potentially beyond the interests or knowledge of historical actors themselves; and (4) *situational history*, in which value-based questions directly structure analysis to produce analyses relevant to the individuals and groups who hold those values.

As we have seen, *historicism* emerged as Leopold von Ranke's alternative to idealist or spiritualized universal history. It reflects a conventional aversion among historians to formal methodology beyond a Rankean commitment to 'scientific' use of the archives. A narrative is constructed to tell 'what really happened' by treating the origins, genesis, and unique character of events in empiricist, self-referential, and seemingly antitheoretical terms. The problem of colligation – that is, selection of events drawn together to cohere as 'history' – is typically resolved by invoking events on the basis of their relation to a larger 'story.' Thus, Leopold von Ranke employed a history of elites – including the church – as the ordering axis, and much more recently, for American history, David Hackett Fischer's *Albion's Seed* used four successive waves of migration of distinct, religiously connected social strata as the axis of an analysis in which 'every period of the past, when understood in its own terms, is immediate to the present' (1989, p. x). But the basis of colligation is in principle open, for example, to the self-understanding of 'one nation under God,' or to an historicized marxism. By some such device, historicism investigates a reality deemed to have an existence independent of the practice of research, while linking that investigation with larger 'moral' stakes. Because historicism is implicitly committed to a value-based ordering principle of colligation, it is subject to ever new constructions of 'history' based on shifts in the ordering principle.

Second, *specific history* is a *verstehende* project that constructs a narrative about lived events in relation to the meanings given them by historical social actors – in anticipation, in unfolding action, and in memory. Because the 'plots' of actual life are manifold and overlapping, the plot of an intrinsic narrative is not determined solely by events, but rather, involves choices by the researcher, who could follow myriad alternative streams of specific history in relation to any given set of events, whether magic in the fourteenth century, household life among Chinese peasants, or the trajectory of a religious social movement, such as I traced in my study of Peoples Temple and Jonestown, *Gone from the Promised Land* (2004). Colligation in specific history thus varies widely in focus, from biography to the study of self-conscious social movements. Across this range, analysis centers on plot, clarified through narrative concerned with what happened and how, given the motives, goals, interactions, understandings, and

misunderstandings of the people involved. Theories relevant to diverse phenomena are deployed in relation to intrinsic narrative and the explanation and interpretation of contingencies, to yield an analytically rigorous account ordered not by the implicit value colligation of historicism, but by actors' meanings as they are asserted *in* history.

Third, *configurational history*, by contrast with specific history, depends on the researcher constructing a (typically analytic) narrative *extrinsic* to events. It operates theoretically by initially identifying the elements, conditions, and developments necessary for the occurrence of a particular 'configurational' social phenomenon, e.g., modern capitalism, an institutional arrangement of religion, or a family structure. The theoretically defined configuration is then used as a basis for generating questions of focused historical analysis, by seeking to identify and more deeply analyze 'break points' at which the fulfillment of conditions and creation of elements that comprise the phenomenon are in play. This strategy is not inherently comparative in the conventional sense, but it involves a strong use of social theory in relation to historical analysis, and is thus favored by historical sociologists (e.g., Max Weber, in his studies of the Protestant ethic, and more recently, Michael Mann) who seek to develop sociologically informed explanations of distinctive historical developments.

Fourth, *situational history* pursues research questions explicitly designed to address moral or political issues, producing knowledge useful for those with special interests in a situation – members of a social movement seeking to advance their cause, or a community buffeted by unwanted social forces. Such research addresses the questions of 'where we stand and are likely to go' (Roth 1976: 310). Lenin's revolutionary tract, *What is to be Done?*, stands as a classic, but even research that does not embrace revolution can combine resolute value commitment and hard-hitting inquiry. Yet ironically, scholars who study religion largely avoid this methodology, perhaps because they fear their research will be dismissed as biased. In such research, 'situation,' defined by value concerns (e.g., over the decline of a religious denomination), structures a distinctive set of questions, and although analytic rigor is paramount, narrative gives special attention to theories, interpretations, and explanations that have timely implications for one course of action over another. Inquiry thus potentially empowers individuals, groups (including religious ones), and even societies, by puzzling out the context, the motives and intentions of protagonists and other actors, and the social processes, conjunctures, and contingencies that shape current situation and future possibilities.

Generalizing Methodologies

In turn, four generalizing methodologies address research questions not easily considered in particularizing research, namely, whether a given account would hold up for other similar cases, and whether different conditions might yield the same or different outcomes. (1) *Universal history* drapes its historical analysis on a master theory or *telos* of history. Given the strong theorization, despite a tendency to focus on a single case, it can be considered a generalizing practice. The other three generalizing practices compare relatively bounded cases. (2) *Theory application* is used to explore how a theorized social process plays out historically in alternative situations. In turn, (3) *analytic generalization*, the favored method of comparative-historical sociology, centers on the logic pioneered by John Stuart Mill. Alternatively, theory can be deemphasized in favor of (4) *contrast-oriented comparison*, in which a substantive question structures comparisons of cases that yield insights and rules of experience rather than the testing of hypotheses.

The first generalizing practice, *universal history*, like situational history, is rarely used by scholars of religion, but for different reasons. It involves an effort to theorize 'history' in its totality, and scholars of religion now typically view such totalizing theories as suspect. The methodology proceeds by specifying an exhaustive general conceptual framework

(such as systems theory) or a temporally dynamic totality (for example, via marxism or world-systems theory, or possibly, a reconstructed social evolutionary theory). Systemic conditions marked by periodization and conjuncture give shape, significance, and developmental import to historical events.

Though totalizing theories stand in disrepute among many scholars today, world-systems analysts rightly observe that an increasingly interconnected world may be subject to encompassing processes that are rightful objects of inquiry. The warrant for this claim approximates astronomy, which studies only one observable universe, nevertheless subject to coherent and predictable processes. Like astronomy, universal history employs a paradigmatic theoretical framework, rarely modifying its fundamental concepts or theorizations, instead focusing on how particular phenomena advance or fail to advance the theorized *telos* of the totality. However, only interconnections constituting the totality are universal. Thus, like other researchers, those committed to universal history can study many phenomena within the totality using another generalizing or particularizing methodology.

In the second generalizing practice, *theory application*, the analyst seeks to bring parallel phenomena into view via narratives that apply a parsimonious theoretical lens to the analysis of cases, as Stark and Finke have done, for example, in their history of American religion (2005). Typically, a historically and contextually bounded social theory dictates the central issues of comparative plot analysis for case narratives, and explanation or interpretation centers on differentiating theoretically informed versus non-theoretical accounts, and on determining whether the non-theoretical accounts require modification or disconfirmation of the theory, or are simply matters that lie outside the theory's domain. The emphasis on close and careful comparison of a small number of cases offers bases for deepening the theorization of explanatory accounts and inductively refining the theory, but generalization typically is undermined by the small number of cases.

Third, *analytic generalization* encompasses the formal methods formulated by Mill and elaborated by Ragin (2000). Here, the researcher empirically tests hypotheses deduced from theories or induced from observations. Examples of research on religion that draw on this methodology include Robert Wuthnow's (1989) study of the Protestant reformation compared to two other ideological movements, and Philip Gorski's (2003) study of religion and state formation in Europe. In these uses of the methodology, and more widely, narrative is structured to offer the basis for adjudication of hypotheses in relation to theories, and the evaluation of alternative explanations and interpretations mediates the process of adjudication. The rigor of this practice approximates the intent of positivism. However, problems of measurement equivalence and sample size can threaten validity. For example, Lieberson (1992) argues that small numbers of cases preclude probabilistic arguments, and the number of variables of interest may overwhelm the cases analyzed, thus making deterministic causal relationships impossible to infer.

However, Emigh (1997) describes the methodological use of even single-case research as a basis for revising theories. And others have suggested a different logic than positivism. Goldstone (2003) points to the value of 'congruence testing' that yields knowledge about patterns shared even by a small number of cases. And Steinmetz (2004) and others hold that close analysis of a small number of cases can yield causal and interpretive knowledge about social processes in themselves and *in situ*. These strategies begin to shift away from analytic generalization, and toward contrast-oriented comparison.

Indeed, many researchers invoke historicity, culture, and contingency as circumstances that draw into question both any 'overly theorized' account of the social world, and any effort to seek analytic generalization by comparing cases that are not actually causally independent of one another. *Contrast-oriented comparison* offers an alternative. Here, explanation and interpretation order inquiry oriented to the production of relatively modest 'bounded generalizations' and 'rules of experience' through contingent and idiographic analysis of sociohistorical phenomena deemed kindred in relation to a theoretical theme. The focus is on how a particular social phenomenon (e.g., proletarianization, fundamentalism) plays out in different (but sometimes connected) sociohistorical contexts. This is basically how Clifford Geertz proceeded in his classic comparative analysis of Islam in Morocco and Indonesia. Geertz, and others who use the methodology, centrally employ narrative to trace the relations between contexts, processes, and outcomes. Because causal independence of cases is not assumed, accounts of genealogies, diffusion, and mutual influence can readily be incorporated into the analysis.

The delineation of these ideal typical research practices notwithstanding, the great practitioners of sociohistorical research have shown us that their craft cannot be adequately reduced to any formalization. Thus, research projects are often more complex than any one of the eight methodologies just described. A given research project will carve out its own distinctive strategy of inquiry, linking research questions, sources of data, and structures and logics of analysis. It may approximate one research practice on one front, and use another methodology to address other questions. For example, a generalizing contrast-oriented comparison might incorporate particularizing studies that use methodologies of specific or configurational history. Such possibilities come into view when the actual range of sociohistorical research on religion is considered.

HISTORICAL AND COMPARATIVE STUDIES OF RELIGION

The sociological study of religion has benefited tremendously from the renaissance of comparative and sociohistorical inquiry since the mid-twentieth century. Research has increased in sophistication, and the old problems of methodologically unreflexive idealism and historicism have become largely eclipsed by clarification and development of alternative methodologies. Yet sociohistorical research on religion has been unevenly distributed – in the academic venues where it is pursued, in its research agendas, and in its methodologies. Indeed, the three are related, as Philip Gorski (2005) has shown by reviewing past and emergent research agendas. In his analysis, sociologists of religion have more often used historical and comparative methods than religion has been incorporated by historical sociologists concerned with the 'classic' topics of state formation, class formation, revolution, and the like.

However, resurgence of religious fundamentalism around the globe has increased the importance of sociohistorical analysis. And indeed, the sociology of religion already was more open to historical analysis than many other subdisciplines of sociology because of its relation to the history of religions, and on the basis of its connections to university religious studies departments and such professional associations as the Society for the Scientific Study of Religion and the American Academy of Religion. Yet the very interdisciplinarity – and interest in specific groups and movements – in religious studies means that the resources of sociology and social theory more generally are sometimes less than fully utilized. Historically oriented sociologists of religion are well positioned to redress this tendency, in part because of the strong exemplars of research that can be drawn upon. Thus, given the challenge of forging a distinctive methodological practice in relation to substantive questions and sources of data, it is useful to examine how actual exemplars in the sociohistorical study of religion are methodologically structured.

To be sure, sociohistorical research on religion is diverse in its methodologies and topical foci, and scholarship often proceeds outside the frame of history *per se*. Some case studies – for example, those of Louis Dumont and M. N. Srinivas on the caste system in India – are distinctly theoretical in their problematics. Other works are not so theoretically oriented, but advance instead largely through the comparative analysis of religion. As noted above, Clifford Geertz's classic study *Islam Observed* (1968) employs a method of contrast-oriented comparison to consider the question of how

religion varies according to its societal context, in Morocco and Indonesia.

It should also be emphasized that qualitative field research can employ comparative methods. Such an approach is unusual, for field researchers typically adopt an attitude similar to historicism, in which a phenomenon is considered unique unto itself, to be understood in its own terms. However, *internal* comparison is sometimes a feature of field research in the sociology of religion, as with Stephen Warner's *New Wine in Old Wineskins* (1988), which examines a schism within a local congregation fueled by renegade evangelicals who begin to meet outside the institutional confines of their mainline Presbyterian church. And some research uses a comparative approach to address theoretical questions. Thus, Penny Edgell Becker (1999) sought to transcend the conservative-liberal continuum as a conceptual basis for differentiating local congregations, by developing a comparative typology centered on organizational structure, form of worship, social forms of congregational life, and other features. This approach – similar to the classic Weberian strategy – allows Becker to examine the degree to which a given congregation approximates the logic of one or more types, how a congregation handles commitments to divergent logics, and what its trajectory is. A Weberian methodology also facilitates comparison of one ideal type with another, as well as comparison of cases within the overall framework (Roth 1976).

Beyond case studies and sociological comparisons in field research, the range of sociohistorical methods in the study of religion can be fruitfully traced in relation to a classic question – the relationship of religion to social change, especially the emergence of modernity. Two broad agendas – somewhat at odds with one another – have been central. On the one hand, analyses of secularization fuel debates concerning whether religion is declining in institutional, social, and cultural significance and the degree to which religion has become permeated by non-religious modern features. On the other hand, there is the debate concerning the significance of religion – especially ascetic and rational Christianity – for the emergence of modernity in its various facets, from the overall character of modernity, to economic institutions, and state and nation structures. In turn, historical studies lend themselves to considering the nemeses of modernity – apocalyptic religious violence and fundamentalism. Although these various agendas are themselves connected in complex debates, it is worthwhile to consider the methodologies employed separately.

Secularization and Historical Studies

On the question of secularization, early functionalist and structuralist theories of modernization tended to encourage a kind of totalization of history via stage systems theories or analysis of evolutionary tendencies. The origins of this approach probably trace to Durkheim's binary account of the shift from mechanical to organic solidarity. However, David Martin's *A General Theory of Secularization* (1978) exemplifies a more nuanced methodology that approximates *contrast-oriented comparison*: his general theory sets up an initial basis for analyzing alternative trajectories of secularization under theoretically specified conditions (e.g., anti-clericalism, civil religion) that map onto world-regions – in England, America, Scandinavia, Latin countries, communist countries, and elsewhere. Martin's agenda could benefit from further historical inquiry, but the basic methodological strategy shows one way of pursuing a theoretical analysis comparatively, thereby taking account of the diverse conditions under which a theorized process occurs. A different approach is the careful *configurational history* by which Hugh McLeod (1974) has explored the social and cultural processes that led to the fading of Victorian religion in London (in good historical fashion, he avoids the conceptual reification of 'secularization').

In the past two decades, secularization theory has been challenged by rational-choice theorists, notably Rodney Stark and his colleagues (e.g., Stark and Bainbridge 1987). For example, Finke and Stark (2004) used a method of *theory application* to analyze shifting markets and preferences for religion over the course of American history. Also, Stark (1996) has applied a number of theories in sociological analyses of history in his book on the first four centuries of Christianity's consolidation.

In the face of the rational-choice challenge, the secularization thesis has been defended for Christian Europe (e.g., by Bruce 2002), while Davie (e.g., 2002) has adopted an intermediate view that asks whether religions tend to operate as public utilities (there when one needs them) or markets (in which people dissatisfied with one product search for another). But as Gorski (2005: 169–71) notes, debates over secularization and its rational-choice alternative have not been strongly informed by close historical-comparative study despite the centrality of historical transformations to the topic. True, a freewheeling discursive consideration of diverse comparative issues has taken place. But the central issue posed by the debate – the relation of religion to modernity – remains open to detailed research using historical-comparative methods. This project becomes all the more relevant in relation to debates over globalization and multiple modernities, and all the more urgent in the face of the rise of militant fundamentalist movements, notably, Islamicist ones. On these fronts, scholars debating secularization have a good deal to learn from the methodological strategies and analytic framings of research problems developed to study other facets of modernity.

The Significance of Religion for Modernity

Whereas secularization theorists and their rational-choice protagonists have centered their debates in sociological theories and definitions – of secularization, religious markets and monopolies, and the like – and focused on religion's waxing and waning, the problem of religion's relationship to modernity has had quite a different character among Weberian scholars and others concerned with gauging the influence of religion on the character of modern social forms, for example, rationalism and work asceticism. Weber's comparative civilizational analyses and his work on inner-worldly asceticism and modernity both centered on religion as a basis for differentiating alternative meaning structures of social organization. His research logic did not strictly follow the approach of John Stuart Mill, oriented toward identifying causal regularities. Rather, Weber favored *contrast-oriented comparison* that concentrated on explaining differences, especially the distinctiveness of Western social institutions. Yet the Weberian interest in religious meanings and social organization does not restrict research to a single methodological practice. Thus, Wolfgang Schluchter (1981; 1989, pt. 2) has formalized the sprawling typologies that Weber laid out in *Economy and Society*. His intellectual reconstruction links Weber's analyses to Parsons's pattern variables (e.g., universalism versus particularism), and yields a typological framework that sketches a *configurational history* of modernity, specifically, a developmental analysis of the emergence of Western rationalism that also continues Weber's practice of contrast-oriented comparison.

Other studies of modernity that bear a Weberian cast are more empirical than Schluchter's almost theoretical construction of historical development. For example, in *Communities of Discourse* (1989), Robert Wuthnow examines the Protestant Reformation along with two other ideological movements important to Europe – the Enlightenment and socialism. His approach uses a comparative logic of *analytic generalization* to examine the interactions of ideology with economic resources and structures of power. In the case of the Reformation, a key factor favoring the movement was the relative independence of the state from countervailing interests in central Europe, northern Europe, and England, compared to other areas, notably eastern Europe, France, and Spain, where landed interests were able to exercise greater influence over the adoption of Reformation ideology. In turn, institutional conditions and social interests in various regions of Europe influenced the selective adoption of Reformation ideas. The consequence of these diverse processes was variation in the degree to which religion became differentiated from state power. Thus, employing a methodology of analytic generalization, Wuthnow contributes not only to a Weberian discussion of religion's consequences for modernity, but through contrast-oriented comparison, reveals alternative trajectories and degrees of secularization.

Other scholarship on religion and modernity differentiates two lines of analysis that Wuthnow fused: (1) religious meaning, its institutional bearers, and its diffusion, adoption, and significance; and (2) macro-historical analyses of religion and state structures.

Religious meanings and institutions

On the first front, there is a venerable tradition of historical and comparative studies concerned with the relationship of the Protestant ethic to economic institutions, and to modern culture more broadly. In the 1950s, debates within Marxism and structural-functionalism framed this line of research. Thus, E. P. Thompson's classic *The Making of the English Working Class* (1963) is an *historicist* Marxist social history that takes account of Methodism's importance for the working classes of England. On the functionalist front, Robert Bellah (1957) used what amounted to a single-case study framed within a methodology of *analytic generalization* to ask whether late industrialization in Japan depended on values that provided a functional equivalent to Protestant inner-worldly asceticism. Another sociologist, Neil Smelser, engaged in *theory application* of Parsonian systems theory to study structural differentiation. In his analysis of the cotton industry and its workers in England, Protestant asceticism became analytically important for how it legitimized entrepreneurial dissatisfaction with production 'bottlenecks' that derived from incomplete systemic function integration of the textile production process (1959, pp. 65–77).

More recent historical studies have employed a variety of methodologies to zero in on modern 'Protestant' meanings, audiences, and their contexts. David Zaret (1985) carried out a social history of the Puritan conception of a 'heavenly contract' between God and believers, in particular addressing the economistic imagery of that contract's relation to salvation and its uneasy alignment with other Puritan ideas, notably predestination. As a good Weberian, Zaret considered covenant theology not just as a debate among religious elites, but in its social and organizational circumstances, analyzing how its development was forged by the interaction between religious virtuosi and lay practitioners. His detailed study of meanings in their social contexts – using a variety of sources of data beyond the conventional analyses of sermons and other clerical works – represents a *specific history*, but one that is framed in relation to theoretical issues originating in historians' debates over the *configurational history* of Protestantism.

Lutz Kaelber (1998) pushes Weberian analysis back to the European medieval period, focusing on lay and heterodoxical practices of rational asceticism, and why their social organizational contexts generally failed to encourage diffusion and institutionalization. Kaelber is very much the sociological historian who makes detailed use of archives. His work shows how a *configurational history* structured as an investigation of the genealogy of inner-worldly asceticism can employ *contrast-oriented comparison* to address key issues en route, for example, about the relation between chronological phases and regional variations of the Waldensian heresy, and the consequences of different formations of asceticism among the Waldenisans versus the Cathars.

At a more general level of analysis, James C. Russell (1994) has synthesized primary sources and secondary analyses to write a *configurational history* of the interaction between early Roman Christianity and the Germanic peoples, whose expectations encouraged a turn toward more magical, heroic, and folk religion, compared to the Church, which he characterizes as mainly world-rejecting in theology and urban in its locus. By carefully developing sociological constructs concerning religious virtuosi, structures of salvation and conversion, and other social phenomena, Russell is able to establish the conceptual benchmarks by which to chart a long-term shift toward the 'Germanization' of early medieval Christianity

that had consequences for modern Roman Catholicism.

Of course, for Weber, the paramount issue about the Protestant ethic concerned its consequences for the character of the self in modern individuals and their ways of experiencing and gearing into the world. One of his great achievements was to demonstrate how to use ideal types as a basis for rigorous analysis of alternative cultural meaning structures that shape identity. Yet Weber's example has been acknowledged more in the breach than in emulation. The reasons are historically complex. For much of the twentieth century, sociologists seeking to legitimate their discipline as a science shied away from cultural analysis, or else sought to reduce culture to yet another 'variable.' Cultural analysis often seemed like a trick of rhetoric that depends on 'enchanting' its audience (Schneider 1993). And indeed, for some of the great cultural analyses in the social sciences – books like Daniel Bell's *The Cultural Contradictions of Capitalism* (1977) – societal self-reflection eclipsed scholarly significance.

The multivalent importance of cultural historical analysis yields a methodological challenge – of whether and how to bridge interpretation and explanation, meaning adequacy and scientific rigor. Cultural historians have many options (Hall 2003a). For religion, one exemplar worthy of note is the study of modern culture by John Carroll, *Puritan, Paranoid, Remissive* (1977). As the title suggests, Carroll has traced a sequence of cultural identity complexes, moving from the Puritan through the Paranoid to, potentially, the establishment of a new cultural persona, the Remissive, who is freed from past burdens of individual and collective guilt to pursue a hedonistic life of self-fulfillment. Although Carroll's study is a typological sketch rather than a full *configurational history*, it is methodologically important for offering a vision of how historical formations of culture and self can be analyzed sociologically by use of Weberian, Freudian, and other conceptualizations that resuscitate specifically religious meaning as an axis for the analysis of modernity and its 'postmodern' developments.

Religion, nation, and state formation

Whereas it is mainly sociologists of religion who have concerned themselves with religious meanings, the relation of culture to nation and state formation has drawn wider attention from historical sociologists. Michael Hechter, for example, studied national solidarity and its connections to cultural boundaries (1975). Yet culture can be a diffuse phenomenon to analyze, and if Weber's analytic framework is a trustworthy guide, a sociological analysis of culture in relation to nation and state can be particularly fruitful if it attends to the social bases of culture creation and transmission, and to its institutional consequences. Though the implications of religion for economic institutions have been long studied and hotly debated, there have been few parallel analyses for nations and states. This situation is now changing, and two recent works suggest methodological approaches.

In *The Disciplinary Revolution*, Philip Gorski (2003: esp. 36, 163) theorizes in a Weberian and Foucauldian fashion that discipline of the Calvinist variety has been important for state formation because it increases social order and administrative efficiency, in part by promoting national cultural integration aligned with state boundaries (a tacit revisiting of Hechter's problematic). To explore this thesis, Gorski in effect uses two methodological practices – *contrast-oriented comparison* and *analytic generalization* to compare two Calvinist cases – the Netherlands from around 1550 to 1700 and Brandenburg-Prussia from around 1640 to 1750 – with each other and with other European cases (2003: 38). The former method allows Gorski to concentrate on the Calvinist cases, both to understand the influence of the historically earlier Dutch case on the later one, and to ferret out the differences in their trajectories based on variations in their societal contexts. The latter method, the comparative method classically formalized by John Stuart Mill, makes it possible to evaluate the thesis about the consequences of Calvinism or its absence for the consolidation of administratively effective modern states.

A second recent study, Anthony Marx's *Faith in Nation* (2003) addresses similar themes in a different way. Marx is concerned to understand nationalism not simply as a phenomenon of modern politics, but rather, as one having its basis in premodern exclusionary politics that allied religion and monarchy. To explore this thesis, Marx uses a practice of *contrast-oriented comparison* to analyze three major cases – Spain, France, and England/Scotland – in relation to a sequence of historical periods in which each formation of nationalism is mediated by opportunities and constraints. His and Gorski's analyses both demonstrate the importance of taking religion seriously in the analysis of nationalism and state formation, and they show how flexible methodologies can bring into view religious organizations and practitioners, religious ideas, and popular religion in their complex relations with state power and national institutions.

Apocalypse and Revolution

Where Gorski and Marx are centrally concerned with the relation of religion to state and nation, a different line of research pursues the connection of religion – often apocalyptic and millennialist religion – to political violence. The cases examined range widely in scale and significance, and the comparison of violent with non-violent groups is important. At one extreme are the small messianic sects driven by fantasies that puncture history, but without significant consequences such as the secret flagellants of Thuringia. At the other end of a continuum, some groups – the movement around Thomas Müntzer, the Mau Mau rebellion, and today, al Qaida – manage to catapult themselves into main currents of history. The central question – of how religion and violence are connected – has a rich tradition of historical research, and it remains of paramount importance today (Hall 2003b).

The practices of historical research that have facilitated study of religion and violence are diverse. Werner Stark's (1967) five-volume 'study of Christendom' certainly deserves attention, not especially for its amalgam of *configurational-historical* and *contrast-oriented comparative* methodologies, but because Stark puts the analysis of violence squarely into the study of the dynamics of church and sect in relation to nationalist and democratizing historical processes. Norman Cohn takes up similar themes but in a different way. His classic study of medieval European millennialist movements, *The Pursuit of the Millennium* (1970), is a loose *configurational history* of apocalypticisms, organized as a series of sometimes interconnected *specific histories* that trace the myriad patterns of millennial eschatology and their social manifestations from ancient Judaism to medieval and early modern Europe. Though Cohn addresses analytic questions along the way – the sociology of the Free Spirit heresy, for example – comparative analysis is left for the most part to a concluding chapter that ferrets out shared conditions under which groups arise, social strata attracted to such groups, and related sociological dynamics.

Bryan Wilson's *Magic and the Millennium* (1973) exemplifies an alternative methodology. It begins with an explicitly sociological typology of the kinds of peoples among whom, and social conditions under which, new religious movements emerge, and the character of meaningful responses (thaumaturgical/magical, versus millennial). This framework then serves as the basis for a *contrast-oriented comparison* that seeds theoretical analysis at various points within subsequent chapters' discussions of specific cases – themselves organized in relation to the book's initial typology. Comparative conclusions avoid strong generalization.

A quite different practice, *specific history*, is used in my (2004) study of the apocalyptic movement of Jim Jones and Peoples Temple. In part, a *verstehende* methodology traces the transformations in meanings given to the ideology of 'revolutionary suicide' in the course of the Temple's confrontation with external opponents. The dynamics unearthed in that study in turn became the basis for an initial sociohistorical model (ideal type) of 'warring apocalypse' that I and my colleagues Philip Schuyler and Sylvaine Trinh later used in

Apocalypse Observed (2000). There, we employed a methodology of *contrast-oriented comparison* to analyze five contemporary cases of collective suicide, in the end, drawing on an inductive method to develop a second model – of 'mystical apocalypse' – to explore the cultural logic of collective suicide in which concerted external opposition was minimal – by Heaven's Gate, and in a different way, by the Solar Temple.

Fundamentalism

When the lens is rotated a bit, a related line of analysis comes into view. 'Fundamentalism' is a fraught term for sociological analysis, since like apocalypticism, its cultural content can vary so much. Thus, the problem of cross-cultural comparison is particularly acute. Among the extensive scholarship on fundamentalism, two studies mark distinctive methodological strategies for dealing with this challenge. Martin Riesebrodt's *Pious Passions* (1993) is predicated on the relative absence of effective comparative research on fundamentalist movements, and therefore proceeds by seeking to develop an initial sociological model based on detailed comparative analysis of ideology, carrier groups, and causes of mobilization within two quite different movements – U.S. Protestant fundamentalism in the 1910s and 1920s, and fundamentalism in Iran during the 1960s and 1970s. The implicit methodology is an inductive form of *analytic generalization* – John Stuart Mill's 'method of agreement' that isolates crucial similarities in a diverse set of cases. The application of this methodology acknowledges differences between the two cases, but nevertheless characterizes shared elements of fundamentalism as 'radical patriarchalism' concerned with moral decay in the family and society, spawned especially under conditions of rapid urbanization.

Riesebrodt develops a general analytic model from close case comparison that portrays fundamentalism as a quintessentially modern phenomenon. By contrast, in *Fundamentalism, Sectarianism, and Revolution*, Eisenstadt (1999) has explored the religiously dualistic and fundamentalist origins of modern radical secular utopianism. He argues that the dualism of Western monotheistic religions is especially prone to utopian millennialism because it posits a radical divide between the mundane world and the utopian world as envisioned by the elect. Eisenstadt identifies the secular progeny of this religious ideology as modern Jacobinism – the ideology that would inaugurate a totalistic transformation of society through violent political action, and he provides a *configurational history* of Jacobinism's relation to fundamentalist religion and apocalyptic eschatology. This configurational history is undergirded by comparative analysis of Judaism, Christianity, and Islam, especially in contrast to other world religions, and fleshed out through *contrast-oriented comparison* of Jacobinism as it plays out in different societal and historical contexts in the modern era.

RELIGION AND HISTORY: TOWARD A SOCIOLOGY OF KNOWLEDGE

This brief and highly selective survey of historical methodologies used in the study of religion demonstrates two general points. First, as Riesebrodt (1993: 196) observed in discussing fundamentalism, religion cannot be summarily glossed by framing its consideration solely in relation to non-religious social theoretical conceptualizations. Certainly religion is amenable to analysis in relation to theories of organizations, social movements, identity formation, and the like. However, it is not reducible to them, for religion is a phenomenon *sui generis*. Indeed, as Durkheim and Weber both well understood, there is much to be said for bringing categories of religious analysis (e.g., the sacred, communion, community, charisma and its routinization, community, ritual, church, sect, schism, and so on) to bear in wider inquiry. Theoretically informed historical inquiry on religion ought to be nurtured and developed, for scholars of religion themselves, and for a wider audience in the human sciences and society-at-large.

Second, although sociohistorical studies of religion range widely in their methodological approaches, some methodologies have been favored more than others. Of course, the present survey reflects my own biases. Though there are many meritorious historicist studies of religion (for example, studies of American religious history), I have not concentrated on them, for historicism as an approach is not particularly methodologically self-conscious; rather, its topics are often framed by historiographic criticism of previous studies. Though some scholars in the humanities have gravitated to an interdisciplinary 'new' historicism, this move seems problematic in light of epistemological critiques associated with the cultural turn (Hall 1999: 220–8). Thus, consideration of historicist studies does not help much in getting at basic methodological issues.

In the wake of the cultural turn, many historians are becoming more reflexive about their methodologies. Fortunately, those interested in religion have a wide range of exemplars demonstrating alternatives to historicism, most notably various studies approximating *specific history* that uses interpretive methods to provide a *verstehende* account of history as it is meaningful to historical actors (among exemplars discussed above, Zaret, Hall), and studies centered in *configurational history* that self-consciously frame historical topics by way of researchers' theoretical or analytic questions (Schluchter, Russell, Carroll, Eisenstadt). Among generalizing studies, a diversity of methods similarly obtains for the study of religion. Although *theory application* confronts a widespread contemporary suspicion of overly theorized accounts of religion, Stark and his associates have done a great deal to demonstrate its potential. That said, the more favored methodology is *analytic generalization*, using either inductive reasoning or hypotheses deduced from theory (Bellah, Wuthnow, Becker, Riesebrodt). Finally, the generalizing approach that enjoys especially frequent use is *contrast-oriented comparison*, for it is designed to take into account conditions of historicity and nuances of cultural meanings that are of central concern in sociohistorical studies of religion.

Of course, many studies encompass more than one logic of research. A given research practice may fold other practices within its discourse, or be constructed as a hybrid that bridges two methodologies – a point demonstrated by Kaelber's (1998) artful balance of configurational history and contrast-oriented comparison and Gorski's (2003) shifts between analytic generalization and contrasting comparison. Notably, the genre of historical analysis that has enjoyed strongest growth in the past quarter century, cultural history, is often carried out as a hybrid of specific and configurational histories, sometimes with important contrast-oriented comparisons (Hall 2003a). Here, a central challenge concerns how to mediate historical particularity and general explanation whilst identifying processes and mechanisms (for approaches, see Biernacki 2000; Hall 2000; Kane 2000).

Yet knowledge is shaped not only by the methodologies employed, but also by methodologies forsworn. In the twentieth century, scholars of religion outside schools of theology generally sought to avoid both universal history – the grand metanarrative of religion and history – and situational history based on value commitments. The reasons were several. Both the modernist urge to separate fact from value and the concern of scholars of religion to gain legitimacy outside religious circles rendered these methodologies suspect. Universal religious history became eclipsed by a general distrust of metanarrative and a strongly secular intellectual culture whose participants shuddered at any thought of religious *telos* or destiny. Situational history became largely the province of scholars aligned with the secular political Left, who asked, as Lenin had, 'What is to be done?'

However, the postmodern condition has changed all this. Both Christian fundamentalists and Islamicists have demonstrated Schleiermacher's point that religion *as* history is not a dead letter. Given these developments, the secularity of modern scholarship has had an unintended consequence. Public intellectuals, who not only adhered to, but embraced, a separation of religion from the public sphere have left postmodern society bereft of the kind

of analysis that Schleiermacher attempted for an earlier era – one that would envision human hopes and destinies by way of a direct engagement of the sacred, not simply in its exegetical sources in ancient religious texts, but in its contemporary social and cultural conditions, challenges, and possibilities. Such a venture might seem anathema to most modernists. But certain thinkers – most notably Jürgen Habermas (1987) – have criticized the binary of fact and value both as an overdrawn empirical description of modern knowledge production, and as an inadequate ethos to guide the production of knowledge. This questioning of the fact-value distinction portends the potential for new relationships between commitment and scholarship. Thus, metanarrative may not be dead. Historian William Hagen (2007) has argued that if metanarrative is taken to encompass 'large scale and long-term historical conceptualizations,' not only is it unavoidable – even in the most micro histories – but researchers would be well served by the use of 'non-tyrannical master narratives, open to falsification and revision.' Reformulated in these terms, universal history can again become an honorable – and important – scholarly project. On a different front, Jeffrey Alexander (1986) and Roger Friedland (2005) seek to advance a 'religious sociology,' one that recognizes religion as inseparable from social life, and therefore places issues about religion at the core of sociology. In substantive analysis, this possibility can be pushed further by arguing, as Adam Seligman (2004) does, that pervasive social and sociological issues – for example, concerning matters of community and of conflict – may be fruitfully addressed from 'outside' secularity, within a religious domain of discourse.

Such new approaches depend upon sociohistorical research, because after all, it is historical possibility that is at stake. For those who share particular values or goals, situational history addresses questions of immediate importance concerning their circumstances and prospects. On the other hand, universal history seeks to discern the larger patterns of history in ways significant to us all. Thus, ironically, a new historical moment recoups the importance of the very methodological practices that lost ground in the modern period. In our era, questions about the historicity of religion have emerged from the quiet shadows. Those who want to say something about these questions will be well served by taking on methodology as central to their calling, for its practice undergirds knowledge.

NOTES

1. See Sharpe (1975), who provides a study of the ancient precursors and modern developments of comparative-historical studies in religion.

2. For a more detailed account of the cultural turn, see Hall 2003a. In Adams *et al.*'s introduction to *Remaking Modernity* (2005), they chart the consequences of the cultural turn for historical and comparative sociology in the U.S., and contributors to the volume survey substantive comparative and historical agendas – especially in the U.S. – under contemporary epistemological conditions of inquiry.

REFERENCES

Adams, Julia, Elisabeth S. Clemens and Ann S. Orloff (eds) 2005. *Remaking Modernity*. Durham, NC: Duke University Press.

Alexander, Jeffrey 1986. 'Rethinking Durkheim's intellectual development II: working out a religious sociology.' *International Sociology* 1: 189–201.

Becker, Penny Edgell 1999. *Congregations in Conflict*. Cambridge: Cambridge University Press.

Bell, Daniel 1977. *The Cultural Contradictions of Capitalism*. New York: Basic.

Bellah, Robert 1957. *Tokugawa Religion*. Glencoe, IL: Free Press.

Bendix, Reinhard 1970. *Embattled Reason*. New York: Oxford University Press.

Biernacki, Richard 2000. 'Language and the shift from signs to practices in cultural inquiry.' *History and Theory* 39: 289–310.

Bruce, Steve 2002. *God is Dead*. Oxford: Blackwell.

Carroll, John 1977. *Puritan, Paranoid, Remissive*. London: Routledge & Kegan Paul.

Cohn, Norman 1970 [1957]. *The Pursuit of the Millennium*. Oxford: Oxford University Press.

Davie, Grace 2002. *Europe: The Exceptional Case*. London: Darton, Longman and Todd.

Durkheim, Emile 1947 [1893]. *The Division of Labor in Society*. New York: Free Press.

Durkheim, Emile 1995 [1912]. *The Elementary Forms of the Religious Life*. Karen Fields, trans. New York: Simon and Schuster.

Eisenstadt, S. N. 1999. *Fundamentalism, Sectarianism, and Revolution: The Jacobin Dimension of Modernity*. Cambridge: Cambridge University Press.

Eliade, Mircea 1963. 'The history of religions in retrospect: 1912–1962.' *Journal of Bible and Religion* 31: 98–109.

Emigh, Rebecca 1997. 'The power of negative thinking: the use of negative case methodology in the development of sociological theory.' *Theory and Society* 26: 649–84.

Febvre, Lucien 1982 [1942]. *The Problem of Unbelief in the Sixteenth Century: The Religion of Rabelais*. Cambridge: Harvard University Press.

Finke, Roger and Rodney Stark 2004 [1992]. *The Churching of America, 1776–1990*, rev. ed. New Brunswick, NJ: Rutgers University Press.

Fischer, David Hackett 1989. *Albion's Seed: Four British Folkways in America*. New York: Oxford University Press.

Friedland, Roger 2005. 'Religious terror and the erotics of exceptional violence.' *Anthropological Yearbook of European Culture* 14: 39–74.

Geertz, Clifford 1968. *Islam Observed*. New Haven, CT: Yale University Press.

Gilbert, Felix 1990. *History: Politics or Culture? Reflections on Ranke and Burckhardt*. Princeton, NJ: Princeton University Press.

Goldstone, Jack 2003. 'Comparative historical analysis and knowledge accumulation in the study of revolutions.' In James Mahoney and Dietrich Reuschemeyer (eds), *Comparative Historical Analysis*. Cambridge: Cambridge University Press, pp. 41–90.

Gorski, Philip S. 2003. *The Disciplinary Revolution*. Chicago: University of Chicago Press.

Gorski, Philip S. 2005. 'The return of the repressed: religion and the political unconscious of historical sociology.' pp. 161–89 in Adams, Clemens, and Orloff 2005.

Habermas, Jürgen 1987 [1981]. *The Theory of Communicative Action, Vol. 2: Lifeworld and System*. Boston: Beacon Press.

Hagen, William 2007. 'Master narratives beyond postmodernity: Germany's "separate path" in historiographical-philosophical light.' *German Studies Review* 30: 1–32.

Hall, John R. 1999. *Cultures of Inquiry: From Epistemology to Discourse in Sociohistorical Research*. Cambridge: Cambridge University Press.

Hall, John R. 2000. 'Cultural meanings and cultural structures in historical explanation.' *History and Theory* 39: 331–47.

Hall, John R. 2003a 'Cultural history is dead long live the Hydra.' pp. 151–67 in Gerard Delanty and Engin Isin (eds), *Handbook for Historical Sociology*. Beverly Hills, CA: Sage.

Hall, John R. 2003b. 'Religion and violence: social processes in comparative perspective.' pp. 359–81 in Michele Dillon (ed.), *Handbook of the Sociology of Religion*. Cambridge: Cambridge University Press.

Hall, John R. 2004 [1987]. *Gone from the Promised Land: Jonestown in American Cultural History*. New Brunswick, NJ: Transaction.

Hall, John R., with Philip Schuyler and Sylvaine Trinh 2000. *Apocalypse Observed*. London: Routledge.

Hechter, Michael 1975. *Internal Colonialism*. London: Routledge & Kegan Paul.

Hume, David 1976 [1757]. *The Natural History of Religion*. Oxford: Clarendon Press.

Iggers, Georg G. 1975. 'The image of Ranke in American and German historical thought.' *History and Theory* 2: 17–40.

Kaelber, Lutz 1998. *Schools of Asceticism: Ideology and Organization in Medieval Religious Communities*. University Park: Penn State University Press.

Kane, Anne 2000. 'Reconstructing culture in historical explanation: narratives as cultural structure and practice.' *History and Theory* 39: 311–30.

Kant, Immanuel 1963 [1784]. 'Idea for a universal history from a cosmopolitan point of view.' pp. 11–26 in *On History*, Lewis W. Beck (ed.) Indianapolis: Bobbs-Merrill.

Kippenberg, Hans G. 2002. *Discovering History in the Modern Age*. Princeton, NJ: Princeton University Press.

Kitagawa, Joseph M. 1959. 'The history of religions in America.' pp. 1–30 in Mircea Eliade and Joseph M. Kitagawa (eds), *The History of Religions: Essays in Methodology*. Chicago: University of Chicago Press.

Kitagawa, Joseph M. 1987. 'The history of religions at Chicago.' Chapter 6, pp. 133–44 in Kitagawa, *The History of Religions*. Atlanta, GA: Scholars Press.

Köhnke, Klaus Christian 1991. *The Rise of Neo-Kantianism*. New York: Cambridge University Press.

Kumar, Krishan 2003. 'Aspects of the Western utopian tradition.' *History of the Human Sciences* 16: 63–77.

Le Roy Ladurie, Emmanuel 1979 [1975]. *Montaillou: The Promised Land of Error*. New York: Random House.

Lieberson, Stanley 1992. 'Small *N*'s and big conclusions: an examination of the reasoning in comparative studies based on a small number of cases.' In Charles C. Ragin and Howard S. Becker (eds) pp. 105–118.

Long, Charles H. 1967. 'Archaism and hermeneutics.' pp. 67–87 in Joseph M. Kitagawa (ed.), *The History of Religions: Essays on the Problem of Understanding*. Chicago: University of Chicago Press.

Manuel, Frank E. 1965. *Shapes of Philosophic History*. Stanford, CA: Stanford University Press.

Martin, David 1978. *A General Theory of Secularization*. Oxford: Blackwell.

Marx, Anthony W. 2003. *Faith in Nation*. Oxford: Oxford University Press.

McLeod, Hugh 1974. *Class and Religion in the Late Victorian City*. London: Croom Helm.

McLeod, Hugh 1996. *Piety and Poverty: Working-class Religion in Berlin, London, and New York, 1870–1914*. New York: Holmes and Meier.

Niebuhr, H. Richard 1929. *The Social Sources of Denominationalism*. New York: Henry Holt.

Oakes, Guy 1988. *Weber and Rickert: Concept Formation in the Cultural Sciences*. Cambridge: MIT Press.

Otto, Rudolf 1923. *The Idea of the Holy*. Oxford: Oxford University Press.

Parsons, Talcott 1937. *The Structure of Social Action*. New York, NY: Free Press.

Patrides, C. A. 1972. *The Grand Design of God*. London: Routledge & Kegan Paul.

Pope, Liston 1942. *Millhands and Preachers*. New Haven, CN.: Yale University Press.

Ragin, Charles C. 2000. *Fuzzy-Set Social Science*. Chicago: University of Chicago Press.

Ragin, Charles C. and Howard S. Becker (eds) 1992. *What is a Case?* New York: Cambridge University Press.

Reill, Peter H. 1975. *The German Enlightenment and the Rise of Historicism*. Berkeley: University of California Press.

Rickert, Heinrich 1986 [1902]. *The Limits of Concept Formation in Natural Science: A Logical Introduction to the Historical Sciences*. New York, NY: Cambridge University Press.

Riesebrodt, Martin 1993. *Pious Passion*. Berkeley: University of California Press.

Roth, Guenther 1976. 'History and sociology in the work of Max Weber.' *British Journal of Sociology* 27: 306–18.

Roth, Guenther, David Lazar and Christof Mauch (eds) 1995. *Weber's Protestant Ethic: Origins, Evidence, Contexts*. Cambridge: Cambridge University Press.

Russell, James C. 1994. *The Germanization of Early Medieval Christianity*. Oxford: Oxford University Press.

Schleiermacher, Friedrich 1996 [1799]. *On Religion: Speeches to its Cultured Dispisers.* Cambridge: Cambridge University Press.

Schluchter, Wolfgang 1981. *The Rise of Western Rationalism: Max Weber's Developmental History.* Berkeley: University of California Press.

Schluchter, Wolfgang 1989. *Rationalism, Religion, and Domination.* Berkeley: University of California Press.

Schluchter, Wolfgang 1996. *Paradoxes of Modernity: Culture and Conduct in the Theory of Max Weber.* Stanford, CA: Stanford University Press.

Schneider, Mark 1993. *Culture and Enchantment.* Chicago: University of Chicago Press.

Seligman, Adam 2004. *Modest Claims: Dialogues and Essays on Tolerance and Tradition.* Notre Dame, IN: University of Notre Dame Press.

Sharpe, Eric J. 1975. *Comparative Religion: A History.* London: Duckworth.

Skocpol, Theda (ed.) 1984a. *Vision and Method in Historical Sociology.* Cambridge: Cambridge University Press.

Skocpol, Theda 1984b. 'Emerging agendas and recurrent strategies in historical sociology.' pp. 356–391 in Theda Skocpol (ed.) *Vision and Method in Historical Sociology.* Cambridge: Cambridge University Press.

Skocpol, Theda and Margaret Somers 1980. 'The uses of comparative history in macrosocial inquiry.' *Comparative Studies in Society and History* 22: 174–97.

Smelser, Neil 1959. *Social Change in the Industrial Revolution.* Chicago: University of Chicago Press.

Stark, Rodney 1996. *The Rise of Christianity: A Sociologist Reconsiders History.* Princeton: Princeton University Press.

Stark, Rodney and Roger Finke 2005. *The Churching of America, 1776–2005* (2nd edn), New Brunswick, NJ: Rutgers University Press.

Stark, Rodney and William Sims Bainbridge 1987. *A Theory of Religion.* New York: Peter Lang.

Stark, Werner 1967. *The Sociology of Religion: A Study of Christendom,* 5 volumes. New York: Fordham University Press.

Steinmetz, George 2004. 'Odious comparisons: incommensurability, the case study, and "small N's" in sociology.' *Sociological Theory* 22: 371–400.

Thompson, E. P. 1963. *The Making of the English Working Class.* New York: Pantheon.

Tilly, Charles 1984. *Big Structures, Large Processes, Huge Comparisons.* New York, NY: Russell Sage.

Troeltsch, Ernst 1912. *Protestantism and Progress: A Historical Study of the Relation of Protestantism to the Modern World.* London: Williams & Norgate.

Troeltsch, Ernst 1972 [1901]. *The Absoluteness of Christianity and the History of Religions.* London: SCM Press.

Troeltsch, Ernst 1991a [1898]. 'Historical and dogmatic method in theology.' pp. 11–32 in Ernst Troeltsch, *Religion in History,* intro. by James Luther Adams. Edinburgh: T&T Clark.

Troeltsch, Ernst 1991b [1904]. 'Modern philosophy of history.' pp. 273–320 in Ernst Troeltsch, *Religion in History,* intro. by James Luther Adams. Edinburgh: T&T Clark.

Troeltsch, Ernst 1992 [1912]. *The Social Teachings of the Christian Churches,* 2 vols. Louisville, KY: Westminster/John Knox Press.

van der Leeuw, Gerhardus 1938 [1933]. *Religion in Essence and Manifestation: A Study in Phenomenology.* London: Allen & Unwin.

Wach, Joachim 1967 [1935]. 'The meaning and task of the history of religions.' pp. 1–19 in Joseph M. Kitagawa (ed.), *The History of Religions: Essays on the Problem of Understanding.* Chicago: University of Chicago Press.

Warner, R. Stephen 1988. *New Wine in Old Wineskins: Evangelicals and Liberals in a Small-town Church.* Berkeley: University of California Press.

Wax, Murray 1960. 'Ancient Judaism and the Protestant ethic.' *American Journal of Sociology* 35: 449–55.

Weber, Max 1949. *The Methodology of the Social Sciences.* New York, NY: Free Press.

Weber, Max 1978. *Economy and Society,* Guenther Roth and Claus Wittich, (eds). Berkeley: University of California Press.

Wilson, Bryan R. 1973. *Magic and the Millennium.* London: Heinemann.

Wuthnow, Robert 1989. *Communities of Discourse,* Cambridge: Harvard University Press.

Zaret, David 1985. *The Heavenly Contract: Ideology and Organization in Pre-revolutionary Puritanism.* Chicago: University of Chicago Press.

PART III

Social Forms and Experiences of Religion

Sociologists can afford to ignore the metaphysical question of whether religious beliefs are actually grounded in transcendental reality. This is the work of mystics, theologians and philosophers. Instead, one of the many tasks of sociologists is to examine the forms in which religious values, beliefs and experiences occur. The five chapters to follow explore some of the most important social forms – or 'vehicles' – of religion. They are the social and cultural devices for producing, expressing and reproducing religion across cultures, space and time. Not only do they 'convey' religion, but they also 'contain' and encapsulate it in distinctive arrangements. Even when religious traditions share underlying patterns of, say, leadership, assembly, worship, and regulation, each tradition tends to displays them in distinctive forms. If it is true, then, that 'the gods have feet of clay,' sociologists of religion are in the business of analysing divine footwear.

The full variety of religion's social forms is too vast and intricate to be compressed into a few chapters, so we have selected five aspects that indicate something of the range of possibilities – at least within the West. They include congregations, Pentecostal and Evangelical mobilisations, new religious movements and sects, New Age, parapsychology and atheistic movements, and civil religion.

Beginning with the formal organisation of religion, **Jay Demerath and Arthur Farnsley** argue in Chapter 9 that the sociological study of congregations has blossomed in recent decades and that congregational forms of organisation are no longer an exclusive property of Christian churches, denominations or sects. Using original data from an investigation of congregations in the city of Indianapolis, Indiana, they note that, like birds of a feather, people from similar social backgrounds tend to 'congregate' together. Other research has documented the growing differentiation of congregations in accordance with their shared background characteristics, principal orientations to the world, and strategies of responding to changes in their social and cultural environments. Demerath and Farnsley's own four-fold typology emphasises how different types of congregation respond to cross-cutting pressures in urban settings. But local congregations of very different types find it increasingly difficult to retain the loyalty of their local parishioners, and they increasingly find themselves in tension with their national denominational bureaucracies. Religious developments in many regions of the world confirm the importance of congregations as basic units of Christian practice. And while Islam, Hinduism and Buddhism all have their own distinctive forms of religious community and sociability, there are growing congregational equivalents even in these traditions.

The case of 'global popular Protestantism' confirms the importance of the congregational form of religion, but **Paul Freston** also argues in Chapter 10 that Christian evangelicalism and the surge of Pentecostalism and fundamentalism around the world deserve sociological analysis for other reasons. In particular, their extraordinarily rapid and pervasive spread into many countries of Latin America, sub-Saharan Africa and Asia has major political implications for democracy and civil order. This new wave of globalising Christianity recalls earlier forms of church missionising beginning some three-hundred years ago, but now the missionaries are likely to come from the global South rather than from Western Europe or North America. And yet the propensity to violence that is such a frequent fundamentalist stereotype is weaker among Christians than some other faith traditions, and recent survey findings indicate that evangelicals' moral and political attitudes do not bear out a US-style 'culture wars' scenario. However, because global evangelicalism seems to be quite differentiated according to its political locale, it is unlikely to promote a new and unified model of global Christendom despite its immense potential for transforming the personal, economic, and political lives of billions across the world's southern hemisphere.

It seems improbable that new religious movements (NRMs) will ever have the same transformative capacity as global evangelicalism. But, as **Thomas Robbins and Phillip Lucas** show in Chapter 11, these movements present sociologists with some exciting opportunities that make it worthwhile – and difficult – to examine them as a distinctive form of contemporary religion. For example, their relative newness brings developmental processes and generational shifts into clear focus; and their relative simplicity of authority structures casts light on leadership issues. At the same time, the sociological study of NRMs faces challenges concerning their definition, their comparability with other forms of religion and their

meaning in theoretical terms. In particular, Robbins and Lucas assess the explanatory usefulness of theoretical ideas about secularisation, globalisation, rational choice, post-modernity and sect-church dynamics in relation to case studies of two different NRMs. They stress the need for sociologists of religion to ensure that their conceptual and explanatory ideas are continually adjusted to fit changing circumstances and to take advantage of intellectual developments in neighbouring fields of study.

Recent developments in the relatively mercurial forms of religion and spirituality associated with the New Age, parapsychology and Transhumanism certainly challenge sociologists of religion to consider whether a re-think of their conventional ideas is required. **William Bainbridge** argues in Chapter 12 that these subtle and shifting new types of consciousness and reflexive practice are more loosely organised than other forms of religion and less resistant to influences coming from the scientific and technological centres of secular culture. Some are merely 'audience cults'; others are 'client cults'; while a third category contains 'cult movements' with the characteristics of fully fledged religious organisations. The many varieties of parapsychology are also shown to take one or more of these three social forms, as illustrated by the Telepathy Developing Circle ritual within the Process Church of the Final Judgment. Bainbridge also assesses various explanations of atheistic beliefs, predicting that 'long-submerged tensions between religion and science are beginning to resurface' in movements such as Transhumanism and Extropianism. His provocative conclusion is that convergence between various fields of cognitive science could herald a significantly greater threat to organised religion because it unifies science as a set of principles in contradiction to religion. On the other hand, we may be entering a period when more innovative religions arise, embracing some of the new scientific ideas – a truly New Age.

The most loosely organised vehicle of religion to be considered in this Part is civil religion. As a form of national self-veneration through its most common religious denominator, its lack of formal organisations or local groups does not mean that civil religion cannot be a carrier of significant nationalist ideas, sentiments and practices in many countries. In fact, **Marcela Cristi and Lorne Dawson** claim in Chapter 13 that civil religion operates in some circumstances as an 'instrument of national unity.' Nonetheless, it can also be a focus for intense controversy. The concept of civil religion has a long history, but it was Robert Bellah's celebrated 1967 essay on 'Civil religion in America' that sparked a continuing debate about the validity of the concept and its applicability to countries other than the US – especially against the background of globalisation, on the one hand, and growing religious diversity, on the other. According to Cristi and Dawson, the debate turns largely on the question of whether civil religion is an effective integrative force on the basis of shared values or a divisive political source of elite manipulation. The US is invariably the reference point for national comparisons with its national days of patriotic celebrations and non-denominational prayers at the beginning of each day in Congress. But research has shown that it is exceptional in many respects and that there are at least three common types of civil religion. The challenge for sociologists of religion is not only to cut through the conceptual confusion but to take proper account of the changes in US society and the effects of globalisation on all national societies. Clearly the prospects for a 'global civil religion' remain remote.

9

Congregations Resurgent

N. J. DEMERATH III AND ARTHUR E. FARNSLEY II

In recent years, few topics in the sociology of religion have enjoyed more attention than congregations, and it is worth wondering why they have sparked a veritable growth industry? Certainly this is not because congregations are a new phenomenon, though we will note that they are now less taken for granted in their older settings and more prominent in new non-Christian religions around the globe. Nor is it because congregations have never been studied before, though we will show how new methodologies allow new types of research on a larger scale. Certainly it is not because they are newly debated, though we will see how the nature of the debate has changed. In the 1960s, many critics saw congregations as an escape from religion's ethical responsibilities in a world crying out for change; today many analysts see congregations as the Maginot line in defending religion's core functions against the onslaught of larger, more impersonal, and more secular forces in increasingly complex societies (cf. Wind and Lewis 1994).

Congregations may be defined in both top-down and bottom-up fashion. Seen from the top down, they are that form of every religion's organization that comes closest to touching and enfolding the individual adherent. Note that informal gatherings for worship, prayer or meditation don't count; congregations entail a formal organizational structure with ties to a larger religious identity, however ephemeral or contested these may be. Meanwhile, seen from the bottom up, they are voluntary religious communities that provide individual adherents their most intimate and potentially influential contact with religious organization. If Peter Berger and Richard Neuhaus (1977) could depict religion generally as a 'mediating institution' between the individual and society, the congregation serves a similar mediating function between the individual and the religion of which it is a part. Congregations also mediate, even buffer, the experiences their members have with other organizations. For instance, many people learn *Roberts Rules of Order* in congregations, a skill they transfer elsewhere. In other cases, congregations provide a familiar 'front door' to multiple other settings ranging from healthcare to family counseling to the arts.

This chapter examines congregations and the literature concerning them historically, typologically, and globally. But, of course, many in the West know congregations to be religion's most local outposts, whether in a city center, a nearby neighborhood, a growing suburb, or a rural hamlet. Because they are especially common within Protestantism, and because Protestantism is especially common within the United States, it makes little sense to map any American community without including the religious congregations within it. To make the point more pointedly, we begin by drawing upon our recent study of religion in the not a-typical American metropolitan area of Indianapolis, Indiana (cf. Farnsley *et al.* 2004). See also Form and Dubrow (2005) for a similar but more ecological portrait of Columbus, Ohio.

AN INDIANA SNAPSHOT OF CONGREGATIONS *IN SITU*

'Anyone wishing a close look at religion's building blocks of the faith traditions will quickly learn that they are not hard to find. In Indianapolis, Indiana, a city of some 850,000 people, there are approximately 1,200 congregations, or one for about every 700 residents. In virtually every neighborhood there is a Catholic parish, a representative sample of congregations from mainline denominations, and several evangelical churches. In some urban neighborhoods, especially African-American neighborhoods, the churches are the defining features of the non-residential landscape. The Martindale-Brightwood neighborhood has nearly 100 churches for its 11,000 residents, a ratio approaching one church for every 100 residents. Religious practitioners understand the congregations' central role. When asked to distill the city's religious life to its essence, one pastor said, "I can best describe religion in Indianapolis as being 'church.' To people in Indianapolis, the size of church and the name of the minister are all important. To "have religion" is to participate in or identify with a congregation." Said another, "my personal experience in Indianapolis is defined best as congregationally-based. I'm very aware of overarching institutions and some attempts to 'network,' but I still sense that 'local churches doing their own thing' summarizes the religious scene".'

Most congregations, considered as distinct, individual units, are homogeneous by comparison to the general population. Their members share ethnicity, race, and social class.

Indianapolis's racial make-up is roughly 76 per cent white, 21 per cent black, 2 per cent Hispanic, and 1 per cent other. Yet in 9 out of 10 congregations, at least 90 per cent of the members are of one race, and most congregations are considerably more racially homogeneous than that. Indianapolis's congregations have, on average, some 400 members and a budget of roughly $250,000. But those averages represent the mean; they are created numbers calculated by spreading the total number of all members and total of all budgets evenly among all the congregations. In real life, most congregations are nowhere near as big as those averages suggest. A small percentage of very large congregations with substantial budgets inflate those averages. At least half of the congregations in Indianapolis have fewer than 150 members, so the majority of congregations are relatively small groups where no more than 100 people gather on the Sabbath to worship. The median budget for congregations is closer to $125,000 than to $250,000 average, and this leaves little after paying a pastor's salary and benefits and the bills for facilities and their upkeep.

Congregations, by their own report, draw fewer than half of their members from the neighborhoods surrounding their houses of worship. Even Catholic parishes, which are arranged as geographic catchment areas, draw substantial numbers from outside their parish boundaries. Clergy, sometimes assumed to live next door to the house of worship, usually commute. Nearly 60 per cent of clergy say, by their own definition, that they live outside the neighborhood where their congregation is located. How, then, do congregations function as the *de facto* centers of religious life, the building blocks of religious community?

Congregations are centers of concurrent interests that overlap with shared race and social class. Members usually share a common history, including family ties. They often have similar interests in schools, property values, and public safety. Once again the sociological truism about 'birds of a feather' holds firm. Congregations are, above all, places where people of similar social characteristics gather to worship, to learn, to teach their children, and to socialize.

Congregations often function as extended families or as the small villages of an earlier epoch. Even larger churches that are complex organizations run by sophisticated management techniques are held together by glue that is both highly personal and interpersonal. St. Christopher Catholic in the Indianapolis suburb of Speedway is an enormous organization, yet it strives to maintain the family metaphor. Said one staff member:

> We have six masses on the weekends now, so we're just bursting at the seams. Since we are so large now – and our philosophy is we want to reach people from womb to tomb – we have over 55 organizations with different types of leadership in each. We try to hit every age group. Now we are a large family, and it's not as intimate as it used to be, but that's the price you pay for growth. I hate saying that large churches are big businesses, but they must be run like one if you're going to make money count and pay your bills. Still, my family made our church a home away from home and my kids all feel the same way. Although my eldest son moved away, he says 'I can't see my kids playing in sports against St. Chris, you know.' He said it just does not feel right. So that's why they all come here. (Farnsley *et al.* 2004, 114–116).

In Indianapolis there can be no question that local congregations have begun to assert their own priorities in charting their own destinies. Correspondingly, ecclesiastical rules and regulations promulgated from points up the religious chain of command have lost some of their legitimacy and credibility. Indeed, in some circles, the struggle between denominations and congregations is a battle over scarce resources. Dividing up the collection plate has always produced its share of disagreements, and they are now increasing.

Even this little bit of local ethnography drawn from one city illustrates the important place of congregations in the social landscape. With that importance in mind, we can shift our attention to a more analytical context that is partly historical and partly conceptual.

THE RISE AND SPECIALIZATION OF CONGREGATIONS IN THE WEST

The congregational phenomenon is largely a development of Western Christendom that is traceable to the sixteenth century Protestant Reformation against Catholicism. Of course, it was Max Weber who chronicled the social implications of the theological change so famously in his *Protestant Ethic and the Spirit of Capitalism.* But another shift was more enduring and more sociological. Protestantism did what every successful movement must; namely, stressing a problem to which it provided the solution. In this case, the problem lay in its new theological emphasis on the individual's direct relationship to God, unmediated by priests or an ecclesiastical hierarchy. Catholic salvation required institutional sponsorship and intervention, but Protestant salvation was solely a matter between individuals and their all-knowing God. Whatever attraction this new Protestant doctrine may have had, it also had a downside.

As Weber knew, there was a loneliness involved in the shift from Catholic ecclesiastical hegemony to Protestant autonomy. Individuals were left on their own to answer to God for their compliance with an ethic that was bleak and demanding – all with their ultimate salvation hanging in the balance. Under such circumstances, it is scarcely surprising that many sought the comforts of community and that congregations emerged as a staple of the new Protestant denominations. The congregational form traveled with these denominations throughout Northern Europe and later in the U.S. The congregation was especially important in the rural areas and small towns of Europe and America where it was often the only gathering point. The U.S.'s particular emphasis on frontier self-reliance and local democracy gave congregational life a further thrust that was later carried back into the new frontiers of urbanization. As the great French observer of America, Alexis de Tocqueville (1848), knew full well, congregations were at the heart of American communities across the land and at every status level. Churches, sects and temples offered a range of social activities and service functions. In addition, they sometimes exerted an ethical influence that energized the local body politic.

But not surprisingly, congregations began to differ. And here too Weber provided the first systematic account with the considerable help of his longtime colleague and sometime lodger, Ernst Troeltsch (1931). Subsequent congregational types flow from their famous 'ideal-typical' distinction between 'church' and 'sect.' 'Churches' were the established religious organizations, sometimes coextensive with the state. Church adherents were generally drawn from the high-status and well-integrated ranks of a community or society, and churches accommodated these members with an educated and professional clergy presiding over a well-managed organization with a fixed liturgy but a relatively flexible doctrine and a social ethic that could adjust to this-worldly needs and changes. 'Sects,' by comparison, were usually set apart from mainstream society and drew from the ranks of the low-status and more marginal members of a community or society. Instead of providing a point of integration with this world, sects stressed a theodicy of escape and compensation in the world beyond and the life to come. Suspicious of the high-status appurtenances of the churches, sects preferred lay leaders to professional clergy and scorned tendencies towards bureaucratization. Here the doctrine was fixed and often literal, while the ritual was flexible, spontaneous and often given to emotional evidences of God's spirit.

The rise of the sociology of religion during the twentieth century revolved around the church-sect distinction to such a degree that there were periodic calls to expunge the phrase from the field's vocabulary. The distinction was elaborated through contributions by many scholars ranging from H. Richard Niebuhr (1929), through Benton Johnson (1963) and Bryan Wilson (1961) to Rodney Stark and William Bainbridge (1985). Although the basic logic remained the same, the term 'churches' became a cover for everything from local congregations (e.g. First Methodist) to denominations (e.g. Methodism), 'institutionalized sects' (e.g. The Church of Latter Day Saints or 'Mormons'), to national 'ecclesia' (e.g. Russian Orthodox Church). At the same time, the category of sects came to include cults, or as they are now more commonly known, 'new religious movements.' The difference between sects and NRMs is that the former represented a return to a given religion's earlier and presumably purer days, whereas the latter championed either a new or newly imported religious vision (Stark and Bainbridge, 1985).

As important as the adding and editing of types have been, the chief American breakthrough was to give the distinction a dynamic dimension beginning with Niebuhr's pioneering work. Thus, while religious organizations generally start as a form of sect, over time it matures into a church. Thomas O'Dea (1961) noted that this was not a simple process and described five basic dilemmas involved in the 'institutionalization' of religion, ranging from an increasingly heterogeneous membership with 'mixed motivations,' to the original shared symbol system's loss of saliency, the loss of a movement's meaning for its members with an increasingly structured organizational form, the tendency for increased legalism to come at the expense of a movement's concrete significance, and the various problems associated with increasing concentrations of power. But perhaps the greatest problem overall is that, in time, the church may become so overzealous in pursuing stability and members that it compromises its founding ideals and alienates a group of members who follow a charismatic leader in breaking away to form a new sect. The scenario is common, and not just in religion. The dynamic occurs in every institutional field from the corporate to the political.

The church-sect distinction did what ideal-types always do by giving concrete status to a distinction that was overdrawn in the first place. To cite one correction not exactly at random, a much younger Demerath (1965) showed that many Protestant congregations had a wider range of member class and status ranks than the distinction would predict but these were related to predictably different patterns of religious involvement – some 'church-type' and some 'sect-type' within the same congregations. However, a different sort of correction shows that not all churches are the same. There has been a steady stream of work showing that the term 'church' covers a wide variety of priorities and agendas, of sinners and saints.

Forms of religious 'polity' have been a long-standing interest of scholars interested in congregations, especially in relation to the larger denominations to which they belong. Traditionally, three types of polity were discerned: (1) the Catholic or Episcopal type in which power flows downward from the ecclesiastical officials at the top of the denominational structure who control everything from the hiring and firing of priests to critical budget decisions, liturgical forms, and doctrinal disputes; (2) The Presbyterian model, in which power is concentrated in regional 'presbyteries' or councils that make the crucial decisions; and finally, (3) the Baptist or Congregational form by which power is concentrated in the congregations themselves as part of a treasured tradition of 'local autonomy.' Of course, this three-fold distinction is another set of ideal-types which tend to blur into one another in reality. Paul Harrison (1959) made the point in his classic study of the American (*viz.* 'northern') Baptist Convention. While its congregations continued to pride themselves on their autonomy, bureaucracy was entering through the denomination's backdoor and imposing a polity that was increasingly top-down.

Meanwhile, another treatment of how church congregations differ came in Roozen et al.'s *Varieties of Religious Presence* (1984). They developed a four-fold typology at the intersection of two dichotomies. The first involves the aforementioned contrast between 'this worldly' versus 'other worldly' orientations; the second distinguishes congregations that are publicly proactive in seeking change versus those content with the status quo. Thus four types emerge: *activist* (this-worldly and publicly proactive), *civic* (this-worldly but not proactive), *evangelical* (otherworldly and proactive), and *sanctuary* (otherworldly but not proactive).

There have, of course, been other helpful categories of congregational activity. Ammerman et al.'s *Congregation and Community* (1997) identifies several congregational strategies to deal with significant changes in their social environment: (a) persistence in the face of change; (b) relocation to new neighborhoods; (c) adaptation to new ideas about gender,

new cultural identities, or new internal structures; and (d) organizational innovation requiring either a new organizational birth or essential rebirth. Congregations are defined as constituent parts of a complex urban environment, and organizational birth, organizational death, and other stages in the organizational life cycle have to be understood relative to the total environment. The book's goal was to consider the response of congregations to major shifts in their immediate communities.

A still more recent addition to the typological repertoire has been Penny (Becker) Edgell's schema in *Congregations in Conflict* (2000). Edgell notes that many congregational studies have come to rely on 'ideoculture', and she focuses on congregations' inner, often idiosyncratic core, studied through the intense lens of ethnography. Applying the insights of an emerging sociological field known as the 'new institutionalism' (cf. Powell and DiMaggio 1991), she seeks patterns in local cultures – what she calls 'bundles of ideas' – that merge with specific practices in individual congregations to form dominant models of and for community life. Edgell's four congregational 'bundles' involve four major congregational orientations as *houses of worship, families, communities,* and *leaders.* Congregations tend to see themselves in all of these terms, but most display a particular penchant for one model or another, especially in times of conflict or crisis.

Finally, we offer one more classification of congregations, not because it supplants earlier work, but because it tries to reflect a different perspective concerning how urban residents define concepts of place or community. Like all of the authors above, most especially Weber himself, we are aware that real-life congregations show the futility of proposing ironclad analytical boxes into which actual organizations will fit. Real congregations sit uneasily among any set of axes. Congregational responses must be fluid in an environment that permits, or even requires, individuals and their organizations to create their own social and cultural centers. Therefore, our research on Indianapolis commends yet another set of four cells. Like their forebears, our types are ideal-typical;

as their creators did, we recognize that every congregation is likely to harbor all four tendencies but with varying weightings.

Again, it makes sense to plot the possibilities of congregational self-centering along two distinct axes. The first axis is by now familiar and runs between congregations that center themselves in *present and this-worldly* concerns and those that orient themselves toward *future and other-worldly* ones. A substantial proportion of congregations, more than half, fall well toward the other-worldly side of this axis. This is not to say that half of all believers fall to that side, because the congregations that take this perspective tend, on average, to be smaller. But when we think about congregations as organizations adjusting to urban realignment, we do well to remember that many of the organizations in question have relatively little interest in the civic community because the bulk of their priorities are focused elsewhere. They align themselves toward the future and toward the Kingdom of God, as opposed to adjusting their activities to the world around them.

The second axis runs between congregations with an *internal* focus on the faith community versus an *external* focus on some aspect of the surrounding social environment. Clearly, every congregation, as a social organization, must be responsive to its members' needs. Moreover, most congregations look beyond themselves at some points as they consider their relationship, and even their mission, to the rest of creation. But there are important differences in degree between congregations at the endpoints of this axis. On one side are those whose primary instinct is to begin with themselves, asking the question, 'who are we?' before looking outward to ask the question, 'where are we and what ought we to do?' On the other side are those who begin with their environment, asking 'where?' and 'what?' in order to define 'who' they are.

Together, these two axes provide four ideal-types of congregational responses, each of which describes a different way that congregations attempt to balance themselves in response to the inward and outward forces of urban change. The question is not whether any congregations look only to the future Kingdom

of God or to the present world around them, nor is it whether they look exclusively 'inside' or 'outside', because all congregations do some of each. The real question is which they do *first*. With these axes in mind, we offer this four-fold typology of congregational response to urban multicentering:

Types of congregational response to multicentering

	This-worldly	Other-worldly
External	Community Outreach	Conversionist
Internal	Customer Service	Cloistered

Community Outreach congregations find their balance in relating to and serving their external environments in this-worldly fashion – perhaps by hosting a soup kitchen, reaching out to an impoverished inner city church, or cooperating with secular agencies to operate a drug recovery center. While *Conversionist* congregations also serve a world outside their doors, they do so by bringing 'the word and the spirit' plus the perceived benefits of conversion to the religiously unaffiliated. Both *Customer Service* and *Cloistered* congregations are more internally directed to the needs of those who are already members. In the customer service case, provision is made for responding to the congregations this-worldly characteristics while serving as 'niches' for particular racial, ethnic, or sexual preferences; these congregations may also respond to a more heterogeneous membership's common this-worldly needs such as pre-school day care, teen-age recreation leagues, a 12-step program for alcoholics, discussion groups or circles of group therapy. Cloistered congregations seek to provide more other-worldly oriented spiritual interventions to pave the way to salvation, including Sunday school, adult Bible study, and prayer meetings.

NEW DIRECTIONS IN STUDYING CONGREGATIONS

Recently work on congregations has taken other paths as new forms of organizational analysis have been deployed by sociologists of religion (cf. Demerath *et al.* 1997; Powell and

DiMaggio 1991). Two recent works have looked at a wide variety of congregations in the process of distilling some common syndromes among them. The Hartford Institute of Religion Research has produced a spate of empirical studies in the area. In addition to the aforementioned work of Roozen *et al.* and the soon-to-be mentioned work of Carl Dudley, Nancy Ammerman has examined congregations as the Pillars of Faith (2005) that uphold the importance of religion in both local communities and the nation at large. Scott Thumma (2007) has done extensive research on the rise of the new 'mega church' congregations where the multitudes are drawn to a range of services and messages that are within the 'customer service' tradition. And Cynthia Woolever and colleagues have conducted a massive study of some 3,000 congregations in the U.S., Australia, England, and New Zealand. Along with Deborah Bruce, Woolever discusses the U.S. findings in *A Field Guide to US Congregations* (2002).

Some excellent studies have focused on the role of congregations in specific locations. Notable among these are Nancy Eiesland's *A Particular Place* (2000) about suburban Atlanta and Omar McRoberts' *Streets of Glory* (2003) about largely black congregations in urban Boston. Still others have focused on the changing organizational styles within specific worship traditions, such as Don Miller's *Reinventing American Protestantism* (1997).

Mark Chaves's work (cf. 2004) offered a striking methodological breakthrough meant to capture the entire range of congregations. The congregations mentioned by the adherents in combined random samples in the General Social Survey of the National Opinion Research Center produced a random sample of congregations that went far beyond earlier research in determining the breadth and depth of the field, especially the many smaller congregations. Using extensive questionnaires with congregation members and key informants allowed Chaves to scotch some popular misconceptions while noting other previously neglected trends. For example, congregations are not typically involved in local politics or the kind of intervention programs promoted by President George W. Bush's 'faith-based initiatives.' Instead, the most prevalent congregational work concerns the cultural production of art and music.

In virtually every Christian faith, there is a widening gap between national denominations and local congregations. Many older 'mainstream' churches have lost their younger generations and become increasingly geriatric in their membership and style. The new religious action occurs in new settings – whether in the world of cults, conservative evangelical churches, or 'mega' congregations that offer their two thousand members and more – often much more – a sense of community that can be both deeply spiritual and sometimes surprisingly secular. These congregational behemoths often bear little resemblance to the churches of yesterday as they struggle on behalf of everything from a ban on abortion to equal rights for homosexuals.

Descriptions of American religion are laced with the congregational motif. It provides one obvious explanation for how the U.S. can be ranked among both the most and least religious peoples. That is, Americans can be towards the top in religious 'form' but towards the bottom in religious 'function.' Since the early nineteenth century, foreign observers have noted how Americans use their religious affiliation and participation to validate and elevate their social standing.

Consider two well-known recent religious movements in the political field, the Moral Majority of the 1980s and the current Christian Coalition. At the outset, this burst of right-wing activism was described as a massive religious movement which would not only elect candidates such as Ronald Reagan but control them once in office. Subsequent evidence suggests that both claims were exaggerated, and sometimes the influence ran unintentionally and ironically in the opposite direction as mainstream voters shrank from the prospect of a new theocracy. As America came to be defined by religious pluralism – a shift from the 'many as one' to the 'one as many' – and as religion lost some of its institutional force vis-à-vis government and its ideological force within an increasingly secular culture, religionists looked to specific communities that shared ethnic, racial, and other socio-demographic characteristics that strengthened their religious coherence. Congregations, the truly local religious organizations where members shared all of those characteristics in the context of a common history, became central to 'lived' religion in America. These were the places where people actually worshipped. This was where they made friends or enemies, celebrated births and deaths. Indeed, it is often lamented but scarcely surprising that 'Sunday morning services are the most segregated time of the week.' To use an old sociological distinction, insofar as these services are 'in-group' celebrations and support mechanisms, it is sadly understandable that they rarely extend their embrace to 'out groups' in the community.

An important chronicler of congregations has been Steven Warner, whose particular research focus has been on immigrant congregations. Warner (1993, 1997) has argued that American religion largely floats on a sea of congregationalism, whether formal or 'de facto,' and has proclaimed this as the basis for a 'new paradigm' for the American (as opposed to the European) sociology of religion.

But it is also true that the ties that bind adherents to congregations have weakened. One can no longer assume that the congregational affiliations of one generation are the same as those of their family's previous generations, and certainly it is less and less the case that 'Once an X, always an X,' though some traditions have greater adhesion than others, especially when they are large enough so that their young members are less apt to find their spouses outside the faith. Given the strength of pluralism, denominational and congregational identities became less compelling, and given the ever-increasing rise of religious illiteracy, such labels made less and less difference – at least within, say, the greater Protestant ranks. Catholics and Jews switch too, though here ties to distinct theological traditions and long-standing cultural traditions matter more.

Religious 'switching' can be easily over-estimated, and there is evidence that when it occurs, the reasons are more secular than sacred, i.e. more a matter of inter-marriage,

residential mobility, needed social services than a matter of doctrine, ritual, or pastor, (cf. Demerath and Yang 1998). At the same time, as Peter Berger (1967) noted some 40 years ago, when religion becomes competitive, congregations are the organizations that bear the brunt of the marketing required to keep members and pay the bills. Not to spoil the story, but such marketing to religious consumers is precisely what happened. Protestant congregations, both liberal and conservative, began to look to American business for models that would help them promote their strengths and appeal to the consumers most likely to constitute their target audience. Denominations still mattered because they offered some assurance by way of 'branding.' Episcopalians and United Church of Christ were most likely to be liberal, to be inclusive (including gays and lesbians), and to attend to ritual. Assemblies of God were likely to be biblically conservative and offered the emotive charismatic experiences such as faith healing and speaking in tongues. Any particular congregation might not fit the mold, but they had reason to stay within accepted parameters or risk having their members switch brands.

CONGREGATIONAL CONSULTANTS

Because supply nearly always rises to satisfy demand, there has arisen a great company of consultants to congregations. Conservative churches were most likely to judge their success or failure in terms of membership growth, since that was the most direct measurement of the degree to which they were spreading a true message and being rewarded by God for it. An entire field of evangelical consulting developed in the 1970s known as the Church Growth Movement.

One of the central features of the Church Growth Movement was the Homogeneous Unit Principle (HUP). Conservatives had always been critics of ecumenical movements like the National and World Councils of Churches because those had been linked to both biblical liberalism and political liberalism, which the conservative churches demonised. Despite those concerns about liberal ecumenism, however, there was a nagging concern that the Gospel message called for inclusion, including racial inclusion, in an environment of universal brotherhood. At the very least, Christ's love extended to everyone.

HUP made clear that the most important thing was that people be led to an individual relationship with Christ, if this required catering to their imperfect predispositions. Men and women could be led to Christ, but in ways that were most comfortable for them, which is to say, with other people most like themselves. So the homogeneity of churches – by race, class, education, and other measures – was portrayed as beneficial for individual salvation, even if such prejudicial segregation was ultimately a necessary evil measured against God's ideal. Better that we be separate now that we might be together one day in God's eternal kingdom.

As American society became ever more multicultural, HUP became an evangelical relic. The church growth movement, however, continued apace. It is worth noting that today such movements are led by international figures like Paul Cho of Korea as well as American gurus such as Peter Wagner of Fuller Seminary.

Meanwhile, liberals never embraced HUP, but they did engage in full-scale management consulting of their own. Members of these churches were, after all, the management classes of American life. Nothing made better sense to them than defining a mission statement, choosing direct, cooperative action – missions in the traditional sense – to carry out that mission statement, and research to identify and then to market to target audiences. They might not always have used such commerce-driven language, but they often came pretty close.

The two names most closely associated with the rise of organizational consulting – either for purposes of community organizing or efficient congregational management – are Carl Dudley and Loren Mead. Dudley is an ordained minister and Alinsky-trained neighborhood organizer dedicated to helping congregations find their appropriate social ministry. Mead is the Episcopal priest whose interest in applying business practices to ministry led to his founding The Alban Institute, the U.S.'s foremost consulting house for congregations, in 1974.

Dudley is perhaps best known for his attempts to make congregational studies relevant to social ministry. Today, he is involved in ministry consulting at Hartford Seminary, a center of congregational research where many of the scholars listed in this chapter have served on the faculty. As noted above, the Hartford Institute of Religious Research is a powerful force in American congregational studies. Dudley's many books include *Basic Steps toward Community Ministry* (1991) and the original *Handbook for Congregational Studies* (1986), which he co-authored with Jackson Carroll and William McKinney. The updated version, *Studying Congregations* (1998), involved many of the same authors, with Ammerman as the new lead editor.

Loren Mead's bibliography contains titles that seem drawn from an MBA course, highlighted by the *The Once and Future Church* (1991). In the mid-1990s Mead stepped down from the presidency of the Alban Institute to pursue retirement as a consultant and author. He was replaced by James Wind. Wind is co-author, with Jackson Carroll and Carl Dudley, of *Carriers of Faith: Lessons from Congregational Studies* (1991). He is also co-editor, with James Lewis of the Louisville Institute, of the two-volume collection *American Congregations* (1994), in many ways the best summary of recent congregational studies, including historical, theological, and sociological analyses.

CONGREGATIONS DISSEMINATED

American religious organization continues to be distinctive in world context, and the congregational emphasis continues to be important. However, the organizational aspect of American religion is not as unique as it was even 25 years ago. The distinctive congregational model has spread around the globe at the same time that it has begun to diversify and even atrophy within the United States itself.

As much as congregations appear to be the distinctive province of Protestantism – and U.S. Protestantism at that – other parallels and equivalencies have begun to develop in recent years. Reform Judaism has a much more congregational focus than Orthodox Judaism, whose temples are more strictly devoted to sex-segregated worship and education than to family and community activity. Gradually the American Catholic parish has taken on more congregational qualities, especially as participation is less tied to neighborhood residence and individuals are allowed to select their churches on other grounds.

Even countries that Americans would think of as defined by the 'European' model of state churches surrounded by sects are host to congregations as a key organizational type. Margaret Harris (1998) provides an account of congregational life within British Judaism as well as Christianity; and Mathew Guest et al. (2004) use congregations to provide multiple lenses on British religious life, ranging from a Welsh case study of evangelicalism to conflict within British Catholicism and the development and maintenance of Quaker identity. A major recent story line has been the declining numbers in Anglican churches around Britain. But here a news report on the latest statistics of declension is apt to be followed by letters from scattered village rectors to the effect that their church attendance has recently increased by 50 per cent (perhaps from 20 to 30 with the arrival of two new families in the parish) and surely this is a harbinger of a revival in the offing. In fact, a similar sequence is now not uncommon with respect to the declining memberships of Liberal Protestant congregations in the U.S.

Congregations continue to redefine the religious realm outside the Euro-American 'west' as well. The congregational model was at the core of the 'Liberation Theology' movement within Latin American Catholicism. A key to this development was a move away from the patriarchal impersonality of large parishes towards the more egalitarian intimacy of 'base communities.' These congregation-like units have been among the most successful Catholic responses to Protestant Pentecostalism's own stress on tightly bonded (and highly feminized) congregations. In somewhat the same spirit in Poland, the political cells of the Solidarity movement gave the Catholic Church new contacts with the people during a decade of cooperation. Now that these contacts have largely disappeared, the Church is suffering the consequences.

The spread of congregations as the basic units of religious worship and community has been both a cause and a consequence of Protestantism's spread from Latin America through Africa, and the Middle East, to both South and East Asia. Paul Freston's chapter in this Handbook charts this development, as does Philip Jenkins' recent book on *The Next Christendom: The Coming of Global Christianity* (2002). But congregation-like units have also been on the rise within other faith traditions that have traditionally made little place for them.

Neither the Islamic mosque nor the Hindu temple functions as a congregation in the Protestant sense. With the family as the key Islamic institution, Muslim ritual life is not grounded in a wider network of social activity and support. Strictly speaking, the mosque is not one of the pillars of Islam, nor is it critical to the prayers that are essential but can be performed anywhere. The mosque is a special locus for prayer alone, and other activities within it are formally proscribed. In practice, mosques can take on educational functions and even serve as a mobilizing vehicle under the leadership of particular imams or mullahs. But traditionally the mosque lacks a sense of full-blown congregational solidarity.

The Hindu temple is more a shrine to a particular god or goddess than a center of lay activity. In fact, Hindu rituals often revolve around the home in their concern for the purification of food and body. Rather than go to the priests, Hindus often have the priests come to them, and it is often said that 'there is nothing two Hindus do together that one Hindu cannot do alone.'

With this in mind, it is perhaps not surprising that other faith traditions have spawned a variety of extra-religious movements that provide more communality. Some are spiritual, some social, some educational, some economic, some political, and some all of the above.

Buddhism has followed several slightly different paths, depending upon which Buddhism is in question. The Theravada Buddhism of Thailand and Southeast Asia is a tradition controlled by monastic monks. Temples are centers of religious observance but not lay organization. Although there is an elaborate ecclesiastical structure in the sangha and some monks have considerable followings, the laity is afforded little by way of a congregational life.

On the other hand, the Mahayana Buddhism of North and East Asia is more oriented to the laity. In China, Buddhist groups are often forced to take a sheltered congregational form as a protection against the party and the state. In Japan, the 'new' and 'new-new' lay Buddhist and Shinto movements have developed clear congregational forms. This characterizes both the most radical of them – the Aum Shinrikyo – and the largest of them, the Soka Gakkai, whose membership is now estimated at anywhere from one-twentieth to one-tenth of all Japanese. The Soka Gakkai's intense recruitment has revolved around nested levels of lay organizations which once offered structured support and identity to rural working-class migrants to urban areas and now perform similar functions for an increasingly middle-class constituency.

In settings where a congregational or other communal grouping is lacking, the faithful may be especially vulnerable to aberrant movements that offer an equivalent to the congregational experience while pursuing more secular and political agendas. This is true of the various organizations within the ranks of India's Hindutva. It is also the case with a number of Muslim extremist movements in countries such as Egypt, Israel, and Pakistan, not to mention the current internal religious wars in Afghanistan and Iraq.

CONCLUSION

The congregation as a type of voluntary religious organization with roots in the traditional Protestant 'sect' is a Western invention most commonly found in North America. The U.S. has no state church and its high religious individualism, fluid social boundaries, and multiple voluntary groups are involved in every conceivable form of social action. America's Protestant colonizers required religious organizations capable of enforcing community boundaries by defining 'us' versus 'them' according to theological, ethnic, and many other status markers. This social ground proved fertile for multiple religious communities locally gathered. It was a seedbed that has produced hundreds of thousands such organizations, each able to provide a locus of identity defined by denominational tradition, social status, geography, or the personal charisma of a founding or sustaining leader.

Congregations or their equivalents now appear across multiple cultures and within a wide variety of faiths. Although we should guard against using a Western lens to interpret non-Western circumstances, there are sound sociological reasons to assume that voluntary religious organizations are well-suited to maintaining belief, building religious community, and providing services in a variety of cultures affected by a globalizing market economy and an expanding bureaucratic state. Put simply, congregations are a good fit for the space occupied by religion in the modern world.

If research into congregations sometimes smacks of defensiveness or boosterism, perhaps this is because many analysts see congregations as a humanizing, personalizing force in an increasingly depersonalizing environment, a place where internal community is created and sustained for folks who no longer find such community in the geography of small towns or the bonds of shared ethnicity. The earliest analysts of church and sect saw congregations as part of a sectarian resistance against the totality of the 'church' in its alliance with mainstream culture. We would argue that today few classical 'churches' exist because religion is so unlikely to be coextensive with the more powerful institutional forces of state and market. In such an environment, congregations offer a truly modern organizational outlet small enough to nurture individual spiritual growth in a local community but large enough to buffer individuals from the larger and more impersonal forces that structure their daily lives.

REFERENCES

Ammerman, N. 2005. *Pillars of Faith*. Berkeley: University of California Press.

Ammerman, N. *et al.* 1998. *Studying Congregations: A New Handbook*. Nashville: Abingdon.

Ammerman N. with A. E. Farnsley *et al.* 1997. *Congregation and Community*. New Brunswick, NJ: Rutgers University Press.

Berger, P. 1967. *The Sacred Canopy*. Garden City, NY: Doubleday.

Berger, P. and R. J. Neuhaus 1977. *To Empower People: The Role of Mediating Structures in Public Policy*. Washington, D.C.: American Enterprise Institute.

Chaves, M. 2004. *Congregations in America*. Cambridge, MA: Harvard University Press.

Demerath, N. J. III 1965. *Social Class in American Protestantism*. Chicago. Rand McNally.

Demerath, N. J. III, P. D. Hall, T. N. Schmitt and R. H. Williams (eds), 1997. *Sacred Companies: Organizational Aspects of Religion and Religious Aspects of Organizations*. New York: Oxford University Press.

Demerath, N. J. III and Y. Yang 1998. 'Switching in American Religion: Denominations, Markets, and Paradigms.' In Margaret Couseneau (ed.), *Religion in a Changing World*. Westport, CT: Praeger.

Dudley, C. 1991. *Basic Steps toward Community Ministry*. Bethesda: Alban Institute.

Dudley, C. *et al.* 1986. *Handbook for Congregational Studies*. Nashville: Abingdon.

Edgell, Becker P. 2000. *Congregations in Conflict: Cultural Models of Religious Life*. New York: Cambridge University Press.

Eiesland, N. 2000. *A Particular Place: Urban Restructuring and Religious Ecology in a Southern Exurb*. New Brunswick, NJ: Rutgers University Press.

Farnsley, A., N. J. Demerath, E. Diamond, M. L. Mapes and E. Wedam. 2004. *Sacred Circles, Public Squares: The Multicentering of American Religion*. Bloomington: Indiana University Press.

Form, William and Joshua Dubrow 2005. Downtown Metropolitan Churches: Ecological Situation and Response. *Journal for the Scientific Study of Religion* 44/3: 271–90.

Guest, M. *et al.* 2004. *Congregational Studies in the UK*. Aldershot: Ashgate Press.

Harris, M. 1998. *Organizing God's Work. Challenges for Churches and Synagogues*. London: Macmillan.

Harrison, P. M. 1959. *Authority and Power in the Free Church Tradition*. Princeton, N.J.: Princeton University Press.

Jenkins, P. 2002. *The Next Christendom: The Coming of Global Christianity*. New York: Oxford University Press.

Johnson, B. 1963. 'On Church and Sect.' *American Sociological Review* 28: 539–49.

Mead, L. 1991. *The Once and Future Church*. Bethesda: Alban Institute.

McRoberts, O. 2003. *Streets of Glory*. Chicago: University of Chicago Press.

Miller, D. 1997. *Reinventing American Protestantism*. Berkeley: University of California Press.

Niebuhr, Richard H. 1929. *The Social Sources of Denominationalism*. New York: Holt.

O'Dea, Thomas 1961. 'Five Dilemmas in the Institutionalization of Religion.' *Journal for the Scientific Study of Religion* 1: 30–9.

Powell, W. W. and P. J. DiMaggio (eds) 1991. *The New Institutionalism in Organizational Analysis*. Chicago: University of Chicago Press.

Roozen, D., W. McKinney and J. Carroll 1984. *Varieties of Religious Presence*. New York: Pilgrim Press.

Stark, R. and W. S. Bainbridge 1985. *The Future of Religion: Secularization, Revival and Cult Formation*. Berkeley: University of California Press.

Thumma, S. and D. Travis 2007. *Beyond Megachurch Myths: What We Can Learn from Americas Largest Churches*. San Francisco: Jossey-Bass.

Tocqueville, Alexis de (1848 [1969]). *Democracy in America*, 2 vols. New York: Harper and Row.

Troeltsch, E. 1931. *The Social Teachings of the Christian Churches* (trans O. Wyon). New York: Macmillan.

Warner, R. S. 1993. 'Work in Progress toward a New Paradigm for the Sociological Study of Religion in the United States.' *American Journal of Sociology* 98 (5): 1044–93.

Warner, R. S. 1997. 'The Place of the Congregation in Contemporary American Religious Configuration.' In Wind and Lewis *op. cit.*, pp. 54–99.

Weber, M. 1910. The *Protestant Ethic and the Spirit of Capitalism*. New York: Scribner's.

Wilson, Bryan R. 1961. *Sects and Society*, London: Heinemann, and Berkeley and Los Angeles: University of California Press.

Wind, J., with J. Carroll and C. Dudley 1991. *Carriers of Faith: Lessons from Congregational Studies*. Louisville: Westminster John Knox Press.

Wind, J. and J. Lewis 1994. *American Congregations* (2 volumes). Chicago: University of Chicago Press.

Woolever, C. and D. Bruce 2002. *A Field Guide to US Congregations*. Diane Publishing Company.

10

Evangelicalism and Fundamentalism: The Politics of Global Popular Protestantism

PAUL FRESTON

'Wherever there are pentecostals, there is trouble'.

The above comment was made at an academic symposium by a leading European scholar of religion, in response to a presentation of mine on global pentecostalism. The comment did not seem to shock the people present, and I was too surprised to do more than murmur my amazement. Later, I wondered what would have been people's reaction if my interlocutor, instead of referring to pentecostals, had said: 'Wherever there are Muslims (or Jews), there is trouble'. There would probably have been a groundswell of ethical disapproval, because it is no longer politically correct to speak that way about Muslims or Jews. But the same comment about pentecostals does not provoke an outcry. Considering that most pentecostals are poor, non-white people from the Third World, that is rather strange.

This chapter is about the political implications of the popular forms of Protestant Christianity in the global south (Latin America, Africa and Asia) of which pentecostals constitute the major segment. This Christianity is variously referred to as 'fundamentalist', 'evangelical' or 'sectarian'. Its global expansion represents a major religious transformation of the last half-century, affecting more established forms of Christianity as well as non-Christian religions, and constituting (along with Islam) perhaps the major grassroots religious presence in poor and volatile regions of the world. For its sheer size, vibrant growth, geographical spread, social, political and cultural effects and potential dangers, this is a key phenomenon of religion and politics at the global level.

We shall look at various aspects of this phenomenon in comparative perspective. The unifying theme is democracy, in a broad sense which includes not only a religion's propensity to oppose dictatorships and deepen democracies, but also its attitudes towards political violence and religious freedom, and the presence or absence of notions of sacred community, sacred territory and divine law. The main question concerns what light is thrown by the globalization of Christianity on the historical correlation between Protestantism and democracy. Historically, democracy has been strongest in countries of a Western Christian tradition (initially Protestant, later Catholic as well). But is that a spurious correlation, dependent on other factors in the West which might not exist in the global south? As Christianity becomes more global it may become easier to separate 'Western' from 'Christian'.

The key theoretical debate is between essentialism and contextualism, i.e. between the weight of traditions and the importance of circumstances. On the one hand, we must question the idea that political consequences can be simply read off from religious doctrine. There may be affinities between certain religious and political doctrines, but many other factors come into play, both within the religious field and from the social context. So we should avoid 'essentialist' ideas such as, for example, that Protestantism is essentially democratic and Islam is essentially undemocratic. Religious traditions are not univocal or immutable; there is always diversity as well as development. On the other hand, we should avoid the opposite conclusion, that religious traditions are epiphenomenal and all show the same internal differences, with any variations being explained by different social contexts.

After the terrorist attacks of September 2001, both these extreme interpretations were common. Some analysts declared Islam to be essentially undemocratic and violent. Others reacted by declaring Islam and Christianity to be as varied as each other in their political manifestations. In discussing global popular Protestantism, I want to navigate between these extremes. Religious traditions *are* important; it is sociological nonsense to say 'all religions are the same'. If we recognize internal differences within major religions (the Christianity of George W. Bush is patently not that of Liberation Theology; the Islam of the Sufis is not that of Al-Qaeda), we can also recognize that each religion's internal diversity is not identical (in range of positions, numbers embracing each position, or the plausibility with which each position can be defended doctrinally). The unique relationship of each religious tradition to sacred scriptures and to concepts of law, territoriality, religious organization and religion-state relations must be thrown into the mix of factors that determine how believers will behave in particular circumstances. At the same time, religious traditions are not *all-important*. How important they are in each context has to be determined empirically, not decided beforehand.

THE GLOBALIZATION OF CHRISTIANITY

Christianity is still often treated as the religion of the developed West. That is problematic today, when it has notable political involvement in the south. While Christianity as a percentage of world population neither declined nor grew during the twentieth century, there was a vital change in its composition. Its areas of recession (Europe and the 'old Commonwealth') were compensated by areas of accession (sub-Saharan Africa, parts of Asia, the Pacific). Christianity is now only 40 per cent European and North American, as opposed to 80 per cent in 1900.

Nevertheless, discussions of religion in global politics are still dominated by Islam and American Christianity, especially the evangelical Protestantism that has achieved visibility (or notoriety!) in the Bush White House. But, after the United States, the countries that now have the largest numbers of practising Protestants are Brazil, China and Nigeria. This is a new reality, and it is important to understand *that* it exists and *what forms* it takes.

Protestantism in the global south is often misleadingly portrayed as largely 'made in the USA'. But in fact it has mostly spread independently of Western initiatives. This autonomous Third World appropriation of Christianity has enabled it largely to transcend historical associations with colonialism, rendering both Western Christian triumphalism and Western post-colonial guilt irrelevant for understanding it and distorting for evaluating its political proclivities. This also points to the need for an appropriate terminology to fit the new reality of Christianity into discussions of global politics which often juxtapose terms such as 'the Islamic world' and 'the West'. Christianity is more and more external to both these categories.

Some recent works have suggested contro-versial hypotheses regarding the political implications of Christianity in the global south. But other works continue to treat Christianity as virtually synonymous with the traditionally Christian countries of the developed West. An example of this would be Norris and Inglehart's (2004) analysis of the data from the World Values Surveys. They do not separate southern Christianity from that of the devel-oped world. It is quite possible that a separate category of 'southern Christian (or Protestant, or Catholic)' would yield quite different results for value systems and attitudes to work, the market and the state. Where does southern Christianity fit into the 'clash' between the West and the Islamic world, which for Norris and Inglehart centres around sexuality and gender equality, and for Huntington (1998) centres around democracy?

Similarly, when Norris and Inglehart con-clude that Protestant societies display the weakest work ethic, they do not mention that the societies examined are overwhelmingly post-industrial and traditionally Protestant, with very weak religious practice. But all of the few 'agrarian' Protestant societies examined (all in Africa) seem to be heavily pro-work. It would be interesting to correlate the work ethic with levels of Protestant practice in diverse countries.

The globalization of Christianity, giving it a huge presence in economically and culturally distinct societies, has increased the variability of its relationship to politics which stemmed originally from its origin as a persecuted sect, the lack of a 'law' in the Christian scriptures and the emphasis on cultural adaptation and the use of vernacular languages. At the same time, Christianity's global spread (not prima-rily due to migration, as with many other religions, but to processes of conversion) has given it a footing as a minority virtually everywhere that it is politically permitted. If Christian minorities were historically located mainly in Muslim societies, with a well-defined *dhimmi* status, and in the colonial period in Africa and Asia were usually under Christian colonial rulers, nowadays Christian minorities find themselves under an immense variety of political systems.

GLOBAL EVANGELICALISM

If the global spread of Catholicism is little known in the West, that of Protestantism is even less so. This is partly because it is fractured and has no global centre to register its activities. It includes not only extensions of Western Protestant denominations (now usually run autonomously), but also huge denominations founded in the global south.

Our focus will be on *evangelical* Protestantism, and in fact most Protestants in the global south would come under this rubric. Compared to Western Protestantism, the Third World version is considerably more evangelical (and indeed largely pentecostal).

What are 'evangelicals'? There is no globally accepted definition, but for our purposes the term refers to a sub-set of Protestants, distin-guished by doctrinal and practical characteris-tics but not by denominational affiliation or even necessarily by self-labelling. Many recent studies have borrowed a working definition from historian David Bebbington (1989: 1), consisting of four emphases: conversionism (need for change of life), activism (missionary efforts), biblicism (special importance to the Bible, though not necessarily the fundamen-talist idea of 'inerrancy'), and crucicentrism (centrality of Christ's sacrifice on the cross). Evangelicals are therefore found in many denominations (including 'mainline' ones such as Anglican, Methodist and Reformed churches, as well as Baptist, Pentecostal and independent churches).

Most southern Protestants are also pente-costal (highly supernaturalistic believers who emphasize the contemporary manifestations of 'gifts of the Holy Spirit' such as speaking in strange tongues to worship God, divine healing, prophecy and exorcism of evil spirits).

Since the term 'evangelical' has become well known globally in conjunction with the American 'religious right', it is important to stress that, even though American missionary efforts are numerous, the vast majority of evangelical growth in the south is not due to them, but rather to indigenous initiatives. While American television evangelists trumpet their own global importance, in reality they are merely the foam on the surface of the river, telling us little about the currents underneath.

Global southern evangelicalism is institutionally divided, strongly practising and fast-growing. In most countries it is over-represented among the poor. It is not a state religion, and rarely has any unofficial privileged relationship with governments; in a few countries, it is discriminated against. Being a voluntary, non-traditional religion composed disproportionately of the poor, it usually does not have strong institutions and its cultural and educational resources are limited. Church divisions make it impossible to establish a normative 'social doctrine'. It often has no international contacts, cutting it off from the history of Christian reflection on politics. It may be an *arriviste* minority inexperienced in the public sphere and still lacking full political legitimacy, but nevertheless confident (even excessively so) about its future.

Evangelicals probably (in a conservative estimate) number 300–400 million people, or 5 per cent or 6 per cent of world population, their importance enhanced by high levels of practice and global distribution. Together with Catholicism (whose 20 per cent of world population includes much more non-practising affiliation), evangelicalism has been a fundamental contributor to the globalization of Christianity which has transformed it into a largely non-white religion, more and more distant from power and wealth.

David Martin (2004: 277) discerns two main lines of evangelical expansion: the attraction of voluntaristic popular Christianity which emphasizes the Spirit, 'spreading in partial alignment with the English language and Anglo-American influence'; and ethnic-minority evangelicalism (especially in Asia), involving 'the emergence of minority self-consciousness which leaps over the pressure exercised by the local majority and links itself to evangelicalism as an expression of transnational modernity'.

The region of most startling expansion is sub-Saharan Africa. Far from independence signalling hard times for the churches, they grew in numbers, organizational depth and social importance. Believers of broadly evangelical characteristics, whether in mainline denominations, pentecostal groups or African Independent Churches, number perhaps 100–150 million.

Another region of growth is Latin America. Long after their arrival in the nineteenth century, non-Catholic churches remained as insignificant as they still are in Latin Europe. But since the 1950s in Brazil and Chile and the 1970s elsewhere, they have grown considerably. The secure hegemony of early twentieth-century Catholicism is now threatened as Protestants have risen to 10 per cent or more of the population (at least 50 million people). Of these, two-thirds are pentecostals. Pentecostalism is associated disproportionately with the poor, less educated and darker-skinned.

While Asia remains by far the least Christianized continent, evangelicalism has done well in certain areas and probably totals some 60 million. The Philippines resembles Latin America in having a Catholic majority and a growing evangelical minority. In South Korea Protestantism numbers 20 per cent of the population and has entered the national mainstream. Evangelical Christianity is also fairly strong among diaspora Chinese. And it has become the dominant religion among several ethnic minorities; there is now a swathe of mini-Christendoms among ethnic minorities from India to Indonesia. In addition, in India it is disproportionately located among the Dalits ('untouchables'). Last but not least, it has grown dramatically in China, both in the official Protestant church and the unregistered churches. If we adopt a fairly conservative estimate of 50 million Christians in China, probably 25–30 million of those would be evangelicals. Some scholars regard China as poised to go through an explosion of Christian adherence similar to that of Africa in the twentieth century.

EVANGELICALISM AND FUNDAMENTALISM

Whether this global popular Protestantism is referred to as 'evangelical' or 'fundamentalist', two comparisons are inevitable. 'Evangelicalism' conjures up the figure of the American religious right which has helped to elect

George Bush, encouraged the invasion of Iraq and supported Israeli expansionism. And 'fundamentalism' invites a comparison with radical Islamism. Is global popular Protestantism an extension of American 'soft power' around the world? Or is it a potential constituency of violent non-state actors? Or could it even be a conflation of these characteristics?

Firstly, it is useful to ponder the term 'fundamentalism' in relation to a globalizing world. I disagree with suggestions (Waters 1995; Beyer 1994) that a globalized world must lead either to religious relativism or to clashing fundamentalisms. Beyer (1990: 393) sees only two options for religion to have any public influence: the 'liberal' option, ecumenical, tolerant and making few really religious demands; and the 'conservative' option which reasserts the religious tradition 'in spite of modernity' and champions the cultural distinctiveness of a particular region, such as the New Christian Right and Islamist movements.

However, besides the relativizing reaction and the fundamentalist reaction, there is also what we might call the conversionist reaction to globalization. Peaceful conversionism is another plausible (and frequent) way of resolving the 'crisis' of identity of a shrinking world. Indeed, it may fit well with the greater seriousness of faith which often accompanies the transformation of religion towards an achieved identity. The dynamic of conversion places evangelicalism in a different relationship to global cultural processes from either pan-religious ecumenism (tending to global homogeneity) or fundamentalism (tending to irreducible pockets of anti-pluralism). As generally a non-traditional religion (in the global south) spreading by conversion, its interests are usually the opposite of those of a reactive fundamentalism. For evangelicalism, pluralism and cultural diffuseness are advantageous, whereas fundamentalisms (and religious nationalisms) constitute its most serious barriers. It may be that evangelicalism flourishes best in a world that is *tranquilly religious*, rather than one that is either *secularized* or *defensively religious*.

The globalization of evangelicalism is largely conversionist rather than diasporic (although the latter also happens, as with African immigrants in Europe). Conversionist and diasporic globalization have different implications. If the de-territorialization and voluntarism usually associated with globalization really do expand, then conversion will become a major phenomenon of the twenty-first century. But works on religion and global politics often suppose a stable situation in terms of religious identities, varying only in the degree of political mobilization of such identities, whereas in fact switching of religion may be rife and may be creating both new conflicts as well as new bases for social cohesion. Since the rise of evangelicalism is usually related to large-scale conversion, it may provide an additional dimension to existing conflicts (Nigeria and North-East India), or it may spark off a transition to a new relationship between state and religion (Latin America), requiring dynamic 'handling' by the state (in legislation, day-to-day treatment and consultation) and society (social attitudes to religious change; who the media consult for a 'religious viewpoint' on issues).

Evangelicalism and fundamentalism have a complex relationship. While there is overlap (some evangelicals can be considered fundamentalists), evangelicalism is an older and broader tendency within Protestantism, while the 'fundamentalist' label has been extended in another direction to include phenomena from other religions. Fundamentalism and evangelicalism relate differently to globalization, the former being more a reactive phenomenon of globalization whereas the latter predates and possibly contributes to it. The *Fundamentalism Project* of the early 1990s illustrates this. The volume on the state defines fundamentalism as 'movements of religiously inspired reaction to aspects of global processes of modernization and secularization ... the struggle to assert or reassert the norms and beliefs of "traditional religion" in the public order' (Marty and Appleby 1993: 2, 5). But evangelicalism is far from traditional in most of the Third World. Guatemalan neo-pentecostalism is studied in the series, but the final volume admits how weakly it fits the *Project's* schema.

Philip Jenkins (2006: 2–12) begins his study of reading the Bible in southern Christianity by asking whether this phenomenon means that the fundamentalists will win on a global scale. There is indeed, he says, great respect for the Bible and often a tendency to literalism. But they are not addressing the same questions as Western fundamentalists (obsessed with 'secular humanism' and 'liberal Christians'), and the greater presence of pentecostalism produces a hermeneutic which is 'feminine, eschatological and organic' and which often unifies things which the West separates, such as social liberation and spiritual deliverance.

Most accounts of American Protestant fundamentalism (e.g. Bruce 2000; Marsden 2006) emphasize peculiarly American factors (local changes; the American system which allows minorities to reproduce themselves). Thus, Marsden says fundamentalist militancy typically arises when proponents of a once-dominant religious culture feel threatened by cultural trends. American fundamentalists romanticize the founders of the republic and often strongly support its foreign wars. As largely a reinvention of white Bible-belt religion, there is little reason to expect it will characterize evangelicalism the world over. The *Fundamentalism Project* concluded that ten movements studied were fundamentalist without qualification; only one (from the US) was Protestant and was highly 'reactive'. Guatemalan pentecostalism was examined, but scored 'absent' on 'reactivity' (Almond *et al.* 1995: 414).

THE HISTORICAL REFERENCE POINTS: PRIMITIVE CHRISTIANITY AND EARLY PROTESTANTISM

Evangelical Christianity, besides its radical biblicism, also sees itself as a return to the purity of the early church. It thus tends to seek justification for its political positions in the scriptures, especially the New Testament. However, early Christianity was a discriminated sect, distant from political power. Not only was its founder executed by the state (unlike the founder of Islam, who governed a state), but it also soon adopted a cultural flexibility which

enabled it to become a cross-cultural voluntary community. Instead of imposing a religious law, it spoke of a law 'written on the heart'. Instead of trying to establish a kingdom, it spoke of a 'kingdom not of this world', which at once enabled believers to belong to any earthly kingdom ('render unto Caesar ...') but also relativized all of them.

This initial distance from, and suspicion of, the state contributed to a lasting political modesty in Christianity. Lacking a definite political recipe, a variety of postures towards the state could be adopted, from eschatological indifference through prophetic critique to conformist legitimation. Not only did early Christianity lack access to power or a body of law to impose on all and sundry; it also lacked any concept of territoriality. In fact, it critiqued the idolatry of territory. This continues to have political implications, even though territoriality remained a 'temptation' which could, if necessary, be justified by Old Testament models of a theocratic 'holy commonwealth'. David Martin (1997: 114–20, 194–201) portrays Christianity as a massive revision of Judaism on a universal scale, but which had to work its way through enormous resistances which partially confiscated it. Thus, this marginalized faith became the official cult of the empire, virtually co-extensive with the social whole and partly reverting to the Old Testament programme. But from early modern times, differentiation and globalization expanded the separation of Church from nation, or faith from land and natural community, and reactivated its original status as a cross-cultural voluntary group. Violence is likely as church separates from nation, since the latter now has the power (invoked by Augustine to curtail religious freedom) to 'compel people to come in'. (This struggle between voluntary church and authoritarian nation-state may partly explain why some observers feel that 'wherever there are pentecostals, there is trouble'.)

Although the magisterial Reformation did not break with the Christendom model, Protestantism did tend to promote tolerance because it fractured the church and weakened all human instances authorized to resolve religious disputes. It also spawned a radical fringe which by the 1640s was breaking the 'Augustinian consensus' (Coffey 2000) on religious persecution. And it was doing so from religious conviction, not from scepticism. Even many sectarians who were intolerant in polemical or ecclesiastical contexts were nevertheless firm supporters of civil tolerance.

CHRISTIANITY AND ISLAM: LAW, TERRITORY AND POWER

Many leading scholars of religion and politics agree that there are differences between Christianity and Islam which transcend their social contexts. While Christianity started on the margins of an existing empire, Islam became the centre of a new empire. Perhaps for that reason, it is not carried by a 'church' distinct from other spheres of life. It also strongly emphasizes a religiously sanctioned body of laws, something absent in Christianity. Another contrast is in Islam's stress on territoriality. This intimate original connection with power, law and territory requires of Islam a theodicy to explain its recent geopolitical humiliations, whereas no such requirement seems to weigh on southern Christians in countries that suffer similar humiliations. But we must remember that no religion is frozen in time, and ideas originally absent can be acquired (as when Christianity acquired territoriality and became Christendom). Thus, Christians living in cultures influenced by non-Christian models of religion-state relations may start to imitate those models (there are hints of an Islamization of Christianity in Nigeria, for example [Freston 2001: 184]). In addition, Christianity's birth distant from power has left it with dangerous voids (e.g. how to relate to other religious groups once in power) which may be filled by Old Testament models or models from surrounding society. While Islam was born with norms of relative tolerance for some religions and regulated intolerance for others, Christianity lacks explicit norms and thus oscillates between extremes of tolerance and intolerance.

Scholars differ (e.g. Juergensmeyer 2001: 40–1 *versus* Bruce 2003: 211) in their evaluation of contemporary Protestant involvement in violence in the global north. Christianity can, evidently, be used to justify violence; like many religions, it offers images of cosmic war which absolutize conflicts and demonize opponents. It has been used (directly by some American Christians and indirectly by the US government) to justify the absolutizing 'war on terror'. But our concern is how much that happens in the global south.

SOUTHERN PROTESTANTISM AND ISLAM

There are several dimensions to the relationship between the two largest religions in the global south: Christianity and Islam.

One of the most influential books on global Christianity, Philip Jenkins' *The Next Christendom* (2002: 190), affirms that 'an increasing share of the world's people is going to identify with one of two religions, either Christianity or Islam, and the two have a long and disastrous record of conflict'. He even foresees a 'coming crusade' of Christians against Muslims, in competition for converts (as people of third religions become scarcer). 'Issues of theocracy and religious law, toleration and minority rights, conversion and apostasy, should be among the most divisive in domestic and international politics for decades to come.' So is politically destabilizing conflict inevitable now that fewer religious 'third options' are available? Will expansionist monotheisms make pluralistic post-colonial nation-states inviable?

POLITICAL DIMENSIONS OF PROSELYTIZATION AND CONVERSION

The legitimacy and regulation of proselytization constitutes a growing political question worldwide (Hackett 2007). However, the growth of southern Christianity is changing the composition of Christian missions

(Freston 2007). While American proselytizers remain numerous, Europeans have diminished sharply, their place being taken by Latin Americans, Africans and Asians. This can affect the debate on the social acceptability and political legitimacy of proselytization, since the new proselytizers are from the oppressed global south and do not carry post-colonial stigma.

In addition, there is now increased interaction among the world religions. Although they have encountered each other before (militarily and peacefully), the encounters were more limited. Today, through the media, diasporas and missions affect more people, even in the heartlands of the respective faiths, and increasingly through peaceful propagation. As the conversionist world religions increasingly target each other's populations, debate over the rights and wrongs of proselytization will become more salient.

The political dimensions of southern Christian proselytistic activities are thus a key dimension of the relationship between Christianity and public life around the world, especially where the churches are fast-growing. In some countries the political system depends heavily on the maintenance of existing religious percentages, making proselytization a threat to political hegemony. How do southern Christian proselytizers see questions of religious freedom and 'appropriate' methods?

Social class comes into play here. In most of the Third World, pentecostal churches have a genuinely popular nature in which both leaders and led are from humble origins. They are distant from cultural and academic power, and often do not conform to 'polite' discourse. In addition, their theology is uncompromising and often seen as intrinsically 'aggressive'.

In increasingly plural societies, it is necessary not only to respect other religions but also to protect them from ridicule and contempt. Yet in general the rising tide of evangelical missionaries from the global south is not, I believe, the final ingredient in a recipe for global religious conflagration. They are, on the whole, engaged in peaceable activities based on the supposition of religious freedom and dialogue. As one Brazilian missionary told me, 'the Protestant reformers went on for centuries doing theology without missions and burning anyone who thought differently'. In other words, he views missions as an antidote to intolerance. This is a far cry from the common idea that missions are related to coercion and the colonization of consciousness. Realistically, we would have to say that both scenarios have happened in the past and will probably happen in the future.

In some pentecostal circles we see a more problematic tendency. Like those pseudo-democrats who want 'one man, one vote, one time', some pentecostal leaders appear to want freedom to 'win' and then close down religious freedom.

Nevertheless, a survey of pentecostals in the United States and nine countries of the global south carried out by the Pew Forum on Religion and Public Life in 2006 paints a more encouraging portrait of ordinary pentecostals. To the question whether it is important that there be freedom for religions other than one's own, pentecostals everywhere were at least as affirmative as the general population of their countries (e.g. 94 per cent of Brazilian pentecostals, compared to a national average of 95 per cent), and in the Philippines even more so (95 per cent compared to 87 per cent).

SOUTHERN CHRISTIANITY AND VIOLENCE

Another dimension of the relationship between Christianity and Islam in the global south concerns political violence, whether related to international terrorism or to more local forms of violence.

The question of a potential connection between Christian poverty and international terrorism leads to the vexed issue of context versus religious tradition. Three leading sociologists (Davie, Heelas and Woodhead 2003: 13) have predicted that, in the world's most impoverished region, which is sub-Saharan Africa, certain forms of 'hard and exclusivistic' Christianity have a serious terrorist potential. All they lack are Al-Qaeda's 'knowledge, skills and technology to be dangerous on an international scale'.

The only movement cited in justification is the Lord's Resistance Army. But their portrayal of this Ugandan militia as an advance guard of 'hard' sub-Saharan Christianity is questionable (the founder is of Catholic origin but has created an eclectic belief system including the Ten Commandments and elements of Islam and traditional Acholi religion, and is funded from Muslim sources, and the movement enjoys no sympathy amongst African Christians in general). But what is the true potential for forms of 'southern' Christianity to become the next constituency of recruits for terrorism?

Political correctness virtually decrees that one admit a similar range of positions as equally feasible within every major religious tradition; that one agree, in short, with what Bruce (2003: 215) calls the 'Pygmalion method': that religion is epiphenomenal and circumstances are everything. If Jerry Falwell and the leader of Hizbollah were to swap places (but not religions) their attitudes to violence would simply be reversed; all major religions are so broad that they can legitimate almost any action. Bruce does not want to go to the opposite extreme adopted by Huntington, whose civilizational blocs are defined largely by religious traditions. Nevertheless, between arguing that religion is absolutely crucial and that it is merely epiphenomenal, it is possible, says Bruce, to argue that there are significant differences between traditions. Apart from separation of church and state, Bruce finds the key difference between Christianity and Islam in the question of 'law', a religiously mandated way of life. Wherever they are found in significant numbers, says Bruce controversially, 'Muslims always want either to take over the state or to secede from it – the goal being the imposition of shariah'. There is nothing comparable in the behaviour of Christians, he claims (2003: 234f.).

One healthy reaction to terrorism in the name of Islam has been to resist the temptation to demonize that religion. But it is also unhelpful to portray Islam as a twin brother to Christianity having a similar diversity of postures and explaining current differences merely as a time-lag ('look at all the similar things Christians have done *in the past*')

caused by the geopolitical humiliation of the Muslim world in recent centuries. It is important to ask whether there are any differences (at least, in the *weight* of each posture within each religion, and the *plausibility* with which each posture can be defended theologically) that stem from the religions themselves.

Does a Christianity with massive grassroots support in the cauldron of the global south become susceptible to the appeal of political violence? Thrust into the same context of poverty and geopolitical humiliation, does it reveal itself as Islam's twin brother?

In coming decades, southern Christianity and 'Euro-Islam' will help us to answer these questions better. But it would seem that the weaker sense of territoriality in Christianity means that, however much it may come to be associated with the poor and oppressed, it will find it hard to generate a broad sense of a 'Christian umma' under threat, a generalized sentiment of belonging to a distinct religiously defined community with a common fate. Thus, there will be no diffused feeling of alienation to underpin a cultural cauldron in which Christian terrorist organizations could emerge and find sufficient recruits and broad enough sympathy (for their causes, if not for their methods).

If not a southern Christian 'umma' using religiously justified geopolitical violence, what about more localized violence based on religion?

Southern evangelicals have indeed used violence. Recent publications (Ranger forthcoming; Lumsdaine 2007) talk of increasing Muslim–Christian conflict in West Africa and South-East Asia. While most of the violence has probably been perpetrated by Muslims, the Christians have been far from blameless. Nigerian bishops have approved taking up arms during inter-religious rioting. Evangelicals have killed Muslims who (they would say) were attacking them. During the guerrilla emergency in the 1980s, Peruvian pentecostals filled the Peasant Patrols formed (sometimes on evangelical initiative) to defend the local community from the Maoist Shining Path guerrillas, in the absence of other support. In their armed action, these pentecostals saw themselves as fighting the anti-Christ (López 2007).

Violence in self-defence is not, of course, incompatible with democracy (especially where the state is weak or absent). But in other contexts, 'self-defence' is construed as necessary against the state itself, e.g. where Protestantism has been adopted by a considerable portion of a small ethnic minority which considers itself oppressed by the post-colonial nation-state. Protestantism has fused significantly with ethnic separatist rebellions among marginal peoples. One example is the Indian state of Nagaland, almost totally Christian and largely Baptist. The main guerrilla group, the National Socialist Council of Nagaland (NSCN), is so influenced by evangelical Christianity that it has an evangelistic music group. The manifesto of the NSCN is imbued with a sense of mission, resulting in a mixture of socialism, democratic centralism, evangelical missionary fervour, a liberal doctrine of religious toleration and a profession of faith in guerrilla warfare. 'It is arms and arms alone that will save our nation' (Freston 2001: 91; for other examples of Protestant involvement in separatist rebellions, see Freston 2001: 82–3, 94–100, 116–18).

Beyond self-defence and armed separatism, can one talk of evangelical terrorists? There was some involvement in the Rwandan genocide of 1994 (after Rwanda had been the scene of one of the great evangelical revivals of the twentieth century). And there are a few cases in Central America of pentecostal vigilante groups, in a context where such groups are proliferating. However, a recent book on religious terrorists (Stern 2003) mentions only three candidates for a category of 'evangelical terrorists', two of which are in the United States. Firstly, the 'Identity Christians' who see Anglo-Saxons as the 'true Israel' and America as a sacred land. As the dominant religion of the racist right, it is not very exportable to the Third World. The second group are the extreme anti-abortionists who have bombed abortion clinics and murdered their staff. This is potentially exportable, and we should only find out how much if most of the Third World were to adopt abortion policies similar to those of the United States. The third group are the Christian militias in some eastern islands

of Indonesia. As the transmigration of Javanese Muslims and the activity of Muslim militias upset the local religious and ethnic balance, Christian militia groups emerged.

What about state violence? Vásquez and Marquardt (2003: 141) inveigh against pentecostalism's 'rhetoric of war', with its language of 'spiritual warfare' and 'crusade', giving as example of the dangers involved the anti-insurgency strategy of the charismatic evangelical general Ríos Montt, president of Guatemala in 1982–83. But that is to underestimate the capacity of pentecostals to comprehend these militant metaphors, and drives a wedge between Ríos Montt and other equally repressive (but non-pentecostal) Central American military presidents. Ríos, in any case, was a recent convert. What is certain, however, is that his pentecostalism did not *prevent* him acting in that way, since he was held in high esteem by his church.

There is a growing tendency on the part of some pentecostals to demonize their religious rivals and social movements they regard as degenerate. Although not necessarily incompatible with peaceful co-existence and democratic life, this is potentially worrying in regions where democratic norms are not soundly embedded.

In short, popular Protestantism in the global south has some connection with violence, but there are few examples not related either to self-defence in the absence of the state, or to ethno-regional separatist movements. Southern Protestants do not have the Islamic concepts of the honour of a sacred community (*umma*) and the defence of a sacred territory (*dar-al-islam*). Nor do they have the geopolitical influence that American evangelicals enjoy. And, as a relatively new religion, only rarely (and then usually only among marginalized minorities) are they connected with ethno-religious conflicts. All these factors minimize their propensity to violence.

A NEW CHRISTENDOM?

Jenkins (2002: 12) foresees a 'new Christendom', a wave of Christian states which may eventually form an African and Latin American axis in which faith is the guiding political ideology. Is there any evidence for this? Or, at least, for attempts to create new 'Christian' nations or states in the global south?

As to predictions of a new Christendom, Sanneh (2003: 39) replies caustically that there is 'little evidence that Christian Africa will repeat the disasters of Christian Europe ... there have been no ecclesiastical courts condemning heretics and witches to death, no bloody battles of doctrine, no territorial aggrandisement by churches, no jihads against infidels, no amputations'. As Sanneh's slide from medieval Christian to modern Muslim deeds indicates, it is not only European Christendom which is the supposed model for future southern Christian deviations, but also radical Islamism. Yet southern Christianity lacks the ecclesiastical unity and political muscle necessary for a reconstituted Christendom, while also lacking the Islamist nostalgia for a glorious past. Almost no southern Christians have political projects similar to those of radical Islamists. This is so even in Zambia (Freston 2004a: 83–91) where the influence of charismatic evangelicalism led to the nation being declared 'Christian' in 1991 by president Chiluba. After his electoral victory (which was not on a specifically religious platform), he had State House 'cleansed' of evil spirits, organized an 'anointing' service modelled on that of King David, and declared Zambia to be a 'Christian nation' in a covenant relationship with God.

While some Christians criticized Chiluba for this, others approved but felt it had not gone far enough. Amongst the latter was Nevers Mumba, a televangelist who ran for president in 2001 for his own political party, promising a 'revolution of morality and prosperity'. It was not good enough, he said, merely to have a Christian president and vice-president; all political positions should be occupied by God-fearing people. His intention was to 'uphold the declaration of Zambia as a Christian nation, with a view to making it more practical'. This did not mean religious discrimination, he explained; rather, it meant leaders with a different character. 'Abuse of office, high levels of selfishness and overall lack of

character in politicians have impeded economic growth ... Good governance cannot be achieved by bad people.'

Mumba was, in any case, heavily defeated at the polls. But we should notice what is *not* going on in Zambia. It is the *nation* that is declared Christian and not the *state*. There is no established church, no legal discrimination of non-Christians in public life and no limitation on religious freedom, much less any Christian 'sharia law'. Even those who lament the inadequate implementation of the 'Christian nation' concept do not advocate such measures. Their proposals are all perfectly compatible with democratic life. Mumba's programme says little about specific laws to make the country more 'Christian', but it does talk a lot about public morality and qualities of leadership. While it makes questionable assumptions about the relationship between personal faith, good governance and national prosperity, there is no idea that a Christian nation should have a 'sharia'. With all the limitations of Zambian Christian politics, this is an encouraging sign for the political future of the Christian south.

And yet there are causes for concern in some charismatic theology, such as the concept of territoriality (and a 'rule of the saints') in versions of 'spiritual warfare' which talk of 'territorial spirits' and are frequently associated with theocratic currents. The sacralisation of power in such concepts (and its consequent demonization when in the hands of non-believers), makes criticism difficult. Introducing territoriality into a pluralistic situation brings dangers. If Tertullian ridiculed the pagans who cried 'away with the Christians to the lions!' whenever the Tiber rose as high as the city walls, today it is 'spiritual warfare' pentecostals who blame such calamities on the particular religious rival or socially 'degenerate' group of their choice.

However, the danger to democracy can be exaggerated: some analysts jump from the discourse to the supposed effects, without any empirical evidence. In practice, the language of demonization functions largely as an internal language of justification, a manicheism of people and not of ideas ('we must elect men of God'). It is possible for people to disagree strongly about things they regard as supremely important (such as the need to convert others, and even exorcise them of demons) and still be good democrats. The popularity of exorcism has to do with the growing concern with evil in many parts of Africa (Ellis and Ter Haar 2004: 42) and Latin America (Birman 2000: 276-8). A spirit idiom is used to express concern with poor governance. By treating older notions of spiritual evil seriously (rather than with poorly concealed disdain), pentecostalism defuses fatalism and leads a cultural revolution (Soares 1993: 43-50; Jenkins 2006: 99).

The American Religious Right and Popular Protestantism in the Global South

If it is important to compare evangelicals with other religio-political actors in the Third World, it is also relevant to compare them with their co-religionists in the global north, and especially in the country often (and largely mistakenly) seen as creator and controller of global evangelicalism: the United States. As American evangelicals have become politically influential in a conservative direction, culminating (so far) in their role in the re-election of George Bush in 2004, does the globalization of evangelical Christianity portend a similar role in the south, including a strengthening of American 'soft power' through a common geopolitical worldview? If not the next constituency of recruits for terrorism, are southern Protestants the polar opposite, creating a global constituency that sees the world through the eyes of American religious right leaders such as Pat Robertson or James Dobson, or at least of the 40 per cent of Bush voters reputed to be evangelicals? Is global Protestant political involvement an offspring of the religious right? Or at least its natural ally? And does it represent an extension of the 'soft power' of the United States?

With regard to being an offspring of the religious right, the bald answer is 'minimally'. The religious right does of course try hard to export its views and would have us believe it is successful. But it is largely wrong. Global Protestant politics cannot be read off from that of white American evangelicals. To give a rather puerile example, no Venezuelan Protestant was willing to assassinate Hugo Chávez at the behest of Pat Robertson!

One line of interpretation of Third World popular Protestantism claims it is 'contributing mightily to the Americanization of global culture', that 'the social product that [Protestants] distribute so successfully around the world is clearly stamped 'Made in USA' and that it promotes an acceptance of American global hegemony (Brouwer et al. 1996: 270–1). In evaluating this, we have to remember this is a phenomenon that spans three continents and several 'generations' of churches, so variations are immense. The 'Americanization' theory obviously builds on certain facts. Southern Protestantism has many foreign contacts; the question is how important they are. In personnel and money, both Catholicism and historical Protestantism are usually far more foreign than pentecostalism. Foreign presence is usually most noticeable in the media, whose efficacy for growth is doubtful. International contacts often do not indicate dependence at all, but rather a source of symbolic legitimacy for fighting local battles.

While Brouwer et al. concentrate on religious globalization from above, it is globalization from below which is more widespread and determinant. Transnational evangelicalism is more and more initiated within the Third World. The 'hard' (orchestrated) Americanization thesis is hard to defend as an account, not of American religious actors' intentions but of global evangelical growth. The 'soft' (emulationist) version of this thesis is still plausible, but close examination of evangelical networks tends more towards a 'complex global flows' explanation.

If not an offspring, what about a natural ally? Here, the answer is more complex. There is considerable alignment on abortion and homosexuality, but less on gender and economics, and still less on geopolitics. Even on abortion and homosexuality, American-style 'culture wars' are not reproduced (except perhaps in South Africa). Most societies (and their laws) are opposed to easy abortion and gay marriage. In addition, most Protestants are poor people in poor countries, on the edge of survival. As they try to reconstruct the family in the midst of mass unemployment, the violence of machismo culture, and the anomie resulting from the transition to mega-cities, they are little attracted to occasional efforts by denominational leaders to involve them in single-issue 'values' politics.

The 2006 Pew Forum survey on pentecostalism asked two questions on abortion. Firstly, whether abortion is ever morally justified. In the US, 64 per cent of pentecostals answered no, well above the 45 per cent of the general population. In all nine southern countries surveyed, an even higher percentage of pentecostals answered no (from 77 per cent in South Korea to 97 per cent in the Philippines). But only in South Korea are pentecostals significantly above the national average as in the US. In Latin America they slightly reinforce the strong general opposition. And in Africa and the Philippines they merely reflect their national average.

The second question concerned legislation: should government interfere with a woman's ability to have an abortion. Global pentecostalism is more nuanced on this than usually imagined. American pentecostals are now in the middle range (54 per cent favouring government intervention, compared to a high of 77 per cent in the Philippines and a low of 37 per cent in Guatemala). But pentecostals in the US and South Korea still stand out as far more favourable to anti-abortion legislation than their national average. Pentecostals elsewhere reflect national opinion closely; and in four countries are below their national average! Little more than a third of Guatemalan pentecostals think government should legislate against abortion.

On gender issues, pentecostals everywhere are more in favour of women as religious leaders than are other Christians and the general populations. As to whether men should have more right to employment than women when jobs are scarce, only 29 per cent of American pentecostals think so, more than the 25 per cent of Kenyan pentecostals but way below the 69 per cent of Filipinos. But compared to their national average, US pentecostals are notably more conservative, whereas southern pentecostals mirror theirs or are slightly more liberal.

On economic policy, southern pentecostals generally reflect national opinion regarding a free market economy (from 89 per cent favourable in Nigeria to 47 per cent in Chile). However, on welfare (whether government should guarantee food and shelter to every citizen) pentecostals everywhere are slightly more favourable than their general populations. And southern pentecostals (from 80 per cent in Kenya to 97 per cent in the Philippines), are always more favourable than their American co-religionists (77 per cent).

Regarding socio-eoconomic questions, evangelicals have shifted somewhat to the left in recent years, especially in Latin America. In part, this is due to changes in the Catholic Church, no longer seen as occupying the left so much. There are also class aspects: in Venezuela, for example, pentecostals tend to be quite favourable to Hugo Chávez, as are other members of the lower classes. And growing involvement in social projects sometimes leads to the perception that many transformations cannot be achieved at the purely individual level. Also, pentecostalism's attraction as a religion of personal salvation means that more and more left-wing militants convert and continue their left-wing militancy.

Even some prosperity preachers, previously thought to be automatically favourable to neoliberalism, have changed their views, realizing that their encouragement of self-employment might be as well served by the left's proposals for strengthening the domestic market and small-scale enterprise as by a recessive neoliberalism which throws people onto the informal market but abandons them there.

Extension of American 'Soft Power'?

Does global Protestantism spread an ideological outlook favourable to US foreign policy? In fact, the 'war on terror' and especially the war in Iraq have revealed a fissure within global evangelicalism. The unpopularity of American foreign policy has meant that the influence of evangelicals on President Bush has sometimes damaged the image of evangelicals locally (as when former president Mário Soares of Portugal spoke of 'fanaticized sects like the evangelicals ... to which Bush belongs').

Our survey of evangelicals should be placed in the context of world opinion. According to a Pew Research Center survey of March 2004 (covering Europe and Muslim countries ['A Year After Iraq War', http://people-press.org/reports/display.php3?ReportID=206]), discontent with US policies had intensified following the invasion of Iraq. Amid doubts about America's real motives, there was broad agreement (except in the US) that the war had hurt rather than helped the 'war on terror'. Similarly, in April 2003 90 per cent of Brazilians were opposed to the invasion of Iraq. Sixty per cent said their view of the US had worsened, and only 2 per cent said it had improved (Datafolha, 6 April 2003, www1.folha.uol.com.br/folha/datafolha). And a 2004 survey concluded that, of 35 nations surveyed, only the Philippines, Poland and Nigeria would clearly back George Bush for re-election (www.fpa.org/newsletter_info2583/newsletter_info.htm).

We should also place our survey of southern evangelicals in the context of American evangelical opinion. Many of its most respected voices blessed the war plans. A poll of February 2003 showed evangelicals were more likely to support a war in Iraq than the American public in general (in Sine 2004). Soon after the invasion, 87 per cent of white evangelicals supported it (Marsh 2006). Many respected leaders viewed it as opening a chance to evangelize Muslims. The president of the National Association of Evangelicals signed an open letter which stated (before the invasion) that 'the threat Iraq and its weapons pose to us and to others is truly grave' (http://www.nae.net/index.cfm?FUSEACTION=editor.page&pageID=17&IDcategory=1). The largest denomination, the Southern Baptist Convention, withdrew from the Baptist World Alliance after the latter had condemned the invasion.

How, then, do Third World evangelicals view the Bush administration's foreign policy? The following overview is admittedly impressionistic. In it, one should take as read a universal condemnation of the terrorist attacks of 2001.

Firstly, what about world bodies within evangelicalism? A World Evangelical Alliance statement of February 2003, when the invasion was imminent, walks a tightrope. 'The WEA is a global, evangelical network ... where no one nation or person is dominant ... We believe that war ... is almost always the worst solution' (statement of 21 Feb 2003, www.worldevangelical.org). The Baptist World Alliance was more direct, classifying the invasion as 'a great sin' (statement of 20 March 2003, http://www.internationalministries.org/update/bwa_war2003.htm).

Our survey of countries will be weighted towards Brazil, which has the largest evangelical community in the world outside the United States. The leading interdenominational evangelical magazine Ultimato has strongly opposed the war, although it does publish letters to the editor which take a different position. It argues that Bush is achieving what 40 years of communist propaganda were unable to, that is, to put the US at odds with the rest of the world. The Iraq war is seen as a pretext to establish a new world order. The magazine favourably cites American evangelist Leighton Ford for his opposition to the war, but denounces the evangelicals who, in its opinion, ally themselves with self-interested politicians who speak cynically of the defence of Christian morality but not against the absurd level of US military spending, the economic imperialism, the exacerbated nationalism, the hypocrisy of alternating free trade and protectionism according to the convenience of American corporations, and of supporting convenient dictatorships and overthrowing inconvenient ones in the name of democracy, and the cowardly 40-year blockade of Cuba.

Interviews in Ultimato with leading Brazilian evangelicals stress the danger of an American mentality which sees itself as the incarnation of good, remembering that Saddam Hussein (like many erstwhile Latin American dictators) was long supported by the US. Behind the rhetoric of disseminating democracy, one finds the desire to control energy resources and consolidate imperial rule.

The neo-conservative doctrine of removing all obstacles to lone global domination makes all states around the world feel threatened. The war will make the world less safe and harm the image of evangelicals everywhere.

How representative is all this? Before the invasion, a television programme with several Brazilian evangelical congressmen discussed the issue. However conservative the parties that these congressmen represented, and however 'unconventional' the pentecostal churches they were members of, they were unanimous in condemning the imminent invasion. In addition, in my research among Brazilian evangelical missionaries abroad I have been struck by how opposed to the Bush administration policies my interlocutors have been. Already during the 2001 war in Afghanistan, the leader of a mission which places professional people in Muslim countries told me: 'American policies are not helping, and American evangelicals are very pro-Israel ... [But] we [Brazilian missionaries] have no difficulty taking a position unfavourable to Israel ... We repudiate the terrorist attacks [of September 2001] ... but we recognise they did not happen in a historical vacuum. The West must reflect on its international policies and abandon the double standard it applies ... We need to show the world that we are moved by a different spirit from the one ... in which prejudices are stronger than respect and dignity.' Even more idealistically, another Brazilian missions leader affirms that 'the Christian community had an opportunity to evangelize the world on September 11th ... If the representative of the greatest Protestant nation had [spoken] of forgiveness and not revenge, the world would really have known the gospel. If he had said, "we forgive what you have done, and we want to ask forgiveness for what we have done to you over the years"...' The president of the leading evangelical student organization in Brazil said that, while he agreed with the standard portrayal of Bush as a leader who has ruined the image of Americans around the world, given munition to those who ridicule Christianity and is a puppet of the arms and oil industries, he feared that Bush's 'insensitive and hypocritical defence of morality' might, in a post-Bush reaction, lead to a weakening of desire for a healthy moral climate.

The majority current in Brazilian evangelicalism seems far closer, on these geopolitical questions, to 'mainstream' Christian currents in the US rather than to American evangelical positions. For Spanish-speaking Latin America, Padilla and Scott (2004) stress the surprising diversity of Latin American churches which pronounced against the war, including many churches thought of as politically conservative or which imagine themselves as 'non-political'. They conclude that not a single Latin American denomination seems to have been in favour, even in the few countries whose governments supported President Bush.

Looking briefly at a few African and Asian countries, we find that a conservative South African political party, based mostly among white and black charismatic churches, the African Christian Democratic Party, strongly opposed the imminent invasion. Its spokesman in parliament said that 'selfish interests and ducking domestic problems' were not good reasons for war. 'The ACDP rejects from a Christian perspective the American "civil religion" that says America is predestined by God to save the world, [which amounts to] a near deification of the US state' (Freston 2004a: 96).

In China (personal communication from Kim-Kwong Chan), which may now have more evangelical Christians than any other country in the world except the United States and Brazil, virtually all Christians followed the standard sentiment of the Chinese population, that the US was bullying the world in its own national interest.

Somewhat different positions predominated in India and the Philippines. In the former country (personal communication from Sushil Aaron), silence seems to have been the main reaction. In the Philippines, however (personal communication from David Lim), many leading evangelicals are pro-Bush, albeit less strongly than before. It should be remembered that Filipinos are one of the few peoples who would have re-elected Bush in 2004.

The Pew survey in 2006 asked whether respondents favoured 'the US-led efforts to fight terrorism'. In all countries surveyed, pentecostals are similar to the national average, except (for obvious reasons) in the half-Christian and half-Muslim country of Nigeria. Only there (71 per cent) and the Philippines (76 per cent) do pentecostals support the 'war on terror' as much as in the US (72 per cent); these two countries are predictable exceptions in the global south since they both suffer internal tension between their Muslim and non-Muslim populations. But in Latin America and South Africa, only around one-third of pentecostals support the 'war on terror', and in South Korea only 16 per cent. In all Latin American countries surveyed, pentecostals are actually slightly less favourable to it than their general populations; so much for the idea that global pentecostalism is helping American 'soft power'!

It is true that this disfavour may be partly due to a desire, especially in countries where evangelicals are a small minority and pluralism is not always respected, to avoid the negative fall-out for their own communities of an association between President Bush's global unpopularity and his well-publicized links with American evangelicals. In any case, this geopolitical divide gives the lie to the idea of Third World evangelicalism as 'global American fundamentalism'.

Christian Zionism in the Third World?

American evangelicals' influence on foreign policy is often considered strongest in its uncompromising support of Israel. This is due to Christian Zionism, a current in modern Christianity which not only reintroduces territoriality but also involves direct conflict with Islam.

Christian Zionism believes that the Jews remain God's chosen people, apart from any possible conversion to Christianity, and that all the land 'from the river of Egypt to the Euphrates' has been given in perpetuity to them. The Jewish temple should be rebuilt in Jerusalem (on the site of the Al-Aqsa mosque). Christian Zionists support Israeli expansionism, believing this will culminate in the battle of Armageddon and the return of Christ. Some would even concur with television evangelist

Pat Robertson's declaration that Yitzhak Rabin's assassination was divine punishment for having signed the Oslo Peace Accords, and Ariel Sharon's stroke was God's retribution for giving up the Gaza Strip.

There are an estimated 25–30 million Christian Zionists in the US (Sizer 2004: 23). Christian Zionism is usually (though not always) linked with a theory of biblical prophetic interpretation known as dispensationalism, which began in Britain in the 1830s but has taken root most strongly in the US. Indeed, there are many 'Judaizing elements' (Martin 1997) in American Protestantism, with its motifs of covenant, promised land and pilgrimage. Such ideas may make it especially susceptible to Christian Zionism.

Does the rise of global evangelicalism mean the globalization of strong support for Christian Zionism? After all, southern believers read the same Old Testament and may be exposed to Christian Zionist literature from the US which tells them that their nations cannot be blessed unless they support Israel.

On the other hand, Christians read the Bible for centuries before anyone thought of a national restoration of the Jews and the dispensationalist schema of interpretation. And there are several reasons why apocalypticism in general and Christian Zionism in particular might not be so important for believers in the global south. Intensity of prophetic interest depends on other priorities; for poor people in the global south, survival issues take precedence over idle speculation. Apocalyptic may be popular for existential comfort but not so much for geopolitical titillation; indeed, as Jenkins says (2006: 128), they may not have to imagine End Times scenarios to make biblical references to persecution real for them. They have no impression of a declining church (which dispensationalism prophesies for the End Times), nor do they resent a loss of cultural hegemony within their own cultures (which they have never had), and much less do they fear a receding geopolitical hegemony for their own countries (which most of them could never dream of having). They have no post-Holocaust feeling of guilt regarding the Jews, and probably have little first-hand contact with Jews. They are more likely to have contact with Arabs, and some of them (e.g. in parts of Latin America) are actually descended from Arab immigrants. They feel less threat from terrorism; indeed, they may entertain feelings of Third World solidarity against 'neo-imperialism'. In the tough conditions of the Third World, the idea of blessing as dependent on support for Israel does not seem as cogent. Even though some denominations cultivate links with the 'Holy Land', the emphasis is more on 'the places where Jesus walked' rather than on current issues (see, for example, the website of the Brazilian neo-pentecostal Universal Church of the Kingdom of God, www.arcauniversal.com.br).

The Pew survey of 2006 asked respondents whether they sympathized more with Israel or the Palestinians. Of course, 'sympathy' for Israel does not necessarily indicate Christian Zionism, but it is the best data we possess. In all ten countries, pentecostals are above their national average in sympathy for Israel. American (60 per cent) and Filipino (67 per cent) pente-costals sympathize very strongly with Israel, considerably above their national averages (41 per cent and 55 per cent respectively). Nigerian, Kenyan and Guatemalan pente-costals are over 40 per cent, but their co-religionists in Brazil, Chile, South Africa and South Korea are below 40 per cent. Even more telling is the sum of the three replies which seem to preclude a Christian Zionist position (sympathy for the Palestinians, both or neither). Only 18 per cent of American pen-tecostals come in those categories, versus 56 per cent of pentecostals in Chile, followed by five other countries between 52 per cent and 46 per cent. Once again, Nigeria (32 per cent) and the Philippines (25 per cent) are the only southern countries whose pentecostals mirror their American brethren.

Protestantism in the global south and democracy

Of the major religions, Protestantism has the longest historical links with religious freedom and democratization. Witte (1993) speaks of three waves of Christian democratizing impulses which accompanied, or even antici-pated, Huntington's (1991) 'three waves' of democratization. The first of Witte's waves was Protestant, in the Northern Europe and North America of the seventeenth and eighteenth centuries. Of course, this first wave was largely an unintended result of the fracturing of the religious field and the experience of wars of religion, rather than the intended result of most Protestant leaders' convictions. Even so, 'most of democracy's original exponents were deeply rooted in verities derived from Christian faith and ethics' (De Gruchy 1995: 49). In addi-tion, 'principled pluralism' was one of the early Protestant postures towards the state. This position, which first achieved political importance in the 1640s with the Levellers in England and Roger Williams in Rhode Island, supplied the theological basis which allowed Protestant sectarian theology to overflow into democratic politics by rejecting any division of the political world between the godly and the ungodly. The situation of Old Testament Israel was seen as entirely exceptional; today, the state should be non-confessional.

Thus, democratization was strengthened not just by Protestant fragmentation (Bruce 2004: 9–10) but also by elements of Protestant teaching and organization (Willaime 1997: 2081; Berger 2004: 78; Anderson 2006: 195). In con-sequence, today's Protestants, wherever they may be, are not usually required to allay fears regarding their religion's ultimate ability to co-exist with democracy.

But in reality, there have always been *Protestantisms* in the plural. Early Protestantism included not only the 'principled pluralist' posi-tion of religious freedom in a non-confessional state, but also the 'Christian nation' idea of the state promoting true religion and morals, and the apolitical 'rejection' of the state. Some non-democratic regimes in modern times have enjoyed Protestant support or at least acquiescence. Protestantism, whether histori-cally in the global north or today in the south, has often been undemocratic at diverse levels: in its internal life, in its attitudes towards other religions, and in its association with undemoc-ratic regimes or with undemocratic political actors. But its historical origins, its theological traditions and its organizational divisions combine to weaken any tendency to theocracy or to a concerted use of political violence.

This is to disagree with those like Bruce (2003: 245, 2004: 18) who believe that 'religion taken seriously is incompatible with democracy' because the godly/ungodly division of the world is incompatible with the principle that all people are essentially of equal worth. Bruce ignores 'principled pluralism' and its importance in the evolution of religious freedom and democratic ideas. Nevertheless, southern Protestantism, which is certainly 'religion taken seriously', does not yet have both feet firmly in the democratic camp, and it often operates in contexts where few other political actors are wholehearted democrats either. In any case, by the late 1990s most scholars of democratic transitions thought religious traditions were largely irrelevant to the outcomes of democratization processes. And while democracy is undoubtedly strongest in countries of a Western Christian tradition, that correlation might not hold if one controlled for other factors (Anderson 2006: 204).

Woodberry and Shah (2004), however, allege that the correlation between democracy and Protestantism does hold in the global south, even controlling for other variables. They talk of compelling cross-national evidence of a causal association between Protestantism and democracy, but a relation that is mediated and contingent. Mediating factors include not only characteristics of Protestant activity (such as the encouragement of education), but also opponents' reactions which often imitate its organizational forms and activities. This means Protestantism's effect on democracy may not be as dramatic as before, as other actors adopt its characteristics. Also, they warn, some strains of global pentecostalism may not have as positive an effect as historical Protestantism (amongst other reasons, because of their smaller emphasis on education).

Thus, there is no blanket answer to whether southern Protestantism is a help or a hindrance to democratization. It arrived in the Third World largely with a critique of Catholic or non-Christian 'confusion' of religion and politics. However, with its numerical burgeoning, the political restraint implied in acceptance of democratic rules is less evident in some quarters. As evangelicalism turned global, it became involved in politics in very diverse settings and was put to a variety of political uses (Freston 2001, 2004a, 2004b). This variety is accentuated by 'local subversion', in which local contextual factors overwhelm the universal heritage of the church; a danger all the greater in churches with local autonomy. Being a decentralized faith, the globalization of evangelicalism may produce a splintering of political perspectives unable to dialogue with each other.

The political implications have been appraised in very varied ways by scholars. On the one side are authors who emphasize the repressive and corporatist nature of many churches (especially the pentecostal ones). Other authors see southern Protestantism as a potential or actual contributor to democracy, whether directly through resistance to authoritarianisms and assistance to democratizing movements, or indirectly through creating the cultural conditions for democratic consolidation (as part of a vibrant civil society, offering a free social space, an experience of solidarity and a new personal identity, as well as responsible participation in the community and, for some, the development of leadership gifts) and, in some versions, through stimulating capitalist forms of economic development.

Theorists who favour the latter interpretation often go back to Tocqueville's study of American democracy in the 1830s. The question is whether global evangelicalism has the characteristics Tocqueville viewed as beneficial to democracy, especially clerical self-restraint in avoiding direct political involvement and doctrines which moderate the people's taste for material well-being. Pentecostalism in the global south has not always done well in maintaining an advisable distance from the vicissitudes of democratic partisanship, or in averting people's gaze from materialistic envy, or in balancing democratic impulsiveness by salutary long-term thinking.

In addition, democratization itself includes both transitions and consolidation. In transitions, pentecostal churches are often not much use. For standing up to dictatorships, it is more helpful to be a traditional, hierarchical, transnational church with elite connections. It is not so easy for a pentecostal church, especially for those with no transnational or elite connections, deprived of intellectual resources and vulnerable to repression. However, in democratic consolidation (the long haul of creating a democratic culture) these churches might be more use because they promote certain activities, encourage economic development, are anti-fatalistic and instill skills of leadership and public speaking. They have certainly provided a significant route for individuals of lower social origin to achieve political visibility (e.g. some pentecostal congressmen in Brazil or Nicaragua).

However, churches may be enveloped in an apocalyptic mentality which regards the world as hopeless. Such withdrawal is not helpful to democratization and may harm it. That mentality is now less common, especially in churches with a slightly higher social level. One now sometimes finds the opposite, a triumphalistic mentality which says believers should govern their countries in the name of God. In some places (Guatemala) it is better-off charismatics, used to a political role, who entertain such ideas. In other places (Brazil) it is the older lower-class pentecostal churches which have grown so much that their leaders become ambitious. Since democracy is the numbers game, they try to transform their religious leadership into political leadership, either to help their own churches by milking the state, or by dreaming of exercising political power themselves, or by electing a 'man of God' as president who will attract divine blessing on the country. That dream has serious anti-democratic potential, but in practice it never happens because they do not control the votes of their members and the denominations never unite behind a single political project. In any case, since they do not have a sharia to implement, their ideas of theocracy generally boil down to little more than their supposed God-given right to rule.

While pentecostals have shown themselves adept at personal transformation, their record in societal transformation has fallen far short, both because of the complexity of social questions and because of the corrupting effect of politics as the supreme focus of power. In fact, the pentecostal self-belief that is positive for personal transformation becomes a liability in politics. And the charismatic ritualism that can produce results at the micro level does not function at the macro level. A 'spiritual warfare' mindset which attributes all a country's problems to the 'wrong people' being in power, and which imagines a manifest destiny for one's own group as incorruptible leaders, is bound to come to grief.

The fragmentation of evangelicalism means that its direct political impact is always smaller than might be hoped or feared. No evangelical neo-Christendom is feasible, however much numerical success the churches might still have. Despite the dangers of corporatism (using the state to strengthen the ecclesiastical institution), there is now a plurality of competing organizations whose actions can politically cancel each other out. These are voluntary communities which people enter or leave at will, and evangelicalism is perceived in many countries as helping to create a vibrant civil society. However, at times it is a civil society bound up in its own limited projects and unable to develop a more universalist reflection on public life such as characterizes, for example, Catholic social doctrine. In some countries the result has been damage to their public image, associating it with political naivety and vulnerability to manipulation, and sometimes with corruption and hunger for power. While fragmentation is beneficial in limiting the danger of theocratic regimes or large-scale conflict, it also increases the possibility of political underachievement compounded by corruption scandals (as have blighted pentecostals in Brazilian politics).

Several questions in the 2006 Pew survey are pertinent for attitudes to democracy. Pentecostals everywhere are affirming (between 84 per cent and 99 per cent) of the importance of honest multiparty elections, similar to or slightly above their national averages. When asked whether, to solve the country's problems, it would be better to have a more participatory government or a strong leader, pentecostals always prefer a participatory government. But in the Philippines, Nigeria, South Africa and Guatemala (following their national tendencies) over 40 per cent would like a strong leader, whereas pentecostals in Brazil, Chile, Kenya and South Korea are less interested (under 30 per cent) in the strong leader solution. In seven countries, pentecostals are less favourable to a strong leader than their general populations, so pentecostal attitudes do not weaken democracy in most of the global south. On the other hand, American pentecostals are more favourable to a strong leader (34 per cent) than their national average of 24 per cent.

When asked whether government should make our country a Christian country or whether there should be separation of church and state, American pentecostals (by a margin of 52 per cent to 36 per cent) prefer the 'Christian country' option, as do pentecostals in Nigeria (58-35) and South Africa (45-37). In all other countries surveyed, pentecostals reject the 'Christian country' idea, notably in Chile (23-62) and Brazil (32-50). However, everywhere except Chile pentecostals are more favourable to the idea than other religious believers in their country. Africa seems the most propitious location for Jenkins' idea that new 'Christian nations' will appear in the global south.

Evangelicalism's emphasis on individual freedom to respond to the religious message results in an opting out of social 'sacred canopies' and the creation of an unending pluralism. The results for democracy are paradoxical. Totalitarian regimes are resisted, as are non-Christian religious nationalisms, but authoritarian regimes which do not impinge on evangelical religion may not be. The evangelical world is too fissured to undergird national-level movements advocating major political change in whatever direction. There have been no national 'Reformations' of Christendom in the Third World as there were in northern Europe, no Protestant state churches.

Evangelicalism is thus less 'use' during phases of democratic transition than it is during the more extended periods of consolidation. Indeed, the evangelical concept of voluntarism and the duty to convince and publicise bears more than a resemblance to Habermas' concept of the public sphere and communicative action. The massive daily practice of convincing, at the grassroots level, even by groups which are not internally democratic, may be important for the quality of democracy that is possible in the public sphere.

Thus, while circumscribed by certain broad parameters, actual evangelical politics is very hard to predict (not only because evangelicalism is decentralized, but because it is now present in so many contexts across the globe). One implication of this localism is that imitation may prevail: local patterns of religion-state relations may be absorbed as evangelicalism gains in political legitimacy. Probably the greatest danger to democracy will come in Africa, especially with the rise of 'Christian nationalism' as the more secular independence movements have lost their lustre. But in Latin America, despite the now-fading heritage of a monolithic Catholic model, the more pluralist present will almost certainly keep evangelicals broadly within the democratic and non-confessional track; and future growth curves will change their composition and push them towards more mainstream politics (in the case of numerical stagnation, by increasing the percentage of birth-members; or in the case of continued expansion, by incorporating other social sectors). In Asia, it is unlikely that evangelicals will be influenced by communist or non-Christian religious nationalist models rather than secular ones. Facing Asian nationalisms, evangelicalism generally represents a democratizing force.

REFERENCES

Almond, Gabriel, Sivan, Emmanuel and Appleby, R. Scott 1995. 'Fundamentalism: Genus and Species'. In Marty, Martin and Appleby, R. Scott (eds), *Fundamentalisms Comprehended*. University of Chicago Press, pp. 399–424.

Anderson, John (ed.) 2006. *Religion, Democracy and Democratization.* London, Routledge.

Bebbington, David 1989. *Evangelicalism in Modern Britain,* London, Unwin Hyman.

Berger, Peter 2004. 'The Global Picture'. *Journal of Democracy* 15: 2, April, pp. 76–80.

Beyer, Peter 1990. 'Privatization and the Public Influence of Religion in Global Society'. In Featherstone, Mike (ed.), *Global Culture,* London, Sage, pp. 373–95.

Beyer, Peter 1994. *Religion and Globalization.* London, Sage.

Birman, Patrícia 2000. 'Whatever Happened to What Used to be the Largest Catholic Country in the World?' *Daedalus* 129, 2, Spring, pp. 271–90.

Brouwer, S. Gifford, P. and Rose, S. 1996. *Exporting the American Gospel: Global Christian Fundamentalism.* London, Routledge.

Bruce, Steve 2000. *Fundamentalism.* Cambridge, Polity.

Bruce, Steve 2003. *Politics and Religion.* Cambridge, Polity.

Bruce, Steve 2004. 'Did Protestantism Create Democracy?' *Democratization* 11, 4 August, pp. 3–20.

Coffey, John 2000. *Persecution and Toleration in Protestant England: 1558–1689.* Harlow, Pearson.

Davie, Grace, Heelas, Paul and Woodhead, Linda (eds) 2003. *Predicting Religion.* Aldershot, Ashgate.

De Gruchy, John 1995. *Christianity and Democracy,* Cambridge University Press.

Ellis, Stephen and Ter Haar, Gerrie 2004. *Worlds of Power.* New York, Oxford University Press.

Freston, Paul 2001. *Evangelicals in Asia, Africa and Latin America.* Cambridge University Press.

Freston, Paul 2004a. *Protestant Political Parties: A Global Survey.* Aldershot, Ashgate.

Freston, Paul 2004b. 'Evangelical Protestantism and Democratization in Contemporary Latin America and Asia'. *Democratization* 11, 4, August, pp. 21–41.

Freston, Paul 2007. 'The Changing Face of Christian Proselytizing: New Actors from the Global South Transforming Old Debates'. In Hackett, Rosalind (ed.), *Proselytization Revisited.* London, Equinox.

Hackett, Rosalind (ed.) 2007. *Proselytization Revisited.* London, Equinox.

Huntington, Samuel 1991. *The Third Wave: Democratization in the late Twentieth Century.* Norman, University of Oklahoma Press.

Huntington, Samuel 1998. *The Clash of Civilizations and the Remaking of World Order.* London, Touchstone.

Jenkins, Philip 2002. *The Next Christendom.* New York, Oxford University Press.

Jenkins, Philip 2006. *The New Faces of Christianity.* New York, Oxford University Press.

Juergensmeyer, Mark 2001. *Terror in the Mind of God.* Berkeley, University of California Press.

López, Darío. 2007. 'Evangelicals and Politics in Fujimori's Peru'. In Freston, Paul (ed.), *Evangelical Christianity and Democracy in Latin America.* New York, Oxford University Press.

Lumsdaine, David (ed.) 2007. *Evangelical Christianity and Democracy in Asia.* New York, Oxford University Press.

Marsden, George 2006. *Fundamentalism and American Culture* (2nd edn). New York, Oxford University Press.

Marsh, Charles 2006. 'Wayward Christian Soldiers'. *New York Times,* 20 January.

Martin, David 1997. *Does Christianity Cause War?* Oxford, Clarendon Press.

Martin, David 2004. 'Evangelical Expansion in Global Society'. In Lewis, Donald (ed.), *Christianity Reborn.* Grand Rapids, Eerdmans, pp. 273–94.

Marty, Martin and Appleby, R. Scott (eds) 1993. *Fundamentalisms and the State.* University of Chicago Press.

Norris, Pippa and Inglehart, Ronald 2004. *Sacred and Secular: Religion and Politics Worldwide.* Cambridge University Press.

Padilla, C. René and Scott, Lindy 2004. *Terrorism and the War in Iraq.* Buenos Aires, Kairos.

Pew Forum on Religion and Public Life 2006. *Spirit and Power: A 10-Country Survey of Pentecostals.* Washington, D.C.

Ranger, Terence (ed.) forthcoming. *Evangelical Christianity and Democracy in Africa.* New York, Oxford University Press.

Sanneh, Lamin 2003. *Whose Religion is Christianity?* Grand Rapids, Eerdmans.

Sine, Tom 2004. 'Divided by a Common Faith'. *Sojourners,* October.

Sizer, Stephen 2004. *Christian Zionism.* Leicester, IVP.

Soares, Luiz Eduardo 1993. 'A Guerra dos Pentecostais contra os Afro-Brasileiros: Dimensões Democráticas do Conflito Religioso no Brasil', *Comunicações do ISER* 44, 43–50.

Stern, Jessica 2003. *Terror in the Name of God.* New York, Ecco.

Vásquez, Manuel and Marquardt, Marie Friedmann 2003. *Globalizing the Sacred.* New Brunswick, Rutgers University Press.

Waters, Malcolm 1995. *Globalization.* London, Routledge.

Willaime, Jean-Paul 1997. 'Les Fondements Religieux du Politique Moderne'. In Lenoir, Frédéric and Tardan-Masquelier, Ysé (eds), *Encyclopédie des Religions vol 2* (2nd edn) Paris, Bayard, pp. 2079–88.

Witte, John (ed.) 1993. *Christianity and Democracy in Global Context*. Boulder, Westview Press.

Woodberry, Robert and Shah, Timothy 2004. 'The Pioneering Protestants', *Journal of Democracy* 15: 2 April, pp. 47–61.

11

From 'Cults' to New Religious Movements: Coherence, Definition, and Conceptual Framing in the Study of New Religious Movements

THOMAS ROBBINS AND PHILLIP CHARLES LUCAS

WHAT IS THE FIELD?

Since the mid-1970s, the study of new religious movements (NRMs) has become a significant and flourishing sub-area within the disciplines of both religious studies and the sociology of religion. Many important studies have been published and some significant theoretical work has been done. In the wake of the 'war on terror,' however, the study of NRMs has had to deal with an increasing shift of public (and academic) attention from 'dangerous cults' to shadowy Jihadist groups such as Al-Qaeda that threaten nations with terrorist attacks. This development has tended to focus scholarly attention on issues of violence and apocalyptic thinking in NRMs, to the detriment of such issues as charismatic authority in NRMs, the social and cultural significance of NRMs, sect to church theory, secularization and NRMs, globalization and NRMs, and recruitment to, and defection from, NRMs. Moreover, it is arguable that the field as a whole is still characterized by a certain ambiguity or incoherence. In our view, a theoretical reconsideration or re-orientation of the field may now be in order.

As James Lewis and Jesper Peterson have recently noted, the 'field of new religious movements' has now become a recognized academic subspecialty. However, 'it is a very odd field of specialization that lacks the adequate internal logic for determining which phenomena fall within its purview' (Lewis and Peterson 2005: 3–4). The basic scope and boundaries of the field do not appear to be definitely settled. There does exist, however, an implicit understanding that the study of NRMs often pertains to a set of familiar groups or 'cults' such as the Unification Church, ISKCON (Hare Krishna), the Children of God (The Family), the Church of Scientology, the Raelians, the Church Universal and Triumphant, and Sokka Gakki. The problem is that some of these groups are now several generations old, i.e., they are not really all that 'new.'

What then is a *new* religious movement or a 'new religion'? How old does a group have to be before it is no longer considered new? Is chronological 'newness' the crucial identifying category or is the vital element some frequent correlate or consequence of 'newness' such as charismatic leadership, rapid organizational change, intensity of member commitment, or tension with society at large? If the latter, does a group cease being a NRM when its charismatic leader dies, when a second generation of members who grew up in the community takes over power, or when the group accommodates itself to societal norms, as, for example, when the Church of Jesus Christ of Latter-day Saints rejected polygamy?

Eileen Barker has argued forcefully that the fact of chronological 'newness' is indeed sociologically significant because chronologically and organizationally 'new' movements tend to share certain typical, important features such as charismatic leadership, a first generation membership of 'converts,' a primary reliance on proselytization rather than birthrate to sustain growth, intense intragroup ties, and a significant degree of tension with mainstream society (Barker 1989, 2004: 88–102). The difficulty with this position arises when these features of 'newness' disappear and the group becomes a stable organization with routinized charisma, solid growth through group birthrates, a conventional means of raising money, and minimal tension with the larger society. Does the group then no longer fall under the purview of NRM study? Are any of these characteristics more important than others? For example, the Unification Church still has its charismatic founder, Rev. Sun Myung Moon, in power. However, the group has become an accepted supporter of, and fellow traveler with Republican conservatives through its publication of the *Washington Times* and its contributions to Republican causes. True, the group's mass marriages still raise eyebrows in the mainstream media, but its packaging of these events as 'rallies to strengthen marriage and family' and its ability to attract mainstream religious and political leaders (such as Neil Bush, George W. Bush's younger brother) to these rallies around the world make it difficult to argue that the marriage ceremonies are evidence of significant tension between the Moonies and the surrounding social environment. In addition, the Unification Church owns a number of conventional businesses throughout the world so that it is no longer dependent on the controversial sale of flowers, books, and other articles in public spaces such as bus depots or airports.

David Bromley makes the additional point that NRM studies (he uses the term New Religion Studies [NRS]) need to 'identify the key analytical dimensions that distinguish types of religious groups and lead toward a conceptualization of newness' (Bromley 2004: 91). He observes that religious studies scholars tend to 'categorize groups on cultural criteria' (Bromley 2004: 91). Thus, for example, J. Gordon Melton has organized his typology of new religious groups according to nineteen families that have historical commonalities, belief system resemblances, and ritual/practice commonalities. Social scientists, on the other hand, emphasize taxonomies of social organization, charismatic authority, and the degree to which social features of a NRM are congruent with 'the structure and interests of dominant institutions' (Bromley 2004: 92; Melton 2004: 73–87).

Bromley proposes a way of defining new religions that incorporates both social and cultural dimensions and subsumes these under the concept of *alignment*. Alignment, in his formulation, is defined as the degree of congruence a group has with the 'dominant culture and dominant institutions' of a particular society (Bromley 2004: 91). This way of defining new religions emphasizes the role of power in understanding what kind of group it is. Bromley posits a continuum along which groups can be classified depending upon their degree of acceptance or contestation by dominant social institutions and their alignment with dominant cultural patterns. This formulation allows him to propose three general categories of religious institution: (1) Dominant religious groups. These are groups 'that are most strongly aligned with dominant cultural patterns and social institutions' (Bromley 2004: 93). They do not challenge the prevailing social order and are thus in a low degree of tension with other dominant groups in society. (2) Sectarian religious groups. These groups reject both the authority and legitimacy of dominant religious institutions and yet claim cultural legitimacy because of their adherence to what they see as the authentic core of the dominant religious tradition's teachings. Sectarian groups create alternative organizations that dominant groups regard as incongruent with mainstream institutions with respect to such elements as specific practices, intensity of commitment, and non-alignment with mainstream legitimating bodies. An example would be the Amish community in the United States. The Amish reject military service, modern technological conveniences, and membership in the National Council of Churches, yet see themselves as authentic heirs of biblical Christianity. (3) New religious groups. These groups lack congruence with both dominant social institutions and dominant cultural patterns. In Melton's taxonomy, they stand outside *dominant* religious 'families,' and in Barker's terms, they are 'new' movement organizations. Because these groups are often rejected by dominant religious and social institutions, they tend to exist in a high degree of tension with the larger social order (Bromley 2004: 94).

Bromley's formulation not only integrates cultural and social elements, but it includes a broader array of groups than encompassed in current NRM studies, which tend to focus on a limited cohort of NRMs in the West. The reason for this broader purview is because Bromley's distinctions work across historical periods and cultures. Since acceptance as a legitimate 'religion' is dependent on cultural setting and historical period, this model allows for the fact that the status of any religious group changes over time; 'legitimate religion' is a contested designation constantly up for renewal or rejection. Thus, for example, the study of Christianity during the first century CE is the study of a sectarian offshoot from Late Temple Judaism. The study of early Buddhism is the study of a new religious group that was incongruent with both dominant social institutions and dominant cultural patterns (rejection of Brahmanistic rites and caste differences, for example).

Another problem lies with the term, 'movement'. Should NRM studies – as a field – cover new subgroups or currents within existing churches (e.g., schismatic movements and parachurch movements)? How about the loose networks, teachers, seminars, books and products subsumed under the designation, 'New Age Movement'? And what about new theological 'schools' (Prosperity Theology) or new tendencies in biblical exegesis? Or political movements that employ religious symbols and rhetoric such as Al-Qaeda or Hamas?

Clearly, the influence and notoriety of the 'usual suspects' in NRM study is on the wane. In the meantime, many other types of groups and movements have emerged that could fall under the purview of NRM study. We have suggested some of these in the above paragraph. Others might include Asian and African 'independent' churches; religio-therapy groups such as Avatar, Mindspring, and Landmark Forum; groups that fall under the Nature Spirituality umbrella, i.e. Wicca, Asatru, goddess spirituality, Pagans, Neo-shamans, and various Druidic orders; and internet or 'virtual' religions.

Perhaps the stated purview of the journal *Nova Religio* could provide a starting point for this redrawing of the boundaries of NRM study. *Nova*'s purview includes religious communities, movements, and phenomena that fall outside the established, or dominant, religious institutions and discourse of a given nation or culture (Lucas 1997: 8). This focus includes, among others, minority religions, new religions, Gnostic and Hermetic groups, millenarian and primitivist groups such as Christian Identity and the Branch Davidians, nationalist NRMs such as Mahikari, metaphysical and Ancient Wisdom movements such as Unity, Spiritualism, and Eckankar, Jewish movements such as Kabbalah Learning Center and the Love Family, African-American and Afro-Caribbean groups such as Father Divine's Peace Mission, Santeria, and Rastafarianism, alternative healing groups, and Marian apparition groups (Lucas 1997: 8). Without a clearer definition of its field of study with clear conceptual parameters, NRM studies may remain somewhat fluid and inchoate as an academic subspecialty. Notwithstanding the present scholarly and public interest in new and minority religions, academic marginality or insignificance may lie in the future for this subfield unless it undertakes more rigorous theoretical elaboration and conceptual boundary setting.

THEORETICAL PERSPECTIVES FOR FRAMING NRM PROLIFERATION, DIVERSITY AND DEVELOPMENT

Much of the theoretical work done in NRM studies has revolved around attempts to 'explain' the rise of NRMs and to provide innovative constructs for interpreting and framing their proliferation, diversity, and notoriety over the past forty or so years. Among the leading theories in this regard are secularization, globalization, rational choice/religious economy, postmodernity/modernization, and sect-to-church theory. Theories regarding conversion and so-called 'brainwashing' have also played a prominent role in NRM studies, but space limitations do not permit discussion of these theories in this chapter.[1]

Secularization

The proliferation of NRMs can be viewed as a repudiation of conventional secularization and disenchantment perspectives, which are arguably incompatible with the ongoing efflorescence of esoteric 'cults' and also with the rise of evangelical and Pentecostal Christianity, and militant Islam. Is the whole idea of secularization simply bankrupt?

Although the conventional theory of secularization has come under heavy criticism, variants of the theory have proved useful in explaining the rise and spread of NRMs in the late twentieth century. In these variant perspectives, the faltering of mainstream churches and faith traditions has created a spiritual vacuum that new groups can fill and exploit.

Religious innovation can thus be seen as both a response to and a repudiation of conventional secularization theory. Indeed, Stark and Bainbridge envision secularization as an *inherently self-limiting process* that engenders a reactive dynamic of spiritual renewal (Stark and Bainbridge 1985). Both secularization and religious renewal are thus viewed as alternating phases of the evolution of a 'religious economy.' This essentially cyclical model, which precludes a linear, fundamental transformation of any particular religious milieu, appears to have provided a persuasive explanation for contemporary religious vitality and societal influence.

It might also be argued that the strongest proponents of conventional secularization theory have been British and European scholars whose perspective may be unduly influenced by the documented decline of state churches in countries like the United Kingdom, Germany, Holland, Denmark, and Sweden. In these cultural milieus, church attendance and membership has indeed dropped precipitously over the past several generations. If secularization is defined as the loss of societal influence for state churches and the concurrent rise of secular philosophies and institutions in Western Europe, there is clearly some validity to the theory. The mistake, however, may be in over-emphasizing state churches to the detriment of the many non-traditional, non-mainstream, new and minority religious groups and movements in their midst. Since these 'alternative' modes of religious activity are not perceived to have the former social influence of state churches, they are often cited merely as proof of the 'privatization' and thus marginalization of religion as a force in society. This is not to say that non-traditional and new religions have been ignored by secularization theorists; quite the contrary is the case. But the strong commitment to various forms of secularization theory by sociologists during the late twentieth century tended to undervalue, in our view, the broader cultural significance of private and alternative modes of religious commitment, including NRMs.

If one looks at a society such as the United States in which there is no state church, conventional secularization theory appears even less convincing. Although some 'mainstream' churches have indeed lost members and societal influence (Presbyterians, Episcopalians, Methodists, United Churches of Christ, for example), other mainstream denominations continue to grow in membership and influence, especially churches such as the Roman Catholics, the Southern Baptists, and the Assemblies of God. Older 'new' religions such as the Church of Jesus Christ of Latter-day Saints and the Seventh-day Adventists continue to grow and expand their memberships and societal influence. The Adventists do so through their respected networks of hospitals and the Mormons through aggressive missionary work, successful penetration into national political life, and strategic ownership of land and businesses. In addition, independent mega-churches such as Willow Creek, the Vineyard Fellowship, and Calvary Chapel have experienced explosive growth and social influence, as have television and radio ministries and religiously based political action groups such as Focus on the Family, the Moral Majority and its offshoots, and Promise-Keepers. Indeed, the influence of conservative and evangelical Christianity on American political and social life has arguably never been stronger than in the present era. All of the preceding evidence still does not take into account the ongoing proliferation of new religious movements, whether 'cult' movements or 'sect' movements.[2] These groups continue to dot the land, notwithstanding their (often) short lifespan.

The above comments with regard to Western Europe and the United States do not take into account other evidence that undermines traditional secularization theory. In particular, the mushrooming growth of independent churches in Africa and Asia, the rise of militant Islam as a potent political and social force in the Fertile Crescent and beyond, and the spectacular surge in membership in Protestant evangelical and Pentecostal churches in Latin America all counter any theory that would argue for a loss of influence for religious worldviews and institutions in the modern world. Secularization as a significant theory in

NRM studies thus survives only in a limited fashion as part of a larger process of religious growth, decline, reformation, and innovation. As older religious institutions lose their influence, secularizing forces may indeed appear ascendant in particular societies or subcultures *at particular times*. What is debatable is whether any society remains wholly secularized over time. As events in the former Soviet Union amply demonstrate, even societies with officially atheistic ideologies are prone to resurgences of religious sentiment over the long duration. Taken as a grand theory of modern religion, the secularization thesis has simply not stood the test of time and has therefore been supplanted by other theories.

Globalization

NRMs are 'global' in the sense that they may frequently be said to represent *transnational fellowship networks*. They may also embody global cultures, i.e., their influence and range have been greatly extended as processes of globalization have accelerated in late modernity (Beckford 2000; Hexham and Poewe 1997).

Globalization may be viewed as involving a number of symbolic and cultural processes or dimensions, which have definite implications for the spread and growth of NRMs. Globalization (or globalism) entails the diffusion of symbolic and communicative networks from places of origin to distant locales throughout the world and across political boundaries. A relevant example is Hinduism, which is associated with the spread of Asian ('Eastern') symbols and practices to the West and the consequent rise of gurus, roshis, and lamas as purveyors of popular spirituality. It can be argued that Hindu-based religious ideas (karma, reincarnation, self-realization) and practices (yoga, meditation, mantras) have saturated Western culture since the mid-1960s, aided by the large-scale immigration of Indians to countries like the United Kingdom, Canada, and the United States and the proliferation of Hindu gurus in Western countries.[3] These teachers often create organizations and institutions to propagate their versions of

Hindu philosophy and spirituality, versions that are often adapted to Western norms and interests. Not only is this diffusion of Hinduism taking place among Westerners, but it also is occurring via ordinary Indians who have migrated to the West in search of economic betterment and opportunity. In some cases, these Indians become supporters of Hindu-based NRMs such as ISKCON and regular attendees at their temples and festivals.

Another example involves the spread of variegated forms of Christianity (especially Pentecostalism and evangelical Protestantism) to Asia, Africa and Latin America. In these cases American versions of Christian belief and practice (for example, speaking in tongues, the 'prosperity gospel,' and television ministries) have been brought to new 'mission fields' and influenced in significant ways the practice of Christianity in cultures very far removed from that of the United States (Cox 2001; Hallum 2003; Gifford 2004). Globalization also denotes an emerging conceptualization of the world as *a single entity or place*. These various aspects of globalization create an impetus for syncretistic religious innovation and diversity. Put another way, the forces of globalization bring together peoples and ideas of widely divergent religious backgrounds, fostering dialogue, accommodation, and innovation that often includes a syncretistic blending together of beliefs and practices into new 'global' faiths (Robertson and Chirico 1985).

New religious movements increasingly find it necessary to *interpret* globalization and its significance and thus to *infuse globality with spiritual meaning*. The meaning systems of a number of movements thus feature conspicuous themes of globality and world unification, e.g., Bahai, Soka Gakkei, Unificationists, Raelians, Watchtower, ISKCON (Barker 1984; Rochford 1985; Beckford 2003, 2004; Palmer 2004b).

It should also be stated that the infusion of religious meaning into globality can sometimes be distinctly negative and demonological, e.g., 'fundamentalist' movements in the U.S. and in the Mideast may be viewed as seeking through political action to *reject or ward off* globalism. They thereby reinforce and

intensify a traditional animus against subversive 'one-worldism,' which is perceived as a threat to traditional beliefs and practices and to traditionalist and localist worldviews.

Globalization, as Roland Robertson and James Beckford have both noted, is accompanied by the relativization of received social and personal identities (Robertson and Chirico 1985; Beckford 1989: 200). As such, it is a social process that fuels a search for new identities. The latter may often be tied to particularistic movement mystiques. The globalist relativization of received individual and social identities may produce a 'fundamentalist' or neo-traditionalist reaction that often entails a primitivist retreat to a traditional deposit of 'truth' and authenticity, which is reinforced by socio-political mobilization. On the other hand, some theorists view 'fundamentalist' religious movements as retreatist and as mere 'defensive reactions against globalization.' Indeed, these fundamentalisms may sometimes attempt to ward off globalizing forces through immersion in a homogenous communal enclave (Castells 1997). This theoretical analysis has been criticized by Beckford as a simplistic and one-sided view that ignores the activist impulse of many 'fundamentalists,' who more and more seek to remove their convictions from the purely private realm and to transform their environment through social action (Beckford 2003: 131–2).

In summary, it might be argued that the conditions of globalization both facilitate and challenge the growth of NRMs. For example, 'cults' have flourished on the global internet, but so has the anticult movement, which has developed a particularly strong internet presence (Beckford 2004: 253–63).[4] Whereas NRMs can easily and inexpensively spread their messages around the world using the 'net,' so too can anticult activists transmit their negative portrayals of 'dangerous and seductive cults' using the same medium. The anticult movement has been signally successful in spreading anticult ideology around the world by making its formulations and warnings non-culture specific. Put another way, anticult activists have been very adept at formulating typologies of cult characteristics that are transnationally applicable. The spread of anticult ideas to governing elites in such countries as France, Russia, Japan, and the Peoples Republic of China shows the success of these efforts (Lucas 2004b: 341–57).

It is our view that the globalization model for interpreting NRMs furnishes a provocative 'large context' frame that yields key insights into the transnational aspirations and ideologies of NRMs, the processes of global diffusion of NRM institutions, and the role of the internet in NRM successes and failures (Richardson 2004). The model has certain shortcomings, however. It over-generalizes and thus directs attention away from key movement attributes that are complex, particularistic and local. NRMs are culture-specific in many ways, and this fact requires that researchers conduct thickly described studies of individual groups (alongside more global interpretations and theory-building) lest essential elements for understanding and interpreting these groups are left undisclosed. Simply put, globalization should not necessarily become the exclusive or dominant frame for the study of NRMs. It may miss too much on the local and particular level (Dawson 1998b: 580–95).

Rational Choice – Religious Economy

'Rational choice' or 'religious economy' models are presently receiving substantial attention. It is worth noting that early formulations of the Stark-Bainbridge 'rational choice' model of religion were developed with specific reference to the growth of NRMs. The Stark-Bainbridge model may thus be viewed as a general, somewhat 'economist' model of religion that has largely arisen from the study of new and emergent movements (Stark and Bainbridge 1985). In its initial elaboration, the rational choice model is a highly systematized and somewhat psychologized theoretical frame for looking at the origin and evolution of NRMs. In this connection, it is interesting that Stark and Bainbridge, perhaps slightly incongruously, have wedded a behavioristic psychology to an explicitly supernaturalistic, substantive (theistic) conception of religion.

The premise of Stark and Bainbridge's social psychology is that human beings are unable to obtain the intense rewards that they greatly desire (e.g., immortality) through direct action. Therefore they tend to accept 'compensators' or promises of future rewards. The most potent anticipations, however, are predicated on explicit supernaturalism. Naturalistic ideologies, in Stark and Bainbridge's view, cannot compete with supernaturalistic religions because the latter are associated with more intense compensators (such as eternal life) than the compensators associated with purely secular ideologies. It is partly for this reason that Stark and Bainbridge see secularization as a self-limiting process that almost automatically engenders religious renewal and revitalization. What their theory envisions is a continuous cycle of secularization and spiritual revitalization whereby dynamic new movements arise, institutionalize, and eventually decline or lose their dynamism and are then supplanted by newer, more fervent movements (Stark and Bainbridge 1985).

Parenthetically, when Stark and Bainbridge initially formulated their theory, there may have been strong objections raised to their basic premise of the superiority of supernaturalist to naturalistic or secular ideologies. They are sociologists, after all. In recent decades, however, certain developments, most notably the fall of the Soviet Union and the diminished appeal of Marxism and communism as theories of social transformation may appear to validate their basic premise. Moreover, militant, Jihadist Islam has now supplanted 'Godless Communism' as the dynamic-but-dangerous ideology that is presumed to menace the United States and the 'Free World.' The intense zeal and growth of Jihadist Islam, with its powerful supernatural compensators, adds further credence to the Stark and Bainbridge theory.

In the view of Stark and his collaborators, established and conventional religions decline because they lack compelling compensators. New, supernaturalist mystiques also possess an intrinsic advantage over 'secular' symbolic structures that are overly accommodated to modernity, such as science, rationality, or secular political ideologies (Stark and Bainbridge 1985).

It may be objected that most NRMs tend to be small and frequently ephemeral compared to traditional or conventional faiths. On the other hand, Christianity, Islam and Buddhism originally began as small sect or cult movements. NRMs might be viewed as part of a revitalization cycle of religion in society: most NRMs fail but some surge forward to ultimately become major or even dominant societal faiths. In the Stark and Bainbridge view, the more audacious a NRM's supernatural claims and promises (thus, its compensators), the more chance it has for long-term success. The success of Mormonism over the past 150 years is eloquent evidence to support this contention. Mormonism provides powerful supernatural compensators for its members: 1. An afterlife of ongoing growth and beatitude with extended family; and 2. The potential to become godlike beings that rule their own planets and planetary systems.

Radically innovative new movements or 'cult movements' are said by Stark and Bainbridge to proliferate where conventional, institutionalized churches are weak. Thus, in the United States cult activity seems highest on the American West Coast and in the 'sun belt.' Europe, conventionally presumed to be highly secularized, might appear to challenge the model; however, according to Stark and Finke, Europe, where churches are indeed weak, 'is awash in cult movements' (Stark and Finke 2000: 55). Indeed, after the fall of the former Soviet Union there was a surge of NRM growth and allegiance in Eastern Europe. To a certain extent this growth continues, in spite of strong countercult and anticult currents in specific Eastern European countries (Shterin 2004: 99–116).

There is a newer 'religious economy' version of rational choice theory, which emphasizes a 'supply side' approach to the sociology of religion. 'Religious demand' is said to be 'very stable over time' such that 'religious change is largely the product of supply-side transformations' (Stark and Finke 2000: 193). 'Hearts and minds' (revivalist sentiments, for example) issues that affect religious *demand* are thus viewed as secondary considerations. What is vital is the *supply* of religion as determined by both the organizational strategies of competing religious groups and the constraints of state regulation. These factors represent a more imperative determinant of religious change than the subjective vicissitudes of demand.

In their economist model, Stark and his collaborators basically envision religious 'firms' operating *competitively* in a market in which each firm seeks to occupy and to consolidate a key 'niche.' Thus, 'it is not church-switching [i.e., changes in the relative demand for various 'brands'] that is the central dynamic in religious change. Rather it is the *shifting of religious firms from niche to niche* that has the greatest impact on the overall religious economy with the consequence that the primary religious suppliers change over time' (Stark and Finke 2000: 196).

For Stark and his collaborators, the degree to which (and manner in which) a religious milieu is subject to state *regulation* is a crucial variable in shaping what we might term the religious 'political economy.' However, there is a pertinent religious variable that is *exclusivity* or the degree to which a religious organization recognizes the legitimacy of religious competition and permits its participants to become involved with competing firms. In a relatively unregulated market *exclusive firms* (which demand exclusive loyalty from participants) tend to be more rewarding to their participants than non-exclusive firms, and the former therefore have a competitive advantage from a Starkian perspective. Perhaps this pattern says something about the psychology of 'homo religiosus' and the attractiveness of elitist or 'morally superior' religious communities. Or perhaps it is simply a matter of the compensators offered by each type of firm. Exclusivist churches and movements tend to offer greater supernatural compensators for their followers and greater assuredness that their followers have chosen the 'one true way.'

Although they are now large, institutionalized and internally differentiated faiths, Judaism, Christianity and Islam were originally exclusive, 'intolerant' firms which appeared initially in a market dominated by relatively non-exclusive firms such as the 'mystery cults' and various versions of civil religion that were focused around local and national pantheons. 'Each [exclusive firm] won because it was a better bargain [for religious consumers] despite requiring higher costs' for devotees (Stark and Finke 2000: 194). Perhaps a more recent example of the competitive advantage of exclusivity is the Sokka Gakkai sect in Japan. It requires an exclusive commitment from devotees (unlike most of its competitors), yet it has grown from a few thousand households in 1951 to over eight million in the mid-90s (Stark and Finke 2000: 194). Ironically, most converts actually come from fairly non-exclusive religious backgrounds.

The recent growth of dynamic and intolerant Christian, Islamic and Hindu fundamentalisms probably entails a similar pattern. In an unregulated market, exclusive firms may have an advantage over non-exclusive competitors. Put another way, religious *competition* in unregulated markets tends to increase the 'efficiency' of religious firms and the commitment of their adherents. Such groups are ultimately strengthened by the need to compete for customers. Competition among multiple religious suppliers tends to increase the available choices for religious consumers and thus compels religious suppliers to be more responsive to consumer needs and more efficient and resourceful.

As stated above, the degree of regulation of the 'religious market' is a key variable affecting religions. In heavily regulated and controlled markets, authorities employ various measures to disable the competitors of favored groups and to *discourage religious pluralism*. In this connection European nations, which purport to have freedom of religion, in actuality 'permit almost unlimited discretion to bureaucrats and parliaments concerning specific policies and decisions to impose sanctions on minority religions,' while not providing the legal safeguards that exist in the U.S. (Stark and Finke 2000: 232). In Germany, some Pentecostal groups are actually denied tax privileges unless they register as sports clubs rather than as churches. In Belgium, a parliamentary commission created a list of dangerous cults without input from the groups themselves at public hearings. It then created a commission to monitor these groups

(Lucas 2004b: 347–8). French politicians responded to the Solar Temple events with the creation of a list of 172 'sects' that had been compiled by the Renseignements Généraux (RG), a secretive government intelligence-gathering agency. The government made it illegal to question the RG's criteria for what constitutes a sect or to question its sources of information (Palmer 2004a: 63–4). Members of particularly disfavored groups, most notably the Church of Scientology, may be denied civil service employment in some parts of Europe (Schoen 2004: 85–98). There are reports of persisting European discrimination against Muslims, although France is making strides to integrate Muslims into approved governmental advisory bodies that protect, for example, Jews and Protestants.

In contrast to Western Europe, religious participation has traditionally been high in the U.S. This may be largely due, according to Stark and Finke, to American deregulation and 'the powerful forces unleashed by a free market religious economy' (Stark and Finke 2000: 221). Deregulation, in their view, fosters pluralism, and both deregulation and pluralism encourage high levels of participation.

Stark and Finke assume that in most societies there are some persons who will prefer to make strong, exclusive commitments to strict, 'uniquely legitimate' groups which do not accept the legitimacy of competing faiths and which generally manifest a high degree of tension with mainstream social and religious institutions. Other persons will gravitate to more tolerant, lax, low-tension groups. In a sense, these are the polar 'niches' of a religious free market, in Stark and Finke's view, and remain as a constant in any religious economy (Stark and Finke 2000: 196–217).

New movements will tend to position themselves in an available 'niche.' But a group's niche in the religious economy may shift over time. There is some tendency over time for high-tension groups to evolve in the direction of lower tension with, and greater accommodation to societal norms. This 'moderating' tendency can have the effect of producing an oversupply of lower tension groups. Such groups are generally characterized by low levels of commitment; many fail while others persist but do not effectively control the behavior of participants. High-demand exclusivist groups exert more control over devotees but the rigorous level of personal sacrifice and commitment expected by leaders can prove too much for many members. These select exclusivist groups thus occupy a fairly small market niche, as few persons are willing to accept their rigid regimentation and excessive demand for personal sacrifice. Given the limited pool of potential recruits, there tends to be an oversupply of such groups; they face fierce competition and manifest a high failure rate (Stark and Finke 2000: 196–217).

Stark and Finke assert that high levels of commitment are most likely to be found in an unregulated market with multiple competing firms. Individuals are empowered to choose the firm which best suits them, while competitive organizations are free to rearrange themselves to meet consumer preferences, and are moreover pressured by market imperatives to make such strategic alterations. They are more likely to proselytize than are firms in a less competitive milieu. The megachurch (defined as a congregation of no less than 2,000 members) phenomenon in the U.S. is an excellent example of this contention. These churches, which deemphasize historical theology and denominational boundaries, do market research to find out what religious 'consumers' want in a church. They then accommodate themselves to these changing needs. Their contemporary programming (including uptempo music), servicing of member needs (for example, singles' groups, 12-step groups, 'Connection cafes') and conservative social message has led to a doubling in the number of these churches (to 1,210) over the past five years (Levy 2006).

According to Stark and Finke, firms which feature *supernaturalist* meaning systems possess an advantage over relatively secularist groups such as today's 'liberal' churches, which are finding it increasingly difficult to market themselves effectively. They observe, 'only vivid conceptions of an active and concerned supernaturalism can generate a vigorous religious action' (Stark and Finke 2000: 258).

The above propositions do not necessarily suggest that high-demand NRMs represent the wave of the future. Indeed, this hardly appears to be the case in Europe, where dynamic but sometimes rather traditional Muslim and Christian sectarian movements appear to be more conspicuous than new religious groups. Stark and Finke argue that 'It is the fear of these [Christian and Islamic] groups that has motivated reactionary, authoritarian laws and policies in Eastern Europe and in the nations of the former Soviet Union' (Stark and Finke 2000: 257). This may be an overstatement, given the draconian European response to the Solar Temple events of the mid-1990s and the anticult measures brought about by resurgent nationalisms in the countries that once made up the former Soviet Union. But it is true that efforts to safeguard society against dynamic, militant Christian and Islamic groups have increased in the wake of 9/11 and the global 'war on terror.' Indeed, we argue that the ecology for new and minority religions throughout the world appears very *unfavorable* for the foreseeable future given the *patterns* of repression and harassment of the past ten years, particularly in Western and Eastern Europe, Central Asia, and the Peoples Republic of China (Lucas 2004b: 341–57).

The rationalization/religious economy model has a number of problems. We have indicated above that certain religious properties such as supernaturalism may enhance the success of religious firms. However, the meaning of the dependent variable of 'success' is not completely clear. Vivid supernaturalism may characterize small close-knit sects with strong bonds between devotees and a tendency to survive and grow. At the same time, however, large institutionalized denominations may evince a somewhat watered down supernaturalism. Such denominations may hold their positions of cultural dominance even when their growth rate slows and they lose the fervency and close intra-group ties of earlier years. Two American denominations, the United Methodists and Roman Catholics, come to mind as examples. There are also cross-cultural complications with the model's applicability. Canada and Australia have witnessed strong NRM growth coincident with generally weak religious (i.e., churchly) commitments. On the other hand, in the United States 'cults' and 'sects' proliferate in a context of stronger general commitment to churches. The weak church-strong sect/cult pattern may have been theoretically over-generalized by Stark *et al.*

Questions have arisen as to whether the United States with its relatively strong churches and weak cultural secularity really (as was once taken for granted) provides a more favorable climate for the growth and proliferation of cults than does more secular Europe, where older churches are weaker compared to the American pattern. An alternative formulation might suggest that NRM growth is a fairly constant phenomenon across cultures, although greater freedom of religion might lead to greater NRM proliferation and diversity. The recent past in Eastern Europe and Russia is evidence for this latter contention; once draconian measures against non-state-sponsored religiosity were lifted in the early 1990s, NRMs, missionary activity, and minority traditions all proliferated to an unprecedented degree.

Postmodernity and Modernization

An additional perspective uses postmodern critiques of contemporary culture as conceptual tools with which to analyze emergence, growth, and distortion in NRMs. This perspective posits that a new and unprecedented phase of socio-cultural development has emerged during the late twentieth century, which has particular implications for new religions.

To begin, the hyper-plural and globalizing dimensions of postmodernity have been identified as encouraging the *worldwide diffusion of alternative worldviews and lifestyles* (and tolerance and receptivity towards such unprecedented diffusion). Put another way, the worldwide diffusion of lifestyles and worldviews that characterizes postmodernity *fosters* cultural conditions that encourage the emergence of new and foreign mystiques and that generate *syncretic* religious formations. This effect can be seen in movements such as the Unification Church and the Holy Order of

Mans (HOOM), which each combined elements from a broad array of religious traditions. In the case of the Unification Church, the Reverend Sun Myung Moon created an original amalgam of traditional Korean shamanism, missionary Presbyterianism, and messianic millennialism, while Earl W. Blighton of HOOM combined theosophical, Rosicrucian, Gnostic, yogic, and traditional Roman Catholic elements into his unique religious system (Barker 1984; Lucas 1995).

The breakdown of the nuclear family and increasing sexual permissiveness are also associated with postmodernity. The fragility of the nuclear family continues a basic trend in late modernity which saw traditional, ethno-religious 'extended families' and homogenous neighborhood settings weakened by enhanced geographical mobility, population shifts to large urban centers from rural areas, and higher levels of education. The undercutting of both nuclear and extended families tends to produce a new search for communal forms that emerge as *family surrogates* for young adults (Dawson 1998c: 53–6).

Another set of postmodern conditions that encourages the proliferation of new groups includes the weakening of ascribed religious ties, the relativization of truth claims and the questioning of metanarratives. These conditions reinforce a growing cultural ethos of *religious individualism* or 'designer religion.' Under these conditions individuals are freer to switch religious affiliations without social censure and to cobble together idiosyncratic religious worldviews and identities that use elements from many religious traditions (Bellah *et al.* 1985; Hammond 1992). Moreover, they arguably erode the cultural power of traditional religious teachings and allow NRMs to emerge and gain at least a small initial following (Sentes and Palmer 2000; Lucas 2004a: 28–48).

These same trends, however, may destabilize new movements and inhibit their consolidation and survival. For example, postmodernity's *radical relativization of truth claims* and hyper-pluralism may encourage the proliferation of diverse groups and movements, but it also makes it difficult for a new movement to establish its putatively unique and superior religious message. This is due to the increased cultural skepticism that accompanies hyper-pluralism and that leads both intellectuals and the public to perceive new religions as socially constructed discourses mainly designed to enhance the cultural influence and financial viability of new organizations and their unscrupulous leaders (Lucas 2004a: 28–48). The postmodern 'hermeneutic of suspicion' that increasingly characterizes societal attitudes toward NRMs is reinforced by sensational episodes of deception, abuse and malfeasance by groups such as the Branch Davidians, the Peoples Temple, Heavens Gate, ISKCON and the Solar Temple (Rochford 1998: 43–69; Bainbridge 2002; Palmer 2004a: 61–74). Thus, cultural patterns that facilitate the *creation* and *emergence* of new groups may also undercut their *consolidation* and *survival*.

A final condition posits that postmodern culture is characterized by a pervasive *domination of simulation* in the sense that contemporary experience is increasingly mediated through *synthetic images* (Baudrillard 1983). Those who become 'masters of the image,' whether politicians, propagandists, media moguls, or television evangelists, can easily damage the legitimacy and public standing of their competitors using advanced telecommunications resources. They can also scapegoat 'deviant' groups in their efforts to maintain moral authority and cultural hegemony. In this context, NRMs must work particularly hard to craft positive public images of themselves (Rochford 1987; Lucas 2004a: 28–48; Palmer 2004b). Because these representations must change in order to adapt to shifting public trends, challenges, and attitudes, they may sometimes diverge rather significantly from the actual internal reality of the group. These problems may lead to identity confusion within new religious communities and to both intra-group and public uncertainty regarding the relation of disseminated group representations to actual reality.

This problem might be profitably understood as a dysfunctional consequence of postmodern *reflexivity*, i.e., the group becomes too aware that it is tactically constructing its own image to meet external exigencies. As a result, rank-and-file members find it more difficult to be confident regarding the timeless and authoritative (e.g., divinely inspired) status of the movement's truth claims. The continual refashioning of the group image to maintain competitiveness in the religious marketplace can also have the effect of undermining group cohesion and collective identity. It therefore becomes more difficult for the leadership to maintain an aura of absolute, timeless spiritual truth and thus to exercise control and authority over the group (Greaves 2004; Lucas 2004a: 28–48).

The critiques of contemporary culture by postmodern theorists such as Jean Baudrillard, Jacques Derrida, Michel Foucault, and Richard Rorty have been largely ignored by scholars of NRMs (but see Beckford 1992, 1996). It is our contention that this inattention to innovative cultural interpretations has robbed NRM studies of powerful conceptual tools with which to interpret and analyze significant dimensions of NRM emergence, growth, and distortion. We recommend a more thorough engagement with these theorists as a way to enlarge the conceptual toolkit available to NRM theorists. This is not to encourage a wholesale adoption of these perspectives, but rather a judicious use of theories and concepts that we believe can yield valuable insights into social and cultural dimensions of NRMs.

Sect-Church Theory

All but one (the religious economy) of the foregoing perspectives might be said to entail causal or *explanatory* constructs in the sense that they purport to reveal what social and cultural factors have fostered the late twentieth-century (and early twenty-first century) proliferation of NRMs, e.g., that groups/movements at least partially reflect the conditions of secularization, globalization, postmodernism, etc. However, our final perspective, which had its inception in an earlier phase of social-scientific theorizing, is rather more a natural history model that identifies recurrent processes and developmental phases featured in the growth of new movements. In this sense it resembles Stark and Bainbridge's rational choice/religious economy theory.

Although in need of serious modification, *sect-church (or church-sect) theory* has for many decades been a mainstay of Anglo-American sociology of religion (Neibuhr 1929; Pope 1942; Wilson 1959; Stark and Bainbridge 1985; Troeltsch 1992). The model identifies recurrent patterns whereby socio-religious ferment has produced emotionally vibrant new sect or cult movements that subsequently undergo processes of institutionalization to produce more respectable and administratively elaborate and hierarchical 'churches' and 'denominations.' The latter have difficulty appealing to the alienated or marginal elements of society, and thus new sects and cults periodically arise to minister to marginal individuals whose needs are not met by state churches or denominations (in the American context). Through the processes of institutionalization and accommodation yesterday's deviant sects (and sometimes cults) have been seen to become tomorrow's conventional, respectable (but less dynamic) churches and denominations.

The past processes of sect conventionalization delineated by sect-church theorists have, as one of the present writers has noted, generally been 'correlated with such long-term factors as a group's rising socioeconomic status and the death of its founding generation ... sect-like movements changed gradually into denominations, but only after the passage of at least fifty to sixty years' (Lucas 1995: 251). However, in the contemporary milieu, it appears that 'conventionalization or co-optation by dominant religious discourses may be taking place within the first generation itself' (Lucas 1995: 251). Moreover, the impetus for such transformation may no longer simply be the death of the founding generation or a gradual rise in socio-economic status. Rather, movement transformation may include: 1. The difficulty of constructing a persuasive, credible, and authentic self-representation in a postmodern world whose ephemerality, hyper-pluralism, and acceleration of time make such attempts at stable identity construction increasingly problematic; 2. The powerful

pressures to conventionalize wielded by electronic-media-savvy religious, anticult, countercult, and socio-political institutions (Lucas 1995: 252); 3. The increasingly repressive legal, political, and religious limits placed on non-conventional religious groups – especially in the wake of 9/11 and the global 'war on terror'; 4. The great difficulty of creating sufficiently impermeable boundaries and sustaining a stable collective identity in a globalizing world that homogenizes, dissolves boundaries, and transmits information with dizzying speed. Finally, today's new movements, unlike yesteryear's 'sects' or sectarian 'churches of the disinherited' are not conspicuous for recruitment of marginal individuals from lower rungs of the socio-economic ladder. Indeed, research indicates that many of those who joined NRMs in Western industrial nations during the late twentieth century came from middle and upper-middle-class backgrounds (Wallis 1977; Barker 1984: 198; Jones 1994; Palmer 1994).

As these observations indicate, sect-church theory must undergo significant updating and modification if it is to contribute to our understanding of developmental processes in contemporary religious movements. Such modifications can extend and elaborate on the pioneering theories of H. R. Neibuhr, Liston Pope, and Bryan Wilson. Like the sectarians they depicted, recruits to today's new religious movements may be 'deprived' or 'disinherited' but not in the simplistic socio-economic or culturally unsophisticated terms once used. Today's NRM recruits may paradoxically find social adjustment through participation in seemingly deviant movements. In this connection, one of the present writers identified 'Eastern' mystical movements in the late 1960s and early 1970s as resocializing 'youth culture' and 'drug culture' recruits in a manner which promoted renewed commitment to prestigious educational and career goals (Robbins 1969: 308–17). More studies are needed to discern the social and psychological profiles of today's NRM recruits. Are there new forms of deprivation or alienation in the postmodern era? Does the loss of influence of state churches and mainstream denominations create a widespread imperative to seek out religious answers wherever they may be found – including sectarian and cult groups? Do the loss of shared public spaces and civil discourse, and the atomization of society create deep-seated needs for emotionally intensive religious communities, whether mainstream or otherwise? Does the 'clash of civilizations' that some theorize lies behind the current war on terror foster a need for new institutions that reinforce religious identities? It is our position that traditional sect-church theory must be continually refined, elaborated, and updated so that it moves beyond narrow studies of mill hands and counterculture youths and begins to grapple with the more complex conditions and populations of postmodern societies.

TRANSFORMATIONS OF POSTMODERN GROUPS: HOOM AND CUT

Two recent studies of contemporary NRMs provide examples of the processes we have discussed in the body of this paper. Particularly interesting in this respect is the tension-fraught transformation of the syncretistic Holy Order of Mans (HOOM) into an Eastern Orthodox sectarian movement. The order emerged in San Francisco as a 'New Age mystery school' teaching an idiosyncratic version of the Western esoteric tradition. It was organized long the lines of Roman Catholic teaching orders such as the Jesuits and Franciscans. The order's founder was Earl Blighton, a retired electrical engineer and social worker who had been affiliated with Spiritualist churches, Rosicrucian groups, the Subramuniya Yoga Order, and the Theosophical Society. Blighton's central message was that the Earth was entering a golden age of spiritual illumination, and that the order had been divinely ordained to prepare the Earth for this new era through the transmission of ancient Christian 'mystery teachings' and 'solar' initiations. HOOM spread rapidly throughout the United States between 1969 and 1974. It established seminaries, mission stations, and training centers in sixty major cities. Members took lifetime vows of poverty, service, obedience, purity, and humility, and

kept all assets in common. Unlike traditional monastic communities, however, the order established its presence in largely urban settings, accepted coeducational membership, and ordained women priests. The early 1970s saw an outreach to lay persons in the form of the Christian Community and Discipleship movements. These movements drew interested families and individuals who wished to study under the renunciate community's auspices while remaining financially independent. Blighton also created the Immaculate Heart Sisters of Mary and Brown Brothers of the Holy Light as celibate suborders dedicated to service work, missionary outreach, and Marian devotional practices. Members of the suborders staffed Raphael Houses, pioneering shelters for victims of domestic violence (Lucas 1995).

Blighton died suddenly in 1974. After several turbulent years of interim leadership, Vincent Rossi assumed leadership of the order in 1978. Rossi's initial public statements reiterated Blighton's mystical and millennial vision and called for members to present the message of Christ in a universal and inclusive manner. The movement's combined membership peaked at about 3,000 in 1977. Following the mass suicides at Jonestown, Guyana, in November 1978, and the resulting public hostility toward non-traditional religions, however, the order's membership began to decline precipitously. The anticult movement capitalized on the public's shock with new efforts to convince politicians and judges to regulate cult movements. The order began to appear on 'cult lists' published by leading countercult groups and to garner negative media coverage for the first time in its history. Rossi responded to this hostile religious ecology with a strong defense of the group's ecumenism, non-sectarianism, and authentic Christian pedigree in various public forums. He also inaugurated a private search within the group for precedents in Christian history for the order's mission and identity. This search was designed to equip members to represent the order in terms acceptable to the Christian mainstream. Rossi's initiatives resulted in the group moving gradually toward a more conventionally Christian public and private identity. After flirtations with evangelical Protestantism and Roman Catholic Thomism, the group began to study a sectarian variant of Eastern Orthodoxy under the guidance of a defrocked Russian monk, Herman Podmoshensky. Working with Podmoshensky, Rossi began to jettison Blighton's eclectic esotericism and adopt in its place Orthodox beliefs and liturgies. This radical shift in value orientations and self-identity entailed mass confusion within the membership and significant defections – particularly among women, whose status and authority declined as the group moved into the Orthodox camp. Rossi also consolidated the order's far-flung communities (which included centers in Germany, England, Spain, and Argentina) into ten large family-centered communities. During the mid-1980s, the order refocused its efforts on the celebration of seasonal festivals, the creation of an alternative private school system, and the preservation of authentic cultural traditions from 'ancient Christianity' (Lucas 1995).

Rossi began negotiations with Orthodox jurisdictions in the United States for official acceptance but was stymied because of his insistence on institutional autonomy. Finally, in 1988, he came to terms with Metropolitan Pangratios Vrionis, the archbishop of the Archdiocese of Queens, New York. The remaining 750 members of the group received re-baptism and changed their name to Christ the Savior Brotherhood (CSB). The brotherhood's new mission was to bring 'the light and truth of Orthodox Christianity to the spirituality of perishing peoples of these darkening and crucial times' (Lucas 1995). CSB had a difficult time establishing itself as a legitimate Orthodox congregation because the Standing Committee of Orthodox Bishops in the Americas did not recognize Pangratios' authority. By the late 1990s the brotherhood had severed ties with Pangratios (who was charged with sodomy with minors) and begun to fracture into individual parishes, each of whom joined with legitimate Orthodox jurisdictions around the country. Today the brotherhood is little more than a legal entity with real estate holdings. Its few remaining members are held together by a nostalgia for a shared past and a commitment to rigorous Eastern Orthodox Christianity (Lucas 2003: 5–23).

A second case study focuses on the controversial, apocalyptic cult movement, Church Universal and Triumphant. The group originally emerged from the theosophical and 'ascended masters' cultic milieu of the 1950s. Founder Mark Prophet followed the teachings of the Saint Germain Foundation and participated in two spin-off groups, the Bridge to Freedom and Lighthouse of Freedom. Each of these groups claimed as its mission the publication of teachings of the Ascended Masters, a group of advanced adepts believed to be responsible for human spiritual evolution. In the 1950s Prophet proclaimed himself the messenger for the Ascended Masters in the dawning Aquarian Age. He founded Summit Lighthouse and began to publish the 'dictations' of the masters in publications such as *Pearls of Freedom*. Summit Lighthouse grew slowly until the late 1960s, when an infusion of counterculture recruits greatly expanded the group's membership and resource base. The Lighthouse established a new international headquarters in Colorado Springs, Colorado, and opened Montessori International to teach the group's children and Ascended Master University (later called Summit University) to give recruits an intensive exposure to Prophet's esoteric teachings (Lucas 2004a).

Mark Prophet died in 1973 and was succeeded by his wife, Elizabeth Clare Prophet. She renamed the group Church Universal and Triumphant in 1974 and moved its headquarters to Pasadena (and later Malibu), California. Prophet became a star of the New Age circuit during the late 1970s and early 1980s, barnstorming the world with her idiosyncratic teachings of anti-communism, mystical nationalism, apocalyptic survivalism, and theosophical enlightenment. Following disputes with neighbors in Malibu, Prophet moved her followers to Paradise Valley, Montana, in 1986. The group settled into a 30,000-acre ranch on the border of Yellowstone National Park and began farming and publishing enterprises as well as seasonal retreats for its international membership. Prophet believed that the ranch was under the protection of the Ascended

Masters, who would allow the group to survive a coming nuclear exchange between the United States and the Soviet Union. In 1989 the church entered the 'shelter cycle,' during which it built fallout shelters in the Grand Teton Mountains and awaited an apocalypse that Prophet claimed was imminent. The failure of these doomsday scenarios to materialize combined with widespread negative publicity, IRS investigations, and weapons smuggling convictions led to growing member defections and declining financial resources for the church. In response, the leadership attempted to recast the church's public image as a benign and 'mainstream' religious group that obeyed the laws, paid its taxes, and looked forward to a glorious New Age of spiritual enlightenment. A new corporate structure emerged in the 1990s involving a more open and responsive leadership style. Unfortunately, the rapid shift in the group's self-representation from an elite, apocalyptic, esoteric movement to a 'customer oriented' purveyor of New Age teachings, goods, and services surprised and confused some of its members. After a number of leadership battles and the retirement of its charismatic prophet because of Alzheimer's disease, many devotees defected from a group which they felt no longer embodied its original spiritual intensity and initiatory ritual practices. The Church Universal and Triumphant soldiers on and has attempted to compensate for the decline of its formerly dominant American contingent by trying to foster spiritual communities worldwide (Whitsel 2003; Lucas 2004a).

These case studies argued that both HOOM and CUT underwent institutionalization and 'conventionalization' processes that played out rather more rapidly than conventional sect-church theory would have predicted. Fundamental transformations in worldview, polity, value orientations, practices, and membership occurred within the first generation of followers rather than over several generations.

The causes for these transformations were directly related to the problems of consolidating a viable group self-representation and protective boundaries in an increasingly hostile postmodern cultural context. Absent such boundaries a stable group identity became problematic and the maintenance of a distinctive religious system – with its non-traditional beliefs and practices – was jeopardized. Each group found it difficult to maintain its integrity in the face of widespread public criticism, member defections, and an increasingly conservative cultural environment. The communities became chameleon-like formations, shifting rhetoric and changing tone and appearance to suit rapid alterations in the cultural landscape. Their millennial and utopian dreams rapidly became implausible and unsustainable and each group took on a more conventional identity in an effort to lessen tension with the dominant society and thus survive in the American religious marketplace (Lucas 2004a). Similar processes have been observed in the Hare Krishna movement, which emerged at the same time as HOOM (Rochford 1997: 2).

As we have already seen, globalization and hyper-pluralism are postmodern conditions that can encourage the initial formation of new movements. New movement formations are also fostered by the postmodern decline of conventional churches, the weakness of ascriptive ties, the precariousness of both the nuclear and extended families, and the syncretizing tendencies associated with telecommunications, international travel, and the internet. Although postmodern culture in many ways encourages the formation of new movements, it clearly (in the ways we have outlined above) impedes their long-term growth and survival. The postmodern pattern for NRMs seems to be 'easy come, easy go.'

It should be acknowledged that the postmodern perspective, or rather the idea that contemporary NRMs should be designated as 'postmodern,' has elicited critical commentary from James Beckford, Lorne Dawson and others. Beckford notes the relative neglect in such discussions of the conspicuous contemporary growth of 'Christian churches and Jewish communities with strict and very conservative outlooks,' as well as those embodying a 'liberal and tolerant spirituality' (Beckford 1992: 17). To denote what contemporary movements have in common, Beckford prefers the designation of 'holistic post-modern'

(Beckford 1992: 17). Thus, 'we should refrain,' adds Lorne Dawson, 'from continuing to identify most, if not all NRMs with some anti-modernist stance' (Dawson 1998a: 139–56). Such an understanding of the term 'postmodern' may be misleading, he adds, in view of the syncretistic blend of 'traditional and modern elements' and of 'conservative and modern impulses' in so many of today's NRMs (Sentes and Palmer 2000; Dawson 1998a: 139–56).

Perhaps a clarification of the term 'postmodern' would address these criticisms. Thus, 'postmodern,' when applied to religious phenomena, would not necessarily be understood as designating a particular ideological stance with regard to modernity, or even a metanarrative that all postmodern groups subscribe to, but rather a cultural context that allows for a wide range of religious formations and organizations, which range from ultra-conservative to ultra-liberal, traditional to experimental, institutional to bio-degradable (transient and ephemeral). The postmodern condition really describes a putative 'ecology' within which religious movements and communities emerge, develop, and decay. Understanding both the more obvious and subtle dimensions of this condition/ecology allows us to assess the challenges and opportunities it presents for new and minority religions. The responses of NRMs to these conditions will vary, to be sure, but in some instances we can observe parallel strategies and initiatives – for example, the creation of sophisticated public relations apparatuses to do battle with negative representations of a group in the mass media.

CONCLUSION

Finally, it is worth noting that the various interpretations of NRM proliferation we have been discussing more or less presuppose (and may only make sense if it is presumed) that new and minority movements have in fact been growing in recent decades and have thus become and continue to be culturally significant. The importance and vitality of contemporary 'NRMs' has been accepted by many observers of the contemporary religious scene, but there have been dissenters. According to Lorne Dawson, 'In the late 1980s the activity of NRMs tapered off, and membership in the relatively well-established groups like Scientology, Krishna Consciousness, and the Unification Church has stabilized well below levels these achieved in the early to mid-seventies.' 'Fewer new religions' notes Dawson, 'are being formed now, and they are attracting fewer followers.' (Dawson 1998a, 1998b) Other commentators, including the present authors, point to continued proliferation of new and minority religious groupings, while acknowledging that the forms these communities take differ in significant ways from those that dominated scholarship during the 1970s and 1980s.

In this connection there has also been dissent from the widely accepted notion that the 1960s and 1970s – the period of the 'counter-culture' – witnessed a striking surge in the number and significance of novel groups. Rodney Stark and his collaborators, for example, have gathered data detailing the proliferation of NRMs in the 'Roaring Twenties' and 'Jazz Age' and affirming the existence of an 'amazing stability in cult activity over the 40 years between 1920 and the 1970s.' This suggests, notes Stark et al., 'the need for more basic theories of cult formation than those suggested by scholars who regard the rise of cults as a *new* phenomenon' (Stark and Finke 2000: 255). In a similar vein, historian R. Lawrence Moore has affirmed that there has never been 'a period in American history when so-called small sects were not growing at a faster clip than denominations then viewed as large and stable.' Moore criticizes sociological and journalistic commentary that has 'assumed that sects and cults ... began to affect religious life in only around 1960' (Moore 1986).

This 'constancy premise' is worth consideration, but it does not challenge the fact that the profusion of NRMs and minority religions in the late twentieth century has been significantly influenced by unprecedented cultural patterns such as postmodernity and globalization, as discussed in the body of this chapter. This influence has more to do with the forms and ideologies of these new groups, as well as cultural and legal challenges, and developmental crises that they face than with raw numbers of recruits – which may have remained constant as a percentage of the general population. Put another way, the cultural context of NRMs and minority religions has undergone seismic shifts during the past sixty years, and the pace of these shifts has accelerated with the advent of global electronic communications technologies, mass emigration of Third World peoples to the Western industrialized democracies, and now the worldwide 'war on terror.' It is the perennial challenge of NRMs to adapt to cultural and social change; our point is that this challenge has become even more acute in the postmodern world.

Finally, as we suggested briefly above, at least a minority of scholars studying new movements are presently considering the possibility that the growth of NRMs has leveled off somewhat and that in future both the study of new movements and expertise in the area may cease to command the premium it has achieved in recent decades. We contend that NRM proliferation will continue at present levels and that the more likely scenario is a shift in interest to groups that exhibit violent or quasi-violent tendencies, for example 'terrorist' and extremist religious formations such as Al-Qaeda, Hamas, Christian Identity, Temple Mount Faithful, and Aum Shinrikyo (see, for example, Cook 2002, 2005; Bonney 2004; Hall 2004; Wessinger 2007; Bjorgo 1995). Clearly, there has been a considerable shift in resources to studies and analyses of these groups at the governmental level, and this is bound to affect funding for academic research and programs. The study of NRMs with violent tendencies has been a growth industry in the U.S. and Canada since the Branch Davidian and Heaven's Gate events, and we foresee this trend continuing as the 'war on terror' expands and dominates national and international agendas and resource allocations (see, for example, Wessinger 2000; Tabor and Gallagher 1995). We also foresee an end to the balkanization of NRM studies, as NRM scholars increase their cooperation and dialogue with scholars in such fields as Islamic studies, social movement studies, political science, criminal studies,

Pagan studies, media studies, Africana studies, folklore studies, anthropology, and Judaica. To the extent that the field of NRM studies can forge alliances with other academic sub-areas, expand its purview, and more clearly define its field of study and theoretical tool kit, it can begin to secure itself a recognized niche within the academy. It can also continue to make a significant contribution to our understanding of religion's role in contemporary cultures.

NOTES

1. The following studies are recommended for those who wish to delve more deeply into conversion and so-called 'brainwashing' theories and debates: Lorne Dawson 1998c, 1996; David Bromley and James T. Richardson 1983; Larry Shinn 1993; James T. Richardson 1993, 1996; and Benjamin Zablocki and Thomas Robbins 2001.

2. A sect movement is an offshoot from an established Christian denomination. Typically, a small group of members become convinced that their denomination has veered away from its original doctrines and values. They break away (and sometimes are expelled) and set about to restore the church to its original purity. The sect movement typically is small and has a very dense social network. There is some degree of tension with the larger society, which it views as corrupt. The Branch Davidians, for example, is a sect movement that is an offshoot of the Seventh-day Adventists. Sect movements tend to have traditional beliefs and practices. A cult movement is a religious community that begins independently of any established denomination or sect movement. Its leaders introduce novel beliefs and practices and may adopt beliefs and practices from other traditions in a piecemeal way. Like sect movements, cult movements typically have small, close-knit memberships and exist in some degree of tension to the surrounding culture (Stark and Bainbridge 1985: 23–9; Stark and Bainbridge 1987: 124).

3. One piece of evidence for this assertion is the new (as of 2005) U.S. television show, My Name is Earl. The show's main character has led a life of crime and one day realizes that his unhappy condition is the result of bad karma. He vows to right all of the wrongs he is responsible for, confident that this will create good karma and a happier life.

4. The anticult movement emerged in the 1970s when concerned parents of children who joined NRMs banded together to 'rescue' their children through various legal and extra-legal means (including 'deprogramming,' a forced removal of the member from their community and attempt to discredit its teachings by intense argumentation). The movement was initially successful in convincing political leaders in the United States to hold hearings on the 'cult' problem. Although they failed to convince these

politicians to pass legislation that would monitor or suppress NRMs, they were successful in popularizing the 'brainwashing' conjecture as an explanation for NRM recruitment of their children. Over time, the movement has disavowed illegal 'deprogramming' and encouraged various forms of post-membership counseling and treatment. The movement continues to hold international meetings and to publish anticult literature. The leading anticult organization today is the International Cultic Studies Association. See Benjamin Zablocki and Thomas Robbins 2001.

REFERENCES

Bainbridge, William Sims 2002. *The Endtime Family: The Children of God*. Albany: SUNY Press.

Barker, Eileen 1984. *The Making of a Moonie: Choice or Brainwashing?* Oxford: Basil Blackwell.

Barker, Eileen 1989. 'New Religious Movements: Their Incidence and Significance.' In Bryan Wilson and Jamie Cresswell (eds). *New Religious Movements*. London: Her Majesty's Stationery Office.

Barker, Eileen 2004. 'What Are We Studying? A Sociological Case for Keeping the "Nova".' *Nova Religio* 8: 88–102.

Baudrillard, Jean 1983. 'The Precession of Simulacra.' In *Simulations*, transl. Paul Foss and Paul Patton. New York: Semiotext(e).

Beckford, James A. 1989. *Religion in Advanced Industrial Society*. London: Routledge.

Beckford, James A. 1992. 'Religion, modernity, and post-modernity.' In *Religion: Contemporary issues*, B. Wilson (ed). London: Bellew Publishing, 11–23.

Beckford, James A. 1996. 'Postmodernity, High Modernity, and New Modernity: Three concepts in search of religion.' In *Postmodernity, Sociology, and Religion*, edited by K. Flanagan and P. C. Jupp, 30–47. New York: St. Martin's Press.

Beckford, James A. 2000. 'Religious Movements and Globalization.' In Robin Cohen and Shirin Rai, *Global Social Movements*. London: Athelone Press.

Beckford, James A. 2003. *Social Theory and Religion*. Cambridge: Cambridge University Press.

Beckford, James A. 2004. 'New Religious Movements and Globalization.' In Phillip Charles Lucas and Thomas Robbins, *New Religious Movements in the 21st Century*. New York: Routledge University Press, 253–63.

Bellah, Robert N., Richard Madsen, William M. Sullivan, Ann Swidler, and Steven N. Tipton 1985. *Habits of the Heart: Individualism and Commitment in American Life*. Berkeley: University of California Press, 1985.

Bjorgo, Tore 1995. *Terror from the Extreme Right*. London: Frank Cass.

Bonney, Richard 2004. *Jihad: From Qur'ân to bin Lâden*. New York: Palgrave Macmillan.

Bromley, David G. 2004. 'Perspective: Whither New Religions Studies?' *Nova Religio* 8: 91.

Bromley, David G. and James T. Richardson (eds) 1983. *The Brainwashing/Deprogramming Controversy: Sociological, Psychological, Legal, and Historical Perspectives*. Lewiston, NY: Edwin Mellen Press.

Castells, Manual 1997. *The Power of Identity*. Oxford: Blackwell, 1997.

Cook, David 2002. 'Suicide Attacks or "Martyrdom Operations" in Contemporary Jihad Literature.' *Nova Religio* 6: 7–44.

Cook, David 2005. *Understanding Jihad*. Berkeley: University of California Press.

Cox, Harvey 2001. *Fire from Heaven: The Rise of Pentecostal Spirituality and the Reshaping of Religion in the 21st Century*. Cambridge, MA: Da Capo Press.

Dawson, Lorne L. 1996. 'Who Joins New Religious Movements and Why: Twenty Years of Research and What Have We Learned?' *Studies in Religion* 25 (2): 193–213.

Dawson, Lorne L. 1998a. 'Anti-Modernism, Modernism and Postmodernism: Struggling with the Cultural Significance of New Religious Movements.' *Sociology of Religion* 59: 131–56.

Dawson, Lorne L. 1998b. 'The Cultural Significance of New Religious Movements and Globalization: A Theoretical Prolegomenon.' *Journal for the Scientific Study of Religion* 37: 580–95.

Dawson, Lorne L. 1998c. *Comprehending Cults: The Sociology of New Religious Movements*. New York: Oxford University Press.

Dawson, Lorne L. 2003. *Cults and New Religious Movements: A Reader*. Oxford: Blackwell.

Gifford, Paul 2004. *Ghana's New Christianity: Pentecostalism in a Globalising African Economy*. Indianapolis: Indiana University Press.

Greaves, Ron 2004. 'From Divine Light Mission to Elan Vital and Beyond: An Exploration of Change and Adaptation.' *Nova Religio* 7: 45–62.

Hall, John 2004. 'Apocalypse 9/11'. In Phillip Charles Lucas and Thomas Robbins (eds) *New Religious Movements in the Twenty-First Century: Legal, Political, and Social Challenges in Global Perspective*. New York: Routledge, 265–82.

Hallum, Anne 2003. 'Ecotheology and Environmental Praxis in Guatemala'. *Nova Religio* 7: 55–70.

Hammond, Phillip 1992. *Religion and Personal Autonomy: The Third Disestablishment in*

America. Columbia: University of South Carolina Press.

Hexham, Irving and Poewe, Karla 1997. *New Religions and Global Cultures*. Boulder, CO: Westview Press.

Jones, Constance A. 1994. 'Church Universal and Triumphant: A Demographic Profile'. In J. R. Lewis and J. G. Melton (eds) *Church Universal and Triumphant in Scholarly Perspective*. Stanford, CA: Center for Academic Publications, 39–53.

Levy, Abe 2006. 'Megachurches Growing in Number and Size'. *San Francisco Chronicle*, February 3.

Lewis, James and Peterson, Jesper 2005. 'Introduction', in J. Lewis and J. Peterson (eds). *Controversial New Religions*. Oxford: Oxford University Press, 3–4.

Lucas, Phillip Charles 1995. *The Odyssey of a New Religion: The Holy Order of MANS from New Age to Orthodoxy*. Bloomington: Indiana University Press.

Lucas, Phillip Charles 1997. 'Introduction and Acknowledgements.' *Nova Religio* 1: 8.

Lucas, Phillip Charles 2003. *Enfants Terribles*: 'The Challenge of Sectarian Converts to Ethnic Orthodox Churches in the United States.' *Nova Religio* 7: 5–23.

Lucas, Phillip Charles 2004a. 'New Religious Movements and the "Acids" of Postmodernity.' *Nova Religio* 8: 28–48.

Lucas, Phillip Charles 2004b. 'The Future of New and Minority Religions in the Twenty-First Century: Religious Freedom under Global Siege.' In Phillip Charles Lucas and Thomas Robbins (eds) *New Religious Movements in the Twenty-First Century: Legal, Political, and Social Challenges in Global Perspective*. New York: Routledge, 341–57.

Melton, J. Gordon 2004. 'Toward a Definition of "New Religion".' *Nova Religio* 8: 73–87.

Moore, R. Laurence 1986. *Religious Outsiders and the Making of Americans*. New York: Oxford University Press.

Neibuhr, H. Richard 1929. *The Social Sources of Denominationalism*. New York: Henry Holt and Co.

Palmer, Susan J. 1994. *Moon Sisters, Krishna Mothers, Rajneesh Lovers: Women's Role in New Religions*. Syracuse, NY: Syracuse University Press.

Palmer, Susan J. 2004a. 'The *Secte* Response to Religious Discrimination: Subversives, Martyrs, or Freedom Fighters in the French Sect Wars?' In Lucas and Robbins, *New Religious Movements in the 21st Century*, 63–64.

Palmer, Susan J. 2004b. *Aliens Adored: Rael's UFO Religion*. New Brunswick, NJ: Rutgers University.

Pope, Liston 1942. *Millhands and Preachers*. New Haven: Yale University Press.

Richardson, James T. 1993. 'A Social Psychological Critique of "Brainwashing" Claims about Recruitment to New Religions'. In D. G. Bromley and J. K. Hadden (eds) *Religion and the Social Order, Vol. 3, The Handbook on Cults and Sects in America*, Part B: 75–97.

Richardson, James T. 1996. '"Brainwashing" Claims and Minority Religions Outside the United States: Cultural Diffusion of a Questionable Concept in the Legal Arena.' *Brigham Young University Law Review* 4: 873–904.

Richardson, James T. 2004. *Regulating Religion: Case Studies from around the Globe*. New York: Kluwer.

Robbins, Thomas 1969. 'Eastern Mysticism and the Resocialization of Drug Users: The Meher Baba Cult.' *Journal for the Scientific Study of Religion* 8: 308–17.

Robertson, Roland and Joan Chirico 1985. 'Humanity, Globalization, and Worldwide Religious Resurgence.' *Sociological Analysis* 46: 219–42.

Rochford, E. Burke 1985. *Hare Krishna in America*. New Brunswick, NJ: Rutgers University Press.

Rochford, E. Burke 1987. 'Dialectical Processes in the Development of Hare Krishna: Tension, Public Definition and Strategy.' In D. Bromley and P. Hammond, *The Future of New Religious Movements*. Macon: Mercer University Press.

Rochford, E. Burke 1997. 'Family Formation, Culture and Change in the Hare Krishna Movement.' *ISKCON Communications Journal* 5: 61–82.

Rochford, E. Burke 1998. 'Child Abuse in the Hare Krishna Movement: 1971–1986.' *ISKCON Communications Journal* Online: 43–69.

Schoen, Brigitte 2004. 'New Religions in Germany: The Publicity of the Public Square.' In Lucas and Robbins, *New Religious Movements in the 21st Century*, 85–95.

Sentes, Bryan and Susan Palmer 2000. 'Presumed Immanent: The Raelians, UFO Religions and the Postmodern Condition.' *Nova Religio* 4: 1.

Shinn, Larry 1993. 'Who Gets to Define Religion? The Conversion/Brainwashing Controversy.' *Religious Studies Review* 19 (3): 195–207.

Shterin, Marat 2004. 'New Religions in the New Russia. In Lucas and Robbins, *New Religious Movements in the 21st Century*, 99–116.

Stark, Rodney and William S. Bainbridge 1985. *The Future of Religion, Secularization, Revival and Cult Formation*. Berkeley: University of California Press.

Stark, Rodney and William S. Bainbridge 1987. *A Theory of Religion*. New York: Peter Lang.

Stark, Rodney and Roger Finke 2000. *Acts of Faith: Explaining the Human Side of Religion*. Berkeley: University of California Press.

Tabor, James D. and Eugene Gallagher 1995. *Why Waco?: Cults and the Battle for Religious Freedom in America*. Berkeley: University of California Press.

Troeltsch, Ernst 1992. Reprint Edition, transl. Olive Wyon. *The Social Teachings of the Christian Churches*. London: Westminster John Knox Press.

Wallis, Roy 1977. *The Road to Total Freedom: A Sociological Analysis of Scientology*. New York: Columbia University Press.

Wessinger, Catherine 2000. *How the Millennium Comes Violently: From Jonestown to Heaven's Gate*. New York: Seven Bridges Press.

Wessinger, Catherine 2007. 'New Religious Movements and Violence.' In Eugene V. Gallagher and W. Michael Ashcraft (eds) *New and Alternative Religious Movements in the United States*. Westport, CT: Praeger.

Whitsel, Bradley 2003. *The Church Universal and Triumphant: Elizabeth Clare Prophet's Apocalyptic Movement*. Syracuse: Syracuse University Press.

Wilson, Bryan R. 1959. 'An Analysis of Sect Development.' *American Sociological Review* 24: 1, 3–15.

Zablocki, Benjamin and Thomas Robbins (eds), 2001. *Misunderstanding Cults: Searching for Objectivity in a Controversial Field*, 2001. Toronto: University of Toronto Press.

12

New Age Religion and Irreligion

WILLIAM SIMS BAINBRIDGE[1]

This chapter scans the periphery of conventional religion, employing unifying themes to consider the New Age Movement, parapsychology, Atheism, and the challenge to religion posed by what E. O. Wilson (1998) calls the *consilience* of science, and what Roco and Bainbridge (2003) call the *convergence* of technology. One theme is the tension between religious authority embodied in traditional denominations and religious traditions, versus the freedom or anarchy represented by a variety of loosely organized parareligious movements, and by people like Atheists and Transhumanists who turn their backs on the supernatural altogether. Another is the function that religion performs for individuals, through both primary and secondary compensation for unavailable but highly desired rewards. A third theme is the progressive consolidation of a secular culture, based partly in science and technology, that is simultaneously libertarian and global, personal and cosmopolitan.

THE NEW AGE

John A. Saliba (2003: 27) has noted that the New Age 'has no central organization and no commonly accepted creed.' However,

J. Gordon Melton (2000) has argued that its historical heart was a millenarian movement that coalesced in the 1960s, when popular culture proclaimed the dawning of the Age of Aquarius. As a distinct movement anticipating the spiritual transformation of the world, Melton says, the New Age reached a peak in the 1980s, then faded afterward. The net result was increased public awareness of alternative spiritual beliefs and practices. The meaning of the term *New Age* is currently ambiguous, and many people do not distinguish it from occult or paranormal phenomena. The nearest thing to a definition is that the New Age is whatever is sold in 'New Age' shops or in the 'New Age' sections of bookstores.

The online bookseller, Amazon.com, includes both New Age and Occult categories within a larger category called Religion and Spirituality. The phenomena covered by New Age are: Astrology, Chakras, Channeling, Divination, Dreams, Meditation, Mental and Spiritual Healing, Mysticism, New Thought, Reincarnation, Self-Help, Theosophy, Urantia, and Visionary Fiction. The Occult category contains: Alchemy, Astral Projection, Auras and Colors, Crop Circles, Cults and Demonism, ESP, Magic, Metaphysical Phenomena, Near-Death Experiences, Occultism, Parapsychology, Rosicrucianism, Satanism, Shamanism,

Spiritualism, Supernatural, UFOs, Unexplained Mysteries, Wicca, and Witchcraft. The Barnes & Noble company uses a somewhat different category system, and Table 12.1 shows the numbers of book titles listed in 30 subcategories of New Age and Alternative Beliefs, as of May 2005.

Each of the Barnes & Noble categories has many subcategories. For example, Astrology has fully 97, from American Federation of Astrologers to Zodiac, including several of the separate planets and constellations, plus special topics like Astrological Geomancy, Ephemerides, and Houses. Note that the Amazon.com and Barnes & Noble classifications mix religious and allegedly non-religious phenomena. What they may have in common is being deviant from the standpoint of the conventional Judeo-Christian tradition in Western societies. Beliefs and practices from Eastern religion are included, but without the sophisticated organizational and cultural context of the societies from which they came.

Consider Astrology. In 1993 and 1994, the General Social Survey asked 2,943 American adults how true each of a set of statements was, including: 'Astrology – the study of star signs – has some scientific truth.' Fully 46.2 per cent said definitely or probably true, 41.8 per cent said definitely or probably not true, and 11.9 per cent failed to decide. Thus, the modal response was the feeling that Astrology has some truth, even though the relevant scientific disciplines (astronomy and perhaps psychology) reject astrology, and the dominant Judeo-Christian-Islamic religious tradition has no place for it either (Bok and Mayall 1941).

In the ancient world, Astronomy was intimately connected to religion, and when the Babylonians named the planets after their gods, they probably imagined that those distant lights in the sky actually were manifestations of their deities (Toulmin and Goodfield 1962). The modern astronomical idea that the planets are lifeless objects unrelated to human purposes was alien to the ancients' way of thought. Most modern astrologers seem to lack a general theory of their art, because few of them take the ancient gods seriously, and they probably do not want to alienate customers who still retain some affinity to a conventional religious tradition.

Except for the mystical principle 'as above, so below,' and non-technical references to the tides caused by the gravity of Moon and Sun, modern astrologers do not explain the physical mechanisms by which the planets could influence our fates (McIntosh 1969). In contrast, some authors connect astrology to Tarot and other interpretive practices as part of a unified symbolic system with which to think about human life and personality, without asserting that the physical planets and stars of astronomy have anything to do with the spiritual planets and constellations of astrology (Gad 1994).

If the phenomena in question here are similar to religion, but in some way different, how are we to conceptualize them? One controversial term that is often applied to them is *cult*.

Table 12.1   *Barnes & Noble titles in 30 subcategories of New Age and alternative beliefs*

2,361	Witchcraft and Magic	353	Tarot	147	Numerology
1,061	Spiritualism	348	Cults	145	Mysticism
1,001	Astrology			135	Anthroposophy
		331	Ghosts & Haunted Places		
916	Mental & Spiritual Healing	316	Supernatural	133	Near-Death & Out of Body Experiences
661	Parapsychology	281	Aliens & UFOs	110	Fraternal Orders: Freemasonry
536	Meditation	261	Angels	103	Sacred Places
517	New Age	228	Reincarnation	64	Atlantis
447	Dreams & Dream Interpretation	183	Alternate Beliefs & Spirituality - Reference	52	Auras & Colors
402	Prophecy	167	New Thought	36	Graphology
356	Fortune Telling & Divination	159	Demonology & Satanism	33	Fraternal Orders: General & Miscellaneous

Dictionaries typically give several definitions, and one found in *Webster's New Collegiate Dictionary* is 'a religion regarded as unorthodox or spurious.' Journalists and public critics of unorthodox religions have used *cult* as a term of opprobrium, implying that a group so called must be spurious, illegitimate, and vile. In reaction to this stigmatization, many scholars have shifted to the phrase *new religious movement*, but this is an awkward term, especially when applied to phenomena that are not new and may not be religious. Stark and Bainbridge (1985) urged scholars to ignore the connotation that journalists give to the word *cult*, and employ it to name supernaturally oriented subcultures with novel or exotic beliefs and practices. Indeed, these phenomena deserve social-scientific study precisely because they reveal many general processes of cultural innovation and variation: *Cult is culture writ small.*

Human culture is the result of social processes of innovation, evaluation, and communication intended to help people achieve desired goals, such as health, security, wealth, and social status. In the pursuit of desired goals, humans frame explanations about how and why rewards can be obtained and costs avoided. Successful explanations are recipes, tactics, instructions, or algorithms for gaining the reward in a series of steps. When a reward is difficult or impossible to attain within the

natural world, humans often imagine ways of seeking it that involve supernatural forces, realms, or beings. Such unproven but hopeful explanations involve *compensators*, essentially promises that must be taken on faith. Table 12.2 lists some definitions that Stark and Bainbridge (1985, 1987) offered for describing and analyzing cults and associated phenomena, in terms of compensators.

The distinction between *religion* (general compensators) and *magic* (specific compensators) merely elaborates the traditional anthropological distinction between these terms (Malinowski 1948). Religion makes big promises, and magic, small ones. For example, religion may promise eternal life, whereas magic offers a supposed cure for a particular disease. The sociological characters of New Age and occult phenomena are clarified by the concepts: cult movement, client cult, and audience cult.

A *cult movement* is a fully fledged religious organization, but one devoted to novel or exotic compensators (beliefs and related practices). Participants are members, and membership typically is exclusive; that is, members do not simultaneously belong to two or more competing religious movements.

A *client cult* is a magical service business, for example uniting a professional astrologer with clients who pay to have their horoscopes cast. The clients may simultaneously visit other cult

---

Table 12.2   *Cult definitions from Stark and Bainbridge (1985, 1987)*

Compensators are postulations of reward according to explanations that are not readily susceptible to unambiguous evaluation.

Compensators which substitute for single, specific rewards are called *specific compensators*.

Compensators which substitute for a cluster of many rewards and for rewards of great scope and value are called *general compensators*.

Supernatural refers to forces beyond or outside nature which can suspend, alter, or ignore physical forces.

Religion refers to systems of general compensators based on supernatural assumptions.

Magic refers to specific compensators that promise to provide desired rewards without regard for evidence concerning the designated means.

Cults are social enterprises primarily engaged in the generation and exchange of novel compensators.

A *cult movement* is a deviant religious organization with novel beliefs and practices.

A *client cult* is a magical service in which practitioners provide specific compensators to clients, often but not necessarily based on supernatural assumptions.

An *audience cult* is a cultural or mass media phenomenon that communicates magical or religious compensators without formal relations between producers and consumers.

practitioners for other magical services, such as Tarot reading or meditation training, and their relations with each other are informal. They are not fellow members of a formal organization.

An *audience cult* is a mythology. The professional myth-maker and his audience may never even meet, as the author of a book about UFOs has no direct social relationship with most readers. In the modern world, audience cults operate largely through the mass media. Thus, the three kinds of cult differ largely in terms of their degree of social organization from high in the case of cult movement (religion), medium in the case of client cults (magic), and low in the case of audience cults (mythology).

This conceptualization can be used to classify cases; for example, the books tallied in Table 12.1 are chiefly audience cult products. It can also be used to analyze processes of change. Sometimes a mythic audience cult can give birth to a magical client cult which evolves into a fully organized religious cult movement. Massimo Introvigne has used this insight to analyze the development of Damanhur, founded by Oberto Airaudi in Italy beginning in the 1970s:

> The birth of Damanhur could be described according to the well-known Stark-Bainbridge typology of audience cults, client cults and cult movements. Damanhur's experience shows that a leader and his or her followers could pass subsequently through the three stages. Damanhur started as an audience cult including the readers of Airaudi's popular books. When Airaudi started a professional career as a 'pranotherapist' and healer, his regular clients moved from the audience cult to the client cult stage. Finally, Airaudi was capable of organizing his clients into a movement, which eventually became communal (Introvigne 1999: 192).

By the late 1990s, Damanhur had grown into a commune of 450 people, with another 300 associate members living in individual homes, and a wider membership of perhaps 1,000 who were studying the ideology. Its unique culture draws upon four chief sources: ancient Egypt, Celtic traditions, Theosophy, and the New Age. For 15 years, the group secretly labored to create a vast underground temple, which was discovered by amazed authorities in 1992. Thus, one of the ways that an audience cult may relate to religion is that it provides the socio-cultural basis for the emergence of a new cult movement. Another way is that an existing cult movement or client cult practitioner may publish books intended to attract potential recruits. For example an astrology book published by Heindel and Heindel in 1922 served to draw adherents to their cult movement, the Rosicrucian Fellowship, that established a small community in Oceanside, California.

Several research studies have explored the relationship between traditional religious commitment and the three degrees of cult organization. One could argue that religious people were especially attracted to the New Age, because it harmonizes with their belief in the supernatural – a positive correlation theory. Or, one could argue that traditionally religious people will reject the New Age, because they are committed to the contradictory set of beliefs promulgated by the denomination to which they belong – a negative correlation theory.

A more sophisticated curvilinear argument says that the New Age will be most popular among somewhat religious people, and least popular among both very religious and non-religious people. Very religious people do not like it because it contradicts their firmly held faith. Very irreligious people do not like it, because they reject the supernatural in general. Somewhat religious people are more accepting, because they are open to religious beliefs but lack doctrinal commitment.

Tobacyk and Milford (1983: 1029) defined paranormal phenomena to include: '... a wide range of beliefs and experiences concerning religion, psi (clairvoyance, precognition, telepathy, and psychokinesis), the occult, witchcraft, superstitions, the supernatural, and extraordinary and extraterrestrial life forms.' In creating a scale to measure these phenomena, they included four statements related to conventional religious belief: 'The soul continues to exist though the body may die.' 'There is a devil.' 'I believe in God.' 'There is a heaven and hell.' However, when Tobacyk and Milford applied the statistical technique called factor analysis to the data, these four items separated out from the others. Thus, conventional religion is distinct from the other topics, even though some connections exist.

Geographic analysis using rather old data on the United States, Canada, and Western Europe has indicated that cult movements and client cults were more common where church membership is relatively low (Stark and Bainbridge 1985; Bainbridge 1989a). One measure of audience cult activity, readership of the occult magazine *Fate*, showed a similar pattern, being less popular where the churches are strong. A questionnaire study of students at the University of Washington showed that 'Born Again' Protestants were far less likely than those with 'no religion' to approve of Yoga, Transcendental Meditation, Tarot reading, 'occult literature' and 'your horoscope' (Bainbridge 1997: 389).

These studies contradict the theory that the New Age and occult correlate positively with religion, and support the negative correlation theory. However, their data may not be sensitive enough to test the curvilinear theory. In a more recent questionnaire study of 1,765 Canadians, Alan Orenstein (2002) found a curvilinear relationship between church attendance and a scale measuring paranormal belief. Among Canadians who seldom if ever attend church, just 27.0 per cent score high on paranormal belief, compared with 34.6 per cent having medium frequency of church attendance, and only 20.6 per cent among those who attend church often.

Another recent study (Bainbridge 2004) analyzed data from 3,909 respondents to an online survey that included 20 putatively New Age statements in an agree-disagree format. A factor analysis grouped fully 15 of these items together, reflecting a high degree of unity. That is, people tended to respond to statements about these varied topics similarly, suggesting that they belong to a more-or-less unified subculture. Twelve of the 15 items were combined to make a reliable index, equally balanced between six items that New Age believers would agree with (positive items), and six they would tend to disagree with (negative items):

Positive statements:
1. There is much truth in astrology – the theory that the stars, the planets, and our birthdays have a lot to do with our destiny in life.
2. Some people can hear from or communicate mentally with someone who has died.
3. Some scientific instruments (e.g., e-meters, psionic machines, and aura cameras) can measure the human spirit.
4. Some people can move or bend objects with their mental powers.
5. Some people really experience telepathy, communication between minds without using the traditional five senses.
6. Scientifically advanced civilizations, such as Atlantis, probably existed on Earth thousands of years ago.

Negative statements:
1. All ancient people were less advanced than modern civilization in science and technology.
2. It's not possible to influence the physical world through the mind alone.
3. Extra-sensory perception (E.S.P.) probably does not exist.
4. Psychic mediums who claim they can communicate with the dead are either frauds or mentally ill.
5. Numerology, biorhythms, and similar attempts to chart a person's life with numbers are worthless.
6. Astrologers, palm readers, Tarot card readers, fortune tellers, and psychics can't really foresee the future.

Respondents were also asked how religious they are on a 7-point scale, from 'extremely non-religious' to 'extremely religious.' Figure 12.1 shows that the relationship to religiousness of four representative beliefs is noticeably curvilinear.

The two solid lines across Figure 12.1 show the percentage agreeing with two positive statements: 'Some people really experience telepathy ...' and 'There is much truth in astrology....' These two lines trace convex (hill-shaped) curves, indicating that people who are somewhat religious agree with these statements more often than people who are either extremely non-religious or extremely religious.

The two dashed lines show the percentage agreeing with two negative statements: 'Extra-sensory perception (E.S.P.) probably does not

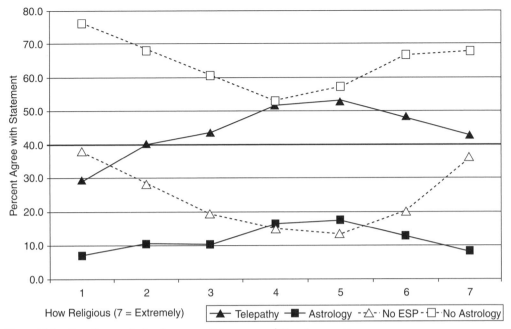

Figure 12.1   *Curvilinear relation between religiousness and New Age acceptance.*

exist.' 'Astrologers, palm readers, Tarot card readers, fortune tellers, and psychics can't really foresee the future.' These lines are concave (valley-shaped), indicating that people in the middle of the religious spectrum are less likely to agree with these negative beliefs. Thus, beliefs associated with the New Age have an ambivalent association with religion, and we see a similar ambivalence in the related cultural phenomena known as *parapsychology*, the *paranormal*, or *wild talents*.

PSEUDOSCIENCE AND PARARELIGION

One of the remarkable facts about standard psychology textbooks is that hardly any of them cover parapsychology, considering it to be a pseudoscience unworthy of mention. Parapsychology could also be described as parareligion, because it postulates essentially supernatural phenomena that satisfy people's desires to transcend the material world. However, many self-identified *parapsychologists*

argue strenuously that their discipline has no connection to religion (Felser 1999). Indeed, K. Ramakrishna Rao rejects any connection to the other topics associated with the occult or New Age:

> The general public often confuses parapsychology with spiritualism, ufology, astrological, palm- and tarot-card readings, hypnotic regression to 'past lives,' and a host of other occult practices. In contradistinction to these practices, however, parapsychology is concerned with 'psychic' abilities that can be studied empirically; that is to say, it is concerned with those abilities that can be studied by observation and experimentation under controlled conditions. Parapsychology, then, is the systematic and scientific study of psi (Rao 1984: 1).

For more than a century, there has been a grand debate between authors who claim that research demonstrates the reality of psi, ESP, and other paranormal phenomena (Rhine 1934, 1971; Beloff 1974; Edge *et al.* 1986), and others who argue that the apparent positive results are the result of error, poor experimental design, and even occasional fraud (Hansel 1966; Alcock 1981; Hyman 1989). In recent years, the parapsychology journals themselves have published a number of studies raising serious questions about the reality of the very phenomena they are dedicated to studying (Milton 1999).

A century ago, scientists were in the process of exploring the electromagnetic spectrum, and the general public was astonished by marvels such as X-Ray photography and radio that exploited wavelengths shorter or longer than the familiar octave that can be seen by the human eye. Thus it was not surprising that many writers imagined that spiritual phenomena might have a physical basis in as-yet undiscovered 'vibrations' or 'rays.' For example, in 1930 Upton Sinclair titled his book about telepathy, *Mental Radio*. At the time, it was reasonable to hope that parapsychology could produce convincing results, and become a recognized branch of the larger discipline of psychology, perhaps based on a well-supported scientific theory of how paranormal phenomena operate. Today, that is a far fetched dream, because progress in physics and neurology did not uncover mechanisms that could account for ESP.

Despite the excuses that psi talents are rare, and that the people with these talents perform unreliably, the phenomenon would have been acknowledged by psychologists by now, if in fact it were real. Psychology is a vast and diverse collection of research approaches and schools of thought, lacking central authority and orthodoxy, so it could not have wrongfully excluded parapsychology for such a long time were there any scientific basis for psi (Kalat 1986).

Books, magazine articles, and television programs about ESP are audience cult artifacts, whereas professional psychics are client cult practitioners. Some cult movements incorporate ESP in their beliefs and practices. For example, the Process Church of the Final Judgement had a training activity called the Telepathy Developing Circle that sought to improve members' intuitive sensitivities (Bainbridge 1978), and that will be described in the next section. Despite its claim to be doing rigorous science, parapsychology tends to focus its experiments on things that are personally meaningful within an individual's private life. For example, many ESP experiments seek to replicate real-life situations in which people sometimes feel they have paranormal experiences, such as hearing the telephone ring and guessing who is calling (Sheldrake and Smart 2003), or sensing that you are being stared at (Evans and Thalbourne 1999).

Psychokinesis, also called *telekinesis*, is the alleged power to move or otherwise affect physical objects at a distance by means of the mind alone. If telepathy is extrasensory perception, psychokinesis is paranormal action. Just as extrasensory perception is abbreviated ESP by parapsychologists, psychokinesis is abbreviated PK. 'Mind over matter' is the principle of magic, whereas Western religions reserve for God the power to affect the real world by force of will alone.

Much stage magic mimics psychokinesis, when a magician levitates a scarf, or teleports a playing card into the pocket of a member of the audience. Many people believed that the magician Yuri Geller possessed the mental power to bend spoons, when he was actually using the misdirection and prestidigitation tricks of a stage magician (Randi 1975; Marks 2000). While Geller performed other kinds of tricks, he was best known for spoon bending. Notice that spoons are ordinary household objects, used by every member of Western societies from earliest childhood, an intimate part of everyday life. A scientist, setting out to investigate whether the human mind can exert forces on physical objects, might never in a million years have thought about experimenting with spoon-bending.

In J. B. Rhine's famous PSI laboratory, a series of psychokinesis experiments were done by asking test subjects to influence rolling dice (L. E. Rhine 1971; Feather and Rhine 1971). Some care was invested in getting well balanced dice, because it is well known that so-called *loaded dice* will roll seven more often than expected by chance. But apparently little thought was given to the question of how PK could make dice come up seven, if indeed PK existed. Supposing the human mind can exert a slight force on physical objects, how can that force control the complex tumbling of a pair of dice? It would be an incredible engineering challenge to design a machine that could force ordinary dice to roll seven, for example by blowing air at them in carefully controlled ways. Merely calculating the rotation, bounces, and final resting position of a pair of dice is an incredibly difficult physical problem, let alone influencing them to give a desired result. But that is the key, actually, *desire*.

Like other forms of pseudoscience and parareligion, psychokinesis is about how people desire the world to be, and those desires are expressed in very human forms. Dice are cultural objects created by humans, and like a spoon they fit in the human hand. We want dice to come up lucky seven, as a metaphor for wanting good fortune in general. Humans want to influence humanly beneficial outcomes, not scientifically measurable ones. Dice are familiar things – found in the typical home – and their symbolism is clear. They are already part of human life, and are personally meaningful.

A great variety of PK experiments have been done, and naturally they vary in whether the methodology carries much humanistic symbolism, but very commonly they ask test subjects to accomplish a humanly desired outcome without having a clear conception of how a mental force could in fact do so. That is, they are experiments in magic.

Some experiments involve living organisms, and thus invoke the symbolism of a life force. For example, parapsychologists experiment with making plants grow more vigorously (Grad 1964), or preventing fungus from growing (Barry 1971). In one study, an experimenter hooked polygraphs to two philodendron plants and asked subjects to mentally 'increase the activity' in one plant but not the other, yet it is not clear what kind of force could do so, unless it is a life force unknown to modern biology (Brier 1971).

A physicist setting out to test PK would probably have designed laboratory instrumentation to measure the pressure of human thought with a finely tuned pendulum or torsion balance in a vacuum chamber, but that would conflict with the magical emphasis on human desires situated in everyday life. One experiment did ask people to influence the movement of a pendulum, but the experimenter commented that frequently the pendulum was covered so the subject could not see it clearly – thus being unable to aim that supposed mental force properly – and the subjects tended to focus on the counter that was supposed to register their successes (Cox 1971). Even in this case, parapsychology obscures the physical mechanism by which the mental force could operate and emphasizes the humanly desired outcome.

In recent years, parapsychologists have made extensive use of computers and other high-tech devices as instrumentation for their experiments. Helmut Schmidt asked research subjects to influence radioactive decay and the generation of electronic noise, each of which was part of a random-number generator that would determine which of a set of lights would flash (Schmidt 1970, 1973; Hyman 1989). Another study had subjects watch an animated dog race on the screen of a computer, and mentally try to make a particular dog win (Roe *et al.* 2003). Quite apart from whether a mental force exists or not, it seems implausible that human beings could aim it into the precise part of the hidden electronic components to affect the measurement device in the desired way. Again, the focus is on a humanly meaningful outcome, not on a clean test of a physical theory.

RELIGIOUS TELEPATHY TRAINING

One of the standard rituals of the Process Church of the Final Judgement, the Telepathy Developing Circle or TDC, will illustrate how the meaning of ESP adapts to the goals and social context of the group that employs it (Bainbridge 1978: 197–202). Conventional religious organizations in modern societies tend to avoid practicing magic, if only because magical beliefs can be disproven empirically and thus risk discrediting the entire belief system. In contrast, religious beliefs like faith in the existence of God and the afterlife are difficult to disconfirm empirically. Telepathy can be tested experimentally, and thus is susceptible to empirical disconfirmation.

The fundamental aim of the Telepathy Developing Circle is to increase the sensitivity and awareness of participants. Processean leaders would explain that a telepath is not a mind reader who steals information from the thoughts of an unwilling victim, but a spiritually advanced person who can discern the mood of a person or group. Telepathy means becoming more aware, increasing sensitivity around other people, around objects, around environments. Telepathy means being able to understand what a person is feeling and going through, without talking about it, just by being near, picking up the person's moods and emotions.

However, the Process always left open the question how much it was dealing in psychology, and how much in religion, how much in natural talents of the human mind, and how much in the supernatural. For example, the Process asserted that God had broken apart into four co-equal gods: Lucifer, Jehovah, Christ, and Satan. Associated with each was a different human personality: Luciferian, Jehovian, Christian, and Satanic. Individual members could decide for themselves whether the gods were real supernatural beings, or metaphors for the different types of humans.

Processeans did tend to agree that two telepaths are capable of extremely intimate communication with each other. A group of telepaths has immense spiritual power which can be channeled either for good or evil. The TDC is designed to emphasize the beneficial aspects of sensitivity, awareness, and non-verbal communication. The following script for a TDC will allow interested readers to try it for themselves, and will illustrate how the supernatural concept of telepathy can be interpreted in actual practice.

An experienced spiritual Guide directs the Circle. Before the gathering, the Guide selects a concept for one of the meditations in the activity. Some actual meditation topics used by the Process in one or another Circle were 'the future of Humanity and your part in it,' 'mass destruction,' 'the end of the world,' and 'self.' If the group faces an important decision, it can become the meditation topic. In the absence of a particular topic, the guide might select one of these 20 emotions as the meditation topic for the evening: Love, Fear, Joy, Sadness, Gratitude, Anger, Pleasure, Pain, Pride, Shame, Desire, Hate, Satisfaction, Frustration, Surprise, Boredom, Lust, Disgust, Excitement, or Indifference. If this Circle is one of a series, the Guide should cycle through all 20 before repeating one.

Depending upon the intensity of the experience and the number of participants, that we will call Novices here, a Telepathy Developing Circle can last from one hour to one and a half hours. The Circle can be done with as few as two people, or as many as three dozen. If more than seven people are present, the group should be divided into subgroups. Ideally, each subgroup should have an even number of people, usually six. One of the activities involves pairs, and if there is an odd number of Novices, the Guide can participate also, to complete the last pair. If this is the first time many of the participants have attended a Circle, the Guide may wish to quote some of the sentences above. If all of the participants have attended several Circles, the Guide may omit some of the instructions below.

Before the Guide enters, participants sit on cushions on the floor, arranged in a circle or a set of circles. The Guide enters and may stand or may sit on a high-backed straight chair, above the participants and able to see them all. The Guide says: 'Welcome. We have gathered to assist each other in developing spiritual sensitivity and awareness. We should not judge each other, but appreciate. We should not criticize, but gently encourage. This will be a safe place to communicate. All hostility, blame, demand, and envy are banished. Prepare to open your minds, your hearts, and your spirits.'

Now the Guide gives the first instruction: 'Begin by meditating on your aims for the evening. What do you wish to give to others? What do you wish to receive from them? Join hands, each of you with the two on either side.' (If there is a single circle, all join hands around. If there are several circles, members of each join hands in a separate ring.) 'Relax. Close your eyes. Make no effort. Let it come. Now begin the meditation.' After a short meditation, the Guide says: 'Come in now. Open your eyes. Release your hands.'

A round of the room follows 'When it is your turn, express the aims that came in your meditation. What do you wish to give? What do you wish to receive?' The Guide then calls each person by name, who answers with a brief phrase (such as: 'to give understanding and receive strength'). The Guide acknowledges whatever each person says, in a warm but dignified tone, using such acknowledgements as: good, right, okay, fine, indeed, sure, true, thank you.

The second part of the activity similarly asks each Novice to speak: 'Now we will have rounds on how your awareness and sensitivity have been during the past week.' (Or, if there are several circles, the Guide can say: 'Now we will have rounds in each of the smaller circles on how your awareness and sensitivity have been during the past week.') 'In turn, each person should say how his or her sensitivity has been developing, what kinds of things have been happening in the realm of emotional communication. Others may ask gentle, encouraging questions, to help the person express what he or she has been experiencing around sensitivity.' During this activity, the Guide may walk around the room, providing encouragement and making sure every person has a chance to say how his or her sensitivity has been.

The Guide says: 'All right? Has everyone finished? Good. Now we will meditate on the emotion of EMOTION (Substituting one of the following for 'EMOTION': Love, Fear, Joy, Sadness, Gratitude, Anger, Pleasure, Pain, Pride, Shame, Desire, Hate, Satisfaction, Frustration, Surprise, Boredom, Lust, Disgust, Excitement, or Indifference.) Close your eyes. Make no effort. Allow the EMOTION within you to rise into your consciousness. Now begin the meditation on EMOTION.' After five or ten minutes, the Guide says: 'Come in now. Open your eyes. We conclude the meditation on EMOTION. Now we will have rounds on what you saw or felt in your meditation on EMOTION.' (Or, if there are several circles, the Guide can say: 'Now we will have rounds in each of the smaller circles on what you saw or felt in your meditation on EMOTION.').

The Guide says: 'All right? Has everyone finished? Good. Did anyone get a particularly strong image around EMOTION?' The Guide encourages individuals to speak out, starting with two or three people the Guide knows will be comfortable speaking, calling on them by name. The Guide should use his or her own 'telepathic abilities' to sense who especially needs to express feelings to the entire group, calling on these individuals by name. The Guide should radiate acceptance, encouraging people to speak and to feel that others have feelings similar to theirs, always acknowledging what people express. The Guide concludes this activity by summing up the feeling in the room around EMOTION.

Next comes a classic psychic practice: 'It is time now for psychometry, so each of you will pair off with another.' The Guide may go around the room, helping people pair off, when possible putting people together who do not know each other well or two people of the opposite sex. 'First, half of you will do a reading on an object belonging to the other person in your pair. It should be something the person has carried, something belonging to that person alone, that has absorbed some of the person's aura. Hold that object to your forehead, and images will flow into your mind. Describe those images to the other person. If the person does not have a suitable object, you may hold hands with them instead. When you are doing the reading, do not worry about whether you are picking up something about the person you are reading, because you will be.

'The main thing is to relax. Do not place any demands on yourself. Just relax and let the images flow in. They will come. If you come up against a block, the block is probably in the person that you are reading, so describe the feelings around the block. If you draw a complete blank, describe what you yourself are feeling, because you will probably be picking it up from the person you are reading. Now begin the psychometry.'

(The Guide may complete the last pair, if there is an odd number of Novices in the group, or may meditate on the vibrations in the room during the psychometry, if there is an even number.) The Guide lets the first psychometry reading go for about ten minutes, then says: 'All right. Bring that reading to a close.' The Guide waits briefly for people to conclude their readings.

The Guide says: 'Now exchange roles in each pair. The person who gave the reading before will receive one now. The person who received the reading before will now take an object belonging to the other, and give a psychometry reading. Remember, if you open your mind and allow the images to flow, they will do so.' The Guide lets the second psychometry reading go for about ten minutes, then says: 'All right. Bring that reading to a close.' The Guide again waits briefly for people to conclude their readings. 'Now let us do a round of the room, about the images you received.' The Guide calls on several participants by name, asking how their readings went, and sympathizing with whatever they express.

The final activity of the TDC follows: 'In conclusion, meditate on what you have achieved during the evening. What did you give to others? What did you receive from them? Join hands, each of you with the two on either side. (If there is a single circle, all join hands around. If there are several circles, members of each join hands in a separate ring.) Relax. Close your eyes. Make no effort. Let it come. Now begin the meditation.' After a short meditation, the Guide says: 'Come in now. Open your eyes. Release your hands.'

The Guide says: 'In your private meditations over the next week, return to the images of this evening. Throughout every day, accept your feelings of EMOTION. Stretch out with your feelings to others. Allow your sensitivity and awareness to grow. The Telepathy Developing Circle is now ended.' The Guide departs. Then the Novices may talk with each other and gradually prepare to leave. The Novices share a quiet, informal social activity with each other, after the TDC.

For the Process, the TDC served several functions. By its very name, it claimed to be developing participants' telepathic powers. Perhaps it developed *empathy* rather than telepathy, encouraging people to use their proverbial five senses to feel the mood and emotions of other people, quite apart from whether a sixth sense exists. Another function was to build emotional bonds between the people, both as a group and as a network of dyads. By allowing people to express their feelings in the group setting, the TDC may also have been building commitment to the group. By couching the communications in paranormal terms, it may have built belief in the doctrines of the group. Indeed, the paranormal definition of the situation may have helped people express feelings and images, by dispelling normal inhibitions. For example, the images that arose in the psychometry activity were defined as real elements of the subject's aura, rather than being the thoughts of the reader, thus freeing the reader of responsibility for them.

The Telepathy Developing Circle encouraged the *willing suspension of disbelief*, rather than demanding belief. This simultaneously facilitated intimate communication among participants, and embedded their feelings within the group's doctrinal structure. As people become emotionally invested in a cult (whether religious, client or audience), suspension of disbelief evolves into belief. The belief may in some mundane, factual sense be incorrect. As it serves functions for individual and group, however, it becomes valued, influential, perhaps even fanatically held. The question then becomes how disbelief could ever become central to a person's view of religion. This is the challenging question of Atheism.

ATHEISM

The social-scientific literature contains few significant studies of Atheism, in part because it is difficult to study a phenomenon that is both rare and unorganized. Historical research has been done within the history of ideas tradition (Campbell 1972; Turner 1985), but it is hard to do field observations of people who never meet for group activities, and even questionnaire research is limited by the cost of obtaining huge numbers of respondents. From 1988 through 2000, the General Social Survey asked 8,027 American adults what they believed about God. Only 2.5 per cent were Atheists who responded, 'I don't believe in God.' Another 4.0 per cent were Agnostics, responding 'I don't know whether there is a God and I don't believe there is any way to find out.'

One would like to use data like this to explore the factors inspiring a small minority of the population to become Atheists, but the 203 Atheistic GSS respondents were polled in six different years, when the survey contained different items, so there are too few cases to run many of the correlations we would wish. The standard GSS demographic items do reveal a few basic facts. Atheists are more common among men (3.7 per cent) than among women (1.7 per cent), and among college graduates (4.0 per cent) than among people who have not completed four years of college (2.1 per cent). Combining the two variables, Atheists constitute 5.1 per cent of male college graduates, but only 1.3 per cent of female non-graduates. Using data from the Eurobarometer surveys, as well as the GSS, Bernadette Hayes (2000) reported that religious independents (including Atheists) tend to be male and well-educated.

Numerous secular intellectuals believe that Atheism is on the rise, as science and other secularizing forces progressively erode both the functions and plausibility of traditional religious faiths. In contrast, Rodney Stark and Roger Finke (2000) have distinguished the level of Atheism in society, which they think may be roughly constant, from the visibility of Atheism in public life, which may vary over time. A key factor may be the degree of repression Atheists experience in different countries and eras.

The GSS contains three items purportedly measuring the willingness of the general population to grant Atheists civil rights, but the items are not precisely about Atheists. All three refer to 'somebody who is against all churches and religion.' One asks, 'If such a person wanted to make a speech in your (city/town/community) against churches and religion, should he be allowed to speak, or not?' The second item asks, 'Should such a person be allowed to teach in a college or university, or not?' And the third inquires, 'If some people in your community suggested that a book he wrote against churches and religion should be taken out of your public library, would you favor removing this book, or not?' Nearly a third (30.6 per cent) of the US population would ban an anti-religion speech, fully 50.3 per cent do

not want such a person teaching in college, and 33.4 per cent want Atheistic books banned from the public library. Nobody today burns Atheists at the stake in Western societies, but in the US an Atheist will frequently interact with people who oppose his right to express his fundamental beliefs. Atheists may be immune to the fear of God, but as potential victims of prejudice they have good reason to fear other people's belief in God.

These observations immediately suggest a perspective for explaining Atheism, namely *control theory* (Hirschi 1969). People will tend to conform to other people's expectations, for example accepting the majority belief in God, unless they are weak in social bonds and thus relatively free to deviate. Of course, this does not explain how the majority got to be religious in the first place. However, given that religiousness is the norm, control theory would explain why some individuals failed to share it. A classic statistical study of schizophrenia found that this form of mental deviance was more common in socially disorganized areas (Faris and Dunham 1939), but the analogy with the mental deviance of Atheism would seem far fetched. Old Australian census data suggest that Atheists are more common among people who have moved away from their region of birth and thus may be weak in the social ties that restrain deviant behavior (Bainbridge 1989b). To date, however, really convincing empirical tests of the control theory of Atheism have not been performed.

A different theory that has some elements in common with control theory suggests that Atheism is encouraged by weakness in social obligations. Religion gains strength from the social obligations people incur in intimate social relationships, because it offers a way of meeting those obligations even when it is impossible for a person to satisfy the needs of other persons in a practical manner (Bainbridge 2002, 2003b). For example, a friend or family member may be dying. Those close to him or her have an obligation to help, but there may be no way they can save the person. Therefore, they offer religious compensators instead. If the dying person expresses some faith in the compensators, then their obligation to help is satisfied by praying God to take the soul of the dying person.

This *social obligation theory* is consistent with the frequent observation that women are less likely to be Atheists, because traditionally (and perhaps biologically) women are more nurturant and take on greater social obligations within the family. A recent study based on a very large international online questionnaire found several pieces of evidence that seemed to support this theory (Bainbridge 2005a). For example, Atheism was more common among childless adults, and less common among adults with two or more children. For other examples, 4,742 people responded to a series of questions, starting: 'How much would you like to do the following activities?' The list included two measures of closeness to family: 'A large family reunion' and 'A family history field trip.' Table 12.3 shows that Atheists are much more common among the people who express negative feelings about family activities.

Social obligation theory is different from control theory, in that it primarily concerns very strong relationships rather than all kinds of stable bonds, and in that it does not take religiousness for granted. Rather, it builds on the compensator theory of religion outlined in Table 12.2, by suggesting that there are two distinguishable processes through which compensators may generate religiousness, the first psychological and the second sociological:

- *Primary compensation* substitutes a compensator for a reward that people desire for themselves.
- *Secondary compensation* substitutes a compensator for a reward that a person is obligated to provide to another person.

One might argue that some people are so satisfied with their lives that they do not need religious compensators: young, healthy, rich people. But this is not a very good explanation of Atheism, because all people are deprived to some extent, and all face the ultimate deprivation of death. Nonetheless a weakened need for primary compensation may facilitate conversion to Atheism when assisted by a lack of need for secondary compensation among people who are deficient in strong social obligations. Other factors may weaken social obligations. A high divorce rate or a low fertility rate will mean that fewer people have family obligations. A high level of economic development provides many impersonal supports, such as health insurance and social services, that reduce interpersonal obligations. A welfare state robs social obligations from its citizens, whether or not it successfully fulfills these obligations itself. And to the extent that secularism weakens religious faith, it also weakens the plausibility of compensators required for secondary compensation.

Nonetheless, people fervently desire things they cannot have. Unlike religion, Atheism promises nothing, unless possibly some pride Atheists may feel in accepting 'the truth' when other people surrender to the wishful thinking of faith in the supernatural. Very recently, a loosely organized but vigorous movement has arisen that is compatible with Atheism yet offers hope comparable to that of religion. A common name for this movement is *Transhumanism*, although the World Transhumanist Association (www.transhumanism.org) is but one of a number of differently named organizations that together constitute the movement. Another term is *Extropian*, coined by the Extropy Institute, that is devoted to 'designing the means for resolving technological and cultural issues of transhumanity' (www.extropy.org). Some observers suggest that Transhumanism is more egalitarian than Extropianism, chiefly on the issue of whether all humans can collectively evolve to a higher

Table 12.3   *Per cent atheist among those who like...*

	Not at all	Not really	Mixed feelings	Would like	Like very much
Family reunion	15.9%	9.8%	9.1%	5.7%	3.4%
Family trip	14.4%	9.8%	7.3%	6.3%	4.9%

level, rather than only a small elite evolving and possibly leaving the human species altogether.

The fundamental principle of Transhumanism is the confidence that science and technology can transform human nature, over the very near future, even perhaps eradicating death (Immortality Institute 2004). For Transhumanists, our species has entered a revolutionary period of transition from human to super-human nature. During the transition, hope in rapid technological progress can substitute for religious faith. After the historical transition, people will have no use for gods, because they will be godlike themselves.

Few Transhumanists beat the drum of Atheism, because they are more interested in promoting the positive things that they believe, rather than refuting the beliefs of others. Yet Transhumanist leaders have expressed concern that religion will attempt to suppress transformative technologies, as it may already be doing with human cloning and stem cell research (Hughes 2004; Bainbridge 2003a, 2005b). Transhumanists and Atheists alike assert that science supports their doctrines.

Science rejects tenets of the New Age and parapsychology, such as astrology and telepathy, yet it does not reject Atheism. Indeed, science is methodologically Atheist, seeing how far it can get in explaining the world without reference to the supernatural. For a century, most scientists have found it impolitic to criticize religion, all the more so after popularly elected governments became the main supporters of pure science. This situation is most acute in the United States, where there is considerable debate over whether the Republican Party has become a vehicle for religious opposition to science, especially social science and socially relevant areas of biology and environmental science, because it seeks to represent the substantial fraction of Americans who are Evangelicals (Larsen 1992; Mooney 2005). An Atheist might argue that it is the obligation of science to test the theories of religion, as it tests all other theories, but in the twentieth century the sciences strenuously avoided taking on that potentially costly challenge. The twenty-first century may tell a different story.

CONVERGENCE OF SECULAR CULTURE

The New Age, paranormal, and Atheist phenomena are taking place in a cultural environment where the long-submerged tensions between religion and science are beginning to resurface. Ideas corrosive of religious faith are already well-developed in diverse areas such as cosmology, evolution, cognitive science, and artificial intelligence. Now, the merging of science and technologies – called *consilience* or *convergence* – closes the loopholes where a 'God of the gaps' might survive. That is, the truce between science and religion has been facilitated by the very fragmentation of science itself, but now secular science is developing a comprehensive model of existence that may more directly challenge religion. At the same time, small but vigorous movements have arisen to promote technologies that challenge religion's monopoly on transcendence and immortality: Transhumanists, Extropians, and related groups. The result may be an environment more conducive to new religious movements, parareligion, and irreligion.

As Stark and Finke (2000) noted, the social and behavioral sciences appear to encourage Atheism, and we are all familiar with Freud's writings against religion, notably *The future of an illusion* (Freud 1927). Several theories of religion have been proposed recently within cognitive science that might have some relevance for Atheism. At this point we can neither integrate them satisfactorily with the compensator theory, nor decide between them on the basis of empirical evidence. However, to the extent that religious faith can be explained without reference to any actual supernatural forces, the existence of such forces becomes less plausible.

To begin with, the dominant model of the mind in cognitive science holds that it is merely the sum of the complex behavior of neurons in the brain. Of course, so simply put, this is merely the old argument that human behavior is the result of brain functions, which has been a challenge to religion for many years (Ray 1863, 1871). However, considerable progress has been achieved in recent years understanding how the brain does in fact function. At the same time, computer and information scientists have made progress duplicating some (but by no means all) of those functions in machines.

A common conception that unites neuroscience and artificial intelligence is *neural networks*, and it has proved possible to model fundamental dynamics of the social-scientific theory of religion in computers (Bainbridge 1995, 2006), which manifestly lack souls. Clearly, cognitive science has a long way to go before it can fully explain human cognitive and emotional phenomena, but researchers in the field are confident that they are on the right track, and that the approach has no need of the concept of *soul*.

Atheism by definition is a belief that God does not exist, but the existence of God is not the only question. The major world religions assume not merely that a supernatural realm exists, but that a portion of each human being is supernatural. Cognitive science may be able to prove that this idea is false. Perhaps more socially important, by applying methods based on neural networks to the treatment of human beings and to technologies that directly serve millions of humans (Stein and Lidik 1998; Quinlan 2003; Schultz 2003), cognitive science may convince a significant segment of the general public that souls do not exist.

Cognitive science has simultaneously offered its own explanations for why people believe in such things as gods or souls. A number of cognitive scientists suggest that evolution placed a sufficiently high priority on humans possessing social skills, that our mind naturally interprets complex phenomena in the non-human world as if they were the result of purposeful action of conscious beings (Pinker 1997; Boyer 2002; Atran 2002; Barrett 2004). If so, humans are innately predisposed to imagine that supernatural beings are responsible for natural processes. If true, this could reinforce the part of the compensator theory that explores how explanations are exchanged between humans, and over time give rise to belief in general compensators based on assumptions about exchanges with supernatural beings.

Very recently, Paul Bloom (2004a, 2004b) has offered a considerable amount and variety of experimental and observational evidence that humans' brains are so constructed that we are bound to be dualists, like the French philosopher René Descartes, believing that we ourselves are somehow separate from our bodies. The human brain is not directly conscious of its own mental processes, and because the brain uses somewhat different modules to handle the social versus physical worlds, we naturally perceive ourselves as both subject and object, thus soul and body. Bloom explicitly argues that his research refutes religion. Of course any body of research may be wrong, but the work of cognitive scientists like Bloom and Pinker is closely integrated with other top-quality research in the field; they have published highly-publicized popular books, and a number of practical applications may also give their ideas very wide currency.

More controversial, but useful as an example of a different research approach, is the work of Eugene d'Aquili and Andrew Newberg (Newberg *et al.* 2001), who have used brain scan methods to seek the structures in the brain that are involved in religious experiences. A core idea of their theory is that a mystical sense of oneness with God can result when what they call the *orientation association area* of the brain experiences sensory deprivation. They claim that this brain module orients the self in space and helps distinguish the self from the rest of the universe. D'Aquili and Newberg have been criticized for failing to use up-to-date brain scan methods, and for ignoring recent literature in the field, but potentially their idea could be integrated into other cognitive science theories that religion is merely an error of perception, an accident of evolution and brain structure. In fact, D'Aquili and Newberg do not argue this. They leave open the possibility that the religious experiences are real, and that evolution may have designed the brain structures to permit religious experiences (either because they are real or because religion benefits humans). This may be another reason their work is controversial within cognitive science yet has generated much interest within theology (d'Aquili and Newberg 2000).

Cognitive science is one of the four fields of science and technology that appear to be merging in what Mihail Roco and I have called *convergence* (Roco and Bainbridge 2003; Roco and Montemagno 2004; Bainbridge and Roco 2005): nanotechnology, biotechnology, information technology, and cognitive science. From their initials, these are called the NBIC fields. Edward O. Wilson (1998; cf. Dennett 1995), has called the unification of the sciences *consilience*, and points out that it poses an entirely new intensity of challenge for religion. Previously, people could ignore the contradictions between science and religion, because science was fragmented, and each piece employed different principles. True unification of science, on the basis of a set of principles that apply across fields and achieve success both in explaining the world and in transforming it, could be extremely inimical to religion, if (as the compensator theory suggests) religion thrives where human comprehension and control are most limited.

Convergence of three of the four fields is already well advanced. Nanoscience examines the structure and behavior of matter at the nanoscale – the size range from 1 to 100 nanometers or billionths of a meter. The nanoscale structures inside the living cell that make biology possible are now being understood as molecular machines. Genetic engineering is based on increasingly rich knowledge about the DNA that carries the code of inheritance and is less than three nanometers across. The smallest components of computer chips are now less than 100 nanometers across, and high-density information storage already depends upon nanotechnology. Biomimetic computing, such as genetic algorithms and evolutionary programming, provide models of how all the complexity of nature could arise mechanistically. At the same time, computers are essential for research and design of both living and non-living creations, notably bioinformatics and nanoinformatics. Through nanotechnology, biotechnology, and information technology, the wonders of nature are being subsumed within human creativity. As people gain the power to create the world anew, they lose faith that a creator must be supernatural.

Convergence with the fourth field, cognitive science, is only now beginning, and the result is likely to be even more profound. Human consciousness is rooted in our biologically evolved neural network that senses and manipulates information through processes at the nanoscale and above. When the rhodopsin pigment in the eye intercepts light, the molecule changes shape by a few nanometers, thereby passing information to the neurons. The neurotransmitter chemicals that communicate across the brain cells are stored in vesicles perhaps 50 nanometers across, and move a similar distance from one neuron to another. Computer vision has yet to duplicate human eyesight, but machines already can see, recognize movement, identify objects, and plan their own path through a complex environment.

Information technology pioneer Ray Kurzweil (1999) may have been overly optimistic when he predicted that machine intelligence will surpass human intelligence before the middle of the twenty-first century, but he was prescient when he called them *spiritual machines*. Consciousness is merely information about existence, processed in an information system that must make decisions and take actions. Whether humans will finally learn the truth about themselves and their universe during this century, it is possible to discern a new vision of ourselves that is emerging in connection with NBIC convergence: Human personalities are dynamic patterns of information. Although embodied in matter – currently in flesh but potentially in silicon – personalities are non-material. *Information* is simply the modern word for *spirit*.

CONCLUSION

Social scientists have suggested that organized religion performs a variety of functions for human beings: providing comfort to desperate individuals, strengthening social solidarity, and supporting morality, among others. To be sure, there remain many empirical questions about how well religion actually performs these functions. For example, church membership apparently deters larceny far better than homicide, thus providing very uneven support for morality (Bainbridge 1989a; Stark and

Bainbridge 1996). However, given that religion performs some of the hypothesized functions at least somewhat well, what would be the consequence if the disorganized faith of the New Age or the faithlessness of Atheism became very popular? The simple answer is that society would suffer. A slightly more complex answer is that an increase in parareligion and Atheism could erode factors like social solidarity that themselves support religion, leading to a feedback loop in which the weakness of organized religion causes even more weakness.

An answer at a higher level of sophistication is that decline of religion as traditionally defined could open opportunities for entirely fresh responses to the challenges of human existence, of which Transhumanism and Extropianism might possibly be foreshadowings. It is unlikely that technology could overcome death and all forms of deprivation in the near future, but the growth of artificial intelligence and genetic engineering could discredit religions that assume souls and deny evolution. Through convergence, the NBIC technologies may have so much impact on everyday life that it is impossible for many people to ignore the materialistic assumptions of the sciences on which they rely. Thus, we may be entering a period when innovative religions arise, embracing some of the new scientific ideas. It remains to be seen whether science-oriented religions or secular culture will be able to create new social forms to support solidarity and morality. If they succeed in doing so in the future, then the term *New Age* will take on an entirely new and more significant meaning.

NOTES

1. The views expressed in this essay do not necessarily represent the views of the National Science Foundation or the United States.

REFERENCES

Alcock, J. E. 1981. *Parapsychology: Science or magic?* Oxford: Pergamon.

Atran, S. 2002. *In gods we trust: The evolutionary landscape of religion.* Oxford: Oxford University Press.

Bainbridge, W. S. 1978. *Satan's power.* Berkeley: University of California Press.

Bainbridge, W. S. 1989a. 'The religious ecology of deviance'. *American Sociological Review* 54: 288–95.

Bainbridge, W. S. 1989b. 'Wandering souls'. In G. K. Zollschan, J. F. Schumaker, and G. F. Walsh (eds), *Exploring the paranormal*, pp. 237–49. Bridport, Dorset, England: Prism.

Bainbridge, W. S. 1995. 'Neural network models of religious belief'. *Sociological Perspectives* 38: 483–95.

Bainbridge, W. S. 1997. 'The New Age'. In *The sociology of religious movements*, pp. 363–91. New York: Routledge.

Bainbridge, W. S. 2002. 'A prophet's reward: Dynamics of religious exchange'. In T. G. Jelen (ed.), *Sacred markets, sacred canopies*, pp. 63–89. Lanham, MD: Rowman and Littlefield.

Bainbridge, W. S. 2003a. 'Religious opposition to cloning'. *Journal of Evolution and Technology*, 13 (www.jetpress.org/volume 13/bainbridge.html).

Bainbridge, W. S. 2003b. 'Sacred algorithms: Exchange theory of religious claims.' In D. Bromley and L. Greil (eds), *Defining religion*, pp. 21–37. Amsterdam: JAI Elsevier.

Bainbridge, W. S. 2004. 'After the New Age'. *Journal for the Scientific Study of Religion* 433: 381–94.

Bainbridge, W. S. 2005a. 'Atheism'. *Interdisciplinary Journal of Research on Religion*, http://www.bepress.com/ijrr/vol1/iss1/art2/.

Bainbridge, W. S. 2005b. 'The Transhuman heresy'. *Journal of Evolution and Technology* (www.jetpress.org/).

Bainbridge, W. S. 2006. *God from the machine.* Lanham, MD: AltaMira.

Bainbridge, W. S. and Roco, M. C. 2005. *Converging technologies for human progress.* Berlin: Springer.

Barrett, J. L. 2004. *Why would anyone believe in God?* Walnut Creek, CA: AltaMira.

Barry, J. 1971. 'Retarding fungus growth by PK'. In J. B. Rhine (ed.). *Progress in parapsychology*, pp. 118–21. Durham, NC: Parapsychology Press.

Beloff, J. (ed.) 1974. *New directions in parapsychology.* Metuchen, NJ: Scarecrow Press.

Bloom, P. 2004a. *Decartes' baby: How the science of child development explains what makes us human.* New York: Basic Books.

Bloom, P. 2004b. 'The duel between body and soul'. *New York Times* 154 52968 September 10: A27.

Bok, B. J. and Mayall, M. W. 1941. 'Scientists look at astrology'. *Scientific Monthly* 523: 233–44.

Boyer, P. 2002. *Religion explained: The evolutionary origins of religious thought*. New York: Basic Books.

Brier, R. 1971. 'PK effect on a plant-polygraph system'. In J. B. Rhine (ed.), *Progress in parapsychology*, pp. 102–17. Durham, NC: Parapsychology Press.

Campbell, C. 1972. *Toward a sociology of irreligion*. New York: Herder and Herder.

Cox, W. E. 1971. 'PK on a pendulum system'. In J. B. Rhine (ed.), *Progress in parapsychology* pp. 97–101. Durham, NC: Parapsychology Press.

d'Aquili, E. and Newberg, A. 2000. 'The neuropsychology of aesthetic, spiritual, and mystical states'. *Zygon* 35: 39–52.

Dennett, D. C. 1995. *Darwin's dangerous idea*. New York: Simon and Schuster.

Edge, H. L., Morris, R. L., Rush, J. H. and Palmer, J. 1986. *Foundations of parapsychology*. Boston: Routledge and Kegan Paul.

Evans, L. and Thalbourne, M. A. 1999. 'The feeling of being stared at: A parapsychological investigation'. *Journal of the American Society for Psychical Research* 93: 309–25.

Faris, Robert E. L. and Dunham, H. W. 1939. *Mental disorders in urban areas*. Chicago: University of Chicago Press.

Feather, S. R. and Rhine, L. E. 1971. 'A helper-hinder comparison'. In J. B. Rhine (ed.), *Progress in parapsychology*, pp. 86–96. Durham, NC: Parapsychology Press.

Felser, J. M. 1999. 'Parapsychology without religion'. *Journal of the American Society for Psychical Research* 93, 259–79.

Freud, S. 1927. *The future of an illusion*. Garden City, New York: Doubleday [1961].

Gad, I. 1994. *Tarot and individuation*. York Beach, Maine: Nicolas-Hays.

Grad, B. 1964. 'A telekinetic effect on plant growth: II experiments involving treatment of saline in stoppered bottles'. *International Journal of Parapsychology* 64: 473–94.

Hansel, C. E. M. 1966. *ESP - a scientific evaluation*. New York: Scribner's.

Hayes, B. C. 2000. 'Religious Independents Within Western Industrialized Nations: A Socio-Demographic Profile'. *Sociology of Religion* 61: 191–207.

Heindel, M. and Heindel, A. F. 1922. *The message of the stars*. Oceanside, CA: Rosicrucian Fellowship.

Hirschi, T. 1969. *Causes of delinquency*. Berkeley, University of California Press.

Hughes, J. H. 2004. *Citizen cyborg*. Cambridge, MA: Westview.

Hyman, R. 1989. *The elusive quarry: A scientific appraisal of psychical research*. Buffalo, NY: Prometheus.

Immortality Institute 2004. *The scientific conquest of death*. Libros En Red.

Introvigne, M. 1999. 'Damanhur: A magical community in Italy'. In B. Wilson and J. Cresswell (eds), *New religious movements: Challenge and response*, pp. 183–94. London: Routledge.

Kalat, J. 1986. *Introduction to psychology*. Belmont, CA: Wadsworth.

Kurzweil, R. 1999. *The age of spiritual machines: When computers exceed human intelligence*. New York: Viking.

Larsen, O. N. 1992. *Milestones and millstones: Social science at the National Science Foundation, 1945–1991*. New Brunswick, NJ: Transaction Publishers.

Malinowski, B. 1948. *Magic, science and religion*. Garden City, New York: Doubleday.

Marks, D. 2000. *The psychology of the psychic*. Amherst, NY: Prometheus.

McIntosh, C. 1969. *The astrologers and their creed*. New York: Praeger.

Melton, J. G. 2000. 'The New Age'. In R. Landes (ed.), *Encyclopedia of millennialism and millennial movements*, pp. 285–88. New York: Routledge.

Milton, J. 1999. 'Should ganzfeld research continue to be crucial in the search for a replicable PSI effect?' *Journal of Parapsychology* 63: 309–33.

Mooney, C. 2005. *The Republican war on science*. New York: Basic Books.

Newberg, A., d'Aquili, E. and Rause, V. 2001. *Why God won't go away*. New York: Ballantine.

Orenstein, A. 2002. 'Religion and Paranormal Belief'. *Journal for the Scientific Study of Religion* 412: 301–11.

Pinker, S. 1997. *How the mind works*. New York: Norton.

Quinlan, P. T. (ed.) 2003. *Connectionist models of development: Developmental processes in real and artificial neural networks*. New York: Psychology Press.

Randi, J. 1975. *The magic of Uri Geller*. New York: Ballantine.

Rao, K. R. (ed.) 1984. *The basic experiments in parapsychology*. Jefferson, NC: McFarland.

Ray, I. 1863. *Mental hygiene*. Boston: Ticknor and Fields.

Ray, I. 1871. *Treatise on the medical jurisprudence of insanity*. Boston: Little, Brown and Company.

Rhine, J. B. 1934. *Extra-sensory perception*. Boston: Bruce Humphries [1964].

Rhine, J. B. (ed.) 1971. *Progress in parapsychology*. Durham, NC: Parapsychology Press.

Rhine, L. E. 1971. 'PK in the laboratory: A survey'. In J. B. Rhine (ed.), *Progress in parapsychology*, pp. 72–85. Durham, NC: Parapsychology Press.

Roco, M. C. and Bainbridge, W. S. (eds) 2003. *Converging technologies for improving human performance*. Dordrecht, Netherlands: Kluwer.

Roco, M. C. and Montemagno, C. D. (eds) 2004. *The coevolution of human potential and converging technologies*. New York: New York Academy of Sciences, Annals of the New York Academy of Sciences, volume 1013.

Roe, C. A., Davey, R. and Stevens, P. 2003. 'Are ESP and PK aspects of a unitary phenomenon? A preliminary test of the relationship between ESP and PK'. *Journal of Parapsychology* 67: 343–66.

Saliba, J. A. 2003. *Understanding new religious movements*. Walnut Creek, CA: Alta Mira.

Schmidt, H. 1970. 'A quantum mechanical random number generator for psi tests'. *Journal of Parapsychology* 34: 219–25.

Schmidt, H. 1973. 'PK tests with a high-speed random number generator'. *Journal of Parapsychology* 37: 105–19.

Schultz, T. R. 2003. *Computational developmental psychology*. Cambridge, MA: MIT Press.

Sheldrake, R. and Smart, P. 2003. 'Videotaped experiments on telephone telepathy'. *Journal of Parapsychology* 67: 147–66.

Sinclair, U. 1930. *Mental radio*. New York: Boni.

Stark, R. and Finke, R. 2000. *Acts of faith*. Berkeley, CA: University of California Press.

Stark, R. and Bainbridge, W. S. 1985. *The future of religion*. Berkeley, CA: University of California Press.

Stark, R. and Bainbridge, W. S. 1987. *A theory of religion*. New York: Lang & Toronto Studies in Religion.

Stark, R. and Bainbridge, W. S. 1996. *Religion, deviance and social control*. New York: Routledge.

Stein, D. J. and Lidik, J. (eds.) 1998. *Neural networks and psychopathology*. Cambridge, UK: Cambridge University Press.

Tobacyk, J. and Milford, G. 1983. 'Belief in paranormal phenomena: Assessment instrument development and implications for personality functioning'. *Journal of Personality and Social Psychology* 44: 1029–37.

Toulmin, S. and Goodfield, J. 1962. *The fabric of the heavens: The development of astronomy and dynamics*. New York: Harper.

Turner, J. 1985. *Without God, without creed: The origins of unbelief in America*. Baltimore, MD: Johns Hopkins University Press.

Wilson, E. O. 1998. *Consilience: The unity of knowledge*. New York: Knopf.

13

Civil Religion in America and in Global Context

MARCELA CRISTI AND LORNE L. DAWSON

Thus stands the cause between God and us. We are entered into a covenant with HIM for his work. We have taken out a commission … For we must consider that we shall be as a city upon a hill. The eyes of all people are upon us (John Winthrop, 1630).

That this Nation, under God, shall have a new birth of freedom – and that the Government of the people, by the people, for the people, shall not perish from the earth (Gettysburg Address, Abraham Lincoln, 1863).

INTRODUCTION

John Winthrop's sermon and Abraham Lincoln's Gettysburg Address are classic expressions of American civil religion, giving voice to the idea that Americans have a special place in history as a people chosen by God to fulfill His will and serve as an example to the rest of the world (Hammond, 1976; Hughey, 1992; Hepler, 1996). The dissenting churches that fled Europe to resettle in America conceived themselves as founding a 'New Israel' devoid of the corruption of the European world. For them, as is commonly observed, America was to be a beacon among nations, a shining example of God's purpose, and the

'trustee' of the blessings of liberty and prosperity for all (Kohn [1944] 1967: 293; Hughey, 1984: 118). To assure the religious liberty that undergirds this promise the Puritan forefathers provided the theological justification for eliminating any sort of religious monopoly in the new world (Hammond, 1974: 125; Rice, 1980: 57). This principle is embodied in the First Amendment of the Constitution of the United States: 'Congress shall make no law respecting an establishment of religion, or prohibiting the free exercise thereof.' By creating the 'wall of separation' between church and state the founding fathers set a social dilemma in place from which the American tradition of civil religion has grown. Since the ethical and moral values of the nation could not be monopolized by any specific church, a different 'civil' religion emerged – a belief system independent of both church and state (Mead, 1974: 66).

Clearly, the great constitutional originality of the American system is disestablishment (Demerath, 2001: 193). But while the separation of church and state is a central principle of American religious and political life, the political realm has historically been imbued with a strong religious dimension (Bellah, 1967).

This relationship is manifested in several ways. Special occasions, such as national holidays and presidential inaugurations, are solemnized with biblical references and invocations of God. Presidents and political statesmen, from Washington onwards, have made appeals to God both to request protection and guidance in times of crisis, and to express gratitude for His blessings. At the opening of legislative sessions and other important public ceremonies it is customary to begin with a prayer. The invocation 'God save the United States and this Honorable Court' is used each time the Supreme Court assembles to hear an argument. American children in school pledge allegiance to 'one nation under God,' and the American motto 'In God We Trust' is engraved on its coins. Presidential speeches are commonly brought to a conclusion with the benediction 'God Bless America,' and biblical quotations or religious symbols are inscribed on various government buildings throughout the land. These and other public religious expressions too numerous to mention are the outward manifestations of American civil religion.

The intimacy of the relation between religion and politics in America has long been recognized. But controversies over the role of religion in public life have become more pronounced in recent decades, placing a strain on both the phenomenon of American civil religion and how sociologists have conceived it. The disputes have focused on everything from school prayers (see Brown and Bowling, 2003; Davis, 1998, 2003c; Hepler, 1996) to the constitutionality of the phrase 'under God' in the Pledge of Allegiance (see Canipe, 2003; Cloud, 2004) to the erection of nativity scenes on public property (Wuthnow, 1996: 82). In a more pluralist and secular America some people believe that religion should be eradicated from public life, just as others are asserting more forcefully than ever that America is a Christian nation, and religion should remain in the public square. The former group asserts that the intrusion of religion in public life is unconstitutional, while the latter claims that the framers of the constitution wanted the nation to be governed by Christian principles

and values. The purpose of the First Amendment, they argue, was to provide freedom from religious oppression, to prevent sectarian fanaticism, and to protect all religions from government interference. It was not intended to eliminate religion from public life. Defenders of an even stricter separation of church and state fear, however, that the civil religious discourse used so often in public life is a ruse for reasserting a *de facto* if not *de jure* religious establishment, legitimizing an evangelical Protestant vision of America.

Clearly, a renegotiation of boundaries between the religious and the political orders is taking place in America and this realignment has recently moved to the forefront of the legal and political agendas of many Americans (McClay, 2004). In these circumstances, the practice of civil religion, normally perceived as an instrument of national unity, has become the focal point of discord and divisiveness.

In this chapter we will briefly outline the genesis of the concept of civil religion, and its application to American history and culture in the highly influential work of Robert N. Bellah. We will then examine the diverse reactions to Bellah's conception of civil religion. Attention will focus in particular on the oft repeated claim that, in theory and practice, the concept of civil religion is fundamentally ambiguous. It is riddled, many argue, with the tensions born of disparate interpretive tendencies, variously conceived as the Puritan and Enlightenment heritages of American political life, the priestly and prophetic expressions of civil religion, and the orthodox versus progressive, or simply conservative and liberal understandings of America and its destiny. Calling on an alternative formulation, drawn from the origins of the concept in the thought of Durkheim and Rousseau, we propose recasting civil religion as a continuum of possibilities for the public expression of religion. This continuum varies from a conception of civil religion as 'culture,' as a spontaneous and integrative social phenomenon, to a conception of civil religion as 'ideology,' as an imposed and manufactured political resource. This approach better serves the critical thrust of contemporary research on civil religion, particularly in contexts other than the United States. We will end with a brief consideration of the comparative literature using the notion of civil religion to explain the social and political uses of religion in other cultures, and some thoughts on the future of research on this topic.

Before proceeding it is wise to note a few things. First, there is a vast literature on this topic and our analysis is necessarily selective and synoptic, but hopefully not unrepresentative of the varied and excellent research available. Second, any attempt to definitively state what civil religion is, to provide 'the' definition of it, is bound to be frustrated by the sheer variety of relevant variables. Nonetheless it is prudent to provide at least an initial and highly generic statement of what we mean. A civil religion is a system of symbols, beliefs, and rites of a reverent and celebratory kind, concerning the myths, history and destiny of a people that is used to establish and express the sacred character of their social identity and the civic and political order associated with it. The elements of this civil religion are commonly derived from, yet institutionally distinct from, existing religious systems. In some instances the civil religion may be the result of strong emotional commitments to political ideals that are elevated to a position of transcendence consonant with religious beliefs, yet without any specific reference to traditional religious systems. As we will see, this form of sacralization can happen in many different ways, but conceptual order can be brought to the plethora of possibilities.[1]

HISTORY OF THE CONCEPT

The notion of civil religion is often traced back to classical antiquity, to the local gods of the Greek city-state, and to Imperial Rome and its religious foundations. It refers to the religious dimension of certain civic ceremonies, collective values and traditions found in any political society (Nisbet, 1988). To this extent, it is 'as old as political society' itself (Henry, 1979: 1). Fustel de Coulanges, in his classic work *The Ancient City* ([1864] 1956), describes the

Greek and Roman city-states as governed by religious notions and organized like a church. Each city had its national religion and a patron deity. Citizens were required to renew the tie of common worship by celebrating together special rites from which non-citizens were excluded. Solemn assemblies, ceremonial festivals and public worship honored the city's myth of origin, and its military prowess and accomplishments. Ritual occasions were used both to inculcate a common morality into citizens' lives, and to reaffirm their sense of solidarity and shared identity. Religion and the political order were fused and indistinguishable.

It is the French philosopher Jean-Jacques Rousseau, however, who first introduced the term 'civil religion' into modern discourse. Rousseau used the term in *The Social Contract* ([1762] 1973) to refer to a public morality regulated by the state. He held that, from a political standpoint, all religions were inadequate to the needs of the modern state. He took an especially dim view of Christianity because he thought it divided citizens' loyalties and distracted them from their civic responsibilities. Yet he feared that loosening the bonds between Christianity and politics might threaten the traditional sources of political legitimacy, and he believed that no state 'has ever been founded without a religious basis.' To resolve the dilemma posed by these conditions, Rousseau postulated a new religious belief system, a 'purely civil profession of faith,' made useful for politics ([1762] 1973: 272). The tenets of this religion, to be fixed by the sovereign, include a belief in the existence of a divinity, in the afterlife, in rewards for the just and punishment for evil, in the sanctity of the social contract, and a love of the country and its laws. Citizens would be forced to accept the canons of this new faith on pain of banishment or death. In Rousseau's view, the social order is 'a sacred right which is the basis of all other rights.' This right, 'does not come from nature.' Rather, it must 'be founded on conventions' ([1762] 1973: 165–6). Civil religion is a central element of the conventions needed to guarantee social order. In short, Rousseau conceives religion in a purely instrumental fashion, as a fundamental prerequisite for government.

He deliberately constructs a creed to encourage civic virtues and a public spirit, and to help maintain the political community by cementing people's allegiance to the state (Cristi, 2001: 20–1). This type of civil religion flourished at the height of the French Revolution, when Robespierre and other Jacobin leaders imposed the Religion of the Supreme Being on France. Dogmas, liturgies, and ceremonies were created by these overzealous adherents of Rousseau's philosophy that had the 'revolutionary state ... as the essence of belief and rite' (Nisbet, 1988: 525).

The contemporary discourse on civil religion does not take Rousseau as its point of departure, however, so much as the sociology of Emile Durkheim ([1912] 1961). Durkheim never used the term civil religion. Nor did he refer to a divinity or a belief in God. But it is his conception of the intimate relationship of religion and society that formatively shaped this field of research. His understanding of the foundations of social integration and allegiance to the state contrasts sharply with that of Rousseau. He believes society to be united by a voluntary, spontaneous, and noncoercive expression of collective identity, which is embodied in a set of beliefs and practices. In his conception, as long as individuals join together to form groups there will always be some common faith between them, since religion is part of the symbolic self-understanding of every society. The very constitution of society is a religious phenomenon, in the sense that a 'society can neither create itself nor recreate itself without at the same time creating an ideal' conception of itself that is traditionally embodied in its religious world view ([1912] 1961: 470). In turn the power that people attribute to the gods and things deemed sacred is actually derived from their participation in the collective consciousness and effervescence of social life. Thus, for Durkheim, religious and civil society are 'coterminous,' to borrow Demerath and Williams' term (1985: 156). In Durkheim's memorable phrase: 'If religion has given birth to all that is essential in society, it is because the idea of society is the soul of religion' ([1912] 1961: 466). In essence religion develops out a pre-existing sense of moral community, and its purpose is to concretely express and legitimate this social solidarity (see Hammond, 1974: 116 and 1980b: 139).

From a Durkheimian perspective, then, civil religion is more of a cultural than a political phenomenon. It is a non-coercive civic faith that emerges naturally from the group and serves to further strengthen its collective identity, rather than an ideology imposed from on high for the presumed greater good of the nation (Cristi, 2001: 12).

AMERICAN CIVIL RELIGION

It was this Durkheimian legacy that informed the contemporary debate on civil religion as initiated by the publication of Robert Bellah's seminal essay 'Civil Religion in America' (1967). Though Bellah notes that the term civil religion is 'of course, Rousseau's,' his orientation is Durkheimian. He emphasizes the non-coercive nature of civil religion, its role as an integrative and legitimating force in society, and its supposed independence from established religions and the state.

Bellah begins his famous article by claiming that 'few have realized that there actually exists alongside of and rather clearly differentiated from the churches an elaborate and well-institutionalized civil religion in America' (1967: 1). He defines American civil religion as a 'genuine apprehension of universal and transcendent religious reality as seen in or, ... as revealed through the experience of the American people' (1967: 12). America's self-understanding is firmly grounded, he asserts, in a universal religion of the nation that endorses a belief in the existence of a God whose laws serve as evaluative standard for judging the nation. He also maintains that since the early days of the nation, Americans have been profoundly influenced by religious and moral understandings, and have interpreted their history essentially in religious terms. In his view, civil religion represents an 'institutionalized' set of 'sacred beliefs' about the nation, which provides Americans with a sense of cohesion and solidarity, especially in times of profound national crisis.

American civil religion, as described by Bellah, is impregnated with biblical imagery: 'Exodus, Chosen People, Promised Land, New Jerusalem, Sacrificial Death and Rebirth' (Bellah, 1967: 18). Like any other religion, it has its own set of sacred rites and symbols, a ceremonial calendar, prophets and martyrs, and sacred texts and places. It is ritually celebrated in various solemn occasions, particularly presidential inaugurations. Holidays such as Memorial Day, the Fourth of July, Thanksgiving, and Veterans Day are all imbued with a special, sacred significance. Its litany of venerated sacrificial martyrs and heroes includes the founding fathers of the nation, President Abraham Lincoln, President John F. Kennedy, Martin Luther King Jr., and the Unknown Soldier. Its most sacred texts are the Declaration of Independence, the Constitution, and the Gettysburg Address. The memorials to Washington, Jefferson, and Lincoln, Arlington Cemetery, and more recently the Vietnam War Memorial, are the hallowed places adorned with the important symbols of the civil religious creed. The ceremonies and visitations associated with these sites provide for the regular renewal and reaffirmation of the American moral vision of itself (Parsons, 2002).

With these descriptive elements in hand, Bellah rightly argues that the principle of church and state separation has never 'denied' Americans the opportunity to attribute a deeply religious meaning to American public life. While civil religion is embedded in religious and moral understandings rooted in the Judeo-Christian tradition, it functions independently and 'alongside' institutionalized religions. It is 'neither sectarian nor in any specific sense Christian' (Bellah, 1967: 8). Yet it is not just some generalized religiosity since its primary referent is the collective consciousness of Americans. Its symbols, though Christian in origin, do not stand for any God, any church, or any denomination in particular. Rather, they are 'uniquely American, transcending denominational or religious differences' (Demerath and Williams, 1985: 157).

Following Durkheim, Bellah claims that any stable and cohesive society rests on a 'common set of moral understandings' about what is collectively accepted as right or wrong. He believes that these moral understandings 'must rest upon a common set of religious understandings.' It is through the collective religious meaning system that people are able to have 'a picture of the universe in terms of which the moral understandings make sense' (1975: ix). The shared religious principles provide both a 'cultural legitimation' of the nation and a basic 'standard of judgement' for criticizing and seeking the perfection of the nation. In his view, there has always been (and perhaps will always be), a certain tension between the spheres of action associated with religion, legitimation, morality, and civic responsibility. Every society has to confront this tension or, put in another way, every society has to find a workable solution to the religio-political problem. Bellah locates civil religion in the dialectical strain of these spheres of action (1980a: viii).

Civil religion does not have constitutional authority, but Bellah notes that historically it has played an active role in matters of public concern. He claims that in American political thought 'sovereignty rests, of course, with the people, but implicitly, and often explicitly, the ultimate sovereignty has been attributed to God' (1967: 4). Presidential inaugurations and political speeches, since the times of the founding fathers, reflect the consistent belief that Americans, personally and collectively, have an 'obligation' to fulfill 'God's will on earth' (1967: 5). What Lincoln referred to as 'our ancient faith' is the belief that the Revolutionary spirit and its 'normative core' – the rights to life, liberty and the pursuit of happiness – are God given and inalienable. God has uniquely blessed the nation and will guide and protect it so that America can champion and defend those rights (Bellah, 1976c: 55–6).

Foreign observers have often remarked on the 'elements of theism and even theocracy' in American political life (Angrosino, 2002: 248). Alexis de Tocqueville, writing about America in the 1830s, was struck by the 'mystical' ways Americans regarded themselves and their history (Nisbet, 1988: 526), and G. K. Chesterton famously remarked that America was 'a nation with the soul of a church' (cited in Mead, 1974: 45).

While skeptical observers may dismiss the use of God talk during inaugural addresses or presidential campaigns as only a 'semblance of piety' designed to win votes or avert losing them, Bellah argues that what people say on public and solemn occasions deserves serious attention. These addresses give voice to a sense of value and purpose 'not made explicit in the course of everyday life' (1967: 2). Bellah uses several examples to illustrate his point. For instance, he quotes from Kennedy's inaugural address: 'the rights of man come not from the generosity of the state but from the hand of God... let us go forth to lead the land we love, asking His blessing and His help, but knowing that here on earth God's work must truly be our own' (1967: 1–2). This public religious spirit, 'expressed in a set of beliefs, symbols and rituals,' and symbolically framed in the founding documents of the nation and reiterated in presidential inaugural addresses and political speeches, is what Bellah calls 'American civil religion' (1967: 4).

This civil religion operates through various institutions and branches of government. The presidency, in particular, is considered to be its most important institutional base (Henderson, 1975; Gamoran, 1990; Cristi, 2001). So too is the public school system. In fact Bellah suggested it may have provided the most significant place 'for the cultic celebration of the civil rituals' (Bellah, 1967: 11; Gehrig, 1981b: 49; and Michaelson, 1970 as well). In general, the social plausibility of the civil religious discourse depends on the creation and maintenance of a set of institutions imbued simultaneously with political and religious significance. In a comparative analysis of civil religion in Mexico and the United States, Hammond (1980a) demonstrates that a true civil religion will only develop if there are sufficient independent organizational vehicles. Elsewhere he has argued that the American legal system has uniquely functioned as such a vehicle as well (1980b, 1989).

In short, Bellah's thesis is that civil religion in America provides religious legitimation to political authority, gives the political process a transcendent goal, serves as a carrier of national identity and self-understanding, and serves as a resource for morally judging the nation.

Civil religion is thus perceived as a spontaneous common civic faith capable of sustaining a pluralistic culture by overriding its religious, ethnic, and social diversity. It is assumed to foster unity and consensus, for its primary function is to generate powerful symbols of national solidarity and encourage Americans to achieve national aspirations and goals.

BELLAH'S GREAT AND TROUBLED LEGACY

The religious identity of American society was noted many times before. It is presaged in John Dewey's classic work *A Common Faith* (1934), Robin Williams's (1951) 'common religion' in America, Lloyd Warner's (1953) analysis of Memorial Day celebrations, and Sidney Mead's ([1967] 1974) discussion of 'the religion of the Republic.' Seymour Martin Lipset posited the existence of an 'American Creed,' a distinct set of values that Americans hold with a quasi-religious fervour (1963: 178), and Will Herberg (1955) spoke of 'the American Way of Life,' a system of beliefs and practices that 'constitutes a faith common to Americans as Americans,' giving the nation an 'overarching sense of unity' (1974: 77). But Bellah's essay resonated, sparking an 'unprecedented burst of excitement' (Wimberley and Swatos, 1998: 94; see Mathisen, 1989: 137).

Indeed, Bellah's essay roused both 'passionate opposition' and 'widespread acceptance' (Bellah, 1978: 16) and went on to become one of the most acclaimed and controversial publications in the sociology of religion. It is difficult to say why. The notoriety of Bellah's esssay may stem simply from his ability to concisely re-articulate past arguments and capture their meaning with an apt new phrase, 'American civil religion.' It may be because he insisted that 'this religion – or perhaps better, this religious dimension – has its own seriousness and integrity and requires the same care in understanding that any other religion does' (Bellah, 1967: 1). Certainly the moral earnestness of the debate over civil religion grew out of the tenor of the times. American institutions were facing a crisis of legitimation in the wake of the social and cultural disturbances of the sixties and the

Nixon years (e.g., the civil rights movement and its attendant riots, the domestic conflict over the Vietnam War, the student rebellions, and the Watergate scandal).

Initial interest in the topic crossed disciplinary boundaries and centered, for the most part, on definitional disputes (e.g., Cutler, 1968; Coleman, 1969; Cherry, 1971; Marty, 1974; Hammond, 1976; West, 1980; Gehrig, 1981b), the clarification of the concept or refinement of its meaning (Jones and Richey, 1974; Garret, 1974; Wilson, 1979), determining if a civil religion actually exists in America, and if so, how it could be empirically identified, and what role it played in people's voting behavior (Thomas and Flippen, 1972; Wimberly *et al.*, 1976; Wimberley, 1976, 1978, 1979, 1980; Christenson and Wimberly, 1978; Jolicouer and Knowles, 1978; Wimberly and Christenson, 1980, 1981, 1982).

Donald Jones and Russell Richey (1974: 15–18), for example, were the first to attempt a conceptual clarification of the term, distinguishing five understandings of the concept: (1) a folk religion, as illustrated by Will Herberg's idea of the 'American Way of Life'; (2) a transcendent universal religion of the nation, as exemplified by Sidney Mead's notion of 'religion of the Republic,' and Bellah's own model; (3) a religious nationalism, which elevates the nation itself to be an object of worship and celebration; (4) a democratic faith, which sacralizes humanistic values such as equality, freedom, and justice as a sort of national creed, but without necessarily referring to a transcendent being; and (5) a Protestant civic piety, which refers to the alliance between Protestantism and nationalism in America – the overall 'Protestant coloring' of the American identity. The five usages reveal the potency of the idea of a 'general religion' (Jones' and Richey's term) of this kind, as well as the perplexing complexity posed by its conceptualization.

The historian John Wilson (1971, 1974) attempted to identify and reduce the ambiguity inherent in Bellah's thesis by examining what he believed were the three most common models implicit in the literature: theological, ceremonial, and structural-functional conceptions of civil religion. In a later publication he proposed four different constructions of what he called public religion in America: social, cultural, political, and theological, using a religious referent to distinguish between the models. His emphasis was on the explicit religious content of civil religion (Wilson, 1979: 149–50). Agreeing with Jones and Richey, he pointed out that Bellah's model was just 'one possible construction of a larger public religion' (Mathisen, 1989: 134). Broadly speaking, however, most scholars accepted Bellah's idea of civil religion as a legitimating and integrative force (Thomas and Flippen, 1972: 218). Consequently, Bellah had either steadfast supporters or friendly critics.

Conceptual differences and definitional discrepancies kept the debate over civil religion alive for a number of years, but eventually attention shifted to identifying the institutional sources of American civil religion and grasping its relationship to broader theoretical models and concerns (Mathisen, 1989: 135). Cole and Hammond (1974) and Hammond (1980b, 1989) placed civil religion in the context of religious pluralism and growing social complexity, and attempted to link it with developments in the legal system. Coleman (1969) and Bellah (1980a) examined it in terms of religious evolution, while Fenn (1978) placed it in the context of secularization theory, and Markoff and Regan (1982) located it within the context of theories of modernization. Others treated popular sports and aspects of popular culture as expressions of civil religion (see Rogers, 1972; Novak, 1976; Sinclair-Faulkner, 1977; Simpson, 1984). Cross-cultural case studies also began to appear. Moodie (1975) examined the civil religion of South Africa, Liebman and Don-Yehiha (1983) that of Israel, and Bellah (1980c; 1980d) and Hammond (1980a) examined civil religion in Japan, Italy, and Mexico.

While explicit academic research on civil religion has waxed and waned, almost four decades later the expression 'civil religion in America' has become part of the accepted vocabulary of social scientists and it is widely used in fields other than the sociology of religion (e.g., Novak, 1992; Selznick, 1992; Beiner, 1993;

Giner, 1993; Kessler, 1994; Frohnen, 1996, Rawls, 1996; DeLue, 1997). As the literature continues to grow the concept has moved beyond the boundaries of America to be embraced around the globe (Regan, 1976; Reynolds, 1977; De Azevedo, 1979; Purdy, 1982; Takayama, 1988; Zuo, 1991; Kim, 1993; Minkenberg, 1997; Cha, 2000; Parsons, 2002). There has also been a resurgence of interest in the concept with the revival of civil religious discourse in the United States after the shocking events of September 11, 2001 (Swatos, 2004: 193).

Bellah spent many years trying to explain what he meant by American civil religion. He expressed both surprise and frustration by the controversy, elaboration, and misinterpretation of the concept. Disheartened by what he called the 'unnecessary reification' of the term, he ceased using it in the late 1980s. But he remained keenly interested, he declared (1989: 147), 'in the substantive issues' addressed by the concept (e.g., see Bellah et al., Habits of the Heart, 1985).

THE TWO CIVIL RELIGIONS IN AMERICA

In the Western world, as Jay Demerath comments, few nations 'can boast such a natural melding of religion and nationhood' as the United States (2001: 236). Yet scholars have noted that civil religion, like any other religion, can work to divide Americans, as well as unite them, as its tenets are interpreted and applied differently.

From the beginning, Bellah (1976c) argued that there was an internal tension in this creed. American civil religion has been buffeted and driven by a clash of what he calls 'two structures of interpretation,' the biblical and utilitarian traditions. Both of these cultural well-springs have nourished the American cultural identity and self-understanding, but their messages tend to diverge.

The biblical tradition has its roots in Puritan theology and republican political practice, and it 'stands, above all, under the archetype of the covenant,' the special relationship thought to

exist between God and the 'New Jerusalem' of America (Bellah, 1976c: 65; Bulman, 1991: 529; Williams, 1999: 8). This tradition, communitarian in nature, is well illustrated by John Winthrop's vision of a holy 'city upon a hill,' and his 'New Order of the Ages' (Novus Ordum Seclorum), as etched upon the Great Seal of the United States (see Kohn [1944] 1967: 291, 293). From colonial times, as George Bancroft, the great American historian of the nineteenth century, demonstrated, the United States has perceived itself as an 'instrument of Providence, its whole history a fulfillment of "Manifest Destiny" and the nearest approximation in all human history to the ideal state' (Nisbet, 1988: 525). Echoes of this view reverberate in American political life to this day.

But the utilitarian tradition has also been present since early in the nation's history. This tradition resonates well with the modern theory of natural rights, as expressed by John Locke. It 'stands, above all, under the archetype of the social contract,' whereby individuals pragmatically give up part of their freedom and unite into commonwealths for the preservation of their own self-interests, especially their property (Bellah, 1976c: 66; 1974b). This tradition is characterized by a 'vigorous individualism' (Bellah and Sullivan, 1981: 42) and in Bellah's words by an 'idolatrous worship of private pleasure and profit' (cited in Watts, 1980: 7). By the mid-nineteenth century, it began to give rise to the 'gospel of work, the gospel of wealth, and the gospel of success' (Bellah, 1976c: 72).

The principles of civil religion, 'certainly liberty and the pursuit of happiness, but also equality and even life – differ [when viewed from] these two perspectives' (Bellah, 1976c: 66). While the tensions between these two visions of America have occasionally been 'obscured,' the dual legacy is reflected in the two most sacred political documents of American civil religion – the Declaration of Independence and the Constitution of the United States. The first expresses virtue and community in the Puritan sense, the other individualism, utilitarianism and self-interest. It seems no accident that there are 'several references to God in the Declaration but none in the Constitution'

(Bellah, 1976c: 70). In Bellah's opinion, these two interpretive tendencies 'are profound and ultimately irreconcilable' (1974b: 116).

The prominent historian of American religion, Martin Marty, has delineated matters somewhat differently, calling on the Weberian distinction between priestly and prophetic religion. As Marty eloquently summarizes, priestly civil religion 'comforts the afflicted,' while prophetic civil religion 'afflicts the comfortable' (Marty, 1974: 145). The priestly interpretation assigns to the United States a special place in the divine scheme of things. America is a chosen nation blessed by God's favor. Under this construct, the nation itself is celebrated and imbued with sacred significance. The prophetic understanding, by contrast, reminds Americans that they will be held accountable before God for their actions (see, Marty, 1974; Wuthnow, 1988a; Mathisen, 1989; Davis, 1997). Thus, the priestly form is 'celebratory,' and the prophetic type is 'challenging and judgmental' (Ungar, 1991: 505). According to Marty, when the discourse of civil religion shifts its focus from the teachings of a transcendent deity to the promise of national self-transcendence, 'the signal of priestly civil religion is raised.' Such a civil religion 'will have as its main priest the president, since he alone stands at the head of all the people ... and he has greatest potential for invoking symbols of power' (1974: 151, 146).[2]

The priestly and prophetic modes roughly correspond in turn to James Davison Hunter's (1991) distinction between two public philosophies competing for dominance in modern America: the orthodox and the progressive, and to Robert Wuthnow's (1988a; 1988b) distinction between conservative and liberal versions of American civil religion as well. These two world views provide conflicting and often incompatible visions of America's destiny. The priestly, orthodox, and conservative account of civil religion, closely identified with the biblical tradition, is explicitly nationalistic, celebrates and legitimates capitalism, and grants the American nation a 'special place in the divine order.' It conceives the nation as 'God's instrument to evangelize the world, gives biblical legitimacy to capitalism, and understands

the American form of government to enjoy lasting legitimacy because it was created by founding fathers ... who were deeply influenced by Judeo-Christian values' (Davis, 1998: 19–20). This is the version of civil religion most often espoused by Christian evangelicals and fundamentalists intent on upholding absolute standards of morality in society. It endorses '"traditional" moral values, and appeals to a generally uncritical acceptance of the correctness and goodness of American values and their influence in the world' (Parsons, 2002: 4). God's laws, set forth in the Bible, are believed to be 'the foundation of all law.' Hence, any law that contradicts biblical teachings is considered unconstitutional (Angrosino, 2002: 261; see also, Pierard and Linder, 1988; Mathisen, 1989; Coleman, 1996; Wuthnow, 1996).

In contrast, the prophetic, progressive, and liberal vision of America assigns a greater role to human agency (Angrosino, 2002: 261), shifting the focus from the nation as such to humanity in general and the special values embodied in American life (Davis, 1998: 20). America's mission is not conceived as 'divine' and Americans are not seen as 'a chosen people.' Rather, if America can play a role on a global scale it is due to its immense blessings, resources and power (Wuthnow, 1988a: 247–51). The liberal rendition emphasizes, however, America's unique commitment to the issues of social and economic justice, international peace, ending global poverty and hunger, and addressing world ecological concerns. Human rights and problems relating to the misuse of power are given a special place. Spokespersons for the liberal version of civil religion are more likely to remind Americans of their 'sins' and failings in these regards, calling on them to uphold the nation's highest ideals.

For Wuthnow (1988a: 254) the conservative and liberal factions in contemporary America have created two different civil religions. Bellah disagrees. He recognizes (or at least did some 30 years ago) that American civil religion may have a different relationship to the republican and liberal traditions of American political life. But, he states, there may be several 'public theologies but only one civil religion.'

Although republicans and liberals 'may differ in their social programs ... they do not necessarily differ in their civil religions' (1976a: 155). More recently, Angrosino has echoed this view claiming that as a resource for judging the behavior of the nation, civil religion transcends the politics of the left and right. It is thus not 'captured either by party politics or by denominational religiosity' (2002: 259). While such statements are debatable, the crucial question remains: Should the phrase 'one nation under God' in the Pledge of Allegiance 'be understood as a proclamation of God's blessing or as a reminder of God's judgement?' (Canipe, 2003: 309). With this ambiguity in mind, references to the conservative-liberal continuum and the priestly and prophetic types have become standard in scholarly examinations of aspects of civil religion in America.

CIVIL RELIGION AS CULTURE AND IDEOLOGY

While there is a wide range of studies on the topic of American civil religion the bulk of the literature fails to note a fundamental theoretical distinction between the variant of civil religion influenced by Durkheim and that proposed by Rousseau. One stresses shared values as the bond of society and focuses on the use of civil religion to promote the non-coercive integration of society. The other emphasizes domination within society and focuses on the manipulation of civil religion in the context of power imbalances and the political interests of different groups in society. In our view, failure to recognize this distinction has produced an over-simplified understanding of civil religion, unnecessarily limiting its utility. To understand why Bellah's model of civil religion is indeed just 'one possible construction of a larger public religion' (Mathisen, 1989: 134), we need to return to the sources of the concept.

Rhys Williams (1996) has argued that two perspectives can be used to explain the sociopolitical significance of religion in general: religion as 'culture' and religion as 'ideology,' and he notes that it is important to see their interactive and complementary natures. Calling on Williams' analysis, Marcela Cristi (2001) argues that civil religion manifests itself in two forms: there is the Durkheimian view of civil religion as 'culture' and the Rousseauan political approach to civil religion as 'ideology.' These types are not polar opposites, but rather definable endpoints of a continuum of blended possibilities.

At one end of the spectrum is the classical Durkheimian position which ascribes sacredness to the group and asserts that each collectivity has a common religion. Here, civil religion is assumed to be a 'cultural given' (Demerath, 1994: 113) or an 'emergent property of social life itself' (Hammond, 1980b: 138). Civil religion as culture has a taken-for-granted character, and it is most manifest during what Swidler (1986) terms 'settled periods.' Its power to shape or direct human action is rather limited. In Geertzian terms, it refers to the 'assumed "givens" of social existence,' what he calls 'primordial attachments' (1973: 259). That is, the 'givenness' that stems from being born into, or being part of a particular community. At the other end of the spectrum, civil religion is conceived in terms of a particular political order, as advocated by Rousseau. It is a premeditated political ideology, constructed by the state and/or its political leaders, and used as a political resource. As an ideology, civil religion tends to develop in times of crisis, abandoning its taken-for-granted character. It has, or at least it is intended to have, a direct influence on public actions and the actions of the public (Swidler, 1986: 282).

Civil religion as culture is a non-coercive faith. It is supposed to be anchored in mutually meaningful rituals and symbols that cement national or group unity. Civil authorities have no power to enforce its doctrine. Allegiance is voluntary, and expressions of loyalty are voluntarily given (e.g., American expressions of civil religion throughout most of the twentieth century). In Durkheimian terms, the core of civil religion is the celebration of the collectivity. By contrast, Rousseau's view of civil religion has little to do with a grassroot consensus. Rather it involves a state-led ideology imposed with various degrees of coercion. When civil religion manifests as ideology, the state has the authority to compel belief and national unity. In its most extreme form, there is little or no freedom as to what individuals can say or do, membership and participation are compulsory, and expressions of loyalty are regularly expected. Soviet Communism, Nazism, Italian Fascism, Franco's Spain, and Pinochet's Chile provide classic examples of civil religion in this more ideological guise.

It does not follow, however, that only dictatorial regimes have Rouseauan civil religions. Democratic societies may employ the machinery of the state (the presidency, political speeches, solemn occasions) or other instruments of coercion (legislation, the judicial and police systems, and education) to pressure people to display patriotism, national solidarity, or support for a particular political program or course of action. Here the symbols and principles of a civic faith are manipulated to serve a political agenda, to legitimize special interests and inspire loyalty among political subordinates and allies. This means that in any given society, including the United States, one may find some degree of each type of civil religion. Political and historic specificity is the hallmark of all kinds of civil religion. Such being the case, different varieties of civil religion may exist not only between societies, but within the same society at different times in their social, political, and religious history (see, e.g., Markoff and Regan, 1982; Cristi and Dawson, 1996).

In the years following Bellah's first essay only a few scholars noted this distinction, let alone discussed its significance (Wilson, 1971; Hammond, 1980b; Demerath and Williams, 1985; Luke, 1987; Giner, 1993; Willaime, 1993; Casanova, 1994; Demerath, 2001).[3]

To avoid mudding the waters some might argue that civil religion should be limited, by definition, to the Durkheimian variety. William Swatos (2004: 195), for example, argues that Bellah may have taken 'language on a holiday' and reshaped Rousseau's concept into something he did not intend, but in the final analysis restoring an understanding of Rousseau's views 'is relatively unhelpful to the course of civil religion scholarship today.' We could not

disagree more. The attempt to identify civil religion exclusively with its Durkheimian heritage unrealistically reduces the intellectual compass of the concept in ways that run counter to the increasingly critical nature of contemporary studies of religion in the United States and comparative contexts. Bellah was describing something real in his original essay, and this helps to account for the persuasive power of the concept of civil religion. But if we cleave too closely to his Durkheimian understanding of this phenomenon we risk undermining the social scientific value of the concept. In the literature, however, it is quite apparent that the concept is employed in a much more generic and elastic sense, especially in comparative or non-American contexts. Here the concept is being used to ferret out and identify similar aspects of the social and political life of other nations and cultures, to address the larger religio-political problematic of social systems. Civil religion is best conceived then, we would argue, as a Weberian ideal type (Weber [1904] 1949). Its primary value is as a heuristic device – a simple fact overlooked too often in applications of the concept. As an ideal type it requires definition, but like the concept of religion itself, it is subject to the push and pull of too exclusive or too inclusive formulations. The Durkheimian criteria, implicitly invoked by Bellah to give definitional substance to civil religion, have the unfortunate effect of muting the full range of the concept. For instance, too often during the so-called 'Golden Years' of the civil religion debate (Mathisen, 1989) the Durkheimian approach was taken at face value. Consequently civil religion was perceived as if it were divorced from political society, or as if it were outside the competence of political leaders and the state. Likewise civil religion was treated, almost by definition, as if it transcended the interests associated with differences in ethnicity, race, gender, and religion.

Some scholars have recognized the immediate problem (e.g., Harding, 1968; Thompson, 1971; Long, 1974). Charles Long noted that civil religion was not always embraced by and did not include the history, values, and experiences of minority groups. American civil religion either 'consciously or unconsciously' had served as an ideological tool to 'enhance, justify, and render sacred the history of European immigrants in this land' (1974: 212). In the process, it had rendered black Americans, Indians, and Jews 'invisible.' He considered the notion of civil religion, together with its narrative and discourse, to be merely a 'mask' hiding the ideological commitments of white America and its discriminatory practices (Long, 1974: 214). Michael Novak (1992) advances a similar argument (see Angrosino, 2002: 249 as well). A few other scholars called attention to the moral ambiguity and potential misuse of civil religion (Bennet, 1979), addressing how demagogues and other political officials could exploit its 'emotional appeal for support of their political causes' (Tanembaum, 1975: 470). Like any form of religion, civil religion may be used to aggravate rather than ameliorate 'sectarian interests' (Cristi and Dawson, 1996; Angrosino, 2002: 253). But the acknowledgment of the political potential of civil religion is limited, and only some researchers have been inclined to pursue the idea that civil religion may be both a spontaneous grassroots phenomenon and a consciously imposed creed manufactured by political leaders (Demerath and Williams, 1985; Demerath, 2001: 9).

Bringing Rousseau's foundational conception of civil religion back into the discourse offers an active corrective to these tendencies in two ways: (1) it highlights the potential for civil religion to be a more elite and coercive phenomenon, and (2) it reasserts the theoretical character of the idea of civil religion, since Rousseau's discussion of civil religion is prescriptive, and not a description of a specific phenomenon at any particular time and place.

The rise of the New Religious Right in the United States as a potent political force has prompted a heightened level of recognition of the relevant issues. As Parsons (2002: 4) writes, 'It is … clear that, especially during the 1980s and early 1990s, there was a concerted attempt by conservative political groups in America to annex the concept of "American civil religion" firmly to their cause.' Condemning the principle of church – state separation, and the recent legal struggles to strengthen this principle,

spokespersons for the religious right (e.g., David Barton and Pat Robertson) have claimed that the wall separating church and state is a nonsensical myth. They have sought to protect and even intensify the outward expressions of civil religion as a means for advancing their evangelical Christian conception of America and the values they associate with this religious worldview. The late Chief Justice of the Supreme Court, William A. Rehnquist, held similar views. Their argument is that the separation principle, as used today, contradicts the original spirit and intent of the founding fathers, for their intention was to form a government based on Christian principles, and to protect the church from state interference, 'not the other way around' (Davis, 2003a: 7; Wuthnow, 1996: 41).[4]

Because civil religion is deeply embedded in the history of the United States, and because it is an 'American cultural reality' (Davis, 1998: 14) expressed in 'a rich tradition of practices that are culturally and judicially accommodated' (Davis, 2003d: 663), it is reasonable to assume that the dispute over which public expressions of religion can be accommodated by the First Amendment will continue for some time. In this regard the liberal and conservative understandings of civil religion have made the issue more complex and difficult to resolve. The U.S. Supreme Court will be increasingly faced with the difficult challenge of assessing when a ritual or custom constitutes a violation of the Constitution, and when to authorize it as a neutral or nonsectarian expression of the nation's religious heritage (Davis, 2003d: 668).

When operating at a national level, then, civil religion gives sacred meaning to national life. It takes place in the public square, where civic life tends to be endowed with a sacred quality by means of collective rituals, symbols, and solemn assemblies. Beliefs and behaviors acquire a sacred dimension. As such, civil religion may be considered a belief system which functions as a surrogate religion in pluralistic contexts, giving meaning to civic and political existence, and expressing the self-identity of a collectivity. Yet, like secular ideologies of all kinds, civil religions may also be used to force an identity on a group and to legitimize an existing political order, or even a particular political agenda, by injecting a transcendental dimension or providing a religious gloss for the justification of various special interests (Cristi, 2001). In this latter sense, civil religion may be no more than a 'cynical use of religion to apply a sacred veneer to a profane reality' (Demerath and Straight, 1997: 207). Given this variation in manifestations, the Durkheimian-Rousseauan distinction is essential when discussing civil religious phenomena anywhere in the world. Drawing this distinction makes it easier to highlight some of the more Rousseauan aspects of civil religions operating even in democratic contexts.

CIVIL RELIGION IN COMPARATIVE PERSPECTIVE

Bellah may have wished to distance himself from the term civil religion, but the concept took on 'a life of its own,' generating an immense literature worldwide.[5] Comparative analyses duly refer to Bellah's work, but they are often confronted with the difficulty of relating the distinguishing features of American civil religion to the variety of more generic forms of religio-political relationships encountered elsewhere (e.g., Regan, 1976; Reynolds, 1977; Cipriani, 1989; Zuo, 1991; Cha, 2000). Researchers can often point to a civil creed, with nationalistic and political significance, that has been given a religious quality through the introduction of specific beliefs, rituals, and public ceremonies, paralleling the situation in the United States. But problems often arise, at least from the vantage point of the largely American paradigm, because the civil religion in question does not exist independently of either the state or a specific dominant religious tradition, or it does not include a belief in God.

But the American case is actually rather exceptional. In the face of existing pluralism, conceived both as an emergent social value and as a developing social fact (see Beckford, 2003: 73–4), and motivated by the religious and political advantages of institutionally protecting that pluralism, the United States sacralized

the values, and the political and legal structures, that afforded this protection. This meant the principle of the separation of church and state became a defining feature of American civil religion. Developing out of different circumstances, from situations where a single religion was dominant or there was cultural warfare between two or more religions, other societies have tended to create civil and political systems premised on the complete disestablishment of religious beliefs and practices, or civil religions designed to assure social order either through the more overt sacralization of a specific political regime, or the *de facto* nationalization of a specific religious tradition. Holding true to the paradigm set by Bellah in the former case it appears that it is relatively easy to conclude, at least in principle, that no civil religion exists, for example in Canada and perhaps Mexico as well. But appearances can be deceiving. In the latter case, the situation is straightforwardly problematic, since a civil religion clearly seems to be present, but not strictly in Bellah's terms of reference.

Working with Bellah's theory in mind, for instance, Hammond (1980a: 62) argues that a true civil religion never developed in Mexico because the sacred and the secular are strictly separated, and there is no set of institutions imbued simultaneously with political and religious significance. He recognizes that Mexico has a 'vibrant nationalism,' but he does not associate it with a civil religion because it is not related to God. Mexican political rhetoric makes no use of transcendental language or any other sacred idea or symbols. Historical circumstances made Mexicans much more ambivalent to the introduction of religious themes into their public ceremonies, political speeches, educational system, and judiciary. The Catholic Church, which backed the losing side in the Mexican Revolution, was purposefully excluded from the affairs of the state (see Stevens, 1975 as well). Coleman and Davis (1978) argue, however, that this analysis places too much weight on the espoused secularism and anticlericalism of Mexican political elites. In practice, they argue, these relatively authoritarian elites tend to call on the quasi-religious mythology of the Mexican Revolution to garner support and exercise social control. They succeed in doing so, moreover, because much of the populace of Mexico is conditioned to certain patterns of interaction with religious authorities that are analogous to the patterns of interaction instituted by the government. Thus civil society in Mexico may not be quite as secular as it first appears.

As indicated, holding too exclusively to Bellah's model is even less helpful in identifying, let alone explaining, the apparent emergence of a civil religious discourse under dictatorial regimes, such as that of Francisco Franco in Spain (Stevens, 1975) or General Augusto Pinochet in Chile. Cristi and Dawson (1996) demonstrate that Pinochet's regime sought to create a 'priestly' civil religion to sacralize and legitimate the political absolutism introduced by the military coup d'état of 1973. The democratically elected government of Salvador Allende was destroyed in the name of a holy war against Marxism. In the years that followed the regime engaged in a systematic campaign of propaganda to cast Pinochet as a messianic figure, the savior of Chilean democracy and the Catholic faith. The regime's struggles with various 'enemies' of the state were symbolically equated with a transcendental view of the destiny of the Chilean people.

Thus, to retain the value of the concept of civil religion as a tool of critical analysis in the social sciences, and hence gain insight into the relationships between religion, nationalism, and politics in much of the rest of the world, we must work with a broader conception, one which recognizes that civil religion can emerge 'from the cultural ground up into the state' or be 'imposed top-down upon the society by the state' (Demerath, 2001: 238).

The orientation to a continuum of forms of civil religion has several theoretical merits. While it renders the concept of civil religion more elastic, it keeps the conceptual focus squarely on the two key determinants of civil religion as a class of social phenomena. First, as both Rousseau and Durkheim stress, civil religions are primarily about the creation and maintenance of 'social order' (as opposed, for example, to the salvation of individuals).

It is this function that differentiates civil religions from other kinds of religion. This is why it is most appropriate to frame a variable conception of civil religion in terms of the degree of conscious political manipulation involved in the creation and operation of any civil religion. This criterion keeps the methodological focus on the use of religion to create, bolster, or even change the social order. Second, while broadening the usage of civil religion, the continuum maintains conceptual clarity because it retains the stress that both Durkheim and Rousseau placed on the truly religious character of civil religions. This emphasis prevents researchers from mistaking all strident forms of nationalism (and other phenomena) for manifestations of civil religion. The tendency to do so undermines the social scientific utility of the concept by eliminating functional equivalents to civil religion. Keeping the focus on the obviously sacred character of the foci of civil religions allows researchers to conceptually and historically differentiate between secular and sacralized forms of nationalism, and chart if and when one sometimes becomes the other.

The latter point is important because it addresses the common and quite understandable tendency to equate the mere presence of some quasi-religious rites within seemingly secular systems of authority and patriotism as evidence of a civil religion. But the presence of such ritualistic practices is a universal feature of social life, and hence insufficient to warrant claiming there is a civil religion.[6] The boundaries of the concept of civil religion are undeniably vague. This is true of many of the basic categories of social analysis (e.g., class, revolution, community, religion), yet it is wise not to deviate too far from the tacit criteria of general usage. Thus when scholars treat professedly secular phenomena, like the civic philosophies and ceremonies of Marxist-Leninist regimes (e.g., McDowell, 1974; Luke, 1987) as instances of civil religion, a measure of caution is in order. These cases are outliers that must be examined on an individual basis to determine if some aspect of their practice has been elevated to the more traditional conceptions of the sacred or transcendent, be it the utopian

Marxist vision of history and the fate of humanity or the personification of the spirit of the revolution in eighteenth-century France or twentieth-century Communist China.

But the situation is problematic. Rousseau, like Bellah, explicitly links the notion of civil religion to belief in a deity and other transcendental elements (e.g., life after death). But the Durkheimian approach, reflecting its roots in Durkheim's theory of religion, is more inclusive. It hinges on a functionalist orientation to systems of beliefs and practices relative to 'sacred' things. The sacred-profane dichotomy is inherently ambiguous, with the emphasis falling on the process of rendering things sacred (i.e., 'set apart and forbidden'), because all manner of things can be deemed sacred. Sacredness is attributed to things; it is not intrinsic to them. Civil religions are systems of beliefs and practices that render aspects of social identity sacred. But what does sacralization entail? This is not the place to resolve this difficult issue. It suffices to say that sacralization entails attributing an ultimate meaning and importance, as well as a sense of permanence, even eternal significance, to whatever is held sacred. We should be able to gauge, with evidence, whether the cluster of phenomena we are studying in any context, such as a nation, involves a measure of sacralization sufficient to establish the presence of a civil religion. The exercise is inevitably interpretive, but it need not be hopelessly open-ended.

In short, we want to keep the creative options of scholars open. Civil religion may either involve straightforwardly relating the fate of a nation to the will of some transcendent being, or it may more indirectly involve achieving a similar level of national self-sacralization through the extreme glorification of some ideals identified with the nation. In some cases political leaders may also become the objects of worship and veneration, achieving a quasi-transcendental status (e.g., George Washington in American culture or Mao Zedong during the Cultural Revolution in China; see Zuo, 1991). But stipulating that civil religion involves a significant measure of systematic sacralization prevents the concept from becoming too porous. Setting the boundary stimulates

a more serious discussion of the ways in which seemingly secular ideologies are sometimes sacralized (e.g., Nazism, see Moltmann, 1986), without opening the door to considering all intense forms of nationalism as forms of civil religion.[7]

With this framework in place we can now further specify that the existing comparative literature suggests there are at least three common types of civil religions: (1) totalitarian, state-directed civil religions, (2) sacralized forms of nationalism, imposed with various degrees of indoctrination and/or coercion, and (3) civil religions manifested as historically specific ideologies promoted by a political or intellectual elite. We are not claiming that these are the only varieties, and in many instances the types overlap, and one variety may be more salient for a time only to be superseded by another.

Totalitarian state-directed civil religions come in two varieties: state-based or church-based, but both forms are characterized by a 'monistic state uncontrolled by civil society' (Markoff and Regan, 1982: 347). In the church-based type, the 'traditionally dominant religion, often supranational,' may act as the civil religion, as in the case of the Islamic republic of Iran and to a lesser extent Saudi Arabia. The most obvious but not the only examples of state-directed civil religions are found either in 'totalitarian regimes or regimes with a recent totalitarian past' (Markoff and Regan, 1982: 347), such as Revolutionary France, Fascist Italy, Nazi Germany, Franco's Spain, Pinochet's Chile, Brazil during the revolutions of 1930 and 1964, China during the Cultural Revolution, and State Shinto in Japan from 1868 to 1945.[8] In totalitarian societies, civil religion is centered on the dictator's ideology becoming in effect a state religion, and sometimes the dictator is deified (e.g., Lenin, Hitler, Mao Zedong). Japan and the former Soviet Union provide examples of very different kinds of state-sponsored civil religions. In the Soviet Union the civil creed took the form of a carefully elaborated state ideology that sacralized the social, economic and political doctrines of Marxism. By contrast, Japan relied on Shintoism, also skillfully crafted by the state, and a small political elite that was eager to industrialize the nation and launch it as a world power (Demerath, 2001: 238). But while the Soviet Union used 'political religion,' or we might say religionized politics, to support the authority of the state, Japan used 'religion politically,' or politicized religion, to achieve the same end (Apter, 1963: 61). Franco's Spain, as Coleman and Davis (1978: 56) note, assigned an explicit religious role to the state, 'and made quasi-religious demands upon citizens,' so that 'one's allegiance to the state became a measure of one's commitment to the "Spaniards" view of themselves as the civilizers and Christianizers of a barbaric and godless world' (Stevens, 1975: 362, cited in Coleman and Davis, 1978: 56). In Chile, Pinochet endowed his mission of *reconstrucción nacional* with divine characteristics, so much so, that one author has referred to the Chilean coup d'état *as 'le coup divin'* (Bastien, 1974; Cristi and Dawson, 1996). In these cases a specific and clearly articulated state ideology was tied to a divine purpose or sacred destiny, explicitly and implicitly, to better mobilize and exert control over the populace.

In sacred nationalism there is either a direct link between the state and the sacred via an established religion, or the nation and its political ideals are sacralized in a more indirect manner by the religious inclinations of its populace. Thus, sacred nationalism focuses on the power of religion, of an organized or more diffuse kind, to legitimize the state. Here the sacred power of the state and the power of religion to legitimize it are one and the same thing. Both in Franco's Spain and in Japan under State Shintoism, there was an overt identification of political and religious allegiances. Franco explicitly justified the repressive apparatus of the state by investing it with religious authority. The measures were necessary to defend Catholicism, to establish a true Christian society, and to combat Satanic Communist forces (i.e., Republicanism). The Spanish state demanded a quasi-religious commitment to the Spanish cause and a fierce loyalty to the nation (Coleman and Davis, 1978: 56–7), to the point that, like during Isabella's Spain, 'treason became heresy, and

heresy treason' (Hammond, 1976: 172). In Japan the emperor was assumed to be linked genealogically to the prehistorical age of the gods, and the Japanese social structure was justified in strictly religious terms (Bellah, 1980c: 29; also Takayama, 1988; 1993).

In a democratic context, Israel's civil religion would also fall under the category of sacred nationalism. Subsequent to the establishment of the State of Israel, after Zionist-socialism was displaced, a 'civil religion of statism' developed to foster the sacrifices needed to build national institutions. Since then, three different kinds of civil religion have emerged in Israel. All three have consciously adopted and adapted traditional symbols of religious Judaism to suit or enhance particular politico-ideological goals (see Liebman and Don-Yehiha, 1983).

Civil religion as an ideology of a political elite is found in contingent circumstances when a civil religious discourse is used to influence the public order for partisan political ends. Specific groups may use religious language and symbols to 'frame ... and legitimate their own particular political and moral visions' (Demerath and Williams, 1985: 166). This may happen both in totalitarian and democratic societies. One might bear in mind the civil religion of South Africa which celebrated and 'elevated the dogmas of the Dutch Reformed Church into political virtue' and provided legitimation for the racist policy of apartheid (Apter, 1963: 65, and Moodie, 1975). If we turn our attention to Europe, we can cite the case of Germany where, since the collapse of the Berlin Wall, the use of religious references and symbols has become more common in political discourses. Indeed, after the unification of 1989–1990, and despite a recognizable trend to secularization in the society, the role of religion in politics significantly increased. Leading statesmen such as Chancellor Kohl attempted to give a religious tinge to the project of unification. Minkenberg has suggested that this increase is the result of a neo-conservative program seeking to use the state and religion to promote a nationalist political agenda (Minkenberg, 1997).

In the United States, during the McCarthy era or the Nixon presidency, civil religion was used as a political tool against a presumed Communist conspiracy and in the defense of the Vietnam War. Bennet (1979: 123fn30); Linder and Pierard (1978: 109); Rouner (1986: 137), and Bellah (1974a: 261–4) have all taken Nixon to task for exploiting appeals to civil religion to rally support for his policies.[9] Likewise, Sheldon Ungar (1991) has shown convincingly how civil religious discourse was manipulated in the United States during the nuclear arms race with the Soviet Union. In his view, a clearly defined civil religious ideology was generated to justify American nuclear monopoly and other military policies. Military superiority came to be viewed as a 'sacred trust,' the outcome of the 'uniqueness' and exceptional 'destiny' of the United States. More recently, President George W. Bush has repeatedly invoked a civil religious discourse to justify the war in Iraq (Cristi, forthcoming), as his father, President George H. Bush adapted the notion of manifest destiny to justify the Persian Gulf War (Coles, 2002).

Political leaders are hardly unique in clothing themselves 'in religious garments.' Politicians worldwide do the same thing (Demerath, 2001: 5).[10] Yet, as Henderson notes (1975: 479), 'the difference between "borrowing" religious language for legitimate purposes, and exploiting that same language for partisan political ends is exceedingly difficult to determine.' But the contention that civil religion is not primarily 'an ideology intended to reinforce the authority of the state or cast a halo over institutions' (Bellah, 1976b: 167), or that it is 'an outlet neither for propaganda nor factional ideology within a state' (Bennet, 1979: 112fn14) will not survive scrutiny. As Marty (1974) concludes, civil religion is 'episodic' and used to fulfill different purposes at different times. To be viable the concept of civil religion must take this state of affairs into account.[11]

Clearly, civil religion manifests itself in different ways in different contexts, and with varying degrees of direct or indirect coercion, or affiliation with organized religion. In its Rousseauan form, it may range from state-sponsored God-talk in support of specific policies, to political witch-hunts, to totalitarianism and political messianism. But while Hammond has argued that civil religions à la Rousseau 'have not routinely developed' and are 'probably quite rare' (1980a: 77), the reverse may actually be more true. It is clear that modern industrial states are no strangers to such phenomena. In the wake of Bellah's famous essay this reality has been commonly overlooked.

THE FUTURE OF RESEARCH ON CIVIL RELIGION

Predicting the future is a fool's errand. Nevertheless, the continued use of any concept is dependent on an estimate of its significance. It seems that research on civil religion in America and around the world will continue to face three basic challenges that will influence this significance: (1) striving for conceptual clarity, (2) coping with the changing character of American society, and (3) coming to grips with the consequences of globalization. These challenges are not new nor are they distinct. But changing circumstances are bringing new considerations to bear on the discourses of civil religion, both the phenomenon and its academic analysis.

The concept of civil religion is intrinsically ambiguous and variable because the phenomenon is, but the sheer volume of literature testifies to its heuristic value. Its future utility, as comparative studies demonstrate, will depend on whether a greater consensus can be achieved about its delineating features. To this end the concept of civil religion needs an identity that is more independent of the American paradigm. We have proposed fashioning an understanding of civil religion that integrates essential elements of its dual intellectual heritage. Reframing civil religion as a continuum of possibilities, ranging from cultural to ideological manifestations, increases the breadth and flexibility of the concept, without sacrificing its integrity. On the contrary, this approach improves and sustains the theoretical focus on the three most important features of civil religion as a distinct form of religious expression.

First, as indicated, an awareness of the range of possibilities highlights the functional foundation of this form of religion, over against others, in meeting the requirements of social order (as opposed to other kinds of more explicitly religious purposes). Second, calling on the dual heritage keeps the focus on phenomena that either have a truly transcendent referent, or have been subject to sacralization in a meaningful way, preventing the concept of civil religion from being sapped of its explanatory power by too loose a usage. Third, the use of a continuum keeps researchers attuned to the intrinsic tie between religion and politics, and not just nationalistic sentiments or aspirations. Civil religion happens in civil and political contexts, and sociological and historical studies show that one cannot exist without the other (i.e., all civil religions are to some extent political).

In many parts of the world, and at many different times in almost all parts of the world, the political half of this relationship has been the source of both the motivation and means of creating and perpetuating civil religions. True in some instances, perhaps the United States foremostly, civil religions have emerged more spontaneously from the celebration of a people's social identity. But the political linkage is never missing nor the potential for manipulation. In fact the success of any nascent civil religion may rely on its elevation to importance in the life of a people through the skillful manipulation of its content by political leaders and elites who can benefit from doing so. This, in fact, is an important question deserving more systematic treatment.

In any event, the dual focus of our approach makes the intrinsically political character of all civil religions apparent to researchers. This is particularly important today in the face of changes in the character of American society and the rest of the world – changes rendering the application of Bellah's more traditional conception increasingly problematic.

For example, the America emerging at the dawn of the twenty-first century is very different from the nation Bellah addressed in his original essay. In 1976 even Bellah wondered if the concept of civil religion 'came to consciousness just when it was ceasing to exist or when its existence had become questionable'

(1976c: 72; see also Ahlstrom, 1972; Wilson, 1986: 118; Wuthnow, 1996: 75). Several religious and social developments in contemporary American society make the persistence of the more cultural form of civil religion problematic: (1) the growing cleavage between those who hold that America is a Christian nation and those who believe that one's identity as a Christian should be more universal (i.e., free of specific affiliation with American interests); (2) the established cleavage between liberal and conservative factions, within both mainline Protestantism and Catholicism, and between them and evangelical Americans, about the very nature of America's 'mission' in the world; (3) the steadily rising number of Americans simply declaring that they have no religious identification, and thus desiring a more secular America; and (4) the substantial and growing number of immigrants coming to America from non Judeo-Christian backgrounds.

Two decades ago Demerath and Williams (1985: 161) questioned whether the social and political implications of differences in ethnicity, gender, race, and religion in America had not 'pushed the nation past the conditions' needed to foster a truly integrative and unifying civil religion. More recently others have raised similar doubts (e.g., Ashbee, 2003; McGraw, 2003). Biblical symbols 'no longer have the legitimacy' they once did, Watts observed (1980: 6, 8), and 'have lost much of their motivational power.' Can Americans learn to successfully incorporate other symbols into a new national myth? Can American civil religion be adapted or reinvented? Or is the identity of Americans heading towards a significant transformation, an identity that is not grounded in religion? Or obversely, are the reports of American civil religion's demise (i.e., a transcendent, Judeo-Christian universal religion of the nation), much exaggerated? Certainly questions like these, whose answers are not self-evident, will stimulate research for decades to come.

Bellah acknowledges that his argument was 'premised on the sociological idea that all politically organized societies have some sort of civil religion' (Bellah, 1974a: 257). On the basis of this Durkheimian assumption, a civil religion is not only an essential but an unavoidable phenomenon (Wilson, 1979: 154). But as Durkheim said, 'the religion of yesterday could not be [that] of tomorrow' ([1898] 1973: 51). Thus, while civil religion is unlikely to disappear, no matter how specific civil religions may wax or wane, its form is not static.

Both Durkheim and Bellah expected a global civil religion to eventually emerge. Bellah stated that the world community needs a 'global concord' for its survival – a global order of civility and justice. In his original essay he alludes to the emergence of a 'transnational sovereignty,' that would require the 'incorporation of vital international symbolism into [American] civil religion, or, perhaps ... it would result in American civil religion becoming simply one part of a new civil religion of the world' (1967: 18). This new civil religion would 'transcend' yet 'include' American ethical commitments and values (Bellah, 1980a: xiv). For Durkheim, the rapid expansion of modern states, combined with the division of labor, will create a diversity of individual experiences that defies the capacity of traditional religions to unite whole societies into moral communities. Soon, he argues, the 'members of a single social group will have nothing in common among themselves except their humanity' (Durkheim [1898] 1973: 51). Consequently, the sacred will be located increasingly in the individual, the human person as the carrier of inalienable rights, dignity and freedom. Traditional religions will be displaced by what he variously called the 'religion of humanity,' the 'cult of the individual,' or the 'cult of man.' This entails the glorification of 'humanity,' not the wants and needs of individuals, but the abstract sense of our common condition and value as individuals. A new body of collective beliefs and practices will arise, endowed with the authority to build the social institutions required to safeguard the individualism enjoyed and sanctified by the citizens of future societies. Durkheim envisioned this new religion as a universal religion capable of embracing, or even substituting for, all other religions (Wallace, 1990: 222). In truth, however, he seems to be describing a new and universal civil religion, one that will likely co-exist, and sometimes clash, with other religions. In fact this civil religion of humanity may be called into existence, much as American civil religion was, by the need to curtail the more oppressive and disruptive features of sectarian and fanatical forms of religion as they re-acquire power in international relations (see e.g., Huntington, 1996; Jenkins, 2002).[12]

The concept of a global civil religion remains rather inchoate, but it warrants the attention of scholars. The global spread of the doctrine of human rights, the shift from national to international laws in the resolution of conflicts, the spread of environmentalism and other global movements such as feminism and gay culture, the success of groups like Doctors Without Borders, Green Peace, and Amnesty International, and hundreds of other international nongovernmental organizations, all seem to lend some support to this vision (Casanova, 2001). Certainly it is in line with the process of 'glocalization' predicted by globalization theory, whereby the realm of the private and the individual, on the one hand, and the truly universal, on the other, will be emphasized as the traditional modern focus on the nation-state and other intermediate social groupings fades (see e.g., Robertson and Chirico, 1985). In studying this fascinating possibility, however, we would urge scholars not to forget the political character of civil religions. Regrettably, we have no reason to believe that the political manipulation of civil religious discourses is limited to national contexts. Expression of the civil religion of humanity must be placed against the full continuum of possible forms of civil religion.

NOTES

1. A Google search for 'civil religion' takes you first to FACSNET, where an extended essay on the topic begins with the following interesting claim: 'Since we first posted our article on American civil religion in October, 2002, it has become among the most demanded pages on FACSNET and has consistently remained in the 'Top 10' most visited pages on the site' (retrieved Feb. 14, 2006).

2. For an historical analysis of presidential inaugural addresses see Toolin (1983) and Pierard and Linder (1988).

For more on American Presidents' religious rhetoric, see Donahue (1975); Henderson (1972, 1975); Hart (1977); Tipton (1984); Adams (1987); Bulman (1991); Linder (1996); Coles (2002), and Davis (2003b).

3. Derek Davis (1998: 12), author of numerous editorials on civil religion in the *Journal of Church and State*, displays a characteristic lack of understanding of Rousseau's ideas. He argues, for instance, that 'Rousseau's civil religion has no transcendental reference point.' Yet the first dogma of Rousseau's civil religion is 'the existence of a mighty, intelligent, and beneficent Divinity, possessed of foresight, and providence' ([1762]1973: 276). Likewise, Hammond (1980a) takes the position that civil religion, in Rousseau's meaning of the term, is independent of both the church and state. But quite the opposite is the case. As Rousseau states, the dogmas of civil religion, 'which the Sovereign should fix, … ought to be few, simple, and exactly worded, without explanation or commentary' ([1762] 1973: 276).

4. Curiously, as some authors have noted, the failure of the legal system to distinguish adequately between civil religion and traditional religion has unwittingly compounded the problem, inadvertently increasing the politicized or ideological character of contemporary support for and expressions of civil religion (Davis, 2003d: 663; Cloud, 2004).

5. To name just a few studies, in a European context (Davie, 2001); the United Kingdom (Bocock, 1985; Wolffe, 1993; Rowbottom, 2001); in Italy (Cipriani, 1989; Ferrara, 1999; Pace, 1999; Rusconi, 1999; Gundle, 2000) and Siena (Parsons, 1997); in Germany (Minkenberg, 1997); in France (Markoff and Regan, 1982; Willaime, 1993); in Eastern Europe (Mestrovic, 1993); in relation to Marxism as a civil religion and Communist states (Zeldin, 1969; McDowell, 1974; Lane, 1979, 1981; Zuo, 1991; Lowe, 2001); and in Poland in particular (Morawska, 1987) and various post-revolutionary Communist systems (Luke, 1987); in relation to other nations around the globe, for example Canada (Cheal, 1978; Kim, 1993); Australia (Crouter, 1990; Black, 1990); Chile (Cristi and Dawson, 1996); Sri Lanka (Seneviratne, 1984); Mexico (Stevens, 1975; Coleman and Davis, 1978; Hammond, 1980a); Brazil (De Azevedo, 1979); Iran (Braswell, 1979); Japan (Bellah, 1980c; Markoff and Regan, 1982; Takayama, 1988, 1993); Korea (Cha, 2000); Thailand (Reynolds, 1977; Markoff and Regan, 1982); Malaysia (Regan, 1976; Markoff and Regan, 1982); Indonesia (Purdy, 1982); Israel (Liebman and Don-Yehiya, 1983, Bidussa, 2000); and South Africa (Moodie, 1975).

6. Civic rituals and ceremonies, such as coronations in England (Shils and Young, 1953), Memorial Day observations in America (Warner, 1953), the funeral of official dignitaries (Cherry, 1970), or other so-called 'present-day totemisms' (Cole and Hammond, 1974: 177) are aspects of the public expression of civil religion. They tend to integrate civil society into the national civil religion or national cult (Bellah, 1967: 11), but the performance of the rites is not sufficient to establish there is a civil religion.

7. The authors of this chapter reflect the interpretive tensions in the field. Cristi favors a more inclusive approach, while Dawson favors a more exclusive one.

8. For revolutionary France see Willaime (1993) and Markoff and Regan (1982: 344); For Italy under Mussolini

see DeGrazia (1981) and Gregor (1969); for Nazi Germany see Moltmann (1986); for Fascist Spain see Stevens (1975) and Coleman and Davis (1978); for Pinochet's Chile see Cristi and Dawson (1996) and Cristi (2001, chapter 5); for Brazil see De Azevedo (1979); for China see Zuo (1991); for pre-1945 Japan see Coleman (1969), Bellah (1980c). For a global comparative view, see Demerath 1994 and 2001.

9. For more on Nixon's public rhetoric, see Henderson (1972), Alley (1972), Donahue (1975), and Wimberley (1980).

10. Renaissance philosopher Niccolo Machiavelli was one of the first thinkers to openly discuss the idea of the political importance of religion. Perhaps the first proto-theory of civil religion *à la Rousseau* is to be found in his writings. Rulers should encourage a religion that 'teaches that he who best serves the State best serves the gods' (Allen, 1960: 459).

11. Bellah (1980a, 1980c), Apter (1963), Coleman (1969), and Hammond (1980b) have tied a blurring of the lines of demarcation between religion and politics to an evolutionary scheme. Any system leaning towards theocracy is viewed as 'archaic.' In early modern societies, the two spheres became differentiated but never totally separated, while modern societies exhibit a high degree of differentiation. Bellah recognizes that the fusion of political and religious power is 'a permanent possibility in human history' and even acknowledges that such regressive tendencies may appear in democratic societies but, overall, he and others tend to confine this solution to the religio-political problem to nations in the process of modernizing or third world countries. In our framework civil religion is never totally divorced from political society, since it seems 'beyond dispute' that the civil religious discourse 'can be employed by the state to mask and sometimes advance raw power' (Goldzwig, 2002: 109). There is no intrinsic link between civil religion and a theory of social, political, and religious evolution.

12. Rousseau also envisioned something like a global civil religion. In *A Discourse on Political Economy* he advocated the idea of a universal general will: 'the great city of the world becomes the body politic, whose general will is always the law of nature, and of which the different states and peoples are individual members' (cited in MacFarlane, 1970: 109).

REFERENCES

Adams, David S. 1987. 'Ronald Reagan's "Revival": Voluntarism As a Theme in Reagan's Civil Religion'. *Sociological Analysis* 48 (1): 17–29.

Ahlstrom, Sidney B. 1972. *A Religious History of the American People*. New Haven: Yale University Press.

Allen, William J. 1960. *A History of Political Thought in Sixteenth Century*. London: Methuen.

Alley, Robert S. 1972. *So Help Me God: Religion and the Presidency*. Richmond, VA: John Knox.

Angrosino, Michael 2002. 'Civil Religion Redux'. *Anthropological Quarterly* 75, 2 (Spring): 239–67.

Apter, David E. 1963. 'Political Religion in the New Nations'. In Clifford Geertz (ed.), *Old Societies and New States* (pp. 57–104). London: Free Press.

Ashbee, Eddie 2003. 'American Identities, Civil Religion and the Political Process'. *Political Studies Association – Annual Conference* 2003, 1–19.

Bastien, Ovide 1974. *Le coup Divin*. Montreal: Editions du Jour.

Beckford, James A. 2003. *Social Theory and Religion*. Cambridge: Cambridge University Press.

Beiner, Ronald 1993. 'Machiavelli, Hobbes, and Rousseau on Civil Religion'. *The Review of Politics* 55 (4): 617–38.

Bellah, Robert N. 1967. 'Civil Religion in America'. *Daedalus: Journal of the American Academy of Arts and Sciences* 96: 1–21.

Bellah, Robert N. 1974a. 'American Civil Religion in the 1970s'. In Russell B. Richey and Donald G. Jones (eds), *American Civil Religion* (pp. 255–72). New York: Harper and Row.

Bellah, Robert N. 1974b. 'Religion and Polity in America'. *Andover Newton Quarterly* 15 (2): 107–21.

Bellah, Robert N. 1975. *The Broken Covenant: American Civil Religion in Times of Trial*. New York: Seabury.

Bellah, Robert N. 1976a. 'Response to the Panel on Civil Religion'. *Sociological Analysis* 37 (2): 153–59.

Bellah, Robert N. 1976b. 'Comment on "Bellah and the New Orthodoxy".' *Sociological Analysis* 37 (2): 167–68.

Bellah, Robert N. 1976c. 'The Revolution and the Civil Religion'. In Jerald C. Brauer (ed.), *Religion and the American Revolution* (pp. 55–73). Philadelphia: Fortress Press.

Bellah, Robert N. 1978. 'Religion and Legitimation in the American Republic'. *Society* 15 (4): 16–23.

Bellah, Robert N. 1980a. 'Introduction'. In Robert N. Bellah and Phillip E. Hammond, *Varieties of Civil Religion* (pp. vii–xv). San Francisco: Harper and Row.

Bellah, Robert N. 1980b. 'Religion and the Legitimation of the American Republic'. In Robert N. Bellah and Phillip E. Hammond, *Varieties of Civil Religion* (pp. 3–23). San Francisco: Harper and Row.

Bellah, Robert N. 1980c. 'The Japanese and American Cases'. In Robert N. Bellah and Phillip E. Hammond, *Varieties of Civil Religion* (pp. 27–39). San Francisco: Harper and Row.

Bellah, Robert N. 1980d. 'The Five Religions of Modern Italy'. In Robert N. Bellah and Phillip E. Hammond, *Varieties of Civil Religion* (pp. 86–118). San Francisco: Harper and Row.

Bellah, Robert N. 1989. 'Comment on "Twenty Years After Bellah"', *Sociological Analysis* 50 (2): 147.

Bellah, Robert N. and William M. Sullivan 1981. 'Democratic Culture or Authoritarian Capitalism?' *Society* 18 (6): 41–50.

Bellah, Robert N., Richard Madsen, William M. Sullivan, Ann Swidler and Steven M. Tipton 1985. *Habits of the Heart: Individualism and Commitment in American Life*. New York: Harper and Row.

Bennet, W. Lance 1979. 'Imitation, ambiguity, and drama in public life: civil religion and the dilemmas of public morality'. *Journal of Politics* 41: 106–33.

Bidussa, David 2000. *Religioni e Societa*, 15, 36 (Jan–Apr): 53–66.

Black, Alan W. 1990. 'The Sociology of Religion in Australia'. *Sociological Analysis* 51 (Supplement): 27–41.

Bocock, R. 1985. 'Religion in Modern Britain'. In R. Bocock and K. (eds), *Religion and Ideology* (pp. 207–33). Manchester: Manchester University Press.

Braswell, George W., Jr 1979. 'Civil Religion in Contemporary Iran'. *Journal of Church and State* 21 (2): 223–46.

Brown, Steven P. and Bowling, Cynthia J. 2003. 'Public Schools and Religious Expression: The Diversity of School District's Policies Regarding Religious Expression'. *Journal of Church and State* 45 (2): 259–81.

Bulman, Raymond F. 1991. 'Myth of Origin, Civil Religion and Presidential Politics'. *Journal of Church and State* 33 (3): 525–39.

Canipe, Lee 2003. 'Under God and Anti-Communist: How the Pledge of Allegiance Got Religion in Cold War America'. *Journal of Church and State*, 45 (2): 305–23.

Casanova, José 1994. *Public Religions in the Modern World*. Chicago: University of Chicago Press.

Casanova, José 2001. '2000: Presidential Address Religion, the New Millennium, and Globalization'. *Sociology of Religion* 62 (4): 415–41.

Cha, Seong Hwan 2000. 'Korean Civil Religion and Modernity'. *Social Compass* 47 (4): 467–85.

Cheal, David 1978. 'Religion and Social Order'. *Canadian Journal of Sociology* 3 (1): 61–9.

Cherry, Conrad 1970. 'American Sacred Ceremonies'. In P. E. Hammond and Benton Johnson (eds), *American Mosaic* (pp. 303–16). New York: Random House.

Cherry, Conrad 1971. *God's New Israel*. Englewood Cliffs, NJ: Prentice-Hall.

Christenson, J. A. and R. C. Wimberley 1978. 'Who is Civil Religious?' *Sociological Analysis* 39: 77–83.

Cipriani, Roberto 1989. '"Diffused Religion" and New Values in Italy'. In J. A. Beckford and T. Luckmann (eds), *The Changing Face of Religion*. London: Sage.

Cloud, Matthew W. 2004. '"One Nation, Under God": Tolerable Acknowledgment of Religion or Unconstitutional Cold War Propaganda Cloaked in American Civil Religion?' *Journal of Church and State* 46 (2): 311–40.

Cole, William A. and Phillip E. Hammond 1974. 'Religious Pluralism, Legal Development, and Societal Complexity: Rudimentary Forms of Civil Religion'. *Journal for the Scientific Study of Religion* 13 (2): 177–89.

Coleman, John A. 1969. 'Civil Religion'. *Sociological Analysis* 30 (1): 67–77.

Coleman, S. 1996. 'Conservative Protestantism in the United States'. In D. Westerlund (ed.), *Questioning the Secular State: The Worldwide Resurgence of Religion in Politics*. London: Hurst.

Coleman, Kenneth M. and Charles L. Davis 1978. 'Civil and Conventional Religion in Secular Authoritarian Regimes: The Case of Mexico'. *Studies in Comparative International Development* 13 (1): 56–76.

Coles, Roberta L. 2002. 'Manifest Destiny Adapted for 1990's War Discourse: Mission and Destiny Intertwined'. *Sociology of Religion* 63 (4): 403–26.

Cristi, Marcela 2001. *From Civil to Political Religion*. Waterloo: Wilfrid Laurier University Press.

Cristi, Marcela (forthcoming). Civil Religion in the United States and George W. Bush's Public Religious Rhetoric. In W. Sweet (ed.), *Before and After Democracy: Philosophy, Religion, and Politics*. Ottawa: University of Ottawa Press.

Cristi, Marcela and Lorne Dawson 1996. 'Civil Religion in Comparative Perspective: Chile Under Pinochet (1973–1989)'. *Social Compass* 43 (3): 319–38.

Crouter, R. 1990. 'Beyond Bellah: American civil religion and the Australian experience'. *Australian Journal of Politics and History* 36: 154–65.

Cutler, Donald R. (ed.) 1968. *The World Year Book of Religion. The Religious Situation*. Vol. 1. Boston: Beacon Press.

Davie, Grace 2001. 'Global Civil Religion: A European Perspective'. *Sociology of Religion* 62 (4): 455–73.

Davis, Derek H. 1997. 'Editorial: Law, Moral, and Civil Religion in America', *Journal of Church and State* 39 (3): 411–25.

Davis, Derek H. 1998. 'Editorial: Civil Religion as a Judicial Doctrine'. *Journal of Church and State* 40 (1): 7–23.

Davis, Derek H. 2003a. 'Editorial: Thomas Jefferson and the "Wall Of Separation" Metaphor'. *Journal of Church and State* 45 (1): 5–14.

Davis, Derek H. 2003b. 'Editorial: Thoughts on the Separation of Church and State under the Administration of President George W. Bush' *Journal of Church and State* 45 (2): 229–35.

Davis, Derek H. 2003c. 'Editorial: Moments of Silence in America's Public Schools: Constitutional and Ethical Considerations'. *Journal of Church and State* 45 (3): 429–42.

Davis, Derek H. 2003d. 'Editorial: The Pledge of Allegiance and American Values'. *Journal of Church and State* 45 (4): 657–68.

De Azevedo, Thales 1979. 'La religion civile'. *Archives de Sciences Sociales des Religions* 47 (1): 7–2.

DeGrazia, Victoria 1981. *The Culture of Consent: Mass Organization of Leisure in Fascist Italy*. New York: Cambridge University Press.

DeLue, Steven M. 1997. *Political Thinking, Political Theory, and Civil Society*. Boston: Allyn and Bacon.

Demerath III, N. J. 1989. 'Religion and Power in the American Experience'. *Society* 26 (2): 29–38.

Demerath III, N. J. 1994. 'The Moth and the Flame: Religion and Power in Comparative Blur'. *Sociology of Religion* 55 (2): 105–17.

Demerath III, N. J. 2001. *Crossing the Gods: World Religions and Worldly Politics*. New Brunswick: Rutgers University Press.

Demerath III, N. J. and Karen S. Straight 1997. 'Lambs among the Lions: America's Culture Wars in Cross-Cultural Perspective'. In Rhys H. Williams (ed.), *Cultural Wars in American Politics: Critical Review of a Popular Myth* (pp. 199–219). New York. Aldine de Gruyter.

Demerath III, N. J. and Rhys H. Williams 1985. 'Civil Religion in an Uncivil Society'. *Annals of the American Academy* 480: 154–65.

Dewey, John 1934. *A Common Faith*. New Haven, Yale University Press.

Donahue, Bernard F. 1975. 'The Political Use of Religious Symbols: A Case Study of the 1972 Presidential Campaign'. *The Review of Politics* 37 (1): 48–65.

Durkheim, Emile [1912] 1961. *The Elementary Forms of Religious Life*. Trans. Joseph Ward Swain. New York: Collier Books.

Durkheim, Emile [1898] 1973. 'Individualism and the Intellectuals'. In Robert N. Bellah (ed.), *Emile Durkheim: On Morality and Society* (pp. 43–57). Chicago: University of Chicago Press.

Fenn, Richard K. 1978. *Toward a Theory of Secularization*. Society for the Scientific Study of Religion, Monograph Series No. 1. Storrs, CT: Society for the Scientific Study of Religion.

Ferrara, Alessandro 1999. 'Reflections on the Notion of Civil Religion'. *Rassegna Italiana di Sociologia* 40, 2 (Apr–June): 209–23.

Frohnen, Bruce 1996. *The New Communitarians and the Crisis of Modern Liberalism*. Kansas: University Press of Kansas.

Fustel de Coulanges, Numa Denis [1864] 1956. *The Ancient City*. New York: Doubleday.

Gamoran, Adam 1990. 'Civil Religion in American Schools'. *Sociological Analysis* 51: 3: 235–56.

Garrett, J. Leo 1974. 'Civil Religion: Clarifying the Semantic Problem'. *Journal of Church and State* (Spring): 187–92.

Geertz, Clifford 1973. *The Interpretations of Culture*. New York: Basic Books.

Gehrig, Gail 1981a. 'The American Civil Religion Debate: A Source for Theory Construction'. *Journal for the Scientific Study of Religion* 20 (1): 51–63.

Gehrig, Gail 1981b. *American Civil Religion: An Assessment*. Society for the Scientific Study of Religion, Monograph Series No. 3. Romeoville, IL: Lewis University.

Giner, Salvador 1993. 'Religión Civil'. *Revista española de investigaciones sociológicas* 61: 23–55.

Goldzwig, Steven R. 2002. 'Official and Unofficial Civil Religious Discourse'. *Journal of Communication and Religion* 25: 102–14.

Gregor, James A. 1969. *Ideology of Fascism: The Rationale of Totalitarianism*. New York: Free Press.

Gundle, Stephen 2000. 'The "Civic Religion" of the Resistance in Post-War Italy'. *Modern Italy* 5, 2 (November): 113–32.

Hammond, Phillip E. 1974. 'Religious Pluralism and Durkheim's Integration Thesis'. In Allan W. Eister (ed.), *Changing Perspectives in the Scientific Study of Religion* (pp. 115–42). New York: John Wiley and Sons.

Hammond, Phillip E. 1976. 'The Sociology of American Civil Religion: A Bibliographic Essay'. *Sociological Analysis* 37 (2): 169–82.

Hammond, Phillip E. 1980a. 'The Conditions for Civil Religion: A Comparison of the United States and Mexico'. In Robert N. Bellah and Phillip E. Hammond (eds), *Varieties of Civil Religion* (pp. 40–85). San Francisco: Harper and Row.

Hammond, Phillip E. 1980b. 'Pluralism and Law in the Formation of American Civil Religion'. In Robert N. Bellah and Phillip E. Hammond (eds), *Varieties of Civil Religion* (pp. 138–63). San Francisco: Harper and Row.

Hammond, Phillip E. 1989. 'Constitutional Faith, Legitimating Myth, and Civil Religion'. *Law and Social Inquiry* 14: 377–91.

Harding, Vincent 1968. 'Black Power and the American Christ'. In F. B. Barbour (ed.), *The Black Power Revolt* (pp. 85–93). New York: Collier.

Hart, Roderick P. (1977). *The Political Pulpit*. West Lafayette, IN: Purdue University.

Henderson, Charles P. 1972. *The Nixon Theology*. New York: Harper and Row.

Henderson, Charles P. 1975. 'Civil religion and the American presidency'. *Religious Education* 70: 473–85.

Henry, Maureen 1979. *The Intoxication of Power: An Analysis of Civil Religion in Relation to Ideology*. London: D. Reidel Publishing.

Hepler, Deborah K. 1996. 'The Constitutional Challenge to American Civil Religion'. *The Kansas Journal of Law & Public Policy* (Winter).

Herberg, Will 1955. *Protestant, Catholic, Jew*. New York: Doubleday.

Herberg, Will 1974. 'American Civil Religion: What it is and Whence it Comes'. In Russell E. Richey and Donald G. Jones (eds), *American Civil Religion* (pp. 76–88). New York: Harper and Row.

Hughey, Michael W. 1984. 'The Political Covenant: Protestant Foundations of the American State'. *State, Culture and Society* 1 (3): 113–56.

Hughey, Michael W. 1992. 'Americanism and its Discontents: Protestantism, Nativism, and Political Heresy in America'. *International Journal of Politics, Culture, and Society* 5 (4): 533–53.

Hunter, James Davison 1991. *Culture Wars: The Struggle to Define America*. New York: Basic Books.

Huntington, Samuel P. 1996. *The Clash of Civilizations and the Remaking of World Order*. New York: Simon and Schuster.

Jenkins, Philip 2002. *The Next Christendom: The Coming of Global Christianity*. New York: Oxford University Press.

Jolicoeur, Pamela and Louis L. Knowles 1978. 'Fraternal Associations and Civil Religion: Scottish rite Freemasonry'. *Review of Religious Research* 20, 3–22.

Jones, Donald G. and Russell E. Richey 1974. 'The Civil Religion Debate'. In Russell E. Richey and Donald G. Jones (eds), *American Civil Religion* (pp. 3–18). New York: Harper and Row.

Kessler, Sanford 1994. *Tocqueville's Civil Religion: American Christianity and the Prospects for Freedom*. Albany: State University of New York Press.

Kim, A. 1993. 'The absence of Pan-Canadian civil religion: plurality, duality, and conflict in symbols of Canadian culture'. *Sociology of Religion* 54: 257–75.

Kohn, Hans [1944] 1967. *The Idea of Nationalism: A Study in Its Origins and Background*. New York: Collier Books.

Lane, Christel 1979. 'Ritual and Ceremony in Contemporary Soviet Society'. *Sociological Review* 27 (2): 253–78.

Lane, Christel 1981. *The Rites of Rulers: Ritual in Industrial Society. The Soviet Case*. Cambridge: Cambridge University Press.

Liebman, Charles S. and Eliazar Don-Yehiya 1983. *Civil Religion in Israel*. Berkeley: University of California Press.

Linder, Robert J. 1996. 'Universal Pastor: President Bill Clinton's Civil Religion'. *Journal of Church and State* 38 (3): 733–49.

Linder, Robert D. and Richard V. Pierard 1978. *Twilight of the Saints: Biblical Christianity and Civil Religion in America*. Downers Grove, IL: Inter Varsity.

Lipset, Seymour Martin 1963. *The First New Nation*. New York: Basic Books.

Long, C. H. 1974. 'Civil rights–Civil Religion: Visible People and Invisible Religion'. In R. E. Richey and D. G. Jones (eds), *American Civil Religion* (pp. 211–21). New York: Harper and Row.

Lowe, Brian M. 2001. 'Soviet and American Civil Religion: A Comparison'. *Journal of Interdisciplinary Studies* 13, 1–2: 73–96.

Luke, Timothy W. 1987. 'Civil Religion and Secularization: Ideological Revitalization in Post-Revolutionary Communist Systems'. *Sociological Forum* 2 (1): 108–34.

Macfarlane, L. J. 1970. *Modern Political Theory*. London: Thomas Nelson and Sons.

Markoff, John and Daniel Regan 1982. 'The Rise and Fall of Civil Religion: Comparative Perspectives'. *Sociological Analysis* 42 (4): 333–54.

Marty, Martin E. 1974. 'Two Kinds of Two Kinds of Civil Religion'. In Russell E. Richey and Donald G. Jones (eds), *American Civil Religion* (pp. 139–57). New York: Harper and Row.

Mathisen, James A. 1989. 'Twenty Years after Bellah: Whatever Happened to American Civil Religion?' *Sociological Analysis* 50: 129–46.

McClay, Wilfred M. 2004. 'The soul of a nation'. *Public Interest* 155 (Spring): 4–20.

McDowell, Jennifer 1974. 'Soviet civil ceremonies'. *Journal for the Scientific Study of Religion* 13 (1): 265–79.

McGraw, Barbara A. 2003. *Rediscovering America's Sacred Ground: Public Religion and Pursuit of the Good in a Pluralistic America*. Albany, NY: State University of New York Press.

Mead, Sidney E. 1974. 'The Nation with the Soul of a Church'. In Russell E. Richey and Donald G. Jones (eds), *American Civil Religion* (pp. 45–75). New York: Harper and Row.

Mestrovic, S. 1993. *The Road from Paradise: Prospects for Democracy in Eastern Europe*. Lexington, Kentucky: University Press of Kentucky.

Michaelson, Robert 1970. *Piety in the Public Schools*. New York: Macmillan.

Minkenberg, Michael 1997. 'Civil Religion and German Unification'. *German Studies Review*, 20 (1): 63–81.

Moltmann, Jürgen 1986. 'Christian Theology and Political Religion'. In Leroy S. Rouner (ed.), *Civil Religion and Political Theology* (pp. 41–58). Notre Dame, IN: University of Notre Dame Press.

Moodie, Dunbar T. 1975. *The Rise of Afrikanerdom: Power, Apartheid, and the Afrikaner Civil Religion*. Berkeley: University of California Press.

Morawska, Ewa 1987. 'Civil Religion versus State Power in Poland'. In Thomas Robbins and Roland Robertson (eds), *Church-State Relations: Tensions and Transitions* (pp. 221–32). New Brunswick, NJ: Transaction Books.

Nisbet, Robert 1988. 'Civil Religion'. In Mircea Eliade (ed.), *The Encyclopedia of Religion*, Vol. 3 (pp. 524–27). New York: Macmillan.

Novak, Michael 1976. *The Joy of Sports*. New York: Basic Books.

Novak, Michael 1992. *Choosing Presidents: Symbols of Political Leadership*. New Brunswick, NJ: Transaction Publishers (originally published 1974).

Pace, Enzo 1999. 'Civil Religion and National Contexts'. *Rassegna Italiana di Sociologia* 40, 2 (Apr-June): 189–207.

Parsons, Gerald 1997. ' "Unità nella diversità": civil religion and the Palio of Siena', *The Italianist* 17: 176–203.

Parsons, Gerald 2002. *Perspectives on Civil Religion*. Aldershot: Ashgate: The Open University.

Pierard, R. V. and R. D. Linder 1988. *Civil Religion and the Presidency*. Grand Rapids: Academie Zondervan.

Purdy, Susan S. 1982. 'The Civil Religion Thesis as It applies to a Pluralistic Society: Pancasila Democracy in Indonesia (1945–1965)'. *Journal of International Affairs* 36 (2): 307–16.

Rawls, John 1996. *Political Liberalism*. New York: Columbia University Press.

Regan, Daniel 1976. 'Islam, Intellectuals and Civil Religion in Malaysia'. *Sociological Analysis* 37 (2): 95–110.

Reynolds, Frank E. 1977. 'Civic Religion and National Community in Thailand'. *Journal of Asian Studies* 36 (2): 267–82.

Rice, Daniel F. 1980. 'Sidney E. Mead and the Problem of "Civil Religion".' *Journal of Church and State* 22 (1): 53–74.

Robertson, Roland and Joann Chirico 1985. 'Humanity, Globalization and Worldwide Religious Resurgence: A Theoretical Exploration'. *Sociological Analysis* 46 (3): 219–42.

Rogers, Cornish 1972. 'Sports, Religion and Politics: The Renewal of an Alliance'. *Christian Century* 5 (April): 392–94.

Rouner, Leroy S. 1986. 'To Be at Home: Civil Religion as Common Bond'. In Leroy S. Rouner (ed.), *Civil Religion and Political Theology* (pp. 125–37). Notre Dame: IN: University of Notre Dame Press.

Rousseau, Jean-Jacques [1762] 1973. *The Social Contract and Discourses*. Trans. G. D. H. Cole. London: J. M. Dent and Sons.

Rowbottom, Anne 2001. 'Subject Positions: Monarchy, Civil Religion and Folk Religion in Britain'. *ActaEthnographica Hungarica* 46, 1–2: 137–52.

Rusconi, Gian Enrico 1999. 'A Substitute for Civil Religion in Italy?' *Rassegna Italiana di Sociologia* 40, 2 (Apr-June): 235–53.

Selznick, Phillip 1992. *The Moral Commonwealth: Social Theory and the Promise of Community*. Berkeley: University of California Press.

Seneviratne, H. L. 1984. 'Continuity of Civil Religion in Sri Lanka'. *Religion*, 14: 1–14.

Shils, Edward and Michael Young 1953. 'The meaning of the Coronation'. *Sociological Review* 1: 218–25.

Simpson, Charles R. 1984. 'Popular Culture as Civil Religion'. *State, Culture, and Society* 1(1): 157–75.

Sinclair-Faulkner, Tom 1977. 'A Puckish Reflection on Religion in Canada'. In *Religion and Culture in Canada/Religion et Culture au Canada* (pp. 383–405). Canadian Corporation for Studies in Religion.

Stevens, Evelyn P. 1975. 'Protest Movement in an Authoritarian Regime'. *Comparative Politics* 7, (3): 361–82.

Swatos, William H. 1998. *Encyclopedia of Religion and Society*. Williams H. Swatos, Jr. (ed.) Walnut Creek, CA: Altamira Press.

Swatos, William H. 2004. Review essay of books on Civil Religion. *Implicit Religion* 7 (2): 193–98.

Swidler, Ann 1986. 'Culture in Action: Symbols and Strategies'. *American Sociological Review* 51: 273–86.

Takayama, Peter K. 1988. 'Revitalization Movement of Modern Japanese Civil Religion'. *Sociological Analysis* 48, 4: 328–41.

Takayama, Peter K. 1993. 'The Revitalization of Japanese Civil Religion'. *Religioni e Societa* 8, 17 (September): 22–35.

Tanembaum, Marc H. 1975. 'Civil Religion: Unifying Force or Idolatry?' *Religious Education* LXX (5), 467–73.

Thomas, Michael C. and Charles C. Flippen 1972. 'American Civil Religion: An Empirical Study'. *Social Forces* 51 (2): 218–25.

Thompson, J. Earl 1971. 'The Reform of the Racist Religion of the Republic'. In Elwyn A. Smith (ed.), *The Religion of the Republic* (pp. 267–85). Philadelphia: Fortress Press.

Tipton, Steven M. 1984. 'Religion and The Moral Rhetoric of Presidential Politics'. *Christian Century* 101: 1010–13.

Toolin, Cynthia 1983. 'American civil religion from 1789–1981: A Content Analysis of Presidential Inaugural Addresses'. *Review of Religious Research* 25: 39–48.

Ungar, Sheldon 1991. 'Civil Religion and the Arms Race'. *Canadian Review of Sociology and Anthropology* 28 (4): 503–24.

Wallace, Ruth A. 1990. 'Emile Durkheim and the Civil Religion Concept'. In Peter Hamilton (ed.), *Emile Durkheim: Critical Assessments* (pp. 220–25). Vol. 4. London: Routledge.

Warner, W. Lloyd 1953. *American Life: Dream and Reality*. Chicago: University of Chicago Press.

Watts, John T. 1980. 'Robert N. Bellah's Theory of America's Eschatological Hope'. *Journal of Church and State* 22, 1 (Winter): 5–22.

Weber, Max [1904] 1949. *The Methodology of the Social Sciences*. Trans. and ed., E. A. Shils and H. A. Finch. New York: The Free Press.

West, Ellis M. 1980. 'A Proposed Neutral Definition of Civil Religion'. *Journal of Church and State* 22 (1): 22–40.

Willaime, Jean-Paul 1993. 'La religion civile à la française et ses métamorphoses.' *Social Compass* 40 (4): 571–80.

Williams, Rhys H. 1996. 'Religion as Political Resource: Culture or Ideology?' *Journal for the Scientific Study of Religion* 35 (4): 368–78.

Williams, Rhys H. 1997. *Cultural Wars in American Politics: Critical Reviews of a Popular Myth*. Rhys H. Williams (ed.). New York: Aldine De Gruyter

Williams, Rhys H. 1999. 'Visions of the Good Society and the Religious Roots of American Political Culture'. *Sociology of Religion* 60 (1): 1–34.

Williams, Robin M. 1951. *American Society: A Sociological Interpretation*. New York: Alfred A. Knopf.

Wilson, John F. 1971. 'The Status of "Civil Religion" in America'. In Elwyn A. Smith (ed.), *The Religion of the Republic* (pp. 1–21). Philadelphia: Fortress Press.

Wilson, John F. 1974. 'A Historian's Approach to Civil Religion'. In Russell E. Richey and Donald G. Jones (eds), *American Civil Religion* (pp. 115–38). New York: Harper and Row.

Wilson, John F. 1979. *Public Religion in American Culture.* Philadelphia: Temple University Press.

Wilson, John F. 1986. 'Common Religion in American Society'. In Leroy S. Rouner (ed.) *Civil Religion and Political Theology* (pp. 111–24). Notre Dame, IN: University of Notre Dame Press.

Wimberley, R. C. 1976. 'Testing the Civil Religion Hypothesis'. *Sociological Analysis* 37: 341–52.

Wimberley, R. C. 1978. 'Dimensions of Commitment'. *Journal for the Scientific Study of Religion* 17: 225–40.

Wimberley, R. C. 1979. 'Continuity in the Measurement of Civil Religion'. *Sociological Analysis* 40: 59–62.

Wimberley, R. C. 1980. 'Civil Religion and the Choice for Nixon in 1972'. *Social Forces* 59: 44–61.

Wimberley, R. C. and J. A. Christenson 1980. 'Civil Religion and Church and State'. *The Sociological Quarterly* 21 (Winter): 35–40.

Wimberley, R. C. and J. A. Christenson 1981. 'Civil Religion and Other Religious Identities'. *Sociological Analysis* 42: 91–100.

Wimberley, R. C. and J. A. Christenson 1982. 'Civil Religion, Social Indicators, and Public Policy'. *Social Indicators Research* 10: 211–23.

Wimberley, R. C. and W. H. Swatos 1998. 'Civil Religion'. In William H. Swatos, Jr. (ed.), *The Encyclopedia of Religion and Society.* London: Altamira Press.

Wimberley, R. C. *et al.* 1976. 'The Civil Religious Dimension'. *Social Forces* 54: 890–900.

Winthrop, John 1630. *'A Model of Christian Charity'.* Online document at: http://www.winthropsociety. org/doc_charity.php

Wolffe, J. 1993. 'The religions of the silent majority'. In G. Parsons (ed.), *The Growth of Religious Diversity: Britain from 1945, Vol I: Traditions* (pp. 305–46). London and New York: Routledge.

Wuthnow, Robert 1988a. *The Restructuring of American Religion.* Princeton, NJ: Princeton University Press.

Wuthnow, Robert 1988b. 'Divided We Fall: America's Two Civil Religions'. *Christian Century,* 115: 395–99.

Wuthnow, Robert 1996. *Christianity and Civil Society: The Contemporary Debate.* Valley Forge, PA: Trinity Press International.

Zeldin, Mary-Barbara 1969. 'The Religious Nature of Russian Marxism'. *Journal for the Scientific Study of Religion* 8 (1): 100–11.

Zuo, Jiping 1991. 'Political Religion: The Case of the Cultural Revolution in China'. *Sociological Analysis* 52 (1): 99–110.

PART IV

Issues of Power and Control in Religious Organisations

The four chapters in this Part of the Handbook aim to take the understanding of religious organisations one stage further. Each chapter focuses on a different type of power and control that may occur in religious organisations. Two are internal such as the power of religious professionals as priests and pastors of mainstream organisations, and an insulated community's capacity to control itself. But two are external such as the outside power and control wielded by the state, and the way outside power characterises the virtual communities of the Internet. Some of the implicated issues have long been high on the sociological agenda; some need to be reconsidered in the light of changing political circumstances, new strategies of 'marketing' religion, and, of course, new information technologies.

The selection, training and career development of religious professionals are key processes in formal religious organisations such as churches and denominations. In Chapter 14 **Paula Nesbitt** provides historical and contemporaneous analyses of the factors that bear on these processes. She also identifies the issues that currently affect both ordained and lay professionals and the organisations in which they work. These include the effects of gendering on clergy careers and the thesis that

the Protestant clerical careers in particular have been feminised, with all the attendant risks that power can be both a blessing and a curse. At the same time, Nesbitt documents the intersection of religious leadership with inequalities based on 'race' and sexual orientation. Role tensions and conflicts, contradictory pressures from forces for professionalisation and deprofessionalisation as well as changes in the supply and demand for clergy are problems in every major faith tradition. They are also problems facing professionals in non-religious organisations, and research is needed to show whether the clergy response is distinctively one of 'exit, voice or loyalty.'

Religious orders – those institutions for people with a strong vocation to a life of worship, prayer, meditation and selfless pursuit of spiritual discipline – are especially interesting to the sociology of religion for what they can reveal about the place of religious *virtuosi* in late modernity. In **Patricia Wittberg's** view, religious orders and schismatic sects may be marginal variants on the periphery of the religious mainstream but they remain connected to the centres of organised religion in various ways. Chapter 15 uses some rational choice ideas to consider factors that lead to the development of orders and sects.

It underlines the importance of heterogeneity in religious markets but also the role of conflicts over religious resources, the tolerance of central religious organisations for diversity, and the degree to which charisma is attributed to them. In structural terms, orders and schismatic sects vary in terms of their relationship to central religious organisations, their internal composition, and their stage of development. Wittberg also stresses their capacity for religious innovation – either by adapting to, or resisting, forces in their socio-cultural environments. In this sense, they are bellwethers or lightning rods for potential disruption to religious traditions, and they offer both alternatives and competition for dominant religious organisations under duress.

Meanwhile, if American churches need help, there is a willing provider standing by. Chapter 16 examines the US Government's effort under President George W. Bush to assist religious organisations in delivering social services within the framework of their faith traditions. **Arthur Farnsley** describes this as a 'renegotiation of institutional boundaries', which raises a number of significant issues for sociologists of religion. Certainly any idea of a clear separation between religion and the state has given way to a more complex notion of an overlapping web of relations between governments at the federal, state and local levels and religious agencies of various kinds. Boundaries between state and religion have been subject to frequent redefinition since the 1980s when the US Government began to encourage religious organisations to provide social services with public money. Provided that religious agencies delivered services with a secular purpose to the public, the long-standing objections to Government backing of religious organisations appeared to be overcome. But beginning in the Clinton administration, the door was opened to dispensing faith as part of the social service package and funding faith for its own sake. This has led to strengthened opposition to the new partnerships and increased pressure on congregations to undertake such new or expanded responsibilities.

All these developments underline the need for sociologists to understand religion in the context of changes taking place at the level of state and government.

Finally, relations between the centre and the periphery of religious traditions have probably become less predictable since access to the Internet and other forms of electronic communication became widely available in many parts of the world. They now form an important dimension of the socio-cultural and technological contexts in which religion operates. As **Douglas Cowan** contends in Chapter 17, sociologists of religion ignore the influence of the Internet at their peril, since it now shapes so many of the activities of religious organisations. Taking the Vatican, the Church of Scientology and the Church of the Flying Spaghetti Monster as case studies, he demonstrates the broad diversity of ways in which ancient, recent and ironic forms of religion have incorporated, refracted or exploited online communication media. It is not simply a question of the Internet being a neutral forum for religion: it is more a question of how usage of the Internet can alter public awareness of religious issues, including the perennial debate about what counts as 'religion'. To this end, Cowan assesses attempts to map the significantly different phenomena of 'religion online' and 'online religion' before broaching the question of whether 'cyber-religion' should be conceptualised as a specific type of religion and, if so, with what distinguishing characteristics. Evidence indicates that an explosion of cyber-religion has taken place since the mid-1990s, but its future remains unclear in view of the persisting 'digital divide' between the world's rich and the poor, the relatively low salience of religious activities among regular users of the Internet and the weakness of the embodied dimension of online communication. Some difficult ethical and methodological issues beset research into religion on the Internet, but sociologists of religion are well placed to accept these challenges and to discover just how far formal and informal religious activities have been affected by the digital revolution.

14

Keepers of the Tradition: Religious Professionals and their Careers

PAULA NESBITT

The emergence of professional religious leadership across a variety of traditions has had a profound consequence on what has been held as sacred, and how religious communities and congregations have practiced their faith. Not only have religious leaders become the authorized keepers of tradition, but the criteria, processes and outcomes of selecting, training, and grooming future leaders have affected how religions develop as organizations and traditions over time.

The rise of professional religious leadership typically has occurred as part of a routinization process that religious movements undergo as they seek to give order and structure to how their religion is lived over generations (Weber 1978) and how it adapts to geographic and cultural migration. Professionalism resolves such questions as, who holds the authority to determine what is a legitimate belief or practice and, more importantly, what is not. Professionalism also regulates who can speak authoritatively for the religion and its historical tradition. Furthermore, it determines who is authorized to interpret doctrine and tradition in the context of changing geographic, cultural or social circumstances so as to maintain consistency with the religion's core precepts.

The implications of religious professionalism are multifold, not only for those interested in becoming leaders, but also for the religious organizations and communities that professional leaders serve. In this chapter, we will analyze various differentiating factors of professional leadership and issues they involve, beginning with the emergence of religious professionalism and the division of religious labor. Our focus primarily will be on the selection, deployment, and careers of ordained clergy, although lay professionals also will be part of our analysis and discussion. The latter part of the chapter will emphasize contemporary issues affecting religious professionals and their denominations such as the ordination and deployment of women clergy, occupational feminization, sexual orientation, clergy role tension and conflict, professionalization and deprofessionalization movements, clergy supply and demand, and abuses of power. The chapter will conclude with implications for the future of religious professionals and areas needing further research.

THE EMERGENCE OF RELIGIOUS PROFESSIONALISM

The word *profession* originally meant the act of taking a religious vow as part of a religious order. To profess was to make a lifelong commitment to uphold the religious tenets and practices, the final step in a lengthy process of discerning one's vocation to monastic life that typically included vows such as poverty, chastity and obedience. A religious vocation was viewed as superior to secular pursuits (cf. Preston 1986). Novices would prove themselves through various criteria at different stages, prior to being allowed to progress to the ultimate act of professing the religious life and attaining the authority that came with this step (cf. Weber 1978). The act of profession, then, separated those legitimated and authorized as religious leaders from others, which Weber (1993) identified as critical to the differentiation and rise of a professional leadership or clergy class from the masses, or laity.

A professional clergy class, according to Weber (1993), initially emerged from a panoply of sorcerers, magicians, and other charismatic leaders. Devotees or disciples who had studied the craft of rituals, teachings and other aspects, and faithfully sought to pass on this body of knowledge, formed a priestly stratum of leadership. A priest in the Weberian context represented an archetypal professional leader who served a religious community or organization by performing its rituals, overseeing and safeguarding a corpus of religious teachings and practices in the service of others. Priestly authority came from the office that one holds, based on others' recognition of that office as a legitimate arbiter of religious practice and tradition. Religions such as Hinduism and Judaism (prior to the destruction of the temple in 70 CE) developed a priestly caste that was set apart through birthright to professionally oversee all matters religious. Other religions recruited from among the ranks of those who showed interest or expertise for leadership. The professionalization process of a religion's leadership is well illustrated in Christianity as that faith organizationally

moved from an itinerant or part-time leadership, often supplemented by secular work, to a professionalized clergy class (see Acts 6: 2–4). Some religions have formed a professional class that remains closely accountable to the laity, where prospective leaders are selected, groomed and affirmed with largely lay input, and where the laity continues to exert substantial influence on designated leaders. Most religions, however, have built at least some bureaucratic layers through which professional leaders take most or all of the responsibility for mentoring, educating and training aspirants for religious careers, and upon whom their subsequent careers depend to a significant extent. In this context, religious authority ultimately becomes tightly consolidated in the hands of administratively chosen religious experts (cf. Weber 1978).

Religious professionals typically solidify into an occupational class having specific shared interests as well as a commitment to their various responsibilities and tasks (Ranson *et al.* 1977). Weber (1993) attributed the development of religious scripture and written doctrine to a professional clergy class. The act of codifying the religious tradition secured the role of priestly leaders as the authentic interpreters, as the arbiters of conflicting interpretations, and the alleviators of skepticism by the laity. Priestly leaders also socialized the laity to support the codified doctrine and teachings through various forms of religious education, exhortation, and ritual obligation. Since priestly leadership emphasized religious guardianship rather than innovation, a professional class was more likely to support the maintenance of the religious tradition and consequently the interests of those who benefit from it (Weber 1993; cf. Lehman 1987a).

Religious professionals have been financially supported in various ways, ranging from those committing themselves to a lifestyle as itinerant monks or preachers, performing services where needed and living off of donations, to rationalized bureaucratic structures where a clergy class receives its livelihood from expected contributions or formal assessments from a congregation's membership or from a centralized regional or organizational office

(Weber 1993; cf. Wuthnow 1994). Economic dependency has further pressed priestly leaders to represent the interests of those to whom they are beholden: their religious community or organization, or where government support is granted, the interests of the state.

A RELIGIOUS DIVISION OF LABOR

The clergy is regarded as the oldest of the three classic learned professions – the other two being medicine and law, which arguably developed from the undifferentiated functions of religious leaders as healers and arbiters of religious law. Historically in many religious traditions, those who sought religious vocations or careers would apprentice to a religious leader or teacher, or join a monastic community that focused on intensive religious education, including scriptural study and ritual practices. As bodies of religious knowledge and scholarship became more detailed and teaching methodologies more formalized, religious schools or seminaries developed in many traditions. Today, in most Christian and Jewish seminaries, students study for several years to earn a professional degree, normally at the Master's level. Following admission, which normally requires recommendations from one or more religious professionals, seminarians undertake a comprehensive curriculum and internships that ensure knowledge of relevant languages, scripture, history, theology, ethics, and various practical skills involving worship and pastoral care. Seminary education also provides the opportunity to accumulate social capital through social networks or ties to other future clergy and religious leaders, as well as religious capital that includes mastery of specialized theoretical and practical knowledge, rituals, and other aspects of religious culture which, taken together, can reinforce the seminarians' emotional commitment to their religion and solidify their professional expertise (Finke and Dougherty 2002). Furthermore, seminary serves to heighten the boundary between professional religious leaders and others.

Many religions have a rite of ordination for professional leaders which formally sets apart those acknowledged to have a professional mastery of religious knowledge and who are authorized to perform certain religious tasks or rites as well as to speak and teach with religious authority. Typically, it follows a process of vocational discernment, mentoring by religious leaders, extended education and practical training. Ordination, which stems from the Latin word *ordināre*, meaning to set into order, has been a controversial term among some Christian and Jewish clergy according to a study by Blohm (2005), primarily in its historical context of setting apart and dividing ordained leaders as clergy from the others, or laity.

Congregationally oriented Protestant denominations typically have a single ordination rite, with the commission given by the local membership. However, to have a congregational ordination recognized elsewhere in the denomination, the process can involve multiple levels of screening by denominational officials and committees, an advanced degree from an approved seminary, internships, examinations, and various other requirements. Christian denominations with an ordered hierarchy typically ordain twice, first to a probationary or preparatory status, which in several denominations is known as the *diaconate*, and then to a final professional status with full standing and authority. In the more hierarchical denominations, a few may ultimately be consecrated as a bishop and possibly elected to a denomination's highest office. Religious organizations also may have multiple ordination tracks and statuses for specialized professional work (Nesbitt 1997).

Among other religious traditions, Buddhist monks and priests also are considered to be ordained. The Jewish rabbinate shares many similarities as an ordained status with Christian ministers and priests by virtue of formally conferring recognition of those who are deemed sufficiently knowledgeable to interpret Jewish law and pass on the tradition, based on their extensive education and mastery of the rabbinical literature. However, some rabbis have viewed the term *ordination* as having a Christian bias, preferring instead the phrase 'getting semichah,' which more closely refers to earning a degree based on one's knowledge (Jacobs 1995, cited in Blohm 2005).

Religion as Vocation

The notion of vocation, which comes from the Latin word *uocare* meaning 'to call,' has been an important part of the discernment process for those in Christianity seeking careers as ordained religious leaders (Weber 1958). Historically stemming from the biblical idea of God's calling people to religious tasks and commitment, such as Moses (Ex. 3–4), the prophets, or the Israelites as a people overall (Is. 41:8–9) and Jesus' calling of his disciples (e.g. Mt. 4:18–22), the commitment to the religious life by entering religious orders was understood to be a divine vocation from the Middle Ages onward (cf. Weber 1958). During the Protestant Reformation, Martin Luther and John Calvin broadened the concept of vocation to include worldly or secular work, based on an interpretation of Christian scripture advocating the priesthood of all believers (1 Pet. 2:9), which resultantly modified the prevailing clerical class structure of priests and laity. Those having the vocation of 'religious gifts' would be ordained or appointed to lead Protestant congregations, although they were to lead lives in close proximity to the laity whom they served, in sharp contrast to monastic traditions.

Today, in most Christian denominations, those seeking a religious career typically claim to have felt a divine call. For some, the notion of a calling has come as a sudden insight or event, while others have perceived it as a gradual yet persistent urging that cannot be ignored (Blohm 2005; Zikmund *et al.* 1998). It is tested in various ways by religious leaders and, if perceived as legitimate, aspirants then are allowed to proceed on a path of supervised training toward a professional vow or commitment. Zikmund *et al.* (1998) found that more than three-fourths of the 4,600 clergy they studied in 15 U.S. Protestant denominations admitted to a sense of having been divinely

called to their careers (cf. Goodwin and Chen 1996). Studies on British Protestant and Anglican clergy have found the call to be a similarly prominent theme (Blohm 2005; Thorne 2000). However, Blohm (2005) suggests that the emphasis on a vocational call may be culturally particular to the British (and North American) context, since it is not particularly important among those on the European Continent.

Protestant congregations in many denominations also have utilized 'the call' as a metaphor for the process of selecting and hiring a minister. Yet, employment processes often resemble those utilized by secular firms seeking to hire management-level employees, which typically involve a detailed job description and its congregational setting, a formalized candidate search, the screening of résumés and, for some denominations, the use of online search engines, followed by intensive rounds of interviews with prospective candidates, then internal discussions as to whether a prospective candidate is a 'good fit' for the organization or setting, before the selected candidate is formally 'called' to the congregation (Nesbitt 1997). Thus, a 'call' functionally invokes a religious overtone to an often highly rationalized and bureaucratized hiring process.

Paradoxically, the concept of a spiritual calling, when utilized for deployment processes, can create sizable dilemmas when aspirations and organizational interests conflict. The 'call' has been widely used as a gatekeeping mechanism by religious organizations to admit or deny applicants based on various external criteria (cf. Zikmund *et al.* 1998). Denominational projections of available openings in congregations, the availability of sufficient resources to pay an adequate fulltime salary, or concerns about recruitment of demographically undesirable candidates based on gender, age, race, ethnicity, or sexual orientation can result in selection decisions made quite apart from an aspirant's sense of calling.

Deployment and Careers

If we consider a career to be a sequence of positions held over the occupational life course, from ordination to the cessation of all occupational activity, analogies can easily be made with secular occupations. Some denominations, such as the Roman Catholic and the Methodist Churches, place their clergy in parishes or congregations and can move them at-will throughout their careers. Clergy in most other religious organizations, however, must find their own position through an array of formal and informal networks. *Formal* networks include advertised openings in denominational media or related sources, computerized placement services that match job openings to potential candidates, and working through a denomination's formal deployment processes that often involve one or more individuals at the regional level who coordinate or broker deployment. Most large Protestant and Jewish organizations have such processes that help to identify and match clergy to position openings. For instance, a Joint Commission on Rabbinic Placement oversees the pulpit search for Conservative rabbis (Fried 2002). *Informal* networks include word-of-mouth referrals, seminary officials and colleagues, family or school classmate social connections, as well as associations of other clergy and laity who may know of openings. For Conservative rabbis, the Rabbinical Assembly serves as both a professional organization and networking opportunity to seek information about placements (Fried 2002). Research on Protestant clergy over the past 30 years has shown that the formal, objective processes such as computerized deployment have been particularly helpful for women and minority-race clergy who either might not be aware of desirable positions or not considered for them if deployment occurred through informal networks alone (Lehman 1980; Zikmund *et al.* 1998). Informal networks have been an important resource for employment among male clergy, although they have been found to be much less effective for women (Lehman 2002; cf. Zikmund *et al.* 1998).

Unlike secular professions, clergy jobs are part of an internal labor market that is bound within their denomination. The primary job sector for clergy has been religious leadership of a self-supporting congregation (cf. Chaves 1991; Zikmund *et al.* 1998). This also represents the modal job in most religious organizations. However, the type of available positions can vary widely by religious tradition and the size of a particular denomination. Beyond leading a congregation, or working on its staff, clergy also may hold positions on administrative staffs in denominational offices and agencies (cf. Chaves 1991), or in seminaries and religious schools. Occasionally crossover can occur in clergy labor markets between denominations that share certain affinities or agreements, where clergy may be employed in a congregation of another denomination (Donovan 1988; Nesbitt 1997). Sometimes clergy and lay professionals may hold religious positions in secular work environments such as chaplaincies in military, prison, campus, or hospital settings; in counseling and social service agencies; or in other organizations where a need is recognized for access to a religious professional. Clergy who work outside the congregation, unless as a denominational executive, tend to have less prestige within their denomination (Nesbitt 1997; cf. Zikmund *et al.* 1998).

Career paths normally begin with an initial placement in a congregation following ordination, either as sole leader of a small congregation or as an associate to the senior leader of a larger congregation (cf. Zikmund *et al.* 1998). Staff positions in large congregations often involve specialization for certain areas of religious work such as education, children and youth programs, pastoral care, or occasionally charitable and outreach programs to serve the wider community. Typically, the first placement is considered to be a transitional position, from which clergy expectedly move to a larger or more prosperous congregation, or to one less so but where they can attain upward mobility by becoming the sole professional leader. Some clergy serve multiple small congregations that are clustered together to form a single job or appointment. This may occur due to an undersupply of clergy or insufficient financial resources to pay a fulltime leader (cf. Blohm 2005). Roman Catholic priests, for instance, may be responsible for sacramental duties at several parishes because of the priest shortage (Wallace 1992).

How clergy are paid and the amount they make also vary by position and denomination. Most Protestant clergy and Jewish rabbis, directly hired by the congregation they serve, typically are paid according to the size and financial resources of the congregation. This can result in sizeable salary disparities among clergy who hold the same job title with similar duties in different congregations. Over the past two decades, several denominations have encouraged the standardization of clergy compensation packages (cf. Waldron 1986; Gilbride et al. 1990), partly to assure that clergy are paid fairly for their work, including contributions to pension and other benefits.

Christopherson's (1994) research found that clergy often feel a tension between secular aspects of a career and the ideals of a religious vocation. This may be particularly acute for male clergy since the types of positions they prefer tend to align with those traditionally associated with career success (cf. Finlay 1996). Within Protestant and Jewish religious organizations, measures of career success have included the relative size and financial resources of one's congregation, the number of clergy and administrative staff one supervises, the extent of membership growth, the amount of compensation received, and one's prestige in the civic community (Lehman 1990; Chapman 1991; Marder 1991; Purdum 1991; Christopherson 1994; cf. Blanton and Morris 1999). Leaders of larger, more prestigious congregations also typically hold more political status within their denomination (cf. Carroll et al. 1983). Although many Protestant clergy perceive their rationale for accepting or remaining in a position based on the notion of divine will or a vocational call (cf. Zikmund et al. 1998), which can affect job mobility and attainment over one's career, other evidence suggests that clergy tend to approach career decisions in ways somewhat similar to secular work, moving to occupational positions of increasing resources, authority and prestige within the job ladder of their denominational structure (e.g. Carroll et al. 1983).

More recently, the age of those entering seminary, being ordained and beginning their clergy careers has risen markedly (e.g. Aleshire 2003, 2005; Zikmund et al. 1998; Blohm 2005). Despite evidence that denominational officials tend to think of clergy deployment in terms of traditional career stages that involve entry-level positions associated with clergy in their 20s and 30s, advancement years of upward job mobility during one's 30s and 40s, career plateau occurring through the early 60s, followed by retirement (Maloney and Hunt 1991), the clergy as a second career has only been found to be problematic for those aspiring to senior-level positions in their denomination (Nesbitt 1997, 1995). Older age has been found to be an asset for working with congregations having middle-aged and older members (Carroll et al. 1983). Resultantly, the clergy as a career tends to be atypical among other professions in its opportunities for those seeking to change careers.

Lay Religious Professionals

Some religions do not ordain their professional leaders. This can arise out of the belief that leadership should be representative of the membership rather than as a distinctive class or status group. Nonetheless, lay professionals similarly are acknowledged to have certain expertise and legitimacy that does grant them a degree of authority and privilege not available to all members. The Salvation Army and The Society of Friends (Quakers) represent two diverse examples within Christianity where leaders are not ordained, although the Salvation Army commissions its lay officers and The Society of Friends *records* what it believes to be an ordination by God (Gibson 1970; cf. Nesbitt 1997). Within Islam, leaders are not ordained. In the Shi'ite tradition, a leader stems from the bloodline of Muhammad, an organizational form that Weber (1978) equated with traditional authority. Sunni leaders, or *imāms,* who lead the prayers in local mosques and function as the overall head of their local religious communities, are selected for their religious knowledge and respect within the religious community (Nasr 1985). The *'ulamā'* however, who are religious scholars having authority on

Islamic life and who are considered to be the custodians of tradition, are broadly recognized as a professional leadership class (Graham and Reinhart 1989). Like ordained clergy in other traditions, they hold the authority to speak for their religious tradition, including the interpretation of Islamic law (*Sharia*) and other matters of religious doctrine and practice.

Even in religions that have ordained clergy, lay professionals may hold powerful positions. More often, they hold staff positions in denominational offices and agencies, specializing in areas such as religious research and scholarship, pastoral care, social welfare services, social justice, administration and development; or in congregations as specialists in religious education, music, or chant. Monahan's (1999b) multidenominational study showed that laity shared a substantial amount of clergy work in many Protestant and Catholic churches. In many denominations, laity can be licensed or appointed to lead a congregation when no ordained clergy are available, although where key sacramental roles exist as in the Roman Catholic and Anglican/Episcopal Churches, they remain the province of clergy (cf. Wallace 1992).

RELIGIOUS PROFESSIONALS
AND SOCIAL INEQUALITY

Although religious professionals as priestly leaders in the Weberian (1993) sense may focus on guarding and transmitting their religious traditions, occasionally they have used charisma to take prophetic stands for social change. Weber (1978) understood this type of leadership as *office charisma*, which is ultimately attached to the credibility of the office one holds, rather than charisma as a pure form of authority that conflicts with rationally organized or bureaucratic leadership. During the latter half of the twentieth century alone, the Rev. Martin Luther King, Jr. provided catalytic leadership during the U.S. Civil Rights movement, attributed to mobilizing more people to action than any other figure in American history (see Morris 1996). Anglican

Archbishop Desmond Tutu played a vital role in South Africa's anti-apartheid movement and the subsequent reconciliation movement; Pope John Paul II visibly supported the struggle of Poland and other countries to break with communism; the Dalai Lama's quest for political freedom in Tibet has been recognized globally. Such prophetic leaders, however, have had the support of the religious groups and organizations they represent. Priestly leaders occasionally have relied on office charisma for reforms about which their religious organizations have been ambivalent or not supported, thereby creating social tension that occasionally has resulted in reprimand, discharge from the position they held, defrocking, excommunication or expulsion.

Some denominations and their congregations insist on their clergy exhibiting office charisma. For instance, the personal charisma of Pentecostal Protestant ministers has been regarded as vital to the community's worship, although the use of charisma is both scrutinized and tested for credibility by the membership and thus closely controlled (Poloma 1989, 1997). Many African American Protestant congregations also have expected their leadership to exert office charisma in making prophetic commitments for racial equality and social change (e.g. Harris 1987). Yet another example involves campus chaplaincies, which have tended to be more liberal than traditional congregations, and where there has been a greater acceptance of clergy speaking prophetically as well as taking action on various social causes and concerns (Demerath and Hammond 1969). This was particularly the case during the 1960s in the U.S., when students faced concerns about the military draft, the Vietnam war, Civil Rights, and what they saw as the inflexibility of institutional boundaries, both secular and religious. Today, however, college chaplains often have been engaged in helping students with little or no religious background learn about their religious traditions and the boundaries upon which religious identity is formed (cf. Poorman 2004).

In the following section, we will explore religious leadership in relation to three different forms of societal inequality and social change.

The first represents the Black Church in the United States, an example of the importance placed on religious leadership as a function of societal segregation and marginality. The second involves an analysis of the emergence of female religious professionals – particularly women clergy – and the extent to which their presence may have affected the clergy overall as an occupation. We will conclude with a brief discussion of ordination and sexual orientation, which has become quite controversial in a number of denominations over the last two decades.

Racism and Religious Leadership: Lessons of the U.S. Black Church

The legacy of slavery, segregation, institutional racism, and socioeconomic inequality has played a crucial part in the prophetic expectations that have been placed on ministers in the Black Church, a phrase that sociologically refers to a range of African American Christian denominations having emerged since the late-eighteenth century in the United States (Lincoln and Mamiya 1990). Ministers have held powerful roles and elevated status in these communities, as head of the only institution where African Americans historically could hold leadership positions in society.

Franklin (1991) has characterized ministers in African American religion in relation to diverse goals, the means they have used to achieve them, and the assumptions of religious authority they hold that inform their actions. *Progressive accommodationists*, traditionally the largest segment, have sought peace and justice through negotiating and working with established interfaith and secular institutions. *Prophetic radicals*, those dissatisfied with the slow gains of the accommodationists and more concerned about economic inequalities of free market capitalism and their effects on the poor, have been more willing to engage in strategies of confrontation. *Redemptive nationalists* have promoted separatism, such as a separate nation that would assure African Americans of their civil and human rights. *Grass-roots revivalists*, characteristic of Protestant Pentecostal

groups and those with storefront churches, have tended to emphasize personal salvation rather than engage in political action, although McRoberts (2003, 1999) argues that these ministers do take an active role in social welfare ministries. The final group, *positive thought materialists* according to Franklin (1991), have emphasized constructive thinking as a route to personal health and success instead of social or political activism. Although as pure types they help to differentiate different leadership orientations, leadership interests don't always fit into discrete categories (cf. McRoberts 2003), or they may shift with societal issues and trends.

In most denominations under the Black Church umbrella, ministers often have been expected to sustain certain prophetic commitments for social change in race relations and the socioeconomic improvement of African American communities. For instance, Lincoln and Mamiya's (1990) national study of 2,150 Black Church congregations found that over 90 per cent of the ministers believed that the Black Church should be politically and socially activist (cf. Pattillo-McCoy 1998). More than three-fourths of laity in another study (Harris 1987) similarly believed that their minister's role should actively include working against oppression, and more than two-thirds wanted their minister to take political leadership in such efforts. Some denominations, however, have focused more on personal salvation and transformation than political activism and change, which at times has created sizable tension within the leadership of the Black Church (McRoberts 2003). Lincoln and Mamiya's (1990) study also points to the ministry's loss of status since the Civil Rights era and to a concern over the future supply of ministers who are similarly talented and motivated as their predecessors.

African American women have a rich legacy as founders and leaders of independent churches, which often has been a result of a lack of opportunities for women's leadership within their traditional church (Baer 1994). Many Black Church congregations have opposed women pastors and preachers despite the strong majority of female participants

(Lincoln and Mamiya 1990; cf. Baer 1994). Pressure to limit preaching ministry to men has been attributed to compensation for the racism that has denied African American men leadership and esteem in other social institutions, although the resultant sexism has limited sharply the job opportunities available to African American women (Gilkes 1989; Goldman 1990; Lincoln and Mamiya 1990; Baer 1994). For instance, Konieczny and Chaves' (2000) study found that women were more likely to lead congregations that were at least 80 per cent African American, were independent of national denominations and that were socioeconomically poorer.

Women as Professional Religious Leaders

Women have found a variety of ways to work as religious professionals, even in restrictive eras and cultures. Traditionally, for Buddhist and Christian women, the religious life as nuns offered them a professional alternative to the traditional roles of marriage and motherhood. Roman Catholic nuns have a long history of running not only their own religious orders but also a range of schools and other institutions that those orders established throughout the world (cf. Wittberg 1994). Protestant women similarly, as missionaries, have had professional religious careers (Smith 1970). Single and widowed Muslim women have made their livelihood as ritual leaders and teachers (Hegland 1997). Women have worked as shamans or religious healers (cf. Lee 1999). They also have founded numerous new religious movements (Wessinger 1993). Yet, as these movements have institutionalized they generally have been taken over by men (e.g. Brereton and Klein 1979).

Weber (1993) observed that religious groups emerging on the social margin have tended to give greater equality to women than those found among more privileged classes. He also noted that as religious groups develop a more formal organizational and leadership structure, with a codified scripture or doctrine, women become excluded from leadership roles.

Carroll *et al.* (1983) have articulated a pattern of women's religious leadership, based on Weber's insights. *Charismatic religious groups* traditionally have provided women important opportunities to found new religious movements and to lead communities that grant leadership based on evident spiritual gifts rather than qualifications and procedures decided upon by a governing body or specified in tradition. *Consolidating and organizing groups*, by contrast, either have developed gender-segregated leadership roles or have excluded women from leadership altogether, based on requirements and procedures that have been formalized and objectified. *Maturing and institutionalizing groups* have offered women leadership roles, but usually those that are marginal or subordinate to senior leadership positions which overwhelmingly are held by men. At times, when women have been given leadership roles, men have guarded their activity to ensure that their religious interpretations conform to those of the male leadership (cf. Stocks 1997).

One of the most significant developments among lay women's professional religious leadership has occurred as a consequence of the shortage of Roman Catholic priests to staff parishes and the need to hire trained lay men and women for the day-to-day administrative, pastoral, and liturgical work. Wallace's (1992) study of lay women pastoral associates found that some parishioners had begun to express their support for the women also being able to perform the sacramental roles traditionally reserved for priests. Eklund's (2006) research further showed that priests acted as gatekeepers for both the amount of authority the women had and for overall parish support for their leadership. This could serve to sustain as well as suppress the women's efforts.

The pattern of women's leadership that Carroll *et al.* (1983) set forth, based on Weberian typology, has been challenged in recent years by the growing number of female elite leaders in large, bureaucratized denominations. Since the 1980s, women have been elected as Anglican/Episcopal, Lutheran, and Methodist bishops, including Presiding Bishop of the Episcopal Church (USA). A female rabbi has led the largest U.S. group of Jewish clergy, Reform Judaism's Central Conference of American Rabbis (Lattin 2003). And, a woman has headed the National Council of Churches (USA). Although it has been argued that a glass ceiling is intact for women leaders in religious organizations (Purvis 1995; Stanley 1996), it has not been categorically impermeable. We now turn to women clergy, where the greatest gender controversies have occurred surrounding their eligibility for ordination and their occupational prospects.

Women's ordination

All religions that ordain their leaders at one time or another have excluded women from the rite (e.g. Carmody 1979). Although there were ordained nuns in Buddhism's early centuries (Goonatilake 1997) and female deacons and priests in some early Christian communities (e.g. Ide 1986; Børresen 1993), women's ordained status disappeared as these religions developed more formal organizational structures and gained prestige in the surrounding society (Carmody 1979; cf. Weber 1993). Contemporary women's ordination, carrying the same status as men, commenced only in the mid-nineteenth century (1853). This occurred in Protestant denominations with a congregational polity, where autonomy and authority resided at the local level (cf. Chaves 1997; Nesbitt 1997). Women ordained in these denominations nonetheless faced significant challenges in finding congregations willing to *call* (hire) them, were paid marginal wages and, if they were successful in making their congregation grow and prosper, typically were replaced by men (Gibson 1970; Tucker 1990). Additional tensions that ordained women faced in those early years ranged from denominational ambivalence and lack of support for their presence to the reversal of women's ordination altogether (cf. Keller 1984; Tucker 1990; Chaves 1997). Women clergy in charismatic-oriented denominations such as Protestant Pentecostalism fared somewhat better occupationally, until these denominations in the 1920s began to shift from a *prophetic* to a more *priestly* orientation.

Women's opportunities correspondingly declined (Barfoot and Sheppard 1980).

A second wave of Protestant denominations opening full ordination to women occurred after World War II. These denominations were more bureaucratically stratified, with strong regional authority structures governed by bishops or other elected leaders (Chaves 1997; Nesbitt 1997). Among the more well-known were the African Methodist Episcopal, Methodist, Presbyterian, Lutheran, and Episcopal/Anglican Church traditions in the U.S. and in several other countries. However, not all sectors of these traditions supported women's ordination, with substantial tension and schism as the result (Darling 1994). During this era, some Jewish denominations also formally opened ordination to women, although the first female rabbi, Regina Jonas, had been ordained privately in 1935 in Germany (Guttmann 1982, cited in Blohm 2005). Women have been counted among Lutheran pastors from Sweden to Japan, Anglican priests from Kenya to Hong Kong, and by the 1990s among Conservative rabbis in North and South America. Yet, in a pattern similar to the late nineteenth century, ordained women still face occupational challenges in obtaining positions on parity with those held by men (Chaves 1997; Nesbitt 1997; Zikmund et al. 1998) and, in cases such as the U.S. Southern Baptist Convention or the Presbyterian Church of Australia, support for women's ordination has been revoked altogether (Ammerman 1990; Lehman 1994).

Not all religions allow women to be ordained. Christian and Jewish Orthodox traditions do not ordain women, nor do some conservative Protestant denominations, although there has been advocacy for doing so (e.g. Greenberg 1984, cited in Blohm 2005; May 1998). The Old Catholic Churches in Europe opened ordination to women in the 1990s (Blohm 2005). The Roman Catholic Church has stood firmly against ordaining women despite movements for women's ordination in Britain, Europe and North America since Vatican II; sizable support for women's ordination among both laity and clergy (e.g. Gallup and Lindsay 1999; Lehman 1994: 37); and an acute shortage of priests in many parts of the world (cf. Schoenherr and Young 1993). In 2002, seven Roman Catholic women were ordained by two retired bishops on a ship in the Danube River (Johnson 2002), analogous to a pattern of extralegal means used to achieve women's ordination by bishops and other supporters in the U.S. Episcopal Church in 1974, in the wake of overt and sustained resistance (Darling 1994). The Catholic women priests were excommunicated one month after ordination (Johnson 2002). At least three Catholic women had been covertly ordained during the Czechoslovakian Communist regime, which was justified as a means to maintain the Church's presence there, although the Vatican has refused to recognize their ordinations (Pomerleau 1992). Some Catholic feminists, however, have been skeptical over supporting Catholic women's ordination and the extent to which a gender integrated priesthood simply would perpetuate a model of leadership and ultimately of church that had been developed by men and served male interests. Rather, they argue that the ordained priesthood – and the Church itself – must be rearticulated in ways that include and sustain feminist values (Ruether 1986; cf. Wallace 1994).

Women clergy: career patterns and perspectives

Studies on women clergy over the past 50 years have shown remarkably consistent findings across geographic locations, denominations and decades. Although Zikmund et al. (1998) did note some improvement in the occupational prospects of U.S. Protestant women clergy, based on their update of an earlier study (Carroll et al. 1983), the occupation was still an 'uphill calling' for women. Broadly, studies on clergy in North America have found that women are several years older than men at the time of ordination, although typically they have the same educational background and other characteristics (e.g. Stevens 1996; Nesbitt 1997; Zikmund et al. 1998). Following ordination, men and women hold similar entry placements, but soon thereafter gender differences emerge in the types of positions that clergy

hold, in salaries and benefits and other aspects of their jobs. Whether women serve as Protestant ministers, Anglican/Episcopal priests or Jewish rabbis, they are more likely to hold a position as *assistant* or *associate* on a congregation's staff (e.g. Marder 1996; Nesbitt 1997; Zikmund et al. 1998). When clergy change jobs, men more often tend to move into positions as solo or senior leaders of congregations while women are more likely to move to another assistant or associate staff position (Nesbitt 1997; Zikmund et al. 1998; Lehman 2002). Evidence also shows that women are paid less than men doing similar work (Marder 1996; Zikmund et al. 1998; Konieczny and Chaves 2000; Lehman 2002), and that women are less likely than men to earn a full-time wage regardless of marital status or children (Zikmund et al. 1998). When women clergy do lead a congregation, it tends to be smaller, with fewer financial resources than those of men (e.g. Nesbitt 1997; Zikmund et al. 1998) – a trend that has persisted since the nineteenth century. Research on women clergy has yielded varying explanations for the challenges that they face. Chaves' (1997) historical comparative study of women's ordination in U.S. Protestantism argues that women's ordination and careers reflect the extent to which a denomination is centralized, its various subcultures that create political influences and pressures, and how the denomination interacts with surrounding secular cultural influences. Denominational stipulations permitting women clergy are loosely coupled with actual practices that are much more restrictive, reflecting the surrounding cultural ethos. He further argues that clergy supply and demand are not correlated with women's ordination. Nesbitt's (1997) longitudinal study of Unitarian Universalist and Episcopal (USA) male and female clergy, makes the case instead that the occupational prospects of women clergy are directly related to changing occupational needs of religious organizations, wrought by low membership growth and financial strain that have created a demand for a part-time and nonstipendiary ordained labor force that has become disproportionately populated by women. She also associates backlash movements against women clergy with concerns over the ensuing prospect of occupational and organizational feminization. Zikmund et al. (1998) document numerous gender inequalities that have persisted in 15 Protestant denominations, finding that women clergy have greater acceptance than in past years, but that men tend to work in larger congregations and earn more than their female colleagues. They argue that women clergy are expanding their ministry beyond congregational and denominational boundaries, and challenging their denominations to rethink their understanding of church and leadership. The findings are remarkably similar in the Nesbitt (1997) and Zikmund et al. (1998) studies despite different methodologies. Chaves' (1997) analysis shows that internal and external forces both legitimate women's ordination and control how it is lived out, and provides an important complement to the other research.

Similar patterns have been identified in research on women clergy in Australia, Britain and the European Continent. Lehman's (1994) comparative study of lay attitudes toward women clergy in two Australian denominations found that support for women clergy faltered when asked to consider a woman to be their senior pastor or leader. Lehman contends that the Australian context shares similarities with research findings on clergy in Britain and the U.S., namely that women more often pastor struggling congregations and are less likely to experience upward career mobility, which he associates with lower support for women in more prestigious clergy roles (Lehman 1980, 1985, 1987b). Other studies on British Protestant clergy found biases against women by male seminary colleagues and in the training process itself (Tidball 1989, cited in Blohm 2005; Furlong 2000). Blohm's (2005) study of Christian and Jewish clergy found a persistence of congregational stereotypes that worked against women ministers, priests and rabbis. Studies of Swedish and Norwegian clergy similarly have found that despite formal church norms prescribing equality for ordained men and women, a substantial sentiment against women clergy has persisted (Stendahl 1985; Hansson 1993; Piper 1995).

As in secular professions, controversy persists as to whether or not a glass ceiling exists in limiting women's opportunities. A *stained glass ceiling* has been argued specifically to limit the number of qualified women who attain high-level positions (Purvis 1995; Stanley 1996). In Konieczny and Chaves' (2000) study of 1,236 U.S. congregations across diverse religious traditions, not only were just 9 per cent headed by women, but as a congregation's size increased the number of female leaders sharply declined, with no women overseeing congregations of more than 1,000 members. Other research confirms that large congregations tend to prefer male clergy (Kammerer 2002; Darling 2003; cf. Lehman 1985, 1994), which directly inhibits women's prospects for upward mobility.

Conversely, it has been argued that a glass ceiling assumes conformity to a certain set of goals (Hitt 2002) and that women should redefine occupational achievement and success on their own terms (Marder 1996). Others have attributed at least some of the gender gap to passive socialization processes and different occupational choices that women have made (e.g. Carroll et al. 1983). For instance, Finlay (1996) found that male Presbyterian (USA) seminarians were more attracted to congregations having a high-status membership, and resultantly were about twice as likely to prefer solo pastorates in growing suburban congregations. Female seminarians, however, were more willing to consider a broader array of positions, including pastorates of congregations in poor communities and chaplaincies. Some women clergy have claimed not to want high-level leadership jobs (Ice 1987; Marder 1996), which often include greater stress and sometimes significantly longer hours. Rather, women may explicitly choose jobs that may fit more easily with childcare or other commitments – positions that may even be part-time or nonstipendiary (cf. Lehman 1985; 2002). Women clergy also have shown greater job satisfaction than men who hold similar positions (McDuff 2001; Zikmund et al. 1998), which suggests that they may have lower intrinsic motivation to seek job change, including the prospect of upward mobility into high-level leadership positions. These disparities, however, can become embedded within different career trajectories that more likely position men than women for accumulating the kind of religious capital that will lead to elite leadership opportunities. It also can result in salary differences, with women serving congregations that are far less able to pay what their male counterparts are making or, in some cases, may not pay a full-time wage. Nonetheless, whether intentional or not, women have modeled more varied interests and career paths.

Women clergy and social change

The prospect of women clergy as change agents has been widely debated. First, as part of the discussion surrounding women's ordination, women with religious authority have been argued to subvert women's subordinate gender roles justified by scripture (Kirk 1957), and to predict major structural change for the religious organization (Fitzpatrick 1993). It also underlies the liberal feminist arguments that once women clergy attain positions of substantive authority in their denominations they will be more likely to act on behalf of women's interests (e.g. Nesbitt 1997; Blohm 2005: 438).

One of the largest assumptions has involved women clergy as harbingers of change through their leadership style. Women have been argued to have a more feminine and relational style (Ice 1987), what Lehman (1993) has called a maximalist perspective in contrast to minimalists who argue that intrinsic gender differences do not exist. Studies on clergy in the United Kingdom and Canada have shown that women see themselves as using a more egalitarian and collaborative style in their ministry (Stevens 1996; Robbins 1998; cf. Nason-Clark 1987). However, studies on several U.S. Protestant denominations have not found strong, consistent gender differences (Lehman 1993; Zikmund et al. 1998). Rather, leadership style has tended to vary more by race and ethnicity than by gender, suggesting the primacy of cultural effects in not only differentiating styles but also in the construction of what is considered to be masculinity and femininity (Lehman 1993). In a study of leadership differences among

male and female Anglican/Episcopal bishops, Nesbitt (2001) found that the male bishops saw the presence of female bishops as a symbolic opportunity for the transformation of the prevalent authoritarian leadership style to a more egalitarian and relational leadership style, which they preferred as well. The women characterized their style as collegial and relational, but did not attribute it to their status as women other than as a byproduct of gender-role socialization experiences and having had to work in nontraditional ways throughout their clergy careers (cf. Stevens 1996), although they did value this style as an opportunity for changing how power was deployed. Male rabbis similarly have perceived the growing number of female rabbis as representing a social change opportunity to broaden the norms and expectations surrounding the rabbinate in ways that allow them to participate in those values and issues often associated with women (Marder 1991).

As denominations have opened their ordination processes to women, concerns often have been raised that the clergy as an occupation would feminize, with an attendant male clergy exodus and diminished interest by young men seeking ordination as well as few laymen participating in their congregations (e.g. Hewitt and Hiatt 1973; Schaller 1987). Since women have been a majority of lay participants in most denominations (see Walter and Davie 1998, cited in Eklund 2006; Gallup and Lindsay 1999), the prospect of a predominately-female clergy would suggest the plausibility of such concerns that women would *take over* their religious organizations. Indeed, women's influx into the ordained clergy rapidly increased during the 1970s and 1980s, both in denominations that had ordained women for a century or more and in those newly opening ordination to women (Chaves 1997; Nesbitt 1997; cf. Carroll 1992: 292; Zikmund et al. 1998), and in the 1990s as the Church of England began to ordain women to the priesthood (see Blohm 2005). As retiring clergy in all denominations have been overwhelmingly male, the new replacement cohorts of clergy, which have reached to over 50 per cent female in some denominations, ultimately predict a changing demographic composition within the clergy over time (Nesbitt 1997; Blohm 2005). Furthermore, denominations that ordain women have experienced sharp declines in the ratio of young men seeking ordination – declining by as much as 55 per cent between 1950 and 1990 in one denomination ordaining women (Nesbitt 1997). However, the occupational prospects for young men have been found to be greater in ordination cohorts with a higher ratio of women (Nesbitt 1997). As women come to represent a greater percentage of clergy in several denominations over time, the occupation is showing effects similar to secular feminized occupations, such as gendered job segregation that benefits the smaller concentrations of men but proportionately few women (cf. Reskin and Roos 1990; Nesbitt 1997; Zikmund et al. 1998).

In sum, male leaders in a range of denominations have accepted women's ordination, but not necessarily granting them parity in opportunities for employment and congregational leadership. Women clergy nonetheless have a broad diversity of ways that they practice their careers. Despite whether an actual glass ceiling exists or not, disparities in the types of positions that women clergy hold, their compensation, and their career trajectories differ in ways that lead to fewer resources and lower compensation over their occupational lifecourse. Furthermore, whether or not women clergy as a critical mass ultimately seek to change the occupation, their demographic concentration over time will create a very different occupational profile in the future of many denominations.

Ordination and Sexual Orientation

Much of mainline Protestantism, Roman Catholicism and Conservative Judaism have been sharply polarized over whether clergy should be ordained without regard to their sexual orientation. Some moderate denominations historically have utilized the standard of celibacy outside of marriage, which effectively sidestepped the sexual *orientation* aspect by framing all sexuality as a matter of *practice* within marriage, although gay and lesbian marriages potentially present a complication to assumptions behind that doctrine. Some religious groups have been more restrictive, prohibiting ordination on the basis of non-heterosexual *orientation*. The few denominations that openly ordain clergy without regard to sexual orientation or a requirement of celibacy outside of heterosexual marriage include Unitarian Universalism, the United Church of Christ (USA), the Metropolitan Community Church, and Reform and Reconstructionist Judaism. *Semi-exclusivist* denominations deeply split over the issue of sexual orientation (Wellman 1999) have affirming or 'reconciling' congregations and movements, such as those found in Presbyterian, Methodist, Lutheran, Disciples of Christ, and American Baptist Churches. More recently, the Roman Catholic Church has moved from a semi-exclusivist to a staunch exclusivist position on the sexual orientation of its clergy, a shift that clearly began in the mid 1980s (cf. Wellman 1999) and was exacerbated in the wake of clergy sexual abuse scandals.

Over the past three decades, gay men and lesbians in committed same-gender relationships have been ordained by clergy leaders or congregations despite their denomination's formal position on the issue. Additionally, some clergy have publicly come out after having lived a heterosexual lifestyle that often included marriage and children (e.g. White 1994). In many denominations, gay and lesbian clergy have great difficulty finding congregational positions or employment within their denomination (Zikmund et al. 1998). Analyzing the 147 female and 64 male clergy in their multidenominational sample who identified as being in a committed same-gender relationship, Zikmund et al. (1998) found no significant differences between gay/lesbian and straight clergy on a range of measures, including the maintenance of boundaries between their work and private lives. However, gay and lesbian clergy did have a slightly greater tendency to be employed in secular positions or to have seriously considered leaving the ministry.

One of the most recent changes in favor of allowing openly gay and lesbian clergy to function in their churches, with far-reaching consequences, was the U.S. Episcopal Church's decision in 2003 to affirm the diocesan election of an openly gay bishop – a move that also traumatized conservative sectors of the denomination as well as conservative churches within the worldwide Anglican Communion (cf. Eames 2004). Thus, despite some moderating trends toward acceptance of gay and lesbian clergy, a sizable amount of opposition or tension remains in most religious organizations.

ISSUES FACING THE CLERGY

The clergy has been called a 'hazardous profession' as well as a 'holy crossfire' (Blackmon and Hart 1990; DeLuca 1980, cited in Blanton and Morris 1999: 331). Clergy and lay religious professionals face numerous issues related to working in religious congregations and organizations. Some involve the organizational environment in which they work, while others have to do with occupational role pressures and professional change. We now turn to a few of the many challenges and possibilities facing religious professionals today.

Role Tensions, Ambiguities and Conflicts

Concerns over role strain, role fragmentation, and the ensuing tensions have been the topic of research among Protestant, Catholic, and Jewish clergy since the 1930s (see Nelson 1985). Blizzard's (1985) multidenominational study of Protestant ministers in the 1950s poignantly showed the disparity between how clergy understood their work as a professional occupation, or what he termed the 'master role,' and the various integrative roles that provided specific occupational self-definition, such as scholar or evangelist. This was further complicated by the numerous practitioner roles associated with specific tasks that ministers were expected to fulfill, namely preacher, pastor, teacher, priest, administrator, and organizer. Not only did heavy time demands weigh on clergy, often pulling them in numerous

directions, but role conflicts also emerged between what ministers viewed as important, given their master and integrative roles, and the other roles that consumed a disproportionate amount of their time. Added pressure of congregational expectations for a high level of expertise in the very different types of practitioner roles and the kinds of knowledge that each represented further added to role tension.

Role strain remains as much of an issue for clergy in congregations today as it was in the 1950s, if not more so. Kuhne and Donaldson's (1995) study of U.S. evangelical ministers showed that in a workweek that averaged 51 hours, they found 41 different work activities each day, with nearly half of these lasting five minutes or less. Such severe time fragmentation and high task load (referring to the number of different activities) both erodes a minister's ability to develop work continuity and contributes to role ambiguity (Monahan 1999a). Both role uncertainty and role conflict have been identified in studies on British Anglican clergy, as well (Francis and Rodger 1996; Heald and Rhodes 1986, cited in Bryman 1996). Blohm's (2005) study of British female rabbis, ministers and priests also affirmed the pervasive feeling of time pressure, role fragmentation, and sometimes unrealistically high expectations from members of their congregation.

Further role conflicts have emerged from the pressures ministers typically have felt to put the needs of members of the congregation before those of their own families. Zikmund et al. (1998) found among Protestant denominations that the emphasis on a spiritual *calling* resulted in expectations that ministers devote virtually all waking hours to their work, with little time left for personal or family life. Additionally, clergy and their families often lived a fishbowl existence, where their personal lives were on display for all to evaluate whether or not they modeled the idealized expectations for clergy (e.g. Mace and Mace 1981). The accumulation of these demands can create a sizable strain on personal and family relationships, although Zikmund et al. (1998) found that the clergy divorce rate was similar to that for the U.S. population overall, and somewhat lower in the conservative denominations of their study.

Work satisfaction, however, has been found to be generally strong among clergy in a range of denominations (cf. Dudley and Cummings 1996; Zikmund *et al.* 1998). Job dissatisfaction among Protestant clergy serving congregations has been associated with experiencing role ambiguity, role conflict and fragmentation (Dudley and Cummings 1996; cf. Jackson and Schuler 1985, cited in Monahan 1999a), feeling the pressures of occupational changes (cf. Coate 1989), and holding more liberal perspectives than a congregation's membership (although being more conservative than a congregation did not have a similar effect, according to Mueller and McDuff's (2004) study). Dissatisfaction has been related to giving serious thought about leaving both a position in the congregation and the ministry altogether (cf. Francis and Rodger 1996; Price 2003; Mueller and McDuff 2004). Ironically, low salaries and benefits are not necessarily a source of significant dissatisfaction when compared to other issues (Mueller and McDuff 2004; cf. Blanton and Morris 1999 for conflicting results).

Brunette-Hill and Finke's (1999) study of U.S. Protestant and Catholic clergy, which built upon Blizzard's (1985) research, found a decline of over 20 hours per week of time that clergy worked (down from 69 hours per week in 1955), most of which was accounted for by fewer pastoral calls and less time spent in local meetings, denominational or ecumenical activities, and with civic organizations. Their study raises important questions about why these shifts have occurred, and whether a declining public involvement of clergy reflect changes in occupational self-understanding, expectations of congregations, or broader societal shifts toward civic disengagement (cf. Putnam 2000).

Professionalization and Deprofessionalization Movements

The clergy has experienced a number of pressures and conflicts that have challenged its professional stature over the past 40 years.

Unlike other professions such as law or medicine that function under a single set of standards or requirements for a given geographical area, different religions have varying standards and requirements for their professional leadership. However, three broad trends can be identified across a range of denominations. The first has to do with professionalization steps to enhance the status of the clergy as an occupation. The second involves various external pressures and internal changes that result in deprofessionalization tendencies. Not surprisingly, a third trend involves efforts to reprofessionalize the clergy. These three steps typically are closely related.

Professionalization movements historically have been related to the growth of an educated middle class (Larson 1977). As average educational levels rise in society, a more highly educated laity has tended to erode some of the power that professional religious leaders traditionally have held. Professionalization movements, similarly, have sought to raise educational standards and other requirements, with many denominations adding new criteria for ordination (Prestwood 1972) and some also developing formal certification programs for lay religious leaders. Educational inflation is particularly evident in mainline Protestantism, where the normal education expected for ordination was raised from a Bachelor's degree to a Master's degree around 1970 (Nesbitt 1997). Although Master's degrees remain normative, doctoral degrees are increasingly common, in large part due to the introduction of an applied, Doctor of Ministry degree that now is offered at a range of seminaries (Nesbitt 1997; Perl and Chang 2000). Professionalization trends in evangelical Protestant denominations not only have included increased education expectations, but knowledge of hi-tech media and organizational growth management skills have been integrated into traditional clergy roles. Pastoral care and counseling as well as spiritual direction have become increasingly professionalized roles for clergy and lay professionals, as a result of third-party insurance and the rise of litigation.

Another aspect of growing professionalization has been the development of clergy associations. These have served as powerful networks within Judaism, Islam, Orthodox Christianity, Roman Catholicism, and Protestantism. Although each denomination self-regulates who is ordained, what the criteria are for professional practice, and means of censuring those clergy who transgress professional boundaries, the clergy associations have had a range of additional functions. Some have formed to link clergy within a single denomination, serving as a forum and as a pressure group for various professional practice concerns such as employment and compensation, or to collaborate on common issues in the community or wider society. In Iran, for instance, the radical Islamic clergy association has endorsed candidates as well as impacting society in other ways (Pipes and Clawson 1993). Another model is exemplified by an African Methodist Episcopal ministers group in Chicago that has worked in the community to get more youth into college and to coordinate their congregations as health screening sites (Ammerman 2001). Other clergy associations have been interfaith, emphasizing social or political action, mutual discussion and support between religious and civic leaders on shared concerns, or on interfaith dialogue as a means to achieve deeper understanding of other religious traditions and practices. Yet others have formed around special interests, such as retired clergy, women clergy, Polish American clergy, or recovering alcoholic clergy. Similarly, professional associations have arisen for chaplains and for lay professionals.

Occupational deprofessionalization

A growing egalitarianism among participants in some denominations has directly decreased lay dependence on professional religious leaders (cf. Monahan 1999b). This and other trends have challenged the professional stature of the clergy. Occupational deprofessionalization trends have been traced as far back as the rise of the secular state, which jeopardized both clerical power and financial support (Douglas 1977). Although clergy of state religions have enjoyed higher status than their secular counterparts, additional pressures have eroded even their professional stature

(Stendahl 1985). Douglas (1977) identifies two additional deprofessionalizing effects: a separation of theological and pastoral functions within liberal Protestantism that occurred in the mid-nineteenth century and the relocation of ministerial virtue from traditional occupational role activities to the character of the individual.

Kleinman (1984) further identified a shift in the occupational self-understanding among mainline U.S. Protestant clergy during the 1960s and 1970s that involved a growing trend for clergy to understand their professional role and its authority in a humanistic perspective. In a shift away from a clerically oriented occupational identity of being set apart, as gatekeepers and brokers of the sacred and its tradition, a humanistic orientation refocuses the occupational master role to enhance the development of ministry among all participants, which theologically is grounded in the scriptural notion of the priesthood of all believers. Kleinman (1984) saw this shift as the crux of a growing professional identity crisis and a deprofessionalization trend within the Protestant ministry. Such changes also can be understood in a context of broader societal shifts that include the demand for a more egalitarian and expressivist approach to religion among those coming of age in the 1960s and subsequently (cf. Tipton 1984; Carroll 1992; Flory and Miller 2000). Blohm (2005) has identified a similar shift among the Anglican and Protestant clergy she interviewed. This shift in the master role from specialist to facilitator has raised concerns over what remains distinctive about professional ministry that cannot be done by nonprofessionals (Carroll 1992: 294).

Deprofessionalization also has been a concern within the rabbinate. The rabbis that Blohm (2005) interviewed had spoken of a declining congregational interest in the rabbi making halachic decisions or seeking the rabbi's advice on life decisions. This ultimately has led to a declining desire for learning about the tradition among congregations ranging from Orthodox to Reform Judaism. Consequently, the rabbinical master role of teacher, as well as arbiter of religious law and tradition, has lost authority and prestige. Blohm's (2005) interviewees also spoke of an *enabling* or facilitating role in the rabbinate, helping others to make their own choices rather than the more traditional role of giving advice. Where role boundaries between clergy and laity lose their distinctiveness, there is likely to be competition (Nelson 1985). Such crises have contributed to congregational conflicts over clergy leadership, and resultant clergy stress (Price 2003).

Reprofessionalization movements

(Re)professionalization movements have sought greater control of religious tasks as a means of professional expertise (cf. Larson 1977). Besides rising educational standards and certification programs, over the past several decades an array of new professional tracks have emerged in several Christian denominations that specialize in training laity, either for professionalized religious leadership or ordained ministry. These tracks have developed distinct professional identities along with circumscribed roles and responsibilities. Perhaps the most well known is the permanent diaconate, more recently called the *professional* diaconate, in Roman Catholic, Anglican (Episcopal), and Methodist traditions. All claim it to be an ancient order of early Christianity (Dunigan 1986). However, its resurgence over the past century creates an alternative supply of clerical labor that either takes over functions that otherwise would have been performed by laity or it relieves clergy in the traditional track from having to perform less prestigious tasks such as pastoral calling, routine education and administration, or community service. Other denominations also have developed professionalized ordained tracks, such as the Unitarian Universalist *minister of religious education* and *community minister* (Nesbitt 1997), and clergy ordained or laity licensed to serve a specific congregation in various denominations. Furthermore, many of the newer tracks often involve part-time or nonstipendiary positions (Nesbitt 1997). In the Church of England, distinct tracks have differentiated full-time stipendiary from part-time and nonstipendiary

clergy (Blohm 2005). Seeking to regiment and control religious work (Wortman 1991) in a time of professional identity transitions and deprofessionalization challenges, the proliferation of clergy tracks represents a movement toward heightened clericalism.

Clericalism has been understood as a means to gauge religious authenticity through attaining hierarchical status as a religious leader (Stendahl 1985), and as such it has served as a means to resist deprofessionalization pressures. Concurrently, it facilitates an emphasis on sacramentalism and ritual that both differentiate clergy tracks from one another but also strengthen the role of clergy as distinct from laity. Stendahl (1985) argues that the Church of Sweden's increase in high-church clericalism came as a response to declining church participation and diminished public prestige of its clergy. Similarly, the growth of the U.S. Episcopal permanent diaconate has been associated with a high-church liturgical movement during the 1950s and 1960s (Stewart and West 1991). Clericalism also has been hypothesized as a means to bolster the status and commitment of lay volunteers (cf. Stewart and West 1991) in ways that allow some laity access to clerical orders without severe disruption to their secular work, as well as to provide a more effective means of social control over their commitment to religious work by virtue of ordination vows (Nesbitt 1997). Taken together, clericalism movements can be useful in bolstering not only the public status of religion in a secularizing milieu but also the internal status of those who govern and administer the religious tradition among its remnant faithful.

Clergy Supply and Demand

Liberal Protestant denominations in the U.S. have experienced a slack clergy labor market over the past 50 years, with a greater supply of clergy than available full-time placements (Chang and Bompadre 1999; Nesbitt 1997). This has resulted in more clergy working in denominational agencies and in placements outside their religious organizations such as hospital, prison, or school chaplaincies, or in the secular workforce. Given that the available supply of clergy has been known to relate to denominational changes (Paul 1964, cited in Ranson *et al.* 1977), conditions of oversupply suggest a connection with the growing number of part-time placements in a number of denominations. Tight congregational budgets, standardization of clergy compensation, and diminished denominational support for struggling congregations have forced many congregations into market solutions for professional labor, namely the use of positions that pay a part-time stipend or that are non-stipendiary. Although this historically has been the situation for small, poor congregations, larger and more affluent congregations also have turned to this solution as a means to maintain programming and services. Conditions of clergy oversupply thus result in a pool of potential candidates who either are unable to find full-time placements, are willing to piece together two or more part-time positions, or for other reasons such as having a secular job or being formally retired, are willing to accept part-time work. Concomitantly, those found to disproportionately hold such positions have been women clergy, retired clergy, one or both spouses of a dual clergy couple, and clergy in alternative ordained tracks (cf. Nesbitt 1997; Zikmund *et al.* 1998; Blohm 2005).

Similarly, clergy *shortages* can affect the occupational structure along with the role content of its positions. Concerns over shortages have involved declines in seminary enrollments, greater interest among seminarians in noncongregational placements, and an increased average age of seminarians that shortens the normative occupational life expectancy from a traditional 40-year span for clergy (Price 2003; cf. Steinfels 1989; Nesbitt 1997). Clergy shortages traditionally have been an issue in remote geographic locations and where congregations cannot offer a fulltime salary, but more recently have included other sites with limited options for the spouse of a clergyperson to pursue a career. Solutions to address regional shortages have ranged in Protestant denominations from the deployment of retirees interested in part-time or interim work to the more frequent steps of licensing of lay local pastors, ordaining clergy to serve specific congregations, and the use of clergy in alternative tracks such as the permanent diaconate (Wortman 1991; Nesbitt 1997).

Clergy shortages: the case of the Catholic Church

The effect of clergy shortages on the traditional parish priestly roles in the Roman Catholic Church is undisputable (cf. Verdieck *et al.* 1996). Since Vatican II, shortages of Roman Catholic priests have become acute in North America and Europe. Schoenherr and Young (1993) predicted that from 1966 to 2005 the number of U.S. diocesan priests would have dropped by 40 per cent – a time when the church had been projected to grow by 65 per cent. Although annual resignations of diocesan priests in the decades just prior to Vatican II had been relatively few (e.g. Schoenherr and Greeley 1974), resignations peaked in 1970 (Hoge 1987) and continued at an elevated level through the 1970s (Schoenherr and Sørensen 1982, cited in Verdieck *et al.* 1996). Most of the shortage, however, has been attributed to sharp declines in ordination rates to the priesthood (Schoenherr and Young 1993). Currently, supply dislocations are being addressed through the recruitment and deployment of young men from less prosperous countries to locations where shortages are most acute, the ordination of married men to the permanent diaconate, and the use of trained lay leadership. Local recruitment efforts to the priesthood have been more problematic. For instance, a study by Hoge *et al.* (2001) found that only about 15 per cent of young adult American Catholics had received encouragement to consider the priesthood or religious orders as a career vocation, and much of this came from their family rather than Church officials. In another study, U.S. Catholic bishops have been found to engage in recruitment for the priesthood, with those having higher results offering a traditional presentation of the priesthood and its leadership role, as well as the unique contribution that it makes

(Yuengert 2001), which itself may contribute to a growing conservatism among recently ordained priests.

Wallace (1992) contends that the ordained permanent diaconate open to married men was revived as an alternative labor supply to help meet parish pastoral needs and to alleviate pressure either for women's ordination or dependence on female lay pastoral leadership. Her research identified some dioceses that chose not to ordain permanent deacons so that parish leadership roles would remain available to laity, especially women. By 1998, about 4 per cent of American Catholic parishes were led by women (Konieczny and Chaves 2000; cf. Wallace 1992). Wallace's (1992) study concludes that the supply dilemma combined with the exclusion of women from ordination may have set off a transformation of the traditional priestly role, and a shift toward democratic decision-making among the laity that challenges traditional hierarchical understandings of religious authority. Regardless of whether solutions to the priest shortage will extend to lifting the celibacy mandate on the priesthood or opening it to women, the Catholic Church's leadership structure is undergoing significant change as it seeks to respond to the supply dilemma.

Augmenting the declining number of clergy, the Catholic Church has experienced a yet greater decline in men and women who profess and remain in religious orders (Stark and Finke 2000). In the U.S., for instance, the number of nuns dropped nearly 50 per cent between 1965 and 1994 (cf. Wittberg 1994; Kelly 1998), the result not only of women leaving, but a yet more precipitous fall in the number of women seeking to enter orders (Ebaugh 1993; Finke 1997). Similar trends also have been evident in Canada, Western Europe, and other industrialized nations (Ebaugh *et al.* 1996; Stark and Finke 2000). For instance, the ratio of nuns to Catholics in countries such as Australia, South Africa, and South Korea declined by 63 to 86 per cent between 1960 and 1990 (Ebaugh *et al.* 1996).

Various explanations for the patterns of decline have ranged from the contraction of Catholic schools and colleges, many of which were staffed and run by women's religious orders, to economic growth in societies that have opened a wider array of secular opportunities for women (Ebaugh *et al.* 1996). Others have pointed to changes set forth by Vatican II that gave more religious roles to the laity, as well as removed both the exclusive benefits and boundary markers that had provided those in religious orders with a distinctive identity and status (cf. Ebaugh 1993; Wittberg 1994; Finke 1997). Many of the Vatican II changes focused on integrating nuns as religious professionals into the secular world, where they lived in secular neighborhoods, dressed in secular attire, and either held church jobs that were actively involved in the secular community or worked in secular institutions altogether. Consequently, less emphasis was placed on the religious community itself as a source of identity, cohesion, or distinctive rewards for those who entered or remained.

Religious orders that have been more traditional in their practices, and make strong demands, have been more successful in recruiting new members (Finke 1997). Such orders have offered a distinctive religious communal lifestyle that differs sharply from the secular world. They also have returned to more traditional symbols such as wearing the habit, putting a greater emphasis on contemplative prayer, and supporting more traditional Church doctrine and hierarchy (Wittberg 1996; Finke 1997). Ebaugh *et al.* (1996) also found a corresponding growth in the ratio of nuns to Catholics in those countries where industrialization has lagged, such as Guatemala. Additionally, some religious orders have grown by opening up lay associate programs for women who are married or otherwise committed to life in the secular world (Ebaugh 1993).

Clergy Sexual Misconduct and Abuse

Religious leaders who are personally involved with a congregation or religious community can become deeply enmeshed in the lives of participants. While their power can be utilized to inspire others or give pastoral support, which can have strong therapeutic value, occasionally power can be used in a manner that becomes coercive, harmful, or abusive. Predictions of priest shortages had not factored into their equation the additional effects of hundreds of Roman Catholic priests removed from parishes in some dioceses as a result of sexual misconduct accusations, settlements and convictions. Referred to as the 'Catholic Watergate' (Yamane 2003), the scandal among Catholic priests has been considered to be the most daunting crisis in the history of the Church (Wiegel 2002, cited in Yamane 2003). Although the abuse by Catholic priests has resulted in steps to put tighter controls on clergy and minimize the prospect of future occurrences (Stammer 2003), concern has been raised over the extent to which the scandals will affect clergy-laity relationships in the longer term, as well as the overall future of the church.

Although Roman Catholic priests have had the most visibility by virtue of the number of cases, sexual abuse has been an issue across a range of religious organizations and traditions. Abuses of power among some gurus in the Hare Krishna movement not only included cases of sexual misconduct but also a range of illegal acts involving drugs, weapons, and death of a dissident follower (Rochford 1998: 104–6). More common has been sexual involvement with adult members of the congregation and the abusive molestation of children. In many denominations today, clergy and lay professionals undergo rigorous background checks and training to minimize the likelihood of such abuses of power. Arguably, the public downfall of Pentecostal televangelists Jimmy Swaggart and Jim Bakker during the late 1980s (Poloma 1989) marked the opening of an era where thousands of cases of sexual misconduct and abuse would not only become public, but many cases would be addressed outside the religious organization, in secular courts, resulting in convictions and settlements. This has resulted in religious professionals increasingly being subject to secular laws governing civil and human rights, with ensuing limitations on occupational and organizational separation from secular oversight.

CONCLUSION: OCCUPATIONAL AND ORGANIZATIONAL TRANSFORMATIONS

The primary roles and responsibilities of religious leaders have varied widely according to religious tradition, although they share a similar form of authority grounded in a formal recognition of their knowledge, expertise, and faithfulness to the religious organization or group they serve. Across sometimes very diverse religious traditions, as migrating groups begin adopting congregational formats, there is a growing normativization of traditional leadership roles and functions (e.g. Abusharaf 1998). Although substantial research has been conducted on the occupation and careers of Protestant and Roman Catholic clergy, and to some extent the Jewish Rabbinate, comparative studies have yet to be done on the leadership of Buddhist, Muslim, and other religious communities as they shift to a congregational form in the wake of migration to a publicly diverse religious environment.

Women have demonstrated strong interest, influence and expertise as religious professionals. Their modeling of nontraditional roles for women, such as ordained clergy, has been transformative for younger women and girls (Stevens 1989; Marder 1991). They also have opened transformative interests among men in reshaping traditional leadership practices to be more inclusive of family commitments and less hierarchical in emphasis (Marder 1991; Nesbitt 2001). As more female religious leaders participate in interfaith settings with others who do not ordain women or grant women leadership opportunities, a role modeling spillover is possible as a contributing factor to social change. In 1998, the presence of 11 female bishops had been anticipated to create a stormy rift at the worldwide Anglican Communion's Lambeth Conference of Bishops, but it turned out to be a nonissue (Nesbitt 2001). Yet, demographic controversies over access to religious leadership often involve an array of other cultural, ideological, and organizational issues, whether the concerns are grounded in race, gender, or sexual orientation. Further research, for instance, needs to be done on gay and lesbian clergy along with the resistances they face, in a manner similar to women's religious leadership, to tease out related linkages and issues as well as those that involve other dynamics and concerns.

The clergy, unlike other professions, is embedded in the context and issues of its host religious organization, however. Their fate rides with that of the gods whom they and their organizations serve (Weber 1993). While there have been numerous lamentations over shifting demographics, more research needs to be done on the extent to which these changes mirror shifts in the interests and needs of the communities they serve. Religious profession-als in most denominations are in the midst of an occupational transformation at the same time that their organizations are undergoing similarly important shifts. As in previous eras, some will address such change by leading emergent sects and new religious movements, while others integrate change with occupa-tional and organizational tradition. The only constant for religious professionals is the inevitable tension between transformation and reform.

REFERENCES

Abusharaf, Rogalia Mustafa 1998. 'Structural Adaptations in an Immigrant Muslim Congregation in New York.' In *Gatherings in Diaspora: Religious Communities and the New Immigration*, R. Stephen Warner and Judith G. Wittner (eds), 236–61. Philadelphia: Temple University Press.

Aleshire, Daniel 2003. 'Sacred Cows and Sacred Callings: The Changing Work of Theological Education.' Paper presented at the Chief Academic Officers Society 2003 Conference: Conversation, Consultation, Cultivation and Care. Association of Theological Schools *http://www.ats.edu/leadership_education/PapersAleshire.asp*.

Aleshire, Daniel 2005. 'Theological Education at Mid-Decade: What the Numbers are Telling Us.' Report. Association of Theological Schools, March 31 (www.ats.edu).

Ammerman, Nancy Tatom 1990. *Baptist Battles: Social Change and Religious Conflict in the Southern Baptist Convention*. New Brunswick: Rutgers University Press.

Ammerman, Nancy Tatom 2001. 'Doing Good in American Communities: Congregations and Service Organizations Working Together.' A research report from the 'Organizing Religious Work Project.' Hartford, CT: Hartford Institute for Religion Research *http://hdl.handle.net/ 2144/19*.

Baer, Hans A. 1994. 'The Limited Empowerment of Women in Black Spiritual Churches: An Alternative Vehicle to Religious Leadership.' In *Gender and Religion*, W. H. Swatos Jr. (ed.), 75–92. New Brunswick, NJ: Transaction.

Barfoot, Charles and Gerald T. Sheppard 1980. 'Prophetic vs. Priestly Religion: The Changing Role of Women Clergy in Classical Pentecostal Churches.' *Review of Religious Research* 22 (1): 2–16.

Blackmon, K. and A. Hart 1990. 'Personal Growth for Clergy.' In *Clergy Assessment and Career Development*, R. Hunt, J. Hinkle, and H. Maloney (eds), 36–42. Nashville, TN: Abingdon Press.

Blanton, Priscilla W. and M. Lane Morris 1999. 'Work-Related Predictors of Physical Symptomatology and Emotional Well-Being Among Clergy and Spouses.' *Review of Religious Research* 40 (4) (June): 331–48.

Blizzard, Samuel 1985 [1956]. *The Protestant Minister: A Behavioral Science Interpretation*. Society for the Scientific Study of Religion Monograph Series, No. 5. Storrs, CT: Society for the Scientific Study of Religion.

Blohm, Uta 2005. *Religious Traditions and Personal Stories: Women Working as Priests, Ministers and Rabbis*. Frankfurt: Peter Lang.

Børresen, K. E. 1993. 'Women's Ordination: Tradition and Inculturation.' *Theology Digest* 40 (1): 15–19.

Brereton, Virginia Lieson and Christa Ressmeyer Klein 1979. 'American Women in Ministry: A History of Protestant Beginning Points.' In *Women of Spirit: Female Leadership in the Jewish and Christian Traditions*. Rosemary Ruether and Eleanor McLaughlin (eds), 302–32. New York: Simon and Schuster.

Brunette-Hill, Sandi and Roger Finke 1999. 'A Time for Every Purpose: Updating and Extending Blizzard's Survey on Clergy Time Allocation' *Review of Religious Research* 41 (Fall): 47–63.

Bryman, Alan 1996. 'The Value of Re-studies in Sociology: The Case of Clergy and Ministers, 1971 to 1985.' In *Psychological Perspectives on Christian Ministry*, Leslie J. Francis and Susan H. Jones (eds), 42–64. Herefordshire: Gracewing.

Carmody, Denise L. 1979. *Women and World Religions.* Nashville: Abingdon Press.

Carroll, Jackson W. 1991. *As One With Authority: Reflective Leadership in Ministry.* Louisville, KY: Westminster/John Knox Press.

Carroll, Jackson W. 1992. 'Toward 2000: Some Futures for Religious Leadership.' *Review of Religious Research.* 33: 289–306.

Carroll, Jackson W., Adair T. Lummis and Barbara Hargrove 1983. *Women of the Cloth: A New Opportunity for the Churches.* San Francisco: Harper & Row.

Chang, Patricia M. Y. and Viviana Bompadre 1999. 'Crowded Pulpits: Observations and Explanations of the Clergy Over Supply in the Protestant Churches, 1950–1993.' *Journal for the Scientific Study of Religion* 38 (3) (September): 398–410.

Chapman, Audrey R. 1991. *Faith, Power, and Politics: Political Ministry in Mainline Churches.* New York: Pilgrim Press.

Chaves, Mark 1991. 'Segmentation in a Religious Labor Market.' *Sociological Analysis* 52 (2) (Summer): 143–58.

Chaves, Mark 1997. *Ordaining Women: Culture and Conflict in Religious Organizations.* Cambridge: Harvard University Press.

Christopherson, Richard W. 1994. 'Calling and Career in Christian Ministry.' *Review of Religious Research* 35 (3) (March): 219–37.

Coate, M. A. 1989. *Clergy Stress: The Hidden Conflicts of Ministry.* London: SPCK.

Darling, Pamela W. 1994. *New Wine: The Story of Women Transforming Leadership and Power in the Episcopal Church.* Cambridge: Cowley.

Darling, Pamela (ed.) 2003. 'Reaching Toward Wholeness II: Highlights of the 21st Century Survey.' New York: Executive Council, Committee on the Status of Women, Episcopal Church U.S.A.

DeLuca, J. 1980. 'The Holy Crossfire: Diagnosis of a Pastor's Position.' *Pastoral Psychology* 28: 233–42.

Demerath, N. J. III and Phillip E. Hammond 1969. *Religion in Social Context: Tradition and Transition.* New York: Random House.

Donovan, Mary S. 1988. *Women Priests in the Episcopal Church: The Experience of the First Decade.* Cincinnati: Forward Movement.

Douglas, Ann 1977. *The Feminization of American Culture.* New York: Alfred A. Knopf.

Dudley, Roger L. and Des Cummings, Jr. 1996. 'Factors Related to Pastoral Morale in the Seventh Day Adventist Church.' In *Psychological Perspectives on Christian Ministry,* Leslie J. Francis and Susan H. Jones (eds), 156–64. Herefordshire: Gracewing.

Dunigan, Francis J. 1986. 'Perception by the Laity of the Restored Permanent Diaconate, Archdiocese of Boston: An Attitude Measurement and Analysis.' Ph.D. diss. Catholic University of America.

Eames, Robin 2004. *The Windsor Report 2004.* London: The Lambeth Commission on Communion, Anglican Communion.

Ebaugh, Helen Rose 1993. *Women in the Vanishing Cloister: Organizational Decline in Catholic Religious Orders in the United States.* New Brunswick, NJ: Rutgers University Press.

Ebaugh, Helen Rose, Jon Lorence and Janet Saltzman Chafetz 1996. 'The Growth and Decline of the Population of Catholic Nuns Cross-Nationally, 1960–1990: A Case of Secularization as Social Structural Change.' *Journal for the Scientific Study of Religion.* 35: 171–83.

Eklund, Elaine Howard 2006. 'Organizational Culture and Women's Leadership: A Study of Six Catholic Parishes.' *Sociology of Religion* 67 (1) (Spring): 81–98.

Finke, Roger 1997. 'An Orderly Return to Tradition: Explaining the Recruitment of Members into Catholic Religious Orders.' *Journal for the Scientific Study of Religion* 36 (2) (June): 218–30.

Finke, Roger and Kevin D. Dougherty 2002. 'The Effects of Professional Training: The Social and Religious Capital Acquired in Seminaries.' *Journal for the Scientific Study of Religion* 41 (1) (March): 103–20.

Finlay, Barbara 1996. 'Do Men and Women Have Different Goals for Ministry? Evidence from Seminarians.' *Sociology of Religion* 57 (3) (Fall): 311–18.

Fitzpatrick, Ruth M. 1993. 'Is There a Valid Basis for a Male Priesthood?' *The Denver Post* 15 August, 1D, 5D.

Flory, Richard W. and Donald E. Miller (eds) 2000. *GenX Religion.* New York: Routledge.

Francis, Leslie J. and Raymond Rodger 1996. 'The Influence of Personality on Clergy Role Prioritization, Role Influences, Conflict and Dissatisfaction with Ministry.' In *Psychological Perspectives on Christian Ministry,* Leslie J. Francis and Susan H. Jones (eds), 65–81. Herefordshire: Gracewing.

Franklin, Robert Michael 1991. 'Clergy and Politics: The Black Experience.' In *Clergy Ethics in a Changing Society: Mapping the Terrain,* James P. Wind *et al.* (eds), 273–94 Louisville, KY: Westminster/John Knox Press.

Fried, Stephen 2002. The New Rabbi. New York: Bantam Books.

Furlong, Monica 2000. *Church of England: The State It's In*. London: Hodder & Stoughton.

Gallup, George J. and D. M. Lindsay 1999. *Surveying the Religious Landscape: Trends in U.S. Religious Beliefs*. Harrisburg: Morehouse Publishing.

Gibson, Elsie 1970. *When the Minister is a Woman*. New York: Holt, Rinehart, and Winston.

Gilbride, Timothy J., Merle L. Griffith and C. David Lundquist 1990. *The Survey of United Methodist Opinion*. Dayton: United Methodist Church, General Council on Ministries, The Office of Research.

Gilkes, Cheryl T. 1989. 'Mother to the Motherless, Father to the Fatherless: Power, Gender, and Community in an Afrocentric Biblical Tradition.' *Semeia*. 47: 57–85.

Goldman, Ari 1990. 'Black Women's Bumpy Path to Church Leadership.' *The New York Times*, 29 July, 1, 28.

Goodwin, Janet L. and Mervin Y. T. Chen 1996. 'From Pastor to Pensioner: A Study of Retired Canadian Protestant Clergy from the Continuity Perspective.' In *Psychological Perspectives on Christian Ministry*, Leslie J. Francis and Susan H. Jones (eds), 206–13. Herefordshire: Gracewing.

Goonatilake, Hema 1997. 'Buddhist Nuns: Protests, Struggle, and the Reinterpretation of Orthodoxy in Sri Lanka.' In *Mixed Blessings: Gender and Religious Fundamentalism Cross Culturally*, Judy Brink and Joan Mencher (eds), 25–39. New York: Routledge.

Graham, William A. and A. K. Reinhart 1989. 'Ulamā.' In *The Perennial Dictionary of World Religions*, Keith Crim (ed.). 772–3. San Francisco: Harper SanFrancisco.

Greenberg, Blu 1984. 'Will There be Orthodox Women Rabbis?' *Judaism* 33: 23–34.

Guttmann, Alexander 1982. 'The Woman Rabbi.' *Journal of Reform Judaism* 29, 3: 21–5.

Hansson, Per 1993. 'Female Ministers in the Church of Sweden. Resistance and Progress.' Paper presented at the Annual Meeting of the Association for the Sociology of Religion. Miami, FL.

Harris, James H. 1987. *Black Ministers and Laity in the Urban Church: An Analysis of Political and Social Expectations*. Lanham, MD: University Press of America.

Heald, G. and R. Rhodes 1986. *Gallup Survey of Church of England Clergymen with Particular Reference to Comparative Differences Between Urban Priority Areas and Elsewhere*. London: General Synod of the Church of England.

Hegland, Mary Elaine 1997. 'A Mixed Blessing: The *Majales* – Shi'a Women's Rituals of Mourning in Northwest Pakistan.' In *Mixed Blessings: Gender and Religious Fundamentalism Cross Culturally*, Judy Brink and Joan Mencher (eds), 179–96. New York and London: Routledge.

Hewitt, Emily C. and Suzanne R. Hiatt 1973. *Women Priests: Yes or No?* New York: Seabury Press.

Hitt, Mary Jane 2002. 'Shape the Debate by the Upside-down Gospel.' In *Women's Path into Ministry: Six Major Studies*, Edward C. Lehman, Jr., 42–3. Pulpit & Pew Research Report, No. 1. Durham, NC: Duke Divinity School.

Hoge, Dean R. 1987. *The Future of Catholic Leadership: Responses to the Priest Shortage*. Kansas City, MO: Sheed and Ward.

Hoge, Dean R., William D. Dinges, Mary Johnson, D. N. D. de N., Juan L. Gonzales, Jr. 2001. *Young Adult Catholics: Religion in the Culture of Choice*. Notre Dame, IN: University of Notre Dame Press.

Ice, Martha L. 1987. *Clergy Women and Their Worldviews: Calling for a New Age*. New York: Praeger.

Ide, Arthur Frederick 1986. *God's Girls: Ordination of Women in the Early Christian & Gnostic Churches*. Garland, TX: Tangelwüld.

Jackson, Susan E. and Randall S. Schuler 1985. 'A Meta-analysis and Conceptual Critique of Research on Role Ambiguity and Role Conflict in Work Settings.' *Organizational Behavior and Human Development Processes* 36: 16–78.

Jacobs, Louis 1995. *The Jewish Religion: A Companion*. Oxford and New York: Oxford University Press.

Johnson, Andrea 2002. 'Ordinations Challenge Juridical Norm of Male Church Leadership.' *NewWomen, NewChurch*, Fall, p. 4.

Kammerer, Charlene P. 2002. 'View from the First Wave.' In *Women's Path into Ministry: Six Major Studies*, Edward C. Lehman, Jr., 44–5. Pulpit & Pew Research Report, No. 1. Durham, NC: Duke Divinity School.

Keller, Rosemary Skinner 1984. 'Women and the Nature of Ministry in the United Methodist Tradition.' *Methodist History* 22: 99–114.

Kelly, James R. 1998. 'Roman Catholicism.' In *Encyclopedia of Religion and Society*, William H. Swatos, Jr. (ed.), 432–9. Walnut Creek, CA: Alta Mira.

Kirk, Kenneth E. 1957. *Beauty and Bands and Other Papers*. Greenwich: Seabury Press.

Kleinman, Sheryl 1984. *Equals Before God: Seminarians as Humanistic Professionals*. Chicago: University of Chicago Press.

Konieczny, Mary Ellen and Mark Chaves 2000. 'Resources, Race, and Female-Headed Congregations in the United States.' *Journal for the Scientific Study of Religion* 39 (3) (September): 261–71.

Kuhne, Gary William and Joe F. Donaldson 1995. 'Balancing Ministry and Management: An Exploratory Study of Pastoral Work Activities.' *Review of Religious Research* 37 (2) (December): 147–63.

Larson, Magali S. 1977. *The Rise of Professionalism: A Sociological Analysis.* Berkeley: University of California Press.

Lattin, Don 2003. 'First Woman to Head Rabbi Group.' *San Francisco Chronicle.* March 21, p. A4.

Lee, Yvonne Young-ja 1999. 'Religion, Culture of *Han* and *Hanpuri*, and Korean *Minjung* Women: An Interdisciplinary Post-colonial Religio-cultural Analysis of the Indigenous Encounter with the Colonial Religions in Korea.' Ph.D. Dissertation, University of Denver and Iliff School of Theology.

Lehman, Edward C., Jr. 1980. 'Placement of Men and Women in the Ministry.' *Review of Religious Research* 22 (1): 18–40.

Lehman, Edward C., Jr. 1985. *Women Clergy: Breaking Through Gender Barriers.* New Brunswick: Transaction Books.

Lehman, Edward C., Jr. 1987a. 'Sexism, Organizational Maintenance, and Localism: A Research Note.' *Sociological Analysis* 48 (3): 274–82.

Lehman, Edward C., Jr. 1987b. *Women Clergy in England: Sexism, Modern Consciousness, and Church Viability.* Lewiston: Edwin Mellen Press.

Lehman, Edward C., Jr. 1990. 'Status Differences Between Types of Ministry: Measurement and Effect.' In *Research in the Social Scientific Study of Religion*, M. L. Lynn and D. O. Moberg (eds), 95–116. Greenwich: JAI Press.

Lehman, Edward C., Jr. 1993. *Gender and Work: The Case of the Clergy.* Albany: State University of New York Press.

Lehman, Edward C., Jr. 1994. *Women in Ministry: Receptivity and Resistance.* Melbourne: The Joint Board of Christian Education.

Lehman, Edward C., Jr. 2002. *Women's Path into Ministry: Six Major Studies.* Pulpit & Pew Research Report, No. 1. Durham, NC: Duke Divinity School.

Lincoln, C. Eric and Lawrence H. Mamiya 1990. *The Black Church in the African American Experience.* Durham and London: Duke University Press.

Malony, H. Newton and Richard A. Hunt 1991. *The Psychology of Clergy.* Harrisburg: Morehouse.

McDuff, Elaine M. 2001. 'The Gender Paradox in Work Satisfaction and the Protestant Clergy.' *Sociology of Religion* 62 (1) (Spring): 1–21.

Mace, D. and V. Mace 1981. 'What's Happening to Clergy Marriages?' In *The Interface of Marriage and the Ministry*, M. Herin (ed.), 37–50. Lake Janaluska, NC: International Growth Center.

Marder, Janet 1991. 'How Women are Changing the Rabbinate.' *Reform Judaism* 19 (4): 4–8, 41.

Marder, Janet 1996. 'Are Women Changing the Rabbinate? A Reform Perspective.' In *Religious Institutions and Women's Leadership: New Roles Inside the Mainstream*, Catherine Wessinger (ed.), 271–90. Columbia: University of South Carolina Press.

May, Melanie A. 1998. 'A Survey of Faith and Order Discussions on the Ordination of Women: A Retrospective Introduction to Future Work.' Paper presented at the Faith and Order Discussions on the Ordination of Women, World Council of Churches. Cambridge, NY (www.wcc-coe.org/wcc/who/vilemov-08-e.html).

McRoberts, Omar M. 1999. 'Understanding the "New" Black Pentecostal Activism: Lessons from Ecumenical Urban Ministries in Boston.' *Sociology of Religion*, 60 (1) (Spring): 47–70.

McRoberts, Omar M. 2003. 'Worldly or Otherworldly? 'Activism' in an Urban Religious District.' In *Handbook of the Sociology of Religion*, Michele Dillon (ed.) 412–22. Cambridge and New York: Cambridge University Press.

Monahan, Suzanne C. 1999a. 'Role Ambiguity among Protestant Clergy: Consequences of the Activated Laity.' *Review of Religious Research* 41 (Fall): 71–94.

Monahan, Suzanne C. 1999b. 'Who Controls Church Work? Organizational Effects on Jurisdictional Boundaries and Disputes in Churches.' *Journal for the Scientific Study of Religion* 38 (3) (September): 370–85.

Morris, Aldon 1996. 'The Black Church in the Civil Rights Movement: the SCLC as the Decentralized, Radical Arm of the Black Church.' In *Disruptive Religion: The Force of Faith in Social Movement Activism*, Christian Smith (ed.), 29–46. New York and London: Routledge.

Mueller, Charles W. and Elaine McDuff 2004. 'Clergy-Congregation Mismatches and Clergy Job Satisfaction.' *Journal for the Scientific Study of Religion* 43 (2) (June): 261–73.

Nason-Clark, Nancy 1987. 'Are Women Changing the Image of Ministry? A Comparison of British and American Realities.' *Review of Religious Research* 28 (4): 330–40.

Nasr, Seyyed Hossein 1985. *Ideals and Realities of Islam.* London: George Allen & Unwin.

Nelson, Hart 1985. 'Introduction. Ministers and their Milieu: Socialization, Clergy Role, and Community.' In *The Protestant Parish Minister: A Behavioral Science Interpretation,* Samuel W. Blizzard, 1–18. Storrs, CT: Society for the Scientific Study of Religion.

Nesbitt, Paula D. 1993. 'Dual Ordination Tracks: Differential Benefits and Costs for Men and Women Clergy.' *Sociology of Religion* 54: 13–30.

Nesbitt, Paula D. 1995. 'First and Second-career Clergy: Influences of Age and Gender on the Career-stage Paradigm.' *Journal for the Scientific Study of Religion* 34 (2) (June): 152–71.

Nesbitt, Paula D. 1997. *Feminization of the Clergy in America: Occupational and Organizational Perspectives.* New York: Oxford University Press.

Nesbitt, Paula D. 2001. 'The Future of Religious Pluralism and Social Policy: Reflections from Lambeth and Beyond.' In *Religion and Social Policy,* Paula D. Nesbitt (ed.) 244–61. Lanham, MD: Alta Mira.

Pattillo-McCoy, Mary 1998. 'Church Culture as a Strategy of Action in the Black Community.' *American Sociological Review* 63 (6): (December): 767–84.

Paul, L. 1964. *The Deployment and Payment of the Clergy.* London: Church Information Office.

Perl, Paul and Patricia M. Y. Chang 2000. 'Credentialism Across Creeds: Clergy Education and Stratification in Protestant Denominations.' *Journal for the Scientific Study of Religion* 39 (2) (June): 170–88.

Piper, Joyce 1995. 'Work Stress among Lutheran Clergy Women in the USA and Norway.' Paper presented at the Joint Annual Meeting of the Society for the Scientific Study of Religion and the Religious Research Association, St. Louis, MO.

Pipes, Daniel and Patrick Clawson 1993. 'Ambitious Iran, Troubled Neighbors.' *Foreign Affairs. America and the World* 72 (1): 124–41.

Poloma, Margaret M. 1989. *The Assemblies of God at the Crossroads.* Knoxville: University of Tennessee Press.

Poloma, Margaret M. 1997. 'The "Toronto Blessings."' Charisma, Institutionalization, and Revival.' *Journal for the Scientific Study of Religion,* 36 (2): 257–71.

Pomerleau, Dolly 1992. *Journey of Hope: A Prophetic Encounter in Czechoslovakia.* Mt. Ranier, MD: Quixote Center.

Poorman, Mark L. 2004. 'A Sign of Hope: Young, Catholic & Curious.' *Commonweal* 131, 20 (November 19): 23 (2).

Preston, Ronald 1986. 'Vocation.' In *The Westminster Dictionary of Christian Ethics,* James F. Childress and John Macquarrie (eds), 650–1. Philadelphia: The Westminster Press.

Prestwood, C. 1972. *The New Breed of Clergy.* Grand Rapids: William B. Eerdmans.

Price, Matthew J. 2003. 'The State of the Clergy.' Research report. New York: Church Pension Group.

Purdum, Stan 1991. 'A Response. What is Success?' *Circuit Rider.* March, 7–8.

Purvis, Sally B. 1995. *The Stained Glass Ceiling: Churches and their Women Pastors.* Louisville, KY: Westminster/John Knox Press.

Putnam, Robert B. 2000. *Bowling Alone: The Collapse and Revival of American Community.* New York: Simon and Schuster.

Ranson, S., A. Bryman and B. Hinings 1977. *Clergy, Ministers and Priests.* London: Routledge & Kegan Paul.

Reskin, Barbara F. and Patricia A. Roos. 1990. *Job Queues, Gender Queues: Explaining Women's Inroads into Male Occupations.* Philadelphia: Temple University Press.

Robbins, Mandy 1998. 'A Different Voice: A Different View.' *Review of Religious Research* 40 (1) (September): 75–80.

Rochford, E. Burke, Jr. 1998. 'Reactions of Hare Krishna Devotees to Scandals of Leaders' Misconduct.' In *Wolves within the Fold: Religious Leadership and Abuses of Power,* Anson Shupe (ed.), 101–17. New Brunswick, NJ: Rutgers University Press.

Ruether, Rosemary Radford 1986. *Women-Church: Theology and Practice.* San Francisco: Harper & Row.

Schaller, Lyle E. 1987. *It's a Different World! The Challenge for Today's Pastor.* Nashville: Abingdon Press.

Schoenherr, Richard A. and Andrew M. Greeley 1974. 'Role Commitment Processes and the American Catholic Priesthood.' *American Sociological Review* 39: 407–25.

Schoenherr, Richard A. and Aage Sørensen 1982. 'Social Change in Religious Organizations: Consequences of Clergy Decline in the U.S. Catholic Church.' *Sociological Analysis* 43: 23–52.

Schoenherr, Richard A. and Lawrence A. Young 1993. *Full Pews and Empty Altars: Demographics of the Priest Shortage in United States Dioceses.* Madison: University of Wisconsin Press.

Smith, Page 1970. *Daughters of the Promised Land: Women in American History*. Boston: Little, Brown and Co.

Stammer, Larry B. 2003. 'Sex-abuse Panel Head Bashes the Bishops.' [*Los Angeles Times*] *San Francisco Chronicle*. June 17, A14.

Stanley, Susie C. 1996. 'The Promise Fulfilled: Women's Ministries in the Wesleyan/Holiness Movement.' In *Religious Institutions and Women's Leadership: New Roles Inside the Mainstream*, Catherine Wessinger (ed.), 139–57. Columbia: University of South Carolina Press.

Stark, Rodney and Roger Finke 2000. 'Catholic Religious Vocations: Decline and Revival.' *Review of Religious Research* 42 (2) (December): 125–45.

Steinfels, Peter 1989. 'Shortage of Qualified New Clergy Causing Alarm for U.S. Religions.' *The Sunday New York Times* 9 July, 1, 22.

Stendahl, Brita 1985. *The Force of Tradition*. Philadelphia: Fortress Press.

Stevens, Lesley 1989. 'Different Voice/Different Voices: Anglican Women in Ministry.' *Review of Religious Research* 30 (3): 262–75.

Stevens, Lesley 1996. 'Different Voice, Different Voices: Anglican Women in Ministry.' In *Psychological Perspectives on Christian Ministry*, Leslie J. Francis and Susan H. Jones (eds), 280–94. Herefordshire: Gracewing.

Stewart, Alexander D. and Margaret S. West 1991. 'The Diaconate: A Call to Serve.' Unpublished paper. New York: The Church Pension Fund.

Stocks, Janet 1997. 'Voices from the Margins: The Evangelical Feminist Negotiation in the Public Debate of a Small Denomination in the United States.' In *Mixed Blessings: Gender and Religious Fundamentalism Cross Culturally*, Judy Brink and Joan Mencher (eds), 59–71. New York and London: Routledge.

Thorne, Helen 2000. *Journey to Priesthood: An In-Depth Study of the First Women Priests in the Church of England*. Ph.D. Dissertation. CCSRG, Department of Theology and Religious Studies, University of Bristol.

Tidball, Dianne 1989. 'Walking a Tightrope – Women Training for Baptist Ministry.' Unpublished M.A. Thesis. London.

Tipton, Steven M. 1984 [1982]. *Getting Saved from the Sixties*. Berkeley: University of California Press.

Tucker, Cynthia G. 1990. *Prophetic Sisterhood: Liberal Women Ministers of the Frontier, 1880–1930*. Boston: Beacon Press.

Verdieck, Mary Jeanne, Joseph J. Shields and Dean R. Hoge 1996. 'Role Commitment Processes Revisited: American Catholic Priests

1970 and 1985.' In *Psychological Perspectives on Christian Ministry*, Leslie J. Francis and Susan H. Jones (eds), 227–42. Herefordshire: Gracewing.

Waldron, Candace 1986. *Women and Resources Audit*. Boston: Episcopal Diocese of Massachusetts.

Wallace, Ruth 1992. *They Call Her Pastor: A New Role for Catholic Women*. Albany: State University of New York Press.

Wallace, Ruth 1994. 'The Social Construction of a New Leadership Role: Catholic Women Pastors.' In *Gender and Religion*, William H. Swatos, Jr. (ed.) 45–52. New Brunswick, NJ: Transaction.

Walter, T. and Grace Davie 1998. 'The Religiosity of Women in the Modern West.' *British Journal of Sociology* 49: 640–60.

Weber, Max 1958. *The Protestant Ethic and the Spirit of Capitalism*. Translated by Talcott Parsons. New York: Charles Scribner's Sons.

Weber, Max 1978 [1925]. *Economy and Society: An Outline of Interpretive Sociology*. Guenther Roth and Claus Wittich (eds). Berkeley: University of California Press.

Weber, Max 1993 [1922]. *The Sociology of Religion*. Translated by Ephraim Fishoff. Boston: Beacon Press.

Wellman, James K., Jr. 1999. 'Introduction: The Debate over Homosexual Ordination: Subcultural Identity Theory in American Religious Organizations.' *Review of Religious Research* 41 (December): 184–206.

Wessinger, Catherine (ed.) 1993. *Women's Leadership in Marginal Religions: Explorations Outside the Mainstream*. Urbana: University of Illinois Press.

White, Mel 1994. *Stranger at the Gate: To Be Gay and Christian in America*. New York: Simon & Schuster.

Wiegel, George 2002. *The Courage to be Catholic: Crisis, Reform, and the Future of the Church*. New York: Basic Books.

Wittberg, Patricia 1994. *The Rise and Fall of Catholic Religious Orders: A Social Movement Perspective*. Albany: State University of New York Press.

Wittberg, Patricia 1996. '"Real" Religious Communities.' In *The Issue of Authenticity in the Study of Religions*, Lewis Carter (ed.) 149–74. JAI Press.

Wortman, Julie A. 1991. 'Dioceses Redefining Roles of Deacons, Priests.' *Episcopal Life*. May, pp. 1, 9.

Wuthnow, Robert 1994. *God and Mammon in America*. New York: Free Press.

Yamane, David 2003. 'Bishops' Political Influence and the Catholic Watergate.' *Sociology of Religion Section Newsletter* 9 (3) (Spring): 1, 4.

Yuengert, Andrew 2001. 'Do Bishops Matter? A Cross-Sectional Study of Ordinations to the US Catholic Diocesan Priesthood.' *Review of Religious Research* 42 (3) (March): 294–312.

Zikmund, Barbara Brown, Adair T. Lummis and Patricia Mei Yin Chang 1998. *Clergy Women: An Uphill Calling.* Louisville: Westminster John Knox Press.

15

Orders and Schisms on the Sacred Periphery

PATRICIA WITTBERG

The role of religion in societies, and in the lives of individuals, has been a central preoccupation of sociologists since the founding of the discipline. According to Durkheim and his successors, religious participation creates and enhances social integration; according to Marx, religion is a pernicious invention of the elite to keep the masses in docile subjugation. For theorists such as Max Weber and J. Milton Yinger, religion provides an essential theodicy to explain why bad things happen to good people, and so enables individuals to cope with the problems of life. For Peter Berger and Thomas Luckmann, religion serves to define and demarcate reality, thus establishing a bulwark against intellectual chaos. For contemporary conflict and social movement theorists, religions provide useful ideological and material resources for the underclass to mobilize in its struggle against the dominant elite.[1]

Since few, if any, modern societies are homogeneous, however, all of these theories must take into account the fact that *whatever role they postulate for religion will be differently enacted in each of a society's varied sub-populations.* It is highly unlikely that a single world-explaining theodicy, a single socially-cohesive ritual practice, or a single empowering/subjugating religious hierarchy would equally satisfy individuals from all of the different classes, ethnicities, ages, genders, or geographic locations in a society. As a result, several variant forms of a given religion may be needed if that religion is to unite individuals within different societal subgroups, to provide their lives with alternative – or even mutually exclusive – meanings, or to support their own collective power *vis-à-vis* others in the society. For example, religious worldviews which require extensive doctrinal expertise to comprehend will be unavailable to the average lay adherent, whose opportunity to acquire such knowledge is limited by time or financial constraints.[2] Theologies which relegate women, peasants, or a particular ethnic group to second-class spiritual status will be less attractive to the members of the stigmatized group. 'Strict' versions of a religion may draw socio-economic strata whose members have little to lose; less-demanding versions may appeal more to the wealthy and successful.[3] In times of rapid social change, successive generational cohorts may also desire different variants of a religion.[4]

Whether these variants remain contained within a single religious tradition or are expelled from it will depend on a host of organizational and ideological factors, both within the larger society and in the religion itself. To a greater or lesser degree, all societies possess a 'center' composed of key values, beliefs, and institutions, as well as of the elites who maintain and propagate them. These center elites are organized into interlocking institutions – business, governmental, educational – which are often, but not always, interconnected 'through a common authority, overlapping personnel, personal relationships, contracts, perceived identities of interest, a sense of affinity with a transcendent whole, and a territorial location possessing symbolic value' (Shils 1975: 4). In some societies, the institutional interlock is complete: elites in one area (e.g. business) also occupy the central positions in government, education, the media, and religion (Farnsley *et al.* 2004). In other societies, or at other times, divisions among these institutional centers may be more pronounced. Additionally, each institutional center may exist in varying degrees of tension with one or dozens of groups which are 'peripheral' to it, whether geographically, economically, or culturally.[5]

In any given religious tradition, therefore, the elites in its center organizations define the official version of its doctrines, rituals, and moral behaviors. The elites of the religious center may overlap with the political and economic elites of the secular center, or they may be in significant tension with them. At the same time, the ecclesiastical center must also deal with the religious needs and desires of groups on the societal periphery (Blasi 2002: 278). The particular social, political, and economic conditions experienced by each of these peripheral groups will influence the type(s) of religious variants they find most attractive – which will most likely *not* be the one promulgated by the center authorities. The theological and organizational characteristics of these marginal variants, and of the sacred center, will determine whether and how peripheral religious expressions remain an accepted – or at least tolerated – part of the central religion, or whether they ultimately separate from it.

This chapter will focus on the religious variants that arise on the periphery of – but still are related to – the center of church and

society.[6] The ideological and structural forces which determine whether such variants remain within a parent church (as 'orders') or break from it (as 'schismatic sects') will be discussed in the first section. For the purposes of this discussion, the term 'order' will refer to any organized group of religious virtuosi (Weber 1958: 287) located outside of the center governing structure of the church but nevertheless retaining a role officially defined and approved by that center. Wach (1944: 173–85) referred to such groups as *ecclesiolae in ecclesia*. Ecclesiolae span a range of organizational distinctiveness: from the devotees of a particular saint or Hindu deity to groups which either periodically or continually engage in a common activity or work for a common goal. Examples might be the base ecclesial communities and house churches among both Protestants and Catholics, as well as the *havurah* and *schtibel* movements in contemporary Judaism and the medieval fraternities providing poor relief or producing a town festival (Henderson 1994; McGuire 2002: 169–70). According to Wach, 'orders' are the most formally organized of these groups, and usually demand their members' primary allegiance while nevertheless remaining connected with the religious center.[7] In contrast, 'schism' will denote that process by which a peripheral group departs from – or is expelled by – the religious center and forms a new and separate sect in opposition to the church from which it sprang (Niebuhr 1929; Troeltsch 1950; Johnson 1957, 1963; Finke and Stark 1992).[8] This section of the chapter will also briefly consider whether the very concepts of 'schism' and 'order' can be generalized to other religious traditions besides Western Christianity – and, for that matter, whether contemporary developments may have rendered these concepts moot within Christianity itself.

In the second section of this chapter, possible variations in peripheral religious groups will be outlined: the market niches filled by the groups, their 'life cycles' of growth and decay, etc. For orders, the differences in their continuing relationship with the denominational center will also be described. Since it has been well documented that both orders and schismatic sects perform a key role in initiating innovative changes within the larger religious landscape,[9] a third and final section will briefly summarize some of these innovations, and will explore the factors conducing to their adoption or rejection by the religious center – and by other peripheral religious groups as well.

FACTORS INFLUENCING THE DEVELOPMENT OF ORDERS AND SCHISMS

The Heterogeneity of Religious Markets

As recent 'Rational Choice' theorists have argued, societies where the religious impulse is not artificially constrained by an ecclesial or governmental center will develop a variety of religious markets within its peripheries.[10] The amount of heterogeneity in the larger society will determine the number of these 'niche markets,' for whom the center's accepted version of religious faith or practice is less attractive. Rural peasants in search of an explanation for capricious weather patterns may prefer a theodicy that emphasizes magically appeasable gods or demons over the more theological and abstract versions prevalent in the center's version. One ethnic group may prefer the cohesion fostered by emotionally expressive worship; another may be extremely uncomfortable in such settings. Upwardly mobile capitalist classes may favor scriptures that elevate self-help and individualism; poorer groups may gravitate toward church-based movements as resources for mobilization or support in time of need.[11]

Peripheral dissatisfaction with the center's official religious belief or practice and preference for an alternative version is often inchoate and unrecognized. The crystallization of religiously variant populations into a self-conscious group usually requires a precipitating event or individual. Rational choice theorists point to the specific efforts of one or more religious entrepreneurs – charismatic individuals who are able, and eager, to articulate a new religious vision and collect a group of followers around it. Since such entrepreneurial leaders

have a greater incentive than the center elites to enlist new adherents, most are more activist in marketing their faith to the periphery.

Often, several entrepreneurial leaders may compete for adherents within the same peripheral niche. The Protestant Reformation furnishes an example of competing schismatic groups in several European countries (Presbyterians vs. Quakers vs. Anglicans in England; Lutherans vs. Pietists vs. Anabaptists in Germany). Protestant sects in Latin America today exhibit the same dynamic (Freston 1993; Green 1993; Chesnut 1997: 172–4). Competition for converts between sect and sect or order and order has often catalyzed efforts to expand and evangelize niche populations in additional peripheries. Of the fifteen largest U.S. agencies supporting overseas missionaries in 1992, all but one were supported by sectarian, rather than mainline, Protestant groups. Likewise, the vast majority of Catholic missionaries have been members of religious orders, who often competed with each other for converts (Finke and Wittberg 2000: 160–1). The chance to engage in such missionary work provided an additional attraction to the order or sect: for women or less-formally educated classes, it offered opportunities to develop their leadership and professional abilities that were rare in the secular world.[12] Labeling these evangelization efforts 'entrepreneurial' or pointing out their personal benefits is not intended to imply that those who engage in them are motivated solely by desires for self-aggrandizement and power – although this may sometimes be the case. It is equally possible, however, that a religious entrepreneur may be sincerely driven by a profoundly felt religious experience. What counts is that, whatever his/her motivation, the religious variant s/he espouses fit the needs or desires of a particular peripheral niche market better than the center's version, and that s/he be particularly devoted to spreading it.

While rational choice theorists may emphasize the efforts of religious entrepreneurs to fill market niches, other researchers attribute schisms to conflicts over religious resources.[13] Such conflicts are especially likely to arise, they maintain, when a religion's center elite attempts to consolidate its power over peripheral groups, or in times of denominational mergers.[14] Conflicts may also occur when the charismatic founder of a religion ages or dies, necessitating 'routinization' of his/her authority. At such times, struggles over resources and power may erupt as potential successors and their followers contend for the founder's mantle (Wallis 1979: 187–90). Finally, some peripheral groups may desire access to a valued spiritual status or practice monopolized by the center; religious variants which provide these groups with access to (e.g.) ordination, theological scholarship, preaching opportunities, or other recognized virtuoso roles may attract a large following from the disenfranchised periphery.[15]

Still another spur to schism might be events in the larger society which lead an ethnic or geographic population formerly intent on assimilating with the societal center to redefine themselves in opposition to it. Once a periphery comes to see itself as a separate group, its members may be reluctant to accept the dominance of the center's religious system and may attach greater significance to their own variant beliefs and practices.

The Center's Tolerance for Diversity

Once constituted as a distinct and self-conscious group, what determines whether a peripheral religious variant remains within the central faith system or separates from it? One factor may be the center's ideological and organizational tolerance for internal diversity (Sutton and Chaves 2004: 177). Several authors have noted that Catholicism, despite its reputation as a religious monopoly, has historically allowed for a wide range of internal variation both in rituals (e.g. the veneration of various local and/or ethnic saints) and – at least until recently – in government.[16] Peripheral groups which might have exited other denominations, therefore, were often retained within Catholicism as religious orders or as lay movements.[17] Many of these espoused particular theological and ritual practices distinct from the practices of the Catholic 'center.'[18] Hinduism has similarly been considered 'tolerant' of internal variation. Many Protestant

denominations, on the other hand – even those which theoretically espoused individual autonomy in matters of faith and practice – have often been fractured by 'culture wars' between center and periphery over doctrinal or moral diversity.[19] According to this model, therefore, the failure of the denominational center to allow sufficient internal variation often pushes peripheral religious groups out of the parent church into schism, while tolerance for diverse beliefs and practices may permit them to stay as encapsulated orders or movements.

These differences in tolerance, however, may not be as clear-cut as they seem. Even 'tolerant' faiths may discriminate in the *kinds* of variation which they will allow on their peripheries. Hinduism has traditionally excluded certain religious variants – Buddhism, for example – while assimilating others (Sharot 2002: 448). Similarly, Catholicism has accepted only some of its peripheral religious groups: for every 'legitimate' religious order or movement approved by Rome, even a cursory reading of church history reveals groups such as the Waldensians, Beguines, or Humiliati – to say nothing of Luther himself – who were rejected and driven from the Church.[20] Ideological tolerance/intolerance for internal variations may also wax and wane over time: the Vatican center's acceptance of variation, especially in governance and ritual practices, has declined markedly in recent years, as has tolerance for diversity within Hinduism. Still further complications may arise if the center and the periphery disagree on the insider/outsider status of the periphery's preferred religious variant: 'There has been a tension between the tendency of Hindus to consider Sikhism as a branch or caste of Hinduism and the demand of Sikhs to be recognized as a separate religious group' (Sharot 2002: 448. See also Mahmood 1997, and Sharot 2001: 103–4).

The Charismatic Characteristics of the Center

In addition to the range of variants tolerated *by* the religious center, the amount of veneration accorded *to* the center by its peripheral populations is also important in determining whether such groups exit or remain within the fold. Protestant Christianity, by definition, has traditionally affirmed the right to exit one's denomination and begin a new, 'purer' church based on the original teachings of Christ. In contrast, Catholic movements seeking a return to apostolic purity might hesitate to break their ties to the sacred center. To leave the 'One True Church' would separate dissidents from the papacy and from two millennia of apostolic succession, the very source of their religious authenticity. Peripheral dissident groups within solidly Catholic regions may thus be more likely to create new religious orders than to break away in schism. Catholic dissidents in more pluralistic religious environments may feel freer to exit but, since a plethora of alternate denominations exist, they may join one of these instead of creating a schismatic Catholic sect of their own.[21]

Linking the faith of the *religious* center to the *societal* center's definition of peoplehood may also inhibit schism: to the extent that one's identity as Orthodox is synonymous with one's identity as a Greek, Russian, or Serb, for example, it may be hard even to conceive of breaking from it.[22] Similarly, the foundational ideal of a pan-Islamic *umma*, which denies the very validity of distinguishing between center and periphery in Islamic society, may render it impossible for Sunni Muslims, at least, to grant legitimacy to attempts at sectarian schism.[23] The concept of the *umma* has taken on added resonance in the European Islamic diaspora, where pan-Islamism provides a foundational identity for deracinated, second-generation immigrants.[24] Due to the value accorded to their sacred or societal centers, therefore, Catholicism and Orthodoxy may have been more likely to retain their peripheries as orders or internal movements, Protestantism to expel them as schismatic sects, and Islam not to recognize the order/sect distinction to begin with.

Whether this will continue to be the case in any of these faith traditions, however, is unclear. The increasing intolerance of Hinduism and Catholicism for internal variation has already been mentioned. Similarly, peripheral Islamist militants have recently begun to deny that their countries' governmental and religious elites are 'true' Muslims, a judgment that is reciprocated by the center in dueling *fatwas*.[25] The Sunni–Shi'ite division is also becoming more acrimonious, with at least some Sunni leaders labeling Shi'ites as heretics.[26] Even ethnically homogeneous faiths such as Eastern Orthodoxy are beginning to experience tensions, in the United States at least, between 'cradle' adherents and new converts, while Orthodox churches in Eastern Europe find themselves resisting the increasingly activist attempts of Protestant evangelicals to convert their flocks.[27] Whether these internal tensions will ultimately lead to formal schisms in Orthodoxy and Islam is currently unclear. Still, although theories of globalization and mass society had once assumed that societies and cultures would become increasingly homogeneous, ideological splits between center and periphery appear to be growing, both in numbers and in acrimony. To the extent that religion is one vehicle for these divisions, faiths without a previous tradition of schism and heresy may soon develop one. And globalizing missionary sects may themselves experience schismatic pressures as adherents from developing countries begin to outnumber those in the faith's home base (Lawson 1998, 1999; Vance 1999: 200–2).

Organizational Factors

In addition to ideological factors such as tolerance of variation and reverence for the sacred center, organizational and structural factors within a religion or denomination may also influence the exit or retention of peripheral religious groups. However, it is not always clear what the outcome of this influence will be. It may be easier for a dissident group to withdraw from a decentralized, congregational-polity denomination such as the Baptists, since no formally constituted hierarchical authority exists to punish them for doing so. On the other hand, similarly decentralized faiths (Sunni Islam, for example) may have retained various competing schools precisely *because* there was no central authority to expel them. Having a religiously authoritative central body may inhibit exit from a denomination, but central authorities may also expel groups that wish to remain. And expelling a peripheral group may be precisely what is needed to feed its growth, to the point that some religious groups may cultivate their identity as a persecuted periphery long after it has ceased to apply to them in any meaningful sense.[28] Other organizational factors, such as whether a potentially dissident group owns its church buildings and land or whether these assets are legally the property of the denominational center, may inhibit or facilitate exit (Templeton and Demerath 1998).

An additional complication may be occurring in the United States, at least, where the recent rise of nondenominational churches may make the whole question of orders and schisms moot. 'Even though they are organized as churches (with buildings, Sunday schools, budgets, choirs, clergy, and committees), [nondenominational churches] are not fully "official religions" – as historically defined. Thus researchers cannot make any general assumptions of what affiliation with such a church means' (McGuire 2002: 103). If it is unclear what it means to be affiliated with a nondenominational church, it will also be unclear what schism from such a 'church' would imply. Similar conceptual vagueness may also arise when considering formal schisms in established denominations. Numerous observers have noted the declining relevance of denominational distinctions within the United States. It is no longer clear to most adherents what the doctrinal and practical differences between being (e.g.) a Methodist or a Presbyterian actually are, beyond the address of a remote central office demanding its yearly assessment.[29] As a result, the traditional dynamics attendant upon severing a periphery's ties to its now-attenuated center may no longer apply, and any dissident congregations which do depart may be less likely to form new, organized sects afterward. Religiously speaking, American society may no longer have a single 'center' from which peripheral groups *can* exit. Or there may be two centers – a declining set of mainline denominations facing a growing, if loosely connected, network of nondenominational churches, parachurch organizations, and alienated individual mainline congregations – in an increasingly acrimonious culture war. Formally organized denominations may no longer be viable in America's highly individualistic religious marketplace. And, therefore, sectarian schisms may become irrelevant as well.

Similarly, the viability of internally encapsulated orders may also be declining within Catholicism, as religious pluralism and individualism increase and Catholics feel freer to 'shop around' for readily available alternatives. This is certainly true in the United States, where the number of men and women in Catholic religious orders has fallen from 214,932 in 1965 to fewer than 91,000 today (Bunson 1999, *Official Catholic Directory* 2005). But solidly Catholic European countries such as Ireland, Spain, and Italy have also shown dramatic declines in both the number and the membership of religious orders.[30] Roman Catholic officials may actually *prefer* that the Church's disruptive peripheral groups exit rather than remaining as religious orders with at least the potential for alternate power and influence *vis-à-vis* the center.

Summary

The number of peripheral religious groups – and whether they break from the center in schism or remain connected to it as orders or lay movements – thus depends on a host of ideological and organizational factors, as well as on precipitating events such as the activities of religious entrepreneurs or the center's consolidation attempts. Furthermore, the ecology of the larger religious field is constantly changing. Over time, peripheral populations grow more distinct or assimilate, governments become more or less tolerant, imported competitors thrive or diminish as threats, successive generations forget the burning issues of their parents, and new 'controversies *du jour*' take center stage. The resulting environmental turbulence not only affects the survival of established sects or orders and the creation of new ones, but also calls into question the very meaning of the conceptual category 'schism' or 'order' itself. Even as it becomes more difficult to define what 'schism' from a nondenominational church might actually mean and as the numbers of religious orders decline within western Catholicism, Salafist or Wahabi movements in Islam are exhibiting *more* schismatic characteristics. It is necessary, therefore, to consider not only the changing mechanisms by which orders or schismatic sects arise on religious peripheries, but also the *kinds* of orders and sects they are (cf. Brock and Harvey, 1987).

VARIETIES OF RELIGIOUS ORDERS AND SCHISMATIC SECTS

Commonalities

Although there could, theoretically, be as many varieties of orders or schismatic sects as there are market niches within the religious periphery to fill, in practice certain commonalities do exist. The ideal type of order or schismatic sect is one that is in some way separated from 'the world,' i.e. from both the secular and the religious center.[31] New sects and orders tend to arise in times of religious and/or civil crisis, resulting in recurrent waves of religious efflorescence alternating with periods in which fewer such groups appear.[32]

Individual groups also exhibit similar 'life cycles.'[33] Both orders and sects tend to experience an enthusiastic beginning distinguished by widespread charismatic manifestations within the leadership or among all of the members. The group exists in high tension with both the religious center and the surrounding secular society (Johnson 1957, 1963; Stark and Finke 2000a: 142–54). A potential order may even be expelled by Church authorities at this point. Upon the death of the founder and the first generation, however, the order or sect undergoes a routinization of its initial fervor, perhaps aggravated by conflict between the deceased leader's successors. If this transition period is successfully navigated, a period of institutionalization and stability ensues.

A differentiation of offices and agencies develops (Chaves 1993; Gorski 2000). Some schismatic sects grow in wealth and status, becoming part of the religious center (Yinger 1970: 261–62; Stark and Finke 2000a: 154–68). At this point, of course, the newly 'denominationalized' sect is itself vulnerable to losing the allegiance of the periphery from which it originated, and a new round of sectarian schism may begin. Some religious orders have experienced a similar life cycle: with stricter Cistercian monasteries splitting off from more lax Benedictine ones; Capuchins from Franciscans, discalced Carmelites from their predecessors. Other orders suffered a more or less gradual decline, followed by ultimate extinction, and new orders arose in their place. However, while individual orders or schismatic sects may have been born, grown, aged, and died, the *cultural template* for such groups has – until recently – continued within the larger religious tradition, constantly giving birth to new orders or new sects that replaced the old (Francis 1950: 440; Stark and Finke 2000a: 206–7).

Variation I: Relationship to the Center

Citing the common characteristics of this cultural template for orders or sects, however, masks a wide range of variations among the individual groups which theoretically conform to it. The first is the organizational distinctiveness of the group itself: how firm is the boundary between it and the center? Within Christianity, at least, schisms draw a clear distinction between the religious center and the breakaway sect. Such schismatic boundary-drawing is almost as old as Christianity itself. Rival Christian groups have contended for occupation of the religious center – and mutually excommunicated each other in the process – since at least the second century (Brown 1988: 110–19; Ehrman 2003). The winner of each round succeeded in defining the losing side as heretical, and thus outside the boundary of 'true' religion. Unless backed by elites in the secular center, these expelled groups usually faded from the religious scene.

Religious orders, by definition, have avoided expulsion and remained connected to the center in greater or lesser degree. Even orders, however, have varied in how distinctly their boundaries *vis-à-vis* the center were drawn, and, as a result, in how difficult or necessary it might be to reconcile any competing claims for the members' allegiance. This was especially the case with the male orders: to what extent were ordained Benedictines, Franciscans, and other religious order priests subject to the local bishop, especially if they staffed parishes within the latter's jurisdiction? Or to what extent did the ordained members of these orders see themselves primarily as parish priests rather than monks or friars (Hennessey 1997)?

Commitment to an order has always co-existed uneasily with the allegiance demanded by the religious center. As a result, faiths with strong centers, such as Roman Catholicism, have taken care to insure that their internal orders remain subordinate to the center's authority.[34] Even *ecclesiolae* that are not full-fledged religious orders, such as the Neocatechumenate or charismatic prayer groups, have been 'reined in' when center authorities feared they were inappropriately usurping their members' loyalty (Allen 2006). Church officials have even attempted to suppress such groups entirely, and have regularly issued decrees forbidding the establishment of any additional ones – usually at the precise time when a new wave of such foundations was beginning.[35] Only when the new orders proved their usefulness – by retaining or attracting peripheral groups otherwise vulnerable to schism, for example, or by bolstering a pope's or bishop's power *vis-à-vis* the state or other clerics – did the central Church authorities officially, if grudgingly, legitimate their existence.[36]

Similarly today, Catholicism's leadership has made little provision for the legitimation of new religious orders, despite the fact that several hundred such groups are being established in various parts of the world.[37] Whenever a new potential order arises in the Catholic Church, bishops have a range of options for how to deal with it. As long as the group remains a 'Private Association of the Christian Faithful,' it does not need any official recognition at all. 'It is well that from the very beginning Church authority may be informed of the project; but prudence may dictate not involving the authority immediately' (Gambari 1991: 17) Alternatively, the bishop might publicly commend the project and appoint an official liaison or supervisor for it, while still requiring it to remain in an unofficial status. Many, if not most, of the new groups within Catholicism have remained at this stage for the entire duration of their existence.

Official Church status begins with a group's formal designation by its bishop as a 'Public Association of the Faithful.' The bishop is considered to be the appropriate judge of the proper time to grant this status. However, there are no established guidelines to help the bishop in this decision – nor, conversely, to protect petitioning groups from the arbitrary application of idiosyncratic standards on the part of different bishops (Gambari 1991: 17, 21). Similarly, there are no published criteria for when a Public Association of the Faithful is ready for the next step – designation as a full-fledged diocesan or papal religious order.

In an attempt to resolve these statutory ambiguities, one ad hoc committee of the U.S. diocesan officials ('Vicars for Religious') responsible for overseeing religious orders attempted to draw up a set of guidelines for when a new group would be eligible for official status:

- The members of the group should live in community for ... at least three years, working out their way of life and writing down their rules.
- After the group has a certain stability – at least three years of living together and at least six members – the group may then ask the diocesan bishop to give it temporary recognition as an Association of the Faithful. This period of temporary recognition shall not last longer than ten years.
- Before making application to the local bishop for formal approval as a [Public] Association of the Faithful, there should be a fair number of members – at least ten – and a long term – at least seven years – of public testimony to their lives (Seif 1994: 189).

However, neither the membership criteria nor the time limits in these guidelines have any legal foundation in Church law. Bishops were free to disregard them at will and have frequently done so.

A second difficulty relates to the ongoing role of the bishop. Officially, he is responsible not only for initially certifying the new public association of the faithful, but also for continuing to guide its spiritual and organizational development until it achieves official status as a full-fledged religious order (Gambari 1991: 18–19). In actuality, however, the bishops have few or no organizational incentives to fulfill this role. In fact, there are disincentives. As the founder of one new religious order put it:

> No one can blame a bishop for trying to avoid extra work. There's so much on the average bishop's plate now that any more would seem cruel. And so, when a new community, following the directions of Canon Law, approaches their [bishop], it's probably natural for him to groan a bit – more work. Unfortunately, many do more than just that. More than a few simply refuse to answer mail – my own experience will attest to that. Then I remember one bishop from New England whom we contacted... who did write back, proudly advising me that he has a policy against accepting any new communities.... He has since gone on to another diocese, where one of his first acts was to disband a new community he inherited when he landed there (Farrell 1992).

Many nascent orders have had to petition scores of bishops before finding one that would allow them to live in his diocese – and even once such an invitation was extended, there was no guarantee it would not later be rescinded. Once present in a diocese, even unofficially, many groups have been kept waiting, sometimes for decades, without being granted official status.

Since clear guidelines for granting official status do not exist, there are widespread inconsistencies from diocese to diocese. This leads to confusion on both sides:

> You can go from chancery office to chancery office and get *vastly* different information, *if* you get any information at all from these people, because they're pretty much in the dark.... They'll *pretend* they know what to do, but – No, really, our vicar for religious is a fine man. But there's nothing out there to tell you what to do (Quoted in Wittberg 1996b: 165).

Some bishops have granted a group its official Public Association status immediately; others require a wait of years. 'Groups' as small as one or two members are recognized in some dioceses; others must wait until they have at least ten or twelve people who have stayed for longer than a year. Some public associations are allowed to accept members who have transferred from established religious orders; others are not. The founders of one new order were told to develop their group's spirituality and ethos (its 'charism') independently, without undergoing any training or mentoring with an established religious order; another group was required to participate in precisely such mentoring for several years before it could be approved (Wittberg 1996b: 165). Some new groups have been restricted in whether they can wear a religious habit, what they can call themselves, or even 'whether a sign can be posted outside or not' (Seif 1994: 191), while others are encouraged to adopt the full accoutrements and practices of a traditional religious order immediately upon their founding. These inconsistencies lose nothing in the telling as they are recounted among the new communities, and the members at times exhibit a sense that at least some Church officials are trying to get rid of them.

In spite of these negative experiences, however, many new Catholic associations perceive their own local Church officials as welcoming and helpful. In addition, the new orders often receive assistance from established orders. The national federations of the Franciscan, Benedictine, and Carmelite orders have assisted numerous new associations within their respective traditions: mentoring their finances, inviting them to workshops and retreats, or interceding for them with Roman authorities. Even the local vicars for religious have been generally well-disposed, despite expressing some reservations about the financial viability and membership stability of the groups under their care (Wittberg 1996b: 169–72).

In contrast to Catholicism, peripheral Protestant movements are more likely to end in schism from the parent denomination than in encapsulation within it, although denominations may vary in whether they immediately expel dissidents or attempt to paper over disagreements for years, or even decades, in order to remain united.[38] Whether a split is interpreted as being due to a niche demand for a different worship style or doctrine, or to the desire of virtuosi for a more rigorous faith, or to a conflict between contending parties over church power and resources, such schisms are 'the primary source of new denominations' in the United States. In subsequent generations, the causes of the original schism may no longer be relevant. Ethnic groups may assimilate, rigorous faith demands may once again attenuate, power balances may shift, and separated denominations which split over these issues may once again merge.

Variation II: Internal Composition

In addition to variations in whether and how a peripheral order or sect relates to its religious center, such groups also vary in their internal composition. Some have appealed primarily to women, others to men. Some have attracted the rural poor, others the rising but disenfranchised middle class, and still others a particular ethnic or racial minority. Within contemporary Catholicism, some religious orders are predominantly young, while others have no members under the age of fifty. This differential attractiveness thus results in orders or sects that are internally homogeneous, but which differ from each other in race, class, or some other characteristic.

While Rational Choice theorists may emphasize attraction to a particular niche as the reason for diversity across sects or orders, another cause might be their original formation from struggles between contending internal factions. Several Catholic religious orders in the United States and Canada owe their existence, not to their doctrinal or ritual appeal for a particular peripheral niche population, but to the secession of (e.g.) Polish-descended sisters from an ethnically German order in which they had occupied an inferior status, or of Francophone sisters from Irish-dominated Canadian orders.[39] Similarly, the formation of the AME and CME denominations was due to African Americans' dissatisfaction, not with

Methodism's central doctrines or worship styles, but with the limited leadership roles and segregated facilities allotted to them in the eighteenth-century Methodist Episcopal churches of New York City and Philadelphia (Lincoln and Mamiya 1990: 49–58; Washington 1972: 36–46). Separating from an established order or denomination thus provided an alternative source of spiritual or temporal power to otherwise powerless groups. Additionally, however, these splits left both groups more ethnically homogeneous internally – and more distinct from each other – than before.

Since it is difficult for any organization, once established, to change its institutionalized goals and operations, the distinctive demographic composition of an order's or a sect's initial market niche fundamentally shapes its subsequent identity and activities.[40] Catholic orders have traditionally addressed some societal or ecclesial disjuncture which was not being filled by the center's version of the faith at the time of their founding. Early monastic orders, for example, arose because some fourth, fifth, and sixth-century Christians wished to model an ideal Christian social order in a time of civil and ecclesial decay (Francis 1950: 437–43; Lawrence 1989: 31). The mendicant friars of the thirteenth and fourteenth centuries evangelized the rising commercial classes in the newly revived medieval cities, whose religious needs and desires were not being met by the stagnant rural monasteries (Little 1978: 173–202). Sixteenth-century 'apostolic' orders focused on renewing the Church to meet the challenges of the Reformation: for male orders such as the Jesuits, this included extensive missionary work; for female orders such as the Ursulines, it included primarily teaching (Rapley 1990: 84).

Over time, the needs and composition of both the religious center and the periphery inevitably change, spawning new under-served (and old over-served) niche markets. With the ascendancy of a new order or sect better adapted to this new environment, established orders or denominations had to conform to the new model of the upstart groups, or else face decline and extinction (Finke and Stark 1992). By the nineteenth century, therefore, the vast majority of Catholic religious orders were of the 'apostolic' variety: the sisters engaged in teaching, nursing, and social service, while the men were occupied primarily with higher education and retreat work. Even formerly monastic and mendicant/evangelizing orders were increasingly adapted to the apostolic model: Benedictine, Franciscan, and Dominican sisters taught and nursed in much the same types of settings as 'apostolic' groups such as the Ursulines or Sisters of Mercy did, while Benedictine monks and Franciscan or Dominican friars ran colleges and worked in parishes. This homogenization was such that, by the end of the nineteenth century, all of the women's orders received constitutions from Rome that were identical except for a single paragraph at the end listing the 'works' they would do, their official title, and the name of their founder (Lozano 1983: 3). Not until after the Second Vatican Council (1963–66) did the monastic and mendicant orders attempt to re-differentiate themselves from the apostolic mold.

Societal and cultural changes in the late twentieth century have again altered the religious environment – and thus the available market niches – for both Catholic orders and Protestant sectarian groups. With the assimilation of the immigrants and the growing bureaucratization of Catholic schools, hospitals, and social agencies, the apostolic orders began to decline in numbers. At the same time, cloistered monastic orders have begun to experience a modest resurgence in Catholicism, and a limited number of such groups were even begun in some Protestant denominations.[41] Interestingly, religious orders in Eastern Orthodoxy and Buddhism appear to be moving in the *opposite* direction: both were primarily monastic and contemplative until the late twentieth century and are now beginning to engage in 'useful' works such as teaching and social service.[42]

Variation III: Stage in Organizational Life Cycle

Another way in which religious orders and schismatic sectarian groups may differ is by occupying various stages in a sort of corporate life cycle. At any one time, some orders or sects may be small, enthusiastic, poor, and growing; others may be large, established, and wealthy; while still others may be shrinking and demoralized, with a largely elderly membership. Numerous scholars have noted that both sects and religious orders typically progress through these stages over a 100 to 200-year period.[43]

Rational Choice theory would postulate that this movement happens because the groups have diluted their distinctive demands in order to appeal to a larger range of potential members, 'thereby moving away from the market niche(s) in which they were originally based,' increasing the number of free riders, and attenuating their original fervor (Stark and Finke 2000a: 205). But this may be only one causal factor in the process. To the extent that the religious environment of any society is turbulent, with niches arising and vanishing over time, sects and orders may simply outlive their appeal (see Kauffman 1991). The birth, growth, and extinction of schismatic sects may thus serve an adaptive function for Protestantism as a whole within this turbulent environment. Catholic religious orders, by undergoing these life cycles within themselves, may spare the larger Church from a similar fate (Finke and Wittberg 2000: 154). It is to the creative and adaptive function of orders and schisms that we now turn.

THE CREATIVE ROLE OF ORDERS AND SCHISMS

Despite their belief that sectarian groups were inferior to more mainstream churches, early scholars noted that it was the former, not the latter, which were the source of creativity and adaptation for the religious field as a whole.[44] Some of these innovations were in worship styles: Luther and Wesley wrote hymns using popular language and melodies; Thomas Aquinas (a Dominican) and Francis of Assisi composed lyric poetry which Catholics still sing today. Other innovations were doctrinal: (e.g.) the early monks' development of asceticism as an alternative for martyrdom, the medieval friars' articulation of a theology for the budding mercantile economy of the thirteenth century, or Luther's doctrine of salvation by faith. Still others were pastoral: the Dominicans perfected the idea of the sermon targeted to a specific audience and even wrote 'how to' books on the subject; the Jesuits invented the idea of a spiritual retreat. The camp meetings of the 'upstart' Protestant sects and the parish missions of nineteenth-century Catholic orders such as the Redemptorists served to re-awaken spiritual fervor in the masses.[45]

Innovation: Adaptation and Resistance

What determines whether the innovations of peripheral sects or orders are adopted by the center? Studies of a variety of religious traditions have claimed, first of all, that the success of peripheral innovations depends on whether the center is open to syncretism and 'bricolage.'[46] Center elites are frequently embedded in larger institutional expectations which may inhibit such change. The increasing professionalization of religious elites may encourage a sort of 'mimetic isomorphism,' whereby denominational officials take their cues from their peers in other established denominations, rather than adopting the innovative alternatives advocated by their own, delegitimated, periphery (Finke 2004: 24; Wuthnow and Cadge 2004: 363).[47] Thus, in contrast to earlier times when seminaries may have been on the cutting edge of denominational change, today's professional training is more likely to discourage clergy from adopting the innovations of peripheral groups (Cherry 1995: 128–51; Carroll et al. 1997: 204–50). At the extreme, center authorities may even choose to allow their denomination to die rather than abandon established theological or pastoral practices respected by their peers for more successful peripheral innovations (Finke and Stark 1992: 98–9). Of course, such a choice insures that peripheral sects will continue to grow and, in time, will supplant the declining elite as a new center.

Elites may also refuse to adopt a peripheral group's innovation, not because it lacks ideological legitimacy, but because it threatens their own power and position. In the face of the center's resistance, the ultimate success of a periphery's innovations may depend on its ability to mobilize adequate material and tactical resources to promote them. However appealing new theologies or practices might be to a potential niche market, they cannot be adopted if the niches never learn of them. Resources needed to reach these markets would include the availability of productive recruitment networks, reliable sources of revenue, access to media or other publicity outlets, and flexible decision-making structures. These may or may not be available to relatively marginalized peripheral groups. Alternatively, a long-established center elite may have grown unused to wielding its power in the face of an organized peripheral insurgency. Ammerman (1990: 168–211), for example, describes the failure of center elites in the Southern Baptist Convention to resist a takeover of the denomination by its fundamentalist periphery.

According to social movement theorists, strengths and weaknesses in its surrounding environment – its 'opportunity structure' – also help determine the success or failure of a peripheral group (Tarrow 1989: 34–5, 83–7). When faced by powerful elite resistance, upstart sects or orders may have to move to areas where the center's reach is weak, or to ally themselves with powerful patrons in the secular center, in order to gain traction for their innovations.[48]

CONCLUSIONS

Religions exist in turbulent and unpredictable environments, which are made increasingly precarious by accelerating technological innovations and widening globalization. As a result, the centers of any denomination or faith tradition must be open to periodic and profound internal changes in order to survive. But numerous organizational studies have cast serious doubt on whether center elites can ever initiate adaptive change sufficient for their survival. Neo-Institutionalists point to interlocking expectations upholding the status quo; sociologists studying internal organizational culture cite the difficulty even of imagining change; critical theorists point to the intransigence of entrenched power elites; organizational ecologists hold that organizational 'dinosaurs' must simply die out and yield the field to competitive upstarts better adapted to the changed environment. In churches as in other organizations, adaptive change occurs in periodic cycles of extinction and resurgence.[49]

Orders and sects have filled precisely this 'upstart' adaptive role within the periphery of Western religious denominations. Without the creative doctrinal, ritual, and pastoral innovations which these groups provide, established churches would become less and less able to provide meaning, belonging, and support to the ever-changing peripheries of their societies. As similar turbulence begins to affect the religious and secular centers of other parts of the world, orders and schisms may become more prevalent even in faith traditions not previously subject to them. On the other hand, environmental turbulence in the postmodern West may have increased to the point that even full-fledged schisms or orders do not have time fully to develop, and a congeries of even more ephemeral nondenominational churches and parachurch movements has taken their place.

This adaptation to a turbulent environment is a constantly contested process. Center elites resist yielding their place to upstart peripheral groups, who must contend with the center – and with each other – for the resources they need to prevail. Elites, too, may be divided, allying with or repudiating peripheral groups as their own interests dictate. It is not simply a matter of the order or sect with the most functionally adaptive innovations being destined to win; the skill and cunning of its leaders, the alliances they can make with powerful patrons and supporters, and their access to networks of recruits and publicists, all play an essential part in the struggle. The study of orders and schisms in all their rich variety, as they arise on the sacred periphery and move – or fail to move – to the religious center, must take into

account the full panoply of forces which they initiate and to which they are subject. It is hoped that this chapter will aid in this effort.

NOTES

1. For the Durkheimian tradition, see Durkheim (1965: 62); Greeley (1972: 108–25) and Turner (1991: xxi). See Marx (1963: 43, 44, 122) for religion as an instrument of oppression; see Yinger (1970: 7); Weber (1958: 275); Meslin (1972) and Wittberg (1996a: 64) for the view that the purpose of religion is to enact a spiritual response to the basic dilemmas of a culture. See Berger and Luckmann (1966); Berger (1967: 24); Luckmann (1967: 23); Malinowski (1944) and Homans (1941) for the role of religion in defining reality. For an example of how religion can provide power resources, see the research by (e.g.) Lincoln and Mamiya (1990); Hunt and Hunt (1977); Nelsen and Nelsen (1975), and Marx (1967: 99–101) on the role of African-American churches in fostering Black militancy.

2. Weber (1963b: 192–3) makes this point. For example, see Finke and Stark (1992: 85–90) on the attraction of 'simple preaching' by uneducated Methodist preachers over the scholarly theological sermons of nineteenth-century Congregationalist and Presbyterian clergy.

3. Stark and Finke (2000a: 198); Argyle and Beit-Hallahmi (1975), and Iannaccone (1988, 1990) all make this point.

4. Mannheim (1952) makes this point about the differing generational worldviews of successive age cohorts; Weber (1958: 270) notes the possibility of generational change in religions. See for example, the movement toward traditionalism among at least some contemporary Catholic youth (Davidson et al. 1997: 145–54).

5. Shils (1975: 3–11) introduces these concepts. However, he considers primarily geographic and socio-economic peripheries. In contrast, this essay will be considering religious peripheries – which may or may not be based on geography or class. A good discussion of interlocking religious and economic elites can be found in Farnsley et al. (2004: 27–30, 50–3, 76). Other peripheries, such as gay/lesbian groups, could also fit this model.

6. This is in contrast to externally originated religious manifestations: 'cults' imported from alien traditions (Johnson 1963, 1971; Stark and Bainbridge 1985) or the faiths of colonial peoples ruled by overlords with a different – or no – religious faith. Imported 'cults' such as the Unification Church or Rastafarianism, as well as colonized religions such as Irish Catholicism under British rule or the Egyptian Coptic church, will not be discussed here, even though both are, admittedly, peripheral to the social and religious centers of their respective societies.

7. Within Roman Catholicism, the term 'order' has a specific canonical meaning. Only a fraction of the religious groups of men, and very few of the women's groups,

are officially 'orders.' While male Benedictines, Franciscans, Dominicans, etc. are orders, only cloistered contemplative nuns can claim this status. Active groups of religious women – teachers, nurses, and the like – are called religious 'congregations' and their members are called 'sisters,' not 'nuns.' To complicate things further, there are additional categories such as 'secular institutes' and 'societies of apostolic life.' In this chapter, however, the word 'order' will be used for all formally organized *ecclesiolae* in Catholicism, as well as for parallel structures within Anglicanism, Eastern Orthodoxy, Hinduism and Buddhism.

8. 'Schism,' too, has had other, variant meanings which are not used here. The 'Great Papal Schism' of the early 1400s stemmed, not from a periphery splitting off from the religious center, but from three competing factions vying for control of this center. The schism between Western and Eastern Orthodox churches (AD 1054) also does not fit the center-periphery schema used here. Some modern cases, too, are ambiguous: the split between the newly merged PC (USA) and dissident congregations of the former PCUS is difficult to fit into the center-periphery model (Templeton and Demerath 1998).

9. A point made by – among others – Troeltsch (1950); Wach (1944); Demerath and Hammond (1969); Gannon (1980); Winter (1980); Stark and Bainbridge (1985); Wittberg (1994); Finke (1997a, 1997b); Demerath *et al.* (1998); and Finke and Wittberg (2000).

10. Stark and Finke (2000a: 193–201); Finke and Stark (1992); Nauta (1994: 48–9). While many critics have disputed other aspects of Rational Choice Theory (see Sharot 2002: 446–7 for a list), its insight about the development of pluralistic alternatives in open religious markets seems to hold true.

11. For tensions between peasant and clerical versions of Catholicism, see Schneider (1990); Behar (1990); Brandes (1990) and Tomasi (1975: 143). Orsi (1985) and Carroll (1989: 31) describe the discomfort of second-generation Irish-Americans when confronted with the worship styles of the newly arrived Italian immigrant Catholics. See McKibben (2005) for the religious preferences of upwardly-mobile classes; see Shirley (1997) and Warren (2001) for the church-based mobilization of the poor. See also the strength of Catholicism in Quebec, Ireland, and Poland, precisely because it served as a vehicle for nationalist resistance to a religiously-alien overlord (Fahey 1992: 254; Abramson 1988).

12. Foley (1992) and Rapley (1990: 21) note this motivation among nuns in eighteenth-century Quebec; Weber (1986: 302); Boyd and Brackenridge (1983: 170); Brereton and Klein (1979: 308–9), and Cnaan *et al.* (1999: 196) note that missionary work was one of the few ways a nineteenth-century Protestant woman could follow a professional career in medicine or social work.

13. Sutton and Chaves (2004) advance this explanation. See Leatham (2003) for an illustration of resource-driven schism in a Mexican millenarian sect.

14. An example of the former might be the schismatic 'Old Catholics,' who broke from Roman Catholicism after the declaration of Papal Infallibility by Vatican Council I.

An example of the latter might be the departure of some Presbyterian congregations after the creation of the PCUSA (Templeton and Demerath 1998).

15. Brown (1988: 787, 143) notes that clerical ascendancy in second- and third-century Christianity had denied virtuoso status to the laity; the monastic and eremitical lives of the early desert fathers and mothers were a reaction to this. Rapley (1990: 5–6) and Buckley (1989: 28) made a similar observation for the virtuoso role of contemplative women in Catholic religious orders. For the appeal of schismatic sects to women, see McNamara (1985: 68) and Pagels (1976: 299) for the Gnostics, Bynum (1987: 123) for the Waldensians, and Rapley (1990: 11–20) for the Protestant reformers. Currently, in Latin America and among the Hispanic population in the United States, evangelical 'sects' offer opportunities for religious leadership to men and women whose class, gender and/or educational status would disqualify them from formal ministry within Catholicism. (See Deck 1994: 412; Martin 1990: 283–4; and Bastian 1998).

16. Finke and Wittberg (2000); Carroll (1996b); Sharot (2002); Iannaccone (1992: 170), and Diotallevi (2002) make this point. This was especially true, Sharot notes, of the medieval Church, whose religious pluralism 'was made possible by the often highly autonomous functioning of the Church's various divisions and branches, such as bishoprics, abbeys, colleges, guilds, religious orders, confraternities, and parishes' (2002: 447. See also Walters 2002: 73–4). Only in the mid-nineteenth century, Carroll (1989: 27) notes, did Church authorities begin to try to standardize and homogenize Catholic theology, ritual, and governance. See also Burns (1992).

17. Weber (1963b: 619–78, 733–57), Troeltsch (1950: 723), and Francis (1950: 440) were the first to point out how important it has been for Catholicism to be able to retain its peripheral virtuosi as a safety valve within the larger institution, thus 'counteracting both sectarianism and license' (Francis 1950: 440). More recently, see also Gannon (1980: 159) and Finke and Wittberg (2000).

18. Carroll (1989: 27–8); Hynes (1989), and Olson (1988: 378–84) describe these rituals and beliefs for peripheral ethnic variants of Catholicism; Orsi (1996: 40–2) charts a similar development for second-generation Catholic laywomen devoted to St. Jude. Tomasi (1975: 152) calls Italian national parishes 'quasi-sects.' Lozano (1983: 7) notes that many Catholic orders also saw themselves as following a parallel calling distinct from the common Christian vocation – a self-perception which many bishops held in suspicion.

19. See Ammerman (1990: 248–52); Farnsley (1994), and Grammich (1999) for examples of this in Baptist churches. See Smith (1998: 210–16) for a discussion of the paradox of Evangelical Protestants espousing both the freedom of individuals to make their own decisions about religious matters and the necessity of using American law and government to enforce 'Christian' principles.

20. Little (1978: 119); McDonnell (1969: 35) and Kaelber (1998) give examples of this uneven process of acceptance/rejection for emerging Catholic religious orders in medieval Europe.

21. Hostie (1983: 279, 282–86) notes that new religious orders have historically been more likely to arise in solidly Catholic countries such as Spain, Italy, or France, and that the density of such new foundations decreases as one moves away from the Catholic center. This does not mean, of course that orders founded in the center cannot move to peripheral areas and even flourish there – witness the membership growth of European religious orders in North America in the nineteenth century and in Southern and Eastern Asia in the late twentieth (Wittberg 1994: 2, 39; 1996a: 6). But they are less likely to *begin* there.

22. This also holds true when faiths are vehicles for nationalist resistance to a religiously-alien colonial overlord. See Beyer (1989: 11); Hynes (1989); Abramson (1988: 8), and Sorrell (1989: 340) who discuss this dynamic for Irish, Polish, and Quèbecois Catholics.

23. Ahmed (2002: 63–4) notes that, while there have been numerous millenarian and reform movements within Islam, as well as many different schools of Koranic interpretation, none of these have ever attempted to exit Islam. Nor, until recently, have the Sunni variants attempted to label other variants schismatic or heretical. Shi'ism, on the other hand, precisely *because* it admits of a center authority, is much more prone to schism.

24. Kepel (1994: 35) makes this point. See also Goody (2004: 97–8); Mayer 2002), and Roy (2005).

25. See Cimino and Mayer (2006); Burt (2003), and Kurzman (2003). Kepel (1994: 31–2) notes that most Islamic militants were peripheral to the Sunni religious center – the ulemas of their respective home countries. Most 'have found their own way into the sacred texts, which they read and interpret without reference to the learned commentaries of the ulemas.' Recently, the new mufti of Syria expressed deep concern about the unrestrained issuing of fatwas by individuals and competing groups (Cimino and Mayer 2006: 2). Among African American Muslims, there are a plethora of sectarian divisions, perhaps as a result of lingering Christian influence on the leadership (Skerry 2005: 20).

26. Wiktorowicz (2005). Ahmed (2002: 57) notes that there are no differences in beliefs between Sunnis and Shi'ites, and that, in the past, neither considered the other to be un-Islamic.

27. See Krindatch (2005: 306) and Gallagher (2005) for Orthodoxy in the United States. See Froese (2004) for religious competition in the post-Soviet states.

28. Frykholm (2004: 15, 17, 20, 34, 184) and Smith (1998: 89, 121–4) illustrate this point within the American Evangelical community. Templeton and Demerath (1998) describe the factors that inhibit a dissatisfied congregation from exiting the PCUSA, as well as the factors that led the denomination's elites to facilitate their departure.

29. Wolfe (2003: 42–9) and Wuthnow (1988: 97) make this point. See Farnsley *et al.* (2004: 4) for the de-centering of religion.

30. See Stark and Finke (2000b) and Ebaugh *et al.* (1996). Church officials may point to booming populations of nuns and priests in religious orders in Africa and Asia. However, many of these, especially the women,

have few options in secular society. And, in Latin America at least, sectarian churches compete in Catholicism for the allegiance of these peripheral groups.

31. Francis (1950: 439–40) makes this point for religious orders; Johnson (1963); Stark (1964); Stark and Bainbridge (1985) and Stark and Finke (2000a: 145) for sectarian groups. See also Gannon (1980: 168–70).

32. Lozano (1983: 46) states that new religious orders 'are born as a result of a return to the Gospel during a period when the church is undergoing powerful pressures.' See Hostie (1983: 289–308); Gannon (1980: 161), and Wittberg (1994: 31–42) for a summary of these 'waves of foundation' for Catholic religious orders. See Hatch (1989) for a discussion of the recurrent periods of schismatic sectarian efflorescence in American Protestantism.

33. Hostie (1983: 82–5) postulates a 100- to 200-year life cycle for Catholic religious orders. See Hostie (1983: 58–69); Knowles (1976); Froese (1985); Hinnebusch (1973: 1311), and Wittberg (1994: 171–94) for a description of these life cycles in Catholic Religious orders. Stark and Finke (2000a: 206–7) note a similar life cycle for Protestant denominations.

34. One official document on new religious orders mentions their subordination to the Church hierarchy or to canon law in at least 66 of its 101 numbered paragraphs (Gambari 1991).

35. This is documented, for different eras, by Lawrence (1989: 228); Padburg (1989: 21), and Rapley (1990: 21), among others. See Lozano (1983: 67–70); Frazee (1982: 263–4); Rapley (1990: 33); McNamara (1996: 317–23, 461–5), and Wittberg (1994: 78–82) for accounts of episcopal and papal suppression of religions orders: Hinnebusch (1973: 1309–10) and O'Malley (1993: 285–96) note that the orders could achieve a certain amount of leverage by playing off bishops against the pope.

36. Rapley (1990: 25) notes that the Jesuits offered the papacy a 'strike force' useful to extend papal authority, but at the price of accepting the very 'mixed' (i.e. non-monastic) hybrid form of religious order the Church had just condemned at the Council of Trent. Similarly, the Daughters of Charity were allowed to exist uncloistered – in defiance of the Trent's decrees – because of the usefulness of their services (Rapley 1990: 86).

37. See Pingault (1989) for the establishment of new religious orders in France; see the Center for the Applied Research on the Apostolate (1999, 2007) for new religious orders in the United States. This official reluctance is in contrast to the historically anomalous situation in the nineteenth century, when bishops actively established religious orders as *center* institutions to assist in the works of the diocese, or to increase their power *vis-à-vis* Rome. (See Wittberg 1994: 86–9 for a summary.)

38. Recent conflicts within the Anglican communion over the ordination of homosexuals would be an example of an extended denominational effort to avoid schism. See Hayes (2004).

39. See Oates (1985: 176); Deacon (1989: 155–60); Thompson (1989, 1992) for these dynamics in the

United States; see Jean (1977: 143–7) and Gahan (1992) for Canada.

40. An entire literature on this exists within the sociology of organizations. See March and Simon (1958); Kaufman (1991); Schein (1991: 14), and Weick (1995: 85, 124–7).

41. See Wittberg (2006) for the effects of the bureaucratization of their institutions on the identity and *raison d'être* of the sponsoring Catholic religious orders and Protestant women's missionary societies. See Wittberg (1996a: 84, 1996b) and Nygren and Ukeritis (1993: 114) for the resurgence of contemplative orders.

42. See Bartholomeusz (1994: 148, 223) and Arai (1999: 145) for the spread of activist religious virtuosity to Buddhism; Sundar (2001: 273) for Hinduism; Stebbing, (2001: 227–8) for Romanian Orthodoxy, and Van Doorn-Harder (1995: 44, 78, 81, 114) for Coptic Christianity.

43. See Troeltsch (1950) and Niebuhr (1929), who make this observation for Protestant sects; see Hostie (1983) for religious orders.

44. See Finke and Wittberg (2000: 155), who cite Troeltsch and Niebuhr in this regard. Silber (1995: 47) makes the same point for the creative role of religious sects and orders in Indian religions.

45. See Miller (1997: 162) for Luther and Wesley; Finke and Wittberg (2000: 163) for Aquinas and Francis of Assisi. See Brown (1988) for the early monks; Little (1978: 176–81) and Lawrence (1989: 251) for the medieval friars. See Little (1978: 187–91) for the Dominicans; O'Malley (1993: 118, 1989: 123) for the Jesuits. See Finke and Stark (1992: 92–6) for the nineteenth-century Protestant revivals. In nineteenth-century Catholicism, as many as 13 religious orders of men were involved in revival work in the U.S. alone (Garraghan 1984, cited in Finke and Wittberg 2000: 161–2). Between 1860 and 1890, the Redemptorists alone conducted 3,955 revivals in Catholic parishes throughout the United States.

46. The term is used by Stadler (2002: 457) to denote instances whereby 'interpretations that have been considered marginal in Jewish hermeneutic tradition, and often suppressed by key rabbinical figures ... are ... introduced into the center of religious discourse, thought, and practice.' Ghozzi (2002: 318) makes a similar observation for the resistance or openness of Islamic ulema elites; Finke (2004: 24) for Christianity, and Wuthnow and Cadge (2004) for Buddhism.

47. An entire literature of neo-institutionalism describes the normative, coercive, and mimetic pressures that may inhibit organizational change (see DiMaggio and Powell 1983; Meyer and Rowan 1977).

48. See Finke and Stark (1992: 66–110) for the movement of Baptists and Methodists to the American frontier. See Wittberg (1994: 97–103) for Catholic orders enlisting secular support.

49. See Kaufman (1991) for a summary of the Organizational Ecology position; see DiMaggio and Powell (1983) for Neo-Institutionalism, Weick (1995) and Schein (1991) for organizational culture.

REFERENCES

Abramson, H. J. 1988. 'Ethnic diversity within Catholicism'. In D. Liptak (ed.) *A church of many cultures*, pp. 1–30. New York: Garland.

Ahmed, A. 2002. *Discovering Islam: Making sense of Muslim history and society*, 2nd edition. London: Routledge.

Allen, J. 2006. 'The Word from Rome: Neocatechumenal Way told to regularize its liturgical practices'. *National Catholic Reporter Online* 5 (17) *http://www.nationalcatholicreporter.org/ word/word122305.htm retrieved Jan.* 12, 2006.

Ammerman, N. T. 1990. *Baptist battles: Social change and religious conflict in the Southern Baptist Convention.* New Brunswick: Rutgers University Press.

Arai, P. K. 1999. *Women living Zen: Japanese Soto Buddhist nuns.* New York: Oxford University Press.

Argyle, M. and B. Beit-Hallahmi 1975. *The social psychology of religions.* London: Routledge and Kegan Paul.

Bartholomeusz, T. J. 1994. *Women under the bo tree: Buddhist nuns in Sri Lanka.* New York: Cambridge University Press.

Bastian, J. P. 1998. 'The new religious map of Latin America: Causes and social effects.' *Cross Currents* (Fall): 330–46.

Behar, R. 1990. 'The struggle for the church: Popular anticlericalism and religiosity in post-Franco Spain'. In E. Badone (ed.), *Religious orthodoxy and popular faith in European society*, pp. 76–112. Princeton, NJ: Princeton University Press.

Berger, Peter 1967. *The sacred canopy: Elements of a sociological theory of religion.* New York: Doubleday.

Berger, P. and T. Luckmann 1966. *The social construction of reality.* New York: Doubleday.

Beyer, P. 1989. 'The evolution of Roman Catholicism in Quebec: A Luhmanian neo-functionalist interpretation'. In R. O'Toole (ed.) *Sociological studies in Roman Catholicism*, pp. 1–26. New York: Macmillan.

Blasi, A. 2001, 2002. 'Presidential address: Marginality as a societal position of religion'. *Sociology of Religion* 63 (3): 267–89.

Boyd, L. A. and R. D. Brakenridge 1983. *Presbyterian women in America: Two centuries of a quest for status.* Westport, CT: Greenwood.

Brandes, S. 1990. 'Conclusion: Reflections on the study of religious orthodoxy and popular faith in Europe'. In E. Badone (ed.), *Religious orthodoxy and popular faith in European society*, pp. 187–99. Princeton, NJ: Princeton University Press.

Brereton, V. L. and C. R. Klein 1979. 'American women in ministry: A history of Protestant beginning points'. In R. Ruether and E. McLaughlin (eds), *Women of spirit: Female leadership in the Jewish and Christian traditions*, pp. 302–32. New York: Simon and Schuster.

Brock, S. P. and S. A. Harvey (eds) 1987. *Holy women of the Syrian orient*. Berkeley: University of California Press.

Brown, P. 1988. *The body and society: Men, women, and sexual renunciation in early Christianity*. New York: Columbia University Press.

Buckley, M. J. 1989. 'Seventeenth century French spirituality: Three figures'. In L. Dupre and D. E. Saliers (eds), *Christian Spirituality III: Post Reformation and Modern*, pp. 28–68. New York: Crossroad.

Bunson, M. (ed.) 1999. *2000 Catholic Almanac*. Huntington, IN: Our Sunday Visitor Publishing Division.

Burns, G. 1992. *The frontiers of Catholicism: The politics of ideology in a liberal world*. Berkeley, CA: University of California Press.

Burt, G. R. 2003. *Islam in the digital age: E-jihad, online fatwas, and cyber-Islamic environments*. London: Pluto Press.

Bynum, C. W. 1987. 'Religious women in the later middle ages'. In J. Riatt (ed.), *Christian spirituality II: High middle ages and reformation*, pp. 121–39. New York: Crossroad.

Carroll, M. P. 1989. 'Italian Catholicism: Making direct contact with the sacred'. In R. O'Toole (ed.), *Sociological studies in Roman Catholicism*, pp. 27–44. New York: Macmillan.

Carroll, M. P. 1996a. 'Stark realities and androcentric/Eurocentric bias in the sociology of religion'. *Sociology of Religion* 57 (3): 225–39.

Carroll, M. P. 1996b. *Veiled threats: The logic of popular Catholicism in Italy*. Baltimore: Johns Hopkins University Press.

Carroll, M. P. 1999. *Irish pilgrimage: Holy wells and popular Catholic devotion*. Baltimore: Johns Hopkins University Press.

Carroll, J. W., B. G. Wheeler, D. O. Aleshire and P. L. Marler 1997. *Being there: Culture and formation in two theological schools*. New York: Oxford University Press.

Center for Applied Research in the Apostolate 1999. *Emerging religious communities in the United States*. Georgetown University: Washington DC.

Center for Applied Research in the Apostolate 2007. *Emerging communities of conscreated life in the United States*. Georgetown University: Washington DC

Chaves, M. 1993. 'Denominations as dual structures: An organizational analysis'. *Sociology of Religion* 54 (2): 147–69.

Cherry, C. 1995. *Hurrying toward Zion: Universities, divinity schools and American Protestantism*. Bloomington, IN: Indiana University Press.

Chesnut, R. A. 1997. *Born again in Brazil: The Pentecostal boom and the pathogens of poverty*. New Brunswick, NJ: Rutgers University Press.

Cimino, R. and J. F. Mayer 2006. 'Dramatic events drive religion in 2005 and beyond'. *Religion Watch* 21 (3): 1–2.

Cnaan, R. with R. J. Wineburg and S. C. Boddie 1999. *The newer deal: Social work and religion in partnership*. New York: Columbia University Press.

Davidson, J. D., A. S. Williams, R. A. Lamanna, J. Stenfetnagel, K. M. Weigert, W. J. Whalen, and P. Wittberg 1997. *The search for common ground: What unites and divides Catholic Americans*. Huntington, IN: Our Sunday Visitor Publishing Division.

Deacon, F. J. 1989. *Handmaids or autonomous women: The charitable activities, institution-building, and communal relationships of Catholic sisters in nineteenth century Wisconsin*. Ph.D. Dissertation, Department of History, University of Wisconsin, Madison.

Deck, A. F. 1994. 'The challenge of evangelical/Pentecostal Christianity to Hispanic Catholicism'. In J. P. Dolan and A. F. Deck (eds), *Hispanic Catholic culture in the U. S.: Issues and concerns*, pp. 409–39. South Bend, IN: University of Notre Dame Press.

Demerath, N. J. III, P. D. Hall, T. Schmitt and R. H. Williams 1998. *Sacred companies: Organizational aspects of religion and religious aspects of organization*. New York: Oxford University Press.

Demerath, N. J. III and P. E. Hammond 1969. *Religion in social context: Tradition and transition*. New York: Random House.

DiMaggio, P. J. and W. W. Powell 1983. 'The iron cage revisited: Institutional isomorphism and collective rationality in organizational fields'. *American Sociological Review* 48: 147–60.

Diotallevi, L. 2002. 'Internal competition in a national religious monopoly: The Catholic effect and the Italian case'. *Sociology of Religion* 63 (2): 137–55.

Durkheim, E. 1965. *Elementary forms of the religious life*. Translated by J. W. Swain. New York: Free Press.

Ebaugh, H. R., J. Lonence and J. S. Chafetz 1996. 'The growth and decline of the population of Catholic nuns cross-nationally, 1960–1990: A case of secularization as social structural change'. *Journal for the Scientific Study of Religion* 35 (2): 171–83.

Ehrman, B. D. 2003. *Lost Christianities: The battles for scripture and the faiths we never knew.* New York: Oxford University Press.

Fahey, T. 1992. 'Catholicism and industrial society in Ireland'. In J. H. Goldthorpe and C. T. Whelan (eds) *The development of industrial society in Ireland.* Proceedings of the British Academy 79: 241–63.

Farnsley, A. E. II. 1994. *Southern Baptist politics: Authority and power in the restructuring of an American denomination.* University Park, PA: The Penn State University Press.

Farnsley, A. E. II, N. J. Demerath III, E. Diamond, M. L. Mapes, E. Wedam 2004. *Sacred circles, public squares: The multicentering of American religion.* Bloomington, IN: Indiana University Press.

Farrell, M. 1992. Interview for the *National Catholic Register*, October 11, 1992. Quotation taken from the unpublished typescript of the interview, provided by the author.

Finke, R. 2004. 'Innovative returns to tradition: Using core teachings as the foundation for innovative accommodation'. *Journal for the Scientific Study of Religion* 43 (1): 19–34.

Finke, R. 1997a. 'An orderly return to tradition: Explaining membership growth in Catholic religious orders'. *Journal for the Scientific Study of Religion* 36 (2): 218–30.

Finke, R. 1997b. 'The consequences of religious competition: Supply-side explanations for religious change'. In L. A. Young (ed.) *Assessing rational choice theories of religion*, pp. 46–55. New York: Routledge.

Finke, R. and R. Stark 1992. *The churching of America, 1776–1990: Winners and losers in our religious economy.* New Brunswick: Rutgers University Press.

Finke, R. and P. Wittberg 2000. 'Organizational revival from within: Explaining revivalism and reform in the Roman Catholic Church'. *Journal for the Scientific Study of Religion* 39 (2): 154–70.

Foley, M. A. 1992. Women as evangelizers in seventeenth century New France. Paper read at the History of Christianity Conference, March 27, 1992, Notre Dame University, Notre Dame, IN.

Francis, E. K. 1950. 'Toward a typology of religious orders'. *American Journal of Sociology* 55 (5): 437–49.

Frazee, C. A. 1982. 'Late Roman and Byzantine legislation on the monastic life from the fourth to the eighth centuries'. *Church History* 51 (5): 263–79.

Freston, P. 1993. 'Brother votes for brother: The new politics of Protestantism in Brazil'. In V. Garrard-Burnett and D. Stoll (eds), *Rethinking Protestantism in Latin America*, pp. 66–110. Philadelphia: Temple University Press.

Froese, P. 2004. 'After atheism: An analysis of religious monopolies in the post-Communist world'. *Sociology of Religion* 65 (1): 57–75.

Froese, W. 1985. 'On reforming the reformed: A study of religious changes and the Premonstratensians in Saxony'. *Church History* 54 (1): 20–8.

Frykholm, A. J. 2004. *Rapture culture: Left behind in evangelical America.* New York: Oxford University Press.

Gahan, E. 1992. 'The demographic evolution of the Sisters of Charity of the Immaculate Conception as an index of Canadian national development'. Paper read at the triennial meeting of the History of Women Religious Conference, June 30, 1992, Tarrytown, New York.

Gallagher, S. 2005. 'Building traditions: Comparing space, ritual, and community in three congregations'. *Review of Religious Research* 47 (1): 70–85.

Gambari, E. 1991. 'Preparatory association of a religious institute', translated by S. M. M. Armato and T. Blessin. Privately printed.

Gannon, T. M. 1980. 'Catholic religious orders in sociological perspective'. In R. P. Scherer (ed.), *American denominational organization: A sociological view.* Pasadena, CA: William Carey Library.

Garraghan, G. J. 1984. *The Jesuits of the middle United States.* Chicago: Loyola University Press.

Ghozzi, K. 2002. 'The study of resilience and decay in ulema groups: Tunisia and Iran as an example'. *Sociology of Religion* 63 (3): 317–34.

Goody, J. 2004. *Islam in Europe.* Cambridge, UK: Polity Press.

Gorski, P. S. 2000. 'Historicizing the secularization debate: Church, state, and society in late medieval and early modern Europe'. *American Sociological Review* 65 (1): 138–67.

Grammich, C. A. 1999. *Local Baptists, local politics: Churches and communities in the middle and uplands South.* Knoxville, TN: University of Tennessee Press.

Greeley, A. 1972. *The denominational society.* Glenview, IL: Scott Foresman.

Green, L. 1993. 'Shifting affiliations: Mayan widows and *evangelicos* in Guatemala'. In V. Garrard-Burnett and D. Stoll (eds), *Rethinking Protestantism in Latin America*, pp. 159–79. Philadelphia: Temple University Press.

Hatch, N. O. 1989. *The democratization of American Christianity*. New Haven: Yale University Press.

Hayes, A. L. 2004. *Anglicans in Canada: Controversies and identity in historical perspective*. Champaign, IL: University of Illinois Press.

Henderson, J. 1994. *Piety and charity in late medieval Florence*. Oxford: Clarendon Press.

Hennessey, P. K. 1997. 'The parochialization of the church and consecrated life'. In Paul K. Hennessey (ed.) *A concert of charisms: Ordained ministry in religious life*, pp. 1–8. New York: Paulist Press.

Hinnebusch, W. 1973. 'How the Dominican order faced its crises'. *Review for Religious* 32 (6): 1307–21.

Homans, G. 1941. 'Anxiety and ritual: The theories of Malinowski and Radcliffe-Brown'. *American Anthropologist* (April: 164–72).

Hostie, R. 1983. *The death and life of religious orders*. Washington DC: Center for Applied Research in the Apostolate.

Hunt, L. L. and J. G. Hunt 1977. 'Black religion as both opiate and inspiration of civil rights militance: Putting Marx's data to the test'. *Social Forces* (Sept): 1–14.

Hynes, E. 1989. 'Nineteenth century Irish Catholicism, farmers' ideology, and national religion: Explorations in cultural explanation'. In R. O'Toole (ed.) *Sociological Studies in Roman Catholicism*, pp. 45–69. New York: Macmillan.

Iannaccone, L. R. 1992. 'The consequences of religious market structure'. *Rationality and Society* 3: 156–77.

Iannaccone, L. R. 1990. 'Religious practice: A human capital approach'. *Journal for the Scientific Study of Religion* 29 (3): 297–314.

Iannaccone, L. R. 1988. 'A formal model of church and sect'. *American Journal of Sociology* 94 (supplement): S241–S268.

Jean, M. 1977. *Evolution des communautés religieuses de femmes au Canada de 1639 à nos jours*. Montréal: Fides.

Johnson, B. 1957. 'A critical appraisal of the church-sect typology'. *American Sociological Review* 22 (1): 88–92.

Johnson, B. 1963. 'On church and sect'. *American Sociological Review* 28 (4): 539–49.

Johnson, B. 1971. 'Church and sect revisited'. *Journal for the Scientific Study of Religion* 10 (2): 124–37.

Kaelber, L. 1998. *Schools of asceticism: Ideology and organization in medieval religious communities*. University Park, PA: The Pennsylvania State University Press.

Kaufman, H. 1991. *Time, chance, and organizations: Natural selection in a perilous environment*. Chatham, NJ: Chatham House Publishers.

Kepel, G. 1994. *The revenge of God: The resurgence of Islam, Christianity, and Judaism in the modern world*. University Park, PA: The Pennsylvania University Press.

Knowles. D. 1976. *Bare ruined choirs: The dissolution of English monasticism*. New York: Cambridge University Press.

Krindatch, A. J. 2005. '"American Orthodoxy" or "Orthodoxy in America?" Profiling the next generation of Eastern Christian clergy in the U.S.A'. *Review of Religious Research* 46 (3): 306–7.

Kurzman, C. 2003. 'Pro-U.S. fatwas'. *Middle East Policy* 10 (3): 155–66.

Lawrence, C. H. 1989. *Medieval monasticism: Forms of religious life in western Europe in the middle ages*, 2nd edition. London: Longmans.

Lawson, R. 1998. 'Broadening the boundaries of church-sect theory: Insights from the evolution of the nonschismatic mission churches of Seventh-day Adventism'. *Journal for the Scientific Study of Religion* 37 (4): 652–72.

Lawson, R. 1999. 'Internal political fallout from the emergence of an immigrant majority: The impact of the transformation of Seventh-day Adventism in metropolitan New York'. *Review of Religious Research* 41 (1): 20–46.

Leatham, M. C. 2003. '"Shaking out the mat:" Schism and organizational transformation at a Mexican ark of the virgin'. *Journal for the Scientific Study of Religion* 42 (2): 175–87.

Lincoln, C. E. and Mamiya, L. H. 1990. *The black church in the African-American experience*. Durham, NC: Duke University Press.

Little, L. K. 1978. *Religious poverty and the profit economy in medieval Europe*. Ithaca, NY: Cornell University Press.

Lozano, J. M. 1983. *Foundresses, founders, and their religious families*. Chicago: Claret Center for Resources in Spirituality.

Luckman, T. 1967. *The invisible religion: The problem of religion in modern society*. New York: Macmillan.

Mahmood, C. K. 1997. 'Hinduism in context: Approaching a religious tradition through external sources'. In S. D. Glazier (ed.) *Anthropology of religion: A handbook* (pp. 305–18). Westport CT: Greenwood Press.

Malinowski, B. 1944. *A scientific theory of culture and other essays*. Chapel Hill, NC: University of North Carolina Press.

Mannheim, K. 1952. 'The problem of generations'. In K. Mannheim, *Essays on the sociology of knowledge* (pp. 276–320). New York: Oxford University Press.

March, J. G. and H. Simon 1958. *Organizations*. New York: John Wiley and Sons.

Martin, D. 1990. *Tongues of fire: The explosion of Protestantism in Latin America*. London: Basil Blackwell.

Marx, G. 1967. *Protest and prejudice*. New York: Harper and Row.

Marx, K. 1963 [1844]. 'Contribution to the critique of Hegel's philosophy of right'. In R. Richey and D. Jones (eds), *Early writings* (pp. 43–59). New York: McGraw-Hill.

Mayer, J-F. 2003. 'Anticonversion laws in India spreading?' *Religion Watch* 18 (6): 8.

Mayer, J-F. 2002. 'Muslims in France: Thriving, but no unity in sight'. *Religion Watch* 17 (8): 6–7.

McDonnell, E. 1969. *The Beguines and Beghards in medieval culture*. New York: Octagon Books.

McGuire, M. B. 2002. *Religion: The social context*, 5th edition. Belmont, CA: Wadsworth.

McKibben, B. 2005. 'The Christian paradox: How a faithful nation gets Jesus wrong'. *Harper's Magazine* (August): 31–7.

McNamara, J. K. 1985. *A new song: Celibate women in the first three Christian centuries*. New York: Harrington Press.

McNamara, J. K. 1996. *Sisters in arms: Catholic nuns through two millennia*. Cambridge, MA: Harvard University Press.

Meslin, M. 1972. 'Le phénomène religieux populaire'. In B. Lacroix and P. Boglioni, (eds), *Les religions populaires: Colloque international 1970* (pp. 4–18). Québec: Presses de l'université de Laval.

Meyer, J. and B. Rowan 1977. 'Institutionalized organizations: Formal structure as myth and ceremony'. *American Journal of Sociology* 83 (2): 340–63.

Miller, D. E. 1977. *Reinventing American Protestantism*. Berkeley, CA: University of California Press.

Morris, J. 1973. *The lady was a bishop*. New York: Macmillan.

Nauta, A. 1994. '"That they all may be one." Can denominationalism die?' *Research in the Social Scientific Study of Religion* 6 (1): 35–52.

Nelsen, H. M. and A. K. Nelsen, 1975. *The black church in the sixties*. Lexington, KY: University Press of Kentucky.

Niebuhr, R. H. 1929. *The social sources of denominationalism*. New York: Henry Holt.

Nygren, D. and M. Ukeritis 1993. *The future of religious orders in the United States: Transformation and commitment*. New York: Praeger

Oates, M. J. 1985. '"The good sisters:" The work and position of Catholic churchwomen in Boston, 1870–1940'. In R. E. Sullivan and J. M. O'Toole (eds), *Catholic Boston: Studies in religion and community*, pp. 117–99. Boston: Archdiocese of Boston.

Official Catholic Directory 2005. New Providence, NJ: P. J. Kenedy and Sons.

Olson, J. S. 1988. 'The Hispanic Catholics'. In D. Liptak (ed.), *A church of many cultures*, pp. 377–97. New York: Garland.

O'Malley, J. 1993. 'The first Jesuits'. Cambridge, MA: Harvard University Press.

O'Malley, J. 1989. 'Early Jesuit spirituality: Spain and Italy.' In L. Dupre and D. E. Saliers (eds), *Christian Spirituality III: Post Reformation and Modern*, pp. 28–68. New York: Crossroad.

Orsi, R. A. 1985. *The Madonna of 115th Street: Faith and community in Italian Harlem, 1880–1950*. New Haven, CT: Yale University Press.

Orsi, R. A. 1996. *Thank you, St. Jude: Women's devotion to the patron saint of hopeless causes*. New Haven: Yale University Press.

Padburg, J. W. 1989. 'The contexts of comings and goings'. In L. Felknor (ed.), *The crisis in religious vocations: An inside view*, pp. 276–320. New York: Paulist Press.

Pagels, E. 1988. *Adam, Eve, and the serpent*. New York: Random House.

Pagels, E. 1976. 'What became of God the mother? Conflicting images of God in early Christianity'. *Signs* 2 (2): 293–303.

Pingault, P. 1989. *Renouveau de l'église: les communautés nouvelles*. Paris: Fayard.

Rapley, E. 1990. *The devotes: Women and church in seventeenth century France*. Montreal: McGill Queens University Press.

Roy, O. 2004. *Globalized Islam: The search for a new Umma*. London: Hurst & Co.

Schein, E. H. 1991. 'The role of the founder in the creation of organizational culture. In P. J. Frost, L. F. Moore, M. R. Louis, C. C. Calhoun, and J. Martin (eds), *Reframing organizational culture*, pp. 14–25. Newbury Park: Sage.

Schneider, J. 1990. 'Spirits and the spirit of capitalism'. In E. Badone (ed.), *Religious orthodoxy and popular faith in European society*, pp. 24–54. Princeton, NJ: Princeton University Press.

Seif, B. 1994. 'Emerging religious communities'. *Sisters Today* 66: 188–94.

Sharot, S. 2001. *A contemporary sociology of world religions: Virtuosi, priests, and popular religion*. Princeton, NJ: Princeton University Press.

Sharot, S. 2002. 'Beyond Christianity: A critique of the rational choice theory of religion from a Weberian and comparative religious perspective'. *Sociology of Religion* 63 (4): 427–54.

Shils, E. 1975. *Center and periphery: Essays in macrosociology*. Chicago: University of Chicago Press.

Shirley, D. 1997. *Community organizing for urban school reform*. Austin: University of Texas Press.

Silber, Ilana Friedrich (1995) *Virtuosity, charisma, and the social order: A comparative sociological study of monasticism in Theravada Buddhism and medieval Catholicism*. New York: Cambridge University Press.

Skerry, P. 2005. 'America's other Muslims'. *The Wilson Quarterly* 29 (4): 16–27.

Smith, C. 1998. *American evangelicalism: Embattled and thriving*. Chicago: University of Chicago Press.

Sorrell, R. S. 1989. 'The *survivance* of French Canadians in New England, 1865–1930'. In D. Liptak (ed.) *A church of many cultures*, pp. 329–347. New York: Garland.

Stadler, N. 2002. 'Is profane work an obstacle to salvation? The case of ultra-Orthodox (Haredi) Jews in contemporary Israel'. *Sociology of Religion* 63 (4): 455–74.

Stark, R. 1964. 'Class, radicalism and religious involvement'. *American Sociological Review* 29: 698–706.

Stark, R. and W. S. Bainbridge 1985. *The future of religion: Secularization, revival and cult formation*. Berkeley: University of California Press.

Stark, R. and Finke, R. 2000a. *Acts of faith: Exploring the human side of religion*. Berkeley, CA: University of California Press.

Stark, R. and Finke, R. 2000b. Catholic religious vocations: Decline and revival. *Review of Religious Research* 42 (2): 125–45.

Stebbing, N. 2001. 'Orthodox Romanian monastic life'. *Religious Life Review* 404: 221–31.

Sundar, P. 2001. Women and philanthropy in India. In K. D. McCarthy (ed.) *Women, philanthropy, and civil society*, pp. 271–86. Bloomington, IN: Indiana University Press.

Sutton, J. R. and M. Chaves 2004. 'Explaining schism in American Protestant Denominations'. *Journal for the Scientific Study of Religion* 43 (2): 171–90.

Tarrow, S. 1989. 'Struggle, politics and reform: Collective action, social movements, and cycles of protest'. Western Societies Program, Occasional paper #2. Ithaca, NY: Cornell University Center for International Studies.

Templeton, Mark N. and N. J. Demerath III 1998. 'The Presbyterian re-formation: Pushes and pulls in an American mainline schism.' In Demerath,

N. J. III, P. D. Hall, T. Schmitt and R. H. Williams (eds) *Sacred companies: Organizational aspects of religion and religious aspects of organization*, pp. 195–207. New York: Oxford University Press.

Thompson, M. S. 1989. 'Sisterhood and power: Class, culture, and ethnicity in the American convent. *Colby Library Quarterly* Fall: 149–75.

Thompson, M. S. 1992 Cultural conundrum: Sisters, ethnicity and the adaptation of American Catholicism'. *Mid-America: A Historical Review* 74 (3): 205–30.

Tomasi, S. M. 1975. *Piety and power: The role of Italian parishes in the New York metropolitan area*. New York: Center for Migration Studies.

Troeltsch, E. 1950. *The social teaching of the Christian churches*, volumes I and II. New York: Macmillan.

Turner, B. S. 1991. *Religion and social theory*, 2nd edition. Newbury Park, CA: Sage.

Van Doorn-Harder, P. (1995) *Contemporary Coptic nuns*. Columbia, SC: University of South Carolina Press.

Vance, L. L. 1999. *Seventh-day Adventism in crisis*. Urbana, IL: University of Illinois Press.

Wach, J. 1944. *Sociology of religion*. Chicago: University of Chicago Press.

Wallis, R. 1979. *Salvation and protest: Studies of social and religious movements*. New York: St. Martins Press.

Walters, B. 2002. 'Women religious virtuosae from the Middle Ages: A case pattern and analytic model of types.' *Sociology of Religion* 63 (1): 69–89.

Warren, M. R. 2001. *Dry bones rattling: Community building to revitalize American democracy*. Princeton: Princeton University Press.

Washington, J. 1972. *Black sects and cults*. Garden City, NJ: Doubleday.

Weber, M. 1958. 'The social psychology of world religions'. In H. H. Gerth and C. W. Mills (eds) *From Max Weber: Essays in sociology* (pp. 267–301). New York: Oxford University Press.

Weber, M. 1963a. *Max Weber*. Tr E. Fischoff. Boston: Beacon Press.

Weber, M. 1963b. *The sociology of religion*. Tr E. Fischoff. Boston: Beacon Press.

Weber, T. P. 1986. 'The Baptist tradition'. In R. L. Numbers and D. W. Amundsen, (eds) *Caring and curing: Health and medicine in the western religious tradition* (pp. 288–316). New York: Macmillan.

Weick, K. 1995. *Sensemaking in organizations*. Thousand Oaks, CA: Sage.

Wiktorowicz, Q. 2005. 'A genealogy of radical Islam'. *Studies in Conflict and Terrorism* 28 (2): 75–98.

Winter, R. D. 1980. 'Protestant mission societies and the other Protestant schism'. In R. P. Scherer (ed.) *American Denominational Organization: A Sociological View*. (pp. 194–224). Pasadena, CA: William Carey Library.

Wittberg, P. 1994. *The rise and fall of Catholic religious orders*. Albany, NY: SUNY Press.

Wittberg, P. 1996a. *Pathways to recreating Catholic religious orders*. Mahwah, NJ: Paulist Press.

Wittberg, P. 1996b. '"Real" religious communities: A study of authentication in new Roman Catholic religious orders'. In L. F. Carter (ed.), *The issue of authenticity in the study of religions* (pp. 149–74). Religion and the Social Order Series, vol. 6. Greenwich, CT: JAI Press.

Wittberg, P. 2006. *From piety to professionalism – and back again? Transformations in organized religious virtuosity*. Latham, MD: Lexington Books.

Wolfe, A. 2003. *The transformation of American religion: How we actually live our faith*. Chicago: University of Chicago Press.

Wuthnow, R. 1988. *The restructuring of American religion: Society and faith since World War II*. Princeton: Princeton University Press.

Wuthnow, R. and Cadge, W. 2004. 'Buddhists and Buddhism in the United States: The scope of influence'. *Journal for the Scientific Study of Religion* 43 (3): 363–80.

Yinger, J. M. 1970. *The scientific study of religion*. New York: Macmillan.

16

Faith-Based Initiatives

ARTHUR E. FARNSLEY II

The term 'faith-based initiatives' refers to a new way of understanding the partnership between government and religious organizations to deliver social services and strengthen community ties. Faith-based initiatives seek to expand that partnership by lowering the barriers between religion and government, making it possible for faith-based organizations to maintain their religious, even sectarian, character while using public funds to deliver services.

By this definition, faith-based initiatives are of primary interest in the American context. To be sure, complex and varied relationships between religion and government exist in virtually every national context. Demerath's *Crossing the Gods: World Religions and Worldly Politics* (2001) highlights the intriguing similarities and differences in those relationships dependent both on the faith traditions and the historical political structures involved.

The affinity between Christianity and the democratic foundations of Western nation-states is a staple of the sociological diet, in Europe as well as in the Americas. Beckford (2005) makes the interesting point that in the United Kingdom, religious difference is so tightly tied to ethnic difference that government's interaction with religion can be understood as an attempt to manage growing diversity. In the United States, however, the

issue comes to a head because of the confluence of two, seemingly disparate, streams: the U.S. is widely noted as the most religious of Western democracies, and the U.S. Constitution explicitly limits the links between religion and government. Faith-based initiatives provide an unusually clear window into this sometimes tense combination.

Faith-based initiatives are a matter of public policy relevant to political scientists and economists, but they also raise several issues of special concern for sociologists of religion. This renegotiation of institutional boundaries provides five key areas for sociological analysis: (1) the changing nature of organizations; (2) the institutional relationship between church and state; (3) the role of mediating institutions, both secular and religious, in American society; (4) the expanding role of congregations; and (5) the increasingly prominent role of conservative evangelicals in public policy.

FAITH-BASED INITIATIVES IN CONTEXT

The United States government works in concert with a variety of other organizations to provide social services of all kinds. In some cases, the federal government uses public revenues and public employees to offer services directly. In other cases, state and local governments are the providers, sometimes with financial assistance from the federal government. Government at all levels pays external, private contractors to provide services for a fee.

Many kinds of religious organizations also provide social services. Most world religions call their followers toward charity and good works. Sometimes this good work is offered *ad hoc* by individuals or congregations; sometimes it is offered through cooperative agencies created specifically for that purpose. A variety of private, secular agencies and organizations also provide social services using revenues from multiple sources.

It is tempting to imagine social services proceeding on three separate tracks – public/ government, private/religious, and private/ secular – but the reality is considerably more complex. Private citizens have both religious and secular reasons for lobbying government to spend public funds in ways they consider worthwhile. Government issues contracts to private service providers, both religious and secular, and has done so for decades. Individuals move back and forth among these institutions as leaders, volunteers, and financial supporters. In societies where the national government assumes the overwhelming share of responsibility for social well-being, the institutional arrangement is truly two-tiered, with government occupying the first level and all other efforts below it in supplemental roles. In the U.S., where there is steady pressure to limit the reach of the national government, the arrangement looks much more like a web in which federal, state, and local government overlaps with both secular and religious private efforts.

As if this mix were not complex enough, it is further complicated by the uneasy relationship between religion and government in the U.S. The First Amendment to the U.S. Constitution states that, 'Congress shall make no law respecting an establishment of religion, or prohibiting the free exercise thereof.' American courts have repeatedly found that when government intersects with religion, governmental activities must have a secular purpose, must not advance any particular religious interest, and must not exclude or marginalize citizens who claim other, or no, religious affiliation.

Faith-based initiatives should be understood in the context of *both* this complex social service web *and* this Constitutional limitation on partnership between religion and government. *What is new, interesting, and controversial about these initiatives is the attempt to strengthen the link between government funding and religious social service offerings by weakening the restrictions imposed by strict interpretations of the First Amendment.*

There is nothing new or especially controversial about government funding for religiously affiliated social service agencies. Religious groups have cared for the poor and unfortunate since America's founding and, especially in the early days, the distinction between local religion and local government was seldom as clearly delineated as the Constitutional restrictions on federal involvement in religion. Over time, state and federal government assumed an ever greater role in service provision, a story much too long and complex to be related here. As government's role increased, the relative role of private providers – both religious and secular – necessarily changed too. Some operated independently, using donations from citizens who were also already paying taxes. Some became contractors hired by the government to provide services on its behalf. Many developed a mixed strategy, using both private and public funds.

Although religious organizations have always been able to use their private funds to deliver any (or no) services as they saw fit, those who became government contractors faced restrictions grounded in First Amendment limits on 'establishment.' Government could not fund activities that were clearly sectarian, such as those aimed at conversion or at strengthening theological beliefs. Congregations – churches, synagogues, mosques, temples – do not usually make this distinction so boldly; their mission is to deliver both material and spiritual comfort as part of the same package. Because it is difficult to separate support for their material missions from support for their spiritual ones, government generally eschewed support for congregations and contracted with large agencies designed specifically to provide services.

But if government tended to shy away from direct involvement with congregations, its support for faith-based social service agencies has long been strong. Over time, government and the faith-based agencies negotiated an understood agreement subject to challenges and tinkering at the edges. Non-profit service agencies could compete for and receive public funding so long as they behaved in a manner consistent with government's secular purposes. Their religious motivation was not an issue so long as their practices conformed to government's non-sectarian standards. These agencies could not, for instance, deny service to clients who were not members of their religion. They could not discriminate in hiring, meaning that they could not deny employment to others who held different, even very different, religious beliefs. They could not evangelize or proselytize, at least not in programs supported by public funds.

The exact location of the boundaries created by these restrictions was subject to constant redefinition as the courts attempted to apply 'establishment' limits to evolving laws and practices. Many faith traditions developed large, bureaucratic agencies that were rooted in their religious beliefs but were operated independently as not-for-profit corporations that conformed to Constitutional requirements. In practice, there was usually little difference between these faith-based non-profit organizations and their secular counterparts, even if their underlying philosophies were sometimes very different. Government contracted with these provider agencies, whether secular or religious, as the situation demanded. For instance, if a Jewish Federation could do a better job of settling Russian, Jewish, immigrants, it could compete for contracts to do so, just as Catholic Charities might claim an advantage in working with certain other ethnic clients. If Lutheran Child and Family Services, the American Friends Service Committee, or a Salvation Army agency could make the case that it was the preferable provider in a given situation, it could receive the government contract so long as its activities did not cross the Constitutional line.

It is crucial to remember that these faith-based agencies working in partnership with government have only ever been a small part of the total religious social service effort. Individuals of faith, their congregations, and their explicitly sectarian agencies use their own funds to provide services of all kinds, from small donations and food pantries to family counseling, job training, and education. Because these efforts are done without government money, they can be as religious, evangelistic, and sectarian as they wish. If private groups want to include scripture reading and evangelization as part of their service delivery, they face no legal restrictions.

HOW CHARITABLE CHOICE CHANGED THE EQUATION

'Faith-based initiatives' represent a fundamental re-negotiation of the limits to partnership between government and religious groups. In the old model described above, government at all levels was cautious in its involvement. Service agencies with religious roots were required to demonstrate that their state-funded programs would be thoroughly non-sectarian. The presumption was that church-state partnerships risked violating the Establishment Clause, so the burden to prove adequate separation was on those who proposed or supported such partnerships. In the new model captured by the term 'faith-based initiative,' government encourages – sometimes even promotes – service provision by agencies with religious roots. Government now presumes these programs are both effective and legally secure; the burden to prove otherwise has shifted to critics who fear government might be supporting religious ideas or practices.

This important change in emphasis began in the 1980s. The Emergency Food and Shelter Program, begun by Congress in 1983, established a coalition that included Catholic Charities, the National Council of Churches of Christ, United Jewish Charities, and the Salvation Army all under the guidance of the Federal Emergency Management Agency.

The Adolescent Family Life Act encouraged 'family members, religious and charitable organizations' to take up the effort to educate teens about sexuality and pregnancy. By 1990, the Child Care and Development Block Grant Act required states to 'maximize' the choices available to eligible parents, including sectarian agencies among those choices (Farris *et al.* 2004).

But the focal point of the change occurred during the Clinton administration in 1996 when Congress passed the Personal Responsibility and Work Opportunities Reconciliation Act (PRWORA) containing the so-called 'charitable choice' provisions. For the first time, federal law made clear the shift from a presumption of church-state caution to one of church-state promotion. Indeed, for several years the changes now known as 'faith-based initiatives' were referred to as 'charitable choice.'

These provisions redefined government's former hesitation about religion as potential discrimination against religious providers and provided new definitions of the Constitutional limits. For instance, state governments that received PRWORA money were not required to hire private contractors but, if they hired any, then they were explicitly required to allow faith-based contractors to compete for those funds. If state law forbade religious groups from participating, then PRWORA funds had to be kept in a separate account for which religious groups could compete. Moreover, these groups could not be discriminated against *because of their religious character.* Eligible religious groups could have sectarian elements in their mission statements and could use those criteria to select officers and board members. They could prefer to hire co-religionists, although state and local anti-discrimination laws might still apply. They could *not* be required to 'remove religious art, icons, scripture, or other symbols.'

The charitable choice provisions did not change the First Amendment's minimal requirements. Religious groups receiving direct funding under this program were expressly prohibited from using them for 'sectarian worship, instruction, or proselytization.'

But the provisions marked the momentous change in emphasis noted above. The old understanding that faith-based agencies had to maintain an essentially non-sectarian character was gone. What supporters of the old model of partnership had considered cautious was defined by proponents of the new model as hostile. In the new model, faith-based groups could keep all of their sectarian character so long as they did not use *direct* government funding for specifically sectarian purposes. And if their funding was indirect, if it came, for instance, from vouchers brought by clients who had a free choice of service providers, then even those minimal restrictions did not apply.

The charitable choice provisions set the new standard, opening the way for a wave of partnerships among government at all levels and religious groups of all kinds. The term 'faith-based' came to be preferred because it covered the widest range of organizations and did not suggest that their activities themselves were strictly religious. So a large, bureaucratic, charitable agency such as Goodwill could be faith-based and so could a small, storefront congregation. The point, especially to supporters of the new changes, was that these groups had religious roots and religious motives – that is, they had a religious base – but they provided services that served a secular, public purpose. 'Faith-based initiatives' came to be the catch-all phrase capable of covering the many programs that developed beyond the specific pool of funds covered by the original Charitable Choice provisions in 1996.

By the 2000 presidential election, candidates Bush and Gore were both promising to expand the partnership between government and faith-based groups. The Bush administration carried through on this promise, though not without setbacks both internal and external to the debate. Internally, the administration faced strong opposition from civil libertarians who favored the older, more cautious model. These critics were leery of the first level of changes enacted as part of sweeping welfare reforms through the 1990s. They were increasingly vocal as the administration sought to expand these reforms. Externally, the disastrous effects of 9/11 forced the administration to put both its energy and its moral capital elsewhere.

Because of this resistance and necessary change in priorities, faith-based initiatives lost steam in Congress and few legislative changes occurred. But the administration pushed ahead, creating faith-based offices in several cabinet departments and directing money toward these efforts where possible. In starkest terms, what could be changed by Executive Order was changed; what could only be done with Congressional approval was not.

But this hardly exhausted the reach of charitable choice and faith-based initiatives. The legal changes already enacted gave state and local government considerable new latitude and potentially new responsibilities. Those who wanted to promote expanded partnerships with religious groups now had much more freedom to do so. Even those who remained cautious now had to worry that any contracting activities that avoided religious groups could be construed as discriminatory. Many states made explicit efforts to educate faith-based groups about their rights to apply as contractors. In some places, a kind of affirmative action *preferring* faith-based providers arose either as a statement of intent or as a precaution.

There are today as many combinations of partnership between government, private/secular, and private/religious providers as there are states and municipalities to manage them. If anything, the web of providers is today even more complex because services have devolved from greater centralized, national control toward state and local levels since the mid-1980s.

The church-state relationship in the U.S. is not, nor has it ever been, 'all or nothing.' Government provided funding for programs with religious underpinnings even when that partnership was defined by caution. Government still does not fund sectarian or evangelistic activities even though the partnership is now defined by advocacy and promotion. The change is one of emphasis based on a revised interpretation of the First Amendment's restrictions.

RELEVANT ISSUES FOR THE SOCIOLOGY OF RELIGION

The sociology of religion offers an unusually good vantage point from which to frame these significant changes in their fullest social context. As noted above, sociologists are especially interested in organizational theory, including the relationship between church and state, the role of mediating institutions, and the changing role of congregations as a type of religious organization. Those more interested in resource mobilization turned their attention to the rising political role of conservative evangelicals.

Organizational Analysis

Sociologists joined a broad interdisciplinary mix as organizational theory was more aggressively applied to religion. Demerath *et al.* (1997) described both how religious groups take on secular characteristics borrowed from political and economic organization and how secular organizations take on certain sacred characteristics. They made the compelling argument that religious organizations were not an isolated case and not necessarily unique.

Their work drew from other organizational theorists outside the sociology of religion, most notably Carl Milofsky, Walter Powell, and Paul DiMaggio, who were already treating congregations and faith-based non-profit groups as constituent elements in neighborhood ecologies (Milofsky 1988). Treating congregations as 'neighborhood organizations' rather than as essentially 'sacred' or 'spiritual' groups represented a major change in thinking about religion's role in public life. Those who studied different kinds of organizations – in the non-profit field, in social work, and in sociology of religion – saw very early the implications of the new government-religion partnership in which local faith-based groups would be treated as neighborhood organizations capable of being alternate providers that could be directed toward community-building or social-service ends.

Two other efforts to take the long, wide view of the changes underway deserve special mention. Thomas Jeavons (1994) attempts to clarify, or at least to highlight, the dualistic position faith communities always occupied. Their members were attracted primarily because these communities met personal needs, but many of those needs pointed them outward toward service. Moreover, the majority of fellow citizens looking on expected congregations to serve, both by creating individuals of character who would serve in other organizational settings and by offering programs of their own. Much of the literature about congregations' roles, to which we return below, drew from this early description.

A second, even more overarching, perspective came later from Robert Wuthnow (2004). Wuthnow analyzes religion's role across the service spectrum, from volunteering to the character and expectations of service recipients to the importance of human and social capital. Echoing Jeavons, he points out essential differences between faith-based non-profits that have adopted a 'service provider model' and congregations that continue to hold a religious-transformation model.

Wuthnow also emphasizes the problem of homogenization raised by Milofsky and the earlier organizational theorists. With more government funding comes ever greater pressure toward uniformity. As others had noted before, Wuthnow emphasizes the social risks of allowing congregations to change their organizational characteristics. As one observer put it, 'Who will do what they used to do?'

Church and State

Thinking about religious organizations and their relationship to other kinds of organization took many shapes. Not surprisingly, church-state issues immediately grabbed, and still command, the bulk of public attention (see Demerath in this volume). Commentators from all sides correctly recognized a major reinterpretation of the Establishment Clause, a new understanding of what Thomas Jefferson called 'the wall of separation between church and state.' Legal scholars and political scientists led the way both in documenting and raising questions about these changes. Ira Lupu and Robert Tuttle (2005) paced the discussion in the legal community, publishing many papers and briefs tracing the case law surrounding the changes. Black *et al.* (2005) surveyed the political machinations aimed at changing laws where possible or instituting executive orders when legal change proved too difficult.

A coalition of think-tanks, public policy institutes, and individual lawyers and academics helped clear the ground for the changes. One of the earliest and most influential contributions came from journalist Marvin Olasky (1992), who claimed social services worsened dramatically as America shifted away from private/religious service provision toward federal/public responsibility. Most prominent among the think-tanks that took up the policy shift was the Center for Public Justice, which not only helped in the formulation of the 1996 'charitable choice' laws, but also provided early guidebooks informing congregations and other organizations of their new 'rights' as potential applicants for funding and reminding governments of their new obligations to ensure non-discrimination for religious groups (Carlson-Theis 2000; Esbeck *et al.* 2004). Other reports followed quickly, detailing the role and responsibilities of faith-based groups (Sherman 2001).

Almost immediately a counter-coalition began to take shape. Americans United for the Separation of Church and State quickly took the lead, but a flurry of books, articles, and reports questioned both the Constitutional legitimacy and the practical efficacy of attempts to shift public funding toward local religious organizations with clearly sectarian practices. Titles like 'Can Churches Save the Cities?' and 'In God They Trust?' became common (Klein 1997; Kramnick and Moore 1997). Social work scholar Robert Wineburg wrote one of the earliest academic challenges to the evolving 'new' partnership model (Wineburg 2000).

Historians were quick to point out that from one point of view the new changes were a matter of degree, not type. Congregations, denominations, and their affiliated service agencies have always been part of the American social service infrastructure (Mapes 2004). The question was not 'if' government could provide funding to faith-based organizations, but what the limits were. Likewise, sociologists recognized that large, overarching institutions like 'church' and 'state' are not so neatly separated in practice as they are in theory. Still, the accumulated changes known as 'faith-based initiatives' could not be dismissed as a minor reinterpretation, either of the Constitution or of established institutional roles. Faith-based initiatives quickly became a fault line in the ongoing culture wars, a symbol of the split between those who wanted to reassert the civic importance of traditionalism and majoritarianism, on the one hand, and those who believed governmental neutrality was best accomplished by leaving religion to individuals and their privately chosen associations. Such a major change in principle, even when accompanied by haphazard changes in practice, signaled other underlying social changes.

Mediating Institutions and Community Renewal

The most pervasive, but in many ways the most abstract, of these changes involves the role of mediating institutions in American life. Whatever else can be said of the neoconservative political resurgence traced to the 1980 presidential election, the reformers have steadily beat the drum for strengthening the role of smaller, local institutions over against the federal government. This is not to say that the federal government has become smaller, at least in budget terms, but that conservative policies have consistently sought to increase local control by families, religious groups, local school systems, and local government. The entire project of welfare reform, most closely associated with the Democratic administration of Bill Clinton, was premised on the idea of 'devolution.' Where possible, the goal was to shift tasks down from the federal level to the smallest, most local level of organization capable of fulfilling the required task.

Berger and Neuhaus's *To Empower People: The Role of Mediating Structures in Public Policy* (1977) was an early manifesto of the changes envisioned. It highlighted the manner by which an expanded federal state alienates individuals and suggested that smaller institutions – families, schools, congregations – could act as effective buffers. This same line of thought runs through much of the early literature touting first Charitable Choice and then faith-based initiatives. Neighborhood reformers like McKnight and Kretzmann (1993) argued that civic planners had focused too much on neighborhoods' liabilities and paid insufficient attention to their assets. Among these assets were the much-ballyhooed 'social capital' made famous by Robert Putnam (2000) and the strength of their mediating institutions, most notably churches and other religious organizations. Henry Cisneros, Secretary for Housing and Urban Development in the Clinton Administration, claimed that congregations were the last, best hope in many depressed neighborhoods (Cisneros 1996). John DiIulio (1997), who later became the first director of President Bush's Office of Faith-Based Initiatives, talked up the advantages of faith-based service provision for urban, especially black-urban, youth.

This mantra – that local congregations could do a better job than welfare bureaucrats – was the reformers' rallying cry. Their arguments rested on three basic assumptions:

(1) That congregations knew their social environments and their individual neighbors – their potential clients – better than other service providers could.
(2) That congregations are smaller and that 'smallness' is better because it allows for greater flexibility and customization of services.
(3) That congregations do not merely provide services, they also provide 'values'. This is tied to the underlying conviction that what poor people need is not simply material assistance, but to become better people.

Each of these assumptions is championed by different reformers and each is challenged from the other side. Critics were especially quick to note the problems that congregations faced both as government contractors and as would-be service providers, despite the fact that most congregations provide some services on a regular basis (Farnsley 2003). But from the sociology of religion's point of view, the most compelling feature of these claims is that congregations became the focal organization. No one was previously arguing about government providing funding to the 'essentially non-sectarian' service groups that had religious roots. Everyone, it seemed, was prepared to argue about congregations as the new locus of service devolution.

The Changing Role of Congregations

In the great academic division of labor, First Amendment issues often fall to the legal and political science communities. Likewise, questions about neighborhoods and mediating institutions interest social workers, economists, and sociologists outside the field of religion. But sociologists of religion, especially those who focus on organizations, stepped to the fore as the role of congregations became a key sticking point in the national debate.

Social work professor Ram Cnaan offered early praise for congregations as part of a large, private safety net. A colleague of both faith-based supporter John DiIulio and faith-based critic Robert Wineburg in some of the earliest research into the topic, Cnaan argued that congregations already do much more than most people realize and should be supported in any way that increases their efforts. He offered broadly optimistic estimates of what congregations were doing and what they could do (Cnaan et al. 2000; Cnaan 2004). Supporter Amy Sherman (2001) worked with various policy think-tanks both to tout the expanding role of congregations and to offer those same groups advice and support.

Students of congregations were quick to challenge the optimistic analysis coming from faith-based supporters. Mark Chaves (2004) used his national survey of congregations to point out that the vast majority of those

organizations were relatively small, had little money to spare, and were generally uninterested in government collaborations. He had also been among the first to note that African-American congregations were statistically much more likely to take advantage of the new partnership opportunities (Chaves and Higgins, 1992). Arthur Farnsley (2003) echoed many of those same findings in his case study of faith-based reforms undertaken in Indianapolis, IN, a city whose mayor was keen to trumpet the success of private community groups.

A number of other sociologists of religion turned at least a little of their attention to the changes. Nancy Ammerman (2005), whose research includes multiple national studies of congregational activities, is especially attuned to the variety of partnerships common to congregations. Without taking a political stand, she says that faith-based initiatives pose a 'challenge,' especially for conservatives who must 'occupy that new territory in a way that enhances rather than diminishes their ability to build bridges' (Ammerman 2005: 264).

The Expanding Public Role of Conservative Evangelicals

Not every sociological analysis of faith-based initiatives focused on organizational aspects, either within types of religious groups or among the many different groups that make up American society. Some sociologists, especially those interested in resource mobilization, turned their attention to the growing strength of the religious group most clearly involved in instituting the new reforms.

A wealth of sociological literature running back into the 1980s described the rise of the 'New Christian Right,' as it was once called, and the increasing public prominence of conservative, evangelical Christians. Anson Shupe (1982) and Jeffrey Hadden (Hadden and Shupe 1986) were discussing the political views of Christian fundamentalists, and their potential social consequences, even before the so-called Reagan Revolution, and long before the rest of the country started thinking about the Moral Majority or red states and blue states.

Sociologists and historians have shared the responsibility for analyzing this significant segment of American society, producing works such as Marsden's *Fundamentalism and American Culture* (1980), Ammerman's *Bible Believers* (1987), Hunter's *American Evangelicalism* (1983), and Smith's more recent *Christian America: What Evangelicals Really Want* (2002).

But it was Hunter who raised the most telling point with his *Culture Wars* (1991), in which he describes a social battle between liberal individualists and conservative traditionalists that creates the principal fault line in American society. Wuthnow's *Restructuring of American Religion* (1988) places that same fault line within, rather than between, some of America's most important religious traditions, especially its denominations.

Sociologists today analyze the religious roots of political cultural disagreement from many different perspectives. Some see lurking cultural boundaries rooted in region, race, and social class. Others see rational choices made by people who favor some sorts of goods, whether personal or social, over others and act accordingly. Some argue for the power of ideology, some about the ability to mobilize resources and forge links between specific sets of ideas and practices. As journalists and political scientists turned toward the notion that political allegiance now hinges on one's attitude toward 'God, Guns, and Gays,' sociologists of religion found a broad audience who wanted to know about the connection between religion, morality, and political involvement.

CONCLUSIONS AND FUTURE DIRECTIONS FOR RESEARCH

Students of American history know that the term 'New Deal' was already in use, but faith-based initiatives represent a reshuffling of their own, albeit on a much smaller scale. Supporters of government funding for faith-based social services have renegotiated the boundaries of church-state separation. The old arrangement presumed any government involvement in religion risked establishment, so would-be contractors had to prove their activities were non-sectarian. The new arrangement presumes social services offered by reputable contractors have legitimate public value. The burden to prove such activities are sectarian, and thus unconstitutional, falls to critics.

What defenders of the old model saw as a cautious desire to ensure government neutrality, critics saw as unjustified hostility toward religion. What supporters of the new model see as a level playing field, critics see as crossing a hard-won Constitutional line keeping church and state safely separate.

Any discussion of the new arrangement must begin with the stipulation that the changes are of degree, not type. The fiction that government never funds religious organizations is deeply ingrained in the popular imagination, but it has never been a reality. Government is a primary funder for many very large service organizations with religious roots. Nothing in the new arrangement changes the firm Constitutional ban on 'establishing' religion; again, a change in degree, not type. But the degree is significant. As with gay marriage, gun control, and abortion rights, there is considerable underlying disagreement in America about the relationship among individual liberty, government responsibility, and the relative role of non-governmental institutions. The Bill of Rights remains the same, but the social context is considerably different.

The sociology of religion has much to say about those contextual differences. First and foremost, the institutions and organizations have changed. Government today plays a much larger role than it did in 1776, 1876, or 1976 (the 'Reagan Revolution's' stated desire to limit government notwithstanding). Congregations play a much different role too. Organizational sociology helps us understand these changes and the effects they have had on our social choices.

Three specific kinds of changes have warranted special attention. Sociologists have been interested in the relationship between religion and government, and organizationally between church and state, from the earliest work of Marx, Weber, and Durkheim. The new arrangement raises questions for Constitutional scholars and political scientists, to be sure, but it sits right in the sociologist's wheelhouse. The role of mediating institutions in America has been, likewise, a foundational interest since the seminal work of Tocqueville. The new church-state arrangement highlighted social changes that had been underway for decades. Finally, congregational studies are a more recent development in which sociologists of religion learned to borrow liberally from organizational theorists. In such a rationalized, bureaucratically directed society, could it possibly be otherwise? The new church-state arrangement provided fertile ground for scholars interested in congregations.

Although organizational questions dominate the literature today, sociologists of religion interested in resource mobilization were writing about the ascendance of conservative evangelicals long before faith-based initiatives came along. In many ways, the story of faith-based initiatives is the story of late twentieth-century conservative evangelicalism writ small. Analysis of that movement, including the role of welfare reform within it, is far from complete, and sociologists of religion will continue to pace the conversation.

Where is future analysis likely to go? That depends, in part, on the future course of public policy. September 11, 2001, the invasion of Afghanistan, and the subsequent invasion of Iraq made it difficult for faith-based initiatives to attract much interest. Religion stories abound in the national media, including stories about conservative evangelicals, but this interesting slice of American institutional order could not sustain ongoing public attention. Even as culture clashes go, with religious conservatives battling civil libertarians, this issue fails to generate the heat thrown off by the abortion and gay marriage controversies. By the middle of his second term, President George W. Bush could hardly afford to waste any political capital on an issue more likely to rile his opponents than to stoke his supporters.

Momentous external events were not the only reason faith-based interest receded. To some degree, both sides lost; and both sides won enough that it was not clear what was left

was worth fighting for. Thanks in part to the steady drumbeat of civil libertarian dissent and non-partisan research that questioned the reforms' efficacy, faith-based initiatives got short shrift in the legislature. President Bush responded by using Executive Order to create offices and programs that did not require Congressional approval. Supporters of the initiatives 'won' because the President delivered the promised programs; critics won by stopping further development where possible. Of course, both sides also 'lost' in the sense that critics were unable to stop the President from using his office and supporters could not enlist enough votes to expand as they hoped.

National interest also receded because the faith-based initiatives, like welfare funding itself, moved down to the state and local level, with governors and state legislators making the decisions. At the local level, even the state level, differences tend to get watered down and covered over. Big-idea groups like the Christian Coalition and the American Civil Liberties Union are relatively weaker. Debates tend to focus on past precedent, best practices, and other pragmatic issues. Thus faith-based initiatives quietly merged into everyday life in the world of government, congregational mission, and social work. As always, the strength or weakness of a state's budget was a very strong factor in determining whether potential reform was desirable or even possible. The relative strength of the majority party or the governor, and the relative homogeneity or diversity of the state's populace, determined how far reformers or critics could try to push the envelope.

Faith-based initiatives are unlikely to push substantive issues like the Iraq war, or more emotional cultural issues like gay marriage, off the front page in the near term. But the changes in church-state definitions are genuine and politicians, pastors, and social workers will all be dealing with them for generations. Religion's public role and its relationship to government as defined in the Constitution have made a real, if somewhat subtle, shift. Sociologists of religion will continue to document the change and analyze its implications.

REFERENCES

Ammerman, Nancy 1987. *The Bible Believers.* New Brunswick: Rutgers University Press.

Ammerman, Nancy 2005. *Pillars of Faith: American Congregations and their Partners.* Berkeley, CA: University of California Press.

Beckford, James 2005. 'Faith Communities and the British State.' Unpublished paper presented at the annual meeting of the American Sociological Association, Philadelphia.

Berger, Peter and R. J. Neuhaus. 1977. *To Empower People: The Role of Mediating Structures in Public Policy.* Washington, DC: American Enterprise Institute.

Black, Amy, Douglas Koopman and David Ryden 2005. *Of Little Faith: The Politics of George W. Bush's Faith-Based Initiatives.* Washington: Georgetown University Press.

Carlson-Theis, Stanley 2000. *Charitable Choice for Welfare and Community Services: An Implementation Guide for State, Local, and Federal Officials.* Center for Public Justice.

Chaves, Mark 2004. *Congregations in America.* Cambridge, MA: Harvard University Press.

Chaves, Mark and Lynn Higgins 1992. 'Comparing the Community Involvement of Black and White Congregations.' *Journal for the Scientific Study of Religion* 31: 425-40.

Cisneros, Henry 1996. 'Higher Ground: Faith Communities and Community Building.' Essay published as brochure by Department of Housing and Urban Development.

Cnaan, Ram, Robert Wineburg and Stephanie Boddie 2000. *The Newer Deal: Social Work and Religion in Partnership.* New York: Columbia University Press.

Cnaan, Ram 2004. *The Invisible Caring Hand: American Congregations and the Provision of Welfare.* New York University Press.

Demerath, N. J. III 2001. *Crossing the Gods: World Religions and Worldly Politics.* New Brunswick, NJ: Rutgers University Press.

Demerath, N. J. III, Peter Dobkin Hall, Terry Schmidt, Rhys Williams (eds) 1997. *Sacred Companies: Organizational Aspects of Religion and Religious Aspects of Organization.* New York: Oxford University Press.

DiIulio, John 1997. 'Lord's Work: Church and the Civil Society Sector' and 'Spiritual Capital Can Save Inner City Youth.' Reports to the Brookings Institution.

Esbeck, Carl, Stanley Carlson-Theis and Ronald Sider 2004. *The Freedom of Faith-Based Organizations to Staff on a Religious Basis.* Center for Public Justice.

Farnsley, Arthur E. II 2003. *Rising Expectations: Urban Congregations Welfare Reform and Community Life.* Bloomington, IN: Indiana University Press.

Farris, Anne, Richard P. Nathan and David J. Wright 2004. *The Expanding Administrative Presidency: George W. Bush and the Faith-Based Initiative.* Roundtable on Religion and Social Policy.

Hadden, Jeffrey K. and Anson Shupe (eds) 1986. *Prophetic Religious Politics: Religion and the Political Order.* NY: Paragon House.

Hunter, James 1983. *American Evangelicalism.* New Brunswick, NJ: University of Rutgers Press.

Hunter, James 1991. *Culture Wars: The Struggle to Define America.* New York: Basic Books.

Jeavons, Thomas. 1994. *When the Bottom Line is Faithfulness: The Management of Christian Service Organizations.* Bloomington, IN: Indiana University Press.

Klein, Joe 1997. 'In God They Trust.' *New Yorker Magazine*, June 16, 40-8.

Kramnick, Isaac and Laurence Moore 1997. 'Can the Churches Save the Cities? Faith-based Services and the Constitution.' *American Prospect* 35: 47-53.

Lupu, Ira and Robert Tuttle 2005. *The State of the Law 2005: Legal Developments Affecting Partnerships Between Government and Faith-Based Organizations.* Albany, NY: Nelson Rockefeller Institute of Government, SUNY.

Mapes, Mary 2004. *A Public Charity: Religion and Social Welfare in Indianapolis, 1929–2002.* Bloomington, IN: Indiana University Press.

Marsden, George 1980. *Fundamentalism and American Culture: The Shaping of 20th Century Evangelicalism.* New York: Oxford University Press.

McKnight, John and John Kretzmann 1993. *Building Communities from the Inside Out: A Path Toward Finding and Mobilizing Community Assets.* Evanston, IL: Northwestern University Press.

Milofsky, Carl (ed.) 1988. *Community Organizations.* New Haven: Yale University Press.

Olasky, Marvin 1992. *The Tragedy of American Compassion.* Washington: Regnery Gateway Press.

Putnam, Robert 2000. *Bowling Alone: The Collapse and Revival of American Community.* New York: Simon and Schuster.

Sherman, Amy 2001. *Charitable Choice Handbook for Ministry Leaders.* Center for Public Justice.

Shupe, Anson D. 1982. *Born Again Politics and the Moral Majority: What Social Surveys Really Show.* NY: Edwin Mellen Press.

Smith, Christian 2002. *Christian America? What Evangelicals Really Want.* Berkeley, CA: University of California Press.

Wineburg, Robert 2000. *A Limited Partnership: The Politics of Religion, Welfare, and Social Service.* New York: Columbia University Press.

Wuthnow, Robert 1988. *The Restructuring of American Religion.* Princeton, NJ: Princeton University Press.

Wuthnow, Robert 2004. *Saving America? Faith Based Services and the Future of Civil Society.* Princeton, NJ: Princeton University Press.

17

Religion on the Internet

DOUGLAS E. COWAN

Claude Lévi-Strauss would be proud. At its most basic level, a computer is Urim and Thummim – yes/no; on/off; open/closed – a set of binary distinctions that has grown into such ever-increasing complexity that the foundations of its technology have been utterly lost to the vast majority of those who use computers on a daily basis, lost in the hype and glitz of its alleged potential, and lost further as it becomes ever more common, ever more deeply embedded in the fabric of our daily lives. Berger and Luckmann (1966), as well, would be proud that the process by which we forget, by which we bury the social construction of reality – externalization, objectivation, and internalization – has been so well and truly demonstrated by the computer and its virtual progeny, the Internet.

Few would contest the claim that one of the most influential technological innovations of the late twentieth century has been the popular emergence of the Internet, especially in its most recognizable form, the World Wide Web. In little more than a decade, the Web has gone from an electronic curiosity, the almost exclusive province of a small population of technological *cogniscenti*, to an integral part of daily life for hundreds of millions of people worldwide. Yet, to say precisely what the Internet 'is,' what social function it serves, or even what those who participate in it are actually doing when they are online is rather more difficult. There is, of course, the technological definition: the World Wide Web is a network of interlinked computers whose purpose is to facilitate the unrestricted flow of information between the varied millions of terminals that constitute that network, and whose principal dictum is 'data must flow' (cf. Abbate 1999; Berners-Lee 2000; Gillies and Cailliau 2000; Hafner and Lyon 1996). At the level of the user, though, within fairly fixed and identifiable limits its function varies. For some it is a necessary tool of employment – whether routing packages for an express shipping service, managing multinational business transactions, auctioning a wide variety of commodities online, or conducting research for an essay on religion and the Internet. For a much larger constituency, it has become an enjoyable pastime, a way to keep in touch with friends and family, interact with like-minded persons around the world, and explore areas of interest that might not otherwise be open to them. For still others, though a significantly smaller group than either of these other two, aspects of Internet use have taken on the character of a lifestyle – online gamers and political Webloggers, for example, who could no more imagine life unconnected to the Internet than they could a day without caffeine, cigarettes, or C-SPAN. Though there may still be some who regard the Internet as little more than a cultural adjunct, sociologists interested in a wide variety of phenomena ignore the influence of the Web only at their peril.

Since the mid-1990s scholars have regularly noted religion's massive online presence (O'Leary 1996) and have tried both to map its contours, and to make sense of the various uses to which religious people are putting this newest of human communication technologies. In this chapter, I would like to survey those attempts at cartography, explore a few of the conceptual frameworks scholars have used to understand the continuum that stretches between religion online and online religion, and suggest the outlines of research that has still to be conducted. To begin, though, consider these three brief vignettes, screenshots of religious life on the World Wide Web. Each reveals salient questions that should be considered by sociologists interested in religion and, or on, the Internet.

THREE VIGNETTES

'The First Areopagus of the Modern Age': The Vatican and the Internet

In 1990 Pope John Paul II called the vast complex of worldwide communications media 'the first Areopagus of the modern age.' Twelve years later, the Pontifical Council for Social Communications issued two documents that directly address the unavoidable reality of the Internet as an integral part of that complex – 'The Church and Internet' and 'Ethics in Internet' (2002a, 2002b). Pointing out in a general way the various benefits and drawbacks of life on the Web – the advantages of increased communication as well as the hazards of communication that is increasingly unregulated – 'Ethics in Internet' stated that the World Wide Web only has positive social value 'if it is used in light of clear, sound ethical principles, especially the virtue of solidarity' (Pontifical Council 2002b). Because the Internet operates

with no obvious controls on the quality of information presented online, this raises the significant question of who determines what constitutes 'clear, sound ethical principles,' and in whose interest the ecclesial gatekeepers of these concepts propose to manage perceived transgressions.

'The Church and Internet,' on the other hand, specifically addresses the role of the World Wide Web in the lived religion of Roman Catholics, and the responsibility of the Church to safeguard the boundaries of acceptable belief and practice that could be challenged by unregulated computer mediation. Most significantly, the report declares unequivocally that 'virtual reality is no substitute for the Real Presence of Christ in the Eucharist, the sacramental reality of the other sacraments, and shared worship in a flesh-and-blood human community. There are no sacraments on the Internet; and even the religious experiences possible there by the grace of God are insufficient apart from real-world interaction with persons of faith' (Pontifical Council 2002a). That is, while many Roman Catholics may be online, online interaction will never replace one's lived Roman Catholicism. Roman Catholics around the world may have become accustomed to hearing Mass on the radio or watching it on television, but the interactivity (or, as some would argue, the illusion of interactivity) presented by the Internet cannot in any way substitute for the physical encounter of the worshipper with the worshipping community.

Despite the proscription contained in 'The Church and Internet,' which would presumably include such devotional practices as the Adoration of the Blessed Sacrament, there are indications that at least some Catholics regard computer-mediated adoration as a significant option in their lives. Unable to travel to a chapel where the Blessed Sacrament has been reserved for devotional adoration, for example, a number of believers are turning to Web sites that upload digital images of the Host. Seeing this as a viable devotional practice, some even report miracles and apparitions associated with their online adoration. Because it lacks the explicit blessing of the Church, however, and following the declarations in 'The Church and Internet,' others regard it as problematic at best, idolatrous at worst (see Cowan 2006).

This single example raises some of the most fundamental questions of religion and the Internet. Are Internet users simply seeking religious information or are they actually attempting to practice some form of computer-mediated faith? What kind of religious activities are people pursuing over the Web, what do those online experiences mean to participants, and is there such a thing as a computer-mediated religious practice that stands as a qualitatively practical substitute for offline religious devotions? What happens when practitioners report what they regard as authentic religious experiences, but the validity of those experiences is denied, sometimes *a priori*, by institutional authorities like the Roman Catholic *magisterium*?

'Propriety Online and the Right to One's Own Belief': The Church of Scientology

When the Internet first emerged as a popular medium of communication in the mid-1990s, enthusiasts regarded the nascent World Wide Web as unregulated territory, a data frontier free from the intervention of government and corporation. Believing that the online world represented a qualitatively different information space than those found offline, users regularly replicated and reposted material from one Web site to another, sometimes citing the original source, but very often not. However utopian this philosophy may have been, in practice it quickly raised the issue of unauthorized reproduction and redistribution of proprietary and, in at least one case, esoteric religious material. If one of the questions raised by online adoration or devotional practice is who determines what is authentic religious experience, the concern here is who controls the right to disseminate religious information.

At the forefront of battles to protect its proprietary material from unauthorized reproduction and distribution over the Internet has been the Church of Scientology (cf. Cowan

2003a, 2004; Grossman 1995, 1997; Lippard and Jacobsen 1995a, 1995b; Peckham 1998). For years prior to the popular emergence of the World Wide Web, Scientologists had tried in a variety of ways to silence or forestall online criticism of the Church's beliefs and activities. They flooded newsgroups with spam postings, employed 'cancelbot' software to automatically delete newsgroup messages containing particular words and phrases, and, in some cases, pursued legal action against Internet service providers and remailers. In 1994, however, particularly sensitive material which had to that point been zealously guarded by the Church suddenly appeared on the Usenet group alt.religion.scientology. Related to the cosmogonic esoterica of Church doctrine and teachings known as the 'Operating Thetan' (OT) levels, this material came to public attention (if not necessarily into the public domain) when a former Scientologist introduced it as part of his defence against a libel suit brought by the Church of Scientology. In short order, though, the OT material was posted on the Internet, where despite a number of efforts by the Church to have it removed it has remained ever since. While many commentators have suggested that a religion has the exclusive right to maintain the propriety of its esoteric teachings and to determine exclusively when and to whom those teachings will be delivered, critics of Scientology have consistently pointed to this material as clear evidence of its fanciful and fraudulent character.

This highlights the issue of religious movement and countermovement on the Internet, of the World Wide Web as a battleground for contending religious (and anti-religious) visions (cf. Introvigne 2000, 2005; Mayer 2000). As I have noted elsewhere (Cowan 2003a, 2004), the Internet appears to favor countermovement activity for a number of reasons. First, the architecture (and, in many ways, the philosophy) of the World Wide Web encourages unrestricted replication of information across multiple Web sites. Anti-Scientologists, for example, quickly picked up the OT material and duplicated it on a number of sites, which both increased the difficulty the Church faced in policing the Internet and occasionally brought the online OT material under the aegis of legal systems that were decidedly unsympathetic to Scientology's position (cf. Brill and Packard 1997; Browne 1998; Horwitz 1997; Kent 1999). Second, because there is no process by which material posted to the Internet is vetted for accuracy – indeed, some enthusiasts promote the Web specifically as a venue for 'instant expertise' (Wright 2000) – because those who search the Web for information are often ill-equipped to gauge the validity of the information presented, and because information that is often wildly inaccurate can be presented online in a very professional-looking manner, the perception of credibility and authority is often conferred on material simply because it is widely replicated. Third, countermovement material is produced for a very specific target audience – those who are already predisposed to believe claims made about suspect groups. This can result in 'a progressively deteriorating epistemic loop, the intellectual rigor of which will continue to degrade over time' (Cowan 2003a: 209), as 'original sources and research become lost in the replication, and the oversimplified portrait of the group under attack comes to represent far more a caricature than an analysis' (Cowan 2004: 268). Finally, religious groups of whatever size have only limited personal, organizational, and financial resources, and for most groups countering Web-based misinformation is at best a secondary agenda. Propagating such information, on the other hand, is the primary agenda of dedicated countermovements, one to which they can and do dedicate the totality of their efforts online.

A related issue concerns popular fears of the Internet as a recruiting tool for new and deviant religious movements. In the wake of the Heaven's Gate suicides in 1997, a number of observers opined that the World Wide Web provided devious religious leaders with a low-cost mechanism for recruiting new members (Brooke 1997; Levy 1997; Markoff 1997; Urban 2000). Though this view has been significantly challenged (cf. Cowan 2005a; Dawson and Hennebry 1999; Robinson 1997), fear of the Internet as a channel for new religious recruitment appears regularly in both secular and religious media (cf. Berger and Ezzy 2004; Clark 2003).

'Touched by His Noodly Appendage': The Church of the Flying Spaghetti Monster

Finally, there is the Internet as a medium for religiously oriented discourse that might never have taken place but for the World Wide Web. Consider, for example, the Church of the Flying Spaghetti Monster. In 2005, outraged at the reintroduction of debates over the teaching of creationism (now called 'Intelligent Design') in Kansas public schools, an unemployed physics graduate named Bobby Henderson wrote a letter to the Kansas State Board of Education outlining an alternative religious cosmogony based on belief in a supreme being known as the Flying Spaghetti Monster, who, according to drawings supplied by Henderson, resembles nothing so much as a plate of *al dente* pasta and meatballs with a pair of eyeballs mounted on bread-stick stalks. Henderson argued that if one religion's creation mythology was going to be taught in public schools, there was no good reason another's cosmogony should not rate equal time in the classroom. Along with the letter, Henderson also constructed a Web site devoted to his satirical faith, complete with downloadable computer graphics about 'the most logical and fastest growing religion on the planet,' a variety of posters, T-shirts, coffee mugs, and even Flying Spaghetti Monster computer games. Within three months, the site was receiving nearly two million hits per day, and has been discussed in mainstream print media as well as a wide variety of Internet chatrooms, discussion forums, and Weblogs.

But for the Kansas Board of Education, the Church of the Flying Spaghetti Monster might never have come into being. It is, after all, a satirical response to what the author regards as an absurd situation. The important point in terms of the current discussion, however, is that but for the World Wide Web as a relatively low-cost venue for the mass dissemination of information few outside the founder's immediate circle of family and friends would ever have known the 'Pastafarian' faith existed, much less have found themselves touched by its chief deity's 'noodly appendage.' What started as a lark has blossomed into a movement that, though not yet a religious movement *per se*, has religious discourse at its heart, finds its chief mode of communication on the Internet, and illustrates a number of issues facing scholars interested in religion on the Internet.

As I will discuss in the following section, to this point much of the research into religion and the Internet has focused on specifically religious uses of the World Wide Web – how religious groups and organizations are promoting themselves online, how that promotion has changed (or not) the nature of the message or experience they seek to communicate, and how successful (or not) that communication has been. Henderson's Church of the Flying Spaghetti Monster highlights the Internet as an important venue for the dissemination of positions that dissent from religion, from its sponsorship in society, and from the power it retains to shape the contours of social life and discourse. This, then, is not the question of religion qua religion on the World Wide Web, but of the Web as a tool to generate social awareness about religiously oriented issues and to contribute to more general discussions about the role of religion in public life. Indeed, it is at this juncture that, although their social penetration remains fairly low, I would expect to see the importance of Weblog contributions to such discussions increase.

Between Religion Online and Online Religion

Before we proceed, it would be useful to mention one of the more important conceptual distinctions in terms of religion on the Internet, one that is either implicit or explicit in each of these examples: the conceptual continuum that runs between 'religion online' and 'online religion,' between *information* about religion that is accessed via computer-mediated networks, and the various ways in which religious

faith is *practiced* over those same networks. Proposed first by Christopher Helland (2000), this concept has been expanded in recognition that these are not opposing positions, but theoretical endpoints on a continuum (cf. Cowan 2005a, 2006; Dawson and Cowan 2004; Hadden and Cowan 2000; Young 2004). A site that provides information about Wicca, for example, its history, beliefs, material culture, and perhaps a listing of Wiccan groups in different countries, but which does not offer either instruction in Wiccan religious practice or online opportunities for practice (such as participation in online ritual), would be considered *religion online*. This moves toward *online religion* when elements of religious practice are incorporated into the Web environment. These include but are hardly limited to online prayer requests and prayer chains; Hindu *puja* and modern Pagan ritual; spiritual counseling and computer-mediated divination; sacramental e-adoration and cyber-monk services from a Zen monastery. Online religion as a fully realized category, however – a 'cyber-religion' – occurs when the entirety of religious activity occurs over the Internet, and will be discussed in more detail below.

MAPPING CYBERSPACE: CATEGORIES OF INTERPRETATION

In necessarily broad strokes, Internet commentators and researchers, both scholarly and lay, have approached the question of 'religion on the Internet' from a number of different perspectives. Although they are hardly discrete categories and while some of the entries in each deal with religion only implicitly (in the sense that their concerns about the Internet apply to all Internet activities more or less equally), to this point four basic approaches have marked the exploration of religion and the World Wide Web. In each, the metaphor of mapping cyberspace is apt because, though they inevitably overlap in some ways, each approach both tightens the focus on particular aspects of religion on the Web and fills in the contours identified by other methods.

From the general to the specific, and though still in their methodological infancy, these approaches include: reconnaissance and survey, construction and maintenance, community and identity, and religious experience and practice.

Asking simply 'What's out there?', the 'guide to' approach provides an initial reconnaissance of the cyberterrain, surveying the wide variety of religious uses of the Internet (e.g., Bedell 2000; Brasher 2001; Bunt 2004; Gold 1997; Helland 2004; Horsfall 2000; Lawrence 2000; NightMare 2001; Raymond 1997). These range from simple congregational homepages listing little more than a location, contact information, and perhaps meeting times, to highly elaborate Web sites that utilize the latest in Internet technology to communicate the organization's message and attract potential participants, both online and off. These initial surveys are important first steps in understanding how different religious traditions have found homes on the Web. Campbell, for example (2004), has described how British Christians use the Web to evangelize participants in nightclub culture, while Prebish (2004) and Kelly (1999a, 1999b) catalog many of the ways in which Buddhism has emerged online. Without deeper analyses, however, the 'guide to' approach can suffer from two fundamental weaknesses: (a) it can easily fall prey to the commercial and enthusiast hyperbole that marks much of the Internet, and (b) the fluidity of the Internet environment and the speed with which it changes render any kind of catalogue approach out of date almost from the moment it is completed.

Industry and enthusiast claims that the world is now 'globally connected,' that the Internet provides 'instantaneous access' to anywhere on the planet, and that the quality and character of this connectivity will change the face of religion as we know it need to be rigorously interrogated as research hypotheses, not accepted as the premises upon which research proceeds. Contrary to much of the rhetoric that surrounds the World Wide Web – especially in highly technologized nations – the world is not nearly so connected as it first appears. Indeed, less than 15 percent of the world's population has Internet access, and in areas where the Internet has achieved the greatest level of social penetration – North America – only slightly more than half of those with access go online on any given day (cf. Castells 2001; Mossberger *et al.* 2003; Norris 2001; Wresch 1996). The most popular use of the Internet remains email, followed by reading news online and using the Web to check the weather (Pew Internet and American Life Project 2005).

In terms of religious use of the Internet, the level of access drops even further. To be sure, the Internet is changing the ways in which millions of people worldwide communicate about their religious beliefs and practices, but whether those religions or their participants have been or will be substantially changed by the Web remains an open and significant question. According to Hoover, Clark, and Rainie, though 38 percent of American Internet users had 'sent, received, or forwarded e-mail with spiritual content,' only 17 percent had used the Web to '[search] for places in their community where they could attend religious services,' and less than half that number reported that they had ever 'made or responded to a prayer request online' (2004: 4). Equally important is the finding that, although 64 percent of those with Internet access in the United States report that they have gone online for religious or spiritual purposes at one time or another (Hoover *et al.* 2004: 4), less than 5 percent do so for those purposes on any given day (Pew Internet and American Life Project 2005: 58).

Moving from a survey of online content to the varied ways in which that content is (or ought to be) produced, the 'how to' approach delineates different facets of Web site construction and maintenance (e.g., Careaga 1999; Careaga and Sweet 2001; Knight and Telesco 2002; McSherry 2002; Telesco and Knight 2001). Though only a portion of this burgeoning literature is aimed at producing religious content on the Internet, and though these are rarely in-depth analyses of Web design or usage, they are important primary data for understanding how members of certain religious traditions both approach the Internet and have suggested to their own religious microcultures how the Web should be used.

A modern Pagan named Ivy, for example, suggests that if participation in an offline ritual group is impractical, then perhaps modern Pagans should 'start your own online coven' (2003: 61). Since a coven is a very particular type of social group – it is not a book club, not a discussion group, and not a chat line – Ivy states that 'the aspect that sets an online coven apart from other online groups is ritual' (2003: 61). While she acknowledges that there are hundreds of modern Pagan email lists and discussion groups, 'neither constitutes a cyber-coven unless they make online ritual part of their activities' (Ivy 2003: 61). For a variety of reasons that I have discussed in detail else-where (Cowan 2005a: 119–51), online Pagan ritual is considerably less common than one might think, and, in fact, the majority of groups that establish themselves as 'covens' on discussion portals such as Yahoo! or MSN do not fit Ivy's principal criterion. Rather, they are online discussion forums for offline ritual working groups, online study, discussion, or chat groups which are often labeled 'covens' by their members, fan sites for television pro-grams such as *Charmed* and *Buffy the Vampire Slayer*, or role-playing game forums that have styled themselves as covens. Beyond the basics of Web site design and construction, 'how to' guides such as these are often most concerned with the creation and maintenance of online community, which leads to the third research approach.

The 'online community and identity' approach poses a number of interrelated ques-tions: Is there such a thing as online religious community, and if so, what does it look like, and how would we know it when we see it? What does this community mean for those who participate, and how does it affect how they see themselves, how they construct their identities, and how they manage relationships, both online and off? If it is not a community, despite the participants' self-description of it as such, then what is it? (See, for example, Bunt 2000, 2003; Campbell 2005; Cowan 2005a; Dawson 2004; Kim 2005; Lövheim and Linderman 2005; MacWilliams 2005; for important perspectives on this, though not directly related to religion on the Internet, see,

for example, Jones 1995, 1997, 1998; Rheingold 1993; Smith and Kollock 1999; Turkle 1995; Wellman and Haythornethwaite 2002).

Some scholars reject the idea that authentic community can ever be established or main-tained through computer-mediated communi-cation (e.g., Lockard 1997; Slouka 1995), while others contend that if what is occurring on the Internet is excluded *a priori*, then perhaps the category itself needs to be reconsidered (e.g., Campbell 2005; Cowan 2005a; Cowan and Hadden 2004; Dawson 2004; Liu 1999; Willson 2000). To this point, one of the most useful contributions to the discussion of online community has been made by Dawson (2004), who proposes a set of empirical 'iden-tifiers' by which researchers could determine whether a religious community is present online or not. Mirroring similar conditions offline, these markers include '(1) interactivity, (2) stability of membership, (3) stability of identity, (4) netizenship and social control, (5) personal concern, and (6) occurrence in a public space' (Dawson 2004: 83). It is important to note here that communities are not binary entities in the sense that there is either a com-munity or there is not. As I have noted else-where, 'it is not the case that something called community either exists or it doesn't, blinking into being when a sufficient number of charac-teristics are present and disappearing the moment it falls below some theoretical thresh-old of viability' (Cowan 2005a: 57). Using these identifiers, however, it is possible to investigate online claims to community and evaluate whether or not the characterization is reasonable.

On Yahoo! and MSN, for example, a number of modern Pagan discussion forums claim to be communities, yet post less than one mes-sage per month per member, and in some cases the majority of messages are posted by only two or three members. Despite explicit claims to being an 'online community' and listing hun-dreds of 'members,' in many cases the vast majority of messages are posted by one or two people, and most of these are repostings from other discussion groups. Despite repeated appeals from list owners, actual discussion is relatively rare. While this group may maintain a stability of membership, a stability of identity, and it may occur in a public space (in that there are no restrictions on membership or access), it fails to meet the more important criteria of interactivity, personal concern, and netizenship (in the sense of a participative responsibility on the part of other members). On the other hand, online discussion groups that are linked in some way to offline groups display considerably more robust community characteristics. In these groups, online communication becomes an extension of, rather than a substitute for, offline community, and groups seem to exhibit higher levels of participation, interactivity, personal concern, and netizenship. While it would be difficult to characterize the first group as a community, despite its self-identification as such, it would be equally difficult to deny the notion of 'community' to the second.

The last approach marks the least-explored region of cyberspace – the 'religious experience.' What makes online activity 'religious,' and how will we know it when we see it? How are participants using the Internet to experiment with, construct, and pursue religious ritual and practice? How do these computer-mediated religious practices relate to parent practices and traditions offline? (On this, see, for example, Apolito 2005; Cowan 2005a, 2006; Dawson 2004; Young 2004).

Although not as abundant as other forms of religion on the World Wide Web, many Internet users are clearly turning to online interaction as a form of religious practice. In some ways their lived religion is migrating from 'real space' to cyberspace, from religion online to online religion. As noted above, Roman Catholics clicking into different Web sites that host a digital image of Host claim to perform computer-mediated adorations of the Blessed Sacrament, some of which even involve the manipulation of multiple Web sites. 'If our computers are working right,' wrote one user to the operators of the adoration site, 'sometimes I can pull up your small chapel window, then 'light' a small candle at Gratefulness.org and have that tiny candle window overlapping your chapel window' (Chapel Webcam Witness Stories). During her period of online adoration, another

user claimed to see 'an image of an angel with head bowed and hands folded appeared on my screen after the exposition. The image appeared to the left of the tabernacle and behind the altar. It looked like an angel on its knees behind the altar adoring the Blessed Sacrament' (Chapel Webcam Witness Stories). Members of a large Hindu temple in the Dallas-Fort Worth area can conduct different computer-mediated *puja*, while similar Web graphics programs allow modern Pagans to construct 'virtual altars' to a wide variety of gods and goddesses. The Christians who operate Digibless.com offer a 'cyber-blessing' service for computer files, data transfers, and email messages, while Web-oriented modern Pagans have created a range of spells and rituals designed both to facilitate computer-mediated Pagan ritual and integrate computer technology into the lived magickal practice of Wiccans and Witches. Telesco and Knight, for example, two popular Pagan authors, have written a number of spells and online rituals designed especially for the computer-literate Pagan. They recommend the 'Antivirus Spell' 'whenever you're scanning your system for viruses, or whenever you're loading in new virus software' (Telesco and Knight 2001: 51); the 'defragmentation' spell features an elaborate offline ritual that 'symbolically supports the restructuring of your system' (Telesco and Knight 2001: 53); and the 'file transfer spell' is designed 'to protect the data as you download it or send it to someone else' (Telesco and Knight 2001: 56).

Clearly, not all co-religionists will regard any of these as authentic religious experiences. What the 'religious experience' approach demands, however, is much closer analysis of the experiences these users claim to have. Instead of simply asking who is doing what online, this approach asks what the online experience means to those who are having it. Claims of an angelic apparition following online adoration of the Blessed Sacrament could be explained away naturalistically as residual retinal stimulation from staring at the computer screen, or technologically as a residual image 'ghosting' on the screen itself. The problem, though, is that naturalistic explanations for offline religious phenomena have been offered for centuries with relatively little impact on the breadth or depth of religious belief. What needs more thorough investigation is (1) what religious experiences users claim to be having online, (2) how they account for those experiences, especially in light of co-religionist criticism or institutional proscription, (3) how those experiences affect their religious lives offline, and (4) whether or not online religious experiences are 'contagious,' that is, will one person reporting an online apparition lead to others reporting the same?

What seems clear at this juncture at least is that no one method should determine how research into the religious usage of or activity on the Internet is conducted. Simply counting the number of Web sites devoted to a particular tradition, for example, tells the researcher nothing about the kind of sites the search returns, how those who constructed the sites intended them to be used and whether their intentions were realized by actual users, or, in many cases, whether the search returns have anything to do with the particular search term at all. Without careful content analyses of the Web sites one finds, for example, it is impossible to know whether the search term 'Goddess' has returned results for sites dealing with the modern Pagan revival of goddess worship, evangelical counter-cult sites dedicated to debunking that revival, fan sites constructed in honor of some musical or cinematic celebrity hyperbolically named a 'goddess,' or cooking sites containing recipes for Green Goddess salad dressing. In the cartography of cyberspace, context is crucial. On the other hand, describing in detail what one finds on a particular Web site is only useful analytically when that description can be set in the much larger contexts of religion on the Internet as a whole and Internet use by that tradition in particular (e.g., Cowan 2005a). The 'religious experience' approach, however, does lead to perhaps the most intriguing aspect of research into religion on the Internet – the possibility of a true 'cyber-religion.'

CYBER-RELIGION: AN 'UN-IDEAL TYPE'?

One of the fundamental theoretical poles around which scholars have tried to conceptualize

religion on the Internet is that of the 'cyber-religion' or true 'online religion,' a religious tradition or group that exists only and completely on the World Wide Web (cf. Campbell 2005; Cowan 2005b; Cowan 2006; Hadden and Cowan 2000; Helland 2000, 2005; Young 2004). In terms of an authentic 'online religion,' however, it is worth asking whether we are attempting to conceptualize what Stark and Bainbridge (1985: 19–20) have referred to as the 'un-ideal type,' a research construct that cannot exist in real life and is, therefore, of limited analytical value. Have discussions over the characterization of 'online religions,' for example, been framed too much in terms of what researchers would like to find, or believe they ought to find, rather than what is actually there? In this regard, consider one recent contribution to these discussions: Højsgaard's analysis of 'cyber-religion' (2005).

'Cyber-Religion': An Initial Exploration

Briefly, Højsgaard defines a 'cyber-religion' as one that is 'mediated or located primarily in cyberspace,' whose 'contents reflect the main features of the postmodern cyber culture,' and which 'is only sparingly organized' (2005: 62). Though some of his conceptual constituents remain vague and it is unclear what it means to be 'located primarily in cyberspace,' Højsgaard's work represents a useful starting point from which to consider the question of a 'cyber-religion.' Using the Google search engine and search combinations of 'cyber,' 'virtual,' 'religion,' and 'religiosity' Højsgaard generated a list of what he characterizes as authentic 'cyber-religions' (2005: 53, n.1), among which were groups such as Digitalism, the Church of the SubGenius, Technosophy, the Church of Virus, and the SpiriTech Virtual Foundation. The sites he includes, however, illustrate three significant and interrelated problems that all research into religion on the Internet must confront: (1) the fragility and fluidity of the online environment relative to the kinds of claims researchers make about the constituents of that environment; (2) adequate conceptualization about the nature of what it means to be 'primarily online'; and (3) the fundamental importance of defining what we mean by 'religion' as a general analytic concept, especially from a sociological perspective.

First, Højsgaard's list clearly demonstrates the fragility and fluidity of cyberspace. Less than a year after the publication of his essay, of the thirteen sites he lists two are defunct, two have not been updated since 2000, two contain little more than the philosophical ramblings of their creators, one provides a variety of links to online religious information, and five are clearly designed to parody religious belief and practice, not emulate it. Only one, Kemetic Orthodoxy, comes close to what might be considered a true online religion, and it moved offline in very significant ways in a very short period of time (cf. Krogh and Pillifant 2004a, 2004b). The fluidity of the Internet also affects research when the domain name for a 'cyber-religion' is either purchased by another Internet content provider or the original provider gets bored and changes the format. One of Højsgaard's 'selected websites with a cyber-religious affiliation' (2005: 53), for example, is 'Cyber-Voodoo,' which has apparently been online since early 2001. A quick check of the site, though, reveals that it is now the product page for something called 'Flaming Hooker Productions,' which markets a variety of T-shirts and other paraphernalia lampooning world leaders such as Kim Jong-Il and Saddam Hussein. There is, in fact, absolutely nothing on the site of even a remotely religious nature.

Second, Højsgaard points to an aspect of the discussion upon which I have written at length (Cowan 2005a). That is, the notion of something being 'located primarily in cyberspace' is analytically unclear at best, and at worst just as hyperbolic and problematic as the idea that we are all now 'globally connected.' In terms of the Web sites he investigates, for example, as long as the operators of the Church of the Subgenius (a) develop their Web product offline prior to uploading, (b) do not allow for the online manipulation of that product by users (that is, users are simply consumers and not participants), and (c) depend almost exclusively on offline referents for the online product to remain meaningful, what part of this product

or process is 'completely and exclusively online'? Perhaps it is from the user perspective, in that Church of the Subgenius is only accessible online, or is only initially accessible online. But even this does not remain online, since there are a plethora of Subgenius items for sale on its Cafepress page, as Højsgaard notes. What happens to online exclusivity as soon as someone orders and begins to wear a T-shirt with the Subgenius logo? Or, even before that, when these items of Subgenius material culture come into being? By definition, T-shirts, ball caps, posters, and bumper stickers cannot exist online; they are exclusively offline phenomena. Indeed, online purchase is only one option; customers can also choose to call a 1-888 number or mail an order form to the Subgenius headquarters at a PO box in Cleveland Heights, Ohio – decidedly mundane options for a full-orbed cyber-religion. Once a self-proclaimed 'cyber-religion' starts hawking coffee mugs, wall clocks, and mousepads, any claim to an exclusive 'virtuality' is rendered a bit gratuitous. Indeed, the 'sacred text' of the Church of the Subgenius was originally published in 1983, a decade before the emergence of the World Wide Web.

Third, and perhaps most importantly, while Højsgaard finds some examples of what he thinks 'cyber-religion' might look like and constructs a theoretical model that describes them (if not necessarily accounts for their existence), his attempt leaves unanswered what he means by 'religion' itself. Definitions, of course, abound in the sociological and anthropological literatures, and I will make no attempt to reprise them here. A few salient aspects ought to be considered, however. According to any definition, for example, is it reasonable to consider a parodistic Web site that purports to be a religion as a way of satirizing other aspects of religious belief and practice an authentic religion itself? What does religious commitment – and by implication religion itself – mean when membership requires no more than the click of a mouse? Claiming more than two-and-a-half million members, for example, users can join the 'religion' of Digitalism simply by submitting an electronic form. Højsgaard's own analysis indicates that the Digitalism Web site has not been updated since 2000, that it contained little more than the author's thoughts on a variety of subjects, and that for the purposes of his own research he relied on an Internet archive site. Further, the 'founder' is quite explicit that there are no requirements for Digitalists. In response to the question, 'Then What???' (2000) the archived site reads: 'It's really up to you. We don't ask you to do anything special but to relax and be yourself. You don't need to pray or do special things every day.' To which we might also add, 'So what?' If one can join a religion simply by clicking a button and nothing further is required, how does this satisfy any substantive or functional definition of religion? Of all the Web sites Højsgaard includes, only one at any point in its history came close to being a 'cyber-religion' – Kemetic Orthodoxy. Also known as the House of Netjer, Kemetic Orthodoxy is 'an Egyptian revival religion that has developed a following largely through the Internet' (Krogh and Pillifant 2004b: 167). Begun originally as an offline group in the early 1990s, Kemetic Orthodoxy moved online in the early 1990s and attracted a few hundred interested visitors to their Web sites, many of whom remain active with the group. In comparison with the other sites Højsgaard considers, their durability has less to do with being a 'cyber-religion,' than with operating both online and off, and with presenting itself as an authentic religion rather than simply a parody.

Cyber-Religion: An Unideal Type?

What would a true 'cyber-religion' look like? Following the criteria set out by modern Pagans who have attempted to create fully-orbed cybercovens, we can identify a number of characteristics, some of which are congruent with attributes ascribed to offline religion, others that are more unique to the online environment. Regardless of its particular beliefs, doctrines, or religious practices, a true 'cyber-religion' or 'online spiritual path' meets the following four criteria, at the very least:

First, not surprisingly, it must be online. An offline faith that has an online presence is simply that. Although Roman Catholics who participate in online adoration of the Blessed Sacrament or Hindus who perform various *puja* via the World Wide Web may find meaning in these activities, these are both predicated on offline referents and function only as adjuncts to these offline traditions. Cyber-religions, on the other hand, may draw their theological and ritual inspiration from offline traditions, but they exist in practice only on the Internet.

More to the point, a cyber-religion must be exclusively online in terms of its social and liturgical interaction. Potential members investigate the cyber-religion through Web sites, chatrooms, and discussion forums; current members use online discussion venues to vet potential members, train and initiate neophytes, and conduct ongoing religious education; doctrinal, liturgical, scriptural, and organizational texts are lodged online, exoteric texts available to all, esoteric perhaps password-protected; and all organizational administration, social interaction, and ritual practice is computer-mediated, whether in a chatroom, a discussion forum, or even a private room in a MUD (Multi-User Domain), MOO (a MUD that is Multiple Object Oriented), or MMORPG (Massive Multiplayer Online Roleplaying Game) – all of which represent the online world in terms of a graphical interface. While members may meet or know each other offline, all the 'business' of the cyber-religion is conducted over the Web. Sociologically, this raises the issue of religious privatization, since the vast majority of users connect to the Internet, surf the Web, and interact online as individuals, not as part of a group. Online interaction calls into question the kind of social solidarity that theorists such as Durkheim regarded as essential to the practice of authentic religion. While there is some evidence that the relationships many people form electronically profoundly affect their religious lives, whether the ephemeral nature of online activity can contribute to the long-term durability of a social network is a problem that has yet to be fully investigated.

Second, a cyber-religion must be identifiable as a religion, not just a grab-bag of icons and text that either parody or parrot offline religious content. Simply uploading a site, proclaiming oneself a saint, prophet, or goddess incarnate, and inviting all those who wish to follow your teachings to 'click-to-join' does not necessarily constitute a religion. Whether we take the definition of religion offered by scholars such as William James ('the belief that there is an unseen order, and that our supreme good lies in harmoniously adjusting ourselves thereto'; [1902] 1999: 61), Peter Berger ('the human enterprise by which a sacred cosmos is established'; 1967: 25), or Catherine Wessinger ('a comprehensive worldview that makes sense of the universe'; 2000: 5), there are at least some criteria that must be satisfied in order for a system of beliefs and practices to be called a religion. If we would not classify something a religion in the offline world, it makes little sense to do so simply because it is online.

Third, religions are social products and cultural institutions, whatever institutional form they take and however unaware participants may be of the ways in which they are produced. Thus, whether through outreach or charisma, a true cyber-religion must have the ability to attract members and to fulfill the religious needs of those members online. What good is being a member if membership means nothing in terms of personal and communal identity, two of the principal social-psychological functions of religious belief, practice, and membership? Here the distinction made by Stark and Bainbridge between audience cults, client cults, and cult movements may be useful (1985: 26–30). An online audience cult would be something like Digitalism. The participant (if we can stretch the concept that far) is a member only insofar as she has clicked-to-join; nothing more is required, and she is free to pursue other spiritual interests at the same time. Client cults offer religious services online, often for a fee, though occasionally not. Online divination sites, for example, or psychic services are the cyber-versions of the client cult. Both of these require relatively little of participants. Online cult movements, on the other hand, what I would consider a threshold for the true cyber-religion, meet all the religious needs of the membership and demand more singular allegiance from members.

Finally, a cyber-religion must exhibit some kind of online durability, and find a way to overcome the fragility and fluidity of the World Wide Web. Obviously, this is not only a function of hardware, software, or Internet service provision, but also and more importantly of the interest, commitment, and creativity of those who would participate. As Højsgaard rightly points out, the Internet does relatively little in and of itself. Whatever its beliefs, rituals, or organizational structures, only people can produce and maintain a religion. Indeed, this may be the hardest of the four criteria to meet. However fantastic it may appear to us at this point, computer-mediated communication is in its technological and social infancy. Despite industry and enthusiast hyperbole, research indicates that it is considerably more difficult to establish and maintain meaningful social relationships exclusively on the Internet than it is when one does so either on and offline or offline entirely. However tantalizing the possibility of online ritual, for a wide variety of reasons, not least of which the fact that we remain ineluctably embodied, successful ritual in cyberspace is far more difficult to achieve than similar rituals held offline. And, lastly, however robust the Internet appears, it is still vulnerable to the vicissitudes of server failure, software and hardware obsolescence, malicious hacker activity, even stormy weather. While a severe thunderstorm might prompt a parishioner to take the car rather than walk to a church meeting, that same storm could easily disrupt Internet communications and end an online meeting before it even begins.

Caveat: The Allure of Covert Research and the Ethics of Disclosure

As religious groups continue to interact online, there will be the temptation for sociological and anthropological researchers to 'blend in with the crowd,' to seek once again the elusive goal of pure covert research (cf. Paccagnella 1997). Offline, my presence as an outsider at a group meeting, worship service, or religious site is immediately apparent. As most researchers have noted however, in online interaction identity is reduced to text and self-presentation, and the salient differences between researcher and researched could easily be disguised. On the one hand, this offers tremendous opportunity for investigations that might not otherwise be possible. On the other, it raises once again the significant issue of ethics in sociological research – especially when that research concerns something as personal, as emotional, and as potentially volatile as religious meaning and practice. As I have pointed out elsewhere, 'I could try to assume the identity of an African-American Wiccan priestess who in mundane life works for the telephone company, but the reality remains that I am a middle-aged, male academic of Scots-Irish descent and no particular religious affiliation' (Cowan 2005a: 174). Internet hyperbole tells us that we can be whoever we want online, that we can change age, sex, race, profession, or physical appearance at will. In terms of research ethics, however, when does this cross the line from identity play to deception and fraud?

RELIGION AND THE INTERNET: PROSPECTS FOR THE FUTURE

In this chapter, we have looked at several brief examples of religion on the Internet, surveyed some of the approaches made by scholars to understand its breadth and depth, and considered in more detail the nature and possibility of a 'cyber-religion.' Ignoring religion on the Internet is akin to ignoring religion on television – whether as a participative practice, a source of information, or a framework for the presentation of entertainment and information texts. Since it is unlikely that either religion or the Internet is going to disappear anytime soon, I would like to conclude by addressing briefly issues related to the future of religion in cyberspace and the sociology of religion online. Specifically, these are: the future of religion and the Internet; technology and technique in the practice of religion; the danger of the computer's 'magic lens.'

The Future of Religion and the Internet

Few things have marked the appearance and speed with which the World Wide Web has penetrated the technologized areas of the world more than the hyperbole and rhetoric – both utopian and dystopian – in which this penetration has been couched. While many take a dystopian view of computer-mediated communication and the power humankind is apparently handing over to it (e.g., Brook and Boal 1995; Brooke 1997; Groothuis 1997; Gutstein 1999; Rushkoff 1995; Slouka 1995; Stoll 1995, 1999), and not a few evangelical Christians saw in the Y2K non-event the approach of a computer-mediated apocalypse (e.g., Hutchings and Spargimino 1998; Jeffrey 1998; Lindsey and Ford 1999; though, on this, see Cowan 2003b), others have greeted the Web with varying degrees of enthusiasm and hope. Modern Pagan Lisa McSherry, for example, who as Lady Maat operates the JaguarMoon Cyber Coven, writes that 'Cyberspace is a technological doorway to the astral plane... Once we enter Cyberspace, we are no longer in the physical plane; we literally stand in a place between the worlds' (2002: 5). Jennifer Cobb, a communications consultant, opines that 'the reality of cyberspace transcends the dualism represented by the objectified mind... it has the potential for opening us to a new way of experiencing the world, a way that relies on a divine reality to give it meaning and substance' (1998: 10). Finally, sociologist Brenda Brasher suggests that 'online religion is the most portentous development for the future of religion to come out of the twentieth century,' and that 'using a computer for online religious activity could become the dominant form of religion and religious experience in the next century' (2001: 17, 19). Notwithstanding the fact that similarly utopian claims were made for the train, the telegraph, the telephone, and television, the dream for the Internet remains that it will break down the walls of misunderstanding that keep humanity separate, and enhance our ability to communicate meaningfully and compassionately with one another.

Each of these, however, ignores fundamental issues related to the computer-mediation of religious communication and experience. First, as I noted above, there is the digital divide, the unavoidable fact that Internet access is as subject to the processes of social stratification as other technological products and that content production is becoming increasingly concentrated in the hands of transnational commercial interests. Second, empirical studies indicate about half of those with Internet access go online on any given day, and when they do, the pursuit of religious knowledge or experience ranks very low on the scale of Web activities. Exchanging email, searching for news, and checking the weather remain the most common activities – which, with its enormous hidden costs, arguably makes the Internet one of the most wasteful of human communication technologies. Third, there is little historical evidence that increased knowledge about differing religious traditions has served to ameliorate human tension and contention – whether those tensions are directly related to religion or not. As I have noted elsewhere, 'those who go online are the same people who interact offline. In fact, just like the "ethnic digital divide," it is clear that the Internet is not blind to all manner of human bias and prejudice' (Cowan 2005a: 14). Finally, there is the reality that we are embodied beings and that lived religious practice is as much about our embodiment as it is our imagination. We cannot live our lives online, and until that technological threshold is crossed offline religion will not be seriously challenged by its online variant.

In 2005, the Pew Internet and American Life Project surveyed more than twelve hundred 'Internet experts' about their predictions for the future of the online environment (Fox *et al.* 2005). Which social and cultural institutions will change most as a result of increased Internet use and social penetration, and which will change the least? In terms of the latter, religion was the most common answer. Barrat i Esteve, for example, argued that 'institutions strongly based on information exchange, like international politics, education, arts or media, will change the most because the internet is directly linked with information management. On the other hand,

religion is above all a personal field and the internet is here a tool with less influence' (Fox *et al.* 2005: 7). While sociologists might question whether 'religion is above all a personal field' – though that balance certainly shifts in the online world – Barrat i Esteve's basic point seems well taken.

This is not to say that there are no benefits to online interaction – obviously, there are. Rather, I would like to suggest that, in order to understand more fully how religion is emerging and developing online, one of the most important functions of the sociology of religion on the Internet is to challenge claims that are often hyperbolic and baseless.

Technology and Technique

Following the rise of the machines during the latter part of the Industrial Revolution, wrote Ellul, 'everything had to be reconsidered in terms of the machine' ([1954] 1964: 5), and in that reconsideration, that reorganization of space and reorientation of life according to the dictates of the machine, *technique* is the key. 'Technique integrates the machine into society' (Ellul [1954] 1964: 5).

In broad strokes, many commentators have asked how computer-mediated communications are affecting the conceptualization and practice of religion by those who have Internet access. Drawing on Ellul here, though, at a more fundamental level we must begin to investigate how the techniques of religious practice are being affected by the technical requirements of computer-mediated communication – perhaps the most obvious example is the consistent privileging of the visual as a marker of reality and authenticity. It is not simply that Internet users are adapting their religious practice to the demands of a machine – however we anthropomorphize that machine – those demands are changing the ways in which some users conceptualize their religious practice and beliefs. *How* we do something becomes an integral part of determining *what* it is that we do. While there are literally hundreds of different online venues for posting prayer requests, sharing the results of one's own prayer, and celebrating the experiences of others, how does that affect one's conceptualization of contact and communication with the divine? On the other hand, how does one engage in online contemplative prayer, online *sesshin* or *koan* practice, online meditation in all its global variety? How can one mechanize – because that is what the online practice of religion requires – the intensely personal spiritual experience of monastic practice? How does the online expression (((hugs))) compare to the feeling of warmth and security that comes from a real human embrace? It may be better than nothing, but how much better remains to be seen and demands to be investigated.

Mechanization of practice also encourages us to ask what is at the heart of our beliefs about a particular thing. If seeing something is the experiential threshold of authentication, if something is real for us because we have seen it, what does it mean to see it onscreen? Although there is a certain absurdity to the suggestion that taking a virtual tour of Temple Square is a realistic substitute for an actual visit, is 'seeing' the Salt Lake City Temple through the lens of a Web camera more 'realistic' than looking at a brochure, a memorial book, or slides of someone's trip? And if so, why? From a technical perspective, for example, there is no way for a user to know whether the onscreen image is 'real' or not. Images can be faked, time and date stamps falsified, information managed to present a particular image, a particular scene, whether or not that scene conforms to reality or not. Yet, we credence these images because we trust that those who have uploaded them mean for them to be taken seriously.

One of the most essential characteristics of computer-mediated communication is that it is and remains *communication*. For religious experience and practice to be authentically a part of the online environment, then, it seems logical that those experiences and practices must be reducible to communicative events. Of course, religion worldwide is replete with such events – sermons, *darshan*, prophecies, and all manner of ritual interactions – but the important point here is that these events are not reducible to their communicative component.

The Magic Lens: Seeing and Not-Seeing Online

Commenting on the 'magic lens' of the computer interface, that small bubble or rectangle that magnifies a certain portion of an image when the user drags it across the larger parent file, Johnson (1997: 88) notes that 'the lens is a tool for discriminating. It filters, and in doing so it keeps many things opaque. The lens acknowledges that surplus information can be just as damaging as information scarcity.' In terms of religion on the Internet, we must be careful that scholars do not become so concerned with mapping cyberspace, with delineating what is there, with using our own particular 'magic lens' to magnify discrete portions of online religious activity and information, that we forget to ask – or at least neglect to foreground – what that same lens misses, what its discrimination renders opaque or invisible. On the one hand, it is not hard to catalogue aspects of religious experience that are missing in the online world – however creative the ways we try to simulate those aspects – but it does not seem that we have asked what it means that those things are missing. For example, are there sufficient clues in the record of online interaction that those who choose to participate in aspects of religious devotion or practice actually fill in the blanks, supplying what is missing in the computer-mediated episode from the broader repertoire of their offline experience? This would hardly be surprising. Cinema audiences have been supplying relevant, often crucial material to film narratives for more than a century. There is no reason to suppose that the same process is not operative in the online experience, and, indeed, close analysis of online religious practice indicates that it is almost always linked in important ways to offline religious referents.

Though he acknowledges that the 'magic lens' may become as common a tool of interface culture as the computer window, Johnson (1997: 90) concludes that 'like so many contemporary interface filters, its value will come less from what it reveals than from what it keeps hidden.' This is also true for religion on the Internet, for the computer itself, the entire screen functions as a magic lens – zooming in on only those aspects of religious belief, practice, life, and culture that are of immediate interest to the user/consumer, and effectively blocking out, in Johnson's words, 'that great, teeming potentiality of data' (1997: 90) that exists beyond the edges of the screen and cannot but press in upon it.

To take just one mundane example, if a worshiper attends church regularly because she likes the music used by a particular congregation and the five-register organ that supports it, that does not mean she is not exposed to all other elements that make up any congregation's particular worship experience. She may love the music, but detest the pastor's preaching style; however, she cannot avoid the latter if she wants to enjoy the former. Online, the magic lens allows her to focus only on those aspects of the religious 'experience' that she wants – though few would dispute that there is an obvious difference between *feeling* the music of a five-register Cassavant Frères while sitting in a well-constructed sanctuary and simply *hearing* a sound file of music played on that same instrument played back through the often tinny speakers of one's home computer.

One way researchers can address this restriction is to refrain from investigating 'religion' as though it were a monolithic, conceptually transparent sociocultural phenomenon, to recognize, as J. Z. Smith has pointed out (1982: 18), that as an analytic category 'religion is solely the creation of the scholar's study.' What is needed now are intentionally comparative studies that do distinguish between the ways different religions can and do use the Internet, and what it is about those different religions that either encourages or restricts their choices. Why are all officially sanctioned Scientology sites so similar, for example? Why is there little if any variation in either the information that is presented or the manner of presentation? It is because Scientology is the quintessentially closed source religion; everything must be transmitted in a form precisely consistent with that laid down by church authorities or it is considered inaccurate, inauthentic, and anathema. No variation of teaching or interpretation is permitted. This insight,

however, is only possible through an understanding of the history of Scientology offline, before any consideration of Scientology's online presence. Consequently, there is a need to conduct research that is informed by a deep understanding of the particular religious tradition at hand. Only then can researchers reasonably and/or responsibly relate what they observe as online activity to the almost inevitably larger, more complex religious parent processes that occur offline. This way, we avoid mistaking something that we may have encountered for the first time online for something that has emerged as a cultural product solely located in cyberspace. In short, we need to move from talking about 'religion on the Internet' (in the sense of religion as a macrocultural phenomenon) to 'religions on the Internet' (which looks at microcultural processes specific to particular religious traditions), and which can then be related to parent traditions offline, and more generally (albeit far more carefully) to larger religious patterns.

REFERENCES

Abbate, J. 1999. *Inventing the internet*. Cambridge, MA: The MIT Press.

Apolito, P. 2005. *The internet and the madonna: Religious visionary experiences on the web*. Chicago & London: The University of Chicago Press.

Bedell, K. 2000. 'Dispatches from the electronic frontier: Explorations of mainline protestant use of the internet'. In J. K. Hadden and D. E. Cowan (eds), *Religion on the internet: Research prospects and promises* (pp. 183–204). London & Amsterdam: JAI Press/Elsevier Science.

Berger, H. A. and Ezzy, D. 2004. 'The internet as virtual spiritual community: Teen witches in the United States and Australia'. In L. L. Dawson and D. E. Cowan (eds), *Religion online: Finding faith on the internet* (pp. 175–88). New York & London: Routledge.

Berger, P. L. 1967. *The sacred canopy: Elements of a sociological theory of religion*. New York: Doubleday/Anchor Press.

Berger, P. and Luckmann, T. 1966. *The social construction of reality: A treatise on the sociology of knowledge*. Harmondsworth, UK: Penguin Books.

Berners-Lee, T. with Fischetti, M. 2000. *Weaving the web: The original design and ultimate destiny of the world wide web.* New York: HarperBusiness.

Brasher, B. E. 2001. *Give me that online religion.* San Francisco: Jossey-Bass.

Brill, A. and Packard, A. 1997. 'Silencing Scientology's critics on the Internet: A mission impossible?' *Communication and the Law* 19 (4), 1–23.

Brook, J. and Boal, I. A. (eds) 1995. *Resisting the virtual life: The culture and politics of information.* San Francisco: City Lights Books.

Brooke, T. 1997. *Virtual gods: The seduction of power and pleasure in cyberspace.* Eugene, OR: Harvest House Publishers.

Browne, M. 1998. 'Should Germany stop worrying and learn to love the octopus? Freedom of religion and the Church of Scientology in Germany and the United States'. *Indiana International & Comparative Law Review* 9, 155–202.

Bunt, G. R. 2000. *Virtually Islamic: Computer-mediated communication and cyber Islamic environments.* Cardiff: University of Wales Press.

Bunt, G. R. 2003. *Islam in the digital age: E-jihad, online fatwas, and cyber Islam environments.* London: Pluto Press.

Bunt, G. R. 2004. 'Rip.burn.pray: Islamic expression online'. In L. L. Dawson and D. E. Cowan (eds), *Religion online: Finding faith on the internet* (pp. 123–34). New York & London: Routledge.

Campbell, H. 2004. 'This is my church': Seeing the internet and club culture as spiritual spaces. In L. L. Dawson and D. E. Cowan (eds), *Religion online: Finding faith on the internet* (pp. 107–21). New York & London: Routledge.

Campbell, H. 2005. *Exploring religious community online: We are one in the network.* New York: Peter Lang.

Careaga, A. 1999. *E-vangelism: Sharing the gospel in cyberspace.* Lafayette, LA: Vital Issues Press.

Careaga, A. and Sweet, L. 2001. *eMinistry: Connecting with the net generation.* Grand Rapids, MI: Kregel Publications.

Castells, M. 2001. *The internet galaxy: Reflections on the internet, business, and society.* Oxford: Oxford University Press.

Chapel Webcam Witness Stories; retrieved from www.monksofadoration.org/webcamst.html, 2 December 2005.

Clark, L. S. 2003. *From angels to aliens: Teenagers, the media, and the supernatural.* Oxford: Oxford University Press.

Cobb, J. 1998. *Cybergrace: The search for God in cyberspace.* New York: Crown Publishers.

Cowan, D. E. 2003a. *Bearing false witness? An introduction to the Christian countercult.* Westport, CT: Praeger Publishers.

Cowan, D. E. 2003b. 'Confronting the failed failure: Y2K and evangelical eschatology in light of the passed millennium'. *Nova Religio* 7 (2), 71–85.

Cowan, D. E. 2004. 'Contested spaces: Movement, countermovement, and e-space propaganda'. In L. L. Dawson and D. E. Cowan (eds), *Religion online: Finding faith on the internet* (pp. 255–71). New York & London: Routledge.

Cowan, D. E. 2005a. *Cyberhenge: Modern pagans on the internet.* New York & London: Routledge.

Cowan, D. E. 2005b. 'Online u-topia: Cyberspace and the mythology of placelessness'. *Journal for the Scientific Study of Religion* 44 (3), 257–63.

Cowan, D. E. 2006. 'The internet and American religious life'. In C. H. Lippy (ed.), *Faith in America: Changes, challenges, and a new spirituality*, vol. 3 (pp. 119–40). Westport, CT: Praeger Publishers.

Cowan, D. E. and Hadden, J. K. 2004. 'Virtually religious: New religious movements and the world wide web'. In J. R. Lewis (ed.), *The Oxford handbook of new religious movements* (pp. 119–40). New York: Oxford University Press.

Dawson, L. L. 2004. 'Religion and the quest for virtual community'. In L. L. Dawson and D. E. Cowan (eds), *Religion online: Finding faith on the internet* (pp. 75–89). New York and London: Routledge.

Dawson, L. L. and Hennebry, J. 1999. 'New religions and the internet: Recruiting in a new public space'. *Journal of Contemporary Religion* 14 (1), 17–39.

Ellul, J. [1954] 1964. *The technological society*, trans. J. Wilkinson. New York: Vintage Books.

Fox, S., Anderson, J. A. and Rainie, L. 2005. *The future of the internet.* Washington, DC: Pew Internet & American Life Project; available online at www.pewinternet.org.

Gillies, J. and Cailliau, R. 2000. *How the web was born.* Oxford: Oxford University Press.

Gold, L. 1997. *Mormons on the internet.* Rocklin, CA: Prima Publishing.

Groothuis, D. 1997. *The soul in cyberspace.* Grand Rapids, MI: Baker Books.

Grossman, W. M. 1995. alt.scientology.war. *Wired* 3 (12); retrieved from www.wired.com/wired/archive/3.12/alt.scientology.war, 25 December 2005.

Grossman, W. M. 1997. *Net.wars.* New York: New York University Press.

Gutstein, D. 1999. *E.con: How the internet undermines democracy.* Toronto: Stoddart.

Hadden, J. K. and Cowan, D. E. 2000. 'The promised land or electronic chaos? Toward understanding religion on the internet'. In J. K. Hadden and D. E. Cowan (eds), *Religion on the internet: Research prospects and promises* (pp. 3–21). London & Amsterdam: JAI Press/Elsevier Science.

Hafner, K. and Lyon, M. 1996. *Where wizards stay up late: The origins of the internet*. New York: Touchstone.

Helland, C. 2000. 'Online-religion/religion-online and virtual communitas'. In J. K. Hadden and D. E. Cowan (eds), *Religion on the internet: Research prospects and promises* (pp. 205–24). London and Amsterdam: JAI Press/Elsevier Science.

Helland, C. 2004. 'Popular religion and the world wide web: A match made in (cyber) heaven'. In L. L. Dawson and D. E. Cowan (eds), *Religion online: Finding faith on the internet* (pp. 23–36). New York & London: Routledge.

Helland, C. 2005. 'Online Religion as Lived Religion: Methodological Issues in the Study of Religious Participation on the Internet'. *Online – Heidelberg Journal of Religions on the Internet* 1 (1); retrieved from *http://online.uni-hd.de*, December 5, 2005.

Højsgaard, M. T. 2005. 'Cyber-religion: On the cutting edge between the virtual and the real'. In M. T. Højsgaard and M. Warburg (eds), *Religion and cyberspace* (pp. 50–63). London & New York: Routledge.

Horwitz, P. 1997. 'Scientology in court: A comparative analysis and some thoughts on selected issues in law and religion'. *DePaul Law Review* 47, 85–154.

Hoover, S. M., Clark, L. S. and Rainie, L. 2004. *Faith Online*. Washington, DC: Pew Internet and American Life Project; available online at www.pewinternet.org.

Horsfall, S. 2000. 'How religious organizations use the internet: A preliminary inquiry'. In J. K. Hadden and D. E. Cowan (eds), *Religion on the internet: Research prospects and promises* (pp. 153–82). London and Amsterdam: JAI Press/Elsevier Science.

Hutchings, N. W. and Spargimino, L. 1998. *Y2K=666?* Oklahoma City: Hearthstone.

Introvigne, M. 2000. "So many evil things": Anti-cult terrorism via the internet'. In J. K. Hadden and D. E. Cowan (eds), *Religion on the internet: Research prospects and promises* (pp. 277–306). London & Amsterdam: JAI Press/Elsevier Science.

Introvigne, M. 2005. 'A symbolic universe: Information terrorism and new religions in cyberspace'. In M. T. Højsgaard and M. Warburg (eds), *Religion and cyberspace* (pp. 102–17). London & New York: Routledge.

Ivy 2003. 'Start your own online coven'. *newWitch* 5 (October), 61–2.

James, William [1902] 1999. *The varieties of religious experience*. New York: Random House/Modern Library.

Jeffrey, G. R. 1998. *The millennium meltdown: The year 2000 computer crisis*. Toronto: Frontier Research.

John Paul II 1990. *Redemptoris missio: On the permanent validity of the church's missionary mandate*. Papal Encyclical (7 December).

Johnson, S. 1997. *Interface culture: How new technology transforms the way we create and communicate*. New York: HarperEdge.

Jones, S. G. (ed.) 1995. *Cybersociety: Computer-mediated communications and community*. Thousand Oaks, CA: Sage Publications.

Jones, S. G. (ed.) 1997. *Virtual culture: Identity & Communication in cybersociety*. London: Sage Publications.

Jones, S. G. (ed.) 1998. *Cybersociety 2.0: Revisiting computer-mediated communication and community*. Thousand Oaks, CA: Sage Publications.

Kelly, D. 1999a. 'Digital dharma.' *The Middle Way: Journal of the Buddhist Society* 74 (1), 57–9.

Kelly, D. 1999b. 'Finding the path on the internet'. *The Middle Way: Journal of the Buddhist Society* 74 (3), 185–87.

Kent, S. A. 1999. 'The globalization of Scientology: Influence, control, and opposition in transnational markets'. *Religion* 29, 147–69.

Kim, M. 2005. 'Online Buddhist community: An alternative religious organization in the information age'. In M. T. Højsgaard and M. Warburg (eds), *Religion and cyberspace* (pp. 138–48). London & New York: Routledge.

Knight, S. and Telesco, P. 2002. *The cyber spellbook: Magick in the virtual world*. Franklin Lakes, NJ: New Page Books.

Krogh, M. C. and Pillifant, B. A. 2004a. 'The house of Netjer: A new religious community online'. In L. L. Dawson and D. E. Cowan (eds), *Religion online: Finding faith on the internet* (pp. 205–19). New York and London: Routledge.

Krogh, M. and Pillifant, B. A. 2004b. 'Kemetic Orthodoxy: Ancient Egyptian religion on the internet – a research note'. *Sociology of Religion* 65 (2), 167–75.

Lawrence, B. B. 2000. *The idiot's guide to religions online*. Indianapolis, IN: Alpha Books.

Levy, S. 1997. 'Blaming the web'. *Newsweek* (7 April), 46.

Lindsey, H. and Ford, C. 1999. *Facing millennial midnight*. Torrance, CA: Western Front.

Lippard, J. and Jacobsen, J. 1995a. 'Scientology v. the internet: Free speech and copyright infringement on the information super-highway', *Skeptic* 3 (3), 35–41.

Lippard, J. and Jacobsen, J. (1995b). 'Scientology loses judgment in internet case.' *Skeptic* 3 (4), 18–19.

Liu, G. Z. 1999. 'Virtual community presence in internet relay chatting'. *Journal of Computer-Mediated Communication* 5 (1); retrieved from *http://jcmc.indiana.edu/vol5/issue1/ liu.html*, 5 December 2005.

Lockard, J. 1997. 'Progressive politics, electronic individualism and the myth of virtual community'. In D. Porter (ed.), *Internet culture* (pp. 219–32). New York: Routledge.

Lövheim, M. and Linderman, A. 2005. 'Constructing religious identity on the internet'. In M. T. Højsgaard and M. Warburg (eds), *Religion and cyberspace* (pp. 121–37). London and New York: Routledge.

MacWilliams, M. 2005. 'Digital Waco: Branch Davidian virtual communities after the Waco tragedy'. In M. T. Højsgaard and M. Warburg (eds), *Religion and cyberspace* (pp. 180–98). London and New York: Routledge.

Markoff, J. 1997. 'Death in a cult: The technology'. *New York Times* (28 March), A20.

Mayer, J-F. 2000. 'Religious movements and the internet: The new frontier of cult controversies'. In J. K. Hadden and D. E. Cowan (eds), *Religion on the internet: Research prospects and promises* (pp. 249–66). London & Amsterdam: JAI Press/Elsevier Science.

McSherry, L. 2002. *The virtual pagan: Exploring Wicca and Paganism through the internet*. Boston and York Beach: Weiser Books.

Mossberger, K., Tobert, C. J. and Stansbury, M. 2003. *Virtual inequality: Beyond the digital divide*. Washington, DC: Georgetown University Press.

NightMare, M. M. 2001. *Witchcraft on the web: Weaving Pagan traditions online*. Toronto, ON: ECW Press.

Norris, P. 2001. *Digital divide: Civic engagement, information poverty, and the internet worldwide*. Cambridge, UK and New York: Cambridge University Press.

O'Leary, S. D. 1996. 'Cyberspace as sacred space: Communicating religion on computer networks.' *Journal of the American Academy of Religion* 64 (4), 781–808.

Paccagnella, L. 1997. 'Getting the seat of your pants dirty: Strategies for ethnographic research on virtual communities.' *Journal of Computer-Mediated Communication* 3 (1); retrieved from *http://cmc.indiana.edu/vol3/issue1/paccagnella.html*, 22 February 2006.

Peckham, M. 1998. 'New dimensions of social movement/countermovement interaction: The case of Scientology and its internet critics.' *Canadian Journal of Sociology/Cahiers Canadiens de Sociologie* 23 (4), 317–47.

Pew Internet and American Life Project 2005. 'Internet: The mainstreaming of online life'. Washington, DC: Pew Internet and American Life Project; available at www.pewinternet.org.

Pontifical Council for Social Communication 2002a. 'The church and internet'. Vatican: Pontifical Council for Social Communications.

Pontifical Council for Social Communication 2002b. 'Ethics in internet'. Vatican: Pontifical Council for Social Communications.

Prebish, C. S. 2004. 'The cybersangha: Buddhism on the internet.' In L. L. Dawson and D. E. Cowan (eds), *Religion online: Finding faith on the internet* (pp. 135–47). New York & London: Routledge.

Raymond, J. 1997. *Catholics on the internet*. Rocklin, CA: Prima Publishing.

Robinson, W. G. 1997. 'Heaven's Gate: The end?', *Journal of Computer-Mediated Communication* 3(3); retrieved from *http://jcmc.indiana.edu/vol3/issue3/robinson.html*, 5 December 2005.

Rheingold, H. 1993. *The virtual community: Homesteading on the electronic frontier*. Cambridge, MA: The MIT Press.

Rushkoff, D. 1995. *Cyberia: Life in the trenches of hyperspace*. New York: HarperSanFrancisco.

Slouka, M. 1995. *War of the worlds: Cyberspace and the high-tech assault on reality*. New York: Basic Books.

Smith, J. Z. 1982. *Imagining religion: From Babylon to Jonestown*. Chicago: University of Chicago Press.

Smith, M. A. and Kollock, P. 1999. *Communities in cyberspace*. London & New York: Routledge.

Stark, Rodney and William Sims Bainbridge (1885). *The Future of Religion: Secularization, Revival, and Cult Formation*. Berkeley and Los Angeles: University of California Press.

Stoll, C. 1995. *Silicon snake oil: Second thoughts on the information highway*. New York and London: Doubleday.

Stoll, C. 1999. *High-tech heretic: Reflections of a computer contrarian*. New York: Anchor.

Telesco, P. and Knight, S. 2001. *The wiccan web: Surfing the magic on the internet*. New York: Citadel Press.

'Then what??' 2000; retrieved from *http://digital-ism.8m.com*, 3 July 2005.

Turkle, S. 1995. *Life on the screen: Identity in the age of the internet*. New York: Touchstone.

Urban, H. B. 2000. 'The devil at Heaven's Gate: Rethinking the study of religion in the age of cyber-space'. *Nova Religio* 3 (2), 269–302.

Wellman, B. and Haythornethwaite, C. (eds) 2002. *The internet in everyday life*. Oxford: Blackwell Publishing.

Wessinger, C. 2000. *How the millennium comes violently: From Jonestown to Heaven's Gate*. New York: Seven Bridges Press.

Willson, M. 2000. 'Community in the abstract: A political and ethical dilemma?'. In D. Bell and B. M. Kennedy (eds), *The Cybercultures Reader* (pp. 644–57). London & New York: Routledge.

Wresch, W. 1996. *Disconnected: Haves and have-nots in the information age*. New Brunswick, NJ: Rutgers University Press.

Wright, S. 2000. 'Instant genius! Just add the net'. *net* (June), 50–8.

Young, G. A. 2004. 'Reading and praying online: The continuity of religion online and online religion in internet Christianity.' In L. L. Dawson and D. E. Cowan (eds), *Religion online: Finding faith on the internet* (pp. 93–106). New York & London: Routledge.

PART V

Religion and Politics

The mutual implication of religion and politics has been a feature of virtually all known civilizations. Given that both of these areas of social and cultural life centre on various forms of power, it is not surprising that the fate of each is at least partially shaped by the other. What *is* truly surprising is that so many people believe that religion and politics can and should be kept separate. Sociologists of religion therefore have the opportunity to demonstrate just how close the relationship between religion and politics can be and just how strong are the flows of mutual influence between them. But these generalisations hardly do justice to the complex and shifting patterns in the nexus between secular and sacred forms of power. Instead, as the following four chapters show, political groups, agencies of the state and social movements are all actors in the drama in which religious and political forces contend, compete and sometimes collide.

Some social scientists claim that globalisation has somehow subverted the sovereignty of states and rendered the idea of separate societies unworkable in the twenty-first century. Relatively little support for these ideas about 'global flows' that bypass states has come from sociologists of religion, most of whom remain fully aware of the extent to which religion needs to be understood in the context of nations and states. For this reason, **Jay Demerath** devotes much of Chapter 18 to the political and legal frameworks which different states provide for the practice of religion in public and private life. The separation of church and state in the US is arguably the most intensely discussed arrangement and is still subject to many different interpretations, which have changed over time. There is no doubt, however, that the US Constitution permits – if not encourages – the powerful involvement of religious forces in American politics. Other countries display different permutations of relations between religion, the state and politics: religious states and religious politics; secular states and secular politics; religious states and secular politics; and secular states and religious politics. Illustrating these four combinations with examples from many parts of the world, Demerath also points out numerous complications and ironies. One of them concerns the propensity of some states and some religions to employ violent methods of pursuing their interests. There is a lively debate among sociologists of religion about the factors that either permit or deter such violence and the infringement of human rights that accompanies it – all in a globalising world.

Historically, religions have contributed heavily to the regulation of social and cultural life.

This is still the case in countries where the state is closely aligned with particular religions as in, for example, Saudi Arabia and Iran. And, as **James Beckford and James Richardson** argue in Chapter 19, self-regulation remains a central function of most religious organisations – with or without the backing of a state. But it is common at the beginning of the twenty-first century for religious institutions to be subject to regulation by state agencies in accordance with constitutions and codes of law, some of which are grounded in international conventions. Nonetheless, the resistance of some religious organisations to regulation by the state is still a contentious issue in some countries, in spite of the fact that constitutional and legal provisions for the freedom of religion are increasingly similar – at least in liberal democracies. By contrast, court systems vary widely in terms of their procedures and prerogatives, thereby reflecting the balance of power in societies between major interest groups. Regional and would-be global efforts to protect the freedom of religion as well as to regulate how it is implemented have met with varying degrees of success. Often the legal forms of regulation play a secondary role in comparison with that of the mass media and public opinion, especially with regard to unpopular religious minorities that are demonised in moral panics. Beckford and Richardson suggest that the regulation of religion has become more controversial in recent decades as a result of, first, the growth of religious diversity in Western societies and, second, the increasing sensitivity of politicians to 'consumer protection' issues with regard to 'privatised religion.' In these circumstances, sociologists cannot afford to ignore the fact that religion is both the subject and the object of regulation and is therefore inevitably politicised.

Another facet of the political significance of religion concerns the pursuit of social change by means of social movements. In Chapter 20, **Sharon Nepstad and Rhys Williams** trace the long history of religious inspirations of conservative and progressive movements for social and cultural change – and the parallel development of sociological thinking about religion's contributions to change at the levels of individual, group and culture. Religion can have a major role in crystallising the ideology and collective identity of social movements, in supplying organisational resources and skills, and in facilitating connections with wider society. This helps to explain why religious figures are so often involved in social movements – as protagonists or antagonists – even if these movements are not themselves predominantly religious. Nepstad and Williams examine three particular movements in an attempt to identify the factors that determine whether religion is a force for the *status quo* or for change: the movement to unionise the workforce in the Southern US after 1945; the liberation movement in El Salvador in the 1970s and 1980s; and the anti-apartheid movement in South Africa from the 1970s onwards. These movements all pursued different grievances in different settings. While different religious interests clashed with each other in all three cases, sociological analysis is able to explain why certain religious interests prevailed over others. The availability of 'free space' for religious mobilisation and of ties to pre-existing organisations was a major factor in the relative success of collective action.

The preceding chapters in this Part analyse the political significance of religion mostly in relation to the state, its welfare policies, the apparatus for regulating religion and the contributions of religion towards social movements. Clearly, politics is also significant at the level of individuals as citizens and voters. **Laura Olson** therefore considers the links between religious affiliations, political preferences and ideological alignments in Chapter 21. Starting with Tocqueville's observation in the 1840s that a political opinion accompanies every religion in the US, she examines the ways in which religious identity shapes Americans' political attitudes and actions. Ideological cleavages between the main Christian churches have long been closely associated with political differences, and recent increases in the level of religious diversity have not changed this pattern. But it is only with the aid of survey data that sociologists have been able to identify the aspects of religion that primarily account for political opinions and allegiances.

This involves separating out the effects of religious believing, belonging and behaving, among other considerations, in shaping political outlooks, voting patterns and opinions on politicised socio-moral issues such as abortion and homosexuality. Olson suggests that it may be an exaggeration to describe Americans as poised on the brink of a 'culture war' between politically polarised 'orthodox' and 'progressive' citizens. This neglects other types of cleavage. Moreover, recent research has emphasised the importance of examining political attitudes in the context of particular issues and events, and the role of high-profile religious leaders is another factor shaping political thought and action. Certainly religio-political groupings other than the 'Christian Right' deserve more careful analysis – for example, traditional vs. non-traditional Catholics, the evangelical religious left, and emergent groupings of Muslims, Hindus and Christians from non-Western backgrounds.

18

Religion and the State; Violence and Human Rights

N. J. DEMERATH III

Sociologists of religion are not often consulted on national and international affairs of state (but see Demerath, 2007 for an imagined exception). Until recently the very idea seemed preposterous. Our lair has been that of the private and the local, of churches, mosques, temples, sects, and cults as the smaller and perhaps lesser communities of the sacred. But lately religion has become increasingly embroiled in the public sphere, and where religion leads, at least a few scholars follow. In country after country, religion has been either shaped by or a shaper of critical state policy, and the conflicts between major faith traditions and the divisions within their ranks have done a great deal to define the world of the twenty-first century. Cases in point are legion and range alphabetically from Afghanistan to the former Yugoslavia with (i)ntermediate stops in, say, India, Iran, Iraq, (Northern) Ireland, and Israel.

This chapter will examine what is to be understood and how it might be approached. It will highlight both old chestnuts and new buds in the literature, while drawing upon and extending some of my earlier writings in the area, especially *Crossing the Gods: World Religions and Worldly Politics* (Demerath, 2001). It will begin with what Americans typically refer to as 'the separation of church and state' and provide some variations on the theme, both in the U.S. and elsewhere around the globe. As we shall see, these variations have had critical consequences first, for inter- and intra-religious violence, and second, for human rights and religious persecution.

SECOND THOUGHTS ON THE TWO CLAUSES OF THE FIRST AMENDMENT

'Congress shall make no law respecting an establishment of religion or prohibiting the free exercise thereof.' This single sentence begins the 'First' of ten amendments to the U.S. Constitution adopted more than 200 hundred years ago in 1791 as its 'Bill of Rights.' As much as Americans might relish the conceit that the idea sprang full-blown from the brow of Thomas Jefferson (or more likely James Madison), it was the result of a long-term historical process. The new nation was eager to avoid the experiences associated with almost 200 years of European religious wars, not to mention more than 150 years of religious rule at the hands of the British, on the one hand, and their own colonial and state religious systems, on the other (cf. Richardson, 2006).

Since its inception, the amendment has been mythically impregnated and variously interpreted (cf. Stokes and Pfeffer, 1964; Wood, 1985; Witte, 2005). Consider, for example, the widespread reference to Jefferson's image of a 'wall of separation' between church and state in a letter he wrote to a group of Baptist clergy in Danbury, Connecticut in 1803. Because Americans are proud of their constitutional heritage, many have taken the Jeffersonian metaphor to heart and regarded the wall as both more unique and less permeable than the facts warrant. As we shall see later, other countries have developed their own forms of 'separation,' though in no country, including the U.S., is the separation absolute.

Clearly the most popular view of the First Amendment celebrates its guarantee of religious freedom for religious individuals and groups seeking to avoid state interference while pursuing their inalienable rights (cf. Adams and Emmerich, 1990; Noonan, 1998). This is certainly a noble and important aspect of the wording, and Richardson (2006) provides a 'socio-legal' analysis of the conditions which favor religious freedom wherever it is found. It has sometimes been argued that religious free exercise is technically unnecessary since it is covered under another First Amendment guarantee concerning freedom of speech. On the other hand, Hammond *et al.* (2004) have sought recently to expand the implications of religious freedom to freedom of conscience.

There is no doubt that the free exercise clause has been important in American history and a beacon to the world. But it is significant that the 'free-exercise clause' follows the so-called (anti- or dis-) 'establishment clause,' which begins the amendment as quoted above. Over time the establishment clause has proved to be the most distinctive part of our constitutional heritage, and a tenet that is rare in other nations around the globe. The over-whelming majority of the world's constitutions proudly (if sometimes inaccurately) proclaim the freedom of religion – or at least of the more private 'religious belief' (cf. Van Moorseven and Ger Van der Tan, 1978; Krislov, 1985; Wilson, 1987;

Noonan, 1998). But in the U.S., it is the establishment clause that has been pivotal and is key to some of the most important church–state litigation of the last half-century concerning issues such as prayer and the teaching of creationism and 'intelligent design' in the public schools, a woman's right to choose an abortion, posting the 'Ten Commandments' in government courthouses, and hosting a Christmas creche on government public property. In such cases, the complaining plaintiffs have sought freedom *from* religion rather than freedom *for* religion.

The common historical wisdom suggests that this clause was intended as a check against bullying religious majorities seeking to use new federal powers to make life difficult for religious minorities. True, this is precisely what 'an establishment of religion' would have entailed, hence what needed to be prevented (cf. Gaustad, 1987; Noll, 1990). But consider another historical interpretation suggested in a forthcoming work by John F. Wilson. The founders were deeply concerned to protect the fledgling federal government, and they realized that two controversial initiatives had the power to bring it down: the first was any effort to end slavery, and the second was any attempt to do away with the powerful religious establishments that were already ensconced at the state level – for example, Congregationalist in Massachusetts and Episcopalian in Virginia. If one reads the establishment clause in this latter context, note how different it seems. Rather than a gauntlet in the face of existing religious officialdoms, it offers assurance that they would not be tampered with – as indeed they were not until 1940 when the Bill of Rights was finally extended to the states, more than a century after Massachusetts had been the last state to abolish its official religious standing in 1833.

Meanwhile, over the last 200 years, the language of the establishment clause has taken on an ever-broadening meaning in the opposite direction (Drakeman, 1991). Gradually judicial interpretations adapted the clause to changing circumstances. The definition of an establishment offense has evolved from large denominations using government powers to muscle small religious groups to perceived government affiliation with or support for either a particular religion or religion in general as opposed to non-religion. It was President Dwight Eisenhower who captured the limits of American religious tolerance when he said he didn't care which God a citizen believed in as long as he had one. If translated into actual policy, this would have been an establishment violation because it amounted to a state official endorsing religion generally. However, one can also imagine establishment violations that involve the opposite, that is, government endorsement of or support for non-religion or what has been called 'secular humanism.' State departures from neutrality on either side of the religious fence are unconstitutional.

And yet there are some well accepted exceptions. Laws concerning the free exercise of religion often have explicit or implicit contingencies concerning the national interest. In the U.S., there are well-established precedents for denying free exercise to practices that endanger the health and welfare of innocent victims, including the children of Christian Scientists who are protected from their parents' decisions to withhold critical medical care. There are also precedents for allowing church–state relationships that might otherwise suggest an 'establishment.' Basically, religious organizations may receive government funds to operate day care centers, hospitals, relief programs, etc. as long as both the intent and the consequences are secular. As the government's social missions have expanded, churches and other religious organizations are often indispensable allies in service provision. This has resulted in not a few winks and nudges over relationships that satisfy the needs of both church and state (cf. Nichols, 1988). As is well-known, the courts have upheld a variety of what have been termed 'civil religious' practices such as the motto 'In God We Trust' on coins and currency, prayers at Presidential inauguration ceremonies and at the beginning of each day's business in the U.S. Congress and virtually every state legislature on the grounds that these are more symbolic than substantive, and the audience is principally one of adults rather than more impressionable students in primary and secondary schools.

Meanwhile, there has always been an uneasy relation between the 'establishment' and 'free exercise' clauses. From a strict legal standpoint, the first decision to be made concerning a potential church–state case is which of the two clauses is most pertinent, since arguments from the two perspectives are often the obverse of each other. For example, consider a recent case in which two Catholic women employed at a greyhound race track in Massachusetts announced that they were taking Christmas day off to celebrate with their families. When the track fired them on the grounds that they had been told in advance that this was its busiest day of the year and their work was very important, the two women secured a lawyer and filed for state compensation because their religious freedom had been violated. This may seem a straightforward free exercise case. However, such claims have generally been rejected. In similar cases, the courts have held that if the state had privileged a religious day off compared to other possible days, especially a religious day off according to one particular faith compared to other possible faiths, it would amount to state support for religion generally, or worse, for one religion in particular. Subsequently, the state's largely Catholic legislature voted to allow every citizen a 'religious' holiday of their own choosing and their own definition. Because the case has yet to find its way into the courts, the last shoe has yet to drop.

One can imagine the ultimate church–state case in which each clause is charged with violating the other. Such a case has never actually materialized but it is not hard to hypothesize. For example, placing limits on any religion's pursuit of becoming established by the state may be an unconstitutional constraint on its free exercise. If a religious denomination is strong enough to marshall control over a governmental unit, isn't it a denial of its religious rights to deny such control? On the other hand, a state guarantee of religious free exercise may itself be an establishment violation. After all, doesn't it single out religion for special standing compared to the free exercise of other beliefs and commitments?

In rare cases such as conscientious objector status during the Vietnam War, religious rights have been extended to those who have no formal religious commitments but hold religious-like convictions. In its 1965 *Seeger* and 1970 *Welsh* decisions, the U.S. Supreme Court extended conscientious objector status to persons who were avowedly not religious but held beliefs that occupied 'in the life of that individual a "place parallel to that filled by God" in traditional religious persons' (*U.S. v. Welsh*, 1970). In some sense, this radical allowance was precedent shattering as it represented the nose of the secular camel in the religious tent. Because its legal implications are daunting, it is not surprising that the Court has seldom returned to the decision. The suggestion that there is only a thin line between formal religion and other sacred cultural tenets, rites, and associations continues to haunt strict constructionists of either law or religion.

This was recently manifest in the case of similarly broad language in the short-lived Religious Freedom Restoration Act (RFRA). The act was passed by Congress in 1993 in response to a narrow 1990 Supreme Court ruling in *Employment Division v. Smith* that allowed the state of Oregon to deny two Native American state employees the religious right to use peyote – an illegal psychotropic plant which had long standing in their rituals. But in a decision involving a Catholic Church's 'freedom' to resist a town zoning ordinance in Boerne, Texas, the Supreme Court struck down RFRA in 1997. The decision not only applied to land use but to a wide variety of dispensations which RFRA had seemingly justified on the basis of personal religious practices. These included prison inmates who petitioned for everything from drug use to conjugal visits as privately important 'religious' rituals. With RFRA defeated, Congress tried again and passed the currently operative bill called the Religious Land Use and Institutionalized Persons Act (RLUIPA), which is currently the federal law of the land awaiting yet another Supreme Court decision when the appropriate case arises on appeal.

Clearly all of this is no simple matter. To the extent that religion is restricted to its conventional forms – whether Buddhist, Catholic, Hindu, Jewish, Muslim, or Protestant – this comes close to requiring an establishment of organized religion through state certification of only recognized churches, sects, faiths. To the extent that religion is left to the definition of each individual, this involves such wide latitude as to stretch 'religion' beyond the point of credibility. In fact, there is no 'substantive' definition of religion to serve as the accepted standard within the American judiciary.

Not long ago, I was asked to serve as an expert witness in a Federal Court case involving a young woman fired as a check-out clerk by a large department store because she wore a small gold ring in a pierced eyebrow. When she replied that this violated her freedom of religion as a member of the Church of Body Modification and later sued on this basis, the case turned on just what constitutes a legitimate religion. Over the past half-century – especially since the Seeger and Welch decisions noted above, there has been a convergence on the issue between the courts, on the one hand, and social science, on the other. In casting a broad net so as to avoid an establishment offense and accommodate the wide variations in religion known to social science, religion could be defined more 'functionally' in terms of three criteria: sacred meanings, ritual enactment, and communal structure, all of which were met by the Church of Body Modification. Alas, the judge finally decided that there were insufficient damages for the case to continue. So much for a possible opportunity to clarify the definitional quandary.

There are two seemingly opposite positions to take on the strained relationship between religious free exercise and establishment. On the one hand, the classic position is that free exercise is so important that some sort of 'established' status should be given to religion in order to protect its freedom. On the other hand, Marci Hamilton has recently argued that 'religion is not an unalloyed good' (cf. Hamilton, 2005, p. 6), and its offenses against the citizenry such as clergy sexual abuse, race and gender discrimination, and narrow views of marriage and abortion require religion to be non-established so that it may be subject to government monitoring and prosecution in the public interest. Given these disparate views, it is hardly surprising that the public at large is varied and conflicted on the issues. There is a consensus on the abstract value of the separation of church and state; in a recent study of Springfield, MA (Demerath and Williams, 1992), some 84 per cent agreed that it was 'a good idea' in principle. But when asked to judge the constitutionality of eleven different religious practices, a mean of some 34.5 per cent answered incorrectly with another 19.8 per cent answering 'not sure.' Jelen and Wilcox (1995) report similar variation, though 'elite' respondents tend to be more in line with prevalent judicial interpretations (and with the establishment clause) than members of their 'mass' sample, who were more inclined to 'accommodate' religion within the establishment and to restrict free exercise to majority Christian groups as opposed to minority sects and non-Christians. But perhaps the most widely misunderstood distinction stemming from the First Amendment involves the difference between religion's separation from politics versus its separation from government or the state. This is the issue to which we turn next.

RELIGION, POLITICS, AND THE STATE IN THE U.S. AND AROUND THE WORLD

As religion has become increasingly involved in politics over the last quarter century in the U.S. and elsewhere around the world, there has been a corresponding increase in calls to ban religion from politics (cf. Thiemann, 1996). The call has become a commonplace of media punditry and political talk shows; it is a frequent weapon used by one political party against another.

Certainly one can imagine the call's appeal. If there is any truth to the cliché that religion and power are a potentially volatile combination, the solution seems obvious. Yet it is one thing to bar religion from state hegemony and quite another to bar religion from political involvement by prohibiting religious candidates from running for office or participating in electoral campaigns. While many assume both are central to the First Amendment, the single sentence refers only to 'Congress,' once elected, not to politicians on the stump. In fact, the one religiously pertinent clause in the original Constitution of 1787 states that '... no religious test shall ever be required as a qualification for any office or public Trust under the United States' (Article VI). Of course, the prohibition also extends by implication to any test for *non*-religion.

American politics is replete with religious candidates of virtually every denominational stripe – clergy as well as laity, elected as well as defeated. Although there are periodic complaints that religion is not welcome in politics (cf. Neuhaus, 1984; Carter, 1992), these generally refer to the public's mood not the government's rules, and they often amount to complaints that a particular type of religion has been politically unsuccessful. It is true that over the nation's history, some denominations such as the Episcopalians have been more successful in gaining high office. But this is more a function of higher social class and its attendant political resources than religion *per se*. In any event, it is precisely at the point that an office seeker becomes an office holder that the First Amendment becomes a major constraint to acting on behalf of one's religion – or irreligion.

The only real constraint on American religious organizations participating in politics is a potential loss of tax exemption – a penalty that the Internal Revenue Service applies to all cultural institutions that would otherwise be exempt. However, the measure is rarely enforced, perhaps because this sanction itself could be construed as an infringement on free exercise, with the prospect of litigation to follow. The most significant recent case involved the campaigning of the Christian Coalition under the aggressive leadership of Pentecostal leader, Pat Robertson, and his recently departed political lieutenant, Ralph Reed. The case moldered for several years in an IRS file, as no case manager seemed eager to create martyrs to bureaucratic religious infringement. When the matter was finally decided, the Coalition's tax exempt status was rescinded, but quietly and with more of a wrist slap than a body blow.

There is little doubt that the founders understood politics as a necessary process of airing competing interests and ideologies. By contrast, the state is a structure of government within which elected politicians serve as temporary office holders under the rules of the Constitution and under the sufferance of the electorate. In fact, leaving politics open to religion while keeping the state closed involves one of the less remarked upon of the celebrated 'checks and balances' in the American constitutional system. Each practice tends to be contingent on the other, much like the relationship between separationism overall and the nation's civil religion described earlier (see also Cristi and Dawson in this volume). Religion can be active in politics precisely because we are protected from its official hegemony; conversely, religion need not have a position within the state because it can air its positions politically. Religious advocates on every side of an issue should be welcome participants in the political contest. But the state's primary obligation is to insure that the rules of the contest are fair to everyone.

It is true that mixing religion and politics can lead to the kind of cultural wars that are as real elsewhere as they are rhetorically inflated in the U.S. (cf. Hunter, 1991). But such intranational religious warfare is rare except when state power hangs in the political balance, as in the cases of Guatemala, Northern Ireland, Egypt, Israel, India, and of course, Afghanistan and Iraq – to name only a few countries that have become battlegrounds. Politics that follow a lawful pattern in the pursuit of well-defined and constitutionally regulated state offices is quite different from a politics of winner-take-all, including the right to re-define the state rather than merely playing a role within it. Similarly, there is a crucial distinction between the state as an enduring, rule-bound apparatus of government that transcends its incumbent officials of the moment versus the state as the momentary and ideologically opportunistic creation of the last conquering politician – i.e. between the state as a long-term end in its own right and the state as a short-term means to more politically particular ends.

As the the U.S. founders understood, because both religion and politics involve competing moral guidelines and ethical priorities, it is only natural that the two should inform – and occasionally inflame – each other. Religious visions can become political agendas, and *vice versa*. Even American public opinion reflects an increasing grasp of the point (cf. Jelen and Wilcox, 1995). But neither the Constitution nor this analysis demands that religion *should* be involved in politics. There are other issues to animate the political zoo. And yet when religion does press for involvement, it is far better to allow it in than to try to keep it out. Banning religious considerations and religious leaders from politics is simply unrealistic. Moreover, the attempt is apt to backfire. When religion is denied a place at the political table, it is likely to create more problems – either as an outraged victim of a repressive political system or as an unmonitored force operating in the political shadows. In short, a politics that excludes religion is no more defensible than a state that establishes religion.

It is perhaps an ironic comment on constitutions generally that many nations have a better record in avoiding establishments that are not constitutionally banned than in nurturing the free exercise that is constitutionally secured. Indeed, what may be most distinctive about the U.S. constitution is not so much its content as the seriousness with which it is regarded. Even Americans who know little of its specifics accord it revered status. In many other countries, constitutions are a changing gloss, and there are some in which a nation's constitutional commitment reflects the sardonic line from a recent American automobile commercial, '(Constitutions) must be good; we've had six of them in the last twelve years.'

Clearly constitutions themselves are an unreliable guide to actual relations between religion and power, even in the U.S. But a different and broader approach is necessary to capture the diversity of relations between religion and power among our comparative cases. They range widely from religious states and state religions to cases where religion lacks either a legal role in politics or cultural standing in the society at large (cf. Marty and Appleby, 1991).

Two distinctions drawn from the above misunderstanding help to make sense of this profusion. The first distinction concerns whether or not religion has a legitimate role in national electoral politics; the second distinction involves whether or not religion is officially established within the formally constituted state or government. Overlapping these distinctions produces four combinations: (1) religious politics with a religious state; (2) non-religious or secular politics and non-religious or secular state; (3) secular politics and a religious state, and finally (4) religious politics with a secular state. As simplistic as these clusters may seem, most countries find at least temporary homes among them.

RELIGIOUS STATES AND RELIGIOUS POLITICS

This combination seems an appropriate starting point because some may regard it as the starting point of Western history, not to mention the most common type among today's non-Western societies. Because such countries are so often depicted as suffused with religion in every aspect of life, a religious state would seem to go hand in hand with religious politics.

In fact, the combination is more the exception than the rule, and this is because it is so volatile. When a religious state is faced with active religious politics, this is because there is some religious disagreement over the state's own religious direction. Under such circumstances, the state's very legitimacy is called into question, and violence may reflect preemptive actions of state control as well as the clash among contending religious parties. If there is a single pattern that lends itself to the most widespread religious and cultural violence, it is this one. And, alas, while the category is rare, it is hardly non-existent.

Among the 'sample' of countries considered in Demerath (2001), several cases qualify here – at least at various points in their histories. Like most other Latin American countries, both *Brazil* and *Guatemala* were once officially Catholic states in a religious political system that involved the subjugation and suppression of indigenous religious alternatives. Formally, both countries had severed these state religious

ties by the end of the nineteenth century; informally, ties have persisted in varying forms. In Brazil, the Catholic ecclesiastical hierarchy is now seeking to reappropriate and renegotiate its seat at the right hand of the state, while at the same time both church and state are engaged in a new religious politics energized by echoing strains of Liberation Theology, on the one hand, and an expanding pentecostal Protestantism, on the other. In Guatemala, the dominant military state has shifted its ostensible religious affiliation from Catholic to Protestant in the last decade, and its indigenous opposition is partly a movement of Mayan religious revitalization.

Perhaps the clearest combination of a religious state with religious politics is *Northern Ireland*. There is no question that the state is perceived in Protestant terms, whether *de jure* as a result of its inclusion within the UK or *de facto* because of the 300 year political dominance of local Protestants. Certainly there is no doubt that politics are riven with religion – at least insofar as they have involved extreme civil religious blocs that are 'culturally,' if not always 'religiously,' Protestant and Catholic. The recent truce and negotiated settlement signal a change in the religious politics, but by no means its end. What was once a small Catholic minority may well become an effective political majority in the next several decades, and Catholics have already begun to make gains through the ballot rather than the bullets of the IRA. This is hastened by the increased out-migration of Protestants with resources who read the new writing on the graffiti emblazoned walls; it is compounded by the frustrations of those less advantaged Protestants remaining behind.

Or consider the case of *Israel*. Many Israelis would protest its categorization as a religious state, arguing that Zionism itself can be seen as a secular movement, and that the state makes ample provision for both secular practices and various non-Judaic faiths, especially Islamic and Christian. At the same time, there is no question that the Israeli state is perceived as Jewish by most Jews and non-Jews alike. Even if this were not the case, Zionism itself may be a sufficiently sacred commitment to qualify as religious in its own terms. Certainly there is no question that Israeli politics often take religious forms. This not only applies to the participation of Muslim Palestinians, including the Hamas, but also to the struggles among various Jewish groups – whether secularists on the left or contesting movements on the right such as the Gush Emunim and the ultra-orthodox Haredim. Former Prime Minister Rabin's assassination makes it clear that the stakes are large and the rates of violence are high.

As all of these countries attest, the combination of a religious state and religious politics has involved some of the most deeply rooted and tragic violence of the modern era. This makes it especially important to consider the alternatives. However, it is one thing to point out the dangers of this combination in the abstract and quite another to prevent countries from sliding towards it in reality. Then too, some of the alternatives have warts of their own.

SECULAR STATES AND SECULAR POLITICS

If the first combination is stereotypically non-Western, this one is associated with the equally common – and equally flawed – stereotype of a fully secularized West. In one sense, it represents a realization of the Enlightenment vision through what has been called the 'secularization of public religion' (Wilson, 1966) or the 'de-sacralization of the state' (Stark and Iannaccone, 1994). The secular-state secular-politics combination is often associated with Western Europe in particular. Apart from the now nominally 'Christian' Democratic and Socialist parties in Germany and France, both countries fall into this category, as does Italy following its revocation of its long-standing concordat with the Catholic Vatican.

Much the same is true if one looks functionally rather than formally at Anglican England or Lutheran Scandinavia. In fact, there are active movements on behalf of religious disestablishment in all of these symbolically religious nations. These are partly efforts to revitalize religion as an autonomous political force, since many church folk now regard the relationship as an inhibiting constraint on their prophetic roles. But then the establishments that survive are often defended principally on non-religious grounds. The Swedish Church still serves as an unofficial census bureau and burial society and still receives state funds after disestablishment in 2000. Many politicians see surviving establishments as non-substantive symbols of cultural continuity and vestigial charm.

Europe does not exhaust the secular-secular category. Its influence is apparent in two additional cases: Turkey and China. *Turkey* had been tilting toward the West throughout the latter days of the Ottoman Empire in the nineteenth century, where there was a special fascination with the secular theology of French positivism. In a sense, Kemal Attaturk both had and ate the Ottoman cake when he seized power in 1921 and carried through one of the most far-reaching and enduring politico-cultural revolutions in the twentieth century. Attaturk was familiar with sociologist Emile Durkheim's argument that an ethical society and effective political culture could be sacred without being religious. Partly as a result, Attaturk banned religion from both government and politics just as he banned irregular verbs and Roman numerals from everyday discourse. For the most part, the reforms have remained, although there have been several instances in which the military has stepped in to preserve secularity, and there is no question that Muslim political interests have begun to mobilize recently. It is characteristic of Turkey that critics and participants alike resist the label of 'fundamentalism' so often applied to neighboring Iran and the formerly Taliban controlled Afghanistan.

China also qualifies as a doubly secular case, again partly on the basis of an imported Western ideology – in this case, of course, Marxist socialism. Actually regime opposition to religion comes and goes, and despite the state's repression of the Falun Gong, there is occasional waggish talk of a 'third opium war' – in this case an intra-Party dispute concerning whether Marx was correct in dismissing religion as the 'opiate of the masses.' Of course, there is truth to the cliché that Marxism itself resembles a religion, not least in the recent 'secularization' of Marxism as a sacred cause. Indeed, one of the reasons why some Chinese leaders have been more accepting of traditional Christian, Buddhist, and Islamic religious communities – as long as they operate on the state's own terms – is a much-lamented void at the core of Chinese society where only money has currency. While some would argue that this is a cue for the re-introduction of Confucianism, this is even less preferable than imported faiths because party cadres see the Confucian tradition as a feudal and anti-revolutionary anachronism, despite its considerable informal persistence. This is a time of transition in China, but not one that portends a serious religionizing of either the state or politics in the near future.

Clearly, the combination of a secular state and secular politics has some empirical standing, and it is in some measure correctly associated with Western post-enlightenment developments. But this does not mean that all cases are confined to the West, or that religion is entirely absent in any instance. Indeed, the combination in pure form runs the risk of cultural lassitude, if not sterility. Many of the above cases reveal persisting strains toward some form of religion or 'sacred' alternative that state administrations seek to dampen, if not drown. While these new religious developments rarely represent major trends, they are also seldom dismissable. So far, then, we have dealt with the two opposing polar combinations: the doubly religious associated with violence and the doubly secular tending toward vacuity. The next two combinations are somewhat more common and a bit less intuitive.

RELIGIOUS STATES AND SECULAR POLITICS

Consider three scenarios that combine a religious state and secular politics. The *first* occurs when state religiousness is an empty symbol rather than a compelling commitment – more an anachronistic form than a contemporary function. In fact, we noted several such countries under the secular-secular rubric, including Anglican England. And even though Sweden was formally religious until 2000, it actually reflected a cultural and political scene that was highly secular. While there were occasional religious issues which drew attention, these were very much the exception rather than the rule.

If this first model of a religious state with secular politics suggests a certain ritualized cover for an indifference to religion, a *second* version involves a religion that is such an important source of state legitimacy that no alternative faith is tolerated. Religion is banned from politics precisely because it is so potentially upsetting as an emotionally charged component of the culture at large. Religious grievances against the state are suppressed, and often any politics of real substance is kept under wraps. These are theocracies represented by some traditionally Catholic Latin American states as well as a number of Islamic hegemonies in the Middle East, for example *Pakistan* at various points in its history. In all of these cases, the state controls the political world very tightly and embraces religion more to control it than to submit to it.

In some ways these first two models of religious states with secular politics are opposites of each other. The first represents religious tokenism in the midst of apathy, while the second reveals an imposed religious order to quell potential religious disorder. Still a *third* version of a religious state and secular politics is a perverse variant on the second. This involves states that carefully construct their own religion to frustrate the political mobilization of a genuine religious alternative.

Indonesia offers a case in point. For more than 50 years, its government has imposed the deliberately crafted syncretic religion of 'pancasila' to bind together Christians, Hindus, Buddhists, and animists – not to mention the 85 per cent of the population who are formally Muslims. Under the now deposed President Suharto, strict electoral rules made it virtually impossible for any one religious group to rise up against the regime, and the state's administrative apparatus ('golkar') also functions as a controlling political structure. In all of this, the object was to stifle the development of the so-called 'Islamic fundamentalists,' whose actual agendas were often more secular than religious.

Thus, the combination of a religious state with secular politics makes for even stranger bedfellows than does politics alone. All three of its scenarios are somewhat procrustean, and the latter two share a sense of unstable vulnerability as a temporary way station for cases caught in transition between the other three basic combinations.

SECULAR STATES AND RELIGIOUS POLITICS

This last combination is another that may seem unlikely at first glance. After all, if a society is able to sustain a government that is basically secular, isn't this because the surrounding culture is itself so secular that there is no real religious action in the first place? Put oppositely, when any society's politics become religiously infected, how can its state structures fail to follow?

Both questions are reasonable, but as we saw earlier, the logic behind a secularly neutral state with a free-ranging religious polity is that each complements and constrains the other. There need be no limits to the free exercise of religion in politics as long as there is a strict prohibition of any religious establishment within the state. Politicians, as politicians, may campaign on – and even vote – their religious consciences; nor is there anything to prevent them from bowing to the bidding of their religious organizations. But state officials and state administrations have a different responsibility. They must remain formally and functionally neutral, and not only in the competition between religions but also in the larger struggle between religion, on the one hand, and secularism, on the other. The overall result should be a contested but vital politics framed by an equitable state that rises above the fray to guarantee fairness to all. At least this describes the constitutional theory and founding enthusiasm behind two countries that constitute the world's largest and oldest democracies respectively;

namely, the *United States* and *India*. When India obtained independence in 1947, it took three years to carefully develop a constitution. The result reflected a number of Western models, including the U.S. itself (cf. Smith, 1963). But while the Indian form of government enjoyed a successful run of almost 30 years with its stability and legitimacy intact, this began to unravel in the 1980s.

A growing complaint within India today is that its Independence leaders were too quick to apply Western secular forms of government to an Eastern cultural reality that required its own unique state response (cf. Said, 1978; Carrier, 1995). The argument holds that a secular state may work well enough in a country like the U.S., but it is discordant within an Indian society that remains so intransigently non-secular at its core. Indeed, the very imposition of Western secularism has served perversely to fan the flames of religious extremism by forcing religious advocates to adopt aggressive measures to make their case – measures that even include communal violence. Some go so far as to suggest that India is not just a deeply religious country but a fundamentally Hindu society that can only be led by a Hindu government. As the argument goes, once Hinduism finds its natural expression in state control, it will revert to its natural historical tolerance of the minority religions in its domain.

And yet this is only one reading of the Indian situation. By no means all Indian influentials and intellectuals have abandoned the secular or religiously neutral state. Many continue to resist both religious and anti-religious models of the state in favor of a more neutral or a-religious reading of the Indian constitution. From this perspective, the cause of the country's 'communal violence' is not that the state is too secular but rather that it is not secular enough – not that the state should use its influence to curb or end religion, but rather that the state should be religiously impartial. From the very outset, religion was implicated in the Indian constitution and the government it conceived. From the beginning there were controversial religious actions, including a state exemption for Muslims to follow Islamic rather than national laws in personal matters, and liberal religious reforms required of Hinduism in such matters as changes in temple administration and a continuation of the British 'reservations policy' as a form of occupational affirmative action for Hindu 'untouchables.'

These exceptions in secular state policy have festered over the years. There is an increasing tendency for state leaders to become involved in such religious conflicts as Hindus vs. Muslims in Ayodyah, Bombay, Gujarat, and Kashmir; Hindus vs. Christians in Orissa; Sikhs vs. Hindus in the Punjab; and southern Tamil rebels mobilizing against Buddhists in Sri Lanka. As concessions made to one group require balancing concessions to its rival, constructing state policy has come to resemble shortening a chair one leg at a time: the results are never quite even, and the seat of power becomes increasingly unstable. The assassinations of both Indira and Rajiv Gandhi offer tragic reminders of the possible consequences.

Of course, religious politics can also lead to violence and tragedies. India is a country in which Hindus and Muslims have long lived cheek by jowl in the same areas of a city and sometimes the same neighborhoods. But periodically these neighborly relations give way to horrific communal violence. Why? One explanation is what might be called the 'spontaneous combustion model,' referring to a tendency for any disparate groups sharing close quarters to be set off by sparks that can lead to conflagrations. A second explanation can be labeled the 'political arson' model by which riots are purposely initiated by 'goondas' in the hire of politicians starting a political campaign and anxious to mobilize supporters. Recent research by observers like Paul Brass (2003) favors the second model as illustrated by right-wing Hindu politicians in city after city in North India. Of course, India is not the only country where political majorities hold a death grip on minorities. Similar scenarios are now occurring in countries like Israel and Iraq.

In a strange way, one's reading of India depends upon one's reading of the United States. Is America a den of constitutionally enforced secularism or a country whose high level of religiosity is only partially inhibited by its constitution? Overall, the United States may be the exception that commends the rule concerning the virtues of a secular state and a religious polity. But it would be both naïve and unseemly to assume that the same combination would work identically for all other nations. Nor is India the only cautionary case.

In *Egypt*, the nation as a whole seems a battleground between a coercive state with an anti-religious ideology of 'secularism,' on the one hand, and small bands of religious extremists, on the other. The scene is not uncommon, and it has surfaced in a variety of other states that have been less than fully successful in their efforts to suppress religious opposition, e.g. the previously described *Indonesia, Turkey,* and *Thailand*.

Post-1989 *Poland* also qualifies as a secular state with religious politics. One might suppose it to be doubly Catholic as a reflection of both its dominant cultural religious alignment and the oft-chronicled alliance of the Church with the Solidarity labor movement in bringing an end to Communist rule. But Catholicism's role has already begun to shift. Many Poles are more 'cultural' than 'religious' Catholics, and the old pattern of opposition to ecclesiastical authority is resurfacing, especially as the Church has sought to pressure the government into outlawing divorce and abortion. While Poland currently illustrates the combination of a secular state with religious politics (cf. Casanova, 1994), it may soon join its European sisters to the West in the doubly secular category as even its politics lose their religious flavor.

Finally, *Japan* is another sharp-edged peg in the round hole of a secular state with religious politics. In fact, Japan is an especially instructive case because it reminds us that our four types rarely fit any country exactly. Like many nations that tend to straddle two or more types, Japan has exemplified all four combinations at various times in its history. First, Japan's Tokugawa period from the early seventeenth to the latter half of the nineteenth century combined religious government (or shogunates) with religious politics in the jousting among various Buddhist, Shinto, and even Christian movements. *Second*, the Meiji restoration in the 1860s ultimately led to a religious state and secular politics as State Shinto came to define the government, and opposing religious voices were stilled. Third, at least for the first three decades following the end of World War II and the adoption of a new constitution, the situation was more that of a secular state with secular politics. *Fourth* and most recently, the combination of a secular state and religious politics has begun to surface, however imperfectly. Formally, the state continues to be secular, although there are signs of a non-militarist, State Shinto recrudescence. Meanwhile, religious politics of a quite different sort involves new roles of 'new' and 'new-new' religious movements over the last decade. The 1995 Aum Shinrikyo's nerve gas attack on the Tokyo subway was a pivotal event. The resulting 'trial of the century' turned out to be a siege for many marginal religious movements who feel tarred by the same stereotypes and sanctions applied to Aum. This is especially true of the Soka Gakkai and its long-standing relation to one of Japan's largest opposition parties (Kasulis, 1991).

So much for a brief exercise in cataloguing the range of relationships between religion, politics, and the state. As nations strain to move from one type to another, we are reminded that a variety of factors are at work – some political and some religious. Even America's heralded church–state separation may be less a matter of law and binding precedent than of broader social, cultural, and institutional patterns (cf. Lipset, 1996).

RELIGIOUS VIOLENCE, HUMAN RIGHTS, AND RELIGIOUS PERSECUTION

In the best of all worlds, the very phrase 'religious violence' would be dismissed as an oxymoron. In reality, of course, it is very real indeed (cf. Appleby, 2000; Juergensmeyer, 1993, 2000; Lawrence, 1990; Riesebrodt, 1990). Two quite different sorts of explanations have emerged to account for it, one cultural and other structural. First, Samuel Huntington (1996) has argued that such violence is increasingly the result of 'clashing civilizations' as political structures become a vestige of the past

overrun by dominantly religious cultures often representing the great faith traditions, most notably and ominously Islam. By somewhat contentious contrast, other scholars have argued that Huntington has been too quick to jettison more conventional structural explanations and religion's relationship to state power. From this perspective, Islam has been hijacked by political movements that give the religion an especially bad name, and while it is true that Islam is vulnerable to such movements, so was Christianity vulnerable to the terrorism of movements like the Ku Klux Klan (cf. Demerath, 2007; Juergensmeyer, 2000). In addition, the very notion of a single seamless civilization sweeping whole nations under its power is far more fiction than fact (cf. Jenkins, 2002; Norris and Ingelhart, 2004). Indeed, the specter of a united and aggressive Islam is greatly overdrawn. The greatest violence in the name of Islam today involves various Islamic factions warring against each other – for example, Taliban vs. other Muslims in Afghanistan, Sunni versus Shiite in the Iraq-Iran border wars of the 1980s, and now within Iraq itself.

This cues a second and more structural account of religious violence that keys on the matters discussed in the previous section. There is a developing consensus among several different scholars that the critical variable involves religion's relationship to state power. Where such power is out of bounds and out of play, very little violence occurs. But where religious traditions or factions with the same tradition either hold state power or compete for it, violence is all-too likely to ensue. I have reached such conclusions following a comparative qualitative project on some fourteen countries around the globe (Demerath, 2001). But similar conclusions are emerging from quantitative research. Israel's Jonathan Fox has mounted several large data sets that allow him to test such propositions (cf. Fox, 2004; Fox and Sandler, 2004). Brian Grim and Roger Finke have availed themselves of another data set with similar results (cf. Grim and Finke, 2006a, b).

Grim and Finke's data derive from a project concerning a different sort of religious violence and a different range of political involvements concerning it. In 1998 the U.S. Congress passed the International Religious Freedom Act (IRFA) providing for annual reports on instances of religious persecution occurring in every country around the world where the U.S. has a diplomatic presence, with a detailed summary to be prepared by the State Department for the House of Representatives Committee on International Relations' Subcommittee on Africa, Global Human Rights and International Operations. The bill passed quickly and unanimously, even though some of its supporters' motives became somewhat suspect. Although the original idea behind such action apparently came from liberal Jewish advocates, it was given special impetus through the House and Senate by a group of conservative Protestants from the Southwest. They saw it as a way of protecting conservative Christian groups from the U.S. proselytizing in Western and Eastern Europe, Africa, Asia, and elsewhere around the globe. These groups have met resistance that was sometimes organized by 'host' governments and was often regarded as persecution.

Not surprisingly, the bill and its subsequent actions have not been universally well received. The legislation seemed inconsistent with other actions of the U.S. Government such as the Bush Administration's use of Congressionally unapproved funds set aside within the Executive Branch for Faith-Based Initiatives, including Christian groups around the world proselytizing at the expense of Islamic, Hindu, Buddhist and other religious communities while providing social services ringed with their own religious constraints with respect to problems such as AIDS and birth control. Countries like China, France and Germany raised strong objections to IFRA's interference with their own internal policies concerning religion. Questions have arisen about the reach of U.S. power, not to mention cross-cultural and cross-national conceptions of internal religious freedom versus external religious predation. However, it is true that the targets of recorded persecutions are often internal themselves and the offenders are by no means dominantly external American evangelists.

Grim and Finke are aware of the cloud under which IRFA began, and the continuing possibility of political bias. In some cases, the embassy assessments are one thing, and the State Department's use of them quite another depending upon its political relations with the country in question While it is true that the first few years of the persecution tallies were somewhat unevenly collected and coded, more recent reports have become more standardized and more rigorous. In any case, Grim and Finke marshal information from some 143 countries with populations exceeding 2 million and, after converting the largely qualitative reports into quantitative form, subject the set to structural equation modeling.

Even though Grim and Finke use quantitative techniques and a 'religious economies' perspective in contrast to my own more qualitative approach anchored in recent church–state theory, our conclusions are strikingly similar to each other and at odds with Huntington's more cultural contentions. By far their most robust predictor of religious persecution is an index of 'government regulation,' though nongovernmental 'social regulation' on the part of majority religions also has a significant indirect effect. Translated into constitutional terms, government regulation of religion might well characterize an established religion keeping its non-established religious competition at bay (cf. Van der Vyver and Witte, 1996; Richardson, 2004). Thus, the finding is consistent with aforementioned strictures against religious establishments and situations where religion is either competing for or actually wielding government power – though, of course, there are a number of countries in which governments regulate and even persecute religion precisely because the governments themselves are non- or anti-religious. Grim and Finke have not yet reported on a third index of 'government favoritism toward religion' that also seems promising in establishment terms.

CONCLUSION

In the final analysis, religion's capital is often best optimized when religion is not a capital religion. That is the pithy version of this chapter's central theme. In reviewing the American tradition of church–state relations, we noted the strange beginnings but growing importance of the First Amendment's 'establishment' clause as opposed to its more commonly cited right of religious 'free exercise.' The chapter described the distinction between religion's often desirable and constitutionally admissible relations with politics as opposed to its undesirable and unconstitutional ties to the state and government. At least this is the case in countries such as the U.S. and India, even though both countries have honored their constitutions in the breach as well as in the observance. Other combinations of a four-fold typology of religion's relations with politics and the state ordered a quick survey of developments in other countries around the world. Finally, the chapter took up recent work in what might be called the sociology of religious violence and persecution. Again operating at a multinational global level, it reviewed cultural and structural explanations, and among the former noted the rash of criticisms provoked by the 'clash of civilizations' thesis.

In all of this, one cannot fail to be struck with how different these questions and answers are from those that characterized the sociology of religion, say, a half-century ago – to take a reference point not exactly at random. When I took my first courses in the field, American research in the sociology of religion was virtually restricted to the United States and largely focused on the local religious scene at that. Now we are moving from the local to the global – or what some would describe as from the local to the loco. In addition, our work has shifted from the personal and the domestic to a concern with politics and violence with larger stakes for us all. It makes one wonder what will have become of the sociology of religion and of humankind generally after another half-century.

REFERENCES

Adams, Arlin M. and Charles Emmerich 1990. *A Nation Dedicated to Religious Liberty: The Constitutional Heritage of the Religious Clauses.* Philadelphia: University of Pennsylvania Press.

Appleby, Scott R. 2000. *The Ambivalence of the Sacred: Religion, Violence and Reconciliation.* New York: Rowan and Littlefield.

Brass, Paul R. 2003. *The Production of Hindu-Muslim Violence in Contemporary India.* Seattle: University of Washington Press.

Carrier, James G. (ed.) 1995. *Occidentalism: Images of the West.* Oxford: Clarendon Press.

Carter, Steven L. 1992. *Culture of Unbelief.* New York: Basic Books.

Casanova, José 1994. *Public Religions in the Modern World.* Chicago: University of Chicago Press.

Demerath, N. J. III 2001. *Crossing the Gods: World Religions and Worldly Politics.* Piscataway, NJ: Rutgers University Press.

Demerath, N. J. 2007. 'Dear President Bush: An Assessment of Religion and Politics in Your Administration for "Posteriority", *Sociology of Religion*, 68:1 (Spring) 5–25.

Demerath, N.J. III and Rhys H. Williams 1992. *A Bridging of Faiths: Religion and Politics in a New England City.* Princeton, NJ: Princeton University Press.

Drakeman, Donald 1991. *Church-State Constitutional Issues: Making Sense of the Establishment Clause.* New York: Greenwood Press.

Fox, Jonathan 2004. *Religion, Civilization, and Civil War.* Oxford: Lexington Books.

Fox, Jonathan and Shmuel Sandler 2004. *Bringing Religion into International Affairs.* New York: Palgrave Macmillan.

Gaustad, Edwin S. 1987. *Faith of Our Fathers: Religion and the New Nation.* San Francisco: Harper and Row.

Grim, Brian J. and Roger Finke 2006a. 'International Religion Indexes. Government Regulation, Government Favoritism, and Social Regulation of Religion,' *Interdisciplinary Journal of Research on Religion*, Vol. 2/1; 2–40.

Grim, Brian J. and Roger Finke 2006b. 'Clashing Civilizations or Regulated Religious Economies: Explaining Cross-National Religious Persecution.' Unpublished manuscript. Pew Forum on Religion and Public Life.

Hamilton, Marci A. 2005. *God vs. the Gavel: Religion and the Rule of Law.* New York: Cambridge University Press.

Hammond, Phillip E., David Machacek and Eric Mazur 2004. *Religion on Trial: How Supreme Court Trends Threaten Freedom of Conscience in America.* Walnut Creek, CA: Alta Mira Press.

Hunter, James D. 1991. *Culture Wars: The Struggle to Define America*. New York: Basic Books.

Huntington, Samuel 1996. *The Clash of Civilizations and the Remaking of World Order*. New York: Simon and Schuster.

Jelen, Ted G. and Clyde Wilcox 1995. *Public Attitudes Toward Church and State*, Armonk, NY: M.E. Sharpe.

Jenkins, Philip 2002. *The Next Christendom: The Coming of Global Christianity*. New York: Oxford University Press.

Juergensmeyer, Mark 1993. *The New Cold War: Religious Nationalism Confronts the Secular State*. Berkeley: University of California Press.

Juergensmeyer, Mark 2000. *Terror in the Mind of God: The Global Rise of Religious Violence*. Berkeley: University of California Press.

Kasulis, W. P. 1991. 'Religion and Politics: Cultural Background of the Soka Gakkai.' In Charles Wei-hsun Fu and Gerald Spiegler (eds), *Movements and Issues in World Religions*. New York: Greenwood Press.

Krislov, Samuel 1985. 'Alternatives to Separation of Church and State in Countries outside the United States.' In James E. Wood, Jr., *Religion and the State*. Waco, TX: Baylor University Press, pp. 421–40.

Lawrence, Bruce 1990. *Defenders of God: The Fundamentalist Revolt Against the Modern Age*. London: I.B. Tauris.

Lipset, Seymour Martin 1996. *American Exceptionalism: A Double-Edged Sword*. New York: W.W. Norton.

Marty, Martin E. and R. Scott Appleby (eds) 1991–1995. *Fundamentalisms Observed*. 5 Vols. Chicago: University of Chicago Press.

Neuhaus, Richard John 1984. *The Naked Public Square: Religion and Democracy in America*. Grand Rapids, MI: Erdmans Publishing Co.

Nichols, J. Bruce 1988. *The Uneasy Alliance*. New York: Oxford University Press.

Noll, Mark (ed.) 1990. *Religion and American Politics: From the Colonial Period to the 1980s*. New York: Oxford University Press.

Noonan, John T. 1998. *The Lustre of Our Country: The American Experience of Religious Freedom*. Berkeley: University of California Press.

Norris, Pippa and Ronald Inglehart 2004. *Sacred and Secular: Religion and Politics Worldwide*. New York: Cambridge University Press.

Richardson, James T. (ed.) 2004. *Regulating Religion: Case Studies from Around the Globe*. New York: Kluwer Academic/Plenum Publishers.

Richardson, James T. 2006. 'The Sociology of Religious freedom: A Structural and Socio-Legal Analysis,' *Sociology of Religion*, 67 (3): 271–94.

Riesebrodt, Martin 1990. *Pious Passion: The Emergence of Modern Fundamentalism in the United States and Iran*. Berkeley: University of California Press.

Said, Edward W. 1978. *Orientalism*. New York: Random House.

Smith, Donald E. 1963. *India as a Secular State*. Princeton, NJ: Princeton University Press.

Stark, Rodney and Lawrence Iannaccone 1994. 'A Supply-Side Reinterpretation of the "Secularization" of Europe'. *Journal of the Scientific Study of Religion*, 33: 230–52.

Stokes, Anson Phelps and Leo Pfeffer 1964. *Church and State in the United States*. Westport, CT: Greenwood Press.

Thiemann, Ronald F. 1996. *Religion in Public Life: A Dilemma for Democracy*. Washington D.C.: Georgetown University Press.

Van der Vyver, Johan and John Witte, Jr. (eds) 1996. *Religious Human Rights in Global Perspective*. The Hague: Martinus NijHoff.

Van Moorseven, Hen C. and Ger Van der Tan 1978. *Written Constitutions: A Comparative Study*. Dobbs Ferry, NY: Oceana Publishers.

Wilson, Bryan R. 1966. *Religion in Secular Society*. London: Penguin Books.

Wilson, John F. (ed.) 1987. *Church and State in America: A Bibliographic Guide*, 2 Vols. Westport, CT: Greenwood Press.

Witte, John, Jr. 2005. *Religion and the American Constitutional Experiment* 2nd Edition. Oxford: Westview Press.

Wood, James E., Jr. 1985. *Religion and the State: Essays in Honor of Leo Pfeffer*. Waco, TX: Baylor University Press.

19

Religion and Regulation

JAMES A. BECKFORD AND JAMES T. RICHARDSON

This chapter will show that religion – just like many other spheres of social life – is the subject and object of regulation. Religion is involved in regulating aspects of social life; and it is an object of regulation by internal and external agencies. Sociological understanding of religion must, therefore, consider issues of regulation but it must also seek fresh approaches that can take account of the shifts that are occurring in the forms of regulation associated with 'the late modern age' (Giddens 1991) or 'new modernity' (Beck 1992). Accordingly, we shall place the topic of religion and regulation in the context of broader questions about the management of risk, diversity and account-ability in advanced industrial or post-industrial societies. Our argument will also be that regulation is far from being a matter only for agencies of the state and that the activities of non-state actors in some countries have become more important since the 1980s (Hutter 2006: 2).

Our analysis of religion and regulation has two sides. On the one hand, it examines the capacity of religious ideas and organisations to regulate thought and action. We shall examine the extent to which religion has been a powerful agent of regulation in various times and places. This includes the 'internal' self-regulation of religions as well as attempts by religious organisations to control the world in

which they operate. On the other hand, religion is subject to control by external agencies such as political or military institutions. The social regulation of religion demands careful analysis not only in terms of underlying inter-ests and social forces but also in terms of its forms and processes. In other words, we shall analyse religion as both an *agent* of regulation and as an *object* of regulation. In addition, we shall consider the attempts made to *resist* both the control of religion and the control exer-cised by religions. This will allow us to place the topic of regulation in a much broader social context than is common in the sociology of religion (cf. Finke 1990; Chaves and Cann 1992; Iannaccone *et al.* 1997; Grim and Finke 2006. But see Bourdieu 1991).

We must sound three notes of caution before our analysis can begin. First, religion clearly amounts to much more than an agent or an object of regulation. Other chapters in this Handbook are an eloquent testimony to the rich diversity of expressions that religion has taken – and continues to take – in many regions of the world. The focus on regulation is merely one way of understanding the social and cultural significance of religion. It is far from being the key to a balanced sociological understanding of religion. But the focus on regulation is still important and timely because religion is directly and indirectly relevant to many of the conflicts and controversies that characterise life in the early twenty-first century (Beckford 2003; Richardson 2004).

The second note of caution is about the word 'religion'. It is a generic term that refers to a wide range of phenomena extending from, at one extreme, entire faith traditions such as Islam or Christianity to, at the other extreme, the personal convictions and commitments of individuals. In between these two extremes there are many different types of religious institutions, organisations, groupings and practices. Although it is convenient to use the word 'religion' as a shorthand way of referring to this vast array of differing values, beliefs, symbols, rituals, teachings, practices, experiences, forms of organisation and ethical rules, we must always keep this sheer diversity in mind. Good sociological analysis of religion requires us to be sensitive to this diversity and to the variable rates at which religious phenomena can change.

The third note of caution is about the complications that arise when the distinction between religious organisations and other agencies is unclear. It sometimes happens, for example, that religious organisations act as proxies for political interests in attempting to regulate social and cultural life. Such cases look like regulation by religion, but they actually mask the influence of non-religious forces. Conversely, of course, some political authorities may appear to be acting independently whilst actually carrying out the wishes of powerful religious organisations. The challenge for social scientists is, therefore, to assess the extent to which religion is a proxy for other interests, and *vice versa*, in any particular circumstance.

The term 'regulation' in this context means the process of directing or controlling things in accordance with rules. Following Hood *et al.* (2001), we can identify three aspects of this process: information gathering, standard setting and behaviour modification. The first involves assembling and evaluating information about the thing to be regulated; the second refers to determining the criteria with which to assess how far regulations are respected or breached; and the third relates to judging

conformity to regulations and, in some cases, applying sanctions in order to punish and/or deter breaches of regulations. The regulation of religion can take many different forms – as does the attempt by religions to regulate aspects of culture and society. Some of them draw upon bodies of law or formalised rules that require interpretation and application by qualified practitioners such as canon lawyers in the Roman Catholic tradition or jurists in various Islamic traditions. Other forms of regulation of religion are in the hands of specialists in, for example, human rights or taxation.

In addition to these technical ways of regulating religion there are less formal – but no less effective – procedures that can have the effect of shaping religions. They include, for example, administrative decisions about the allocation of public funds to religious groups or the stereotypes of religious personnel that appear in the mass media. In all these different ways, religion is subject to attempts to control, canalise, categorise or certify its beliefs, expressions, practices and forms of organisation. It follows that some of these regulatory practices actually favour religion over non-religion, while other practices accord advantages or privileges to some religions but not to all.[1] No less relevant to this chapter are the attempts to regulate thoughts, feelings, actions, policies, property and organisations in the name of religions. But we should add that regulation of religion – and regulation by religion – is not always successful or complete. For our purposes, then, *attempts* to exercise regulation are no less interesting in themselves than are the cases in which regulation actually succeeds. Similarly, the *resistance* to regulation deserves more careful consideration than it usually receives in the sociology of religion.

The chapter is in four main parts. It will begin by considering the variety of ways in which religions regulate themselves with differing degrees of success. Forms of religious self-regulation include the codification of beliefs, tests of orthodoxy, the training and certification of leaders, and the disciplining of deviants. The second section will analyse the ways in which external forces and agencies regulate religions. Codes of law, state constitutions, anti-religious forces, and the mass media can all have the effect of regulating religious belief, practice and organisation. The third section will focus on attempts that are made in the name of religion to regulate aspects of personal and social life. They include sexuality, the human body, the family, education, culture, social welfare, economics and politics. The fourth and final section will place changes in the regulation of religion in the context of broad social processes such as globalisation, the perception of risks, sensitivity to consumer protection, and the emergence of international norms of religious freedom.

SELF-REGULATION OF RELIGION

We have deliberately refrained from trying to define religion, preferring to acknowledge that there is no agreement either in public life or in sociology about the term's meaning. It is equally important to recognise that the meaning of religion is itself a matter of regulation in some circumstances. For example, the rules governing the eligibility on grounds of religion for the status of 'conscientious objector' and, consequently, exemption from combat duties in the military are a good example of how controversial the regulation of religion can be. So, rather than pre-empt the question, we shall simply accept that the definition of religion is subject to public and academic debate and – sometimes – dispute (Beckford 1999, 2003).

Despite the lack of universal agreement about the definition of religion, it is clear that most systems of belief and practice that claim to be religious are subject to their own rules. Self-regulation covers a wide range of phenomena but is particularly interesting from a sociological perspective for what it reveals about the variety of ways in which religions seek to control their practices and their practitioners. For the purpose of analysis, we shall examine two interrelated aspects of the self-regulation of religion.

(1) First, there are rules that constitute particular religions. These *constitutive* rules mark the outer limits of what counts as the religion in question. That is, they ideally determine what the main features of the religion actually are. At the most basic level, each religion's constitutive rules provide answers to questions about its distinctive beliefs, practices and organisational forms. They are usually nested in 'founding myths' or narrative accounts of relations between divinities and human beings which, in turn, frame accounts of the origins and history of the religion. As a rule, some degree of belief in these accounts is regarded as a condition for being identified or self-identified with the religion. Many, but not all, religions show reverence for codified versions of these and other beliefs in the form of sacred texts, buildings, landscapes, calendars, uniforms, rituals and music. Again, rules govern their legitimate uses.

Further codification of the constitutive rules has taken place in many religions by means of theological, philosophical, historical and other forms of scholarship. Monasteries, universities, seminaries, theological colleges, doctrinal commissions, ecumenical councils and committees of jurists or scholars have all fostered this kind of codifying – and critical – work. They have produced creeds, statements of faith, dogma and codes of sacred law – as well as the disputes between different traditions and schools that have punctuated the history of all religions. The long-term effect of these disputes varies with the form of governance: it is more disruptive in highly centralised types of religious organisation than in more loosely structured organisations or faith traditions. Disputes are just as likely to centre on rules governing rituals and other practices as on questions of belief and teaching.

The importance attached by many, but not all religious traditions, to the control of belief and practice is matched by the centrality of agencies within religious organisations for inculcating basic principles and norms. The reproduction of 'correct' belief and practice requires extensive investment in teaching and testing. Part of this involves the preparation and diffusion of sacred texts and teaching materials – either in printed forms or, increasingly, in the form of video cassettes, DVDs and online documents. No less important is the training and deployment of teachers, cate-chists, preachers and evangelists. In turn, this requires seminaries, training colleges, mis-sionary organisations and communications specialists.

Admission to strict religious organisations is usually dependent on displaying knowledge of their essential truths. Testing candidates for admission by examining their knowledge and their moral qualities is, therefore, an integral aspect of the self-regulation of religions. Formal certification of suitability for member-ship and for varying degrees of responsibility for teaching or healing may also occur in strict organisations. By contrast, some other faith traditions such as Islam require new believers to make a public profession of their conviction that 'None has the right to be worshipped but Allah, and Muhammad is the Messenger of Allah' and to understand what this means. Ritual symbolisation of new members' cross-ing the boundary line between outsider and insider often accompanies such professions of faith. 'Initiation' rituals, particularly in some primal or indigenous traditions, may even entail strenuous trials of physical or psycholog-ical worthiness. In all these cases, rules govern the acceptable forms of profession of faith and of ritually symbolising admission to a faith tradition.

(2) If constitutive rules provide the frame-work of principles that mark each religion as unique and self-contained, the *regulatory* rules are concerned with monitoring and, if neces-sary, correcting the thoughts, feelings and actions of each religion's office holders and practitioners. Admittedly, the distinction between constitutive and regulatory rules is not water-tight. It is merely an aid to understand-ing the complexity of self-regulation. In prac-tice, the two types of rules are interdependent.

The authority to detect and punish infringe-ments of constitutive rules also varies with the type of organisation. For example, the Roman Catholic Church's Congregation for the Doctrine of the Faith[2] is a highly formal body of cardinals, at the very heart of its worldwide organisation, for regulating the Church's doctrines and morals. By compari-son, Islam, Hinduism and Buddhism lack single authoritative organisations for regulat-ing their national and transnational activities. Nevertheless, certain scholars, seminars, uni-versities, mosques, temples and monasteries are able to shape and to influence the values, principles and norms that regulate the devel-opment of these faith traditions. Competition, tension, disagreement and conflict are common between the various regulatory bodies particu-larly when they try to deny the legitimacy or the validity of their competitors' versions of orthodoxy or conformity to the religions' claims to truth. In some cases the process of schism occurs when different factions fail to resolve fundamental disagreements about a religion's constitutive rules.

Again, religions vary widely in terms of the degree of formality with which they regulate their activities and respond to alleged breaches of their rules. Many Christian organisations have central agencies for deciding whether their rules have been broken and, if so, how to discipline the culprits. Cases range from 'clergy malfeasance' (Shupe 1995, 1998) to accusa-tions of heresy (Richardson 1975; Givens 1997). Other religious traditions depend less on formal disciplinary procedures and more on local, *ad hoc* judgements issued by self-appointed guardians of doctrinal truth or moral probity. But in all cases the concern of religious organisations is to preserve the integrity of their principles and to prevent errors and abuses from undermining it. Retaining control over the uses of their key myths, symbols and ideas is also a major con-cern of religious organisations that are worried by the prospect of their sacred truths being stolen or misused by others.

The number of places in the world where religious authorities can still legitimately impose a death penalty for a breach of reli-gious rules decreased throughout the twenti-eth century. This form of punishment is now limited to certain countries in the Middle East, North Africa and South East Asia where Islam remains the dominant religion. In fact, *threats* to kill heretics or apostates occur more widely in the world and more frequently but without the force of secular law. It is much more common nowadays for religious authorities, particularly in liberal democratic regimes, to discipline their rule breakers by censure, removal of the authority to teach or preach, temporary or permanent expulsion in the form of, for example, excommunication, disfellowshipment or 'shunning'. The effect of these penalties can be especially hard on people with no friends or relatives outside the religious organisation that banned them from participation.

Resistance to attempts at self-regulation in religions can take various forms of dissidence or defection. It may involve direct challenges to the authority of religious organisations to control, for example, the production of knowledge in theological faculties or political alliances between wealthy interests and elite clergy. It may also stimulate the cultivation and spread of atheism, rationalism, free thought and anticlericalism. Less dramatically, dissidents may simply refuse to comply with rules governing certain beliefs or practices whilst remaining compliant in other respects. For example, many Catholics in various parts of the world seem reluctant to obey the Vatican's strictures against 'artificial' methods of contraception but they still choose to conform to other requirements of the Catholic Church. In the last resort, defectors not only reject the regulations of particular religious organisations but also remove themselves from the jurisdiction of such organisations. This may take the collective form of schism (Wilson 1971) or the individual form of disaffiliation (Mauss 1969; Richardson *et al.* 1986). The act of apostasy is more radical than disaffiliation if it involves denouncing the religious organisation from which the apostate has defected (Bromley 1998).

REGULATION BY RELIGION

From a sociological point of view, beliefs about transcendent realities or divine powers are rarely an end in themselves. Religious beliefs invariably have implications for the conduct of life (Runciman 1969). For example, they can imply that individuals should strive to do certain things and to avoid doing others.

The prescriptions and the proscriptions that are inseparable from religious beliefs can apply to individuals, groups, categories of people, entire societies or the whole of humanity. But in each case, the argument is the same: religious belief is integral to regulation of thought and conduct. In principle, many religious believers insist that nothing should fall outside the realm of religious regulation. In practice, however, the situation is often different in the sense that religious prescriptions and proscriptions can be challenged, changed, ignored or rejected. Furthermore, regulation by religion is only one of many other forms of actual or would-be regulation.

Regulation by religion takes many different forms. A simple, but effective, way of thinking sociologically about them is to identify the main sources of the rules that religious organisations regard as authoritative. There is, in fact, a continuum between the two extremes of external and internal sources of authority. Adapting the terms devised by Heelas and Woodhead (2005: 61), some types of religion expect their followers to make their lives conform to external 'God-given rules and roles'. By contrast, the major source of authority for other types of religion is 'their inner feelings, convictions, instincts and judgements'. The distinction between external and internal sources of authority is, of course, a simplified exaggeration of complex realities. In practice, regulation by religion draws on combinations of external and internal sources of authority. But for our purposes it is helpful to organise our discussion in terms of the two extreme positions.

External

The 'external' source of the most explicit statements of religious rules usually lies in texts widely regarded as sacred. Such laws, codes and entreaties vary widely in form and content, but their normative force commonly flows from the belief that they were dictated, handed down or inspired by divine powers. Some of the best known codes include the Laws of Manu (*c.* 1500 BCE), the Torah, the Ten Commandments, the Qur'an and the Shariah, and the Book of Mormon.

The mere existence of sacred rules in the form of normative texts is not enough to regulate conduct. In addition, formal religious institutions such as churches, monastic orders or theological academies create organisations and functions with the responsibility of applying the rules. This involves finding ways of disseminating the rules as widely as possible, integrating the rules into religious ceremonies, making the rules central to courses of training for religious professionals, and setting up procedures and bodies that can enforce the rules. It is no coincidence that religion and education are bedfellows in every faith tradition.

No less important than these formal schemes for enforcing rules in the name of religion are the less formal processes whereby cultures and societies become imbued with religious ethics. These processes include, for example, shaping the content of religious education in schools, influencing public policies, guiding the development of economic ethics in business, trade unions and political parties, affecting the evolution of criminal and civil law, ensuring that artists, architects, novelists, musicians and playwrights respect religious ethics in their creative works, and so on. Some of these processes are scattered and subtle. Other processes of control by means of, for example, laws against blasphemy or heresy can be blunt and brutal. Such attempts at control operate in isolation from political and economic forces. But their effect is plain to see in the religiously inspired regulation of whole swaths of life in settings as different as late medieval Christendom, early modern Japan or Iran in the early twenty-first century.

The capacity of religions to regulate social life may be diffused through many different processes and institutions, but the effect is achieved by identifiable agencies working directly or indirectly for religious organisations. They include religious agencies in the fields of education, health care, social welfare, sport, and the care of the young, the elderly and vulnerable people. In addition, they include religious publishers, broadcasters, programme makers, lobbyists and website owners.

Some of these agencies provide services exclusively for members of particular religions, but their impact on the wider society should not be overlooked.

Furthermore, it is common for religions to spawn voluntary associations, campaigning groups and lobbying organisations with the aim of influencing political programmes and public policies. Some of the high profile examples of religious contributions towards change in public policies include the many 'temperance' groups that have campaigned at various times against the sale and distribution of alcoholic drinks (Gusfield 1963) or illegal drugs, the even larger number of religious groups that have long protested against warfare (Epstein 1990) or capital punishment (Haines 1996) and the current mobilisations – supported by widely differing religions – against the availability of abortion in all but the most extreme cases (Williams and Blackburn 1996). Support for these different campaigns comes largely from religious sources and is motivated by the desire to regulate or, ideally, to abolish, the use of alcohol, illegal drugs, weapons of war and abortion. Other campaigns by religious organisations to regulate human life – especially its physical and genetic components – are currently focused on euthanasia, experimentation with human embryos, surrogate motherhood, genetic therapy, the use of condoms to control the spread of AIDS, and organ transplantation. Controversy surrounds religious groups such as Jehovah's Witnesses or the Church of Scientology that oppose such routine medical treatments as, respectively, blood transfusions and psychiatric care.

Most of these campaigns to regulate what they regard as major social and moral problems take place on the margins of mainstream politics and political parties, but the campaigners' grievances are sometimes pursued by individual politicians and political parties as well. Indeed, the overlap between religion and politics has been – and continues to be – extensive in many places. Orthodox Christian churches throughout Greece, the Balkans and Eastern Europe, for example, are heavily involved in local and national politics; some political parties and movements in Israel define themselves in terms of Judaism; Islamic political movements and parties are powerful throughout the Middle East, North Africa, Central Asia, South Asia, and South East Asia; and Christian Democrat parties controlled legislatures and governments in a number of West European countries in the latter half of the twentieth century (Fogarty 1957; Madeley 1991). In all of these cases, religion serves as a major source of ideological legitimacy and motivation, thereby helping to shape both public and private life – and, in some places, to control it. The Islamic Republic of Iran and the Kingdom of Saudi Arabia provide the clearest examples of religious regulation over all aspects of society and culture. Many other regimes still subject their citizens to regulations that are formally in accordance with the teachings of, for example, the Roman Catholic Church (in Ireland, Poland and Spain), Orthodox Churches (in Greece, Serbia and Russia), Islam (in Pakistan, Malaysia and Indonesia) and Buddhism (in Thailand). A variety of constitutions, concordats and codes of law underpin the regulatory powers of religion.

Nevertheless, resistance to the religious basis of regulation was a feature of the revolutionary movements that overturned monarchical or colonial regimes in the USA (1776), France (1789), Mexico (1910), Russia (1918), Turkey (1923) and Cuba (1959). The constitutional separation of religion and state has also taken effect without revolution in countries as diverse as India, Japan and Sweden. And even in countries where religion remains closely allied to the state – as in Denmark or the UK – secularist opponents agitate for a complete separation or, at least, a reduction of religion's capacity to regulate citizens' lives.

Internal

By definition, the internal or subjective sources of regulation by religion do not derive their main force from codes of sacred law or other revealed forms of truth. Instead, they arise from insights into truths regarded as immanent in nature, history or humanity. Although these inner truths may be formulated in books,

poems, music, dance, art or drama they are only authoritative to the extent that individuals freely choose to follow them in daily life. It is less a question of obedience to external rules – and more a question of seeking to align one's personal life with recipes for achieving tranquillity, healing or balance. The emphasis is therefore on voluntary decisions to experiment with ideas and practices that claim to produce desired states of body, mind and spirit. Admittedly, gurus, teachers, therapists and trainers may indicate paths to follow in the search for inner truth; but they usually act as exemplars rather than as law-givers or judges. Their practice is more likely to be guided by subjective ideas of appropriateness and self-reflexive discipline.

The growing popularity of being 'spiritual but not religious' (Fuller 2001) or of cultivating subjective forms of spirituality and religion (Heelas and Woodhead 2005) does not signal the end of regulation by religion. It simply means that different 'technologies of subjectivity' (Rose 1999) or 'interiority' (Foucault 1985: 63–7) come into play. They include ideas, practices, ways of talking and forms of social interaction that call forth certain notions of what the self is – and of how it can flourish. For example, rituals that challenge participants to experience the 'goddess within' or to share their deepest feelings with other members of a group help to shape their awareness of themselves as particular kinds of people. Such rituals address participants as 'capable-of-being-empowered' or as 'open' and 'sensitive' beings. Healing rituals can be particularly powerful occasions for shaping the self by showing that it is possible to become a different, i.e. 'healed' or 'whole', person by choosing to make oneself open to healing powers.

In fact, one of the attractions of 'subjective religion' is that it offers freedom from the constraints of organised or formal religion. But the subjective freedom or autonomy on offer is available only on condition that the individual conceives of his or her 'self' as being susceptible to 'growth' or 'choice'. In other words, regulation by external constraint or compulsion gives way to a more subtle process that shapes the individual's sense of self in such a way that it becomes 'naturally' susceptible to self-improvement, self-transformation and self-monitoring in accordance with the expertise claimed for particular 'technologies of subjectivity'. In the words of Nikolas Rose (1999: 93):

> ... the norm of autonomy produces an intense and continuous self-scrutiny, self-dissatisfaction and self-evaluation in terms of the vocabularies and explanations of expertise. In striving to live our autonomous lives, to discover who we really are, to realize our potentials and shape our lifestyles, we become tied to the project of our own identity and bound in new ways into the pedagogies of expertise.

Nevertheless, teachers, therapists and gurus who market their products and services are subject to external regulation by statutory agencies responsible for governing, for example, health and safety, financial accountability, consumer protection and child protection. In addition, those individuals who are approved by voluntary organisations as teachers or therapists are also accountable for their actions in terms of codes of ethical practice.

The heated controversies that sometimes erupt along the border between statutory regulation and voluntary control usually arise from claims that the latter is incapable of dealing adequately with problems that allegedly put the well-being of individual practitioners or consumers in jeopardy. The next section will examine statutory regulation in greater detail.

REGULATION AND RESISTANCE

In modern societies the most visible and usual method of exerting control over religious groups and religious expression is via legal constraints, i.e. laws and constitutional provisions enforced by police and other governmental authorities, including the courts. However, there are other less obvious but important ways of exerting control, as will be described herein. Before discussing more subtle methods of social control we will discuss the arena of legal constraints, adopting some perspectives and ideas derived from the Sociology of Law,

integrating them with relevant theories from the Sociology of Religion.

Constitutional Provisions

Modern societies have constitutions, demonstrating the growth of 'constitutionalism' in the modern era (Arjomand 2003; Go 2003; Scheppele 2004). The spread of constitutionalism around the globe has been a major development in recent decades, demonstrating the power of political leaders holding certain views about what should be the proper order or arrangement of global political and economic realms. Interestingly, virtually all these constitutions include provisions dealing with religion (Richardson 2006a). Most constitutions in Western societies offer guarantees for religious freedom and separation of church and state, although some, particularly in Islamic societies, appear to establish what are, in effect, theocratic states.

What the widely mimicked basic documents in Western societies indicate is that religion should not interfere with the political and economic realms, and that individuals should not be forced to be beholden to a specific religious tradition. The idea of churches as mediating structures for individuals in modern society is weakened considerably in the face of provisions guaranteeing individual religious freedom and choice. Individuals are seemingly left to their own devices in modern Western societies, and religious groups are to be subservient to political and economic interests, as well.

The specific language of these basic constitutional documents is of import, even if the provisions dealing with religious freedom and disestablishment are not understood or enforced uniformly throughout the world. An idealised view of a constitution is that it represents the basic values of society, and therefore should be the underpinning for the legal structure of society, the laws and practices of which are designed to implement values apparent in the constitution. A more realistic (and perhaps cynical) view is that constitutions often play a public image role dictated by those in power in a given society as the constitution is being written and later interpreted. From this perspective, constitutions may include provisions that are designed to convey selected messages to those external to the society and even citizens of the society about how the society should be viewed. Those messages may be misleading as to the true state of affairs in the society, but the messages are still of import.

Thus we saw during the era of the Soviet Union provisions guaranteeing religious freedom written into constitutions of Soviet Bloc countries, belying the extreme persecution of religious groups that was occurring on the ground in many of those societies (Bociurkiw 1989). And in China we see a constitution that guarantees religious freedom to all 'normal religions', with the key term being the meaning of 'normal'. It turns out that normal religion in China means religious organisations set up by the state, with state-selected leadership. This designation is accompanied by severe persecution of 'non-normal' (not state approved) religious groups, including evangelical Christians, Tibetan Buddhism, the Falun Gong, and other non-approved religious groups (Edelman and Richardson 2003; Yang in this volume).

Even in Western Europe and the United States we note significant differences in the understandings of religious freedom and the role of the state *vis-à-vis* religion, and such understandings can change in important ways over time (see relevant chapters in Richardson 2004). In Western Europe we find crucial differences between and among societies all of which claim to be modern Western style democracies. All European societies take a somewhat 'managerial' posture towards religion and religious groups, a product of a somewhat paternalistic attitude towards their citizenries.

France, for instance, is supposedly a secular state which affords, especially in recent times, little official tolerance for high demand religions such as the Jehovah's Witnesses and other minority faiths. But, at the same time, France is definitely a Catholic nation, with special understandings allowing a privileged role for Catholicism. Meanwhile across the border in Italy and Switzerland there are more relaxed attitudes towards minority faiths, and about

the involvement of religion in public life. Similarly, The Netherlands and Scandinavian nations seem much more tolerant of religious differences, although in recent times concern about Islam has tested the levels of tolerance in these and other Western societies. But in Belgium it is apparent that the French attitude towards minority faiths has had a major impact, leading Belgium to attempt to exert more control over minority faiths than is the case in most European countries. In Germany there is yet another traditional approach to regulating religion, with there being two major official state churches, with special privileges, as well as guarantees of religious freedom for other faiths. Yet some of those other faiths chaff under the arrangement and have been seeking for years a legal status similar to that held by the Catholic and Lutheran religious organisations. The Jehovah's Witnesses won such a status in Land Berlin in 2006 after 16 years of litigation.

The United States Constitution guarantees freedom of religion and separation of church and state, and was the first constitution to include those now much-copied concepts (Richardson 2006b, c). However, interpretations of those provisions have varied considerably over the two plus centuries since those words were written. Indeed, there has been a recent controversy associated with US Supreme Court rulings that have shifted from a position where those clauses concerning disestablishment and religious freedom were considered quite sacrosanct to one where religious freedoms are more carefully circumscribed and approached in a much more European management style. The former position of the Court was that any state regulation of religion must pass a 'compelling interest' test before regulation was allowed. In 1993, however, a controversial decision changed the formal position dramatically, allowing regulation of religion if a law allowing such was otherwise neutral on its face towards religious groups and practices. More recently, the Court under new Chief Justice John Roberts, has moved, with a decision involving use of an hallucinogenic tea by a small Brazilian religious group, somewhat back towards the traditional position, at least as far as federal laws affecting religion are concerned.

In former Soviet Bloc countries there is also variation in terms of constitutional statements concerning religion, particularly in how such statements are applied. All constitutions in these countries in Eastern and Central Europe espouse religious freedom, with guarantees that minority faiths will be protected, if for no other reason than the emulation of Western Europe and the desire to become a part of the European Union and the Council of Europe. What happens in those nations varies greatly, however, as reports on the treatment of minority faiths in some of those societies demonstrate that the situation is less than ideal (see Borowik and Babinski 1997; Sajo and Avineri 1999; relevant chapters in Richardson 2004; and Borowik in this volume). Hungary is perhaps the most Western in its approach, and minority religions flourish there, even with considerable recognition and support from the state. This posture seems congruent with Hungary's much more pluralistic history. Russia is towards the other extreme, while also harkening back to its historical context of a nation with a 1,000 year history of domination by the Russian Orthodox Church. The promise of the early 1990s of significant change in how religion was being regulated in a more tolerant and open manner gave way fairly rapidly to a situation of far-reaching domination by the Russia Orthodox Church. As to the other former Soviet Bloc countries, there are almost as many postures towards regulation of religion as there are nations.

Laws

Theories from the Sociology of Law suggest that usually laws are passed which serve the interests of the more powerful in society (Black 1976). However, law making is a continual dialectic process, and seldom is the legal structure of a society static for long periods of time (Chambliss and Zatz 1993). What is the law at one point in time can change drastically in a short period, depending on many circumstances and variables operating within a given historical context (Richardson 2000). This dialectic process can be well illustrated by laws concerning religion, as is the role of status in exerting control over religious expression (Richardson 2001, 2004, 2005).

As noted, ideally constitutions are thought to reflect the values of a society. In turn one would expect those values to be elaborated in the specific laws of a given society. If a society's constitution guarantees religious freedom, supposedly allowing religious groups and individuals to practise their faith without state interference, then laws would be expected that would enable religious groups to act on that basic guarantee. Thus, for instance, religious groups in such a society should be able to rent and own facilities in which to practise their faith, and citizens should be allowed to change religious affiliations if they desire, with no penalty enforced by the state. If a society's constitution speaks of separation of church and state, then supposedly laws would be developed that treat various religious groups similarly or at least neutrally in terms of their access to public funds and other privileges.

However, if a constitution delineates a close relationship between a religion and the state, then there would be laws allowing for such things as public funds to flow to the chosen religious group, and representatives of that group being allowed special privileges in terms of tax status, access to military and prison populations, and other indications of a special relationship between chosen church and state. Non-privileged religious groups might balk at being treated as less than equal, but there may not be much that could be done about the situation, barring effective interference from powerful entities external to the society or successful campaigns within a society that alter the political situation and lead to another 'resolution' within the dialectic law-making processes of that society.

Courts

Court systems vary greatly in terms of the degree of autonomy afforded them within societies. The same circumstances that allow powerful interests in a society to dictate terms and interpretations of constitutional provisions and specific laws also can sometimes dominate judicial systems. Indeed, if powerful interest groups in a society cannot dominate the judicial system of the society, then this demonstrates limitations on the power of those institutional interests (Richardson 2001).

In modern Western societies it is usually economic and political entities that dominate other institutional structures, including religion. In these typical situations the courts may support views of the powerful interests that limit religious freedom of groups and individuals. In some non-Western societies dominated by Islam the courts may be nothing more than extensions of the political apparatus of a theocratic state. Thus the court systems in societies can become an important tool in efforts to regulate religion.

However, the dialectic processes referred to earlier also apply to the ways laws are interpreted and applied. Thus, there may be circumstances where religious groups prevail in Western societies against seemingly more powerful forces. And, there may be situations where the prevailing values in an Islamic state do not completely dictate the outcomes of a situation involving controversy over religious practices. Such situations usually would involve the intervention of more powerful external or internal entities on behalf of the religious group or individual practitioner. The actions of such 'third party partisans' (Black and Baumgartner 1999; Richardson 2004) might be exemplified within the US by the American Civil Liberties Union or a major political party intervening in court proceedings in ways that affected the outcome of a case in a manner favourable to a minority faith or the interests of a religious constituency. Another example of third party intervention that has had some impact on public opinion outside China (even if not internally with Chinese courts) is the actions of Amnesty International concerning treatment of the Falun Gong in that country.

Third parties can also intervene in ways detrimental to the interests of politically weak religious groups, and those intervenors might include more dominant religious organisations. Thus in Russia we have since about 1990 a concerted effort by the Russian Orthodox Church to limit the activities not only of minority faiths – particularly newer ones from the West – but also of longer established ones such as the Jehovah's Witnesses (Shterin and Richardson 2000, 2002). Those efforts have included quite overt actions meant to influence decisions of the courts in Russia in cases involving minority religious groups. Such efforts have not always been completely successful, but nonetheless they have been made, and are usually effective, demonstrating a general lack of autonomy of the court system in Russia.

One fairly recent judicial development, although with roots going back nearly a century in Europe, is the rise of constitutional courts, particularly in former communist countries of Eastern and Central Europe (Richardson 2006a). These courts were established with the express purpose of enforcing provisions of the new constitutions that were developed with the fall of the Soviet Union. Indeed, the establishment of a constitutional court was considered a strong sign that a former member of the Soviet Bloc was ready to join the European Union and the Council of Europe. These new constitutional courts have been able to enforce some rather basic and universal values about human and civil rights in some of these countries, although the pattern has been spotty at best. In Hungary the Constitutional Court of the 1990s made a number of decisions that reinforced the position of religious groups in public life in that country and allowed protections for minority faiths as well (Schanda 2002). However, in some other former Soviet dominated countries the situation has been different. In Russia, for instance, the Constitutional Court has been severely limited in power, and thus unable to act decisively as the ultimate authority concerning constitutionally based protections for human and civil rights in that society. Nevertheless, in recent years the Court has made a few decisions that demonstrate a growing confidence and degree of autonomy (Scheppele 2003).

Global and Regional Regulation Efforts

It is common to view religious regulation from the perspective of a world dominated by nation states. This view is largely correct and quite useful in understanding what is happening in most societies, given the relative autonomy of nation states in today's world. Nations determine to a large extent what occurs within their borders concerning religion and religious groups. However, there is another perspective worthy of consideration given the globalisation that has occurred in recent times. There are universal values and norms concerning human and civil rights that have evolved over the decades since World War II, and there are organisational entities whose major focus is to enforce and implement those values and norms (Donnelly 1999).

The United Nations is one such body which has taken special note of problems concerning religion and religious freedom on occasion. The Council of Europe is another such body which has established what is arguably the most influential court in the world concerned with human rights issues. The European Court of Human Rights has developed a significant record in recent years of supporting religious freedom (Evans 2001). This activity was a long time coming, as the first decision finding a violation of Article 9 of the European Convention Concerning Human and Civil Rights guaranteeing religious freedom did not occur until 1993 (Richardson 1995b). However, since that time a number of decision have been rendered that found violations of Article 9 and related articles.

The pattern of decisions of the Court is an interesting one in that most of the decisions involve the Jehovah's Witnesses seeking to defend themselves as they proselytise and refuse to serve in the military or accept blood transfusions, and most decisions involve Greece and a few countries in the former Soviet Bloc (Richardson and Garay 2004). The Court may be developing a pattern where the older members of the Council of Europe are allowed a considerable measure of respect for their internal decisions concerning religion, whereas newer members of the Council of Europe are not afforded this same degree of latitude.

Another example of regional or global regulation concerns efforts of the US State Department to evaluate the state of religious freedom in countries around the globe. The International Religious Freedom Act, passed during the Clinton administration, requires annual reports to be made that deal with actions concerning limitations on religious freedom in all societies with which the US has relationships (Sadat 2002). The Act contains enforcement mechanisms which allow the President to curtail aid and other relations with a country found in violation of religious freedom. Recent State Department reports have condemned China and other countries for violations of religious freedom. Occasionally, even countries friendly towards the US such as Germany and Japan are criticised in this report, but there have seldom been any consequences of note as a result of these annual reports. Thus this regulatory effort has not had much impact, but has led to considerable criticism of the US for producing such reports.

Media and Regulation

As mentioned, there are less obvious but quite effective ways of exerting control over religious groups than through use of the legal system. The mass media play a major role in social control of deviant behaviour, including actions of religious groups that transgress societal values. Some religious entities, particularly newer ones, may be defined as controversial and violative of normative values of society, and the mass media broadcast and interpret information about the alleged transgressions to the public. Indeed, it may be the case that the media play a primary role in the regulation of religion, with other mechanisms of social control and regulation, including the legal system, following the lead of mass media coverage concerning an activity or group that has attracted attention.

This view of the role of the media is at odds with an idealised view that posits the mass media in modern democratic societies as simply reporting the news in an objective manner in order to have an informed citizenry.

Instead, the mass media are viewed as an important element of social control mechanisms in all modern societies. This view then shifts the issue to discerning the values of those who control this important institution.

On occasion there appears to be overt and direct control of the mass media by political institutions, as in societies such as communist China, in the former Soviet Union, or in Iran. In Western democracies the mass media usually have somewhat more independence from political structures, but this does not mean that the media fail to express the values of the dominant culture in coverage of religion. Thus we usually see the Catholic Church granted great respect in the mass media of countries such as France, Italy, Poland, or Hungary, but treated with much less respect by media in Russia, where Catholicism is considered by many to be an interloper in territory controlled by historical right by the Russian Orthodox Church, or in China, where the authority of the Pope is not accepted by Chinese authorities.

In virtually all modern societies newer religious groups are viewed with suspicion and reported by the mass media with sometimes quite biased coverage (Beckford and Coles 1988; van Driel and Richardson 1988; Richardson 1996; Robbins and Lucas in this volume). The coverage varies, of course, depending on the degree of control exerted by other institutions over the mass media and the view of those controlling media outlets about a given religious group or practice. Thus in China there has been a relentless state directed media campaign to discredit practitioners of the Falun Gong. Such coverage helps justify the severe actions of the state towards Falun Gong, and sends a message to Chinese citizens concerning the official view of this movement (and other forms of deviant behaviour as well). In Iran, media coverage of the Baha'i faith serves to justify the perennial persecution of members of that religious tradition.

In Western democracies the efforts at regulation through media coverage are more subtle but can be very effective. There can be an unacknowledged effect of a confluence of values among various parties involved with regulating religion. Political and religious leaders with a vested interest in maintaining the status quo in the realm of religion can express their values in various ways, including through the media, which are often a willing partner in exerting control over unorthodox religious groups and activities. Journalists also have personal values, of course, even if they like to claim that their values are not expressed in their stories (Richardson and van Driel 1997). When the personal values of journalists, including editors and owners of media outlets, align with those of other dominant institutional structures in society this can bode ill for anyone or any group viewed as outside the bounds of normal society.

Media treatments of unpopular religious groups can justify quite violent actions against such groups even in Western democracies. Such was the case with the Branch Davidians episode occurring at Waco in 1993 (Beckford 1994; Shupe and Hadden 1995). In that tragic episode it was clear that representatives of the media were willing to work closely with government officials to portray the Davidians in a very negative light. Media representatives have since expressed concern at the heavy controls exerted over media activities at Mt Carmel outside of Waco, Texas (Richardson 1995a), but at the time it was plainly the case that the mass media were simply parroting what government officials wanted them to say. The overall effect of this cooperation between the media and state officials was for American citizens to express high levels of support for governmental actions at Mt Carmel, even including the ultimate attack that led to the burning of the compound where dozens of women and children were killed in the conflagration.

Less overtly violent actions concerning controversial religious groups have been justified through media presentations that portray such groups in negative ways. Within the US this can be demonstrated by the manner in which the mass media so quickly adopted the 'cult brainwashing' interpretation of participation in new religious groups of the 1960s and 1970s (Richardson 1993). This effective cultural product was exported over the ensuing decades to, and adopted by, other societies including France and even China and former

Soviet societies such as Russia. France was particularly effective at promoting this negative perspective on minority faiths within its borders and in a number of other countries, including China (Richardson and Introvigne 2001).

The 'cult brainwashing' view includes definitions of newer religious groups as 'cults' (a term with strong negative connotations) which 'brainwash' people into joining and use 'mind control' to make them stay in the groups. Such a view defines newer religious groups so labelled and characterised as outside the pale of normal protections afforded religious expression within American culture or other societies espousing religious freedom. The First Amendment to the US Constitution guaranteeing religious freedom was not thought by many to be applicable to 'cults' (Bromley and Breschel 1992). Instead, for a time in the 1960s and 1970s it was deemed acceptable in the US to take overt 'self-help' (Black 1999) action against such groups, sometimes even including the kidnapping and deprogramming of adult members of such groups. This media-promoted view of newer religious groups also served in the US as the basis of a number of civil court actions against the groups, a tactic that was successful for years until the judicial system belatedly issued rulings precluding such actions on the grounds that 'brainwashing' based claims were not supported by scientific studies of participation (Anthony 1990; Ginsburg and Richardson 1998; Anthony and Robbins 2004).

Anti-Cult and Counter-Cult Movements

A common reaction to the rise of newer or controversial faiths is the development of movements and organisations opposing them (Shupe and Bromley 1980, 1994). Such oppositional groups, which are a specific form of NGO, may be situated in one society or may be transnational. These organisations attempt to encourage official sanctions against the group by government officials, as well as other activities that exhort others to exert control over the target groups. We have seen in the US and elsewhere the development of organisations typically made up of ex-members of religious groups such as Jehovah's Witnesses, Mormons (Latter Day Saints), and Christian Scientists. These oppositional groups disseminate information about the religions to any who are interested, using whatever means they have available. A special focus is on disseminating press releases to the mass media, representatives of which are often quite willing to treat such information as factual, making use of it in publications of various kinds. In contemporary times the activities of these oppositional groups include use of the internet, which is a haven for dissidents and apostates from various religious groups. Looking for information on the internet about nearly any religious group will result in sites being found which are adamantly opposed to the specific groups as well as some sites that are opposed to particular categories of religious groups or religion in general (Dawson and Cowan 2004).

Of particular note for our purposes is the development of Anti-Cult movements (ACMs) and Counter-Cult movements (CCMs) (Introvigne 1999) in the US and elsewhere whose function is to oppose, and encourage others to oppose, some of the major New Religious Movements (NRMs) such as Scientology, The Unification Church, the Hare Krishna, The Children of God (now The Family), and others. The distinction is not always clear between ACMs and CCMs, but ACMs tend to be more secular oriented organisations which claim not to oppose religious movements themselves, but to take issue with some of their tactics such as the claimed use of 'brainwashing' and 'mind control'. CCM organisations are opposed to the beliefs of the NRMs, claiming that they are teaching a false religion. These organisations, though small, have been quite effective in spreading their message of opposition, in part because the ideological position of such groups usually comports well with the basic cultural values of dominant groups in society. Those dominant class members who occupy positions in major institutional structures of society are prone to accept the ACM and CCM messages which resonate with their values and self-interest. Thus, these counter-movement organisations have often seen their information accepted by the media and taken at face value by political and religious leaders in society, as well as by the courts (Anthony 1990; Richardson 1991).

Moral Panics and the Media

Moral panics are powerful devices of social control, and serve to justify rigorous regulation of religious groups when they are the targets of a moral panic. The term 'moral panic' was developed in the 1970s in deviance studies to refer to situations involving an exaggerated response to some issue or activity that had become a concern in a society (Cohen 1972). Since then the term has been used to refer to the social construction of a number of different issues or social problems that have become a focus of the media and other institutional interests in society. In recent decades there have been moral panics about child sex abuse, missing children, violent juvenile delinquents, and a number of other issues that were initially defined as social problems. For an issue or activity to move from the status of a social problem to that of a moral panic means that a significant escalation of concern has been achieved. Scholars are now studying how this escalation occurs, and under what conditions. Moral panics about NRMs have been central to this research (Richardson and Introvigne 2007).

Eric Goode and Nachman Ben-Yehuda (1994) list six major elements or actors that play a role in establishing a moral panic. Not surprisingly, they list 'the press' as the primary actor, followed by the public, law enforcement, politicians and legislators, 'action groups', and 'folk devils'. They also discuss what they call the 'disaster analogy' which they claim is used in moral panic construction to help make a case that the social problem targeted is thought of in terms of a disaster that is being visited upon the populace. The term 'action group' fits well the ACM and CCM organisations referred to above. Those organisations have managed to promote their message well with the usually receptive mass media outlets. This symbiotic-like relationship between the media and ACMs and CCMs has been a major factor in the

development of the moral panic about NRMs that swept through a number of Western and non-Western countries. The campaign has found its share of 'folk devils' (defined by Goode and Ben-Yehuda 1994: 28, as 'the personification of evil') on which to focus attention. For the moral panic about NRMs the term has included such personages as the Reverend Sun Myung Moon and David Berg of the Children of God, as well as more recent examples such as David Koresh of the Branch Davidians and Shoko Asahara, the leader of Aum Shinrikyo responsible for the sarin gas attacks made in Tokyo as well as a number of other violent actions.

Obviously, if religious groups are successfully defined as the subject of a moral panic, then social control of such groups is made much easier. Normal rules do not apply when dealing with groups headed by 'folk devils' and supported by unverified 'folk statistics' that claim to document the depth and degree of the problem. Religious groups which find themselves defined in such a manner are often virtually helpless when dominant groups in society act against them. The infamous 'dingo case' in Australia demonstrates this kind of effect. The Chamberlain couple were accused and found guilty of killing their daughter who apparently had been taken by a dingo (Richardson 1996, 2001). What happened with this matter shows the level of hysteria that can develop when a somewhat strange (to many people) religious group is involved (Seventh Day Adventists). Many other instances involving small or controversial religious groups could be cited as well, such as the moral panic in the US concerning the 'Moonies' that eventually contributed to the Reverend Moon being found guilty of tax evasion and sentenced to federal prison (Richardson 1992). It is noteworthy that in both the 'dingo case' and the Reverend Moon tax case, the courts played a major role only after a high level of hysteria had been fomented in the general public by extensive media coverage. These episodes clearly demonstrate that the rules of evidence and other judicial procedures can be amazingly flexible when the court is functioning in a normative mode, enforcing the values of society through its rulings (Richardson 2001). Regulation of religious groups and personages is quite effective when all segments of a society have been convinced that an evil is being visited upon a society, and that it must be controlled.

EMERGING DILEMMAS

Several discussions of contemporary religious changes and their implications for public policies have a bearing on the regulation of religion – and of regulation by religion. In this sense, the study of religion and regulation opens up an interesting – albeit unusual – perspective on some of the major themes in the sociology of religion. The following two sub-sections will explore dilemmas concerning regulation and religion that arise from growing tensions between changes in religion and changes in modes of regulation.

De-Regulation and Religious Vitality

A growing trend among sociologists of religion is to argue that the level of religious vitality – as measured by, for example, rates of participation in religious activities, membership of religious groups, or financial support for religious organisations – is likely to be higher in societies where agencies of the state do not significantly regulate the markets for religion (Lechner in this volume). Thus, countries that foster a free market in religion are expected to have high levels of religious vitality because they supposedly encourage healthy competition and opportunities for religious innovation. By contrast, countries which have state-sponsored religious organisations or which subsidise some – but not necessarily all – religious activities are expected to depress the level of religious vitality by inducing 'lazy monopolies', by deterring competition between different religious groups or by imposing excessively high start-up costs of new religious ventures.

Empirical research has tended to confirm these broad theoretical generalisations (Grim and Finke 2006; McCleary and Barro 2006) whilst also generating some interesting

reservations and variations. For example, countries with predominantly Roman Catholic populations tend to have higher rates of religious vitality than would be predicted by the 'free market' theory. And in the case of a country such as China, which forcefully controls religious activity, the effect is not to eliminate all religion but to produce a complicated structure of (a) officially permitted religion, (b) officially banned religion, and (c) a 'grey' market of 'activities with ambiguous legal status' (Yang 2006: 97). Another refinement of the argument about the vitality of relatively unregulated religious markets has shown that 'state regulation of religion is a more important variable than religious pluralism in explaining religious vitality' (Chaves and Cann 1992: 285; see also Norris and Inglehart 2004: 24). In other words, the mere fact of religious diversity is not necessarily associated with religious vitality.

The argument that religion flourishes when regulation by agencies of the state is at a low level was confirmed by Gill (2001: 132), but he added that 'scholars have yet to explain the variation in levels of religious regulation across nations'. In fact, Norris and Inglehart (2004: 24) devised a 20-point Religious Freedom Index precisely to test the theoretical idea that regulation of religion by state agencies depresses the level of participation in religious activities. Their analysis of data from the World Values Survey and the European Values Survey showed that 'the relationship [between regulation and religion] is weak and the correlation may be spurious' in nearly 80 countries. They went on to specify that, in the particular case of post-communist countries in Europe, 'religious pluralism and religious freedom have a negative relationship with participation'. Their provocative conclusion is that 'societies with the *greatest* state regulation of religion have the greatest religious participation and the strongest faith in God' (Norris and Inglehart 2004: 230, emphasis original).

Nevertheless, a more recent analysis of cross-national data from 196 countries and territories suggested that high levels of regulation of religion were positively correlated with high levels of religious persecution (Grim and Finke 2006). Indeed, Grim (2005: 114) has claimed that 'Religious regulation was found to be the strongest predictor of religious persecution even when controlling for other possible explanations'. The most general implication of Grim's findings is that 'a free and unregulated religious marketplace is in the best interests of religion' (2005: 120).

On the other hand, opposition to a free market in religion is detectable to varying degrees in all regions of Europe as well as in other parts of the world, but politicians, officials and public opinion in France have gone further than in most other countries – except perhaps Saudi Arabia, Russia, Iran and China – in articulating and implementing policies designed to ensure that the freedom of religion does not prejudice 'free thinking' and republican solidarity. In particular, France currently mobilises statutory and voluntary agencies in a 'struggle' against 'sectarian aberrations' (*les dérives sectaires*) – partly to punish religious groups that allegedly take advantage of vulnerable people's psychological weaknesses, and partly to prevent such abuse from taking place. The French Republic's doctrine of *laïcité* has a mission to strengthen rational, free thought and thereby to safeguard the freedom of citizens to decide for themselves whether they wish to practise religion in their private life (Beckford 2004).

In short, there is strong tension between, on the one hand, the claim that deregulation of religion increases religious vitality and religious freedom and, on the other, the assertion that deregulation leads to abuses of religion, threats to the freedom of thought and attacks on the cohesiveness of society. The dilemma for policy makers is how to resolve the tension. This task is made more complex by the fact that issues of religious freedom and perceived threats from religious extremism cut across national boundaries. In other words, there is a global dimension to the regulation of religion – and to the resistance against such regulation.

Individualisation, Subjectivisation and Consumer Protection

Religion in advanced industrial societies has undergone processes of privatisation,

individualisation and subjectivisation. Each of these terms emphasises a different facet of a general trend towards patterns of beliefs, feelings, actions and social relations that reflect the growing importance of personal choice in matters of religion. All of these changes are firmly nested in theories of modernisation and its more recent forms of 'new modernity', 'late modernity', 'postmodernity' and 'ultra modernity' (Willaime 2006); and they all seem to indicate that religious freedom, religious diversity and religious pluralism (the positive evaluation of diversity) flourish alongside privatised and individualised religion. Nevertheless, this picture of recent changes in religion is one-sided. Admittedly, the picture is supported by extensive evidence (summarised in Heelas and Woodhead 2005), but it conceals the fact that privatised and individualised forms of religion are part of expanding *markets* of religion and that the 'consumers' of marketised religion are at risk of deception, exploitation and abuse. The second dilemma that arises from recent trends in religion in advanced industrial societies therefore concerns the extent to which legislators and public policy makers are prepared to allow the marketisation of religion to proceed without regulation.

In David Lyon's (2000: 10) words, 'The demise of regulated, institutional religion seems to open space for all manner of alternatives, as varied as they are unpredictable'. The process may involve piecing together items taken from highly disparate origins (often known by the French term '*bricolage*'); and the outcome may be hybrid or syncretistic forms of religion which juxtapose or blend these items in idiosyncratic combinations. Some of them draw inventively on traditions, while others are more radically original. What they all share in common is the conviction that individuals voluntarily and freely choose their particular beliefs, practices and allegiances.

On the other hand, the growth of freedom in religious choice in many countries means that supposedly autonomous individuals are increasingly exposed to the marketing practices of religious organisations seeking to increase their share of the market. This is an aspect of what Beck and Beck-Gernsheim

(2002: 203) call 'institutional individualiza-tion'. It simultaneously frees individuals from tradition and makes them dependent on markets, thereby confining free choice to increasingly standardised or packaged prod-ucts. Entrepreneurial and – in some cases – exploitative organisations try to supply reli-gious 'goods' to potential consumers whose sense of loyalty or obligation to traditional or conventional forms of religion is weak or non-existent. In itself, this entrepreneurialism in religion is far from new but it has benefited hugely from technological and social changes in recent decades. Beginning in the 1960s, the availability of credit cards, photocopiers, fax machines, computers, video recording, mobile phones, the internet and satellite communica-tion has assisted the virtually world-wide mar-keting of religion.[3] At the same time, relatively cheap forms of transport, extensive migration and social mobility have also tended to increase the number of people statistically 'at risk' of encountering new suppliers of religious goods. The result is that consumers of religion enjoy greater freedom of choice *and* that suppliers are better able to influence their choice by skilful marketing and branding of their goods.

The extent to which the supply of marke-tised religious goods is subject to regulation by agencies of the state varies widely from coun-try to country. Regulation of religion in the USA, for example, is relatively light (Richardson 2006b), but conditions are nevertheless imposed on the kind of religious (and non-religious) material that can be legally broadcast or sent through the post. It also controls all offers to cure medical problems on the strength of reli-gious beliefs. Moreover, some local authorities regulate door-to-door evangelism as well as the use of public space – such as airports and train stations – for the purpose of proselytis-ing. And access by religious groups to state-funded institutions such as hospitals, schools, prisons and military establishments must con-form to certain regulations. Very few of these regulations are applicable only to religion in isolation, but the fact is that the American reli-gious market – probably the least regulated in the world – is nevertheless subject to a range of controls. As we explained earlier in this chapter, the US Supreme Court has changed its position since 1990 and seems to have reverted to a position that provides strong protection for religious freedom. In fact, some critics of current legislation claim that religious groups now benefit from too many protections or exemptions (Henriques 2006).

The growth of religious freedom goes hand in hand, then, with increasing pressure on govern-ments to protect the consumers of marketised religion against exploitation. This is a relatively unexplored feature of 'risk society' (Beck 1992) in the sense that knowledge about the frequency and probability of the potentially harmful effects of all human activities is, in theory, available to agencies of the state. Religion is no exception, especially in the wake of the violent incidents that have cost thousands of lives either as a result of criminal activity in religious groups or as a consequence of the harassment and bad policing to which some groups have been subjected. Gathering 'intelligence' and expertise about the risks allegedly associated with strong religious convictions is becoming a routine aspect of work in government departments responsible for criminal justice, security and social cohesion. At the same time, civil society contains growing numbers of organisations and campaigns that monitor the activities of religious groups consid-ered to be potentially or actually problematic. Most of them fall into the categories of 'cult watching', 'anti-cult' or 'counter-cult' organisa-tions (Barker 2002). Some of these organisations receive support for their work from agencies of the state and can, therefore, be said to perform a type of 'delegated' regulation. This primarily involves collecting information and offering to forward it to statutory authorities but it can also include disseminating information to the mass media or trying to mediate between religious groups and people with a grievance against them.

Liberal democracies face the dilemma of trying to strike an acceptable balance between the risks of harm perceived to be associated with religion and the risks associated with what might look like intrusion into a suppos-edly private area of life. 'Managing' those risks is central to governance in the early twenty-first century.

CONCLUSION

Issues concerning regulation and religion have been growing in importance since the mid-twentieth century. In some respects, these issues have also affected other social institutions such as business, education, the family and healthcare as well as politics and public protests. One of the key features of late modern societies has, in fact, been the increasing capacity of systems of regulation to control more and more spheres of social life – and to be more accountable for doing so.

The prominence enjoyed by regimes of regulation is related in complex ways to social and cultural changes affecting all societies in a rapidly globalising world. It would take too long to discuss all these changes here, but the most salient include the spread of the internet to virtually all parts of the world and all realms of human activity, the widespread juridification (Teubner 1998) of regulation in response to the perceived need for social protection, the near-instantaneous penetration of global media of communications into any event or situation deemed newsworthy, and the rise in status of formal 'expertise' in the management of perceived risks and problems. In combination, these changes – and others too numerous to mention here – have not only extended the reach of regulation but have also raised awareness of new risks supposedly requiring regulation (Beck 1992).

This chapter has shown that religion is subject to self-regulation as well as to regulation by external agencies. It is also resistant to some attempts to regulate it; and, in turn, it seeks to regulate aspects of social life in accordance with its own values. On the other hand, religion also gives rise to issues about regulation that are relatively specific to itself and that require closer investigation in future research. These issues are diverse but they all reflect the fact that social change has rendered religion more susceptible to calls for enhanced regulation or self-regulation (Richardson 2004). Three factors deserve special consideration.

First, the growth of religious diversity is probably the most important factor in this respect (Champion 1999; Beckford 2003).

Diversification of religion is closely associated with processes of globalisation, marketisation and 'institutional individualization' (Beck and Beck-Gernsheim 2002). The collapse of communist regimes in Central and Eastern Europe in the early 1990s triggered particularly acute concerns about the rapid expansion of an entirely new and uncontrolled religious market (Richardson 2004; Borowik in this volume). The partial marketisation of religion in the People's Republic of China has already sparked some difficulties (see Yang in this volume).

Second, concerns about the uses of religion in connection with acts of violence and terrorism have forced issues about regulation and religion much higher up the political agenda – especially since the attacks launched against the USA on 11 September 2001 and subsequently against public transport systems in Madrid and London. Other incidents in Japan, India and the Middle East have also intensified this concern (Juergensmeyer 2000; Reader 2000; Kepel 2006). Some of them involve violent attacks on religious groups.

Third, developments in medicine, genetics and bioethics have not only raised the profile of religion as a source of demands for closer regulation of research and therapies but have also prompted questions about the need to consider tougher regulation of therapies based on religion (Sloan et al. 1999; Guinn 2006). Long-running debates about abortion, euthanasia and blood transfusion are now paralleled by equally contentious discussion of religious ideas about cloning (Palmer 2004), gene therapies and so-called New Age healing. These developments represent an extension of disputes about the limits of consumer protection, patient protection and even child protection. Religious ideas and interests are at the centre of these disputes about regulation.

NOTES

1. Control over publicly funded chaplaincies in prisons, health care institutions and the military is a good illustration of the unevenness that exists in many countries between the negative and positive aspects of the regulation of religion.

2. This is the successor to the medieval Inquisition and the early modern Holy Office.

3. Opponents of various religious groups have also profited from access to the internet. See Mayer 2003; Cowan 2004.

REFERENCES

Anthony, D. 1990. 'Religious movements and brainwashing litigation: Evaluating key testimony'. In T. Robbins and D. Anthony (eds), *In Gods We Trust*. New Brunswick, NJ: Transaction Books: 295–344.

Anthony, D. and T. Robbins 2004. 'Pseudoscience versus minority religions: An evaluation of the brainwashing theories of Jean-Marie Abgrall'. In J. T. Richardson (ed.), *Regulating Religion*. New York: Kluwer: 127–50.

Arjomand, S. A. 2003. 'Law, political reconstruction, and constitutional politics'. *International Sociology* 18: 7–32.

Barker, E. V. 2002. 'Watching for violence: a comparative analysis of the roles of five types of cult-watching groups'. In D. G. Bromley and J. G. Melton (eds) *Cults, Religion and Violence*. New York: Cambridge University Press: 123–48.

Beck, U. 1992. *Risk Society. Towards a New Modernity*. London: Sage.

Beck, U. and E. Beck-Gernsheim 2002. *Individualization*. London: Sage.

Beckford, James A. 1989. *Religion and Advanced Industrial Society*. London: Unwin-Hyman.

Beckford, James A. 1994. 'The media and new religious movements.' In J. Lewis (ed.), *From the Ashes: Making Sense of Waco*. Lanham, MD: Rowan and Littlefield: 143–49.

Beckford, James A. 1999. 'The politics of defining religion in secular society: from a taken-for-granted institution to a contested resource'. In Platvoet, J. G. and Molendijk, A. L. (eds), *The Pragmatics of Defining Religion: Contexts, Concepts and Conflicts*. Leiden: E. J. Brill: 23–40.

Beckford, James A. 2003. *Social Theory & Religion*. Cambridge: Cambridge University Press.

Beckford, James A. 2004. '"Laïcité", "dystopia", and the reaction to new religious movements in France'. In Richardson, J. T. (ed.) *Regulating Religion. Case Studies from Around the Globe*. New York: Kluwer/Plenum: 27–40.

Beckford, James A. and Melanie Coles 1988. 'British and American responses to new religious movements'. *Bulletin of the John Rylands University Library of Manchester* 70: 209–24.

Black, D. 1976. *The Behavior of Law*. New York: Academic Press.

Black, D. 1999. *The Social Structure of Right and Wrong*. New York: Academic Press.

Black, D. and M. P. Baumgartner 1999. 'Toward a theory of the third party'. In D. Black (ed.). *The Social Structure of Right and Wrong*. New York: Academic Press: 95–124.

Bociurkiw, B. R. 1989. In J. E. Wood (ed.), *Readings on Church and State*. Waco, TX: Dawson Institute for Church State Studies: 303–18.

Borowik, I. and G. Babinski 1997. *New Religious Phenomena in Central and Eastern Europe*. Krakow: Nomos.

Bourdieu, Pierre 1991. 'Genesis and structure of the religious field'. *Comparative Social Research* 13: 1–44.

Bromley, David G. (ed.) 1998. *The Politics of Religious Apostasy: the Role of Apostates in the Transformation of Religious Movements*. Westport, CT: Praeger.

Bromley, D. and E. Breschel 1992. 'General Population and Institutional Elite Support for Social Control of New Religious Movements'. *Behavioral Sciences & Law* 10: 39–52.

Champion, F. 1999. 'The diversity of religious pluralism'. *MOST Journal on Multicultural Societies* 1 (2). Online document at: *http://www.unesco.org/most/v11n2cha.htm*.

Chambliss, W. J. and M. S. Zatz 1993. *Making Law*. Bloomington: Indiana University Press.

Chaves, M. and D. E. Cann 1992. 'Regulation, pluralism, and market structure: explaining religion's vitality'. *Rationality and Society* 4: 272–90.

Cohen, S. 1972. *Folk Devils and Moral Panics: The Creation of Mods and Rockers*. London: MacGibbon and Kee.

Cowan, D. E. 2004. 'Contested spaces: movement, countermovement, and e-space propaganda'. In L. L. Dawson and D. E. Cowan (eds) *Religion Online. Finding Faith on the Internet*. New York: Routledge: 255–71.

Dawson, L. and D. Cowan 2004. *Religion Online: Finding Faith on the Internet*. New York: Routledge.

Donnelly, J. 1999. 'The Social Construction of International Human Rights'. In T. Moore and N. Wheeler (eds). *Human Rights in Global Politics*. Cambridge: Cambridge University Press: 71–102.

Edelman, B. and J. T. Richardson 2003. 'Falun Gong and the Law: Development of Legal Social Control in China'. *Nova Religio* 6: 312–31.

Epstein, B. 1990. 'The politics of moral witness: religion and nonviolent direct action'. In S. Marullo and J. Lofland (eds) *Peace Action in the Eighties*.

New Brunswick, NJ: Rutgers University Press: 106–24.

Evans, C. 2001. *Freedom of Religion under the European Convention on Human Rights*. Oxford: Oxford University Press.

Finke, R. 1990. 'Religious deregulation: origins and consequences'. *Journal of Church and State* 32 (3): 609–26.

Fogarty, M. 1957. *Christian Democracy in Western Europe, 1820–1953*. South Bend, IN: University of Notre Dame Press.

Foucault, M. 1985. *The History of Sexuality. Vol 2 The Use of Pleasure*. New York: Random House.

Fuller, R. C. 2001. *Spiritual but not Religious*. New York: Oxford University Press.

Giddens, A. 1991. *Modernity and Self-Identity. Self and Society in the Late Modern Age*. Cambridge: Polity Press.

Gill, Anthony 2001. 'Religion and comparative politics', *Annual Review of Political Science* 4: 117–38.

Ginsburg, G. P. and J. T. Richardson 1998. '"Brainwashing" evidence in light of *Daubert*'. In H. Reece (ed.), *Law and Science*. Oxford: Oxford University Press: 265–88.

Givens, T. L. 1997. *Mormons, Myths, and the Construction of Heresy*. New York City: Oxford University Press.

Go, J. 2003. 'A Globalizing Constitutionalism: Views from the Postcolony, 1945-2000'. *International Sociology* 18: 71–95.

Goode, E. and N. Ben-Yehuda 1994. *Moral Panics: The Social Construction of Deviance*. Cambridge: Blackwell.

Grim, B. 2005. 'Religious regulation's impact on religious persecution: the effects of de facto and de jure religious regulation', Unpublished PhD dissertation, the Pennsylvania State University.

Grim, B. and R. Finke 2006. 'International religion indexes: government regulation, government favoritism, and social regulation of religion', *Interdisciplinary Journal of Research on Religion* 2: 2–40.

Guinn, David E. (ed.) 2006. *Handbook of Bioethics and Religion*. New York, Oxford University Press.

Gusfield, J. 1963. *Symbolic Crusade: Status Politics and the Temperance Movement*. Urbana, IL: University of Illinois.

Haines, H. 1996. *Against Capital Punishment. The Anti-Death Penalty Movement in America, 1972-1994*. New York: Oxford University Press.

Heelas, P. and L. Woodhead 2005. *The Spiritual Revolution*. Oxford: Blackwell.

Henriques, Diana B. 2006. 'As exemptions grow, religion outweighs regulation'. *New York Times*, 8 October.

Hood, C., H. Rothstein and R. Baldwin 2001. *The Government of Risk*. Oxford: Oxford University Press.

Hutter, B. M. 2006. 'The role of non-state actors in regulation'. Discussion paper no. 37. London: London School of Economics, Centre for Analysis of Risk and Regulation.

Iannaccone, L., R. Finke and R. Stark 1997. 'Deregulating religion: supply-side stories of trends and change in the religious marketplace', *Economic Inquiry* 35: 350–64.

Introvigne, M. 1999. 'The secular anti-cult and the religious counter-cult movement: Strange bedfellows and future enemies?' In R. Towler (ed.), *New Religions and the New Europe*. Aaarhus, Denmark: Aaarhus University Press: 32–54.

Juergensmeyer, M. 2000. *Terror in the Mind of God. The Global Rise of Religious Violence*. Berkeley, CA: University of California Press.

Kepel, G. 2006. *Jihad: The Trail of Political Islam*. Oxford: I.B. Tauris.

Lyon, D. 2000. *Jesus in Disneyland. Religion in Postmodern Times*. Cambridge: Polity.

Madeley, J. 1991. 'Politics and religion in Western Europe'. In G. Moyser (ed.) *Religion and Politics in the Modern World*. London: Routledge: 28–66.

Mauss, A. L. 1969. 'Dimensions of religious defection'. *Review of Religious Research* 10: 128–35.

Mayer, J.-F. 2003. 'Religion and the Internet: The global marketplace.' In J. A. Beckford and J. T. Richardson (eds) *Challenging Religion*. London: Routledge: 36–46.

McCleary, Rachel M. and Robert J. Barro 2006. 'Religion and political economy in an international panel', *Journal for the Scientific Study of Religion* 45 (2): 149–75.

Norris, P. and R. Inglehart 2004. *Sacred and Secular. Religion and Politics Worldwide*. Cambridge: Cambridge University Press.

Palmer, Susan J. 2004. *Aliens Adored: Rael's UFO Religion*. New Brunswick, NJ: Rutgers University Press.

Reader, I. 2000. *Religious Violence in Contemporary Japan*. Honolulu: University of Hawai'i Press.

Richardson, James T. 1975. 'New forms of deviancy in a fundamentalist church: a case study'. *Review of Religious Research* 16: 134–42.

Richardson, J. T. 1991. 'Cult/brainwashing cases and the freedom of religion'. *Journal of Church and State* 33: 55–74.

Richardson, J. T. 1992. 'Public opinion and the tax evasion trial of Reverend Moon'. *Behavioral Sciences & Law* 10: 53–65.

Richardson, J. T. 1993. 'A social psychological critique of brainwashing claims'. In J. Hadden and

D. Bromley (eds), *Handbook of Cults and Sects in America*. Greenwich, CT: JAI Pess: 75–97.

Richardson, J. T. 1995a. 'Manufacturing consent about Koresh'. In S. Wright (ed.), *Armageddon in Waco*. Chicago: University of Chicago Press: 153–76.

Richardson, J. T. 1995b. 'Minority religions, religious freedom, and the pan-European political and judicial institutions'. *Journal of Church and State* 37: 39–60.

Richardson, J. T. 1996. '"Brainwashing" claims and minority religions outside the Untied States: Cultural diffusion of a questionable legal concept'. *Brigham Young University Law Review* 1996: 873–904.

Richardson, J. T. 2000. 'Discretion and discrimination in legal cases involving controversial religious groups and allegations of ritual abuse'. In R. Ahdar (ed.), *Law and Religion*. Aldershot, UK: Ashgate: 11–132.

Richardson, J. T. 2001. 'Law, social control, and minority religions'. In P. Côté (ed.), *Frontier Religions in Public Space*. Ottawa: University of Ottawa Press: 139–68.

Richardson, James T. (ed.) 2004. *Regulating Religion. Case Studies from around the Globe*. New York: Kluwer.

Richardson, J. T. 2005. 'Law'. In H. R. Ebaugh (ed.), *Handbook of Religion and Social Institutions*. New York: Springer: 227–40.

Richardson, J. T. 2006a. 'Religion, constitutional courts, and democracy in former communist countries'. *The Annals of the American Academy of Political and Social Science* 603: 129–38.

Richardson, J. T. 2006b. 'Religion in public space: A theoretical perspective and comparison of Russia, Japan and the United States'. *Religion-Staat-Gesellschaft* 7 (1): 45–61.

Richardson, J. T. 2006c. 'The sociology of religious freedom: A structural and socio-legal analysis'. *Sociology of Religion* 67: 271–94.

Richardson, J. T. and Alain Garay 2004. 'The European Court of Human Rights and Former Communist Countries'. In D. M. Jerolimov, S. Zrinscak, and I. Borowik (eds), *Religion and Patterns of Social Transformation*. Zageb: Institute for Social Reseach: 223–43.

Richardson, J. T. and M. Introvigne 2001. '"Brainwashing" theories in European parliamentary and administrative reports on "cults" and "sects"', *Journal for the Scientific Study of Religion* 40: 143–68.

Richardson, J. T. and M. Introvigne 2007. 'New religious movements, counter movements, moral panics, and the media'. In D. G. Bromley (ed.) *Teaching New Religious Movements*. New York Oxford University Press: 91–111.

Richardson, James T., Jan van der Lans and Frans Derks 1986. 'Leaving and labelling: voluntary and coerced disaffiliation from religious social movements', *Research in Social Movements, Conflicts and Change* 9: 97–126.

Richardson, J. T. and B. van Driel 1997. 'Journalists; attitudes toward new religious movements'. *Review of Religious Research* 39: 116–36.

Rose, N. 1999. *Powers of Freedom*. Cambridge: Cambridge University Press.

Runciman, W. G. 1969. 'The sociological explanation of "religious" beliefs'. *Archives Européennes de Sociologie* (10) 2: 149–91.

Sadat, L. N. 2002. 'Religious freedom and American foreign policy: The United States Commission on International Religious Freedom'. *New England Journal of International and Comparative Law* 9: 1–15.

Sajo, A. and S. Avineri 1999. *The Law of Religious Identity: Models for Post-Communism*. The Hague: Kluwer.

Schanda, B. 2002. *Legislation on Church-State Relations in Hungary*. Budapest: Ministry of Cultural Heritage.

Scheppele, K. 2003. 'Constitutional negotiations: Political contexts of judicial activism in post-Soviet Europe'. *International Sociology* 18: 219–38.

Scheppele, K. 2004. 'Constitutional ethnography: An introduction'. *Law & Society Review* 38: 389–406.

Shterin, M. and J. T. Richardson 2000. 'Effects of the Western anti-cult movement on development of laws concerning religion in post-communist Russia'. *Journal of Church and State* 42: 247–71.

Shterin, M. and J. T. Richardson 2002. 'The *Yakunin v. Dworkin* trial and emerging religious pluralism in Russia'. *Religion in Eastern Europe* 22: 1–38.

Shupe, A. 1995. *In the Name of All that's Holy: a Theory of Clergy Malfeasance*. Westport, CT: Praeger.

Shupe, A. (ed.) 1998. *Wolves Within the Fold: Religious Leadership and Abuse of Power*. New Brunswick, NJ: Rutgers University Press.

Shupe, A. and D. Bromley 1980. *The New Vigilantes: Anti-Cultists and the New Religions*. Beverly Hills, CA: Sage.

Shupe, A. and D. Bromley 1994. *Anti-Cult Movements in Cross-Cultural Perspective*. New York: Garland.

Shupe, A. and J. Hadden 1995. 'Cops, news copy, and public opinion: Legitimacy and the social construction of evil in Waco'. In S. Wright (ed.) *Armageddon in Waco*. Chicago: University of Chicago Press: 177–202.

Sloan, R. P., E. Bagiella and T. Powell 1999. 'Religion, spirituality and medicine'. *The Lancet* 353 (February 20): 664–67.

Teubner, G. 1998. 'Juridification: concepts, aspects, limits, solutions'. In R. Baldwin, C. Scott and Hood C. (eds) *A Reader on Regulation*. Oxford: Oxford University Press.

Van Driel, B. and J. T. Richardson 1988. 'Print media coverage of new religious movements: A longitudinal study.' *Journal of Communication* 38: 37–61.

Willaime, J-P. 2006. 'Religion in ultramodernity'. In James A. Beckford and John Walliss (eds) *Theorising Religion. Classical and Contemporary Debates.* Aldershot: Ashgate: 32–43.

Williams, R. H. and J. Blackburn 1996. 'Many are called but few obey: ideological commitment and activism in Operation Rescue'. In Smith, C. (ed.) *Disruptive Religion. The Force of Faith in Social Movement Activism.* New York: Routledge: 167–85.

Wilson, J. 1971. 'The sociology of schism', *A Sociological Yearbook of Religion in Britain* 4: 1–20.

Yang, Fenggang 2006. 'The red, black, and gray markets of religion in China'. *Sociological Quarterly* 47: 93–122.

20

Religion in Rebellion, Resistance, and Social Movements[1]

SHARON ERICKSON NEPSTAD AND RHYS H. WILLIAMS

The connections, both theoretically and empirically, between religion and social change have occupied many of sociology's most prominent thinkers. Sociology was born with the advent of Europe's industrial society, and religion's role in those societal-wide changes was deemed important even by social theorists not personally religious – in many cases especially by thinkers and writers not personally religious.

But sociology has many of its intellectual roots in the Enlightenment and generally privileges reason over emotion, empiricism over revelation, and progress over tradition. Further, many established religious authorities were hostile to the development and spread of the scientific study of society, in part due to their conviction that moral philosophy was the best way to order social relations, and in part due to their institutional interests in being societal arbiters themselves. Thus, in many sociological perspectives, religion is typically part of the social formation that supports tradition and order, rather than promoting change and innovation. At the same time, sociology was also enormously influenced by conservative responses to the Enlightenment. The emphasis on communities over individuals, the importance of culture and ritual in social life, and the key organizing role that institutions play in maintaining social order are ideas recognizable to sociologists and all implicate religion.

Thus, as a result of the social and intellectual contexts of sociology's inception, much of its early analysis of religion centered on the latter's contributions to social change *or* resistance to it. In contemporary sociology, a particularly salient aspect of that relationship has been the intersecting subdisciplines of the sociologies of religion and social movements. In this chapter, we: (1) examine briefly the theoretical perspectives that assign religion major roles in social solidarity and social change; (2) review briefly the major approaches to the study of collective action in contemporary American sociology; and, (3) review some empirical literature on religion and social movements that illustrate our theoretical points.

RELIGION AS SOLIDARITY AND STASIS

For our purposes here, we lay out two major theoretical statements regarding religion as the source of social coherence and order. First, is of course Emile Durkheim's in *The Elementary Forms of Religious Life* (1912/1995). Durkheim offers a case for 'social solidarity'; that is, religion is the ideational and emotional consequence of humans acting together in society. Periods of collective effervescence produce intense emotions of being connected to others and to the collective as a whole. Religion is the articulation of social connection and collective identification. Durkheim's is, in essence, a 'social organization' approach to religion, in which social relations and their facticity are the source of the 'transcendent.' This need not be resistant to change, but the emphasis on order and the way in which religion connects the present to the past make it a powerful force for tradition.

A similar, but nonetheless distinct, approach is found in the work of Clifford Geertz (1973). He offers an approach to religion that emphasizes the meanings and symbols that humans use to make sense of the world and communicate with each other. In his famous essay on 'Religion as a Cultural System,' and in empirical work on religion in several different societies, Geertz focused on how religious understandings provide humans with a way to put themselves and others meaningfully in the world. Relations between humans and the divine, relations between humans and the natural world, and relations among humans in society are all made possible, and intelligible, by a shared cultural system that can be defined as 'religion.' Cultural chaos and social disintegration are held at bay through sense-making systems that are anchored in a uniquely transcendent reality. Geertz's is a 'culturalist' approach to religion, in every sense of the word.

Many scholars have noted, both approvingly and as critique, that these approaches to religion are heavily focused on religion as a conservative force in society – one that privileges order and can justify extant social arrangements. Clearly, religions often claim to offer timeless and non-changing truths, and often function to connect past, present, and future times into a seamless whole. This can support the assumption that the world as it is – including the social world – reflects divine intention or master plan. Further, the focus on religion

and order easily implies that tampering with social order (or for that matter, with received religious traditions) can lead to social instability. Occasionally religion justifies the world – especially the political world – explicitly, as with doctrines such as the 'Divine Right of Kings' in the late eighteenth-century Europe, or with 'priestly' forms of American Civil Religion (see, e.g., Demerath and Williams 1985), but it is often indirect, as with the Marxian critique of religion for making people politically quiescent, and focused on eternal, otherworldly rewards.

RELIGION AS AN AGENT OF SOCIAL CHANGE

While religion often plays a significant role in codifying, transmitting, and legitimating the extant, religion has also been a force for social change at some points in history and in some societies. The most developed theoretical approach to these dynamics in the classical sociological canon is in Max Weber's (1904–05/1996) examination of the development of capitalism in the West. Of course, Weber is often credited, or damned, with the argument that Protestantism caused capitalism – a breathtaking thesis about the power of religion to cause social change. What is more important to us here is the process or mechanism through which Weber imagined Protestantism doing this.[2]

Weber re-constructed the world of sixteenth-century Calvinism, particularly focused on sermons and the theology of predestination they contained. Empathetically imagining himself in that social time and place, Weber envisioned living within that cultural and religious worldview. He reasoned that the uncertainty of salvation in that theology would engender religious and psychic angst. One way to deal with that dilemma would be to engage in worldly actions that would seem to indicate one was among the elect. The worldly action that followed – a vocational calling regarding work and an ascetic avoidance of consumption – led to capital accumulation and economic change. Fundamentally, therefore, Weber credited religious beliefs with the power to propel social change through their abilities to motivate individuals to engage in highly moralized, self-sacrificial, and perhaps even risky behaviors (given the thorough integration of religion into life in this period, Collins [1996: xii] notes that religion was a *social practice*, not just disembodied belief).

Thus, individually oriented and religiously motivated behavior is one path through which religion contributes to social change. In another example of how religious actions can have unexpected consequences for social change, Weber analyzed the dynamics of charismatic leadership, and the organizational dilemmas confronting religious groups by their need to routinize charisma. Charismatic leadership, by definition, is a relationship that stretches or even breaks the boundaries of established social and cultural authority. The challenge to 'the world as it is' is built into the connection between a charismatic leader and his or her followers. And movements, religious or otherwise, that try to harness that charisma after the first generation passes engage in a form of social change with that very action. Thus, the transcendent character of charismatic authority was built into the heart of Weber's theory of institutional change. In this sense, 'prophetic' religion is a consistent challenge to existing social and political arrangements.

Of course, religiously motivated actions can take many forms, among them short-lived collectivities such as crowds or mobs as well as more organized movements. And religious movements such as millenarian revivals or cults have often been considered as the *products* of cultural pathologies or the breakdown of routinized social transmission mechanisms, as well as a *source* of change (see Kniss and Burns 2004).

Religion can also work as a more collective cultural force in fostering change. On one hand, this is due to a quality of religious life that does not take the existing world as the ultimate reality. Beliefs, practices, rituals, and group participation are religious elements that can question, or help produce challenges to, the way the world is organized. Anthropologist David Kertzer (1988) makes just this point in his examination of ritual and power. He duly notes the role of religion in creating legitimacy, and in 'mystifying' political and social relationships. But, he maintains, these properties can work for social movement challengers just as they do for the status quo. Rituals and symbols, he notes, have the 'virtue of ambiguity' and can be multi-vocal in their interpretation. Further, ritual helps create 'solidarity without consensus' (1988: 67), meaning that participants can feel connected to each other enough to act collectively without all having to agree on all beliefs or ideas: 'solidarity is produced by people acting together, not by people thinking together' (1988: 76).

That religion's solidarity-building functions could challenge power was integral to Antonio Gramsci's (1991) understanding of 'hegemony.' While hegemonic cultural forces are crucial to supporting those who hold social power, developing a 'counter-hegemony' is a concomitantly critical component of social change. Gramsci argued that religion can contribute to the emergence of such counter-hegemonic ideologies since religious groups are semi-autonomous from other social institutions and thus provide a free space where alternative perspectives can be discussed. However, for alternative views to develop into a viable oppositional force, Gramsci argued that two other conditions were necessary: the emergence of leaders from the aggrieved population, and mechanisms for reinforcing insurgent beliefs over time. As Billings (1990) notes, religious organizations typically build such 'structures of support' into their practices, sustaining beliefs through various rituals. These same practices can be used to strengthen counter-hegemonic ideologies. Moreover, religious institutions may provide the space for new leaders to emerge who can persuade others to act upon their insurgent views. Consequently, we see that religion plays a role in social change at the individual, group, and cultural levels of analysis.

Not all social change is intentional, nor were most classical sociological theorists much concerned with what contemporary sociologists would call 'social movements.' But we engaged in the foregoing discussion to show how deeply sociological concern with religion has been connected with sociological concern with changes in society. We now narrow our substantive focus and bring our discussion into the sociological present, by turning to a brief examination of one particular agent of social change: social and political movements.

THE DYNAMICS OF COLLECTIVE ACTION

The sociological study of social and political movements has spent most of its intellectual energy on the problems of movement genesis, and member recruitment/mobilization. How movements arise in society has been the basic problematic, with the existence of collective action the thing that needs to be explained. Various 'schools' of thought have dominated social movement scholarship at various times, usually with a slightly shifting focus. Some schools give pride of explanatory place to organizational dynamics, an approach usually referred to as 'resource mobilization.' Others to the development of grievances among populations, and the cultural work that mobilizers do to turn grievances into motivations for protest; the 'framing' literature has generally emphasized this. Still others examine the surrounding social conditions that are considered either more or less favorable to movement emergence – often called the 'political opportunity structure' theory.

While we have learned a great deal about movement emergence in this way, the focus has had some costs in terms of analytic myopia. For one thing, focusing on movements as the thing to explain treats the lack of movement activity – and the social stasis that it seems to represent – as the societal norm. This is plausible if social movements become a thing apart, a time of special action from self-consciously movement-identified actors. On the other hand, if we think of collective action as a standard part of the human experience, and calls for social change as the norm rather than the exception, our analytic attention shifts to the socio-cultural dynamics that all forms of collective action must negotiate in order to sustain themselves.[3]

Admittedly, this theoretical assumption has its own pitfalls. While it may be true that collective action is a constant in human social life, explicitly organized attempts at socio-political change are rarer. And while participation in social movements may often be 'politics by other means' – usually through demonstrations and protests among people who do not have a hand on the society's institutionalized levers of power – not all collective action is coolly calculated or strategically rational. Not all collective action is self-consciously geared toward change or toward resisting it. We do want to be able to account for why it sometimes is, and why some movements grow larger, spread farther, last longer, and effect more change than others.

It is exactly because of that last goal – to understand variation in collective action movements – that we urge a moratorium on emendations of theoretical schools of movement emergence. Better, we claim, to look at the dynamics of collective action, particularly that geared toward creating or resisting social change, and understand them as existing on continua that vary based on both social circumstances and the active decisions made by the people involved.

For example, Williams (1994) analyzed religious movements in terms of three basic dynamics that all attempts at collective action must engage and negotiate. There are: (a) issues of ideology and movement culture; (b) issues of organization (which includes the garnering and deployment of material and cultural resources); and, (3) issues of negotiating the social and cultural environment in which collective action takes place. McAdam et al. (1996) offer a similar tripartite scheme, calling attention to framing processes, mobilizing structures, and opportunity structures, respectively. A longer discussion of how this conceptualization of the three dynamics is different from our own would require a different essay. Suffice it to say that McAdam et al. remain concerned primarily with explaining why movements, as discrete political actors, emerge and engage in contentious politics with the state, while we are less concerned with movement emergence as the central problem, and do not limit ourselves to collective action aimed at overt *political* change. We consider each of the three analytic foci in turn.

Ideology and Movement Culture

Acting collectively for change requires that people become motivated to try to and change – or try to resist some change to – their social world. A social condition must be defined as both wrong and changeable – as unjust grievances that can and should be addressed. Motivation and mobilization must be defined and articulated in a clear and convincing language that resonates both with those who share a potential grievance, and with those who may not, but who may be sympathetic to movement activity. Whether the definition of grievances and the motives for change *precede* or *emerge from* collective action is an active debate in the scholarly literature. But in either case there are ideological needs for grievance definition, public rhetoric, and legitimacy. Relatedly, if people are to act together, rather than just as isolated individuals, they must feel they have something in common with others, and want to work with them to accomplish their joint ends. This requires elements of a 'culture' that can produce solidarity among movement members, the collective and individual motivations to act, and the rituals and identity claims that makes this collectivity and its actions meaningful for participants. Religious beliefs, moral worldviews, and religious identities are not the only resources for those engaging in – or hoping to engage in – collective action, but they can be among the most potent.

Organization and Organizing

If collective action is going to be maintained over time and not dissipate too easily, it will require some type of organization. A set of leaders always emerges, resources such as money, members, and rhetorical symbols must be gathered, and decisions made about distributing them. Some social movements respond to these demands by founding formal organizations, often with the purpose of harnessing the charismatic action that helped initiate mobilization, and some with a quasi-bureaucratic structure. If a movement wants to found formal organizations to sustain their action, those organizations often turn 'participants' into 'members' and find some way of marking membership and cementing loyalty. In addition, such practical infrastructural needs as meeting spaces, financial resources, and communication networks among members must be established and sustained. Even if these things are not codified into a bureaucratic organizational structure, some forms of organization and coordination must be generated and maintained over time. As above, religious institutions possess many of these organizational features that may be available for use, or may be useful templates for movement groups to adopt.

Social and Cultural Environments

While collective action may be constant in society, some time periods are more likely to produce definable social movements than are others. And even when a social movement has all the necessary ideological and organizational characteristics needed to flourish, it doesn't always succeed in accomplishing its aims. Thus, the nature of the social context and larger society is crucial to understand. For analytic purposes the societal environment can be thought of as having both institutional and cultural fields within which collective action takes place. The health and distribution of the economy, the relative openness of the polity and the status of religion in societal legal institutions (e.g., Richardson 2004), and the connections between political power and institutional religion all shape the likelihood of religiously based social movements. Further, the extent to which a culture is permeated with religious meanings (what Demerath 2001, calls 'cultural religion'), the strength of collective and individual emotions that accompany religious convictions, and how the content of religious meanings open or close certain avenues of action, affect movement activity.

It should be clear, given these three areas of social dynamics, why religion is so often a factor in efforts at protest, resistance, rebellion, and social change. Religion's cultural and institutional properties, along with its various roles in different types of societies, mean that it is often implicated in the struggle for social change. A variety of scholars have specifically explored religion's contribution to social movements (e.g., Beckford 1989: Chapter 6; Nepstad 2004; Smith 1996; Williams 1996, 2003), sometimes focusing on one of these dimensions, sometimes trying to integrate them. To illustrate these dynamics more concretely, we offer three empirical cases in which religion was central to the dynamics of contention. In each case, some religious elements supported the social movement challenge while other elements opposed it. We hold up issues of ideology and culture, organization, and social environment as a way of showing some of the ways religious collective action intersects with, shapes, and is shaped by, social forces.

RELIGION, RESISTANCE, AND SOCIAL QUIESCENCE

If religion can both foster resistance and strengthen the established social order – as our theoretical overview has demonstrated – then what are the circumstances under which religion will likely become a progressive or conservative force? To explore this question empirically, we examine unionization battles in the southern United States, the liberation movement in El Salvador, and the effort to dismantle the racial apartheid system in South Africa. This type of comparative approach has several advantages. First, it provides theoretical leverage; since religion was both a force for and against social change in each of these struggles, we can discern the conditions under which religion has a mobilizing or a suppressing effect. Second, by examining movements in different geographic regions, we hope to minimize the tendency to construct theories that primarily reflect the developed world. Third, these cases entail challenges to different types

of social injustices – from economic exploitation to human rights abuses to racial segregation. While we believe that the diversity of cases enhances the generalizability of our findings, we also recognize that Christianity is the primary religion involved in each case. Although this poses certain limitations, it nonetheless provides a constant across our cases and thus it is a useful starting point for assessing some of the factors that influence whether religion fosters or hinders resistance movements.

Labor Struggles in the United States

We begin with Dwight Billing's (1990) study of U.S. labor struggles in the early twentieth century. Billings examines Protestantism's support for the unionization of coal miners in Appalachia as well as its anti-union stance in the textile mills of North Carolina. Through careful comparative analysis, Billings discerns several factors that explain why religion facilitated social change in one instance but promoted social quiescence in the other. Before discussing these factors, we briefly summarize Billings' cases.

Several major labor conflicts arose in the textile mills in the North Carolina Piedmont region between 1928 and 1931. The post-war market decline, combined with increased competition, led mill owners to slash wages and lay off workers. Simultaneously, employers demanded increased worker output, prompting several thousand employees of the Loray plant to strike spontaneously. Taking note of this action, organizers from the National Textile Workers Union (NTWU) office in New England sent several staff members to provide leadership and direction to the strikers. But within weeks, the numbers of strikers dropped to less than 200 while the number of union opponents in the community expanded. Leading this anti-union sentiment were many church members and ministers who considered the NTWU organizers to be an atheistic menace. Since the local pastors' salaries were paid by mill owners (who had built and sponsored their churches), ministers aligned themselves with the mill companies and discouraged congregational members from participating in the strike. The pastors even refused to condemn police attacks against the strikers, which resulted in several deaths. Ultimately, then, the strike failed. Workers did not win any significant concessions and in the trials that followed the conflict, 'all persons accused of killing strikers were acquitted, while workers accused of conspiracy and murder were found guilty' (Billings 1990: 13). In this instance, religion encouraged quiescence and strengthened the status quo.

During the same time period, religion had a notably different influence on strikes that occurred in Appalachian coal mines. Billings notes that workers in both the textile and coal industries had remarkably similar economic and cultural backgrounds and shared an evangelical Protestant heritage that emerged from the rural South. Moreover, like the mill owners, coal operators built and supported the local churches and encouraged ministers to denounce unions. During the strikes, most of the local pastors aligned themselves with management.

Despite the parallels to the Piedmont case, Appalachian coal miners did not heed the conservative teachings of their pastors. Instead, many openly denounced the ministers for siding with coal operators and up to 90 percent of miners stopped attending company-sponsored churches (Billings 1990: 17). Soon, some of the militant workers emerged as lay pastors and miners held their own religious services. These 'miner-ministers' used this free space to promote a religious culture of resistance that fostered an insurgent mindset and a willingness to strike for union recognition. Moreover, these alternative religious services provided a context where biblical teachings were given new meaning, granting religious legitimacy to labor struggles. For instance, miners altered lyrics of traditional hymns to link faith with union activism. Corbin (1981: 164) records the words of one hymn that was frequently sung by the miners: 'When you hear of a thing that's called union / You know that they're happy and free / For Christ has a union in heaven / How beautiful a union must be.' This oppositional religious culture fostered labor activism and, in some cases, lay pastors worked directly as organizers with the National Miners' Union and the United Mine Workers Association (Garland 1983; Hevener 1978). As a result, miners were able to sustain their struggle for union recognition while the efforts of their textile mill counterparts collapsed in just a few weeks.

These two cases appear very similar, so why did they result in such divergent outcomes? Why did religion effectively blunt labor activism in the Carolina textile mills while fueling resistance in the Appalachian coal industry? To explain these distinct religious dynamics, Billings discusses several factors including: organizational form, the role of culture and ideology, the broader historical context, and relational ties to employers.

One of the critical differences in these cases is that the coal miners were able to develop an alternative religious organization while textile workers did not. Both groups initially found that the churches would not support their struggle because of their financial dependence on company owners, and in each case ordained pastors uncritically accepted the practices of capitalism. So why did coal miners believe they had the right to reject the views of their ministers and conduct their own church services? According to Billings, this reflects the distinct religious history of the southern backcountry. He observed, 'The [miner-minister's] authority was rooted in frontier religious traditions that recognized the legitimate role of lay ministers' (1990: 17). Out of necessity, the region had historically allowed non-ordained individuals to lead services and act as religious authorities. This norm empowered miners to form alternative pro-union churches rather than comply with the teachings of pro-company ministers.

While the presence of autonomous religious institutions was essential, it does not in itself account for the differential outcomes in these two labor struggles. To get a more complete understanding of how they fomented resistance in the Appalachian case, we must examine what occurred within these alternative churches. Billings argues that the miners' services functioned as a 'free space' that aided the labor struggle in three key ways. First, it provided a context where an oppositional religious culture and critical consciousness was cultivated. Second, the pro-union rituals and music in these alternative services helped sustain this insurgent mindset and reinforce union commitment among the miners. In other words, these autonomous religious groups functioned as a 'plausibility structure' (Berger 1969) that continually reinforced the belief in the necessity for action, which, in turn, kept the labor struggle going. Finally, these autonomous religious groups provided a context for the emergence of indigenous leaders who were known and trusted by their co-workers.

In the Piedmont mills, no comparable free space existed. Authorities and mill owners 'effectively ... destroy[ed] any autonomous space and institutions which the working class could claim as their own – in which independent leadership could emerge and develop, in which popular traditions could be sustained, or in which workers could compare and analyze their experience as working people' (Boyte 1972: 23). Without this, there was a limited capacity to develop oppositional culture, insurgent consciousness, and a commitment to sustained activism. Billings notes that some oppositional religious practices did initially arise and that textile mill strikers thought of their struggle in religious terms. Yet lacking a context where these practices could be routinely enacted and beliefs reinforced, this oppositional religion quickly dissipated.

In addition to free spaces, Billings argues that the relationships that workers had to established unions also explains the different outcomes in these cases. Although the United Mine Workers of America (UMWA) had not done any organizing in the Appalachian coal industry, it had been active in other coal mining areas in the south. The UMWA was willing and able to provide resources to the Appalachian strikers but what was particularly important is that they were sensitive to the religious commitments of the miners. In contrast, there' was no comparable union in southern textile industries at that time. The New England-based National Textile Workers Union (NTWU) did try to assist the Piedmont workers by sending in professional organizers

but they committed a serious error when they expressed disdain for mill employees' religiosity, considering it false consciousness that needed to be eliminated. According to one account, an NTWU organizer kicked a Bible out of the hands of a worker, stating that no one believed in that book anymore (Pope 1942). Thus Billings concludes 'Striking workers in Gastonia [North Carolina], who initially may have suspected that their God was on their side, found no support.... If textile militants found little sympathy for their religious beliefs among their leaders, they found even less support from the wider environment.... A potentially autonomous expression of opposition was thus silenced' (1990: 22).

Finally, the type of relational ties that workers had to company owners also made a difference in the outcome of these two cases. The Carolina textile industry was built by wealthy cotton planters who portrayed themselves as the patrons of impoverished white sharecroppers. As planters became industrialists, they continued this type of paternalistic relationship, promising jobs for white sharecroppers in exchange for their loyalty. In fact, Billings notes that mill workers only challenged owners when they failed to live up to their end of the agreement; this indicates that many employees bought into the image of mill owners as benevolent patrons. Additionally, the highly mechanized nature of mills meant that owners' responsibility was often masked by the perception that machines directed and dictated most of the day-to-day work in the mills. Only when managers or owners interfered by imposing demands (such as faster paces) did workers deem them responsible for their state of affairs. The image and relationship between employer and employees, therefore, contributed to social quiescence in this case. The relationship between Appalachian coal miners and coal company owners was markedly different. There was no prior patron relationship as in the Carolina textile mills, since most miners had been independent subsistence farmers before working in the coal mines and were accustomed to working autonomously. They felt no sense of loyalty, therefore, to company owners and were willing to challenge them.

In short, Billings presents us with two labor struggles that, at the outset, look remarkably similar. Yet his closer probe enables us to see that the role of religion in these unionization efforts varied because of differences in: (1) historical factors that legitimized lay ministers (or failed to do so); (2) the presence of autonomous free spaces that could foster an oppositional religious culture; (3) ties to pre-existing unions that were sensitive to the religious sensibilities of these Southerners; and (4) the historical context of worker-employer relationships.

The Liberation Movement in El Salvador

The struggle for human rights, land reform, and economic change in El Salvador in the 1970s–1980s presents another case where religion both facilitated and impeded social change. El Salvador's social problems emerged from a long colonial history that created a situation of extreme inequality, with a small segment of the population owning most of the land and controlling the nation's political institutions. In response to this concentration of wealth and privilege, numerous popular organizations emerged in the 1970s. Eventually, a broad popular opposition movement coalesced around a progressive political agenda. As this liberation movement expanded, the military became highly repressive, using abductions, torture, and assassinations to intimidate activists (Berryman 1984; Peterson 1997; Smith 1996; Wood 2003).

During this period, the Catholic Church in El Salvador was divided over the nation's social conflicts. On one side, a sizeable number of poor Catholics in the so-called popular church were supportive of or involved in the struggle for liberation; on the other side, some Catholics (including many church authorities) sought to maintain tradition and the status quo. The same variables that we used to examine U.S. labor struggles – organization, ideology and culture, and historical context – help us to understand how the church was both an impetus and an obstacle to social change in El Salvador.

The roots of El Salvador's progressive popular church are found in two important events in twentieth-century church history. The Second Vatican Council (1962–1965) opened Roman Catholicism to the modern world, updating anachronistic practices and encouraging new forms of worship and ministry. As part of this new impetus, the Pope called priests and nuns in Latin America to move out to the countryside and into urban barrios to live among the poor. The initial goal was to learn about the needs of the masses in order to win them back to the church after many years of neglect; the real effect, however, was on the clergy who were transformed by seeing the suffering and exploitation of the people. These priests and nuns quickly recognized that the church had to address the material and social concerns of the poor, not just their spiritual needs, and doing so would require a restructuring of church practices and theology (Berryman 1986; Lernoux 1980).

This burgeoning social justice sentiment was reinforced by the Latin American Bishops Conference held in Medellín, Colombia in 1968. At this meeting, church leaders discussed ways of addressing poverty and implementing the lessons of the Vatican II Council. They also wrestled with the implications of liberation theology, which holds that Christian mission must include efforts to change oppressive social structures and people of faith must take a 'preferential option for the poor.' As the conference concluded, the bishops released a document denouncing the dehumanizing consequences of economic exploitation and indigence, and they called upon Christians to work for a just social order and the authentic liberation of the people. The bishops proclaimed that the poor have the right to challenge injustices and that social change would only occur through the organization and action of the popular sectors (Smith 1991; Nepstad 2004).

Immediately after the Medellín conference, Archbishop Chávez of El Salvador began to implement these ideas by encouraging the formation of base Christian communities – small, lay communities where participants pray, read scripture, and discuss the gospel's meaning in light of contemporary political and economic conditions. Between 1970 and 1976, seven training centers were established to teach lay leaders (known as catechists) how to conduct worship and facilitate discussion and Bible study. They often received training in health care, agriculture, and community organizing as well. By the end of the 1970s, 15,000 catechists had been trained and hundreds of base communities were established (Montgomery 1982a). The skills these religious lay leaders developed often transferred to political activism as thousands of catechists and members of base Christian communities participated in various organizations working for liberation (Berryman 1984). One analyst concluded:

> The rapid growth of the popular organizations of the left in El Salvador cannot be explained without taking into account the role of the CEBs [base Christian communities] in organizing and *concienticizing* the people. Similarly, the strength of the revolutionary leadership at the grass roots cannot be explained without recognizing that dozens, if not hundreds, of revolutionary leaders acquired their organizational skills through their training as catechists (Montgomery 1982a: 220).

As the popular church expanded and became more involved in progressive social movements, conservative Catholics attempted to stop this development. Wealthy Catholics and most members of the church hierarchy were opposed to the liberation movement (with a couple of notable exceptions such as Archbishop Oscar Romero); they feared that popular church members were becoming too political and too radical. This segment of the Catholic Church justified and supported the government's repressive policies as a necessary means of preventing the spread of communism. Conservative Catholic support for the military regime was evident in numerous ways. For example, the bishop of Santa Ana, Monsignor Marco René Revelo, went to a Salvadoran Air Force base to bless some newly purchased war planes, even though the military's dismal human rights record was well known (Montgomery 1982a). Others were subtler, stating that the church should only address spiritual matters and leave political concerns to the government and the army. Eventually, conservative opposition to the liberation movement grew so strong that the church became deeply divided.

How could these two segments of El Salvador's Catholic Church take such different positions on the nation's conflicts? Clearly, the division reflected distinct class interests. Most traditional Catholics had no incentive to challenge the status quo since it benefited them. Many were wealthy individuals who had much to lose if the liberation movement succeeded in transforming the economic, social and political institutions of the country (Berryman 1984). Even some members of the church hierarchy had vested interests in maintaining the social structure. Monsignor Pedro Aparicio, for instance, had a large estate that had been given to him by a former president of El Salvador and subsequently the bishop mostly sided with the wealthy landed class. Others, such as Monsignor Alvarez, a colonel and chaplain for the military, had institutional forms of power and prestige at stake (Montgomery 1982a). In contrast, poor Salvadorans had a great deal to gain from the liberation movement – namely, an end to human rights abuses and economic exploitation, and greater political input.

These class interests, however, cannot sufficiently explain the emergence of El Salvador's faith-based resistance since the masses had long desired an end to their poverty and oppression. Similar to the U.S. labor struggles described by Billings, one of the critical factors that helps explain why this movement emerged in the 1970s was the presence of an autonomous religious structure. Once base Christian communities were formed, the poor had free spaces where they could discuss their suffering and develop a critical consciousness. For example, in these base communities, the priest's traditional homily was replaced by group dialogue and reflection on biblical passages. This provided opportunities for reinterpreting scripture to support the liberation struggle. The following transcript reveals how this practice helped one group find political meaning in the biblical story of Christ multiplying the loaves and fishes to feed the crowd that had gathered to hear him preach (Scharper and Scharper 1984: 42):

> Julio: The apostles think there isn't any food, and it seems to me that's the way it is now. We all say we don't have any food. It's that a few people have it all. If it was all shared around, we'd be all eating what those few who have the food are now eating, and I think we'd all have enough.

Alejandro: As I see it, the same thing didn't happen to Jesus that almost always happens to the church: that it's nothing but words – that we must do good and all that. But when people are hungry, nothing is done to solve the problem. Christ not only uses words, talking to them all day about the kingdom of God, but he feeds them through his disciples. He doesn't send them away hungry. Christ's gospel also feeds you. But many bishops and priests think it's only to save your soul and not to change the economic situation of society.

Felipe: A lot of people think things are the way they are because God wants them to be that way. He made people rich and poor, and until he wants it nothing's going to change. And that's not true. He's given us the order to change things. We have to feed the hungry, and God will give us the power to make miracles as he gave it to his disciples.

Not only did base Christian communities foster oppositional views, they also sustained them with rituals. In many religious services, music reinforced beliefs and commitment. Just as miners incorporated pro-union lyrics into familiar hymns, El Salvador's popular church emphasized the importance of organizing and political work in their music. For instance, the following hymn was sung in many Salvadoran base communities: 'When the poor believe in the poor / That's when we'll be free to sing/ When the poor seek out the poor / And we're all for organization / Then will come our liberation' (as quoted in Nepstad 1996: 113).

While the popular church's oppositional religious culture contributed to the liberation impulse in El Salvador, efforts to put faith into action were facilitated by connections to pre-existing groups. Ties to established organizations are valuable because they can contribute human and material resources to incipient movements (McAdam 1982; Morris 1984). This was true in El Salvador, as Montgomery (1982b) notes that some of the earliest base Christian communities regularly met with representatives of labor unions, student groups, and teachers' organizations at the Basilica of the Sacred Heart in San Salvador. In 1974, these groups combined their experience and resources to form the first mass popular organizations – a coalition known as the United Popular Action. The Jesuit Central America University also assisted the burgeoning liberation movement. Professors conducted research

into issues and policies that the movement supported, such as land reform, and the university produced a weekly newsletter that gave voice to popular organizations and provided alternative sources of information (Montgomery 1982a).

Additionally, historical developments shaped both the liberation movement in the popular church as well as the traditional stance of conservative Catholics in El Salvador. Vatican II and the Latin American Bishops Council gave impetus to the formation of base Christian communities, granting legitimacy to lay leaders and the struggle for social change. Yet the election of a new pope in 1978 strengthened the position of traditional Catholics. Pope John Paul II was born and raised in Poland, where he saw first-hand the repressive effects of Soviet domination, compelling him to take a strong anti-communist stance. When he assumed the papacy, John Paul II was pleased with the revitalization of faith in Latin America but he also believed the popular church was too closely linked to a particular political agenda and had strayed from the authentic teachings of the Catholic Church. This was evident when he visited Nicaragua in 1983, where he sternly admonished several priests who held key positions in the new revolutionary Sandinista government. When the pope arrived at the airport in Managua, Father Ernesto Cardenal, who was Minister of Culture and had been an important advocate and proponent of Nicaragua's popular church and liberation struggle, was there to greet him. Yet when Father Cardenal dropped to his knees and attempted to kiss the pope's ring, John Paul II pulled away saying, 'You'd better put your relationship with the church in order' (Randall 1983: 33–4). Later, in an outdoor mass attended by 800,000 Nicaraguans, the pope chastised members of the popular church who asked him to pray for those who had died in the revolutionary war. El Salvador's conservative Catholics viewed the pope's actions as clear, unequivocal support for their position and a public condemnation of the religiously based liberation movement.

In short, El Salvador's popular church was able to mobilize and expand in the 1970s due to several factors. First, the emergence of base Christian communities meant that the poor had autonomous free spaces where they could develop leadership skills, discuss their suffering, and develop counter-hegemonic views. These communities also functioned as a support structure that, through various rituals, reinforced oppositional religious views and political commitments. Second, the Vatican II and the Medellín conference marked an important break from the historical position of the Latin American church that had encouraged the poor to accept their lot in life. These events gave legitimacy to this religious movement for liberation. Finally, ties to established organizations, such as labor unions and university groups, provided valuable resources that helped members of the popular church put their convictions into action. Yet the counter-movement of conservative Catholics was also strong due to historical changes – namely, the appointment of a new anti-communist pope – as well as the resources available to them through their wealthy constituents and the traditional church. Thus some of the same factors that facilitate religiously based progressive movements can also help mobilize opposing forces.

Racial Apartheid in South Africa

The conflict over South Africa's policy of racial segregation provides a third case for analyzing religion's role in challenging or maintaining societal structures and practices. Since roughly 80 percent of South Africa's population identifies as Christian (Renick 1991) and numerous denominational groups were involved in the anti-apartheid struggle, we will limit our focus to the Dutch Reformed Church. This religious tradition had a very important, albeit contradictory, influence on twentieth-century South African racial policies. The earliest European settlers in South Africa were Dutch Calvinists (called Afrikaners or Boers) who used their religious beliefs to justify the creation of apartheid policies and support for the Nationalist Party that implemented them. They also initiated mission projects among the indigenous population, which led to the

formation of the Dutch Reformed Church in Africa (DRCA). This black segment of the church was fairly quiescent until the 1970s, when it became a leading force in challenging the South African government and the system of apartheid. Since the white Dutch Reformed Church (DRC) and the black Dutch Reformed Church (DRCA) held such divergent views, a closer look at this case will enable us to see how the same religious institution can generate opposing movements.

While many religious groups support the status quo by their silent acceptance of societal institutions, the Afrikaner DRC was a vocal, driving force behind South African racial policies. Ken Jubber observed, 'The Church played a vital role in placing on the statute books laws dealing with the prohibition of mixed marriages and immorality, residential segregations, separate amenities, influx control, job reservation, and separate universities' (1985: 282). How did the white DRC come to advocate such blatantly racist policies? The collective action literature again provides insight by pointing our attention toward organizational, cultural, and contextual factors.

Dutch Calvinists immigrated to the South African Cape in the seventeenth and eighteenth centuries and many viewed their tumultuous voyage through stormy seas as one that replicated the journey of ancient Israelites to the promised land (Villa-Vicencio 1978). As they settled and began to prosper, their Calvinist beliefs led them to interpret their well-being as an indication that they were chosen by God and were faithfully following God's will (not uncommon for settler societies; see the comparative examination by Akenson 1992).

The nineteenth century, however, brought dramatic changes as the British occupied the Cape. They put into place a British administration, established English as the official language, and granted legal equality for all free persons regardless of race. A few years later, the British abolished slavery in South Africa, causing significant financial losses among many Dutch settlers. Thus British control of South Africa generated Afrikaner resentment for economic, political, and cultural reasons; consequently, many moved to the Transvaal region of the Cape in what became known as the Great Trek (Renick 1991). At one point in the trek, roughly 500 Afrikaners were surrounded by 15,000 Zulus. The Afrikaners prayed for protection and made a covenant with God, pledging to commemorate the event each year and build a temple in honor of this saving act. On December 16, 1838, the Zulus attacked. By the end of the day, 3,000 Zulus had been killed but the Afrikaners suffered only 3 deaths. This event, known as the Vow of Covenant at Blood River, was seen as further confirmation that Afrikaners had God's favor (Templin 1984).

The British-Afrikaner conflict erupted again at the end of the nineteenth century when gold and diamonds were discovered in the Transvaal and the British attempted to annex this Afrikaner republic. In a three-year Anglo-Boer War, 100,000 Afrikaners were forcibly relocated into civilian concentration camps where more than 25 percent of them died. Eventually, the British prevailed and annexed the Transvaal. To make sense of their defeat, Afrikaners turned to the Exodus story in which the Israelites were enslaved by the Egyptians. Just as God sent Moses to liberate them from Pharaoh, the Afrikaners believed that God had not abandoned them but would one day liberate and vindicate them. When British rule ended in 1948 and the Afrikaner National Party came to power, the Dutch Reformed pastor who took over as Prime Minister declared it the fulfillment of God's promise: 'The history of the Afrikaner reveals a determination and definiteness of purpose which makes one feel that Afrikanerdom is not the work of man but a creation of God' (Carr 2001: 53–4).

These historical events provided the basis for the white Dutch Reformed Church's theology of racial segregation. Afrikaners believed that their survival was dependent upon their ability to preserve their religious and cultural identity. Perceiving themselves as God's chosen people, they felt an obligation to protect this identity through racial separation. Moreover, they maintained that segregation is biblically mandated. Specifically, they argue that in Genesis 10, Noah's three sons became the fathers of different nations after the flood. When these nations united in an attempt to

usurp God's power by building the tower of Babel, God responded by confusing their speech and scattering the groups. Afrikaner theologians argue that this act constitutes 'spiritual diversification' of the human race and an act of judgment. On this basis, the DRC formally adopted a doctrine of 'autogeneous development' in 1974, which called upon the government to enact legislation that would keep racial groups separate from one another. The synod stated, '[A]s a church we have always worked purposefully for the separation of races. In this regard apartheid can rightfully be called a church policy' (Matheba 2001: 114).

This unusual interpretation of scripture and the support that it generated for the apartheid policies of South Africa's Nationalist Party certainly marks a departure from traditional Protestant Christianity. How did such unconventional, oppressive views arise? Just as religious free spaces can foster oppositional beliefs and progressive movements, the organizational autonomy of South Africa's DRC facilitated the emergence of these regressive views. Early on, the Afrikaner church in South Africa declared its independence from the DRC in Holland and quickly established its own seminaries where theology was constructed in a 'hermeneutical vacuum' (Carr 2001). Ken Jubber (1985: 277) observed:

> The organization of the Reformed Church, unlike that of the Roman Catholic Church for example, has never been strongly internationally centralized or controlled. In addition it has not had a single arbitrator or pontificator as far as theology is concerned. It has accepted that the Bible does not prescribe a specific church structure.... Consistent with the Reformed tradition, the Dutch Reformed Church accepted that Jesus Christ was the only head of the Church. Because of this, the Church strove to be as un-hierarchic as possible and to counter the inevitable tendencies towards hierarchy, institution and bureaucracy.... Two important results flowed from the way the Church was organized. Firstly ... [t]he absence of a single authoritative voice encouraged diverse interpretations of scripture. Secondly, factors such as the Church's relative isolation, sovereignty, limited locale, lack of hierarchy, social homogeneity, and close congregational ties allowed it to be strongly determined by local events and the changing fortunes and interests of its members.

This religious autonomy and isolation – combined with the economic and political interests of Afrikaners – not only provided a fertile context for the rise of apartheid theology, it also created space for the development of rituals that would reinforce these beliefs. Similar to the labor struggles in the U.S. and the liberation movement in El Salvador, these cultural practices sustained views over time. As noted, a key ritual is the annual celebration of 'Covenant Day' commemorating the defeat of the Zulu at Blood River; this ritual reminds Afrikaners that they have withstood difficult circumstances because they are God's chosen people.

Given its vehement support for segregation, it is ironic that the white Dutch Reformed Church indirectly generated opposition to apartheid in the late twentieth century when black Calvinists called people to resist Nationalist Party policies. The black Dutch Reformed Church of Africa was formed in the nineteenth century when white DRC members faced a dilemma in terms of reconciling their segregationist beliefs with the influx of black converts who sought to join the church as a result of DRC mission efforts. Eventually, most white congregations began holding independent services for black members and in 1881 a separate 'daughter' church was officially established (Jubber 1985). Although born out of racism, these black DRCA congregations functioned as free spaces, allowing an oppositional culture and consciousness to arise, albeit nearly a century later.

In the latter part of the twentieth century black Calvinists helped mobilize the fight against apartheid. A significant contribution to this movement came from theologians at the DRC's seminary for 'coloureds' at the University of the Western Cape. Inspired by black theology in the U.S., these religious scholars drew links to their own situation. One of the most influential figures was Allan Boesak, a black DRCA pastor who served as the University of the Western Cape's campus minister (Kinghorn 1997). In 1976, Boesak published a fiery book on black power, *Farewell to Innocence*, which led the Dutch Reformed Church for Coloureds to release the 1982 Belhar Confession condemning apartheid as a heresy (Klaaren 1997). This document, released in

conjunction with the Alliance of Black Reformed Christians in Southern Africa, proclaimed: 'We unequivocally declare that apartheid is a sin, and that the moral and theological justification of it is a travesty of the Gospel ...' (Walshe 1997: 388).

Black Calvinists also reinterpreted the very symbols and stories that their white counterparts used to justify apartheid and Afrikaner dominance. This is possible because, as Kertzer (1988) states, symbols and rituals can be multivocal in their interpretation. The Exodus story – which the white DRC used to describe their past oppression and eventual liberation from British rule – was seen by the black DRCA as a promise for their future. Boesak proclaimed, 'Israel has experienced Yahweh's power in his sensitivity to their cries of pain and suffering and in the ten plagues; in the exodus and in the closing of the waters of the Red Sea.... This God will rise up; this God will deliver us from the hands of those evil men who think and do violence to God's defenceless people' (Boesak and Villa-Vicencio 1986: 152, 35). Even the Covenant celebration was given new meaning as black Calvinists transformed it into a day for the church to commit itself to reconciliation and unity. Hence Renick argues that 'symbols such as ... the Covenant and the Exodus – symbols, ironically, planted in the religious psyche of blacks by the Afrikaners themselves – are being reinfused with liberating potential by black Calvinists' (1991: 140).

When the white DRC formed separate congregations and educational institutions for its black members, they inadvertently created free spaces that cultivated a theology of black power and a culture of resistance. This also provided a context where black leaders emerged who, over time, established ties to faith-based organizations in the broader international community. Much as African-American pastors in the U.S. civil rights movement were able to tap into wider religious networks for various forms of support (Morris 1984), black Calvinist leaders helped the anti-apartheid movement through worldwide ministerial connections. For example, in the 1980s, Boesak (who by then was the moderator of South Africa's Dutch Reformed Church for

Coloureds) was elected as the president of the World Alliance of Reformed Churches (WARC). This gave him a platform for discussing apartheid and he quickly realized that international interest in the black South African struggle could make a critical difference. At the 1982 WARC conference, he brought South African apartheid to the forefront of discussion; as a result, WARC suspended the white Afrikaner church's membership and called for a *status confessionis,* 'a state of affairs in which the very essence of Christianity is threatened and a new confession of faith is called for' (Kinghorn 1997: 153). This provided an important source of moral support to the religiously based anti-apartheid struggle.

Black Calvinists also won significant material support for the anti-apartheid struggle through their ties to the ecumenical South African Council of Churches and its international counterpart, the World Council of Churches (WCC). In the 1960s, the WCC established a 'Programme to Combat Racism' that was designed to lend support to anti-racism groups and liberation movements. The WCC subsequently provided funding for various outreach programs in South Africa and it also sponsored conferences in Harare, Zimbabwe (1985) and Lusaka, Zambia (1987) where South African church representatives and members of exiled organizations such as the African National Congress met to discuss anti-apartheid theology and strategies to dismantle the segregationist Nationalist Party regime (Walshe 1997).

Additionally, various historical events thrust church leaders to the forefront of the anti-apartheid movement. In the late 1970s, the South African government began banning various black consciousness groups and arresting numerous black political leaders. This effectively eliminated the strategic direction of the movement and thus black religious leaders felt an obligation to step in to help fill the gap. Then, in July of 1985, the Nationalist Party imposed a partial State of Emergency. Within a year of this declaration, over 30,000 anti-apartheid activists were detained and nearly 1,200 political deaths were recorded (Borer 1996: 130–1). As a result, the South African

Council of Churches (including the DRCA) called together 150 local theologians to discuss the appropriate Christian response to these escalating levels of state-sponsored repression. Out of this meeting came *The Kairos Document,* which stated that praying for a regime change was not sufficient. The document argued that Christians must directly confront the oppressive apartheid system; people of faith would need to disobey the government in order to obey God. After it was released, church leaders all over the country responded to the Kairos challenge by sponsoring illegal protest marches. In Cape Town, Allan Boesak co-organized a march of 300 religious leaders who delivered a petition to parliament demanding a complete withdrawal of police from black townships. As the faith-based anti-apartheid struggle grew more active and militant, the government took a harsher stance with Christian activists. Throughout the 1980s and into the early 1990s, clergy and laity were being closely monitored, attacked, harassed, arrested, and in some instances, tortured. This repression further radicalized black religious activists (Borer 1996).

In short, the black Dutch Reformed Church's efforts to dismantle South Africa's apartheid regime were facilitated by organizational, cultural, and contextual factors. First, the DRC's commitment to racial segregation led to the creation of autonomous organizations for black and 'coloured' members. This provided the free space for a religious culture of resistance to arise and black leaders to emerge. Second, ties to other faith-based groups, such as the World Alliance of Reformed Churches and the World Council of Churches, brought in critical moral, human, and material support. Finally, various historical events set the stage for religious leaders to step into political roles within the anti-apartheid movement.

CONCLUSIONS

We have used labor struggles in the Southern United States, the liberation movement in El Salvador, and the struggle over South Africa's apartheid to illustrate three important ways in which religious institutions and religious cultural systems contribute to social movement protest and resistance. Religion provides important organizational resources such as networks of members, meeting spaces, fund-raising capacities, recognized leadership, and free spaces that can promote the development of organizing skills and oppositional consciousness. Religious cultures offer theological and ideological critiques of existing societal arrangements, and cultural elements such as music, symbols, rituals, and collective identities that shape solidarity and help participants stay committed to the cause and each other. Finally, religion often has a uniquely legitimate place in the institutional and cultural fields of a society. Religious actors are often granted the benefit of the doubt, and can take the moral high ground in political disputes. Political authorities often have trouble persecuting activist clergy, and risk making them mobilizing martyrs if they do.

Although our analysis is limited to three cases, the literature on faith-based resistance in other parts of the world indicates that religion's capacity to foster protest and revolt is indeed widespread. Not surprisingly, significant scholarly attention has recently focused on Islamic political movements in the Middle East including Afghanistan (Marsden 1998), Algeria (Roberts 1988), Palestine (Abu-Amr 1994), Turkey (Yavuz 2003), Iran (Keddie 1983; Salehi 1996), Egypt (Kepel 1986), Pakistan (Nasr 1994), Bahrain, Yemen, and Saudia Arabia (Wiktorowicz 2004). The role of religion in Latin American social movements is also well documented, particularly in Brazil (Adriance 1995; Bruneau 1982; Burdick 1993), Chile (Lowden 1996; Smith 1982), Guatemala (Bermúdez 1985; Berryman 1994) and Nicaragua (Berryman 1984; Dodson and O'Shaughnessy 1990; Kirk 1992; Mulligan 1991; Randall 1983).

Even in relatively secular Europe, numerous studies have explored the role of Christianity in Northern Ireland's conflict (Dillon 1997; Dunlop 1995; McVeigh 1989; O'Brien 1994), in Poland's Solidarity movement (Kubik 1994; Osa 1996; Szajkowski 1983; Weigel 1992), and in the democratization of East Germany

(Burgess 1997; Hadjar 2003; Pfaff 2001). Another example of the near universal capacity of religion to foment collective action is Marty and Appleby's (1994) edited volume on comparative fundamentalist movements. Chapters in this volume cover movements from almost every continent and involving all the major world religions. While not all the movements they consider are directly engaged in trying to transform the public sphere – some are 'defensive' movements that just want to keep the modern world out of their enclave – the substantive examples show that attempts at both fostering and resisting change display many analytic similarities. Religion can engender or nurture movement culture, organizations, and a receptive social environment.

In examining the episodes of collective action we analyzed here, no one element can completely explain or predict the occurrence of religiously based collective action. This is all the more true when one moves to social contexts where Christianity is not the dominant religious culture. And yet, as noted above, there are dynamics to collective action that span many differences in time, place, and culture. While the trend in social movement theorizing for many years was to emphasize one set of factors to the neglect of others, it is clear that there needs to be some complementarity – or perhaps an additive relationship – before these elements result in a protest movement. As we have also noted, these factors can also shape a religious response that reinforces the status quo and suppresses dissent. But we want to stress that we view collective action as a constant in human society; for us, the question is not how does collective action emerge, but rather, how does the collective action that constantly swirls around social actors – such as religious groups or established institutions – become angled in such a way that it challenges extant societal relationships and sustains that challenge over time. Religion's important role in this is no longer overlooked by scholars of either religion or social movements. Now we need to explore this in more historical depth and with greater sensitivity to the coalescence of facilitating factors.

NOTES

1. We are equal co-authors; our names are listed alphabetically. We thank Jim Beckford and Jay Demerath for feedback on an earlier draft. Williams also thanks the Charles Phelps Taft Research Center at the University of Cincinnati for the fellowship year in which this was written.

2. Stark (2004) calls for an end to 'ancestor worship' in the sociology of religion, and is particularly critical of sociology's big three – Marx, Weber, and Durkheim. Nonetheless, their thought is useful for us, in that they illustrate influential theoretical approaches to understanding religion, worldly power, and the relations between the two. Given how important to Stark's own theory of religion is the uncertainty over salvation and the effects of religious beliefs on worldly action, one might think he would look more kindly on the Weberian theoretical project, if not on all the empirical conclusions.

3. Meyer and Tarrow (1997) argue for what they call a 'social movement society' – their thesis is that developed democracies have currently institutionalized social movements as a dimension of contentious politics. We would push that insight a bit further, arguing for 'collective action' in many forms rather than just formally organized social movements involved in state-based politics.

REFERENCES

Abu-Amr, Ziad 1994. *Islamic Fundamentalism in the West Bank and Gaza: Muslim Brotherhood and Islamic Jihad*. Bloomington: Indiana University Press.

Adriance, Madeleine Cousineau 1995. *Promised Land: Base Christian Communities and the Struggle for the Amazon*. Albany: State University of New York Press.

Akenson, Donald H. 1992. *God's Peoples: Covenant and Land in South Africa, Israel, and Ulster*. Ithaca, NY: Cornell University Press.

Beckford, James A. 1989. *Religion and Advanced Industrial Society*. London: Unwin Hyman.

Berger, Peter 1969. *A Rumor of Angels*. Garden City, NY: Doubleday.

Bermúdez, Fernando 1985. *Death and Resurrection in Guatemala*. Maryknoll, NY: Orbis Books.

Berryman, Phillip 1984. *The Religious Roots of Rebellion: Christians in Central American Revolutions*. Maryknoll, NY: Orbis Books.

Berryman, Phillip 1986. 'El Salvador: From Evangelization to Insurrection.' Pp. 58–78 in Daniel Levine.

Berryman, Phillip (ed.) 1986. *Religion and Political Conflict in Latin America*. Chapel Hill: University of North Carolina Press.

Berryman, Phillip 1994. *Stubborn Hope: Religion, Politics, and Revolution in Central America*. New York: Orbis Books.

Billings, Dwight B. 1990. 'Religion as Opposition: A Gramscian Analysis.' *American Journal of Sociology* 96 (1): 1–31.

Boesak, Allan and Charles Villa-Vicencio 1986. *A Call for an End to Unjust Rule*. Edinburgh: Saint Andrew Press.

Borer, Tristan Ann 1996. 'Church Leadership, State Repression, and the "Spiral of Involvement" in the South African Anti-apartheid Movement, 1983–1990.' Pp. 125–43 in *Disruptive Religion: The Force of Faith in Social Movement Activism*. Edited by Christian Smith. New York: Routledge.

Boyte, Harry 1972. 'The Textile Industry: Keel of Southern Industrialization.' *Radical America* 6: 4–49.

Bruneau, Thomas 1982. *The Catholic Church in Brazil: The Politics of Religion*. Austin: University of Texas Press.

Burdick, John 1993. *Looking for God in Brazil: The Progressive Catholic Church in Urban Brazil's Religious Arena*. Berkeley: University of California Press.

Burgess, John P. 1997. *The East German Church and the End of Communism*. New York: Oxford University Press.

Carr, Thomas K. 2001. 'Apartheid and Hermeneutics: Biblical Interpretations, Neo-Calvinism, and the Afrikaner Sense of Self (1926–86).' Pp. 49–65 in *Religious Fundamentalism in Developing Countries*, edited by Santosh Saha and Thomas Carr. Westport, CT: Greenwood Press.

Collins, Randall 1996. 'Introduction.' Pp. vii–xxxiii in *The Protestant Ethic and the Spirit of Capitalism*, by Max Weber. Translated by Talcott Parsons, introduction by Randall Collins. Los Angeles: Roxbury.

Corbin, David 1981. *Life, Work, and Rebellion in the Coal Fields: The Southern West Virginia Miners, 1880–1930*. Urbana: University of Illinois Press.

Demerath, N. J. III 2001. *Crossing the Gods: World Religions and Worldly Politics*. New Brunswick, NJ: Rutgers University Press.

Demerath, N. J. III and Rhys H. Williams 1985. 'Civil Religion in an Uncivil Society.' *The Annals* 480: 154–66.

Dillon, Martin 1997. *God and the Gun: The Church and Irish Terrorism*. New York: Routledge.

Dodson, Michael and Laura Nuzzi O'Shaughnessy 1990. *Nicaragua's Other Revolution: Religious Faith and Political Struggle*. Chapel Hill: University of North Carolina Press.

Dunlop, John 1995. *A Precarious Belonging: Presbyterians and the Conflict in Ireland*. Belfast: Blackstaff Press.

Durkheim, Emile 1912 [1995]. *The Elementary Forms of Religious Life*. Translated and with an introduction by Karen E. Fields. New York: The Free Press.

Garland, Jim 1983. *Welcome the Traveler Home*. Lexington: University of Kentucky Press.

Geertz, Clifford 1973. *The Interpretation of Cultures*. New York: Basic Books.

Gramsci, Antonio 1991. *Selections from Cultural Writings*. Edited by David Forgacs and Geoffrey Nowell-Smith. Cambridge, MA: Harvard University Press.

Hadjar, Andreas 2003. 'Nonviolent Political Protest in East Germany in the 1980s: Protestant Church, Opposition Groups, and the People.' *German Politics* 12 (3): 107–28.

Hevener, John W. 1978. *Which Side Are You On? The Harlan County Miners, 1931–1939*. Urbana: University of Illinois Press.

Jubber, Ken 1985. 'The Prodigal Church: South Africa's Dutch Reformed Church and the Apartheid Policy.' *Social Compass* 32: 273–85.

Keddie, Nikki R. 1983. *Religion and Politics in Iran: Shi'ism from Quietism to Revolution*. New Haven: Yale University Press.

Kepel, Gilles 1986. *Muslim Extremism in Egypt: The Prophet and the Pharoah*. Berkeley and Los Angeles: University of California Press.

Kertzer, David I. 1988. *Ritual, Politics, and Power*. New Haven, CT: Yale University Press.

Kinghorn, Johann 1997. 'Modernization and Apartheid: The Afrikaner Churches.' Pp. 135–54 in *Christianity in South Africa: A Political, Social, and Cultural History*. Edited by Richard Elphick and Rodney Davenport. Berkeley: University of California Press.

Kirk, John M. 1992. *Politics and the Catholic Church in Nicaragua*. Gainesville, FL: University of Florida Press.

Klaaren, Eugene M. 1997. 'Creation and Apartheid: South African Theology since 1948.' Pp. 370–82 in *Christianity in South Africa: A Political, Social, and Cultural History*. Edited by Richard Elphick and Rodney Davenport. Berkeley: University of California Press.

Kniss, Fred and Gene Burns 2004. 'Religious Movements.' Pp. 694–716 in *The Blackwell Companion to Social Movements*, D. Snow, S. Soule, and H. Kriesi, eds. Malden, MA: Blackwell Publishing.

Kubik, Jan 1994. *The Power of Symbols Against the Symbol of Power: The Rise of Solidarity and the Fall of State Socialism in Poland*. University Park: Pennsylvania State University Press.

Lernoux, Penny 1980. *Cry of the People*. New York: Penguin Books.

Lowden, Pamela 1996. *Moral Opposition to Authoritarian Rule in Chile, 1973–1990*. New York: St. Martin's Press.

Marsden, Peter 1998. *The Taliban: War, Religion, and the New World Order in Afghanistan*. London: Oxford University Press.

Marty, Martin E. and R. Scott Appleby (eds) 1994. *Accounting for Fundamentalisms: The Dynamic Character of Movements*. Chicago: University of Chicago Press.

Matheba, Gampi 2001. 'Religion and Political Violence in Apartheid South Africa.' *Journal of Cultural Studies* 3 (1): 108–23.

McAdam, Doug 1982. *Political Process and the Development of Black Insurgency, 1930–1970*. Chicago: University of Chicago Press.

McAdam, Doug, John McCarthy, Mayer N. Zald (eds) 1996. *Comparative Perspectives on Social Movements: Political Opportunities, Mobilizing Structures, and Cultural Framings*. New York: Cambridge University Press.

McVeigh, Joseph 1989. *A Wounded Church: Religion, Politics and Justice in Ireland*. Dublin: Mercier Press.

Meyer, David S. and Sidney Tarrow (eds) 1997. *The Social Movement Society: Contentious Politics for a New Century*. Lanham, MD: Rowman and Littlefield.

Montgomery, Tommie Sue 1982a. 'Cross and Rifle: Revolution and the Church in El Salvador and Nicaragua.' *Journal of International Affairs* 36: 209–21.

Montgomery, Tommie Sue 1982b. *Revolution in El Salvador: Origins and Evolution*. Boulder, CO: Westview Press.

Morris, Aldon 1984. *The Origins of the Civil Rights Movement: Black Communities Organizing for Change*. New York: The Free Press.

Mulligan, Joseph 1991. *The Nicaraguan Church and the Revolution*. Kansas City, MO: Sheed and Ward.

Nasr, Seyyed Vali Reza 1994. *The Vanguard of the Islamic Revolution: The Jama'at-i Islami of Pakistan*. Berkeley: University of California Press.

Nepstad, Sharon Erickson 1996. 'Popular Religion, Protest, and Revolt: The Emergence of Political Insurgency in the Nicaraguan and Salvadoran Churches of the 1960s–1980s.' Pp. 105–24 in *Disruptive Religion: The Force of Faith in Social Movement Activism*. Edited by Christian S. Smith. New York: Routledge.

Nepstad, Sharon Erickson 2004. *Convictions of the Soul: Religion, Culture, and Agency in the Central America Solidarity Movement.* New York: Oxford University Press.

O'Brien, Conor Cruise 1994. *Ancestral Voices: Religion and Nationalism in Ireland.* Dublin: Poolbeg Press.

Osa, Mary Jane 1996. 'Pastoral Mobilization and Contention: The Religious Foundations of The Solidarity Movement in Poland.' Pp. 67–85 in *Disruptive Religion: The Force of Faith in Social Movement Activism*, edited by Christian Smith. New York: Routledge.

Peterson, Anna 1997. *Martyrdom and the Politics of Religion: Progressive Catholicism in El Salvador's Civil War.* Albany: State University of New York Press.

Pfaff, Steven 2001. 'The Politics of Peace in the GDR: The Independent Peace Movement, the Church, and the Origins of the East German Opposition.' *Peace and Change* 26 (3): 280–300.

Pope, Liston 1942. *Millhands and Preachers.* New Haven, CT: Yale University Press.

Randall, Margaret 1983. *Christians in the Nicaraguan Revolution.* Vancouver: New Star Books.

Renick, Timothy M. 1991. 'From Apartheid to Liberation: Calvinism and the Shaping of Ethical Belief in South Africa.' *Sociological Focus* 24 (2): 129–43.

Richardson, James T. (ed.) 2004. *Regulating Religion: Case Studies from Around the Globe.* New York: Kluwer.

Roberts, Hugh 1988. 'Radical Islamism and the Dilemma of Algerian Nationalism: The Embattled Arians of Algiers.' *Third World Quarterly* 10 (2): 567–75.

Salehi, M. M. 1996. 'Radical Islamic Insurgency in the Iranian Revolution of 1978–1979.' Pp. 47–63 in *Disruptive Religion: The Force of Faith in Social Movement Activism*, edited by Christian Smith. New York: Routledge.

Scharper, Philip and Sally Scharper 1984. *The Gospel in Art by the Peasants of Solentiname.* Maryknoll, NY: Orbis Books.

Szajkowski, Bogdan 1983. *Next to God ... Poland, Politics, and Religion in Contemporary Poland.* New York: St. Martin's Press.

Smith, Brian 1982. *The Church and Politics in Chile.* Princeton, NJ: Princeton University Press.

Smith, Christian 1991. *The Emergence of Liberation Theology: Radical Religion and Social Movement Theory.* Chicago: University of Chicago Press.

Smith, Christian 1996. *Resisting Reagan: The U.S.-Central America Peace Movement.* Chicago: University of Chicago Press.

Stark, Rodney 2004. 'Putting an End to Ancestor Worship.' *Journal for the Scientific Study of Religion* 43 (4): 465–75.

Templin, J. Alton 1984. *Ideology on a Frontier: The Theological Foundation of Afrikaner Nationalism, 1652–1920.* Westport, CT: Greenwood Press.

Villa-Vicencio, Charles 1978. 'A Rationale for Repression: The Theology of Apartheid.' *Christianity and Crisis*, March 13. Pp. 45–49.

Walshe, Peter 1997. 'Christianity and the Anti-Apartheid Struggle: The Prophetic Voice within Divided Churches.' Pp. 383–99 in *Christianity in South Africa: A Political, Social, and Cultural History.* Edited by Richard Elphick and Rodney Davenport. Berkeley: University of California Press.

Weber, Max 1904–05 [1996]. *The Protestant Ethic and the Spirit of Capitalism.* Translated by Talcott Parsons, introduction by Randall Collins. Los Angeles: Roxbury.

Weigel, George 1992. *The Final Revolution: The Resistance Church and the Collapse of Communism.* New York: Oxford University Press.

Wiktorowicz, Quintan (ed.) 2004. *Islamic Activism: A Social Movement Theory Approach.* Bloomington, IN.: Indiana University Press.

Williams, Rhys H. 1994. 'Movement Dynamics and Social Change: Transforming Fundamentalist Ideology and Organizations.' Pp. 785–833 in *Accounting for Fundamentalisms: The Dynamic Character of Movements.* Edited by M. E. Marty and R. S. Appleby. Chicago: University of Chicago Press.

Williams, Rhys H. 1996. 'Religion as Political Resource: Culture or Ideology?' *Journal for the Scientific Study of Religion* (December) 35 (4): 368–78.

Williams, Rhys H. 2003. 'Religious Social Movements in the Public Sphere: Organization, Ideology, and Activism.' Pp. 315–30 in *Handbook of the Sociology of Religion*, M. Dillon (ed.) (New York: Cambridge University Press).

Wood, Elisabeth Jean 2003. *Insurgent Collective Action and Civil War in El Salvador.* New York: Cambridge University Press.

Yavuz, M. Hakan 2003. *Islamic Political Identity in Turkey.* New York: Oxford University Press.

21

Religious Affiliations, Political Preferences, and Ideological Alignments

LAURA R. OLSON[1]

Already the events of the twenty-first century have provided ample evidence of the fact that Americans – much more than people in other parts of the developed world (Norris and Inglehart 2004) – connect their religious and political views rather closely. For example, in a 2004 debate with John Kerry, President George W. Bush stated: 'My faith plays ... a big part in my life.... And that's been part of my foreign policy.... My principles that I make decisions on are a part of me, and religion is a part of me' (Commission on Presidential Debates 2004). The same year, evangelical Protestants and traditional Catholics were widely credited for Bush's reelection (Cooperman and Edsall 2004). The Bush-Cheney campaign had worked diligently to mobilize conservative Christians, who evidently turned out to vote for Bush in droves (Green *et al.* 2004; Pew Forum 2004). Meanwhile, Americans are deeply divided over a range of socio-moral issues, from homosexuality to abortion to gambling to physician-assisted suicide, and there is growing evidence that religious differences create public opinion cleavages regarding these issues (Green *et al.* 1996; Kohut *et al.* 2000;

Olson, Cadge, and Harrison 2006). How and why do religion and politics intersect so profoundly in a country that is supposedly steeped in the principle of church-state separation? How and why does Americans' approach to religion and politics differ so dramatically from that of their counterparts in other developed countries?

A time-honored norm of common courtesy in the United States is that one should discuss neither religion nor politics, much less the two in combination, in polite company. Nonetheless, the close connection between religion and politics is an inexorable ingredient of American culture. Alexis de Tocqueville was among the first to recognize the profundity of the bond between religion and politics in America. After observing America's young democracy during his four-year visit in the 1830s, Tocqueville wrote: 'By the side of every religion is to be found a political opinion, which is connected with it by affinity.... [Religion's] indirect influence appears to me to be ... considerable, and it never instructs the Americans more fully in the art of being free than when it says nothing of freedom' (1840/1945: 100).

Tocqueville's observation was – and continues to be – keen. Religious freedom grew and prospered in the early years of the American Republic, in large part because the framers of the United States Constitution ensured that no single faith would ever enjoy a monopoly over others. The notion that a country could exist without an established church was revolutionary in the eighteenth century. Every European country had an established faith (such as the Roman Catholic Church, the Church of England, and the Greek Orthodox Church). Although the notion of the divine right of kings was already being debunked, the major world powers of the eighteenth century nevertheless justified their colonial imperialism at least in part through religious justifications. The United States, however, would have none of this; its early colonists had been religious refugees, after all, and would not tolerate any governmental imposition of particular religious viewpoints (Witte 2005).

By eschewing religious establishment and guaranteeing free exercise rights, the framers created a religious milieu in the U.S. that encouraged the flowering of both traditional faiths and new religious movements. The religious diversity that the First Amendment helped to engender has strengthened and preserved organized religion on the whole in the United States (Finke and Stark 1992; Fowler 1989; Stark and Finke 2000). Despite – or perhaps because of – the constitutional principle of church-state separation, religion and politics have each informed the other[2] in profound and lasting ways since the colonial era. The same cannot be said of European countries. Established churches are now moribund in most of Europe and secularism is increasingly replacing religiosity (Berger 1999; Norris and Inglehart 2004; Stark and Finke 2000; Stark and Iannaccone 1994).

Thus we cannot achieve a thoroughgoing knowledge of the sociology of religion without an understanding of the many intersections (some of them quite convoluted) between religion and politics – particularly in the United States, since it is such a religious outlier (Norris and Inglehart 2004). This chapter is specifically concerned with the ways in which religious identity shapes individuals' political attitudes and actions. In the pages that follow, I shall examine scholarship on the relationship between religion and political attitudes and ideologies with an emphasis on the situation in the United States. My emphasis on the U.S. is motivated both by the country's unusually high levels of religiosity – and by American politicians' frequent public connection of religion and politics – but also by the fact that relatively few cross-national empirical studies of religion and politics have been undertaken (but see Berger 1999; Demerath 2003; Norris and Inglehart 2004; Jelen and Wilcox 2002). I chart the recent history of scholarly inquiry in this area, paying special attention to the nature of religious cleavages in American political attitudes and voting behavior. Then I explore emerging issues in the study of religion and political alignment, including the increasing relevance of the concept of political context, the political roles played by religious leaders, and the consequences of our heavy scholarly focus on the American Christian right. I conclude by calling for further research on several underexplored aspects of the relationship between religion and politics.

A BRIEF HISTORY OF THE FIELD

Early studies of religion and politics were few and far between. Before the 1980s, empirical political scientists ignored religion, and sociologists of religion focused little attention on politics. The emergence of evangelical Protestants as a political force, however, led scholars to turn their attention to questions of how and why religion and politics are relevant to one another, particularly in the United States. The increased attention given to religion and politics by the American media since the early 1980s finally spurred a small group of political scientists (some of whom were motivated by personal religious convictions: Leege 2003) to launch empirical studies of religion and politics. Substantive emphasis was first placed on the voting behavior and policy agenda of evangelical Protestants on the heels of the Moral

Majority's appearance on the American political scene (Guth 1983; Liebman and Wuthnow 1983). The net then widened to encompass Catholics (Leege 1988; Welch and Leege 1988, 1991), African American Protestants (Harris 1999; Lincoln and Mamiya 1990), and Jews (Maisel and Forman 2001). In 1983 an organized section of the American Political Science Association was founded specifically to further the study of religion and politics (see Leege 2003 for a lengthier account of these developments). Before long, courses on religion and politics were being offered at colleges and universities across the United States, and thorough texts were written on the subject (for the most recent updates, see Fowler *et al.* 2004; Reichley 2002; Wald 2003). Political scientists and sociologists also began securing grants from major public and private funding organizations for research on religion and politics (see Leege 2003).

Systematic research on religion and politics has now proceeded apace for two decades. Debates rage about the extent to which the framers of the U.S. Constitution were religious men who wished to establish a Christian nation as well as about the specific meaning of church-state separation in the United States (Dreisbach 2003; Jelen and Wilcox 1995; Witte 2005). Scholars also have noticed that religion affects the behavior of members of Congress (Benson and Williams 1982) and political party activists (Layman 2001) and that presidents as different as Abraham Lincoln, Jimmy Carter, and George W. Bush have used religious rhetoric to their advantage for electoral gain, policy influence, and the justification of military action (Leege *et al.* 2002). Meanwhile, the study of the average American citizen's religious and political orientations occupies researchers who note that both voting behavior and public opinion on key socio-moral issues are informed by religious affiliation, belief, and behavior (Green *et al.* 1996; Kohut *et al.* 2000; Wald *et al.* 1988, 1990). Studies also have documented the fact that throughout American history, religious interest groups have worked to bring their policy agendas to bear in Washington, D.C. (Hertzke 1988; Hofrenning 1995). Such interests span every major religious tradition and

offer messages ranging from left-wing calls for social justice to conservative Prohibition-era campaigns and late-twentieth-century Christian Right politics. As the religious diversity of the United States continues to grow (Roof 1999; Wuthnow 2005), so too does the range of religious voices demanding the government's attention. This increasing religious diversity, coupled with the enhanced role religion seems to have been playing in American politics in recent years, makes fully developed scholarly analysis of all facets of the religion-politics connection all the more essential.

We need look no further than the newspaper for substantive research questions and justifications for inquiry in the field of religion and politics. In fact, the 'news of the day' has given rise to some of our most distinguished studies. The Civil Rights Movement of the 1950s and 1960s relied heavily on the organizational foundation of African American churches, as demonstrated by Fredrick Harris (1999). In the wake of the Second Vatican Council, Catholic bishops became deeply involved in American politics, as documented by Timothy Byrnes (1991). The political mobilization of white evangelical Protestants was studied in detail by a variety of scholars, most notably Clyde Wilcox (1987, 1992, 1996). The 1988 presidential primaries featured two high-profile clergy as candidates – Democrat Jesse Jackson and Republican Pat Robertson; these two ministers soon became the subject of a sweeping study of the politics of populism by Allen Hertzke (1993). The 1990s witnessed a turn of the religion-politics connection in the U.S. to the local level, as documented by Melissa Deckman (2004) and others (Green *et al.* 2000, 2003; Rozell and Wilcox 1995, 1997). And the twenty-first century already has provided much new fodder for scholars of religion and politics in America, from the study of religion and terrorism (Demerath 2003; Juergensmeyer 2000; Stern 2004) to the institution of the White House Office of Faith-Based and Community Initiatives (Black *et al.* 2004), and from the U.S. response to religious persecution abroad (Hertzke 2004) to the 'God gap' that appears to be bifurcating the American electorate into two categories: religious Republicans and secular

Democrats (Kohut *et al.* 2000; Layman 2001; Layman and Green 2005).

One major challenge facing scholars of religion and politics has been the paucity of appropriate survey items by which to measure religious tradition and religiosity in valid and reliable ways. Today, the National Opinion Research Center's General Social Survey contains some useful religion items, as do the University of Michigan's National Election Studies. Political scientists Lyman Kellstedt and David Leege led pioneering work to develop suitable survey items, making it their mission to ensure that scholars would be able to study religion's impact on elections and public opinion with the best possible measures (Green *et al.* 1996; Leege and Kellstedt 1993). Motivated by the earlier methodological contributions of sociologists Charles Glock and Rodney Stark (1966), Kellstedt and Leege led the way in overseeing the improvement of survey items on religion, particularly those included in the National Election Studies. Furthermore, over the past twenty years, political scientist Ronald Inglehart has undertaken the enormous four-wave World Values Survey, which provides comparative perspective on a range of matters that touch on the relationship between religion and politics (see Inglehart 1990; Norris and Inglehart 2004). Most recently, the discipline of political science has been gradually incorporating religious measures into broader empirical studies of political attitudes and behavior (see Putnam 2000; Verba *et al.* 1995).

HOW DOES RELIGION CREATE POLITICAL CLEAVAGES?

If religion is politically relevant, then religious factors must somehow separate citizens into politically distinct categories. The specific nature of these cleaving religious factors has been open to debate. Is it the case that religious *affiliation* is the most politically relevant cleaving factor? Alternatively, to what extent do other factors, such as religious belief and behavior, create politically distinct groups of citizens? Here I focus solely on Americans, as it

is they who, in comparison with people in other countries of the developed world, bring their religious beliefs most directly to bear upon their political lives (Norris and Inglehart 2004).

Belonging, Believing, Behaving

Initially, scholars believed that ecclesiastical lines of division were most politically relevant in the United States. Sociologist Will Herberg (1955) categorized American religions into three basic ecclesiastical groups – Protestants, Catholics, and Jews – and scholars assumed that political affiliations fell neatly in line with these groupings for many decades (see also Lenski 1961). White Protestants were thought to be rather uniformly Republican, whereas both Catholics and Jews were portrayed as roundly Democratic. These characterizations were not baseless; indeed, political affiliation did break along these affiliational lines for much of the twentieth century. The principal explanation for this political cleavage, however, is not explicitly *religious* in nature. Although elements of Catholic and Jewish theology did resonate with the Democratic Party's concern for the underdog and the disadvantaged (Layman 2001; Leege *et al.* 2002; Maisel and Forman 2001), so too did the mainline Protestant Social Gospel (Wuthnow 1988) – and mainline Protestants were not Democrats. Far more politically relevant was the fact that white Protestants formed the basis of the American establishment for most of its first two centuries of existence, whereas Catholics and Jews were viewed with some suspicion because their religious beliefs and practices lay outside the perceived mainstream. Thus Catholics and Jews were themselves underdogs, so it was only natural for them to identify with the party that portrayed itself as the champion of the disadvantaged. As xenophobia receded in the second half of the twentieth century and both Catholics and Jews assimilated even more fully into American society, ecclesiastical dividing points became less socially – and therefore politically – relevant (Wuthnow 1988). If it was no longer a major stigma not to be Protestant, there would naturally be fewer feelings of shared grievance among Catholics and Jews, and therefore it is not surprising that these two groups (particularly Catholics) have displayed less internal political cohesion over the past several decades (Layman 2001).

In recent times, the once hard-and-fast political division between Protestants and Catholics has all but disappeared. In a significant deviation from their strong Democratic allegiance during the Camelot era, Catholics are now swing voters; most evangelical Protestants are Republicans, but mainline Protestants are increasingly leaning in a Democratic direction (Fowler *et al.* 2004; Green *et al.* 2004; Kohut *et al.* 2000; Layman 2001; Layman and Green 2005; Manza and Brooks 1999, 2002; Reichley 2002). While religious *affiliation* may not be a perfect predictor of political behavior on its own, religious *commitment* is highly correlated with Americans' political attitudes, outlooks, and actions (Kohut *et al.* 2000). Political scientist John Green and his colleagues (Green *et al.* 2004; Green *et al.* 1996; Guth *et al.* 1997) have led the way in explaining that religion must be understood in a threefold fashion: belonging (affiliation), believing (specific theological and eschatological beliefs), and behaving (religious practices). There is increasing evidence that when it comes to political beliefs and behavior, there are two Americas: those for whom religion is highly salient, and those for whom it is not. Simply put, Americans across religious traditions who display high levels of religiosity (as measured by frequent worship attendance, prayer, and other religious activities, as well as high levels of self-reported religious commitment) are markedly conservative on a range of policy issues (Fiorina 2005; Kohut *et al.* 2000) and Republican in their voting behavior (Kohut *et al.* 2000; Layman 2001) as compared with Americans for whom religion is not a high priority.

The political cleavage that separates Americans with high levels of religious commitment from those who are less involved in religious life has been termed the 'God gap.' Robert Wuthnow (1988) was the first to propose that American religion could no longer be understood thoroughly on the basis of the traditional (Herberg 1955; Lenski 1961) 'Protestant-Catholic-Jew' framework. Extensive societal changes caused two dominant religious orientations to emerge in the United States by the end of World War II: (1) a conservative (some might say orthodox) religious witness, and (2) a more liberal (theologically and morally relativist) approach to religion. Wuthnow demonstrates that this dichotomy appears *within* all major American religious families. Therefore, it becomes most politically relevant to compare individuals who are highly committed to their religion – whatever their religious affiliation may be – to those who report moderate to low religious commitment.

Religion and Public Opinion on Socio-moral Issues

The foregoing discussion raises the question of how religion affects American public opinion on key socio-moral issues, especially matters such as abortion and homosexuality. On the whole, public opinion on socio-moral issues in the United States is correlated with religion, but not always with religious affiliation alone. What tends to be even more significant in models of public opinion about abortion and homosexuality is the strength of individuals' religious commitment, as measured by the orthodoxy of their religious beliefs and the frequency of their participation in religious activities. Religious orientations also shape individuals' perceptions of which types of political issues are of greatest importance. Andrew Kohut and his colleagues (2000) report that committed evangelical Protestants are far more likely than any other religious group to say that 'social, sexual, and cultural issues' are most important. In recent years, committed Catholics have joined committed evangelicals in their concern about this set of issues (Kohut *et al.* 2000). Pope John Paul II (1995, 1997) spoke and wrote often against a worldwide 'culture of death' in which abortion, euthanasia, and homosexuality are widely accepted. This message has evidently resonated with many traditional American Catholics, who have frequently heard their priests and bishops repeat John Paul's teaching about the culture of death and call instead for a 'culture of life.' Committed Catholics are more morally conservative now than they have been in the past (Kohut *et al.* 2000).

Religion and public opinion on abortion has been studied widely (Cook *et al.* 1992; Dillon 1996; Grindstaff 1994; Jelen 1992; Hoffman and Miller 1997; Welch *et al.* 1995). Recently, Morris Fiorina (2005) has demonstrated that public opinion on abortion does not vary dramatically by religious tradition, even though on the whole, Catholics and evangelical Protestants tend to oppose abortion while mainline Protestants, Jews, and secular individuals typically support abortion rights (Cook *et al.* 1992). In fact, opinion on abortion is nearly as stable as partisanship in the American electorate (Wilcox and Norrander 2001). Nevertheless, religion – especially when operationalized to include level of religious *commitment* (Cook *et al.* 1992; Evans 2002; Emerson 1996; Fowler *et al.* 2004) – has been shown to affect attitudes toward abortion at the aggregate level. In particular, committed evangelical Protestants and Catholics espouse highly conservative attitudes toward abortion, and the effect of religious commitment even mitigates the effect of high educational attainment (Evans 2002; Peterson 2001).

Recent studies of religion and public opinion toward homosexuality have shown that religious affiliation and religiosity are both highly correlated with opposition to gay rights. Religious affiliation has an especially strong impact: Jews, mainline Protestants, and secular individuals have the most liberal attitudes about homosexuality. Catholics and moderate Protestants espouse more tolerant attitudes, and evangelical Protestants have the most conservative attitudes (Cochran and Beeghley 1991; Fisher *et al.* 1994; Glenn and Weaver 1979; Herek and Glunt 1993; Kirkpatrick 1993). Religiosity, as measured by the frequency of attendance at religious services, is also a significant predictor of individuals' opinions about gay rights. People who display the highest levels of religiosity also espouse the most conservative attitudes toward homosexuality (Cochran and Beeghley 1991; Fiorina 2005;

Fisher *et al.* 1994; Fowler *et al.* 2004; Herek and Glunt 1993). A comprehensive study of religion and attitudes toward gay marriage and civil unions (Olson *et al.* 2006) demonstrates that religious variables outperform even demographic measures in models of attitudes toward same-sex unions. Protestants are more likely than members of other faith traditions to oppose same-sex unions, and individuals with conservative attitudes toward morality and secularism and (to a lesser extent) those who participate actively in religious life, are more likely to oppose such unions.

Religion and Voting Behavior

Just as religion shapes public opinion about socio-moral issues, it also shapes voting behavior (Fowler *et al.* 2004; Kohut *et al.* 2000; Green *et al.* 2004; Layman 2001; Reichley 2002). Of course the relationship between religion and voting behavior is no longer described easily using the old Protestant-Catholic-Jew framework; as is the case with public opinion on socio-moral issues, believing and behaving are equally important factors in the shaping of religion's connection to voting. As discussed above, the 'God gap' phenomenon has created a meaningful electoral cleavage that separates 'the churched' from 'the unchurched.' Individuals with high levels of religious commitment tend to support Republican candidates, while secular individuals vote more frequently for Democrats.

In the United States, religion now affects voting behavior most visibly via the allegiance of committed evangelical Protestants and traditionalist Catholics to the Republican Party and its candidates. Table 21.1 displays the strong religious cleavages that characterized Americans' voting behavior in the 2004 presidential election. Evangelicals supported George W. Bush at higher rates than did adherents of any other major American religious tradition. Mainline Protestants and Catholics appear on the surface to be swing voters, but there is also clear evidence of the 'God gap,' as *traditionalist* (theologically conservative and highly committed) mainline Protestants and

Table 21.1   *Religion and the 2004 American Presidential Vote*

	Vote Choice		
	Bush	*Kerry*	*Turnout*
Entire Electorate	51	49	61
Evangelical Protestant (all)	78	22	63
Traditionalist evangelical Protestant	*88*	*12*	*69*
Mainline Protestant (all)	50	50	69
Traditionalist mainline Protestant	*68*	*32*	*78*
Latino Protestant	63	37	49
African American Protestant	17	83	50
Catholic (all non-Latino)	53	47	67
Traditionalist Catholic	*72*	*28*	*77*
Latino Catholic	31	69	43
Other Christians	80	20	60
Jews	27	73	87
Other non-Christian faiths	23	77	62
No religious affiliation	28	72	52

Source: Green *et al.* (2004). Data are from the Fourth National Survey of Religion and Politics, Post-Election Sample (N=2,730, November–December 2004, University of Akron). All numbers presented are percentages.

Catholics supported Bush at rates almost equal to those of evangelical Protestants. The turnout rates of Protestant and Catholic traditionalists alike were very high (these groups' turnout rates were eclipsed only by that of Jews, but Jews comprise only a tiny fraction of the American electorate). Not only do religious traditionalists feel connected to the Republican Party, they are evidently also highly mobilized to appear at the polling place on Election Day to cast their ballots for Republican candidates.

In appealing to his committed evangelical Protestant and Catholic constituencies, George W. Bush has repeatedly alluded to Pope John Paul II's teachings about the culture of death. Like the late pope, Bush has asked that Americans instead embrace a 'culture of life' (Fletcher 2005). He first used this language in a 2000 debate with Albert Gore:

> I think what the next president ought to do is to promote a culture of life in America. Life of the elderly and life of those women all across the country. Life of the unborn. As a matter of fact, I think a noble goal for this country is that every child, born or unborn, need to be protected by law and welcomed to life (Commission on Presidential Debates 2000).

The phrase 'culture of life' later appeared in the 2004 Republican Party platform as well (Republican Party 2004). On balance, the

Republicans appear to be doing a more effective job than the Democrats of articulating the ways in which their policy program connects to the agenda of 'religious' Americans.

Culture War?

In part because public opinion and voting behavior seem to bear a relationship to religious factors, a recurring theme in the religion and politics literature in recent years has been the debate over the so-called 'culture war' that is supposedly being waged over the definition of morality in American society. In 1991, sociologist James Davison Hunter published his controversial *Culture Wars: The Struggle to Define America*. In this book and elsewhere (see Hunter 1994), Hunter argues that over the past several decades, American liberals and conservatives have polarized around socio-moral issues. Dissension over such issues, according to Hunter, has evolved into warlike conflict that cuts across religious lines. In essence his assertion is that there is little basic, cultural-level consensus in the United States over the foundational issues of how people ought to relate to each other.

Hunter argues that two major combatants are entrenched in the culture war. On one side are the 'orthodox,' a group who rely on religious orthodoxy to explain their views. Their understanding of the world is traditional; they consciously reject many modern (and postmodern) ideas about social interaction. Standing in opposition to the orthodox are the 'progressives,' who reject religious orthodoxy and value human potential and reason in its stead. Some might label them 'secular humanists'; however, Hunter's progressives are not by definition anti-religious, they are just not religiously orthodox. Each side in the culture war distrusts and criticizes the other. For Hunter, the culture war is rooted in fundamentally incompatible definitions of such basic concepts as morality, truth, good, obligation, and community. He notes that many of the specific issues being contested deal with the human body, which leads him to observe in a later book (Hunter 1994) that the human body is more than just an organism; it has social and cultural meaning and significance. If this is so, American conflict over the meaning and significance of the human body may be a profound statement about the presence of a much deeper, yet somehow unarticulated, division in American society.

The culture war thesis is obviously compelling and has warranted a great deal of analysis. However, as a variety of scholars have demonstrated, not all people take up sides along the lines of the culture war rubric. Scholars of public opinion consistently have demonstrated that while an orthodox-progressive cleavage may appear in public opinion on some issues, this cleavage clearly has not superseded other cleavages (Davis and Robinson 1997; Demerath and Yang 1997; Fiorina 2004; Jelen 1997; Williams 1997). Nor has there been convincing evidence of increased polarization of political views in the mass public (DiMaggio *et al.* 1996; Evans *et al.* 2001; Fiorina 2004; Miller and Hoffman 1999). In fairness to Hunter, challenges based on studies of mass behavior may miss his point: the culture war is a war between elite-level *activists* who wish to shape the culture. Those on the sidelines of the battle should not be expected to display the same single-minded dedication or polarization.

EMERGING ISSUES IN THE STUDY OF RELIGION AND POLITICAL ALIGNMENT

In recent years, the field of religion and politics has diversified and deepened. Political scientists and sociologists alike have made important strides toward expanding our empirical understanding of the relationship between religion and politics, especially the political attitudes, behavior, and strategies of specific religious groups. Nevertheless, some scholars insist that the religion and politics field has generated far too little distinctive empirical theory (Campbell 2004; Leege *et al.* 1991; Olson and Jelen 1998; Wald *et al.* 2004). As I see it, theoretical innovation in this field is likely to proceed from at least three major frontiers in religion and politics research: the inclusion of the notion of political context in our work, the study of the concept of religious leadership, and an expansion of our horizons beyond substantive investigation of the Christian right.

The Relevance of Political Context

Religion and politics scholarship was limited until recently by a narrow emphasis on the 'belonging' aspect of religion: the beliefs and actions of specific religious groups. Our recent fascination with the question of the culture war only magnifies this tendency, because at root Hunter's thesis marks an attempt to fit large groups of American citizens into a neat two-fold typology. Social phenomena, particularly religion and politics, do not often lend themselves to elegant theorization.

Religion is an enormously complex social construct that implies many different things to different observers. At heart, though, religion reflects a set of interactions that take place every day, and at every possible level, between faith forces and (for our purposes) the world of politics. In this sense, religion is an empirical variable, so we should expect the connections between religion and politics to look and act differently in different contexts. One should not expect public religion and politics to intersect in exactly the same manner in different cities (such as, say, Atlanta and Seattle) or in different countries (such as, say, the United States and Germany). The connections between religion and politics also vary with neighborhood and regional characteristics such as socio-economic status (Crawford and Olson 2001; Olson 2000).

Context accounts for variation among large sectors of society and comes in many forms, such as religious, political, national, socio-economic, urban, and rural. Context is the means by which it is possible to show that 'social groups are politically relevant not only because members share common characteristics, but also because social interaction within the group makes the members aware of their commonalities' (Huckfeldt 1986: 5). Through an understanding of the extent to which the relationships between religion and politics vary in different contexts, progress is being made toward a broader appreciation of the totality of the interaction between religion and American politics.

Pippa Norris and Ronald Inglehart (2004) have illustrated the ways in which national cultures create different sorts of contexts for religio-political interaction. They argue: 'Each society's historical legacy of predominant religious traditions will help shape adherence to particular religious values, beliefs, and practices' (Norris and Inglehart 2004: 28). They classify religious cultures worldwide following an ecclesiastical rubric (Protestant, Catholic, Orthodox, Muslim, and Eastern), but they are also interested in exploring the ways in which these religious cultures intersect with the type of society – postindustrial, industrial, or agrarian – supported by a given nation-state. These contexts have enormous political significance worldwide, as Norris and Inglehart clearly demonstrate.

The notion of context can also lead us to a richer understanding of the voting behavior and political attitudes of members of certain religious groups. Recent research has shown that religious congregations are themselves contexts that can facilitate political learning and mobilization (Djupe and Grant 2001; Gilbert 1993; Putnam 2000; Verba et al. 1995;

Wald et al. 1988, 1990). Scholars who have employed the notion of context have suggested that the links between religion and politics are ultimately rooted in people's particular religious experiences. The overall political tenor of faith communities (churches, synagogues, or even prayer groups) often plays a more important role in shaping group members' political behavior than their own personal worldviews (Wald et al. 1988). Moreover, some faith communities are more politically cohesive than others. Group members may be bound together in many ways; one of their common bonds is that they often share political information (Wald et al. 1990). Participation in religious congregations also engenders 'civic skills' that are directly transferable to the political realm (Verba et al. 1995).

There is even appreciable political variation within religious communities. The ecclesiastical perspective would suggest that all members of a particular Baptist congregation would have similar political outlooks. Yet contextual research has shown that the political outlooks of group members are most profoundly influenced by the specific 'discussion partners' (friends) with whom they choose to associate most closely (Gilbert 1993).

The notion of context also fosters a better understanding of the organized political activism of specific faith groups. Above all, the time-bound nature of political context (Zeitgeist) shapes faith groups' decisions about the extent and direction of their collective political activity (Fowler et al. 2004). When Jerry Falwell founded the Moral Majority, it marked the end of an era of political disengagement by a large sector of the American religious population. But only a subset of white evangelicals took part in, or even supported, Falwell's political efforts (Jelen 1993; Wilcox 1987, 1996). There was something unique about the Zeitgeist of the late 1970s that led some (but by no means all) evangelicals into a very public political engagement. So too there was something about the Zeitgeist of the early 1960s that led some (but by no means all) liberal Protestants to rally around the civil rights cause (Chappell 2004; Findlay 1993; Friedland 1998). Context also shapes faith groups' political activities at the local level. This is illustrated by the simple fact that some churches organize for political activity while others do not. For example, a United Methodist congregation on one side of town might be deeply involved in anti-abortion protesting and other forms of activism, while its counterpart on the other side of town might shun politics altogether.

As Paul Djupe and Christopher Gilbert (2003) have explained, various contextual factors also constrain the actions of religious leaders. Djupe and Gilbert show that clergy's political leadership is shaped by three broad contextual factors: their congregations, their religious traditions, and their community. For instance, clergy serving in socio-economically disadvantaged neighborhoods may look out of their office windows and see drug deals taking place, violent crimes being committed, and homeless people struggling to survive. The same would not be true for clergy serving in more affluent areas; they deal instead with people who are faced with an entirely different set of personal and social challenges. The vast differences separating these two socio-economic contexts translate into differences in political choices on the part of the clergy whose churches are located within them. Members of churches that are located in affluent areas are often very politically involved and active in their communities, either on their own or through various organizations. Their clergy may have no incentive to provide these people with a stimulus for political involvement. On the other hand, members of churches that are located in disadvantaged neighborhoods may spend more of their time concerning themselves with basic survival needs (or at least encountering others with such concerns). Pastors of disadvantaged congregations therefore sometimes have an incentive to engage in political activity on behalf of the people in the neighborhoods that surround them (Crawford and Olson 2001; Olson 2000).

Finally, the notion of context can help us come to grips with the matter of the culture war. Why is it that some individuals become engaged in culture war-like conflicts while others do not? Why is it that the culture war has *not* yet torn American society apart at the seams? For some Americans, of course, the culture war rubric makes sense. Certainly there is conflict over socio-moral issues that simply cannot be resolved because of the incredible divergence of political viewpoints among Americans. Ironically, though, part of what keeps American society *together* is the very same divergence and diversity that created the culture war.

Robert Booth Fowler (1989) has advanced the theory that the diversity of American culture (which gives rise to the culture war) has an unconventional partnership with religion whereby each *benefits* the other. Fowler argues that no social institution in the United States is able to provide people who live in every possible context with meaning, community, and moral values as efficiently as religion. The rest of American culture – its political system, its economic system, even its morality – is highly individualistic. Individuals are thus isolated and left to fend for themselves.

Religion, according to Fowler, survives and thrives in the United States because it offers a temporary alternative to the isolation of modern life. American religion, in all its many incarnations, acts as a social refuge. In a highly individualistic and often confusing society, people seek meaning, they seek togetherness, and they seek community. Instead of searching for conflict, they turn instead to religion for shelter from the storm of everyday life. And because of religious freedom, they are able to do so in a myriad of contexts. Most significantly, the very culture that causes people to turn to religion for meaning and protection serves to sustain religion.

The Study of Religious Leadership

Leadership is a concept of enduring importance in both political science and sociology because both fields concern themselves with the study of social structures and their ramifications for people's everyday lives. Without some form of leadership, of course, no complex social structure could exist over the long term. As such, both political scientists and sociologists maintain a keen and necessary interest in the concept of leadership – the forms it takes, the effects it has on other individuals, and the changes that leaders can and do bring to social structures themselves.

Organized religion is no different from other complex social structures in its need for leadership. Religion is, by its very nature, dependent on leadership of the divine sort. It is logical, then, that nearly all organized religions in the world today feature organizational leadership structure of one kind or another. After several early studies (Campbell and Pettigrew 1959; Hadden 1969; Quinley 1974; Stark *et al.* 1971), the field lay largely dormant until the 1990s. In the last decade, however, scholars' interest in the political roles of religious leaders has experienced great renewal. Of course the array of candidates for the title 'religious leader' is wide and diverse. We should not assume that leadership emanates from the top only; grassroots religious leadership, as the Civil Rights Movement so profoundly demonstrates (see Morris 1984), can move mountains as well. And clergy are not alone as organizational elites. Religious leaders also include officials who outrank clergy in the hierarchy of their religious tradition, as well as by seminary faculties and interest group leaders.

How effective are clergy and other religious leaders when they attempt to influence politics? Ted Jelen (2001) recently observed, astutely, that both the amount and consequences of political activity by clergy (and by extension, other religious leaders) are themselves both *variables* and thus difficult matters for broad theorization. James Guth echoes Jelen: 'The most obdurate problem is discovering the *consequences* of [clergy's political] activity…. Assessing influence has always been notoriously risky…. Clergy influence is especially difficult to gauge, given the great variety of targets and the multiple possibilities for impact' (2001: 41).

In his discussion of future directions for research on religious leaders, Guth (2001) argues that one of the biggest gaps in the literature is that we simply do not have a good typology of the sorts of political actions clergy take. Indeed this is the case, and the same is true of lay leaders. Fortunately, the political activities of denominational officials and interest group leaders are much easier to track, because in many instances they have specifically defined political roles. Arriving at a comprehensive typology of the political actions taken by either clergy or laity, however, is a thornier matter. Clergy, of course, have long been interested and involved in American politics in ways that span the gamut from running for elective office to organizing study groups about controversial issues in their congregations. Clergy have enormous potential to mobilize others for political action, as they have a steady 'captive audience' and the force of moral suasion due to the position they hold as religious elites.

We must begin with a tractable definition of political activity. Elsewhere (Olson *et al.* 2005), my colleagues and I define political activity as activities taken to influence the distribution of resources or the development and enforcement of shared values in the larger community. We emphasize that these activities range from those commonly seen as political (such as electoral activities) to those often viewed as social-service activities (such as providing a service to the community without government assistance). We note that some of these activities might take place within the congregation (a sermon on a political issue), but that more often such activities relate somehow to the world outside of the congregation. The activities seek to influence collective decision-making, resource distribution, or enforcement of values beyond the membership of the congregation.

To make sense of the broad range of possible political activities available to clergy (and by extension, other religious leaders), we examine two dimensions of political strategies: *where* clergy act and *how* clergy act. We know, of course, that both dimensions are constrained by contextual factors unique to each clergyperson's work situation (Djupe and Gilbert 2003). The first distinction divides activities into those conducted within the congregation (which are primarily designed to influence the political attitudes and behaviors of congregation members) versus activities that directly involve clergy in influencing resource allocation or value enforcement. Guth and his colleagues (1997) distinguish the first type of action as 'cue giving' and the second as 'direct action.' Cue-giving activities rely on clergy's use of their teaching and leadership authority within their congregations. Direct action, on the other hand, finds clergy acting to influence resource distribution or enforcement of values outside of the congregation.

Each religious leader must decide on his or her own whether it is appropriate to take political action, to inspire others to act, or both. This still leaves open the question of what kind of political action to take. Political activities may be divided into four types of political strategies, based on their relationship to government: electoral activities, advocacy, partnership, and gap filling (see also Crawford 1995). *Electoral* activities (such as campaigning, running for office, or contributing money to candidates) influence collective decision-making by shaping the selection of the individuals who will make government decisions. *Advocacy* (such as protesting, contacting political officials, or forming congregational study groups on issues) seeks to affect collective decision-making by influencing government officials or shaping public opinion.

Most analyses of political action focus on electoral and advocacy activities. However, clergy, and many other nonprofit professionals, also have access to two other political strategies: partnership and gap filling. *Partnership* activities involve working with a government entity to address some problem or provide some service. Examples of partnership activities include working on a community policing task force, serving on a community development corporation board that receives government funding, or being a member of a mayoral task force on race relations. Partnership options available to clergy continue to expand as government officials from the White House to City Hall increasingly turn to faith-based initiatives as an option in addressing social problems. The final type of political action, *gap filling*, involves working within the community to influence the distribution of resources or the enforcement of values directly – without government assistance. These actions 'fill in gaps' by providing services

that government does not adequately provide. A rabbi working in a soup kitchen, for example, changes the distribution of food in her community and thus shapes politics in that community. A minister walking the streets to talk with gang members changes the enforcement of values in the community. In short, there are a plethora of political activities in which religious leaders may choose to engage. Further expanding and fleshing out the typology proposed here and elsewhere in my recent work would be an extremely valuable contribution to the study of religious leadership.

Looking Beyond the Christian Right

Over the past several decades, scholars and journalists alike have paid substantial attention to the phenomenon of the American Christian Right. This movement of politically engaged evangelical Protestants, which came into being rather suddenly in the late 1970s, has had its partisanship, voting behavior, issue agendas, participation patterns, and interest group activism studied in great detail. Attention to the Christian Right is well placed, as its emergence as a political force transformed American politics in myriad ways (Green *et al.* 1996; Moen 1992; Oldfield 1996). The movement is now mature and well institutionalized (Green *et al.* 2003), and it demonstrated its political clout rather impressively in the 2004 American presidential election (Cooperman and Edsall 2004; Green *et al.* 2004; Pew Forum 2004).

The Christian Right was born in 1979 – and scholars became interested in it – when a fundamentalist religious broadcaster, Rev. Jerry Falwell, founded the Moral Majority. Even though the Moral Majority did not achieve many concrete policy victories, it did succeed in returning a range of socio-moral issues to the American policy agenda in the wake of 1960s-era social change (Moen 1989). The Moral Majority and other like-minded religious interest groups also succeeded in mobilizing large numbers of evangelical Protestants to vote for Republican candidates (Liebman and Wuthnow 1983), which subsequently contributed to a large-scale partisan realignment in the American South (Feldman 2005;

Layman 2001; Leege *et al.* 2002; Oldfield 1996; Wilcox 1992, 1996; Woodard 2006). The Christian Right reorganized in the wake of the mid-1980s televangelism scandals around the 1988 presidential candidacy of another religious broadcaster, Rev. Marion 'Pat' Robertson. Robertson did surprisingly well in early Republican caucuses and primaries, but ultimately dropped out of the race for the Republican nomination (Hertzke 1993). He quickly moved to organize his campaign supporters and other Americans who had supported the now-defunct Moral Majority to form a new interest group, Christian Coalition. Christian Coalition became one of the most powerful interest groups in Washington, D.C. during the first half of the 1990s (Wilcox 1996). More recently, Christian Coalition has fallen on difficult times and is now a shadow of its former self in Washington. Instead of replacing Christian Coalition with another powerful, national-level interest group, the Christian Right movement has diversified and gained a strong foothold in local-level politics (Deckman 2004; Green *et al.* 2003).

The literature on the Christian Right is voluminous and extremely useful; little has been left undocumented about its rise and political maturation process. Nonetheless, the keen focus scholars have placed on this movement has led (almost by necessity) to a comparative paucity of research on other religio-political movements in the United States (but see Smith 1996a, 1996b). For example, far more research needs to be undertaken to explore the reasons why traditional Catholics – but not conservative African American Protestants – seem to have linked arms in recent years with the Christian Right. Perhaps most urgently, we need an answer to the question of whether there is any semblance of a 'religious Left' in the United States. Does a religious Left exist, or are the Christian Right's main opponents (to employ the culture war rubric) secular?

The religious left today is difficult to describe because it is anything but a unified political movement. As Martin Marty (1999) has observed, '[Perhaps] the religious left flies stealthily low and gets unnoticed. Or [maybe] there is not much of a religious left about which to speak.' To the extent that it exists at all, it is a loosely knit coalition of religious people who approach politics from a liberal/progressive vantage point. 'There is no one entity called "the religious left".... [Instead] many different groups ... advocate a range of issues with common themes of peace, justice, and support for the disenfranchised' (Alpert 2000: 2). Intertwining themes of liberalism – theological and political – would seem to define the religious left, but very little broad-based research has been done in recent years about what might constitute such a religio-political movement.

Coincidentally, these two forms of liberalism work to increase the diversity and lack of cohesion that characterize the religious left. Theological liberalism in particular means that differences in religious viewpoints are not just tolerated, but celebrated. And while political liberalism has seemed to attach to religious liberalism over the years, it is incorrect to assume that all theological liberals are political liberals. In fact, the *evangelical* left is a growing component of the broader religious left, yet almost no evangelicals would be considered theological liberals.

A reasonably large body of work has been undertaken that examines relatively narrow aspects of a more progressive religio-political witness. Several works have explored the role of religious people's involvement in the Civil Rights Movement (Chappell 2004; Findlay 1993; Friedland 1998; Harris 1999; Morris 1984). Other studies have explored the role of religious people in antipoverty programs in American cities (Hart 2001; Warren 2001; Wood 2002). However, these threads have not been pulled together in recent years (but see Olson Forthcoming). It is important for the future of the field of religion and politics to look beyond the headline-making Christian Right (vital though that movement is to understanding religion's role in American politics).

LOOKING TO THE FUTURE

Since the 1980s, political scientists and sociologists have taken important steps toward a more complete understanding of the many interconnections between religion and politics, but there are still many miles left to travel.

There has been great success in this field in an inductive, cumulative sense. In particular, we have learned a great deal about the empirical realities of major American religious groups' encounters with the political world.

The foundation formed by the studies of the past several decades positions us well to move forward in this new century with a firm basis for the broader study of religion and politics. Such breadth will be crucial for the continued development of political scientists' understanding of religion and its intersections with government and politics. Several specific themes should be emphasized in the next few decades of research on religion and politics.

First, future research needs to explore concrete policy implications of the relationship between religion and politics in the United States. The extant literature on religion and politics is rather silent on many of the ways in which public policy is (or is not) shaped by the demands of politically active religious groups. Existing literature also tends to overlook the broader cultural implications of having religious groups among the chorus of American interest groups. The boundaries of culturally acceptable public policy are shaped in part by the fact that religious groups actively assert their political presence in the United States. Although in some ways American society might appear secular, Americans are in fact more conservative on many socio-moral issues than their counterparts in other developed countries (Norris and Inglehart 2004). Scholars need to approach the challenge of understanding American exceptionalism through a broader cultural lens.

Second, there is a significant substantive gap in the literature on American religion and politics that can no longer be overlooked: we do not adequately understand the politics of non-European and non-Christian religious traditions. Because it is a nation of immigrants, and thanks to the religious freedom afforded by the First Amendment, the United States has always been a bastion of religious experimentation and diversity. At the dawn of the twenty-first century, the United States is continuing to accommodate itself to even greater religious diversity. Despite a large literature documenting African American churches' crucial role in the Civil Rights Movement and its after-effects (Harris 1999; Lincoln and Mamiya 1990; Morris 1984), we need more studies of the unique ways in which African Americans marry religion and politics. Meanwhile, immigrants from East Asia (Yang 1999) and Latinos (Espinosa et al. 2005a, 2005b) are bringing their own unique interpretations of Christianity to the table in the United States. Latinos in particular are a growing swing constituency in American electoral politics; Table 21.1 shows that a majority of Latino Protestants voted for President George W. Bush, and exit polls indicated that 44 percent of Latinos on the whole followed suit (Edison and Mitofsky 2004). In part this political conservatism flows from evangelical Protestant and traditional Catholic religious convictions. New immigrants – particularly those from Latin America, Asia, and Africa – also have facilitated the growth of non-Western faith traditions (Ebaugh and Chafetz 2000; Haddad et al. 2003; Warner and Wittner 1998). Despite some anti-Muslim sentiment in the post-September 11 America, Islam is flourishing in the United States (Leonard 2003). So too are Buddhism (Cadge 2004) and other polytheistic faiths, especially Hinduism. Sociologists have undertaken most of the research on religion and immigration to date; work that incorporates political variables must also be added to this small but growing corpus.

It is important that we do not lose sight of the symbolic nature of the religion-politics connection – and for future research, this will mean employing diverse theoretical approaches and research methodologies. Despite the constitutional separation of church and state, religion and politics regularly intertwine in symbolic ways via prophetic narratives offered by both governmental and religious elites that either reinforce or challenge the notion of 'civil religion' (Bellah 1967). Civil religion theory suggests that many Americans share a set of shared spiritual values and beliefs that portray the United States as unique, transcendent, and touched by the hand of God. Civil religion is not a doctrinal faith; more accurately it is a public theology that celebrates democracy and hearkens back to the Puritans' image of America as a 'shining city on a hill.' Rhetorical analysis and in-depth observation are most appropriate for addressing such material.

As the culture war thesis teaches us, the study of religion and politics in the United States cannot be separated from the need to understand public discourses about contentious issues. Among these issues are religious liberty, welfare reform, the recent governmental 'faith-based initiatives,' homosexuality, and environmentalism. We must also further acknowledge the enormous religious diversity not only of the United States but also of the entire world, and study it in its full range of detail. It is especially important for scholars to incorporate narratives from outside of the standard classifications of white Christianity in exploring these contentious matters.

It is also essential that scholars recognize and interpret the ways in which the religion-politics connection was shaped and transformed by the events of September 11, 2001 and more broadly by post-cold war international relations. That day's attacks on the United States highlighted the impulse many Americans have to turn to faith (both concretely and symbolically) to deal with crises (both public and private). The events of September 11 show that we need further cross-national research on religion and politics to understand where the United States stands in comparison to other countries in terms of secularism and tolerance of religious diversity. Understanding 9/11 also requires further study of the circumstances under which religiosity, particularly when it takes a fundamentalist turn, can motivate violence (Almond *et al.* 2003; Berger 1999; Demerath 2003; Juergensmeyer 2000; Marty and Appleby 1993; Stern 2004). Finally, our understanding of religion and politics in international context would be enhanced by the application of the culture wars thesis (Hunter 1991) in countries where an ongoing culture war is hardly debatable, including India, Iraq, Israel, and Northern Ireland.

NOTES

1. I would like to thank Jim Beckford and Jay Demerath for their helpful guidance and suggestions as I prepared this chapter.

2. In this chapter, I assume that the direction of causation is typically from religion to politics rather than *vice versa.*

REFERENCES

Almond, Gabriel A., R. Scott Appleby and Emmanuel Sivan 2003. *Strong Religion: The Rise of Fundamentalisms around the World.* Chicago: University of Chicago Press.

Alpert, Rebecca T. (ed.) 2000. *Voices of the Religious Left: A Contemporary Sourcebook.* Philadelphia: Temple University Press.

Bellah, Robert N. 1967. 'Civil Religion in America.' *Daedalus* 96: 1–21.

Benson, Peter L. and Dorothy L. Williams 1982. *Religion on Capitol Hill: Myths and Realities.* New York: Oxford University Press.

Berger, Peter L. (ed.) 1999. *The Desecularization of the World: Resurgent Religion and World Politics.* Grand Rapids, MI: Eerdmans.

Black, Amy E., Douglas L. Koopman and David K. Ryden 2004. *Of Little Faith: The Politics of George W. Bush's Faith-Based Initiatives.* Washington, DC: Georgetown University Press.

Byrnes, Timothy A. 1991. *Catholic Bishops in American Politics.* Princeton, NJ: Princeton University Press.

Cadge, Wendy 2004. *Heartwood: The First Generation of Theravada Buddhism in the United States.* Chicago: University of Chicago Press.

Campbell, David E. 2004. 'Putting Religion into Context by Putting Context into the Study of Religion: The 1960 and 2000 Presidential Elections.' Presented at the Annual Meeting of the Southern Political Science Association, New Orleans.

Campbell, Ernest Q. and Thomas F. Pettigrew 1959. *Christians in Racial Crisis.* Washington, DC: Public Affairs Press.

Chappell, David L. 2004. *A Stone of Hope: Prophetic Religion and the Death of Jim Crow.* Chapel Hill: University of North Carolina Press.

Cochran, John K. and Leonard Beeghley 1991. 'The Influence of Religion on Attitudes toward Nonmarital Sexuality: A Preliminary Assessment of Reference Group Therapy.' *Journal for the Scientific Study of Religion* 30: 45–62.

Commission on Presidential Debates 2000. 'Debate Transcript: The First Gore-Bush Presidential Debate.' *http://www.debates.org/pages/trans2000a.html.*

Commission on Presidential Debates 2004. 'Debate Transcript: The Third Bush-Kerry Presidential Debate.' *http://www.debates.org/pages/trans2004d.html*.

Cook, Elizabeth Adell, Ted G. Jelen and Clyde Wilcox 1992. *Between Two Absolutes: Public Opinion and the Politics of Abortion*. Boulder, CO: Westview.

Cooperman, Allen and Thomas B. Edsall 2004 'Evangelicals Say They Led Charge for the GOP.' *The Washington Post* (7 November): A1.

Crawford, Sue E. S. 1995. 'Clergy at Work in the Secular City.' Ph.D. diss., Indiana University.

Crawford, Sue E. S. and Laura R. Olson (eds) 2001. *Christian Clergy in American Politics*. Baltimore: Johns Hopkins University Press.

Davis, Nancy J. and Robert V. Robinson 1997. 'A War for America's Soul? The American Religious Landscape.' In *Culture Wars in American Politics: Critical Review of a Popular Myth* (ed.) Rhys H. Williams. New York: Aldine de Gruyter.

Deckman, Melissa M. 2004. *School Board Battles: The Christian Right in Local Politics*. Washington, DC: Georgetown University Press.

Demerath, N. J. III 2003. *Crossing the Gods: World Religions and Worldly Politics*. New Brunswick, NJ: Rutgers University Press.

Demerath, N. J. III and Yonge Yang 1997. 'What American Culture War? A View from the Trenches as Opposed to the Command Posts and the Press Corps.' In *Culture Wars in American Politics: Critical Review of a Popular Myth* (ed.) Rhys H. Williams. New York: Aldine de Gruyter.

Dillon, Michele 1996. 'Cultural Differences in the Abortion Discourse of the Catholic Church: Evidence from Four Countries.' *Sociology of Religion* 57: 25–39.

DiMaggio, Paul J., John H. Evans and Bethany Bryson 1996. 'Have Americans' Social Attitudes Become More Polarized?' *American Journal of Sociology* 102: 690–755.

Djupe, Paul A. and Christopher P. Gilbert 2003. *The Prophetic Pulpit: Clergy, Churches, and Communities in American Politics*. Lanham, MD: Rowman and Littlefield.

Djupe, Paul A. and J. Tobin Grant 2001. 'Religious Institutions and Political Participation in America.' *Journal for the Scientific Study of Religion* 40: 303–14.

Dreisbach, Daniel L. 2003. *Thomas Jefferson and the Wall of Separation Between Church and State*. New York: New York University Press.

Ebaugh, Helen Rose Fuchs and Janet Saltzman Chafetz 2000. *Religion and the New Immigrants: Continuities and Adaptations in Immigrant Congregations*. Walnut Creek, CA: Alta Mira.

Edison Media Research and Mitofsky International 2004. November 2 National Election Exit Polls *http://www.exit-poll.net*.

Emerson, Michael O. 1996. 'Through Tinted Glasses: Religion, Worldviews, and Abortion Attitudes.' *Journal for the Scientific Study of Religion* 35: 41–55.

Espinosa, Gastón, Virgilio Elizondo and Jesse Miranda (eds) 2005a. *Latino Religions and Civic Activism in the United States*. New York: Oxford University Press.

Espinosa, Gastón, Virgilio Elizondo and Jesse Miranda, (eds) 2005b. *Latino Religions and Politics in American Public Life*. New York: Oxford University Press.

Evans, John H. 2002. 'Polarization in Abortion Attitudes in U.S. Religious Traditions, 1972–1998.' *Sociological Forum* 17: 397–422.

Evans, John H., Bethany Bryson and Paul DiMaggio 2001. 'Opinion Polarization: Important Contributions, Necessary Limitations.' *American Journal of Sociology* 106: 944–60.

Feldman, Glenn (ed.) 2005. *Politics and Religion in the White South*. Lexington: University Press of Kentucky.

Findlay, James F. 1993. *Church People in the Struggle: The National Council of Churches and the Black Freedom Movement, 1950–1970*. New York: Oxford University Press.

Finke, Roger and Rodney Stark 1992. *The Churching of America, 1776–1990: Winners and Losers in Our Religious Economy*. New Brunswick, NJ: Rutgers University Press.

Fiorina, Morris P. 2005. *Culture War? The Myth of a Polarized America*. New York: Pearson Longman.

Fisher, Randy D., Donna Derison, Chester F. I. Polley, Jennifer Cadman and Dana Johnston 1994. 'Religiousness, Religious Orientation, and Attitudes towards Gays and Lesbians.' *Journal of Applied Social Psychology* 24: 614–30.

Fletcher, Michael A. 2005. 'Bush Hails Progress toward "Culture of Life".' *The Washington Post* (25 January): A3.

Fowler, Robert Booth 1989. *Unconventional Partners: Religion and Liberal Culture in the United States*. Grand Rapids, MI: Eerdmans.

Fowler, Robert Booth, Allen D. Hertzke, Laura R. Olson and Kevin R. den Dulk. 2004. *Religion and Politics in America: Faith, Culture, and Strategic Choices* (3rd edn.) Boulder, CO: Westview.

Friedland, Michael B. 1998. *Lift Up Your Voice Like a Trumpet: White Clergy and the Civil Rights and*

Antiwar Movements, 1954–1973. Chapel Hill: University of North Carolina Press.

Gilbert, Christopher P. 1993. *The Impact of Churches on Political Behavior: An Empirical Study.* Westport, CT: Greenwood.

Glenn, Norval D. and Charles N. Weaver 1979. 'Attitudes toward Premartial, Extramarital, and Homosexual Relations in the U.S. in the 1970s'. *Journal of Sex Research* 15: 108–18.

Glock, Charles Y. and Rodney Stark 1966. *Christian Beliefs and Anti-Semitism.* New York: Harper and Row.

Green, John C., James L. Guth, Corwin E. Smidt and Lyman A. Kellstedt 1996. *Religion and the Culture Wars: Dispatches from the Front.* Lanham, MD: Rowman and Littlefield.

Green, John C., Mark J. Rozell and Clyde Wilcox (ed.) 2000. *Prayers in the Precincts: The Christian Right in the 1998 Elections.* Washington, DC: Georgetown University Press.

Green, John C., Mark J. Rozell and Clyde Wilcox (ed.) 2003. *The Christian Right in American Politics: Marching to the Millennium.* Washington, DC: Georgetown University Press.

Green, John C., Corwin E. Smidt, James L. Guth and Lyman A. Kellstedt 2004. 'The American Religious Landscape and the 2004 Presidential Vote'. *http://www.uakron.edu/bliss/research.php.*

Grindstaff, Laura 1994. 'Abortion and the Popular Press: Mapping Media Discourse from *Roe* to *Webster*'. In *Abortion Politics in the United States and Canada* (eds) Ted G. Jelen and Marthe A. Chandler. Westport, CT: Praeger.

Guth, James L. 1983. 'Preachers and Politics: Varieties of Activism among Southern Baptist Ministers'. In *Religion and Politics in the South: Mass and Elite Perspectives* (eds) Tod A. Baker, Robert P. Steed, and Laurence W. Moreland. New York: Praeger.

Guth, James L. 2001. 'Reflections on the Status of Research on Clergy in Politics'. In *Christian Clergy in American Politics* (eds) Sue E. S. Crawford and Laura R. Olson. Baltimore: Johns Hopkins University Press.

Guth, James L., John C. Green, Corwin E. Smidt, Lyman A. Kellstedt and Margaret M. Poloma 1997. *The Bully Pulpit: The Politics of Protestant Clergy.* Lawrence: University Press of Kansas.

Haddad, Yvonne Yazbeck, Jane I. Smith and John L. Esposito (eds) 2003. *Religion and Immigration: Christian, Jewish, and Muslim Experiences in the United States.* Walnut Creek, CA: Alta Mira.

Hadden, Jeffrey K. 1969. *The Gathering Storm in the Churches.* Garden City, NY: Doubleday.

Harris, Fredrick C. 1999. *Something Within: Religion in African American Political Activism.* New York: Oxford University Press.

Hart, Stephen 2001. *Cultural Dilemmas of Progressive Politics.* Chicago: University of Chicago Press.

Herberg, Will 1955. *Protestant-Catholic-Jew: An Essay in American Religious Sociology.* Garden City, NY: Doubleday.

Herek, Gregory M. and Eric K. Glunt 1993. 'Interpersonal Contact and Heterosexuals' Attitudes toward Gay Men: Results from a National Survey'. *Journal of Sex Research* 30: 239–44.

Hertzke, Allen D. 1988. *Representing God in Washington: The Role of Religious Lobbies in the American Polity.* Knoxville: University of Tennessee Press.

Hertzke, Allen D. 1993. *Echoes of Discontent: Jesse Jackson, Pat Robertson, and the Resurgence of Populism.* Washington, DC: CQ Press.

Hertzke, Allen D. 2004. *Freeing God's Children: The Unlikely Alliance for Global Human Rights.* Lanham, MD: Rowman and Littlefield.

Hoffman, John P. and Alan S. Miller 1997. 'Social and Political Attitudes among Religious Groups: Convergence and Divergence over Time'. *Journal for the Scientific Study of Religion* 36: 52–70.

Hofrenning, Daniel J. B. 1995. *In Washington But Not of It: The Prophetic Politics of Religious Lobbyists.* Philadelphia: Temple University Press.

Huckfeldt, Robert 1986. *Politics in Context: Assimilation and Conflict in Urban Neighborhoods.* New York: Agathon.

Hunter, James Davison 1991. *Culture Wars: The Struggle to Define America.* New York: Basic Books.

Hunter, James Davison 1994. *Before the Shooting Begins: Searching for Democracy in America's Culture War.* New York: Free Press.

Inglehart, Ronald 1990. *Culture Shift in Advanced Industrial Society.* Princeton, NJ: Princeton University Press.

Jelen, Ted G. 1992. 'The Clergy and Abortion'. *Review of Religious Research* 34: 132–51.

Jelen, Ted G. 1993. 'The Political Consequences of Religious Group Attitudes'. *Journal of Politics* 55: 178–93.

Jelen, Ted. G. 1997. 'Culture Wars and the Party System: Religion and Realignment, 1972–1993'. In *Culture Wars in American Politics: Critical Review of a Popular Myth* (ed.) Rhys H. Williams. New York: Aldine de Gruyter.

Jelen, Ted G. 2001. 'Notes for a Theory of Clergy as Political Leaders'. In *Christian Clergy in American Politics* (ed.) Sue E. S. Crawford and Laura R. Olson. Baltimore: Johns Hopkins University Press.

Jelen, Ted G. and Clyde Wilcox 1995. *Public Attitudes Toward Church and State*. Armonk, NY: M. E. Sharpe.

Jelen, Ted G. and Clyde Wilcox (ed.) 2002. *Religion and Politics in Comparative Perspective: The One, the Few, and the Many*. New York: Cambridge University Press.

John Paul II 1995. *Evangelium Vitae*. http://www.vatican.va/holy_father/john_paul_ii/encyclicals/documents/hf_jp-ii_enc_25031995_evangelium-vitae_en.html.

John Paul II 1997. *The Theology of the Body According to John Paul II: Human Love in the Divine Plan*. Boston: Pauline Books and Media.

Juergensmeyer, Mark 2000. *Terror in the Mind of God: The Global Rise of Religious Violence*. Berkeley: University of California Press.

Kirkpatrick, Lee 1993. 'Fundamentalism, Christian Orthodoxy, and Intrinsic Religious Orientation as Predictors of Discriminatory Attitudes.' *Journal for the Scientific Study of Religion* 32: 256–68.

Kohut, Andrew, John C. Green, Scott Keeter and Robert C. Toth 2000. *The Diminishing Divide: Religion's Changing Role in American Politics*. Washington, DC: Brookings Institution.

Layman, Geoffrey 2001. *The Great Divide: Religious and Cultural Conflict in American Party Politics*. New York: Columbia University Press.

Layman, Geoffrey C. and John C. Green 2005. 'Wars and Rumors of Wars: The Contexts of Cultural Conflict in American Political Behavior.' *British Journal of Political Science* 36: 61–89.

Leege, David C. 1988. 'Catholics and the Civic Order: Parish Participation, Politics, and Civic Participation.' *Review of Politics* 50: 704–31.

Leege, David C. 2003. 'Methodological Advances in the Study of American Religion and Politics.' Presented at the Annual Meeting of the American Political Science Association, Philadelphia.

Leege, David C. and Lyman A. Kellstedt (ed.) 1993. *Rediscovering the Religious Factor in American Politics*. Armonk, NY: M. E. Sharpe.

Leege, David C. Joel A. Lieske and Kenneth D. Wald 1991. 'Toward Cultural Theories of American Political Behavior: Religion, Ethnicity and Race, and Class Outlook.' In *Political Science: Looking to the Future*, vol. 3 (ed.) William J. Crotty. Evanston, IL: Northwestern University Press.

Leege, David C., Kenneth D. Wald, Brian S. Krueger and Paul D. Mueller 2002. *The Politics of Cultural Differences*. Princeton, NJ: Princeton University Press.

Lenski, Gerhard 1961. *The Religious Factor: A Sociological Study of Religion's Impact on Politics,*

Economics, and Family Life. Garden City, NY: Doubleday.

Leonard, Karen Isaksen 2003. *Muslims in the U.S.: The State of Research*. New York: Russell Sage Foundation.

Liebman, Robert C. and Robert Wuthnow (ed.) 1983. *The New Christian Right: Mobilization and Legitimation*. New York: Aldine de Gruyter.

Lincoln, C. Eric and Lawrence H. Mamiya 1990. *The Black Church in the African American Experience*. Durham, NC: Duke University Press.

Maisel, L. Sandy and Ira N. Forman 2001. *Jews in American Politics*. Lanham, MD: Rowman and Littlefield.

Manza, Jeff and Clem Brooks 1999. *Social Cleavages and Political Change: Voter Alignments and U.S. Party Coalitions*. New York: Oxford University Press.

Manza, Jeff and Clem Brooks 2002. 'The Changing Political Fortunes of Mainline Protestants.' In Robert Wuthnow and John H. Evans (eds) *The Quiet Hand of God: Faith-Based Activism and the Public Role of Mainline Protestantism*. Berkeley: University of California Press.

Marty, Martin E. 1999. 'Who is the Religious Left?' *Sightings* (April 30): 1.

Marty, Martin E. and R. Scott Appleby (eds) 1993. *Fundamentalisms and the State: Remaking Polities, Economies, and Militance*. Chicago: University of Chicago Press.

Miller, Alan S. and John P. Hoffmann 1999. 'The Growing Divisiveness: Culture Wars or a War of Words?' *Social Forces* 78: 721–46.

Moen, Matthew C. 1989. *The Christian Right and Congress*. Tuscaloosa: University of Alabama Press.

Moen, Matthew C. 1992. *The Transformation of the Christian Right*. Tuscaloosa: University of Alabama Press.

Morris, Aldon D. 1984. *The Origins of the Civil Rights Movement: Black Communities Mobilizing for Change*. New York: Free Press.

Norris, Pippa and Ronald Inglehart 2004. *Sacred and Secular: Religion and Politics Worldwide*. New York: Cambridge University Press.

Oldfield, Duane M. 1996. *The Right and the Righteous: The Christian Right Confronts the Republican Party*. Lanham, MD: Rowman and Littlefield.

Olson, Laura R. 2000. *Filled with Spirit and Power: Protestant Clergy in Politics*. Albany, NY: State University of New York Press.

Olson, Laura R. 2002. 'Toward a Contextual Appreciation of Religion and Politics.' In *Religion, Politics, and the American Experience:*

Reflections on Religion and American Public Life (ed.) Edith L. Blumhofer. Tuscaloosa: University of Alabama Press.

Olson, Laura R. Forthcoming. *Generals without an Army: The Protestant Left in American Politics.* Washington, DC: Georgetown University Press.

Olson, Laura R., Wendy Cadge and James T. Harrison 2006. 'Religion and Public Opinion about Same-Sex Marriage.' *Social Science Quarterly* 87: 340–60.

Olson, Laura R., Sue E. S. Crawford and Melissa M. Deckman 2005. *Women with a Mission: Religion, Gender, and the Politics of Women Clergy.* Tuscaloosa: University of Alabama Press.

Olson, Laura R. and Ted G. Jelen 1998. *Religion and Political Behavior: A Critical Analysis and Annotated Bibliography.* Westport, CT: Greenwood.

Petersen, Larry R. 2001. 'Religion, Plausibility Structures, and Education's Effects on Attitudes toward Abortion.' *Journal for the Scientific Study of Religion* 40: 187–204.

Pew Forum on Religion and Public Life 2004. 'How the Faithful Voted.' *http://pewforum.org/events/index.php?EventID=64.*

Putnam, Robert D. 2000. *Bowling Alone: The Collapse and Revival of American Community.* New York: Simon and Schuster.

Quinley, Harold E. 1974. *The Prophetic Clergy: Social Activism among Protestant Ministers.* New York: Wiley.

Reichley, A. James 2002. *Faith in Politics.* Washington, DC: Brookings Institution.

Republican Party 2004. 'A Safer World and a More Hopeful America.' *http://www.gop.com/media/2004 platform.pdf.*

Roof, Wade Clark 1999. *Spiritual Marketplace: Baby Boomers and the Remaking of American Religion.* Princeton, NJ: Princeton University Press.

Rozell, Mark J. and Clyde Wilcox (ed.) 1995. *God at the Grass Roots 1994.* Lanham, MD: Rowman and Littlefield.

Rozell, Mark J. and Clyde Wilcox (ed.) 1997. *God at the Grass Roots 1996.* Lanham, MD: Rowman and Littlefield.

Smith, Christian (ed.) 1996a. *Disruptive Religion: The Force of Faith in Social-Movement Activism.* New York: Routledge.

Smith, Christian 1996b. *Resisting Reagan: The U.S. Central America Peace Movement.* Chicago: University of Chicago Press.

Stark, Rodney and Roger Finke 2000. *Acts of Faith: Explaining the Human Side of Religion.* Berkeley: University of California Press.

Stark, Rodney, Bruce D. Foster, Charles Y. Glock and Harold E. Quinley 1971. *Wayward Shepherds: Prejudice and the Protestant Clergy.* New York: Harper and Row.

Stark, Rodney and Laurence Iannaccone 1994. 'A Supply-Side Reinterpretation of the "Secularization" of Europe.' *Journal for the Scientific Study of Religion* 36: 230–52.

Stern, Jessica 2004. *Terror in the Name of God: Why Religious Militants Kill.* New York: HarperCollins.

Tocqueville, Alexis de 1840/1945. *Democracy in America,* The Henry Reeve Text (ed.) Francis Bowen and Phillips Bradley. New York: Knopf.

Verba, Sidney, Kay Lehman Schlozman and Henry E. Brady 1995. *Voice and Equality: Civic Voluntarism in American Politics.* Cambridge, MA: Harvard University Press.

Wald, Kenneth D. 2003. *Religion and Politics in the United States* (4th edn.) Lanham, MD: Rowman and Littlefield.

Wald, Kenneth D., Dennis E. Owen and Samuel S. Hill 1988. 'Churches as Political Communities.' *American Political Science Review* 82: 531–48.

Wald, Kenneth D., Dennis E. Owen and Samuel S. Hill 1990. 'Political Cohesion in Churches.' *Journal of Politics* 52: 197–15.

Wald, Kenneth D., Adam L. Silverman and Kevin Fridy 2005. 'Making Sense of Religion in Political Life.' *Annual Review of Political Science* 8: 121–43.

Warner, R. Stephen and Judith G. Wittner (ed.) 1998. *Gatherings in Diaspora: Religious Communities and the New Immigration.* Philadelphia: Temple University Press.

Warren, Mark R. 2001. *Dry Bones Rattling: Community Building to Revitalize American Democracy.* Princeton: Princeton University Press.

Welch, Michael R. and David C. Leege 1988. 'Religious Predictors of Catholic Parishioners' Sociopolitical Attitudes: Devotional Style, Closeness to God, Imagery, and Agentic/Communal Religious Identity.' *Journal for the Scientific Study of Religion* 27: 536–52.

Welch, Michael R. and David C. Leege 1991. 'Dual Reference Groups and Political Orientations: An Examination of Evangelically Oriented Catholics.' *American Journal of Political Science* 35: 28–56.

Welch, Michael R., David C. Leege and James C. Cavendish 1995. 'Attitudes toward Abortion among U.S. Catholics: Another Case of Symbolic Politics?' *Social Science Quarterly* 76: 142–57.

Wilcox, Clyde 1987. 'Popular Support for the Moral Majority in 1980: A Second Look.' *Social Science Quarterly* 68: 157–66.

Wilcox, Clyde 1992. *God's Warriors: The Christian Right in Twentieth Century America*. Baltimore: Johns Hopkins University Press.

Wilcox, Clyde 1996. *Onward Christian Soldiers? The Religious Right in American Politics*. Boulder, CO: Westview.

Wilcox, Clyde and Barbara Norrander 2001. 'Of Mood and Morals: The Dynamics of Opinion on Abortion and Gay Rights.' In *Understanding Public Opinion*, (2nd edn.) (ed.) Barbara Norrander and Clyde Wilcox. Washington, DC: CQ Press.

Williams, Rhys H. (ed.) 1997. *Culture Wars in American Politics: Critical Reviews of a Popular Myth*. New York: Aldine de Gruyter.

Witte, John 2005. *Religion and the American Constitutional Experiment* (2nd edn.). Boulder, CO: Westview.

Wood, Richard L. 2002. *Faith in Action: Religion, Race, and Democratic Organizing in America*. Chicago: University of Chicago Press.

Woodard, J. David 2006. *The New Southern Politics*. Boulder, CO: Lynne Rienner.

Wuthnow, Robert 1988. *The Restructuring of American Religion*. Princeton, NJ: Princeton University Press.

Wuthnow, Robert 2005. *America and the Challenges of Religious Diversity*. Princeton, NJ: Princeton University Press.

Yang, Fenggang 1999. *Chinese Christians in America: Conversion, Assimilation, and Adhesive Identities*. State College, PA: Pennsylvania State University Press.

PART VI

Individual Religious Behaviour in Social Context

Religion can be an intensely subjective experience that is concentrated in intimate moments of prayer, learning or meditation in spite of the fact that its other expressions include collective worship, membership in formal organisations, participation in communal institutions such as schools, seminaries and hospitals, and sentiments of loyalty to shared traditions. Sociologists of religion need to keep the subjective and the collective dimensions of religion in simultaneous focus if they are to grasp either's significance. Clearly these two dimensions are not mutually exclusive. They are actively intertwined in everyday life, and each helps to fashion the other in the sense that collective forces shape individual thought, feeling and action, while individuals play a part in forging collective phenomena. The four chapters in this Part explore the interplay between individual religious behaviour and its social contexts.

The study of individuals' religious beliefs lies at the heart of the sociology of religion and is one of the keys to religious continuity and change. Yet, as **Pierre Bréchon** demonstrates in Chapter 22, sociologists face formidable methodological challenges in attempting to generate good quality, relevant information about individuals' beliefs and values. Moreover, the

methodological task is even more taxing when the aim is to produce cross-national comparisons of individual religiosity – comparisons especially important in an age of globalisation and regional re-alignment. Bréchon discusses at length the problems with conceptual issues and empirical indicators that have to be resolved before cross-national surveys can be effective. Using examples from a number of international social survey programmes, he explains both the difficulties and the workable solutions that have been adopted in the use of, for example, synthetic attitude scales and measures of religious socialisation. The fact that some international surveys have included questions on religion on more than one occasion since 1981 means that changes over time can be plotted and debated in the context of theoretical scenarios about modernisation, secularisation, privatisation and religious renewal. In the case of Central and Eastern Europe, for example, Bréchon's interpretation of survey data shows how complicated the picture has become since 1990. He also argues that the restructuring of religion in Western Europe reflects strong national variations, generational effects and confessional differences.

Cross-national surveys enable sociologists of religion to place the religiosity of individuals in contexts that help to explain rates of continuity and change in beliefs and practices, but an understanding of how religion can be interwoven with ethnicity usually requires approaches that are better attuned to the lived realities of particular peoples, nations and societies. As **Peter Kivisto** explains in Chapter 23, relations between ethnicity and religion are of great interest to sociologists not only because of the association with voluntary or enforced migration and settlement but also because they concern indigenous peoples and ethno-national groupings. In short, ethnicity – referring to shared belief in common descent irrespective, in some cases, of blood relationships – is a social construct in which religion's role may vary from a bit part to the lead. As a form of identity somewhere between kinship and nationality, it has the potential to mobilise collective action and is therefore potentially complementary to religious identity as in the case of Americans who call themselves Swedish Lutherans, German Jews, Dutch Reformed, Serbian Orthodox, Polish Catholics, Black Baptists or Native Americans. In varying degrees, each of these 'religio-ethnic' categories combines ethnicity and religion, although Kivisto warns against any attempt to infer 'essential' or fixed identities. He also entertains the possibility that the ethnic and religious components of these combined categories may change at different speeds – a consideration that directly concerns members of the 'immigrant congregations' of Christians from Korea, China, the Philippines, etc. in recent decades. The current and future development of immigrant congregations is particularly interesting for what it may reveal about theological trends, the prospects of assimilation, the likelihood of secularisation, the creation of transnational networks between societies of origin and settlement, and the investment of time and money in church-based communities. All these possibilities will affect the general question of how the assimilation of migrants into the US will take place – if at all. Religion is therefore a major factor shaping the outcome of immigration, although the potential for tension between the religious and the ethnic aspects of identity should not be ignored.

The capacity that ethnicity and religion have for mutual reinforcement is a potentially powerful source of religious identities, but another – partly independent – influence on the religiosity of individuals comes from their socialisation as children and young adults. Indeed, the family is the social institution which has the most long-lasting effect on most people's religious beliefs, feelings and allegiances. But, as **John Bartkowski** observes in Chapter 24, these effects do not always conform to expectations. For example, the findings of recent extensive research on conservative Protestants' patterns of child-rearing are partly paradoxical. Within a predominantly conservative model of child–parent relations that endorses physical punishment, parents are also encouraged to develop an expressive and nurturant style of parenting that favours praising and hugging children more often than do non-conservative parents. Children brought up in families following this parenting style do not appear to be at greater risk of emotional or behavioural problems than their peers in non-conservative families. In settings other than conservative Protestantism, research suggests that the children of actively religious parents tend to develop well unless their families frequently argue about religion. Bartkowski adds that most American teenagers claim a religious affiliation, and socialisation in religious groups has clear effects on their behavioural patterns. On the other hand, the rate of religious affiliation declined by 10 per cent between 1976 and 1996, and American teenagers tend not to display deep understanding of their faith. More research is needed on cross-faith and cross-national samples of parents and children as well as on the influence of the media and online communication on teenagers' religiosity.

This is the point at which to underline the importance of generations, cohorts and age as yet further components of the social context shaping individual religious behaviour. As **Michele Dillon** explains in Chapter 25, sociologists need to distinguish between the life experiences of people born in different cohorts (years or spans of several years) or generations (sets of birth cohorts amounting to about twenty years) if they are to understand the social factors that shape continuity and change in religious conduct. High-level generalisations about the effects on religion of, for example, modernisation or secularisation have to be scrutinised in the light of the experiences of particular age groups, cohorts and generations. In addition, the effects of ageing intersect with these other factors to produce rich and complex characterisations of religion among, say, Baby Boomers, Generation X or the category of people born in the 1980s. For example, case study data from Americans born in two cohorts in the 1920s showed that religiousness did not increase in a linear fashion over the life course but went into relative decline between adolescence and late middle adulthood before increasing significantly thereafter. Dillon adds that focusing on the interplay between the effects of ageing, cohort, historical period and generation is a useful corrective to simplistic notions of religious change.

22

Cross-National Comparisons of Individual Religiosity

PIERRE BRÉCHON

Sociology and the social sciences more broadly aspire to understand and explain social phenomena.* This kind of aspiration means that it is necessary to be able to compare groups and social situations across time and space. For example, comparisons may be made between very small geographical areas (such as local communities or regions of a single nation) or much bigger areas (e.g. countries). By means of comparisons we can obviously discover some points in common and some points of difference between the outlooks of different groups. We can also discover the immense richness of institutions, thoughts and human conduct, and this makes it possible to devise theories about how societies work and about the factors that make them what they are.

Although comparison is of great importance to the social sciences, it is also very difficult to achieve. We have waited a very long time for some reliable tools for making comparisons. Admittedly, it was possible to compare statistics (Durkheim's[1] pioneering work on suicide at the end of the nineteenth century comes to mind), but they were few in number and often comparable only with great difficulty because there was no agreed tradition of measurement between countries.[2] This is why

comparison has always been heavily supplemented by the travellers' tales[3] or by in-depth monographs from which general implications for a country's culture could be drawn.

The growth of quantitative investigations opened up new possibilities for comparison, especially from the end of the 1970s. This marked the beginning of major international surveys using a common questionnaire administered in a large number of countries. The Eurobarometer studies, carried out every six months by the Commission of the European Community from September 1973 onwards, are a good case in point. Their primary aim was to discover the facts about public opinion in the different countries of the European Community and, more precisely, to measure carefully the state of feelings and opinions in Europe about the different policies enacted by the Commission. This survey generally contained only one or two indicators of religion among its socio-demographic variables and unfortunately these questions now seem to have disappeared.

Few surveys that use replication of a large number of identical indicators over time are about the field of religion.[4] But this is the case with the three phases of the European Values

Survey (EVS) conducted in 1981, 1990 and 1999 (next in 2008). This work was subsequently taken up again in other countries, on the initiative of Ronald Inglehart, under the name of the World Values Survey (WVS) using a mainly identical questionnaire.[5] This has therefore given us religious indicators – which are in principle comparative – for about 80 countries in the world. Obviously, the more countries are involved, the more likely it is that serious methodological problems will occur. In certain countries where survey traditions are not firmly established and the level of education is low, the reliability of samples can turn out to be dubious. The translation of questions into different languages is another problem that can weaken the comparability of results. It is possible that some differences may not be real sociological differences but may merely have to do with the different meanings of the words used in different languages. In addition, there are some theoretical questions about the conditions of comparability; and it can be argued that only countries being close enough to each other in culture could really be compared. None of these limitations – albeit real – should be exaggerated. Even though we must always be careful about our use of data, the interpretations based on the findings of international surveys prove that this approach to research is of great value.

Another international survey programme, the International Social Survey Programme (ISSP), began in 1985. Every year a national module of the survey is conducted on a particular theme in about 40 countries. Religion was the subject of the surveys in 1991 and 1998; and a new wave will be carried out in 2008. A survey specifically on religion was implemented in 11 European countries at the end of the 1990s on the topic of Religious and Moral Pluralism (RAMP). The RAMP survey was only conducted on one occasion with a very long questionnaire dealing simultaneously with all beliefs (in the hope of measuring their complexity beyond the realms already marked out by major institutions) and with different forms of expressing spirituality. The questionnaire also contained indicators about moral and political attitudes.[6] The remainder of this chapter will highlight the findings from the EVS because it enables us to make the best comparisons across time and space.

We need to inspect the notion of 'individual religiosity' before beginning to present some of the findings from the EVS. There is no point here in going back over the big debate about the definition of religion[7] which has divided sociologists of religion into, on the one hand, those who support substantive definitions for being narrower and referring to a super-human realm – if not to divinities – and, on the other, those who support broader, functional definitions that only deal with the different functions fulfilled by religions. The term 'religiosity' is preferred to that of 'religion' because it signals a readiness to take account of religious matters in all their dimensions and a refusal to confine them to an institutional definition bearing the hallmark of any particular religious faith. Studying 'individual' religiosity does not mean neglecting the sociological approach in favour of a psychological one. The relation between individuals and religious matters is in fact largely social. It depends on the socialisation, the education and the social context in which each of us lives. Of course, all individuals carry the social with them.

From the point of view of our empirical approach, individual religiosity can only really emerge from the way in which quantitative surveys measure the relation with religion. The implicit definition of individual religiosity lies in the indicators that are used. So, it is true that the survey tradition has been influenced by the major Christian institutions. Surveys always have some conservative characteristics, and they are slow to adapt to social change because the people who control questionnaires often prefer to keep using questions that are not perfect but that are comparable over time rather than trying to devise new indicators.

We shall begin by thinking about the different dimensions of religiosity as well as about the main indicators used in surveys to measure them. Then we shall display some synthetic attitude scales and point out the importance of religious socialisation. After that we shall try to explain changes in religiosity since the 1980s and we shall discuss whether the same tendencies are observed in Western and Eastern Europe.

THE DIFFERENT DIMENSIONS OF INDIVIDUAL RELIGIOSITY

It is well known that the classical approach is to distinguish five dimensions of religiosity (Glock 1961; Stark and Glock 1968):

- the experiential dimension refers to the religious feelings that an individual experiences, especially the sense of being in communication with the divine;
- the ideological dimension concerns beliefs and ideas about the divine;
- the intellectual dimension relates to knowledge of doctrines;
- the ritual dimension deals with the religious acts that individuals carry out;
- finally, the consequential dimension involves individuals' attitudes and conduct in all spheres of life in so far as they are connected to their religious beliefs, practices and experiences.

This way of dividing things up is debatable. First, as the authors acknowledge, these dimensions cannot be completely separated from each other. We know, for example, that for many believers participation in worship services – which belongs to the ritual dimension – is also an experience of communication with their God. Moreover, it is certainly easier to study the first dimension by using qualitative material, especially by means of interviews which enable researchers to collect the personal experiences and feelings of individuals. Nevertheless, it is still possible to identify a few indicators, used in surveys, which pick up this dimension. We should also add that it is difficult to separate the ideological and intellectual dimensions: very few people, apart from theologians and intellectuals familiar with religious organisations, possess accurate knowledge of their religious doctrines. By contrast, everyone can have ideas and beliefs that are more or less structured,

positive or negative, about the existence and forms of a super-human world. The final dimension is measured in terms of the influence that religious variables exert on other spheres of life and is not, therefore, really a dimension of religion at all.

In fact, the five classical dimensions can be reduced to three: the basic expressions of religiosity are feelings, beliefs and practices. The content of these three dimensions varies widely depending on whether individuals are – or are not – strongly integrated into a religious faith. In other words, it depends on how closely they are involved in this religion. Religiosity is much more diverse these days and less 'contained' than previously by the major religious institutions. It is only minorities in numerous European countries who are strongly involved in a religious faith; but these minorities are distinctive for having powerful religious experiences, for holding to definite religious beliefs and a super-empirical explanation of the world, and for performing a lot of devotional practices either as individuals or in groups. This degree of participation and involvement in religious affairs often has consequences for the whole life of these individuals.[8] The question therefore arises of whether a single, synthetic dimension – stretching from firm religiosity to definite non-religiosity – would not give sociologists a simple way of locating individuals in terms of their religiosity.

THE MAIN INDICATORS IN USE IN INTERNATIONAL SURVEYS

There are quite a lot of indicators of religiosity in the EVS and ISSP surveys (Bréchon 1999, 2002a). It would be tedious to describe them all, but we can try to see how they are connected to the dimensions that have already been mentioned.

Several questions deal with individuals' religious feelings. Thus, a very simple question in the EVS asks individuals whether they perceive themselves as religious, not religious or staunch atheists.[9] The ISSP survey contains a similar question but with seven options that range from 'extremely religious' to 'extremely non-religious'. Another EVS question refers to the importance of religion in the individual's life (ranging from 'very important' to 'not at all important'). Yet another question – this time dichotomous – asks individuals 'Do you find you get comfort and strength from religion or not?'

The EVS survey first takes the 'belief' dimension into account by measuring belief in God by means of three questions. The first asks whether the individual believes in God ('Do you believe in God, yes or no?'); the second offers four alternative choices:

- 'There is a personal God'.
- 'There is some sort of spirit or life force'.
- 'I don't really know what to think'.
- 'I don't think there is any sort of spirit, God or life force'.

A third question gets at the importance of God in life by asking individuals to place themselves on a scale from 1 ('not at all important') to 10 ('very important'). This question permits many more nuances of meaning than the previous ones.

The measurement of beliefs clearly applies to other religious beliefs, some of which are linked to the world of Christianity, as in 'I believe in hell, heaven or sin'.[10] But other questions are broader than the Christian world, as in the case of belief in life after death, which exists in many religious systems and which can be associated with ideas that are very different from each other. One specific question in the EVS concerns belief in reincarnation,[11] which can trace its origins back to a world of Asian beliefs. Finally, some beliefs arise from the para-sciences or from popular religion such as believing in telepathy,[12] 'to have a lucky charm as a mascot or a talisman', 'to believe that a lucky charm can protect or help' (with answers on a ten-point scale ranging from 'not at all' to 'very much').

There has not been much development of the dimension of practices in international surveys. It always contains a measure of the attendance at religious services; and the EVS includes two questions on prayer: 'Do you take some moments of prayer, meditation or contemplation or something like that?' (yes or no) and 'How often do you pray to God?' with a scale of intensity going from 'every day' to 'never'. A measure of the demand for rites of passage can also be attached to this dimension: is it important or not to have a religious service for birth, marriage and death. But these questions measure the demand for social rituals to mark the major events of life rather than a true religious expectation.

Certain questions do not necessarily fit very well into the dimensions that we have set out here. This is the case with everything to do with the religious situation of the individual, its formal definition, its specification. The most classical question about belonging to a religious faith (acknowledging that one is a member or a former member of a denomination), which is probably the most frequently asked question about religion in surveys, does not really measure a religious experience or a belief or a practice. Moreover, this question can sometimes convey attachment to a culture, to a nation or to an origin just as much as to a religion. Some of the questions in the ISSP that deal with religious socialisation and attendance at services during youth or with parents' religion and their frequency of attendance at services are also to do with definitional specification and are very interesting to know about in order to assess the degree to which religious attitudes are reproduced between generations.

Measuring trust in churches – and more generally everything that concerns their image – belongs to a dimension for assessing religious institutions that Stark and Glock did not take into account.

The above discussion of a few questions shows clearly that, in the field of religion just as in other fields covered by quantitative surveys, statistical indicators are very rough. Compared with the complexity of the thought system of an individual, quantitative indicators are highly reductionist. Sometimes they can only offer two possible responses. But this is not meaningless. In any case, the same problem very often arises in democratic regimes at the time of elections. Many citizens hold nuanced political positions and hesitate when they choose a candidate or reply 'yes' or 'no' to a referendum (often on highly technical-grounds). However, this very reductionist choice is considered legitimate by political actors and by citizens themselves. And socio-logical studies of elections show that this sim-plistic choice is not meaningless even though its meanings may be multiple. Votes can be considered as indicators which assess political opinion at a given moment.

The same argument holds for religion. All individuals can have doubts about their beliefs and highly complex or ambiguous positions; and a non-directive interview has the great advantage of revealing this complexity in the field of beliefs. But a quantitative indicator of a belief in, for example, the existence of God makes no less sense. There is a strong expecta-tion that the individual will make a decision and will leave hesitation behind. He or she can refuse to answer, choose a middling response which sometimes amounts to a posi-tion of safety and a way of avoiding involvement, or answer with a compromise which only imperfectly reflects their attitude. But, finally, and in statistical terms, the bulk of responses makes sense.

Studies of the interrelationships with other variables show that belief in God, measured with this fragile tool, is unevenly distributed in the population of various countries. The big advantage of these rough indicators is that they enable sociologists to carry out detailed studies of the field of beliefs in a group and to make some comparisons across time (does this group believe more, or less, than previously?) or space (comparisons between different groups). Obviously, certain questions can nevertheless be better than others in their wording or in the opportunities that they give the interviewees to express themselves. For this reason dichoto-mous questions are particularly questionable when it comes to religion because they impose a highly restrictive binary logic. Anyway, every question has its own limitations and can be discussed critically. Having a number of indicators to measure the same dimension is a way of responding to the limitations of each indicator.

Table 22.1 gives a concrete illustration – for the 15-member EU, the USA and Canada – of what has just been said. The fact of feeling religious or not religious may be related to very different types of thinking, which depend on the individuals' conception of religion. The many meanings of the term 'religious' still do not strip the question of its value. The first point to note is that few West Europeans call themselves convinced atheists. Strong opp-osition to the idea of divinity and religion remains rare, even in France – the country on which the tradition of opposition to religion has left the strongest mark. According to EVS survey responses, the fact of calling oneself religious is very often connected with belief in God (only 9 per cent of West Europeans who state that they do not believe in God describe themselves as religious). This ques-tion also reveals that declaring that one is religious and a member of a faith group are quite closely linked, but a substantial minority calls itself religious while still denying that it belongs to a faith (20 per cent of people with no religious belonging call themselves religious). Conversely, 21 per cent of people who report that they belong to a faith also call themselves non-religious (this percentage is as high as 52 per cent in Sweden). This is a sign of the declining impact of the religious institutions that have lost a part of their power to define a country's religious field.

Nevertheless, the question about belonging to a faith enables sociologists to classify European countries (Lambert 2002). The Scandinavian countries, located on the left of the Table, come from the Protestant tradition in which belonging to a faith remains very high, although they have very low levels of attendance at religious services. In these coun-tries belonging is very often linked to a form of membership that is more cultural and national than properly religious. The other indicators in Table 22.1 show, nonetheless, that fairly size-able differences exist among these countries, with Denmark and above all Finland looking less detached than Sweden from the world of religion.

The next countries in the Table – the Netherlands, Great Britain[13] and Germany – are

Table 22.1 *Religious feeling, denomination, religious practices and beliefs in God (European and World Values Survey, 1999)*

	Sweden	Denmark	Finland	Netherlands	Great Britain	Germany	France	Belgium	Spain	Austria	Italy	Portugal	Ireland	Greece	Europe of 15	Canada	USA
A religious person	37	71	62	63	37	52	44	62	56	75	83	85	71	81	**57**	72	81
Not a religious person	52	17	28	30	48	34	37	26	33	18	11	9	23	15	**31**	22	16
Convinced atheist	6	5	3	6	5	7	14	8	6	2	3	3	2	2	**6**	4	1
Catholic	1	1	–	24	13	32	53	55	81	79	81	85	87	1	**46**	37	23
Protestant or Anglican	71	87	84	17	51	40	2	3	1	6	–	–	2	–	**22**	23	26
Other	4	2	3	5	19	4	3	6	–	2	–	2	2	96	**8**	7	26
Do not belong	24	11	13	54	18	24	43	37	18	14	18	12	9	3	**24**	31	20
Service once a month	9	12	14	26	19	30	12	28	36	42	54	51	67	43	**30**	35	60
Take moments for prayer	44	50	72	70	47	52	40	61	61	67	77	72	82	62	**57**	79	89
To pray once a week	–	20	41	34	29	34	20	36	41	44	62	62	69	64	**37**	57	77
Believe in God: yes	47	62	74	60	61	62	56	66	81	83	88	93	93	91	**69**	85	94
There is a personal God	16	24	49	23	28	34	21	29	46	31	70	77	63	70	**40**	–	–
Some sort of spirit or life force	52	36	31	49	37	31	31	34	27	51	19	15	25	17	**30**	–	–
God important in one's life (8-10)	17	14	36	25	26	28	20	31	34	46	58	63	55	68	**34**	57	77

Interpretation: 37% of Swedes say they are a religious person, 52 % not a religious person and 6% a convinced atheist. 9% of Swedes attend religious services at least once a month, 47% say they take moments for prayer and 52% not a religious person, 47% say they believe in God.

dual faith countries which, however, display very different relations with religious institutions. The crisis of institutions, especially Catholicism, has been severe in the Netherlands, and this explains the very high number of people who report that they do not belong to any religion (the highest rate in Europe). The Netherlands is a country where certain forms of religious feeling continue to survive (38 per cent of those who do not belong describe themselves as religious); it is also a country where dynamic minorities are active in or around the major religious institutions, but a great deal of restructuring of religion is going on at a remove from traditional Christianity. Germany remains a country where the major religious institutions maintain organic ties with the state and where the movement towards disaffiliation is still limited.

Countries belonging to the Catholic tradition are arranged next in Table 22.1 in order of their level of secularisation: France and Belgium, Spain, Austria, Italy, Portugal and Ireland. It is in the three latter Catholic countries that institutional religion seems best able to resist secularisation even though it could be shown, by comparing levels of religiosity in different generations, that their young people are noticeably less affected by Catholicism than are older people.

Greece is the only country in Western Europe from the Orthodox tradition. All the data indicate that traditional religion is still very vibrant there.

The final two columns on the right of Table 22.1 point to the fact that the World Values Survey questionnaire is not completely identical to the EVS questionnaire, and this rules out the possibility of making comparisons on certain indicators. In spite of this difficulty, it is clear that Canada, notwithstanding the powerful religious revolution that affected it 40 years ago, is still a fairly religious country and that the USA displays high levels of religiosity which are, however, comparable with those of Ireland. There does not appear, then, to be any real American religious exceptionalism compared with secularised Europe.[14] There is no European exceptionalism either,[15] with Europe undergoing a process of secularisation

while the rest of the world is supposed to be undergoing a return of religion. In fact, Europe is too diverse to be analysed as a single entity. The level of religiosity varies widely between European countries; and the levels are not all the same in the different geographical regions.

The complexity of religious worlds also emerges clearly from Table 22.1. Two-thirds of Europeans continue to report belief in God but only 40 per cent say that they believe in a personal God – in general closer to the Christian God – and 30 per cent in a spirit God or vital force. The content that these individuals give to these terms can, of course, vary from person to person, and this explains why, among convinced atheists, 2 per cent describe themselves as believing in a personal God and 19 per cent in a spirit or vital force. The results of the Swiss surveys mentioned above (Campiche 1992, 2004) can help us to understand this apparent contradiction. In 1999, 53 per cent of the Swiss reported that they were 'completely' or 'rather' in agreement with the statement that 'God is nothing other than what is positive in humanity'. Only 42 per cent had given this answer in the 1989 survey. This seems to show a progressive widening of immanent ideas of God.

According to Table 22.2, beliefs in life after death are less widespread in all countries than simple belief in God. Only 53 per cent of Catholics and 42 per cent of Protestants believe in life after death, which is yet another indication of the individualisation and de-institutionalisation of believing. Belief in hell and belief in heaven are statistically very closely related (Cramer's V of 0.73), even though the former is rarer than the latter. This conveys the optimistic character of religious ideas in modern society, whereas Christianity had previously elaborated a pedagogy of fear. It used to be imperative to follow a rule of life that was in line with Catholic teachings in order to reach heaven and avoid the damnation of hell, but the Christian world has now become much more relaxed: God-given salvation is a hope for all people. It seems easier, for Christians themselves, to admit believing in heaven rather than in hell. As for belief in reincarnation, it is only weakly related to the

Table 22.2 Beliefs in life after death, hell, heaven, reincarnation, telepathy and lucky charms (European and World Values Survey, 1999)

	Sweden	Denmark	Finland	Netherlands	Great Britain	Germany	France	Belgium	Spain	Austria	Italy	Portugal	Ireland	Greece	Europe of 15	Canada	USA
Life after death	39	32	45	46	43	34	38	40	40	50	61	37	68	50	**43**	65	75
Hell	9	9	25	13	28	18	18	18	27	16	42	31	46	46	**25**	47	71
Heaven	28	16	50	35	45	28	28	31	42	38	50	50	77	53	**38**	70	84
Reincarnation	19	15	15	20	–	17	25	17	16	19	15	24	19	19	**16**	–	–
Telepathy	43	31	39	49	34	25	35	34	21	41	32	25	32	44	**32**	–	–
Lucky charms (mean)	2.4	2.4	2.1	2.3	2.3	2.9	2.5	2.5	2.3	3.1	2.2	2.7	2.7	3.4	**2.6**	–	–

Interpretation: 39% of Swedes believe in life after death, and 9% in hell.

previous beliefs (Cramer's V = 0.11 with hell and 0.15 with heaven), and this clearly shows that it does not generally belong to the same realm of meanings, even though a minority can believe simultaneously in heaven, hell and reincarnation.

Belief in telepathy has practically no connection to belief in heaven and hell; and it is only weakly linked to belief in God. But it is moderately strongly related to belief in life after death (Cramer's V = 0.26) and to reincarnation (Cramer's V = 0.33). Thus, telepathy, as a belief, is poorly defined and weakly articulated with Christian ideas of believing. The same is true for belief in the efficacy of lucky charms, which is unrelated to beliefs in the Christian world and is slightly related only to telepathy (V = 0.22) and reincarnation (V = 0.20).

What emerges from this discussion is that all indicators have their limitations and are debatable. Nonetheless, they are robust since analysis of the intersections between each indicator and a range of independent variables would show that the answers reflect a logic – or several logics. As the indicators are numerous and as they all have their limitations, it is important to try to work by constructing attitude scales.

THE CONSTRUCTION OF SYNTHETIC ATTITUDE SCALES

A first scale, on belief in God, can be constructed on the basis of the three questions mentioned above: belief in God – yes or no; four positions; and the importance of God in one's life. There are very strong correlations between these questions, and this enables us to build a first scale by adding the scores together.[16] In Europe, therefore, we can separate out a category of 24 per cent of people who have almost no belief in God; 41 per cent who have medium beliefs, and 33 per cent whose beliefs are strong.

The same procedure can also be used to construct a scale of practices by amalgamating attendance at services, taking a moment for prayer and meditation, as well as the intensity of prayer.[17] This gives us four more or less equal categories of the population in terms of their level of religious practice in groups or alone.

A third scale on the intensity of religious feelings is built on the basis of the three questions about the feeling of being religious, the importance of religion in life, and religion bringing strength and comfort.[18] People with strong religious feelings amount to 35 per cent, while 34 per cent have moderate feelings, and 18 per cent weak feelings.

The final scale concerns trust in churches[19]: 25 per cent display strong trust, 43 per cent moderate trust, and 32 per cent no trust at all.

The discussion will begin with the interrelationships between the scales themselves (Table 22.3). The level of belief in God is extremely high among church attenders and those who have strong religious feelings. On the contrary, it is weak among non-attenders and people who do not report having religious feelings. What emerges is that the scales are strongly interrelated. The more people believe in God, the more they attend church, and the more they also have an interest in religion; trust in churches is a little less tightly linked to the other three scales. Even though the more people believe in God, the more they trust churches, there is a minority who do not trust

Table 22.3 *Relationship between the scale of beliefs in God and the scales of practices, religious feeling and trust in churches (Western Europe, EVS 1999)*

Beliefs in God	Religious practices				Religious feeling			Trust in churches			Mean
	− −	−	+	+ +	weak	moderate	strong	not at all	moderate	strong	
Weak	65	25	2	0	74	23	1	52	18	3	**24**
Moderate	33	63	51	17	25	61	26	39	50	29	**41**
Strong	2	12	47	83	1	16	74	10	32	67	**33**

Interpretation: 65% of Europeans with the lowest level of religious practices also have the lowest level of beliefs in God.

in churches but nevertheless strongly believe in God. This involves a minority of believers who are highly critical towards religious institutions.

This is yet another illustration of the point that the interpretation of data must constantly take account of two apparently opposing positions. On the one hand, it is indisputable that overall patterns of meaning exist in religious ideas and behaviours. We are not dealing with an entirely atomised world where every individual might have his or her own meaning system. Religious and non-religious attitudes display an overall logic. On the other hand, it is possible to show that there are also minority logics and sub-groups whose attitudes are complex, if not apparently contradictory. A particularly good case in point concerns those people who describe themselves as convinced atheists and nevertheless hold certain religious beliefs.

Now it's time to consider the differences that the major socio-demographic factors introduce into religious attitudes (Table 22.4). What clearly emerges is that the differences in religiosity between men and women remain quite sharp: women have more belief in God, they practise their religion more, they feel more religious and have a little more trust in churches, although the difference between them and men is weaker on this last criterion. The explanation for this phenomenon does not lie only in women's lower rate of participation in employment. The table shows that a gap in religiosity continues to exist between men and women who are all in employment, but it is smaller than for the population as a whole. One possible explanation is that the fact of having a job and being involved in professional life makes some women leave the traditional world of the family behind, thereby helping to relativise and weaken their level of religiosity. But the gender differences persist because religiosity fits deeply rooted values which are at the heart of the early socialisation and which change only slowly. We also confirmed that these differences in religiosity cannot be explained by a higher average age among women. When age is controlled, differences persist. Once again, however,

changes and a weakening of differences are observable among the younger generations. But educational levels cannot explain away the differences in religiosity either. Among young people between the ages of eighteen and thirty-four who have completed higher education, differences of religiosity according to gender remain stable. These differences are not inherent, of course, but they are deeply rooted and do not disappear under the impact of education or of sharing any youth culture.

Independently of gender, religiosity clearly tends to decline among young people. They have fewer beliefs in God than older people; they are less 'practising'; they feel religious less often; and they display less trust in religious institutions. We need to consider however, whether the difference is a matter of age, of period or of generation. If it was an effect of age, young people would be less religious by virtue of adopting values linked to their life cycle: in theory, they would display the carefreeness of youth and they would not think about the meaning of life or the possible existence of another world because they would not yet have had to confront the problem of their mortality – unlike older people. They would be expected to become more religious as they got older. But if, according to the second hypothesis, it was an effect of period, all generations would undergo the same rate of change together as a result of the change of values from one period to another – depending on whether religion was declining or returning. If, as a third hypothesis, it was an effect of generation, religious orientations would be rather unchanging throughout life and tied to a deeply internalised value system. It would follow that, if the younger generations are less religious and if they have not been brought up religiously, there is every statistical likelihood that they will remain so for the rest of their life.[20] If we want to decide between these three types of effect, we will have to begin by comparing our data at several different points in time in order to check whether the age cohorts of 1981 have become more – or less – religious as they aged.

Table 22.4 also shows that religiosity tends to be a little weaker among people who have

Table 22.4 Relationship between the scales of religiosity and some socio-demographic variables (Western Europe, EVS 1999)

	Beliefs in God			Religious practices				Religious feeling			Trust in churches		
	weak	moderate	strong	– –	–	+	++	weak	moderate	strong	not at all	moderate	strong
Male	30	42	28	34	28	20	18	26	42	32	35	43	22
Female	20	41	40	21	24	24	32	16	36	48	29	43	28
Employed man	31	41	28	35	29	19	17	28	43	30	36	44	20
Man without employment	28	43	29	33	28	24	20	23	41	36	34	41	25
Employed woman	24	44	32	25	27	24	25	21	41	39	33	44	22
Woman without employment	17	38	45	17	21	24	37	13	33	54	25	43	32
18–34 years old	30	44	26	32	31	21	16	28	43	29	36	46	18
35–54 years old	26	42	32	28	27	22	23	22	41	37	34	43	23
55 years and over	18	38	44	21	20	23	37	12	33	54	25	41	35
Short education (till 16 years)	22	41	38	27	23	22	28	18	37	45	31	40	29
Medium education (17–20 years)	27	42	31	29	26	23	22	24	40	37	33	45	22
Long education (21 years and +)	29	43	29	26	32	20	22	23	43	34	32	48	21
Farmer	12	41	47	18	18	37	27	8	32	60	24	42	34
Craftsman, shopkeeper	24	42	35	24	29	21	26	19	42	40	31	46	24
Executive	25	39	36	22	29	20	30	20	38	43	30	45	25
Intermediary profession	29	44	28	29	29	21	21	23	41	36	33	46	22
Employee	28	41	31	28	25	25	22	22	41	38	32	41	27
Worker	26	43	32	33	24	20	22	24	39	37	35	41	24
Low income –	23	36	41	26	22	23	29	19	33	48	27	41	31
Low income +	26	41	33	30	25	22	23	23	38	39	32	42	27
High income –	26	44	31	28	27	21	24	23	39	38	33	42	25
High income +	27	43	31	25	29	21	25	20	44	36	32	45	23
Catholic	8	44	48	12	24	27	38	6	37	57	19	47	34
Protestant	25	50	25	27	30	25	18	19	50	31	31	47	23
Other	10	32	58	12	22	24	42	9	22	69	22	39	39
Does not belong	61	31	8	62	27	9	2	54	39	7	61	34	6

Interpretation: Beliefs in God are weak among 30% of men, moderate among 42% and strong among 28%.

spent many years in education. That would confirm the commonly advanced hypothesis that the acquisition of knowledge and access to modern science would make it more difficult to support the idea of a super-human religious world. But we have to remember that age and level of education are linked. Young people also have more qualifications than older people, so it is worth pondering whether the determining variable is age or educational level. When age is controlled, the Tables of our four attitude scales display the same structure: a modest effect attributable to length of education is apparent only for people of 55 and older. Religiosity is low among young people, regardless of their educational level. Access to knowledge may have slightly encouraged the rejection of religion in the distant past, but this no longer seems to be the case today.

Concerning the current or past social background of individuals, farmers – admittedly few in number in Europe today – emerge as a specific category: they display a religiosity that is decidedly more robust than that of other social categories. It is also noticeable that the religiosity of craftsmen, shopkeepers and higher executives tends to be stronger than among intermediary professions, employees and workers. These tendencies are most clearly evident, however, in the first three scales (beliefs in God, religious practices and feeling religious) but only weakly for trust in churches. It is only among farmers that trust in churches is higher.

According to Table 22.3, the first three scales are very strongly linked, and Table 22.4 brings out the parallels between the correlations obtained for socio-demographic variables with each of the three scales. This shows that, when looking for one single synthetic indicator of religiosity in order to discover, for example, the links between religiosity and other dimensions of values – without wanting to conduct detailed investigations of the little groups which end up in paradoxical situations, positive or negative, on the different scales – there is freedom to choose any one of the scales. This is confirmation of what several authors have pointed out, notably Wolfgang Jagodzinski and Karel Dobbelaere (1995). Using data from the 1981

and 1990 EVS, they regarded answers to the question about attendance at religious services as a good indicator of overall religiosity. They examined, country by country, the intersections between this indicator and three variables: the importance of God in one's life, the feeling of being religious, non-religious or a convinced atheist, and the number of religious beliefs held by each respondent (God, soul, sin, life after death, heaven, the devil and hell). Their way of proceeding was therefore close to ours. Having also noted some very strong correlations they came to the conclusion that 'church attendance can be classified as an excellent indirect indicator of church religiosity' (Jagodzinski and Dobbelaere 1995: 90).

Whenever the possibility arises, in national or international quantitative surveys, of accurately measuring the different dimensions of religiosity, it is highly important to do so because this is how we can assess the complexity of situations and demonstrate the existence of minority sub-groups. But in studies that are not to do with the sociology of religion and where there is an opportunity to insert into a questionnaire only one synthetic indicator as a potential explanatory variable of widely differing attitudes, the simple indicator of frequency of attendance at religious services – coupled, if possible, with a statement of membership of a religious denomination – provides an acceptable measure of religious attitudes.[21] This shows that the direct or indirect influence of the major religious institutions is still plain to see in religiosity. The individualisation of religion is far from being total.

THE IMPORTANCE OF RELIGIOUS SOCIALISATION

The EVS question about the frequency of attendance at religious services at the age of 12 years is a good illustration of this point about the lingering influence of the major churches on individuals. This indicator is a measure of the importance of religious socialisation during youth. Table 22.5 shows that 16 per cent of Europeans report that they went to

Table 22.5   Relationship between attending religious services at 12 years old and age, denomination and frequency of current attendance at worship (Western Europe, EVS 1999)

	Age				Denomination				Current worship attendance			Mean
	18–29 years	30–44 years	45–59 years	60 years and +	Catholic	Protestant	other	do not belong	monthly	less often	almost never	
More than once a week	9	12	19	25	23	9	18	8	29	14	9	16
Once a week	35	39	46	47	53	33	45	26	56	45	31	42
Once a month or holy days	23	21	15	14	15	27	20	16	12	31	15	18
Almost never, never	32	29	20	15	9	31	17	51	3	11	46	24

Interpretation: Among young people of 18 to 29 years old, 9% attended a religious service more than once a week when they were 12 years old, 35% once a week, etc.

religious services more than once a week when they were young – and 42 per cent once a week. However, a quarter of the population practically never went to a place of worship. It seems that, between childhood and the time of the survey, frequency of visits to places of worship drops substantially (these days 30 per cent of Europeans go to services at least once a month). This can be explained by a life-cycle effect: parents may wish to give their children a religious and moral education – and even to make them attend schools run by religious institutions where attendance at religious services is more or less obligatory. It should be normal, then, to find high rates of attendance for 12 year olds which then drop lower when they become adults and no long feel a strong need to pay regular visits to places of worship.

This gap between church attendance at 12 years old and during adulthood can also be explained, however, by an aspect of secularisation. Indeed attendance at worship at 12 years old is decidedly less common in younger generations than in older ones (Table 22.5 reveals that 72 per cent of people aged 60 and above used to be weekly attenders at the age of 12, compared to only 44 per cent of today's 18 to 29 year olds). It is possible that parents, who share religious beliefs and values less often and less intensely, come to the view that it is less important than it used to be to make their children share these beliefs and values as well.

Attendance at worship during childhood also varies by religious denomination (Table 22.5) and national traditions (first part of Table 22.6). During their youth, Catholics were decidedly more frequent visitors to churches than Protestants; and they continue to be more assiduous. That can be explained in terms of differences in theology: Catholicism has always placed a much higher value on regular attendance at worship than Protestantism. This is because, normally, a good Catholic ought – or used to feel obliged – to attend mass weekly.[22] The mass is a communal gathering and a moment of encounter and of potential communion with God. The Catholic strategy for transmitting religiosity – not only by insisting on weekly attendance at mass but also by having a more centralised and hierarchical

organisation with a theology that is generally more critical towards the world and modernity – seems to give more conclusive results in the sense that the levels of Catholics' religiosity on the four attitude scales are higher than those of Protestants (bottom of Table 22.4).

Obviously, this simple distinction between Catholics and Protestants is crude. Depending on the countries, Protestantism and even Catholicism may be diverse; and the type of educational system in a country can do more – or less – to promote socialisation in religious values. It is in countries with a Catholic tradition, such as Ireland, Italy and Belgium, that attendance at mass was most frequent during childhood (Table 22.6). By contrast, in Scandinavia weekly attendance at worship seems to have been very rare. Clearly, religious socialisation can operate through many different channels: groups for catechism, family discussions and prayer, various para-religious educational movements, etc. But children's attendance at worship seems to produce powerful effects on the structuring of a religious world and the assimilation of religious values for the rest of life. Table 22.5 shows that there is a close relation between the rate of respondents' attendance at religious services today and the level of their religious practice when they were 12 years of age: 85 per cent of monthly attenders used to go to religious services at least once a week when they were 12 years old. If religious practice in childhood is no guarantee of adult practice (and 40 per cent of people who practically never, or never, go to church used to go each week in their childhood), it is rare among adults who did not have any religious socialisation when they were children. Religious socialisation remains, then, a highly important component of individual religiosity, even though there is no warrant for talking about determinism. A typology will show this better.

A four-fold typology can be constructed on the basis of two dichotomous variables: (a) religious practice at 12 years of age (divided into two groups of weekly attenders and those who attended less frequently or never); and (b) religious identity as measured on the basis of ten indicators concerning belief in God, practice and religious feeling.[23] This dichotomous scale

Table 22.6 *Attendance at religious services at 12 years old and typology of religious evolution (EVS 1999)*

	Denmark	Finland	Netherlands	Great Britain	Germany	France	Belgium	Spain	Austria	Italy	Portugal	Ireland	Greece	Europe of 15
More than once a week	2	1	20	17	6	10	23	17	12	35	14	25	12	16
Once a week	8	5	33	36	32	47	49	46	52	51	57	70	54	42
Once a month or holy days	32	43	16	12	32	13	11	18	24	10	11	3	30	18
Almost never, never	58	51	31	35	30	30	17	19	12	5	19	2	3	24
Distanced from religion	5	1	20	27	12	35	35	24	17	19	10	21	8	21
Strong religious transmission	5	5	33	26	26	22	37	39	48	66	60	74	59	37
Transmission of weak religiosity	66	45	35	40	45	37	21	29	23	9	13	4	17	32
Closer to religious values	24	49	12	7	17	6	7	7	13	6	16	2	16	11

Interpretation: 2% of Danes attended religious services more than once a week when they were 12 years old, and 58% attended almost never or never.

enables us to distinguish between strong and weak religiosity.

Thus, we create the following four categories (see the lower half of Table 22.6):

- Weekly attenders at 12 years of age whose religiosity is weak today. They can be considered as having at least *distanced* themselves *from* the religious values of their childhood. They amount to 21 per cent of the sample.
- Weekly attenders at 12 years of age whose religiosity remains strong today. They amount to 37 per cent of the sample and can be identified as a pattern of *strong religious transmission*.
- Those who did not attend church much at 12 years of age and who still display weak religiosity. They amount to 32 per cent of the sample and are deemed equivalent to the *transmission of weak religiosity*.
- Those who did not attend Church much at 12 years of age but have strong religiosity today. They amount to 11 per cent of the sample and seem to have grown *closer to religious values*.

Most people fall into the two central categories, which display a degree of continuity – or at least constancy – in the individual's journey through life;[24] another quite important category distances itself from religion, and this is no surprise in a Europe familiar with secularisation processes; the smallest category – as might be expected – is the one where there has been a degree of growth in religiosity.

Of course, this device is far from perfect since it measures religious socialisation at 12 years of age by means of a single indicator and because it divides current religiosity into only two categories whereas, quite obviously, it can take very different forms and degrees of intensity.[25] Nevertheless, this imperfect device enables us to measure national differences as well as to assess the extent of continuity and change in religious journeys through life at the European level. The transmission of strong religiosity occurs much more frequently in countries steeped in ancient Catholic or Orthodox traditions which have most successfully withstood secularisation (Ireland, Italy, Portugal, Greece and Austria). The transmission of weak religiosity takes place principally in countries where secularisation has been under way for a long time (Denmark, Finland and Germany). Belgium and France are countries where putting a distance between oneself and religion appears to be a powerful process between childhood and adulthood. These countries belong to the Catholic tradition where children's religious practice used to be taken for granted in past generations but where secularisation has been powerful since the 1960s. The case of Finland is quite special: although children's religious practice there has been very low for a very long time, some forms of religiosity seem to hold steady.

CHANGES OVER TIME IN THE INDICATORS OF RELIGIOSITY, FROM 1981 TO 1999

Sociologists of religion have discussed the secularisation thesis at length (see, for example, Berger 1967; Martin 1978; Dobbelaere 1981, 2002; Norris and Inglehart, 2004). To begin with, it received strong support from many of them. The major religious systems were supposedly losing their dominance over public institutions and societies; Europe was to be de-christianised; and the de-institutionalisation of religion would mean that it would be less regulated by institutions than in the past. In the eyes of some sociologists, secularisation is a process that goes as far as to challenge the very existence of religious thinking: rational modernity was supposed to progressively undermine and render obsolete all religious thought and belief. After the tendency to fail to see any religion anywhere any more, some sociologists in the 1980s and 1990s tended, rather, to see it everywhere again. We were supposedly witnessing the return of religion[26] in the form of 'new religious movements', a 'New Age' or, more recently, a renewal of identity religions among ethnic minorities. We are definitely not pretending to present a complete overview of this debate here – even in a summary form. It is simply a question of drawing attention to what the data from the EVS – which are the only surveys to provide quantitative comparisons over a period of 18 years – allow us to say about fluctuations in religiosity.

Jean Stoetzel (1983) used the first wave of surveys to show that younger generations were much less religious than older ones. He remained careful about the interpretation, however, insisting on an explanation in terms of life-cycle (as generations get older and closer to death, they were expected to become more religious) but also suggesting an explanation on the basis of generational differences (with young generations being progressively more de-christianised).[27]

Data from the second wave, in 1990, showed that the gaps between generations remained wide and that changes in the same indicators pointed, rather, to a decline in religious values among people of the same age, thereby verifying the secularisation thesis (Ashford and Timms 1992; Halman and Riis 1999). Yves Lambert (1995) was heading in the same direction by noting that the baby-boomers (born after 1946) were the first generation for which this decline of religious values could be observed. This decline increased in later generations, including young people in 1990. The downward movement of the main indicators of religiosity between 1981 and 1990 was the result of both the renewal of generations (with elderly religious generations being replaced by much less religious younger generations) and of a period effect (with religiosity crumbling away in all generations). Lambert pointed out, however, that some indicators (belief in life after death, in heaven and in hell) seemed to be on the rise again among young people. His conclusion wondered whether 'we were not witnessing a growing distinction between spirituality and institutional religion, with increasing concerns with the former and with a decline of other concerns' (Lambert 1995: 111). We would then be entering a post-Christian era, when the major beliefs of Christianity would convey less and less meaning for Europeans but when more vague concerns with the meaning of life might develop.

When the same Yves Lambert (2002, 2004a) analyses the data from the latest wave of the EVS he considers that a turning point had been reached between 1990 and 1999. The secularisation tendencies are still there but they were counter-balanced by two other phenomena: the growth of 'believing without belonging', according to Grace Davie's (1994) expression (i.e. a form of religiosity among people who do not admit to any loyalty to a particular religious faith), and even the growing strength of religiosity among Christians. Across the whole of the population of the nine countries of Western Europe for which we have comparable data for 1981, 1990 and 1999,[28] the downward tendency of religious indicators remains the dominant feature.[29] The feeling of being religious, for example, goes down from 62 per cent in 1981 to 56 per cent in 1999; membership of a religion goes from 85 to 75 per cent; monthly attendance at religious services goes from 36 to 30 per cent; trust in churches from 51 to 43 per cent; and belief in God from 74 to 68 per cent. The only three indicators to go up are belief in a personal God (from 30 to 38 per cent), agreement with the statement that churches respond adequately to individuals' spiritual problems (from 44 to 52 per cent), and belief in hell (from 22 to 25 per cent).

Of course, it is open to debate whether this growth in only three indicators should be considered significant. An increase of three points in the belief in hell could be regarded as stability more than growth; the fact that churches respond to spiritual needs can be regarded as having little significance since even an atheist could acknowledge that it is the role of churches to respond to their members' spiritual needs; the 8 point increase in belief in a personal God is a more troubling sign – albeit difficult to interpret since the other indicators that can be included in the same attitude scale have not undergone the same change, as we shall see.

If we stop looking at the population as a whole and concentrate, instead, on changes among young people between the age of 18 and 29, the picture is quite different. Now, the changes occurring among young people can – with caution – be considered as heralding future phenomena, which are likely to grow in importance in the decades to follow.

Staying with Yves Lambert's calculations, among young people only four indicators are in decline, nine are static, while 11 show an increase. Among these 11 increases, as we argued above, some may appear to have little significance (for example, the growth from 3 to 4 points in the attachment to holding religious ceremonies to mark birth, marriages or deaths, which is an indication of the need for social rituals rather than religion). But other indicators are more significant: belief in a personal God (up from 24 to 31 per cent), in life after death (from 38 to 44 per cent), in hell (from 16 to 23 per cent) and in heaven (from 30 to 35 per cent). Overall, the gaps between generations seem to shrink between 1981 and 1999. In 1999 young people remained less religious than older people, but the difference between them had shrunk.

Still following up Yves Lambert's analysis, let us try to be more specific about the three tendencies which, according to him, are characteristic of the current situation of young people. The tendency towards secularisation or leaving religion behind is mainly evident in the fall in membership of religions and in the decline of worship practices. It is the most institutional aspect of religion which is still tending to recede among young people in Europe.

The second tendency – the spread of believing without belonging – is open to two interpretations. On the one hand, certain religious indicators which are not tied to the Christian world and which point to a search for spirituality either hold up well (for example, 47 per cent of young people in 1981 and 48 per cent in 1999 reported that they 'take some moments of prayer, meditation or contemplation or something like that' or increase (belief in life after death). On the other hand, in a way that is probably more significant, there is a growth of religiosity among people who state that they do not belong to a faith.[30] Among those with no religion, then, belief in God goes up from 20 to 27 per cent, and in life after death from 19 to 27 per cent. Not belonging to a denomination is now less likely to imply an absence of religious belief than in the past. In this sense, a distinction can be made between 'those who do not belong' and

'convinced atheists' who are obviously more estranged from all religiosity and who also have a different value system (Bréchon 2003). This 'off-piste' religion, to use Yves Lambert's expression, is much more common in the more secularised countries or those where a severe crisis of religious institutions has occurred – such as the Netherlands (54 per cent of young Dutch people without religion say that they take a moment for prayer, meditation or contemplation).

The third tendency concerns the internal 'recovery of Christianity' that is noticeable mostly on the basis of indicators such as belief in a personal God, in life after death or the various forms of trust in churches. This tendency is clearer among young Catholics than young Protestants. Yves Lambert calculated the percentage of young Christians who meet the core criteria for minimal personal attachment to Christianity (such as attendance at services – leaving aside social or family ceremonies – at least once a year, belief in God, belief in sin and belief in life after death). This minimal core went from 24 per cent of young European Christians in 1981 to 28 per cent in 1999 (33 per cent among young Catholics and 13 per cent among young Protestants in 1999). I think this shows that the tendency towards an internal 'recovery' is actually limited when progress in the core that is regarded as minimal attachment to Christianity only grows by 4 points and when it only concerns a good quarter of young Christians.

It must be added that the changes vary widely by country. Decline is dominant in Great Britain, Spain and Ireland; and recovery is more noticeable in Italy, Portugal, Denmark and Sweden. It is impossible to find a single explanation that fits all these differences in development. Spain and Ireland can be considered as countries where the Catholicism which, up to that point, had held out well against the process of secularisation, was rapidly losing its influence. But, by contrast, Italy and Portugal – also relatively unsecularised countries – were registering the growing strength of religiosity among young people. And in countries with a long history of secularisation, the secularising tendency was getting stronger in Great Britain

Table 22.7   *Attendance at religious services once a month by birth cohort (EVS, 9 comparable Western European countries for 1981, 1990, 1999)*

	1981	1990	1999
From 1973 to 1981	–	–	19
From 1964 to 1972	–	21	23
From 1955 to 1963	24	21	26
From 1946 to 1954	26	27	29
From 1937 to 1945	36	37	40
From 1928 to 1936	40	43	44
From 1919 to 1927	44	53	46
From 1910 to 1918	48	57	–
From 1901 to 1909	52	–	–
Mean	**36**	**33**	**30**

Interpretation: in 1981, 24% of Europeans born between 1955 and 1963, who were then between 18 and 26 years old, attended a religious service at least once a month. In 1999, in the same birth cohort, then 36 to 44 years old, 26% went to services at least once a month.

and was being reversed in Denmark and Sweden for reasons that remain puzzling.

All these analyses are based on changes over time among indicators for the population as a whole as well as for young people. We know whether there is decline or progress but without taking precise account of the changes for each cohort. It is interesting to show what such an analysis might contribute.[31] It provides strong support for the tendency towards secularisation, as seen in Table 22.7, for example, which deals with the six point drop in rates of monthly religious practice over a period of 18 years. The explanation is basically to do with the renewal of generations, with the elderly generations being replaced by young generations that are decidedly less likely to practise religion. Table 22.8 presents an identical structure: trust in churches falls by 7 points as an effect of generation. Each generation is

very stable, but the young generations show much less trust than the older ones in churches.[32] Overall change stems from generational renewal. A similar Table structure could be revealed for the subjective feeling of being religious: an overall drop of 6 points (from 63 to 57 per cent) is basically due to the fact that older generations used to feel much more religious and that they have been replaced by young generations that identify themselves less with religious values.

The tendency towards the development of believing without belonging and of restructured beliefs – based on beliefs only loosely linked to any particular religious world – is particularly clear in the indicator of belief in life after death (Table 22.9). The overall level can be regarded as stable (43 per cent in 1981 and 45 per cent in 1999), but there is quite a pronounced progression among younger generations.

Table 22.8   *A great deal or quite a lot of confidence in the church by birth cohort (EVS, 9 comparable Western European countries)*

	1981	1990	1999
From 1973 to 1981	–	–	35
From 1964 to 1972	–	34	37
From 1955 to 1963	36	37	38
From 1946 to 1954	38	41	44
From 1937 to 1945	52	51	52
From 1928 to 1936	57	58	60
From 1919 to 1927	64	65	61
From 1910 to 1918	69	73	–
From 1901 to 1909	72	–	–
Mean	**52**	**48**	**45**

Table 22.9   *Belief in life after death by birth cohort (EVS, 9 comparable Western European countries)*

	1981	1990	1999
From 1973 to 1981	–	–	45
From 1964 to 1972	–	40	46
From 1955 to 1963	38	39	45
From 1946 to 1954	39	39	43
From 1937 to 1945	44	42	46
From 1928 to 1936	44	47	43
From 1919 to 1927	47	48	45
From 1910 to 1918	51	57	–
From 1901 to 1909	48	–	–
Mean	**43**	**43**	**45**

As a result, the gap between ages for this variable had disappeared by 1999 – unlike for preceding variables. Belief in life after death can be asserted just as well by traditional believers who cling to Christian ideas as by people who are making a new religious world for themselves. The same question is asked in the ISSP survey but with a scale of four responses (instead of being 'yes' or 'no'). Thus, a distinction can be made between those who are very confident about life after death and those who think that it is only probable. The data for 1998 show clearly that what is making quite strong progress among young people is the probability rather than the certainty of life after death (Bréchon 2001a). There is a warrant for thinking that some young people are open to religious beliefs and that they would even like to be able to believe that what they experience as good in life can be pursued afterwards. They find it hard to believe that we are mortal; and they want to believe in the possibility of a life after death without, however, identifying the forms that it would take, without having a clear idea about it, and without formalising a sure and certain religious belief. What we can see, therefore, is more a matter of patching together uncertain beliefs – sometimes on the very edge of religion – rather than a return of the religion of past times.

Can we really detect in the survey data a third tendency, a Christian recovery? I am doubtful. As we have seen, some indicators clearly demonstrate Christian decline (belonging, attendance at services, etc.), but it is more difficult to interpret others, especially changes in the belief in God. According to the 'yes' or 'no' question, there was a drop in the belief in God from 75 per cent in 1981 to 70 per cent in 1999. And this decline is explicable – as before – mainly by the lower extent of believing among the younger generations. On the other hand, belief in a personal God went up, especially among young people; and a noticeable increase was recorded for all generations between 1981 and 1999 (Table 22.10). The effect of age or of period is stronger than that of the renewal of generations (which was heading downwards in the opposite direction). The whole problem is to understand what this increase means: perhaps believing in a personal God no longer means – as it did in the past – attesting to a belief in the Christian God. That said, the question about the importance of God in one's life (on a scale of 10) may provide some additional information when the change between 1990 and 1999 is considered (Table 22.11).[33] The average is stable, with God being considered important (8 to 10 points on the scale) by a third of the sample. Again, this stability is the outcome of two contrary movements: a renewal of generations, the most recent of which accorded less importance to God, and an effect of age or of period (almost all generations accorded a little more importance to God in their life in 1999 than in 1990).

In point of fact, we do not have indicators that clearly identify Christian beliefs in our attempts to test fully the hypothesis of a Christian recovery. For example, indicators of belief in the resurrection or the divine nature of Jesus Christ are not available. The rise of the belief in hell among young people between 1981 and 1999 (from 16 to 23 per cent) or in

Table 22.10   *Belief in a personal God by birth cohort (EVS, 9 comparable Western European countries)*

	1981	1990	1999
From 1973 to 1981	–	–	32
From 1964 to 1972	–	28	35
From 1955 to 1963	23	28	35
From 1946 to 1954	24	31	39
From 1937 to 1945	31	40	46
From 1928 to 1936	32	43	49
From 1919 to 1927	39	48	48
From 1910 to 1918	38	58	–
From 1901 to 1909	42	–	–
Mean	**31**	**37**	**39**

heaven (from 30 to 35 per cent) is astonishing, but again, can it be interpreted as Christian renewal? Obviously, the hypothesis of a renewal of Christianity cannot be discarded. But, for the moment, support for the hypothesis seems to rest entirely on significant increases in only a few indicators that are difficult to interpret – and which could also be explained by the development of restructured and individualised beliefs at some distance from Christianity.

CHANGE IN CENTRAL AND EASTERN EUROPE

Still using the EVS surveys, Yves Lambert (2004a, b, 2005) compares the data for 1999 and 1990 and shows that the three tendencies identified in Western Europe also exist in the East. But he argues that the growing strength of religiosity in Eastern Europe was more intense and, in almost every country, higher among the younger generation than others. Communism

did not wipe out religions; and the percentage of staunch atheists is still particularly weak in the countries of Central and Eastern Europe, whereas the percentages of people with no membership of a faith are high (except in Poland, Romania and Croatia).

If countries are classified according to their religious tradition and level of religiosity, a first group is of countries with a Catholic tradition where religiosity is overall high, with differences, nevertheless, between a very Catholic Poland (where religiosity was stable between 1990 and 1999) and less religious Lithuania and Slovenia. A second group of countries can be regarded as pluri-confessional with moderate religiosity (decreasing from Latvia to Hungary, the former Czechoslovakia, the former East Germany and Estonia). A third group consists of countries with Orthodox majorities (with Romania being decidedly more religious than Russia[34] and Bulgaria).

Siniša Zrinščak (2004) analyses some of the indicators in the 1999 EVS and shows that there are big differences of religiosity between countries. He distinguishes a first group of

Table 22.11   *Belief that God is important in one's life (from 8 to 10 positions) by birth cohort (EVS, 9 comparable Western European countries)*

	1990	1999
From 1973 to 1981	–	21
From 1964 to 1972	19	27
From 1955 to 1963	22	28
From 1946 to 1954	25	33
From 1937 to 1945	34	42
From 1928 to 1936	41	45
From 1919 to 1927	48	48
From 1910 to 1918	61	–
Mean	**32**	**33**

Table 22.12   *Dimensions of religiosity, for young and old people, in Central and Eastern European countries (EVS, 1999)*

	Poland		Croatia		Lithuania		Slovakia		Slovenia		Latvia	
	18 29	60 and +	18 29	60 and +	18 29	60 and +	18 29	60 and +	18 29	60 and +	18 29	60 and +
A religious person	91	95	75	85	62	92	69	90	60	76	65	79
Catholic	91	95	83	87	68	84	55	74	61	81	18	23
Protestant	3	1	1	0	2	2	9	17	1	2	12	30
Orthodox	0	1	0	0	1	7	1	1	3	1	12	20
Do not belong	6	2	15	9	29	5	34	8	35	17	56	26
Services once a month	74	84	46	58	17	65	41	67	24	44	11	22
Moment of prayer	82	90	68	80	46	82	55	81	38	63	61	65
God scale: strong	73	87	39	55	33	78	31	64	11	38	14	30
Church scale: strong	32	62	30	54	23	67	35	64	20	39	21	35
Life after death	76	76	62	52	46	78	52	69	34	34	38	35
Reincarnation	26	12	26	10	30	26	19	11	26	6	35	18
Telepathy	41	22	41	21	50	32	38	23	32	15	50	31
Lucky charms (mean)	7.1	8.1	3.9	3.8	4.5	3.1	3.9	3.3	3.8	2.7	5.3	4.1

Interpretation: 91% of Poles from 18 to 29 years old say they are a religious person.

countries where the return of religion is currently stronger. They are countries that had experienced the most thorough anti-religious repression. Thus, Latvia, Estonia, Russia, Ukraine, Belarus and Bulgaria display rates of religious practice today that are higher than when the respondents were 12 years old, but these rates remain generally weak (except in Belarus and Bulgaria). The distinctive characteristic of a second group of countries is that their industrialisation and secularisation have a long history (Czech Republic, Hungary, Slovenia – even Slovakia). In spite of a tendency towards the revitalisation of religion in the 1980s, the level of religiosity there is rather moderate (and even very low in the Czech Republic). Secularisation seems to have actually occurred along with the rapid modernisation of the 1990s; and on average, people's religious practice is lower than when they were 12 years old. Finally, in countries where religion was most firmly anchored in society and was one with national identity (as in Poland, Lithuania, Croatia and Romania), religion provided a powerful support for resistance to communism; and religiosity declined less under communism. Religiosity remains strong, and there is not much difference between the respondents' level of religious practice at the age of 12 and today.

Without denying that quite a lot of indicators of religion went up, especially among young

people between 1990 and 1999, we should not forget that powerful generational differences could be seen in 1999 – just as in Western Europe. With reference to the traditional indicators of religiosity, young people were clearly less religious than older people. Table 22.12 puts the phenomenon in a clear light by contrasting the 18 to 29 year olds to those of 60 years and over in the three groups of countries (Catholic tradition, mixed, Orthodox – arranged from the most to the least religious). The subjective feeling of being religious is often noticeably weaker among the 18 to 29 year olds except in the very religious Poland and, by contrast, in the quite secularised Ukraine.[35] The percentage of people saying that they belong to no faith is greater among young people in every country except, again, in Poland and Romania. It reaches a record high level in Estonia (86 per cent) and in the Czech Republic (80 per cent). Attendance at religious services at least once a month is also less common in the younger generations. It drops by 10 points among young Poles but plummets by 48 points in Lithuania. Only in Bulgaria, where Orthodox practice is close to the average, does the rate of attendance at services hold up. Prayer, meditation or contemplation – which could be part of Christian practices but also of a wide range of diverse spiritualities – is equally weaker among young people (except in Latvia). The scale of beliefs in God (constructed as previously

Hungary		Estonia		Czech Republic		Romania		Bulgaria		Russia		Ukraine	
18 29	60 and +	18 29	60 and +	18 29	60 and +	18 29	60 and +	18 29	60 and +	18 29	60 and +	18 29	60 and +
46	78	28	53	32	58	75	88	38	64	58	72	67	72
33	51	0	1	14	49	9	7	0	0	0	0	1	1
9	24	8	25	4	7	2	2	1	1	1	0	4	1
0	1	5	12	0	0	85	87	51	74	38	62	35	53
58	24	86	61	80	43	3	3	39	16	57	34	52	37
10	30	5	22	9	24	34	59	23	25	7	14	12	22
45	79	41	60	33	51	87	97	30	48	25	51	40	57
23	53	9	24	9	25	54	67	24	38	20	40	31	48
15	42	11	26	9	28	49	66	14	22	26	42	28	47
34	34	31	22	40	32	63	46	33	34	36	27	35	28
27	11	39	15	30	8	25	10	35	16	35	16	28	14
48	28	45	34	69	48	59	28	37	19	54	22	49	22
3.1	1.8	4.4	3.3	4.1	2.9	6.5	7.6	2.9	1.7	4.0	3.3	4.0	2.6

explained for Western Europe) brings the same linkage to light. Beliefs in God are decidedly lower among young people in all countries. The scale of trust in churches also varies widely by generation. And even in the very Catholic Poland the church appears to come in for criticism and not to be regarded by young people as responsive to the different needs of the population. On all the previous indicators, the same pattern emerges: young people seem much less religious than their elders. Having become adults after the collapse of communist regimes and being socialised in a context of democratic transition, of openings to the West, of return to religious freedoms and sometimes to national traditions of the past – despite all that, young people still have not re-discovered strong religiosity. Although they are sometimes a little more religious than the young people of 1990, they are much less so than the older generations.

However, a few indicators – the same as for Western Europe – display a different pattern of relations. In 11 of the 13 countries, young people believe in life after death as much as, or more than, their elders. They also believe markedly more in reincarnation, showing levels of belief equivalent to belief in life after death in countries with weak religiosity. Belief in telepathy is also very common among young people, reaching as high as 69 per cent among young Czechs who are nevertheless at a considerable remove from the worlds of religion.

This is a new type of belief which may fit together with widely differing experiences and may claim to be scientifically proven or provable eventually. The belief that a lucky charm like a mascot or a talisman can help or protect people, in the form of a scale from 1 (total non-belief) to 10 (strongest belief), is also more common among young people in 11 out of the 13 countries. The most notable exception occurs in the very Catholic country of Poland, which seems highly receptive to this popular belief and where elderly people seem to believe in lucky charms even more than young people.

As for Western Europe, the overall impression is that religious belief is shifting and being loosely re-structured. Development is strong among these beliefs that have weak links with the world of Christianity and are in some cases borrowed from rival worlds, from the Asian world, from para-scientific or popular worlds – more as possibilities than certainties.

FINALLY, HOW TO EXPLAIN DIFFERENCES IN RELIGIOSITY?

Of course, it is possible to offer explanations in terms of the level of economic development. The argument would be that the economic modernisation of a country would undermine the foundations of the religious world and that the institutions and systems of traditional beliefs would not manage to survive in this context. And religion itself would become problematic in a modernised world. Considerable of empirical evidence can obviously be found to support this thesis: for example, the low level of religiosity in the highly developed North of Europe and the relative preservation of religious traditions in certain less developed countries of Europe such as Catholic Portugal and Orthodox Greece. But a large number of counter-examples come to mind. Thus, Italy has undergone a lot of development, but religiosity there remains strong and may even be growing among young people. Austria enjoys a level of development comparable with that of Germany but is much more religious. In Central Europe, Slovenia is relatively developed but has kept a fairly high level of religiosity. And obviously, the United States has often been put forward – and rightly so – as a case to challenge the thesis that modernity is necessarily unfavourable to religion. In fact, it is clear that a country's economic transformation progressively modifies individuals' value systems; and it is also possible that existing value systems can promote or slow down a country's economic development. There is nothing mechanical or automatic about these processes.

In its confrontation with modernity, religion – like all value systems – is undergoing restructuring. The values of individualisation are making advances everywhere and undermining traditional systems of thought. Institutional religion is finding it really hard to hold its ground because individuals want to define themselves and they claim their originality. But the opportunities for diversity, originality, restructuring and tinkering with religion are extensive.

This general movement of potentially restructuring religion takes different forms in accordance with each country's history and cultural traditions, which, overall, have a stronger determining effect on religion than does the level of economic development. There is a good fit between each country and its history and tradition of relations between religious institutions and the state. Opposition to religions and their exclusion from the public sphere were particularly severe in France, and this may help to explain the powerful secularisation of this Catholic country. By contrast, the majority religious institution in some countries embodies the national sentiment and can have more or less institutionalised relations with the state. But that was accompanied by powerful secularisation in the Nordic countries, whereas in Greece the Orthodox tradition has managed to hold its own. The type of Christianity that has developed in each country has probably shaped the decline of traditional religions as well as the type of religious restructuring. Traditional religiosity seems better able to hold steady in Catholic and Orthodox countries – just as much in the West as in the East of Europe – than in Protestant countries. And obviously, the type of Protestantisms and of Catholicisms must also be borne in mind, since each Christian religion can play the card of being open to the world or, on the other hand, of being closed in on its traditional forms. The forms and rhythms of modernisation may also have effects on religiosity. The modernising revolution of Canada in the 1960s or of Spain in the 1980s following a democratic process of transition, helps us to understand the process of very rapid secularisation.

NOTES

* Many thanks to James A. Beckford for the very effective translation of this text.

1. Emile Durkheim produced a theory for explaining the social by the social. The suicidal character of a society is basically explained by the strength of the social bonds that hold individuals together. See Durkheim 1895, 1897.

2. Durkheim compared 'ecological' statistics (i.e. for the entire collectivity) rather than rates for individuals. But he sometimes drew conclusions about individuals from the collective rates. For example, he knew that the suicide rate was higher in the Swiss cantons where Protestants formed a majority than where Catholics were in the majority, so he inferred that more Protestants than Catholics take their own life. But this is debatable. There is always a risk of committing the 'ecological fallacy'. See Robinson 1950. Isambert 1973 showed that Protestant cantons were also more likely to be urbanised and that the explanation could lie in this phenomenon rather than in religion itself.

3. Alexis de Tocqueville, for example, wrote: 'In every case, at the head of any new undertaking, where in France you would find the government or in England some territorial magnate, in the United States you are sure to find an association' (1969 [1840]: 513).

4. There are some very good national surveys but they tend to use country-specific questionnaires which are not therefore comparable. In the case of Switzerland, for example, there are the two volumes edited by Roland Campiche 1992 and 2004; for France, Michelat, Potel, Sutter and Maître 1991 present the findings of a survey in 1986; and the findings of a survey in 1994 are available in Michelat, Potel and Sutter 2003.

5. The first wave of the World Values Survey took place in 1981–1983, then in 1990–1991, in 1995–1997 and in 1999–2000. See Inglehart 2004 for the recent data incorporating countries from the world and European surveys. Comparative sociological interpretations can be found in Inglehart 2003 and Norris and Inglehart, 2004.

6. Several articles in *Research in the Social Scientific Study of Religion* 13, 2003 report findings from the RAMP project. See also Billiet *et al.* 2003.

7. See Lambert 1991.

8. An analysis of the 1998 ISSP survey in Western Europe showed that strong involvement in Christianity – regardless of whether it was Catholicism or Protestantism – led people to adopt a system of values that was very different from that of people with no religion. See Bréchon 2002b.

9. 'Independently of whether you go to church or not, would you say that you are a religious person, not a religious person, a convinced atheist?'.

10. Heaven and hell have very often figured in pictorial representations, but this is less true of sin – except around original sin. Sin is an abstract notion and is difficult to define. These three questions (about belief in hell, heaven or sin) are open to critical discussion both for being dichotomous and for the lack of precision in the belief in question. Nevertheless, strong statistical associations between the three variables suggest that all three of them belong to the world of Christian ideas.

11. Owing to the various meanings of 'reincarnation' and its possible confusion with the resurrection of the dead among certain Christians (according to earlier surveys), the wording of the question was made more precise in 1999: 'Do you believe in reincarnation, that we are born into this world again?'.

12. If respondents report that they believe in telepathy, it normally means that they know what it is. This term refers to the transmission of thought and the possibility of communicating between people at a distance. The religious dimension of this term can be stronger or weaker.

13. It is very difficult to compare data from the United Kingdom with those of other European countries as far as belonging to a faith is concerned since this country does not include in its 1999 questionnaire the filter question 'Do you belong to a religious denomination?' before asking what religion the respondent belongs to. It is well known that this lack of a filter has the effect of reducing the number of people who say they do not belong to any religion.

14. Religious pluralism is much more advanced in the USA, where the image of a flourishing competitive religious market is often brought to mind. Everyone is supposed to choose his or her religion and to change it in accordance with changes in what is on offer from religious groups, whilst demand is assumed to be nearly constant. See Stark and Bainbridge 1985; Iannaccone 1988, *Social Compass* 2006. The findings from quantitative American surveys show that younger generations are less religious than older ones, just as in all European countries. Like Ireland and Poland, the USA is still very religious but likely to experience some decline. On the puzzle of secularisation in the United States and Western Europe, see Norris and Inglehart 2004.

15. Davie 2002 reckons that religion is often considered anti-modern in Europe, while modernity actually makes the spread of diversity, especially religious diversity, possible.

16. As the importance of God in one's life is on a scale of 10, from 1 ('not at all important') to 10 ('very important'), the scores for the yes or no question and the question offering one of four positions have been inverted so that the calculation makes sense. They have also been recoded to give them more or less equal weighting in the scale. The scale goes up to 26 for the most believing (10 on the importance of God, 8 on belief in God, and 8 again on a personal God). Once the scale has been constructed like this it is then re-worked in order to identify the following three major categories: weak (up to 10), medium (from 11 to 22) and strong (from 23 to 26) believers.

17. Here again, addition of scores is the basis for the scale, with attendance at services going from 1 to 8, and the intensity of prayer from 1 to 7, and the fact of praying or meditating – a yes or no question – being scored 3 for yes and 6 for no. So, the scale goes from 5 to 21. It is re-structured into four categories: from 5 to 8 for strong practice, 9 to 13, 14 to 19, and finally 20 to 21 for virtually no practice.

18. There are three positions for the feeling of being religious, four for the importance of religion in life, and two for strength or comfort from religion. The scale, which goes from 3 to 9, is re-structured into three categories of 'strong' (3–4), 'moderate' (5–7) and 'weak' (8–9) religious feeling.

19. The scale is based on five indicators: 'to have a great deal or quite a lot of trust in the church', 'to think that your church (or 'the' churches, for those who do not belong to any) is (are) giving adequate answers to the moral problems and needs of individuals', 'the problem of family life', 'people's spiritual needs', and 'the social problems facing our country today'. People giving 4 or 5 positive answers are categorised as displaying lots of trust; 1 to 3 as qualified trust; and 0 as no trust at all.

20. This is not incompatible with *individual* changes of religious orientation which either make up for each other or, because of their weakness, allow the specificity of each generation to survive.

21. Michelat 1990 has often shown, for France, that the degree of integration in Catholicism – ranging from

regularly practising Catholic to 'no religion' – amounted to a valid synthetic variable. This dimension, even today, is still the one that best explains voting behaviour in France. This indicator of religious practice is actually an indirect measure of the strength of integration in a religious worldview.

22. The rule of weekly attendance is regularly repeated in Roman documents, and still appears in 2005 in the Compendium of the Catechism of the Catholic Church with a preface by Pope Benedict XVI. But in several European countries, this norm nowadays receives much less emphasis from clergy and bishops than some decades ago.

23. The ten indicators are: attendance at religious services at least once a month; being a member of a religious organisation; taking time for prayer, meditation or contemplation; praying to God at least once a week; defining oneself as a religious person; saying that religion is very, or quite, important in one's life; saying that one finds strength and comfort in religion; finding God important in one's life (with 8 to 10 points on a scale of 10); belief in a personal God or a vital force; and belief in life after death. Respondents with scores of 0 to 4 are categorised as having 'weak' religiosity; those with scores between 5 and 10 are categorised as having 'strong' religiosity.

24. The strength of the category where weak religiosity seems to have been transmitted tells us a lot about the current state of secularisation.

25. Using data from the 1990 EVS I constructed a similar typology on the basis of a religious identity scale and yes or no answers to the question 'Were you brought up religiously?'. Bréchon 1997.

26. Theorists of secularisation sometimes change their position completely, notably Peter Berger 2001. See also Hervieu-Léger 1999.

27. As Stoetzel had access only to data at one moment in time he could not really go beyond hypotheses. This underlines the importance of repeating the same survey in order to have longitudinal data.

28. Belgium, Denmark, France, Ireland, Italy, Spain, the Netherlands, United Kingdom, and West Germany.

29. Yves Lambert calculated that twelve indicators were declining, nine were stable and three were increasing.

30. I analysed the same phenomenon on the basis of the ISSP surveys in Bréchon 2001a.

31. See Bréchon 2004. Cohort analyses over time were conducted only for the nine European countries where comparative data for 1981 to 1999 were available: West Germany, Belgium, Denmark, Spain, France, Ireland, Italy, the Netherlands and the United Kingdom. Unfortunately, these analyses could not be performed with the attitude scales previously established. This was partly because some variables were missing in 1981 and partly because of minute differences in the same question.

32. Unlike Table 22.7 where, for each new wave of investigation, the 18 to 29 years olds are less likely to practise religion, there is no gap in the level of trust among young generations: the level is the same for the young people of 1981, 1990 and 1999 (read the Table diagonally). So, the indicator is constant over 18 years among young people but it is decidedly lower than for older generations.

33. This question has existed since 1981, but there was a very high and unexplained number of 'no answer' responses in the first wave (18 per cent in 1981 but only 2 per cent in 1990). These 'no answer' responses often come from elderly people and Catholics. It does not seem possible to compare this question on the three dates.

34. Concerning Russia, see Agadjanian 2006.

35. Ukraine is a country where Orthodoxy is deeply divided. Powerful religious competitiveness does not seem to promote much religious vitality. The divisions are often politico-religious between the Ukrainian Orthodox Church of the Kiev Patriarchate, the Ukrainian Orthodox Church of the Moscow Patriarchate, the Autocephalous Ukrainian Orthodox Church and the Ukrainian Uniate Church.

REFERENCES

Agadjanian, A. 2006. 'The Search for Privacy and the Return of a Great Narrative: Religion in a Post-Communist Society', *Social Compass* 53 (2): 169–84.

Ashford, S. and Timms, N. 1992. 'The Unchurching of Europe', in *What Europe thinks? A Study of Western European Values*. Aldershot: Ashgate.

Berger, P. 1967. *The Sacred Canopy: Elements of a Sociological Theory of Religion*. New York: Doubleday.

Berger, P. *et al.* 2001. *Le réenchantement du monde*. Paris: Bayard.

Billiet, J., Dobbelaere, K., Riis, O., Vilaça, H., Voyé, L. and Welkenhuysen-Gybels, J. 2003. 'Church Commitment and some consequences in Western and Central Europe', *Research in the Social Scientific Study of Religion* 14: 129–59.

Bréchon, P. 1997. 'Identité religieuse des jeunes en Europe'. In R. J. Campiche (ed.), *Cultures jeunes et religions en Europe*. Paris: Cerf: 47–96.

Bréchon, P. 1999. 'The measurement of religious beliefs in international surveys'. In N. Tos, P. Ph. Molher and B. Malnar (eds), *Modern society and values. A comparative analysis based on ISSP Project*. Ljubljana: Faculty of Social Sciences: 291–315.

Bréchon, P. 2001a. 'L'univers des croyances religieuses. La Suisse comparée à ses voisins (Allemagne, Autriche, France, Italie)'. In *International Social Survey Programme: religion et valeurs, problémes de méthode et comparaison internationale*. Lausanne: Université de Lausanne et Institut d'éthique sociale de la FEPS, *Cahier de l'Observatoire des religions en Suisse*, 1: 39–57.

Bréchon, P. 2001b. 'L'évolution du religieux', *Futuribles*, 260: 39–48.

Bréchon, P. 2002a. 'Mesurer les croyances religieuses'. In J-M. Donegani, S. Duchesne and F. Haegel (eds), *Aux frontières des attitudes: entre le politique et le religieux. Textes en hommage à Guy Michelat*. Paris: L'Harmattan: 153–72.

Bréchon, P. 2002b. 'Influence de l'intégration religieuse sur les attitudes: analyse comparative européenne', *Revue française de sociologie* 43 (3): 461–83. [In English translation as 'Influence of religious integration on attitudes: a comparative analysis of European countries', *Revue française de sociologie*, 2004, 45, Supplement: 27–49].

Bréchon, P. 2003. 'Integration into Catholicism and Protestantism in Europe: The Impact on Moral and Political Values'. In L. Halman and O. Riis (eds), *Religion in secularizing society. The European's Religion at the end of the 20th* century, Leiden: Brill: 114–61.

Bréchon, P. 2004. 'L'héritage chrétien de l'Europe occidentale: qu'en ont fait les nouvelles générations?', *Social Compass* 51 (2): 203–19.

Campiche, R. 1992. *Croire en Suisse(s). Analyse des résultats de l'enquête menée en 1988–1989 sur la religion des Suisses*. Lausanne: Age d'homme.

Campiche, R. 2004. *Les deux visages de la religion. Fascination et désenchantement*. Genéve: Labor et Fides.

Davie, G. 1994. *Religion in Britain since 1945. Believing without Belonging*. Oxford: Blackwell.

Davie, G. 2002. *Europe: the exceptional case. Parameters of faith in the modern world*. London: Darton, Longman and Todd.

Dobbelaere, K. 1981. 'Secularization: a Multidimensional Concept', *Current Sociology* 29 (2): 1–216.

Dobbelaere, K. 2002. *Secularization: An Analysis at Three Levels*, Brussels: P.I.E.-Peter Lang.

Durkheim, E. 1895. *Les règles de la méthode sociologique*. Paris: F. Alcan.

Durkheim, E. 1897. *Le suicide*, Paris: F. Alcan.

Glock, C. 1961. 'Y a-t-il un réveil religieux aux Etats-Unis?', *Archives de sociologie des religions* 12: 35–52.

Halman, L. and Riis, O. (eds) 1999. *Religion in secularizing society*. Tilburg: Tilburg University Press.

Hervieu-Léger, D. 1999. *Le pèlerin et le converti. La religion en mouvement*. Paris: Flammarion.

Iannaccone, L. 1988. 'A formal model of church and sect', *American Journal of Sociology* 94, Supplement: 241–68.

Inglehart, R. 2003 (ed.). *Human Values and Social Change*. London and Boston: Brill.

Inglehart, R. 2004. *Human beliefs and values: a cross-cultural sourcebook based on the 1999-2002 values surveys*. Mexico City: Siglo Veintiuno Editors.

Isambert, F-A. 1973. *Une nouvelle civilisation? Hommage á Georges Friedmann*. Paris: Gallimard.

Jagodsinski, W. and Dobbelaere, K. 1995. 'Secularization and Church religiosity', In J. W. Van Deth and E. Scarbrough (eds), *The Impact of Values*. Oxford: Oxford University Press: 76–119.

Lambert, Y. 1991. 'La "Tour de babel" des définitions de la religion'. *Social Compass* 38 (1): 73–85.

Lambert, Y. 1995. 'Vers une ère post-chrétienne?'. *Futuribles* 200: 85–111.

Lambert, Y. 2002. 'Religion: L'Europe à un tournant', *Futuribles* 277: 129–59.

Lambert, Y. 2004a. 'A Turning Point in Religious Evolution in Europe', *Journal of Contemporary Religion* 19 (1): 29–45.

Lambert, Y. 2004b. 'Des changements dans l'évolution religieuse de l'Europe et de la Russie', *Revue française de sociologie* 45 (2): 307–38.

Lambert, Y. 2005. 'Un regain religieux chez les jeunes d'Europe de l'Ouest et de l'Est'. In O. Galland and B. Roudet (eds), *Les jeunes Européens et leurs valeurs*. Paris: La découverte/INJEP: 65–91.

Martin, D. 1978. *A General Theory of Secularization*. Oxford: Blackwell.

Michelat, G. 1990. 'L'identité catholique des Français, II. Appartenance et socialisation religieuses', *Revue française de sociologie* 31 (4): 365–88.

Michelat, G. Potel, J. and Sutter, J. 2003. *L'héritage chrétien en disgrâce*. Paris: L'Harmattan.

Michelat, G., Potel, J., Sutter, J. and Maître, J. 1991. *Les Français sont-ils encore catholiques ?* Paris: Cerf.

Norris, P. and Inglehart, R. 2004. *Sacred and Secular. Religion and Politics Worldwide*. Cambridge: Cambridge University Press.

Robinson, W. S. 1950. 'Ecological correlations and behavior of individuals'. *American Sociological Review* 15: 351–57.

Social Compass 2006. *Salvation Goods and the Religious Markets*, (Jörg Stolz ed.), 53 (1).

Stark, R. and Bainbridge, W.S. 1985. *The Future of Religion. Secularisation, Revival and Cult formation*. Berkeley, CA: University of California Press.

Stark, R. and Glock, C. 1968. *American Piety: the Nature of Religious Commitment*. Berkeley, CA: University of California Press.

Stoetzel, J. 1983. *Les valeurs du temps présent: une enquête européenne*. Paris: PUF.

Tocqueville, Alexis de 1969. *Democracy in America*, 2 vols, Garden City, NY: Doubleday & Co. (edited by J.P. Mayer) [*De la démocratie en Amérique*, 1st edition 1840].

Zrinščak, S. 2004. 'Generations and atheism: Patterns of response to Communist rule among different generations and countries', *Social compass* 51 (2): 221–34.

23

Rethinking the Relationship Between Ethnicity and Religion

PETER KIVISTO

Given the growing ethnic and religious diversity of the advanced industrial nations, it is not surprising that sociologists of religion have in recent years become increasingly interested in exploring once again the intersections of ethnicity and religion in an era of globalization. The consequence of the mass migration of people from the nations of the South and East to those of the North and West, the salience of this topic has stimulated a substantial expansion of research agendas by both sociologists of religion and immigration studies scholars. The relationship between these two modes of identity and communal affiliation is not a new topic in the field, and as a result, today's researchers are able to build on a tradition of empirical inquiry and conceptual developments deriving from both the sociology of religion and from ethnic and immigration studies. This is particularly the case in the United States, where considerable attention in the past has been devoted to the religion of immigrants during the last great migratory wave, as well as to the religion of the black descendants of slaves. At the same time, given certain limitations to the lessons that can be learned from past efforts and due to some of the novel

features of the present moment, we are indeed presented with, as Robert Wuthnow (2004) puts it, 'the challenge of diversity.'

In this chapter, I will argue that there is a need to rearticulate the sociology of religion's commonly employed ideal-typical formulation of the relationship between ethnicity and religion. In making this case, two recent developments are of particular relevance to that task, R. Stephen Warner's (1993) 'new paradigm' for the study of religion and more broadly construed empirical and theoretical trends in immigration studies. In addition, the relevance of Rogers Brubaker's (2004) idea of 'ethnicity without groups' for this task will be examined. What follows, then, represents an effort to both take stock of how sociologists have framed the relationship and an indication of what I consider to be some of the key empirical lacunae and conceptual issues that ought to be considered in the future.

Before proceeding, the following points are helpful in explaining the particular path taken herein. First, as will quickly become clear, the United States is the primary geographic focus. There are a few reasons for this, including the fact that this is the literature I know best and simply due to the fact that the number of articles and books produced in recent years in this single nation has grown dramatically. However, there is another reason as well: it is my sense that much of the development of contemporary research agendas and theoretical work has occurred in the US, for better or worse given the enduring question about whether or not we ought to frame the American experience in terms of exceptionalism.

Second, the bulk of the discussion focuses on immigrant groups. Such groups, obviously, do not constitute all ethnic groups. Rather, they are but one of a subset of various ethnic groups (Kivisto and Ng 2005: 29–41). The other subsets include indigenous peoples (e.g., First Nations Peoples in Canada and Aboriginals in Australia), ethno-national groups (e.g., Scots in the United Kingdom and Basques in Spain), and the involuntary migrants caught up generations ago in the international slave trade (i.e., African Americans).

The reason for the decision to concentrate on immigrant groups is similar to that suggested above in justifying the US focus of the chapter: sociologists of religion have devoted far more attention in recent years to immigrant religions than they have to the religions of these other subsets. For instance, there are only 52 articles listed in Sociological Abstracts dealing with the religions of indigenous peoples, and in the majority of these cases the articles are concerned with developing nations. Ethno-nationalism and religion yields 114 results, primarily focusing on Russia and Eastern Europe, Asia, and Africa. Of the 238 results under the rubric African American religion, a majority of the articles are concerned with the social psychological dimension, exploring for example, the ability of religious belief to reduce levels of stress and to enhance feelings of well-being. Many of these articles are concerned with such phenomena in general terms. Typically, race is used as one of a number of standard demographic variables to be examined, with a typical article reporting on differences between blacks and whites. In contrast, there were 1,017 articles concerned with immigration and religion and a substantial majority of those articles focused specifically on the US.

CONCEPTUALIZING AND PROBLEMATIZING THE SUBJECT

Before turning to an examination of recent research on immigrant religions, it is necessary to first enter into a discussion of the ways that the connections between ethnicity and religion have been conceptualized in the past. According to both Nathan Glazer and Daniel Patrick Moynihan in the introduction to their edited volume *Ethnicity* (1975: 1) and Werner Sollors in *Beyond Ethnicity* (1986: 21–4), the term ethnicity is of rather recent vintage. Sollors contends that it became part of the language of sociology only with the appearance of W. Lloyd Warner's Yankee City series, the classic study of Newburyport, Massachusetts, that inquired into the processes of adjustment and absorption of the second- and third-generation offspring of immigrants who arrived between the last two decades of the nineteenth century and the passage of immigration restriction legislation in 1924. Not long after the Yankee City works appeared Everett C. Hughes (1971 [1948]: 153) characterized the term 'ethnic group' as 'a colorless catch-all much used by anthropologists and sociologists.'

But what exactly do the terms 'ethnic,' 'ethnicity,' and 'ethnic group' signify? In fact, an earlier and oft-quoted formulation derives from Weber (1978: 389), who defined ethnic groups as 'those human groups that entertain a subjective belief in their common descent because of similarities of physical type or of customs or both, or because of memories of colonization and migration.' He goes on to contend that the belief may or may not be grounded in 'an objective blood relationship.' There are three pertinent features to this definition that are worth highlighting. First, the ethnic group is a social construct – and thus not an ascriptive given – that emanates from the sentiments and beliefs of its constituent members. Second, racial groups are construed as a subset of the ethnic groups. Though more implicit, to the extent that religious affiliation is an aspect of shared customs, religious identities at least in some instances can be viewed as reinforcing ethnic identities. Conceptually, ethnic groups and religious groups can be overlapping, intersecting, or unconnected. Third, the emphasis on those claiming group membership as the sole arbiters of defining the ethnic group fails to appreciate the role of others in imposing group identities on the less powerful and more marginalized sectors of a society (surprisingly given Weber's usual attentiveness to power in social relations).

It is common to compare the ethnic group to the kinship group. Weber did so (1978: 389) by contending that, 'Ethnic membership differs from the kinship group precisely by being a presumed identity, not a group with concrete social action, like the latter.' Although this is not an entirely transparent claim, one assumes that the reason for making the comparison in the first place is because of the assumption that the two types of affiliation bear a family resemblance. This is clearly what E. K. Francis (1947) thought when he defined the ethnic group as a subtype of *Gemeinschaft* groups, defining it in terms of its involuntary nature and the emotive bonds between members. In so doing, he contended that these two features of the ethnic group mean that, although a secondary group, it bears some of the characteristic features of the most important primary group, the family. In a somewhat different take, Craig Calhoun (1997: 40) has sought to position the ethnic group in 'an intermediary position between kinship and nationality.'

In yet another attempt to construct a parsimonious definition of the ethnic group that built on Weber while attending to its problematic features, Christiano *et al.* (2002: 155) proposed the following formulation: 'ethnic groups are composed of people who are presumed, by members of the group itself and by outsiders, to have a shared collective origin and history, and a common set of cultural attributes that serve to establish boundaries between the group and the larger society.' This definition does not directly address race, but one can use this definition to locate racial groups as a subset of ethnic groups – or to speak of 'racialized ethnicity.' Left unaddressed is how it is that a group becomes a group. This was an issue that Weber (1978: 389) was aware of when he noted that 'ethnic membership does

not constitute a group; it only facilitates group formation …' The sociological question then becomes, how is group formation facilitated?

Although posed somewhat differently, this is the question that Rogers Brubaker (2004; see also Brubaker 2003; Calhoun 2003) addresses in his brief on behalf of treating 'ethnicity without groups.' In making his case, he takes aim at two targets: what he calls 'groupism' and aspects or versions of the social constructionist model (though he is himself a social constructionist). Addressing the first of these targets, the central complaint is that it constitutes a form of essentialism, one that encourages a perspective that treats ethnicity as a substance or entity rather than in 'relational, processual, dynamic, eventful, and disaggregated terms' (Brubaker 2004: 11). His proposal is indebted to the theoretical perspective of Bourdieu, seeking to replace both a groupist and an individualistic orientation with a new analytical vocabulary. In so doing, he aspires to revitalize social constructionism.

In order to do so, Brubaker (2004: 64–87) sketches the outline of what it might mean to treat 'ethnicity as cognition.' He contends that, 'What cognitive perspectives suggest, in short, is that race, ethnicity, and nation are not entities in the world but ways of seeing the world' (Brubaker 2004: 81). More specifically, he is interested in exploring a topic rooted in Durkheimian theory, categorization, for '[w]ithout categories, the world would be a "blooming, buzzing confusion"' (Brubaker 2004: 71). While much of his work is designed to specify what a research program might look like and whom it might borrow from, he does make one observation relevant to the topic at hand. Referring to the debate within ethnic studies between primordialists (Geertz 1973; Shils 1975; van den Berghe 1981) and circumstantialists (Glazer and Moynihan 1975; Gleason 1983), he contends that contrary to the common assumption, they ought to be viewed as 'complementary rather than mutually exclusive' (Brubaker 2004: 83).

At a moment in sociology when social constructivism frames this debate, the typical assessment of primordialism is to dismiss it as yet another instance of essentialism.

However, Brubaker cautions, this represents a misreading of primordialism. Referring specifically to the seminal work of Geertz (1963), he stresses that what is considered to be a primordial attachment to the givens of cultural life are in fact imputed or 'presumed' givens by social actors and not by social scientists. As Brubaker (2004: 83) sums up, 'In fact, on the primordialist account, it is participants, not the analysts, who are the real primordialists, treating ethnicity as naturally given and immutable.' The task at hand for future research agendas is to – making use of the work of cognitive psychologists and cognitive anthropologists – begin to understand when and under what circumstances participants latch onto 'the givens' and when they abandon or ignore them.

Despite Brubaker's efforts, it is unlikely that sociologists will soon abandon the idea of ethnic groups. At the very least, it serves as a useful shorthand for the constructivist consequences resulting from the claims-making strategies of social actors, those perceived to be within and those without particular ethnic boundaries. The value of Brubaker's complaint is that it does manage to call attention to the fact that ethnicity ought to be perceived as a highly variable and complex phenomenon subject to historical transmutations and transformations.

Linking Ethnicity and Religion

This is evident in efforts to categorize the varied ways that ethnicity and religion can be related to each other. Sociologists of ethnicity have long referred to some ethnic groups as 'religio-ethnic.' To fall into this category, a group would be defined in such a manner that its members' religious identity and ethnic affiliation are deeply embedded in each other, and in combination they serve to define the group (Abramson 1975). Whereas German immigrants to the United States would not be defined as a religio-ethnic group, Jews are often considered to be the paradigmatic instance of such a group. Other groups that would readily be included in this categorization are the Amish and Hutterites. However, this is a more

complicated relationship than the term might suggest, as the Jewish case attests. Does being a Jew depend on being a religiously observant Jew, or can an atheist, freethinker, or convert to Christianity be a Jew. What about individuals who convert to Judaism? From Brubaker's perspective, it would be argued that the answer to the question depends entirely on the claims-making success of various actors, individual and collective, in the process of advancing alternative definitions of the situation in competition with other claims-makers. As such, any religio-ethnic label amounts to an ongoing accomplishment requiring persistent efforts aimed at maintaining the connection between religion and ethnicity. In other words, the label is always historically contingent.

Harold Abramson (1980), in an entry on 'Religion' in the *Harvard Encyclopedia of American Ethnic Groups,* made the following assertion:

> Religion becomes a major and consequential reason for the development of ethnicity. The Armenian Orthodox, the Chinese Buddhists, the Finnish Lutherans, the German Jews, the Scottish Presbyterians, the Sephardic Jews, the Southern Baptists, the Spanish-speaking Catholics, and the Utah Mormons are only a few of the groups in which ethnicity and religion are inextricably linked.

Given what Abramson considers to be the rather broadly conceived linkage between religion and ethnicity in the American case – primarily a consequence of being a settler nation where a vast majority of the population is composed of immigrants and their offspring – he moves beyond the earlier singular notion of religio-ethnic as an adequate concept to capture that variability by postulating four types of relationship see Figure 23.1.

The first type most closely approximates what the original term means. In this type, religion serves as the 'major foundation' of ethnicity. The examples he cites are Jews, Hutterites, Amish, and Mormons (Abramson 1980: 869). Leave aside the fact that the Mormons are a suspect example, for it is not clear in what ways they ought to be treated as an ethic group at all. What he appears to have in mind is a sense of ethnic peoplehood inextricably rooted in a particular religion.

In the second type, 'a particular ethnic group may be grounded in a relatively unique religion, but one that has a more marked association with a distinct territory or homeland, a particular language, or an evolving sense of nationality' (Abramson 1980: 870). The examples cited include Dutch Reformed, the Church of England, the Serbian Orthodox, and Scottish Presbyterianism. Implied in the effort to distinguish this type from the preceding one is the assumption that the relationship between religion and ethnicity is more historically circumstantial than is the case for the first type. In other words, the linkage is somewhat looser and more subject to change, particularly to erosion.

The third type is, according to Abramson, the most common. It refers to a situation in which a number of distinct ethnic groups share a common religious tradition. This would include the Nordic groups and Germans who shaped American Lutheranism, the Irish, Polish, Italian, Mexican, and other groups who are major constituent components of Roman Catholicism in the United States, black and white Baptists, and more recently the many nations that together form the composite Islamic population of the nation (Abramson 1980: 870). The final type is considered to represent the smallest of the four. Here the relationship is very loose, as religion plays a very small and insignificant part in the definition of an ethnic identity. The examples pointed to include the Romany, a tiny group in the United States, and American Indians. The latter can be debated, but it is not clear if Abramson means the traditional religions of Indian tribal units or is thinking about the fact that a sizeable segment of the Native American population has over time converted to Christianity.

As is the case with such typologies, it is designed to offer a snapshot at a particular point in time. As such, there is a static quality to this schema. It is not capable of capturing the changes that have occurred over time. Given their derivation, such ideal types are necessarily historically variable, and as such when the gap between the ideal and real become too pronounced, it becomes necessary to revise or reformulate the type. Religious change during the last half of the past century has called into question the continuing utility of these types. Take, for instance, Lutherans. While it is certainly true that almost all Lutherans in the United States up to the first half of the twentieth century could trace their origins to one of the Nordic countries or to Germany, and even today one can detect the significance of the linkage between ethnic background and Lutheranism, in fact much has changed. First, outreach efforts to both African Americans and Hispanic and Asian immigrants have resulted in increasing the ethnic diversity of the denomination (Granquist 2003). However, far more significant has been the impact of intermarriage between Nordics or Germans and others of European ancestry. Thus, the typical Lutheran congregation today looks considerably more pan-European than in the past.

IDEAL TYPE	CHARACTERISTICS	EXAMPLE
Ethnic Fusion	Powerful linkage	Amish
Ethnic Religion	Ethnicity reinforces religion	Greek Orthodox
Religious Ethnicity	Religion shapes ethnicity	Irish Catholic
Ethnic Autonomy	Weak linkage	Romany

Figure 23.1 *Summary of the Abramson and Hammond/Warner Typology*

Adopting and modifying, rather than substantively revisiting, Abramson's typology, Phillip Hammond and Kee Warner (1993) attempted to take stock of the ways that the relationship between religion and ethnicity had been transformed by the end of the last century. As such they sought to link process to structure. They depicted two processes working in tandem to effect a progressive loosening of the ties that had heretofore linked religion to ethnicity: assimilation and secularization. Contending that both ethnicity and religion are 'vulnerable to forces that diminish their social importance,' they consider assimilation and secularization to be accurate characterizations of parallel declines in salience of these two aspects of identity, attributing both to the advance of individualism in the society at large (Hammond and Warner 1993: 56–7).

Within this general perspective, they turn to the Abramson typology, giving names to the three types they consider relevant to the American scene (the fourth type, the most inconsequential in the original formulation, is simply ignored). The type wherein religion is the major foundation of ethnicity is called 'ethnic fusion.' Such groups may succeed in maintaining the powerful linkage between religion and ethnicity. But they do so at a price, which is that the 'very strength [of the bond] may keep such groups small and insulated' (Hammond and Warner 1993: 59). If we exclude Mormons as an inappropriate group for this type, what is obvious about these groups (Hutterites, Amish, and Jews) is that they represent examples of non-proselytizing religions. As such, they represent a side stream in the larger currents of American religion.

For this reason, Hammond and Warner focus on the other two types, which they defined as ethnic religion (e.g., Greek Orthodox and Dutch Reformed) and religious ethnicity (e.g., Irish, Italian, and Polish Catholics). They note a crucial differentiating characteristic of ethnic versus religious identity: the former is perceived to be inheritable, while the latter is not. As they point out, although the salience of ethnicity might erode and even disappear, it is unlikely that people would engage in ethnic switching. Such, of course, is not the case with religious affiliation. Nonetheless, they contend that the evidence they bring to bear suggests that assimilation and secularization are mutually reinforcing processes. Moreover, they think that both are occurring in all of the groups they examined, though the rate of change varies based on whether or not the groups are the victims of discriminatory exclusion and marginalization. When groups are so victimized, the pace of both assimilation and secularization is slowed. Finally, they contend that in the future the connection between religion and ethnicity will erode, due chiefly to the fact that as religion increasingly becomes a matter of individual choice, 'ethnicity, along with other background characteristics, will have a declining effect in determining religious identity' (Hammond and Warner 1993: 66).

A curious feature of this study is that, despite framing it in terms of the impacts of the dual processes of assimilation and secularization, in fact there is nothing in the data that are employed that would permit an examination of whether or not secularization is occurring. It does address standard measures of assimilation (evidence of mixed versus single ancestry, in-group or out-group marriage, and a measure of the level of subjective attachment to people from one's ancestral background). However, no similar measures are included that could be construed as measuring the relative social significance of religion for respondents. Thus, although the authors can make a case that the role of ethnicity in determining religious identity has declined, they cannot argue on the basis of the data that religious identity itself has eroded.

Assimilation and the New Paradigm

This raises a critical question: what if assimilation is occurring in American society but secularization is not? This is the prospect implicitly raised by R. Stephen Warner (1993) in his influential essay on the emergence of a new paradigm for the study of American religion, which coincidentally was published the same year as the Hammond and Warner article.

Stressing here (Warner 1993: 1055) and else-where (Warner 1997, 2005; Lechner 1997) that he is sketching out the contours of a paradigm shift and has not yet developed a new theory, Warner's target is the old secularization para-digm that he associates in particular with the early work of Peter Berger (1967, 1970). Warner is, of course, not the first person to critique secularization theory (Hadden 1987). Nor is he the first to search for a new model, for rational choice theorists have earlier made their case (Bainbridge and Stark 1984; Finke and Stark 1988; Iannaccone 1992) for an approach to religion modeled after economic markets.

In Warner's critique of the old paradigm, he makes two central points. First, it is predicated on a perspective that is chiefly psychological and cultural in character (see also, Hirschman 2004). Inasmuch as this is the case, it is insuffi-ciently attentive to institutional analysis. Second, although it purports to offer a general theory of religion, in fact it reflects the European biases of its proponents, who have tended to be of European origin and who have implicitly treated religious change in Europe as a synecdoche for change elsewhere, or at least everywhere that modernization was occurring (Warner 1993: 1046; see also Christiano et al. 2002: 67–8). In contrast, the new paradigm, despite other differences among those whom he sees as advocates for an alternative to the old, places a premium on institutional analysis. In Warner's formulation, the paradigm is intended to lay the ground-work for constructing a theory of American religion rather than a general theory of religion. Warner advocates, in effect, what Merton long ago called middle-range theory.

The key to the new paradigm, he contends, is not, as some of the above-noted figures might propose, an economic model. Rather, the new paradigm is defined 'by the idea that disestablishment is the norm' (Warner 1993: 1053). That being said, the idea of the market is relevant to the paradigm. Warner views the 'sacred canopy' framework of the old paradigm as being shaped by the idea of religious monopoly that structured European history from Constantine forward. In contrast, the new paradigm sees in the Second Great Awakening

in nineteenth-century America the contours of the distinctive pattern of American religious history. Borrowing from the new institutional-ism, he argues that competition between reli-gious groups seeking their market share in an essentially laissez-faire contest that stimulates innovative responses to societal change rep-resents an 'institutionally specific cultural system' (Friedland and Alford 1991: 234). Such a system creates a 'social space for cultural pluralism' (Warner 1993: 1058).

In this regard, Warner (2005: 109) has recently suggested that his take on the new par-adigm bears a family resemblance to rational choice theory, but ought not to be confused with it. He seeks to correct those who in his estimation have misread his essay and so concluded (Christiano et al. 2002: 42). At the same time, he does not seek to replace, but to complement rational choice. His idea of a plu-ralistic religious market speaks to the supply side of the equation, and here the insights of a rational choice perspective are germane. However, he is not convinced, in contrast to figures such as Stark and Finke (2000) and Iannaccone (1990), that rational choice theory can adequately address the demand side of the equation.

To address this issue, Warner has recently proposed introducing the concept of ambiva-lence into the new paradigm, borrowing from Smelser (1998: 5), who employs a Freudian-inspired conceptualization of the term that treats it as an affective state characterized by holding simultaneously two opposed emotions toward an object: attraction and repulsion, love and hate. Ambivalence is at the root of obsessive/compulsive disorders, but it is also evident where no obvious pathology is present. In particular, situations of dependency are sites for the generation of ambivalence, with the child/parent relationship being the most obvi-ous and universal example. Smelser (1998: 6) writes that, 'Because ambivalence is such a *powerful, persistent, unresolvable, volatile, generalizable,* and *anxiety-provoking* feature of the human condition, people defend against experiencing it in many ways.' Turning to Freud's summary of the options people have available to them, Smelser identifies the following potential responses: repression, reversion, displacement, projection, and splitting. Referring to Albert Hirschman's (1970) work, Smelser notes that actors can respond to their ambivalent relationships in three ways: by exit (which stresses the negative side of ambivalence), loyalty (which represses the negative side), and voice (which seeks to steer a middle course between the positive and negative).

One can make three observations about importing ambivalence into the new paradigm. First, Warner is supplementing the institutional focus of the original formulation with a psychological underpinning. In doing so, he makes a move that draws him closer to the old paradigm, which he had criticized for being insufficiently sociological because it stressed psychological factors impacting religion. Second, the paradigm has shifted from a case on behalf of American exceptionalism, which necessarily makes it something other than a general theory of religion to one that, at least in part because of the universal nature of ambivalence, moves beyond the specificities of the American experience. Third, Warner does not make a move from a psychoanalytic perspective on ambivalence to a sociological one, ignoring, for example, the approaches of Merton (1976) or Levine (1985). He does, however, seek to illustrate the ways that individuals react to ambivalence by using examples derived from his research on immigrant religion.

IMMIGRANT RELIGION

In addition to his role in articulating the new paradigm, Warner is one of the most prominent sociologists of religion to have advanced the study of the post-1965 immigrants and religion (Warner 1998a, 1998b), a topic that he turned to during the 1990s but remained an underdeveloped research area at the time the new paradigm was first formulated (Warner 1998a). Since then a substantial body of research has been produced, beginning with one of the earliest collaborative projects, the New Ethnic and Immigrant Congregations Project (NEICP), directed by Warner with

methodological assistance provided by Judith Wittner (Warner and Wittner 1998). This project sought to reflect something of the diversity of the new immigrants' religious identities. Thus, it included immigrant faiths that existed within the parameters of the Protestant-Catholic-Jewish religious pantheon described in the 1950s by Will Herberg (1955), including Mayan Catholics, Korean and Chinese Protestants, Mexican Pentecostals, and Iranian Jews. However, it also included adherents to major world religions that had only a limited historical presence in the U.S, such as Indian Hindus and a multi-ethnic Muslim congregation. Moreover, it also included practitioners of new religious movements such as Rastafarians from Jamaica and syncretistic Haitians committed to both Vodou and Catholicism.

This research program was followed by similar comparative projects, such as the Religion, Ethnicity and New Immigrants Research (RENIR) project directed by Helen Rose Ebaugh and Janet Saltzman Chafetz (2000). Unlike the NEICP study, where the case studies were conducted in various locales throughout the country, RENIR was a community study that focused solely on the Houston area. The more recently completed project, under the directorship of Karen I. Leonard et al. (2005) derives its case studies from across the nation. Like the Warner and Wittner study, there is an evident desire to be as expansive as possible within the confines of funding and other constraints on the project. In short, these collaborative projects and similar individual studies have sought to tap into the growing diversity of the American religious scene. In so doing, they have begun to redress the heretofore marginalization of the study of religion in immigration studies (Kivisto 1993, 1995; Christiano 1991).

Given that desire to carve out a new research field, it is useful to consider briefly in what ways and to what extent American religion has been transformed due to the arrival of the post-1965 immigrants. There are two ways of responding, one that looks at the extent to which the new immigrants differ from the native population and the other at the size of these groups as a percentage of the population as a whole. According to the findings of the New Immigrant Survey Pilot (NIS-P), two-thirds of the new immigrants are Christian. While this means that a sizeable majority fall within the nation's traditional religious patterns, this figure also indicates that the new immigrants are less likely to be Christian than the population at large, where 82 percent report being Christian. In addition, the percentage of immigrant Christians who are Catholic is considerably higher than the general population – 42 percent versus 22 percent (Jasso *et al.* 2003: 218).

Members of non-Judeo-Christian religions are four times larger among the ranks of the new immigrants than among the native born, and they are slightly more inclined to report no religious preferences (Jasso *et al.* 2003: 218). While becoming proportionally larger, these groups began with very small numbers and thus despite substantial growth they remain a very small percentage of the overall population. Thus, although there were three to four times more members of non-traditional faiths in the US at the end of the last century compared to 1970, they constitute less than 3 percent of the total population (Smith 2002a: 582). Within this framework, Muslims probably represent no more than 1 percent of the population (Smith 2002b: 414).

Despite their relatively small size, the new immigrants are in many ways recasting the religious landscape. For one thing, immigration continues and this means that in the future Catholics will likely continue to arrive in larger numbers than Protestants, while non-traditional religions will also continue to grow. Moreover, given the concentrations of the new immigrants in certain states and major cities, their impact is also concentrated. The bottom line is that, contrary to the somewhat misleading title of Diana Eck's (2001) book, the nation has not changed from being a 'Christian country' to becoming 'the world's most religiously diverse nation.' Rather, it simultaneously remains a predominantly (though slightly less so) Christian nation and has become an even more religiously pluralistic society.

Four Recurring Themes

With this in mind, what are the major themes that have been explored by the scholars of the new immigrants and religion? Warner (1998a: 14–27) identifies four themes that structured the NEICP project. The first involves the role that religion plays in the efforts of immigrants to renegotiate their identities in the process of adjusting to and claiming a place in the land of settlement. The second theme, related to the first, is that immigrants' abilities to negotiate their identities is predicated on the nature of the relationship they have with the host society in general and with religious host communities in particular. Thus, some immigrants seek to embrace while others seek to distance themselves from their 'proximal host' (a concept Warner borrows from Mittelberg and Waters 1992). The third theme is that immigrant religions typically involve institutional reframing such that the religious institutions from the homeland are recast in the congregational mold characteristic of the disestablishment pattern deeply embedded in American religious history. Warner distinguishes the congregational form from two other types of church polity, the episcopal and presbyterian, defining it as 'a local *voluntary religious association* [emphasis in the original], usually culturally homogeneous and often legally constituted as a non-profit corporation controlled by its laity and administered by a professional clergy.' The religious environment that new immigrants enter is one in which many religious organizations have over the course of time adopted the congregational form, including Presbyterians and Catholics among Christian groups, and among non-Christians by Jews (Warner 1998a: 21). The fourth theme concerns issues related to the internal differentiation within congregations. Two topics in particular have constituted the primary foci of research agendas: the redefinition of gender roles and generational change. All of these themes are concerned – implicitly or explicitly – with the ways in which and the extent to which immigrant groups become incorporated into the larger society's mainstream (Alba and Nee 2003).

An examination of the programmatic overviews of other collaborative projects or edited collections on immigrant religions reveals that these are recurring themes, even if not articulated in quite the same terms (Orsi 1999; Yoo 1999; Ebaugh and Chafetz 2000; Kwon *et al.* 2001; Min and Kim 2002; Haddad *et al.* 2003; Carnes and Yang 2004; Leonard *et al.* 2005). At the same time, these themes have been further refined and elaborated. This is evident in the Fenggang Yang and Helen Rose Ebaugh's (2001) survey of recent research. They illustrate, for instance, the widespread agreement with Warner about the centrality of the congregational form, pointing to research that has studied such aspects of this institutional type as its structural characteristics, its voluntary nature, the role of lay leadership, the expansion of services to members, the emergence of organizational networks, and the adaptation of rituals to a congregational format. They also point to the fact that the levels of financial, social, and human capital immigrants possess and the nature of the reception they receive from the host society are crucial variables in determining their location in American society either in the mainstream or on the margins.

At the same time, Yang and Ebaugh (2001: 278–81) identify two other research themes not evident in Warner's formulation. The first involves what they term 'returning to theological foundations,' which they contend is a pervasive response to the multicultural character of American society. The returning to roots can take various forms, ranging from an inward rejection of 'the world' and an affirmation of an insular conservatism (and in this regard, being akin to fundamentalism) to a more self-reflexive casting off or purging of a theological system from various historically-grounded cultural practices that are deemed to be non-essential to the core tenets of the faith. The second topic Yang and Ebaugh (2001: 281–83) address is 'including other peoples,' by which they mean the shift from ethnically exclusive religions to more universalistic ones. While this might mean the inclusion of native-born Americans into non-traditional religions such as Buddhism or Islam, it also means – more

significantly – the willingness to move from ethnic religions organizations to panethnic or cosmopolitan ones.

Religion and Transnational Migration

Recently an additional theme has been introduced in the study of immigrant religion: transnationalism. Given the centrality at the moment of the term in immigration studies in general and increasingly in research on immigrant religion in particular, it merits sustained attention. Transnationalism is a term that began to be applied to immigration studies in the early 1990s, initially at the initiative of cultural anthropologists Nina Glick Schiller and associates (Basch *et al.* 1994; Glick Schiller *et al.* 1995; Glick Schiller 1997, 1999), but further developed and refined by others, in particular by sociologist Alejandro Portes (1996a,b, 1998; Portes *et al.* 1999) and political scientist Thomas Faist (1998, 2000). Transnationalism refers to 'the processes by which immigrants forge and sustain multi-stranded relations that link together their societies of origin and settlement' (Basch *et al.* 1994: 7), which means that transnational immigrants 'live aspects of their social, economic, and political lives in at least two settings' (Levitt 2003: 850).

In some of its earliest formulations, it was presumed that due to new communication technologies and advanced modes of travel, transnationalism served to distinguish contemporary immigrants from those in the past; today's immigrants were transnational while immigrants in the past quickly severed their homeland ties. Second, it was assumed that transnationalism was a widespread phenomenon among immigrant groups. Finally, it was claimed that transnational ties were likely to persist over time and across generations. All three of these assumptions have been challenged on empirical and conceptual grounds, and in the process transnationalism is now generally seen as one possible mode of immigrant incorporation that applies to some but not all immigrants. Moreover, it may be far more temporally limited than first imagined, with some suspecting that it is primarily a phenomenon of the immigrant generation (Foner 2000; Kivisto 2001, 2003; Morawska 2001; Waldinger and Fitzgerald 2004).

Distinguishing three types of transnationalism – economic, political, and sociocultural – Portes and his associates have conducted the most empirically rigorous examinations of the scope and range of the first two types. In the case of economic transnationalism, they have concluded that the proportion of new immigrants who can be classified as transnational entrepreneurs probably does not exceed 3 percent (Portes et al. 2002). While the number of transnational labor migrants is no doubt considerably higher, at the moment we do not have a good read on the number of workers who divide their work lives between two or more nations, but it is clearly more likely for Mexicans and some immigrants from the Caribbean than for Asian-origin migrants. In the case of political transnationalism, Guarnizo et al. (2003) deflate the claim that such border-crossing activities are widespread and growing. In fact, only a small minority of contemporary immigrants regularly engage in transnational political activities. This is true despite the dramatic increase in dual citizenship (Kivisto and Faist 2007). In both instances, there is no attempt to deny the significance of transnationalism, but rather to locate it in terms of complex modes of immigrant incorporation.

Religious transnationalism as a critical aspect of sociocultural transnationalism has only recently begun to receive the scholarly attention that it merits. As Levitt (2003: 849) observes, there are two ways that one can speak about religious transnationalism, one involving immigrants and the other concerned with 'the ways in which global or world religions create a transnational civil society that challenges nation-states and security interests as they have been traditionally understood.' Of course, in concrete instances, these two modes of religious transnationalism can often be expected to be intertwined (Levitt 2004).

Members of the immigrant generation often seek to transplant their religious heritages in the new homeland in an effort to counter the alienating, or uprooting, character of the migration experience. Codified in particular by the highly influential works of Oscar Handlin (1952) and Will Herberg (1955), a substantial body of literature on the last great migratory wave in the US emerged that treated religion in terms of its capacity to provide psychological compensation for individuals living in an alien, confusing, and often hostile world (Hirschman 2004). One way of preserving the particularistic, generally ethnic, character of a religious heritage was to bring religious leaders from the homeland to the immigrant community. Perhaps the paradigmatic instance of this practice were the Irish, who imported large numbers of priests and nuns from Ireland, thereby making it possible to not only create a Catholic presence in the US that was constructed in the image of the Church in Ireland, but also to achieve a position of hegemony within the American Catholic community (often to the dismay of other Catholic groups, particularly the Poles and the Italians). There is often a one-way quality to this process of transplantation.

Although there is abundant evidence to suggest that immigrants in the past did what they could to remain connected with the homeland, this was often difficult. In the first place, limited resources conspired against it, along with the inherent limitations of existing modes of communication (the letter being the chief vehicle) and transportation. However, there was another factor making ongoing involvement with the homeland difficult. Elites, political and cultural, tended to be quite hostile to emigrants, who were depicted as traitors to the homeland. This included religious elites. The net result was that the movement of religious cultures was essentially a one-way street, from the homeland to the land of settlement. Given the limitations of the capacity to draw on the resources and even the memories of the homeland over time, the result was that the linkages between religion and ethnic ancestry loosened, particularly for the second generation and beyond, Marcus Lee Hansen's (1938) claim about third generation return notwithstanding.

Much has changed between the last migratory wave and the present one, and it is for this reason that the idea of transnational religion is beginning to receive attention. Among the key features of today's immigrants is the fact that they are able to stay in touch with those who remained behind, chiefly due to phone cards and relatively cheap telephone costs and the internet. They are also able to take advantage of improved and generally affordable transportation systems, ranging from cheap airfares to distant lands to chartered buses in the case of immigrants from Mexico. In addition, religious elites in the homeland are no longer inclined to be hostile to emigrants, but instead often attempt to facilitate ongoing contacts (Fitzgerald 2004). For their part, the immigrants frequently take an active interest in homeland religious practices and institutions. This can entail pilgrimages to religious sites in the land of origin and the sending of remittances to help sustain religious institutions.

Cecelia Menjívar's (2000; see also Menjívar 2006) insightful comparison of Catholic and evangelical Protestant Salvadorans illustrates both the potential for and the limitations of religious transnationalism, which in this case suggested that transnational religion has a greater presence among Protestants rather than Catholics. Manuel Vásquez and Marie Friedmann Marquardt's (2003: 119–44) work has examined the back-and-forth character of Pentecostal churches in El Salvador that have been used to combat drug trafficking gangs. Like the gangs themselves, the churches are transnational, operating both in the US and El Salvador. Yet another example is Peggy Levitt's (2001: 159–79) study of the transnational religious practices of Dominicans from the village of Miraflores residing in the Jamaica Plain section of Boston. In this case, the Dominicans have to confront a US religious establishment intent on promoting a pan-Latino Catholicism, at the expense of a distinctly Dominican version, resulting over time in changing beliefs and practices. This, in turn, has had an impact on religion in Miraflores, where remittances have helped to revitalize religious life in the community, while simultaneously introducing there some of the changes embraced earlier by the immigrant enclave in Boston. These are but a few of the products of research projects that have used the transnational paradigm to explore the interplay between origins and destinations in shaping the religious identities, practices, and institutions of both migrants and non-migrants alike (see also, Vertovec 1997; Peterson et al. 2001; Ebaugh and Chafetz 2002; McAlister 2002; Ebaugh 2004; Kurien 2004).

Scholars of late nineteenth and early twentieth century immigrants have paid relatively little attention to the transnational character of immigrant religion. However, as with other forms of transnationalism, there is no reason to conclude that it was absent. Rather, one can assume that Ewa Morawska's (2001: 193) general characterization of substantial numbers of these immigrants as 'closet transnationalists' is applicable to religion as much as to other realms of social life. That being said, Nancy Foner (2005: 69–70) points to factors that make transnationalism more likely today than in the past. In addition to factors noted earlier, she cites the expansion of a global economy, the increase in the incidence of and tolerance of dual citizenship, and greater levels of tolerance and acceptance of ethnic difference. All of these can contribute, directly or indirectly, to religious transnationalism (Levitt 2003, 2004).

As long as immigration levels remain high, transnantionalism remains one possible type of religious adaptation to the migratory experience. From the vantage of scholarship, one of the differences between the last and current migratory waves is that the former ended with the passage of immigrant restriction legislation in 1924. Thus, as the third generation and beyond came of age, newcomers no longer infused the ethnic communities they grew up in and thus they increasingly lost touch with the homeland. The forces of Americanization no longer contended with the counterforces of homeland traditions and values. While this is a possibility in the future, at this moment it would appear that the cross-party political coalition necessary to impose similarly draconian restrictive legislation is unlikely to emerge.

However, more significant at present is the matter of whether or not transnationalism will persist across generations. This question ought to be located in terms of a problematic feature of much work framed in terms of the transnational paradigm, namely that it assumes that the factors that have made transnationalism possible will continue to operate, thereby making likely the prospect that second, third, and beyond generations can, too, be transnationals. The underlying reason for this assumption is that transnationalism is an alternative to assimilation. As such, this perspective resembles an earlier theoretical alternative, cultural pluralism. Andrew Greeley's work is a prime example of the cultural pluralist model. In challenging the claim that European ethnics were assimilating, in spite of the fact that his empirical findings yielded decidedly mixed results, he offered the highly qualified criticism of assimilation theory: 'to some extent some dimensions of the ethnic culture do indeed survive and enable us to predict some aspects of … behavior' (Greeley 1974: 319). His main conclusion was that ethnic persistence continues as a result of cultural transmission across generations, which he viewed as a refutation of assimilation theory.

Missing from Greeley's account was any appreciation of the larger structural context of ethnic attitudes. His research was conducted at a time when membership in ethnic institutions declined dramatically, ethnic neighborhoods had eroded considerably, language loyalty waned, inter-ethnic marriages reach all-time highs, and the 'ethnic factor' appeared to play a declining role in shaping individual life chances. Why did he not focus on these profound changes? The reason, I believe, is twofold. First, by embracing cultural pluralism as an alternative analytical stance to assimilation, he articulated a research agenda that sought out evidence of the persistence of ethnicity, without providing an adequate theoretical framework for interpreting indications of persistence. Secondly, the very nature of the agenda tended to obscure from consideration changes that would call into question the pluralist framework.

The advocates of cultural pluralism in the recent past and transnationalism today might fairly respond that the same problem occurs when one employs the assimilationist stance. And, indeed, this is true if we stake out these analytic positions as either/or alternatives. When we do so, we create something akin to Köhler's Goblet-and-Faces drawing: some viewers can see only one or the other of these visual objects and nobody can see both at the same time. The debates pitting cultural pluralism and assimilation in ethnic studies research during the 1970s and 1980s had this character to them. What got them off the mark were efforts to integrate evidence of persistence with evidence of change, as in discussions of symbolic ethnicity (Gans 1979) and ethnic options (Waters 1990) – both locating pluralism, either explicitly or implicitly, within an assimilationist framework.

While many exponents of transnationalism seek to pit it against assimilation in a parallel fashion to pluralists in the recent past, Portes for one embraces both transnationalism and assimilation. However, he is averse to theoretical efforts aimed at integrating transnationalism and assimilation, especially if it means that the former will be absorbed into the latter in a theory of incorporation. Thus, in his work on transnationalism, Portes treats it as an alternative paradigm to assimilation. On the other hand, in another research track he has been intent on reviving and reframing assimilation. This informs the conceptual framework of his work with Rubén Rumbaut on the immigrant second generation (Portes and Rumbaut 2001). In this work, whether the offspring will assimilate is not the issue; rather, operating with the concept of segmented assimilation, the question they seek to explore is into what sector of society components of the second generation will assimilate.

Portes exhibits an aversion to the development of a synthetic theory of immigrant incorporation. This is a perplexing stance given that in his work on transnationalism he appears to recognize the fact that the future of transnationalism depends in no small part on the form and content of assimilation, while at the same time assimilation is quite capable of being influenced by the impact of transnationalism. Portes has gone so far as to contend that transnationalism might actually stimulate ethnic incorporation (Portes *et al.* 2002). This is reminiscent of what Barbara Ballis Lal (1990: 3) has referred to as the 'ethnicity paradox,' namely that ethnic consciousness and actions shaped by ethnic ties have the capacity to facilitate 'participation in mainstream American life.' This was a central theme that she saw deriving from Robert E. Park's classic formulation of assimilation. At times, without so naming it, Portes appears to think that there is a contemporary counterpart – which one might call the 'transnational paradox' – at play. Interestingly, despite his reluctance to promote a theoretical approach that seeks to integrate transnationalism and assimilation, he offers the same conceptual tools to promote these dual research agendas: social capital, network analysis, and embeddedness.

Religion and Incorporation

Whether they seek primarily to transplant their religious heritage in a new setting or attempt to forge a transnational religious space, it is clear that for many contemporary immigrants, like their earlier counterparts (Miller and Marzik 1977), religion is a central site for the dual task of remaining connected to the past while simultaneously preparing for the future. In this regard, Charles Hirschman (2004: 1228) contends that, 'The centrality of religion to immigrant communities can be summarized as the search for refuge, respectability, and resources.' Refuge has both psychological and socioeconomic dimensions insofar as religious institutions function to protect newcomers from the alienating and disorienting aspects of their situation while also countering the negative impact of an often-hostile social world.

Respectability refers to the capacity of religion to serve as a source for status claims, both within and outside of the ethnic community. As with Weber's understanding of the role of Protestant sects in America a century ago, membership in religious institutions can be used by members as a proxy for moral worthiness. Not only does membership have the potential for providing valuable social

networks, but also it can be the basis for the generation of trust. Finally, in pointing to resources Hirschman is referring to the fact that American religious organizations tend to offer a wide array of non-religious support to members. He notes that:

> Almost all studies of contemporary immigrant churches and temples describe the multiple services provided to newcomers. Immigrants and their families go to church to acquire information about housing, employment opportunities, and other problems. Churches sponsor classes to help immigrants learn English, deal with their Americanized children, and acquire benefits for their aging parents. Young immigrants or the second generation can go to church for help with their homework, for social activities, and to meet prospective marriage partners who will likely meet with parental approval (Hirschman 2004: 1229).

Given the multiple functions performed by immigrant religious institutions, it is not surprising that both in the past and at present they have been a prominent feature of ethnic communities. In this regard, for many members of the immigrant generation – people who are closest to their ancestral roots – the connection between ethnicity and religion is apparent. The unanswered question is whether that connection can be expected to persist over time and across generations (Min and Kim 2005).

As research agendas increasingly turn from the immigrant generation to the second and third generations, the salience of this question will increase. As that occurs, recognizing certain lacunae in current research efforts is required in order not to draw unwarranted conclusions. First, there is a general assumption that immigrants are more religious in the land of destination than they were in the nation of origin. Linked to this is the assumption that religious institutions play a central role in immigrant communities. Both of these need further empirical confirmation than is available at present. What we know little about at the moment are those in contemporary immigrant communities who are not religious. Not only does this mean that we don't know what percentages are and are not religiously affiliated, but we don't know the relationship between the two sectors of the community. Do they have a cooperative, distant, or conflictual relationship?

In beginning to answer these questions, scholarship on the past can be instructive. For example, there is abundant evidence that the three main Catholic groups in America – the Irish, Italians, and Poles – had different attitudes about religious belief and practice, with the Italians not sharing the devotionalism of the other two groups. Or in another case, the Finnish ethnic community was split essentially in two between 'church' and 'red' Finns, replete with a system of dual institutions designed to serve various constituencies in the divided community. We need to expand our research agendas to promote comparative research between groups and to study in a more sustained way internal conflicts within communities, including conflicts between co-religionists and between the religious and irreligious. The question at hand today is what exactly is the role and place of religion within particular post-1965 immigrant communities? Put in general terms, what is called for in work on contemporary immigrants is an effort to adequately locate religion within the larger matrix of the ethnic community.

Another assumption that needs further reflection concerns the claim made by Warner and endorsed by most sociologists of immigrant religion that when religions are transplanted to the US, they tend to take on congregational form. While this may well be the case, it is also true that most research to date – primarily conducted using ethnographic methods – has concentrated on congregations as strategic research sites. Whether this is because it is the most important place to study religion or the most convenient is not necessarily clear. In other words, other forms of religious practice, especially forms that focus on the family, have not received the attention they perhaps deserve. When we better understand the extent to which the congregational form takes hold, we will also be in a position to know whether attempts to make sense of persistence and change are best undertaken by studying congregations, or whether we need to look elsewhere as well.

ASSIMILATION AND THE FUTURE OF ETHNIC RELIGION

Assimilation is not an inevitable process, but it is a powerful one. It is also a multi-faceted and variable process that need not be linear or unidirectional. Thus, cultural assimilation takes places unless strenuous efforts are undertaken to prevent it from happening. Those religious groups that have succeeded in preventing cultural assimilation, such as the Amish and Hasidic Jews, are few and far between. On the other hand, some groups manage to become structurally assimilated quickly while for others it occurs either slowly or to only a very limited extent.

Two factors have proved capable of serving as powerful brakes on structural assimilation: race and religion. In regard to race, ethnic groups defined as non-white have confronted and continue to confront the impact of racism that serves to prevent or limit assimilation. Nowhere is this more evident than in the case of African Americans. Residential segregation, educational segregation, occupational discrimination, and low levels of intermarriage structured black/white relations for most of American history, beginning with the era of slavery and continuing through the century-long Jim Crow era. Although much has changed since the civil rights movement of the 1950s and 1960s, there is abundant sociological evidence to indicate that the 'American dilemma' is far from being resolved (Smelser et al. 2001).

The limits to structural assimilation within black America at the beginning of the twenty-first century can be seen in the fact that despite modest increases in the integration of historically white churches, most blacks are members of predominantly black congregations. C. Eric Lincoln and Lawrence Mamiya (1990) have argued that several decades after the civil rights movement and the end of Jim Crow, the black church remains the most important extrafamilial institution in the community, intimately connected to all facets of African American life. This assessment has been reinforced by Cheryl Townsend Gilkes (1998; for a more qualified assessment, see McRoberts 2003). She points out that unlike mainline white churches, black churches have not experienced declines in membership. In addition, middle-class blacks that have moved out of segregated neighborhoods as part of the process of upward mobility have maintained their congregational ties to poorer neighborhoods to a far greater extent than whites. Gilkes (1998: 109) writes that, 'the church became the site for personal, social, and cultural integration and reintegration as class configurations changed.'

On the other hand, those deemed to be or who have managed to become white found opportunities open to structural assimilation (Roediger 2005). Thus, European-origin immigrants who by no later than World War II were all construed to be white witnessed the steady erosion of their ethnic churches. In many instances, the clerical leadership sought to prepare their members for the impact of assimilation. Thus, it was not uncommon for such leaders to inform the laity that they needed to distinguish between their religious and their ethnic heritages and furthermore that they ought to appreciate that the former needed to be protected, while it was permissible to allow Americanization to undermine ethnic allegiances. Within Lutheran America, for example, efforts were underway as early as the 1920s to merge the ethnic Lutheran churches into a larger American church body. The Catholic Church often exhibited a willingness to engage in ethnic social engineering. Ever-rising levels of intermarriage aided the erosion of the ethnic character of such churches. Ruby Jo Reeves Kennedy's (1944) 'triple melting pot' thesis, which informed Herberg's (1955) work, saw this process occurring within and not among the distinct communities of Protestants, Catholics, and Jews. Whether or not assimilation took precisely this form a half-century ago has been the subject of debate (Peach 1980); what is evident today is that even if this was how the structural assimilation of white ethnics took place in the past, it is clearly the case today that the boundaries between Protestants and Catholics has dramatically eroded, and more recently this is also the case with Jews and Christians.

The second obstacle to structural assimilation – religion – has deep historical roots revealing that in practice race and religion are often intertwined. Thus, in the first half of the nineteenth century the Irish were defined as non-white and they were also vilified for their Catholicism, which was viewed as inherently authoritarian, thus posing a threat to democracy. Other Catholic ethnic groups confronted similar hostility. However, anti-Catholicism was never as intense or virulent as anti-Semitism, and thus it was Jews in particular who – falling outside of Christianity – faced the most opposition to their presence in America due to their religious beliefs (Higham 1970). It was Herberg's conviction that in the aftermath of World War II, a new religious tolerance replaced the older hostilities. It was within this climate of tolerance and ecumenism that the WASP hegemony of an earlier era gave way to the idea that the nation's religious roots were to be defined in terms of three distinctive religions existing under what came to be defined as the shared canopy of the Judeo-Christian tradition. Once this happened, the boundaries dividing these three religious communities became considerably more porous.

In the ensuing half century, a new racial formation has begun to emerge, though it remains framed by the older dichotomous black/white divide. In the past, this meant that all groups not perceived to be white ended up on the black side of the divide, and thus the divide was posed in terms of non-white/white. Some, such as Herbert Gans (1979) have speculated about the possibility of a new racial formation in which the black/white divide is cast in terms of black/non-black. There is certainly evidence that many new immigrants today seek to distance themselves culturally and socially from blacks. They want to end up on the non-black side of the divide, for even if they are not defined as whites, they are at least on the side of the divide where whites, too, are located. Mia Tuan's (1999) claim that Asians may be becoming 'honorary whites' is an example of what this shift might portend.

At the same time that the racial formation is being redefined, questions arise about the way that growing religious diversity will be located in terms of the ongoing project of defining a national identity. Put bluntly, if the US has been defined for a half century as a Judeo-Christian nation, what does this mean for adherents of that other Abrahamic religion, Islam? This, of course, is an even more salient question after 9/11. Moreover, how might members of other faiths – including the major religions Hinduism and Buddhism – fit in? What are the terms of inclusion imposed by the mainstream society? What is the price that outsiders are prepared to pay in order to structurally assimilate? Will they, instead, opt to remain outsiders in order to protect their religious heritage? How successful will they be in preventing their children and grandchildren from opting for assimilation?

CODA

These and related questions constitute central issues to be explored in future research agendas that are aimed in various ways at getting at the complex and variable relationship between ethnicity and religion. In this chapter, I have attempted to indicate that at the moment, the most significant cutting-edge developments are occurring in the study of immigrant religion. In this research, three major conceptual frameworks are increasingly deployed. From the sociology of religion, the first is Warner's 'new paradigm.' The other two derive from immigration studies: transnationalism and assimilation. Just as Warner insists that he has outlined and further developed a paradigm, and not yet a theory of religion, it can similarly be said that both transnationalism and assimilation are paradigms and not theories. What this means is that in addition to the further expansion of empirical research, there is a need to clarify and refine these concepts. To make this task more complicated, and to suggest something of the challenge ahead, research will benefit from comparative studies that look beyond the US to other advanced industrial nations (as an illustration of some of the issues involved, see Kastoryano 2004).

The first stumbling block to cross-national comparative research is that the new paradigm is explicitly defined as applying to the US and is not intended to promote a general theory of religion. In interjecting the idea of ambivalence, Warner has (perhaps unintentionally) begun to move beyond the particularities of the US. One starting point for such a reconsideration is a recognition of the fact that although the lingering influence of a long history of religious monopoly in Europe is a reality, tolerance of other faiths is at least in principle adhered to and such nations are like the US insofar as they have experienced the expansion of religious diversity in recent years. Second, transnationalism as a concept has suffered by conceptual inflation and by the fact that scholars have not yet agreed upon a shared definition. This is due to the fact that the concept is quite new, and I think the process of refinement is well underway. Finally, assimilation is a concept that originated to make sense of ethnic relations in the US. The term, if not necessarily the idea underlying it, does not travel well because it comes with considerable ideological baggage. Nevertheless, efforts aimed at rethinking assimilation (even when it is sometimes labeled something else, such as incorporation or inclusion) have increasingly been presented with an aim to developing a concept applicable to all of the advanced industrial nations and not only the US.

In both the conduct of research and in efforts aimed at theory development, it is well to recall Brubaker's case against 'groupism.' To the extent that we proceed as he would have us means that we will maintain a keen appreciation of the fact that ethnicity and religion have the capacity to be intimately linked and mutually reinforcing, but that such linkages are historically contingent and neither necessarily permanent nor inevitable.

REFERENCES

Abramson, Harold 1975. 'The Religioethnic Factor and the American Experience.' *Ethnicity* 2 (July): 165–77.

Abramson, Harold 1980. 'Religion.' Pp. 869–75 in Stephan Thernstrom, Ann Orlov and Oscar Handlin (eds), *Harvard Encyclopedia of American Ethnic Groups*. Cambridge, MA: Harvard University Press.

Alba, Richard and Victor Nee 2003. *Remaking the American Mainstream: Assimilation and Contemporary Immigration*. Cambridge, MA: Harvard University Press.

Bainbridge, William Sims and Rodney Stark 1984. 'Formal Explanation of Religion: A Progress Report.' *Sociological Analysis* 41: 137–43.

Basch, Linda, Nina Glick Schiller and Christina Szanton Blanc 1994. *Nations Unbound: Transnational Projects, Postcolonial Predicaments, and Deterritorialized Nation-States*. Basel, Switzerland: Gordon and Breach.

Berger, Peter 1967. *The Sacred Canopy*. Garden City, NY: Doubleday Anchor.

Berger, Peter 1970. *A Rumor of Angels: Modern Society and a Rediscovery of the Supernatural*. Garden City, NY: Doubleday Anchor.

Brubaker, Rogers 2003. 'Neither Individualism nor "Groupism": A Reply to Craig Calhoun.' *Ethnicities* 3(4): 553–7.

Brubaker, Rogers 2004. *Ethnicity without Groups*. Cambridge, MA: Harvard University Press.

Calhoun, Craig 1997. *Nationalism*. Minneapolis: University of Minnesota Press.

Calhoun, Craig 2003. 'The Variability of Belonging: A Reply to Rogers Brubaker.' *Ethnicities* 3 (4): 558–68.

Carnes, Tony and Fenggang Yang (eds) 2004. *Asian American Religions: The Making and Remaking of Borders and Boundaries*. New York: New York University Press.

Christiano, Kevin 1991. 'The Church and the New Immigrants.' Pp. 169–86 in Helen Rose Ebaugh (ed.), *Vatican II and U.S. Catholicism: Twenty-five Years Later*. Greenwich, CT: JAI Press.

Christiano, Kevin J., William H. Swatos, Jr. and Peter Kivisto 2002. *Sociology of Religion: Contemporary Developments*. Walnut Creek, CA: AltaMira Press.

Ebaugh, Helen Rose 2004. 'Religion across Borders: Transnational Religious Ties.' *Asian Journal of Social Science* 32 (2): 216–31.

Ebaugh, Helen Rose and Janet Saltzman Chafetz (eds) 2000. *Religion and the New Immigrants: Continuities and Adaptations in Immigrant Congregations*. Walnut Creek, CA: AltaMira Press.

Ebaugh, Helen Rose and Janet Saltzman Chafetz (eds) 2002. *Religion Across Borders: Transnational Religious Networks*. Walnut Creek, CA: AltaMira Press.

Eck, Diana L. 2001. *A New Religious America: How a 'Christian Country' Has Now Become the World's Most Religious Diverse Nation*. New York and San Francisco: HarperSanFrancisco.

Faist, Thomas 1998. 'Transnational Social Spaces Out of International Migration: Evolution,Significance, and Future Prospects.' *Arch. Europ. Socio.* 39 (2): 213–47.

Faist, Thomas 2000. *The Volume and Dynamics of International Migration and Transnational Social Spaces*. Oxford, UK: Oxford University Press.

Finke, Roger and Rodney Stark 1988. 'Religious Economies and Sacred Canopies.' *American Sociological Review* 53 (1): 41–9.

Fitzgerald, David 2004. 'Transnationalist or Nationalist? Mexican Catholic Emigration Policies, 1920-2004.' Paper presented at the American Sociological Association Annual Meeting, August 13, in Philadelphia, PA.

Foner, Nancy 2000. *From Ellis Island to JFK: New York's Two Great Waves of Immigration*. New Haven, CT: Yale University Press.

Foner, Nancy 2005. *In a New Land: A Comparative View of Immigration*. New York: New York University Press.

Francis, E. K. 1947. 'The Nature of the Ethnic Group.' *American Sociological Review* 52 (5): 393–400.

Friedland, Roger and Robert R. Alford 1991. 'Bringing Society Back In: Symbols, Practices, and Institutional Contradictions.' Pp. 232–63 in Walter Powell and Paul J. DiMaggio (eds), *The New Institutionalism in Organizational Analysis*. Chicago: University of Chicago Press.

Gans, Herbert 1979. 'Symbolic Ethnicity: The Future of Ethnic Groups and Cultures in America.' *Ethnic and Racial Studies* 2 (1): 1–20.

Geertz, Clifford 1963. 'The Integrative Revolution.' Pp. 105–57 in Clifford Geertz (ed.), *Old Societies and New States: The Quest for Modernity in Asia and Africa*. New York: Free Press.

Geertz, Clifford 1973. *The Interpretation of Cultures: Selected Essays*. New York: Basic Books.

Gilkes, Cheryl Townsend 1998. 'Plenty Good Room: Adaptation in a Changing Black Church.' *Annals* 558: 101–21.

Glazer, Nathan and Daniel P. Moynihan (eds) 1975. *Ethnicity: Theory and Experience*. Cambridge, MA: MIT Press and Harvard University Press.

Gleason, Philip 1983. 'Identifying Identity: A Semantic History.' *Journal of American History* 16 (1): 20–46.

Glick Schiller, Nina 1997. 'The Situation of Transnational Studies.' *Identities* 4 (2): 155–66.

Glick Schiller, Nina 1999. 'Transmigrants and Nation-States: Something Old and Something

New in the U.S. Immigrant Experience.' Pp. 94–119 in Charles Hirschman, Philip Kasinitz, and Josh De Wind (eds), *The Handbook of International Migration: The American Experience.* New York: Russell Sage Foundation.

Glick Schiller, Nina, Linda Basch and Christina Szanton Blanc 1995. 'From Immigrant to Transmigrant: Theorizing Transnational Migration.' *Anthropological Quarterly* 68 (1): 48–63.

Granquist, Mark 2003. 'North American Lutheranism and the New Ethnics.' Pp. 166–86 in Richard Cimino (ed.), *Lutherans Today: American Lutheranism in the 21st Century.* Grand Rapids, MI: William B. Eerdmans Publishing.

Greeley, Andrew. 1974. *Ethnicity in the United States: A Preliminary Reconnaissance.* New York: John Wiley and Sons.

Guarnizo, Luis Eduardo, Alejandro Portes, and William Haller 2003. 'Assimilation and Transnationalism: Determinants of Transnational Action among Contemporary Migrants.' *American Journal of Sociology* 108 (6): 1211–48.

Haddad, Yvonne Yazbeck, Jane I. Smith, and John L. Esposito (eds) 2003. *Religion and Immigration: Christian, Jewish, and Muslim Experiences in the United States.* Walnut Creek, CA: AltaMira Press.

Hadden, Jeffrey 1987. 'Toward Desacralizing Secularization Theory.' *Social Forces* 65 (March): 587–611.

Hammond, Phillip E. and Kee Warner 1993. 'Religion and Ethnicity in Late-Twentieth Century America.' *Annals* 527 (May): 55–66.

Handlin, Oscar 1952. *The Uprooted.* Boston: Little, Brown.

Hansen, Marcus Lee 1938. *The Problem of the Third Generation Immigrant.* Rock Island, IL: Augustana Historical Society.

Herberg, Will 1955. *Protestant-Catholic-Jew.* Garden City, NY: Anchor Doubleday.

Higham, John 1970. *Strangers in the Land.* New York: Atheneum.

Hirschman, Albert O. 1970. *Exit, Voice, and Loyalty: Responses to Decline in Firms, Organizations, and States.* Cambridge, MA: Harvard University Press.

Hirschman, Charles 2004. 'The Role of Religion in the Origins and Adaptation of Immigrant Groups in the United States.' *International Migration Review* 38 (3): 1206–33.

Hughes, Everett C. 1971 [1948]. *The Sociological Eye: Selected Papers.* Chicago: Aldine.

Iannaccone, Lawrence 1990. 'Religious Practice: A Human Capital Approach.' *Journal for the Scientific Study of Religion* 29 (3): 297–314.

Iannaccone, Lawrence 1992. 'Religious Markets and the Economics of Religion.' *Sociological Compass* 39: 123–31.

Jasso, Guillermina, Douglas S. Massey, Mark R. Rozenzweig and James P. Smith 2003. 'Exploring the Religious Preferences of Recent Immigrants to the United States: Evidence from the New Immigrant Survey Pilot.' Pp. 217–53 in Yvonne Yazbeck Haddad, Jane I. Smith, and John L. Esposito (eds), *Religion and Immigration: Christian, Jewish, and Muslim Experiences in the United States.* Walnut Creek, CA: AltaMira Press.

Kastoryano, Riva 2004. 'Religion and Incorporation: Islam in France and Germany.' *International Migration Review* 38 (3): 1234–55.

Kennedy, Ruby Jo Reeves 1944. Single or Triple Melting Pot? Intermarriage Trends in New Haven, 1870-1940. *American Journal of Sociology* 49 (4): 331–9.

Kivisto, Peter 1993. 'Religion and the New Immigrants.' Pp. 92–108 in William H. Swatos, Jr. (ed.), *A Future for Religion? New Paradigms for Social Analysis.* Newbury Park, CA: Sage.

Kivisto, Peter 2001. 'Theorizing Transnational Immigration: A Critical Review of Current Efforts.' *Ethnic and Racial Studies* 24 (4): 549–77.

Kivisto, Peter 2003. 'Social Spaces, Transnational Immigrant Communities, and the Politics of Incorporation.' *Ethnicities* 3 (1): 5–28.

Kivisto, Peter and Wendy Ng 2005. *Americans All: Race and Ethnic Relations in Historical, Structural, and Comparative Perspectives.* Los Angeles: CA: Roxbury Publishing.

Kivisto, Peter and Thomas Faist 2007. *The Future of Citizenship.* Malden, MA: Blackwell Publishing.

Kurien, Prema 2004. 'Multiculturalism, Immigrant Religion, and Diasporic Nationalism: The Development of an American Hinduism.' *Social Problems* 51 (3): 362–85.

Kwon, Ho-Youn, Kwang Chung Kim and R. Stephen Warner (eds) 2001. *Korean Americans and Their Religions: Pilgrims and Missionaries from Different Shores.* University Park: Pennsylvania State University Press.

Lal, Barbara Ballis 1990. *The Romance of Culture in an Urban Civilization.* London: Routledge.

Lechner, Frank J. 1997. 'The "New Paradigm" in the Sociology of Religion: Comment on Warner.' *American Journal of Sociology* 103 (1): 182–92.

Leonard, Karen I., Alex Stepick, Manuel A. Vasquez and Jennifer Holdaway (eds) 2005. *Immigrant Faiths: Transforming Religious Life in America.* Walnut Creek, CA: AltaMira Press.

Levine, Donald N. 1985. *The Flight from Ambiguity: Essays in Social and Cultural Theory.* Chicago: University of Chicago Press.

Levitt, Peggy 2001. *The Transnational Villagers.* Berkeley: University of California Press.

Levitt, Peggy 2003. 'You Know, Abraham Was Really the First Immigrant: Religion and Transnational Migration.' *International Migration Review* 37 (3): 847–73.

Levitt, Peggy 2004. 'Redefining the Boundaries of Belonging: The Institutional Character of Transnational Religious Life.' *Sociology of Religion* 65 (1): 1–18.

Lincoln, C. Eric and Lawrence A. Mamiya 1990. *The Black Church in the African American Experience.* Durham, NC: Duke University Press.

McAlister, Elizabeth 2002. *Rara!: Vodou, Power, and Performance in Haiti and its Diaspora.* Berkeley: University of California Press.

McRoberts, Omar M. 2003. *Streets of Glory: Church and Community in a Black Urban Neighborhood.* Chicago: University of Chicago Press.

Menjívar, Cecilia 2000. *Fragmented Ties: Salvadoran Immigrant Networks in America.* Berkeley: University of California Press.

Menjívar, Cecilia 2006. 'Liminal Legality: Salvadoran and Guatemalan Immigrants' Lives in the United States.' *American Journal of Sociology* 111 (4): 999–1037.

Merton, Robert K. 1976. *Sociological Ambivalence and Other Essays.* New York: The Free Press.

Miller, Randall M. and Thomas D. Marzik, (eds) 1977. *Immigrants and Religion in Urban America.* Philadelphia, PA: Temple University Press.

Min, Pyong Gap and Jung Ka Kim (eds) 2002. *Religions in Asian America: Building Faith Communities.* Walnut Creek, CA: AltaMira Press.

Min, Pyong Gap and Dae Young Kim 2005. 'Intergenerational Transmission of Religion and Culture: Korean Protestants in the U.S.' *Sociology of Religion* 66 (3): 263–82.

Mittelberg, David and Mary C. Waters 1992. 'The Process of Ethnogenesis among Haitian and Israeli Immigrants in the United States.' *Ethnic and Racial Studies* 15 (4): 412–35.

Morawska, Ewa 2001. 'Immigrants, Transnationalism, and Ethnicization: A Comparison of This Great Wave and the Last.' Pp. 175–212 in Gary Gerstle and John Mollenkopf (eds), *E Pluribus Unum? Contemporary and Historical Perspectives on Immigrant Political Incorporation.* New York: Russell Sage Foundation.

Orsi, Robert A. (ed.) 1999. *Gods of the City: Religion and the American Urban Landscape.* Bloomington: Indiana University Press.

Peach, Ceri 1980. 'Which Triple Melting Pot? A Re-examination of Ethnic Intermarriage in New Haven, 1900–1950.' *Ethnic and Racial Studies* 3 (1): 1–16.

Peterson, Anna L., Manuel A. Vásquez and Philip J. Williams 2001. *Christianity, Social Change, and Globalization in the Americas.* New Brunswick, NJ: Rutgers University Press.

Portes, Alejandro 1996a. 'Global Villagers: The Rise of Transnational Communities.' *American Prospect* 25: 74–7.

Portes, Alejandro 1996b. 'Transnational Communities: Their Emergence and Significance in the Contemporary World-System.' Pp. 151–68 in Roberto Patricio Korzeniewicz and William C. Smith (eds), *Latin America in the World-Economy.* Westport, CT: Greenwood Press.

Portes, Alejandro 1998. 'Divergent Destinies: Immigration, the Second Generation, and the Rise of Transnational Communities.' Pp. 33–57 in Peter H. Schuck and Rainer Munz (eds), *Paths to Inclusion: The Integration of Migrants in the United States and Germany.* New York: Berghahn Books.

Portes, Alejandro, Luis E. Guarnizo and Patricia Landolt 1999. 'The Study of Transnationalism: Pitfalls and Promise of an Emergent Research Field.' *Ethnic and Racial Studies* 22 (2): 217–37.

Portes Alejandro, William J. Haller and Luis Eduardo Guarnizo 2002. 'Transnational Entrepreneurs: An Alternative Form of Immigrant Economic Adaptation.' *American Sociological Review* 67 (2): 278–98.

Portes, Alejandro and Rubén Rumbaut 2001. *Legacies: The Story of the Immigrant Second Generation.* Berkeley and New York: University of California Press and Russell Sage Foundation.

Roediger, David R. 2005. *Working Toward Whiteness: How America's Immigrants Became White, The Strange Journey from Ellis Island to the Suburbs.* New York: Basic Books.

Shils, Edward 1975. *Center and Periphery: Essays in Macrosociology.* Chicago: University of Chicago Press.

Smelser, Neil J. 1998. 'The Rational and the Ambivalent in the Social Sciences.' *American Sociological Review* 63 (1): 1–16.

Smelser Neil J., William Julius Wilson and Faith Mitchell (eds.) 2001. *America Becoming: Racial Trends and Their Consequences,* vol. I and II. Washington, DC: National Academy Press.

Smith, Tom W. 2002a. 'Religious Diversity in America: The Emergence of Muslims, Buddhists, Hindus, and Others.' *Journal for the Scientific Study of Religion* 41 (3): 577–85.

Smith, Tom W. 2002b. 'The Muslim Population of the United States: The Methodology of Estimates.' *The Public Opinion Quarterly* 66 (3): 404–17.

Sollors, Werner 1986. *Beyond Ethnicity: Consent and Descent in American Culture.* New York: Oxford University Press.

Stark, Rodney and Roger Finke 2000. *Acts of Faith: Explaining the Human Side of Religion.* Berkeley; University of California Press.

Tuan, Mia 1999. *Forever Foreigners or Honorary Whites? The Asian Ethnic Experience.* New Brunswick, NJ: Rutgers University Press.

van den Berghe, Pierre L. 1981. *The Ethnic Phenomenon.* New York: Elsevier.

Vásquez, Manuel A. and Marie Friedmann Marquardt 2003. *Globalizing the Sacred: Religion across the Americas.* New Brunswick, NJ: Rutgers University Press.

Vertovec, Steven 1997. 'Three Meanings of Diaspora Exemplified among South Asian Religions.' *Diaspora* 6 (3): 277–99.

Waldinger, Roger and David Fitzgerald 2004. 'Transnationalism in Question.' *American Journal of Sociology* 109 (5): 1177–95.

Warner, R. Stephen 1993. 'Work in Progress toward a New Paradigm for the Sociological Study of Religion in the United States.' *American Journal of Sociology* 98 (5): 1044–93.

Warner, R. Stephen 1997. 'A Paradigm is Not a Theory: Reply to Lechner.' *American Journal of Sociology* 103 (1): 192–98.

Warner, R. Stephen 1998a. 'Religion and Migration in the United States.' *Social Compass*, 45 (1): 123–34.

Warner, R. Stephen 1998b. 'Approaching Religious Diversity: Barriers, Byways, and Beginnings.' *Sociology of Religion* 59 (3): 193–215.

Warner, R. Stephen 2005. 'Enlisting Smelser's Theory of Ambivalence to Maintain Progress in Sociology of Religion's New Paradigm.' Pp. 105–22 in R. Stephen Warner, *A Church of Our Own: Disestablishment and Diversity in American Religion.* New Brunswick, NJ: Rutgers University Press.

Warner, R. Stephen and Judith G. Wittner (eds) 1998. *Gatherings in the Diaspora: Religious Communities and the New Immigration.* Philadelphia, PA: Temple University Press.

Waters, Mary 1990. *Ethnic Options: Choosing Identities in America.* Berkeley: University of California Press.

Weber, Max 1978. *Economy and Society*, vol. 1. Berkeley: University of California Press.

Wuthnow, Robert 2004. 'The Challenge of Diversity.' *Journal for the Scientific Study of Religion* 43 (2): 159–70.

Yang, Fenggang and Helen Rose Ebaugh 2001. 'Transformations in New Immigrant Religions and Their Global Implications.' *American Sociological Review* 66 (2): 269–88.

Yoo, David K (ed.) 1999. *New Spiritual Homes: Religion and Asian Americans.* Honolulu: University of Hawaii Press.

24

Religious Socialization among American Youth: How Faith Shapes Parents, Children, and Adolescents

JOHN P. BARTKOWSKI

In the last fifteen years, a great deal of attention has been paid to the role of religion in socializing young people. This chapter reviews several different genres of research that have emerged within this growing body of scholarship in an attempt to draw some general insights about the contours and effects of religious socialization among youngsters from early childhood to adolescence. The chapter begins by reviewing scholarship related to conservative Protestant parenting. This research points to a paradox in evangelical childrearing, such that conservative Protestant parents utilize an unusual mix of physical discipline and positive emotion work in the home. Next, the rather small but significant literature on the developmental effects of religion on youngsters of primary school age is considered. Although there is much more work that needs to be conducted on this front, early studies suggest that religion, particularly in a cohesive family environment, can have a positive developmental effect on young children. Finally, the chapter considers the rapidly growing body of research on religion among American teens. This scholarship generally shows that religion is important to American

teens and influences many facets of their lives; however, adolescents are rarely able to exhibit an articulate understanding of faith, a pattern that raises questions about the depth of religious attachment among teens.

Before proceeding with the review, several caveats are in order. First, the review provided here is designed to be illustrative rather than exhaustive. As such, key themes in research on the religious socialization of young people are highlighted here in a way that undoubtedly overlooks particular studies that may be breaking new ground or genres of research that are still under development. Second, because the methods for studying religious socialization among the young have improved a great deal during the past several years, a strategic choice has been made to focus more pointedly on recent studies than those that are decades old. While early studies paved the way for some of the work that is conducted today, space limitations and increasing methodological sophistication lead me to focus on contemporary research rather than the earliest studies in the field. Finally, while sociologists readily acknowledge that socialization is a lifelong process, I have chosen to focus on the religious socialization of young people because so much research has emerged on this topic of late. Religious socialization processes that occur later in life such as adult conversion or the influence of religion on family formation are beyond the scope of this chapter.

RELIGION AND PARENTING: THE CONSERVATIVE PROTESTANT PARADOX

A good deal of research published during the past fifteen years has highlighted the paradoxical nature of conservative Protestant (or evangelical) parenting. Conservative Protestantism is defined by its members' (1) commitment to an inerrantist view of the Bible (i.e., the Bible is God's word and contains prepositional truths to guide daily living), (2) a belief in the fundamental sinfulness of all human persons (i.e., human depravity is seen as a result of original sin), and (3) an understanding of salvation as a product of a born-again experience (i.e., acceptance of Jesus Christ as one's personal savior).

A number of studies have examined the rhetoric of leading conservative Protestant parenting experts that is disseminated through best-selling childrearing books sold through countless Christian bookstores. James Dobson, founder and president of Focus on the Family, is the most visible of such commentators, having authored a series of books that boast millions of copies sold or in print. The parenting advice contained in such manuals is quite distinctive from that offered in secular childrearing tracts that are widely available through mainstream secular bookstores. Upon comparison with secular parenting advice manuals, the most distinctive aspects of evangelical childrearing texts are (1) a hierarchical vision of the human family and, in particular, the parent–child relationship, and (2) an endorsement of corporal punishment as a legitimate means of child discipline (Bartkowski and Ellison 1995; Ellison 1996).

What specific forms of advice do conservative Protestant parenting experts provide to their (presumably evangelical) readers? At first blush, evangelical parenting ideologies seem rather authoritarian (Bartkowski 1995; Wilcox 1998, 2004). Elite evangelicals champion obedience to parental authority and control of youngsters' behavior through the use of physical discipline (Bartkowski and Ellison 1995; Ellison and Bartkowski 1997; Ellison and Sherkat 1993a, b; Ellision et al. 1996a, b). Many of these authors argue that God created the family not as a democracy but instead as an institution defined by clear lines of hierarchy and authority. Consequently, they argue that just as human beings must learn to submit to God's authority in order to gain salvation, small children must be taught to submit to the authority of their parents. These authors contend that if submission is not learned early in life, the sinful nature that all persons have inherited from Adam and Eve will dominate with ruinous consequences in one's earthly life and the hereafter. These authors argue that God has charged parents with 'shaping the will' of their youngsters. Indeed, the parent–child relationship is seen as the paradigm from which youngsters will develop attitudes toward other authority figures, such as teachers in school, supervisors in the workplace, and ultimately God.

According to conservative Protestant parenting specialists, the Bible provides clear direction about appropriate disciplinary strategies for shaping the child's will. These experts encourage parents to use physical discipline to teach young children right from wrong at an early age (Bartkowski and Ellison 1995; Ellison and Bartkowski 1997; Ellison and Sherkat 1993a), and scriptural support for this form of discipline is found throughout these manuals, including Proverbs 13:24 – 'He that spares the rod hates his son; he that loves his son chastens him,' and Proverbs 22:15 – 'Foolishness is bound in the heart of a child; but the rod of correction shall drive it far from him.' In contrast to the secular view of spanking as harsh and potentially abusive, corporal punishment in conservative Protestant discourse is described as a manifestation of love. According to this line of reasoning, parents that genuinely care for their children will not shy away from using corporal punishment as a means of correction.

Evangelical parenting experts urge parents to use an actual rod such as a wooden spoon or switch to spank their children. In fact, they propose a detailed methodology for administering physical discipline (Ellison and Bartkowski 1997). While the use of a 'rod of chastisement' would seem to border on barbarism to non-evangelicals, conservative Protestant luminaries view it as a 'neutral object' designed to depersonalize discipline. Thus, the rod of correction is distinguished from the 'loving hand' of the parent. The use of a rod is part of a broader commitment to a deliberate, controlled, and restrained form of child discipline (Bartkowski 1995; Ellison and Bartkowski 1997). Consequently, caregivers are told to administer punishment when children willfully defy parental authority or household rules. Upon determining that a child is willfully defiant, parents are urged to inflict sufficient pain immediately with a rod on the child's buttocks. Indeed, some commentators go so far as to suggest that this portion of the child's body was purposefully crafted by God to receive such correction from parents because a strategically targeted punishment can inflict pain without physical injury. Parents are reminded of the biblical passage found in Hebrews 12:11, 'No discipline seems pleasant at the time, but [is instead] painful. Later on, however, it produces a harvest of righteousness and peace for those who have been trained by it.'

The logic of traditional parental authority found in conservative Protestant childrearing advice manuals is interwoven with a countervailing logic that promotes expressive and nurturant parenting. Thus, elite evangelical support about the importance of children's obedience and parents' use of corporal punishment is coupled with strong encouragement for parental affirmation of children. In this way, parents are admonished against assuming an overbearing demeanor or harming the child's spirit. This emphasis on nurturant parenting stresses parental tenderness, and resonates with other scriptural passages, such as that found in the fourth verse of Ephesians 6, which parents are told 'not [to] exasperate your children; instead, bring them up in the training and instruction of the Lord.' This motif of tenderness is also manifested in frequent references concerning the need for parents to affirm their children through practices that sociologists would describe as 'positive emotion work' (e.g., hugging, praising, and expressing affection) (Wilcox 1998, 2004). Once again, God's relationship with the Christian believer is viewed as paradigmatic for the parent–child relationship. Evangelical commentators reason that because God's love is expansive enough to chastise those who have sinned even while mercy is extended to those who repent (e.g., Hebrews 12:6), parents are expected to couple chastisement with forgiveness, and mercy with justice. Strong recommendations for paternal involvement in childrearing also fit within this progressive strand of evangelical parenting. Although conservative Protestant commentators generally endorse a patriarchal family structure, this particular brand of patriarchy places a premium on paternal responsibility and involvement rather than male dominance (Bartkowski 2001, 2004; Bartkowski and Xu 2000; Wilcox 2002, 2004). Thus, conservative Protestant parenting advice dovetails quite nicely with the New Father ideal in contemporary American society.

Empirical research on the attitudes and practices of evangelical caregivers demonstrates that the advice of conservative Protestant parenting specialists is being acted upon in many households affiliated with this religious subculture (Bartkowski et al. 2000), thereby calling into question claims of a broad Catholic-Protestant convergence in childrearing orientations (Alwin 1986). Research using nationally representative data reveal that conservative Protestants are significantly more likely than their non-evangelical counterparts to support the view that 'it is sometimes necessary to discipline a child with a good, hard spanking' (Ellison and Sherkat 1993a; see also Grasmick et al. 1991). Indeed, support for corporal punishment is closely linked with the distinctive evangelical beliefs in the inerrancy of the Bible, the depravity of human nature, and punishment as a legitimate response to sin. Moreover, conservative Protestants are more likely to value children's obedience to parental authority, whereas their non-evangelical counterparts tend to value autonomy and self-direction in youngsters (Ellison and Sherkat 1993b). And perhaps most tellingly, evangelical parents report actually spanking their toddlers and preschoolers much more often than other parents (Ellison et al. 1996a, b). This practice is linked closely with inerrantist beliefs about the Bible. In short, children in conservative Protestant households are more likely to have parents who are committed to children's submission to parental authority, who believe that corporal punishment is justified in the face of children's misconduct, and who administer physical punishment more frequently.

Yet, despite elite evangelicals' enthusiasm for upholding parental authority in the home, research also reveals that conservative Protestant parents are attuned to the countervailing logic of expressive caregiving embedded within best-selling Christian childrearing manuals (Bartkowski and Wilcox 2000; Bartkowski and Xu 2000; Wilcox 1998; see Bartkowski et al. 2000 for review). Survey research reveals that evangelical mothers praise and hug their children more often than their non-evangelical counterparts (Wilcox 1998). What's more, evangelical fathers are quite inclined to engage in this kind of expressive parenting (Bartkowski and Xu 2000; Wilcox 1998, 2004). Moreover, consistent with admonitions against verbal outbursts found in conservative Protestant parenting manuals, evangelical parents are significantly less inclined to use yelling as a means of disciplining their youngsters (Bartkowski and Wilcox 2000).

Evidence of progressive parenting practices within evangelical households is also found in the generally higher level of paternal involvement within such homes. Evangelical fathers are, in fact, more involved with their children than their peers in other faith traditions (Bartkowski and Xu 2000; Wilcox 2002). Conservative Protestant fathers evince higher levels of involvement with their youngsters across a number of self-reported survey measures, such as having dinner with their children and volunteering for youth activities such as soccer and Scouts. When compared with their non-evangelical peers, conservative Protestant fathers are also more likely to shoulder more of the supervisory responsibilities of raising school-aged children, such as monitoring their children's chores, homework, and television viewing.

The current research, then, paints a paradoxical portrait of childrearing within conservative Protestant families. Traditional forms of discipline such as the valuation of children's obedience and the more frequent use of corporal punishment have indeed been observed in such families. Yet, these practices are coupled with a panoply of progressive childrearing practices, such as more frequent parental hugging and praising of youngsters, less parental yelling, and greater paternal involvement. Evangelical childrearing practices, then, seem to confound longstanding sociological typologies that aim to fit parents neatly into 'authoritarian,' 'authoritative,' and 'permissive' categories. The mélange of childrearing practices within this subculture can be best characterized as 'neo-traditional.'

THE FRUITS OF FAITH: THE EFFECTS OF RELIGIOUS SOCIALIZATION ON YOUNG CHILDREN

Having examined the contours of religious (specifically, evangelical) parenting to this point, what can be said about the effects of religious socialization among youngsters? In what follows, I explore the small yet important body of research on child outcomes associated with religious socialization. I begin by detailing the effects of conservative Protestant childrearing on the development of evangelical youngsters. I then turn to research on the broader effects of religion on children's social psychological development.

A large body of social scientific research links corporal punishment with a series of negative consequences for youngsters, including emotional distress, low self-esteem, aggression, and academic underachievement. Given the higher rates of corporal punishment found in conservative Protestant homes (noted above), are evangelical youngsters at special risk for such developmental problems? Although there is only preliminary evidence available on this front, evangelical child discipline has been shown to produce distinctive developmental outcomes (Ellison et al. 1999). Ellison and colleagues (1999) used nationally representative data to compare the incidence of emotional and behavioral problems approximately five years after initial reports of physical punishment (i.e., during grade school) for both evangelical and non-evangelical children. They also accounted for recent episodes of corporal punishment by parents with children of grade school age. Harmful effects so spanking were not observed for evangelical children in this study. Interestingly, evangelical children who were not spanked at either point in time (i.e., as toddlers or in grade school) actually exhibited greater risk of emotional and behavioral problems than their evangelical peers who were spanked.

Why would spanking be less harmful or not harmful at all for evangelical children? Several possible explanations have been entertained (Ellison et al. 1999). First, as noted above, corporal punishment is one part of a broader set of parenting behaviors. It is possible that the positive aspects of evangelical family life noted above offset the negative effects typically associated with physical punishment. Second, higher levels of social and cultural support for physical discipline within evangelical communities (among family members, pastors, youth ministers, and fellow congregants) might give spanking a different cultural meaning for parents and youth. The subculture of conservative Protestantism might lead evangelical children to expect spanking and to interpret this form of discipline as a sign of parental love and concern rather than parental rejection or harshness. Third, evangelical parents may administer corporal punishment quite differently than other parents. As described above, evangelical writers have rendered detailed advice on when, where, and how to administer corporal punishment, and strongly admonish parents against uncontrolled, abusive discipline or lashing out in anger against

children (Bartkowski 1995; Ellison and Bartkowski 1997). Given such advice, evangelical parents might be unusual in their consistent and reasoned application of corporal punishment (Gershoff et al. 1999).

Turning from conservative Protestantism to the broader effects of religion on child development, what type of research has been conducted on child outcomes of youngsters raised by religious parents (broadly defined)? Where religion in general is concerned, there is mounting – though not unequivocal – evidence that faith is a valuable developmental asset for young children. Admittedly, there is surprisingly limited research on this score, likely because of disciplinary biases against religion in the fields of psychology, sociology, and child development. But what have we learned to date?

For quite some time, there was one single published study of religion and child development among American youngsters. That study was conducted with data drawn from a convenience sample of parents and children, the latter of whom were preschoolers enrolled in a Head Start program (Strayhorn et al. 1990). Significantly, the authors of this study called attention to the non-existent prior research on religion and child development (Strayhorn et al. 1990: 35), a circumstance that others observed over one decade after that initial study's publication (Bridges and Moore 2002). Respondents in the Strayhorn et al. (1990) study were predominantly black, low-income mothers of Head Start enrollees. Parental religiosity was measured through a twelve-item scale adapted from previously published research, and included the following measures: (1) a subjective measure of the parent's personal religiosity, (2) the frequency of personal scripture study, (3) the frequency of personal prayer, (4) the frequency of asking God for strength when facing temptation, (5) the frequency of asking God for help in making everyday decisions, (6) the typical frequency of attendance at religious worship services, (7) the general proportion of income donated to a religious organization, (8) the frequency of serving in a church responsibility (e.g., teaching a religious class, serving as a leader in one's local congregation), (9) closeness of the parent's relationship with God, (10) the frequency of experiencing God's approval for good deeds, (11) the frequency of experiencing God's disapproval for undesirable acts, and (12) the degree to which a religious goal or purpose gives direction to life.

Children's behavior was gauged by a number of measures, including researchers' ratings of videotaped parent–child interactions and researchers' assessments of children's classroom behaviors using a preschool behavior assessment survey. While the sampling design in this study was less than ideal from a sociological perspective (that is, a non-random, unrepresentative sample), multiple measures of parental religiosity and multiple contexts for data collection (videotaped parent–child interactions, children's classroom behavior) were commendable. Parental religiosity proved to be associated with a number of positive factors for adults in the Strayhorn et al. (1990) study (e.g., parental mental health, social support, and positive parenting practices), but the religiousness of parents was not significantly associated with children's behavior.

Should we then surmise that parental religiosity is largely ineffectual in the socialization of young children? In a word, no. More recent and rigorous studies have revealed significant connections between parental religiosity and developmental outcomes in children. Miller and colleagues conducted an intriguing longitudinal study of the linkages between religiosity (denominational affiliation, worship service attendance, and importance of religion) and depression for mothers and their offspring (Miller et al. 1997). Miller and colleagues found that religion can, in some circumstances, inhibit the intergenerational transmission of major depression disorders. Specifically, major depressive disorders were significantly less likely to be transmitted across generations when mothers and offspring were concordant on worship service attendance. However, these findings were manifested only for mothers who did not initially exhibit maternal depression. For mothers that did exhibit maternal depression upon initial clinical assessments, offspring were more likely to have a major depressive disorder at ten-year follow-up when mothers

and offspring were concordant on religious importance. Thus, the effects of religion were not wholly positive in this study, though the non-random nature of the sample again raises concerns about the generalizability of findings.

In the latest study on religion and child development, researchers used data from the 2000 wave of the Early Childhood Longitudinal Study, a nationally representative sample of young children beginning primary school featuring a number of different measures of parental religiosity (Bartkowski et al. 2007). Attendance frequency items for each parent were used to explore the independent effects of mothers' and fathers' frequency of worship service attendance on child development. The researchers were also able to examine the effects of religious homogamy among couples, thereby measuring the degree to which the couple attended together or exhibited attendance disparities. Finally, two novel measures (frequency of parent–child talks about religion and frequency of spousal arguments about religion) were used to examine the effects of the family's religious environment on child development. Child development domains explored in this study ranged widely and were generated through both parent and teacher ratings of children's dispositions and behaviors, including such outcomes as self-control, interpersonal skills, internalizing behaviors, externalizing behaviors, and approaches to learning.

In this particular study, the religious attendance of parents (individually) and especially couples (together) proved to have a strong positive effect on children's dispositions and behaviors across a wide range of developmental domains. Despite these generally positive findings, the authors cautioned that the family's religious environment could function as a help or hindrance for children's development. Frequent parent–child discussions about religion generally yielded positive effects on child development, while the effects associated with family arguments about religion were deleterious for children. The authors concluded that generic homogamy (i.e., religious similarity among couples regardless of level of religiosity) was a noteworthy but less important factor in child development than the overall amount of religious capital that a couple can jointly generate within the family. Despite this study's use of nationally representative data to explore the effects of religion on child development, this study suffered from some important limitations. Most notably, a cross-sectional investigation cannot explore possible selection effects that might explain the connection between parental religiosity and children's developmental capacities. It is possible that the parents of youngsters who have more self-control and are better behaved would find worship service attendance a more hospitable climate than parents with children who frequently misbehave. Parents with more poorly behaved children might feel uncomfortable or unwelcome at worship services, where skills such as sitting still and remaining quiet might be expected by fellow congregants. Until such issues are adjudicated, though, this study provides compelling evidence that parents' (and especially couples') embeddedness in religious networks is good for children, while household arguments about religion have a negative impact of the developmental trajectories of youngsters.

Why would religion have such pronounced effects on the development of young children? Religion has been shown to enhance the parent–child bond for both mothers (Pearce and Axinn 1998) and fathers (Bartkowski and Xu 2000; King 2003; Smith and Kim 2003; Wilcox 2002). And while the precise connections between parental religiosity and religiosity in children are not well understood, it is clear that religion and spirituality are meaningful to many children. A growing body of scholarship has examined the contours and correlates of religious and spiritual development among youngsters from early childhood through pre-adolescence. This line of research has underscored the sophisticated nature of children's religious beliefs (see Boyatzis 2003), and has highlighted variations in youngsters' spiritual development (including God images) by age, gender, and denomination (e.g., Nucci and Turiel 1993; Richert and Barrett 2005; Tirri et al. 2005). Yet other research demonstrates an elective affinity between religion and family, such that a principal concern of religious communities entails the provision of resources

that promote family cohesion and effective parenting (e.g., Hertel and Donahue 1995; Mahoney 2005; Marks 2004; Ratcliff 1992; Smith and Kim 2003; see Mahoney et al. 2003 for review).

In a more general sense, scholars have begun to point to religion's 'sanctification' of family relationships (Mahoney 2005; Mahoney et al. 2001; Mahoney et al. 2003; see also Marks 2004; Pargament and Mahoney 2005). This line of research demonstrates that religion can imbue family relationships with meaning and significance. As Mahoney and colleagues (2003: 221) have argued: 'Religion is distinctive because it incorporates people's perceptions of the "sacred" into the search for significant goals and values ... The sacred refers to the holy, those things that are "set apart" from the ordinary and deserve veneration and respect ... Indeed, part of the power of religion lies in its ability to infuse spiritual character and significance into a broad range of worldly concerns,' including those in the home. Hence, religion functions as a cultural resource that a family can use to enhance cohesion, resolve conflicts, and pursue collectively desired goals. Thus, Mahoney and colleagues explain, 'Although religious traditions offer diverse prescriptive statements about what constitutes a "good" family member, a central theme [of sanctified family relations] emanates from most religions,' and they note that 'Judeo-Christian religions portray the burdens and pleasures of parenting as opportunities to model and deepen one's understanding of God's love, patience, and commitment, and frame the parental role as a sacred calling that requires personal sacrifices' (Mahoney et al. 2003: 222–23; see also Swank et al. 2000). In short, to the extent that religion sacralizes family relationships and casts parental responsibilities as convenantal, it is not surprising that the developmental outcomes of children raised in religious families is decidedly different from those raised in non-religious homes. This is not to say that religious families are without challenges, difficulties, or problems. But such research does suggest that religious families have an additional repertoire of resources to draw on in raising their children, and the tools that faith communities provide seem to make a difference in the socialization of young children.

RELIGION AMONG AMERICAN TEENS: THE CONTOURS AND INFLUENCE OF ADOLESCENT FAITH

Does the distinctive influence of religion on children's socialization endure as young people move into adolescence? Does religion exert any discernible influence on the attitudes and behaviors of teenagers? After decades of only scant research on youth religiosity (e.g., Cornwall 1988; Nelson and Potvin 1980; Wuthnow 1976), scholarship on religion among teens has recently exploded (see Regnerus et al. 2003; Smith et al. 2003 for reviews). What does such research reveal?

Taking first the contours of teenage religiosity and spirituality, the available survey evidence suggests that religion occupies a formidable place in the lives of American teens. Data consistently reveal that about 85 percent of teens claim a denominational affiliation (e.g., Smith 2005; Smith and Faris 2002a). Just over 50 percent of teens claim a Protestant affiliation (most commonly Baptist, Christian [likely, evangelical], Methodist, and independent/non-denominational), while about a quarter of teens are Catholic. Thus, claims of 'spiritual seeking' bereft of organized religious ties among American youth seem to be exaggerated (Smith 2005). Religion among American teens, like that among adults, takes a decidedly denominational form (Smith 2005); and teens are generally not alienated from or hostile toward organized religion (Smith et al. 2003).

Yet, is this propensity to claim a denominational affiliation simply a superficial form of religiosity? Or does it give way to more deeply seeded beliefs and practices? Current survey evidence suggests that many teens take religion quite seriously. Data from one wave of Monitoring the Future (1996) demonstrate that about 60 percent of high school seniors report that religion is important in their lives,

with about one in every three claiming that religion is 'very important' to them (Smith and Faris 2002a). This figure contrasts markedly with the scant 15 percent of high school seniors who say that religion is 'not important' to them (Smith and Faris 2002a). Religious salience does vary by denominational affiliation, such that youth affiliated with more theologically conservative traditions tend to rate their faith as more important to them (Smith et al. 2003). Data from the initial wave of the National Study of Youth and Religion (NSYR), the most comprehensive survey of its kind, further underscore the importance of faith to young Americans. More than half of respondents to this survey (collected in 2002–2003) report that their faith was 'extremely important' or 'very important' in shaping their daily lives (Smith 2005). Only 7 percent of NSYR respondents reported that their faith was 'not at all important.' A whopping 84 percent of NSYR respondents reported that they believe in God, while only 12 percent and 3 percent, respectively, claim an agnostic or atheistic orientation (Smith 2005). Sixty-five percent of NSYR respondents view God as a personal being who is involved in people's lives (Smith 2005).

Recent survey data reveal that religious predispositions among youth are not idle beliefs. Rather, young people seem to act on their faith. Nearly one-third of all high school seniors surveyed in the 1996 wave of Monitoring the Future attend religious services once per week or more often (Smith and Faris 2002a). NSYR data reveal a more detailed portrait, showing that conservative Protestant and Latter-day Saint (LDS) teens attend at extremely high rates when compared with other religiously active youth. Indeed, about 40 percent of conservative Protestant youngsters and 70 percent of LDS teens attend religious services once per week or more. This pattern is generally consistent with higher rates of religious attendance among teens affiliated with more conservative faith traditions (Smith et al. 2002).

According to the 1996 wave of Monitoring the Future, approximately one in five twelfth graders is actively involved in church youth group activities (Smith and Faris 2002a). Over half (56 percent) of high school seniors report ever having participated in a church youth group; and about one-quarter of them report having been involved with religious youth groups for four or more years (Smith and Faris 2002a). Long-term participation in church youth programs far eclipses teen involvement in extracurricular activities, boys or girls clubs, and community youth organizations. Evidence from the National Study of Youth and Religion underscores the importance of religious youth groups in general, with 38 percent of teens surveyed claiming current involvement. Here again, there are initial indications of noteworthy denominational variations. Youth groups are particularly prominent in the lives of conservative Protestants (56 percent currently involved) and Latter-day Saints (72 percent currently involved). Previous research has shown that religious organizations are a key conduit for social capital, civic engagement, and social benevolence for adults (e.g., Ammerman 1997; Park and Smith 2000; Putnam 2000; Regnerus et al. 1998; Wuthnow 1999). And, consistent with such findings, initial indications suggest that faith communities play a similar role for young people as well (Smith 2005; Smith and Faris 2002a; Wagener et al. 2003).

Recent attention has also turned to historical trends in youth religiosity, though this work is in its early stages and consists largely of descriptive analyses. Longitudinal analyses reveal that the propensity for youth to claim a denominational affiliation is pervasive and relatively stable (Smith et al. 2002). Broad comparisons of denominational families with Monitoring the Future data reveal that Protestant affiliations among American high school seniors have declined by 10 percent from 1976 to 1996. The percent of young people claiming a Catholic affiliation and Jewish affiliation during these decades changed slightly, with a decline of 1 percent for Catholics and an increase of 1 percent for Jews. Those claiming an 'other' religious affiliation (different than those identified above) increased by 5 percent and those claiming no affiliation also grew by 5 percent. On balance, then, denominational affiliation has remained a central facet of religiosity among American teens from 1976–1996, with the greatest amount of change occurring among Protestants, those affiliated with non-mainstream faiths, and those who are unaffiliated.

Univariate trend analyses demonstrate that worship service attendance among high school seniors has been fairly stable from 1976 to 1996, with slight declines evidenced among the percent of teens that report weekly attendance and a slight growth in the percent of teens that report never or rarely attending (Smith et al. 2002). (Denominational variations in these attendance trends have not been investigated to date, and deserve further exploration.) The importance of religion has also remained stable among high school seniors, with a slight trend toward polarization such that 'not important' and 'very important' responses have increased somewhat over time (Smith et al. 2003).

Relatively little change over time (1976–1996) is exhibited by youth concerning their general affect toward organized religion (Smith et al. 2003). High school seniors consistently agree with their parents' religious views, render a generally positive evaluation of religious institutions, express a desire for religious institutions to be influential in society, and have given or would give financially to religious organizations provided they have the monetary means to do so.

Beyond the contours of youth religiosity, what effect does faith have on the lives of American teenagers? Current evidence suggests that religious communities play a major role in providing adolescents with positive adult role models, pro-social peer associations, and meaningful social skills that often insulate religious youth from risks commonly faced by teens (e.g., Bartkowski and Xu 2007; Cnaan et al. 2004; Hoge and O'Conner 2004; King and Furrow 2004; Meier 2003; Regnerus et al. 2004; Smith 2003a, b, c, 2005; Smith and Faris 2002a, b; Smith and Kim 2003; Smith et al. 2002, 2003; Wagener et al. 2003; Wallace and Forman 1997; see Regnerus et al. 2003; Smith 2003b for reviews). Religious youth, and especially those that are highly active in their faith (i.e., frequent attenders) are less likely to engage in risky behaviors such as drug use (e.g., Bartkowski and Xu 2007) or early and promiscuous sexual activity (e.g., Meier 2003, Regnerus 2007), two of the most prominent forms of risk faced by adolescents today. Moreover, religious youth are more apt to be civically engaged (e.g., involved in youth groups) and render service to their communities (Smith 2005). The protective effects of religion for teenagers are especially pronounced when faith commitments are shared across generations between parents and children (Pearce and Haynie 2004; Regnerus 2003).

Several different explanations have been offered to explain the protective effects that religious involvement confers on teenagers, and can generally be grouped into three categories: (1) moral order, (2) learned competencies, and (3) social and organizational ties (Smith 2005: 240–51). Religious involvement provides youth with moral directives (e.g., self-control, virtuous action) that are likely to have a strong influence on teens' life choices. Religion also provides a ground for cultivating particular capacities such as leadership skills or coping strategies that might help youth navigate the challenges and vagaries of adolescence while developing character and a positive self-image. Finally, youth embedded within religious institutions have a deep reservoir of social capital available to them (intergenerational ties, community linkages), and would be more likely to situate within an interlocking set of relationships with various adults that foster network closure (mutual guidance and oversight of youth by a range of adults sharing similar values).

This generally positive portrait of religion in the lives of American teens is counterbalanced, however, by a series of less sanguine findings. Religion is not good for teens under all circumstances. There are tradition-specific and domain-specific effects of religion on the life chances of young people, and such effects are not uniformly positive. For example, recent research has revealed that parents' theological conservatism (operationalized as a commitment to biblical inerrancy) can significantly hinder children's educational attainment, especially for female children who do not hold the parents' theologically conservative convictions (Sherkat and Darnell 1999). Such findings have led researchers to conclude that there is 'strong evidence that fundamentalist parents regard education with enmity, and would only support religiously motivated education. Indeed, even if fundamentalist parents are unaware of their children's religious deviance, they may generate a household climate that is hostile to educational pursuits and thereby influence the educational options their children consider' (Sherkat and Darnell 1999: 30).

Another series of findings suggests that while the involvement of youth in formal religious groups is pronounced and often generates positive effects for religious teens, the depth of youth attachment to religion is not terribly strong in most faith traditions. With the exceptions of Mormons and some evangelicals, 'adolescent religious and spiritual understanding and concern seem to be generally very weak. Most U.S. teens have a difficult to impossible time explaining what they believe, what it means, and what the implications of their beliefs are for their lives ... [and few] can articulate little more than what seem to be the most paltry, trivial, or tangential beliefs' (Smith 2005: 262). This lack of depth in religious conviction has given way to what one expert on teen religiosity, Christian Smith (2005), has dubbed 'Moralistic Therapeutic Deism,' the dominant creed among American teens. Moralistic Therapeutic Deism is a generic belief in a God who wants people to be good and fair to one another and who will provide assistance as requested but who does not exact any serious demands on believers. God (and, more broadly, religion) thus becomes a mean to an end – and that end is self-fulfillment – rather than a source of moral authority. This contemporary creed is linked with American individualism and consumerism while creating a narcissistic orientation toward deity in which 'God is something like a combination Divine Butler and Cosmic Therapist: he is always on call, takes care of any problems that arise, professionally helps his people to feel better about themselves, and does not become too personally involved in the process' (Smith 2005: 165). Thus, while it is clear that religion confers many protective benefits on American adolescents, some observers argue that the quality of religious socialization among U.S. teens leaves much to be desired.

CONCLUSION

This chapter has reviewed current research on the religious socialization of young people, with a particular focus on the distinctive patterns of conservative Protestant parenting, the effects of religious socialization among young children, and the contours and outcomes of teenage religiosity. Just as religion has a pronounced influence on American society and culture, faith is a strong influence in the lives of many young people. The treatment of young people within the home and the social opportunities that they face outside of it are shaped by the religiosity of their parents and by youngsters' own faith convictions. Overall, then, such research suggests that religion remains a key institutional conduit for the socialization of young people.

Perhaps the most notable take-away lesson from this review of various literatures on the religious socialization of young people is this: Religion is a complex agent of socialization, one characterized by contradictory tendencies and countervailing forces. Conservative Protestants spank their children more than other parents and value children's submission to parental authority, but are also more prone to hug and praise their kids while yelling at them less. Such paradoxical childrearing patterns defy the conventional parenting typology (authoritative, authoritarian, and permissive parenting) long embraced in the social scientific community. Conservative Protestant parents confound this typology by creatively melding elements of the first two parenting styles.

Where child development is concerned, the current research demonstrates that religion can be both an asset for children, particularly when couples attend frequently, and a liability,

such as when couples argue frequently about religion. In this way, then, religion cannot be reduced to a wholly positive or uniformly negative influence on child development. Moreover, the positive influences of religious belonging for children of primary school age are evidenced more strongly in some social domains (the home) than others (schools), though there do seem to be some trans-institutional effects when both parents are highly active in their faith tradition. Attention needs to be paid to such wrinkles and nuances if the effects of religious socialization in particular contexts are to be ascertained with any precision.

Finally, research on religion among American teens is also characterized by complex findings. On the one hand, religion seems to be a powerful agent of socialization for U.S. teens, such that affiliation is commonplace and religion is generally deemed to be quite important to adolescents. Moreover, religion seems to provide various protections against social risks faced by teens, including drug use and early sexual activity. Yet, on the other hand, most teens' understandings of their faith are not very deep. Rather, the dominant religious creed of American society is that of Moralistic Therapeutic Deism, a superficial, generic set of beliefs that are not too demanding and that resonate with contemporary individualism and consumerism. Ironically, religion is at once influential and not personally meaningful to the majority of American teens.

Undoubtedly, there is more ground to be plowed in exploring the contours and effects of religious socialization among young people. Comparative research on parenting across different faith traditions is one of the most promising avenues for future research on the religious socialization of the young. Unfortunately, there is very little solid empirical research on parenting and youth socialization in non-Christian (and even non-U.S.) contexts, a bias in the scholarship that has been noted elsewhere (Stewart and Bond 2002). One study that has countered this general pattern of neglect is a comparative analysis of parenting in Christian, Jewish, Mormon, and Muslim families (Marks 2004).

This qualitative study used interview data with parents in each of these traditions to explore the meaning of religious practices in the home, as well as the perceived benefits and difficulties associated with the religious socialization of children. This study revealed that, despite the obvious doctrinal differences across these faith traditions, religious parents shared a number of characteristics in common. Interviewed parents (1) recognized the need to teach by example or 'practice what they preach' (belief-behavior congruence) to promote effective religious socialization, (2) acknowledged the vital role that religion can play in promoting family cohesion, whether through candlelight vigils, Sabbath meals, or other family rituals, and (3) identified the costs of family religious practices, including children's unwillingness to participate and, among parents in non-mainstream traditions, the intraceable American religious culture that often impinges on the ritual observances of non-Christian groups (e.g., Muslim Ramadan, Jewish Sabbath). Clearly, more comparative research of this sort, and on religious parenting outside the United States, is needed.

An additional line of inquiry that should be pursued is the role of new media (particularly the internet, iPods, and the like) in the religious socialization of young people. Young people today are rabid consumers of new media, and there are signs that religious groups are utilizing new media tools to spread their message (Brasher 2004), even where young people are concerned (see Clark 2003). Religious home schooling programs use DVD technology and interactive online exercises to simulate classroom environments in a more sophisticated fashion than in years past. At the same time, chat rooms and online dating sites for youth affiliated with particular faith traditions, or those with a general interest in spiritual matters, have proliferated. Researchers would be wise to keep their finger on the pulse of such changes, while examining the influence of such technological innovations on the religious and spiritual sensibilities of the young.

Regardless of the directions pursued concerning research on the religious socialization of young people, work on this front should proceed with an awareness of the paradoxical nature of religion, and an appreciation for the context-specific contours and effects of religious socialization. Moreover, it would seem that inasmuch as religious socialization occurs through the daily interactions of young people with their parents, siblings, and peers, the time is ripe for methodological approaches (e.g., ethnographic research, in-depth case studies, online research) that are designed to examine the complex cultural processes that underlay the broad patterns reviewed here. Until that time, there is much to be gained from understanding that religion plays a critical, yet terribly complex, role in the socialization of young people.

REFERENCES

Alwin, Duane F. 1986. 'Religion and Parental Childrearing Orientations: Evidence of a Catholic-Protestant Convergence'. *American Journal of Sociology* 92: 412–40.

Ammerman, Nancy T. 1997. *Congregation and Community*. New Brunswick, NJ: Rutgers University Press.

Bartkowski, John P. 1995. 'Spare the Rod ..., or Spare the Child? Divergent Perspectives on Conservative Protestant Child Discipline'. *Review of Religious Research* 37: 97–116.

Bartkowski, John P. 2001. *Remaking the Godly Marriage: Gender Negotiation in Evangelical Families*. New Brunswick, NJ: Rutgers University Press.

Bartkowski, John P. 2004. *The Promise Keepers: Servants, Soldiers, and Godly Men*. New Brunswick, NJ: Rutgers University Press.

Bartkowski, John P. and Christopher G. Ellison 1995. 'Divergent Models of Childrearing: Conservative Protestants vs. the Mainstream Experts'. *Sociology of Religion* 56: 21–34.

Bartkowski, John P., W. Bradford Wilcox and Christopher G. Ellison 2000. 'Charting the Paradoxes of Evangelical Family Life: Gender and Parenting in Conservative Protestant Households'. *Family Ministry* 14: 9–21.

Bartkowski, John P. and W. Bradford Wilcox 2000. 'Conservative Protestant Child Discipline: The Case of Parental Yelling'. *Social Forces* 79: 865–91.

Bartkowski, John P. and Xiaohe Xu 2000. 'Distant Patriarchs or Expressive Dads? The Discourse and Practice of Fathering in Conservative

Protestant Families'. *The Sociological Quarterly* 41: 465–85.

Bartkowski, John P. and Xiaohe Xu 2007. 'Religion, Social Capital, and Teen Drug Use: A Preliminary Investigation'. *American Journal of Preventive Medicine* (in press).

Bartkowski, John P., Xiaohe Xu and Martin L. Levin 2007. 'The Impact of Religion on Child Development: Evidence from the Early Childhood Longitudinal Study'. *Social Science Research (in press)*.

Boyatzis, Chris 2003. 'Religious and Spiritual Development: An Introduction'. *Review of Religious Research* 44: 213–19.

Brasher, Brenda E. 2004. *Give Me That Online Religion*. New Brunswick, NJ: Rutgers University Press.

Bridges, Lisa J. and Kristin A. Moore 2002. 'Religion and Spirituality in Childhood and Adolescence' (Child Trends Publication #2002–39). Washington, D.C.: Child Trends.

Clark, Lynn Schofield 2003. *From Angels to Aliens: Teenagers, the Media, and the Supernatural*. New York: Oxford University Press.

Cnaan, Ram A., Richard J. Gelles and Jill W. Sinha 2004. 'Youth and Religion: The Gameboy Generation Goes to "Church"'. *Social Indicators Research* 68: 175–200.

Cornwall, Marie 1988. 'The Influence of Three Agents of Socialization'. Pp. 207–31 in *The Religion and Family Connection*, Volume 16, edited by Darwin L. Thomas. Provo, UT: Brigham Young University Press.

Ellison, Christopher G. 1996. 'Conservative Protestantism and the Corporal Punishment of Children: Clarifying the Issues'. *Journal for the Scientific Study of Religion* 35: 1–16.

Ellison, Christopher G. and John P. Bartkowski 1997. 'Religion and the Legitimation of Violence: The Case of Conservative Protestantism and Corporal Punishment'. Pp. 45–67 in *The Web of Violence: From Interpersonal to Global*, edited by Lester R. Kurtz and Jennifer L. Turpin. Urbana, IL: University of Illinois Press.

Ellison, Christopher G., John P. Bartkowski and Michelle L. Segal. 1996a. 'Conservative Protestantism and the Parental Use of Corporal Punishment'. *Social Forces* 74: 1003–28.

Ellison, Christopher G., John P. Bartkowski and Michelle L. Segal. 1996b. 'Do Conservative Protestant Parents Spank More Often? Further Evidence from the National Survey of Families and Households'. *Social Science Quarterly* 77: 663–73.

Ellison, Christopher G., Marc A. Musick and George W. Holden 1999. 'The Effects of Corporal Punishment on Young Children: Are They Less Harmful for Conservative Protestants?' Paper presented at the annual meetings of the Society for the Scientific Study of Religion, Boston, Massachusetts.

Ellison, Christopher G. and Darren E. Sherkat 1993a. 'Obedience and Autonomy: Religion and Parental Values Reconsidered'. *Journal for the Scientific Study of Religion* 32: 313–29.

Ellison, Christopher G. and Darren E. Sherkat 1993b. Conservative Protestantism and Support for Corporal Punishment. *American Sociological Review* 58: 131–44.

Gershoff, Elizabeth Thompson, Pamela C. Miller and George W. Holden 1999. 'Parenting Influences from the Pulpit: Religious Affiliation as a Determinant of Parental Corporal Punishment'. *Journal of Family Psychology* 13: 307–20.

Grasmick, Harold, Robert Bursik and M'lou Kimpel 1991. 'Protestant Fundamentalism and Attitudes toward Corporal Punishment of Children'. *Violence and Victims* 6: 283–97.

Hertel, Bradley R. and Michael J. Donahue 1995. 'Parental Influences on God Images among Children: Testing Durkheim's Metaphoric Parallelism'. *Journal for the Scientific Study of Religion* 34: 186–99.

Hoge, Dean R. and Thomas P. O'Conner 2004. 'Denominational Identity from Age Sixteen to Age Thirty-eight'. *Sociology of Religion* 65: 77–85.

King, Valarie 2003. 'The Influence of Religion on Fathers' Relationships with Their Children'. *Journal of Marriage and Family* 65: 382–95.

King, Pamela Ebstyne and James L. Furrow 2004. 'Religion as a Resource for Positive Youth Development: Religion, Social Capital, and Moral Outcomes'. *Developmental Psychology* 40: 703–13.

Mahoney, Annette 2005. 'Religion and Conflict in Marital and parent–child Relationships'. *Journal of Social Issues* 61: 689–706.

Mahoney, Annette, Kenneth I. Pargament, Nalini Tarakeshwar and Aaron B. Swank 2001. 'Religion in the Home in the 1980s and 90s: Meta-analyses and Conceptual Analyses of Links between Religion, Marriage, and Parenting'. *Journal of Family Psychology* 15: 559–96.

Mahoney, Annette, Kenneth I. Pargament, Aaron Murray-Swank and Nichole Murray-Swank 2003. 'Religion and the Sanctification of Family Relationships'. *Review of Religious Research* 44: 220–36.

Marks, Loren 2004. 'Sacred Practices in Highly Religious Families: Christian, Jewish, Mormon, and Muslim Perspectives'. *Family Process* 43: 217–31.

Meier, Ann M. 2003. 'Adolescents' Transition to First Intercourse, Religiosity, and Attitudes about Sex'. *Social Forces* 81: 1031–52.

Miller, Lisa, Virginia Warner, Priya Wickramaratne and Myrna Weissman 1997. 'Religiosity and Depression: Ten-Year Follow-up of Depressed Mothers and Offspring'. *Journal of the American Academy of Child and Adolescent Psychiatry* 36: 1416–25.

Nelson, Hart M. and Raymond H. Potvin 1980. 'Toward Disestablishment: New patterns of Social Class, Denomination, and Religiosity among Youth?' *Review of Religious Research* 22: 137–54.

Nucci, Larry and Elliot Turiel 1993. 'God's Word, Religious Rules, and Their Relation to Christian and Jewish Children's Concepts of Morality'. *Child Development* 64: 1475–91.

Pargament, Kenneth I. and Annette Mahoney 2005. 'Sacred Matters: Sanctification as a Vital Topic for the Psychology of Religion'. *International Journal for the Psychology of Religion* 15: 179–98.

Park, Jerry Z. and Christian Smith 2000. '"To Whom Much Has Been Given …": Religious Capital and Community Voluntarism among Churchgoing Protestants' *Journal for the Scientific Study of Religion* 39: 272–87.

Pearce, Lisa D and William G. Axin 1998. 'The Impact of Family Religious Life on the Quality of Mother-Child Relations'. *American Sociological Review* 63: 810–28.

Pearce, Lisa D. and Dana L. Haynie 2004. 'Intergenerational Religious Dynamics and Adolescent Delinquency'. *Social Forces* 82: 1553–72.

Putnam, Robert D. 2000. *Bowling Alone: The Collapse and Revival of American Community*. New York: Simon & Schuster.

Ratcliff, Donald 1992. 'Baby Faith: Infants, Toddlers, and Religion'. *Religious Education* 87: 117–26.

Regnerus, Mark 2000. 'Shaping Schooling Success: Religious Socialization and Educational Outcomes in Urban Public Schools'. *Journal for the Scientific Study of Religion* 39: 363–70.

Regnerus, Mark 2003. 'Linked Lives, Faith, and Behavior: Intergenerational Religious Influence on Adolescent Delinquency'. *Journal for the Scientific Study of Religion* 42: 189–203.

Regnerus, Mark 2007. *Forbidden Fruit: Sex and Religion in the Lives of American Teenagers*. New York: Oxford University Press.

Regnerus, Mark, Christian Smith and Melissa Fritsch 2003. 'Religion in the Lives of American Adolescents: A Review of the Literature'. A Research Report of the National Study of Youth and Religion, Number 3. Chapel Hill, NC: The National Study of Youth and Religion www.youthandreligion.org.

Regnerus, Mark, Christian Smith and David Sikkink 1998. 'Who Gives to the Poor? The Influence of Religious Tradition and Political Location on the Personal Generosity of Americans toward the Poor'. *Journal for the Scientific Study of Religion* 37: 481–93.

Regnerus, Mark D., Christian Smith and Brad Smith 2004. 'Social Context in the Development of Adolescent Religiosity'. *Applied Developmental Science* 8: 27–38.

Richert, Rebekah A. and Justin L. Barrett 2005. 'Do You See What I See? Young Children's Assumptions about God's Perceptual Abilities'. *International Journal for the Psychology of Religion* 15: 283–95.

Sherkat, Darren E. and Alfred Darnell 1999. 'The Effect of Parents' Fundamentalism on Children's Educational Attainment: Examining Differences by Gender and Children's Fundamentalism'. *Journal for the Scientific Study of Religion* 38: 23–35.

Smith, Christian 2003a. 'Religious Participation and Network Closure among American Adolescents'. *Journal for the Scientific Study of Religion* 42: 259–67.

Smith, Christian 2003b. 'Theorizing Religious Effects among American Adolescents'. *Journal for the Scientific Study of Religion* 42: 17–30.

Smith, Christian 2003c. 'Religious Participation and Parental Moral Expectations and Supervision of American Youth'. *Review of Religious Research* 44: 414–24.

Smith, Christian (with Melinda Lundquist Denton) 2005. *Soul Searching: The Religious and Spiritual Lives of American Teenagers*. New York: Oxford University Press.

Smith, Christian, Melinda Lundquist Denton, Robert Faris and Mark Regnerus 2002. 'Mapping American Adolescent Religious Participation'. *Journal for the Scientific Study of Religion* 41: 597–612.

Smith, Christian and Robert Faris 2002a. 'Religion and American Adolescent Delinquency, Risk Behaviors and Constructive Social Activities: A Research Report of the National Study of Youth and Religion', Number 1. Chapel Hill, NC: The National Study of Youth and Religion (www.youthandreligion.org).

Smith, Christian and Robert Faris 2002b. 'Religion and the Life Attitudes and Self-images of

American Adolescents: A Research Report of the National Study of Youth and Religion', Number 2. Chapel Hill, NC: The National Study of Youth and Religion (www.youthandreligion.org).

Smith, Christian, Robert Faris, Melinda Lundquist Denton and Mark Regnerus 2003. 'Mapping American Adolescent Subjective Religiosity and Attitudes of Alienation toward Religion: A Research Report'. *Sociology of Religion* 64: 111–33.

Smith, Christian and Phillip Kim 2003. 'Family Religious Involvement and the Quality of Parental Relationships for Families with Early Adolescents. A Research Report of the National Study of Youth and Religion', Number 5. Chapel Hill, NC: The National Study of Youth and Religion (www.youthandreligion.org).

Stewart, Sunita Mahtani and Michael Harris Bond 2002. 'A Critical Look at Parenting Research from the Mainstream: Problems Uncovered While Adapting Western Research to Non-Western Cultures'. *British Journal of Developmental Psychology* 20: 379–92.

Strayhorn, Joseph M., Carla S. Weidman and David Larson 1990. 'A Measure of Religiousness, and Its Relation to Parent and Child Mental Health Variables'. *Journal of Community Psychology* 18: 34–43.

Swank, Aaron B., Annette Mahoney and Kenneth I. Pargament 2000. 'A Sacred Trust: Parenting and the Spiritual Realm'. Paper presented at the annual meeting of the American Psychological Association. Washington, D.C.

Tirri, Kirsi, Mary K. Talent-Runnels and Petri Noklainen 2005. 'A Cross-cultural Study of Pre-adolescents' Moral, Religious, and Spiritual Questions'. *British Journal of Religious Education* 27: 207–14.

Wagener, Linda Mans, James L. Furrow, Pamela Ebstyne King, Nancy Leffert and Peter Benson 2003. 'Religious Involvement and Developmental Resources in Youth'. *Review of Religious Research* 44: 271–84.

Wallace, John, Jr. and Tyrone Forman 1997. 'Religion's Role in Promoting Health and Reducing Risk among American Youth'. *Health Education and Behavior* 25: 721–41.

Wilcox, W. Bradford 1998. 'Conservative Protestant Parenting: Authoritarian or Authoritative?' *American Sociological Review* 63, 796–809.

Wilcox, W. Bradford 2002. 'Religion, Convention, and Paternal Involvement'. *Journal of Marriage and Family*. 64: 780–93.

Wilcox, W. Bradford 2004. *Soft Patriarchs, New Men: How Christianity Shapes Husbands and Fathers*. Chicago: University of Chicago Press.

Wuthnow, Robert 1976. 'Recent Patterns of Secularization'. *American Sociological Review* 41: 850–67.

Wuthnow, Robert 1999. 'Mobilizing Civic Engagement: The Changing Impact of Religious Involvement.' Pp. 331–63 in *Civic Engagement in American Democracy* (eds) Theda Skocpol and M. P. Fiorina. Washington, D.C.: Brookings Institution Press.

25

Age, Generation, and Cohort in American Religion and Spirituality

MICHELE DILLON[1]

The purpose of this chapter is to highlight how age, generation, and cohort matter in shaping how people construe and practice religion. I confine my empirical focus to American society because as illuminated in particular by a generational lens, religion is heavily contextualized by the social, historical, and cultural circumstances in which it is construed and practiced. The many differences in the nature and place of religion in the United States compared to Western Europe, for example, both historically and in contemporary times (Warner, 1993; Davie, 2003), suggest that it is more sensible to use the space allotted to consider the complexities attendant on the interplay of age, generation and cohort in one societal context rather than comparatively, though readers familiar with other countries will be able to make inferences as to how these age and generational implications take effect elsewhere.

I begin with a general overview of the sociological relevance of age, generation, and cohort, and then discuss how their consideration complicates any simple model of religious change. I follow this with a review of the links between religion and aging. In the second half

of the chapter, I broaden the focus to consider the generational narrative of American religion. Here, I highlight how cohort or generational succession produces change as well as intra-family variation in religious habits and attitudes. The chapter concludes with a review of the inter-generational differences in religion evident among contemporary cohorts and I also take note of the broad cultural continuities in how Americans construe religion across generations.

THE SOCIOLOGICAL RELEVANCE OF AGE, GENERATION, AND COHORT

With the publication of Karl Mannheim's (1927/1952) seminal essay on the critical significance of the social and historical context in which ideas originate and get elaborated, sociologists began to recognize that different birth cohorts and generations inherit, experience, and learn to think about the social world in different ways. The relevance of social context to the cultivation and development of specific ways of apprehending the world was already underscored in Karl Marx's writings on ideology and in Max Weber's on culture and stratification. But Mannheim highlighted the sociological importance of attentiveness to a discrete generational consciousness or identity and opened the path for social scientists to map the dynamic connections between the temporal progress of individual lives and macro societal change. We can investigate whether in fact the social and historical context impacts how individuals think and what they know and what they do by looking for evidence of generational variation in attitudes and behavior. It is thus customary for sociologists to generalize about the Depression Era generation, the World War II generation, the Baby Boomers, Generation X, and so on.

Generational frames are particularly valuable for the sociology of religion because they offer discrete, historically meaningful time frames by which to track and tap into the multiple ways in which religion may vary from one social and historical context to another. Equally important, they also enable sociologists to illustrate how within a given historical period, different generations construe religion, thus highlighting that religion is invariably multi-layered and differentiated, and that it evolves in varying ways over time and across social conditions and circumstances.

Related to generational differences are cohort differences. Birth cohort typically refers to all individuals born in a single year of birth or born within the span of a specified number of years. Although cohort and generation are closely related, and some social scientists may even use the terms interchangeably, it is customary to regard generation as encompassing several birth cohorts. In a defining article, 'The cohort as a concept in the study of social change,' Norman Ryder (1965) argued that the cohort is a more precisely defined temporal unit from which generations are constructed; for Ryder, cohorts provide the fundamental mechanism by which social change is introduced into a population. New birth cohorts replace the cohorts of older age individuals and this demographic process of population replacement inevitably introduces social change because the same socio-historical events impact

younger cohorts differently than older cohorts and these differential effects can persist across the life course. That each generation can claim a discrete chronological and social history is well captured by the scholarly and popular acknowledgment of inter-generational family dynamics; the recognition that each generation can comprise a relatively broad span of birth years and that the younger or the older generation's expectations and consciousness are shaped by different social and cultural circumstances.

It is true, of course, that regardless of age, different generations simultaneously experience the same historically or culturally significant events that occur within a given period. Nevertheless, the perception and impact of these events will likely vary by age. Age is not simply a number, but a signifier of how much history and cultural memory the individual has already acquired, and is intertwined with generational expectations and social roles whose obligations and experiences also shape how the individual sees and makes sense of the world. Developmental psychologists argue that individuals develop a more settled identity structure as they age (Levinson, 1996), as they progress across the life course and negotiate its various events and transitions. This means that at any given moment in history younger cohorts are more likely than older cohorts to be influenced by particular social and cultural events such that they incorporate their impact into their own (relatively unsettled) identity.

Thus, for example, even though World War II is a historically momentous event that impacted a large aggregate of twentieth-century lives, it had a more formative impact on the cohort who served in the war (and their spouses) than on those who were older or who were too young to serve. Similarly, the cultural upheavals of the 1960s were witnessed by many people, but they exerted a much more critical impact on college-age cohorts than on their younger-age siblings or on their parents and grandparents. A generational focus thus retrieves a core sociological point, namely that social context matters and, therefore, the socio-biographical location in which objective historical events are experienced will necessarily differentiate their perception and impact among the population aggregate who experienced the event. In other words, a generational perspective gives pause to generalizing claims about historical epochs; as I will note later, even the American Puritan era, though typically portrayed in homogeneous terms, was experienced differently by its different generations.

The sociological importance of differentiating between generation and cohort becomes especially relevant in discussing the social experiences of birth cohorts who, though born just a few years apart, nevertheless encounter very different social worlds, and by extension generational experiences, due to the coincidence of their age and the timing of specific institutional and historical events; birth cohorts in the early and late 1920s are a good case in point (as I will discuss in a later section). Clearly there is no simple logic by which to draw a line between cohort and generation; these categorizations – whether to use single birth cohort years or to group birth years in a particular cohort order, and whether generations should be narrowly or broadly encompassing of cohorts, are questions whose answers must be guided by the theoretical questions and statistical methodology informing the research at hand.

Demographers typically group birth cohorts by decades coinciding with the Census years (e.g., Myers, 2004), whereas generations usually encompass a 15 to 20 year span. Thus cultural reference to the Baby Boomer generation typically includes all those born between 1946 and 1965 even though it also makes good socio-demographic sense to demarcate the early boomers (born 1946–1955) from the late boomers (born 1956–1965). Using a shorter span of birth years, Generation X refers to those born between 1966 and 1975, and Generation Y, 1976–1985 (Myers, 2004, 6). If, on the other hand, one is interested in examining how the social experiences of individuals born prior to World War II are different from successive cohorts, it makes sense to consider combining several birth cohorts as comprising a single generation, as indeed Putnam (2000: 254) does in referring to these cohorts as America's 'long civic generation,' i.e., those who were born

between 1910 and 1940 and who show substantially more social and community involvement than successive cohorts.

Independent of cohort and generation as categories for mapping social change, age, of course, is also a major source of social variation. Family, work, volunteering and other social roles are age-graded as are religious rites and ceremonies. Age is, most fundamentally, the marker of an individual's chronological life, demarcating maturation and developmental progress through the life cycle. Although age can stand alone as an independent variable predicting various outcomes, it is generally more fruitful to integrate age with cohort or generation; namely, the extent to which the coincidence of being of a particular age at a particular time in history provides a different generational experience and consciousness than had the individual belonged to a different birth cohort. Clearly, to be a 21-year-old in 2006 is to experience a very different societal context than a 21-year-old would have experienced in 1986 or 1966 or 1946.

It is customary to map age onto stages or phases in the life course such as adolescence, early adulthood, mid-life, and late adulthood. Each of these stages confront the individual with specific identity tasks (cf. Erikson, 1950) whose successful achievement is critical to ensuring that the individual functions as a purposeful and productive member of society. Nevertheless, the cultural expectations linked to age-specific behavior shift to some extent with large-scale structural and historical changes, and within families, may also be shaped by birth order. In contemporary times, with the economic pressures of globalization and job deskilling, the role of college student is no longer necessarily associated with the moratorium from adult responsibilities typically found between adolescence and early adulthood. Instead, increasing numbers of traditional-age (late adolescence) college students work while attending college, and increasing numbers of older age students return to college in mid-life in order to acquire new job-related skills. And, it is also increasingly common today to see older age retirees attending college in the post-retirement phase for purely intellectual fulfillment, taking advantage of their comparatively greater affluence and health relative to earlier generations of older age Americans. Clearly, then, the social and cultural context can moderate our expectations of age-related behavior and hence the critical importance of considering the generational context in which aging occurs. Yet, at the same time, there is evidence that some age-related attitudes and behaviors persist irrespective of birth cohort, generational experiences or historical era (e.g., the importance given to children's religious socialization by successive generations of parents).

AGE, GENERATION, AND COHORT IN THE MOSAIC OF RELIGIOUS CHANGE

The dominant thrust of sociological and demographic analyses is to present social change as progressive and linear. As Dowell Myers (2004: 6) has commented, 'Throughout American history, the presumption has been that each generation enjoys a higher socioeconomic status than the last.' Yet, of course, as Myers (2004: 8) points out, this progressive story was seriously disrupted by the Great Depression and in recent decades by economic problems (such as inflation, recession, and the high cost of home ownership) that were particularly burdensome to the late Baby Boomers (those born between 1956 and 1965) and currently to Generation X (those born during the following decade). Nonetheless, the presumption is that 'each decade a new cohort enters adulthood and is launched on its trajectory from a (usually) higher starting point' (Myers, 2004: 10).

If demographers see cohort succession in terms of upward socio-economic trajectories, sociologists of religion tend to expect cohort succession to produce a progressive decline in religious engagement. The strong hold of secularization theory and its core assumption that religion declines with modernization has framed how sociologists from Max Weber and Emile Durkheim onward think about religion and social change. The tenaciousness of this

assumption has been abetted by the relative paucity of historical data on the religious habits and attitudes of ordinary people prior to the 1940s when opinion polling began and started a tradition of attentiveness to religious attitudes and behavior. Consequently, sociologists tend to use relatively narrow time frames (and narrow geographical frames) in assessing secularization and omit consideration of the social, cultural and political factors that variously influence religious expression in different historical periods (see Gorski, 2003 for a critique). This truncated historical perspective distorts understanding of the changing place of religion in individual lives and in society across time. And from a secularization perspective, this distortion can be particularly misleading because current cross-sectional trends are usually compared with cross-sectional trends from the 1950s, a period when levels of church activity were at a peak.

Introducing cohort considerations further complicates the assessment of whether and how religion changes over time. Current trends and historical patterns are themselves subject to varying demographic forces that can variously impact the amount of religious activity observed at any given time (see Hout, 2003). Clearly, some cohorts are born during a period of decreased or of heightened religious activity in the society as a whole and this socio-cultural context will shape the trajectory of the subsequent religious involvement across the life course of the cohort members (see Hout and Greeley, 1987). Americans who entered adulthood in the early 1980s, for example, a time of increased societal interest in religion, and of an evangelical resurgence in particular, may be more likely than those who were young adults in the 1970s to become religiously involved and to maintain that commitment across adulthood independent of any aging, life course, or historical effects.

The cohort effect of this greater religiousness, moreover, will further reverberate on other cohorts as a result of the multiple dynamics of cross-generational religious influences. Because adult children influence the religious commitments of their aging parents (Sherkat, 2003), this can contribute to a general increase in the religious involvement of the older (parents) cohort. And, these effects will not die as the 1980s' cohort dies. Because grandparents exert a critical socializing influence on grandchildren (King and Elder, 1999), an effect that will likely become more visible with the increased longevity and functional ability of older age individuals, we might well expect that the religiousness of the grandchildren of the 1980s' cohort (or of any other comparatively more, or less, religious cohort) will be influenced too, and so on. Indeed whether as a function of family socialization, or more generally of the sociological coincidence between age and social roles, there is some evidence that an individual's religious involvement at any given time in adulthood is likely to parallel that of their parents when they were of the same age or phase in the life course (the religious life cycle hypothesis; e.g., Greeley, 1980), though these patterns are also contingent on historical and cohort effects. In any event, each cohort's religious baseline will impact the cohort's aggregate life course patterns of religiousness as well as reverberating on other, older and younger, cohorts.

Another way in which cohort matters is the variability in the demographic characteristics of specific cohorts, a variability that both directly and indirectly impacts religious engagement. Most fundamentally, some cohorts are numerically bigger (or smaller) than others, and some cohorts will have cohort-specific marriage, divorce, and fertility trends. These demographic factors, in turn, impact levels of religious engagement in all sorts of interrelated ways. Religious activity tends to be especially pronounced during the early adulthood, family-formation phase of the life course, and is further contingent on the age of parents and whether they are still married, single or divorced (e.g., Chaves, 1991; Stolzenberg et al., 1995; Myers, 1996;). Consequently, for any given cohort, change in such basic demographic trends as age of first marriage and fertility and divorce rates can produce significant shifts in aggregate patterns of religious engagement.

The culturally embedded American tradition of sending school-age children to Sunday school regardless of the parents' level of religious involvement (Dillon and Wink, 2007), means that an increase in the population of children should increase demand for religious services and a subsequent decrease should result in the opposite trend. Similarly, the currently observed increase in the proportion of evangelicals in the United States is largely due to the higher fertility rates of religious conservatives than a result of religious switching from other denominations (Hout, 2003; Hout et al., 2001). Shifts in denominational membership and religious activity are further prompted by aggregate changes in regional migration and especially, immigration, given the pronounced ethnic contours of American religion marked by earlier and new generations of immigrants.

These examples underscore that any increases or decreases in religious preferences and activity should not mechanistically be interpreted as evidence of a surge in religiosity or conversely of secularization. Such trends, rather, would have to be contextualized with regard to demographic changes as well as in regard to historically specific events and other societal factors.

The importance of considering religious trends in terms of both cohort variation and historical and cultural developments is well demonstrated by Hout and Fischer (2002). They document a significant two-fold increase from 7 to 14 per cent within a ten-year period in the proportion of American adults who report no religious preference (from 1991 to 1998). They find that recent cohorts are more likely than earlier cohorts to have been raised without any religion (p. 169), a pattern that produces a cohort replacement (and secularization) effect that contributes to fewer people currently having a religious preference. At the same time, however, Hout and Fischer (2002) also find that the decline in religiously affiliated Americans is not driven by cohort succession alone. In other words, the increase in religious disaffiliation was a more general trend, true of younger and older cohorts alike. And, because it occurred in the 1990s and not before, Hout and Fischer link it to the cultural conflicts that revolved around religion in the 1990s. They argue that these church-associated political conflicts made political liberals and moderates less inclined to identify with churches and institutionalized religion. Further, because those who have disaffiliated from church have nevertheless maintained their religious and spiritual beliefs, Hout and Fischer argue that the trend toward disaffiliation should not simply be seen as evidence of secularization.

RELIGION AND AGING: BRINGING BACK COHORT AND CONTEXT

A core question for social scientists is whether the process of aging impacts religious involvement. The research findings in this area are somewhat inconclusive. On the one hand, large cross-sectional studies using data gathered across various age groups at a particular point in time present a map of American religiosity indicating that religiousness increases with age. Thus, older age individuals report higher levels of religious participation than younger age individuals (Hout and Greeley, 1987) though there is some uncertainty as to when religious involvement peaks. The public opinion data analyzed by Hout and Greeley (1987) suggest that the steepest rate of increase in religiousness occurs between ages 45 and 55, with Protestants peaking in their 40s and Catholics after age 60. In contrast, Rossi's (2001) survey data indicate that the sharpest increase occurs when individuals are in their 50s and 60s. In any case there is a strong presumption that, as summarized by Gallup, 'Religion's importance intensifies as people grow older' (Gallup and Lindsay, 1999: 74).

The presumption of a positive relation between aging and religiousness, however, is somewhat misleading. Such trends (e.g., Gallup and Lindsay, 1999) are typically based on the conflation of age group (as a category) with aging (as a process), thus ignoring the influence of cohort on aging (with the exception of Hout and Greeley, 1987; Hout and Fischer, 2002). It tends to be assumed that the 50 to 65-year-olds who show greater religious involvement at a given time than those who are in their 40s at the same interview time have become more religious with age, i.e., that their religiousness

has increased as a result of aging. What is frequently omitted from consideration is whether these 50 to 65-year-olds were less (or similarly, or more) religious when they were in their 40s. Cross-sectional designs do not have multi-time follow-up data and while individuals' retrospective accounts of religiousness at earlier times in their lives lend support to the age-increased religiosity thesis, they are compromised somewhat by memory, cultural changes, and social desirability biases.

The finding that different age groups have different levels of religiousness is easy to interpret as an effect of the aging process alone, rather than the outcome of a mix of cohort, historical and aging effects. But essentially it simply tells us that at a particular moment in time, different age categories have different levels of religiousness. The impression of an aging effect is, of course, further encouraged by the fact that studies customarily find that older age categories have progressively higher levels of involvement than younger age groups. And, even though aggregate shifts occur in the population composition of older age categories, the cohort succession, secularization assumption would predict that the older age category (irrespective of its size) would invariably be more religious than younger cohorts. (Beyond individual level data, however, an increase in the older age population should, following the religion and aging hypothesis, result in more religious activity in the society as a whole, and similarly a proportionate reduction in the older age population should produce a contrary trend; once again, demographic factors complicate the assessment of secularization.)

Unlike cross-sectional studies, longitudinal studies avoid the problem of comparing different age cohorts, but they have other limitations. Typically, because of the financial and logistical challenges in following the same individuals over time, longitudinal studies use relatively small and homogeneous samples, and they too have produced mixed results on the relation between religion and aging. Data from a 40-year follow-up study of male graduates of Amherst College (Shand, 1990) suggest stability in adult religiousness, whereas the Terman study of intellectually gifted individuals

(McCullough and Polak, 2007), shows an inverted U-curve trajectory with religiousness increasing from early to middle adulthood and then declining from age 50 onward. The generalizability of the patterns in these studies is limited, however, because of the specialized composition of their samples (male college graduates and intellectually gifted people, respectively), whose religiousness may be quite different than commonly found in socially mixed, community samples.

Disentangling age, cohort and generational or historical effects on religious participation is clearly complicated, and as Hout and Greeley discuss (1987: 327) its methodology lacks final resolution. I would, however, like to illustrate the interplay between age, generation and cohort using as a case study data from a study established in California in the 1920s (by the Institute of Human Development [IHD] at the University of California, Berkeley). The IHD study is especially well suited to this purpose. It has long-term longitudinal data gathered over 60 years from a heterogeneous community sample that is differentiated by gender, denomination (Protestant/Catholic), and social class.

Importantly for our purposes, a further source of variation is that the study participants also come from two different birth cohorts; one-third of the sample was born in 1920–21 and two-thirds were born in 1928–29. Though eight years, a half-generation, may not strike as too-likely a source of generational variation, the social experiences of individuals born in the early 1920s were substantially different from those born in the late 1920s. Those born in the early years of the decade are children of the Great Depression (Elder, 1974), they entered military service in World War II upon graduation from High School, and encountered the cultural turmoil of the late-1960s when, approaching age 50, their adult identity was well settled. By contrast, those born in the late 1920s avoided the childhood deprivation associated with the Depression, they graduated from High School just as World War II was ending, and they were on the cusp of middle age (age 40) as the cultural changes and religious transformation of the

late-1960s unfolded. The timing of these various events in the life course of individuals born less than ten years apart resulted in significant differences in their life experiences and accordingly it makes good sociological sense to regard those born in the 1920s as representing not only different birth cohorts but also different generations.

Another advantage of the IHD study is that it allows us to compare different types of religious engagement across time. Social scientists frequently emphasize the importance of paying attention to the multidimensionality of religion; yet many study designs allow attentiveness to only one aspect of religion, typically church participation. Because the IHD study gathered extensive in-depth interview data on religious beliefs, attitudes and practices at each of five interview times from adolescence through late adulthood it has been possible to code the data for both church-centered religiousness and for more individualized or non-institutionalized spiritual seeking. Being able to explore how both religiousness and spiritual seeking intertwine with age, cohort and historical change illuminates the complexity of religion in America as well as the ways in which its expression is shaped by different cohorts and socio-historical forces.

In the IHD study, religiousness did not follow a straightforward, linear upward trend across the life course.[2] Instead, the pattern of change was captured by a quadratic function, meaning that it was best described as a U-curve with levels of religiousness highest in adolescence and late adulthood and dipping in the middle years (Dillon and Wink, 2007). The mean level of religiousness among the study participants as a whole decreased from adolescence to early adulthood (age 30s), and from early to middle adulthood (age 40s). It then reached a plateau between middle and late middle adulthood (age mid 50s/early 60s), before increasing significantly from late middle to late adulthood (age late 60s/mid 70s).

The general U-curve pattern of change in religiousness over the life course was true of both cohorts (born 1920–21; 1928–29), of Catholics and Protestants, and of men and women. This suggests that the ebb and flow in religiousness over time was most likely driven by general social forces that cut across the demographic characteristics of the sample. The exact timing of the dip in religiousness varied, however, in terms of these variables and points to the importance not simply of age but the social and historical context in which aging occurs.

The cohort difference in the timing of individuals' dip in religiousness points to the relevance of specific generational or historical experiences in shaping religious involvement. Although both cohorts showed a U-curve pattern of change, the younger participants (born in 1928–29) had declined in religiousness by early adulthood (age 30s; 1958) whereas the older participants (born 1920–21) tended not to decline until middle adulthood (age late 40s; 1970). The two cohorts did not differ significantly in religiousness in adolescence. But, the older study participants had very different experiences in late adolescence (e.g., the Depression) and early adulthood (e.g., participation in World War II) than their younger peers though they differed in age by only eight years. It may well be that as a result of their particular socio-historical experiences, the older cohort maintained a greater commitment to established social institutions and traditions, including religion, and thus were slower than the younger cohort to decrease their religious involvement.

In late adulthood, nevertheless, members of the older and younger cohorts had similar levels of religiousness. This again suggests that religiousness is a function of social context – the free time available during the post-retirement period with the absence of burdensome work and extensive family responsibilities makes it easier for older age individuals to include church involvement as part of their schedules. In any event, the surge in religiousness did not appear to be driven by the existential concerns associated with impending mortality. If this were a motivator, we would have expected the older cohort, who as a group had by late adulthood experienced more illness and bereavement in their lives than the younger cohort, to be comparatively more religious as a way of coping with the losses and fears

of older age. And nor was religiousness related to fear of death among either cohort (Wink and Scott, 2005). In sum, the similar level of religiousness for both cohorts in late adulthood suggests that the relatively greater imminence of mortality was not a major driver of the general increase in religiousness in late adulthood.

The comparison of change among Protestants and Catholics in the IHD study highlighted the relevance of historical and institutional events. The only significant difference in the pattern of change between Catholics and Protestants occurred in the 12-year interval between 1970 and 1982 (from middle to late middle adulthood). During this time, the Protestants showed little change in religiousness but Catholics declined significantly. The decline among Catholics was largely concentrated among those who were relatively less religious rather than moderately or more highly involved, with a doubling from middle to late middle adulthood in the percentage of individuals who were not religious (21 per cent versus 42 per cent). In comparison, the proportion of Catholics with moderate to high religious involvement showed little change during this time (38 per cent versus 33 per cent).

The significant mid-life decline in religiousness evident among IHD Catholics captures a more general Catholic historical effect. It coincided with the disaffection among American Catholics as a whole regarding the Church's ban on contraception issued in 1968 (*Humanae Vitae*), and the Vatican's unwillingness to continue reforms initiated by the Second Vatican Council. The pattern of Catholic decline in church attendance starting in 1969 and followed by a stabilization in lower church attendance by the mid-1970s is well documented (Greeley, 1985; Hout and Greeley, 1987). Similarly, in the IHD study, Catholics (and Protestants) increased in religiousness by late adulthood, and for the Catholics this was sufficient to bring their involvement largely back on par with their early adulthood commitment.

The social context informing the relation between religion and aging is further highlighted by the different timing of men and women's dip in religiousness. Men's drop in religiousness set in earlier than that for women with the significant decline occurring between adolescence and early adulthood (age 30s). Women's religiousness, by contrast, did not dip until middle adulthood (age 40s) and the decline was not as precipitous as in the case of men. Because the study participants tended to marry early and have children at a young age, the mid-life decline in women's religiousness largely coincided with children leaving home and the attendant absence of child socialization pressures.

The timing of women's drop in religiousness fits with the findings from other studies that point to the critical cultural role that the religious socialization of children exerts on increasing the religious involvement of parents, especially mothers. This responsibility was especially pronounced for the IHD women who, reflecting the more traditional gender social roles confronted by their generation, were by and large not in the labor force in the 1950s and 60s when their children were young. Consequently, whereas many of the men felt free to drop out of church early on in adulthood, women's slower pace of religious detachment was largely influenced by the pull of child socialization pressures. Earlier cross-sectional research (e.g., Fichter, 1952) and recent retrospective findings from elderly individuals (Ingersoll Dayton et al., 2002), as well as findings from the baby boom generation (Roof, 1999), point to a similar pattern of decline in parental religiousness once children leave home.

Across the sample as a whole, birth order was unrelated to religiousness. Within cohort, however, it was a source of variation. Contrary to the expectation that first-born children are more conscientious and thus tend to be more religiously involved than later-born siblings (cf. Saroglou and Fiasse, 2003), this was not the case in the IHD study despite the fact that religiousness and conscientiousness were positively related (Dillon and Wink, 2007). It was not the first-born, but the later-born, who tended to be more religious in late adulthood and this was especially true of women in the younger cohort. What exactly about early family experiences, personality, and the larger social context accounts for this pattern remains unclear and suggests that the relation between birth-order and religiousness deserves further exploration using other samples (see Saroglou and Fiasse, 2003).

In sum, the IHD findings clearly indicate that religiousness changes with age but the changes observed are not a function of either age or of aging *per se*. The patterns in the data highlight that the relation between religion and age is contingent on the interplay between cohort, historical period and generational social context (e.g., social roles associated with parenting, retirement, etc.). Moreover, while change occurs, it is also true that there is a certain stability in religiousness over the life course. Eyeing the life course as a whole, it is remarkable that despite a pattern of statistically significant change from one time period to another, the level of religiousness among the IHD participants in late adulthood was not significantly different from the level in early adulthood. In other words, at the end of the life course the IHD study participants completed a full circle and manifested the same degree of religiousness as 40 years earlier when in their 30s. Thus while the increase in religiousness from late middle to late adulthood would, taken on its own, be indicative of the fact that people become more religious in old age, when seen in a longer light, it is more indicative of stability than increase. In short, had there been data for the study participants for just two time periods, early and late adulthood, their religiousness could have been graphed essentially as a straight line. This perception of stability in religiousness is reinforced by the fact that across all the time points the magnitude of change from one time to another, even when significant, tended to be small; the magnitude of change for all of the statistically significant effects did not exceed one quarter of a standard deviation (Dillon and Wink, 2007). We can conclude from the IHD data, therefore, that the relation between religiousness and aging is relatively stable across adulthood and yet contingent on the social and historical contexts in which people move as they age and encounter different phases of the life course.

Spiritual Seeking

The IHD study participants, born in the 1920s, are the generational parents of the baby boomers, the generation who has led the way in embracing the non-institutionalized forms of spiritual seeking that have become so prevalent in America since the 1960s (discussed in more detail in a later section). The post-60s' shift in American religion, however, was also evident among this older generation, and in ways that again help to illustrate the interplay between cohort and historical effects. The IHD study participants showed a general increase in spiritual seeking over time, and one that was especially pronounced in the second half of adulthood. Using a practice-oriented definition, spiritual seekers' average scores increased significantly from their 40s (interviews conducted in 1970) to their 50s (1982), and especially from their 50s to their 70s (1997–2000). The presence of a generalized increase in spiritual seeking – true of men and women, members of both cohorts, and Protestants and Catholics (Wink and Dillon, 2002) – supports the hypothesis that aging has an effect on individuals' spiritual concerns, thus making spiritual engagement a more salient part of life as people move from middle to late adulthood.

Clearly, however, the post-mid-life trajectory in the IHD data also had a definite social and cultural logic. The study participants entered middle adulthood in the late 1960s and consequently their negotiation of mid-life identity during this time of cultural upheaval may have primed their openness to the new currents that were taking hold in America's vastly expanding spiritual marketplace (Roof, 1999). These newly accessible spiritual resources could be drawn on to enhance a preexisting disposition toward a journey of self-discovery. Or, independent of any inner psychological process, the public accessibility of these new resources may have generated a new spiritual awareness among individuals who were attracted to these innovative elements in the popular culture. Moreover, the fact that the vast majority of the IHD study participants were living in California, the cauldron of new forms of spirituality, greatly enhanced their access to spiritual ferment and exploration. Thus the greater salience of spiritual seeking for the study participants from late middle age onward most likely had as much to do with an expanded spiritual marketplace and geographical context as with chronological age or phase in the life course.

The historical or cultural explanation for the post-mid-life increase in spiritual seeking is strengthened by the fact that it was the younger cohort (those born in 1928–29) who showed the steeper increase in spirituality. The younger participants were in their early 40s at the time of the 1970 interview. From a maturation perspective, therefore, they were less likely to have had a settled adult identity (cf. Levinson, 1996), compared to the older participants who, born in 1920–21, were approaching age 50. This developmental difference, in turn, would make it more likely for the younger cohort to be open to, and influenced by, the cultural changes of the 1960s. Indeed, analyses of the study participants' personality data show that at mid-life (1970), but not in early adulthood (1958), members of the younger cohort were more likely than the older cohort to show evidence of identity exploration (Dillon and Wink, 2007). Giving emphasis to the significance of historical-cultural context in aiding the post-mid-life spiritual growth of individuals does not negate the psychological maturational thesis (e.g., Sinnott, 1994) that the post-mid-life phase in the life-course necessitates an adaptive shift in an individual's identity toward non-material or spiritual concerns. It simply affirms the fact that individual lives take shape in particular socio-historical and cultural contexts, and that these contexts are bounded in quite specific ways by birth cohort and generation.

Overall, the IHD findings on religiousness, spiritual seeking, and aging indicate the relevance of cohort, historical and institutional events (e.g., Vatican II; the 1960s), and the generational context in which people execute their social roles as forces accounting for age-related changes in religious and spiritual behavior. Age matters, but it is its intertwining with the social context in which aging happens – the varying social roles associated with different phases in the life course and their coincidence with the timing of particular historical and cultural events – that more fully fleshes out why age functions as it does. The IHD study participants were relatively similar demographically in terms of marriage and family patterns – most married and did so around the same age and had children within a relatively similar span of time. Such within-cohort homogeneity is not characteristic of all cohorts, and certainly with the increased rates of cohabitation, divorce and single parenthood, is uncharacteristic of recent cohorts. Studies using a broader mix of cohorts (and indeed greater racial and regional diversity) may well find that age and phase in the life course do not map as neatly together as was true for the IHD participants. Hence the patterns observed between aging and various forms of religious engagement may well vary for different cohorts, and these patterns will be further contingent on the specific historical and cultural context informing those cohorts' lives.

AMERICAN RELIGIOUS HISTORY AS A GENERATIONAL NARRATIVE

The history of American religion quite easily falls into a narrative of successive generations. The framing and sequencing of important events and developments and their intertwined connection with the dominant figures that have made an indelible imprint on the evolution of American religion makes for a story of intergenerational influences, counter-influences, and adaptive innovations. We readily think of American history in terms of John Winthrop and the Puritan settler generation, of the post-Revolutionary generation who carved a populist freedom in the everyday practice of religion, of the revival generations who made the First and, later, the Second Great Awakenings so momentous, of the Catholic immigrant generation who literally built a powerful church, of the Moral Reform and Social Gospel generations who with different methods tried to improve American society,

of the Fundamentalist generation who resisted scientific and modernist influences, and in more recent times, the 1950s generation who so zealously embraced religion and the 1960s generation who redefined the meanings of religious freedom both within and beyond the church.

Thinking about American religion in terms of generations accomplishes two things. One, it draws attention to the fact that religion is invariably shaped by the particular cultural mood and social conditions of any given historical time period; different times give rise to different errands (to adapt Perry Miller's phrasing). And second, it can cultivate a genealogy of religion which recognizes that the articulation of religion takes on different accents for different generations *simultaneously*. Thus, although time progresses in a linear manner, religious change does not necessarily follow a progressive linear pattern of decline or, indeed, of resurgence. A generational perspective thus allows for a greater appreciation both of the dynamic ebb and flow of religion across time as well as for its diverse multi-generational expression at any one time. A generational narrative, therefore, will likely complicate historical narratives that tell either a purely progressive or a purely defensive story of religious change.

The very beginnings of American history attest to the significance of generation in shaping religious beliefs and practices. We rightly think of the Colonial settlers as serious and devout Christians committed, in the words of John Winthrop (1630/1965: 77), to building an honorable society that would be seen as a city upon a hill. But less than 50 years after Winthrop's culturally decisive sermon, clergy and elders at the Boston Formal Synod in 1679 lamented among other failings, the 'much visible decay of godliness, contentiousness in the churches, and violation of the Sabbath' (Miller, 1964: 5–6). Indeed, it was not long at all before the first settlers encountered the inter-generational dilemma that history attests confronts all generations: namely, how to ensure that the religiosity of the next generation remains as pure as they believe their own to be. The historian Mark Noll (1992/2003: 48) describes the Puritans' inter-generational challenge:

As the 1640s gave way to the 1650s, more and more children of the earliest settlers failed to experience God's grace in the same fashion as their parents, and hence they did not seek full membership in the churches. The problem became acute when these children began to marry and have children of their own. Under the Puritans' Reformed theology, converted people had the privilege of bringing their infant children to be baptized as a seal of God's covenant grace. Now, however, many of those who had been baptized as infants were not stepping forth on their own to confess Christ. Yet they wanted to have their children baptized. The Puritan dilemma was delicate: leaders wished to preserve the church for genuine believers, but they also wanted to keep as many as possible under the influence of the church. Their solution was to propose a 'halfway' covenant whereby second-generation New Englanders could bring their third-generation children for baptism and a halfway membership. Participation in the Lord's Supper remained a privilege for those who could testify to a specific work of God's grace in their lives.

This generational story offers three lessons. One, the fact that the Puritans had to resort to 'halfway' solutions in order to preserve their religious beliefs and practices trans-generationally offers a much needed caution to cultural observers who lament the dilution of contemporary religion. The lightening of the cloak of religious obligation certainly takes on varying expressions but it is not a new phenomenon. Religious activity in times past was not always as pure as some contemporary observers frequently argue and who confidently do so even in the absence of empirical evidence against which to assess the validity of the claim. Thus a recent study concludes that contemporary American teenagers have a faith that 'seems qualitatively quite different from the faith of the same [Christian] traditions in previous eras' (Smith and Denton, 2005: 154). Such claims deserve more nuance in light of the generational dynamics that have long characterized American religion.

Second, the Puritan experience underscores that the autonomous adaptation and creative reshaping of religion to meet the needs of successive generations is in large part what enables religion to maintain its social significance across time. And, third, it reminds us that while our sequencing of historical periods is a valuable heuristic in demarcating and making comparisons across different socio-historical contexts, it can suppress the inter-generational

and other social differences that invariably characterize religion (as well as other aspects of everyday life).

The community studies conducted by the Lynds in the American Mid-West in the 1920s and 1930s also point to how generational influences and cohort replacement processes push social and religious change. The Lynds documented a community in which there were many (Christian) churches, religious affiliation was an assumed part of individual and family identity, and attendance at Sunday services as well as weekly prayer meetings and Bible classes was quite normative. The church was also a center for social activities ranging from organized church dinners, young people's athletic and social groups, and even dances in church halls. This picture of a church-centered communal life also bore traces, however, of a diminishing religious dominance. We can easily contrast the Lynds' portrait with that offered by Alexis de Tocqueville during his American travels almost 100 years earlier ([1840] 1946: 143). De Tocqueville's journalistic eye described the Sabbath as the day on which 'all noises cease; a deep tranquility, say rather the solemn calm of meditation, succeeds the turmoil of the week, and the soul resumes possession and contemplation of itself.' The solemnity of the Sabbath was noticeably well in decline, however, at the turn of the twentieth century. The Lynds found that 'although the tradition is that 'every one goes to church,' a count of actual church attendance contradicted this assumption. Similarly, they argued, that while 'in theory, religious beliefs dominate all other activities in Middletown, large regions of Middletown's life appear uncontrolled by them' (Lynd and Lynd 1929: 358, 406).

Competition between religious and secular activities was evident not only in the churches' accommodation of non-religious social events (e.g., athletics, dances) but also in the increased prevalence of secular activities being held on Sundays and in other ways undermining the prominence of religious activities in daily life. This trend did not emerge from nowhere; evidence suggests that recreational activities were challenging religious activities at least as early as the 1890s (Lynd and Lynd, 1929: 339–43). Clearly, the increased secularization of the Sabbath was driven by larger modernizing changes in society, and especially by the expansion of leisure activities made accessible by technological innovations such as the invention of the car, a direct effect of which was to make family car-rides and picnics on Sunday more attractive than church and Sunday school. In-depth interviews conducted with California adolescents and their parents in the 1930s and 40s (from the IHD study discussed earlier) gave voice to this new threat to the dominance of church. One upper-class Protestant father, though he himself was not religious, was very critical of the inability of churches to stem the attraction of non-religious activities. He complained: 'The automobile has done a terrible thing to the church, and I'd like to see the tendency for people to go for a Sunday ride instead of to church corrected' (Dillon and Wink, 2007: 29).

GENERATIONAL DYNAMICS WITHIN FAMILIES

These examples of how cohort replacement produces inter-generational change in religion support the secularization presumption that modernization produces a progressive historical decline in the obligations and prominence of religion. But intra-family generational dynamics also shape the nature of religious activity in more complicated ways than this thesis fully recognizes. Secularization resulting from the process of cohort-replacement would lead us to expect the younger generation or younger cohorts to be less religious than their parents or the older generation. In American society, the smoothness of this flow is restrained by the long-persistent cultural emphasis on the value of children's religious socialization. Accordingly, at any given historical moment in America, we find inter-generational variation in family church habits, and this is a variation that inverts the straightforward motion of secularization via generational or cohort succession. The Lynds, for example, found that

while Middletown children prayed and were sent regularly to Sunday school, many of the parents were not religiously active (1929: 341). Pointing to the effect of cohort replacement, many Middletown mothers acknowledged that they were placing less emphasis on church loyalty in their children's socialization than they themselves had been taught by their parents (ibid.: 323). Yet, the impact of this cohort or generational change on religion is not all-encompassing because this apparently less religious cohort of mothers chose to send their children to Sunday school rather than choosing not to send them, thus preserving the salience of religious activity for these younger cohorts.

A similar pattern of intra-family variability in church habits was apparent in Northern California in the 1930s and 40s. Most of the IHD study participants – who were adolescents during the 1930s and 40s – attended Sunday school and church during childhood and most were still involved in church during adolescence. The majority of the parents, too, were attending church; yet, close to a third of them were not religiously active during their children's adolescence (Dillon and Wink, 2007). Nonetheless, regardless of their own varying levels of religiousness almost all of the parents (90 per cent) saw to it that their children went to church or Sunday school, a pattern that underscores the trans-generational credibility long given to religious socialization and Sunday school in American society (cf. Boylan, 1988).

More recently, survey data from the 1990s shows that a substantial one-third of individuals whose parents had no religious preference were themselves brought up with a religious affiliation (Hout and Fischer, 2002: 185). Family religiousness is undoubtedly the most powerful predictor of adolescent and subsequent adulthood religiousness (e.g., Myers, 1996). Nevertheless, as these examples of intra-family variation suggest, we should not automatically assume that if children are in church, so too are their parents, and nor should we assume that if parents are unchurched, so too are their children. The current and historical evidence suggests a more nuanced picture. Like the

Puritan settlers who devised half-way strategies to maintain their grandchildren within the church, early- and late-twentieth century parents make half-way accommodations to ensure the religious socialization of their children – many send their children to church and Sunday school while they themselves go about other (non-religious) activities.

GENERATIONAL DIFFERENCES IN RELIGION

So far, I have drawn attention to how generational factors variously shape the practice of religion within historical eras and within families. But how does generational membership itself differentiate religious beliefs and practices? In other words, are there religious differences evident between successive generations of Americans as they progress through history? The short answer to this question is 'Yes, there are.' It is to these generational differences in religion that I now turn and to illustrate both I use the Baby Boom generation as a benchmark comparator.

When social scientists embark on generational comparisons they inevitably focus on the Baby Boom generation comprised of the post-World War II, populous cohorts born between 1946 and 1965. The Baby Boomers are a pivotal generation not solely because of the demographic implications of their large size but also on account of the historical timing of their lives: their coming of age during the momentous economic, social, cultural and religious transformations set in motion in the post-war period and accelerated in the 1960s and 1970s. As Wade Clark Roof (1993, 1999) has extensively documented, the Baby Boomers are the vanguard generation responsible for 'remaking American religion' and transforming American culture more generally.

The changes in the religious landscape were driven in part by specific structural and institutional developments. Salient among these was the substantial increase in the number of Asian immigrants settling in the United States following the liberalization of immigration laws (1965), and in the process making non-Western religious practices more accessible to Americans (Roof, 1999). An important socio-demographic shift was the increase in the number of women entering the labor force, thus reducing the time and energy available to women to maintain their dominant role in church and in other voluntary organizations and activities (cf. Putnam, 2000). Changes in religious institutions themselves also contributed to the reshaping of religion. In the Catholic Church, for example, Vatican II affirmed a wide array of doctrinal and institutional changes that markedly transformed the religious socialization of young Catholics and the church experiences of all Catholics irrespective of age.

The main engine of change, however, was cultural. In the 1960s, 'the nature of freedom itself was contested and redefined' (Wuthnow, 1998: 53–4). This new understanding of freedom was applied to all domains of everyday life, and it was the Baby Boomers who led the charge in putting it into practice. Specifically in regard to religion, the 60s expanded the freedom of the individual to exercise his or her own authority in regard to religion (see also Greeley, 1985; Roof, 1993), and accordingly 'marked a turning point in American religious life' (Roof and McKinney, 1987: 11). The post-1960s accent on individual autonomy contrasts with the iconic image of the 1950s as an era of social conformity, a time in American society when 'Organizational Man' crystallized the conventionality imposed by external authorities on everyday life. Thus not coincidentally, church attendance and deference to religion and other institutional forces were at a historical peak in the 1950s as the parents of the Baby Boomers settled comfortably into the suburban affluence that had been spurred on by post-war social and economic developments.[3] But in the 1960s, the number of Americans reporting no religious affiliation significantly increased (from 2–3 to 6–7 per cent; Glenn, 1987) and church attendance and deference to institutionalized religious authority declined significantly (Hout and Greeley, 1987).

Studies discussing the increased freedom and individualism in post-1960s religion modeled by the Baby Boom generation give particular emphasis to three related ways in which this gets expressed. Several scholars focus on the fact that religion is treated as an individualized consumer-like choice akin to other life style choices (e.g., Warner, 1993; Wuthnow, 1998; Roof, 1999). Other studies document an increased detachment from denominational identity and affiliation (e.g., Bellah et al., 1985; Roof, 1999; Hout and Fischer, 2002); and, others comment on the autonomy of everyday morality from the authority of religious dogma in favor of a more diffuse, Golden Rule morality (e.g., Hoge et al., 1994; Ammerman, 1997; Roof, 1999).

As part of the decline in the authority of church-based or institutionalized religion there has been a notable increase in the prevalence of highly active spiritual seekers (Roof, 1993, 1999; Wuthnow, 1998), a religious style modeled by, though not exclusive to, the Baby Boom generation (as discussed earlier, older age Americans also engage in spiritual seeking). With roots in American Transcendentalism (e.g., Fuller, 2001), spiritual seekers emphasize experiential sacred meanings and look for these in practices that may have little to do with traditional church-centered beliefs and rituals. Instead they variously seek the sacred by negotiating among Western and Eastern religious practices, Pagan and Celtic traditions, and through New Age, ecological, and therapeutic practices (e.g., yoga).

With the Baby Boomers as the 'lead cohort' in reshaping American religion, Roof identifies the primary inter-generational religious differences as lying between those born prior to World War II and those born after it. He notes that this pattern of differences (in strength of religious preference, valuing of faith etc.) is larger than any differences among either the wide cohort span of Baby Boomers or subsequent cohorts (those born since the mid-1960s). Roof summarizes the pre/post-war inter-generational dynamic thus: 'Older generations remain more loyal to institutions and doctrinal beliefs whereas younger generations register higher scores on experiential measures not directly related to "church religion" (Roof, 1998: 52). Therefore, while there has been an increase across cohorts in the proportion of Americans who describe themselves as spiritual and not religious, this is particularly characteristic of the boomer generation and its successor cohorts.

Hout and Fischer's (2002: 183) detailed cohort analyses confirm that generational succession is attenuating church-centered religious attachment. They find that 'cohorts born prior to 1935 are more religious than those that came after, each cohort from 1935 to 1950 is increasingly less religious than the one right before it, and those born after 1950 are at the same (low) level of religious attachment as the 1950 cohort.' More specifically, Fischer and Hout (2006) find a clear generational trend indicating that more recent birth cohorts are less likely to attend church than those born earlier in the twentieth century, and that those in recent cohorts who grow up unchurched are less likely than earlier cohorts of religiously unaffiliated Americans to become church members in adulthood (upon marriage, for example).

Inter-generational differences in attachment to religious institutions become especially apparent when the spotlight is focused on specific denominational groups. Among Catholics, for example, the largest religious denomination in America, studies indicate substantial inter-generational differences. The survey research of D'Antonio et al. (2001) identifies Catholics in terms of pre-Vatican II, Vatican II, and post-Vatican II generations. Coincidentally, the Vatican II generation, defined as those born between 1941 and 1960, closely matches with the Baby Boomer cohorts. Baby Boomer Catholics, therefore, had their formative young adulthood directly impacted conjointly by the cultural turmoil of the 60s and the enormous transformation and turmoil (in regard to contraception, for example) in the church.

D'Antonio et al. find several points of commonality between the Vatican II and the pre-Vatican II generation, and between the Vatican II and the post-Vatican II generation. However, there are significant differences among all three in regard to commitment to Catholicism (2001: 83), with commitment progressively decreasing for each successive generation, and similarly, a negative relation between generation and those who are likely to say that the individual (and not the church hierarchy) is the locus of authority on sexual and related matters (e.g., abortion and homosexuality). As D'Antonio *et al.* make clear, although the biggest generational differences among Catholics are between the pre-Vatican II and subsequent generations, 'there also are sizable differences between the Vatican II and post-Vatican II generations .... from compliance with traditional teaching to greater autonomy' (2001: 129).

The emphasis on individual autonomy in how the Baby Boomer and successor cohorts construe religion, spirituality, and personal morality has been widely criticized for what some sociologists see as self-indulgence. Most notably, Bellah *et al.* (1985) regard the increased trend toward spiritual seeking as self-centered, therapeutic, and narcissistic and as undermining Americans' long historical commitment to creating participative and socially responsible civic communities. Bellah's concerns find support in Robert Putnam's (2000: 257–58) findings which show that Baby Boomers and later cohorts of Americans are significantly more disengaged from social, community and political activities than early twentieth century cohorts. Yet, as Putnam notes, these trends have no single cause; as societies undergo change (increased education, mass media) and as successive generations have different cultural and historical experiences, we should be surprised if these structural and cultural differences did not impact the social commitments and life styles of different generations.

The religious individualism associated with the decline in religious affiliation and church attachment, however, may not be as detrimental to the preservation of social and communal ties as observers fear. There is some evidence that Baby Boomer spirituality is not as self-centered as suggested in media images and cultural critiques. Roof (1999: 163, 269), for example, shows that middle aged Baby Boomers who have had spiritual experiences are more likely to value self-giving than those who have not. Openness to self-growth, Roof argues, translates into a predisposition toward more

generative personal and social relations on the part of individuals who are spiritually engaged.

This thesis is supported by research among older age cohorts (born in the 1920s). Using the IHD data, Dillon and Wink show that spiritual seeking, if measured as disciplined engagement in intentional spiritual practices (e.g., meditation) and not simply as a self-report personal descriptor, is also related to altruism and concern for the welfare of others. For example, in late adulthood (age late 60s/mid-70s), high scorers on either church-centered religiousness or on a more individualized spiritual seeking were equally likely to engage in social activism on behalf of such causes as homelessness (Dillon and Wink, 2007; Dillon *et al.* 2003). Although the relation between spiritual seeking and social responsibility found among older age cohorts may be a function of the socio-historical context in which their lives unfolded – they are, after all, members of the long civic generation in America – it is nonetheless evident that a disciplined spiritual seeking can, similar to church-centered participation, lead to the development of a social perspective and awareness that focuses attention on the needs of other individuals and groups. The different interests and orientations that characterize church-centered individuals and spiritual seekers mean that their care-giving will likely vary in where and how it is expressed. From the perspective of social change, however, it is prudent not to automatically assume that a decline in church affiliation or involvement will necessarily lead to a decline in social commitment.

Given the emerging evidence of a generational shift in contemporary American society toward non-church centered religion it is clearly important for social scientists to systematically assess the social implications of newer forms of religious/spiritual engagement. Most of the research on religion and civic and social involvement, however, compares church-goers with non-church-goers (e.g., Putnam, 2000), and/or uses a definition of spirituality that relies on a self-report personal descriptor (as in the General Social Survey; Hout and Fischer, 2002). Such self-report descriptors of spirituality do not require the same behavioral threshold that is customarily used in assessing traditional religious involvement (e.g., church attendance). Consequently, these studies do not fully discriminate between the truly non-religious and non-spiritual individuals and those individuals who may not go to church but who are serious or disciplined about their spirituality beyond simply describing them-selves as spiritual. Research that uses a prac-tice-oriented definition of spiritual seeking (e.g., Wink and Dillon, 2003) paralleling the behavioral indicators typically used in assess-ing religiousness, has been fruitful in distin-guishing among different types of religious engagement (religiousness and/or spiritual seeking) as well as between people who are religious or spiritual and those who have no religious or spiritual interests. This differentia-tion provides a more multi-layered pattern of findings for altruism, social responsibility and other behavioral outcomes than simply com-paring church attendance with non-attendance. It thus allows for a more multi-dimensional assessment of religion and generational and social change.

GENERATIONAL CONTINUITIES

Notwithstanding the compelling empirical evidence that cohort and generational succes-sion change the American religious landscape, it is important also to acknowledge the gen-erational continuities in the construal and practice of religion across time. I draw atten-tion to generational continuities because they are historically and sociologically interesting in their own right; providing greater texture to our understanding of American religion and social history, and giving pause to the emphasis on linear change that so pervades sociological and cultural narratives.

From the perspective of generational change and its impact on religion as a life course phenomenon, the IHD findings – coming from the generational parents of the Baby Boomers – offer a caution against over-stating the uniqueness of the life course religious

trajectories of the Baby Boomers and indeed of the Baby Boomers' children. Roof (1999: 233–4) found that the Baby Boomers too dropped out of church as their children matured and left home, and he suggests that because the Baby Boomers' mid-life decline in religiousness set in at an earlier mid-life age than is assumed for previous cohorts, it may signal a major generational change and a long-term decline in the significance of insti-tutionalized religion for them and successive cohorts. However, the fact that the gen-erational parents of the boomers, the IHD participants, reduced their church-centered religiousness in mid-life but then subsequently resumed church involvement by late adult-hood suggests that a similar pattern may well characterize the religiousness of the boomers as they too move into late adulthood, notwith-standing their different, generationally specific experiences. It is also noteworthy in this regard that the church attendance patterns of current youth, the Baby Boomers' children, share some remarkable similarities to the adolescent reli-gious habits of their grandparents' generation as suggested by the religiousness of the IHD study participants when they were adolescents in the 1930s and 40s.[4]

Similarly, there are several continuities apparent in the cultural construal of religion trans-generationally. The theme of individual freedom that is so pivotal to contemporary American religion has long had some presence in the vocabulary of earlier generations. Most notably, as Nathan Hatch's (1989) important study of the 'democratization of Christianity' underscores, the early nineteenth century was renowned for its emphasis on individual reli-gious autonomy. It was a time when individual conscience and the common sense of ordinary people to think for themselves took priority over the dictates of church leaders and educated religious elites. Indeed Hatch's observations about that period could well be applied to the 1960s. He argues:

> The American Revolution and the beliefs flowing from it created a cultural ferment over the meaning of freedom. Turmoil swirled around the crucial issues of authority, organization, and leadership. Above all the Revolution dramatically expanded the circle of people

who considered themselves capable of thinking for themselves about issues of freedom, equality, sovereignty, and representation. Respect for authority, tradition, station, and education eroded. Ordinary people moved toward these new horizons aided by a powerful new vocabulary, a rhetoric of liberty that would not have occurred to them were it not for the Revolution .... The correct solution to any institutional problem, political, legal, or religious, would have to appear to be the people's choice (1989: 6).

Therefore, while studies today rightly emphasize the autonomy with which contemporary Americans regard religion, it is worthwhile to keep in mind that earlier generations also used a rhetoric of liberty and some took a highly individualized approach to religion. Interview data from the IHD longitudinal study of Americans born in the 1920s uncovered much evidence of individual autonomy in how they too regarded religion (Dillon and Wink, 2007). Their interviews from the 1950s are especially illuminating of the cultural and generational continuities in American religion. In the late 1950s, the study participants were then in their 30s and at a stage in the life course when almost all of them were married and with young school-age children. This family-centered phase in the life course coincided, moreover, with the heightened salience of institutionalized religion in American society more generally as Cold War politics encouraged the counter-posing of American faith and religiosity against godless Communism. Nonetheless, a majority of the study participants (54 per cent) spoke of religion using a consumer choice vocabulary that clearly anticipated the expanded autonomy of choice associated with post-1960s religion. These individuals talked about religion in terms of preferences not beliefs, about shopping around for a church that they liked, about going to different churches because they offered different satisfactions, or conversely, that because the services provided were basically interchangeable, the specific church chosen was irrelevant. The language the participants used in talking about church stressed pragmatism, satisfaction, and convenience rather than theological content or denominational tradition, for example. Moreover, whether someone was highly religious or only marginally so did

not impact their likelihood of using this vocabulary. These findings thus suggest that the idea of religion as a consumer choice was quite pervasive in the 1950s, and rather than being reflective of a casual approach to religion was part and parcel of how many ordinary Americans construed religion.

Similarly, although many scholars comment on the uncoupling today of morality from theology and the articulation of a diffuse Golden Rule ethos (e.g., Hoge *et al.*, 1994: 111–13; Smith and Denton, 2005), historical data also show that a Golden Rule morality has much deeper roots in American culture than simply being a post-1960s' or Baby Boomer morality. The parents of the IHD study participants were born toward the end of the nineteenth century, and interviews with these parents conducted in the 1930s and 40s are characterized by frequent allusions to the Golden Rule. Similarly, in the 1950s, several of the study participants themselves also spontaneously used Golden Rule language (29 per cent; at age 30s in 1958), and did so irrespective of their varying levels of religious commitment. The IHD participants' use of this language was not an aberration. Will Herberg (1955/1960: 73), the well-renowned observer of American 50s religion, argued at the time that the tendency of Americans to assert their practical commitment to following the Golden Rule 'would seem to offer a better insight into the basic religion of the American people than any figures as to their formal beliefs can provide.'

The presence of a Golden Rule ethos in the remarks of Americans born at least as early as the late nineteenth century highlights that the uncoupling of everyday morality from an explicit religious theology is a characteristic of American religion that reaches back over several generations. Because the Golden Rule is found in Christianity and also across other religious and secular philosophies, it is difficult to untangle the extent to which the appeal of the Golden Rule in American culture derives from purely religious or non-religious sources. It is interesting, however, that it was a much earlier generation of policy makers and church leaders who intentionally sought to institutionalize non-denominational or non-sectarian moral teachings in the curricula of public schools and of Sunday schools. In the late nineteenth century, this more diffuse though biblically based morality was seen as less divisive than emphasizing specific dogmas and was regarded as a way to foster American national unity in the wake of the Civil War and in response to the increasing ethnic pluralism (cf. Boylan, 1988; McGreevy, 2003).

Thus while it is understandable that observers lament the paucity of theological content in the moral views expressed by contemporary generations of parents (e.g., Hoge *et al.*, 1994) and teenagers (e.g., Smith and Denton, 2005: 118–71), a longer historical perspective gives pause to the assumption that this is solely a post-1960s phenomenon. The benign expectations currently associated with the rhetoric of a Golden Rule morality may well be unintended, but their original non-sectarian spirit was the brainchild of serious moral leaders intent on knitting the common good.

CONCLUSION

In closing, it should be apparent that generation, cohort, and age are all important factors in tracking and understanding religion both as an individual and as a societal phenomenon. Including these frames in sociological analyses can only enhance awareness of the dynamic nature of religion as it is lived and changes across varying life course, social, historical, and cultural contexts. We must be careful, however, not to use age, generation and cohort in a reductionistic manner that favors either a simple progressive or regressive narrative of religious change. Greater recognition of a generational logic complicates the secularization thesis that has been so influential in sociology. Its tendency to assume a progressive decline in the relevance of religion in modernized societies, and the related assumption that current generations are less attached to religion and more autonomous in their religious views and behavior than their forebears were, betray a limited understanding both of religion and of social history. Although there are many

substantial inter-generational differences evident in the march of religion through time, there are also trans-generational continuities in how Americans from diverse cohorts construe religion. Researchers need to be more attentive to recognizing that in any given period they are unlikely to find religious uniformity but a more complicated, mixed bag that variously includes evidence and counter-evidence of the hold of religion. Any portrait of religious change, moreover, is unlikely to derive solely from the logic of cohort or generational succession *per se* but will also be driven by the particular ways in which generational succession intertwines with important demographic, social and cultural changes.

NOTES

1. I appreciate the helpful comments of James Beckford and Jay Demerath on an earlier draft of this chapter.

2. I have been using the IHD data for the last few years. The IHD study participants were interviewed extensively in adolescence (1934 and 1943), and four times in adulthood: 1958 (age 30s), 1970 (age 40s), 1982 (age late 50s and early 60s), and 1997–2000 (age late 60s and mid 70s). Separate interviews were also conducted with the participants' parents in the 1930s and 1940s. Attrition in the study has been low; after an initial fall-off between adolescence and early adulthood, the numbers who participated in the adulthood interviews were remarkably consistent (approx. N = 240). Approximately 90 per cent of the original sample who were still alive and contactable were interviewed in late adulthood (N = 184). The IHD participants differ from the general American population in that they come from California, have higher levels of education and income, almost all are White and most are mainline Protestant or Catholic. Yet, notwithstanding these differences, they closely resemble similar age Americans on other important social variables such as household structure, church attendance, and political affiliation. Further details about the sample, the measures of church-based religiousness and spiritual seeking, and the results reviewed in this section can be found in Dillon and Wink, 2007.

3. Gallup poll data (Gallup and Lindsay, 1999: 15) show, for example, that weekly church attendance in America was higher in 1958 (49 per cent) than in 1939 (41 per cent), 1975 (40 per cent), 1989 (43 per cent), 1994 (42 per cent), or 1998 (40 per cent).

4. As adolescents in the 1930s and 40s, only 13 per cent of the IHD participants had no religion. Conversely, 55 per cent demonstrated high religious involvement, and 32 per cent were somewhat involved (Dillon and Wink, 2007).

A recent nationwide study of 13 to 17-year-old American adolescents found that a majority, 52 per cent, attends religious services at least twice a month, 29 per cent do so occasionally, and 18 per cent never attend church (Smith and Denton, 2005).

REFERENCES

Ammerman, N. 1997. 'Golden Rule Christianity: Lived Religion in the American Mainstream'. In D. Hall (ed.), *Lived Religion in America* (pp. 196–216). Princeton: Princeton University Press.

Bellah, R., Madsen, R., Sullivan, W., Swidler, A. and Tipton, S. 1985. *Habits of the Heart: Individualism and Commitment in American Life*. Berkeley, CA: University of California Press.

Boylan, A. 1988. *Sunday School: The Formation of an American Institution, 1790–1880*. New Haven, CT: Yale University Press.

Chaves, M. 1991. 'Family Structure and Protestant Church Attendance: The Sociological Basis of Cohort and Age Effects'. *Journal for the Scientific Study of Religion* 30, 501–14.

D'Antonio, W., Davison, J. Hoge D. and Meyer, K. 2001. *American Catholics: Gender, Generation, and Commitment*. Walnut Creek, CA: Alta Mira.

Davie, G. 2003. 'The Evolution of the Sociology of Religion'. In M. Dillon (ed.), *Handbook of the Sociology of Religion* (pp. 61–75). New York: Cambridge University Press.

De Tocqueville, A. [1840] 1946. *Democracy in America*. Volume Two. New York: Knopf.

Dillon, M. and Wink, P. 2007. *In the Course of a Lifetime: Tracing Religious Belief, Practice and Change*. Berkeley: University of California Press.

Dillon, M., Wink, P. and Fay, K. 2003. 'Is Spirituality Detrimental to Generativity?' *Journal for the Scientific Study of Religion*, 42 427–42.

Elder, G. 1974. *Children of the Great Depression*. Chicago: University of Chicago.

Erikson, E. 1950. *Childhood and Society* New York: Norton.

Fichter, J. 1952. 'The Profile of Catholic Religious Life'. *American Journal of Sociology* 145–49.

Fischer, C. and Hout M. (2006). *Century of Difference*. New York: Russell Sage Foundation.

Fuller, R. C. 2001. *Spiritual, but not Religious*. New York: Oxford University Press.

Gallup, G. and Lindsay, D. M. 1999. *Surveying the Religious Landscape: Trends in U.S. Beliefs*. Harrisburg, PA: Morehouse.

Glenn, N. 1987. 'The trend in "no religion" respondents to U.S. national surveys, late 1950s to early 1980s, *Public Opinion Quarterly* 51, 292–314.

Gorski, P. 2003. 'Historicizing the Secularization Debate: An Agenda for Research'. In M. Dillon (ed.), *Handbook of the Sociology of Religion* (pp. 110–22). New York: Cambridge University Press.

Greeley, A. 1980. *The Young Catholic Family*. Chicago: Thomas More Press.

Greeley A. 1985. *American Catholics Since the Council: An Unauthorized Report*. Chicago: Thomas More.

Hatch, N. 1989. *The Democratization of American Christianity*. New Haven: Yale University Press.

Herberg, W. 1960. *Protestant-Catholic-Jew: An Essay in American Religious Sociology*. Chicago: University of Chicago Press.

Hoge, D., Johnson, B. and Luidens, D. 1994. *Vanishing Boundaries: The Religion of Mainline Protestant Baby Boomers*. Louisville, KY: Westminster/John Knox Press.

Hout, M. 2003. 'Demographic Methods for the Sociology of Religion'. In M. Dillon (ed.), *Handbook of the Sociology of Religion* (pp. 79–84). New York: Cambridge University Press.

Hout, M. and Fischer, C. 2002. 'Explaining the Rise of Americans with No Religious Preferences: Politics and Generations'. *American Sociological Review* 67, 65–190.

Hout, M. and Greeley, A 1987. 'The Center Doesn't Hold: Church Attendance in the United States, 1940–1984'. *American Sociological Review* 52, 325–45.

Hout, M., Greeley, A. and Wilde, M. J. 2001. 'The Demographic Imperative in Religious Change in the United States'. *American Journal of Sociology* 63, 113–19.

Ingersoll-Dayton, B., Krause, N. and Morgan, D. 2002. 'Religious Trajectories and Transitions Over the Life Course'. *International Journal of Aging and Human Development* 55, 51–70.

King, V. and Elder, G. 1999. 'Are Religious Grandparents More Involved Grandparents?', *Journal of Gerontology* 54B(6), S317–S328.

Levinson, D. 1996. *The Seasons of a Woman's Life*. New York: Ballantine.

Lynd, R. and Lynd, H. 1929. *Middletown: A Study in Contemporary America Culture*. New York: Harcourt, Brace.

Mannheim, K. [1927] 1952. 'The problem of generations'. In P. Kecskemeti (ed.), *Essays on the Sociology of Knowledge* (pp. 276–322). London: Routledge and Kegan Paul.

McCullough, M. and Polak, E. (2007). 'Religion in the post-retirement period'. In J. James and P. Wink (eds). *The Crown of Life*. Springer.

McGreevy, J. 2003. *Catholicism and American Freedom: A History*. New York: Norton.

Miller, P. [1956] 1964. *Errand into the Wilderness*. Cambridge, MA: Harvard University Press.

Myers, S. 1996. 'Families and the Inheritance of Religiosity'. *American Sociological Review* 61, 858–66.

Myers, D. 2004. *The American People, Census 2000: Cohorts and Socioeconomic Progress*. New York: Russell Sage Foundation.

Noll, M. 1992. *A History of Christianity in the United States and Canada*. Grand Rapids, MI: Eerdmans.

Putnam, R. 2000. *Bowling Alone: The Collapse and Revival of American Community*. New York: Simon and Schuster.

Roof, W. C. 1993. *A Generation of Seekers: The Spiritual Journeys of the Baby Boom Generation*. San Francisco: Harper and Row.

Roof, W. C. 1999. *Spiritual Marketplace: Baby Boomers and the Remaking of American Religion*. Princeton, NJ: Princeton University Press.

Roof, W. C. and McKinney, W. 1987. *American Mainline Religion*. New Brunswick, NJ: Rutgers University Press.

Rossi, A. S. 2001. *Caring and Doing for Others*. Chicago: University of Chicago Press.

Ryder, N. 1965. 'The cohort as a concept in the study of social change'. *American Sociological Review* 30, 843–61.

Saroglou, V. and Fiasse, L. 2003. 'Birth Order, Personality, and Religion'. *Personality and Individual Differences* 35, 19–29.

Shand, J. 1990. 'A Forty Year Follow-Up of the Religious Beliefs and Attitudes of a Sample of Amherst College Grads'. In M. L. Lynn and D. O. Moberg (eds), *Research in the Social Scientific Study of Religion* (pp. 117–36). Greenwich, CT: JAI Press.

Sherkat, D. 2003. 'Religious Socialization: Sources of Influence and Influences of Agency'. In M. Dillon (ed.), *Handbook of the Sociology of Religion* (pp. 151–63). New York: Cambridge University Press.

Sinnott, Jan 1994. Development and Yearning: Cognitive Aspects of Spiritual Development. *Journal of Adult Development* 1: 91–9.

Smith, C. and Denton, M. L. 2005. *Soul Searching: The Religious and Spiritual Lives of American Teenagers*. New York: Oxford University Press.

Stolzenberg, R., Blair-Loy, M. and Waite, L. 1995. 'Age and Family Life Cycle Effects on Church Membership'. *American Sociological Review* 60, 84–103.

Warner, R. S. 1993. 'Work in Progress Toward a New Paradigm for the Sociological Study of Religion in the United States'. *American Journal of Sociology* 98, 1044–93.

Wink, P. and Dillon, M. 2002. 'Spiritual Development Across the Adult Life Course: Findings From a Longitudinal Study'. *Journal of Adult Development* 9, 79–94.

Wink, P. and Dillon, M. 2003. 'Religiousness, Spirituality, and Psychosocial Functioning in Late Adulthood'. *Psychology and Aging* 18, 916–24.

Wink, Paul and Scott, Julia 2005. 'Does Religiousness Buffer against the Fear of Death and Dying in Late Adulthood?' *Journal of Gerontology: Psychological Sciences* 60B: 207–14.

Winthrop, J. [1630] 1965. 'A model of Christian Charity'. In E. Morgan (ed.), *Puritan Political Ideas* (pp. 75–93). Indianapolis: Bobbs-Merrill.

Wuthnow, R. 1998. *After Heaven: Spirituality in America Since the 1950s*. Berkeley: University of California Press.

Religion, Self-Identity and the Life-Course

Most chapters in the Handbook up to this point have been about religion in relation to theoretical ideas, methods of research, forms of organisation, interaction with politics, and individual beliefs and actions. But the chapters in Part VII head in a new direction. They examine the various processes by which personal identification with religions waxes or wanes – with the emphasis firmly on the social, bodily and emotional contexts in which religious identities are moulded. They show that religion is clearly gendered, embodied, emotive and situated in changing forms of the life-course.

Beginning with an overview of theories about religion and identity, **Arthur Greil and Lynn Davidman** argue in Chapter 26 that self-identity cannot be divorced from social and cultural life. While considering the evolution of psychological approaches to identity and religion, they emphasise the more recent shift from thinking about identity as a matter of individual psychology to a more sociological conception of identity as the result of interaction between self and others. The contributions of symbolic interactionism, social identity theory and narrative notions of identity have all helped explain both change and continuity in religious identification. Indeed, many sociological debates about the evolution

of modernity have highlighted its impact on religious identity as one of a growing number of potential identities. Similarly, studies of conservative forms of religion and of processes of conversion, commitment, and disaffiliation have all stressed identity's centrality. Recent investigations of new 'immigrant congregations', generational changes in religious practice and the tensions between religious identity and other sources of identity such as sexuality or lifestyle display a continuing concern with the negotiation of religious identity in the midst of rapid social change.

Linda Woodhead opens Chapter 27 with the claim that sociologists of religion were relatively slow to recognise the significance of gender as a factor shaping religious ideas, identities, sentiments and practices. But she acknowledges that a recent shift of focus away from essentialist notions of sex and gender towards 'masculinities' and 'femininities' has created exciting opportunities for understanding the multiple identities that make up religious identities. Power – cutting across inequalities of class, ethnicity and 'race' – is a key to the understanding of religion's variable relations with the gender order in society. The four types of relationship between religion and gender that Woodhead explores are: consolidating, tactical, questing and counter-cultural. Developing a highly original argument, she then analyses the gendering of secularisation and indicates other topics in the sociology of religion that deserve re-examination from the point of view of their association with the gender order. They include the definition of 'religion', the interpretation of religious practices, the geography of the sacred, and the selection of research methods. By delving beneath the male-dominated surface of religion as it is commonly organised and symbolically represented, sociologists of religion can gain insight into new problems and fresh perspectives on old ones. This is particularly relevant to understanding the positioning of different religious groups in relation to issues such as homosexuality, abortion and the veiling of Muslim women – all of which give rise to anxieties about gender.

In another argument that aims to fill an important gap in the sociology of religion, **Philip Mellor** mounts a challenge in Chapter 28 to the tendency to ignore the fact that there is a bodily dimension to being religious. His central claim is that the embodied experience of religion deserves more careful attention. This is an area in which the sociology of religion has a potentially major contribution to make towards the enhancement of debates about interaction between human beings, their bodies, experiences, emotions and the socio-cultural forces that shape the interaction. Six models of embodiment point the way towards a more refined understanding of the place of religion in this interaction. Illustrating his argument mostly with examples drawn from charismatic forms of Christianity, Mellor shows how sociology's general lack of attention to embodiment can be remedied by attending to the body as: emotional, permeable, learning, mimetic, mindful and global. In this way, the complex interplay between religion, culture, the body, emotions and experience can be brought to the foreground of sociological consciousness and methodically examined. The chapter's provocative conclusion is that

the disposition of many sociologists to regard religion as a secondary or purely reactive product of social, economic or political factors can be overcome by giving due recognition to the irreducible properties of human embodiment. This helps to frame religion as a potentially creative and relatively independent way of engaging with the socio-cultural world.

Recent changes in the nature of the socio-cultural world lie at the heart of Chapter 29 where **Stephen Hunt** traces their implications for the place of religion in the individual's life-course. He shows that the time-honoured practice of thinking about human maturation in terms of the life-cycle is now giving way to the idea of a less predictable and less sequential model of a personally chosen life-course. This shift – in perception as well as social reality – is congruent with some authoritative characterisations of the increasingly self-reflexive 'project' of the self in late-modernity or post-modernity. The expectation is that individuals construct forms of religiosity that reflect their experiences of the life-course that they have chosen. Whereas religious rites of passage, for example, used to be associated with age-related stages of the life-cycle, the tendency nowadays is for the significance of fixed age categories to be reduced in favour of more self-reflexive negotiation of the meaning of experience in terms of personal projects that require less collective celebration. The decline of family life-cycle rites is particularly damaging for the religious socialisation of young children, although the impact may be refracted differently by differences of social class and gender. Hunt also outlines the implications of these changes for the religious outlooks, experiences and practices of people at all the main stages of life, concluding with a discussion of the changing relations between religion, dying, death and bereavement among different ethnic groups. This is one of the areas where the sociology of religion undoubtedly gets to grips with what Durkheim called 'the serious life'.

26

Religion and Identity

ARTHUR L. GREIL AND LYNN DAVIDMAN

The interplay between religion and identity has been a core theme in the sociology of religion since the classical period, although it is not always described in those terms. One could argue that a major theme in Durkheim's (1966) sociology of religion is the role of communal ritual in fostering personal and social identity. If the provision of meaning and belonging are two of the most important functions of religion (Greeley 1972; McGuire 1992), then it is clear that religion is intimately bound up with people's identity, their sense of who they 'really' are. In fact, Hans Mol (1976) goes so far as to make identity the key concept in his definition of religion. For Mol, religion is the 'sacralization of identity.'

Writers like Durkheim, Weber, and Simmel could not have used 'identity' in its modern sense, because it was not available to them as a social scientific term. According to Gleason (1983), the term did not really become part of the social scientific lexicon until the 1960s. Gleason identifies both psychological and sociological sources for the incorporation of identity into the social science vocabulary. Erikson (1968) used the terms 'identity' and 'ego-identity' to refer to a 'sense of invigorating continuity and sameness,' the development of which is the primary task of adolescence. In this view,

the achievement of a mature identity is a necessary condition to successful development.

At the same time, sociologists informed by the symbolic interactionist tradition, including Erving Goffman (1959, 1963b) and Peter Berger (1963), began using the word 'identity' as a synonym for or as an aspect of the concept of 'self' first developed by William James (1890) and later elaborated by Charles Horton Cooley (1902) and George Herbert Mead (1934). In this view, 'identity' is the sense of who one is as a social being and is a dynamic product of interaction with significant others. Another sociological source of the term 'identity' was the study of ethnic groups and immigration, where first Oscar Handlin (1951) and then Will Herberg (1956) used the term to connote identification with a collectivity. Within a very short period, this became perhaps the most frequent sociological meaning of identity as other sociologists, as well as political scientists, began using identity to refer to an attachment to social categories, particularly race and ethnicity, but also to gender and sexual identity (Cerulo 1997; Howard 2000; Sanders 2002). The term caught on so rapidly and was used in such a variety of ways that, by the 1970s, scholars were complaining that it was too imprecise to have any scholarly traction

(Coles 1972). More recently, Brubaker and Cooper (2000) have recommended that 'identity' be abandoned by sociologists.

The call to abandon identity has apparently not been heeded. There are by now a great many works that consider the relationship between religion and identity, but few of them do this in a theoretically informed way (Ammerman 2003). The study of religion and identity has also been hampered by the existence within the sociological literature of different and often inconsistent uses of the identity concept. It is our intention in this chapter to proceed, first, with some theoretical elaboration of what different theorists mean by 'identity.' We then go on to discuss the variety of ways in which sociologists have examined the relationship between religion and identity. In our view, sociological accounts of the transformation of religion under conditions of modernity provide a convenient narrative framework for organizing a diverse array of studies on religion and identity into a coherent story.

IDENTITY AND RELIGIOUS MATURITY: PSYCHOLOGICAL APPROACHES

Although all social scientific approaches to identity see it as a theoretical link between the self and the larger community, it is possible to distinguish approaches which focus more on identity as an attribute of individuals from those which place the essence of identity in the on-going interaction between self and others. This latter conception of identity has been more relevant to the sociology of religion and, although we will briefly discuss the former approach, we will devote considerably more attention to the second, more sociological perspective.

Several studies on religion and identity, primarily by psychologists, build on the concept of ego-identity developed by Erikson (1968). In Erikson's psychoanalytic conception, individuals pass through eight stages of development. In each stage, the ego is presented with a dilemma that must be resolved in a satisfactory manner if it is to continue to move to full maturity. The dichotomy characteristic of adolescence is the challenge of identity versus identity diffusion. Successful navigation through the period of adolescence results in the achievement of a feeling of uniqueness, a sense of continuity over time, and a state of ego completeness. While Erickson's ego identity is, in large part, an intra-psychic state, it clearly has a social dimension insofar as the achievement of a healthy identity depends on identification with the values of a group. Although he was working within the psychoanalytic tradition, Erikson was particularly sensitive to the interpenetration between the developing personality and the history, culture, and structure of the social environment.

Erikson's conception of identity has been subjected to the criticisms that it is imprecise and hard to operationalize. Marcia's (1966) elaboration of Erikson's conception of identity has proven more amenable to empirical research. Marcia identified four identity statuses: achievement (characterized by a commitment to a value orientation following a period of self-exploration), foreclosure (characterized by a premature commitment in the absence of self-exploration); moratorium (characterized by self-exploration in the absence of firm commitment), and diffusion (characterized by an absence of both commitment and self-exploration). Berzonsky (1989, 1992, 1994), who conceptualizes identity not so much as a developmental outcome as a style of thinking about oneself, developed an instrument, the 'Identity Style Inventory,' in order to assess identity-processing orientations as being 'normative,' 'informational,' or 'diffuse/avoidant.'

Some psychologists of religion have employed these concepts and measures in an attempt to predict religious maturity. Allport (Allport and Ross 1967) set the tone for the study of religious maturity with his distinction between an 'intrinsic' religious orientation, which serves as an overarching motivation for individuals concerned to realize their values in their daily action, and an 'extrinsic' religious orientation, characteristic of individuals whose religiosity serves as a means to other ends, such as social acceptance. While Allport originally conceived of intrinsic religiosity as more mature than extrinsic religiosity, others (Batson *et al.* 1993) have pointed out that extrinsic religiosity may be linked with blind conformity and a lack of compassion for others outside the community. Batson and his associates (Batson and Schoenrade 1991a,b) have developed the concept of 'religion as quest' to express their sense that mature religiosity is characterized by an open-minded, personal search for meaning.

Watson, Morris, and their colleagues (Watson *et al.* 1992, 1998) have criticized the religion as quest concept because it appears to be associated, not with religious maturity and healthy identity styles, but with identity confusion and a lack of concern with religion. In a recent study of undergraduates, Watson and Morris (2005) made use of a measure called the 'Spiritual Experience Inventory' to explore the connection between identity styles and religious maturity. These authors found that 'spiritual openness' was positively associated with religion as quest, a diffuse/avoidant identity style, and extrinsic religiosity and negatively associated with identity commitment, normative identity style, intrinsic religiosity, and religious interest. 'Spiritual support' was associated with higher levels of identity commitment, informational and normative identity styles, intolerance of ambiguity, and religious interest but with lower levels of 'religion as quest' and a diffuse/avoidant identity style. Watson and Morris conclude that the attempt to associate certain identity styles with religious maturity is fraught with challenges in that both of their measures of spiritual experience were associated with psychological weaknesses as well as strengths. The attempt to use the concept of identity to predict and explain the quality of religious experience is a decidedly minority tradition within the social scientific study of religion.

A second minority tradition within the social scientific study of religion and identity combines concerns about identity formation and religious orientation with an interest in moral reasoning in the tradition of Lawrence Kohlberg. While Kohlberg's developmental model of moral reasoning was formulated in part as an attempt to account for moral behavior, it has become clear that there is not a one-to-one correspondence between moral reasoning and moral action (Blasi 1980, 2004; Jennings *et al.* 1983). Blasi (1980) has suggested that the sense of oneself as a moral person may be a key factor mediating the relationship between moral reasoning and moral behavior. Blasi argues that those with integrated identities are more likely to feel responsible for acting in accordance with their moral values. Within this tradition, MacLean *et al.* (2004) have looked at the relationships among moral reasoning, identity integration, religious orientation, and altruistic behavior. In a study of sixty undergraduates, McLean *et al.* found a high correlation between all variables. They conclude from their hierarchical regression analysis that moral reasoning is the strongest predictor of altruism but that identity integration and religious orientation function as mediating variables. The authors speculate that it might be profitable to conceptualize an intrinsic religious orientation as a measure of identity integration in the religious domain.

SOCIOLOGICAL APPROACHES TO RELIGION AND IDENTITY

The Symbolic Interactionist Tradition: Identity and Self

The bulk of scholarly writing on religion and identity relies more on the symbolic interactionist conception of identity than on Erickson's more psychoanalytic and developmental approach. While terms like identity integration and identity status suggest a concern with the quality of psychological functioning, the symbolic interactionist tradition is more concerned with accounting for the content of identity and with describing the identity construction process. Fundamental to the symbolic interactionist concept of the self are the twin notions of the social nature of the self and the reflexivity of the self. Building on William James' (1890) conception of the 'social self' and Charles Horton Cooley's (1902) 'looking glass self,' George Herbert Mead (1934) conceived of the self as a malleable and continuous process emerging out of interaction with significant others through 'taking the role of the other.' In this view, the self is crucially shaped by the expectations of others and the roles into which one has been cast. But the symbolic interactionist self is not the mere reflection of the expectations of others. Symbolic Interactions conceive of the self as reflexive; the self is seen as having an objective aspect – the 'me,' which is the reflection of the expectations and judgments of others – and a subjective aspect – the 'I,' which responds creatively and spontaneously to the me. As symbolic interactionists use the term, 'identity' is treated either as a synonym for self or as an aspect of self. McAdams (1997) refers to identity as being synonymous with the me, the sense we have of ourselves as an objective reality to which the I, the subjective aspect of self, responds.

To our knowledge, Erving Goffman is the first scholar to use identity in its symbolic interactionist sense as an aspect of self. Goffman's view of self appears to be dualistic. On the one hand, in such works as *The Presentation of Self in Everyday Life* (1959), *Behavior in Public Places* (1963a), and *Relations in Public* (1968), he seems to regard self as a performance, an individual achievement, or even as the creation of deliberate artifice. On the other hand, in works like *Stigma* (1963b), and *Asylums* (1961), he seems to take a more structural view of self, seeing it responding to structural features of interaction. It is in these works that he employs the term 'identity.' In *Stigma*, whose subtitle is 'The Management of Spoiled Identity,' Goffman examines the way in which individuals with 'abominations of the body,' 'blemishes of character' or 'tribal stigma' (including membership in an ethnic or religious category) perceive and respond to negative regard from others. In *Asylums*, he describes the process by which 'inmates' of such total institutions as asylums, prisons, and convents are stripped of their 'identity kits,' the resources they employ in everyday life to maintain a stable and positive sense of self. Although he is not generally considered a sociologist

of religion, Birrell (1981) points out that Goffman (1967) clearly builds upon Durkheim's (1964) analysis of religious ritual in his analysis of the role played by the rituals of everyday life in maintaining the sacredness of the self.

While most of those working in the symbolic interactionist tradition employ ethnographic research techniques, Kuhn and McPartland (1954) and others in the 'Iowa School' have taken a more quantitative approach to questions of self and identity. These authors pioneered the use of the 'Twenty Statements Test,' which elicits spontaneous answers to the question 'Who am I?' as a means of measuring identity. Kuhn and McPartland asserted that individuals' 'self-attitudes' reflect social-structural realities and tested this assumption with a study of religious identification. They found that religious identities are likely to be more salient among members of sectarian, or 'differentialistic,' groups than among members of more mainstream groups.

Identity Theory

Stryker (1980; Stryker and Serpe 1982; Stryker and Burke 2000; see also McCall and Simmons 1966) developed Identity Theory in an attempt to formally link identity and social structure through the concept of role. For identity theory, identity is the pivotal concept linking social structure with individual behavior; thus the prediction of behavior requires an analysis of the relationship between self and social structure. Since everyone has multiple roles and, therefore, multiple role identities, the key question for identity theory becomes discovering which identities get translated into behavior. In this tradition, role behavior is determined by identity salience (Callero 1985) – the probability that an identity will be invoked across a variety of situations – and by role commitment – the degree to which people's relationships to others in their networks depend on possessing a particular identity and playing a certain role.

Stryker and Serpe (1982) test identity theory with a study of religious behavior, finding that the salience of religious identities predicts the level of involvement in religious organizations. These authors do not address the factors that make religion more salient to some individuals than to others in this study. Reasoning that religion is likely to be more salient for clergy and elders than for rank-and-file congregation members, Krause *et al.* (1998) hypothesized that clergy and elders would be more affected by both the emotional support and the negative interactions they encounter in church. They found this to be the case in a study of a national sample of American Presbyterians. Peek (2005) has analyzed the process by which religious identity becomes salient for Muslim immigrants to the United States.

As noted above, one issue raised by the symbolic interactionist perspective and by identity theory is the question of whether identity is unitary or multiple. Since individuals interact with different others and play many roles, the perspective implies that one has multiple identities. As William James (1890, 1: 294) wrote, 'a man has as many social selves as there are individuals who recognize him and carry an image of him in their minds.' But this is at odds with what is usually implied by the concept of identity and by the phenomenological reality that we 'feel' as if we are one person and that we experience conflicting identities as a source of personal crisis. Identity theory forces us to ask how it is possible to have multiple identities while still believing ourselves to be unitary individuals.

Social Identity Theory

The focus in identity theory is on interpersonal or individual identity; it asks how individuals see themselves in relation to role partners (Thoits and Virshup 1997). Social Identity Theory, on the other hand, concentrates on categorical or group identity. As Thoits and Virshup express it, identity theory focuses on the 'me,' while social identity theory focuses on the 'we.' As formulated by Tajfel, Hogg, and others (Hogg 1992, 1993; Hogg and Abrams 1988; Tajfel 1969, 1970; Tajfel and Turner 1979), social identity theory is intended to be a social psychological theory of intergroup processes and the social self. Social identity theory emphasizes the importance for self-definitions of membership in social categories. In social identity theory, membership in a social category becomes the crucial basis for behavior and self-regulation via the processes of depersonalization and self-verification.

The primary emphasis in social identity theory is on such basic social categories as ethnicity, race, and gender. Less attention has been paid to religious identity except insofar as this can be conceptualized as a type of ethnicity. One notable exception can be found in the work of Seul (1999) who specifically applies social identity theory to religious identity in his effort to explain the frequent presence of religion as a marker dividing groups in conflict. The notion of group identity featured by social identity theorists appears to be related to Greeley's Durkheimian (1966) assertion that one of the primary functions of religion is the provision of belonging. In *The Denominational Society*, Greeley (1972; see also Hammond 1988; Swatos 1981) argues that denominationalism in the United States gained its strength from the fact that denominations came to serve as a source of community for immigrants and their children. Earlier, Herberg (1956) argued that Protestantism, Catholicism, and Judaism, had come to serve as 'super-ethnic groups' in American society, serving to give Americans a category smaller than the nation but larger than the local community with which to identify. The voluminous literature on Jewish identity (Cohen 1983, 1997; Dashefsky 1972; Dashefsky and Shapiro 1974; Heilman 1996; Himmelfarb 1980; Lazerwitz 1978; Rebhun 2004) appears to employ a conception of identity that focuses on identification with a collectivity.

The use of identity to refer to identification with a social category raises the question of why certain social categories are so often the basis of identification with a collective. Much writing on identity and 'identity politics' takes the 'primordialist' position that people naturally identify with people like themselves. Isaacs (1975) asserts that identity is inherently group identity and that religion, national origins, race, and language are important because they are highly visible symbols of group identity. Van den Berghe (1981) advances the sociobiological argument that humans are genetically predisposed to identify with others like themselves as a result of group selection processes. Others (Glazer and Moynihan 1975; Patterson 1975; Waters 1990) take a position that has been variously called 'utilitarianism,' 'optionalism,' or 'circumstantialism.' This position argues that there is nothing natural or inevitable about the categories into which group identities often cluster. Rather, the opponents of primordialism argue that people identify with social categories when it appears to be in their interest to do so. If the primordialists are right, we are left with questions concerning why people do not always respond the way we might expect based on their group memberships and why one category rather than another comes to serve as the basis of social identity in a given situation. What, for example, determines, whether immigrants from the Middle East will identify as Arabs or as Muslims? If the circumstantialists are right, we need to know more about the social construction of identity and the process by which identity categories come to exert power over individuals and groups.

The Concept of Personal Identity

Both the 'role identity' of identity theory and the 'categorical identity' of social identity theory are related to a conception of a 'social self' (Brewer and Gardner 1996), but both approaches recognize – even if they don't dwell on it – a more personal, individuated self. In addition to identifying themselves in terms of roles and of group and category memberships, individuals also ask 'What makes me unique?' (Reid and Deaux 1996). It is this notion of a personal self or personal identity that has been of primary concern to Western philosophers and psychologists since the time of Locke.

As Charles Taylor (1989) ably argues, the question of identity is always intimately connected to the moral question of 'What is the good?' According to Taylor, when we ask ourselves, 'What sort of person am I?,' we are asking an evaluative question. We are, in effect, asking ourselves if we are the kind of people who merit our own approval. More recently, Hitlin (2003) has taken a similar tack in arguing that personal identity is intimately connected to values. Since questions about morality and values are often answered in a religious idiom, a focus on personal identity leads us to consider the important role of religion when it comes to questions of identity. Peter Berger's (1967) argument that the function of religion is to sanctify one's cosmos is, in essence, an argument that personal identity is intimately tied in to one's conception of the sacred. Those who employ functional definitions of religion as whatever is of ultimate concern to the individual are, for all practical purposes, linking religion to the personal identity process by definition. When Thomas Luckmann (1967) defines religion as the 'capacity of the human organism to transcend its biological nature through the construction of objective, morally binding and all-embracing universes of meaning,' he is implicitly defining religion as the ground for identity. Mol (1976) makes this same point more explicitly when he defines religion as the 'sacralization of identity.' Seul (1999) posits that it is because religion lies so close to the core of people's identities that it is so often the basis for in-group identification and intergroup conflict.

One issue raised by a focus on personal identity is the question of stability versus mobility. Symbolic interactionism and identity theory suggest that identity must shift with changes in reference others and changes of roles; yet we have a sense that our identity persists over time. Without this sense of continuity, the question of who I am as a unique individual has no meaning. Social identity theory suggests that identity is relatively stable, but this makes the question of religious conversion and other shifts in identity problematic. A focus on personal identity forces us to ask how an individual can have a sense of self that is simultaneously changing and persistent.

Identity as Narrative

This overview of social scientific theories of identity has posed three questions provoked by the perspectives we have discussed thus far:

1. How is it possible for one to have multiple identities and yet perceive oneself as an integral individual who has an identity?
2. What determines which roles and which category memberships become salient in particular social situations?
3. How is it possible to have a sense of oneself as having an identity if identity is always changing?

Perhaps these issues may be in part resolved by a conception of identity as narrative. Ammerman (2003) has criticized the literature on religion and identity for its lack of attention to theories of identity and has suggested that the narrative theory of identity propounded by Somers (1994) can serve as a good foundation for studies of identity and religion.

For Somers, the problem with using the concept of identity to refer to membership in a social category as so many sociologists do is that this seems to assert the primordial importance of ascribed, 'essentialist,' categories in determining human behavior at the expense of an appreciation for human agency. Somers argues that people are not impelled to act in accordance with their membership in class, gender, or other categories; rather they use these categories of experience as materials with which to construct their own ontological narratives and, thus, their identities. According to McAdams (1997), when we think of identity as a story we tell about ourselves we have a way to understand how people can maintain a sense of themselves as coherent entities, even as they balance multiple identities in the context of continually changing social circumstances. Anthony Giddens (1991) defines identity tersely as 'the ability to keep a narrative going.'

In *Talk of Love*, Anne Swidler (2000) describes culture, not as a unitary set of values and rules, but as a toolkit from which people can choose the appropriate implements with which to construct solutions to the problems they encounter in everyday life. In this view, culture is not a rationally organized set of axioms and corollaries, but a series of 'recipes' upon which people can call in specific situations (Schutz 1967). Swidler shows how the people she interviewed switched almost effortlessly between two logically incompatible cultural repertoires to describe their relationships. The notion of love as a voluntary working relationship between two autonomous beings derives its plausibility from the voluntary and contingent nature of American marriage in a time when divorce is common, while the notion of love as a binding commitment derives its plausibility from the legal realities of marriage. Perhaps it is not unreasonable to conceptualize identity as a toolkit as well. In order to make decisions about how to act in a given situation, individuals must draw from their repertoire of stories about who 'they really are' in order to decide upon a course of action. What is constant about identity in this view is not that the stories we tell ourselves about ourselves remain the same or are even consistent with one another, but rather the fact of narrativity itself.

RELIGION AND IDENTITY: THE DOMINANT SOCIOLOGICAL CONCEPTUAL NARRATIVE

It strikes us that one useful way to organize the wide range of studies in religion and identity into a coherent story is to discuss them in the context of one popular sociological narrative: the transition from traditional to modern societies. The relationship between identity and modernity has been a central sociological problem since the development of the discipline. Emile Durkheim (1964) described pre-modern societies as being characterized as held together by a 'mechanical solidarity' born of a sameness that derived from many individuals being socialized to the same ascribed roles and seeing themselves as essentially similar to one another. Modern societies, Durkheim argued, are characterized by 'organic solidarity,' whereby individuals who have the freedom to learn different roles and develop independent identities are connected to one another, not by their sameness, but by their interdependence. Organic solidarity, while it brings with it a challenge to the strength of the *conscience collective*, also carries with it the possibility of freedom, since social actors can now choose what to do and who to be.

Georg Simmel (1955: 149) followed Durkheim's lead in contrasting the individualism of modernity with traditional affiliations with the group that 'absorbed the whole man.' Simmel viewed people in pre-modern societies as being constrained by overlapping social circles, while the intersecting social circles of modernity leave people free to become unique individuals. While Durkheim and Simmel are among those who deserve credit for identifying traditional society with constraint and modern society with choice, it was anthropologist Ralph Linton (1936) who popularized the terms 'achievement' and 'ascription' as descriptors of the presumed dichotomy between modern and pre-modern roles and identity. In *The Social System*, Talcott Parsons (1951) highlights ascription and achievement as one of the five sets of dichotomies, or 'pattern variables,' individuals use to orient themselves in the social world. Ascribed characteristics – which people consider to be fixed, immutable or inherited – typify pre-modern societies, whereas achieved characteristics – which 'place the accent on the performances of the incumbent in his qualities or attributes independently of any specifically expected performances' – are the hallmark of modern societies (Parsons 1951: 111).

The last half of the twentieth century has brought such extensive changes to modern societies that many commentators no longer speak of 'modernity', but of 'post-modernity' or 'late-modernity.' Nonetheless, more recent discussions of the nature of identity in modern societies seem more like a variation on traditional sociological discourse than a radically different analysis. For example, Giddens (1991) describes the societies of 'high modernity' as being characterized by 'chronic mutability' (p. 21), by abstract systems, by mediated experience, by a sense of risk, and by a 'puzzling diversity of options and possibilities' (p. 3). Under such conditions, Giddens writes, self-identity becomes a reflexively organized endeavor. The self is no longer an entity but a project. In high modernity, individuals continually refer to experts for lifestyle advice and constantly retool their identities. In a situation of multiple choices and uncertainty, people tend to avoid moral questions at the same time that they experience the threat of existential meaninglessness. Another student of identity in post-modernity, the psychologist Kenneth Gergen (1991), describes a situation of 'social saturation,' which gives rise to a mutable and fragmented self.

Herbert Gans has created the concepts of 'symbolic ethnicity' and 'symbolic religiosity' in an effort to make similar points about the malleability and contingency of contemporary identities in the context of questions about assimilation and the maintenance of ethnic identity in American society. Gans (1979) introduced the concept of 'symbolic ethnicity' in an effort to describe a new form of ethnicity that was expressive and flexible rather than fixed. For Gans, symbolic ethnicity represents the evolution of ethnicity from an instrumental and ascribed necessity into an 'identity marker.' The new function of ethnicity, in this view, was to give people a 'peg' on which to hang their identities in an increasingly large and impersonal society. Building on the symbolic ethnicity idea, Mary Waters (1990) has emphasized the individual and 'optional' nature of this new ethnic form. Ethnicity is still an important component of American identity, according to Waters, but it has become an optional, personally chosen identity marker rather than the totally ascribed characteristic it was for the first and second generations of immigrants. More recently, Gans (1994) has introduced the term 'symbolic religiosity' to makes the case that religion functions in a similar way for some people in modern society.

The sociological narrative of the effects of the transition from tradition to modernity on identity has been a major theme in the sociology of religion over the past fifty years. Peter Berger, whose ideas constituted the dominant paradigm in the sociology of religion for a generation, claimed that, while religion in traditional societies presents itself to the individual as a preexisting and not-to be-questioned fact, religion in modernity is characterized by pluralism, privatization, and the recognition that religion is a social construction. In *The Sacred Canopy*, Berger (1967) argued that an awareness of multiple worldviews and the accompanying sense that religion is a matter of personal choice would weaken the hold religion had on modern consciousness. Berger's view of modern identity sounds a lot like the ideas formulated later by Giddens; for Berger (1974), modern identity is striking in that it is peculiarly open, peculiarly differentiated, peculiarly individuated, and peculiarly reflective. Although Berger's 'secularization thesis' has now been rejected by most sociologists, including Berger himself, the notion that religious identity in modernity is a matter of individual choice has survived the transition to the 'new paradigm.'

R. Stephen Warner, who coined the term 'new paradigm' as a label for the post-secularization sociology of religion, agrees with Berger that religious identity loses its ascribed, taken-for-granted character under contemporary conditions. Warner asserts that 'religion need not represent something in which people are primordially rooted. Religious affiliation in the United States is not tribal' (1993: 1078). Warner, however, challenges Berger's assumption that the element of choice – the ability to accomplish one's religious identity – weakens religious commitment. In fact, he asserted, choice might well strengthen religious identity, since the very act of choosing a religion and its beliefs and practices among various competing alternatives may add agency and meaning to one's commitment. Phillip Hammond (1988) makes a similar argument when he posits that America is seeing a shift from a 'collective-expressive' religious identity to an 'individual-expressive' mode. Hammond asserts that both religion and ethnicity retain their significance for identity but that the nature of the significance they have is changing.

In their attempt to capture the transformation of religious identity in contemporary American society, Roof and McKinney (1987) have spoken of a 'new voluntarism.' Roof and McKinney find evidence for the new voluntarism in the highest rate ever of denominational switching, among Protestants, showing that individuals feel less constrained to conform to the patterns of religious behavior they have 'inherited' from their parents. They also find support for the existence of the new voluntarism in the tendency of people to pick and choose what they will and will not practice and believe within a religious tradition as well as the tendency to 'mix and match' among traditions. Finally, they see the increasing trend toward viewing religiosity as separate from and more important than church attendance as an indicator of the new voluntarism. Perhaps the most extreme exemplar of the new voluntarism is Sheila Larson, the woman described by Bellah *et al.* (1985) in *Habits of the Heart*, who claimed to have her own private religion, which she called 'Sheilaism.' In a more recent work, Roof (1993) describes Baby Boomers as a 'generation of seekers.'

Robert Wuthnow (1988) similarly embraces the view of contemporary America as an arena where individuals search for individualized meanings they cannot find in fixed traditions. Comparing the religious scene of the mid-twentieth century America that Will Herberg described in *Protestant, Catholic, and Jew* (1956) to that of the present, Wuthnow (Wuthnow *et al.* 1992) describes a shift from ascription to achievement in American religious identities. He argues that Americans have moved from a spirituality of 'dwelling' in a prescribed religious space to a spirituality of 'seeking' (1998). Concomitant with this trend has been a decline in the significance of traditional religious institutions and a proliferation of special purpose religious groups. The increasing tendency for people to see themselves as 'spiritual but not religious' may be part of this trend.

Thus, Warner, Hammond, Roof and McKinney, and Wuthnow all see contemporary Americans as religious seekers engaging in practices through which they enact their freely chosen religious commitments and identities, thereby escaping the limits of ascription.

Luckmann's (1967) discussion of the privatization of religion and Bailey's (1983) work on implicit religion can both be seen as part of this same broad tradition. It is obvious, then, that current scholarly writing on religion and identity is consistent with the longstanding sociological tradition of associating premodernity with ascription, structure, and stable identity and modernity with achievement, fluidity, and shifting identities. For both scholars of religion and theorists of identity in general, identity in modernity has become a *project* in which individuals cobble together a self out of multiple sources through a process that Lévi-Strauss (1966) referred to as *bricolage*. Contemporary American religiosity, we are told is an individualistic affair, where no single community defines us. Instead, we draw from multiple sources to construct unique and fluid religious narratives (Ammerman 2003).

SPECIFICATIONS AND DISSENTS

While most contemporary case studies of religion and identity do not directly challenge the dominant narrative theme of the transition of religious identity from a stable, ascribed, and collective form to a dynamic, individuated, and achieved form, they do seem oriented toward fleshing out nuances, variations, and apparent exceptions. Giddens (1991) argues that, because the reflexive, malleable, and contingent nature of modern self-identity brings with it the constantly looming threat of personal meaninglessness, it is possible to observe many instances of what he terms 'the return of the repressed.' Among the examples of the resurgence of collective, more stable bases for self-identity, Giddens specifically mentions the appeal of religious fundamentalism. Many researchers have explained the appeal of strict, encapsulated or 'enclave' religious groups as a response to the fluid, tentative, differentiated identity of late modernity.

The 1970s and 1980s saw a sharp increase in scholarship on the identity change process, largely as a result of increased sociological interest in new religious movements (Greil and Rudy 1984a; Richardson 1978; Snow and Phillips 1980; Snow and Machalek 1984). Travisano's (1970: 60) definition of conversion as a 'radical reorganization of identity, meaning, and life' is well known. Most sociological studies of religious identity change have focused on converts, individuals who have left the loosely structured role options of modern society for the more tightly structured roles of a sectarian religious group (Barker 1984; Galanter 1989; Richardson *et al.* 1979). While earlier studies concentrated on developing 'process models,' of the stages through which converts typically pass (Downton 1979; Lofland and Stark 1965), more recent studies have focused on the micro-structural dynamics of the conversion process. People who join new religious movements or sectarian groups generally engage in intensive interaction with members of the group and limit their contact with those outside the group (Greil and Rudy 1983, 1984b; Snow and Machalek 1984). Greil and Rudy (1984b) describe groups that try to change people – whether or not they define themselves as religious – as 'social cocoons' that try to encapsulate their members physically, socially, and ideologically in an attempt to shield them from the influence of the larger society and to foster identity change within the confines of group boundaries. Although they recognize the importance of structural factors, conversion scholars have emphasized that converts must be regarded, not as passive objects of structural conditions, but active agents in their own conversions (Balch 1980; Bromley 1997; Bromley and Shupe 1979; Richardson 1978; Straus 1976, 1979).

Although most studies have focused on the processes of conversion, there have also been studies of disaffiliation from religious communities (Beckford 1978; Bromley 1991, 1997; Davidman and Greil 2007; Jacobs 1987, 1989; Rothbaum 1988; Wright 1984, 1988). As Shaffir (1997) has pointed out, much of this work has centered on people who grew up in the open secular society, joined an encapsulated group, and then returned from the tightly structured roles of the group to the loosely structured choices with which they grew up. In many ways, the process of dis-affiliation, which depends upon a breakdown in encapsulation, is the structural mirror image of conversion, which involves insulation from the outside world (Wright 1987). Conversion entails identification with group members and the goals of the group; disaffiliation requires disidentification from group members, goals, and leaders. The different structural contexts in which the process of affiliation and disaffiliation take place result in some systematic differences in their dynamics. As Beckford (1985: 174) writes, 'There is little in the way of a cultural script for the passage of a person from being a member of an intense religious group to being a non-member.'

Research on the identity change process typically involves the analysis of retrospective accounts after the fact (Beckford 1978; Davidman 1991; Greil and Rudy 1984a; Lofland 1978; Snow and Machalek 1984; Yamane 2000). Yamane has argued in the more general context of the study of religious experience that it is important for scholars to recognize that conversion accounts must not be understood as literal descriptions of what has actually happened but as narratives, stories constructed to explain and present one's experience of transition in a meaningful way to one's self and to others (Beckford 1978: 260). Some scholars have gone so far as to argue that we can learn nothing about the actual process of conversion from narratives. In the view of these scholars, conversion narratives are not referential, but constitutive; they should be viewed, not as a description of conversion, but as an *enactment* of conversion (Stromberg 1993). Rephrasing this argument in terms employed by Somers (1994), these authors are making the claim that conversion narratives should be read, not as a 'mode of representation' but only as an 'ontological act' by which individuals constitute their social identities. We would argue that, although narratives of identity change are properly understood as creative constructions, they may nevertheless provide insight into the actual process of identity reconstruction.

The Continuing Identity Salience of Religious Organizations

Some writers who have looked at the identity functions of tightly knit religious organizations have focused on groups that are seen as somewhat more mainstream (Manning 1999). Some scholars (Ammerman 1987; Armstrong 2000; Fields 1991; Hewitt 1989) have interpreted the appeal of fundamentalism as providing a firmer anchor for identity than is generally available under conditions of late modernity. Davidman (1990, 1991) has analyzed the appeal of the more structured roles of Orthodox Judaism for contemporary American Jewish women. Neitz (1987) has studied the process by which 'low salience' Catholics embrace a Charismatic Catholic identity. A number of researchers have examined the growing tendency toward embracing an Evangelical Christian identity (Gallagher 2003; Hunter 1983; Smith 1998; Stacey 1990). Smith (1998) uses his survey data on American Evangelicals to argue against Berger's (1967) assertion that the pluralism associated with modernity inevitably threatens religious identity. In fact, Smith asserts that awareness of the threat of modernity and the concomitant sense of being in a battle with the forces of secularism serve to strengthen Evangelical identity. Such writers as Bartkowski (2001), Hunter (1983), Shibley (1996) and Stacey (1990) have argued that it is a serious mistake to interpret evangelicalism and other conservative religions as simply shoring up identity against the threats of modernity. Rather, these authors argue that conservative religion will only exert its appeal to the extent that it can rework tradition and incorporate elements of modern identity. The image that these studies paint is neither a picture of individuals stubbornly hanging on to traditional identity in the face of modernity nor of succumbing to the threats modernity poses to identity; rather we see the creative adaptation of traditional identities to new circumstances.

Recent years have also seen the emergence of a tradition of scholarship that emphasizes the role that religious organizations play in helping new immigrants navigate the vicissitudes of identity in a new society (Kim 2000; Lawson 1999; Peña and Freehill 1998; Warner and Wittner 1998; Yang 1999). In a study of Muslim university students, Peek (2005) describes the process by which her respondents shifted over time from seeing their Muslim heritage as an ascribed identity to seeing it is a freely chosen declaration of their religious and ethnic identity. Read and Bartkowski (2000) analyze the role of the veil as a means of negotiating gender and religious identities among a sample of women in Austin, Texas. In a study of second generation Korean Americans, Chong (1998) examines the way in which the Korean ethnic Church serves in the construction and maintenance of Korean ethnic identity.

Other researchers are looking at questions of religious identity among an earlier generation of immigrants. Hoge (2000) has recently argued that Jews and Catholics in American society confront similar identity issues. Both groups have entered the mainstream of American society and are facing the challenge of trying to fully integrate into American life while retaining a distinct identity, producing much anxiety among their leaders. Some Catholics (Dillon 1999; Ecklund 2005) are confronted with the task of trying to reinterpret their tradition in a way that allows them to think of themselves as good Catholics at the same time as they have embraced mainstream American ideas about leadership, gender, sexuality and the autonomy of the individual. There are by now a large number of studies on the ways in which Jewish identity has been transformed by and adapted to American society (Cohen 1983, 1997; Dashefsky 1972; Dashefsky and Shapiro 1974; Heilman 1996; Himmelfarb 1980; Lazerwitz 1978; Rebhun 2004).

The ways in which case studies of religion and identity have served to add texture to the sociological conceptual narrative of the effect of modernity on religious identity are well illustrated by a recent study of American Jews and Buddhists. In this study, Cadge and Davidman (2006) challenge the notion that ascription and achievement are conceptually distinct, dichotomous ways of constructing religious identities. Although choice is often portrayed as a central characteristic of religion in contemporary America, the respondents Cadge and Davidman study clearly combined ideas of ascription and achievement in their narratives of religious identity. Rather than seeing their religious identities as either ascribed as a result of birth or achieved as a result of conscious choices, their respondents combined notions of ascription and achievement in making sense of their identities.

Another theme found in the contemporary study of religion and identity revolves around people who struggle to balance two apparently incongruous identities. Thumma (1991) has analyzed the ways in which members of Good News, a gay conservative Christian organization, collectively reinterpret their faith in order to construct a positive identity out of apparently incompatible aspects of their selves. In his study of identity negotiation among gay Jews, Schnoor (2006) distinguishes four types among his respondents: Jewish lifestylers, gay lifestylers, gay-Jewish 'commuters,' and gay-Jewish integrators. Other analyses have focused on attempts to balance feminist identities against identities as Catholics (Ecklund 2005) or Jews (Dufour 2000). Dufour describes the achievement of a Jewish feminist identity as the outcome of a creative process of 'sifting' through available options.

CONCLUSIONS

Sociologists of religion have always been concerned with questions of identity, but they are now more likely than ever to use the term 'identity.' This increase in explicit attention to the concept of 'identity' appears to be a consequence of changes in the nature of religion in late modernity. As religious identity becomes more voluntaristic and reflexive, concerns about the construction and maintenance of religious identity are coming to the fore. The version of 'identity' that sociologists of religion are embracing in their study of contemporary religious identity is one that emphasizes the social construction of identity and the conception of identity as narrative. Thus, sociologists are employing 'identity' in a way that emphasizes agency in the sociological study of religion at the same time as they recognize the influence of social structure on identity.

REFERENCES

Allport, Gordon W. and J. Michael Ross 1967. 'Personal Religious Orientation and Prejudice.' *Journal of Personality and Social Psychology* 5: 432–43.

Ammerman, Nancy T. 1987. *Bible Believers: Fundamentalists in the Modern World.* New Brunswick, NJ: Rutgers University Press.

Ammerman, Nancy T. 2003. 'Religious Identity and Religious Institutions.' Pp. 207–24 in *Handbook of the Sociology of Religion,* edited by Michele Dillon. Cambridge: Cambridge University Press.

Armstrong, Karen 2000. *The Battle for God.* New York: Knopf.

Bailey, Edward 1983. 'The Implicit Religion of Contemporary Society: An Orientation and Plea for its Study.' *Religion* 13: 69–83.

Balch, Robert 1980. 'Looking Behind the Scenes in a Religious Cult: Implications for the Study of Conversion.' *Sociological Analysis* 41: 137–43.

Barker, Eileen 1984. *The Making of a Moonie: Brainwashing or Choice.* Oxford: Blackwell.

Bartkowski, John 2001. *Remaking the Godly Marriage: Gender Negotiation in Evangelical Families.* New Brunswick, NJ: Rutgers University Press.

Batson, C. Daniel and Patricia A. Schoenrade 1991. 'Measuring Religion as Quest: 1. Validity Concerns.' *Journal for the Scientific Study of Religion* 30: 416–29.

Batson, C. Daniel and Patricia A. Schoenrade 1991. 'Measuring Religion as Quest: 2. Validity Concerns.' *Journal for the Scientific Study of Religion* 30: 430–47.

Batson, C. Daniel, Patricia A. Schoenrade and W. Larry Ventis 1993. *Religion and the Individual.* New York: Oxford University Press.

Beckford, James 1978. 'Accounting for Conversion.' *British Journal of Sociology* 29: 249–62.

Beckford, James 1985. *Cult Controversies: The Societal Responses to New Religious Movements.* New York: Tavistock.

Bellah, Robert, Richard Madsen, William Sullivan, Anne Swidler and Steven Tipton 1985. *Habits of the Heart: Individualism and Commitment in American Life.* Berkeley: University of California Press.

Berger, Peter L. 1963. *Invitation to Sociology: A Humanistic Approach.* Englewood Cliffs, NJ: Doubleday.

Berger, Peter L. 1967. *The Sacred Canopy: Elements of a Sociological Theory of Religion.* Garden City, NY: Doubleday.

Berger, Peter L. 1974. 'Modern Identity: Crisis and Continuity.' Pp. 159–81 in *The Cultural Drama: Modern Identities and Social Ferment,* edited by Wilton S. Dillon. Washington: Smithsonian Institution Press.

Berzonsky, Michael D. 1989. 'Identity Style: Conception and Measurement.' *Journal of Adolescent Research* 4: 268–82.

Berzonsky, Michael D. 1992. 'Identity Style and Coping Strategies.' *Journal of Personality* 40: 771–8.

Berzonsky, Michael D. 1994. 'Self-Identity: The Relationship between Process and Content.' *Journal of Research in Personality* 28: 453–60.

Birrell, Susan 1981. 'Sport as Ritual: Interpretations from Durkheim to Goffman.' *Social Forces* 60: 354–76.

Blasi, Augusto 1980. 'Bridging Moral Cognition and Moral Action: A Critical Review of the Literature.' *Psychological Bulletin* 88: 1–45.

Blasi, Augusto 2004. 'Moral Functioning: Moral Understanding and Personality.' Pp. 335–47 in *Moral Development, Self, and Identity,* edited by Daniel K. Lapsley and Darcia Narvaez. Mahwah, NJ: Lawrence Erlbaum Associates.

Brewer, Marilyn B. and Wendi Gardner 1996. 'Who Is This "We"? Levels of Collective Identity and Self Representations.' *Journal of Personality and Social Psychology* 71: 83–93.

Bromley, David G. 1991. 'Unraveling Religious Disaffiliation: The Meaning and Significance of Falling from the Faith.' *Counseling and Values* 36: 164–85.

Bromley, David G. 1997. 'Falling from the New Faiths: Toward an Integrated Model of Religious Affiliation/Disaffiliation'. Pp. 31–60 in *Leaving Religion and Religious Life,* edited by Mordechai Bar-Lev and William Shaffir. Vol. 7 of *Religion and the Social Order,* edited by David G. Bromley. Greenwich, CT: JAI Press.

Bromley, David G. and Anson D. Shupe, Jr. 1979. 'Just a Few Years Seems Like a Lifetime: A Role Theory Approach to Participation in Religious Movements.' Pp. 159–85 in *Research in Social Movements, Conflict, and Change,* edited by Lewis Kriesberg.

Brubaker, Rogers and Frederick Cooper 2000. 'Beyond 'Identity.' *Theory and Society* 29: 1–47.

Cadge, Wendy and Lynn Davidman 2006. 'Ascription, Choice, and the Construction of Religious Identities in the Contemporary United States.' *Journal for the Scientific Study of Religion* 45: 23–38.

Callero, Peter L. 1985. 'Role Identity Salience' *Social Psychological Quarterly* 48: 203–14.

Cerulo, Karen A. 1997. 'Identity Construction: New Issues, New Directions.' *Annual Review of Sociology* 23: 385–409.

Chong, Kelly H. 1998. 'What it Means to be a Christian: The Role of Religion in the Construction of Ethnic Identity and Boundary among Second-Generation Korean Americans.' *Sociology of Religion* 59: 259–86.

Cohen, Steven M. 1983. *American Modernity and Jewish Identity.* New York: Tavistock.

Cohen, Steven M. 1997. *Religious Stability and Ethnic Decline: Emerging Patterns of Jewish Identity in the United States.* Jerusalem: Hebrew University Melton Center for Jewish Education in the Diaspora.

Coles, Robert 1972. Review of *Dimensions of a New Identity,* by Erik H. Erikson. *New Republic* (June 8): 23.

Cooley, Charles Horton 1902. *Human Nature and Social Order.* New York: Scribner's.

Dashefsky, Arnold 1972. 'And the Search Goes On: The Meaning of Religio-Ethnic Identity and Identification.' *Sociological Analysis* 33: 239–45

Dashefsky, Arnold and Howard M. Shapiro 1974. *Ethnic Identification among American Jews.* Lanham, MD: University Press of America.

Davidman, Lynn 1990. 'Accommodation and Resistance: A Comparison of Two Contemporary Jewish Groups.' *Sociological Analysis* 51: 35–51.

Davidman, Lynn 1991. *Tradition in a Rootless World: Women Turn to Orthodox Judaism.* Berkeley: University of California Press.

Davidman, Lynn and Arthur L. Greil 2007. 'Characters in Search of a Script: The Exit Narratives of Formerly Ultra-Orthodox Jews.' *Journal for the Scientific Study of Religion* 46(2): 201–16.

Dillon, Michele 1999. *Catholic Identity: Balancing Reason, Faith, and Power.* Cambridge: Cambridge University Press.

Downton, James 1979. *Sacred Journeys: The Conversion of Young Americans to Divine Light Mission.* New York: Columbia University Press.

Dufour, Lynn Resnick 2000. 'Sifting through Tradition: The Creation of Jewish Feminist Identities.' *Journal for the Scientific Study of Religion* 39: 90–106.

Durkheim, Emile 1964. *The Division of Labor in Society.* Glencoe: Free Press.

Durkheim, Emile 1966. *The Elementary Forms of the Religious Life.* London: Allen and Unwin.

Ecklund, Elaine Howard 2005. 'Different Identity Accounts for Catholic Women.' *Review of Religious Research* 47: 135–49.

Erikson, Erik H. 1968. *Identity: Youth and Crisis.* New York: Norton.

Fields, Echo E. 1991. 'Understanding Activist Fundamentalism: Capitalist Crisis and the Colonization of the Lifeworld.'

Galanter, Mark 1989. *Cults, Faith, Healing, and Coercion.* New York: Oxford University Press.

Gallagher, Sally 2003. *Evangelical Identity and Gendered Family Life.* New Brunswick, NJ: Rutgers University Press.

Gans, Herbert J. 1979. 'Symbolic Ethnicity: The Future of Ethnic Groups and Cultures in America.' *Ethnic and Racial Studies* 2: 1–20.

Gans, Herbert J. 1994. 'Symbolic Ethnicity and Symbolic Religiosity: Towards a Comparison of Ethnic and Religious Acculturation.' *Ethnic and Racial Studies* 17: 576–92.

Gergen, Kenneth J. 1991. *The Saturated Self: Dilemmas of Identity in Contemporary Life.* New York: Basic.

Giddens, Anthony 1991. *Modernity and Self-Identity: Self and Society in the Late Modern Age.* Stanford, CA: Stanford University Press.

Glazer, Nathan and Daniel P. Moynihan (eds) 1975. *Ethnicity: Theory and Experience.* Cambridge: Harvard University Press.

Gleason, Philip 1983. 'Identifying Identity: A Semantic History.' *The Journal of American History* 69: 910–31.

Goffman, Erving 1959. *The Presentation of Self in Everyday Life.* Garden City, NY: Doubleday.

Goffman, Erving 1961. *Asylums: Essays on the Social Situation of Mental Patients and Other Inmates.* Harmondsworth: Penguin, 1968.

Goffman, Erving 1963a. *Behavior in Public Places: Notes on the Social Organization of Gatherings.* New York: Free Press.

Goffman, Erving 1963b. *Stigma: Notes on the Management of Spoiled Identity.* Englewood Cliffs, NJ: Prentice Hall.

Goffman, Erving 1967. *Interaction Ritual: Essays on Face-to-Face Behavior.* New York: Anchor.

Goffman, Erving 1968. *Relations in Public.* New York: Harper Colophon.

Greeley, Andrew M. 1972. *The Denominational Society.* Glenville, IL: Aldine de Gruyter.

Greil, Arthur L. and David R. Rudy 1983. 'Conversion to the Worldview of Alcoholics Anonymous: A Refinement of Conversion Theory.' *Qualitative Sociology* 6: 5–28.

Greil, Arthur L. and David R. Rudy 1984a. 'What Have We Learned from Process Models of Conversion?: An Examination of Ten Case Studies.' *Sociological Focus* 17: 305–23.

Greil, Arthur L. and David R. Rudy 1984b. 'Social Cocoons: Encapsulation and Identity Transformation.' *Sociological Inquiry* 54: 260–78.

Hammond, Phillip E. 1988. 'Religion and the Persistence of Identity.' *Journal for the Scientific Study of Religion* 27: 1–11.

Handlin, Oscar 1951. *The Uprooted: the Epic Story of the Great Migrations that Made the American People.* Boston: Little, Brown.

Heilman, Samuel C. 1996. *Portrait of American Jews: The Last Half of the 20th Century.* Seattle: University of Washington Press.

Herberg, Will 1956. *Protestant-Catholic-Jew: An Essay in American Religious Sociology.* Garden City, NY: Doubleday.

Hewitt, John P. 1989. *Dilemmas of the American Self.* Philadelphia: Temple University Press.

Himmelfarb, Harold S. 1980. 'The Study of American Jewish Identification: How it is Defined, Measured, Obtained, Sustained and Lost.' *Journal for the Scientific Study of Religion* 19: 48–60.

Hitlin, Steven 2003. 'Values as the Core of Personal Identity: Drawing Links between Two Theories of Self.' *Social Psychological Quarterly* 66: 118–37.

Hoge, Dean 2000. 'Jewish Identity and Catholic Identity: Findings and Analogies.' Paper presented at the annual meeting of the Religious Research Association, Houston, TX.

Hogg, Michael A. 1992. *The Social Psychology of Group Cohesiveness: From Attraction to Social Identity.* London: Harvester Wheatsheaf.

Hogg, Michael A. 1993. 'Group Cohesiveness: A Critical Review and Some New Directions.' *European Review of Social Psychology* 4: 85–111.

Hogg, Michael A. and Dominic Abrams 1988. *Social Identifications: A Social Psychology of Intergroup Relations and Group Processes.* London: Routledge.

Howard, Judith A. 2000. 'Social Psychology of Identities.' *Annual Review of Sociology* 26: 367–93.

Hunter, James D. 1983. *American Evangelicism: Conservative Religion and the Quandary of Modernity.* New Brunswick, NJ: Rutgers University Press.

Isaacs, Harold R. 1975. *Idols of the Tribe: Group Identity and Political Change.* New York: Harper Colophon.

Jacobs, Janet Liebman 1987. 'Deconversion from Religious Movements: An Analysis of Charismatic Bonding and Spiritual Commitment.' *Journal for the Scientific Study of Religion* 26: 294–308.

Jacobs, Janet Liebman 1989. *Divine Disenchantment: Deconverting from New Religions.* Bloomington: Indiana University Press.

James, William 1890. *Principles of Psychology.* New York: Holt, Rinehart, and Winston.

Jennings, W.S., R. Kilkenny and L. Kohlberg 1983. 'Moral Development Theory and Practice for Youthful and Adult Offenders. Pp. 281–355 in *Personality Theory, Moral Development and Criminal Behavior,* edited by W. S. Laufer and J. M. Day. Lexington, MA: Lexington Books.

Kim, Andrew E. 2000. 'Korean Religious Culture and its Affinity to Christianity: The Rise of Protestant Christianity in South Korea.' *Sociology of Religion* 61: 117–33.

Krause, Neal, Christopher G. Ellison and Keith M. Wulff 1998. 'Church-Based Emotional Support, Negative Interaction, and Psychological Well-Being: Findings from a National Sample of Presbyterians.' *Journal for the Sociology of Religion* 37: 725–41.

Kuhn, Manfred H. and Thomas S. McPartland 1954. *American Sociological Review* 19: 68–76.

Lawson, Ronald 1999. 'When Immigrants Take Over: The Impact of Immigrant Growth on American Seventh day Adventism's Trajectory from Sect to Denomination.' *Journal for the Scientific Study of Religion* 38: 83–102.

Lazerwitz, Bernard 1978. 'An Approach to the Components and Consequences of Jewish Identification.' *Contemporary Jewry* 4: 3–8.

Lévi-Strauss, Claude 1966. *The Savage Mind.* Chicago: University of Chicago Press.

Linton, Ralph 1936. *The Study of Man.* New York: Appleton-Century-Crofts.

Lofland, John 1978. 'Becoming a World Saver Revisited.' Pp. 10–23 in *Conversion Careers: In and Out of the New Religions.* Beverly Hills, CA: Sage.

Lofland, John and Rodney Stark 1965. 'Becoming a World-Saver: A Theory of Conversion to a Deviant Perspective.' *American Sociological Review* 30: 863–74.

Luckmann, Thomas 1967. *The Invisible Religion: The Problem of Religion in Modern Society.* New York: Macmillan.

MacLean, A. Michael, Lawrence J. Walker, and M. Kyle Matsuba 2004. 'Transcendence and the Moral Self: Identity Integration, Religion, and Moral Life.' *Journal for the Scientific Study of Religion* 43: 429–37.

Manning, Christel J. 1999. *God gave Us the Right: Conservative Catholic, Evangelical Protestant, and Orthodox Jewish Women Grapple with Feminism.* New Brunswick, NJ: Rutgers University Press.

Marcia, James 1966. 'Development and Validation of Ego Identity Status.' *Journal of Personality and Social Psychology* 3: 551–8.

McAdams, Dan P. 1997. 'The Case for Unity in the (Post) Modern Self: A Modest Proposal.' Pp. 46–78 in *Self and Identity: Fundamental Issues*, edited by Richard D. Ashmore and Lee Jussim. New York: Oxford University Press.

McCall, George J. and J. L. Simmons 1966. *Identities and Interactions*. New York: Free Press.

McGuire, Meredith 1992. *Religion: The Social Context* (3rd edn.). Belmont, CA: Wadsworth.

Mead, George H. 1934. *Mind, Self, and Society*. Chicago: University of Chicago Press.

Mol, Hans J. 1976. *Identity and the Sacred: A Sketch for a New Social-Scientific Theory of Religion*. Oxford: Blackwell.

Neitz, Mary Jo. 1987. *Charisma and Community: A Study of Religious Commitment within the Charismatic Renewal*. New Brunswick, NJ: Transaction Books.

Parsons, Talcott 1951. *The Social System*. Glencoe, IL: Free Press.

Patterson, Orlando 1975. 'Context and Choice in Ethnic Allegiance: A Theoretical Framework and Caribbean Case Study.' Pp. 304–49 in *Ethnicity: Theory and Experience*, edited by Nathan Glazer and Daniel P. Moynihan. Cambridge: Harvard University Press.

Peña, Milagros and Lisa M. Freehill 1998. 'Latina Religious Practice: Analyzing Cultural Dimensions in Measures of Religiosity.' *Journal for the Scientific Study of Religion* 37: 12–31.

Peek, Lori 2005. 'Becoming Muslim: The Development of a Religious Identity.' *Sociology of Religion* 66: 252–42.

Read, Jen'nan Ghazal and John P. Bartkowski 2000. '"To Veil or Not to Veil?" A Case Study of Identity Negotiation among Muslim Women in Austin, Texas.' *Gender & Society* 14: 395–417.

Rebhun, Uzi 2004. 'Jewish Identity in America: Structural Analyses of Attitudes and Behavior.' *Review of Religious Research* 46: 42–63.

Reid, Anne and Kay Deaux 1996. 'Relationship between Social and Personal Identity.' *Journal of Personality and Social Psychology* 70: 1084–91.

Richardson, James T. (ed.) 1978. *Conversion Careers: In and Out of the New Religions*. Beverly Hills: Sage.

Richardson, James T., Mary White Stewart and Robert B. Simmonds 1979. *Organized Miracles: A Study of a Contemporary, Youth, Communal, Fundamentalist Organization*. New Brunswick: Transaction.

Roof, Wade Clark and William McKinney 1987. *American Mainline Religion*. New Brunswick, NJ: Rutgers University Press.

Roof, Wade Clark 1993. *Generation of Seekers: The Spiritual Journeys of the Baby Boom Generation*. With the Assistance of Bruce Greer *et al.* San Francisco: Harper.

Rothbaum, Susan 1988. 'Between Two Worlds: Issues of Separation and Identity after Leaving a Religious Community. Pp. 205–28 in *Falling from the Faith*, edited by David G. Bromley. Newbury Park: Sage.

Sanders, Jimy M. 2002. 'Ethnic Boundaries and Identities in Plural Societies.' *American Review of Sociology* 28: 327–57.

Schnoor, Randal F. 2006. 'Being Gay and Jewish: Negotiating Intersecting Identities.' *Sociology of Religion* 67: 43–60.

Schutz, Alfred 1967. *The Phenomenology of the Social World*. Evanston, IL: Northwestern University Press.

Seul, Jeffery R. 1999. '"Ours Is the Way of God": Religion, Identity, and Intergroup Conflict.' *Journal of Peace Research* 36: 553–69.

Shaffir, William 1997. 'Disaffiliation: The Experiences of Haredi Jews. Pp. 205–28 in *Leaving Religion and Religious Life*,' edited by Mordechai Bar-Lev and William Shaffir. Vol. 7 of *Religion and the Social Order*, edited by David G. Bromley. Greenwich, CT: *JAI* Press.

Shibley, Mark A. 1996. *Resurgent Evangelicalism in the United States: Mapping Cultural Change since 1970*. Columbia: University of South Carolina Press.

Simmel, Georg 1955. *Conflict and the Web of Group Affiliations*. K. H. Wolff and R. Bendix, trans, foreword by Everett C. Hughes. New York: Free Press.

Smith, Christian with Michael Emerson, Sally Gallagher, Paul Kennedy, and David Sikkink 1998. *American Evangelicalism: Embattled and Thriving*. Chicago: University of Chicago Press.

Snow, David and Richard Machalek 1984. 'The Sociology of Conversion.' Pp. 167–90 in *The Annual Review of Sociology*, edited by Ralph H. Turner and James F. Short. Palo Alto, CA: Annual Reviews.

Snow, David and Cynthia Phillips 1980. 'The Lofland-Stark Conversion Model: A Critical Reassessment.' *Social Problems* 27: 420–37.

Somers, Margaret R. 1994. 'The Narrative Constitution of Identity: A Relational and Network Approach.' *Theory and Society* 23: 605–49.

Stacey, Judith 1990. *Brave New Families: Stories of Domestic Upheaval in the Late Twentieth Century America*. New York: Basic.

Straus, Roger A. 1976. 'Changing Oneself: Seekers and the Creative Transformation of Life Experience.' Pp. 252–72 in *Doing Social Life*, edited by John Lofland. New York: Wiley.

Straus, Roger A. 1979. 'Religious Conversion as a Personal and Collective Accomplishment.' *Sociological Analysis* 40: 158–65.

Stromberg, Peter G. 1993. *Language and Self-Transformation: A study of the Christian Conversion Narrative*. Cambridge: Cambridge University Press.

Stryker, Sheldon 1980. *Symbolic Interactionism: A Social Structural Version*. Menlo Park, CA: Benjamin Cummings.

Stryker, Sheldon and Peter J. Burke 2000. 'The Past, Present, and Future of an Identity Theory.' *Social Psychological Quarterly* 63: 284–97.

Stryker, Sheldon and Richard T. Serpe 1982. 'Commitment, Identity Salience, and Role Behavior: A Theory and Research Example.' Pp. 199–218 in *Personality, Roles, and Social Behavior,* edited by William Ickes and Eric S. Knowles. New York: Springer-Verlag.

Swatos, William 1981. 'Beyond Denominationalism.' *Journal for the Scientific Study of Religion* 20: 217–27.

Swidler, Ann 2000. *Talk of Love: How Culture Matters*. Chicago: University of Chicago Press.

Tajfel, Henri 1969. 'Cognitive Aspects of Prejudice.' *Journal of Science Issues* 25: 79–97.

Tajfel, Henri 1970. 'Experiments in Group Discrimination.' *Scientific American* 223: 96–102.

Tajfel, Henri and John C. Turner 1979. 'An Integrative Theory of Intergroup Conflict.' Pp. 33–47 in *The Social Psychology of Intergroup Relations,* edited by W. G. Austin and S. Worchel. Monterey: Brooks-Cole.

Taylor, Charles 1989. *Sources of the Self: The Making of the Modern Identity*. Cambridge: Harvard University Press.

Thoits, Peggy A. and Lauren K. Virshup 1997. 'Me's and We's: Forms and Functions of Social Identities.' Pp. 106–33 in *Self and Identity: Fundamental Issues,* Richard Ashmore and Lee Jussim. New York: Oxford University Press.

Thumma, Scott 1991. 'Negotiating a Religious Identity: The Case of the Gay Evangelical.' *Sociological Analysis* 52: 333–47.

Travisano, Richard 1970. 'Alternation and Conversion as Qualitatively Different Transformations.' Pp. 137–48 in *Social Psychology through Symbolic Interaction*, edited by Gregory Stone and Harvey Farberman. New York: Wiley.

Van den Berghe, Pierre 1981. *The Ethnic Phenomenon*. New York: Elsevier.

Warner, R. Stephen 1993. 'Work in Progress toward a New Paradigm for the Sociological Study of Religion in the United States.' *American Journal of Sociology* 98: 1044–93.

Warner R. Stephen and Judith G. Wittner (eds) 1998. *Gatherings in the Diaspora: Religious Communities and the New Immigration*. Philadelphia: Temple University Press.

Watson, Paul J. and Ronald J. Morris 2005. 'Spiritual Experience and Identity: Relationships with Religious Orientation, Religious Interest, and Intolerance of Ambiguity.' *Review of Religious Research* 46: 371–9.

Watson, Paul J., Ronald J. Morris, Ralph W. Hood. Jr., J. Trevor Milliron and Nancy L. Stutz 1992. 'Quest and Identity within a Religious Ideological Surround.' *Journal of Psychology and Theology* 20: 376–88.

Watson, Paul J., Ronald J. Morris, Ralph W. Hood. Jr., J. Trevor Milliron and Nancy L. Stutz 1998. 'Religious Orientation, Identity, and the Quest for Meaning in Ethics within an Ideological Surround.' *International Journal for the Psychology of Religion* 8: 149–64.

Waters, Mary 1990. *Ethnic Options*. Berkeley: University of California Press.

Wright, Stuart A. 1984. 'Post-Involvement Attitudes of Voluntary Defectors from Controversial New Religious Movements.' *Journal for the Scientific Study of Religion* 23: 172–82.

Wright, Stuart A. 1987. *Leaving Cults: The Dynamics of Defection*. Washington: Society for the Scientific Study of Religion.

Wright, Stuart A. 1988. 'Leaving New Religious Movements: Issues, Theory, and Research.' Pp. 106–21 in *Falling from the Faith*, edited by David G. Bromley. Newbury Park: Sage.

Wuthnow, Robert 1988. *The Restructuring of American Religion: Society and Faith Since World War II*. Princeton, NJ: Princeton University Press.

Wuthnow, Robert 1998. *After Heaven: Spirituality in America Since the 1950s*. Berkeley: University of California Press.

Wuthnow, Robert, Martin Marty, Philip Gleason and Deborah Dash Moore 1992. 'Sources of Personal Identity: Religion, Ethnicity, and the American Cultural Situation.' *Religion and American Culture* 2: 1–22.

Yamane, David 2000. 'Narrative and Religious Experience.' *Journal for the Scientific Study of Religion* 61: 171–89.

Yang, Fenggang 1999. *Chinese Christians in America: Conversion, Assimilation, and Adhesive Identity*. University Park: Penn State University Press.

27

Gender Differences in Religious Practice and Significance

LINDA WOODHEAD

For reasons which merit separate analysis, the Sociology of Religion has lagged behind many other fields in taking gender seriously. Whilst small-scale, ethnographic studies have been most likely to recognise the significance of gender, dominant theoretical frameworks within the Sociology of Religion often remain gender-blind. Although there has been some debate about why women, in the West at least, are more religious than men,[1] this has largely taken place in isolation from what are still considered to be the 'big' issues in the sociological analysis of religion, most notably issues concerning the growth and decline of religion in modern societies.

This inattention to gender contrasts with the liveliness of gender studies within the academy in recent decades. There have been a number of significant advances in theorising gender, most notably in three related areas. First, the idea that a distinction can be drawn between a biologically-given 'sex' and a socially-constructed 'gender' has been widely discredited. Historical studies like Laqueur (1990) demonstrate that sex is historically and culturally variable, with the modern idea of two separate sexes representing a shift away from the longer-established Western view that

there is a single male sex, of which the female is an inferior manifestation. The 'sex and gender' model has also been undermined by a model of sex/gender as produced in and by social processes and performances (Butler, 1999), or as a form of 'social embodiment' (Connell, 2002). The latter view stresses the mutual constitution of bodies and social processes, such that it is impossible to prise them apart, whilst the former tends to reduce the bodily to the social. Second, rejection of the 'sex and gender' model is bound up with a rejection of the idea that there are 'two spheres' of masculinity and femininity or male and female. Psychological research on sex difference has failed to find any large or universal differences between men and women (for a summary see Kimmel, 2000), and there is a growing awareness that in different cultural contexts gender can be viewed as one or as many, rather than as binary. Finally, these developments have rendered talk about 'sex roles' – a term which implies a sex and gender model – problematic. The idea that individuals are socialised into sex roles in childhood has been supplemented by the idea that sex/gender differences are continually negotiated throughout the life-course, in a process which is active as well as passive. Thus investigation into 'femininities' and 'masculinities' is replacing study of 'sex roles', one consequence of which is to move the research agenda away from a concentration on 'women' alone.

Cumulatively, these developments have led to a shift away from the so-called 'essentialism' of the 1970s and early 1980s which set 'women' against 'men', towards a view which prefers to stress the multiple 'differences' which go to make up identities. This shift has rendered talk of 'patriarchy' suspect, since the idea that men systematically dominate, oppress and exploit women is challenged by the view that society is structured by a complex set of differences (ethnic, racial, gendered, class-based), and that both men and women occupy and negotiate a range of different positions within this complex matrix. Under the towering influence of Michel Foucault many writers dismiss the idea of power as a possession which is unequally distributed in society, above all between men and women, in favour of a picture of power as constantly negotiated in the small, ceaseless, real-time interactions between individuals. There is, however, a countervailing move by others who believe that the stress on 'capillary' rather than 'arterial' power has gone too far (for example, Sayer 2004; Skeggs, 1997, 2004), and that talk of 'differences' must not be allowed to mask the massive and consolidated inequalities of power which still structure contemporary societies – including, pre-eminently, that between men and women.

This, then, is the lively tradition of debate with which the Sociology of Religion has thus far entered into only limited dialogue. As I will illustrate in this chapter, there have been a number of significant sociological contributions to the study of religion and gender in recent decades, which have nevertheless failed to make a significant impact upon the wider field of gender studies.[2] Even within the Sociology of Religion itself, those who engage with gender issues have failed to convince many of their colleagues that such a move is not an optional extra or an interesting specialisation, but an essential corrective to the gender-blindness which has, until now, restricted the discipline's field of vision. The argument still

has to be won that removal of these blinkers has consequences for the entire discipline – its methods, its theories, its critical tools and concepts, its focus, its areas of concentration, its specialisations, its hierarchies, its institutional forms and material practices.

One consequence of this patchy and partial interaction is that there is as yet no agreed 'syllabus' in the sociological study of religion and gender, no tried and tested way of approaching the subject, no theory or theories of religion and gender. Of necessity then, this chapter cannot simply summarise the 'state of the art' and suggest how it can or should develop in the future – it must also try to fill in some of the gaps. It will approach this task, first, by sketching a theoretical framework for understanding religion and gender, and then by substantiating the theory by reference to some key studies of aspects of religion and gender. Next, the significance of gender for the sociological study of religion will be illustrated in relation to classic theories of secularisation. The chapter will end with a brief sketch of additional areas in which attention to gender has the potential to disrupt and reform agendas in the sociological study of religion.

STARTING POINTS FOR A THEORY OF GENDER AND RELIGION

To take gender seriously in the study of religion means taking power seriously as well. Although the theme of power has been neglected in recent sociological thinking about religion (Beckford, 1983), classical Sociology investigated relations between religion and economic power (for example, Weber, 1992 [orig. 1904–1905]), religion and class (for example Halévy, 1949), and religion and political power (still a topic of interest – see the work of Martin, 1977, 2005 and Norris and Inglehart, 2004, for example). Religion and gender – and arguably religion and ethnicity – is the missing element in this programme. A theoretical account of the relations between religion and gender requires an acknowledgement that both serve to represent, embody and distribute power within society, plus an account of how these two systems of distribution may relate to one another.

Gender and Power

Attention to gender demands attention to power because gender is inseparably bound up with the unequal distribution of power in society. Recent developments in gender theory have, if anything, reinforced awareness of the significance of the unequal distribution of power between the sexes by seeing it as constitutive of sex/gender itself. By denying that the construction of sex/gender has a material basis in biologically-given bodies (at least over and above basic reproductive differences), gender theory has shifted the focus onto systematic structural inequalities between men and women as the basis of sex/gender difference. It is social inequality which creates the idea that there are two opposed sexes, male and female, characterised by the different characteristics we label 'masculine' and 'feminine', and not the other way round. To imagine that inherent differences between men and women result in the gender division of labour and other inequalities is the exact inverse of what is really the case. As MacInnes (1998) argues, inequality creates masculinity and femininity as ideologies which serve to mask and legitimate social inequality.

This is not to deny that gender is experienced and constructed differently in different social and geographical locations, with ethnic, racial and class identifications serving to modify its influence. Although acknowledgement of such differences undermines the idea of patriarchy as a single system of oppression of all women by all men, it is compatible with a recognition that the workplace, the home, the political arena, the legal system, and mass culture are organised in mutually-reinforcing ways which, though various and ever-changing, nevertheless result in women being disadvantaged and disempowered relative to men across the globe (Connell, 2002: 97–114). Clearly different theorists have different ways of explaining how gender-based patterns of inequality

are generated and sustained, and different authors may assign priority to different factors. The widespread cultural turn in gender studies in recent decades has seen some shift of concentration from material factors such as gender difference in the workplace to cultural factors such as the influence of film, television and other popular cultural representations of masculinity and femininity (Evans, 2003). Yet there is still widespread agreement about the interconnection of a wide range of processes in the production and reproduction of gender difference, and wherever they choose to concentrate their attentions, feminist theorists tend to agree that such processes reflect and reproduce not just 'difference', but the unequal distribution of power on the basis of gender (Walby, 1990, 1997).

Religion and Power

If gender is a complex and interlocking set of power relations constituted in the historical process (Bourdieu, 2001), then it is possible to speak of the 'gender order' of a society, despite the impossibility of ever disentangling the full complexities of this order. Religion not only takes its place within this order, it is a constitutive part of it, though it may play a range of different roles and occupy a number of different positions.

Religion's constitutive contribution to power relations within society is best understood by viewing religion itself as a system of power. As I have argued in relation to Christianity (Woodhead, 2004), religion is the social expression of engagement with a source of power which is unique to religion ('sacred power'), but religion also involves interaction with 'secular' sources of power, both social (cultural, political, economic, military) and socio-personal (emotional, physical, intellectual, aesthetic). Although it can have independent force, the potency of sacred power is enhanced through alignment with secular power (e.g. there is a close historical relationship between the power of the Christian God and the wealth and political influence of the church, or between the success of 'holistic' therapies and their ability to enhance emotional wellbeing). There are many possible permutations of sacred and secular power, many different ways in which they can reinforce or repudiate one another. To view religion simply as a benign 'sacred canopy' over society (Berger, 1967) is to ignore the ways in which religion(s) can and do play active roles in: reinforcing and legitimating dominant power interests; generating resistance to dominant power; resourcing groups with little social power; resourcing reconfigurations of power. A group which has a great deal of social power may call on sacred power to enhance, extend, legitimate and normalise that power (for example, the Frankish dynasty in medieval Europe, or George W. Bush's Republican Party in the USA). Conversely, a group which has little social power can draw on sacred power to improve its access to secular power in a way which would not otherwise be possible (for example, early Christian communities in the second and third centuries, women-dominated holistic self-spiritualities today, see Heelas and Woodhead, 2005).

THEORISING RELIGION AND GENDER

Once power is highlighted, it is easy to see how religion and gender can and do interact. By way of symbolic and material practices religion can reinforce existing gendered distributions of power or try to change them. At any one time a religion will exist in a particular structural relation to the gender order of the society of which it is part. But the existing relationship is only a snapshot in an on-going dynamic that is shaped by many factors, including the religion's own gender strategy. Given that gendered distributions of power are integral to the wider inequalities of social power which define all known societies, this gives us two main variables to consider. One, the way in which religion is situated in relation to existing distributions of secular power: religion's *situation* in relation to gender. Two, the way in which religion is mobilised in relation to existing distributions of secular power: religion's *strategy* in relation to gender.

Expressing this diagrammatically (see Figure 27.1), we can draw a vertical axis which runs from 'mainstream' to 'marginal' religion and a horizontal axis which starts with religion as 'confirmatory' and moves to religion as 'challenging'. 'Mainstream' religion is integral to the existing distribution of power in society and socially respectable. 'Marginal' religion sits at more of an angle to the social and gender order, and will therefore be treated as socially deviant by those who accept the dominant distribution of power. 'Confirmatory' religion seeks to legitimate, reinforce, and sacralise the existing distribution of power in society, particularly the existing gender order, whilst 'challenging' religion seeks to ameliorate, resist or change this order. The two axes give us four 'cells', which represent the four main ways in which religion (as a distribution of power) may relate to gender (as a distribution of power) – and hence four main 'types' of religion in relation to gender.

First, religion can be integral to the existing gender order, and can serve to reproduce and legitimate gender inequality for those who practise the religion and those who fall within its penumbra ('consolidating'). Second, religion can be integral to the existing gender order, but can be used to give access to power from 'inside' and use it in ways which may be subversive of the existing gender order ('tactical'). Third, religion may be marginal to the existing gendered distribution of power, but used as a means of access to that power from the outside, without necessarily intending to disrupt the distribution of that power ('questing'). Finally, religion may be situated in a marginal relation to the gendered distribution of power, and may be used to try to contest, disrupt and redistribute that distribution ('counter-cultural').

This typology does not assume that there is necessarily a static single 'gender order' in a society, for the unit of analysis may vary from a nation-state to a region or ethnic group. It is, however, assumed that within such a unit there will at any one time be a prevailing distribution of power between genders which can be labelled 'mainstream', and alternatives to it which are currently 'marginal'. In most known

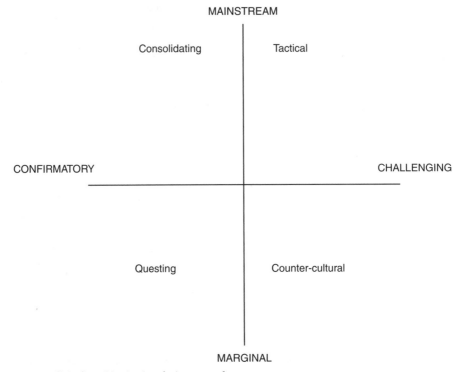

Figure 27.1 *Religion's positioning in relation to gender*

societies the mainstream distribution has been one which has favoured men over women. However, the nature of that unequal distribution varies considerably over time and place, and in some societies – as, for example, in many contemporary Western societies – gender relations may be in a state of considerable flux, such that mainstream position(s) are relatively precarious. Neither does this typology assume that there is necessarily a dominant religious order within a society, or that all members of a religion will assume identical positions in relation to gender. Thus, for example, within a single Christian congregation or denomination the religious activities of some members may 'consolidate' the existing gender order (those who do not question the 'sanctified' version of masculine domination which is presented in official church teachings, institutional arrangements and liturgical practice, for example), whilst the religious activities of others may fall into the 'tactical' category (for example, women who ignore a good deal of official church teaching,

create groups in church for women's mutual support, and use these groups to claim both sacred and political power, see Winter *et al.* 1994), whilst still others may be 'questing' (for example, those who use churches sporadically, and sometimes enter them simply to enjoy the sacred space and use it for their own personal and spiritual purposes which do not, however, disrupt the status quo).

This typology directs attention not only to gender orders in society, but also to the gender order(s) inherent in a religion or religious group. In order to investigate the latter it is necessary to pay attention not only to cultural factors, such as teachings and visual representations, but to the entire inner landscape of a religion. Early feminist explorations of religion, from Cady Stanton to Mary Daly, focused almost exclusively on the explicit and implicit teachings about men and women, masculinity and femininity, which were to be found in religions' sacred texts (Clark, 1997; Juschka, 2001). Important though these are to gendered distributions of power, their real-world significance can only be assessed in relation to the patterned practices, institutional frameworks and material contexts in which they take their place and gain their significance. Explicit directives about the different nature, capabilities, duties and obligations of the sexes may be unnecessary if assumptions about gender are already deeply embedded in the everyday practices and institutional arrangements of a religion and the society to which it belongs. It is when such practices are called into question that teachings may need to be made more explicit – as is apparent today in much conservative religion across the globe (Woodhead, 2006a).

Thus religion's implications in a gendered distribution of power cannot simply be read off from its cultural symbols, important though these are. Even representations of the sacred do not necessarily have a one-to-one relationship with gender order. We can think of such representations as running along a spectrum of possibilities, from those which identify sacred power with a supernatural being or beings and their authorised representatives ('priests') on the one hand, to those which identify the sacred with life itself, and thus with the inner 'spiritual' core of each and every living being on the other (Woodhead and Heelas, 2000). In the former 'religions of difference', sacred power is tightly concentrated and controlled, whereas in the latter 'spiritualities of life' it is more diffuse and accessible. Clearly the former has a natural affinity with forms of social and religious organisation in which power is hierarchically distributed, with the few ruling over the many, whilst the latter has a closer fit with flatter, more egalitarian distributions of power. Given the pervasive social norm of male dominance, it is not surprising to find that religions of difference – particularly monotheistic ones – tend to identify concentrated sacred power with masculinity. Thus in the case of a hierarchical, male-dominated society, we might expect to find a hierarchical, monotheistic religion which sacralises male power, in a 'consolidating' relationship with the prevailing gender order. Likewise, we might expect a 'countercultural' religion which opposes masculine domination to reject a male deity in favour of a female deity, polytheism, pantheism, or a more amorphous mysticism – all of which bring sacred power into closer relation with women. As a number of the studies reviewed below indicate, however, relationships between representation and social enactment should be explored rather than assumed, for in practice a range of possible and sometimes surprising relationships are possible.

STUDIES OF RELIGION AND GENDER

Consolidating

Religion's central role in consolidating gender difference and inequality was recognised, explored and critiqued by nineteenth-century feminists like Elizabeth Cady Stanton and her revising committee in *The Woman's Bible* (1985 [orig. 1895–1898]). This tradition of feminist critique was revived with second-wave feminism and lives on into the present day in the work of influential feminist writers like Mary Daly. Although its focus falls on historic texts rather than present realities, this intellectual trajectory has influenced many later attempts to approach the topic of religion and gender from a more sociological point of view. So too have historical studies of the consolidating relations between religious and gender inequality in a range of contexts: from early Christianity and Judaism (e.g. Kraemer and D'Angelo, 1990; Elm, 1994), through the medieval period (e.g. Bynum, 1987, 1991), to early modern (e.g. Davidoff and Hall, 2002) and industrial society (e.g. Ginzberg, 1990; Brown, 2002; Summers, 2000).

In a more fully sociological mode, the continuing link between religion and gender inequality has been demonstrated on a world scale by Ronald Inglehart and Pippa Norris' (2003) analysis of the World Values and European Values Surveys carried out between 1995 and 2001. The study finds that levels of gender equality across different countries are related not only to economic growth and legal-institutional reforms, but to cultural factors – above all, religiosity. Thus cross-sectional differences in support for gender equality vary even between societies at similar levels of development, and depend upon degree of religiosity and the type of religious values. Inglehart and Norris conclude that, 'religion matters, not only for cultural attitudes but for the opportunities and constraints on women's lives, such as the ratio of females to males in educational enrolment, the female adult literacy rate, the use of contraception, and the UNDP Gender-Related Development Index, as well as for opportunities for women in the paid workforce and in parliamentary representation' (2003: 69). This is not, however, a question of religious men simply imposing religious attitudes upon women, for traditional sexual values tend to be shared by both sexes in the same type of society, and women tend to display higher levels of religiosity than men (greatly in industrial society, somewhat in post-industrial society, less in agrarian society, 2003: 58).

Although intensifying secularisation is positively correlated with growing gender equality, religion's continuing ability to consolidate gender inequality remains evident in post-industrial societies in the West. If anything, this role seems to have become more prominent in the religious sphere as acceptance of the goal of gender equality becomes more widespread in society as a whole (Woodhead, 2006a). Thus the second half of the twentieth century has seen important moves within Christianity, Judaism and Islam to consolidate identity around a defence of 'traditional' roles for men and women which involve male headship and female domesticity. Although this tendency is evident across the spectrum of religious commitment – from the more moderate to the more traditionalist – in the former it may be a function of standing still whilst cultural and sexual values liberalise, whilst in the latter there is a more active drive to consolidate highly differentiated and unequal gender roles. DeBerg (1990) and Bendroth (1993) convincingly demonstrate that hostility to changing gender roles and the rise of feminism was a central factor in the rise of Christian fundamentalism in the USA, and that consolidation of 'traditional' gender roles is as essential and

defining a component of fundamentalism as belief in God and theological ideas (Brasher, 1998: 11).

Sociological studies of 'consolidating' forms of conservative religion have been preoccupied with the issue of why women affiliate with groups which sacralise gender difference and inequality. Lynn Davidman's (1991) study of women affiliating to Orthodox Judaism in the USA suggests that women are attracted because of, rather than in spite of, the traditional gender roles on offer: what attracts women is the way in which such religion offers a clear alternative to the confusing and contradictory roles open to women in late modern society. In particular, the role of wife and mother within a nuclear family appeals, and women in conservative religions are happy to make this their primary identity, rather than being caught in a confusion of domestic and professional roles (even when they continue in paid work). What becomes emblematic for Davidman's women is the (idealised) experience of the warm, close, family gathering around the Shabbat table, with candles, food, mutual love and support (1991: 116–20).

But it is not merely the sacred female role which can prove attractive to women who affiliate with conservative, consolidating forms of religion – so too can the sacred male role. Davidman's data suggests that women are attracted by the whole package of nuclear familial domesticity which is advocated by contemporary forms of Orthodox Judaism, including the idea of a husband who will be a companionate protector-provider and protect women from the dangers posed by family breakdown. This too can be seen as a reaction against prevailing gender norms, in particular against recent modes of masculinity which de-emphasise paternal responsibility (what Ehrenreich [1983] characterises as the 'flight from commitment'), or which legitimate male violence (Dworkin [1983] explains women's flight to fundamentalism as motivated by a futile desire to seek male protection against male violence). In the context of developing countries in the southern hemisphere Martin (1988) notes that women's attraction to Pentecostal Christianity has much to do with the benefits that accrue to them and their children from a stable household unit with a committed father whose conversion to Christianity also involves conversion from *machismo*. Shifting the register more clearly from the real to the ideal, Clark-King (2004) finds Christianity in the northwest of England providing working-class women with an idealised provider-protector figure in God the Father, and an idealised husband/lover in Jesus Christ.

The ways in which religion and hegemonic masculinities consolidate one another remain relatively ill-explored, with the majority of sociological studies of religion and gender focusing on 'marked' femininity rather than 'unmarked' masculinity. This is beginning to change as masculinity becomes more prominent in gender studies (e.g. Connell, 1995; Kimmel and Messner, 1998), and as the active role of religion in the construction and consolidation of masculinity becomes more evident. Movements like Promise Keepers and events like the Million Man March in the USA have helped provoke scholarly awareness of the importance of conservative Christianity in consolidating certain patriarchal modes of masculinity, most notably a paternalistic role. This is not simply a repristination of a 'traditional' mode of Christian patriarchy, since it gives emphasis to new 'expressive' and relational imperatives which are said to be binding on men as well as women (Williams, 2000), but it is certainly a rallying cry to reclaim a man's divine right to rule over his family and to expect his wife and children to serve and obey him, not least by way of unpaid labour in the household (Eldén, 2002). Such developments take place against a background which has seen a shift from what Walby (1990) calls the 'private patriarchy' which held sway in advanced industrial societies right through to the 1950s towards a 'public patriarchy' (see below). The former, which operates an exclusionary patriarchal strategy and relies on 'household production as the main site of women's oppression' (1990: 24), has been consolidated historically by religions like Christianity and Judaism. Fundamentalist religion across the globe retains loyalty to private patriarchy in the contemporary context, whilst being willing to make some accommodation to the shift towards a public patriarchy in which women's labour is exploited across a wider range of sites, including the paid workforce. The corresponding shifts and accommodations made by 'mainstream' and more liberal forms of religion remain to be studied.

Tactical

Whereas consolidating forms of religion accept, reinforce and sacralise the dominant gender order – and vice versa – tactical forms work within such orders but push beyond them. In Kandiyoti's (1988) terms, they 'bargain with patriarchy', accepting prevailing patterns of meaning and power-distribution, but maximising their advantage for those who are disadvantaged by them. They can never fatally undermine the prevailing distribution of power, for to do so would be to undermine the source of power to which they seek greater access. Since such a stance is most likely to emerge within a religious group rather than to give rise to a religion as such, it may be more accurate to speak of a tactical trajectory within religion, rather than a tactical type. For obvious reasons, it is those who are disempowered by the prevailing gender order – usually women – who are most likely to be involved in such a trajectory.

Two recent studies of women in conservative Christian congregations and networks in the USA religions reveal the continuing importance of tactical religion. In her research in two conservative mega-churches, Brasher (1998) discovers that their appeal to women – who make up about 50 per cent of the congregations – does not lie primarily in the large weekly Sunday worship service led by male pastors which scholars have traditionally assumed to be the central ritual and social event of congregational life. Rather, women have created what is in many respects a parallel religious association, in which small women-only groups which meet on a regular weekly or more-than-weekly basis form the basic social unit. Such 'female enclaves'

(1998: 5) fall under the oversight of women responsible for women's ministry, and have considerable autonomy. Whilst their explicit focus is often around Bible study, their characteristic activities do not resemble 'traditional' Bible studies in which an authorised (male) interpreter offers an intellectual commentary upon the scriptures. Rather, activities and interpretations are shaped by women's own agendas, and often focus on personal and family issues, providing an opportunity for the exploration, expression, healing and disciplining of emotions. Such groups become life-support systems, in which women listen to, care for, and give practical support to one another, almost entirely independent of the formal male-dominated power structures of the church. Also, women make use of congregational space to set up a wide variety of additional, often very practical, support structures which provide a variety of services including child-care and marital support.

Griffith's (1997) study of the evangelical-charismatic 'Women's Aglow' movement also finds that women simultaneously accept the sanctification of female domesticity and male headship, whilst making use of their parallel female religious organisation to deal with the high costs of their subordination. Like Brasher she finds women participating in male-approved discourses and activities, but bending these to their own uses. Women worship a perfect husband and lover, Jesus Christ, whilst struggling to improve and cope with the disappointments and high costs of their actual marital and familial duties. They support one another as they cope with problems with their children, spousal infidelity and cruelty, low self-esteem and everyday unhappiness. Like Brasher's parallel female congregational activities, Women's Aglow operates within a territory which is ultimately under male control, but which in practice offers women considerable autonomy, and some positions of quite significant public action and authority for leaders within the movement. It seems no coincidence that both examples arise within evangelical-charismatic territory, since charismatic Christianity loosens the ties between sacred power and ecclesiastical office, and makes

sacred power in the guise of 'the Spirit' more widely available – to women as well as men. Nevertheless, such power remains linked to the authority of Father, Son, husband and pastor. As such, it can be appropriated to empower women, but not to overturn the male dominance which it symbolises and supports.

The tactical trajectory within more traditional forms of church Christianity, both Protestant and Catholic, has been less carefully investigated – at least in the twentieth and twenty-first centuries. However, a cluster of pioneering studies of women in late nineteenth-century Britain and America demonstrates the importance of tactical religion at the origins of modern feminism. Studies like Welter (1976), Rendall (1985), Banks (1986), Morgan (1999) and Mumm (1999) show that although churches in industrial society played a central role in the consolidation of a rigid gender division and a doctrine of 'separate spheres', religion also provided middle class women with ideological and practical means to combat coercive forms of male power (by reference to scriptural injunctions, and by way of temperance movements), to enter into the civil and public spheres (through charitable, mission and temperance work), and to extend domestic roles, like maternal care, into more public duties. The massive expansion of Catholic female religious orders, often dedicated to a profession such as teaching, nursing or mission, has also been investigated in this light (see, for example, Walsh, 2002). Although the rise of 'secular' feminism and improvements in women's legal, political, and economic status have gradually undermined the basis and necessity of many such tactical developments of Western religion, a number of small-scale studies continue to point to ways in which women use mainline church Christianity for purposes often far removed from the intentions and meanings supplied by an official, male-dominated leadership. Thus Ozorak (1996) finds that a reason male dominance of ecclesiastical power-structures does not necessarily deter female involvement is that the women interviewed do not seek the same benefits from church adherence as men. Whereas the latter often seek institutional office, economic reward and social capital, women are more likely to seek the personal and emotional benefits which derive from the supportive relationships they forge in ecclesiastical contexts.

Clearly tactical religion carves out and flourishes in women-only spaces which gain the protection of male-dominated religion, but escape its immediate supervision. They can never wholly step outside the authority of the religion, however, since their existence is ultimately dependent upon it. An interesting case arises when ecclesiastical authorities actively oppose a tactical trajectory, as the Roman Catholic church has done in relation to its movements for the ordination of women. Although continuing to ally themselves with the same source of sacred power, such movements may gain independent impetus as a result, and sections may splinter off to form counter-cultural religious movements.

Questing

Questing forms of religion begin from a position marginal to the dominant gender order, but use sacred power in ways which aim at personal (or occasionally group) transformation and movement towards a position of greater advantage within the existing gender order. The aim is not to change this order so much as to improve one's position – and wellbeing – within it.

Some forms of questing religion seek worldly benefits for the individual or group, the most striking examples being those which involve the use of magic and spells aimed not solely at achieving an enhanced inner emotional or physical state, but some favourable change in external circumstances. As one would expect, given their power disadvantage, women are more likely to make use of sacred power in this way than men. This is still the case in contemporary Western societies where there has been a notable revival and popularisation of magic practices, particularly since the 1980s (Partridge, 2004). Such revival has generally taken the form of a revival of interest in witchcraft which, in its more 'magical'

manifestations, is increasingly common amongst teenagers, especially girls (Berger and Ezzy, 2007). Spells, both invented and scripted in popular books, may be directed at attaining power over a love object, though teenagers who become more seriously involved in witchcraft tend to reject such spells as tampering with another's will. They are more likely to use spells for practical benefits for self or others, including healing and (in Britain rather than the UK!) invisibility. Such aims tacitly accept the dominant gender order, whilst seeking to shift the balance of power within it, or at least allow the actor to maximise her advantage within it. Other forms of Wicca and neo-paganism more generally, especially those practised by adults in small groups and organised networks, are more likely to fall into the counter-cultural category discussed below.

The most prevalent form of questing religion in late industrial societies is that which became known as 'New Age' in the 1980s, but which has proliferated since then, and is now better referred to as subjective-life spirituality or self-spirituality (Heelas and Woodhead, 2005; Houtman and Aupers, 2006). Such terms point to a central concern with sacralising and enhancing inner life. At one end of the spectrum of such spirituality lie dedicated ritual groups including those which make up the neo-pagan movement (see below), but the forms of self-spirituality most likely to fall into the questing category are those which often describe themselves as 'holistic', by virtue of their concern with 'mind, body and spirit'. Holistic self-spirituality takes a variety of social forms, ranging from individual reading and practice, to one-to-one encounters (such as Reiki, and explicitly spiritual forms of homeopathy and aromatherapy) to group meetings (such as Yoga, Buddhism, Greenspirit), and larger workshops and festivals. It is increasingly incorporated into workplace trainings, nursing and education. Looking at one-to-one and group practices in the UK, Heelas and Woodhead (2005) find that a full 80 per cent of those involved, both as practitioners and clients, are female. Woodhead (2006b) and Houtman and Aupers (2006) offer explanations for this gender imbalance which appeal to the unresolved clash between 'traditional' female roles based around domestic labour and the new, more masculinised roles, which become available to women as they enter the paid workforce in increasing numbers. Self-spiritualities address this condition by encouraging the construction of new modes of selfhood in which identity is not dictated by social position and expectation, but discovered from within. Although this project of selfhood *may* have socially radical implications (see below), it is more likely to render women successful in coping with the contradictions and costs of the unequal distribution of power and unpaid care work in contemporary Western societies than in changing in these conditions.

One further interesting example of borderline quest religion concerns the men's mythopoeic movement, which looks to figures like Robert Bly for inspiration (Connell, 1995: 206–11). Although not a straightforwardly religious group, this certainly has elements of a religion. It makes self-conscious use of myth and ritual practices to help men engender new forms of inner strength and identity in which they recover the 'lost masculine'. It can be classified as questing because it is marginal both to the dominant Judaeo-Christian religious order and, at least in its own estimation, to the dominant gender order – since it believes that women's growing social power threatens the position of men.

Counter-cultural

Religion which is counter-cultural with regard to gender is not only marginal to the existing gender order, but actively opposes it and strives to change it and forge alternatives. Here sacred power becomes a central resource in the attempt to establish more equal distributions of power between the sexes.

One of the most influential and most studied contemporary examples of such counter-cultural religion is what is broadly referred to as the goddess feminist movement. In different ways and by different means, those involved with this movement seek to honour

the 'divine feminine' in their own lives and in society. Although goddess feminism falls into the broad category of subjective-life spirituality discussed above, and into the narrower sub-category of neo-paganism, it differs from much holistic self-spirituality by virtue of its greater emphasis on ritual practice and the more cohesive communities which develop around such practice, and it qualifies neo-paganism through its concentration on the divine feminine and its commitment to female empowerment. Many goddess feminists are happy to reclaim the title of 'witch', and to describe their religion as 'Wicca'.

The single most influential figure in goddess feminism is the writer, activist and witch Starhawk, whose most influential book remains *The Spiral Dance. A Rebirth of the Ancient Religion of the Great Goddess* (1979). As Salomonsen (2002) argues, both this eminently practical guide to the living of a divinely-empowered life and its author are best understood in relation to the Reclaiming community of witches in San Francisco, of which Starhawk is a founding member. Salomonsen's study of the Reclaiming witches leaves little doubt about their counter-cultural stance with regard to gender and power. Although there are male members of the movement, women dominate. There is an explicit commitment not merely to gender equality but to female empowerment. 'Traditional' forms of religion and religious organisation are critiqued from a feminist standpoint, and a self-conscious attempt is made to forge new forms of organisation, practice and communal living which provide a new model not only for religion and personal life, but for society. Ritual practice is central to all these aims. It brings the whole Reclaiming community together at certain points of the year for large ritual gatherings, and is central to the life of the autonomous small groups, 'cells', 'circles' or 'covens' of up to fifteen people which form the building blocks of the Reclaiming community. Both rituals and religious commitment are focused not around transcendent forms of masculinity, but either around personal lives and journeys, or around nature and natural cycles. The effect is not to subordinate the female self to an overarching order of male-defined dogma, organisation and divinity, but to empower in relation to others and to (sacred) nature. As Reclaiming's mission statement – replete with the language of power – puts it:

> RECLAIMING means:
> We reclaim the Goddess: the immanent life force, the connecting pattern to all being.
> We reclaim the creative and healing power of women…
> We reclaim our personal power, and transform blocked energies into freedom, intimacy and strength to change…
> We use the word 'Witch' as an affirmation of women's power to shape reality. (Salomonsen, 2002: 40–1)

Whereas holistic subjective-life spirituality of the questing type is chiefly concerned with inner personal healing and/or transformation, some goddess feminism clearly has, in addition, a more overtly political agenda. Salomonsen distinguishes between 'utopian' and 'generic' witches. For the latter Wicca has personal reference, whereas for the former, including Starhawk, it is 'a religious and social gospel for the transformation of the world' (2002: 97). Utopian goddess feminists may make experiments in alternative living, including establishing new eco-communities, and often play an active part in political protest – as in the protests against the siting of a nuclear power plant at Diabolo Canyon in California in 1981 which gave rise to the Reclaiming community, or at the Greenham Common airbase in England in 1981–1991, in protest against nuclear weaponry.

RELIGION AND GENDER IN ADVANCED INDUSTRIAL CONTEXT

Although the typology proposed here is applicable to different times and places, the specificities of relation between religion and gender order are always specific to a particular social context. In the case of most of the studies discussed above, the context is that of late modernity/advanced industrial society. A brief sketch of the latter's gendered profile sets the preceding discussion in context, and paves the way for the discussion of religious decline which follows.

Although late modernity is often defined in social, political and cultural terms which are gender-blind, it can also be defined in terms of its unique gender order. This begins with the 'sexual revolution' of the 'sixties', which represents a sharp reaction against the gender order of the immediate post-war period. The latter had involved a nostalgic return to (or re-invention of) domestic values, with a desire to return to 'the home' – which meant, in practice, a nuclear family structured around clearly demarcated gender roles in which women had responsibility for home, childcare and 'husbandcare', and men went out to earn the 'family wage' (May, 1988). Taking place against a backdrop of disrupted gender roles (due in part to occupational and sexual permissiveness during the war), political threat (the cold war), and a new economic framework (paternalistic welfare states), men and women entered into a paternalistic pact whereby husbands, backed by the state, promised life-long protection and provision for families, and wives provided free domestic labour. Conscious of the costs and restrictions of these roles, baby boomers with the opportunities to do so rebelled against them in favour of new, more 'liberated' sex and gender roles for both men and women. Second-wave feminism combined with the new opportunities for women to enter the paid workforce to disrupt the expectation that femininity was identical with wifehood and motherhood and that it consisted in the dutiful discharge of the labour of care for low pay or no pay. Masculinity also loosened its ties with dutiful paternalism, as a male flight from life-long commitment to marriage and children got underway.

Although these changes in gender relations were profound and unsettling, the result in terms of the distribution of power between the sexes has been less revolutionary. Glendon (1985), analysing shifts in the family and property, argues that women now suffer from a 'triple burden', whereby they have to earn a wage, carry the bulk of domestic and childcare duties, and bear the costs of the rising divorce rate which leaves mothers 'holding the baby'. Arlie Hochschild's (2003) study of working couples comes to similar conclusions.

Other studies concentrate on the new sexual demands which have been placed on women, with bodily presentation and sexual attractiveness to men coming to acquire a new premium in the deregulated sexual marketplace (Dworkin, 1981; Walby, 1990; Paul, 2005). There are obvious costs for men under this gender order as well, including unstable ties to children, increased competition from women at lower and middle levels of the workplace, heightened demands to 'perform' and assert dominant masculinity, new uncertainties about appropriate male roles.

Given that religions in the West, most notably Christianity and Judaism, played a central role in consolidating masculine dominance right through to the 1950s (a decade which witnessed a significant upturn in church attendance), the shift in gender relations since the 1960s presents considerable dangers as well as opportunities. The tendency has been for both Protestant and Catholic churches to hold onto an ideal of 'traditional' family values, where that is taken to mean the nuclear family, compulsory heterosexuality, and divinely-inscribed gender difference. Images of a paternalistic God appropriate to a welfare era have been slow to fade (Nicholls, 1989), as has an ethic of selfless care whose effect is to reinforce women's domestic roles and male paternalism. The result, as we have seen, is a persistence or reinvigoration of the consolidating role for much contemporary religion in the West, sometimes with significant political support, as in the USA today. At the same time, as has also been noted, this tendency may be used by women for tactical purposes whose result is to tip the balance of power more in their favour than would otherwise be the case. The severe disruption of gender relations after the 1950s also forms the backdrop for the contemporary upsurge of questing forms of religion which start from outside consolidating forms of religion, but make use of sacred power to try to achieve a more favourable position within the existing gender order. By contrast, counter-cultural forms of religion seek to consolidate gains for women and minimise the losses by bringing about permanent change which will dissolve essentialist ideas about male-female

hierarchical difference, and replace them with a social order in which power is no longer unequally distributed along gender lines.

GENDERING SECULARISATION

As the preceding discussion hints, attention to religion's implication in the ordering and disordering of gender relations is capable of yielding new insights about the process of secularisation – and 'sacralisation' – in modern contexts.

Classical theories of secularisation arise out of reflection on the ways in which changes associated with the transition to urban industrial society have a corrosive effect on traditional forms of religious belonging and activity. They are limited not only by their focus on the industrial phase of modernisation, but by their lack of attention to gender difference. They are consequently far more plausible as accounts of the religious implications of the male experience of industrial modernisation than of female experience of modernisation (industrial and later). Whether they emphasise the secularising effect of societalisation, functional differentiation, rationalisation, or the revolutionising of production, they focus on the situation of men uprooted from the more stable and cohesive social settings of small towns or villages and propelled into the anonymous, impersonal context of the modern city and workplace structured by the imperatives of efficient production. Leaving behind enchanted worlds imbued with sacred meaning and significance, modern man enters an 'iron cage' stripped of religious meaning and moral value.

Since one of the most central and defining aspects of industrial modernity was its sharp division of productive and reproductive labour between a feminised domestic sphere and a masculinised public sphere, women's version of industrial modernisation takes a significantly different form from men's. Since women were excluded by a variety of means from participation in the public world of economically rewarded work, as well as from political power, they were confined not to an iron cage of rational efficiency but to a soft cage of domesticity. Whether their labour consisted solely of unpaid care for home and family, as was typical for the middle classes, or also involved low paid domestic work for others or piece work within the home, as was more typical of working class experience, it was different in kind from male labour (and was consequently legitimated by the new 'two sex' model of humanity in which men and women appeared different in kind rather than merely in quality from one another). As a result, women were less likely to suffer as serious a dislocation from previous patterns of meaning and sociality as men. In Hochschild's (2003: 250) words, women became 'urbanising peasants', preserving rituals, customs and material cultures – including those associated with religion – and helping to ease male transition into modernity as a result. Home becomes for men a haven not only of care but of continuity, an enchanted place maintained by women's labour, which makes it possible to survive the rigours of rationalised work.

Rather than simply being evacuated from the modern context, religion is therefore relocated. Although still under the ultimate control of a male father God and male 'religious professionals' (as they increasingly become), religion becomes women's work, closely associated with the domestic sphere. As both literary critics and historians have documented (Douglas, 1977; Welter, 1976; Ginzberg, 1990), Christianity becomes increasingly feminised during the course of the nineteenth century in many north American and European societies, not only in terms of its teachings, imagery and gender ideology, but also in terms of its most active constituency. The much-heralded male crisis of faith in the Victorian era therefore takes place alongside an upsurge of female piety, with the result that the nineteenth century became not the *least* but probably the *most* Christian century of all time, not only in terms of cultural influence but also in terms of churchgoing. Viewed in terms of the theoretical framework offered above, Christianity succeeds both as a consolidating *and* tactical religion. It consolidates by

sanctifying women's domestic labours, offering a female identity which dignifies women's spiritual and moral standing, erecting class distinctions on the basis of Christian virtue, and reinforcing an ideology of separate spheres. And it offers tactical means for some women to negotiate not only greater power and protection, but routes into civic and public life (see above).[3]

Precisely because religion became so implicated within the gender order of industrial modernity, however, it would be extremely vulnerable to challenges and changes to this order. As Brown (2002) argues, the fact that femininity had become so closely identified with a particular brand of nineteenth-century piety meant that the decline of the former led inevitably to the decline of the latter. Christian femininity was challenged by a range of factors, not least by feminist action and sentiment from the late nineteenth century onwards. Nevertheless, Christian ideals of feminine care, self-sacrifice, piety, domesticity and spiritual and moral responsibility for husband and family proved resilient in many quarters, both inside and outside the churches, so much so that the 1950s could witness the revival of commitment to 'traditional family values' mentioned in the previous section, and with it a brief flurry of church growth. Such growth was short-lived, however, and was quickly followed by the onset of a phase of decline steeper than that which had preceded it. This late modern phase of secularisation set in during the 1970s and has continued to the present day in most European societies, in Canada, and, to a lesser extent, in the USA (Heelas and Woodhead, 2005: 50–60).

Although classical theories of secularisation are unable to explain the speeding up of secularisation after the 1960s, the gendered perspective proposed here would expect the far-reaching shifts in gender relations at the time to have exactly such a momentous impact on a religion so closely identified with the gender order of industrial society. Such shifts include not only the rise of a new feminist agenda committed to equality between the sexes, but – above all – a combination of political, social and economic changes which lead to women entering the paid workforce in ever-increasing numbers (Wharton, 2005). The simplest way of expressing the consequences for religion would be to say that women enter the iron cage around a century later than men, but when they do so the corrosive effect on their commitment to religion is similar. This is over-simple, however, because even if we ignore the fact that women enter the workplace during a later phase of capitalism, their experience of work is both similar and different from men's experience. Not only do women tend to cluster in different occupations than men, including the caring professions, and to be more likely than men to work part-time, they also continue to carry out far more unpaid domestic care work than men. The consequences for religion, as illustrated by the studies discussed earlier in this chapter, are complex.

For men, the transition to late modernity has been less traumatic, not only because they continue to be supported by women's traditional work of care, but because masculinist modes of autonomous, competitive selfhood adapted to the demands of late capitalism have a long-established social currency. However, insofar as the latter now break from the paternalistic modes of masculinity which dominated the era of paternalistic state and industrial enterprise, and which fitted neatly with church-endorsed modes of modern family life, this has also been corrosive of Christian commitment. With its sacred paternalism and emphasis on the gentle virtues, Christianity has always had an uneasy relationship with forms of 'hegemonic masculinity' centred on sexual and physical prowess, material success, and 'hardness'. The repristination of the latter in recent times, not only in the form of 'new laddishness', but on a wider socio-economic scale with the sanction of entrepreunerial capitalism, may well be a further factor in the continuing secularisation of many Western societies.

BROADENING AGENDAS

Although space does not permit any serious exploration of additional agendas which greater

attention to gender within the sociology of religion is beginning to open up, it is useful to survey briefly some of the most important in order to indicate their range and potential significance.

This chapter has attempted to show how a move away from gender-blindness profoundly affects the way in which we think about religion and its relation to the social order, so much so that it impacts upon even the most foundational theories within the Sociology of Religion, namely theories of secularisation. By the same token, the move from gender-blindness is likely to lead to serious re-examination of foundational concepts within the field, including the concept of 'religion' itself.

Although enshrined in the very name of the discipline, the concept of religion has received less critical examination in the Sociology of Religion than in Religious Studies, Psychology of Religion and Anthropology. Almost four decades ago Thomas Luckmann (1967) argued that the concept was used in a way which rendered the Christian tradition normative: 'Religion becomes a social fact either as ritual (institutionalised religious conduct) or doctrine (institutionalised religious ideas)[...] The discipline, thereby, accepts the self-interpretations – and the ideology – of religious institutions as valid definitions of the range of their subject matter (1967: 22; 26). Luckmann's suggestion still has bite, a bite which becomes even sharper when extended to include the point that it is the most androcentric aspects of Christianity which seem to shape sociological presuppositions about what counts as 'real' religion. This is particularly clear in the way in which new forms of religion which bear structural resemblances to church Christianity became the subject of serious scholarly investigation in the latter part of the twentieth century, under the heading of 'New Religious Movements', whilst forms of self-spirituality which involve larger numbers of women and do not conform to the implicit norm of 'real religion' have been routinely ignored, dismissed or even criticised by many sociologists of religion (Woodhead, 2007).[4]

The tendency to render male practice normative in understandings of what counts as religious is also evident in deep sociological assumptions about what counts as sacred, as ritual, as scripture, as belief, as religious practice, as a religious professional, a religious organisation, and so on. Studies of religion by social historians which widen their focus to include women's activities often take in a much broader range of phenomena than fall within the purview of established sociological theorising and research (see for example Williams' [1999] study of religion in Southwark). Detailed qualitative research is also extending our understanding of 'women's religion', whether that be Christianity or some other form of religious or spiritual practice (see for example McGuire, 1988, 1994, 1997; Jenkins 1999; Chambers, 2005). Sered's (1994) comparative study of religions in which women are dominant finds that although there are no universal patterns, women's religions tend to be characterised by greater concern with 'this-worldly' matters including bodily and emotional wellbeing (health and healing) and the quality of intimate and familial relationships, and to be more centred around the home, preparation of food, and sometimes the natural world. Such a conclusion is not surprising, given the widespread gender division of labour which leaves women in most societies with greater responsibility than men for bodily and emotional care, for the maintenance of affective and kin relationships, and for domestic concerns in general. What is more surprising is the way in which activities whose religious significance has previously been overlooked start to appear in a new light once a gender-critical perspective is applied (Nason-Clark and Neitz, 2001). A recent example is furnished by Day's (2005) study of an evangelical women's prayer group, which began by assuming that the ten minutes of formal prayer at the end of the meeting was the religious element before realising that it was the preceding activities of coffee drinking and 'chat' about friends and family which actually constituted the ritual and religious work of the group. As Sered (1994: 286) puts it, patterns which are institutionalised and esteemed in female-dominated religions tend, in other contexts, to be 'subsumed under the categories of "folk-lore", "superstition", "syncretism", "heresy", or simply, "ladies' auxiliary"'.

As well as impacting upon frameworks, theories and concepts within the Sociology of Religion, a gendered perspective may therefore start to shift the field's focus towards topics which have previously received little attention. In very general terms one may speak of a shift of concern from the 'higher' to the 'lower' or more 'mundane' aspects of religion, including the body, emotions, space and place. Gender-critical developments in other fields are starting to have an impact, with cultural geography's recent attention to geographies of space and emotional geographies, for example, beginning to influence the sociological study of religion, sometimes by way of the mediating influence of Religious Studies (see, for example, Knott (2005) on religion and space). Although general sociological interest in negotiations of identity and selfhood has been slow to influence the Sociology of Religion, there are some recent indications of growing interest in linkages between religion, ethnicity, gender and class. Recent work on 'diasporic' identities which pays attention to religion, including that by geographers like Dwyer (2000) and anthropologists like Werbner (2003), is beginning to influence the Sociology of Religion, and may also have the effect of directing greater attention to religion and ethnicity, and loosening the discipline's almost exclusive concern with Western religions (including those, like Pentecostal Christianity, which now have a global reach). Even in relation to topics in which there has already been some concentration of interest by sociologists of religion, perhaps most notably religion, the family and sexuality, there is still a very great deal of work to be done in bringing these into closer relation with gender (a task begun by Marler, 1995; Neitz, 2001; Becker, 2001).

These developments also have methodological implications. With the exception of Ingelhart and Norris' work, all the studies of religion and gender cited in this chapter use qualitative rather than quantitative methods. Most are small-scale studies which use some mix of fieldwork and interview. It is debatable whether or not this is mere coincidence. Sometimes it is suggested that large-scale quantitative surveys are part of a masculinist scientific project which views the researcher as disinterestedly scrutinising the beliefs and actions of research 'subjects' in a way which requires little or no contact between them, and maintains the superior status of the former. The scientist generates hypotheses which observation confirms or disconfirms, with research subjects serving merely as 'data' who cannot influence hypothesis-generation or even conceptual formulations. At the opposite extreme of the methodological spectrum is 'feminist' research which involves prolonged face-to-face contact with research participants, treats them as partners in the research process, makes explicit acknowledgement of the situated interests of all those involved, generates and reforms hypothesis in an on-going participatory fashion, and has an explicit commitment to expose and work towards the elimination of structural inequalities (Harding, 1987; Reinharz, 1992; Olesen 2005).

In reality these alternatives are probably caricatures. Any qualitative study which goes beyond a single case is likely to have some quantitative element, and most quantitative studies have a significant qualitative element (including the use of interviews, which inform survey questions, and can impact upon hypotheses). Some of the most prestigious projects in sociological research on religion in the last few decades depend upon cross-sectional survey research with follow-up interviews (e.g. Roof 1993, 1999; Wuthnow 1996, 2003; Ammerman, 1997), and may be described as 'mixed' or 'multiplied' method.[5] Nevertheless, it remains true that the more quantitative studies have, so far, failed to advance our understanding of religion and gender. There may be several reasons for this, many of them contingent. One is simply that the resources and expertise required to undertake large-scale quantitative research are more likely to be controlled by men than by women, and until recently have been unlikely to have been made available for gender-critical studies (particularly when funding comes from private institutions with some stake in the existing gender order). In addition, it is well recognised that the 'gendering' of academic

disciplines results in a clustering of men in the 'hard' sciences, including statistical research, and in the greater prestige of the latter. By the same token the skills of empathy and communication essential to qualitative research tend to be devalued and regarded as 'natural' rather than as acquired through rigorous training (as is true of 'women's work' in general). As women become more prominent in the academy, and as a gender-critical approach affects its funding regimes, such contingent causes of methodological gender-blindness may be expected to ease. The one thing that may not change is what appears to be the greater potential of qualitative research to be critical about existing intellectual agendas and to help set new agendas, by virtue of its ability to become so immersed in the life-world of research participants that it can 'change the subject' (Fulkerson, 1994).

The most visible face of religion is always its 'male face', not only because men will be able to give greater prominence to the organisational forms and activities in which they have most power, but also because religion is represented – in the academy, the media, civic and political life – in a way which renders male-dominated activities and organisations most visible. Methods which represent themselves as 'objective' and 'scientific' mask their political effect, which is to perpetuate male domination by rendering it normal. What is clear from the work reviewed above is that by taking different routes, using different methods – or the same methods to different effect – asking different questions, seeking out different activities and discourses, and being more self-conscious about political and personal interests in research, it is possible for sociologists to probe beneath the presenting surface of religion to make new discoveries.

CONCLUSION

This chapter discusses a selection of recent studies which have put gender onto the agenda of the Sociology of Religion. Such studies highlight some of the ways in which gender affects religious practice and significance, and raise awareness of the close and often constitutive relations between religion and gender. Taking the latter realisation as its starting point, the chapter proposes a theoretical approach to the sociological study of religion and gender which distinguishes the main ways in which religion may locate itself in relation to a prevailing gender order. This approach draws attention to the importance of power in the study of religion and in society, for it reminds us that both religion and gender are centrally implicated in unequal distributions of power, and that their interplays serve and seek to reinforce existing distributions of power or to change them – in various ways and by various means.

Although the sociological study of religion has been slow to abandon its gender-blindness, the studies considered here suggest that this situation is beginning to change. The magnitude of the change should not be exaggerated; at the present time one is likely to find one member of a faculty working on gender, one paper in an edited collection dedicated to the topic, one stream on gender at a conference on the Sociology of Religion, and so on. The belief that attention to gender can and should inform and enrich all study of religion is not yet firmly established. Changes in the academy may continue to effect change, not only as gender becomes entrenched in bordering fields, but as the gender balance begins to shift within the academic study of religion. Equally important may be the changes in religion and society which force attention to religion's relations with gender. Whether we are looking at campaigns against homosexuality and abortion, controversies over veiling, attempts to return to 'traditional family values', religiously-inspired terrorism and violence, or radical utopian eco-feminist movements, it is no longer easy to overlook the ways in which contexts of gender change and anxiety have flushed out religion's central and abiding concern with gender roles and relations, and revealed it as one of the key sites in society for the defence or negotiation of unequal distributions of power.

NOTES

1. The evidence for women's greater religious commitment is now extensive, and is summarised in Argyle and Beit-Hallahmi (1975), Francis (1997) and Walter and Davie (1998). Most of this evidence concerns women's involvement in Christianity. There is also growing evidence of women's disproportionate involvement in new forms of spirituality in the West (Heelas and Woodhead, 2005; Houtman and Aupers, 2006). Some debate has centred on Rodney Stark's argument that this can be explained by women's greater risk-aversion, whilst others have explored relations between gender orientation and being religious (e.g. Thompson and Remmes, 2002).

2. The one writer in the broad area of religious studies who has been, and still is, regularly cited in gender studies – albeit these days often as an example of 'essentialist' reductionism – is Mary Daly. Despite her wide-ranging critique of the world's religions in books like *Gyn/Ecology* (1979) she does not claim to be engaged in the sociological study of religion.

3. One could also mention the various forms of marginal religion which flourished in the nineteenth century, and which sought either to negotiate an advantageous position within the gender order (questing), or to overturn that order (counter-cultural) – for example, the Mormons, Shakers and Theosophists.

4. This is not to deny that some scholars of NRMs have adopted a gender-critical perspective. See, for example, Jacobs (1991) and Palmer (1994).

5. 'Multiplied' because their interviews take on a quantitative dimension by virtue of their number and overall representativeness. I owe the latter point to Dr David Voas, University of Manchester (conversation).

REFERENCES

Argyle, Michael and Benjamin Beit-Hallahmi 1975. *The Social Psychology of Religion.* London: Routledge.

Ammerman, Nancy 1997. *Congregation and Community*. New Brunswick, NJ: Rutgers University Press.

Banks, Olive 1986. *Becoming a Feminist. The Social Origins of 'First Wave' Feminism*. Sussex: Wheatsheaf Books.

Becker, Penny Edgell 2001. 'Boundaries and Silences in a Post-Feminist Sociology'. In Nancy Nason-Clark and Mary Jo Neitz (eds), *Feminist Narratives and the Sociology of Religion*. Lanham, Oxford: Alta Mira Press.

Beckford, James 1983. 'The Restoration of "Power" to the Sociology of Religion', *Sociological Analysis* 44 (1): 11–31.

Bendroth, Margaret L. 1993. *Fundamentalism and Gender: 1875 to the Present*. New Haven: Yale University Press.

Berger, Helen A. and Douglas Ezzy 2007. *Finding Witchcraft, Magic and the Self: Teenage Witches in the United States, England, and Australia*. New Brunswick, NJ: Rutgers University Press.

Berger, Peter L 1967. *The Sacred Canopy. Elements of a Sociological Theory of Religion*. Garden City, New York: Doubleday.

Bourdieu, Pierre 2001. *Masculine Domination*. Cambridge: Polity.

Brasher, Brenda 1998. *Godly Women. Fundamentalism and Female Power*. New Brunswick, NJ; London: Rutgers University Press.

Brown, Callum 2002. *The Death of Christian Britain. Understanding Secularisation, 1800–2000*. London: New York: Routledge.

Butler, Judith 1999. *Gender Trouble: Feminism and the Subversion of Identity*. New York: Routledge.

Bynum, Caroline Walker 1987. *Holy Feast and Holy Fast. The Religious Significance of Food to Medieval Women*. Berkeley: University of California Press.

Bynum, Caroline Walker 1991. *Fragmentation and Redemption. Essays on Gender and the Human Body in Medieval Religion*. New York: Zone Books.

Chambers, Paul 2005. *Religion, Secularization and Social Change in Wales: Congregational Studies in a post-Christian Society*. Cardiff: University of Wales Press.

Clark, Elizabeth A. (ed.) 1997. *Women and Religion. The Original Sourcebook of Women in Christian Thought*. Revised and expanded edition. HarperSanFrancisco.

Clark-King, Ellen 2004. *Theology by Heart. Women, the Church and God*. Peterborough: Epworth.

Connell, R. W. 1995. *Masculinities* (2nd edn.). Cambridge: Polity.

Connell, R. W. 2002. *Gender*. Cambridge: Polity.

Daly, Mary 1979. *Gyn/Ecology. The Metaethics of Radical Feminism*. London: Women's Press.

Davidman, Lynn 1991. *Tradition in a Rootless World. Women Turn to Orthodox Judaism*. Berkeley and Los Angeles: University of California Press.

Davidoff, Leonore and Catherine Hall 2002. *Family Fortunes. Men and Women of the English Middle Class, 1780–1850*. London: Routledge.

Day, Abby 2005. 'Doing Theodicy: An Empirical Study of a Women's Prayer Group'. *Journal of Contemporary Religion* 20 (3): 343–56.

DeBerg, Betty A. 1990. *Ungodly Women: Gender and the First Wave of American Fundamentalism*. Minneapolis: Fortress.

Douglas, Anne 1977. *The Feminization of American Culture*. New York: Knopf.

Dworkin, Andrea 1981. *Pornography: Men Possessing Women*. London: Women's Press.

Dworkin, Andrea 1983. *Right Wing Women: The Politics of Domesticated Females*. London: Women's Press.

Dwyer, Claire 2000. 'Negotiating Diasporic Identities: Young British South Asian Muslim Women'. *Women's Studies International Forum* 23 (4): 475–86.

Ehrenreich, Barbara 1983. *The Hearts of Men. American Dreams and the Flight from Commitment*. London: Pluto.

Eldén, Sara 2002. 'Gender Politics in Conservative Men's Movements: Beyond Complexity, Ambiguity and Pragmatism'. *NORA: Nordic Journal of Women's Studies* 10 (1): 38–48.

Elm, Susannah 1994. *Virgins of God: The Making of Asceticism in Late Antiquity*. Oxford; (New York): Oxford University Press.

Evans, Mary 2003. *Gender and Social Theory*. Buckingham, UK; Philadelphia: Open University Press.

Francis, Leslie 1997. 'The Psychology of Gender Differences in Religion: A Review of Empirical Research'. *Religion* 27 (1): 68–96.

Fulkerson, Mary McClintock 1994. *Changing the Subject. Women's Discourses and Feminist Theology*. Minneapolis: Fortress Press.

Ginzberg, Lori 1990. *Women and the Work of Benevolence. Morality, Politics and Class in the Nineteenth-Century United States*. New Haven: Yale University Press.

Glendon, Mary Ann 1985. *The New Family and the New Property*. Toronto: Butterworth.

Griffith, R. Marie 1997. *God's Daughters: Evangelical Women and the Power of Submission*. Berkeley: University of California Press.

Halévy, Élie 1949. *England in 1815*. London: Benn.

Harding, Sandra (ed.) 1987. *Feminism and Methodology*. Bloomington: Indiana University Press.

Heelas, Paul and Linda Woodhead 2005. *The Spiritual Revolution. Why Religion is Giving Way to Spirituality*. Oxford: Blackwell.

Hochschild, Arlie R., with Anne Machung 2003. *The Second Shift*. Updated edition. New York: Penguin.

Houtman, Dick and Stef Aupers 2006. 'The Spiritual Revolution and the New Age Gender Puzzle: The Sacralisation of the Self in Late Modernity, 1980–2000', in Giselle Vincett, Sonya Sharma, and Kristin Aune (eds), *Women and Religion in* the West: Challenging Secularization. Aldershot: Ashgate, forthcoming.

Ingelhart, Ronald and Pippa Norris 2003. Rising Tide. Gender Equality and Cultural Change Around the World. Cambridge: Cambridge University Press.

Jacobs, Janet 1991. 'Gender and Power in New Religious Movements. A Feminist Discourse on the Social Scientific Study of Religion', Religion 21: 345–56.

Jenkins, Tim 1999. Religion in English Everyday Life. An Ethnographic Approach. New York: Berghahn.

Juschka, Darlene M. (ed.) 2001. Feminism in the Study of Religion. A Reader. London, New York: Continuum.

Kandiyoti, Deniz 1988. 'Bargaining with Patriarchy'. Gender and Society 2 (September): 274–90.

Kimmel, Michael S. 2000. The Gendered Society. New York: Oxford University Press.

Kimmel, Michael S. and Michael A. Messner 1998. Men's Lives (4th edn). Boston: Allyn and Bacon.

Knott, Kim 2005. The Location of Religion. A Spatial Analysis. London: Oakville: Equinox.

Kraemer, Ross Shepard and Mary Rose D'Angelo (eds) 1990. Women and Christian Origins: A Reader. New York: Oxford University Press.

Laqueur, Thomas W. 1990. Making Sex: Body and Gender from the Greeks to Freud. Cambridge, MA: Harvard University Press.

Luckmann, Thomas 1967. The Invisible Religion. London: Collier-Macmillan.

MacInnes, John 1998. The End of Masculinity. The Confusion of Sexual Genesis and Sexual Difference in Modern Society. Buckingham, UK; Philadelphia: Open University Press.

Marler, Penny L. 1995. 'Lost in the Fifties: The Changing Family and the Nostalgic Church'. Nancy Ammerman and Wade C. Roof (eds), Work, Family and Faith in Contemporary Society. New York and London: Routledge.

Martin, Bernice 1998. 'From Pre- to Postmodernity in Latin America: The Case of Pentecostalism'. In Paul Heelas (ed.), Religion, Modernity and Postmodernity. Oxford, UK; Malden USA: Blackwell.

Martin, David 1977. A General Theory of Secularization. Oxford: Blackwell.

Martin, David 2005. On Secularization: Towards a Revised General Theory. Aldershot: Ashgate.

May, Elaine Tyler 1988. Homeward Bound. American Families in the Cold War Era. New York: Basic Books.

McGuire, Meredith B. 1988. Ritual Healing in Suburban America. New Brunswick: Rutgers University Press.

McGuire, Meredith B. 1994. 'Gendered Spirituality and Quasi-Religious Ritual'. In. A. Greil and T. Robbins (eds). Religion and the Social Order: Research on Theory and Quasi-Religion. Vol. 4: Between Sacred and Secular. Greenwich, CT: JAI Press.

McGuire, Meredith B. 1997. 'Mapping Contemporary American Spirituality: A Sociological Perspective', Christian Spirituality Bulletin 5 (1): 1–8.

Morgan, Sue 1999. A Passion for Purity: Ellice Hopkins and the Politics of Gender in the Late Victorian Church. Bristol: CCSRG Monograph 2, University of Bristol.

Mumm, Susan 1999. Stolen Daughters, Virgin Mothers: Anglican Sisterhoods in Victorian Britain. London: Leicester University Press.

Nason-Clark, Nancy and Neitz, Mary Jo (eds) 2001. Feminist Narratives and the Sociology of Religion. Lanham; Oxford: AltaMira Press.

Neitz, Mary Jo 2001. 'Queering the Dragonfest: Changing Sexualities in a Post-Patriarchal Religion'. In Nancy Nason-Clark and Mary Jo Neitz (eds), Feminist Narratives and the Sociology of Religion. Lanham, Oxford: AltaMira Press.

Nicholls, David 1989. Deity and Domination. Images of God and the State in the Nineteenth and Twentieth Centuries. London: Routledge.

Norris, Pippa and Ronald Inglehart 2004. Sacred and Secular. Religion and Politics Worldwide. Cambridge: Cambridge University Press.

Olesen, Virginia 2005. 'Early Millennial Feminist Qualitative Research. Challenges and Contours'. In Norman K. Denzin and Yvonna S. Lincoln (eds), The Sage Handbook of Qualitative Research (3rd edn). Thousand Oaks, London, New Delhi: Sage.

Ozorak, Elizabeth Weiss 1996. 'The Power but not the Glory. How Women Empower Themselves Through Religion'. Journal for the Social Scientific Study of Religion 35 (1): 17–29.

Palmer, Susan Jean 1994. Moon Sisters, Krishna Mothers, Rajneesh Lovers. Women's Roles in New Religions. New York: Syracuse.

Partridge, Christopher 2004. The Re-enchantment of the West. Volume 1. London; New York: T & T Clark, Continuum.

Paul, Pamela 2005. Pornified. How Porn is Transforming our Lives, our Relationships and our Families. New York: Time Books.

Reinharz, Shulamith with the assistance of Lynn Davidmann 1992. Feminist Methods in Social Research. New York: Oxford University Press.

Rendall, Jane 1985. The Origins of Modern Feminism. Women in Britain, France and the United States, 1780–1860. Basingstoke: Macmillan.

Roof, Wade Clark 1993. *A Generation of Seekers. The Spiritual Journeys of the Baby Boom Generation.* New York: HarperSanFrancisco.

Roof, Wade Clark 1999. *Spiritual Marketplace. Baby Boomers and the Remaking of American Religion.* Princeton, NJ: Princeton University Press.

Salomonsen, Jone 2002. *Enchanted Feminism. The Reclaiming Witches of San Francisco.* London and New York: Routledge.

Sayer, Andrew 2004. 'Seeking the Geographies of Power'. *Economy and Society* 33 (2): 255–70.

Sered, Susan Starr 1994. *Priestess, Mother, Sacred Sister. Religions Dominated by Women.* London and New York: Oxford University Press.

Skeggs, Beverley 1997. *Formations of Class and Gender. Becoming Respectable.* London: Sage.

Skeggs, Beverley 2004. *Class, Self, Culture.* London: Routledge.

Stanton, Elizabeth Cady 1985. *The Woman's Bible.* Abridged edition. Edinburgh: Polygon.

Starhawk 1979. *The Spiral Dance: A Rebirth of the Ancient Religion of the Great Goddess.* San Francisco: Harper and Row.

Summers, Anne 2000. *Female Lives, Moral States. Women, Religion and Public Life in Britain, 1800–1930.* Newbury: Threshold Press.

Thompson, Edward H. Jr and Kathryn R. Remmes. 2002 'Does Masculinity Thwart being Religious? An Examination of Older Men's Religiousness', *Journal for the Scientific Study of Religion* 41 (3): 521–32.

Voas, David 2005. 'The Gender Gap in Religiosity: Evidence from European surveys'. Paper presented at the annual conference of the British Sociological Association Sociology of Religion Study Group, Lancaster, England, 13 April.

Walby, Sylvia 1990. *Theorizing Patriarchy.* Oxford: Blackwell.

Walby, Sylvia 1997. *Gender Transformations.* London; New York: Routledge.

Walsh, Barbara 2002. *Roman Catholic Nuns in England and Wales, 1800–1937.* Dublin: Irish Academic Press.

Walter, Tony and Grace Davie. 1998. 'The Religiosity of Women in the Modern West', *British Journal of Sociology* 49 (4): 640–69.

Weber, Max 1992. *The Protestant Ethic and the Spirit of Capitalism.* Translated by Talcott Parsons with an introduction by Anthony Giddens. London, New York: Routledge.

Welter, Barbara 1976. *Dimity Convictions. The American Woman in the Nineteenth Century.* Athens: Ohio University Press.

Werbner, Pnina 2003. *Pilgrims of Love. The Anthropology of a Global Sufi Cult.* London: Hurst; Bloomington: Indiana.

Wharton, Amy S. 2005. *The Sociology of Gender. An Introduction to Theory and Research.* Malden, MA: Blackwell.

Williams, Rhys H. 2000. 'Promise Keepers: A Comment on Religion and Social Movements'. *Sociology of Religion* 91 (10): 1–10.

Williams, Sarah C. 1999. *Religious Belief and Popular Culture in Southwark, c.1880–1939.* Oxford, New York: Oxford University Press.

Winter, Miriam, Adair Lummis and Allison Stokes 1994. *Deflecting in Place: Women Claiming Responsibility for their own Spiritual Lives.* New York: Crossroads.

Woodhead, Linda 2004. *An Introduction to Christianity.* Cambridge: Cambridge University Press.

Woodhead, Linda 2006a. 'Sex and Secularisation', in Gerard Loughlin (ed.), *Queer Theology: Rethinking the Western Body.* Oxford, UK; Malden USA: Blackwell, forthcoming.

Woodhead, Linda 2006b. 'Why So Many Women in Holistic Spirituality?'. In Kieran Flanagan and Peter Jupp (eds), *The Sociology of Spirituality.* Aldershot: Ashgate, forthcoming.

Woodhead, Linda 2007. 'Real Religion and Fuzzy Spirituality. Questioning some Deep Assumptions in the Sociology of Religion', in Stef Aupers and Dick Houtman (eds), *Religions of Modernity: Sacralizing the Self and the Digital* (forthcoming).

Woodhead, Linda and Paul Heelas 2000. *Religion in Modern Times. An Interpretive Anthology.* Oxford: Blackwell.

Wuthnow, Robert 1996. *Sharing the Journey. Support Groups and America's New Quest for a Community.* London: The Free Press.

Wuthnow, Robert 2003. *All in Sync: How Music and Art are Revitalizing American Religion.* Berkeley, Los Angeles and London: University of California Press.

28

Embodiment, Emotion and Religious Experience: Religion, Culture and the Charismatic Body

PHILIP A. MELLOR

What does it mean to be 'religious'? This is the most basic theoretical question that confronts anyone attempting to study religious phenomena, and one that sociologists have sought to answer in various ways. They have stressed the relative importance of either beliefs or practices, established tight or loose boundaries between religions and other social or cultural phenomena, and diverged sharply over issues such as the degree to which religiosity shapes, or is shaped by, its social and cultural context. What has often been neglected, however, is the fact that religion is an *embodied* phenomenon: not only does its meaningfulness for individuals, and its various forms of social and cultural import, depend upon human bodies that are able to believe and act in particular ways, but it can also be stated that all religions, though in different ways, consciously seek to shape bodily experiences, actions and ways of thinking.

Though there have been exceptions, the relative neglect of religious *experience* as an object of sociological study is significant here, since this most obviously directs our attention to embodiment. What I shall suggest, in fact,

is that a focus on experience can help illuminate the embodied nature of beliefs and practices too, as well as other issues to do with the specific character, boundaries and cultural contexts of religious life. Although some religious forms emphasise the importance of experience more than others, just as some stress belief above practice or vice versa, the experiential aspects of being religious cannot ultimately be isolated from, or subordinated to, beliefs and practices. All three aspects of being religious are intimately, and inextricably, related to the inherent capacities and potentialities of bodies, and the varied patterns of social and cultural shaping to which they are necessarily subject. The purpose of this chapter is to make a contribution towards the development of the systematic analysis of these relationships.

The arguments offered here are made possible by the burgeoning literature in the sociology of the body over the last few decades. This has, of course, resulted in innumerable theoretical approaches to the subject, many of which are incommensurate, and of more or less usefulness for the study of religion. After acknowledging continuing difficulties in approaches to the body and how these relate to religion, however, I structure the rest of this chapter with regard to six models of embodiment that, taken together, can offer a productive way forward for future studies. The presentation of each model involves a critical account of the key theoretical arguments, and suggestions about how these can help illuminate the character and function of specifically religious phenomena. These six models are focused on the following issues: (1) the primacy of the *emotional* dimensions of embodiment; (2) the *permeability* of bodies with regard to outside forces; (3) the *learning* capacities of bodies; (4) the power of *mimetic* models with regard to religious experience; (5) the *mindful* character of bodies in the sense that cognitive factors have to be seen as fully integrated into embodied experience; and (6) the *global* nature of bodies. In the latter case, I use the word 'global' in two senses: first, in the sense that all human beings share the same embodied potentialities and properties; and second, in the sense that aspects of globalisation offer new opportunities for appreciating the complex relations between embodied potentialities and cultural processes.

Throughout these discussions I have elected to draw principally upon 'charismatic' forms of Christianity, loosely understood, to illuminate the theoretical arguments associated with each model. Experiences of 'Spirit possession', 'trance' and other altered states of consciousness have been traced not only to the 'pentecostal' Christian churches of the 'Acts of the Apostles' in the Bible but also to Jesus himself (Davies, 1995). The late twentieth-century development of Christian forms centred on intense experiences of being filled with the Holy Spirit, however, manifest in speaking in 'tongues', sacred 'swoons' and gifts of healing, are notable for a number of reasons. First, they are of general sociological interest: such forms are growing so rapidly across the world today, particularly in the Southern hemisphere, that there have been claims of a 'new reformation' (Jenkins, 2002: 7; Cox, 1995). Second, although the models of embodiment developed in this

chapter could, with modifications, be applied to any form of religion, charismatic forms are of particular interest in that they have an especially strong focus on the experiential dimensions of Christianity, and can be seen as part of a broader resurgence of emotionally or experientially centred forms of community (McGuire, 1982; Hervieu-Léger, 1993; Hunt, 2001; Gumbel, 2002; Watling, 2005). A third factor that makes charismatic Christianity of particular interest, however, is the fact that, as a global phenomenon, it offers valuable insights into embodiment, religion and culture that might not be possible otherwise. As Beckford (2003: 207) notes, in fact, one of the key points of interest about charismatic Christianity as a global phenomenon, which has not been discussed critically in the major studies of it, is that specific forms of embodiment recur across a range of otherwise very different cultures. Through the models outlined in this chapter, I shall attempt to fill the gap in this literature.

Initially, however, it is important to note how problematic the notion of the 'body' has been in sociology, even within contemporary body studies. Indeed, the characteristic ambivalence shown towards religion by many mainstream sociologists has also been evident with regard to the body, in that it has often been defined by its relationship to other social and cultural phenomena rather than with regard to its own distinct properties. It is in this sense that we can talk of the *absent/present* body.

THE ABSENT/PRESENT BODY

The latter decades of the twentieth century saw a remarkable growth in the sociological interest in the body, though a significant feature of this interest has been the fact that, despite its apparent ubiquity, the body has remained an elusive, indeterminate phenomenon (Leder, 1990; Shilling, 1993, 2005). One way of accounting for this 'absence/presence' is by noting that the body's significance was usually emphasised in relation to a range of other, more established, concerns. These included the commodification of the body in consumer culture, feminist analyses of gender and sex, and technological and governmental attempts to regulate and control bodies (Shilling, 2005: 2; see Featherstone, 1991; Grosz, 1994; Turner, 1984, 1991). Although such studies did much to foster sociological interest in the body, the focus on representations or images of bodies, analysed in relation to determinative social, cultural or political processes, often meant that bodies became strangely empty of any real material, sensual, emotional and cognitive characteristics.

More positively, however, despite these limitations, the body was seen as something centrally implicated in debates about modernity, post-modernity and, increasingly, globalisation processes. It is in this context that many of these body studies returned to classical sociological theories of modernity and found within them an attention to embodied factors that remained highly relevant to the present, particularly with regard to the critique of the cognitivist and rationalist dimensions of post-Enlightenment Western thought (Turner, 1984; Shilling 1993; Grosz, 1994; Mellor and Shilling, 1997).

This sociological interest in the 'corporeal constituents' of modernity mirrored similar developments in anthropological studies, where critiques of Western cognitivism combined fruitfully with data on non-Western peoples, as well as fresh studies of pre-modern European cultures, to map out the various ways in which sense experiences and cultures have interacted across a huge range of different contexts (Howes, 1991; Classen, 1993). This renewed interest in the body also gave rise to new visions of the sociological importance of religion, focused especially upon the embodied dimensions of ritual, disciplinary regulations of the body by religious institutions, and the ways in which religious developments have served to reshape and reform the experience of embodiment across Western history (Asad, 1983, 1988; McGuire, 1990; Turner, 1991; Bell, 1992; Mellor and Shilling, 1997). The close relationship between the emergence of body studies and the resurgence of sociological interest in religion was not accidental,

however, but indicative of the fact that these subjects had been inextricably entwined for a number of the classical sociological theorists.

It is undoubtedly the case that, throughout the twentieth century, the secularisation thesis, in its many variants, constituted the dominant theoretical paradigm in the sociology of religion, and that this fostered the increasing marginality of religion to the core theoretical and substantive foci of sociology in general. The arguments of Max Weber (1991), one of the major 'founding figures' of sociology, concerning the increasing rationalisation and disenchantment of the modern world, were decisive influences in this regard. None the less, re-reading Weber's work today, it is clear that his arguments about the social and cultural effects of the Reformation are not simply to do with transformations in 'beliefs', but with a 're-formation' of embodiment involving the disciplining, regulation and individualisation of bodies markedly different to the Catholic engagement with human embodiment in the medieval period (Mellor and Shilling, 1997). It is also notable that Weber's (1968) notion of 'charisma', which offers the counterpoint to rationalisation in his account of social creativity and control, is expressive of specific experiences, power and authority that come through the body. Although he stressed the waning significance of charisma as rationalisation processes developed (Weber, 1968: 1146-9), this is now increasingly questioned, just as his account of the 'disenchantment' of the world is now considered problematic.

Lindholm (1990), for example, explores the continuing significance of charisma as a source of social creativity in various contexts. He also notes that 'charisma', in Weber's work, and 'collective effervescence', in that of Émile Durkheim, have similar roles in that both are embodied sources of social creativity. The former locates this creativity within individuals, however, while the latter associates it with groups. Weber took the notion of charisma from Christianity, where it had referred to 'the gift of grace'. This could take various forms, though was associated particularly with the charisma of ordination, conferred by a bishop through the laying on of hands. In this context, contrary to Weber's understanding, the contagious features of charisma are not associated only with specific individuals, but are embodied transformations of a more collective nature, and make sense more in terms of Durkheim's (1995: 326) understanding of consecrations as the diffusion of sacred contagion through physical contact. For Durkheim (1995: 328), the 'founding figure' of French sociology and, along with Weber, a hugely important influence upon the sociological study of religion, the spreading of a pattern of emotional contagion that reconfigures the experience of the body is 'the very process through which sacredness is acquired'.

Weber's account of the increasingly rationalised bodies of modernity continues to exercise an influence. In reassessing the role of the body in relation to religion, culture and society today, however, it is clear that the absence/presence of the body in recent sociological thought is not only intimately tied to the absence/presence of religion, but also that both forms of 'absence' might reflect an overestimation of the degree to which social and cultural changes can transform basic human potentialities and characteristics. In this regard, it is worth noting that those sociological studies of the body that have a constructionist orientation, where the body is seen as a site for the interplay of social and cultural forces (Haraway, 1991; Butler, 1993; see Foucault, 1977), are now increasingly challenged by attempts to develop more substantial visions of embodiment, centred on phenomenological, realist or pragmatist accounts of the 'lived body' (Bourdieu, 1984; Leder, 1990; Crossley, 1995; Archer, 1995; Mellor, 2004; Shilling, 2005). The amount of attention devoted to religion in such studies continues to vary a great deal, but their attempts to make sense of the embodied bases of society and culture are of potentially great value to students of religion, though this is especially so with regard to the renewed interest in the work of Durkheim.

In this light, the idea that modernisation, and, by extension, globalising processes, necessarily render religion a phenomenon of marginal significance to contemporary social and cultural life, and therefore to sociological

analysis, looks increasingly problematic theoretically, even aside from empirical factors. Indeed, two arguments can be suggested. First, if social and cultural life has some sort of embodied basis, then however radical social and cultural changes might appear to be, these can only be possible or sustainable in so far as they make sense in relation to the embodied potentialities and characteristics of human beings. Second, if these potentialities and characteristics are intimately tied to religious phenomena, as Durkheim suggests, then making sense of society and culture necessarily involves the study of religion (see Maffesoli, 1996; Janssen and Verheggen, 1997; Mellor and Shilling, 1997; Shilling and Mellor, 2001; Rawls, 2001; Mellor, 2004).

These two arguments are, of course, of a generalised and contentious nature, and developing them in more detail must involve the consideration of a number of models of religion and embodiment that might offer a productive basis for further reflection and study. In the following sections, however, I outline the six models that are, I suggest, indicative of some of the most useful analyses of the embodied basis of religion and culture, and particularly helpful in terms of providing building blocks for further development.

(1) The Emotional Body

The notion of an emotional body is an important starting point, since all the other models I consider can be seen as developments of, or supplements to, it. Williams and Bendelow (1998) have suggested that emotions have often enjoyed a somewhat 'ethereal' existence in sociological thought, despite the rise of body studies, but it has long been accepted that emotion plays a particularly significant role in religious experience. In this regard, it is worth noting that, alongside the upsurge of interest in the embodied dimensions of the Durkheimian tradition, the work of William James, an immensely important figure at the turn of the twentieth century for the shaping of the modern study of psychology, has again begun to interest sociologists.

Like Durkheim, James (1907) emphasises the primacy of embodied experience in social and cultural life, and both can be said to offer arguments for 'the authenticity and validity of religious belief premised on religious experience' (Barbalet, 2004: 348). Both, furthermore, stress the emotional nature of this experience, and the embodied predispositions of human beings to experience strong emotional states of various sorts. Where they differ is that, in contrast to Durkheim's focus on the collective stimulation and regulation of emotion through either unpredictable patterns of contagion or institutionalised forms of ritual (Mellor, 1998), James is concerned with the emotional experiences of individuals and sees collective forms as secondary to, and derivative of, these. His definition of religion as 'the feelings, acts and experiences of individual men in their solitude' is indicative of the apparent gulf between his position and that of Durkheim (James, 1907: 30–1).

None the less, Barbalet's (2004) adoption of James as an important resource for the contemporary sociology of the emotions dismisses earlier accounts of the divergences between him and Durkheim (e.g. Lukes, 1974: 460), and emphasises their fundamental similarity with regard to the idea that social phenomena, including religious beliefs and scientific arguments, have their basis in the human capacities for emotional arousal. As Barbalet (2004: 341) suggests, for James, reason, volition and emotion are not only intimately related to each other, but emotion is the primary factor, since conceptual or sensual faculties are essentially meaningless to us without the 'emotional pertinency' that allows us to care about anything or to act in a particular way (see James, 1897: 117, 83). Referring us to Durkheim's (1995: 392ff.) discussion of piacular rites, Barbalet (2004: 350) notes that his argument that bodily actions and gestures create the emotional states characteristic of these rites, rather than thoughts of the deceased, is entirely consistent with James's social psychology of emotions, even if James is more interested in individual bodily processes than collective engagements with these.

Looking at charismatic religiosity it is indeed clear that the apparent theoretical gulf

between James and Durkheim starts to looks bridgeable. It is generally acknowledged, for example, that this religiosity has a highly *personalist* character, in the sense that it is focused on the transformation of individuals through powerful religious experiences. Although it has been suggested that charismatic Christianity encourages individuals to find their way to God through all five senses (Poewe, 1994: 249; Coleman, 2000: 68), it is clear that the foundation for this experiential focus is an intensely emotional encounter with Christ and the Holy Spirit (Percy, 1996: 67). Here, it is worth noting that James refers us to Jonathan Edwards's *Treatise on Religious Affections*, which not only offered support for his emotionally and experientially centred view of religion, but also came to exercise a decisive influence upon modern evangelical, Pentecostal and charismatic churches (Noll, 2001: 262).

For Edwards, as for contemporary charismatics, true religion is a phenomenon of the heart rather than the mind, based on an experience that was close to an actual sensation (Schröder, 2000: 194). This has led some commentators to associate charismatic Christianity with the modern privatisation of religion (Wilson, 1988: 204; Percy, 1996: 145). Bruce (2002), in fact, argues that in 'giving a much higher place to personal experience than to shared doctrines' it expresses a more culturally pervasive ethic of 'personal fulfilment' (see also Davies, 1984: 144). Not only do these highly personal experiences offer the inductive basis for the affirmation of a community life, however, but the range of extreme physical and emotional symptoms individuals experience as they encounter the power of the Holy Spirit are *collectively nurtured* (Percy, 1996: 100). Rather than simply endorsing James's view of religion, this nurturing of specific experiences in group settings, where powerful encounters with the Holy Spirit are both expected and collectively interpreted, as well as the apparently 'contagious' circulation of phenomena such as speaking in 'tongues', fainting, intense body heat and extreme exuberance, are more suggestive of Durkheim's (1995) account of the collective effervescence at the heart of religious life, and its recurrent structuring and mediation through ritual processes.

Discussing the hugely successful '*Alpha Course*', for example, which, after its initial development in London, has gone on to become a major evangelising and renewal programme across a range of churches in Europe and the US, Watling (2005: 92) notes that it has cognitive features, in the sense that it aims to educate individuals into the basic truths of Christianity, but that 'its underlying intention is to create an emotional experience which encourages personal identification with Christianity'. In this regard, the *Alpha* Course has much in common with other charismatic forms of Christian evangelisation, such as the 'Toronto Blessing' associated with John Wimber and the 'Vineyard' churches. The more extreme range of physical phenomena associated with the Toronto Blessing, which also became a worldwide form of Christian 'renewal', including hysterical 'holy laughter', roaring like animals, and other bizarre bodily gestures and expressions, suggest a much more chaotic and 'spontaneous' worship environment than that offered by *Alpha*. It is also clear, however, that, even in such extreme examples, certain experiences and expressions are only possible on the basis of subtly structured collective processes (Percy, 1996; Lyon, 2000).

In the light of these examples, it is clear that intensely personal religious experiences and patterns of collective emotional stimulation need not have the dichotomous relationship that a superficial reading of the arguments of James and Durkheim might imply. None the less, Barbalet's eagerness to resolve their theoretical differences obscures remaining questions about how individuals come to experience forms of emotional intensity that have a religiously *specific* character: James's (1907: 512) association of these with unconscious elements within the self is clearly unable to make much difference between, for example, distinctively Christian or Muslim religious experiences. As Spickard (1993: 110) suggests, discussing sociological utilisations of a Jamesian approach to charismatic Christianity (e.g. Poloma, 1989), this is a major weakness of his account of religious experience.

More generally, it is a weakness in its understanding of human embodiment. In contrast, the dominant model of embodiment within the Durkheimian tradition can be characterised as one that emphasises the *permeability* of bodies, in the sense that they have an inherent susceptibility to transformation by social energies or forces in specific settings.

(2) The Permeable Body

Csordas (1994: 277) has argued that Marcel Mauss's essays on the 'person' (1950a) and on the 'body' (1950b) are entirely independent of each other, reflecting a broader Western duality he was unable to resolve, but this is misleading. The continuity between Mauss's views of the body and the person rests on the fact that, in the Durkheimian tradition, of which Mauss became the leader following the death of Durkheim, both can be seen as 'permeable' rather than as bounded material or existential totalities. While the immense power of social forces to permeate bodies is strongly emphasised, it is also acknowledged that this is constrained by bodies' natural dispositions. It might be said that this tradition offers a vision of bodies that are socially *constituted* rather than socially *constructed*.

Mauss's (1950b) discussion of 'body techniques' and Hertz's (1973) of the cross-cultural pre-eminence of the right hand offer anthropologically informed studies that can help clarify this distinction. The argument of Hertz (1973: 89), an early Durkheimian who died in World War I, is that, despite the physical resemblance of left and right hands, in nearly all societies they are treated with an astonishing inequality, which he analyses in relation to Durkheim's sacred/profane dualism. What Hertz is *not* doing is arguing that the distinction between right and left is either socially or biologically determined. What he argues is that most humans appear to have an embodied predisposition towards right-handedness: it is upon the basis of this that social forces serve to sacralise all that is 'right' and denigrate all that is 'left'. This embodied predisposition cannot be socially deconstructed entirely: musicians, for example, can retrain the left hand out of its socially reinforced relative 'uselessness', but left-handed people living in societies that have striven to coerce them into right-handedness continue to have a preference for the left. In short, even though the vast array of practices, beliefs, ideas and values attributed to right and left are clearly distinctively social phenomena, the distinction between right and left is not entirely socially constructed: it is socially *constituted* through the societal engagement with real embodied human predispositions that constrain the constructions that can be developed upon them (Mellor, 2004: 56).

Mauss's (1950b) discussion of body techniques, along with developments of similar ideas by Bourdieu (1977) and Elias (1987, 1991), are of note in that this process of body constitution is articulated with reference to the notion of a *habitus*. Techniques of the body refer to how people learn to relate to and deploy their bodies, a process that is often unconscious but involves practice and accomplishment, and results in bodies acquiring particular identities and histories. Elias's analysis of the transformations in manners and etiquette in Western history builds on this idea, emphasising how the embodied *habitus* of individuals is highly permeable with regard to large-scale social processes. Similarly, Bourdieu discusses the pre-cognitive, embodied predispositions which promote particular forms of orientation to the world, organise each generation's senses and bodily experiences into particular hierarchies, and predispose people towards particular ways of knowing and acting (Mellor and Shilling, 1997: 20).

Csordas (1994: 7) has drawn upon Bourdieu's notion of the *habitus*, with its view of the body as 'the principle generating and unifying all practices' (Bourdieu, 1977: 124), to account for how the bodies of both Christian healers and patients are 'socially informed' by a broader charismatic culture (Csordas, 1994: 107). In a similar vein, he also defines the Catholic charismatic practice of 'resting in the Spirit', a kind of 'sacred swoon' generally referred to as 'slaying in the Spirit' by Protestant charismatics, as a technique of the body in Mauss's sense (Csordas, 1994: 231–2).

While both Elias and Bourdieu are attentive to transformations in the habitus over large stretches of time, however, Bourdieu's (1977: 124) work, in particular, has a strong socially determinist character and his vision of the 'socially informed body' offers little scope for a sensitivity to how actions and interactions can lead to the development of new orientations to the body. Csordas (1994: 108) attempts to circumvent this determinism by noting the possibilities for elaborating upon habitual practices and experiences that can arise in 'the performative flow of a healing event', but there are limits, perhaps, to how successful this can be within Bourdieu's framework.

A brief consideration of quite different, yet clearly related, examples of how Christianity has engaged with the 'permeability' of bodies points towards greater creative possibilities. In a Roman Catholic context, the Eucharist incorporates the Body of Christ (body/bread, blood/wine) as *food* into the body of the individual, while incorporating the individual into the Body of Christ (i.e. the Church) (Mellor and Shilling, 1997: 68). This re-formation of the body, in its two senses, links human permeability to the transformative possibilities of the Incarnation. In broad terms, of course, Protestant forms of Christianity have tended to be less overtly ritualistic in their forms of religious expression. None the less, not only have most 'mainline' Protestant churches retained the Eucharistic ritual in some form, but, as Sack's (2000) discussion of 'Whitebread Protestants' in the US amply demonstrates, the highly ritualised construction of religious, political and ethical forms of solidarity through the bodily incorporation of food remains central to large areas of contemporary American culture.

A related, though somewhat divergent, pattern of bodily incorporation is evident in certain forms of charismatic Christianity, though Christ (as food) is ingested not through the Eucharistic ritual or by imbibing 'the Spirit' but through reading the Bible. Here, Coleman (2000: 127–9) discusses how members of the Swedish 'Word of Life' church 'describe the process of reading the Bible as a form of ingestion akin to eating'. Furthermore, the language used to describe religious experience is also understood to *cause* and to *constitute* experience, since 'eating' the Word involves the physical ingestion of Christ into the materiality of the body and not just the acceptance of Christ in cognitive or psychological terms (Coleman, 2000: 127–9). In contrast to the Catholic model, the charismatic focus on the Bible reconfigures the religious meanings of bodily senses (Christ is ingested not through the mouth, but through the eyes or the ears), and downplays any notion of sacramental efficacy, but in each case the reception of Christ is made possible by the permeability of bodies.

These creative engagements with the body are only possible in so far as people are in a particular *habitus* that allows them to acquire specific skills, orientations and aptitudes, but the acquisition of such things cannot be explained simply as a process whereby the indeterminate potentialities of bodies are given specific shape by cultural norms, beliefs or concepts. The cultural shaping of bodies is, of course, immensely important, but attention must also be paid to the properties of bodies themselves, since this cultural shaping is both made possible and constrained by the inherent characteristics of bodies. In this regard, a focus on the *learning* body helps direct our attention to the ways in which embodiment structures the acquisition of knowledge, as well as being structured by it.

(3) The Learning Body

Mauss's (2003) study of prayer defines it as a *ritual*: since speech is a social act, prayer is a socially structured form of action closely allied to collective regulations concerning the body, such as posture, kneeling, sitting, and prostrating, which shape the consciousnesses and experiences of individuals in specific ways. Thus, discussing the invocation at the beginning of the Lord's Prayer, he argues that it is 'not just the effusion of a soul, a cry which expresses a feeling', but 'the fruit of the work of centuries', while Christians who 'abandon themselves to the Spirit' in an apparently free and individual manner are actually submitting

themselves to the spirit of the church (Mauss, 2003: 33). In arguing this, he claims that he is not denying the felt authenticity of individual prayer, but emphasising the social reality that allows individual mental and bodily states to be shaped in particular ways (Mauss, 2003: 36). This view of prayer helps account for what Beckford (2003: 189) has called the 'instrumental' dimensions of charismatic religiosity. At the heart of the *Alpha* Course, for example, is the experientially focused 'Holy Spirit Weekend', where individuals have the opportunity to 'abandon themselves to the Spirit' in the manner Mauss suggests, but this 'abandonment' is very carefully prepared for in the earlier parts of the course, while the weekend itself is a structured pattern of prayers, videos and discussions helping individuals to become sufficiently open to bodily, psychological and spiritual transformation that they can receive the outpouring of the Holy Spirit that is the culmination of the course (Watling, 2005: 98).

Although she does not draw directly upon Mauss's study, Norris's (2005) discussion of the embodied basis of religious experience can be read as an extension of his arguments, revolving around the central question of how it is that intensely personal, often indescribable, religious experiences can be learned. Emphasising that religious phenomena such as states of prayer are primarily 'somatic states, transmitted and learned through the body', she sees embodiment as the medium through which collectively sanctioned religious norms come to reshape individual consciousness, the senses and the emotions (Norris, 2005: 182). Consequently, she claims that the development of particular emotions and experiences is one of the major ways in which religious tradition is transmitted, and, like Mauss, emphasises the primacy of ritual in this process, since repetition is one of the key ways in which certain kinds of knowledge become embedded in the body (Norris, 2005: 187; Levin, 1985: 209–20). Through repetition, certain forms of knowledge become constitutive of the body; a process that may develop quite gradually, but also in sudden leaps as the body becomes attuned to achieving certain types of experiences. This latter point suggests that bodies have their own dynamics that to some extent structure the learning processes individuals subject them to.

Here, it is worth going back to James (1907: 206), who refers us to Starbuck's comparison of the alternation between periods of steady progress and sudden, rapid forms of development in the bodily awareness and knowledge of athletes with the pattern of conversion to religious life. This captures something about embodiment similar to Czikszentmihalyi's (1975) notion of 'flow', where the practitioners of various sports, medical procedures or religious disciplines are no longer consciously deploying techniques, but experience a total immersion in what they are doing. Neitz and Spickard (1990), in fact, have used this notion of the 'flow' to capture the experiences of the loss of self, and the immersion in something transcendent, that characterises various forms of religious practices. It also implies, however, that the instrumental efficacy of culturally acquired techniques ultimately depends upon bodies able to achieve such 'peak experiences' (Spickard, 1993: 113). In this regard, phenomenologically oriented visions of the learning body tend to have a much stronger emphasis on the inherent emotional and sensual characteristics of bodies than that evident in the work of Mauss.

For Merleau-Ponty (1962, 1974), for example, the phenomenological analysis of the body explicitly prioritises the natural over the cultural, in the sense that the sensory characteristics and practical abilities of our bodies constitute the ground and the medium through which our experiences of ourselves, others and the world become possible (Archer, 2000: 128; see Crossley, 1994, 1995). This confronts directly the constructionist arguments of writers such as Proudfoot (1985), who not only argues that all forms of experience are determined by linguistic, cultural and historical factors, but also goes so far as to claim that there is no 'common humanity' against which the plurality of cultural constructions of experience can be measured (see also Neitz, 1987; Asad, 1993). It also illuminates the weaknesses in Yamane's (2000) argument that sociologists cannot study

'religious experience', only retrospective linguistic representations of it: what such studies do, in giving such analytical weight to language, is ignore the degree to which our bodies never cease to be the media through which all experience, knowledge and meaning are constituted. As Archer (2000: 11) suggests, 'physiological embodiment does not sit well with social constructionism ... social constructions may be placed upon it, but the body is stubbornly resistant to being dissolved into the discursive'. This is so because the body adapts to natural and social environments even before we have acquired language, and because physical responses related to pleasure, pain, desire and need continue throughout our lives to challenge the constructionist overemphasis on language (Archer, 2000: 316).

Csordas's (1994) study of charismatic Christianity has drawn on Merleau-Ponty's notion of bodily being-in-the-world, combined with Bourdieu's account of the *habitus*, in order to account for the intimate relationship between embodied experience and its inevitable immersion in systems of cultural meaning. Archer's discussion of religion goes beyond Merleau-Ponty, however. For her, religion arises on the basis of practice: it entails a 'feel for' the sacred rather than a prepositional knowledge about it, an exercise of spiritual 'know how' rather than a cognitive acceptance of abstract principles. This challenges the Enlightenment's *logocentric* view of human beings, in cutting through the distinction between reason and emotions: as she expresses it, 'unless we are already affective beings, then no amount of knowledge could move us to anything' (Archer, 2000: 185).

Following this line of thought, religion is 'a codification of practice, and thus there is no such thing as a non-liturgical religion' (Archer, 2000: 184). This codification gives rise to developments in art, music, architecture, artefacts and other cultural forms, while the institutionalisation of a 'Church' is usually connected to the development of a 'priesthood' to act as custodians of codified practice (Archer, 2000: 185). These developments impact back upon practical activity, elaborating new forms of embodied relations and new bodily practices, but the essence of religion remains fully embodied. In this light, Archer (2000: 186) notes that the practice of Christian life as an embodied commitment of the whole person 'is distorted if fragmented into a cognitive-propositional "grammar of assent" and a modern Decalogue of prescribed behaviour'. Rather, the real centre of Christian life is in the bodily disciplines of prayer, pilgrimage and contemplation and, especially, in the corporeal reception of the Body of Christ in the Eucharist.

This view of Christian life is, of course, implicitly Catholic, and charismatic Protestants would dispute the idea that all religion is 'liturgical', even though their worship and healing services are highly ritualised (Csordas, 1994). More broadly, however, the charismatic focus on the practical, existential and emotional aspects of bodily being, not only in 'worship' settings but also in all areas of life, is consistent with Archer's account. Furthermore, her particular concern for the importance of 'personal experience' is also highly relevant to charismatic forms of religion.

Although Rawls (2001), amongst others, has identified an orientation towards practical action as a key feature of Durkheim's arguments, Archer's focus on the learning body is, to some extent, defined in opposition to what she sees as his overemphasis upon the social. Indeed, she asserts the importance of allowing for the possibility of 'authentic personal experience' which, rather than simply arising on the basis of social causes, facilitates an individual's ability to filter the social practices that are sought or shunned, and which thereby makes a significant difference to their 'chosen way of being in the social world' (Archer, 1995: 292). For Archer, in fact, human embodiment predisposes individuals towards a 'fundamentally evaluative' engagement with the world, stimulating an 'inner conversation' constitutive of our 'concrete singularity' (Archer, 2000: 318–19). Csordas's (1994) discussion of the thoroughly reflexive processes through which charismatic self-identities are established is indicative of the importance of Archer's point here.

As valuable as this interest in the 'inner conversation' of individuals is, however, there is the danger that individuals can appear to be a little too self-contained: our 'concrete singularity' as individuals is, as she would acknowledge, a 'work in progress' rather than a given fact, and, even amongst those who have a highly developed sense of their own identity, the ability to 'filter' social forces through a strong evaluative orientation is not always as evident as Archer seems to imply. In this regard, and building on the idea of a learning body *and* the fact that the body remains permeable to social and cultural forces throughout our lives, the notion of the *mimetic* body offers a further productive theoretical model for making sense of the relationships between religion, embodiment and culture.

(4) The Mimetic Body

It has been noted that the body learns to be religious through the imitation of others, particularly as these mimetic actions become increasingly habitual through patterns of repetition that succeed in 'layering, compounding and shaping present experience' (Norris, 2005: 191), but mimesis, in general, has highly ambiguous social and cultural consequences. The foremost theorist of mimesis in this regard is René Girard (1977, 1987, 2001). For him, mimetic desire is a key aspect of what it is to be human, particularly with regard to the freedom to make choices about our preferences and actions since, if our desires were fixed upon predetermined objects, they would be merely a particular form of instinct (Girard, 2001: 15). Consequently, the malleability of human desires opens us up to collective patterns of contagion, just as it also allows for their religious re-formation. It is this that accounts for the embodied basis of both those harmonious and violent energies that Durkheim (1995: 412) sees as part of the 'ambiguity' of the sacred.

For Girard, the objects of human desire are shaped collectively: we have an embodied predisposition to desire what others desire; something that can be immensely rewarding, but which can also lead to progressively more intense cycles of mimetic contagion

(Girard, 1987: 26). It is on this basis that he argues that, because mimetic contagion can threaten to overwhelm and destroy a social group, it is often the case that the group protects itself through the sacrifice of a surrogate victim or 'scapegoat', a sacrificial substitution that must be concealed in order for the sacrifice to have its intended effect of restoring harmony and order (Girard, 1977: 4–5). None the less, Girard is also interested in a mimetic retraining of bodies that can have more harmonious, but equally dramatic, social and cultural consequences. In reference to the way in which the New Testament presents Jesus Christ as the primary mimetic model for all humans to follow, for example, he notes that the text is acutely sensitive to the potentially dangerous consequences of the human predisposition towards mimesis. Discussing Jesus' treatment of the woman taken in adultery (John, 8: 3–11), in fact, he notes how Jesus breaks up the mob about to stone her to death by saying 'Let him who is without sin among you be the first to throw the stone at her'. As he suggests, that first stone is the most difficult to throw precisely because 'it is the only one without a *model*' (Girard, 2001: 56). In broader terms, however, the New Testament urges the modelling of human desire upon the desire of Jesus Christ to be the perfect image of God: we are invited to 'imitate his own imitation' (Girard, 2001: 13).

This focus on mimesis adds a further dimension to the consideration of how individuals learn to be religious. In the New Testament, as Longenecker (2003: 70) suggests, the Apostle Paul 'parades Christ-likeness as the essential characteristic of Christian living', but he also attacks those who live according to 'the lusts of their hearts', thereby 'dishonouring' their bodies (Romans, 1: 24–26), since these are expressive of what Girard calls violent mimetic rivalry (see also Jewett, 2003: 93). Thus, Paul fiercely repudiates those early Christians who sought to accommodate the gospel to 'enlightened philosophical ideas about the transcendence of crass bodily existence' (Hays, 2001: 126; see 1 Corinthians, 15: 12–19), because, if Christ was God *incarnate* as an embodied, fully human being, then human embodiment contains religious potentialities that can be developed through the imitation of him. None the less, these can only be achieved by a re-formation of the body: humans must abandon their 'old nature' and become 'imitators of God' who talk, walk, desire, feel and think in a way that is entirely at odds with their previous modes of being (Ephesians, 4: 22, 5: 1).

Such attempts at bodily re-formation have been a key feature of Christian history: Bynum (1987, 1991), for example, discusses the exploration of the religious potentialities of the body through the imitation of Christ in the medieval period, and the experiences of religious 'ecstasy' often characteristic of them. In this perspective, Bruce's (2002: 180) claim that the charismatic emphasis on experience is 'novel' in Christian history is misleading: rather, this emphasis manifests new elaborations of a tradition of engaging with embodiment that is not only well established but central to Christianity's incarnational focus. It is this focus, in fact, that explains why bodily states of health and illness, and not just psychological problems, as Bruce (2002: 182) suggests, continue to be so important for charismatic Christians, since the body is understood to exemplify divine favour (Coleman, 2000: 130). Again, it is possible to note continuities with the medieval Christian view that evil was manifest in sick bodies (Classen, 1993), as well as with the Biblical accounts of Jesus' healing miracles (e.g. Mark, 9: 24–29). More broadly, however, such phenomena can be associated with a renewal of attempts at the 'imitation of Christ', where individuals commit themselves to the 're-forming' of the constitution, experiences and conduct of human bodies in the light of the incarnational revelation of Christ as the Word of God.

Watling (2005: 101), for example, notes that the ultimate aim of *Alpha* is to enable individuals to '*embody* the attitudes of Jesus' and become Christ-like (Watling, 2005: 101), while an even more distinctively contemporary example of the charismatic Christian engagement with embodiment, concerns a painting displayed amongst the Swedish Word of Life community that shows Christ with the physique of a body-builder (Coleman, 2000: 147).

Coleman notes the prevalence in sermons of the theme of the 'spiritual body-builder', exemplified in this depiction, and its notable variance with regard to conventional images of the suffering Christ. Drawing upon Harré's (1989) account of body-building as a process wherein individual body parts can be isolated and worked on individually and rationally in pursuit of an aesthetic vision of the ideal body, Coleman (2000: 149) notes that Word of Life members display a similar attempt to refashion the flesh through a form of mimesis where Christ's perfect body is the model for a form of spiritual 'pumping iron'.

Such phenomena are not entirely novel, however: late nineteenth-century forms of 'muscular Christianity', as well as the links between sports and contemporary evangelical groups such as the 'Promise Keepers', indicate the established potency of this model of Christian embodiment (Hall, 1994; Higgs, 1995; Clausen, 1999; Ladd and Mathisen, 2002). More broadly, attempts to depict charismatic churches as being radically at odds with traditional Christianity can be misleading. Discussing Wimber's charismatic theology, for example, Percy (1996: 99) notes the emphasis on the Incarnation as the 'embodiment of power', and argues that it ignores the weakness and suffering of Christ. Csordas (1994: 25) has interpreted Catholic charismatic healing rituals in a similar way: rather than 'embracing suffering and self-mortification as an imitation of Christ's passion', charismatics have participated in a broader, late-twentieth-century shift towards 'the relief of suffering through divine healing as practiced by Jesus in the gospels' (see also Favazza, 1982). None the less, the emotionally intense empowerment of individuals through the Holy Spirit, the much discussed 'tongues of fire' central to many contemporary forms of Pentecostal and charismatic Christianity (Martin, 1990), actually marks the birth of the post-crucifixion and resurrection church (Acts, 2: 1–5). Furthermore, if a key feature of the charismatic movement is its repudiation of the Enlightenment's mind/body dualism (Robeck, 2000), then this arguably finds a warrant in the Pauline New Testament writings.

It is also worth noting that, even in the medieval period, where the mimetic power of Christ's *suffering* body for Christians was especially potent, the hardships, torture and violence that Christians inflicted or had inflicted on their bodies were accompanied by miraculous signs and wonders, as well as an empowerment of individuals that made them immune to pain (Burke, 1983; Hamilton, 1986). Despite differences with earlier Christian models, then, charismatic Christianity also exhibits continuities: the imitation of Christ through 'spiritual body-building' might look highly unorthodox on first glance, but the mimetic power of Christ and the mimetic potentialities of bodies are similarly evident in the asceticism of earlier Christian forms (see Brown, 1988: 442).

In Girard's terms, we might say that specifically *Christian* religious experience only becomes possible through the adoption of Christ as mimetic model in place of the endlessly variable models that characterise human cultures. This extends and adds to the notions of the 'permeable body' and the 'learning body' discussed earlier: bodies always remain permeable with regard to collective forces, in the sense that mimesis is an unavoidable feature of embodied being, but religious life involves the adoption of *particular* mimetic models that reconstitute human experience and action in specific ways. This reconstitution is not simply the gradual accumulation of practical knowledge developed through embodied action and the 'internal conversation', but a more radical reshaping of the embodied *habitus*.

A further implication of the notion of the mimetic body, indeed, is that the attempt to account for religious experience simply with regard to emotional energies of various sorts is inadequate: the desire to imitate a figure such as Jesus Christ, however emotionally intense and rich, is clearly an experiential and practical phenomenon involving cognitive aspects of various sorts, including theological, conceptual and traditional elements as well as the existential challenges and assurances that this sort of religious commitment entails. In short, while the focus on embodment necessarily involves a rejection of the idea that religions can be explained primarily with regard to a cognitive system of abstract beliefs, it is equally unsatisfactory to ignore the important role that cognitive factors play within the embodied experience of religion. Further to this, the notion of the *mindful* body can be a useful supplement to the models considered already.

(5) The Mindful Body

Across Western history, as in contemporary sociological and cultural theory, questions about the changing role of embodied factors in religious life have been dealt with in different ways. The term 'carnal knowing', for example, has been used by Miles (1992) to indicate the intimate links between thinking, sensing and understanding in early medieval Christianity. It expressed the idea that the body was not experienced as something separate from the mind, let alone subordinate to it. This account of what can be called the 'mindful' body was focused on a very specific period of Western history, however, and has since been contrasted with the 'cognitive apprehension' of the Protestant Reformation, where ritual became devalued, the body's emotions and senses were often seen as obstacles to the development of faith, and issues of belief became even more central to the general understanding of what constitutes Christian religious experience (Mellor and Shilling, 1997: 25). In ideal typical terms, the shift from carnal knowing to cognitive apprehension can be taken as a useful indicator of real changes in how Western societies experienced and conceptualised human embodiment, but it is also a massive simplification in that it ignores the complex intertwining of 'carnal' and 'cognitive' factors in all cultures and across all times. In this regard, current debates about the neurobiological aspects of religious experience and practice can be helpful in establishing a more complex understanding of embodied experience.

The sociological engagement with neurobiology is not new, but goes back to Durkheim, who argued that the 'psychic life' or 'spirituality' of the individual is an emergent totality,

rather than a simple aggregation, of the biological and mental components of embodied life (Durkheim, 1974: 34). It has been suggested that Durkheim's arguments are consistent with twenty-first century philosophies of the mind (Sawyer, 2002), but, Norris, in common with a number of other contemporary writers, has drawn upon the work of neurobiologists in a far more detailed way in order to understand the biological processes inherent to religious experience. Damasio (1999: 79–80; 2003: 57–8), for example, is held to illuminate how a combination of the electrochemical messages conveyed via nerve pathways, chemicals conveyed by the blood, and the secretion of certain chemical substances in particular regions of the brain construct a 'body landscape' that is highly responsive to specific forms of 'emotion-triggering', especially when repeated exposure to certain stimuli is able to 'amplify' recollections of earlier chains of events within the brain's sensory processing systems (Norris, 2005: 193–4). On the basis of such work, Norris (2005: 196) argues that, while emotions themselves and the religious 'triggers' for them are culturally specific, the biological processes within the brain that allow bodies to be taught to have religious experiences are common to all humans.

Such arguments help us to understand how it is that repeated exposure to, or immersion within, certain forms of religious practice can trigger experiential states unavailable to the novice, or to someone outside that particular religious tradition. The danger with them, however, is that they can render specifically religious factors relatively insignificant in comparison with neurobiological processes. This is evident in Hammond's (2003) reassessment of Durkheim's notion of social solidarity in the light of developments in evolutionary neurophysiology. He discusses, for example, how religious experiences 'piggyback' upon reward mechanisms emergent from the evolutionary development of humans, stimulating certain types of hormone production, and activating or dampening different types of brain activity (Hammond, 2003: 360). Like Norris, Hammond (2003: 373) claims to offer a 'non-reductive' approach, arguing that 'sociological tradition and modern neurosciences can be fused into a new synthesis', but neurobiological phenomena come to have the determinative role in this analysis of religious experience, rather than seeing them as component features of a more complex phenomenon that includes distinctively social phenomena, the highly variable contents of different forms of religious belief and practice, and the self-reflexivity of individuals. All of these render the reduction of religious feeling to neurobiological arousal and reward mechanisms highly problematic.

Indeed, it should be noted that, while sociologists and other scholars of religion have drawn upon neurobiological studies to make strong claims about the embodied basis of religion, neurobiologists themselves tend to be much more cautious. Thus, Azari et al. (2001: 1649) point out that 'For more than a century, the nature of religious experience has been a topic of considerable scholarship and debate, yet virtually nothing is known about its biological foundations'. Developed on the basis of a detailed empirical study of neuroimaging patterns in the brains of a group of German evangelicals, their own, modest, though significant, conclusion is that cognitive processes play a very important part in religious experience, reinforcing earlier claims in the psychology of religion that the authority and 'force' of religious experience is determined not simply by felt immediacy, but by a causal claim regarding the religious source of the experience. Building upon this study, Azari and Birnbacher (2004) have argued that religious experience is a complex phenomenon embracing cognitive and emotional aspects.

The major problem with non-cognitive theories of religious experience, according to them, is that they fail to explain why some forms of stimuli produce emotional responses while others do not: if human emotions have a non-cognitive core, then certain types of arousal should be automatic, but this is clearly not the case (Azari and Birnbacher, 2004: 904). Cognitive theories, however, which claim that the specificity of emotional experiences is determined solely by a cognitive appraisal of various forms of bodily arousal, ignore the degree to which certain affective dimensions of embodied experience remain resistant to cognitive control (Azari and Birnbacher, 2004: 907). Drawing upon Kutschera's (1990) argument that 'believing in' God is different from 'believing that' God exists, Azari and Birnbacher (2004: 909–10) emphasise that 'religious belief differs from factual belief by its emotional quality', but also stress that the 'belief that' God exists necessarily forms a key component of the 'belief in' Him: this allows them to reject James's (1907) association of religious experience with 'pure' feelings, while also establishing the centrality of emotion to diverse forms of religious experience.

In the light of these arguments, it is clear that religious experiences cannot be located in a particular set of brain functions, or in 'emotion' or 'cognition' exclusively, since they are *emergent* phenomena constituted through the complex interrelations between biological, social and religious phenomena. Further to this, the meanings given to states of bodily arousal by individual subjects are crucial in the shaping of religious experiences (Azari and Birnbacher, 2004: 911). This helps to account for how it is that certain mimetic models, such as Christ, can come to have such a powerful role in reshaping human experience: the highly emotional character of the charismatic engagement with Christ as mimetic model cannot be separated from the cognitive dimensions of embodiment that allow an experience to be meaningful as *Christian* religious experience. It is for this reason that a study of the embodied character of religious experience must be as attentive to the textual, doctrinal, and conceptual aspects of religious life as its practical, ritualistic or performative dimensions.

For Christians of different periods the primary authoritative source for models of how to be religious has, of course, been the Bible. In the light of a theoretical account of embodiment that was doubtful of the significance of cognitive in relation to emotional elements of religion, it might be expected that Biblical authority would be weaker amongst Christians forms with a strong experiential focus, but this is not so. Just as seventeenth and eighteenth-century Pietism, with its strong focus on religious experience, developed out the Lutheran emphasis on *sola scriptura*, and analogous attempts to realise the experiential power of the early church emerged in biblically centred Reformed and Methodist contexts (Enger, 2000), so too contemporary charismatic Christianity is very strongly centred on the Bible. Bruce (2002: 179), for one, has questioned whether this is really as meaningful as it appears to be, arguing that the prioritisation of experience renders doctrinal and scriptural sources open to such diverse interpretations that charismatic Christianity marks a decisive break with the biblical focus of Protestantism, but this argument rests on an unsustainably sharp distinction between cognitive and emotional engagements with the Bible. In the Bible itself, Paul refers to how Christ 'will change our lowly body to be like his glorious body' (Philippians, 3: 21), and charismatics understand the Bible, since it contains the Word of God, to have the power to bring about this transformation. As Coleman (2000: 118) suggests, for these Christians, the words of the Bible and an experience of 'spiritually charged physicality' are not opposed to each other, but are mutually constitutive: the words of the Bible have to be *embodied*, in a 'dramatisation' of the power of the Word to reshape human life and experience (see Peacock, 1984: 108).

Rather than polarising 'minds' and 'bodies', then, the notion of a 'mindful body' draws attention to their interconnectedness: religious experience is a complex, emergent phenomenon wherein both emotion and cognition have important, interconnected roles to play. The permeable, learning and mimetic potentialities of bodies are also key parts of this pattern of emergence, however, since they help us account for how it is that the emotional and cognitive aspects of religious experience are not simply expressions of biological predispositions, but are constituted within, and constitutive of, a particular religious *habitus*. Furthermore, understanding the embodied basis of religious experience in these terms might go some way towards accounting for the question that, as, Beckford (2003: 207) has suggested, has been notable by its absence in the major studies of charismatic Christianity,

namely, how is it that specifically charismatic forms of embodiment 'occur in virtually all of the culturally different regions of the world where charismatic Christianity is practised'? It is to this question that I now turn.

(6) The Global Body

Several writers have claimed charismatic Christianity for 'post-modernity', suggesting that the embodied basis of the religious transformations it manifests directly confronts a modern epistemological focus on the cognitive character of knowledge, and can therefore be seen as part of a broader 'resacralisation' of the contemporary world (e.g. McGuire, 1982). Such claims are not entirely satisfactory, however, not least because many theories of post-modernity tend to perpetuate modern ambiguities about religion and embodiment. Indeed, the 'absence/presence' of both religion and the body continues to be evident in many theories of post-modernity, where a neo-Nietzschean fascination with the 'Death of God', rather than religious practice in the world today, coexists with notions of 'bodies without organs' or 'mutant' hyper-real simulations of the human (see Deleuze, 1977; Baudrillard, 1988; Braidotti, 1994).

The rejection of a 'species-specific' model of globalisation by Urry (2000), in favour of a focus on human/technological 'hybrids' constituted through information flows, manifests the same sort of tendency, in that the dissipation of bodies into global information flows is matched by the marginalisation and virtualisation of religion. Even in studies that take religion and embodiment more seriously, however, there is still a sense that, even if they are not entirely empty categories to be filled by culture, they are essentially reactive to, rather than productive of, cultural changes. In an interesting account of the Toronto Blessing, for example, Lyon (2000: 109–110) associates its experiential theology with the way post-modern culture has encouraged 'fitness' to supersede health in a commodification of bodies that allows them to becomes sites for the dramas of constructing and reconstructing self-identity; in this respect, the extravagant emotionality and physicality of charismatic worship is part of a broader reconstruction of the body as a cultural artifact.

Such arguments clearly have merits, in the sense that the charismatic focus on the body may indeed have features in common with broader contemporary cultural engagements with embodiment, but the danger is that bodies, and religion, lose any substantive reality of their own and become defined largely through the degree to which they fit, or can be made to fit, into broader categories developed by social and cultural theorists. This is relevant not only to the notion of 'post-modernity', or in Meštrović's (1997) case, 'postemotional society', but to that of 'modernity' too. Beckford (2003: 189), for example, has argued that charismatic Christianity is actually 'resolutely modern' in its serious-mindedness, its assertion of absolute truth, and, in particular, its implicit instrumental rationality, but, again, this looks problematic. All three of these characteristics are to be found in various 'non-modern' contexts: for example, the medieval exploration of the religious potentialities of the body through the imitation of the suffering of Christ was, arguably, as thoroughly instrumentalised as the body techniques employed by contemporary charismatics.

For the focus on the cultural shaping of bodies to be genuinely illuminating it must be contextualised within an attention to the fact that it is a common human species that populates different cultural contexts. Where the analytical import of this fact is denied (e.g. Proudfoot, 1985), we can have no basis upon which to analyse the various commonalities, as well as the differences, that mark particular cultural engagements with bodies, nor can we assess the relative fruitfulness of these diverse engagements. Here, it is not simply a question of acknowledging various 'basic emotions' that appear to have a trans-cultural character (Lindholm, 2004), but also of attempting to make sense of the cognitive and mimetic dimensions of embodiment that allow religious models, theologies and concepts, along with specific body techniques, to constitute highly specific forms of religious experience.

In this context, the charismatic engagement with the Bible is particularly notable, not least because it directs our attention to the productive, rather than reactive, dimensions of embodied religious experience in relation to existing cultural forms.

Noll's (2001: 87) study of evangelical Christianity treats Pentecostal and charismatic forms as parts of the broader evangelical movement, which he defines as 'culturally adaptive biblical experientialism' (see also Lehmann, 1996). Not only is the Bible the source of the authoritative models that shape Christian life, and that have to be engaged with experientially to the degree that the individual is 'born-again' (Noll, 2001: 2), but it also facilitates the emergence of a Christian *habitus* that can be thoroughly immersed in and yet transcendent of particular cultures. In other words, the fact that this Biblical experientialism is 'culturally adaptive' does not signal an uncritical assimilation to broader cultural patterns. Indeed, as Noll (2001: 269) suggests, in terms of its general attitude towards prevailing cultural norms, the 'history of modern evangelicalism could be written as a chronicle of calculated offense'. For Noll, rather, its adaptive qualities have an instrumental character, signalling its readiness to use all available means, such as satellite technology, to spread its biblical experientialism. For Cox (1995: 147), on the other hand, its adaptive characteristics are far more substantial, containing a 'phenomenal power to embrace and transform anything it meets in the cultures to which it travels' (see also Coleman, 2000: 68).

Contrary perspectives, which emphasise the culturally *reactive* character of religious phenomena, remain influential. For Castells (1998: 382–6), for example, 'culturally adaptive Biblical experimentalism' amounts to little more than the emergence of 'resistance identities' that take up the Bible as 'a banner of despair' in the face of uncontrollable global changes, expressing an ultimately futile attempt to 'opt out' of global society. Two things can be noted, however. First, there appears to be little 'despair' amongst these charismatic Christians: their experiential focus is manifest in feelings of joy, empowerment and personal transformation (Percy, 1996). Second, they are hardly 'opting out' of globalisation; they exhibit a particularly powerful manifestation of how a religious movement can constitute itself as a global phenomenon (Poewe, 1994). Here, more complex models of globalisation, which exhibit a greater sensitivity to its creative possibilities for religions, are of much more value.

Robertson (1992) and Beyer (1994, 2003), for example, have analysed globalisation as a phenomenon that transcends the logic of either 'modernity' or 'post-modernity', focusing instead on the diverse patterns of universality and particularity manifest in forms of 'glocalisation'. Here, the nature of religion in the contemporary world cannot be accounted for with regard to either universal, hegemonic cultural models and institutional structures, or to the endlessly diverse patterns of pluralism valorised in much post-modern theorising: on the contrary, as Beyer (2003: 361) suggests, the global success of religious forms such as Pentecostal and charismatic forms of Christianity is expressive of the way in which globalisation now facilitates the 'multiple particularisation' of universal religious practices, texts, models, and structures. Neither Robertson nor Beyer has explicitly addressed the significance of the body in relation to globalisation processes: Coleman (2000: 51), in fact, has criticised Robertson for having an overly cognitive focus that ignores the broader embodied dimensions of globalisation. None the less, the notion of 'glocalisation' seems particularly pertinent to the subject of embodiment, since bodies are universal in the sense that all humans have them, yet they are inevitably 'particularised' not only in that they are individual, but also in terms of the fact that embodied experience is shaped within a specific *habitus*.

The idea that we now live in a world where the global and the local are simultaneously constitutive of each other can, therefore, offer a potentially fruitful way of extending existing models of embodiment in sociology, particularly in terms of accounting for the cross-cultural success of forms such as charismatic Christianity, which are highly flexible in terms

of their interaction with particular cultures, yet are also expressive of an engagement with universal embodied potentialities that is able to generate common religious experiences. It is in this sense that Poewe (1994: 249) has identified charismatic Christianity as an inherently global phenomenon precisely because it is 'iconic'; that is, this form of religion engages with, and is able to shape actively, common embodied characteristics (see also Coleman, 2000: 68). Thus, rather than simply reacting to, let alone 'resisting', globalisation processes, charismatic Christianity is representative of the potentially productive and creative ways in which religions can engage not only with social and cultural processes, but with the inherent properties of bodies: it is the fruitful combination of these two patterns of engagement which accounts for the global spread of the same charismatic experience of the body.

CONCLUSION

Charismatic Christianity clearly has a specific character, as do the globalising processes characteristic of the contemporary world, but reflection upon the embodied bases of their interrelationships can help illuminate broader problems concerning the complex connections between religion, culture and the body. The immense importance of emotional factors is of particular note here, not only with regard to the 'permeability' of individuals in terms of patterns of 'sacred contagion', but also in relation to the cultivation of certain emotional experiences through specific body techniques. These, along with the mimetic models that shape patterns of religious identification, and the mutually reinforcing role of cognition and emotion in religious experience, point to the centrality of embodied issues in the constitution of religious belief, practice and experience, and the complexity of their relationships with other social and cultural phenomena.

Further to this, a key feature of the focus on religion as an embodied phenomenon is that, in its best forms, it resists the logic of social or cultural constructionism, and not only moves beyond the peculiarly 'absent/present' body of certain forms of social and cultural theory, but also rescues religion from a similar state. The suggestion that charismatic Christianity manifests a type of 'resistance identity' is merely one example of a broader theoretical tendency to identify religion as something of only secondary significance in relation to other social or cultural phenomena. In contrast, analysing religion as a phenomenon that can engage with common human potentialities, and thereby embrace and transform all sorts of existing cultural forms, enables us to identify an embodied basis for religious creativity and its relative independence with regard to the large-scale social and cultural transformations that habitually preoccupy sociologists.

Despite recognising the common human potentialities and properties of bodies, however, a further key feature of this embodied focus is that it helps account for the ways in which very *particular*, often very different, religious experiences and identities are able to emerge. The fact that some of these can have a global character, and that all of them can be understood as engaging with common human features, does not justify ignoring their differences. The models of embodiment outlined in this chapter offer a basis for accounting for these differences as well as for common features, and, therefore, in broader terms, point towards the immense value of focusing upon the nature and consequences of human embodiment for the sociological analysis of religion.

REFERENCES

Archer, M. S. 1995. *Realist Social Theory*. Cambridge: Cambridge University Press.

Archer, M.S. 2000. *Being Human*. Cambridge: Cambridge University Press.

Asad, T. 1983. 'Notes on body pain and truth in medieval Christian ritual', *Economy and Society* 12 (3): 287–327.

Asad, T. 1988. 'On ritual and discipline in medieval Christian monasticism', *Economy and Society* 16 (2): 159–203.

Asad, T. 1993. *Genealogies of Religion*. Baltimore: John Hopkins University Press.

Azari, N. P. *et al.* 2001. 'Short Communication: Neural correlates of religious experience', *European Journal of Neuroscience* 13: 1649–52.

Azari, N. P. and D. Birnbacher 2004. 'The role of cognition and feeling in religious experience', *Zygon* 39 (4): 901–17.

Barbalet, J. 2004. 'William James: Pragmatism, Social Psychology and Emotions', *European Journal of Social Theory* 7 (3): 337–53.

Barbalet, J. 2005. 'Smith's *Sentiments* and Wright's *Passions* (1601): the beginnings of sociology', *British Journal of Sociology* 56 (2): 171–89.

Baudrillard, J. 1988. *The Ecstasy of Communication*. New York: Semiotext(e).

Beckford, J. A. 2003. *Social Theory and Religion*. Cambridge: Cambridge University Press.

Bell, C. 1992. *Ritual Theory, Ritual Practice*. Oxford: Oxford University Press.

Beyer, P. 1994. *Religion and Globalisation*. London: Sage.

Beyer, P. 2003. 'De-centring Religious Singularity: The Globalisation of Christianity as a Case in Point', *Numen* 50 (4): 357–86.

Bourdieu, P. 1977. *Outline of a Theory of Practice*. Cambridge: Cambridge University Press.

Bourdieu, P. 1984. *Distinction*. London: Routledge.

Braidotti, R. 1994. *Nomadic Subjects*. New York: Columbia.

Brown, P. 1988. *The Body and Society*. London: Faber.

Bruce, S. 2002. *God is Dead*. Oxford: Blackwell.

Burke, P. 1983. *Popular Culture in Early Modern Europe*. London: Temple Smith.

Butler, J. 1993. *Bodies That Matter*. London: Routledge.

Bynum, C. W. 1987. *Holy Feast and Holy Fast*. Berkeley: University of California Press.

Bynum, C. W. 1991. *Fragmentation and Redemption*. New York: Zone.

Castells, M. 1998. *End of Millennium*. Oxford: Blackwell.

Classen, C. 1993. *Worlds of Sense*. London: Routledge.

Claussen, D. S. (ed.) 1999. *The Promise Keepers: Essays in masculinity and Christianity*. Jefferson, NC: McFarland.

Coleman, S. 2000. *The Globalisation of Charismatic Christianity*. Cambridge: Cambridge University Press.

Cox, H. 1995. *Fire From Heaven*. Reading, MA Addison-Wesley.

Crossley, N. 1994. *The Politics of Subjectivity*. Aldershot: Avebury.

Crossley, N. 1995. 'Merleau-Ponty, the elusive body and carnal sociology', *Body and Society* 1 (1): 43–63.

Csordas, T. J. 1994. *The Sacred Self*. Berkeley, CA: University of California Press.

Czikszentmihalyi, M. 1975. *Beyond Boredom and Anxiety*. San Francisco: Jossey-Bass.

Damasio, A. 1999. *The Feeling of What Happens*. New York: Harcourt.

Damasio, A. 2003. *Looking for Spinoza*. New York: Harcourt.

Davies, D. 1984. 'The charismatic ethic and post-industrialism'. In Martin, D. and Mullen, P. (eds) *Strange Gifts? A Guide to Charismatic Renewal*. Oxford: Blackwell.

Davies, S. 1995. *Jesus the Healer: Possession, Trance, and the Origins of Christianity*. New York: Continuum Press.

Deleuze, G. 1977. *Nietzsche et la philosophie*. Paris: Presses Universitaires de France.

Durkheim, E. 1974. 'Individual and Collective Representations', in *Sociology and Philosophy*. New York: Free Press.

Durkheim, E. 1995. *The Elementary Forms of Religious Life*. New York: Free Press.

Elias, N. 1987. 'The changing balance of power between the sexes – a process-sociological study: the example of the ancient Roman state', *Theory, Culture and Society* 4: 287–316.

Elias, N. 1991. *Symbol Emancipation*. London: Sage.

Enger, T. 2000. 'Pietism'. In Hastings, A., Mason, A. and Pyper, H. (eds) *The Oxford Companion to Christian Thought*. Oxford: Oxford University Press.

Favazza, A. 1982. 'Modern Christian Healing of Mental Illness', *American Journal of Psychiatry* 139: 728–735.

Featherstone, M. 1991. *Consumer Culture and Postmodernism*. London: Sage.

Foucault, M. 1977. *Language, Counter-Memory, Practice*. Oxford: Blackwell.

Giddens, A. 1984. *The Constitution of Society*. Cambridge: Polity.

Girard, R. 1977. *Violence and the Sacred*. Baltimore: Johns Hopkins University Press.

Girard, R. 1987. *Things Hidden Since the Foundation of the World*. London: Continuum.

Girard, R. 2001. *I See Satan Fall Like Lightning*. New York: Orbis.

Grosz, E. 1994. *Virtual Bodies*, London: Routledge.

Gumbel, N. 2002. *Questions of Life*. Eastbourne: Kingsway.

Hall, D. (ed.) 1994. *Muscular Christianity: Embodying the Victorian Age*. Cambridge: Cambridge University Press.

Hamilton, B. 1986. *Religion in the Medieval West*. London: Edwin Arnold.

Hammond, M. 2003. 'The Enhancement Imperative: The Evolutionary Neurophysiology of Durkheimian Solidarity', *Sociological Theory* 21 (4): 359–74.

Haraway, D. 1991. *Simians, Cyborgs and Women*. London: Free Association Books.

Harré, R. 1989. 'Perfections and Imperfections of Form: Cults of the Body and their Aesthetic Underpinnings', *International Journal of Moral and Social Studies*, 4: 183-94.

Hays, R. B. 2001. 'Why Do You Stand Looking Up Toward Heaven? New Testament Eschatology at the Turn of the Millenium'. In Buckley, J. and Gregory Jones, L. (eds) *Theology and Eschatology*. Oxford: Blackwell.

Hertz, R. 1973. 'The Pre-eminence of the Right Hand: A Study in Religious Polarity'. In Needham, R. (ed.) *Right and Left*. Chicago: University of Chicago Press.

Hervieu-Léger, D. 1993. 'Present-Day Emotional Renewals: The End of Secularisation or the End of Religion?'. In Swatos, W. H. (ed.) *A Future for Religion*. London: Sage.

Higgs, R. 1995. *God in the Stadium: Sports and Religion in America*. Lexington: University of Kentucky.

Howes, D. 1991. *The Varieties of Sensory Experience*. Toronto: University of Toronto Press.

Hunt, S. 2001. *Anyone for Alpha?* London: Darton, Longman and Todd.

James, W. 1897. *The Will to Believe and Other Essays in Popular Psychology*, New York: Longmans, Green and Co.

James, W. 1907. *The Varieties of Religious Experience*, New York: Longmans, Green and Co.

Janssen, J. and Verheggen, T. 1997. 'The double centre of gravity in Durkheim's symbol theory: bringing the symbolism of the body back in', *Sociological Theory* 15 (3): 294–306.

Jenkins, P. 2002. *The Next Christendom*. Oxford: Oxford University Press.

Jewett, R. 2003. 'Romans'. In Dunn, J. D. G. (ed.) *The Cambridge Companion to St Paul*. Cambridge: Cambridge University Press.

Kutschera, F. 1990. *Verunft und Glaube*. Berlin: Gruyter.

Ladd, T. and Mathisen, J. A. 2002. *Muscular Christianity: Evangelical Protestants and the Development of American Sports*. Grand Rapids, MI: Baker Books.

Leder, D. 1990. *The Absent Body*. Chicago: University of Chicago Press.

Lehmann, D. 1996. *Struggle for the Spirit*. Cambridge: Polity.

Levin, D. M. 1985. *The Body's Recollection of Being*. London: Routledge.

Lindholm, C. 1990. *Charisma*. Oxford: Blackwell.

Lindholm, C. 2004. 'Creating an Anthropology of Emotion'. In Casey, C. and Edgerton, R. (eds) *A Companion to Psychological Anthropology*. Oxford: Blackwell.

Longenecker, B. 2003. 'Galatians'. In Dunn, J. D. G. (ed.) *The Cambridge Companion to St Paul*. Cambridge: Cambridge University Press.

Lukes, S. 1974. *Emile Durkheim*. Harmondsworth: Penguin.

Lyon, D. 2000. *Jesus in Disneyland*. Cambridge: Polity.

McGuire, M. B. 1982. *Pentecostal Catholics*. Philadelphia: Temple University Press.

McGuire, M. B. 1990. 'Religion and the Body: Rematerializing the human body in the social sciences of religion', *Journal for the Scientific Study of Religion* 29 (3): 283–96.

Maffesoli, M. 1996. *The Time of the Tribes*. London: Sage.

Martin, D. 1990. *Tongues of Fire*. Oxford: Blackwell.

Mauss, M. 1950a. 'Une catégorie de l'esprit humain: La notion de la personne, celle du "moi"', *Sociologie et Anthropologie*. Paris: Presses Univeraires de France.

Mauss, M. 1950b. 'Les techniques du corps', *Sociologie et Anthropologie*. Paris: Presses Univeraires de France.

Mauss, M. 2003. *On Prayer*. Oxford: Berghahn Books.

Mellor, P. A. 1998. 'Sacred Contagion and Social Vitality: Collective Effervescence in *Les formes élémentaires de la vie religieuse*', *Durkheimian Studies*, 4: 87–114.

Mellor, P. A. 2004. *Religion, Realism and Social Theory*. London: Sage.

Mellor, P. A. and Shilling, C. 1997. *Re-forming the Body*. London: Sage.

Merleau-Ponty, M. 1962. *The Phenomenology of Perception*. London: Routledge and Kegan Paul.

Merleau-Ponty, M. 1974. *Phenomenology, Language and Society*. London: Heinemann.

Meštrović, S. G. 1997. *Postemotional Society*. London: Sage.

Miles, M. 1992. *Carnal Knowing*. Tunbridge Wells: Burns and Oates.

Neitz, M. J. 1987. *Charisma and Community*. New Brunswick: Transaction.

Neitz, M. J. and J. V. Spickard 1990. 'Steps Toward a Sociology of Experience', *Sociological Analysis* 51: 15–33.

Noll, M. 2001. *American Evangelical Christianity*. Oxford: Blackwell.

Norris, R. S. 2005. 'Examining the structure and role of emotion: Contributions of neurobiology to the study of embodied religious experience', *Zygon* 40 (1): 181–99.

Peacock, J. 1984. 'Religion and Life History: An Exploration in Psychology'. In Brunner, E. (ed.) *Text, Play and Story*. Prospect Heights: Waveland.

Percy, M. 1996. *Words, Wonder and Power*. London: SPCK.

Poewe, K. 1994. *Charismatic Christianity as a Global Culture*. Columbia: University of South Carolina Press.

Poloma, M. 1989. *The Assemblies of God at the Crossroads*. Knoxville: University of Tennessee Press.

Proudfoot, W. 1985. *Religious Experience*. Berkeley: University of California Press.

Rawls, A. W. 2001. 'Durkheim's Treatment of Practice', *Journal of Classical Sociology* 1 (1): 33–68.

Robeck, C. M. 2000. 'Pentecostalism'. In Hastings, A., Mason, A. and Pyper, H. (eds) *The Oxford Companion to Christian Thought*. Oxford: Oxford University Press.

Robertson, R. 1992. *Globalisation*. London: Sage.

Sack, D. 2000. *Whitebread Protestants: Food and Religion in American Culture*. New York: St. Martin's Press/Palgrave.

Sawyer, R. K. 2002. 'Durkheim's Dilemma: Toward a Sociology of Emergence', *Sociological Theory* 20 (2): 227–47.

Schröder, C. 2000. 'Edwards, Jonathan'. In Hastings, A., Mason, A. and Pyper, H. (eds) *The Oxford Companion to Christian Thought*. Oxford: Oxford University Press.

Shilling, C. 1993. *The Body and Social Theory*. London: Sage.

Shilling, C. 2005. *The Body in Culture, Technology and Society*. London: Sage.

Shilling, C. and Mellor, P. A. 2001. *The Sociological Ambition*. London: Sage.

Spickard, J. V. 1993. 'For a Sociology of Religious Experience'. In Swatos, W. H. (ed.) *A Future for Religion*. London: Sage.

Turner, B. S. 1984. *The Body and Society*. London: Sage.

Turner, B. S. 1991. *Religion and Social Theory*. London: Sage.

Urry, J. 2000. *Sociology Beyond Societies*. London: Routledge.

Watling, T. 2005. '"Experiencing" *Alpha*: Finding and Embodying the Spirit and Being Transformed – Empowerment and Control in a ("Charismatic") Christian Worldview', *Journal of Contemporary Religion* 20 (1): 91–108.

Weber, M. 1968. *Economy and Society*. London: University of California Press.

Weber, M. 1991. *The Protestant Ethic and the Spirit of Capitalism*. London: Harper Collins.

Williams, S. J. and Bendelow, G. 1998. 'Introduction'. In Bendelow, G. and S. J. Williams, (eds) *Emotions in Social Life*. London: Routledge.

Wilson, B. R. 1988. 'The functions of religion: a re-appraisal', *Religion* 18: 199–216.

Yamane, D. 2000. 'Narrative and Religious Experience', *Sociology of Religion* 61 (2): 171–89.

29

Religion as a Factor in Life and Death through the Life-Course

STEPHEN J. HUNT

This chapter is concerned with one of the more intricate dimensions of contemporary religion: its significance throughout the life-course. Levels of religiosity and spirituality, as numerous sociological studies have shown, vary considerably for individuals throughout their lives. While this is an observation that can be made of many previous societies and those of today that are frequently described as less 'developed', variation is complicated by the fact that in the secular West religion is not a compulsory aspect of social experience. Rather, it is increasingly rendered a matter of personal choice and not infrequently void of rigorous community pressures of religious socialization. People are thus free to choose for themselves a religious faith or none at all and, if they do so, to apply it at various times in the life-course according to personal needs and circumstances.

If the matter of choice in matters of religious faith renders an overview of the subject in relation to the life-course a challenging prospect, the sociological enquiry is further compounded by other cross-cutting factors which will inform the discussion of this chapter. Perhaps the most obvious is the changing nature of the life-course itself. One repercussion is that the complexity of social experience

has led to the abandonment of the notion of the 'life cycle' which suggests a fair amount of predictability related to features of social life including the significance of religion. Today, this predictive element, for various reasons, is more and more elusive. Contemporary societies are extraordinarily complex in terms of social organization. Moreover, economic, cultural and technological changes continue apace and undermine taken-for-granted assumptions regarding the so-called 'stages' of life and matters of religiosity. While such transformations are increasingly significant, religion in the life-course is rendered even more multifaceted by more familiar sociological concerns, namely, the continuing relevance of social status, ethnicity, gender, cohort differences, and regional variation. All such variables will be integrated in the survey below with reference to recent sociological research and theoretical speculations.

FROM LIFE-CYCLE TO THE LIFE-COURSE

Throughout the social sciences the once popular 'life-cycle' approach largely took as its premise the notion that the life-span displayed a particular character and followed a basic and predictable sequence. Put succinctly, the life-cycle referred to ways of examining the duration of human existence in the societal context, taken as a whole, in terms of a succession of phases related to maturation, physiological change and the correlated alterations of self-image and transforming social roles which they engendered. Elaborate models, such as that of Erikson (1951), integrated physical, social, and psychological variables but at the same time allowed for considerable cultural variation. These models proved to be highly influential not only for anthropological scholarship but in relevant sociological specialisms of a comparative nature. Many of these relevant works identified similar 'stages' of societal development and their pertinence in terms of religious rites and practice found in pre-industrial and small scale societies.

For several decades the legitimacy of the life-cycle framework in anthropological accounts impressively enhanced cross-cultural studies in the area of religious belief and performance. Such an approach also influenced academic appraisals of the life-cycle in contemporary Western societies, but with important modifications which often highlighted the repercussions for aspects of religiosity. Historians and sociologists alike recognized that the advent of modernity brought a more complex life-cycle, providing a fresh meaning to some stages of life such as childhood (cf. Ariès 1965), while laying down new ones including adolescence and youth (cf. Eisenstadt 1956). The demographic changes of the nineteenth century brought a gradual differentiation in age groups and allowed a greater specialization in age-related functions, although they were by no means complete by the end of that century. The principal source of this transformation was the onset of the industrial-capitalist order and its diffused Protestant ethic which encouraged the growth of bureaucracies identified not only by, as Max Weber (1978) explored at length, certain 'internal' arrangements such as a pervading rationalism, hierarchy and a division of labour, but regularized control of social relations of time and space. These social changes implemented a regularity and regimentation that was most evident in production and organization – enhancing secularizing processes and reducing aspects of religiosity to the private sphere.

A coherent and predictable life-cycle, as a structured round of human experience, reached its greatest density in the mid-twentieth century. This increasingly inflexible 'modern' life-cycle encouraged fresh theoretical frameworks, including perhaps most famously that developed by Levinson et al. (1978), which furnished finely tuned models outlining the complex stages of life in Western industrial societies. Yet, while notions of 'modernity' permeated sociological writings for generations as a coherent and unchanging typology, it proved to be unsustainable across the broad discipline by the end of the twentieth century. Subsequently, throughout the sociological mainstream, the concept of the life-cycle has largely been rendered superfluous, while that of the 'life-course' is currently increasingly employed as a descriptive and analytical tool. The rapidly changing nature of contemporary society, alongside insights provided by comparative surveys which emphasize variety rather than commonality, continuingly reduced the significance of the life-cycle as a working paradigm. Similarly, the recognition of the life-cycle approach as constituting an inherent part of medical ideology and the cultural legacy of post-colonial anthropology added to its demise in the sociological vocabulary including the sub-discipline of the Sociology of Religion. While the life-cycle paradigm has fallen into disuse, there are currently various and sometimes contrasting ways by which sociology has engaged the subject of the life-course and the relevance of religiosity in what is increasingly designated 'late' or 'post-modernity'.

LATE/POST-MODERNITY AND THE LIFE-COURSE

Anthony Giddens uses a variety of terms such as 'late', 'high', or 'reflexive modernity' in describing the emerging social condition. In doing so, he discusses socio-cultural developments which suggest an outgrowth of those features that forged modernity, particularly reflexive identity and self, consumption, and the culture of choice, all of which have implications for the life-course. According to Giddens, conceptions of the life-course now allow for the anticipation of risks and future possibilities. Here there is an underlying denial of fate that comes with a rational mode of cognition. Nothing is inevitable; there are no 'divine scripts'. Every aspect of human life is potentially improvable and can be rendered more effective. Reflexivity, as a core element of cultural ordering, impacts selfhood in that it entails the constant monitoring of the individual's life in order to enhance human wellbeing.

According to Giddens, in the emerging social environment individuals are increasingly willing to change their beliefs, practices, and locus of belonging in the light of new experience and knowledge. This would seem to run against the embrace of a traditional, static and inherited supernatural belief system at the heart of cultural expressions and by way of structuring aspects of religiosity throughout the life-course. Indeed, in *The Consequences of Modernity* (1990), Giddens suggests that religion struggles to retain its influence since, in the context of late-modernity, aspects of social life are manifestly incompatible with religious faith as a pervasive influence upon day-to-day existence. However, in *Modernity and Self-Identity* (1991), Giddens contends that late-modernity may nevertheless provide the condition for the resurgence of religiosity. The individual sense of self is, in fact, conducive to a fairly widespread concern for spirituality throughout the life-course. While tradition and predictability decline, rational reflexivity means that individuals may undertake more conscious and informed choices throughout the duration of the life span concerning who they are and what they wish to become. In an age of uncertainty religion, especially in its more conservative forms which cogently addresses issues of self, may therefore thrive in such an environment. Furthermore, what Giddens calls 'existential questions' tend to be

separated from everyday life in late-modernity. The sequestration of experience means that, for many people, direct contact with events and situations which link the individual's life-course to broad issues of morality and finitude are rare and fleeting. Personal meaningless may thus encourage a search for a faith which brings a sense of fulfillment.

The notion of post-modernity undoubtedly implies a somewhat different view of social change and its implication for the life-course compared to that of 'modernity' or 'late-modernity'. Nonetheless, there is little agreement among theorists concerning the meaning of post-modernity. Hence, rather different approaches, or at least emphasis, may be observed in current theorizing especially in relation to dimensions of religiosity throughout the life-course. Bauman (1992), for example, in his analysis of the contemporary condition, identifies a collapse of meta-narratives including both singular religious and rationalized worldviews. The consequence is a 'crisis' of meaning for socially atomized individuals who may increasingly search for the ultimate significance that only religion can satisfactorily answer. If such a crisis cannot be addressed within the context of traditional religion that passes from one generation to the next and enduring across the life-course, then it will be addressed by forms of quasi-religions or new expressions of religion which display a strong moral content.

Paul Heelas argues in a similar vein. For Heelas, post-modernity brings a measure of de-traditionalization – a demise of the pressures of socialization and social structures such as the family – ushers in a utilitarian selfhood. This is evident in contemporary forms of religiosity such as the New Age movement and 'self-religions' which dismiss the grounds upon which historical religions were one based (Heelas 1996). The construction of the self has thus become *the* project of a culture of post-modernity. Hence, traditional forms of religion give way to those congruent with contemporary culture, above all, that of all-pervading consumerism and choice. Indeed, it is the consumerist culture which is particularly conducive to the growth of innovating new religions which often constitute a mix 'n' match religiosity. If such theorizing is correct, then individuals plausibly construct forms of religiosity congruent with their experiences throughout the life-course.

While conceptualizations of late- or post-modernity compete for legitimacy, and rival theoretical underpinnings are discernible, there remains considerable overlap between these perspectives. Perhaps, above all, there is a general and shared recognition that individuals do not pass through such clearly demarcated stages of life as in previous social orders whether designated 'traditional' or 'modern'. For instance, it is now an arduous task to stipulate where childhood ends and adolescence begins and whether associated age norms, including religious norms, where they exist, still hold, although it is apparent that to one degree or another some cultural expectations remain. What is abundantly lacking is a structural rigidity which, in turn, undermines generalized statements regarding levels and expressions of religiosity through what is arguable now best described as loosely structured and diverse 'phases of life'.

To be sure, not all of the recent scholarly works have entirely abandoned concerns traditionally associated with a life-cycle paradigm. The various 'stages' of life are still frequently viewed as continuingly providing an area of interest in shaping aspects of religiosity and thus habitually inform a good deal of recent sociological literature whatever theoretical approach endorsed. Nonetheless, the interest in dimensions of faith during the various stages-of-life have been supplemented by a growing awareness of the implications of variety, plurality, fragmentation, discontinuity, and life-style choice in encouraging differing levels of religiosity. Indeed, the complexities and sometimes the contradictions of the life-course, in Western societies at least, have ushered in a fresh and burgeoning interest in the implications of religious expression by way of belief, belonging, and practice.

RITES OF PASSAGE

One aspect of the Western life-course seemingly facing demise in late/post-modernity is the universal phenomenon of rites of passage which are now reduced to mostly optional, rather than compulsory aspects of social experience. Previously, such rites were a primary aspect of a structured life-cycle and helped establish collective identity and moral integration. In pre-modern cultures such ceremonial rituals were essentially related to simple forms of social differentiation and dimensions of religious socialization – over time as well as spatially. Without a doubt a core theme of anthropological studies of religion in these societies largely related to those rituals designating the transition of one clearly demarcated stage of life to another, whether biologically defined such as birth, puberty, pregnancy and death, or those socially constructed with marriage perhaps constituting the foremost instance. Compared to contemporary societies, pre-industrial communities displayed a less complex and relatively undifferentiated 'cycle-of-life' and typically involved merely a transition from pre-adult to adult stages. Such transitions marked a simple distinction that was largely unchanging over the generations and where rites of passage constituted community imposed expressions of religiosity in the individual's experience of the life-span.

These transitions of life proved open to differing interpretations that stressed both social and psychological dimensions. The Structural Functionalism of Radcliffe-Browne (1952) focused on 'ritual prohibition' concerning objects, places, and people that were to be avoided and subject to taboo and social boundaries. In this context, rituals emphasized collective values and enhanced a sense of community belonging typified by rites surrounding marriage since the institution brought a degree of social continuity. Other works, exemplified by that of Van Gennep (1908), indicated how rites of passage often related to interpretations of biological changes and their social implications, as well as psychological adaptation to culturally constructed institutions. It followed that religious meaning and taboo status were, more often than not, attached to these transitions especially when they were associated with what amounted to 'life crises'. Such 'crises' were precipitated by a significant individual and collective sense of uncertainty that resulted from experiences such as pregnancy and childbirth – events which required psychological and social adjustment.

In the past, as in numerous less developed societies today, rites of passage were often tied to one of the most important forms of social stratification; age-sets and related categories. Unlike Western societies, social structures and culture in pre-industrial societies were usually static or underwent transformation very gradually. The generations that passed through the age categories were invariably subject to similar social processes. This is far less the case in the contemporary West where life experiences are extraordinarily diverse and where the notion of age cohort is seemingly more relevant and denotes those born in a distinct historical period. It is the historical timing of an age cohort which frequently forges very different experiences when compared to past or later generations. Such a contrast serves to highlight the fact that pre-industrial societies were built upon a high degree of predictability despite the precariousness of material human existence. In short, social members anticipated with assurance which age-sets they would belong to in the years to come and what this entailed by way of expected modes of age-related norms.

In contemporary sociological theorizing there is a growing inclination to play down the significance of age categories. The meaning of being 'young', 'middle-aged', or 'retired' is perceived in many scholarly accounts as open to interpretation and negotiation, by way of identity construction, throughout an increasingly varied life-course. Furthermore, shifting age categories and lengthening life expectancy means that they are no longer clearly defined 'stages' of life with accompanying modes of behaviour. Rather, such stages are now increasingly the subject of negotiation as to how they are experienced and lived out in terms of life-styles options. These developments invariably prove important given the fact that the various stages of life were once commonly associated with fairly distinct and non-divergent religious values and beliefs. Today it is ever

more arduous to forge generalizations regarding age categories and broad religious orientations. This is not to suggest they are entirely obsolete since empirical studies continue to establish a link between religiosity and age, and such a relationship forms much of the discussion below. Nonetheless, it is the larger picture which must be appraised, one where religious socialization is of decreasing importance and where a culture of choice has become recognized as a cultural development which cuts across generational boundaries.

Certain developments identified with the onset of modernity had previously eaten away at one essential dimension of religiosity: the significance of rites of passage. This is evident in Bryan Wilson's elucidation of the theme of secularization which contended that religion would invariably decline with an underpinning rational-orientation of social life on the one hand, and a reduction in common values and the breakdown of collectivities that upheld shared religious conviction on the other (Wilson 1976). This decline of community in modern industrial society resulted from high levels of social and geographical mobility and consequent changes in the nature of social control. It followed that the authoritative moral and religious foundation of well-integrated communities could no longer be upheld and was evident in the demise of the rites of passage. Hence, the decline of rituals related to the essential 'turning points' of life, alongside church attendance and other forms of religious observance, provided the evidence of ongoing and relentless secularization. Paradoxically, then, the same modernity which increased the number of 'stages' of life, also stripped them of rites of passage. Rationalism and science secured many of the 'crisis' of human existence: childbirth lost most of its dangers and the survival of the immediate post-natal years became more predictable as the environment was increasingly mastered. In turn, the majority of the population of Western societies could look forward to fulfilling an ever-extending life-span. Hence, in the context of modernity many of the social and psychological underpinnings to the rites of passage were eroded, not least of all the uncertainty and unpredictability of everyday life.

The reduction in the appeal of such rites and ceremonies among the populations of North American and Western Europe is evident by various indices. England is a good example (given its level of secularity between the evidently more 'religious' USA and the highly secularized Scandinavian countries). In England, in 1880, practically all newborns were baptized (albeit after an appreciable length of time after which their survival was anticipated as likely). During the mid-1970s there were 428 baptisms per 1000 live births compared to 554 in 1960. The basis on which infant baptism statistics were calculated altered in England after 1979 but the decline continued. In the Anglican Church, from 1885 to 1950, the number of baptisms fluctuated between 60 and 67 per cent. In 1922, this figure declined to 53 per cent of the population and by 1993 to a mere 27 per cent. At the same time, there has been a discernible reduction in the number of marriages conducted in the Anglican Church. In 1929, 56 per cent of marriages in England and Wales were performed in the church setting compared with 37 per cent in 1979. Thereafter, there was a further reduction in church weddings to 31 per cent in the year 2000.

Arguably the steady demise of such religious ceremonies is because, for various reasons, the great 'milestones' of life are of decreasing significance. The fall of the infant mortality rate may mean that parents and close kin are less inclined to give a specifically religious significance to the arrival of newborns. Simultaneously, a number of social institutions, such as marriage, are decreasingly subject to social pressure and reduced to a matter of preference. Also true is that the continuingly relative popularity of the social institution of marriage indicates levels of secularity since it is frequently emptied of religious relevance evident through the church wedding rite. Indicative of this is the List of Approved Premises, produced by the Office for National Statistics in Britain, which encompasses a register of legitimate non-religious sites for weddings other than places of worship. They include zoos, soccer grounds, museums, golf clubs and restaurants.

Divorce statistics also indicate that marriage is not necessarily a life-long commitment.

It is no longer perceived as 'made in heaven' and witnessed in the sight of God. Similarly, marriage annulment may reflect an increasing secularity and provides a symbol of growing rationality and individualism (Gibson 1994). Just as individuals rationally choose to enter into marriage and select a partner in instrumental terms, divorce may be equally pragmatically decided upon. This is reflected too in divorce legislation where the philosophy of 'till death do us part' is replaced by a range of rational-secular legitimations for marital annulment typified by notion of 'the irretrievable breakdown of marriage'.

More recent accounts of the demise of rites of passage have found scope in late/post-modern theorizing. In Anthony Giddens' interpretation, rites of passage are undermined by the reflexive 'project' of late-modernity that extinguishes clearly formulated stages of life. For Giddens, part of such a project is a personalized life-course largely derived from recognition that individualism as a cultural value and a general orientation is paramount. However, individualism merges with other observable developments that undermine coherent rites of passage. Giddens constructs his argument on the observation that today the experience of living the life-span potential is virtually guaranteed. This allows the individual to predict the future, calculate risks, and plan ahead with a view to possibilities and alternatives in mind. S/he can thus negotiate optional courses of action through making present decisions from a large number of choices offered. Such reflexive calculation does not remain at the individual level since social institutions and processes undercut traditional habits and customs demonstrated by religious practice. In this environment rites of passage are subsequently rendered superfluous (Giddens 1991).

In post-modernist accounts, scholars such as Bauman (1992) see the life-course as characterized by a number of overlapping, often disparate conditions associated with the blurring of traditional chronological boundaries and the integration of formally segregated periods of life. Fixed definitions of childhood, middle age, and old age are eroded under pressure from two cultural directions that have accompanied the profound shifts in the political economy of labour: flexible retirement and traditionally structured forms of stratification typified by social class. Moreover, among the far-reaching repercussions of contemporary culture is the prospect of an endless life which has been revived through images of perpetual youth and the blurring of traditional life-course boundaries.

Despite the theoretical conjectures, there remains a confusing picture regarding the demise of rites of passage. Some rituals remain, albeit in the form of social conventions rather than as explicit expression of religiosity. This may explain why, in many Western countries, the proportion of people preferring church weddings, baptisms and funerals remains higher than the number of members or regular congregational attenders. It may be surmised that while individuals opt for such religious settings, they probably do not do so for intrinsically religious reasons. Plausibly it is the ritual and ceremony that is important, not the 'religious' content. Hence, major life events may still psychologically require markers of change but are increasingly stripped of their essentially religious significance.

Undoubtedly, in the pluralist contemporary Western setting rites of passage may still be observable among religious groups which display rituals marking some form of spiritual or communal transition. This would include baptism in Christian churches, while for ethnic-religious collectives they remain important as with the bar mitzvahs among Jews which represents the transition from childhood to adulthood. Yet, even in many explicitly religious spheres such rites have discernibly experienced an ongoing decline. Evidence of this is the near disappearance of 'churching' – a long-held tradition in many churches where women were prohibited from returning to the congregation until a month after giving birth. Despite such evidence, the 1999 European Values Survey more than hinted at unexpected changes which were plausibly indicative of the complexities of late/post-modernity: the attachment to ceremonies for birth, marriage and death was on the rise among young people and perhaps indicated a small revival for some

forms of Christianity in a number of Western European countries (Lambert 2004: 33).

THE LIFE-COURSE AND EARLY RELIGIOUS SOCIALIZATION

While the decline of rites of passage may point to the demise of the life-cycle as an increasingly redundant framework, an enduring remnant of this approach in the field of sociology is related to the implications of religious socialization through the various 'phases' of life. There are conventionally various significant agencies of such socialization. Despite its declining significance the family remains a core social institution which impacts religious belief and practice throughout life: establishing patterns of religiosity and structuring continuities across the generations (hence, the enduring popularity of the so-called 'family life-cycle' approach). Furthermore, through early socialization, the needs and tasks that an individual is frequently compelled to address during different phases of the family life-course is understood to determine his/her level and expression of faith.

The significance of religious activity during childhood would seem to demonstrate the significance of family influences. Certainly, parents' religious behaviour is still proven to determine to what extent beliefs are internalized and rendered central to the lives of their children later in life (cf. Pearce and Axinn 1998). At the very least children tend to assimilate the broad religious cultures of their families and religion, as a system of meaning, can be a key influence on many later life-course events such as accepting the role of housewife (Sherkat 2000), the legitimacy of pre-marital sex (Thorton and Camburn 1987), and attitudes towards voluntary childlessness (Pearce 2002). Yet, while extant sociological findings suggest that religion should be studied and measured as a life-long process that is linked to childhood experience in particular, there is a general recognition that levels of belief and practice undoubtedly have the potential to change throughout life.

Where parents are successful in transmitting a faith to their children and provide role models in attending religious institutions, there is much less likelihood that their off-spring will relinquish attendance at a later stage of the life-course. This tendency has been explored by various studies. For example, Hunsberger (1983) found that church-leavers are inclined to report there has been less emphasis placed on religion in their families while they were growing up than church remainers. Today, however, the complex contemporary family structure complicates the picture. In a two-parent family, only one parent may choose to go to church. The other may be a non-believer, belong to another denomination, or even another faith. Sandomirsky and Wilson (1990) have indicated that the result of this kind of cross-pressure is more likely to lead a child to withdraw from religious commitments altogether than it is for him/her to choose one parent's religion over another. Plausibly, such factors may be accentuated in the so-called 'restructured' or 'blended' family which results from the increasingly common re-marriage situation. Indeed, the breakdown of family structures and the complexities of family life today may suggest that religious socialization is undermined in various far-reaching respects.

It is also evident that the precise variables involved throughout social learning in respect of religiosity are multifaceted and cross-cutting. One dimension is the cohort effect. The evidence of Roof and Gesch's survey (1995), by way of illustration, suggests that there are changing attitudes to religious socialization among the parents of the so-called Baby-Boom generation. The principle of individual choice is now prevalent even inside the family, with nearly half the parents of this generation surveyed advocating that family members should decide for themselves regarding religious matters, rather than necessarily following the beliefs of their parents and attending church as a family unit. At the same time, the experience of family socialization is also likely to be mediated through religious beliefs and practices arising through the observation of role models and by practising

new modes of religious behaviour. The importance of gender suggests itself here. Since men's religious roles are apt to be less institutionalized or socially defined than women's, the involvement of males in religious organizations may depend more on non-religious factors typified by changes in family structure over the life-course. Subsequently, this may lead to a greater or lesser involvement in religious practice and affiliation from an early age (Wilson and Sherkat 1994).

Neither gender differences nor the cohort effect, however, may necessarily account for reduced levels of religious socialization. Rather, an ongoing process of secularization may diminish its impact. In this regard, Tilley (2003), using data from the British Election Studies and the Household Panel Study, points out that sex-specific influences and family formation cannot themselves comprehensively account for differences between age groups in church attendance: both childrearing and marriage are only weak predictors of differences in religious behaviour. Indeed, Tilley argues that the evidence proves that generational differences are primarily responsible for both age disparities and the large decline over time in church attendance. People born before 1940 have similar levels of church attendance irrespective of family formation, as do those born after 1950. The latter group, and the transitional cohort of the 1940s generation, were growing up and coming of age in the 1960s and onwards – a time of considerable social change that reduced attendance generally. Moreover, Tilley concludes that one of the main reasons for the overall demise in church attendance is that newer generations, raised in a societal environment of declining attendance, are much less likely to be churchgoers than older cohorts.

The impact of the social learning of aspects of religiosity is not, of course, confined to the influence of the family throughout the life-course. The importance of social learning within religious groupings in the formative childhood years continues to be confirmed by recent research. For instance, O'Conner et al.'s (2002) sizeable survey of over two hundred adults of different denominations in the USA found that measurements of personal spirituality including private prayer, attending Bible classes and reading religious material, are linked to denominational background in the formative years and inform such activities as church youth group participation and attending church with one's spouse in later life. It is clearly the more traditionalist and sectarian forms of religion that are strictest in early religious socialization. This may at least partly explain the apparent success of conservative churches in the USA. Hence, it has been calculated that the high level of church growth experienced by fundamentalist Baptists is less traceable to evangelism, and much more to do with their higher birth rate and the evident ability to retain their children within the church through rigorous religious socialization (Smith 1992).

In much the same way as the strong community nature of sectarian forms of religiosity informs early socialization, ethnic communities frequently remain more meticulous in sustaining religious beliefs and practices, although there are major variations. For example, attitudes towards female dress and gender roles, which are generally proscribed by religious regulation, are often virtually unchanged between Muslim parents and their children, while Sikh and Hindu children are sometimes observably more flexible than their parents in adapting to Western conventions. Muslim parents also appear to be a good deal more stringent in their parental control of their offspring into the teenage years and enforcing attitudes towards traditionally arranged marriages (cf. Nielson 1982). While variations in religious adherence may be put down to differing degrees of socialization within the family, they may be simultaneously re-enforced by the existence of ethnic and faith-based schools outside of mainstream education. It has been the creation of such specialized institutions, deemed as desirable by many major faith communities in a perceived threatening secular environment, which has led to sensitive debates in many Western educational systems and inform broader issues of cultural assimilation.

The matter of formal traditional Christian schooling, as pertinent to the religious socialization processes of the general population, has also attracted a measure of interest. Gunnoe and Moore (2002) found that religious schooling throughout childhood was a crucial predictor of young adult religiosity, providing evidence for the importance of explicit religious training during the formative years of middle childhood. Nonetheless, some traditional aspects of early religious education within the broad populace are in measurable decline. Perhaps the most obvious is the demise of the Sunday school movement. This institution which originated in the nineteenth century, with its focus on specifically Christian knowledge, was felt by many churches to be necessary in an increasingly secular and differentiated society. At the peak of their influence in the late nineteenth and early twentieth centuries the Sunday schools reached a very large number of young people and a very high proportion of their age group. In 1911 over half the children in England and Wales attended Sunday school. This figure was down to 20 per cent in 1961 and had further reduced to 14 per cent in 1989. By the year 2000 fewer than 10 per cent of children attended a Sunday school (Brown 2001). In his account of the repercussions of decline, Davies suggests that the demise of the Sunday school movement means that in terms of the Christian faith an 'entire culture had been lost' (Davies 2004: 66).

Christian based youth organizations have also experienced a reversal in fortunes. In this regard, the number of Scouts and Guides meeting in churches throughout Britain decreased by 15.8 per cent between 1987 and 1993. This trend had, however, been set in motion several decades earlier. The Church of England's report, *Youth A Part*, attributed this to a general social trend of 'similar patterns of declining attendance … in secular organisations' (1996: 13). The report took comfort in what it believed was the sensitivity and commitment of many young people to the issues of justice, peace and the environment but stopped short of attributing such sympathy to any meaningful religious conviction.

EARLY ADULTHOOD

While little research has been conducted on the religious socialization and levels of religiosity during childhood, a good number of surveys, particularly in the USA, have illuminated various patterns of belief and behaviour during the periods of adolescence and youth. Despite evident variation, young adulthood appears to be a period when religious practice and commitment, if not belief, decline. Stoetzel (1983: 231–2) contends that the overall evidence points towards a tendency which suggests that the older the person, the stronger the probability they are religious in their opinions, beliefs and observances. This means, inversely, that the younger the person, the more likely they are to be irreligious. It follows that irreligion reaches its peak around the age of thirty years old. This particular profile can be explained largely by life-course effects with the initial decline attributed to the autonomy of young people resisting religious socialization as they are exposed to competing social influences, ideas and worldviews, notably in institutions of higher education and the pressures of peer group conformity, the result of which may be the forging of a fresh social identity. This undoubtedly reflects an actual inversion in the relative influence of parents' religious socialization versus peers as youth move outside their family's residence at a formative stage of the life-course.

The picture is, however, a complex one which suggests that such processes are circumvented by generalized changing trends in religiosity and the transformation of its meaning which may, or may not, be subject to cohort influences. In the nine countries surveyed by the 1999 European Values Survey, the rate of self-definition as 'a religious person' among young people who declared to have no religious conviction, increased from 14 per cent from 1981 to 22 per cent in 1999. In addition, the survey disclosed that the young person's belief in God rose from 20 per cent to 29 per cent, while the acceptance of life after death increased from 19 per cent to 28 per cent. The survey also

discerned an underlying principal tendency: an increase in 'believing without belonging' and a growth in the percentage of those who never belonged to a formal religion. Somewhat paradoxically, the EVS found that on the increase was the belief that churches bring answers to spiritual needs (if not social problems), although the conviction of the significance of individual sin still continued to have less and less attraction.

A second concern of the sociological enquiry regarding youth is to establish a baseline for longitudinal research on religious influences on people's later life in much the same way that child socialization is deemed as influential. The evidence is, once more, far from straightforward. Nonetheless, the longitudinal study in the USA by Gunnoe and Moore (2002) considered predictors of religiosity among older youth through eight areas: childhood training, religious schooling, cognitive ability, psychodynamic need, parenting style, role models, the family life-cycle, and background demographics. Predictors were assessed when participants were 7–11 and 11–16 years of age. Levels of religiosity were further analyzed when participants reached the period of youth (designated as between 17 and 22 years old). According to Gunnoe and Moore, the best predictors of youth were found to be ethnicity and church attendance by the peer group during the high school period. Other indicators included residence in the Southern United States, gender, religious schooling during childhood, maternal religiosity and the importance mothers placed on childhood religious training, and an interaction variable identifying mothers who were very supportive in religious participation.

Young adulthood is most certainly a demographically dense period of life in which many decisions are made and events occur that influence the rest of the life-course. Hence, a further interest of sociologists of religion regarding youth is in considering the implications of this stage of life as one in which a degree of convergence is likely to take place such as biological change, identity formation, peer group activity, and changing relations within the family. This has led to a fair number of sociological, as well as psychological studies in North America which have sought to establish a link between religious faith and the promotion of positive, healthy outcomes in the lives of adolescents. It is clear that various measures of religiosity are associated with a range of positive, desirable consequences across diverse areas of concern. These have included avoidance of drug, alcohol and tobacco use, lower levels of delinquency and suicide (cf. Donahue and Benson 1995), depression, and a sense of hopelessness (cf. Wright *et al.* 1993). Life satisfaction, involvement with families, and skills in solving health-related problems (cf. Varon and Riley 1999), avoidance of risky sexual behaviour (cf. Lammers *et al.* 2000), level of academic achievement (cf. Muller and Ellison 2001), effective coping with problems (cf. Balk 1991) and political and civic involvement (cf. Serow and Dreyden 1990) are also associated with higher levels of religiosity among younger adults.

MATURE ADULTHOOD

Although contemporary sociological accounts identify new social roles and obligations as a common feature of all phases of the life-course, mature adult life beyond the stage of youth would appear to bring them in abundance. This may have considerable implications with changing aspects of religiosity. Certainly, for those that survive the period of youth with a religious faith, experiences of life discontinuities and change, in many ways synonymous with late or post-modernity, may impact levels of religious beliefs and practices in both positive and negative ways. For one thing, change is disruptive of established routine. It follows that studies have tended to suggest that if people have forged a place for church-going in their routine, but when their habits are subsequently overturned by change, may find there is no longer any space in their lives for attendance.

Equally, work obligations and schedule changes can make Sunday church-going and other observances difficult to fulfil. In this regard, Richter and Francis' (1998) study in

Britain indicates that younger adults brought up in church life may leave as a result of the distractions the secular world has to offer, alongside challenging work commitments and family responsibilities. While Richter and Francis identify such commitments as often temporary, and conjecture that a return to church life remains possible, the matter of priorities are suggested in the choice of obligations undertaken. Compressing church duties into a life-style full with other options and responsibilities is seemingly not a prospect which the younger adult often relishes. Furthermore, low levels of religious activity may be related to highly stressful events and include death of a spouse, divorce, illness, unemployment and moving house, all of which may lead to a decline in institutional participation (Richter and Francis 1998: 67–75)

Adapting to the responsibilities of mature adulthood, on the other hand, may engender continuing or even increasing aspects of religiosity. Thus, not all of the changes associated with the onset of adulthood necessarily mean leaving church or neglecting other forms of religious commitment. Some may lead to opportunities to engage or re-engage in religious activity – encouraged by a 'fresh start' of which moving home is perhaps the most obvious (Roof and Hadaway 1979: 199). Moreover, in mature adulthood, and with family responsibilities of their own, individuals may treat their parents as role models (although parental over-enthusiasm can have a negative effect (Wilson and Sherkat 1994)) since church-going may fit into what constitutes the 'good parent' (Roof 1994: 151) – once again suggesting the impact of early religious socialization.

Nor does adulthood necessarily amount to personal dilemma and instability. Indeed, it may stimulate the search for identity no less than in the phase of youth. Levinson *et al.*'s model (1978) of the life-course, previously mentioned, suggests that rather than turmoil, the thirties and forties constitute a time of settling down. Godden (1982), from a more phenomenological perspective, maintains that this hypothesis raises the question as to the ways in which the younger adult's concern about establishing vocation and family makes a difference to his/her faith commitment. For Godden, the burden of relating to his/her past and living towards the future includes a process of self-understanding and insight that is necessary if the adult is to enjoy productive, responsible relations with others. In short, s/he must integrate relearned information into a more balanced view of self and deal with any potential or actual 'crises of life' which shatter old images of self and beliefs about how things are. Nevertheless, the transition to adult maturity can be fairly smooth. It follows that enhanced religious faith is not necessarily in response to some 'crisis' but may develop naturally as part of the ageing process and give way to a blossoming of interest in ideology, philosophy and a religious worldview as part of the establishment of the mature adult identity relating to the profound questioning of the meaning and purpose of one's existence. The theoretical basis for this hypothesis is that the more roles one plays, the more diverse life experience are, and that this broadening of personal perspective has a positive relationship on faith. Another factor, Godden speculates, may be that the more roles one plays, the greater the task of organizing these roles into a coherent, unified life structure. If one is successful, then the stronger one's 'constitutive imagination' and religious faith is likely to be.

As part of a well-documented area, studies have suggested that discontinuity and negative change may, in fact, stimulate levels of religiosity. Indeed, the subject of religiosity and adverse life situation has recently interested those sociologists embracing the rational-choice paradigm. For example, Iannaccone (1990) argues that those who were most active in a religious group and invest time, energy, and emotional support in religious activity, were the most likely to use their fostered 'religious capital' to respond to life situations. This is supported by a measure of empirical work. It has been established in numerous research surveys that people who *already* identify strongly with their religion and/or express it regularly are more likely to turn to religious or spiritual sources for comfort and inspiration when faced with health and other personal problems.

While relatively few studies systematically examine religion consolation, there is a large body of research on religiosity that provides useful insights into the likelihood of religious solace in adulthood. This literature on consolatory religiosity may be especially helpful for anticipating variations in belief and practice due to the stage of the life-course reached and its relation to status characteristics. Thus studies indicate that the propensity to use religion as a coping resource may be particularly strong among individuals confronting negative change, disability, illness, and death. This tendency, however, may be more discernible among certain social groupings. For instance, Ellison and Taylor's (1996) representative sample of African Americans, a constituency historically at the lower end of the social spectrum, found that negative events, including illness episodes, heighten religious coping mechanisms. The research revealed that those of this ethnic group who are forced to manage with illness, chronic conditions, and injuries are five times more likely to turn to prayer as a coping strategy than those who deal with problems unrelated to health and bereavement.

Little research has been conducted on gender differences in seeking religious comfort. Ferraro and Kelley-Moore (2002) have sought to rectify this by examining the extent to which physical and mental problems precipitate seeking religious consolation among males and females. In line with earlier works, their findings indicate that seeking religious compensation is most likely among those who identify with and practise a religion, suggesting that such consolation intensifies among religious persons. Chronic (non-serious) conditions were associated with increased religious seeking over time. Cancer was associated with higher levels of religiosity especially among women, while depression tended to be related to a greater seeking of religious solace among both sexes. The results indicate that women are more likely than men to seek religious consolation, but men seek religious relief for a wider range of health and situational problems such as loss of employment. However, there was no support in this survey for the hypothesis that religion and health problems would interact in shaping religious consolation in any coherent or predictable way.

Although religious and spiritual beliefs and practices have been frequently associated with greater psychological wellbeing among illness populations, little is known about the specific benefits that individuals perceive they receive from such recourse. Throwing light on the subject are the findings of Siegel and Schrimshaw (2002) via their interview of 63 older HIV-infected adults who reported a variety of benefits from their religious beliefs and practices. The study revealed that religion evokes calming emotions and feelings; offers strength, empowerment and control; eases the emotional burden of illness; provides social support and a sense of belonging; furthers spiritual enhancement through a personal relationship with God; facilitates meaning and acceptance of the illness; helps preserve health; relieves fear and uncertainty of death; and facilitates self-acceptance and reduces self-blame. All of these perceived benefits suggest potential mechanisms by which religion and spirituality may impact social and psychological adjustment.

LATER LIFE

A number of studies suggest that religion is of more central importance in the lives of older people compared to younger generations (cf. Gray and Moberg 1977), while other works have found the association questionable (cf. Steinitz 1980). Inconclusive findings must also be supplemented by the observation that the nature of 'being religious' may be understood to be multi-dimensional, so that what constitutes the scope and breadth of religiousness among older adults continues to be debated as it is with younger age cohorts (Futterman and Koenig 1995).

Common sense might suggest that age is positively associated with spirituality and 'turning to' religion. Thus, older people may be more likely to seek religious comfort, especially when facing the ageing process itself. Yet, while the link between older age categories and increasing levels of religiosity is fairly well established, it remains unclear, once again, whether this represents an ageing or cohort effect (Moberg 1997). The latter is given to mean that the elderly generation today was more religious as an earlier age cohort compared to subsequent cohorts as a result of distinct historical factors or the broader development of an increasing secular society. It may well be, that older individuals, and older women in particular, regard church activity as central to their lives, perhaps by force of custom. Evidence for this comes from Peter Brierley in a chapter in his book, entitled *Bleeding to Death* (1999), which shows that for each of his earlier three English surveys it was possible to estimate the age profile structure of the various denominations and suggest that, with the exception of Pentecostal churches recruiting mainly from the Afro-Caribbean population, church-goers over some two decades have proved to be considerably older than non-attenders. This would seem to be even more the tendency in recent years. For example, in 1999, 29 per cent of attenders in the Church of England were over the age of 65 and displayed a further demographic feature in that they tended to be female.

Not dissimilar patterns are observable in the USA. An analysis of Gallop Poll data collected from 1992 to 1999 would seem to confirm that religious involvement increases in the later stages of life (Gallop and Lindsay 2000). Among other findings, it disclosed that of the 18 to 29 years old polled, 45 per cent reported that religion remains 'very important'. This percentage increases steadily with age to 55 per cent for those 30–49 years old, 70 per cent for those 50 and older, and 77 per cent among those 75 and older. Patterns are similar for older adults' involvement in religious services. This is particularly noteworthy because some older adults are inevitably no longer physically able to attend religious observances (Ainlay et al. 1992).

Other surveys, focusing on indices of belief as well as participation, complicate the picture. The most recent European Values Survey (1999) indicated that older generations in

Western Europe, those born before 1946, displayed a minor revival in religiosity although more limited and excluded belief in God. Those born before 1928 have scarcely changed their convictions at all – if not in terms of belonging, then certainly by way of the perceived positive aspects of church life and belief in a personal God. Individuals born after 1964 would appear to reverse decline apart from the areas of belonging, religious practice, and belief in sin. This is a clear change, at least across many indices, in comparison to the 1970s and 1980s when people displayed decreasing levels of religiosity, and when the gap with the older generations underwent change. Among the young, the reversal began in the 1980s with beliefs in the life after death spread to others areas of religious conviction (Lambert 2004).

Studies also indicate that older age cohorts are less likely to embrace new forms of religion and spirituality than younger ones. Older people have not only lived through less secular times, but were more subject to traditional forms of religious socialization which, in the case of North America and Western Europe, meant one form or another of Christianity. Religious pluralism and the pursuit of fresh and innovating forms of spirituality are thus more identifiable with the preferences of more recent generations. For example Berger *et al.* (2003) found that the subscription to various forms of neo-Paganism was more evident among those aged between 30 and 49 years old, than those over 50. In their sample, Berger *et al.* found that the former constituted nearly 80 per cent of active pagans, compared to just over 10 per cent of the latter.

In gauging the significance of religion in later life, we may distinguish between its impact in mid-life compared to both earlier life and old age. Religious activity may vary in mid-life as compared to other periods of adulthood. Those reaching mid-life frequently find that they are faced by new challenges and social roles. This may mean that middle-age is a time of increasing religious involvement for some and this apparent religious resurgence among those over 40 years old is generally attributed to the increased religiosity once

children are raised, career established, retirement assured, and with the increasing proximity of death (Stoetzel 1983: 94). In the USA, in 1980, the overall pattern in adult church attendance indicated a steady increase from the late 'teens to a peak in the late 50s to early 60s, followed by a slight decline in later old age which can largely be put down to physical incapacitation (Atchley 1980: 330–40). These figures, however, do not necessarily reflect greater religious sentiment among middle-aged people, but could be viewed as a reflection of changing patterns of involvement in voluntary associations especially when their children leave home or, alternatively, reflect career patterns when work becomes less significant. Thus involvement in church life plausibly increases as commitment to such activities as work-related, sport-related and school service associations reduces over the same period.

Gender differences in religiosity are also discernible in later life and cut across common patterns of belief and activity. While variation is observable at a generalized level in mid-life, as in previous stages of life, some studies show that the gender gap in religiosity in fact narrows with older age categories (cf. Levin *et al.* 1994). It remains unclear, however, whether such a convergence is largely due to higher religious seeking among men who reach older age, the premature death of non-religious men which exaggerates tendencies, or some combination of the two (Strawbridge *et al.* 1997).

The time of middle-age is often regarded as a period of 'identity crisis', not unlike the teenage years, and one brought about by biological changes and altering social obligations. While acknowledging that this 'crisis' may at least partly be a medicalized construct, belief and belonging plausibly helps establish a new sense of identity, interest and status. Certainly, a long-standing, rather commonsense view is that the attraction of religious belonging, particularly for women of this age, is possibly linked to the loss of socially ascribed gender roles as well as natural changes in reproductive capacities. The broad argument is that all of these changes require psychological adjustment to which an increasing level of religiosity lends itself. These assumptions, however, are not easily substantiated and have to be supplemented by the fact that women of all age groups are inclined to be over-represented in many expressions of religion and the variables often advanced for this tendency cannot easily be substantiated (Walter and Davie 1998).

Theorists have increasingly acknowledged that as men move forward into mid-life they also experience transformations in identity, self-belief, and behaviour (Whitbourne 1999). There are observably implications here for aspects of religiosity. Paralleling the growing sociological interest in masculinities and male studies, recent surveys have provided more information concerning the hitherto under-researched area of older men's religiosity. Payne (1994), for example, has thrown light on the propensity for a more mature 'faith' to emerge in men's later life. Prior to mid-life, according to Payne, men's religiousness largely entails pro-church involvement and the translation of their faith outwards into 'acts of justice' – the social application of faith. Payne observes that, over time, however, men's religiousness shifts from ritualistic participation and a rational/logic religious orientation to a more earnest spiritual journey and an introspective disposition.

A further study by Thompson and Remmes (2002) discovered that before entering later life, men with a 'feminine orientation' have a greater religious involvement than other males. This would appear to confirm earlier works which suggested that lower rates of religiosity, by various indexes, are due to men equating religiosity with femininity (cf. Francis and Wilcox 1996). In their sample of older men from three Massachusetts counties, Thompson and Remmes found that gender orientation, more than masculine ideology, was likely to be a reliable predictor of older men's religiousness. A feminist orientation, so it would seem, is a significant determinant of their religious participation, commitment and intrinsic orientation. Older men who define self in traditional masculine terms, however, tended to engage in a 'quest religiosity'. These finding are discussed by Thompson and Remmes in their research paper in terms of how masculinity is at times a barrier to men's

private devotion and at other times can be a trigger to a religious quest. Thus, if growing older did not impact on men's view of the world and themselves, then it could be argued that older males with a developed feminine orientation would be more religiously involved. It could also be assumed that older men who adhere to a traditional masculine ideology will me more irreligious.

For those moving beyond mid-life a further dimension of the ageing effect is that the involvement of the elderly in religious organizations may indicate increasing social marginalization. Retirement in contemporary society effectively means, for many older people, leaving the public sphere. Thus, for this age category the basis of identity and self-worth is largely derived from the private sphere – family, leisure, perhaps religious activity. Increased emphasis on the religious foundation of individual identity, then, may represent, for older people, an attempt to transform the previous cultural emphasis on work and parenthood to a fresh self-valuation based on spiritual growth (Christiano 1987). Nonetheless, the emergence for a sizeable proportion of the population of a Third Age (Laslett 1994) of increasing affluence, flexible retirement and life-style choice for many people before 'deep' old age invariably confuses the link between religious belief and older age categories. Speculatively speaking, the improving economic situation of this growing section of the population, alongside their increasing political power through the 'grey vote', may break the link between old age and religion as some kind of compensator for social marginalization (Hunt 2005: 200).

One of the most common interpretations of the implications of ageing for religiosity is premised on the awareness of finitude – that the proximity to death heightens interest in 'making peace with one's maker' (Thorson 1983). For this reason belief in an after-life may be especially evident in later stages in the life-course, in so far as older people typically display higher levels of belief in a life after death. However, as Finney notes in his survey Finding Faith Today, bereavement and suffering, often associated with old age, are among the factors reported in finding faith at any time in the life-course.

Moreover, while it may well be that the ageing process and bereavement of family and peers is accentuated in old age, it could equally lead to a loss of faith (Finney 1995: 50).

The alleged relationship between approaching death and religiosity has constituted a fairly distinct body of academic knowledge. It is, however, something of an under-researched area amongst sociologists and gerontologists alike even in the USA where religious attitudes to life appear to be more common than many Western European countries. The research that has been conducted in this area has tended to take various trajectories. A general finding, nonetheless, is that religious belief reduces fear of death.

From a sociological perspective differing degrees and types of religious commitment on the approach of death remain strongly evident. For instance, Kalish and Reynolds (1976) found that strong religious believers were rated lowest on death anxiety, but those with 'confused' religious beliefs were rated higher than agnostics or atheists. They also found that old people differed from other age groups in the opinions expressed concerning preparation for their own death. When asked to imagine they had been told that their deaths would occur within thirty days and to report what changes would be made in their lives as a result, older people were more likely to say that they would not change their life-style but they would nonetheless concentrate on aspects of the contemplative 'inner life' in preparation for the end of their lives

In a more psychological vein, a comparative study by von Franz (1986), developing the psychoanalytic theories of Jung, stressed that the unconscious 'beliefs' in a life after death become more significant from middle-age onwards, but are especially important as death approaches. Unconscious beliefs, especially expressed as dreams, prepare individuals for the hereafter – often pointing to imbalances in attitudes which need to be corrected and constitute something approaching a life review. Such a review allows older people to come to terms with the past in differing respects. In this way religion, once again, may enhance psychological and social well-being. For example,

consistent with the work of earlier investigators, the findings of nation-wide research in the USA by Krause and Ellison (2003) disclosed the tendency of older people, coming to a realization of their own mortality, to be concerned with distressing events in earlier life. Those who forgive others in later life tend to enjoy a greater sense of psychological wellbeing than older people who are less willing to forgive transgressors for the things they have inflicted upon them.

DEATH AND THE AFTER-LIFE

Inspiring a good deal of anthropological work embracing the largely obsolete life-cycle approach to religiosity was Malinowski's seminal anthropological account of the people of the Trobriand Islands (Malinowski 1954). Malinowski indicated that religion was particularly significant during certain times, in particular, situations of individual emotional stress that threatened collective solidarity and sentiment. Contexts which produced these emotions included crises such as birth, puberty, marriage and death. Malinowski noticed that in all pre-industrial societies life crises are surrounded with religious ritual. Death was the most disruptive of these events since it severed strong personal attachments and thwarted human designs. This is why he regarded the ability to deal with the problems associated with death as probably the main source of religious belief. Thus, through funeral ceremonies, mourning is expressed and belief in immortality articulated – in a sense denying the fact of death itself and subsequently comforting the bereaved. Indeed, the significance of religiosity in the bereavement process signifies a particular type of discontinuity. Death means the cessation of someone's life and the end of the relationship that the deceased shared with others. Moreover, it brings a unique form of psychological challenge since death is final.

Recent sociological studies have tended to emphasize the failure of traditional funerals, stressing orthodox Christian beliefs of the after-life, are not always congruent with those of the general population. In short, they fail to provide the functions associated with pre-industrial societies. At the same time, contemporary culture is often identified as void of meaning and insufficiently deals with the mourning process because it is unable to provide sufficient guidelines in these areas. This plausibly explains the rise of 'alternative' funerals that are underscored by the value of 'choice' and, increasingly, the 'alternative' means little or no religious element apart from that concocted by relatives of the deceased from a pick 'n' mix 'spirituality' (Walter 1999a).

Perceptions of death in Western cultures, moreover, profoundly reflect social change – not least of all as a result of increasing secularity and the declining communal context of religiosity (cf. Ariès 1974). Firstly, death, as the last rites of passage, is not a public event. Rather, it is a private experience and is likely to take place within the institutional setting of the hospital, hospice or home for the elderly. Secondly, Western culture is age and death-denying. Where there is an emphasis on prolonging life, of consuming strategies to retain youth, there is an inability to tolerate death in a post-modern culture orientated towards perpetual happiness (Featherstone 1982). Thirdly, there exists a contradiction and dilemma generated by the death denying culture – one which displays profound difficulty in accepting the reality of death on the one hand, while sustaining a familiarity with 'real' death through media images and the 'celluloid death' of fiction. These cultural complexities have impacted both mourning processes and beliefs in the after-life.

Enduring perceptions of death and processes of mourning, alongside proscribed forms of funeral arrangements, are nevertheless evident among ethnic minorities. For various faith communities ways of disposing of the dead provide a means for rooting their identity in Western soil and these have frequently become part of legal and political controversies (cf. Harte 1994). Furthermore, in pluralist Western societies there are numerous difficulties facing ethnic communities in observing preparations regarding funerals (cf. Volt 1991). Ideally for Muslims, by way of illustration, the corpse is ritually bathed before death, a task that is traditionally performed by family members who belong to the same gender as the deceased. The only acceptable way of disposing of a body in the eyes of the majority of Muslims is through burial underground with the head facing the Kaba in Mecca. Religious doctrine also dictates that a person is ideally to be buried within a day of their death. In practice, in the Western context, burials are often delayed by several days. There are other limitations. Joining in a funeral procession is considered a collective duty: if there are sufficient people accompanying the body to the cemetery individual Muslims are duty-bound to join in. In the streets of modern cities the observance of this rule is increasingly rare.

By contrast, cremation is the ideal disposal of the corpse for Hindus. At death, the family prepares the body of the deceased, carries it in a procession to the cremation grounds, and recites specific prayers while the body is cremated. The god of death is called upon to give the deceased an honoured place among the ancestors, and other deities are also invoked to intercede on behalf of the departed. Once cremated, the ashes and bones of the deceased are either committed to a holy river or buried. After the funeral, the family members, being in a state of ritual impurity, proceed to a brook or river to purify themselves with ritual baths. Because of the difficulties in performing many such rituals associated with the traditional Hindu life-course, modifications may be observable within the Western context (cf. Shattuck 1999).

For ethnic faith communities, after-life beliefs remain fairly traditional although they obviously vary considerably. Beliefs outside of such collectives are, however, undergoing transformation. In mainstream culture, despite secularization processes, belief in an after-life appears to be fairly buoyant. Yet for many people this belief is a tentative one, and the content of the after-life remains vague. For a sizeable number of young adults, in particular, there may be a refusal to rule out an after-life, though they would not go so far as to say they positively believe one actually exists. This is a generation which finds itself in the culture of relativism that is associated with post-modernity, one which does not trust religion but also no longer has faith in science. In short, it is an age group that keeps an open mind on the subject of life after death (Walter 1999b).

The precise range of beliefs regarding the after-life, held by the populations of Western societies, has proved to have been of considerable interest to sociologists of religion over several decades. Recent surveys suggest that orthodox Christian beliefs remain evident but they are supplemented by a range of alternatives. In his research in Britain, Douglas Davies (1997) identified five options of a possible after-life which respondents discerned fairly easily to distinguish between. In his sample of 1603 individuals Davies found that 29 per cent believed nothing happens after death; 43 per cent that the soul passes on to another world; 8 per cent that the body awaits resurrection; 12 per cent believed in reincarnation as something or someone else; and 22 per cent that what occurs after death 'is in God's hands'. The striking figure relates to reincarnation beliefs, a notion traditionally alien to Western culture. Earlier research in the USA by a Gallop opinion poll had established such belief as high as 20 per cent when respondents answered 'yes' to the question 'Do you believe in reincarnation?'. In this research the pollsters presented those asked with the option of replying 'yes', 'no', or 'don't know' to the possibility of reincarnation (Gallop 1999: 137–8).

Walter and Waterhouse (1999) discovered in their survey that those in Britain who answered the question 'yes' to whether they believed in reincarnation far outnumbered those who belonged to such religions as Hinduism, Sikhism and Buddhism formally teaching reincarnation or rebirth. Reincarnation therefore is not part of a well-established and communally held folk-religion in most Western societies. This means that belief in reincarnation is not something that has been formally codified by the culture and conventional religion of the indigenous population.

Indeed, the notions involved are under-developed and rarely seem to distinctly originate in any particular world religion. Walter and Waterhouse also argue that after-life beliefs are becoming semi-detached from other religious beliefs and almost entirely detached from morality, hence there is no overriding fear of future retribution for actions in this life.

A number of Walter and Waterhouse's findings were reflected in the European Values Survey of 1981 and 1990. The surveys asked respondents whether they believed in life after death, and found those answering 'yes' constituted around 40 per cent of the sample This figure had changed little over the decades. Moreover, the EVS data indicated that those who believed in an after-life tended to be religious according to other measurements. However, these surveys also contained more specific questions about what the after-life was supposed to actually entail. For instance, it showed that whereas belief in heaven remained fairly buoyant (at around 30–50 per cent across Western European countries), belief in hell had definitely gone out of fashion. Lambert (2004), interpreting the 1999 EVS data, nonetheless suggests an increasing belief in the after-life in terms of death, heaven and re-incarnation, among young people.

One conjecture offered by Lambert, in his analysis of the 1999 EVS data, is that an over-valuation of self-realization as a Western cultural attribute may have increased beliefs in the after-life, especially belief in reincarnation. Hence, Lambert asks the question whether a link should be drawn between the return of belief in life after death, as evident in recent EVS surveys, with the pessimistic outlook of contemporary culture. In short, is it possible that the excessive individualism of late-modernity may have run its course and subsequently made death even less an acceptable proposition? If so, this plausibly explains the increasing belief in reincarnation particularly since it allows the chance to live one's life again and the opportunity to learn lessons from previous existences. On the other hand, the belief in reincarnation reflects the current individualized concern with meaning, ethics, identity, and faith which all constitute part of an autonomous spiritual quest or what Lambert calls 'pluralistic secularization'.

SUMMARY

The evidence regarding after-life beliefs indicates that one important shifting dimension of the life-course is its increasing subjection to transforming aspects of religiosity or, as often now preferred in contemporary sociological literature, 'spiritualities'. This is an important consideration. Numerous scholars have long expressed concern about the types of religious measurements and definitions used to develop generalizations about religiosity over the life-course. Today, the matter of measurement and definition has become imperative. While the life-course continues to undergo considerable change and is no longer identifiable with predictable 'stages' and attendant dimensions of religiosity, the nature of religion itself is undergoing an observable transformation. Side-stepping, for the moment, the debate as to whether religion as a social phenomenon is undergoing a general decline – a decline at least evident by the demise of rites of passage – the evidence points towards a disengagement from its institutional expression and perhaps religious ceremonies. This trend is also supplemented by an increasing recourse to a mix and match individualized form of spirituality. It follows that the traditional indexes of religion across the life-course have become increasingly less cogent and thus renders comparative analysis less plausible. The significance of this eclectic and fluid component of religiosity throughout the contemporary life-course is not one comprehensively explored in extant sociological surveys, although it has opened up fresh possible paths for research. Typical of this is the burgeoning field of child spirituality. Such research has been innovating not least of all in that it has tended to move away from discernible aspects of religious socialization and towards the subjective individual experiences during this period of early life (cf. Duff 2003).

Due to transforming aspects of religiosity, as well as the broad themes discussed above in this chapter, it is evident that the subject of the significance of religion throughout the life-course remains a widely debated if, in some respects at least, under-researched area. To be sure, some themes, such as age and religiosity, remain perennial concerns, as does the impact of the enduring variables of ethnicity, gender and, perhaps to an increasingly lesser extent, social class. Other areas, notably the link between religion and life discontinuities are clearly other expanding concerns of the sociology of religion, in addition to the growing recognition of implications of the cohort effect. A further interest is the disparity in levels of belief across different Western societies which do, in turn, suggest that if a decline in religious faith is taking place, then it is by no means a linear and predictable process in what is increasingly designated late- or post-modernity.

Clearly, sociological theorizing around such socio-cultural transformations would seem to complicate a number of the core issues that have long preoccupied scholars. Thus it might be glibly asserted that both continuity and change are observable in various indices life-course religiosity. Nonetheless, the evidence points to both. Continuity is evident in that religion remains an important aspect of the life-course for at least some social constituencies in an increasingly secular and pluralistic society, not least of all among faith communities, although these collectives clearly face their own dilemmas and questions of cultural assimilation remain of sociological interest. Change, however, is certainly discernible in Western societies today. Perhaps, above all, discontinuity is increasingly recognized as spurring disruption to the life-course. Alongside choice and the increasing evidence of dimensions of the consumerist ethic in religiosity, the consequences of discontinuity ensure that the study of the life-course in respect of religiosity, as with other dimensions of contemporary social and cultural life, will remain a vibrant and significant area for further research in the sociological enterprise.

REFERENCES

Ainlay, S., Singleton, R. Jr. and Swigert, V. 1992. 'Aging and Religious Participation: Reconsidering the Effects of Health', *Journal for the Scientific Study of Religion* 31: 175–88.

Ariès, P. 1965. *Centuries of Childhood*, London: Cape.

Ariès, P. 1974. *Western Attitudes Towards Death: From the Middle Ages to the Present*. Baltimore, MD: Johns Hopkins Press.

Atchley, R. 1980. *The Social Forces in Later Life*. Belmont, CA: Wadsworth.

Balk, D. 1991. 'Sibling Death, Adolescent Bereavement, and Religion', *Death Studies* 15: 1–20.

Bauman, M. 1992. *Postmodernity and Its Discontents*. New York: New York University Press.

Berger, H., Leach, E. and Shaffer, L. 2003. *Voices from the Pagan Census: A National Survey of Witches and Neo-Pagans in the United States*. Columbia, SC: University of South Carolina Press.

Brierley, P. 1999. *Bleeding to Death,* London: MARC Europe.

Brown, S. 2001. *The Death of Christian Britain*, London: Routledge.

Christiano, K. 1987. 'Church as a Family Surrogate', *Journal for the Scientific Study of Religion* 25 (3): 339–54.

Church of England 1996. *Youth A Part: Young People and the Church*. London: Church House Publishing.

Davies, C. 2004. *The Strange Death of Moral Britain*, New Brunswick: Transaction.

Davies, D. 1997. 'Contemporary Belief in Life After Death'. In P. Jupp and T. Rogers (eds) *Interpreting Death: Christian Theology and Pastoral Practice*. London: Cassell.

Donahue, M. and Benson, P. 1995. 'Religion and Well-being of Adolescents', *Journal of Social Issues* 51: 145–60.

Duff, L. 2003. 'Spiritual Development and Education: A Contemplative View', *International Journal of Children's Spirituality* 8 (3): 227–37.

Ellison, C. and Taylor, R. 1996. 'Turning to Prayer: Social and Situational Antecedents of Religious Coping Among African Americans', *Review of Religious Research* 38: 111–31.

Eisenstadt, S. 1956. *From Generation to Generation*. Basingstoke: Collier-Macmillan.

Erikson, E. 1951. *Identity and the Life-Cycle*. London: Norton.

Featherstone, M. 1982. 'The Body in Consumer Culture', *Theory Culture and Society* 1 (2): 18–31.

Ferraro, K. and Kelley-Moore, J. 2002. 'Religious Consolation Among Men and Women: Do Health Problems Spur Seeking?', *Journal for the Scientific Study of Religion* 39 (2): 220–44.

Finney, J. 1995. *Finding Faith Today: How Does It Happen?*, Swindon: British Bible Society.

Francies, L. and Wilcox, C. 1996. 'Religion and Gender Orientation', *Personality and Individual Differences* 15: 43–59.

Franz, von, M. 1986. *On Dreams and Dreaming: A Jungian Perspective*. Boston: Shambhala.

Futterman, A. and Koenig, H. 1995. 'Measuring Religiosity in Later Life: What Can Gerontology Learn from the Sociology and Psychology of Religion?'. Paper presented at the Conference on the Methodological Advances in the Study of Religion, Health and Aging, Bethesda, MD.

Gallop, G. 1999. *The Spiritual Life of Young Americans: Approaching the Year 2000*. Princeton, NJ: Heoerge H. Gallop International Institute.

Gallop, G. and Lindsay, D. 2000. *Surveying the Religious Landscape: Trends in U.S. Beliefs*. New York: Morehouse Publishing.

Gennep, A. Van 1908. *Les Rites de Passage*. London: Routledge.

Gibson, C. 1994. *Dissolving Wedlock*. London: Routledge.

Giddens, A. 1990. *The Consequences of Modernity*, Cambridge: Polity Press.

Giddens, A. 1991. *Modernity and Self-Identity: Self and Society in the Late Modern Age*. Cambridge: Polity Press.

Godden, W. 1982. 'Responses from an Adult Developmental Perspective', K. Stokes (ed.) *Faith Development in the Adult Life Cycle*. New York: W. H. Sadlier.

Gray, R. and Moberg, D. 1977. *The Church and the Older Person*. Grand Rapids, MI: Eedmans.

Gunnoe, M. L. and K. A. Moore 2002. 'Predictors of Religiosity Among Youth Aged 17–22: A Longitudal Study of the National Survey of Children', *Journal for the Scientific Study of Religion* 41 (4): 613–22.

Harte, J. 1994. 'Law After Death, or "Whose Body Is It?" The Legal Framework for the Disposal of the Dead'. In *Ritual Remembrance: Responses to Death in Human Societies*, J. Davies (ed.). Sheffield: Sheffield Academic Press.

Heelas, P. 1996. *The New Age Movement: The Celebration of the Self and the Sacralization of Modernity*. Oxford: Blackwells.

Hunsberger, B. 1983. 'Apostasy: A Social Learning Perspective', *Review of Religious Research* 44 (3): 569–80.

Hunt, S. 2005. *The Life Course: A Sociological Introduction*. Basingstoke: Palgrave.

Iannacone, L. 1990. 'Religious Practice: A Human Capital Approach', *Journal for the Scientific Study of Religion* 29: 297–314.

Kalish, R. A. and Reynolds, D. K. 1976. *Death and Ethnicity: A Psychocultural Study*. Los Angeles: University of Southern California Press.

Krause, N. and Ellison, C. 2003. 'Forgiveness by God, Forgiveness of Others, and Psychological Well-Being in Late Life', *Journal for the Scientific Study of Religion* 42 (1): 77–93.

Lambert, Y. 2004. 'A Turning Point in Religious Evolution in Europe', *Journal of Contemporary Religion* 19 (1): 204–15.

Lammers, C., Ireland, M., Resnick, M. and Blum, R. 2000. 'Influences on Adolescents' Decision to Postpone Onset of Sexual Intercourse: A Survival Analysis of Virginity Among Youths Aged 13 to 18 Years', *Journal of Adolescent Health* 26: 42–48.

Laslett, P. 1994. *Fresh Map of Life: Emergence of the Third Age*. Basingstoke: MacMillan.

Levin, J., Robert, T. and Chatters, M. 1994. 'Race and Gender Differences in Religiosity Among Older Adults: Findings From Four National Surveys', *Journal of Gerontology: Social Sciences* 49: 137–45.

Levinson, D., Darrow, C., Klein, C., Levinson, M. and Braxton, M. 1978. *The Seasons of Man*. New York: Alfred A. Knopf.

Malinowski, B. 1954. *Magic, Science and Religion*. London: Souvenir Press.

Moberg, D. 1997. 'Religion and Ageing'. In K. Ferraro (ed.) *Gerontology: Perspectives and Issues*. New York: Springer Press.

Muller, C. and Ellison, C. 2001. 'Religious Involvement, Social Capital, and Adolescents' Academic Progress: Evidence from the National Longitudinal Study of 1988', *Sociological Focus* 34: 155–83.

Nielson, G. 1982. 'Islamic Communities in Britain'. In P. Badman (ed.) *Religion, State, and Society in Modern Britain*. Lampeter: The Edwin Mellen Press.

O'Connor, T., Hoge, D. and Alexander, E. 2002. 'The Relative Influence of Youth and Adult Experience on Personal Spirituality and Church Involvement', *Journal for the Scientific Study of Religion* 41 (4): 723–32.

Payne, B. 1994. 'Faith and Development in Older Men'. In E. Thompson (ed.) *Older Men's Lives*. Thousand Oaks, CA: Sage.

Pearce, L. 2002. 'The Influence of Early Life Course Religious Exposure on Young Adults' Dispositions Towards Childbearing', *Journal for the Scientific Study of Religion* 41 (2): 325–40.

Pearce, L. and Axinn, W. 1998. 'The Impact of Family Religious Life on Mother-Child Relations', *American Sociological Review* 63: 810–28.

Radcliffe-Brown, A. 1952. 'Religion and Society' in *idem, Structure and Function in Primative Society*. London: Cohen and West.

Richter, P. and Francis, L. 1998. *Gone But Not Forgotten*. London: Darton, Longman and Todd.

Roof, W. 1994. *A Generation of Seekers: The Spiritual Journey of the Baby Boom Generation*, San Francisco: Harper and Row.

Roof, W. and Gesch, L. 1995. 'Changing Patterns of Work, Family and Religion'. In N. Ammerman and W. Roof (eds) *Work, Family and Religion in Contemporary Society*. New York: Routledge.

Roof, W. and Hadaway, C. 1979. 'Denominational Switching in the Seventies: Going Beyond Glock and Stark', *Journal for the Scientific Study of Religion*, 18: 363–77.

Sandomirsky, S. and Wilson, J. 1990. 'Processes of Disaffiliation: Religious Mobility Among Men and Women', *Social Forces* 68: 1211–29.

Serow, R. and Dreyden, J. 1990. 'Community Service Among College and University Students: Individual and Institutional Relationships', *Adolescence* 25: 553–66.

Siegel, K. and Shrimshaw, E. 2002. 'The Perceived Benefits of Religious and Spiritual Coping Among Older Adults Living with HIV/AIDS', *Journal for the Scientific Study of Religion* 41 (1); 87–101.

Shattuck, C. 1999. *Hinduism*. London: Routledge.

Sherkat, D. 2000. '"That They Be Keepers of the Home": The Effects of Conservative Religion on Early and Late Transition into Housewifery', *Review of Religious Research* 41 (3): 344–58.

Smith, T. 1992. 'Are Conservative Churches Really Growing?', *Review of Religious Research* 33 (1): 305–59.

Steinitz, L. 1980. 'Religiosity, Well-Being, and Weltanschauung Among the Elderly', *Journal for the Scientific Study of Religion* 19 (1): 60–7.

Stoetzel, J. 1983. *Les Valeurs du Temps Présent: une Enquête Européenne*. Paris: Presses Universitaires de France.

Strawbridge, W., Cohen, R., Shema, S. and Kaplan, G. 1997. 'Frequent Attendance at Religious Services and Mortality Over 28 Years', *American Journal of Public Health* 87: 957–61.

Thompson, E. Jr. and Remmes, R. 2002. 'Does Masculinity Thwart Being Religious? An Examination of Older Men's Religiousness', *Journal for the Scientific Study of Religion* 41 (3): 521–32.

Thorson, J. 1983. 'Spiritual Well-being in a Secular Society', *Generations* 8: 10–11.

Thorton, A. and Camburg, D. 1987. 'The Influence of the Family on Pre-marital Sexual Attitudes and Behaviour', *Demography* 24 (3): 323–40.

Tilley, J. 2003. 'Secularization and Aging in Britain: Does Family Formation Cause Greater Religiosity', *Journal for the Scientific Study of Religion* 42 (2): 269–78.

Varon, S. and Riley, A. 1999. 'Relationship Between Maternal Church Attendance and Adolescent Mental Health and Social Functioning', *Psychiatric Services* 50: 799–805.

Volt, J. 1991. *Muslims of America*, New York: Oxford University Press.

Walter, T. 1999a. *On Bereavement: The Culture of Grief*. Buckingham: Open University Press.

Walter, T. 1999b. 'Popular Afterlife Beliefs in the Modern West'. In P. Badman and C. Becker (eds) *Death and Eternal Life in the World Religions*, London: Paragon.

Walter, T. and Davie, G. 1998. 'The Religiosity of Women in the Modern West', *British Journal of Sociology* 49 (4): 639–60.

Walter, T. and Waterhouse, H. 1999. 'A Very Private Belief: Reincarnation in Contemporary England', *Sociology* 60 (2): 187–97.

Weber, M. 1978. *Economy and Society: An Outline of Interpretive Sociology*, G. Roth and C. Wittch (eds). Berkeley, CA: University of California Press.

Whitbourne, S. 1999. 'Identity and Adaptation to the Ageing Process'. In C. Ryff and V. Marshall (eds) *The Self and Society in Aging Processes*. New York: Springer, 122–49.

Wilson, B. 1976. *Contemporary Transformations of Religion*. London: Oxford University Press.

Wilson, J. and Sherkat, D. 1994. 'Return to the Fold', *Journal for the Scientific Study of Religion* 60: 84–103.

Wright, L., Frost, C. and Wisecarver, S. 1992. 'Church Attendance, Meaningfulness of Religion, and Depressive Symptomatology Among Adolescents', *Journal of Youth and Adolescence* 22: 559–68.

Wright, L., Frost, C. and Wisecarver, S. 1993. 'Church Attendance, Meaningfulness of Religion, and Depressive Symptomatology Among Adolescents', *Journal of Youth and Adolescence* 22: 559–68.

PART VIII

Case Studies from Around the World

This final Part of the Handbook stands apart from its predecessors. The following five chapters reflect critically on some of the most significant features of religion in five countries or regions that have received less attention here and elsewhere in the sociology of religion than they deserve. All of them discuss problems in simply adopting concepts and explanations used to explain religion in Western liberal democracies. The fact that our theories do not always travel well is a needed corrective in a world that sometimes seems drunk on globalisation but starved for local specifics.

Chapter 30, by **Fenggang Yang**, analyses the highly distinctive, tripartite marketisation of religion that has developed in China since the late 1970s and shares a scepticism towards rational choice thinking about the presumed association between religious markets, de-regulation and pluralism. In the context of China's 'religious oligopoly', the state keeps all religious activity under close surveillance whilst permitting only five 'official' religions to operate publicly in a 'red' market. Meanwhile, a 'black' market of officially banned religions continues to function with great difficulty; and a 'grey' market of religions with ambiguous legal status enjoys a precarious existence on the margins of public life. Yang analyses two

contrasting cases and their respective strategies for survival and – modest – success. Contrary to rational choice theory, the expansion of a particular Buddhist community not far from Beijing cannot be explained in terms of ideological strictness or exclusiveness. Its success is due to the leader's personal skills, the marketability of his 'brand' of Buddhism, the support of wealthy overseas supporters and, most importantly, the backing of political authorities who came to realise the community's potential for generating economic wealth from tourism and the 'heritage' business. By contrast, Yang shows that a remote Christian church that was subject to harsh discrimination for many years has survived by studiously conforming to all regulations and by honouring the patriotic rhetoric demanded by political authorities. Attempts to eradicate or suppress the Christian group have failed, but official suspicion of 'foreign' religion remains strong, thereby confirming Yang's insistence that marketisation of religion in China should not be confused with pluralisation.

A form of marketisation also began to take place in Central and Eastern Europe (CEE) after the collapse of communist regimes in the early 1990s. But, as **Irena Borowik** explains in Chapter 31, politicians and the courts have sought to control the liberalisation of religion and the revitalisation of religious beliefs, practices and organisations, while continuing the state suppression inflicted to varying degrees since the mid-1940s. Since Christian Orthodoxy, Roman Catholicism and Protestantism have been long aligned with political, ethnic and national divisions in CEE, it is not surprising that religion is once again at the centre of conflicts. Each of these main religious traditions now grapples with explaining its history under communism and competing with other older faiths and with new religious movements. Borowik also points out that research on current levels and types of religiosity in the CEE countries seems inconsistent – at least at first glance. On the one hand, rates of religious participation have risen significantly since the early 1990s; on the other hand, the rates are much lower for younger generations, thereby suggesting that the strong resurgence of religion may be short-lived. In any case, Borowik insists that it is necessary to distinguish between three types of individual religiosity: cultural, core, and 'being religious in one's own way' – all developing unevenly. For all their differences, the CEE countries form a fascinating laboratory for examining religious phenomena such as secularisation and religion-state relations.

Strong links between ethnic, religious and national identifications also loom large in **Stephen Sharot**'s analysis in Chapter 32 of Judaism in Israel since the state's foundation in 1948 and during the bitter conflict that continues to crescendo between the state and its Palestinian minority. He describes the growing hostilities between and among Muslim, Christian, and Jewish 'ethno-nationalisms' as increasingly religious, and this includes the deepening acrimonious disputes between religious and secular Jews. The Israeli state has no official religion, but religion looms large in the public and political realm. At the same time, secularisation is also reflected in the differentiation of secular and religious spheres, declining rates of religious beliefs, and marginalisation of religion to the private world. Secularism, civil religion, extreme Jewish orthopraxy and nationalistic Zionist messianism all co-exist

uneasily in Israel, and their tensions have only intensified with continuing waves of culturally clashing immigrants from different regions of the world. Sharot's chapter sounds a warning to sociologists of religion against taking secularisation for granted and assuming that privatisation is the master trend of religious change in the twenty-first century.

Shortly before Israel became a sovereign state, Japan acquired a new, post-World War II constitution that placed strict limits on the place of religion in the state's affairs. But **Susumu Shimazono** contends in Chapter 33 that the distinction between religion and non-religion is blurred in the Japanese context. He calls into question a number of Western assumptions about the definition of religion and, in particular, raises the politically sensitive issue of how far the Shinto tradition should be considered 'religious'. The difficulty lies in deciding whether the pre-war system of 'State Shinto' was really demolished in 1945 if the practice of Emperor worship remains in place and if worship in neighbourhood shrines retains an element of veneration for the Japanese state. Much depends on how 'State Shinto' is defined; and the heart of this issue involves questions about the sacredness of the Emperor and the State. Shimazono adopts a broad definition of 'State shinto' and shows that it persists in the many quotidian rites commonly performed but also that it has grown stronger and more politically assertive since the 1970s. Indeed, the political mobilisation of Shinto in Japan resembles that of other right-wing religio-nationalist movements in the US, Israel, Russia and India. Shimazono's chapter provides a needed re-thinking of our understanding of religion and its possible imbrication with politics and the state.

Finally, in Chapter 34, **Roberto Blancarte** challenges sociologists of religion in another fashion through his focus on the notion of popular religion and its relations with the predominantly Catholic mainstream of Mexican religion. Long after Mexico emerged from colonisation, began to 'modernise', and displayed the unquestionably Western-originated features of laicity and church-state separation, many of its pre-Hispanic beliefs and practices are still alive, thereby problematising Western assumptions about secularisation. Moreover, because popular religion has had a significant impact on social and political life in Mexico, it is quite different from its equivalents in other countries. Blancarte asks to what extent Mexican popular religion is compatible with pluralism and especially with the increasing and increasingly diverse surge of Protestantism. He argues that Protestantism is better considered as a form of religious dissidence than an expression of modernity, and notes that despite their occasionally authoritarian character, Protestant movements display continuities with popular religion and newer forms of communitarianism. Meanwhile, notions of laicity and secularisation apply more to the political sphere than to the everyday life of individuals. Sociologists of religion are invited to look at their own countries in the conceptual mirror held up to them by Mexico.

30

Oligopoly Dynamics: Official Religions in China

FENGGANG YANG

In the economic approach to the study of religious change, the nature of religious economies is commonly dichotomized into monopoly and free market. According to Stark and Finke (2000), a religious monopoly, enforced by state regulation, breeds a lazy clergy and consequently a less religiously mobilized population. Conversely, in a deregulated market, that is, a free market, religious pluralism tends to prevail over monopoly. 'To the degree that religious economies are unregulated and competitive, overall levels of religious participation will be high' (Stark and Finke 2000: 199).

This simplistic conceptualization has two problems. First, critics (Bruce 2000; Beaman 2003) have pointed out that there is no completely unregulated market, and that state regulations can be either *against* religion or *for* religion. In the U.S., for example, the First Amendment establishes basic rules; and zoning, tax, and other regulations are also pertinent to religious organizations. In this sense, there is no 'unregulated' religious economy. Nonetheless, it is important to note that U.S. regulations are not intended to restrict any particular faith, but to ensure equal competition and free religious exercise, although the reality may fall short of the ideal (Beaman 2003; Beyer 2003; Gill 2003). *Equal treatment to all religions, instead of freedom from regulation, should be considered the most important measure of religious freedom.*

Second, Stark and Finke link together the terms 'unregulated and competitive' in categorizing certain religious economies, but how about religious economies that are both regulated *and* competitive? Conceptually, this is probably the case for oligopoly economies, in which only a select few religions are permitted and the rest are suppressed. Indeed, most countries fall into this category nowadays. Oligopoly is certainly not monopoly, nor can it be equated to pluralism or to a *laissez-faire* free market. Given their prevalence in today's world, the dynamics of oligopoly economies of religion deserve much more careful examination. Under oligopoly regulation, how do the officially sanctioned religions operate? Is there inter-religious competition? What kind of religious groups grow or decline?

Elsewhere (Yang 2006) I have articulated a triple market model to account for the religious economy of China and similar economies under heavy regulation. I argue that 'heavy regulation leads not to religious reduction, but to complication of the religious market, resulting in a tripartite market with different dynamics' (Yang 2006: 97): a red market (officially permitted religions), a black market (officially banned religions), and a gray market (religions with an ambiguous legal/illegal status). A red market comprises all legal or officially permitted religious organizations, believers, and religious activities. It is 'red' because the officially sanctioned religions are stained with the official Communist ideology, as reflected in the rhetoric of clergy, the theological discourse, and the practices of these religious groups. The red market is a typical case of oligopoly, in which only a few religions are permitted and heavily regulated.

In this chapter I will elaborate on the red market religions in China. I will first describe the general status of the officially permitted religions and on the government's control apparatus, and then present two cases – a Buddhist temple and a Protestant church.[1] These descriptions will reveal the dynamics of state favoritism, religious competition, and patterns of religious survivals and revivals. Simply put, state favoritism might have contributed to the revival of Buddhism, but state discrimination has not stopped the rapid growth of Christianity. Indeed, state repression might be a factor contributing to the popularity of Christianity in the Chinese populace.

THE RELIGIOUS OLIGOPOLY OF CHINA

Following the establishment of the People's Republic of China (PRC) in 1949, atheist ideology compelled the Chinese Communist Party (CCP) to impose control over religion. Foreign missionaries were expelled, cultic or heterodox sects were banned, and major religions that were difficult to eliminate were co-opted into 'patriotic' associations. Through tremendous government maneuvers, the China Protestant Three-Self[2] Patriotic Movement Committee was established in 1954; the China

Buddhist Association in 1955; the China Islamic Association in 1957; the China Daoist Association in 1957; and the China Catholic Laity Patriotic Committee in 1957, which later became the China Catholic Patriotic Committee. Soon after that, existing denominational and sectarian systems were banned. Amalgamation was imposed upon each of the five religions.

Limited Tolerance and Broad Restriction

Following 13 years of banning all religion from the mid-1960s to the late 1970s, the CCP reverted to its previous policy of limited tolerance toward religion. In 1982, the CCP issued the edict 'The Basic Viewpoint and Policy on Religious Affairs during the Socialist Period of Our Country', widely known as 'Document No. 19', which has served as the basis for religious policy until today (Yang 2004). This fundamental document grants legal existence to Buddhism, Daoism, Islam, Protestantism, and Catholicism under the government-sanctioned 'patriotic' associations, but not to any group outside the five religious associations, nor to other religions. Denominationalism within a religion is prohibited. Document 19 proscribes proselytizing outside approved religious premises, and insists that atheist propaganda must be disseminated unremittingly. In line with this Document, the PRC Constitution of 1982 reaffirms freedom of religious belief, but clearly stipulates that only certain religious activities are protected. Since 1982, the CCP and the government have distributed circulars, enacted ordinances, and issued administrative orders (Potter 2003) that aim to tighten control over religion.

The control apparatus of religion involves several government ministries and bureaus, including the Ministry of Public Security (police), the Ministry of State Security, the Ministry of Civil Affairs, and the Religious Affairs Bureau (also known as State Administration of Religious Affairs), and the United Front Department (UFD) of the CCP Central Committee. The UFD has a division on religious affairs, which is supposed to frame religious policies and to rally religious leaders around the CCP. The day-to-day administration of religious affairs is in the hands of the Religious Affairs Bureau (RAB). The RAB operates downwards from the central through provincial and prefecture levels down to county governments, sometimes combined with the Commission of Ethnic Affairs at the provincial and county levels. At provincial and lower levels, the RAB chief is often an associate director of the CCP's United Front Department.

RAB oversees and manages all day-to-day religion-related affairs, including approving the opening of temples, churches, and mosques, approving special religious gatherings and activities, and approving the appointment of leaders in the religious associations. In practice, the RAB usually rules through the religious associations. The associations of the five official religions are nongovernmental organizations in name but they function as an extension and delegation of RAB. For example, in principle, the provincial-level Three-Self Patriotic Movement Committee (TSPM) holds the power to ordain ministers, but no one can be ordained without prior approval from the provincial RAB. The prefecture- or county-level TSPM appoints the senior pastor of local churches, but the appointment must be first approved by the same level RAB. More importantly, the national, provincial, prefecture, and county level TSPMs are separate organizations independent from each other. That is, the local TSPMs are not under the leadership of the provincial or national TSPMs. TSPMs report to the RAB on the same level and the one immediately above. When a church plans to organize meetings or activities involving people beyond the local administrative region, it has to apply to the higher-level RAB. That is, if the activity involves people from another county, it has to be approved by the prefecture RAB; if from another prefecture, then from the provincial RAB; if from another province, then from the state RAB. This applies to all five religions.

The RAB plays the central role in dealing with religious believers and organizations, and it cooperates with other government agencies in reinforcing religious regulations. Religious associations must also register with the Ministry of Civil Affairs, but the registration must be stamped first by the RAB. The Ministry of Public Security deals with all illegal religious activities, including any illegal activities of the five official religions and all activities of all other religions. Like political activists and dissident groups, some religious groups and active leaders are also watched by the Ministry of State Security (MSS). Since the early 1990s, the Chinese authorities have made it an integral part of religious policy to guard against infiltration by foreign religious organizations and foreign political entities that are suspected of using religion as a means of political infiltration.

It is clear that the red market is not an open market, nor a free market. Only five religions are permitted. Many restrictions are imposed on government-sanctioned churches, temples, and mosques. They include 'monitoring by the state, required political study for pastors [and other religious ecclesiastics], certain restrictions on acceptable topics for preaching and intervention in church personnel matters' (Bays 2003: 492). Some restrictions are explicit in law, others are implicit in CCP circulars, and many are arbitrarily decided by local officials. Explicitly, Article 36 of the Constitution of the PRC (in effect since 1982) maintains: The state protects normal religious activities. No one may make use of religion to engage in activities that disrupt public order, impair the health of citizens, or interfere with the educational system of the state. A key word here is 'normal'. 'Normal' religious activities are defined by the officials in charge. What is normal in other countries may not be normal in the eyes of the Chinese authorities. For example, the religious education of children is common in most countries. In China, however, providing religious education to children under the age of 18 is mostly prohibited. In principle, Christian churches cannot lawfully hold Sunday school for children. Similarly, churches are not allowed to baptize young people under the age of 18.

Of course, exceptions can be made when politically necessary, such as when a child was recognized as the reincarnation of the Tibetan Buddhist Panchen Lama. Religious initiation and education have been permitted for several boy lamas. In 2001, Christians filed a law suit against the local RAB in Wenzhou, Zhejiang, contending for equal rights to comparable religious practice for their children (Pomfret 2002), but the ban is still in effect. In the red market of religion, Chinese authorities do not treat all officially permitted religions equally.

The Size of the Red Market of Religion

It is difficult to know how many believers there are in the five permitted religions because the Chinese authorities usually guard such numbers as state secrets similar to military secrets. Nonetheless, responding to pressures and inquiries from foreign governments and Western media organizations – and reacting to criticisms from international human rights groups and religious organizations – the Chinese government has provided some religious statistics. The Chinese government's *White Paper: Freedom of Religious Belief in China* (1997) states:

> According to incomplete statistics, there are over 100 million followers of various religious faiths, more than 85,000 sites for religious activities, some 300,000 clergy and over 3,000 religious organizations throughout China. In addition, there are 74 religious schools and colleges run by religious organizations for training clerical personnel.
>
> –Buddhism has a history of 2,000 years in China. Currently China has 13,000-some Buddhist temples and about 200,000 Buddhist monks and nuns. Among them are 120,000 lamas and nuns, more than 1,700 Living Buddhas, and 3,000-some temples of Tibetan Buddhism and nearly 10,000 Bhiksu and senior monks and more than 1,600 temples of Pali Buddhism.
>
> –Taoism, native to China, has a history of more than 1,700 years. China now has over 1,500 Taoist temples and more than 25,000 Taoist priests and nuns.
>
> –Islam was introduced into China in the seventh century. Nowadays in China there are ten national minorities, including the Hui and Uygur, with a total population of 18 million, whose faith is Islam. Their 30,000-odd mosques are served by 40,000 Imams and Akhunds.
>
> –Catholicism was introduced into China intermittently in the seventh century, but it had not spread widely until

after the Opium War in 1840. At present, China has four million Catholics, 4,000 clergy and more than 4,600 churches and meeting houses.

> –Protestantism was first brought to China in the early 19th century and spread widely after the Opium War. There are about 10 million Protestants, more than 18,000 clergy, more than 12,000 churches and 25,000-some meeting places throughout China.

These numbers are believed to be based on a religious census conducted jointly by the State RAB and the Central UFD in 1995, the details of which have not been released to the public. Since then, the Chinese government has been reluctant to update the statistics, although some government officials and religious leaders acknowledge the rapid increase of most religions.

Actually, these numbers are guesstimates at best, fabrications at worst, serious undercounts for certain. Because of the Communist desire for reducing religion, local government officials tend to under-report the numbers of religious believers. As a matter of fact, Ye Xiaowen, the head of the State RAB since 1995, acknowledged this ubiquitous problem in a speech at the CCP Central School in Beijing. According to him, a major problem of gathering accurate statistics is that, as a rule of the political game, 'the numbers come from the cadres; and the cadres come from the numbers'. More precisely, local officials who report negative or lower growth of religion are more likely to get promoted (Ye [1997] 2000: 9).

Meanwhile, it is difficult to count religious believers. Buddhism and Daoism do not have a clear membership system. A Buddhist or Daoist believer does not *belong* to a particular temple, may patronize several temples, or may just practice at home. Although Protestant and Catholic churches have had clear definitions of membership, congregational leaders are often discouraged from reporting the real numbers because of the government's hostile policies toward Christianity. Many churches do not even keep baptismal records, so that baptized Christians are not easily identifiable by the authorities.

Nonetheless, when we examine official statistics over the past several decades (see Table 30.1), we can still see some broad trends.

Table 30.1   *Official statistics of five religions in China*

	Catholic Believers (million)	Protestant Believers (million)	Islamic Population (million)[4]	Buddhist Believers (million)	Daoist Believers (million)
Early 1950s[a, 2]	2.7	0.7	8.0		
1956[b]	3.0	0.8	10.0	Several tens of millions[3]	10.0[3]
1982[a]	3.0	3.0	10.0		
1991[c]	3.5	4.5	17.0		
1995[d]	4.0	10.0	18.0		
	Clergy[5]	Clergy	Clergy	Monks/Nuns	Monks/Nuns
1982[a]	3,400	5,900	20,000	27,000	2,600
1995[d]	4,300	18,000	40,000	200,000	25,700
	Churches and meeting points[6]	Churches and meeting points	Mosques	Temples	Temples
1995[d]	4,377	37,000	36,200	13,000	1,557

Sources: a. Document No. 19; b. Luo (2001)[1]; c. White Paper on the Status of Human Rights in China; d. Li (1999)[1].

Notes:

1. Li (1999) and Luo (2001) are officials of the CCP United Front Department.

2. The numbers of the early 1950s are consistent with nongovernmental and non-Chinese publications.

3. No number of Buddhist and Daoist believers is given in most of the years because there is no membership system. The only estimates in 1956 were uttered by the late Chairman Mao Zedong in a published conversation.

4. The number of Muslims is the total population of 10 ethnic minorities that consider Islam as their ethnic religion, although many do not practice or believe.

5. The professional ecclesiastics of different religions are not totally comparable because Buddhist and Daoist monks and nuns may not interact with lay believers, whereas Catholic priests, Protestant pastors, and Islamic imams are ministering to the laity.

6. The religious venues of different religions also have very different functions: Churches and mosques are buildings for regular weekly lay gathering, whereas many temples are monasteries in the mountains that receive occasional pilgrims, and some of them are secluded for hermits with few or no outside visitors. The so-called Protestant and Catholic meeting points are mostly congregations with simple, shabby buildings, not necessarily small congregations.

The numbers of believers listed for 1956 and 1982 deserve particular attention. The 1956 figures are the last official count before the enforced disbanding of denominations, followed by 13 years of efforts to eradicate all religion (1966–1979). The official count in 1982 shows that the numbers of Catholics and Muslims remained the same, while the number of Protestant Christians increased 3.75 times from 800,000 to 3,000,000.

It is widely known that many religious people have stayed away from the red market but engaged in the black and gray markets (Yang 2006). The China Buddhist Association leaders sometimes claim more than 100 million Buddhists. Catholics inside and outside China often estimate the number of Chinese Catholics at 10 to 12 millions. Estimates of Protestants vary widely, from 50 million to over 100 million. The population of 10 ethnic minority groups that subscribe to Islam is about 22 million today, although many of them may not practice the religion.

Specific cases clearly reveal the dynamics of the red market religions. In the next two sections I will describe a Buddhist temple and a Christian church, both of which are government approved religious venues. The Christian church faces many more obstacles to carrying out its normal religious activities, whereas the Buddhist temple has managed to expand rapidly under government support.

A THRIVING BUDDHIST TEMPLE

Bailin is a Buddhist temple located in Zhaoxian, Hebei, about 300 kilometers (186 miles) south of Beijing. Before 1988, all the temple buildings except a pagoda (*stupa*) were destroyed. Since 1988, a number of buildings have been constructed one after another, culminating with the grandeur of the Ten-Thousand Buddha Hall completed in 2003. Within 15 years, a site of ruins was transformed into a sublime Buddhist center with a 14-acre (80 mu) compound of magnificent buildings in the traditional Buddhist style of architecture. The number of residential monks has reached around 150, and their outlook and ritual performance have impressed many domestic and international Buddhist believers.

Moreover, Bailin has functioned as the center of Buddhist revivals in the whole Province of Hebei and beyond. By the end of 1987, the whole province had only two Buddhist temples open for religious services; their shabby halls and tatty living quarters were in desperate need of renovation, but the small income from devotees and tourism was not enough even to support the daily life of the few ailing monks who tended the temples. In the whole province, no more than 4,000 lay Buddhist believers had taken *guiyi*, a formal rite of conversion comparable to baptism for Christians. From that point on, however, Buddhist growth in Hebei has been nothing but extraordinary. For example, within the space of two days in May 1988, 461 people in the county of Renxian in Southern Hebei took the *guiyi* rite under the Bailin Abbot, the Venerable Jing Hui (*Chan* Magazine[3] 1990, 4). On 8 January 1995, over a thousand people took the rite at the Bailin Temple (*Chan* Magazine 1995, 2). More and more temples were reopened, restored, or rebuilt throughout Hebei Province. By the end of 2003, there were over 580 Buddhist monks and nuns stationed at over 280 Buddhist temples open for religious services. Hebei suddenly became one of the provinces with a very active Buddhist Sangha (monks and nuns) and lay believers, attracting pilgrims from beyond Hebei and China.

How did the Bailin Temple achieve such expansion within a mere 15 years? How could it lead revivals throughout the whole province? In the sociological literature on religious growth and decline, the dominant supply-side model argues that in an unregulated religious market, strict and competitive groups tend to grow (see Finke and Stark 1992; Finke and Iannaccone 1993; Iannaccone 1994; Finke 1997; Stark and Finke 2000). However, the thriving Bailin Temple is not strict, for it has offered Summer Camps free of charge to participants. Nor is its doctrine in high tension with the surrounding culture. To the contrary, Jing Hui has proclaimed a brand of Buddhism that clearly accommodates the ruling CCP and its Communist ideology. He emphasizes living harmoniously with other people, rather than challenging others.

To explain the success of the Bailin Buddhist Temple in today's China, it is necessary to include – but go beyond – institutional factors as well as individuals' tactics. The major factors in its success include the able leadership of the well-connected and well-positioned Venerable Jing Hui, his articulation and promotion of a marketable brand of Buddhism – the Life Chan – with innovative slogans and practices, the financial support of wealthy overseas and domestic donors, and most importantly, the political support of government officials.

The Leadership of the Sangha

Traditional Chinese Buddhism has been a Sangha-centered religion. Following the Mahàyàna tradition, the Sangha is composed of celibate monks and nuns living at the temple-monastery to carry out their own practices, to tend the statues of Buddhas and Bodhisattvas, and to perform rituals for lay worshippers. Some of the lay believers may take the conversion rite of *guiyi*, but they do not belong to, or formally affiliate with, a temple. Lay believers who are attracted by the Sangha, especially by the abbot, may patronize the temple by making donations to the monks or to funds for the construction of temple buildings. Most lay believers go to a temple to make personal requests, and their donations tend to be small and spontaneous. Therefore, a temple's existence and expansion depend less on the number of regular attenders at the temple and more on a few wealthy and generous donors. A charismatic abbot is thus critical for a temple's survival and growth.

The Venerable Master Jing Hui is the indispensable magnet in the success story of the Bailin Temple. He is an entrepreneurial monk who has mobilized multiple resources for his endeavors to revitalize Buddhism. Born in 1933 in Hubei Province in South-Central China, he was abandoned by his parents in dire poverty when he was only 18 months old. Reared at a Buddhist nunnery, he became a novice monk at age 15. A few years later, he took refuge as a disciple of the Venerable Master Xu Yun, the most revered Buddhist monk in modern China. In 1956, the Chinese Buddhist Academy was established. Jing Hui entered the first class, and upon graduation he was admitted to its graduate program. His talents and diligence were recognized by his classmates and teachers. However, sharing the fate of most clergymen in the 1950s and 1960s, in due time Jing Hui was persecuted and sent to a camp for reeducation through labor. During the brutal Cultural Revolution period, Jing Hui was even forced to return to a secular life in his hometown in Hubei Province. Not until 1979, when the CCP's religious policy reverted from eradication of religion to limited toleration, was he able to return to the religious life.

Before coming to Hebei Province, Jing Hui worked as the chief editor of the *Fa Yin* (Voice of Dharma), the official magazine of the Buddhist Association of China. Working at the magazine and being involved in the operation of the Buddhist Association of China for nearly a decade, Jing Hui gained remarkable experience and unusual access to various resources.

First of all, this mannerly monk was able to develop personal relationships with various important people, including very senior monks throughout the country, foreign Buddhist leaders, overseas lay Buddhist patrons, and government officials in charge of religious affairs. The political, religious, and financial support of these people was essential for the revitalization of the Bailin Temple.

Secondly, the nature of his work editing the magazine made it both necessary and possible for Jing Hui to become a scholar, knowledgeable about the Buddhist theories, ideas, and practices of various sects and senior monks, as well as about modern developments of Buddhism in China and other societies. Working in this important position helped Jing Hui develop a thorough understanding of political dynamics and policy subtleties. The chief editor of the official magazine is the ultimate gatekeeper of the information flow within the Chinese Buddhist community. He was responsible for publishing articles that were both appealing to Buddhist believers and acceptable to the CCP authorities.

In October 1987, he accompanied a Japanese Buddhist delegation of over 100 people to visit the lonely *stupa* in Zhaoxian. The pilgrims expressed the wish to restore the Bailin Temple. They had even raised some funds in Japan for the restoration work. Soon after, coincidently, representatives of the Hebei Province's CCP's United Front Department (UFD) and the Religious Affairs Bureau (RAB) went to Beijing to invite Jing Hui to come to establish the Hebei Buddhist Association. Zhao Puchu, the President of the Buddhist Association of China, commissioned Jing Hui to go and establish the Hebei Buddhist Association and revitalize the Bailin Temple and the Linji Temple, another renowned Buddhist temple in Hebei Province. With Zhao's endorsement and evident support from people with some political clout, Jing Hui accepted the challenge and came to Shijiazhuang, the capital of Hebei Province, in January 1988. Soon after, the Hebei Buddhist Association was organized, and Jing Hui became its President.

Before going to Hebei, Jing Hui had attracted some highly educated young people as followers or disciples through the *Fa Yin* magazine. Following the 1989 Tiananmen Square incident, when the student-led pro-democracy movement was crushed by tanks, many college-educated young people began to turn to religion to search for personal salvation and national direction. Whereas some urban young people have converted to Christianity (Yang 2005), a number of college graduates have become Buddhist monks and nuns. Jing Hui has attracted several such highly educated young people who have become his disciples. Overall, it is said that about a third of the Bailin Sangha have had a college education.

A Marketable Brand of Buddhism

In late dynastic China, Buddhism became a religion very much detached from the world. The teachings focused on sufferings in the world and on how to become free from these sufferings through chanting, rituals, and secluded meditation. Most of the temples were monasteries deep in the mountains. Along with its increasing withdrawal from the world, Buddhism declined in Ming and Qing Dynasties. However, throughout its long history, some Buddhists have emphasized helping others to achieve enlightenment and to engage with the world. The Chan sect especially underscores gaining enlightenment in daily life.

In modern times, some Buddhist laymen and monks hoped to reform traditional Buddhism and make it more relevant in social life. The most influential Buddhist reformer in the first half of the twentieth century was the Venerable Master Tai Xu (1890–1947). He advocated 'Buddhism in the World' (*renjian fojiao*). He also instigated such reforms as establishing Buddhist academies on the model of Christian seminaries and operating charity projects on the model of Christian missionary works. One of the most notable contemporary leaders of reformed Buddhism has been the Venerable Master Hsing Yun (1927–), who developed the Foguangshan sect and led it in establishing many temples in Taiwan, Southeast Asia, and North America. He refers to his brand of Buddhism as 'Buddhism of Life' or 'Humanist Buddhism' (*rensheng fojiao* or *renben fojiao*). In March-April 1989, Hsing Yun made his first visit to mainland China, together with a 70-person delegation. Jing Hui, representing the Buddhist Association of China, was among the few who accompanied Hsing Yun and his delegation on their four-week pilgrimage journey throughout China.

After coming to Bailin Temple, Jing Hui developed his own distinct brand of Buddhism – the Life Chan (*sheng huo chan*). In the 'Life Chan Pronouncement', published in the *Chan* magazine, he states that learning Buddhism, practicing cultivation, and living life should be combined into an organic unity. 'It is

Buddhism with Chinese cultural characteristics' (*Chan* Magazine 1993, 1). He further articulated:

> The ultimate goal of Life Chan is 'a life of enlightenment, a life of dedication' (*jue wu ren sheng, feng xian ren sheng*) …. 'A life of enlightenment' is continuous improvement of the quality of oneself … and 'a life of dedication' is continuous effort to harmonize self-other relations. (*Chan* Magazine 2002: 6)

To promote his brand of Buddhism, the Life Chan, Bailin Temple has been holding the annual Life Chan Summer Camp since 1993. The week-long camp includes traditional Buddhist practices such as morning and evening chanting, sitting-still meditation, and walking meditation. It also has innovative activities appealing to intellectuals, such as lectures and discussion sessions with scholars and the more scholastic monks. In addition, it incorporates the modernized ritual of passing on the candlelight at an evening service, which has been popularized by Hsing Yun and his Foguangshan sect in Taiwan. The Life Chan Summer Camp has been a great success, with up to 500 participants in recent years, the maximum the temple could accommodate. It has also become known as the signature activity of the Bailin Temple, highly praised by the participants, top leaders of the Buddhist Association of China, overseas and domestic Buddhist clergy, and university scholars of Buddhist studies.

The summer camp has been free of charge for participants, and the funding has come from donations by Hong Kong Buddhist business people. In fact, the summer camp has been the most effective means for Bailin Temple to attract financial support for its physical expansion. Between 1993 and 2003, the Bailin Temple doubled in size by acquiring adjacent land.

Political Support by the Authorities

Both the Sangha leadership and having a marketable brand of Buddhist ideas and practices have been important for Bailin Temple's revitalization. But the most critical factor for its success has been the political support of government officials.

First of all, without the permission of the authorities, there would have been no reconstruction of the Bailin Temple. After all, the old Bailin Temple had been largely destroyed before the Communists took power, thus it fell outside the range of 'implementing the religious policy' after 1979. The post-1979 religious policy has been very much restricted to restoring temples, churches, and mosques to the level immediately before the Cultural Revolution or that of the late 1950s at best. The Bailin Temple was not on the 1983 list of 'major temples' designated for restoration as religious venues, which includes only two Buddhist temples in Hebei – Linji in Zhengding and Puning in Chengde. Nonetheless, the Bailin Temple was granted permission for restoration – indeed, not only permitted, but also actively encouraged and supported by the authorities at all levels.

Although there were very few Buddhist believers in Hebei in the 1980s, the Hebei government provided firm and persistent support for Jing Hui in his efforts to develop Buddhism in Hebei. The Hebei RAB actively and insistently recruited Jing Hui, covered the expenses of his initial activities in Hebei, and directed the local county government to 'return' the site of the Bailin Temple to the newly established Hebei Buddhist Association. Since then, the Hebei RAB has sent representatives to every major activity of the Bailin Temple, including every ceremony of ground-breaking and dedication of the buildings, every Life Chan Summer Camp, and other major gatherings. Furthermore, provincial support has gone up in rank, including the most powerful Provincial CCP Secretary.

Similarly important for the success of Bailin Temple is the support of the local government of Zhaoxian County. The county government's support has been mostly motivated by the perceived economic benefits, including attracting overseas Buddhist businessmen to invest in the county. Beginning in 2001, a 33,000 square-meter (eight acre) commercial plaza has been developed across from the Bailin Temple. It was designated as one of the major economic development projects of Shijiazhuang Prefecture and Zhaoxian County. It boasts of being the country's largest wholesale center for artefacts used in Buddhism, such as statues, incenses, construction materials, musical instruments, clothes, etc. How many economic benefits for the county have been generated by the temple-related projects remains to be studied.

The most important support for the Bailin Temple, however, comes from officials of the central government. Without the open encouragement of the highest authorities, the Bailin Temple would have been unable to hold the large-scale, high-profile, cross-provincial activity of the Life Chan Summer Camp. Without tacit backing by the highest authorities, Bailin Temple would have been unable to sustain criticisms from inside the Buddhist community and from Communist ideologues. Abbot Jing Hui acknowledges:

> Consistent support by the government is the fundamental assurance and guarantee for the expansion of our activities. This is because the Life Chan Summer Camp is a very sensitive activity. Many college students have participated in it. Some people raised criticisms, saying that Buddhism was competing with the Communist Party for the next generation. This view was brought to the Central United Front Department and the State Religious Affairs Bureau. In response, they [the officials] did some explanations... The State Religious Affairs Bureau, the Hebei Religious Affairs Bureau, and the United Front Department did a lot of work. They have indeed given us powerful support.

The support of the central government also manifests itself in publishing positive news reports in the *China Religions* magazine, the official publication of the State Religious Affairs Bureau, and other state media. They have also arranged to have China Central Television make a special news report about the Bailin Temple. But the most effective support is through the visits of high-ranking officials. On 15 April 1999, the Chairman of the Chinese People's Political Consultative Conference and Politburo member, Li Ruihuan, visited Bailin Temple. On 1 April 2000, Vice Premier Qian Qishen came. On 5 November 2001, President Jiang Zemin, accompanied by top military and party officials, made a visit. Jing Hui told us that there were some difficulties early on:

> Things gradually began to turn better after the dedication of the Hall of the Universal Illuminating Light in 1992.

The really important moment was after completing the Guanyin Hall in 1995, when the Provincial Party Secretary made a visit. From then on it has really turned better... On 5 November 2001, President Jiang Zemin came to visit us. The situation turned unprecedentedly better. His visit itself was a very great support to us. It was not only helpful for us here, but also helpful for the whole Buddhist community.

Why does the central government support the Bailin Temple? There might be some interest in the positive moral functions of Buddhism during the transition toward a market economy. However, the more important reasons to support the Bailin Temple appear to be political. One concerns the outside world: Bailin Temple is used as a showcase of China's freedom of religion. The other concerns managing religious affairs: Bailin Temple is used as a model of religious accommodation to the socialist society under CCP rule.

First, China has been constantly criticized by Western countries for its bad human rights record, including its restriction of religious freedom. To answer Western criticisms, the Chinese government published the *White Paper about Freedom of Religious Beliefs* in 1997 and several other white papers about the human rights situation in China. It has also invited foreign delegations of religious leaders to visit religious sites in China. The Bailin Temple in the 1990s became an excellent showcase for the purpose of international public relations. Not only do Japanese pilgrims continue to make frequent visits to the Bailin Temple, but European and American delegations have now also been brought there. During a recent visit, the Politburo member Li Changchun made this remark: 'We should more often arrange for foreigners to come here to see, to let them know, the real status of religion in China.'

Second, since 1979, restrictions on religious organizations have increased (Potter 2003; Kindopp and Hamrin 2004), but restrictive regulations and severe suppression have not been effective in curtailing religious revivals. Adopting an alternative strategy since the mid-1990s, the authorities have tried hard to co-opt religious organizations – 'actively guide the religions to accommodate the socialist society.' The authorities have encouraged religious leaders to develop new theologies suitable for the socialist system under CCP rule.

Given this situation, it was indeed delightful for the CCP leaders to find that Jing Hui's Life Chan appeals to Buddhist believers. They hope that other Buddhist leaders will follow his example, and wish that other religions would model themselves on the Bailin Temple's approach. In practice, on 23 August 2004, a group of 66 Catholic leaders participating in a national seminar led by Bishop Ma Yinglin was taken to the Bailin Temple.

Meanwhile, the Bailin Temple Sangha has deliberately and frequently expressed patriotism. At major gatherings, the first item of the ritual procedure has always been to play the national anthem. The Bailin monks have also learned to repeat 'love the country and love the religion,' with 'love the country' preceding 'love the religion.' In the long speech given at the Third Conference of the Board of Directors of Hebei Buddhist Association on 29 November 2001, Jing Hui made repeated calls for patriotism, insisting that the Life Chan is fully compatible with the CCP's idealism:

It is totally possible to make Buddhism accommodate socialist society. The Buddha told us, the most fundamental principle of spreading the dharma is 'the proper theory for the right moment'. The proper theory for the right moment requires us to combine the Buddhist dharma with the particular social reality and mental reality, to serve the fundamental goal of purifying human hearts, and solemnizing the nation (*Chan Magazine* 2002: 2).

Jing Hui also equates the ideal Communist Society to the 'Pure Land' in Buddhism, saying that it is the best social system that humans have ever devised. Such words are certainly music to the ears of the CCP leaders who are in pressing need for affirmation of Communist society's ideological goals and for popular support of its leadership. In comparison, Christians in China are less generous in giving lip-service to the ruling Chinese Communist Party and its ideology.

A PERSEVERING VILLAGE CHURCH

Until recently, the rapid growth of Christianity in China since the 1980s had occurred mostly in rural areas (Leung 1999). The Wu Village (Wuzhuang, a pseudonym) is a remote village in the southeast corner of Gansu bordering Shaanxi Province. From Lanzhou, the capital of Gansu Province, it takes more than five hours by train to reach the city of Tianshui, and one more hour to get to the village by local train or two more hours by bus through the spiraling mountain roads. It takes about 18 hours by train from Tianshui to Beijing.

Christianity was first brought to the Tianshui area by British missionaries of the China Inland Mission at the end of the nineteenth century. In 1898, the Wuzhuang Christian Church was formed by over 30 converts. By 1949, when the People's Republic of China was founded, there were more than 200 believers in Wuzhuang.

In 1958, the church buildings were confiscated and occupied by the village government as its office and as the elementary school. In 1962, as the political climate became less tense, about 40 members came together and began Sunday worship services at the then elementary school. The building was used by the school on weekdays and by the church on Sundays. Beginning in Spring 1964, however, all religious activities were banned in the whole of Tianshui Prefecture, as well as in many other parts of the country. During the Cultural Revolution (1966–1976), several Wuzhuang Christian leaders were persecuted and jailed, including Deacon Wu Ende, who was in prison from 1966 to 1973 and who later became an independent evangelist.

In the 1970s, Wuzhuang Christians clandestinely gathered at homes in the night. In Summer 1975, two young men were baptized in the Wei River behind the village, the first baptisms in two decades. Many more people followed in their footsteps in the next few years. After secretly celebrating Christmas in 1978, they began Sunday worship services in the daytime – semi-openly – although still illegally. By 1980, the number of Christians in Wuzhuang had reached 300.

In 1982, Wuzhuang Christians succeeded in getting back one of three church properties, the one that had been used as the Village Committee Office. A new Village Committee Office compound was then constructed across

from the church; four loudspeakers were installed on top of its room. Wuzhuang Christianity began a period of rapid growth so that by 2000 there were at least a thousand Christians in Wuzhuang, who amounted to about a third of the total village population of 3,129.

Claiming the Anti-Imperialist Heritage

In 1982, religious tolerance was formally reinstated in 'Document No. 19.' Wuzhuang Christians took the circular to the local government bureaus and petitioned to get the buildings back. Only after showing this CCP document did the local government officials consent. In the process, the Beidao District TSPM Committee mediated between the government bureaus and Wuzhuang Christians, eventually reaching a compromise – returning one of the three church properties.

In the process of petitioning to reopen the church, besides leveraging with 'Document No. 19,' Wuzhuang Christians had to offer persuasive justifications that pleased the authorities. Above all, they had to acknowledge repeatedly the legitimate authority of the Chinese Communist Party. In their oral and written presentations, church leaders had to praise the greatness of the past and present CCP leadership, the glory of the CCP's history, and the correctness of the current CCP policies. Moreover, they had to recite the officially imposed slogan 'love our country, love our religion' (*ai guo ai jiao*), with 'love our country' preceding 'love our religion,' although many TSPM leaders did not feel comfortable singing such praises to the CCP and the state.

Wuzhuang Christians do not find all patriotic rhetoric difficult to say. Besides submission to the CCP and the state, patriotism in the official discourse also includes anti-imperialism. Wuzhuang Christians have had little difficulty about elaborating on this. In petitioning for the return of their church buildings, the leaders handed to the authorities a copy of the church history as narrated by Elder Wu Shengrong, which includes this anti-imperialist story: In 1920, after Wuzhuang Christians had built a sanctuary, a British missionary offered a donation and asked the church to give the deed to the China Inland Mission.

> At that time, our Elder Wu Buyi realized that it was the imperialists' trick to control our church. We firmly refused it, so that their planned plot failed. That was probably the first case of all the churches [in this area] in which a foreign swindle effort was of no avail.

The description of this incident was well liked by the TSPM and CCP authorities, for it was later included in the official publications, *History of Christianity in Tianshui* and *History of Christianity in Gansu Province*, as an example of Chinese believers' patriotism in their struggles against Western missionaries. As a matter of fact, that incident was the precursor of the Christian Independence Movement (*jidujiao zili yundong*), which spread throughout China in the second quarter of the twentieth century. The Wuzhuang Church History continues:

> In the year 1927, when the National Revolutionary Movement was at its climax, Brother Tong Lin-ge of Tianshui initiated the independence movement of the Chinese churches from the control of Western missionaries. He called Chinese believers to establish Chinese indigenous churches with four measures: Self-governing, self-supporting, self-evangelizing, and self-standing (zili, independence). So our village church became the 'Independent Christian Church of China' and formally cut off all ties with foreign missionaries. The imperialists' control of our church passed into history.

However, in spite of the heritage of Christian independence, Chinese authorities continue to treat Protestant and Catholic Christians with greater suspicion than other religious believers in regard to their political loyalty. Christians are still referred to as believers of a 'foreign religion.' The CCP worries that Chinese Christians may be used by foreign hostile forces that seek to 'peacefully subvert the socialist system.'

In 1991, the CCP circulated *Document No. 6 –* 'A Further Notice to Better Deal with Religious Affairs'. It declares that China faces two kinds of political threats related to religion. First, 'overseas enemy forces have always been using religion as an important tool for their strategic goal of "peaceful subversion", infiltrating China and causing damage to our country.' Second, 'the separatists are also making use of religion, attacking the leadership of the Party and the socialist system, threatening the unity of the country and harmony among the ethnic groups.' While Tibetan Buddhism and Uygur Islam are the references for the second threat, Protestantism and Catholicism are the focus of the first threat. Anti-infiltration has become a major concern of the authorities in regard to Christianity.

Within this social and political context, and to ensure continuous legal existence, Christian leaders of the government-approved churches must repeatedly reiterate their patriotism and political loyalty to the Chinese Communist Party, but they are only willing to do so to a certain extent.

'Give to Caesar What Is Caesar's, Give to God What is God's'

Besides the anti-imperialist heritage, Wuzhuang Christians also stress that they do love the Chinese nation and are good citizens. They would quote what Jesus said, 'give to Caesar what is Caesar's, and to God what is God's' (Matthew 22: 21). An often preached message to the congregation is 'all those who believe in the Lord are obedient to the laws and regulations.' Indeed, the accountant of the Wuzhuang Village Committee confirmed that 'These Jesus believers are all honest, good fellows, and really easy to deal with.' This pattern of civic obedience and social charity among Christians has been reported by several studies published in China (Xu and Li 1991; Jing 1995; Wang 1987).

However, obedience to the government does not mean that Wuzhuang Christians are willing to abandon their faith. Rather, it means that as long as they are given the space to practice their religion, they will be good citizens. While they are willing to 'give to Caesar what is Caesar's' they also insist on 'giving to God what is God's.'

The Chinese authorities unquestionably demand political loyalty above all else, including religious piety toward God. Li Dezhu, the

Deputy Minister of the Central United Front Department of the CCP, once said, 'In regard to religion, when the national and the people's interests are violated, there is but one principle to follow: Stand by the interests of the nation and the people. No ambiguity is permitted on this point. No damage to the state is allowed with whatever excuses' (Li 1996: 13). Such a demand places Christians in the government-approved churches in an impossible situation, forcing them to choose between compromising their faith and going against the authorities.

Fortunately, Christians do not have to deal with this problem everyday. In the reform era, it seems that as long as Christian leaders reiterate patriotic slogans and show respect to the CCP authorities on formal occasions, they do not have to take the slogan 'love the state first' to heart or change anything in their religious beliefs and practices. The current leader, Elder Liu Guizhu, said, 'The authorities often hold meetings to emphasize the importance of "loving our country and loving our religion". But as I see it, these meetings are nothing but formality and superficiality.'

It is interesting to note Elder Liu's name. His given name is Guizhu, which in Chinese literally means 'belongs to the Lord.' It is a name that Chinese Christians can immediately recognize for its Christian identity. However, he is known to the government officials as Liu Guozhu, which in Chinese means 'a pillar of the state' or 'a pillar of the nation,' a commonly recognizable patriotic name. Among Wuzhuang Christians, Elder Liu is known only as Guizhu, his Christian identity. He also referred to himself as Guizhu when we talked with him. It appears to us that to accommodate the authorities' demand for patriotism, Elder Liu chose to use the patriotic name 'a pillar of the state/nation' for the formal registration of the church and for official occasions. This kind of acknowledgement of political loyalty may seem superficial, but that seems to be good enough for government officials.

Keeping State Intrusion at Arm's Length

Government's control over religious organizations has been less effective in the rural areas than in cities. Urban churches are more easily and closely supervised by government officials. For example, following official guidelines or hints, ministers at the churches in Tianshui City have avoided preaching on certain topics. Pastor Wei of the Beidao Church told us:

> There *are* some topics that are not suitable to talk about at the present. The Religious Affairs Bureau has given me hints against topics like the doomsday, the final judgment, and the creation of the world. I should talk about them as little as possible, if at all. But we hold that, if it is in the Bible, we should talk about it. I am against the so-called 'construction of theological thinking'. That stuff belongs to the unbelieving type.

The 'construction of theological thinking' is a theological movement promoted by Bishop Ding Guangxun, the chief leader of the TSPM in the reform era. Bishop Ding has spoken on various occasions and published the *Collection of Ding Guangxun* in 1998. His central idea is to make Christianity compatible with the socialist society under Communist rule, which would be achieved by emphasizing the notion of love above everything else. Underground Christians have rejected this idea as giving up faith in Christ. Some aboveground church leaders have also resisted the movement as blurring distinctions between Christians and non-Christians. Both underground Christians and aboveground critics say that the importance of 'justification by faith' should not be compromised for whatever reasons.

Pastor Wei, who had been imprisoned as a young man for three years in a 'reform-through-labor camp' in Xinjiang, has been Chairman of the Beidao District TSPM Committee since the TSPM was reopened in 1982. While he was determined to resist this particular ideological movement for the 'construction of theological thinking,' his non-cooperation had obviously generated heavy pressure on him. He has had to prepare himself psychologically to step down if the situation became worse.

In comparison, the leaders of the village church in Wuzhuang have felt little such pressure. First, they really have no position to lose. Their leadership status has been attained very much through members' trust nourished over a long time. Even if an official title of Eldership or Deaconship were removed by an order from above, that would not take away their influence and trust among the members. Second, the TSPM and government officials have made infrequent visits to this remote village. Therefore, the indirect hints or even explicit guidelines of the RAB have made little impact on the content or mode of the pulpit message delivered at the Wuzhuang Church.

Nonetheless, Wuzhuang Christians conform as much as possible to the requirements of the Religious Affairs Bureau and the Three-Self Patriotic Movement Committee. This manifests itself in many routine arrangements of church affairs such as holding regular meetings to study state policies, regulations, and laws and having a 'fixed place' to hold activities, 'fixed persons' in leadership and membership and 'fixed areas' for ministry. The 'three fixes' are to restrict evangelization across administrative borders. Apparently, the Wuzhuang Church has observed this regulation even though they do not like it.

However, Wu Ende, the former deacon who was jailed for six years during the Cultural Revolution, traveled around the Tianshui Prefecture to evangelize in his new status as a layman. In fact, tens of thousands of nameless evangelists have been active in the vast rural areas since the 1970s. Believers call them 'brothers' and 'sisters,' 'uncles' and 'aunts' (Aikman 2003). These nameless evangelists have led the revivals in rural areas, which have multiplied the number of Christians in China in the last few decades. Wu Ende was just one of them. Since he does not hold a position at the church, the authorities could not impose pressure on the church to stop his evangelization.

Another example of the Wuzhuang Church's conformity to official requirements concerned the appointment of an Elder. State regulations require church Elders and Deacons to obtain the approval of the higher level TSPM committee and the RAB. When the Wuzhuang Church was to elect Elders and Deacons in 1996, the Beidao TSPM under the instruction of the Beidao RAB handpicked a Wuzhuang believer, Wu Shenzhao, and appointed him as one of the three Elders. The TSPM and RAB wanted Wu Shenzhao to keep an eye on the church and report any violation of regulations. He was used as a means of state control. The Wuzhuang Church acquiesced to the appointment. While the rest of the church leaders and lay members have been careful not to antagonize Wu Shenzhao, they have managed to circumvent his power and influence effectively by distancing themselves from him. Most of the church affairs have been decided by the senior Elder, Liu Guizhu. Believers would not go to Wu Shenzhao for anything important to church life.

Facing the Village Communist Chiefs

While the village church has managed to keep state intrusions from above at arm's length, Wuzhuang Christians have to face fellow villagers day by day. In this ancient village that has a majority of Wu families, clan ties are actually not very strong. The power of the village has been in the hands of the Chinese Communist Party cadres. Although Christians comprise one-third of the village population, they have no share in the political power. They have stayed away from village politics in the hope that this would avert interference with their religious practice from other villagers. However, their unbending beliefs set off open antagonism from the village Party chief. While their faith gave them the strength to endure in silence, the Party chief's abuses, the larger political atmosphere for social stability ensured their peaceful existence in the village.

Without a clan temple (*ci tang*) or long-term clan association in the village, the CCP authorities retain the actual political power. With a population of over three thousand, Wuzhuang is considered a large village and entitled to have five official positions. The most powerful is the Secretary of the CCP Village Branch (*cun zhishu*), followed by the Chairman of the Village Committee (*cun weihui zhuren*), the Vice Chairman of the Village Committee, the Director of Agricultural Production (*shezhang*), and the Accountant. The villagers are organized into eight Production Brigades (*shengchan dui*). Although about a third of the villagers are

Christian, no Christian has ever held any of the five administrative positions; and only one of the current eight brigade leaders is a Christian. The Party Secretary position naturally requires CCP membership, and the CCP Constitution has been clear that CCP members must uphold atheism. The Party cadres at the village do not like to share power with Christians. First, they are not compatible in ideology. Second, Christians do not smoke or drink, which would make the CCP cadres feel uncomfortable on social occasions or at the dinner table.

However, Wuzhuang Christians have expressed little desire to occupy any of the official positions. According to church leaders, Christians have been afraid of being corrupted and committing sins against God if they stepped into the quagmire of power. They have also been afraid of being suspected of having political ambition. In the current ideological and political conditions, Christians have to show no interest in politics at all to avoid inviting trouble.

Even though Wuzhuang Christians have tried hard to avoid problems, they have nevertheless stumbled into various troubles. The most difficult ones in the reform era involved the *laoshuji*, the previous Party Secretary of the village. His antagonism toward the church started in the mid-1980s when the authorities decided to endorse and foster the folk practice of worshipping Fuxi – the progenitor of Chinese civilization – in restored temple buildings and during festivals that would attract tourists and contribute towards solidarity among Chinese at home and abroad. The *laoshuji* imposed a temple tax on all villagers in order to help finance Fuxi worship, but Christians refused to comply.

They told him that as believers in God they would not be involved in any idol worship. Uncle Fu explained to us: 'If it were charity for disaster relief, we all would be willing to contribute. But we absolutely will not give any money for idolatry.' Indeed, Wuzhuang Christians have noticeably stayed away from the festivals on Guatai Mountain. Their refusal angered *laoshuji*. He took it as a sign of the lack of submission to his power as the Party Secretary. He also felt a loss of face in front of his fellow

Temple Management Council members. In the following years, instead of collecting a separate temple tax from each household, *laoshuji* ordered it to be lumped together with other taxes and fees. Because there were so many items of taxes and fees without clear explanations, villagers commonly could not tell which item was for what purpose. Christians suspected that the lump sum taxes might include the temple tax, but they never could confirm it, thus they did not confront *laoshuji* regarding it. The only thing they could do was to pray to God to stop the whole Fuxi worship thing.

After the incident of tax resistance, *laoshuji* became openly antagonistic to Wuzhuang Christians. He intentionally and regularly turned on the loudspeakers on the roof of the Village Committee Office when the church was holding a worship service or some other gathering. He would broadcast revolutionary songs or Qinqiang opera at the highest possible volume. The Christians simply kept quiet about the very intrusive loudspeakers.

In 1995, as church membership increased, the Wuzhuang Church renovated and enlarged the sanctuary, added a chapel, and replaced the worn-out mud walls of the yard with new brick walls. They also built a covered gate, on top of which they erected a tall cross in bright red. The cross faces the loudspeakers silently, yet sturdily. It is a symbol of perseverance and determination. The renovated church visibly outshone the Village Committee Office across the street. This made *laoshuji* unhappy. Moreover, adding oil to the fire, a *feng shui* master in the village told him that the taller church gate overshadowed the Village Committee Office, which would bring bad luck to the Village Committee. This made *laoshuji* depressed. He made several attempts to stop its erection or to destroy it. He asked the town government to send officials to Wuzhuang and to issue an order to tear down the walls and gate. Some officials came and inspected the church. Surprisingly, however, they told *laoshuji* that having the new walls and gate was not a big deal. They ignored his request and left, which enraged him. After that, in addition to turning on the loudspeakers, he sometimes stood in front of the Village

Committee Office and swore at Christians as they were walking into the church. The Christians simply ignored his provocation and went to their gathering. During some evening services, *laoshuji* walked into the church and ordered the group to leave, accusing the crowd of disturbing the neighbors' sleep. The Christians simply acquiesced 'because we believe the Lord will redress the injustices for us.' Two months after interrupting a revival meeting in July 1998, however, *laoshuji* died suddenly and unexpectedly. According to Elder Liu,

> Even nonbelievers felt that it was very strange. They said that it was because he offended our God. It was God's punishment of him. After that, many people became fearful [of the Christian God]. In the past some nonbelievers would curse us in front of us or behind our backs. But they dared no more.

Not only did average villagers seem to have learned the lesson of not insulting Christians, the new Party Secretary also resorted to assuagement. At Christmas 1998, he led all the village cadres to the church and conveyed greetings to Christians on this special occasion of their most important festival. He also brought a gilt board to the church, on which were inscribed the words 'everlasting friendship' (*youyi chang cun*). Under his new leadership, the loudspeaker has also come on less frequently.

The new Party Secretary's efforts at assuagement do not signify any change of the overall religious policy. As a new chief of the village, he needed to consolidate his power. He knew that Christians were cooperative citizens on civic matters. He understood that it would do no good to antagonize this large mass of Christian villagers. The goodwill visit and the gilt board were gestures intended to end the bad relations under the old Party Secretary.

DISCUSSION AND CONCLUSION

In the red market of religion in China, political submission to the government and theological accommodation to the ruling ideology are preconditions for a group's legal existence. In the oligopoly where equal treatment of all religions is not the norm, state favoritism is probably inevitable. The two case studies show that the Chinese authorities have shown favoritism toward Buddhism and imposed greater restrictions on Christianity. As a result, the Buddhists seem to be more willing to embrace Communist ideology and subscribe to the current political rhetoric, whereas the village Christians are acquiescent to the authorities but also trying to keep some distance from the ideology and politics in general. Having lived through the more difficult years of attempted eradication and suppression, Christians have learned to live in peace without giving up their faith. Indeed, Wuzhuang Christians feel genuinely grateful for the improved political condition nowadays. After all, the overall situation has indeed improved in comparison with the earlier decades under Communist Party rule. It is still far from the ideal of religious freedom, but the social space for religious practice has enlarged.

The survival and perseverance of the Wuzhuang Christian Church show that reform-era China has followed a religious policy of tolerance with restrictions, but the restrictions have not been very effective. In order to attain and maintain a status of legal existence, the church has had to resort to the patriotic rhetoric imposed by the authorities, conform to numerous ordinances and guidelines, and acquiesce to the appointment of a church elder by the Religious Affairs Bureau through the Three-Self Patriotic Movement Committee. Nonetheless, the Wuzhuang Church has managed to keep state intrusions at arm's length. Wuzhuang Christians have exercised extraordinary forbearance, especially in dealing with the village Communist Party chief. State discrimination has not stopped the rapid growth of Christianity. Interestingly, because many Chinese perceive the government as corrupt and regard the Communist ideology with disbelief, state repression of Christianity is probably a factor contributing to the popularity of Christianity in the Chinese populace.

Unlike the struggling village church, the success of the Bailin Buddhist Temple has resulted largely from explicit support by government officials at central, provincial and county levels. However, oligopoly is not monopoly. Political support itself is not enough to guarantee Buddhist revivals. In addition to winning the political support of the authorities, Abbot Jing Hui has also tried hard to maintain his legitimacy in orthodox Buddhism. In this regard, inheriting the ancient Bailin Temple that had been eminent for a distinctive tradition of Zhaozhou Chan is very helpful. Meanwhile, Jing Hui has repeatedly emphasized his discipleship status under the Venerable Xu Yun, who was probably the most revered monk among the Buddhist Sangha and laity in modern China. These claims of religious capital have helped the Bailin Temple to market his brand of Life Chan Buddhism.

The apparent blooming of the Bailin Temple is not a result of fair competition in a free market. Instead, the authorities have provided consistent support. If such support is lacking, an even more famous Buddhist temple would not have been able to thrive. Indeed, the more famous Linji Temple, which is located in the same prefecture but in a different county, has not been as successful. Linji Temple in Zhengding is known as the original temple of an important Chan sect – the Linji sect – and thus it enjoys a more prestigious status within Buddhism. It was one of the only two Buddhist temples in Hebei Province that were included in the 1983 list of 'major temples' designated for restoration as religious venues. That list was suggested by the Buddhist Association of China, approved by the State Religious Affairs Bureau, and decreed by the State Council, which is the highest cabinet of the Chinese government. When Venerable Jing Hui was sent to Hebei Province, the President of the Buddhist Association of China commissioned him to restore both Bailin Temple and Linji Temple. However, Linji Temple has retained its shabby halls. The key obstacle is that the County Government of Zhengding has not provided the same kind of political and other support as the Zhaoxian Government. In Zhengding, there is a large population of Muslims, and the Religious Affairs Bureau director of Zhengding was from the *hui* ethnic group. *Hui* is one of the ten ethnic groups that subscribe

to Islam. Similarly, Jing Hui's effort to spread Buddhism in Cangzhou Prefecture, where there are many Muslims and Catholics, has not been very successful.

Also telling is the failed revival effort of Venerable Jing Hui in Baoding City. Upon arrival in Hebei, one of Jing Hui's first assigned tasks was to organize the Buddhist association for the Prefecture of Baoding, which happens to be the very center of underground Catholics in China (Madsen 1998, 2003). Several Baoding Municipal and Prefecture bureaus blocked attempts to return and restore the Great Compassion Hall (*da ci ge*) for religious services. One of the arguments was that the Great Compassion Hall was not a functional temple in the 1950s and 1960s, so that it was not within the scope of 'implementing the religious policy' meant to return pre-Cultural Revolution religious properties to religious organizations. Therefore, lacking political support at the local level makes Buddhist growth impossible.

As a temple in a highly regulated economy, the success of the Bailin Temple has clear limitations. While the Life Chan doctrine pleases the authorities, other Buddhists regard it as a compromise and have criticized the Bailin activities, although the criticisms were muted after President Jiang Zemin's visit in 2001. Another limitation is that Bailin is not a local congregation. Most of the participants of the signature activity – the Life Chan Summer Camp – come from afar, often from other provinces. Most of the major donors have been overseas Chinese Buddhist businesspeople. How long the Bailin Temple can maintain the continuous support of these distant devotees remains to be seen.

Meanwhile, economic marketization is now well underway in most of China, and this has led to further relaxation of state control over the private life of citizens. In the more market-driven coastal provinces, Christians and others seem to enjoy greater freedom to practice their religion. Moreover, to follow international norms, the authorities have made 'rule by law' or the 'rule of law' an official goal in deepening reforms. Although these reforms have been 'two steps forward and one step backward,' things seem to have been moving in the direction of greater freedom. Taking a broad and long-term view, we have seen – and will likely see more – progress toward greater freedom of religion in China. The oligopoly of five religions increasingly faces challenges from both domestic and international forces in the globalization era. As long as China maintains its orientation toward a market economy and global integration, it is only a matter of time before the authorities have to open up the religious market toward other religious groups outside the five 'patriotic' associations and toward other religions.

NOTES

1. The case studies come from my collaborative work with Dedong Wei (Yang and Wei 2005) and Jianbo Huang (Huang and Yang 2005) of Renmin University of China. I would like to acknowledge and thank them for their fieldwork contribution.

2. The Three-Selfs are self-administration, self-support, and self-propagation.

3. *Chan* magazine is the official publication of the Hebei Buddhist Association. The full texts of every issue have been online at *http://www.chancn.com/magazine/index.asp* (accessed on September 13, 2004). Citations to this magazine will be indicated by the year and issue number only.

REFERENCES

Aikman, David 2003. *Jesus in Beijing: How Christianity Is Transforming China and Changing the Global Balance of Power.* Washington, DC: Regnery.

Bays, Daniel H. 2003. 'Chinese Protestant Christianity Today.' *The China Quarterly* 174 (2): 488–504.

Beaman, Lori G. 2003. 'The Myth of Pluralism, Diversity and Vigor: The Constitutional Privilege of Protestantism in the United States and Canada.' *Journal for the Scientific Study of Religion* 42 (3): 311–25.

Beyer, Peter 2003. 'Constitutional Privilege and Constituting Pluralism: Religious Freedom in National, Global, and Legal Context.' *Journal for the Scientific Study of Religion* 42 (3): 333–40.

Bruce, Steve 2000. 'The Supply-Side Model of Religion: The Nordic and Baltic States.' *Journal for the Scientific Study of Religion* 39 (1): 32–49.

Finke, Roger 1997. 'The Consequences of Religious Competition: Supply-Side Explanations for Religious Change.' Pp. 45–64 in *Assessing Rational Choice Theories of religion*, edited by L. A. Young. New York: Routledge.

Finke, Roger and Rodney Stark 1992. *The Churching of America, 1776–1990: Winners and Losers in Our Religious Economy.* New Brunswick, NJ: Rutgers University Press.

Finke, Roger and Laurence R. Iannaccone 1993. 'Supply-Side Explanations for Religious Change.' *The Annals of the American Association for Political and Social Science* 527: 27–39.

Gill, Anthony J. 2003. 'Lost in the Supermarket: Comments on Beaman, Religious Pluralism, and What It Means to Be Free.' *Journal for the Scientific Study of Religion* 42 (3): 327–32.

Huang, Jianbo and Fenggang Yang 2005. 'The Cross Faces the Loudspeakers: A Village Church Perseveres under State Power.' Pp. 41–62 in *State, Market, and Religions in Chinese Societies*, edited by Fenggang Yang and Joseph B. Tamney. Leiden, The Netherlands, and Boston, MA: Brill Academic Publishers.

Iannaccone, Laurence R. 1994. 'Why Strict Churches Are Strong.' *American Journal of Sociology* 99: 1180–1211.

Jing, Jiuwei 1995. 'A Trip to West Yunnan.' *Heavenly Breeze* (Nanjing) 154 of the joint edition: 1.

Kindopp, Jason and Carol Lee Hamrin 2004. *God and Caesar in China: Policy Implications of Church–State Tensions.* Washington, DC: Brookings Institution Press.

Leung, Ka-lun 1999. *The Rural Churches of Mainland China Since 1978.* Hong Kong: Alliance Bible Seminary Press.

Li, Dezhu 1996. 'Hold on to "Love our Country, Love our Religion; Unite and Make Progress" and Strengthen the Self-Construction of the Religious Organizations in order to Make Religion Compatible to Socialist Society.' Pp. 11–14 in *Love Our Country, Love Our Religion; Unite and Make Progress—Symposium in Northeast of the Religious Organization Leaders*, edited by Central United Front Department. Beijing: Hua Wen Press.

Li, Pingye 1999. '90 Niandai Zhongguo Zongjiao Fazhan Zhuangkuang Baogao' (A Report of the Status of Religious Development in China in the 1990s). *Journal of Christian Culture (Beijing)* 2: 201–22.

Luo, Guangwu 2001. *1949–1999 Xin Zhongguo Zongjiao Gongzuo Dashi Gailan (A Brief Overview of Major Events of Religious Affairs in*

New China 1949–1999). Beijing, China: Huawen Press.

Madsen, Richard 1998. *China's Catholics: Tragedy and Hope in an Emerging Civil Society*. Los Angeles and Berkeley: University of California Press.

Madsen, Richard 2003. 'Catholic Revival during the Reform Era.' *The China Quarterly* 174 (2): 468–87.

Pomfret, John 2002. 'Evangelicals on the Rise in Land of Mao Despite Crackdowns, Protestant Religious Groups Flourishing in China.' *Washington Post*, December 24, p. A01.

Potter, Pitman B. 2003. 'Belief in Control: Regulation of Religion in China.' *The China Quarterly* 174 (2): 317–37.

Stark, Rodney and Roger Finke 2000. *Acts of Faith: Explaining the Human Side of Religion*. Berkeley and Los Angeles: University of California Press.

Wang, Jingwen 1987. 'The True Light of Christ Shining on the Mountain Village.' *Heavenly Breeze* 60: 23.

Xu, Hongbin and Sun Li 1991. 'An Investigation of the Present Situation of Religion in Yixing.' *Contemporary Studies of Religion* 6: 48–52.

Yang, Fenggang 2004. 'Between Secularist Ideology and Desecularizing Reality: The Birth and Growth of Religious Research in Communist China.' *Sociology of Religion* 65 (2): 101–19.

Yang, Fenggang 2005. 'Lost in the Market, Saved at McDonald's: Conversion to Christianity in Urban China.' *Journal for the Scientific Study of Religion* 44 (4): 423–41.

Yang, Fenggang 2006. 'The Red, Black, and Gray Markets of Religion in China.' *Sociological Quarterly* 47: 93–122.

Yang, Fenggang and Dedong Wei 2005. 'The Bailin Buddhist Temple: Thriving under Communism.' Pp. 63–86 in *State, Market, and Religions in Chinese Societies*, edited by Fenggang Yang and Joseph B. Tamney. Leiden, The Netherlands, and Boston, MA: Brill Academic Publishers.

Ye, Xiaowen [1997] 2000. 'Dangqian Woguo de Zongjiao Wenti – Guanyu Zongjiao Wu Xing de zai Tantao' (Current Issues of Religion in Our Country – A Reexamination of the Five Characteristics of Religion). Pp. 1–27 in *Annual of Religious Research in China, 1997–1998*, edited by Cao Zhongjian. Beijing, China: Religious Culture Press

31

The Religious Landscape of Central and Eastern Europe after Communism

IRENA BOROWIK

Speeches of the Past

All Christian realms will come to an end and will unite into the one single realm of our sovereign, that is, into the Russian realm, according to the prophetic books. Both Romes fell, the third endures, and a fourth there will not be.[1]

The monk Filoteus from the Monastery in Pskov,
XVI Century

The speech of the Patriarch of the Russian Orthodox Church after Stalin's death before the religious service linked to his burial included:

... the Great Commander of our nation is no longer with us, Iosif Vissarionovitch Stalin. There is no more great, moral and social power; (...) there is no sphere of life that was not penetrated by the deep insight of the Great Leader. As a genius he discovered things that were invisible and inaccessible to the ordinary mind. (...) We proclaim the eternal memory of our beloved and unforgettable Iosif Vissarionowitch with a prayer and passionate love (Stricker 1995: 383–84).

Speech of the Present

I have said it more than once, and I shall continue to repeat it: Catholics have an obligation to vote for a Catholic; Christian for Christian, Muslim for Muslim, Jew for Jew, Mason for Mason, Communist for Communist: each must vote for him who best represents his views.

Bishop Józef Michalik on the 1991 parliamentary
elections in Poland[2]

INTRODUCTION

There are five important reasons for distinguishing Central and Eastern Europe (CEE) from the rest of Europe when discussing the role of religion. First, Christianity arrived in the majority of the countries representing this part of the continent later than in the West of the continent. Slavs were Christianised between the sixth and sixteenth centuries, and the Baltic tribes later still, between the thirteenth and fifteenth century. This means that remnants of Paganism survived for longer in this part of Europe, forming a kind of 'double faith' (*dwuwirje*) in the sense of the co-existence between Christianity and Slavic cults for a significant period until the sixteenth century.

Second, Christianity was promoted at the same time in two different ways from two different centres. On the one hand, the Byzantine,

Eastern rite, with its specific attachment to liturgy, was accepted in Eastern Europe where Orthodoxy prevails today in countries such as Belarus, Bulgaria, Macedonia, Moldova, Romania, Russia, Serbia, Montenegro and Ukraine. On the other hand, the parallel wave of Western, Latin Christianity came to the Central part of the region and is currently dominant in Croatia,[3] the Czech Republic, Hungary, Lithuania, Slovakia, Slovenia, and Poland. Two Baltic states, Latvia and Estonia, are predominantly Protestant. Lutheranism triumphed there in the sixteenth century Reformation and it has remained the dominant faith tradition. Muslims form a significant part of the population in Albania (alongside significant numbers of Christians from both the Catholic and Orthodox traditions) as well as in Bosnia and Herzegovina. Other Muslims include an influential minority of Crimean Tatars who live on the Crimean Peninsula in Ukraine.

Third, religions were consolidated in CEE during the same processes in which national identity and traditions of statehood were created. Historians have shown that the differences in Christianity between Eastern and Western traditions, between Byzantine or Roman rites, and between Orthodox or Latin forms signified not only different modes of religious faith but also different types of political identity, state organisation, style of life, rule of law, ceremonies of political and economic elites, and so on (Dujtsev 1997: 111). The Christianisation of countries in this region of Europe entailed a parallel process of constructing states, nationalities and national identity, each of which reflected either the Latin or the Byzantine tradition. To varying degrees, religious and national identities were not only important in history but are still strongly interrelated in Eastern Europe. One of the typical elements of national identity was opposition to the 'Other', which was different partly because of differences in religion. One's 'own' religion supported national and ethnic pride in fighting legitimate battles and wars against the 'other'. It also provided mystical justification for giving priority to one's 'own' nation. CEE countries were similar to the rest of the world in regarding

Jews as typical prototypes of the 'other', but it was also common for neighbours to play the same role of the 'other' and the 'stranger'.

One of the major points in common between the CEE countries – but which also separates them from countries in Western Europe – is related to religion. Babinski's (1997: 97–8) comparison of the processes whereby modern nations emerged in the nineteenth century in Western and Eastern Europe emphasises the fact that religion did not serve as a line of ethnic division and conflict in Western Europe; nor was it a factor in nation building. No religion was associated with any particular nation or national consciousness. By contrast, in Eastern Europe where religious dominance was associated with political, economic or cultural struggles for independence and was

> usually connected with rather clear religious differences between the dominant political oppressor and the national groups demanding their independence. And what was of particular importance, national differences and national conflicts were growing not only between oppressing imperial powers on one side and national groups struggling for independence on the other, but also between the oppressed nations and national groups (Babiński 1997: 98).

For instance, not only were Poles, Ukrainians, Belorussians, Lithuanians oppressed by the Russian Empire, but in addition each nation built up strong negative stereotypes of the other nations and perceived them as potential enemies of their own independence. In all cases religion served as a tool for the integration of identity, the clarification of political and cultural goals and the differentiation of each nation from the others.

Two important factors shaped the specific role played by Catholicism in Poland, by Greek-Catholicism in the Ukraine, and by Orthodoxy in Russia or Bulgaria: the historical link between religious and national identity; and the Church's role in preserving national identity at times of persecution.[4] Poland provides a good illustration of this point. Throughout the difficult periods of history when the Poles did not have their own state – or when the state was subordinated to the Soviet Empire (which was not accepted by the majority of Poles) – the Catholic Church was the only social institution capable of preserving Poland's language, traditions and memories of its glorious past. In effect, the Church and religion integrated the whole society and shielded it against any possible differentiation on the basis of education, social class, environment, and so on. The history of the Poles' struggle for an independent state conferred on Catholicism the status of a Polish civil religion (Morawska 1984: 29–34; Borowik 2004) in which religious and national symbols of patriotism constituted the inseparable elements of Polishness, leading to the well known stereotype of Poles as Catholics. After World War II, being Catholic meant being anti-communist. According to Hank Johnson (1989) Catholicism amounted to a religio-oppositional subculture which was eminently well symbolised by the 'Polish' Pope.[5] The universal message of Catholicism in Poland was specifically pared down to the particular role of religion and the Church in preserving national identity and struggling for the country's independence. All these factors had a major influence on religious socialisation, which relied mainly on two institutions: the family[6] and the Church. Since religious instruction had been removed from the curriculum of state schools – and since the mass media carried no religious programmes – the Church could not officially present its position in public life; and in general (with the exception of Poland) public discussion of religion was not allowed. The church buildings with their altars therefore became the principal setting for anti-communist demonstrations; and sermons became the most common weapon of anti-communist speakers.

To take a different example, the pluralism of the Ukrainian religious landscape is often cited as a reason for making close comparisons with Western Europe and for arguing that Ukraine really belongs to the Western European tradition. Emphasis was placed not only on differentiation from Russia but also on the country's differences from Catholic Lithuania and from Protestant Latvia and Estonia – which all differed from Orthodox Russia. This aspect of religion was also evident in Croatia where emphasis was placed on differentiation from Serbia and – at the same time – on belonging to Western Catholic culture. All these examples show that religion has historically served – and still serves – as a tool of building and preserving identity as well as playing a crucial role in the interrelationship with politics.

Communism artificially froze ethnic and national animosities by constructing 'internationalism' and a new type of a man, namely, 'Soviet man', one of whose *expected* characteristics was a complete lack of attachment to such 'remote' objects of emotion as ethnic or national ties. Soviet people were expected to love each other without regard for international boundaries and without taking any differences into consideration. The fact that these ideological concepts were widespread but not actually shared by the inhabitants of Central and Eastern Europe, who still harboured secret animosities, goes a long way towards explaining why confrontations between ethnic and national groups in the post-communist dissolution of some former states have been so violent. Ideas about 'great nations' are also powerful drivers of the transformations that have occurred in the region. Borders – no less in the past than in the present – cut across religious and political divisions and provoke mutual misunderstandings.[7] In addition, new borders and borderlands have appeared.[8]

The fourth factor that unifies the countries of Central and Eastern Europe lies in the historical and political fortunes experienced by the region in recent decades. Unlike any other time or place, this region has been subjected to the powerful anti-religious forces of Communism and anti-religious totalitarian regimes. Strong anti-religious sentiments, active struggles against Christian and other religious traditions, and the promotion of atheism were first implemented in the Soviet Union and subsequently in the other countries of the Eastern bloc. The consequences included specific difficulties for all those who were institutionally involved in service to the churches, a risk to the life of ordinary believers, and the necessity for 'underground' faith and prayers. The humiliation of religion – symbolised by turning churches and monasteries into museums of atheism and by making jokes about believers – was a part of the shared experience of countries in Central and Eastern Europe. Persecuting religion was part of the persecution of freedom; and the struggle against it was part of the fight for the defence of human rights.

The fifth component of the experiences shared by the countries of Central and Eastern Europe is the collapse of communism. The process of transformation has been rapid in all these countries since the collapse of communism in 1989 and the dissolution of the Soviet Union in 1991. Some of the symbolic phrases and images that capture the beginning of that transformational period include: Gorbatchev's *pieriestroika*, the dismantling of the Berlin wall, the round table in Poland (Zukrowska 1995), 'the Velvet Revolution' in Czechoslovakia, and the death sentence carried out in public on the Romanian communist leader Ceausescu. Transformation has affected all areas of social and individual life, including politics, the economy, the market, life style, education and science, social policy and medicine. Nothing has escaped transformation; and obviously religion is part of these changes. Religious institutions are involved in the processes taking place in all important fields of social life; and at the same time they are objects of the changes themselves.

DIFFERENTIATION OF THE RELIGIOUS FIELD IN CENTRAL AND EASTERN EUROPE

In spite of these – and possibly some other less important – similarities among the countries of Central and Eastern Europe, there are also some striking differences between them. The post-communist lands could be roughly divided into three groupings: Eastern Europe under Orthodox domination; the Central region of post-communist Europe under Catholic domination; and the North of the region where Protestantism dominates in two Baltic states. There are also wide variations between the CEE countries in terms of their religious composition. Certain countries, for example Belarus, Croatia and Poland, are almost homogeneous in religion, whereas others, such as Albania and Ukraine, are more diverse. In addition, many countries have sizeable and influential minorities that include the Orthodox (mostly Russians) in the Baltic states, Catholics in Ukraine, and Reformed Protestants in Hungary. All these very basic elements of religious structures in every country are part of specific relations between Church and state. They have an impact on the presence of religion in social life and they influence social relations between specific religious groups – not only minorities and majorities but also dominant and marginal traditions. To bring this picture up to date, it is important to mention that new religious movements started to operate much more actively after the collapse of communism, thereby making the religious scene in the region resemble some other regions of the world – but with the additional and crucial difference that radical social transformation began there in 1989.

Very important differences, mostly at the civilisational level, follow from the fact of belonging either to Eastern or Western Christianity. In brief, the most important differences relate to the way of approaching beliefs (dogma), religious organisation and the influence of religion on everyday life. Orthodoxy emphasises immanence, while Western Christianity emphasises transcendence. The image of God is different: it is 'apophatic'[9] in the Western Christian tradition but 'kathaphatic'[10] in Eastern Christianity. The Orthodox tradition, drawing from Pseudo-Dionysius the Areopagite, describes God in phrases indicating that nothing could be said about His nature and features. Orthodoxy is a-historical and a-temporal, while Western Christianity is well adapted to time and history. The central role of dogma in Roman Catholicism is comparable to the equally central position of liturgical contemplation in Eastern Christianity or of discursive religious reflection in Protestant churches.[11]

Orthodoxy and Catholicism differ significantly in respect of their forms of ecclesiastical organisation. In the case of Roman Catholicism, the structure of the Church is hierarchical and is supported by dogma concerning the infalli-bility of the Pope. Relations between the Holy See and the local churches are vertical. Orthodoxy, by comparison, is organised in 14 local churches enjoying self-governance (autocephaly) and independence from each other within a framework of 'horizontal' relations. Protestant churches also lack a common, vertical, central organisation and are independent from each other. Catholicism has a tradition of its own centrally governed policy of remaining independent from secular powers, whereas the Orthodox tradition involves long-term subordination to secular rulers. These differences result in different sociologically significant models of exercising institutional power and control and of mutual relations of influence between the secular sectors of societies and religion. Among Christian traditions, Catholicism has the best organisational framework for acting at the global level.

The religiosity of those who belong to Eastern Christianity is described in terms of 'bytovoje christianstwo', which means that religion is a non-reflexive and inseparable part of the way of life. The Orthodox religious consciousness typically displays an inclination towards mysticism and is supported by the significance attached to such institutions as 'starcy' (charismatic individuals with a status close to that of saints, who give spiritual advice and help in illness) and 'jurodivi' (sanctified but psychically disturbed people who are convinced that the sacred speaks through them). Religiosity of the Western type is more closely linked to dogmas and is related to the significance of religious institutions under-pinned by regular catecheses.

Taking into account the differential impact of religion on the formation of Western and Eastern European cultures reveals a difference of attitudes towards the process of rationalisation. As Max Weber (1963: 20–8) pointed out, the rationality of European culture is founded on the notion of transcendence in the Judeo-Christian tradition. The formulation of dogmas, their precision and their continuing development, are regarded as the rationalisation of religion. The great complexity of the world

and the complexity of theological thought are mutual reflections of the relevance of religious and social developments (Luhmann 1984: 48–9). The Orthodox world, plunging from a feudal system directly into communist ideology and totalitarian policy – which was in many senses a continuation of the feudal order – has not undergone full modernisation since the collapse of the Soviet bloc. Although this short-cut definitely took place, it is also true that the Orthodox faith, as a spiritual foundation of Eastern European culture, lacked the structural and functional motivation to create mechanisms of rationalisation similar to those of Western Europe which had been strengthened by the Reformation.

Some of the features that are typical of Western culture – such as individualisation, pluralism, the central position of the individual, and negotiation as an exercise of inter-subjectivity – are replaced in Eastern culture by the power of the collectivity, charismatic and authoritarian leadership in politics, and arguments about power instead of the power of arguments. Nevertheless, Grace Davie is right to say that 'Countries that belonged, and continue to belong, to Western rather than Orthodox Christianity may well find it easier to realize their political and economic aspirations. Despite their real economic difficulties, their aim is to re-establish Western traditions; they are not learning something totally new' (2000: 4). By contrast, the Orthodox countries of Eastern Europe are indeed learning (or not?) something new.

One of the extraordinarily important and mysterious questions about Central and Eastern Europe is 'What has happened to the collective memory of formerly communist societies?'. And what has happened to the memory of individuals? The special importance of this question relates to ambiguous but rapid changes that took place in the field of religion very soon after the collapse of communism. Although the intensity and the direction of these changes vary widely between countries of the region, one generalisation holds true: societies that seemed to be atheistic turned to religion. This reinforced the importance of the past – but in new terms. What happened to religions under communist persecution? Is the past still present in contemporary features and problems of religion?

THE SOCIALIST/COMMUNIST PAST. THE CHURCHES AND THEIR BELIEVERS

Some thinkers are fully convinced that communism should be considered 'not as a social system but as religion . . . fanatically hostile to every religion and to Christianity first of all. It wants to be religion by itself and to replace Christianity; it pretends to find an answer to religious questions of human spirit, to give a sense to human life' (Berdiaiev 1995: 129). Communism competed fanatically with religion and offered – as A. Walicki (1995) put it metaphorically – *the Leap to the Kingdom of Freedom*. From the perspective of an economic theory of religion, communism intended to convert religious compensators into rewards offering salvation on earth – and achievable in historically predictable processes and time-frames. It should be stressed that the past requires understanding; and this is one of the important tasks for sociologists studying Central and Eastern Europe. It became clear that, in spite of the attractions of this concept, using force and persecution to convince people that 'the old religion' was nothing but a useless obstacle to the building of 'a new man' and 'a new society' became – not for the first time in history – a way of justifying something as 'obligatory' in the circumstances of a revolution.

The religions and churches of Central and Eastern Europe experienced differing degrees of intensity of persecution. The most intensive in negative terms took place in the Soviet Union and Albania, where being visibly religious or even keeping religious literature, such as the Holy Bible, at home meant putting one's life at risk. Very strong pressure was applied to religious leaders in Hungary and Czechoslovakia. Much 'softer' ways of dealing with religion were implemented in Bulgaria, and to some extent there was co-operation in the Orthodox territories of Serbia and in Cernogora in Yugoslavia and Romania.

The communist regime was unable to fight religion in Poland or did not wish to resort to such extreme measures. Religion in general and the dominant Catholic Church in particular were persecuted in Poland to a lower degree than in other countries of the region.

The political leaders in most countries more or less 'accurately' copied the actions undertaken by Lenin after victory in the October Revolution. The French Revolution had not only shaped the pattern that Lenin followed in fighting religion but it also embodied his ideal. Probably for this reason the first steps of the process related to the legal position of the churches. As early as the 4th of December 1917 the Orthodox Church was 'nationalised' in the sense that the state became the owner of all properties, lands, seminaries, schools, and monasteries belonging to the Church. The decree of 20th January 1918 secularised the state and the education system by separating the state and schools from the Church. Subsequently, religious marriage ceremonies were abolished; and the bank accounts of religious institutions were closed. Lenin tried to use – to some extent successfully – the strategy of favouring religious minorities in order to weaken the dominant religious body, i.e. the Orthodox Church. All these steps, one by one, were followed in the countries of Central Europe after World War II: secularisation, the nationalisation of church properties, the liquidation of the legal status of religious bodies, the mobilisation of 'pro-socialist' priests, and the favouring of religious minorities. The main aim of this early stage of anti-religious action was to dissolve the fundamentals of religious activity and religious organisation. Success of the action automatically implied that the social significance of the churches, the social response to their teachings, and their religious activities were all weakened. The possibility of mobilising believers was significantly reduced because the networks of religious organisations had been rapidly undermined. Only in Poland was this basic problem overcome. This is because the country had long had a religious network of anti-state activity that was based on the structure and power of the Roman Catholic Church and had been elaborated over 200 years of partitions and the absence of an independent state. In the other countries of the region Lenin's strategy was quite a successful way of quickly undermining the position of the Churches.

On the other hand, Christian churches took different approaches to the confrontation with communism as an ideology and as a totalitarian type of regime. One of the most influential factors in this policy was the organisational and structural tradition of Church-state relations. This was more positive – as far as the survival of religion was concerned – in predominantly Catholic countries and rather negative in countries where the Orthodox and Protestant churches defended their own position. In the former, the universality of the Church was put to such good use that its international leaders were able to bring different countries together and thereby to speak on behalf of people imprisoned behind the Berlin wall. The Catholic Church had also been prepared by past reforms – for example the eleventh and twelfth century reforms of the papacy – and by conflicts between the papacy and secular powers. In fact – as Kloczowski (1998) emphasises – one of the most important aspects of the Gregorian reforms had been the division of secular and ecclesiastical powers. In addition, historians of Christianity are correct to argue that in the Western world the Pope's authority – the image of Peter's successor – was important in helping to integrate Western Latin Christianity (Kloczowski 1998: 156–61). This tradition helped Catholic Churches to gain more independence from secular power, and that experience was much more significant in countries where religion was persecuted.

In structural terms, the papacy forged good conditions for opposition, by using – to borrow Jan Kubik's (1994) phrase – the power of religious symbols melded with national ones against symbols of power. By comparison, the Orthodox tradition of having strong links and close ties between state and Church made it easier to justify the submission of the Church to the state as well as Church co-operation with the state, whatever the state was. Structurally, Orthodox churches have quite weak relations with each other and – more importantly – they did not have instruments for influencing the position of the Church in any particular country. Orthodox churches, in respect to these two considerations, could be described as closer to Protestant churches and very different from the Catholic Church. The subordination to the state of the Protestant churches in Estonia, Latvia and Eastern Germany[12] was not accidental and was much easier than for Catholic churches. For our point of view, these structural differences contributed significantly to the much higher losses of Orthodoxy than Catholicism in confrontation with communism. Catholicism had a strong tradition of opposing the state as well as a powerful international and organisational structure that mobilised an external centre of power and an international milieu in defence of local churches.

The effects of anti-religious propaganda and of the activity of communist states seem to have a bigger impact on religious institutions than on subjective religiosity. From this perspective, no church in any country of Central and Eastern Europe reflects seriously on its communist past.[13] The past was rarely heroic, and this is probably why the majority of actors from that time prefer not to talk, not to remember, not to remain – just to let go.

Analysis of the most general features of the changes taking place in the last 15 years requires a distinction between two levels or fields. On the one hand, there is the institutional field where structural changes in churches and religious organisations occur, including the new conditions in which they operate within a framework formed by states liberated from communism or newly created as a result of the collapse of communism. On the other hand, there is the presence of religion at the level of individuals and society. This refers to changes in religiosity, including the relation of individuals to religion, religious identification, problems of belonging, beliefs, and so on. The next two sections will analyse changes at the institutional level and at the level of individual religiosity.

RELIGION IN CENTRAL AND EASTERN EUROPE AT THE INSTITUTIONAL LEVEL

One of the simplest indicators of religious vitality is the number of churches, religious denominations, groups and movements registered in every country. Looked at from this point of view, the extent of change appears to be enormous. The number of religious bodies registered by the state and operating in countries of CEE increased rapidly and visibly. In Russia, for example, the number of registered religious organisations jumped from 19 in 1990 to 54 in 1996. The number of registered religious communities – such as parishes or local groups – was over 15,000 at that point. After a change of the law in Russia, all religious communities were obliged to re-register; and 20 of them – along with 215 religious organisations – succeeded in obtaining re-registration.[14] In Poland on the eve of the collapse of the communist system there were 37 religious organisations (Urban 1994: 101). By the end of the 1990s this number had increased to 152 (Borowik 2000b: 92) and, by the end of 2005, to 160.[15]

In a country as large as Russia the tendencies towards growth in religious organisations are mainly to do with traditional Russian sects, pagans and Evangelical groups.[16] These tendencies do not mean that the religious structure is going to change in favour of these particular religions. The increase is concentrated in certain social milieux, and it is unlikely that pagans or indigenous religious movements will prevail over the traditionally strongest faith communities of Orthodoxy and Islam. A very striking example is Hungary, where the 35 denominations registered in 1990 had grown to 135 by the end of 2002 (Török 2003: 132).

The other influential feature is the sheer variety of religions present in the CEE region. The most important, dominant churches and the minority religions all continue to play important roles. For instance, among the Orthodox churches the biggest and the most influential is the Russian Orthodox Church (ROC), with the Moscow Patriarchate as the governing centre and with Patriarch Aleksey II as its head. Its jurisdiction extends over the whole former USSR, encompassing Ukraine, Belarus and other countries of the former Soviet Union.[17] Orthodox believers form significant minorities in many former Soviet republics which are currently independent states, such as Lithuania, Latvia, Estonia or Kazakhstan. The Orthodox are typically found among ethnic Russians whose families have been re-located to these territories at various times since the October Revolution of 1917.[18]

As elsewhere in the world, the number of Evangelical and Pentecostal groups has been growing rapidly (Lubaschenko 1996: 314–16; Prusak and Borscev, 1996: 112). Jehovah's Witnesses are also active, while the number of Jewish communities is declining in Eastern Europe mainly as a result of emigration to Israel and other countries. The presence and the activities of many New Religious Movements in CEE countries are significant not because of their statistical strength but because they constitute a challenge for the traditional religions. They are also a test for the democratic quality of the state's procedures as well as a matter for discussion in the mass-media and public opinion. These topics are interesting in themselves and are often on the agenda of scholars working in the field of religion.

One of the most significant changes affecting religion after the collapse of communism in CEE countries concerns its institutional aspect and, more precisely, the legal status of churches that did not have rights in the past. All countries in the region have introduced significant changes in this field.[19] The first stage of the change was directly inspired by feelings of freedom and a strong need to give them expression. Religious freedom was associated with human freedom in general and was understood as the right of people and institutions to practise religion. This was the point at which the majority of CEE countries introduced liberal laws that provided a framework for the activities of religious groups. 'Liberal' in this context means that it was easy to satisfy the requirements for obtaining registration and acquiring legal status, including privileges in relation to the tax system or to military service and charity work.

It took some time to reach the next stage. After roughly five years of development, the laws were discussed and revised in the light of questions about issues such as equality of status for all religions and religious groups in society and the limits of state control over new religious movements. According to Eileen Barker's (1997: 60) summary, 'Minority religions have been treated with suspicion and discriminated against throughout the world and throughout history, and their fate in postcommunist societies is no exception'. The answers given to these questions are unclear not only for members of societies involved in religion in various ways but also for scholars. Some scholars are convinced that 'the old' traditions deserve more social trust because they have proved themselves throughout many years of activity in some countries (Tomka 1999: 58). But others contend that, in the eyes of the law, all religious groups should be equal and that there is no need for states to control religious groups more than any others or to impose separate conditions on them (Barker 1997: 54). Some scholars are personally involved in anti-cult groups fighting not so much against the principle of religious freedom as such but, rather, against particular religious groups and their activities. However, published research findings show that these problems appeared to be much more acute in the early years of transformation, while in recent years it has been possible to identify some stability in the 'religious market'. The law concerning religion is effective, and even in the Russian Federation, where a new and more restrictive version of the law was introduced in September 1997 in the face of widespread opposition and criticism, the level of religious re-registration appeared to be higher than expected.[20] Nevertheless – as Marat Shterin (2000: 423) concluded – although the new law reflected a compromise between various trends and players in Russian politics and religious life, it could still be said that 'the Law serves to institutionalise prejudice against a large number of religious minorities'.

The other very important dimension of institutional religion relates to the policies of Churches and their relation to social actors such as states and societies – including civil society, education, gender, welfare problems and the mass-media. All these areas of life in CEE countries were dominated by new arrangements. The unprecedented possibilities included holding public debates on issues in which religion was involved, the fact that the dominant Churches – even if they did not have their own media such as radio and TV – could still have easy access to the media, and developing their own educational networks ranging from primary schools to universities. That signified a fundamental change not only in the aims of actors in religious institutions but also in the forms of their activities and their presence in society; it also changed the possibilities of influencing them. If it is possible to treat post-communist countries as if they amounted to a single place, one generalisation could be made: the public presence of religion is one of the most visible and important changes to have followed the collapse of Communism. Although Churches took different approaches to confronting transformation and the rapid modernisation that accompanied it – including the emancipation of women, pluralistic life styles, values and other elements – nevertheless, the main point is that rather conservative ways of approaching them tended to prevail.

THE RELIGIOSITY OF POST-COMMUNIST SOCIETIES

Sociologists of religion have various problems with interpreting the changes that have occurred in the field of religion in CEE countries. How to categorise the changes? Do they amount to 'the return of religion'? Has there been a 'religious revival'? Or is there a spiritual revival? How to assess the numbers of people who are religious? The starting point for all these problems is the simple fact that it is very difficult – if not impossible – to appraise the past, the degree of 'atheisation', or the influence of communist ideology that competed with religion. As Siniša Zrinščak (2004: 232) correctly observed, all that can be said is 'that atheism as an official ideology reinforced secular manifestations of social change, while it is impossible to say to what extent'. What is clear is that subsystems of social life such as the law, education, culture and politics were more successfully and obviously secularised or 'atheised' than human consciousness. This is what makes it so difficult to recognise what the present situation is and to interpret it properly.

The important questions to be answered relate to religiosity among individuals and in social life. Unfortunately, even an issue as simple as religious belonging seems to defy understanding. How, indeed, can one assess and measure religious commitment in countries where people who are engaged in 'do-it-yourself religion'[21] are in the majority? Or, to take the example of Ukraine, people used to say that they were religious and that they were Orthodox without being members of any Church. Indeed, in apparent contradiction of this, some of them even said that they were actually 'Orthodox unbelievers'. None of this has changed.

Research on religiosity is among the most advanced, and changes in religiosity are monitored in the majority of the countries in the CEE region. There has also been a tendency in recent years towards a growth of interest in organising and participating in international, comparative research projects which permit the testing of theoretical frameworks such as secularisation theories, rational choice theory or, more rarely, Luckmann's privatisation thesis (Pollack 2003; Norris and Inglehart 2004). Data specifically collected in research projects on religion[22] and data gathered in such international projects as the European Values Survey or the International Social Survey Programme are deployed in testing these theoretical ideas. The generalisations arising from these projects and the interpretations of their data seem to go in two different directions: first, a growing number of respondents are reporting their religiosity in most countries of the CEE region, and this means that many more people than previously are finding various ways of declaring their personal attraction to religion and to being religious. Andrew Greeley (2004: 93) argues that in the case of Russia we are witnessing 'the most dramatic religious revival in human history'. Moreover, Miklos Tomka (2004: 56) argues that an increase in religiosity has been observed among younger people in almost all

post-soviet countries in the last ten years. But, second, Pippa Norris and Ronald Inglehart (2004) draw exactly the opposite conclusion about the younger generation, concluding that religiosity was stronger among the older generation in all post-communist societies. According to them, this proves 'the pattern that is predicted by the theory of secularization and existential security' (Norris and Inglehart 2004: 119). Similarly, Olaf Müller (2004: 71) reached the same conclusion. His analysis refers to the future as well, since he believes that 'there is a lot of evidence that a huge increase in traditional forms of religiosity in most East European countries cannot be expected'.

Conclusive interpretation of religious changes in CEE countries on the basis of local and international research is clearly not possible. As a result, there are significant doubts about the appropriateness of the term 'religious revival' for explaining these changes. Some authors are convinced that, in this process of change, traditional Christian religion and churches, specifically in Eastern Europe, are proving to be too weak. As Włodzimierz Pawluczuk (1998: 127) put it, 'the search for metaphysics to legitimize everyday life and politics takes place . . . on the basis of neo-pagan images and thoughts, in amorphous, non-formal structures that could be labelled "post-modern neo-paganism"'. Other commentators describe it as eclecticism similar to that observed in Western Europe (Borowik 2002).

Looking at the CEE region as a whole – and with some unavoidable simplification – it is possible to discern three dominant types of religious orientations alongside varying levels of indifference to religion:

1. Cultural religiosity. Religion, as an aspect of identity, was sometimes lost or questioned under communism, but also survived under communism in other cases. This category includes people who claim to belong to a religious tradition but in the majority of cases without strong attachment to the religious institutions, and with no interest in the details of religious truth or religiously legitimised moral rules. Nevertheless, this category shares a general belief in God.

Culturally religious people may claim in interviews that, before the collapse of communism, they did not believe in God but that they currently do. 'Belonging without believing' is a phrase that could describe this type of orientation. Different countries of the region display different proportions of people who fall into this category and different contexts. In the predominantly Orthodox part of Eastern Europe they would form a majority of the population. Their religious values are seen more as a cultural heritage from the past. In Tomka's (2002: 549) words, religion is simply a cultural reference with, or without, a relation to the transcendental.

2. Core religiosity. This category includes all those people who were deeply involved in religion in the past or who converted to religion in recent years. Interesting examples could be found in those countries of Eastern Europe where religion was strongly persecuted under communist rule and where some people were active in Communist Party affairs. For instance, among Orthodox believers 'core religiosity' is more frequent among women – especially older rather than younger women. A related phenomenon is the development of groups strongly opposed to ecumenism (Mitrokhin 2004: 228–32). A similar category includes those who understand and practise religion in deeply personal terms, as was well expressed by a believer who claimed that 'God moved my heart' (Borowick 2000a: 80).

3. 'Being religious in one's own way'. This orientation towards piecing together one's own religiosity is not based on institutional affiliation but it is popular and is likely to develop further in the future. As Ludmila Skokova's biographical approach has shown, there is a tendency among religiously oriented young people in Ukraine to leave taken-for-granted religiosity or atheism (in the past) behind and, instead, to re-orient themselves towards a religiosity of personal choice (Skokova 2004: 132).

The clear conclusion is that religion in Central and Eastern Europe is now much more visible than it was during Soviet times. It is visible in the streets, in architecture and – most importantly – in the mass media. In many countries of the region this trend towards 'visibility' is accompanied by growing interest *in* religion. This means that publications about religions, discussions and visits to sites associated with saints (but not religious practices or church attendance) are popular. As Eileen Barker (1997) pointed out, the felt need to describe oneself as religious in Eastern European societies is now comparable to the emphasis on belonging to the Communist Party in the past. Just as 'it was advisable to be a card carrying member of the Communist Party, so, after the collapse of communism, it might be helpful to be seen to attend the "right" church to meet with the "right" people in order to demonstrate that one was a true Christian supporter of the National Church' (Barker 1997: 47).[23]

IN PLACE OF A CONCLUSION: THE MAIN TASKS AND PROMISES FOR THE FUTURE

Another very frequently asked question about the role of religion and churches in CEE countries concerns their relations with politics in the post-communist era (Smrke 1996). What is specific about these relations in comparison to other regions? The answers are complex, but it is generally true that connections between religion and politics – including a major role for the state – are stronger and more direct in CEE countries. Nevertheless, there are wide differences that require fine conceptual distinctions, although – it must be noted – the opinions of sociologists of religion are divided about the 'proper' or most useful ways of modelling these relations in particular countries. Some scholars are critical of the close relations between the dominant Church and the state in some countries as well as of the direct impact of religion on politics in, for instance, Russia. At the same time, others contend that religion and churches could help to make politics more moral, as has happened in Ukraine. Miklós Tomka (1999: 62), for example, is convinced that, in spite of the problematic aspects of political and social activity, 'there are distinct social expectations for the contributions of churches in the social regeneration of East-Central Europe'. But this is not self-evidently true, and it does not address the related problem of how religions may be implicated in the political divisions and orientations in the post-communist part of Europe. Political parties oriented towards the left are quite strong in all CEE countries, but anti-religious rhetoric is no longer heavily used. It is usually replaced by forms of pragmatic co-operation that seem to be acceptable to both political and religious actors. The underdevelopment of civil society may also help to explain the lack of clear orientations in the politics-religion nexus. But even in a country as religious as Poland – or perhaps precisely because Poland is a very religious society – there is strong opposition to the involvement of the Roman Catholic Church and its clergy in politics (Borowik 2002: 249).

Religious and national mythologies are manipulated in war and are an extremely un-reflexive way of mobilising people, according to Velikonja (2003). Moreover, religiosity can flourish rapidly in conditions of conflict. In Bosnia-Herzegovina between 1988 and 1999, for example, the level of self-reported personal religiosity rose among all national groups. The increases were from 55.8 per cent to 89.5 per cent among Croats; from 37.3 per cent to 78.3 per cent among Bosniaks; and from 18.6 per cent to 81.6 per cent among Serbs in the Doboj region in 2000 (Velikonja 2003: 261).

Disputes are rife about the significance of religion for post-communist societies in CEE countries – in terms of the strength with which individual religiosity is 'recovering'. Perhaps the weaknesses of the sociology of religion are more evident in this region than elsewhere since these countries are a kind of sociological 'laboratory' where an experiment is taking place. It involves a series of dramatic changes that began with revolution and the installation of regimes exercising totalitarian anti-religious power; they were then followed by an unexpected turn towards democracy and the freedom of religion. These strong divisions, sharp turns and rapid changes might have been expected to facilitate research and analysis

of the religious situation, since the evidence was so clear. Unfortunately, this has not happened. It has actually been impossible to prove that the process of 'atheisation' produced expected effects on the societies under consideration. Nor has it been possible to claim that religiosity has returned or revived in general terms. And to the surprise of many, it seems to me that the general picture of religion in Central and Eastern Europe bears a significant number of similarities to developments in Western Europe, namely, the de-institutionalisation of religion, the subjectivisation of religious choice, the growth of '*bricolage*' (or do-it-yourself religion), and the individualisation of religion. The factor that is most distinctive of Central and Eastern Europe, as it recovers from its communist past, is the strong presence of religion in the political field and the growing strength of the institutional power exercised by the dominant churches. This is the picture in most – if not all – of the CEE countries.

NOTES

1. Originally it was published in Malinin (1901: 45). Translation in J. Meyendorff (1996: 136).
2. 'Pismo Okólne' (PO) [General Circulars] was a publication of the Polish Episcopate, containing official statements, documents and bishops' letters, aimed at churchgoers.
3. Christianity arrived much earlier in some countries. For instance present-day Croatia was part of the Roman Empire, and Christianity was accepted there as early as the second century CE. Slovenians were Christianised in the sixth and seventh centuries, although they did not have their own state until recent times.
4. Persecutions have taken different forms: in Bulgaria, years of Ottoman, Islamic domination; in Poland, partitions of the country; and in Ukraine, the liquidation of the Greek-Catholic Church, which was symbolic for the formation of the nation. In all these and other cases, religion served as an emotional bond among those who felt that they belonged to the nation. Ukraine is an especially interesting case as it has no homogeneity in religion: both Greek-Catholicism and Orthodoxy are 'Ukrainian' religion. Moreover, Ukrainian scholars working on religion emphasise the differences between 'Moscow' and 'Kiev' Orthodoxy, arguing that the Kievan tradition is 'more westernized' (Sagan 2004: 172–4). In many non-Orthodox countries under communism religion also provided ideas

for opposing communism and Soviet domination, as for instance in predominantly Catholic Lithuania, Hungary and Slovakia.

5. In January 2006 I visited a Polish town on the Baltic coast, Kolobrzeg, which is situated close to the Polish-German border. During a tour of the city a professional guide explained details of the historical cathedral, mentioning that the Pope had given it the status of a basilica. When I asked him 'which pope?', he looked at me in complete astonishment and replied: 'obviously, our Pope!'.

6. The family became the most important vehicle of religious tradition not only in Poland but in other communist countries as well. The special role of grandmothers should be mentioned here as, thanks to them, religion was preserved in Eastern Europe by a dwindling population. Nevertheless, the rate of decline in the number of baptised people was lower than it would otherwise have been because of their activities and because they took their grandchildren to church without informing the children's parents. Indeed, it would have been much more risky for the children's parents to do this than it was for the generation of grandparents.

7. For instance, before the mid-fifteenth century one of the ways to 'push' the borders of the Latin tradition further to the East was to boost the work of the Dominican order in innumerable towns throughout the Eastern territory such as Podolie, Wolhynie and Ruthenie (Delacroix-Besnier 1999).

8. The war in the former Yugoslavia provides some striking examples. Orthodox Serbs and Muslim Bosniaks, for instance, have moved out of the territory of present-day Croatia. It currently has a tiny Orthodox minority (0.1 per cent of the population) and virtually no Muslims, whereas the census of 1991 showed that there had previously been 76.5 per cent of Catholics, 11.1 per cent of Orthodox, and 1.2 per cent of Muslims (Črpić and Zrinščak 2005: 52–6). The statistics are eloquent testimony to the changes; and so is the landscape where, 15 years after the fighting, the houses vacated by Serbs still stand empty with broken windows. The landscape is a dramatic shadow of the past and visible proof of the shifting of borders.

9. See Ware 1997: 63. This involves restricting statements about God to what may be said about Him and refraining from what cannot be said about Him.

10. This involves seeking a deeper understanding of God through such sensory experiences as feelings, visions and images.

11. Does this have any significance from a sociological point of view? It certainly does. From a Weberian point of view, societies where God is considered immanent are likely to be less rationalised and less secularised than Western societies with a more transcendent image of God. Following Niklas Luhmann's (1999) view that developments of religious dogmatics reflect developments of societal contingencies (and modernities), Eastern European societies, which tend to be dominated by Orthodoxy, were and are less modernised and less contingent. There is a risk of dangerous oversimplification in this discussion. But to put the question another way – does religious doctrine and the way of expressing it have to reflect the spirit of society and

vice versa? Doctrine and the way of teaching it shape a society's most profound ways of perceiving and expressing the world. Luhmann (1999: 99) was convinced that religious leaders tried to achieve coherence between religious doctrine and the type of society in which it was developed. Different expressions of doctrine and different societies – in both Western and Eastern Europe – show a tendency to search for coherence. It could be said that in Catholic – and even more so in Protestant – societies this tendency takes the form of reflection (dogmas are ideal forms of reflection) on social life from 'above' by means of doctrine, teaching and rational ethics. By contrast, Eastern Orthodox societies try to implement reflection 'from below' in the hard-to-define forms of so-called 'Eastern mysticism', 'spirituality' or what Russians call *bytovoje christianstwo*. This represents a kind of 'lived Christianity', which is an indissoluble mixture of religion, magic, folk traditions and *habitus* in everyday life.

12. Goeckel (1990: 21) shows how dramatic the decline was in Eastern Germany between 1952 and 1969. It could be compared to the decline in the Orthodox countries of the Soviet Union.

13. A lot of examples could be given here. Poland became aware, in the spring and summer of 2005, that a significant number of priests had apparently been collaborators of the communist system and that some of them had probably been very close to Pope John Paul II. This emerged from documents in the Institute of National Memory (Instytut Pamięci Narodowej), where the files of communist security agents are stored. The bishops of the Roman Catholic Church remained silent about it, while the mass-media were full of the story every day. Another example concerns the answer that the Patriarch Aleksey II gave on 25th April to a question from journalists about the life of the Church in the past and whether it had become easier or more difficult. His answer was anything but direct. The patriarch presented examples of his duties and life and of the places where he had served during communist times and then concluded: 'It is only outsiders who have the impression that, in comparison to the Soviet epoch, the life of the Church is easy and simple today ... There are problems in life today. Church people confirm that they still experience problems today, as in the past. Atheism has not disappeared yet' (www. mospat). Then the Patriarch cited the example of the difficulties that beset the introduction of a subject called 'The Principles of Orthodox culture' into the curriculum of state schools in the Russian Federation. Putting emphasis on the present-day problems enabled him to ignore the journalists' intention of asking about the past. The past tends to be portrayed in personal terms, and in terms of the Church as an institution suffering losses and being persecuted. Collaboration with the communists is not mentioned. It seems that for many reasons the Orthodox churches of Eastern Europe prefer to cast a silence over the past.

14. The nature of the statistics renders sociological analysis difficult, because the number of communities does not tell us anything about the number of individual believers. Communities can vary widely in size. In this

respect, a large number of small communities could easily create the impression that membership of a given religion was expanding rapidly.

15. The number of registered religious communities could result from the combination of two components: on the one hand, more or less liberal conditions for registration in alliance with a particular administrative practice in a society and, on the other hand, religious vitality (www.mswia.gov.pl) [accessed 25.03.2006].

16. 'The fastest growing groups are indigenous Russian sects – the Church of the Last Testament (the followers of Vissarion, based in Krasnoyarsk region) and the Church of the Sovereign Mother of God (previously known as the Bogorodichny Tsentr and led by Ioann Bereslavsky). Although both of these groups are small – with 15 and 28 organisations respectively – they have grown sevenfold since 1996. The next fastest increase has been enjoyed by the pagans, whose organisations have increased by almost sixfold to 41. After them come the fastest growing Christian Churches – the Full Gospel Church (with 62 organisations) and the Pentecostals, who have both increased approximately fourfold' (Fagan 2006).

17. The statistics of the ROC for 2002–2004 were as follows: 11,525 parishes were registered on Russian territory, 10,384 in Ukraine, 1,265 in Belarus, 1,080 in Moldova, 233 in Kazakhstan, and 93 in the other former Soviet republics such as Kyrgyzstan, Uzbekistan, Tajikistan and Turkmenistan. As far as the number of religious communities is concerned, the second largest Orthodox Church in Eastern Europe is the Ukrainian Orthodox Church of the Kiev Patriarchate (UOC-KP) with 3,395 registered communities, followed by the Ukrainian Autocephalous Orthodox Church (UAOC) with 1,156 registered communities (Mitrokhin 2004: 416).

18. In some of the countries that emerged from the collapse of communism – for instance the Baltic states or Ukraine – ethnic Russians amount to 30 per cent of the population. They are also heavily involved in national politics not only in respect of religious matters but also in connection with problems concerning citizenship, knowledge of the national language and the local status of the Russian language, the education system, and so on. All these problems are strongly overshadowed by the anti-Russian sentiment that is apparent in some regions such as the Western Ukraine or the Baltic States. Their opponents consider that Russians, as a people, are the successors of the Soviet Union.

19. Local and international conferences about these legal issues have resulted in publications in local languages concerning, for instance, Ukraine (Zdioruk 1996) and Croatia (Grubišič 1997) as well as in English (Borowik 1999). More specific publications on this topic include Tőrők 2003.

20. With regard to the principles of democracy, probably the worst situation is in Belarus where the state has a list of groups that allegedly do not qualify for registration and are not allowed to operate. It is not clear how this list was drawn up; and it functions secretly in the sense that it has never been published or justified by any state or scholarly body.

21. In the case of Hungary, for example, Tomka (1997: 222) estimated that 55 per cent of people described themselves as 'believers on their own' in 1997.

22. Some research projects are devoted specifically to religion and international comparisons. Two post-communist countries, Hungary and Poland, were involved in the RAMP Project (Religious and Moral Pluralism), and the *Aufbruch* Research Project (Pastorales Forum, Vienna) includes a growing number of post-communist countries.

23. Barker distinguishes the following types of groups in terms of their relation to religion: 'revivalists', 'belongers-not-believers', 'believers-not-belongers', 'religious seekers', 'New Age seekers' and 'consumerists' (Barker 1997: 46–8).

REFERENCES

Babiński, G. 1997, 'Borderland Identity. Religious and National Identification in the Polish-Ukrainian Borderland'. In I. Borowik and G. Babiński (eds) *New Religious Phenomena in Central and Eastern Europe*. Krakow: Nomos Publishing House: 93–113.

Barker, E. 1997. *But Who's Going to Win? National and Minority Religions in Post-Communist Society*. In I. Borowik and G. Babiński (eds) *New Religious Phenomena in Central and Eastern Europe*. Krakow: Nomos Publishing House: 25–62.

Berdiaiev, N. A. 1995. *Istoki i smysl russkogo kommunisma* (Sources and Meaning of Russian Communism). Paris: YMCA – Press (first published in German in 1937. First English edition *The Origin Of Russian Communism* trans. by R. M. French. London: G. Bles, 1937).

Borowik, I. (ed.) 1999, *Church-State Relations in Central and Eastern Europe*. Kraków: Nomos Publishing House.

Borowik, I. 2000a. 'Young Adult Catholics in Contemporary Poland'. In J. Fulton, A. M. Abela, I. Borowik, T. Dowling, P. Long Marler and L. Tomasi, *Young Catholics at the Millennium. The religion and Morality of Young Adults in Western Countries*. Dublin: University College Dublin Press: 70–90.

Borowik, I. 2000b. *Odbudowywanie pamieci. Przemiany religijne w Srodkowo-Wschodniej Europie po upadku komunizmu.* (The Rebuilding of Memory. Religious Change in Central and Eastern Europe after the Fall of Communism). Kraków: I. Borowik and G. Babiński (eds) *New Religious Phenomena in Central and Eastern Europe*, Krakow: Nomos Publishing House.

Borowik, I. 2002. 'Between Orthodoxy and Eclectism: On the Religious Transformation of

Russia, Belarus and Ukraine', *Social Compass* 49 (4): 497–508.

Borowik, I. 2004. 'Religion and Civil Society in Poland in the Process of Democratic Transformation'. In D. Marinović-Jeromlimov, S. Zriščak and I. Borowik (eds), *Religion and Patterns of Social Transformation.* Zagreb: Institute for Social Research: 125–141.

Črpić, G. and S. Zrinščak 2005. 'Between identity and Everyday life'. In J. Baloban (ed.), *In Search of Identity. A Comparative Study of Values: Croatia and Europe.* Zagreb: Golden marketing – Tehnička knjiga: 19–83.

Davie, G. 2000. *Religion in Modern Europe. A Memory Mutates.* Oxford: Oxford University Press.

Delacroix-Besnier, C. 1999. 'Les Dominicains en Europe du centre-est (Rhutenie, Podolje, Moldavie): flux et reflux du catholicisme (1370-1430)'. In J. Kłoczowski (ed.), *Christianity in East Central Europe. Late Middle Ages.* Lublin: Instytut Europy Środkowo-Wschodniej: 72–85.

Dujtsev, I. 1997. 'Wpływ Bizancjum na kulturę słowian po upadku Imperium', (Influence of Byzantium on the Slavs culture after the collapse of Imperium). In J. Kłoczowski (ed.), *Chrześcijaństwo Rusi Kijowskiej, Bialorusi, Ukrainy I Rosji (X-XVII wiek)* (Christianity of Kievan Rus, Belarus, Ukraine and Russia [X-XVII centuries]). Kraków: PAU: 116–28.

Fagan, G. 2006. 'Russia: Re-Registration Figures For Religious Organizations', online document at: *http://www.starlightsite.co.uk/keston/kns/2001 /010402RU.htm* (accessed 02.06.2006).

Goeckel, R. F. 1990. *The Lutheran Church and the East German State. Political Conflict and Change under Ulbricht and Honecker.* Ithaca, NY: Cornell University Press.

Greeley, A. 2004. *Religion in Europe at the End of the Second Millennium.* New Brunswick, NJ, Transaction Publishers.

Grubišić, I. (ed.) 1997. *Crkva i država u drustvima u tranziciji* (The Church and the State in Transforming Societies). Split: Knjižnica Dijalog.

Johnson, H. 1989. 'Toward an Explanation of Church Opposition to Authoritarian Regimes: Religio-Oppositional Subcultures in Poland and Catalonia'. *Journal for the Scientific Study of Religion* 28 (4): 493–508.

Kubik, J. 1994. *The Power of Symbols against the Symbols of Power: The Rise of Solidarity and the Fall of State Socialism in Poland.* Philadelphia: Pennsylvania State University.

Kłoczowsaki, J. 1998. *Młodsza Europa. Europa Środkowo-Wschodnia w kręgu cywilizacji chrześcijańskiej średniowiecza* (The Younger Europe. Central and Eastern Europe in the circle of Christian civilization). Warszawa: PIW.

Lubaschenko, W. I. 1996. *Istoria protestantismu w Ukraini* (History of Protestantism in Ukraine). Kiev: Polis.

Luhmann, Niklas 1984. *Religious Dogmatics and the Evolution of Society.* New York: Edwin Mellen Press.

Luhmann, N. 1999. *Funkcja religii* (Function of Religion), Kraków: Nomos.

Malinin, V. 1901. *Starets Eleazarova Monastyria Filofei i ego poslania.* Appendix, Kiev.

Meyendorff, J. 1996. *Rome, Constantinopole, Moscow. Historical and Theological Studies,* Jordanville.

Michalik, J. 1991. 'Letter of the Bishop' *Pismo Okólne* (General Circulars) 42, 1991.

Mitrokhin, M. 2004. *Russkaia Pravoslavnaia Tserkov. Sovriemiennoie sostojanie i aktualnyje problemy* (The Russian Orthodox Church. Contemporary Situation and Current Problems). Moskow: Novoie Litieraturnoie Obozrienie.

Morawska, E. 1984. 'Civil Religion vs. State Power in Poland. In *Society* (21) 4: 29–34.

Müller, O. 2004. 'Religiosity in Central and Eastern Europe: results from the PCE Survey'. In D. Marinović-Jeromlimov, S. Zrinščak and I. Borowik (eds) *Religion and Patterns of Social Transformation.* Zagreb: Institute for Social Research: 61–79.

Norris, P. and Inglehart, R. 2004. *Sacred and Secular. Religion and Politics Worldwide.* Cambridge: Cambridge University Press.

Pawluczuk, W. 1998. *Polityka i mistyka na Ukrainie* (Politics and Mystics in Ukraine). Kraków: Nomos Publishing House: 93–113.

Pollack, D. 2003. 'Religiousness Inside and Outside of the Church in Selected Post-Communist Countries of Central and Eastern Europe', *Social Compass* 50 (3): 321–34.

Prusak, M. M. and Borscev, W. W. (eds) 1996. *Religioznyje objedinienia Rossijskoj Federacii. Spravocniuk.* Moskow: Respublika.

Sagan, A. 2004. *Wsielenskie prawoslaw'ja. Sut', istortia, sutsasnyj stan* (The Worldly Orthodoxy. The idea, history and present position). Kyjiw: Swit znan'.

Skokova, L. 2004. *Identyfikacja religijna w autobiograficznych przekazach mlodziezy: próba interpretacji socjologicznej* (Religious Identification in Autobiographies of Youth: The Attempt of

Sociological Interpretation), *Studia Socjologiczne* (Sociological Studies) 4: 109–35.

Shterin, M. 2000. 'Church-State Relationships and Religious Legislation in Russia in the 1990s'. In M. Kotiranta (ed.), *Religious Transition in Russia*, Helsinki: Kikimora Publications: 218–50.

Smrke, M. 1996. *Religija in Politika. Spremembe v deželah prehoda* (Religion and Politics. Change in the Land of Transition), Ljubljana: Znavstveno in politicistično središče.

Stricker, G. 1995. *Russkaia Pravoslavnaia Tserkov v sovietskoie vriemia*, (The Russian Orthodox Church in Soviet Times) Moskwa: Propilei.

Tomka, M. 1997. 'Hungarian Post-World War II. Religious development and the present Challenge of New Churches and New Religious Movements'. In Borowik I. and G. Babiński (eds), *New Religious Phenomena in Central and Eastern Europe*. Kraków: NOMOS Publishing House: 203–35.

Tomka, M. 1999. 'Religion, Church, State and Civil Society in East-Central Europe'. In I. Borowik (ed.), *Church-State Relations in Central and Eastern Europe*. Kraków: Zakład Wydawniczy NOMOS.

Tomka, M. 2002. 'Tendances de la religiosité et de l'orientation vers les Eglises en Europe de l'Est', *Social Compass* 49 (4): 537–52.

Tomka, M. 2004. 'Comparing Countries by their Religiosity in Eastern Europe'. In D. Marinović-Jeromlimov, S. Zrinščak and I. Borowik (eds) *Religion and Patterns of Social Transformation*, Zagreb: Institute for Social Research: 49–61.

Török, P. 2003. *Hungarian Church-State Relationships*, Budapest, Studies of Hungarian Institute for Sociology of Religion.

Urban, K. 1994. *Mniejszości religijne w Polsce 1945–1991. Zarys Statystyczny*. (Religious Minorities in Poland. Statistical review). Kraków: Zakład Wydawniczy Nomos.

Velikonja, M. 2003. *Religious Separation and Political Intolerance in Bosnia-Herzegovina*. Texas: Texas A&M University Press.

Walicki, A. 1996. *Marksizm i skok do królestwa wolności. Dzieje komunistycznej utopii*. Warszawa: PWN. (Published in English as *Marxism and the Leap to the Kingdom of Freedom. The Rise and Fall of the Communist Utopia*, 1995 Stanford Junior University).

Ware, T. (Bishop Kallistos of Diokleia) 1997. *The Orthodox Church*. Harmondsworth: Penguin Books.

Weber Max 1963. The Sociology of Religion. London: Lowe & Brydon.

Zdioruk, S. 1996 (ed.) *Swoboda wiriwiznannia. Cerkva i Derzawa w Ukrajini* (The Freedom of Religion. The Church and the State in Ukraine). Kyjiw: 'Prawo'.

Zrinščak, Siniša 2004. 'Generations and Atheism: Patterns of Response to Communist Rule among Different Generations and Countries', *Social Compass* 51 (2): 221–34.

Żukrowska, K. 1995. 'Poland: Changes for the Better'. In: B. Góralczyk *et al.* (eds) *In Pursuit of Europe. Transformations of Post-Communist States 1989–1994*. Warsaw: PAN.

32

Judaism in Israel: Public Religion, Neo-Traditionalism, Messianism, and Ethno-Religious Conflict

STEPHEN SHAROT

RELIGIONS IN ISRAEL/PALESTINE

Religion is a crucial factor in the political and ethno-national divisions among Israeli Jews and Palestinian Arabs who claim rights of settlement and political sovereignty over a territory viewed by both as their homeland. Jews, Christians and Muslims can claim a long uninterrupted presence in Israel/Palestine over most of the last 20 centuries. There have, of course, been significant changes in the relative and absolute size of the religious populations. Following the prominence of the Jewish population during the early period and of the Christians during the Byzantine period between the second and sixth centuries, the rise of Islam saw the emergence of a Muslim majority after the seventh century. This lasted through 1947 when the population of Palestine approached two million; about 60 per cent were Muslims, 32 per cent Jews, and 7 per cent Christians.

With the establishment of the State of Israel in 1948 and the ensuing war between Israel and the Arab states, most of the Arab population fled or were expelled from the areas of the new state. About 150,000 Arabs or 19 per cent of the total Israeli population remained after these events and, of these, 21 per cent were Christians who had been treated more favorably than Muslims by the Israeli authorities. The ratio of Arabs within the boundaries of the Jewish state has changed little; in 2005, out of a population of nearly seven million, the Arabs constituted 20 per cent of the population but, as a consequence of the higher Muslim birth rate and Christian emigration, the Christians now represented less than 10 per cent of the Arab population and 2.1 per cent of the population of the state. Although the Arab Christians were prominent for some time in the secular political parties of Arab-Palestinian nationalism, their position declined with the rise of Islamic movements in the 1980s and 1990s and the rise of tension between Christians and Muslims. Another religious rift within the Arab Israeli population is between the Druze, who are the only Arab group who commonly serve in the Israeli army, and other Arabs.

The 1967 war extended Israeli rule over the whole of Palestine, and in the year 2000, when the total population of the conquered territories approached three million, 94 per cent of the population were Arabs, of whom only about 1.5 per cent were Christians, and 6 per cent were Jews. The withdrawal of Israel from the Gaza Strip, where Jewish residents constituted less than 1 per cent of the population, has freed more than one million Arabs, nearly all Muslims, from Israeli rule. Jewish settlers in the West Bank constitute 9 per cent of its population, and most are concentrated in areas close to the 1967 borders. The number of Christians in the West Bank has declined as many have emigrated, especially following the *intifadas* (uprisings) and the rise of the Islamist groups, Hamas and Islamic Jihad (DellaPergoa, 2001; Tsimhoni, 2001).

The proportional decline and political marginalization of Christian Arabs in Israel and Palestine is one consequence of the increased prominence of religion in the ethno-national identity of Palestinian Muslims. Although the religious factor was by no means the sole explanation of the success of the Islamic party Hamas in the elections of the Palestinian Authority in 2006, it clearly played a part. Hamas has embraced Palestinian national symbols but it has endowed them with Islamic meaning. Its ultimate goal is the establishment of an Islamic society and state, and unlike the PLO, which depicts the struggle as one between Palestinians and Zionists, Hamas views the conflict as one between Islam and Judaism, or Muslims and Jews. Its sanctification of Palestine as a holy Islamic land is justified by God's choice of the al-Aqsa Mosque in Jerusalem as the place for the ascension of the Prophet Muhammad to heaven and the designation of Palestine as a *waqf* by the Caliph `Umar ibn al-Khatab. As a *waqf* Palestine is considered to belong to the entire Muslim nation until the day of resurrection, and no Muslim party or leadership has the right to concede even an inch of that land (Litvak, 1996; Mishal and Sela, 2000).

Since the October or Yom Kippur War in 1973 the prominence of ultranationalist religious Jews in the Jewish settlement of the occupied territories and their refusal to countenance any compromise over the sacred *Eretz Yisrael* (Land of Israel) has also contributed to the identification of the Israeli Jewish-Palestinian conflict as a religious one. However, the division within the Israeli Jewish population between religious and secular sectors has become focal to the increasingly acrimonious debate and violent clashes among Israeli Jews over withdrawal from the occupied territories. The question of the boundaries of the Israeli state has become an issue of the very nature of that state: whether it has a religious foundation which requires that it retains Jewish sovereignty over the sacred Land of Israel or whether it is civic in nature, serving a population which is largely but not exclusively Jewish in a given territory.

PUBLIC RELIGION AND SECULARIZATION

The religious developments and divisions of the Israeli Jewish population are the focus of this paper and are analyzed within a conceptual framework of the sociology of religion. Such an analysis has not been common among Israeli sociologists who have tended to analyze religion in Israel from the perspective of other sub-disciplines such as ethnicity and political sociology. In an attempt to explain why the sociology of religion has not developed in Israel, it has been argued that, whereas post-classical sociology of religion has been developed by American sociologists who focus on religion as a private, voluntary realm, most Israeli sociologists conceptualize religion as a public realm, tied to the state (Kopelowitz and Israel-Shamsian, 2005).

It is true that Jewish Israelis, and secular Israelis in particular, conceive of religion as shaped by a state-sponsored religious establishment. There is no formal state religion in Israel, but the state gives its official recognition and financial support to particular religious communities, Jewish, Islamic and Christian, whose religious authorities and courts are empowered to deal with matters of personal status and family law, such as marriage, divorce and alimony, that are binding on all members of the communities. The Jewish religious authorities who have the sole state-sanctioned authority to deal with these matters with respect to Israeli Jews are the Orthodox or, a more appropriate term in the context of Judaism, Orthoprax rabbinate. As a formally proclaimed 'Jewish state' with Jews making up four-fifths of the population, Jewish religious symbols and ritual are prominent in the public sphere and are generally taken-for-granted by Israeli Jews, including secular Jews who practice little or nothing of religion at the private, voluntary level (Liebman, 1997a; Samet, 1979; Tabory, 1981; Sharot, 1995: 21; Waxman, 2004).

Privatization of religion has been conceptualized by sociologists of religion as a dimension of secularization, and the prominence of public forms of religion in Israel poses questions of secularization in Israeli society. In comparison with many Western societies, and especially with the United States, a significant sector of Israeli Jews identifies as secularist and is highly critical of religious institutions. On the other hand, religion is a major social and political force in Israeli society: religious political parties and movements have both responded to, and had considerable impact on, political policies and the Jewish-Palestinian/Arab conflict. In order to make sense of these diverse trends and their relationships, it is necessary to approach secularization as a multi-dimensional phenomenon.

Among the multi-dimensional frameworks for the analysis of secularization, the framework suggested by Jose Casanova (1994) is particularly helpful for my purposes because it was formulated with particular reference to the importance of public religion. Three dimensions of secularization are distinguished: firstly, the differentiation of secular spheres from religious norms and institutions; secondly, a decline of religious beliefs and practices; and thirdly, the marginalization of religion to a privatized sphere. The first dimension, differentiation, is common to all Western societies, but of particular relevance here is the variation among societies with respect to the differentiation of nationalist ideologies from religion and the differentiation of state and religion.

The second dimension, the decline of religious beliefs and practices, is less encompassing of Western societies than differentiation, and, as Casanova notes, the more the religious institutions resisted differentiation, the more there has been religious decline. The third dimension, privatization, has been a historical trend in many societies, but Casanova emphasizes that, unlike differentiation, it is not a modern structural trend. It is an 'historical option' found particularly in those societies that have experienced religious decline, and in recent decades there have been important trends of deprivatization.

There has been little discussion of deprivatization in Israel because there has been little cognizance of privatization; the prominence of public religion in Israel has been taken-for-granted both by the Israeli public and by most Israeli sociologists. The following account of religion in Israel, organized according to the dimensions of differentiation, decline and privatization, analyzes both secularization and counter-secularization trends within each of the dimensions.

DIFFERENTIATION AND UNDIFFERENTIATION

The state of Israel was founded by secularized Jews from Europe who established institutions differentiated from religion in accord with Western models, but a number of factors limited the differentiation of national and religious values and political and religious institutions. Firstly, the new state was formed as a 'Jewish state,' and given the integral link between Judaism and the Jewish people, national symbols drew upon the religious tradition. Secondly, the dominant ideology of the state founders included secularized forms of traditional religious ideas such as messianism. And thirdly, the political strategy of the secular founders included accommodations to the ultra-Orthoprax and religious Zionist sectors and, at a later date, to the predominantly non-secular Jewish immigrants from North Africa and Asia.

A Jewish State and its Symbols

The most basic reason for the prominence of public religion in Israel is that the Israeli state was founded as a 'Jewish' state, and the vast majority of its Jewish citizens have identified with it on this ethno-national and, because of the historical correspondence of the Jewish people and Judaism, religious basis. The Declaration of Independence left open the interpretation of who is Jewish in the 'Jewish state.' If 'Jewish' was to be interpreted in secular nationalist terms, a person's simple declaration that he or she was Jewish would have been sufficient to secure citizenship. Such a possibility was rejected by subsequent laws and government agencies which have defined a Jew according to the *halachic* (religious law) formulation: 'a person born of a Jewish mother, or who converted to Judaism, and is not a member of another religion.' Although the religious parties have been prominent in equating Jewish nationality with the religious definition of the Jew, this formulation was supported by the secular political leadership who rejected a liberal Western definition of citizenship in favor of a definition which, although religious, provided a primordial foundation for national classification and identity (Shafir and Peled, 2002: 145–7).

Although mainstream Zionists thinkers from Herzl onward stressed that the future state for Jews would follow the liberal principle of extending equal rights to all its citizens, the principle of universal civil equality stated in the Declaration of Independence has been subordinated in practice to the particularistic character of a Jewish state (Cohen, 1995: 204–5). A fusion of religion and state was signaled by the choice of the state's symbols. As the official symbol of the state, a motif of seven stars, symbolizing secular Enlightenment, was rejected in favor of the seven-pronged candelabra which played an important role in the Temple rites of antiquity. The colors of the national flag are blue and white, the traditional colors of the prayer shawl, and the flag's blues stripes on the white background follow that of the shawl (Etzioni-Halevy, 2002: 87; Ezrahi, 2004: 256–8).

Socialist Zionism as a 'Secular Religion'

Somewhat paradoxically the prominence of public religion in Israel followed from the goal of the most important Jewish groups in the Zionist settlement in Palestine and the establishment of the state to create a Jewish society in which a secularized nationalism would replace religion as identity and culture. The early Zionist immigrants, who came to be known as the *halutzim* (pioneers), were mostly from Eastern Europe where, around the turn of the nineteenth century, they had adopted radically secularist-socialist nationalist identities. Most had grown up in religious homes and were familiar with the beliefs and practices of the tradition, but they had come to reject religion as a repressive force keeping the Jews in chains. Some accused religion of usurping the true bases of national identity, land, language and the state, and as they constructed a national identity as 'New Hebrews' or 'Israelis' they insisted on a clear differentiation of nationality and religion, signaled by substituting the 'people of Israel' for God when they drew upon biblical and traditional literature. Their problem was that, if they were to retain some degree of continuity with the past of the people with whom they identified, they had to acknowledge and deal with the fact that their nation's past was bound to religion (Sharot, 1998; Knaani, 1975; Diamond, 1986: 15–19; Luz, 1988 xii–xiii).

The attempts to differentiate between religion and nation, and – once the state was established – between religion and state, were beset by forces which limited that differentiation or resulted in de-differentiation. For the secularist Jews there was tension between their goals of transforming Jewish culture into a secular nationalism and settling Jews within the territory of Zion or *Eretz Israel* (Land of Israel) which was to be the territory of an independent state (Kimmerling, 2001: 186–7). Although some Western European Jews had considered other territories, particularly Uganda, as possible areas for a separate Jewish political entity, Eastern European Zionists had rejected such schemes and insisted on 'Zion' as the only possible site for a Jewish state. The moral right of Jews to immigrate and settle was expressed in the term 'Land of Israel' which implied an essential link between a geographical place, 'the Land,' and the Jewish people, 'Israel' (Almog, 2000: 14).

Like other emergent nation states, the particular territory of the Jewish nation was a pivotal factor and was sacralized in Zionism. The territorial ethos was inculcated in the socialization and educational practices instituted in the pre-state Jewish settlement, the *Yishuv*: an emphasis on nature, geography and agriculture in the school syllabi, and frequent cross-country treks which were termed 'spiritual journeys.' The landscape was mystified in art, and archaeology became an important discipline which located and recovered ancient, particularly Israelite, settlements (Ben-Ari and Bilu, 1987: 231–2). Zion, however, was the land that the religion taught had been promised to the Jews by God, and the return to Zion had remained the promise of Jewish messianism throughout the almost two thousand years in *galut* (exile) (On messianism in Jewish history see Sharot, 1982). The sacralization of the land by secular Zionism was difficult, if not impossible, to dissociate from its sacred status within traditional religion.

The Zionist pioneers saw themselves as realizing, in a secular fashion, the diaspora dreams of redemption, messianism, and the realization of God's kingdom on earth. In place of the passive expectation of redemption that Jews traditionally believed would come with the arrival of the messiah, the pioneers saw themselves as leading the nation in its self-redemption. God and a personal messiah had no part in this epic of national liberation, but metaphysical and deterministic elements remained. The return to Zion was a 'miracle' or a 'miraculous stage in history,' and there was a 'law of redemption' that determined the progress of Jewish history. Expressions like 'rebirth,' 'the dawn of redemption,' 'the lost generation of slavery and first of redemption' reoccurred in the writings and speeches of the pioneers, and many believed that they were 'building the Third Temple' in the political sense (Almog, 2000: 41–3).

As the negation of diasporic history, Zionist redemption was viewed as a renewal of the Jewish or Israelite history of Antiquity (Zerubavel, 1995: 4–23). The major text for the account of Antiquity was the *Tanach* (Old Testament Bible) which became for secular Zionists part and parcel of their rejection of *galut* (exile). Judaism in the diaspora had become focused on the Talmud, particularly the Babylonian Talmud and the rabbinical responsa, and the Bible had been relegated to the margins by rabbinical Judaism. For the socialist Zionists, the Bible, stripped of its supernatural elements, told of the glorious past of the Israeli people, it linked that past to their present, and it justified their socialism and the Jewish right of settlement. The recent and contemporary history of the conquest and settlement of the land and the victories over the British and Arab adversaries were presented as actualizations of Biblical stories. Non-Marxist Jewish socialists claimed that the origins of socialist ideas were to be found in the Bible, especially in the books of Isaiah and Amos (Shapira, 1998: 261–2; Almog, 2000: 27, 45; Kimmerling, 2001: 191).

The link between the biblical past and the Zionist present was reinforced by the observance of sacred holidays, both traditional holidays, refashioned by Zionism, and new holidays which celebrated socialist ideology (May Day) and commemorated events of modern Zionist history (Balfour Declaration Day, Tel Chai Day). The most important holidays remained the traditional ones, observed according to their dates in the traditional Jewish calendar, but transformed to conform to the secular and nationalist values of Zionism. The adoption of traditional holidays was a selective one; those holidays that dwelt on national conflicts and celebrated the victories of ancient Hebrews over their enemies were the most prominent (*Hanukkah*, Passover, *Purim*), while important holidays of traditional Judaism which lacked these themes were largely ignored (*Yom Kippur, Tish'a be-Av*). The commemorative accounts of the holidays focused on human rather than divine agency. The traditional *Hanukkah*, Festival of Lights, which celebrated the rededication of the Temple in 165 BCE and the miraculous resupply of oil sufficient for lighting the

Temple's lamps over eight days, was replaced by an exclusive focus on the Maccabee's heroism and victory over the Seleucids (Zerubavel, 1995: 216–18).

Whereas important holiday rituals were traditionally observed by families in their homes, in the Zionist versions they became communal rituals that mobilized individuals to identify with the community and nation. The emphasis on communally-focused rituals was especially evident in the kibbutzim, the agricultural settlements established on communistic principles, where traditional holidays were reintroduced in forms that expressed kibbutz values and their way of life with an emphasis on the connection of the holidays to the agricultural cycle. *Shavuot*, traditionally a celebration of the giving of the Torah, was the first of the holidays to be reinstated in the kibbutzim where it was renewed as a celebration of the first crops (Lilker, 1982). Secular Zionists made little effort to transform rituals that focused on the individual, and many continued to observe the rites of passage, often in their traditional forms. Circumcision was performed on practically all newborn males, although some dispensed with the religious ceremony. Most boys had a barmitvah, and no secular versions were devised for the marriage ceremony (Shapira, 1998: 264)

Compromise and Accommodation; the Ultra-Orthodox, Religious Zionists, and Jews from North Africa and Asia

The distaste of the Socialist Zionists of the early *aliyot* toward religion was reinforced by their perceptions of the Old *Yishuv* (Old Settlement) which they regarded as an extension of exile in the Land of Israel (Zerubavel, 1995: 33–4). The Jews of the Old *Yishuv*, predominantly of European origins, led a life regulated by, and devoted to the study of, the Torah or religious law. Their immigration had been motivated solely by religious considerations; they sought a way of life that was not threatened by the *Haskalah* (Jewish Enlightenment) and other secular trends in Europe, and without the worldly pressures of having to make a living.

They depended on a system of economic contributions from the diaspora communities, and they saw in their economic inactivity and material dependence on others an expression of the highest Jewish values: an opportunity to devote themselves to prayer and religious study. The secularist immigrants saw the Old *Yishuv* as a deformed and parasitical society, and they were seen in turn by the Old *Yishuv* as the worst representations of all that was evil and dangerous in Zionism (Friedman, 1977; Knaani, 1975; Azili, 1984).

During the period of the British mandate, changes occurred in the attitude of many Orthoprax Jews towards Zionism, and although the majority of the ultra-Orthoprax remained non-Zionist or anti-Zionist, a *modus vivendi* developed between the more moderate Orthoprax, including an increasing number of religious Zionists, and the secular Zionist leadership. *Mizrachi*, the political party of the religious Zionists, which later changed its name to *Mafdal* (National Religious Party), was established in 1902 as a faction within the World Zionist Organization, and in the *Yishuv* its leaders cooperated with the secular Zionists and gave *de facto* recognition to the secular-led society. The *Mizrachi* leaders saw the party's main role as upholding the essential precepts of Judaism within the public sphere, and after World War I they formulated the statement: 'The private sphere is not our concern, but rather the public violation of religious precepts.' Although, at first, the secular Zionist leadership tried to ignore the demands of the religious Zionists, such as obligatory *kashrut* (dietary laws) in restaurants, they accepted that the Sabbath should be recognized as a day of rest, and they became more compromising in order to preserve unity and avoid alienating religiously observant workers (Kolatt, 1998: 277, 290, 297).

The most important party representing the ultra-Orthoprax was *Agudat Israel* (Union of Israel) which was established in Europe in 1912 as an anti-Zionist religious movement with the aim of protecting the semi-autonomous political and legal status of traditional Jewish life and opposing secularization and secularism. *Agudat Israel* vehemently opposed Zionism as an ideology, but it supported efforts to settle Jews in Palestine as a means of easing the plight of diaspora Jews, and it entered into negotiation with secular Zionists in order to ensure the religious autonomy of its sector. This stance continued after the establishment of the state, although they declared that they were still living in exile and that a true Jewish state had to await the coming of the messiah. The more extreme ultra-Orthodox groups, *Edah Haredit* and *Neturei Karta* rejected cooperation with secular Zionists and any recognition of the new state (Kopelowitz, 2001: 173, 177; Liebman and Cohen, 1997: 59; Liebman and Don-Yehiya, 1984: 86).

Although the secular Zionists were by far the most dominant and powerful sector in the *Yishuv,* their political leaders sought a compromise with the religious sectors in order to obtain their support, or at least neutralize their opposition, to the founding of the state. *Agudat Israel* had threatened to appear separately before the United Nations fact-finding commission for Palestine if its demands were not met. In a letter to *Agudat Israel*, signed by David Ben-Gurion and two others, promises were made with respect to the Orthoprax control of religion in the public sphere, and assurances were made that the principal arrangements that prevailed in the *Yishuv* would be maintained in the new state. These arrangements covered Saturday as the national day of rest, the observance of dietary laws in public institutions, the exclusive jurisdiction of Orthoprax religious courts over marriage and divorce, and the autonomy of the religious educational system. The arrangements were enacted into the laws of the new state, such as the Rabbinical Courts Jurisdiction (Marriage and Divorce) Law of 1953, and the State Education Law which established two state systems, one secular and one religious, the latter under the *de facto* control of *Mizrachi* (Liebman and Don-Yehiya, 1984; Evron, 1995: 194–5; Sheleg, 2000: 284–5; Shafir and Peled, 2002: 140–1).

The secular political leaders accommodated the ultra-Orthoprax by allowing them considerable institutional, albeit state financed, autonomy, but they could not hope to include the ultra-Orthoprax under a unified symbol system. A unified symbol system to unite the majority of Israeli Jews was conceived as an imperative as the population became more heterogeneous in their cultural backgrounds. Of particular importance was the immigration of large numbers of Jews from North Africa and Asia in the first two decades of the state.

In contrast with both the secular Zionists and non-Zionist Orthoprax Jews from Europe, many immigrants from the Middle East saw Zionism and the establishment of the state as affirmations of the religious tradition that they had upheld in their countries of origin. Some interpreted their immigration or *aliyah* (ascent) in traditional messianic terms. These were communities from the Middle East, such as Yemenite and those from the rural areas of Morocco and Tunisia, whose traditional religious life had remained substantially intact prior to the immigration. Among other communities, secularization had made inroads, but in most cases it was moderate in comparison with secularized European Jews, and this also meant that there was no militant ultra-Orthopraxy with a self-conscious task of defending the tradition (Deshen and Zenner, 1982; Ben-Rafael and Sharot, 1991: 27–8; Sharot, 1995: 21).

Zionist-Socialism had been the most important 'civil religion' of the New *Yishuv*, but it held no attraction for immigrants from Muslim countries and it was replaced in the newly founded state by *Mumluachtiyut* (Statism) that equated the state with the highest moral order and affirmed, in a selective manner, elements of the Jewish tradition. In the first years of the state, class and statist symbols coexisted in labor Zionist circles, but as Statism became the civil religion the socialist rhetoric was toned down, the symbols of Statism (national flag, menorah) replaced the older class symbols (red flag, International), and Independence Day became the major holiday. In an attempt to appeal to immigrants from North Africa and Asia, *Mapai*, the dominant labor party, created a religious subsystem within the labor movement, further moderating the Labor Zionist attitude toward religion (Liebman and Don-Yehiya, 1983: 82–3, 88–94, 109, 113).

STABLE, DECLINING, AND STRENGTHENED RELIGION

Stable Religion

Surveys of religiosity conducted in Israel give a somewhat misleading impression that little has changed over time in the religious practice of Israeli Jews. A survey published in 1963 included some rough measures of levels of religious observance; respondents were asked whether they observed all the *mitzvot* (commandments), most of them, to some extent, or not at all. The distribution is remarkably similar to the distributions found by subsequent surveys asking similar questions, including the last large-scale survey conducted in 1999 (see Table 32.1).

About a third of the population report that they observe all or most of the *mitzvot*, about one-quarter report that they do not observe the *mitzvot*, and about two-fifths report partial observance. Surveys that asked whether respondents were 'secular' or 'non-religious' reported higher percentages in those categories than those surveys which asked if respondents were entirely non-observant. This is congruent with findings that show that many respondents who identity as 'secular' or 'non-religious' observe certain popular religious holiday practices such as lighting *Hanukkah* candles or participating in the Passover *Seder* meal (Antonovsky, 1963; Ben-Meir and Kedem, 1979; Goldscheider and Friedlander, 1983; Kedem, 1995; Levy *et al.*, 1993, 2002).

Three of the surveys (Ben-Meir and Kedem, 1979; Levy *et al.*, 1991, 1999) provide more detailed data on identification, observances and beliefs, and these data reinforce the impression that little has changed over time (see Table 32.2).

A classification of identification with respect to religion, widely used in everyday discourse as well as in surveys, distinguishes *dati* (religious), *mesoriti* (traditional), and *lo-dati* (non-religious) or *hiloni* (secular). A further distinction made among Israelis and in some surveys with respect to the religious sector is between the *haredi* or ultra-Orthoprax, denoting a segregative life style as well as a strict level of observance, and the *dati* or Orthoprax. These identifications are generally understood to refer to, and have been found to correspond with, levels of religious observance: *haredi* and *dati*, strict levels, *mesoriti*, moderate levels, and *hiloni*, low levels or non-observance. Over the time period covered by the surveys, the percentage of 'religious' remains unchanged at 17 per cent to 18 per cent, the 'traditional' appears to have declined somewhat in the 1990s from 43 per cent in 1991 to 35 per cent in 1999, and the 'non-religious' (including the 'anti-religious') has increased somewhat from 42 per cent in 1979 and 43 per cent in 1991 to 48 per cent in 1999.

The distribution and pattern of observance indicates a continuum of religiosity rather than any clear-cut polarization between religious and non-religious Jews, and this pattern has not undergone any significant change over the years. Certain practices, such as not traveling on the Sabbath, are observed by a minority: 22 per cent in 1968 and 27 per cent in 1999. About half of the population observe such practices as reciting a blessing over a cup of wine on the Sabbath eve (38 per cent in 1968, 51 per cent in 1999) and lighting candles with a blessing on the Sabbath (53 per cent in 1968, 51 per cent in 1999). Some practices are observed by the majority, such as fasting on Yom Kippur (74 per cent in 1968, 67 per cent in 1999), lighting *Hanukkah* candles (88 per cent in 1968,

Table 32.1 *Respondents' proclaimed level of observance of the* mitzvot

Year of survey	1962	1969	1982	1988	1991	1999
Complete observance	15	12	14	10	14	16
Observance to a large extent	15	14	20	18	24	20
Some observance	46	48	41	40	41	43
No observance	24	26	25	32	21	21

Source: Percentages: abstracted from Kedem, 1995; Levy *et al.*, 1993, 2002.

Table 32.2   *Identities, practices, and beliefs*

Year of survey	1968	1991	1999
Identities			
Religious (including haredim)	17	18	17
Traditional	41	42	35
Non-Religious (including anti-religious)	42	43	48
Practices			
Not travel on Sabbath	22	26	27
Light candles on Sabbath with blessing	53	51	51
Fast on Day of Atonement	74	71	67
Light Hanukkah candles	88	72	71
Participate in Passover Seder meal	99	78	85
Beliefs			
In God	64	63	65
In coming of messiah	36	39	36
In divine origins of Torah	56	47	51

Source: Percentages: abstracted from Ben-Meir and Kedem, 1979; Levy *et al.*, 1993, 2002.

71 per cent in 1999), and participating in the *Seder* night Passover meal (99 per cent in 1968, 85 per cent in 1999). However, if there is a trend, it is in the direction of polarization; the minority with strict levels of observance has increased in size while the practices observed by the majority have become somewhat less popular. Among the 'non-religious' sector there are indications, although no exact figures, of a decline in the religious observance of the rites of passage. Over 90 per cent of Jewish parents circumcise their newborn sons, but an increasing number have only the medical procedure without the religious ceremony. In 2001 the Ministry of Health issued permission for medical practitioners to perform the procedure whereas previously only a *mohel*, a religious practitioner, was officially entitled to do so. There are increases in the celebration of the *bar mitzvah* without a religious ceremony and marriages without a religious ceremony, and a number of non-religious burial sites have been established (Etzioni-Halevy, 2002: 92–5).

The distribution of responses to questions on beliefs have remained the same: 64 per cent in 1968 and 65 per cent in 1999 expressed a belief in God; 36 per cent in 1968 and in 1999 stated that they believed in the coming of the messiah; 56 per cent in 1968 believed that the Torah was given to Moses on Mount Sinai and 51 per cent in 1999 believed that the Torah precepts are divine commandments (Ben-Meir and Kedem, 1979; Levy *et al.*, 2002). A survey

carried out in 2006 found considerable differences between Israeli Jews and Israeli Arabs with respect to religious beliefs: 66 per cent of the Jews and 93 per cent of the Arabs said that they believed in God 'now and always'; 53 per cent of the Jews and 95 per cent of the Arabs believed that man had been created by God; 43 per cent of the Jews and 78 per cent of the Arabs believed in paradise and hell. Among the Jews, religious beliefs corresponded closely to religious identifications with respect to religion. For example, belief in the messiah was stated by all respondents who identified as *haredi*, by 83 per cent of the 'religious,' by 47 per cent of the 'traditional,' and by 10 per cent of the 'secular' (Ya'ar, 2006).

What might perplex outsiders is that the percentages of Israeli Jews who observe certain religious practices, such as lighting *Hanukkah* candles and participating in the Passover meal, are higher than the percentage who believe in God. Many Israeli Jews might be described as conforming to a pattern of observing without believing which contrasts with the pattern in Britain of 'believing without belonging' (Davie, 1994). Quite a number of Israelis carry out a number of practices, not because of a belief in their divine origins or as a religious obligation, but because they are conforming to common practices that express a Jewish-Israeli national identity. However, the way that secular Jews carry out the practices often differs substantially from their observance by religious and *mesoriti* Jews. For example, when secular Israelis celebrate the Passover meal they do not read all the traditional text, they omit some of the traditional symbols, and they introduce meanings of an ironic or sarcastic nature into the text (Deshen, 1997).

The statistics on religiosity, indicating a continuum of levels of observance rather than a dichotomous pattern, obscure differences with regard to the meanings of practices. Almost all of the strictly or mostly observant say that their acceptance of the *halacha* (code of religious law) is the source of authority for their observance; they observe 'because it is a commandment.' The reasons given by the less observant for their observance are instrumental or sentimental in nature: 'this is what Jews do,' 'this is the way it was done in my home,' 'it is more hygienic.' Many who fast on *Yom Kippur* do not do so in order to beg forgiveness for their sins but as an identity performance as well as for a number of idiosyncratic reasons. Ninety-eight per cent of Israeli Jews attach a *mezuzah* to the entrance of their homes, but for many this is a declaration of national allegiance rather than one of faith.

Since many of the 'somewhat observant' do not believe in the divine origin of the commandments, they have no problem in selecting a few practices that meet their needs of identity and community, and the ceremonies are performed with little or no reference to what the religious law enjoins. Many who light candles on the Sabbath eve do so after sundown, and ignore the religious stipulation that it should be carried out before sundown (Katz, 1997: 79–80; Susser, 1997; Etzioni-Halevy, 2002: 52). It should not be presumed, therefore, that the absence of clear boundaries between levels of observance and the fact that even the self-defined 'nonobservers' actually observe a few practices removes the basis for a religious-secular division. There is an important division, between those for whom the religious commandments represent an absolute and supreme authority, determining an entire way of life, and those who celebrate a few elements of the tradition as non-compulsory and personally chosen folk customs (Schweid, 1997). However, few nonobservers

today justify their nonobservance as a matter of principle or by reference to a militant secularist ideology. They are more likely to explain it by a lack of interest or the absence of observance in their families of origin (Deshen, 1997). It is secularization without secularism.

Declining Religion

The statistics which give an impression of a stable distribution of religiosity over the years hide trends of secularization and counter-secularization. One secularization trend is the decline in the observance of *mitzvot* among Jews from North Africa and Asia, from the immigrant to the second generation. With respect to the relationship between religious observance, geographical origins, and generational changes, the findings of the 1999 survey (Levy *et al.*, 2002) reinforces what has been shown in previous surveys (see Table 32.3).

First, it shows that Israelis born in Africa or Asia have much higher levels of observance and are far less likely to identify as non-religious or anti-religious than those born in the West. Second, there are no significant differences between the observance and identity patterns of the Western-born first generation and the Israeli-born with Western born fathers. With regard to certain popular holidays (Passover, *Hanukkah*) the second generation of Western origin demonstrate slightly higher levels of observance than the first generation. Third, apart from the most popular holidays, the level of observance of the second generation, Israeli born with African/Asian fathers is lower than that of the first generation, African/Asian born. Fourthly, following from the above, the differences between the second generation of Asian/African origins and the second generation of Western origins is less than the differences between the first generation categories (for earlier similar findings see Antonovsky, 1963; Matras, 1964; Bensimon, 1968; Herman, 1970; Goldscheider and Friedlander, 1983; Ayalon *et al.*, 1986). Fifthly, the levels of practice and belief of the more recent immigrants from the former Soviet Union, who now account for one-fifth

Table 32.3   *Identities, practices, and beliefs by origins in 1999*

| Birthplace: Respondent | N. Africa/Asia | Israel | West | Israel | |
Father	N. Africa/Asia	N. Africa/Asia	West	West	Former Soviet Union
Identity					
Haredi	6	3	4	7	–
Religious	22	14	8	10	2
Traditional	53	50	24	16	22
Non-Religious	19	31	59	62	70
Anti-Religious	–	2	6	5	6
Practices					
Separate meat & milk dishes	65	55	29	30	17
Fast on Yom Kippur	88	80	54	50	41
Light Hanukkah candles	84	79	61	66	40
Participate in Passover Seder meal	93	93	73	84	26
Beliefs					
In God	86	78	52	49	32
In coming of the messiah	55	45	22	23	10
Divine origins of Torah	74	64	35	34	23

Source: Percentages: abstracted from Levy *et al.*, 2002.

of the Israeli Jewish population, is consistently lower than that of all other categories. Even the most popular practices are celebrated by 40 per cent or less of former Soviet Union Jews.

There is a considerable overlap in Israel between geographical origins and socio-economic status as measured by education and occupation, but, apart from the study by Ayalon *et al.* (1986) of four groups of origin (from Morocco, Iraq, Poland, Rumania), there has been almost no analysis of the independent effects of socio-economic status on religiosity. Controlling for geographical origins and other variables, Ayalon *et al.*, found that higher occupational prestige reduced religiosity among those of Moroccan and Iraqi origins, especially among the Iraqis, and had no effect on religiosity among those of European origin. A regression analysis demonstrated that fathers' religiosity was the most important determinant of respondents' religiosity, but Jews from Morocco and Iraq, who had lived longer in Israel or had moved into higher socio-economic strata in which those of Western origin were overrepresented, were likely to have lower levels of religiosity (see also Kedem and Bar-Lev, 1983).

One might have expected that the intergenerational declines within the Asian/African category and the low observance levels of the more recent immigrants from the former Soviet Union would have reduced the overall levels of religiosity of Israeli Jews over time. In fact, as we have seen, surveys have continued to show a remarkably stable distribution. At least part of the answer to this puzzle is that the decline of religiosity has been in sectors with birth rates considerable lower than those in the Orthoprax and especially the ultra-Orthoprax sector in which the birth rate is more than three times that of the secular population.

Another secularization trend, of which there is little indication in the statistics on religious observance and belief, is the adoption of secular leisure patterns by a large sector of the younger generation of Jews who identify as *datiim* (religious). In contrast with the ultra-Orthoprax or *haredim* who reject the secular world and are either non-Zionist or anti-Zionist, the majority of Israelis who identify as *datiim* support Zionism, particularly in its religious forms, and have adopted a compartmentalized response to the secular world; their observance of the *mitzvot* is compartmentalized from their acceptance of secular education and modern styles of living. Many religious Jews live in neighborhoods and apartment buildings with secular Jews, and although a study of a mixed Tel Aviv suburb showed that the friendships of religious Jews tend to be restricted to other religious Jews (Tabory, 1989), among the younger generation there appears to be a greater openness to friendships, including romantic attachments, with secular Jews.

The Zionist or nationalist religious have always been open to the influence of secular culture, but in recent years this influence has widened to secular patterns of behavior which the religious norms and educational institutions of this sector have sought to avoid. The consumption of secular culture among the nationalist religious population in the past was justified by an emphasis on 'high culture' such as classical music, and the tendency was to reject frequenting popular places of entertainment. This has changed as religious youth are now to be seen in cinemas, pubs and dance halls where, in contradiction to religious norms, the sexes mix and dance together. Certain pubs cater to a young religious clientele who have their own popular music groups and appreciate satires on life in religious society, but others have moved into realms formerly confined to secular youth, such as backpacking to India, south-east Asia, and South America. One attempt by the religious establishment to keep these trends under their institutional auspices was their encouragement of the formation in the late 1980s of a college of film and television for religious students. The intention of the college's founders was to develop media that would convey religious messages, and when some students' films included critical representations of religious society, such as its treatment of women, a concerned administration imposed a stricter censorship (Sheleg, 2000: 54–63).

Trends within the nationalist religious sector are not in a single direction and many within the sector have sought to strengthen their boundaries with the secular population. This is one of the counter-secularization trends discussed in the following section.

Strengthened Religion

Counter-secularization in Israeli society is evident in developments among Israeli Jews of Asian/North African origins, the nationalist religious sector, and the ultra-Orthoprax or *haredim*. Beginning with the Jews from Asia and North Africa, it would be misleading to conclude from the decline of the observance of the stricter *mitzvot* that the trend among them is simply one of secularization. It is significant that there has been almost no change from the first to the second generations of Asian/North African origins in the proportion (about half) who identify as *mesoriti* (traditional). This large sector is often overlooked by Israeli public discourse that tends to divide the Israeli Jewish population into two camps – religious and secular.

Most of those Israeli Jews who identify as *mesoriti* emphasize their ties to the religious tradition, the tradition of their parents, but select rituals from that tradition with little concern for *halachic* standards and consistency. They may, for example, go to synagogue on Sabbath morning and travel to the sea or to a park on Sabbath afternoon. The term *mesoriti* has highly favorable connotations for Jews of Asian/North African origins but it is not presented as an alternative stance to the Orthoprax establishment which, although they largely ignore its decrees, they accept as the legitimate religious authority (Deshen, 1994; Shokeid, 1985).

'Tradition' denotes for Israeli Jews of Asian/North African origins the ties of religion to family and communities of origin. Whereas among Israelis of European origins ethnic synagogues based on country of origin rarely continued beyond the immigrant generation, among Middle Eastern Israelis they have continued in the second generation, especially in the lower strata (Ben-Rafael and Sharot, 1991: 78–80). The close relationship of religion and ethnic community among Jews from North Africa is clearly indicated in the revival of the veneration of saints and the pilgrimages (*hillulot*) to the tombs of saints on the anniversary of their deaths.

Whereas the worship of saints had been central to the communal religion of Jews in North Africa, in Israel the saints' anniversaries were celebrated at first by small numbers in houses and neighborhood synagogues. What began as small family gatherings became in the 1970s and 1980s grand, massive events, with some *hillulot* drawing thousands who come to pray, to light candles, to eat, drink and dance, and to seek help from the saints to cure illnesses and overcome infertility. The celebrations attract not only the older generation who remember the custom in North Africa but also the Israeli-born younger generation (Ben-Ari and Bilu, 1987; Weingrod, 1990; Bilu 2004).

The popularity of the *hillulot* is not part of a comprehensive revival of the traditional culture of Jews from North Africa. It is a religious activity which is amenable to a pattern of religiosity that is not highly demanding in terms of daily observance but provides strong mystical and magical meanings within a traditional ambience. Weingrod (1990) suggests that the celebration is not so much a reaction to modernization as a consequence of it. After a rise in living standards, and having undergone considerable acculturation to the dominant secular values and patterns of behavior of Israeli society, Jews from North African now feel secure enough to assert their specific identities as Moroccan or Tunisian Jews. As an occasion for the gathering together of considerable numbers to celebrate a part of their cultural heritage, the *hillula* allows North African Jews to express their ethnic identity, solidarity and power. However, it would be unwise to interpret saint worship as simply an expression of ethnicity and ignore its importance as a focal religious event, not only for those for whom it is part of a traditional way of life, which they seek to follow in many other ways, but also for those who continue to respect the heritage of their family and community even though they have abandoned a large part of the religious tradition (Sharot, 1996).

A less ambiguous counter trend to secularization than the *hillulot* is the growth and increased strength of the ultra-Orthoprax or *haredim* who, according to different definitions of *haredi*, constitute between 6 and 10 per cent of the Israeli Jewish population (Caplan, 2003: 228). *Haredi* is a Hebrew epithet meaning a God-fearing devotee. The term was used in the past to denote any Jews who was punctilious about religion, but in the last 50 years it has been increasingly used to designate those Jews who go beyond Orthopraxy. *Haredim* conform to a comprehensive and enveloping system of religious law which they believe was the way of life of the vast majority of European Jews prior to the incursions of modernity. Although ultra-Orthopraxy has spread to Sephardim or Jews of North African/Asian origins in recent years, most *haredim* are Ashkenazim and trace their diaspora origins to the Jewish communities of Eastern Europe which, prior to the incursions of secularism, provide their models of emulation, an emulation which extends to distinctive clothes and appearance. The men grow beards and dangling sideburns and many wear long black topcoats and wide-brimmed black hats. Women's dress is governed by rules of modesty: arms are covered at least to the elbows, dresses and skirts cover most of the legs, and dark stockings are worn. Women have their heads shaved at marriage, after which they wear a head scarf or wig. Conspicuous by their appearance, the *haredim* live in separate neighborhoods and conduct much of their lives within the confines of their own autonomous or semi-autonomous institutions (Sharot, 1982: 192–5; Friedman, 1986).

Following World War II the future of ultra-Orthoprax Judaism had seemed bleak; most of the traditionalist communities of Eastern Europe were destroyed by the Holocaust, and it was expected that the defections to secular society would accelerate in the open societies of the West and Israel. Instead, the last decades of the twentieth century saw a considerable strengthening and growth of the ultra-Orthoprax communities, both in the West and in Israel. By building an enveloping system of socialization and education, separated from the wider society, the *haredim* succeeded in retaining the vast majority of those born within the communities, and, as a consequence of high birth rates, they have grown in numbers and spread in Israel from their centers in Jerusalem and Tel Aviv to an increasing number of neighborhoods and towns (Shilhav and Friedman, 1985).

Haredim depict the Eastern European Jewish communities of the past as the ideal model and their communities today as a faithful expression of that ideal. In fact, the success of the present-day *haredi* society as a neo-traditionalist society can be attributed to its differences from the traditional societies of the past which are now cast in the mold of the present (Heilman and Friedman, 1991: 212–13; Sharot, 1992; Soloveitchick, 1994: 212). From a religiosity in the Eastern European communities transmitted by the family and local community, religiosity in the contemporary *haredi* population is rooted in texts and transmitted by the schools and *yeshivot*, the post-school religious educational institutions which have become the focal institutions of the community. In the Eastern European communities, the family and the school (*heder*) taught a rudimentary knowledge of the religious texts necessary for the appropriate observance of the *mitzvot*. Scholarship was an important value and basis for status, but the *yeshivot* instructed only a small proportion, the scholarly elite of the community. In contrast, the contemporary community is a 'society of learners' in which a large proportion of the male population attends the *yeshivot* for many years.

After the Holocaust, when only a few thousand children were in the *haredi* educational system, the *yeshivot* were seen by *haredim* as the principal means by which a Torah-based society could be rebuilt and the youth kept apart from the secular world. Unlike the former Eastern European communities, the traditional way of life could no longer be taken for granted and had to be constructed on the basis of voluntary communities in which there was a more overt commitment to a strictly religious way of life. Within an encompassing framework, males are expected to devote long years to Talmud learning, a way of life that is presented as requiring great effort and devotion and as absolutely essential for the survival of the Jewish people. Removed from the concerns of earning a living and often sheltered from the pressures of families, *yeshiva* students stress stringent interpretations of the religious law. The tradition of written codes has gained in strength at the expense of folk traditions anchored in families and local communities, and younger *haredim* often supersede their

fathers in their religious knowledge and strict conformity to the *halacha* (Friedman, 1987; Soloveitchick, 1994: 202–6, 216–17).

Long years in the *yeshivot* has also limited the participation of *haredim* in the army and the work force; few are conscripted, and the proportion of *haredi* men (aged 25–54) not working because of full-time *yeshiva* attendance rose from 41 per cent in 1980 to 60 per cent by 1996 (Berman, 2000: 914–15; Stadler, 2002: 456). Stadler (2002) has shown that withdrawal from the work force has been legitimized within the *yeshivot* by drawing upon and emphasizing particular religious interpretations of work and earning income that were previously considered of little importance in rabbinical interpretative traditions. The traditional rabbinical emphasis on hard work and activism in the world has been replaced by interpretations that stress the role of miraculous events in economic maintenance, the need to abandon profane work in order to worship God, and the devaluation of work as a distraction from the higher calling of study and as an obstacle to salvation.

Considerable resources are required, not only to cover the running costs of the *yeshivot*, but also to cover the living expenses of the students and, when they marry and have children, their families. Wives are often the major income-earners during the years when their husbands are studying, but their limited education and frequent child-bearing restricts their earnings. Although there are rich *haredim*, especially in the United States, who contribute to the support of the Israeli *yeshivot*, it is Israel's welfare state that has been a necessary condition for the support of this system. Only about one-quarter of *yeshiva* graduates participate in the job market; as a consequence of the elementary nature of their non-religious education and their self-segregation, occupational possibilities are limited to religious roles (teachers, ritual slaughterers, circumcisers) and small shops and businesses. Competition over the limited opportunities results in low incomes; many families are below the poverty line, and half of the income of *haredim* comes from public support compared with one-seventh of the income of the non-*haredi* population

(Sheleg, 2000: 128–30). In recent years a few *haredi* organizations have been founded to provide non-religious education and professional instruction, particularly in the areas of computer studies, but such developments have provided opportunities for only a small proportion.

Not all young *haredi* males are suited to many years in the *yeshivot*, and the non-legitimization of army service, together with the related restrictions on entering the work force, have left little alternative apart from idleness and petty crime for a small but increasing number of marginal *haredi* youth (Sheleg, 2000: 133–5, 157–8). At the other end of the social scale in the *haredi* community are what have been termed the 'yuppie *haredim*,' a wealthy sector living in spacious apartments in new *haredi* areas. The majority of these have entered the professions, mostly private businesses, particularly in accounting and computers (Sheleg, 2000: 147). This stratum has been in the forefront of the penetration into *haredi* society of consumerism and entertainment, a trend against which chastity committees of the community have fought, plastering the walls of *haredi* neighborhoods with notices against women's fashions, such as loud colors, close fitting clothes, short skirts, modern-style wigs, and wigs made of natural hair. On the grounds that norms of modesty and the separation of the sexes are difficult to uphold at large events, there has been opposition to concerts of popular *hassidic* singers. Most cases of opposition to the penetration of leisure activities have had, at best, limited effect, and the would-be regulators have had to be satisfied with forms of compromise (Sheleg, 2000: 141–6).

Most of the growth of the *haredi* population is a consequence of high birth rates. However, the ultra-Orthoprax way of life has attracted small but significant numbers from three sectors of the Israeli Jewish population: *mesoritiim* of North African/Asian origins, religious nationalists of mainly Western origins, and Jews from secular backgrounds. What has been termed the 'haredization' of Sephardic Jews of North African/Asian origins has been associated with the success of SHAS (Sephardi Religious Party), established in 1983, the first *haredi* party led and supported by Jews of North African/Asian origins. Although the majority of its supporters are not *haredim*, SHAS is a consequence of, and has contributed to, a process of haredization among Jews of North African/Asian origins. SHAS obtains its highest levels of support in the economically depressed 'development' towns with high concentrations of Jews from North Africa. These are the same areas where the most important saint shrines are to be found, but in comparison with the *hillulot* which represent a renewal of a tradition anchored in family and community, haredization involves the adoption of a tradition of written codes.

In the first years of its existence a large proportion of SHAS voters were *haredim*, many having transferred their support from *Agudat Israel* to SHAS. The party grew by attracting non-*haredi* voters, especially *masoriti* identifiers who had never previously voted for a *haredi* party. The emergence of SHAS as an independent party was related to the discrimination against, and haughtiness to, the *haredim* of North African/Asian origins by the Ashkenazi *haredim*, but the major message of SHAS is that the secular Ashkenazi Zionist establishment took away the heritage of Middle Eastern Jews and drove many into lives of poverty, crime, and drugs. SHAS has canalized social and economic grievances into an ethno-religious program and presented itself as the party of a true Judaism, superior to that of the Ashkenazim, and a true Zionism, far superior to that of the secular parties (Fisher and Beckerman, 2001: 326–38. See also Peled, 1998; Cohen, 2001.).

SHAS has encouraged haredization among its followers and among the children who are educated within its independent school system and who are encouraged to continue a religious education in *yeshivot*. The extent of haredization among Jews of North African/Asian origins is difficult to estimate, but it appears that only a minority of SHAS supporters have made the transition from *mesoritiyut* (traditionalism) to becoming either *datiim* or *haredim*. There has also been some haredization within the religious nationalist sector of mainly Western origins which is part of a counter-trend to the one described earlier of the penetration of secular culture, especially leisure activities, into that sector. This haredization, together with the move toward radical nationalism of some *haredim*, has resulted in a new identity label, *haredi leumi* (nationalist *haredi*).

Not all the religious nationalists who have become more stringent in religious practice have become *haredim*. They emphasize, however, the need to remain separated from the secular population and to retain strict religious norms, especially with respect to the division of the sexes. Many *dati* families have shown an increased preference to concentrate in their own neighborhoods, and distance from the secular atmosphere of the large cities was one consideration in the establishment of religious settlements in the West Bank. *Ariel*, a youth religious movement which strictly separates boys and girls, was established as an alternative to *Bnei Akiva*, the long-established religious youth movement which has been criticized for allowing the mixing of sexes. Some parents, dissatisfied with the education provided by the religious sector of the state school system, send their children to elitist religious schools. Class and ethnic factors are also a consideration here since large proportions of the pupils in many of the state religious schools come from low socio-economic and North African/Asian *mesoriti* backgrounds (Sheleg, 2000: 91–2, 96–9; Etzioni-Halevy, 2002: 56).

In comparison with the *mesoritiim* of North African/Asian origins and the religious nationalists who become *haredim*, the process of *teshuvah* or 'repentance' of Israeli Jews from secular backgrounds represents a more radical change or transformation in identity and way of life. Beginning after the 1967 war and increasingly after the 1973 war the number of *baalei teshuvah*, 'returnees' to Judaism from secular or non-Orthoprax backgrounds, is modest compared with the natural growth of the *haredim*, but the phenomenon generated great interest and has been widely discussed in Israel (Beit-Hallahmi, 1992: 49–72). The first *baalei teshuvah* in Israel were mostly youth from America who turned to ultra-Orthoprax Judaism following upon the counter-culture

and its religious offshoots in the late 1960s and early 1970s. Special *yeshivot* were established for the Americans, and when a wave of Israeli-born *baalei teshuvah* occurred in the middle 1970s, the framework of special *yeshivot* was extended to incorporate them (Sheleg, 2000: 177–83).

Studies of *baalei teshuvah* of middle-class backgrounds have shown that their dispositions toward the wider society are similar to those members of the 'world-rejecting' types of new religious movements, but in contrast with a NRM *teshuvah* is understood as a 'homecoming,' or as a 'return to the fold,' whereby the returnee recovers the true self that had temporarily gone astray (Aviad, 1983; Danzger, 1989). Within the *yeshivot* the criticisms of, and need to withdraw from, secular society are reinforced. The message is that the adoption of Western culture was a betrayal of Judaism and that the *yeshivot* are a major force in the battle for the survival of the Jewish people.

For the *haredi* community the *baalei teshuvah* provide evidence of the rightness of their way of life and their increasing strength. However, although the majority of *baalei teshuvah* have assimilated for the most part into *haredi* society, reservations toward them, especially with respect to *shiduchim* (arranged marriages), remain. Marriages are viewed as between families, not only between a couple, and established *haredi* families do not approve of their children marrying into families whose religiosity is in question, even if the prospective spouse is stringently religious. As a consequence, and perhaps also because of their own preferences, the majority of *baalei teshuvah* marry among themselves (Sheleg, 2000: 183–5).

PRIVATIZATION AND PUBLIC RELIGION

Privatization and 'Post-Zionism'

Privatization in the Israeli context has occurred within the 'secular religion' of Zionism and the civil religion of the state. This is a change within the secular rather than the religious sectors of the population, and it has been associated with the emergence of 'post-Zionism,' the replacement of the institutions and collectivistic ideology and ceremonies of Socialist or Labor Zionism by a market-driven economy and consumer-oriented society. The economic expansion that followed the 1967 war was seen by many as accelerating the decline of the communalism that had characterized the *Yishuv* and early state, but the term 'post-Zionism' has been applied to the period since the mid-1980s when the institutions founded by the Labor movement collapsed, restrictions on markets were lifted, the capitalist stratum improved its position by taking advantage of the greater opportunities in the more open economy, and inequality widened. Western patterns of consumerism rapidly advanced as signaled by the many new shopping malls, the spread of American franchises like McDonald's, and the introduction in the 1990s of commercial television channels and cable and satellite television (Silberstein, 1999: 94, 195; Ram, 2004: 313–16).

Zionist calls for the sacrifice of individual preferences and private needs for those of the collective lost their persuasive power, and the collectivistic rituals of Zionism were no longer appropriate to the new style of life. The turn to individualistic values and a nuclear family focus were particularly evident in those sectors, such as the *kibbutzim*, where collectivism has taken its most manifest forms. At a more general level, the celebrations of civil religion were transformed into private events. Independence Day, for example, was no longer celebrated by processions and other communal events but by private parties and family barbecues in public parks (Liebman, 1997b: 102; Etzioni-Halevy, 2002: 88–9).

The major constituency of post-Zionism, which includes liberal values and dovish positions with regard to foreign policy and the territories, is predominantly middle class and secular. Higher income encourages a secular life style in some respects; purchasing private cars enable travel on the Sabbath (public transport is not available in most of Israel on the Sabbath), and consumption is now possible in the increasing number of shops, restaurants, and entertainment venues open on the Sabbath

(Etzioni-Halevy, 2002: 60). The religious population were not unaffected by the growth of consumerism and commercialized leisure, but privatization in religion has not been extensive.

Conservative and Reform Judaism

As indicated, the prominence of public religion in Israel is associated with the Orthoprax establishment, and this establishment has used its position to obstruct and delegitimize the Conservative and Reform movements in Judaism. Largely removed from public practice, the Conservative and Reform movement in Israel facilitate the privatization of religion, but their influence in this direction is limited by their small size. In the early 2000s the Conservative movement with 52 congregations and the Reform movement with 28 congregations had a combined membership of some 15,000 who take part in congregational activities on a regular basis. In contrast with the United States, where the Reform and Conservative movements are far larger than the Orthoprax, the members of the non-Orthoprax movements in Israel constitute a minute percentage of regular synagogue worshippers. Whereas in the United States affiliation to a synagogue or temple is the most important means of expressing Jewish identity, most Israeli Jews feel little need to affiliate with a synagogue in order to identify ethnically or nationally as Jews. Association with a synagogue is mainly confined, therefore, to highly observant Jews who are mostly Orthoprax (Tabory, 2004).

The Conservative and Reform movements have sought to attract Israelis who identify as 'traditional' or 'non-religious,' but they have met with limited success. For the *mesoritiim*, the dominant identity among Jews of North African/Asian origins, religion is Orthopraxy, even though they choose not to be bound by its laws. As long as they can practice Orthopraxy in their own way, they support it as the official and public representation of Judaism, and because they hold to the *mesoret* (tradition), the 'new' forms of Conservative and Reform have no appeal (Cohen and Susser, 2000: 132).

Many non-religious Israelis of European origin are sympathetic towards the non-Orthoprax movements as part of their opposition to the Orthoprax establishment. Some turn to the movements for the celebration of the rites of *bar mitzvah* and *bat mitzvah* which, unlike marriage ceremonies, have no implications for civil status, but sympathy and infrequent celebrations rarely extend to membership. For most non-religious Israelis, the ethno-national and identity functions of religion are sufficiently provided for by civil or public religion (Tabory, 2004).

New Religious Movements

Jewish Israelis retain their Jewish identity and its associations with Judaism even when they seek a privatized form of religion outside Judaism. The attraction of new religious movements to Israeli Jews was a post-1973 development. 'Cult movements,' requiring high levels of obligation and participation, remained small and marginal: in the early 1980s, when NRMs in Israel were at their peak, there were about 20 movements with a joint membership that probably never rose about 3,000. However, 'client cults' of a quasi-religious character, particularly Human Potential and psychotherapeutic organizations, have attracted a large clientele of mostly 'non-religious' Jews who observe a few Jewish religious practices in secularized forms. In addition to Transcendental Meditation which at one time boasted many Israeli practitioners, organizations such as *est* (Erhard Seminar Training), I Am, and Landmark Education have attracted thousands to their encounter groups and psychotherapeutic sessions (Beit-Hallahmi, 1992: 11–48, 101–31). Movements with more recognizable religious features and more highly involved and committed memberships, such as ISKCON, have met with fierce, sometimes violent, persecution by *haredim*. Coverage in the secular media has also been almost wholly negative. The movements are perceived, not only as threats to the family, but also as challenges to the very basis of the Israeli state and society: its Jewish religious and national identity (Zeidman-Dvir and Sharot, 1992).

'DEPRIVATIZATION' AND THE RELIGIOUS-SECULAR DIVISION

Although most Israeli Jews, including the majority of the 'non-religious,' continue to support the notion of Israel as a Jewish state, the nature of its Jewish identity has become an increasingly divisive issue among different sectors of the Israeli Jewish populations in recent years, and religion has been central to this division. It makes little sense to refer to 'deprivatization' of religion in Israel because privatization was never extensive, but religion and politics have become even more intertwined in recent decades with the greater overlap between divergent political positions and secular and religious world views. Conflicts between religious and secular sectors of the population over the allocation of resources have become secondary to conflict over fundamental questions of the Jewish identity of the state and its territorial boundaries. Two trends are of importance here. Firstly, the transformation of the religious Zionist population into a movement emphasizing the Jewish settlement of the occupied territories as the most central part of the messianic process of redemption of the Jewish people. Secondly, the greater political involvement and political hawkishness of the ultra-Orthoprax.

Religious Zionism; Nationalism and Messianism

Religious Zionism presents a prominent case of counter-privatization with its emphasis on the relevance of Judaism beyond the spheres of home and synagogue into the civic and political realms. This is a case of political schemes and policies grounded in religious messianism with far-reaching effects on Israeli society and the Jewish-Palestinian conflict.

The emergence of a radical, activistic messianism within religious Zionism provided a solution to the tensions and paradoxes within a movement which attempted to combine Orthopraxy and modern Zionism, two ideological streams represented by groups fundamentally in opposition to each other. The exponent of a messianic religious Zionism during the period of the *Yishuv* was Rabbi Abraham Issac Kook (1865–1935) who defined Zionism as a wholly sacred phenomenon that was furthering the process of redemption. For Kook, the secularist Zionists who did not keep the *mitzvot* but who sought to redeem the Jewish people from exile were at a higher level of sacredness than the anti-Zionist Orthoprax Jews. Kook was appointed by the British mandate authorities, with the consent of the Zionist establishment, as the Ashkenazi chief rabbi (1921–1935), but his teachings were not widely known and even among the religious Zionists he had little influence during his lifetime (Friedman, 1977: 92–102; Sharot, 1982: 226–7).

After the establishment of the state, Kook's son, Rabbi Zvi Yehuda Kook, took the sanctification of Jewish nationalism further than his father. He pronounced that the sovereign Jewish state was part of redemption, that the state's symbols, such as the flag and anthem, were media for the worship of God, and that the process of redemption required Jewish control over the entire Land of Israel (Aran, 1997). Prior to the 1967 war, the influence of Kook's teaching was confined mainly to his *yeshiva*, *Mercaz HaRav*, but this changed with the conquest of Judea and Samaria (the West Bank) when a new dimension was added to Kook's emphasis on the sacredness of the Land of Israel and its relationship to the messianic hope. Some religious Zionists referred to the 1967 victory as the beginning of redemption and the euphoria following the victory encouraged hopes, soon discarded, that they could convert secular Jews to their beliefs. Although some religious Jews described the victory as a miracle, for most Israelites the war served to confirm the image of a society that had undergone successful modernization and whose efficiency and rationality, at both the technological and social levels, had defeated the tradition-bound Arabs.

The 1973 war shattered the feelings of confidence and optimism of secular Israel. The questioning and criticism that followed the war went beyond the loss of authority and credibility of the Labor establishment and extended to new appraisals of the meanings of Zionism and the Israeli state. Religious Zionists interpreted the war as one of the 'birth pangs of the messiah' and as a warning to the Jewish people to take their part in the process of redemption. Secular Israelis had failed to continue to energize the redemption process and it was now the role of the religious Zionists to lead the nation in its divine mission and to act as pioneers in the settlement of the conquered territories. Recognition of the need to organize to promote their goals led to the establishment of *Gush Emunim* (Bloc of the Faithful) in February 1974. The Gush was an extra-parliamentary movement but it was represented within the *Mafdal* (National Religious Party) by what became known as the Young Guard who rebelled against the established leadership and succeeded in replacing the party's moderate politics by policies that focused on settlement and a hawkish, non-compromising stand over the territories (Sharot, 1982: 233–7; Aran, 1991; Kopelowitz, 2001: 178–9).

The major component in the messianism of *Gush Emunim* was that Jewish sovereignty and settlement over the whole of the Land of Israel was the present decisive state in the attainment of redemption. It was not so much *Gush Emunim's* messianic interpretation of the Jewish state that was new, but rather its insistence on the importance of the borders in the historical process and the enthusiasm and dedication of its supporters in settling the land which they saw as a sacrament and a *tikkun*, a mending of the cosmos.

The first *Gush* settlements in the West Bank during the last years of the Labor government usually started as illegal activities which drew public support and succeeded in obtaining concessions from the government. The movement's settlement activities were legalized and given a boost when the Likud party came to power in 1977. During the first Likud government the *Gush* continued to be the major force behind the settlement process as it established many small settlements, thinly distributed over an extensive territory. The second Likud government changed the settlement pattern by building large urban settlements or suburbs which provided inexpensive housing near to the high density central zone. Most residents of the government-sponsored settlements were attracted by the opportunity to improve their quality of life at a relatively low cost and were indifferent to the messianism of the *Gush*. These developments weakened the *Gush* as an organization especially as its leaders had not developed hierarchical structures linking national and local levels or formulated procedures for appointments and decision making. The *Gush* came to function primarily as a concept symbolizing a firm commitment to the Greater Land of Israel and its settlements, but its leaders were appointed to key executive positions in most of the new municipalities and regional councils of the occupied territories, and the vast sums of money distributed by the government to the settlement authorities gave them a formidable financial and political base (Shafir, 1985; Aran, 1991: 282; Sprinzak, 1991: 129–32; Don-Yehiya, 1994: 285–7).

The *Gush* saw itself as the heir apparent of the pioneering spirit that had characterized secular Zionism in the past, and it continued to reach out to secular Jews, moderating its religious language, to join them in 'the restoration of Zionist fulfillment.' Secular supporters of the *Gush* did not share the messianic beliefs but the *Gush's* language of redemption and its emphasis on the sacredness of the land resonated with what had been the secular messianism of Socialist Zionism. Some secular Jews in the labor camp, including members of the kibbutzim, looked back on the intense ideological spirit and activism of the pioneering period with nostalgia and saw a revival of that spirit in the *Gush*. Secular Zionists had secularized and nationalized religious messianism, and they could find an affinity with the fusion of religious messianism and nationalism in the *Gush* (Kohn, 1976: 11–20; Sharot, 1982: 233; Sprinzak, 1991: 302).

A partial affinity also existed between the religio-politics of the *Gush* and what has been termed the 'New Civil Religion' that developed after the 1967 war and became more important after the 1973 war. The new civil religion emphasized the unity of all Jews, the centrality of the Holocaust, and the Jews as an isolated nation confronting a hostile world. An emphasis on the

ties of the Jews to the conquered territories, especially 'Judea and Samaria' with its biblical associations, invoked a penetration of religious symbols and holy places, of which the Western Wall was the most important (Liebman and Don-Yehiya, 1983: 123–66). The incorporation of traditional religious symbols by secular politicians was particularly evident in the Likud party whose leaders clothed their hawkish politics in religious imagery and language (Heilman, 1997: 339).

The close relationship of religious Zionism with the governing Likud party took a knock when Menachem Begin signed the Camp David accords in 1979 and presided over the withdrawal from Sinai and the evacuation of Jewish settlements along the Yamit strip in northern Sinai in April 1982. As has been the case of other messianic movements, responses to the failure or partial disconfirmation of prophecy included a weakening of messianic hopes among some and a more intense messianism among others. One group of what was labeled the *Machteret* (Underground) justified their plan to blow up the mosques on the Temple Mount as a preparation for the rebuilding of the Temple in the process of redemption. Members of the Underground, who were arrested and imprisoned in 1984, had hoped that their action would incite a holy war against Israel in which God would be obliged to intervene on behalf of the Jews and thereby hasten the final stages of redemption. The implicit assumption was that God could be directed by humans, and one member asserted that it was Man rather than God who had the central role in redemption (Aran, 1991: 267; Don-Yehiya, 1994: 278–82; Liebman and Cohen, 1997: 71).

Although the majority of religious Zionists did not support the actions of the Underground, the peace agreement with Egypt began a reformulation among them of the place of secular Jews and the state in the process of redemption. The theology that had been formulated by the Kooks, father and son, was that the secularists were advancing the divine mission despite their non-observance of the *mitzvot*, but the willingness of the secular politicians to withdraw from territory and uproot Jewish settlements contradicted this notion and opened them up to the charge of enemies of God, a charge that developed among the more extreme elements of religious Zionism. The state had been seen as a core factor in the process of redemption, and the question now arose of the right to oppose the state if its policy contravened the principle of the Greater Land of Israel and the unlimited right of Jews to settle anywhere on that Land.

These questions became more acute when the Labor party was returned to power under Yitzhak Rabin in 1992 and the Oslo accords were signed with the PLO followed by a peace treaty with Jordan. Rabbinical rulings that it was a sin to relinquish Jewish sovereignty over the Holy Land were a clear indication that the secular leaders could no longer be considered to be acting according to the divine plan. Further rabbinical rulings that territorial withdrawals were endangering the lives of Jews could be interpreted as an invitation to adopt a Jewish law that states that someone who put the life of a Jew in danger or hands Jews over to their enemies may be punished or killed. After assassinating Yitzhak Rabin on the 4th November, 1994, Yigal Amir justified his action in such terms (Heilman, 1997: 349, 353–4; Don-Yehiya, 1994: 275–7).

The question of the place of the state in the sphere of redemption has arisen in an acute form with the withdrawal from, and dismantling of Jewish settlements in Gaza and northern Shomron. The sense of betrayal among religious Zionists was compounded by the fact that the pull-out was initiated by Ariel Sharon who had been a staunch supporter of settlement and one of the most important secular allies of the *Gush*. Attempts to prevent the dismantling of the settlements included mass demonstrations and marches, stopping traffic on major roads by barricades of demonstrators and burning tires, calling on soldiers and police to disobey orders, and stigmatizing government policy by comparing the 'expulsion' of Jews from their homes with the Nazi persecution. These actions come from religious Zionists who had encouraged their children to volunteer for army combat units and who had seen the state as 'a foundation of the throne of God in the world.'

Following the dismantlement of settlements a number of religious Zionists have expressed doubts that the state of Israel represents the beginning of the process of redemption of the Jewish people. The question has arisen of what takes precedence, loyalty to the state or loyalty to the land, and a survey undertaken after the dismantlement of settlements found that half of the religious Jews who had settled in the West Bank now felt 'less Israeli.' Some religious Zionists continue to sanctify the state but claim that the political and military elites have betrayed that sanctity. They have concluded that their alliance with secular Zionism is at an end and that a new alliance should be forged with the *haredim* (Sheleg, 2005; *Ha'aretz* May 1, 2006).

Politicization of the Haredim

The proposal among some religious Zionists of an alliance with the *haredim* is an indication of the changes that have occurred since the period of the *Yishuv* when the *haredim* accused the religious Zionists of a false messianism which could only delay redemption (Raanan, 1980: 18–23; Sharot, 1982: 225–6). Most *haredim* accommodated to the idea and then the actuality of a Jewish state dominated by secular Jews, but they claimed that, in the religious realm, Jews in Israel were still living in exile (Liebman and Cohen, 1997: 59). In order to ensure the religious autonomy of its constituency and the resources necessary for living the religious life, the major *haredi* party, *Agudat Israel*, participated in parliamentary politics and cooperated with non-religious Jews. Its stance shifted to hostility when its autonomy or fundamental religious principles were threatened, and in 1952 it withdrew from the coalition following the government's decision to draft women into the army. From outside the government, *haredi* politicians continued to trade their support in return for benefits, but they remained largely impassive or neutral toward politics, such as foreign policy, that did not affect their particular interests. Their political influence was also limited by their small representation in the Knesset; whereas, in the early decades of the state, the National Religious Party consistently received ten to twelve seats in the Knesset, the *haredi* parties received from four to six (Cohen and Susser, 2000: 48–9; Kopelowitz, 2001: 174; Shafir and Peled, 2002: 141–2).

Agudat Israel's self-imposed ban on entering the government lasted until 1977 when it entered the Likud-led coalition. The party was now in a better position to exercise influence and gain benefits for its constituency because, whereas prior to 1977 the dominant Labor party had not been dependent on its coalition partners to stay in power, after 1977 neither of the two largest parties, Likud and Labor, was generally able to form a coalition without the support of the religious parties. The position of the *haredi* parties improved further when their electoral support grew, overtaking that of the NRP which saw a sharp drop in its support. The Ashkenazi *haredi* party, now named *Yahadut Hatorah* (United Torah Judaism), has in recent elections received five to six mandates while *SHAS's* mandates rose from 10 in 1996 to 17 in 1999 and then dropped to 11 in 2003 and 12 in 2006.

At the same time as they have increased their representation, the *haredi* parties have undergone a transformation from generally moderate positions on foreign and security issues to supporting hawkish positions. Although the majority of *haredim* continue to distance themselves from Zionism and the symbols and rituals of the state, a number of factors have disposed them to hawkishness over territory and relationships with the Palestinians. Firstly, continued Israeli control of the conquered territories ensures access to the Holy Places such as the Western Wall, the Tomb of the Patriarchs and Matriarchs in Hebron, and Rachel's Tomb (Etzioni-Halevy, 2002: 129). Secondly, the *haredim* have benefited from the highly subsidized housing in new *haredi* neighborhoods in the occupied territories. Thirdly, the belief that non-Jews are bent on destroying Jews is deeply embedded in their religious culture, and Arab hostility is attributed with theological and even cosmic significance. And fourthly, Labor and dovish 'left-wing' parties are viewed by them as the major carriers of secularism and alien non-Jewish values which they see as the causes of permissiveness, sinful behavior, and social deterioration (Cohen and Susser, 2000: 53, 57, 60–1).

The heightened prominence of the *haredim* in the public sphere, the large sums allotted to their institutions and welfare, and their confrontational tactics have been met by anti-*haredi* sentiments which found political expression in *Shinui* (Change), a party with a belligerent, anti-*haredi* position which increased its seats in the Knesset from six in 1999 to 15 in 2003. *Shinui* failed, however, to make significant changes to the status quo on religious issues, and after a split in the party neither faction succeeded to receive any mandates in the 2006 elections.

Although *Shinui* was a centrist-right rather than dovish party, the political cleavage between hawks ('right-wing') and doves ('left-wing') among Israeli Jews has come to overlap considerably with the division between religious and secular Jews. Of course, this overlap is by no means total. A dovish section of religious Zionists, represented by the political faction *Meimad* broke from the NRP in the late 1980s; it did not succeed as an independent political party and in 1999 it joined the Labor party. There are more secular hawks than religious doves, but the small radical right parties that have attempted to combine secular and religious Jews have had little success, and the most hawkish of the secular parties have remained on the political margins.

The largest 'right-wing' party, Likud, has always been dominated by secular politicians of mainly European origins, but a significant part of its electoral strength comes from the disproportionate support of Jews from North African/Asian origin who identify predominantly as *mesoritiim*. Labor voters, in comparison, are disproportionately secular and of European origins. However, the recent policy of partial withdrawal from occupied territories by the Likud government has reinforced the impression of a division within the Israeli Jewish population between secular doves and religious hawks. The struggle between the two camps goes beyond the territorial issue which may be viewed as one aspect of the wider struggle over the identity of the state. For secular Jews withdrawal from conquered territories is a necessary condition for retaining a Jewish state in accord with Western and democratic values. For religious Jews, whose goal is a *halachic* state, the loss of what they regard as sacred territory is a diminution of the state's Jewishness (Cohen and Susser, 2000: 64–7, 71; Etzioni-Halevy, 2002: 6–22, 118–30).

CONCLUSION

Secularization in one dimension can contribute to secularization in another, but it can also limit secularization in another dimension. The limited privatization of religion in Israel is, in part, a consequence of the attempts by the secularist founders of the new *Yishuv* and new state to differentiate their national Jewish identity from religion. The historical unity of Judaism with the Jewish people and the secularists' settlement on religiously defined sacred space limited this differentiation; the secularists' own 'secular religion' was expressed in terms of messianism and redemption, and in choosing the symbols of the 'Jewish' state, they only had recourse to a symbolic system grounded in a religious tradition.

Two related consequences followed from the process of differentiation and its limitations: the prominence of public religion, and the virtual monopolization of Orthoprax religion. The early waves of immigration came from Eastern Europe, and Israel followed the Eastern European Jewish pattern of a division between secular and religious Jews rather than the Western, particularly United States, pattern of division into different religious denominations (Orthodox, Conservative, Reform). Israeli Jews who are only partially observant or observe a few secularized versions of religious ceremonies have felt no need for alternative forms to Orthoprax religion. 'Traditionalists,' who largely originate from the comparatively tolerant Jewish religious traditions of North Africa and Asia, have not attempted to give ideological legitimation or organizational expression to their non-Orthoprax patterns of observance, and the 'secular' or 'non-religious,' who largely originate from Europe, express their Jewish identity in national-political terms which include secularized renditions of symbols historically grounded in religion.

Although the 'traditionalist' pattern remains important, trends in religiosity have strengthened both the secular and religious sectors. Among Jews of North African and Asian origin, the economically and socially mobile are less observant of the religious tradition than their parents, but *SHAS*, a *haredi* party, draws its support from those who remain in economically deprived neighborhoods and 'development towns,' and some of these supporters have gravitated toward the Orthoprax or ultra-Orthoprax. The nationalist religious sector has also displayed divergent patterns; on the one hand, the influence of commercialized leisure patterns, especially among the youth, and on the other hand, a stricter segregation from the secular population together with greater religious stringency and, in some cases, haredization.

The *haredim* have attracted some Jews, including secular Jews, into their communities, but their growth has been mainly a result of a very high birth rate, and their success in retaining most of those born within the communities is a consequence of their post-World War II restructuring, making the *yeshivot* their core institutions. There have been recent signs of cracks in the *hasidic* walls of segregation as consumerism has penetrated their communities, especially the wealthy stratum, and institutions have been established for training in the secular professions in an attempt to enter the work force and reduce dependence on the state.

The trend toward polarization of religious and secular sectors is less the result of divergent trends in religiosity than of an increasing convergence of religious and political divisions. Among religious Zionists the move towards greater segregation and religious stringency has been combined with political radicalization grounded in messianism. Unlike the religious Zionists, the *haredim* do not attach messianic meanings to the State of Israel or the settlement of the territories, but they have also taken a militant hawkish position on the conflict with the Palestinians. These developments, together with some withdrawal among the secular right-wing from the more hawkish positions, have made the political dividing line between hawks and doves among Israeli Jews increasingly religious vs. secular. As political and religious positions have become one, it is not surprising that religious trends representing the privatization of religion remain weak.

REFERENCES

Almog, O. 2000. *The sabra; the creation of the new Jew*. Berkeley: University of California Press.

Antonovsky, A. 1963. 'Israeli political-social attitudes'. *Amot* 6, 11–22 (in Hebrew).

Aran, G. 1991. 'Jewish Zionist fundamentalism: the bloc of the faithful in Israel (Gush Emunim)'. In M. E. Marty and R. S. Appleby (eds), *Fundamentalisms observed* (pp. 265–344). Chicago: University of Chicago Press.

Aran, G. 1997. 'The father, the son, and the holy land; the spiritual authorities of Jewish-Zionist fundamentalism in Israel'. In R. S. Appleby (ed.), *Spokesmen for the despised; fundamentalist leaders of the middle east* (pp. 294–327). Chicago: University of Chicago Press.

Aviad, J. 1983. *Return to Judaism; religious renewal in Israel*. Chicago: University of Chicago Press.

Ayalon, H., E. Ben-Rafael and S. Sharot 1986. 'Secularization and the diminishing decline of religion'. *Review of Religious Research* 27 (3), 193–207.

Azili, A. 1984. *The attitude of HaShomer Hatzair to religion and tradition (1920–1948)*. Givat Haviva: Documentation and Research Center (in Hebrew).

Beit-Hallahmi, B. 1992. *Despair and deliverance; private salvation in contemporary Israel*. Albany: State University of New York Press.

Ben-Ari, E. and Bilu, Y. 1987. 'Saints' sanctuaries in Israeli development towns: on a mechanism of urban transformation'. *Urban Anthropology* 16, 244–72.

Ben-Meir, Y. and P. Kedem 1979. 'Index of religiosity of the Jewish population of Israel' *Megamot* 14, 353–62 (in Hebrew).

Ben-Rafael, E. and S. Sharot 1991. *Ethnicity, religion, and class in Israeli society*. Cambridge: Cambridge University Press.

Bensimon, D. 1968. 'Pratique religieuse des Juifs d'Afrique du nord en France et en Israel'. *Archives de Sociologie des Religions* 26, 81–96.

Berman, E. 2000. 'Sect, subsidy and sacrifice: An economist's view of Ultra-Orthodox Jews'. *Quarterly Journal of Economics*, CXV (3), 905–53.

Bilu, Y. 2004. 'The sanctification of space in Israel; civil religion and folk Judaism'. In U. Rebhun and C. I. Waxman (eds), *Jews in Israel; contemporary social and cultural patterns* (371–93). Hanover: Brandeis University Press.

Bilu, Y. and E. Ben-Ari 1997. 'Epilogue (three years later)'. In E. Ben-Ari and Y. Bilu (eds), *Grasping land; space and place in contemporary Israeli discourse and experience* (231–35). Albany: State University of New York Press.

Caplan, K. 2003. 'Investigating the haredi society in Israel: characteristics, achievements, challenges'. In K. Caplan and E. Sivan (eds), *Israeli haredim: integration without assimilation?* (pp. 224–77). Jerusalem: Van Leer Institute & Hakibbutz Hameuchad Publishing House (in Hebrew).

Casanova, J. 1994. *Public religions in the modern world*. Chicago: University of Chicago Press.

Cohen, E. 1995. 'Israel as a post-Zionist society'. In R. Wistrich and D. Ohana (eds), *The shaping of Israeli identity; myth, memory and trauma* (pp. 203–14). London: Frank Cass.

Cohen, A. 2001. 'Shas and the secular-religion division'. In Y. Peled (ed.), *Shas - the challenge of Israeliness* (pp. 75–101). Tel Aviv: Miskal (in Hebrew).

Cohen, A. and B. Susser 2000. *Israel and the politics of Jewish identity: the secular-religious impasse*. Baltimore: The Johns Hopkins University Press.

Danzger, M. H. 1989. *Returning to tradition: the contemporary revival of orthodox Judaism*. New Haven: Yale University Press.

Davie, G. 1994. *Religion in Britain since 1945: believing without belonging*. Oxford: Blackwell.

DellaPergola, S. 2001. 'Demography in Israel/Palestine: Trends, prospects, policy implication'. Salvador de Bahia: IUSSP XXIV General Population Conference.

Deshen, S. 1994. 'The religiosity of the mizrachim: public, rabbis and faith'. *Alpayim*, 9, 44–58 (in Hebrew).

Deshen, S. 1997. 'The Passover celebrations of secular Israelis'. *Megamot* 38 (4), 528–40 (in Hebrew).

Deshen, S. and W. P. Zenner (eds) 1982. *Jewish societies in the middle east: community, culture, and authority*. Washington, DC: University Press of America.

Diamond, J. S. 1986. *Homeland or holy land? The 'Canaanite' critique of Israel*. Bloomington: Indiana University Press.

Don-Yehiya, E. 1994. 'The book and the sword: the nationalist yeshivot and political radicalism in Israel'. In M. E. Marty and R. S. Appleby (eds), *Accounting for fundamentalism* (pp. 264–302). Chicago: University of Chicago Press.

Etzioni-Halevy, E. 2002. *The divided people; can Israel's breakup be stopped*. Lanham: Lexington Books.

Evron, B. 1995. *Jewish state or Israeli nation?* Bloomington: Indiana University Press.

Ezrachi, E. 2004. 'The quest for spirituality among secular Israelis'. In U. Rebhun and C. I. Waxman (eds), *Jews in Israel; contemporary social and cultural patterns* (pp. 315–28). Hanover: Brandeis University Press.

Fisher, S. and Z. Beckerman 2001. 'Church or sect'. In Y. Peled (ed.), *Shas - the challenge of Israeliness* (pp. 321–42). Tel Aviv: Miskal (in Hebrew).

Friedman, M. 1977. *Society and religion: the non-Zionist orthodox in Eretz Israel, 1918–1936*. Jerusalem: Yat Izhak Ben-Zvi Publications. (in Hebrew).

Friedman, M. 1986. 'Haredim confront the modern city'. *Studies in Contemporary Jewry* 2, 74–96.

Friedman, M. 1987. 'Life tradition and book tradition in the development of ultraorthodox Judaism'. In H. E. Goldberg (ed.), *Judaism viewed from within and from without*. Albany: State University of New York Press.

Goldscheider, C. and D. Friedlander 1983. 'Religiosity patterns in Israel'. *American Jewish Year Book* 83, 3–39.

Heilman, S. C. 1997. 'Guides of the faithful; contemporary religious Zionist rabbis'. In R. S. Appleby (ed.), *Spokesmen for the despised; fundamentalist leaders of the Middle East* (pp. 328–62). Chicago: University of Chicago Press.

Heilman, S. C. and M. Friedman. 1991. 'Religious fundamentalism and religious Jews: the case of the haredim'. In M. E. Marty and R. S. Appleby (eds), *Fundamentalisms observed* (pp. 197–264). Chicago: University of Chicago Press.

Herman, S. J. 1970. *Israelis and Jews: the continuity of an identity*. New York: Random House.

Katz, E. 1997. 'Behavioral and phenomenological Jewishness'. In C. S. Liebman and E. Katz (eds), *The Jewishness of Israelis* (pp. 71–83). Albany: State University of New York.

Kedem, P. 1995. 'Dimensions of Jewish religiosity'. In S. Deshen, C. S. Liebman, and M. Shokeid (eds), *Israeli Judaism* (pp. 33–59). New Brunswick: Transaction Publishers.

Kedem, P. and M. Bar-Lev 1983. 'Is giving up traditional religious culture part of the price to be paid for acquiring higher education?: adaptation of academic western culture by Jewish Israeli university students of Middle Eastern origin'. *Higher Education* 12, 373–88.

Kimmerling, B. 2001. *The invention and decline of Israeliness*. Berkeley: University of California Press.

Kohn, M. 1976. *Who's afraid of Gush Emunim?* Jerusalem: Jerusalem Post.

Kolatt, I. 1998. 'Religion, society, and state during the period of the national home'. In S. Almog, J. Reinharz and A. Shapira (eds), *Zionism and Religion* (pp. 273–301). Hanover: Brandeis University Press.

Kopelowitz, E. 2001. 'Religious politics and Israel's ethnic democracy'. *Israel Studies* 6 (3), 166–90.

Kopelowitz, E. and Y. Israel-Shamsian 2005. 'Why has a sociology of religion not developed in Israel? A look at the influence of socio-political environment on the study of religion: a research note'. *Sociology of Religion* 66 (1), 71–84.

Knaani, D. 1975. *The labor second aliyah and its attitude toward religion and tradition*. Tel Aviv: Sifriat Po'alim (in Hebrew).

Levy, S., H. Levinsohn and E. Katz 1993. *Beliefs, observances and social interaction among Israeli Jews*. Jerusalem: Louis Guttman Israel Institute of Applied Social Research.

Levy, S., H. Levinsohn and E. Katz 2002. *Beliefs, maintaining tradition, and values of Jews in Israel 2000*. Jerusalem: Guttman Center, Israeli Institute for Democracy, and Avi Chai (in Hebrew).

Liebman, C. S. 1997a. 'Religion and modernity: the special case of Israel'. In C. S. Liebman and Katz, E. (eds), *The Jewishness of Israelis* (pp. 85–102). Albany: State University of New York.

Liebman C. S. 1997b. *Religion, democracy and Israeli society*. Amsterdam: Harwood Academic Publishers.

Liebman, C. S. and A. Cohen 1997. 'A case of fundamentalism in contemporary Israel'. In C. S. Liebman (ed.), *Religion, democracy and Israeli society* (pp. 57–76). Amsterdam: Harwood Academic Publishers.

Liebman, C. S. and E. Don-Yehiya 1983. *Civil religion in Israel: traditional Judaism and political culture in the Jewish state*. Berkeley: University of California Press.

Liebman, C. S. and E. Don-Yehiya 1984. *Religion and politics in Israel*. Bloomington: Indiana University Press.

Lilker, S. 1982. *Kibbutz Judaism; a new tradition in the making*. New York: Herzl Press.

Litvak, M. 1996. 'The Islamization of Palestinian identity: The case of Hamas'. Tel Aviv: Moshe Dayan Center for Middle Eastern and African Studies.

Luz, E. 1988. *Parallels meet; religion and nationalism in the early Zionist movement (1882–1904)*. Philadelphia: Jewish Publication Society.

Matras, J. 1964. 'Religious observance and family formation in Israel: some intergenerational changes'. *American Journal of Sociology* 69, 464–75.

Mishal, S. and A. Sela 2000. *The Palestinian Hamas; Vision, violence, and coexistence*. New York: Columbia University Press.

Peled, Y. 1998. 'Towards a redefinition of Jewish nationalism in Israel: the enigma of Shas'. *Ethnic and Racial Studies* 21 (4), 703–27.

Raanan, Z. 1980. *Gush Emunim*. Tel Aviv: Sifriyat Hapoalim (in Hebrew).

Ram, U. 2004. 'The state of the nation: contemporary challenges to Zionism in Israel'. In A. Kemp, D. Newman, U. Ram and O. Yiftachel (eds), *Israelis in conflict; hegemonies, identities and challenges* (pp. 305–20). Brighton: Sussex Academic Press.

Samet, M. 1979. *Religion and state in Israel*. Jerusalem: Hebrew University (in Hebrew).

Schweid, E. 1997. 'Is there really no alienation and polarization?'. In C. S. Liebman and E. Katz (eds), *The Jewishness of Israelis* (151–8). Albany: State University of New York.

Shafir, G. 1985. 'Institutional and spontaneous settlement drives: did Gush Emunim make a difference?'. In D. Newman (ed.), *The impact of Gush Emunim: politics and settlement in the west bank* (pp. 153–171). London: Croom Helm.

Shafir, G. and Y. Peled 2002. *Being Israeli; the dynamics of multiple citizenship*. Cambridge: Cambridge University Press.

Shapira, A. 1998. 'The religious motifs of the labor movement'. In S. Almog, J. Reinharz and A. Shapira (eds), *Zionism and religion* (pp. 251–72). Hanover: Brandeis University Press.

Sharot, S. 1982. *Messianism, mysticism, and magic; a sociological analysis of Jewish religious movements*. Chapel Hill: University of North Carolina Press.

Sharot, S. 1992. 'Neotraditionalism; religious fundamentalism in modern societies'. In B. R. Wilson (ed.), *All Souls Seminars in the Sociology of Religion* (pp. 24–45). London: Bellew Publishing Company.

Sharot, S. 1995. 'Sociological analyses of religion'. In S. Deshen, C. S. Liebman and M. Shokeid (eds), *Israeli Judaism* (pp. 19–32). New Brunswick: Transaction.

Sharot, S. 1996. 'Traditional, modern, or postmodern? Recent religious developments among the Jews in Israel'. In K. Flanagan and P. Jupp (eds), *Postmodernity, sociology and religion* (pp. 118–33). London: Macmillan.

Sharot, S. 1998. 'Judaism and Jewish ethnicity: changing interrelationships and differentiations in the diaspora and Israel'. In E. Krausz and G. Tulea (eds), *Jewish survival; the identity problem at the close of the twentieth century* (pp. 87–105). New Brunswick: Transaction Publishers.

Sheleg, Y. 2000. *The new religious Jews: recent developments among observant Jews in Israel*. Jerusalem: Keter Publishing House (in Hebrew).

Sheleg, Y. 2005. 'The insult of religious Zionism'. *Haaretz* newspaper, 25/07/2005.

Shilhav, J. and M. Friedman 1985. *Growth and segregation - the ultra-orthodox community of Jerusalem*. Jerusalem: Jerusalem Institute for Israel Studies.

Shokeid, M. 1985. 'Cultural ethnicity in Israel: the case of Middle-Eastern Jews' religiosity'. *AJS Review*, 9, 247–71.

Silberstein, L. J. 1999. *The postzionism debates*. New York: Routledge.

Soloveitchick, H. 1994. 'Migration, acculturation, and the new role of texts in the haredi world'. In M. E. Marty and R. S. Appleby (eds), *Accounting for fundamentalisms: the dynamic character of movements* (pp. 197–235). Chicago: University of Chicago Press.

Sprinzak, E. 1991. *The ascendance of Israel's radical right*. New York: Oxford University Press.

Stadler, N. 2002. 'Is profane work an obstacle to salvation? The case of ultra orthodox (haredi) Jews in contemporary Israel'. *Sociology of Religion* 63 (4), 455–74.

Susser, B. 1997. Comments on the Guttman Report. In C. S. Liebman and E. Katz (eds), *The Jewishness of Israelis* (pp. 166–71). Albany: State University of New York.

Tabory, E. 1981. 'State and religion: religious conflict among Jews in Israel'. *Church and State* 23, 275–83.

Tabory, E. 1989. 'Residential integration and religious segregation in an Israeli neighborhood'. *International Journal of Intercultural Relations* 13, 19–35.

Tabory, E. 2004. 'The Israel Reform and Conservative movements and the market for liberal Judaism'. In U. Rebhun and C. I. Waxman (eds), *Jews in Israel; contemporary social and cultural patterns* (pp. 285–314). Hanover: Brandeis University Press.

Tsimhoni, D. 2000. 'Israel and the territories – Disappearance'. *The Middle East Quarterly* 8 (1), ejournal.

Waxman, C. I. 2004. 'Religion in the Israeli public square'. In U. Rebhun and C. I. Waxman (eds), *Jews in Israel; contemporary social and cultural patterns* (pp. 221–39). Hanover: Brandeis University Press.

Weingrod, A. 1990. *The saint of Beersheba*. Albany: State University of New York Press.

Ya'ar, E. 2006. *Science and technology in Israeli consciousness*. Tel Aviv: Shmuel Neeman Institute (in Hebrew).

Zeidman-Dvir, N. and S. Sharot 1992. 'The response of Israeli society to new religious movements: ISKCON and teshuvah'. *Journal for the Scientific Study of Religion* 31 (3), 279–95.

Zerubavel, Y. 1995. *Recovered roots; collective memory and the making of Israeli national tradition*. Chicago: University of Chicago Press.

33

State Shinto and Religion in Post-War Japan

SUSUMU SHIMAZONO

This chapter raises questions about the most appropriate conceptual framework for explaining some aspects of the constellation of 'religions' in Japan today. It also makes connections between this topic and the general issue of the relationship between the state and religions. More particularly, the main aim is to explain how the Japanese state is related to Shinto.

The definition of Shinto and of State Shinto has become a key issue in the sociology of religion in Japan in recent decades. This is partly because there is a growing awareness that the Western norm of secularism does not fit well with the situation in Japan. Shinto tends to be understood as a set of customs and a way of life. This is why resistance has been growing to a strict separation of the state and Shinto, which can be regarded as an ancient tradition of the Japanese people. By contrast, some Buddhists, Christians, liberals and leftists are critical of this essentialist and nationalist conception of Japanese culture. Sociologists of religion cannot help being involved in this debate about whether Shinto is merely one of Japan's religions or something more profoundly rooted in Japanese culture and therefore beyond the diversity of religions.

In short, this chapter will indicate just how difficult and controversial the distinction between 'religion' and 'non-religion' can be, especially in a country with few historical precedents for such a distinction. As a result, sociologists of Japanese religion have to face the challenge of deciding whether the term 'religion' means the same for them as it does for scholars of religion elsewhere in the world.

Japan has a wide variety of religions. Buddhism, Shinto, Christianity, the New Religions and folk religion usually figure in discussions of religion in Japan. There is also widespread recognition that a policy of freedom of religion was adopted after World War II. But if we look carefully at the present-day relationship between the Japanese state and religions, the question arises of whether all religions have the same status in the eyes of the state and whether the state is really neutral in matters of religion. Indeed, the state not only has a special relationship with Shinto but it is also integrated by it. In these circumstances, can we say that Japanese society is completely secular? This question is inseparable from the idea that modern democratic states must be secularist. But, as the anthropologist, Talal Asad (2003), has argued, the norm of secularism – which is taken for granted in some Western countries – should be understood as something created by their particular histories. In the Japanese context the key to understanding this issue is the notion of 'State Shinto'.

SHINTO, STATE SHINTO AND SHRINE SHINTO

Following the end of World War II on 15 August 1945, all the institutions associated with religion in Japan underwent tremendous change. The framework for this change was laid down by the Allied General Headquarters in the form of the so-called Shinto Directive of December 1945, which was based on the fundamental policy that emerged from the American occupation strategy. This document's directives finally achieved legal expression in the provisions of the Japanese Constitution – promulgated in November 1946 – in so far as they related to the Emperor and religion.

Some commentators have summarised the reform of institutions brought about by the Shinto Directive as the dismantling of State Shinto and the establishment of religious freedom. There is no agreement, however, about the effect of this reform because the meaning of State Shinto had not always been clear. In contemporary Western terminology, 'religions' tend to be understood as consisting of groups of people who believe in doctrines, practise rituals and other activities, and make use of facilities related to them. But Shinto does not conform to this Western concept of religion.

Japan has about 80,000 Shinto shrines (*jinja* in Japanese), most of which belong to the *Jinja Honcho* or the Association of Shinto Shrines. This association and all the shrines belonging to it are known as Shrine Shinto (*jinja Shinto*); and in some circumstances Shrine Shinto is equated with Shinto *per se*. But there is another very important component of Shinto which is sometimes overlooked in descriptions of religions in Japan today. I am referring to the aspect of Shinto that is related to the Emperor system. The Imperial Palace in Tokyo has a large Shinto compound of three altars (*kashikodokoro, koreiden and shinden*) which are quite similar to Shinto shrines but are not defined as such. The ritual system which is associated with these altars supports the veneration of the Emperor by the Japanese people. In law, however, it is not considered as having anything to do with the state because it concerns the private rituals of the Imperial family. Nevertheless, I take it to be an important aspect of Shinto today, despite the fact that no specific religious group represents it. This is one of the difficulties of knowing how to define Shinto – but it is also part of the more basic difficulty of defining 'religion' itself (Asad 1993, 2003).

Before I can begin to discuss the place of State Shinto and Shrine Shinto in post-war Japan, I need to give a brief historical account of how modern Shinto evolved. In 1867 revolutionary forces defeated the Shogun regime[1] and established the new Japan based on worship of the Emperor. The Meiji Restoration marked the beginning of modern Japan under the formal leadership of the newly installed Meiji Emperor, who also played the role of the highest priest in Shinto rites. The new Meiji government began with the intention of adopting Shinto as the state religion. They wanted to revive the belief that the Emperor was the descendant of the Goddess Amaterasu – the supreme deity of Shinto mythology – and they established various rituals and other practices connected to Shinto and Emperor worship. The Emperor and his family also began the systematic practice of Shinto rituals, which came to be known later as 'Imperial House Shinto'. Furthermore, the Meiji government tried to revitalise local shrines which, in most cases, had become subordinate to Buddhist temples. This policy was partly successful, but Buddhists and other local people soon put up stiff resistance to it. The Western idea of religious freedom also began to exercise some influence when it was imported by political leaders, elite scholars and Buddhist intellectuals.

The Meiji government was forced to make some compromises as early as the 1870s. The outcome was that Shinto facilities and groups were divided into the two categories of (a) Shrine Shinto (considered as the facilities for public rites but not as religion) and (b) Sect Shinto (considered as religions with the same legal status as Buddhism and Christianity). Shrine Shinto was regarded as a public non-religious organisation and was treated as transcending religions. The state considered that Shinto priests, at least those who served at the larger shrines, had a special status almost on a par with public servants. The chief shrine of Shrine Shinto – the Ise Shrine whose main deity is the Goddess Amaterasu, the ancestor of the Imperial House – became the central sacred place for the state. Yet, this was not considered incompatible with the freedom of religion, since all shrines, including the Ise Shrine, were defined as places for the celebration of state rituals rather than religious practices.

This is how the rituals of the Imperial House came to be closely associated with the rituals of the Ise Shrine located on the Kii peninsula about 160 miles south-west of Tokyo. In the process they occupied a central position in Shrine Shinto, being promulgated not only by Shinto shrines but also by schools, military organisations and the mass media. In fact, many local Shinto shrines had little to do with the mythology of State Shinto and worship of the Emperor. They were the location of annual festivals for celebrating local communities and for praying for their prosperity. The people who visited local Shinto shrines were mainly concerned with the local affairs of their village or town as well as with praying for their own well-being and that of their family.

In later years, however, particularly during the Asian-Pacific War between 1931 and 1945, worship of the Emperor became more and more closely associated with Shrine Shinto in efforts to promote the system of sacred and divine kingship centred on the Showa Emperor, Hirohito.[2] Religious groups were forced to join in worship of the Emperor. The alternative was for them to be persecuted, with their leaders being imprisoned and with their religious activities being completely suppressed. Not only Shinto shrines but the entire system of Emperor worship were also forced on the people. Before 1945, some scholars defined State Shinto as the combination of Emperor worship and Shrine Shinto. Their definition included the ritual system of the Imperial House as well as the ideology centred on divine kingship, but this was not the opinion of the majority. Official terminology defines State Shinto as Shrine Shinto understood as the rituals of the state: not as religion.

THE REALITY OF THE 'DISSOLUTION OF STATE SHINTO'

Given the complexity of Shinto, it is essential here to analyse the concept of State Shinto carefully and to understand its place in the constellation of religions in contemporary Japanese society. The religious scene in Japan after World War II can be characterised by the official dissolution of State Shinto and the establishment of freedom of belief. Until Japan's defeat in 1945 State Shinto enjoyed high status as the public institution that offered the sacred concepts and practices that governed the nation, whereas the other religions had to be content with subordinate status. State Shinto was dissolved at the end of the war, and all religious organisations – including traditional Shrine Shinto – were given the same position; and all citizens obtained the freedom to believe in any religion. It was the Shinto Directive[3] that pushed through these dramatic changes in the country's religious structure.

This account of events is accurate, but it overlooks the fact that there are wide differences in the understanding of the term 'State Shinto' (Shimazono 2001b, 2001c, 2005) and, not surprisingly, of what the 'dissolution of State Shinto' means. More than 60 years after the war ended, interpretations of 'State Shinto' remain confused. The term is often used in people's expression of their personal or one-sided views, but it is rare to find a well-balanced, general statement of its meaning.

Discussions of State Shinto fall into roughly two types, each one reflecting a different point of view. Scholars in Religious Studies and the Sociology of Religion tend to consider the system of Emperor worship as an important component of State Shinto. By contrast, many scholars in Shinto studies and historians consider State Shinto to be nothing more than all of Shrine Shinto at a time when, unlike other religions, it enjoyed a special relationship with the Japanese state (Murakami 1970; Ashizu 1987; Sakamoto 1994).

The reasons for this confusion lie mainly in the Shinto Directive itself (Ohara 1993; Nitta 1997). The Directive's official title clearly reflected the intention to dissolve State Shinto. The definition of the term given in the latter half of the document is as follows:

> The term State Shinto within the meaning of this directive will refer to that branch of Shinto (*Kokka* Shinto or *Jinja* Shinto) which by official acts of the Japanese Government has been differentiated from the religion of Sect Shinto (*Shuha* Shinto or *Kyoha* Shinto), and has been classified as a non-religious national cult commonly known as State Shinto, or National Shinto or Shrine Shinto.

According to this definition, 'State Shinto' meant Shrine (*Jinja*) Shinto; and 'the dissolution of State Shinto' referred to the process of turning Shrine Shinto into non-State Shinto, or of separating Shrine Shinto from the Japanese state. This seems to suggest that the separation between the state and the shrines was expected to bring about the freedom of religion for the Japanese people, i.e. freedom of thought and belief in the sphere of religion in Japan's national life.

On the other hand, the Shinto Directive also made many other points. Above all, it aimed to 'prevent recurrence of the perversion of Shinto theory and beliefs into militaristic and ultra-nationalistic propaganda designed to delude the Japanese people and lead them into wars of aggression'; and it provided a range of measures for achieving this aim. The Directive considered that this 'ideological distortion' of Shinto included the idea that 'the Emperor of Japan is superior to the heads of other states because of ancestry, descent, or special origin'. The concept of the Unique National Polity (or Unique National Structure, *kokutai* in Japanese) was also an inseparable part of this ideology. But even if Shinto had been distorted by this 'ideology', the Directive gave no indication of

how it was related to 'State Shinto'. Although the dissolution of State Shinto was supposed to be understood in such a way that it included liberation from this ideological distortion of Shinto as a direct consequence of the Directive's wording, the document failed to make it clear whether this understanding was indeed correct.

Another implication of the definition of State Shinto given in the Directive was that it made little reference to Imperial House Shinto and its religious rites, which had often been considered as essential components of State Shinto. It was not clear what had happened to the relationship between the Emperor and Shinto rites. Since the Meiji Restoration of 1867, Imperial House Shinto had been highly valued as important rites for maintaining national order. But how far had these rites changed? And to what extent had their significance been weakened? The answers to these questions are the key to understanding whether 'State Shinto' had really been dissolved and, if so, in what respects. There may be many reasons why this point is often omitted from recent discussions of State Shinto, but one of them is that the Directive's administrative terminology defined State Shinto narrowly as Shrine Shinto.

In view of the fact that the Directive's definition of State Shinto is so narrow that it causes confusion, I think it is more realistic to define it more broadly (Shimazono 2001b, 2005). My broader definition is therefore counter-posed to Murakami's (1970) simplistic use of 'State Shinto'. When I use this term I refer to Shinto-inspired ideas and practices that are mainly propagated by agencies of the Japanese state or government in connection with attempts to integrate the nation and to strengthen the sense of national loyalty – and which are accepted by many of the Japanese people.

This sense of the term 'State Shinto' preserves an important space for Imperial House rites and Imperial House Shinto. In the pre-war system, Imperial House rites were national events – so much so, in fact, that festivals and public holidays were conducted in accordance with Imperial House rites. Paying respect to the Emperor implied that the public could participate in the world in which the Imperial House rites were spiritually grounded. Imperial House rites are conducted in the name of the Emperor, who is a descendant of Amaterasu Omikami – the principal female deity of Shinto who is believed to be the progenetrix of the Imperial line. The Japanese people therefore have a connection with the nationalistic world of gods through their worship of the Emperor, who has the character of a priest-king. The idea that 'the Emperor of Japan is superior to the heads of any other states because of ancestry, descent or special origin' has a strong connection with the principle that all of the Japanese people can be involved in the Imperial House rites and that reverence for the Emperor is considered fundamental to national identity. What the Shinto Directive considers to be 'ideological distortion' is inseparably bound up with the cosmological system of 'the unity of the rites, state and indoctrination' that was promoted by the state after the Meiji Restoration and that accorded a high status to Imperial House rites. To understand the history of Shinto, to compare Japanese society with others, and to grasp the whole picture of the cosmological and ideological structure of the modern Japanese state, it is essential to view State Shinto from a broad perspective (Shimazono 2001c).

The question now arises of how the meaning of State Shinto, in this broad sense, changed after the structural reforms of 1945. How far was it dissolved? And to what extent did it survive? If it still persists today, what does it really amount to? What role do Imperial House Shinto and its rites play in State Shinto now? How does reverence for the Emperor and the concept of national polity differ from the pre-war situation? What is the position today of Shrine Shinto now that it has become a religious organisation? Many accounts of these separate issues have been published, but few attempts have been made to provide an overview of them. My sketch of this general overview of State Shinto in a broad sense after World War II will attempt to answer questions about its meaning in the eyes of Japanese

people today. It is an essential part of the work of reconstructing the history of religions in modern Japan.

POST-WAR IMPERIAL HOUSE RITES

What changes occurred in the system of Imperial House rites after World War II? As mentioned above, the Shinto Directive made few references to them aside from distinguishing them from Shrine Shinto rites. It also considered them to be a private matter for the Imperial House and therefore outside the framework of the public's freedom of belief. If 'religion' is regarded as a set of doctrines and rites practised by a religious community, prohibiting any specific religion from having a special relation with the state is at the centre of concerns about guaranteeing the freedom of belief. The Shinto Directive deals directly with these concerns but without including Imperial House Shinto or its rites in the framework of 'religion' or 'Shinto' provided by the Directive. Even if the rites performed inside the Imperial House belong to 'Shinto,' the assumption is that the Imperial House is free to decide whether to perform them or not. They are not subject to the restrictions that bear on the relationship between a religious organisation and the state. In fact, the Imperial House continues to perform Shinto rites which have enormous meaning for the Japanese public. The Directive takes an optimistic view of the relationship between Imperial House rites and Shinto.

According to Ohara Yasuo[4] (1993: 120), who made a comprehensive study of the Shinto Directive and the process of implementing it in practice, 'While the General Headquarters (GHQ) intended to wipe out the holiness of the Emperor and the people's Emperor worship, it seems that it considered that this kind of consciousness had little linkage with the Imperial House rites'. Belief in the 'priest-king' was discussed among GHQ officers at the time the Shinto Directive was issued. W. K. Bunce of the Civil Information and Education Section (CIE), who had been in charge of formulating the Directive, received a report from the

Allied Forces Translation and Interpretation Section (ATIS) in October 1945 indicating that people should be free to choose whether to believe in the Priest-King. As a result, he did not consider that this belief was dangerous as long as people were free to make a choice about it and as long as it was not politically enforced (Ohara 1993: 10–12). In the light of this understanding, the existing Imperial House rites were largely preserved. If a system was to be set up to ensure that no group could use the rites for political purposes, Imperial House rites would remain matters of private belief which would presumably not exercise much influence over people's lives.

It is highly likely that Bunce's view was deliberately reflected in General Douglas MacArthur's attempt to govern the occupation by using the authority of the Emperor. Ohara (1993: 160) argued that the GHQ responded mildly to Imperial House rites partly because it did not see any threat or danger in them, but in addition 'there may have been a sensitive consideration of the Emperor by supreme commander MacArthur'.

The time when the policy was agreed to allow Imperial House rites to continue coincides with the period when General MacArthur was finally coming to the conclusion that it would be wise to maintain the authority of the Emperor. Considerable influence was exercised over General MacArthur by Warrant Officer Bonner F. Fellers. Bonner's memorandum to MacArthur on 2 October 1945 repeatedly stated that the GHQ should appreciate popular religious respect and affection for the Emperor, and suggested that the Emperor should not be charged with responsibility for the war. According to Dower (1999: 298–99)

> It is a fundamental American concept that the people of any nation have the inherent right to choose their own government. Were the Japanese given this opportunity, they would select the Emperor as the symbolic head of the state. The masses are especially devoted to Hirohito. They feel that his addressing the people personally made him unprecedentedly close to them.

With regard to its approach to State Shinto, GHQ attempted to reduce the potential for shock and dissatisfaction among the Japanese people by framing the Shinto Directive in such

a way that it was kind to the Imperial Family and the Imperial House rites. Inadvertently, this helped to ensure that confusion about the meaning of State Shinto is still with us.

In fact, GHQ's decision to exclude Imperial House rites from the important political issue of State Shinto gave rise to many questions and problems at a later date. Many of these problems about the status of the Imperial House rites emerged when attempts were made to revive State Shinto. The present situation of State Shinto can only be understood if topics such as the following are examined in detail: (i) the daily and seasonal rites in the Imperial House, (ii) the rites of passage for the Emperor and other family members, (iii) the Three Sacred Treasures and Imperial Graves, and (iv) the relationship with *Jinja* Shinto.

(i) Daily and Seasonal Rites in the Imperial House

The Imperial Palace in Tokyo houses the three altars known as the *Kashikodokoro* (Place of Awe), *Koreiden* (Imperial Ancestors' Altar) and *Shinden* (the Deities' Altar). Every morning at the Place of Awe a male court ritualist recites a prayer for the Emperor, while several women court ritualists undertake a purification procedure, give 'rice offerings', and ring the bell. Both male and female court ritualists then make daily offerings of rice balls, fish, seaweed, *sake*, etc. Following this, a chamberlain makes a bow on behalf of the Emperor in the sanctum. These rites are held earlier than usual on the 1st, 11th and 21st day of each month, when the Emperor himself often bows in worship. Ritualists are regarded as employees of the Imperial House and are paid from the budgeted allowances for its private expenditure, but chamberlains are employees of the government. In all, more than 20 kinds of seasonal rituals are held each year. At minor rites, the Emperor simply makes a bow but he actually presides over major rites. Many Imperial House rites correspond to those held at the Ise Shrine and at other Shinto shrines that belong to the Association of Shinto Shrines across the country. Since they are regarded as 'court events', however, or as private occasions for the Emperor's family, they are not publicly reported by the media. The events that are reported in the media are non-religious events such as the Emperor's Birthday. Although no public announcement is made, those who have an attachment to, or an interest in, the Emperor are well aware of the fact that he and his family are strict in their performance of Shinto rites.

(ii) Rites of Passage for the Emperor and Other Family Members

Funerals of emperors and empresses – as well as the wedding ceremonies of the Crown Prince and other members of the Imperial Family – are occasions when the public can see the relationship between the Imperial Family and Imperial House rites. Controversy surrounds these occasions because holding them in the Shinto style is contrary to the principle of the separation of religions and the state. There is no denying that some of the Shinto rites and rituals conducted these days display the characteristics of state events. Nevertheless, the principle of religion/state separation is honoured in a narrow sense in so far as the National Treasury does not make budgetary allocations for these events related to the Imperial House – unlike other government-sponsored, non-religious public events.

(iii) The Three Sacred Treasures and Imperial Graves

Three Sacred Treasures symbolise the Emperor's status as a deity. The original sacred mirror (*yata no kagami*) is enshrined at the Ise Shrine, and its replica is housed in the Place of Awe in the Imperial Palace; the sacred sword (*ameno murakumo no tsurugi*, later re-named *kusanagi no tsurugi*) is enshrined in Atsuta Shrine, while its replica and the curved jewels – as well as the seal (*yasakani no magatama*) – are stored in the Room of the Sword and Seal next to the bedroom of the Emperor and Empress. The practice of transporting the sacred sword

and the seal along with the Emperor on journeys was suspended in 1947 and revived in 1974. Since then, the sacred sword and the seal have accompanied the Emperor whenever he visits the Ise Shrine and on other important occasions. Nearly 900 locations have been designated without firm evidence as Imperial Graves – and respected as holy places – since the Meiji period. Critical voices are often heard on this topic.

(iv) Relationship with Shrine Shinto

The post-war system in Japan has a rule that, even though Imperial House rites are still conducted and have not been 'dissolved', they are not associated with Shrine Shinto as a religious organisation. Admittedly, the relationship between the Imperial House and Shrine Shinto has undergone major changes since the war, so that there are now fewer occasions when the Emperor visits shrines for the purpose of worship in his public capacity or performs a leading role in rites at shrines. Nevertheless, there is no denying that Ise Shrine has the character of the ancestral mausoleum of the Imperial House. It is natural to consider it as the original facility of the Place of Awe in the Imperial Palace. The Emperor's visits to Ise Shrine have profound meaning as Shinto events in association with the state; and the involvement of the Imperial House in the most important Shinto event at Ise Shrine – when parts of the existing shrine are dismantled and a new shrine is dedicated every 20 years – is gradually assuming greater importance. For example, a ceremony at which the Imperial envoy presents offerings from the Emperor is held during the three main annual festivals at Ise Shrine, namely, the festival for the deities tasting the new rice as well as rites at the end of June and December. Moreover, a female member of the Imperial Family or other relatives (currently the daughter of the Showa Emperor) serves as the chief ritualist. These events take place as private affairs of the Imperial House without drawing on its official budget, but it can be argued that in reality the Imperial House is conducting State Shinto events and that they preserve a strong connection between the Imperial House and Shrine Shinto.

THE ASSOCIATION OF SHINTO SHRINES AS A RELIGIOUS ORGANISATION

Not many academic studies of Shrine Shinto as a religious organisation have been undertaken since World War II, but the historical reports published by the Association of Shinto Shrines – the umbrella organisation of Shinto shrines across Japan – are useful points of reference (Jinja Shimpo-sha 1971, 1986; National Association of Shinto Shrines 1976). The findings of sociological research by Morioka (1975) and Ishii (1998) have been published, but they do not discuss the relationship between the Association and the Japanese state. Some scholars of political history have also focused their investigations on the 'Emperor system' as a political system without paying attention to the political aspects of Shrine Shinto as a religious organisation (Watanabe 1990; Ruoff 2001). In fact, the Association of Shinto Shrines as a religious entity has been a blind spot in historical research.

After the Shinto Directive, Shrine Shinto lost its position as part of the state and ceased to be State Shinto in the narrow sense, as used in legal and administrative history. Shinto shrines all over Japan were re-organised as non-governmental organisations and became members of a religious organisation with the name of the Association of Shinto Shrines. This association has developed as a politically oriented organisation having the state and the Emperor as its main preoccupations rather than as a force for uniting folk beliefs in shrines at a national level. With belief oriented towards State Shinto (in the broad sense of the term) as its religious principle, the Association adopted the aim of strengthening both reverence for the Emperor within a Shinto frame of reference and partnership between the Emperor and shrines. The Association has promoted its activities as a religious organisation by pouring greater energy into enhancing the status of State Shinto in people's lives instead of activating Shrine Shinto at the civil level.

The term 'Shrine Shinto' may evoke in Japanese minds images of shrines across the country, and it is easy to understand that worshippers may not necessarily feel that they are revering the Emperor. But in the Association, reverence for the Emperor, the Imperial House and the Grand Shrine of Ise is the highest aim; and it constitutes the axis of its belief system. A brief review of the Association's doctrinal statements will help to explain its background and belief system.

Initially, people claiming to support a non-doctrinal principle formed a majority among the Association's members, but others thought that unified 'standards' should be laid down (Association of Shinto Shrines 1971, 1976). The original description of 'standards' – which really means 'doctrines' – can be found in the Rules that the Association adopted at the time of its foundation in February 1946. They continued to enhance the 'standards' until, in 1980, the Charter of the Association of Shinto Shrines was formulated. The Charter's first three articles are a concise description of the Association's belief system:

Article 1: The Association of Shinto Shrines shall place value on tradition, promote rites and rituals, and enhance moral principles, pray for the permanent prosperity of the Emperor's reign, and at the same time, contribute to peace in the world.

Article 2:
(1) The Association of Shinto Shrines shall revere the Grand Shrine of Ise as its head shrine, and shall sincerely devote itself to the work of the Grand Shrine.
(2) The Association of Shinto Shrines shall be engaged in services for the prosperity of all Shinto shrines and shall convey the gods' power of commanding love and respect.

Article 3: The Association of Shinto Shrines shall initiate an educational doctrine of revering the gods and respecting the Emperor, and uphold the platform for its practice. It shall train Shinto priests, and educate parishioners and followers.

The things that the Association intends to propagate appear to be far removed from the sentiments of many of those who visit shrines to make wishes for the New Year or to wish for good health. The Association strongly advocates reverence towards the Emperor and the Ise Shrine; and it argues that all shrines in Japan should be integrated under the Grand Shrine of Ise and the Emperor. With this type of Shinto belief, the Association is rightly regarded as pursuing a form of Shinto that leans towards State Shinto in its broad meaning.

In fact, routine religious activities at Shinto shrines do not centre on politics. Ishii's (1998) discussion of Shrine Shinto from the viewpoint of local people draws a completely different picture of it in the post-war period. He shows that shrines have functioned mainly as places to pray for this-worldly benefits and to celebrate the well-being and prosperity of families and communities – even companies. On the other hand, Nakano (2003) discusses the legal and institutional reforms of post-war Japan and the political activities of the New Religions without examining those of the Association of Shinto Shrines. This is in sharp contrast to the Association itself, which has been constantly pursuing a religious mission strongly oriented towards politics, as it intends to lead the nation in a particular spiritual direction. While mobilising shrines all over Japan under its umbrella, the Association is active as a political and religious organisation that champions State Shinto as its belief.

Evidence of the political and religious activities of the Association of Shinto Shrines can be seen by looking back on the many political actions of which it was a major supporter. Jinja Shimpo-sha, publisher of the Association's newspaper, *Jinja Shimpo*, also published *The History of Modern Shrine Shinto* (1986). Towards the end of the section on 'The activities of the shrine community after the Shinto Directive', this book describes the movement in its early days as a 'movement to demonstrate the real status of the Ise Shrine'. The passage begins with:

> The Shrine community in postwar days attempted to change the spiritual climate of the Japanese, who had been poisoned by the Shinto Directive. The first movement was to rectify the attitude of the state toward the Grand Shrine of Ise, in what was called the Grand Shrine System Rectification Movement. Needless to say, Ise Shrine is the shrine to conduct rites for the Emperor and enshrines the sacred mirror bestowed by the founder of the Imperial family. Its relations with the Imperial family and the state have continued for 2000 years from far back in ancient days to the occupation period after the Great East Asia War, and they have not changed at all. However, the relations between this valuable shrine and the Imperial House and the state were discontinued by the policy of the Allied Occupation Forces after the war, and the Grand Shrine of Ise became a private religious corporation. Needless to say, this status degrades the real status of the Shrine, and it is a matter of natural course that the demand for restoration of its original and real status has grown among the people after the end of the Occupation. It is precisely a movement to rectify the shrine system, which resulted in clarifying the movement's focus of spiritual concern, that is, the inseparable relationship between the Emperor and the Grand Shrine of Ise. This was made clear in October 1960 by the then Prime Minister Ikeda's reply (Jinja Shimpo-sha 1986: 277).

The book then goes on to describe the movements to revive 'Empire Day',[5] to restore the habit of transporting the Sacred Sword and the Seal along with the Emperor on his travels outside the Imperial Palace, and to preserve the Yasukuni Shrine as a state facility. It enshrines those who died fighting in wars for the sake of Emperors and the Japanese state since the mid-nineteenth century.

The section of the book entitled 'Confusion of political and educational problems' takes up two further issues that are highly sensitive. One case concerns a ceremony for purifying a building site in Tsu City, while the other is about the relationship between the Japanese self-defence forces and Shinto. All of these issues are connected to constitutional questions about the separation of religion and the state in Japan. The Association of Shinto Shrines demanded that an agency of the state must be permitted to participate not only in rites at the Ise Shrine and the Yasukuni Shrine but also in celebrations of the Emperor's holiness. The book gives additional examples of advocacy led by the Association such as the 'national spiritual enhancement movement' of 1967, the establishment of its 'political situation headquarters' in 1969 and the foundation of the Shinto Political League in the same year. Successful outcomes of the League's campaigning are said to include the movement to make it legal to use the reign-name in dates – on official documents from 1972 to 1979 – which count years from the enthronement of each Emperor in place of the phrase 'Christian (or common) era', and the movement to protect the Emperor's dignity against the offence of *lèse majesté*.

In other words, there can be no doubt that the Association of Shinto Shrines is putting its energy into political campaigns. It is acknowledged to have made some astonishing advances in connection with the political issue concerning the status of the Emperor after the war. Kenneth Ruoff's (2001) argument in *The People's Emperor* is that the concept of the Emperor in post-war Japan as the symbol of the state and of national unity has gradually taken root. It means that the monarchy will be maintained, while the Emperor's political functions will be kept neutral. The Association has a religious motive for insisting that the Emperor's political functions should be strengthened. It is a leading organisation in the political movement to raise the status of the Emperor much higher than that of a merely symbolic being with the support of the majority of Japanese people. Ruoff (2001: 194) cites a telling example: 'Between 1977 and 1979, the offices of the Association of Shinto Shrines resembled a war room when it was campaigning among Local Assemblies for the Bill demanding legalisation of the use of the reign-name'.

Nevertheless, Ruoff's assessment of the Association's contributions to campaigns for strengthening the Emperor's status or for stirring up nationalism is ambiguous. Taking the examples of its campaign to restore state sponsorship of the Yasukuni Shrine and to revive the offence of *lèse majesté*, he concludes that 'precisely because groups such as the Association of Shinto Shrines stood to the right of the mainstream, many of their campaigns have failed' (Ruoff 2001: 187). On the other hand, he also acknowledges the successful cases of establishing the National Foundation Day (a revival of Empire Day) and of enacting the use of the reign-name:

> I do not interpret the postwar Japanese state to be neutral – it tended to lean to the right . . . This association's views often contrasted with those of the LDP, not to mention the left-wing parties. Like the far right Christian Coalition in the United States, the Association of Shinto Shrines occupies a place in civil society between the individual citizen and the state. And similarly to the Christian Coalition in the late 1980s and 1990s, the Association of Shinto Shrines has shown itself capable of manufacturing popular support for some of its programs . . . Still, although many LDP[6] politicians courted the support of groups such as the Association of Shinto Shrines, which could deliver votes and contributions, only fragments of the association's platform ever found their way into law. Foundation Day and the reign-name system were two such fragments (Ruoff 2001: 200).

The Association of Shinto Shrines is primarily active as a political force in Japan. Its political aim is to revive State Shinto by promoting nationalism and reverence for the Emperor. It is not too much to claim that the majority of its account of the activities of Shrine Shinto after the Shinto Directive in its own *History of Modern Shrine Shinto* is devoted to describing the political movement to support reverence for the Emperor and the restoration of State Shinto.

LATENT IMPERIAL HOUSE RITES AND STATE SHINTO

As I noted earlier, State Shinto may have been 'dissolved' immediately after World War II, but it is not extinct. In fact, State Shinto in the post-war period has retained two religio-political projects which have become central to its plans for revitalising itself. One is the Imperial House rites; and the other is the campaign, promoted by the Association of Shinto Shrines, to increase reverence for the Emperor. Although the former is partly hidden from view, the latter is the organisation or movement seeking to expand the State Shinto-oriented system that places importance on Imperial House rites. Taken together, these two projects constitute the core of today's State Shinto within the current framework of law.

The 'movement' aspect of State Shinto consists mainly of shrines affiliated to the Association of Shinto Shrines as well as some other organisations and individuals from many walks of life. The famous novelist,

Mishima Yukio, was a polemicist for State Shinto in post-war Japan but he had come from a community that differed sharply from that of Shrine Shinto. In addition to Mishima, other activists in the post-war State Shinto movement came from a wide range of social backgrounds. Any voices advocating governmental commitment to the Yasukuni Shrine can be considered supportive of the restoration of State Shinto. What is clear is that the volume of support for State Shinto is much stronger now than it was around 1970 when Mishima committed suicide with the intention of performing an act of heroism (Watanabe 1990). A new trend is emerging among discourses about Shinto and State Shinto: it involves discussion of uniquely Japanese culture in a self-assertive and aggressive way (Shimazono 1995, 2001a), in extreme cases claiming that the essence of the Japanese religious mind-set is to be found in reverence for the Emperor.

As an example of this new trend in advocacy of State Shinto, I shall analyse the discourse used by Nakanishi Terumasa (2005: 18–19, 30–1), a professor of Political Science at Kyoto University:

In Japan, people are required to be 'honest and pure at heart' or to be a 'non-double-faced personality'... It is the 'Emperor' who embodies such Japanese mind in the simplest, and most visible way.

It is true that the Emperor is the guardian of Japanese culture, and a person who typifies it. However, it is not only the cultural aspect that is sought in the Emperor. As repeatedly mentioned in the conversation with Fukuda Kazuya in this book, what the Japanese should become conscious about is the Emperor as a religious being. (The term 'religion' does not express the Japanese mentality, but with no proper alternative, it is used for the time being.) Looking back on the genealogy of the Emperor, we will go into the mythological world. The Emperor conducts rites every day and night praying for the prosperity of the country and the well-being of the nation. Because of this, the Emperor is able to embody the state and perform the role of integrating the nation. It is important that we should be firmly aware of this fact in our view of the Emperor. What he does is not simply a cultural activity but a political activity in a broader sense, which leads the state [governance]. Here lies the very *raison d'être* of the Emperor. And for this reason, the Imperial House is respected. It is this aspect of the Emperor, I think, that the contemporary Japanese have forgotten. Once they realize this, they will be straightforwardly moved, and thankfulness will come up in their minds. Because it is the immovable 'Japanese mind'.

This type of discourse elicits quite a positive response in Japan at the beginning of the twenty-first century. As Ruoff (2001) suggests, it has much in common with the discourse of religious rightists in the USA and of other religio-political communalist and nationalist movements in various regions of the world. This chapter has confirmed that the source of the discourse lies in State Shinto, which, under the state's leadership, played an important role in the modernising process in Japan in the mid-nineteenth century as well as today. State Shinto evolved as an actor in the hidden Imperial House rites and as a voluntary State Shinto movement in the latter half of the twentieth century after being reformed by the Shinto Directive immediately after World War II. There is, of course, a difference between the nature of pre-war State Shinto under the state's control and the nature of today's State Shinto as expressed in hidden Imperial House rites and in a voluntary movement. But continuity between them is also apparent. State Shinto has not been rendered extinct: it has not even been dissolved.

CONCLUSION

It is essential to re-examine the long-accepted understanding that, after 1945, Japan was compelled by the Allied Forces and the international community to separate religion and state. This is partly true and partly false. Scholars were unable to describe the real state of affairs because they uncritically accepted the conceptual distinction between politics and religion. Because Shinto was understood to fall within the category of 'religion', as consisting of Shinto shrines, scholars tended to fail to see Imperial House rites as an important component of the state. Thus, it has been widely accepted that State Shinto was dissolved and had become extinct just after the end of the World War II. In reality, however, State Shinto has survived to play an important part in post-war Japan and has even been gaining more influence in recent times. In order to correct these misunderstandings about the religious system of post-war Japan we need to re-think such basic concepts as religion, Shinto and State Shinto.

NOTES

1. Shoguns were the leading Samurai warriors who effectively ruled Japan for most of the medieval and early modern period, while emperors exercised only symbolic authority.

2. Showa (Illustrious Peace) is the name chosen to identify the reign of Emperor Hirohito from 1926 to 1989. The current Emperor's reign-name is Heisei.

3. 'The abolition of governmental sponsorship, support, perpetuation, control and dissemination of State Shinto' (*kokka Shinto, jinja Shinto*), issued by the General Headquarters of the Allied Forces (GHQ) in December 1945.

4. Names in this chapter follow the Japanese convention of placing the family name before the personal name.

5. To celebrate the accession of the Jimmu Emperor in, according to legend, 660 BCE.

6. Liberal Democratic Party.

REFERENCES

Asad, Talal 1993. *Genealogies of Religion: Discipline and Reasons of Power in Christianity and Islam,* Baltimore, MD: The Johns Hopkins University Press.

Asad, Talal 2003. *Formations of the Secular: Christianity, Islam, Modernity*, Stanford, CA: Stanford University Press.

Ashizu, Uzuhiko 1987. *Kokka Shinto towa Nandattanoka* (What was State Shinto?), Tokyo: Jinja Shimpo-sha.

Association of Shinto Shrines, Bureau of Education in the Department of Edification (ed.) 1951. *Jinja Honcho 5-nen Shi* (Five Year History of the Association of Shinto Shrines). Tokyo: Jinja Honcho.

Association of Shinto Shrines, Central Institute for Training (ed.) 1971, 1976. *Jinja Honcho Shiko* (Historic Notes about the Association of Shinto Shrines). Tokyo: Jinja Honcho Chuo Kenshu-jo.

Association of Shinto Shrines, Central Institute for Training (ed.) 1976. *Jinja Honcho Shiko* (Historic Notes about the Association of Shinto Shrines). Tokyo: Jinja Honcho Chuo Kenshu-jo.

Association of Shinto Shrines, Research Office for Doctrinal Studies (ed.) 1980. *Jinja Honcho Kensho no Kaisetsu* (Explanation of the Charter of the Association of Shinto Shrines). Tokyo: Jinja Honcho.

Dower, John W. 1999. *Embracing Defeat: Japan in the Wake of World War II,* New York: Norton.

Ishii, Kenji 1998. *Sengo no Shakai Hendo to Jinja Shinto* (Postwar Social Changes and Shrine Shinto) Tokyo: Taimei-do.

Jinja Shimpo-sha, Research Office for Religion and State (ed.) 1976, 1982, 1986. *Zoho Kaitei Kindai Jinja Shinto Shi* (Revised and Enlarged edition of The Modern History of Shrine Shinto), Tokyo: Jina Shinpo-sha.

Jinja Shimpo-sha, Research Office for Religion and State 1971. *Shinto Shirei to Sengo no Shinto* (Shinto Directive and Postwar Shinto). Tokyo: Jina Shinpo-sha.

Morioka, Kiyomi 1975. *Religion in Changing Japanese Society*. Tokyo: University of Tokyo Press.

Murakami, Shigeyoshi 1970. *Kokka Shinto* (State Shinto). Tokyo: Iwanami Shoten.

Murakami, Shigeyoshi 1977. *Tenno no Saishi* (Emperor's rites), Tokyo: Iwanami Shoten.

Nakanishi, Terumasa 2005. 'Josho: Naze Nippon ni Tenno to iu sonzai ga hitsuyoka (Prelude: Why is the entity of the Emperor necessary in Japan?)'. In Nakanishi, Terumasa and Fukuda, Kazuya *Koshitsu no Hongi* (Significance of the Imperial House). Tokyo: PHP Institute.

Nakano, Tsuyoshi 2003. *Sengo Nihon no Shukyo to Seiji* (Religion and Politics in Postwar Japan), Tokyo: Taimei-do.

Nitta, Hitoshi 1997. *Kindai Seikyo Kankei no Kisoteki Kenkyu* (Fundamental Study on the Relation between Religions and Politics in the Modern Times). Tokyo: Taimeido.

Ohara, Yasuo 1993. *Shinto Shirei no Kenkyu* (Study on the Shinto Directive). Tokyo: Hara Shobo.

Ruoff, Kenneth, J. 2001. *The People's Emperor: Democracy and the Japanese Monarchy 1945-1995.* Boston: Harvard University Asia Center.

Sakamoto, Koremaru 1994. *Kokka Shinto Keisei Katei no Kenkyu* (Study on the Formation Process of State Shinto). Tokyo: Iwanami Shoten.

Shimazono, Susumu 1995. 'Nihonjinron to Shukyo (Observation on the Japanese and Religions)'. In *Tokyo Daigaku Shukyogaku Nempo* (Annual Report on Religious Studies of Tokyo University) No. 13.

Shimazono, Susumu 2001a. *Postmodern no Shin Shukyo* (New Religions in Postmodern Age) Tokyo: Tokyo Do Shuppan.

Shimazono, Susumu 2001b. 'Kokka Shinto to Kindai Nippon no Shukyo (State Shinto and Modern

Japan)' in *Shukyo Kenkyu* (Religious Studies), No. 329.

Shimazono, Susumu 2001c. 'Sosetsu 19 seiki Nippon no Shukyo Kozo no Henyo (Transformation of the Religious Structure in Japan in the Nineteenth Century)'. In Komori Yoichi, Sakai Naoki, Shimazono Susumu, Chino, Kaori, Narita Ryuichi and Yoshimi Shun'ya (eds), *Iwanami Koza: Kindai Nippon no Bunkashi*

2: Kosumologii no Kinsei (Iwanami Lecture Series: Cultural History of Modern Japan 2: 'Cosmology in Early Modern Times').

Shimazono, Susumu 2005. 'State Shinto and the Religious Structure of Modern Japan', *Journal of the American Academy of Religion* 73 (4): 1077-98.

Watanabe, Osamu 1990. *Sengo Seijishi no naka no Tennosei* (The Emperor System in postwar Political History). Tokyo: Aoki Shoten.

34

Mexico: A Mirror for the Sociology of Religion

ROBERTO J. BLANCARTE

One of the good reasons for analyzing Mexico's religion and society is the fact that the country (and in fact the entire region of Latin America) is simultaneously host to both a Western *and* a non-Western society. Indeed, the question of whether Mexico and Latin America constitute 'the extreme West,' 'the other West', a 'semi-Western' society or simply another world that we have not yet been able to explain is widely discussed. The fact that different cultures coexist in Mexico and that there are syncretistic and *'mestizo'* cultures – as well as combinations of them – convinces some scholars to adopt a different perspective from the 'paradigms' that govern European and North American sociology of religion. In this respect, Mexico is not only an exotic curiosity or an example of religious backwardness but it is also an important case study of attempts to universalize concepts in the sociology of religion field.

Mexico, like many other Latin American or Caribbean countries, experiences modernity or post-modernity with all the ambivalence and paradoxes of any country that was colonized and partially Westernized not only by Spaniards but also by the Portuguese and the Flemish. From the beginning of the sixteenth century, the wider region was colonized by the British, the Germans and the French. There has also been discussion about the impact, extent and depth of Christianity in the so-called New World. On the other hand, we have a similar debate about the persistence, strength and capacity to adapt – or to resist – of local cultures and religions. In theory, this approach should be extended not only to colonized countries but also to European lands where Christianity was established on the ruins of other religions in, for example, the Celtic regions, Eastern Europe or the Nordic countries. But in practice, it is in Latin America that the idea of the subsistence or persistence of ancient religious beliefs and practices beneath a thinner or thicker Christian cultural overlay has been studied most intensely.

Regardless of whether we consider it a more or less Westernized country, Mexico could and should be a perfect reminder that theories devised to explain particular situations are not always automatically applicable in general. Furthermore, in order to achieve global reach, concepts and theories should incorporate particular experiences. Theory construction can then become a two-way process, not only in the sense of a dialogue between theory and empirical data – between analysis and facts – but also between the different experiences of Western, semi-Western and non-Western societies. We are not advocating a nationalist or 'local' perspective on religion and its socio-logical study. In fact, much of the theoretical questioning about Euro-centric or Western-centric approaches to the sociology of religion has come from scholars in developed countries (see Spickard 1998, 2000, 2001). Rather, I perceive this as a permanent dialogue between different perspectives in an attempt to create universal tools for a broader understanding of religion in the world. We could call this a 'system of cultural mirrors in social sciences' that would seek to elaborate new universal paradigms, theories and concepts.

In any assessment of the religious situation in Mexico, we have to question or at least to reconsider some of the theoretical frameworks or paradigms used in the sociology of religion. We shall show, for example, that the study of secularization, conversions, rituals and practices, popular religion, pluralism, toler-ance, 'laicism,' church-state relations and other related subjects in Mexico and Latin American countries can become – if not necessarily a new source of paradigms – at least a mirror in which Western societies can see themselves. It is hoped that this process of reflecting back on Western societies will eventually challenge received and unquestioned ideas in the sociology of religion.

THE LEGACY OF THE PRE-HISPANIC WORLD AND THE COLONIAL PERIOD IN MEXICO AND LATIN AMERICA

For the last five centuries, religions in Mexico and Latin America have thrived under an apparent and contradictory monopoly of 'salvation goods' at the institutional level, and a profuse diversity of religious expressions that coexist, intertwine and feed on that monopoly. Resistance, adjust-ment, and integration are but a few of the options used by this set of religious expressions – particularly during the Colonial Period (1521–1821) but nowadays as well – to find a relationship with the dominant system of beliefs.

In pre-Hispanic times, religion occupied a central place in the life of the peoples of the region called 'Mesoamérica.'[1] Their daily life, familial relationships, wars, magical proce-dures, therapeutics and medicine, social struc-ture, priesthood organization and 'cosmovision' depended on their religious conceptions.[2] Central to this religious vision in Mesoamerica is the 'Cosmic Tree' that served as a link between the world of human existence, the lower world and the 'upper world,' and as a road for the gods to travel from one to the other. In this conception, astrology, architec-ture, mathematics, agriculture and the calendar were intimately related.

The violence of evangelization had a big impact on the outlook of the indigenous people. Pre-Hispanic people were familiar with the destruction of the images of the vanquished and subordination of their deities to the conquering gods: but not to the total extermination of ancient beliefs. At the begin-ning of the Conquest they thought that the old and new deities might be compatible but they very soon discovered that Christian priests were talking about the exclusive truth of their own beliefs.

The colonization that followed brought about fundamental changes in the religious panorama, although there was a rapid process of incorpora-tion and adaptation. Catholic Mendicant Orders (mainly Franciscans, Dominicans and Augustinians) had a central role in the evange-lization of the Indians. Millions of natives were lightly converted to Christianity by a few hun-dred priests and friars. As in other historical examples, the new gods and deities (including the Virgin and the saints) replaced the old divini-ties. Furthermore, many worship sites witnessed the mere replacement of old idols by new deities (with the Virgin Mary of Guadalupe from the Tepeyac and the Christ of Chalma being the most paradigmatic though certainly not the only instances). There was also an intense process of replacing deities with Patron Saints in every community. Christianity became a central element in the life of indigenous peoples, as it was among the Spaniards. Thus, religion occupied a fundamental place in the daily life of settlers in New Spain (later called Mexico).

Three essential characteristics of religion in colonial times determined the role of religion in the centuries that followed:

(1) The concentration of the Church in very specific regions (Center and West) of the country generated scarce pastoral care and a type of Catholicism that was centered on ritualism rather than doctrine.

(2) The subsequent development of popular Catholicism with a markedly autonomous and at times anticlerical tendency.

(3) Religion was under the control and management of the State – another common feature of the Pre-Hispanic and colonial eras that would determine, from my point of view, the place that institutionalized religion would occupy in the future. Just as in the Aztec or Inca world, where priests were part of the power structure and ensured the reproduction of their 'cosmovision,' thereby replicating the central power of the Tlatoani[3] and of the ruling caste, Patronage led to the integration of the Church into the State during the colonial period. The Church was a branch of the colonial administration, and the Crown was entitled to intervene in the Church's internal affairs in the Americas. Evidence of this lies in the fact that if historians wish to consult documents on the colonial Latin American Church they have to go to Seville's Indies Archives – not the Vatican – where all the documentation relating to the colonial administration is located. The Catholic Church in the Americas, ruled by the kings of Spain, was thus part of the socio-political and administrative network by means of which the Crown ruled over Spaniards, creoles, *mestizos* and the other castes that populated the continent.

POPULAR RELIGION AND SOCIO-POLITICAL IMPACT

The result of this historical process in Mexico is a type of religiosity broadly called 'popular religion.' This form of religiosity is, to a certain extent, the most important manifestation of religion in the country because it encompasses the vast majority of Mexicans and is found not only in Catholicism but also among Evangelicals, Traditionalists and members of non-Christian religions.

The concept of 'popular religion' has many meanings, depending on the cultural area even in the same religion. In France, for example, 'according to a well established custom, those who say "popular religion" in general appeal to the living, the "sensitive" the "festive" practices (in particular the four seasons of life) the popular beliefs that are heterodox or archaic, the faith of the common people, the cult of intercessors, the magico-religious gestures, the superstitions' (Lambert 1985: 16). 'Popular' in English also refers to something widespread and widely followed, but in the case of Mexico and Latin America the term refers to the religion of the lower classes, the masses or, as the French say, 'le petit peuple.' We should be very careful, then, about how we use the concept and the kind of reality to which it refers. In any case, French scholars have discussed at length the meaning of the concept and its components. Unfortunately, the knowledge and analysis emerging from different schools of thought about popular religion are unevenly disseminated. Different approaches to the same subject often converge in the end but only after many years. For example, a chapter about magico-popular religion by the Chilean sociologist of religion, Cristián Parker (2006), outlines four components of a theoretical approach to present-day popular religion: (1) Transcending 'ecclesio-centrism' and considering communal mysticism, (2) Understanding the religion-magic continuum, (3) Understanding the creativity of the religious subject, and (4) Situating the new syncretisms in the context of globalizing culture. Parker stresses the need to place the focus 'on practices in respect of actors in existential situation, not just the situation of institutions' and 'the analysis of religious phenomena from the point of view of the subject': not as 'the passive consumers of religious beliefs and rituals' (Parker 2006: 65, 68).

In fact, some scholars had already emphasized the need to understand the capacity of the masses to produce popular religion. As Danièle Hervieu-Léger (1986: 134) put it, quoting Yves Lambert's book on Limerzel:

> The premeditated actions, the deliberate strategies, the system of references of faithful Catholics, have a function which is not confined to accompanying the practices by translating and legitimating them. The Christian masses have the capacity to produce, to assimilate, to select and to reinterpret the system of references elaborated by religious professionals, in keeping with the concrete conditions in which they try to maintain or improve their situation.

Parker's (2006: 60) main argument is that 'new forms of religious expressions are breathing new life into magical or popular practices which, according to "scientistic" opinion, should have disappeared by the middle of the last century.' Parker affirms the 'limits of Western rationalism' based in the works of four classical authors (Troeltsch, Weber, Durkheim and Mauss). The 'new' approach, although very pertinent and useful concerning contemporary magical beliefs, does not seem to take into account a number of advances in Western sociology in the latter half of the twentieth century concerning popular religion (see González Martínez 2002). In any case, ideas tend to converge after some years. The question is how – and how far – to apply them. At the same time, the capacity to produce, assimilate, select and translate the official religious system varies according to every particular national or regional experience.

In Mexico, popular religiosity also has a social and political impact that has rarely been explored. Of particular relevance are the many different ways in which the various ecclesiastical and political forces of the country interpret popular religiosity. These interpretations have produced multiple versions of what constitutes the 'essence' of culture and national identity. Constitutional articles and legislation in matters of religion are a direct consequence of this way of thinking about national culture, of which religious belief is a central component.

Consequently, defining the extent to which the Mexican or Latin American people are religious, what the characteristics of that religiosity are, and how these beliefs translate into socio-political behaviors is an essential way of assessing how much religion counts for in these societies. In this respect, it is of capital importance to ascertain how deeply Christianity has permeated Latin-American countries in the last 500 years, and how capable the Catholic Church has been of influencing legislation and public policies in this region.

The notion of popular religion refers us back to the distinction between an allegedly 'educated' religion and a popular religion that is more oriented towards ritualism than towards doctrinal orthodoxy. From this perspective, popular religion would be the price to pay – as well as the gap to close – in order to complete the process of adopting another culture. Furthermore, we employ this distinction to differentiate the religion professed by the upper classes from that professed by the masses. In the case of Latin America, this would be the same as separating the religion of the white people from that of culturally assimilated *mestizos* and impoverished and socially marginalized Indians and African-Americans. In Mexico, the term 'popular religion' refers to the religion of Indians and the many underprivileged *mestizos*. This is why, on occasion, popular religion also applies to the piety of ordinary people, as manifested in traditional ceremonies and festivities.

Furthermore, some commentators consider that popular religion has become a mechanism of resistance and, for others, a way of integrating into the culture and the dominant religion. The extensive development of confraternities and religious festivities in Colonial Spanish America illustrates the ambiguity and ambivalence of this process. In recent decades, the notion that popular religion was a mechanism of resistance was supported by a social conception of Christianity linked to 'Liberation Theology.' Inasmuch as this movement was openly repressed by the Holy See, the idea that popular religion was equivalent to resistance to political or ecclesiastical power flourished among many followers of that school of thought. Understanding popular religion as a form of resistance, considering the autonomy and even anti-clerical standing of popular religious practices, has given way to new interpretations of the phenomenon.

Therefore, popular religion is not only the religion of the lower classes but is also the faith professed by many who are struggling to recover partial control of salvation goods. However, it is not always possible to talk about a religious pole that is completely separate and autonomous from the clergy or ecclesiastical hierarchy. Indeed, this phenomenon is much more complex than that. For instance, the development of Catholic confraternities in the colonial period was the result of a specific institutional initiative by the Catholic hierarchy – therefore not an example of secular autonomy. These confraternities were often the most important means for lay people to demonstrate their commitment to the Church. Other more 'ecclesiastical' manifestations of popular religiosity, such as pilgrimages, can in some circumstances produce expressions of strong autonomy.

Finally, some scholars consider that popular religion is incompatible with secularization processes because it is frequently regarded as a vestige or residue of past beliefs or old regimes, thus constituting an obstacle to society's process of rationalization. In fact, the process of eradicating religious superstitions and endless festivities was initiated by the enlightened clergy of Spanish America in the last third of the eighteenth century. Leaving aside recent questioning of secularization, historians and sociologists can agree on the need for demystifying the Christianization of the Western world as a finished process because 'especially for entire masses, the forced process of de-Christianization reveals that in fact Christianization never really took place or that it occurred in combination with all sorts of beliefs and pagan practices, thus weakening religious observance [mass attendance] which was, anyway, much less unanimous, at least in certain regions, than might be thought' (Hervieu-Léger 1986: 104).

Could we think that this myth of the Christianization of medieval Europe has its counterpart in the myth of the Christianization of colonial Latin America? Actually, the difference between the two is very wide. For instance, the Christianity that arrived in Spanish America was reformed and utopian. In addition, the social context was different because of the relationship between Christianity and religions that were powerful military forces. However, it is important to question the alleged and almost absolute moral and cultural control that the Catholic Church exercised over believers as well as its social and political influence over institutional affairs insofar as it might help us to explain the early dissemination and wide spread of anticlericalism and laicism in most Latin-American nations.

From this point of view, it is important to ask whether the religiosity of Latin Americans – whom the Holy See has sought to identify with Roman Catholicism – remains central to culture and national identity in the twenty-first century in a region where a secular tradition has been rooted at least since the nineteenth century and where pluralism is on the increase. This question has become the focus of a contemporary debate regarding what type of legal regime should prevail and what role religions should play.

RELIGIOUS PLURALISM AND THE PARADIGM OF MODERNITY

The notion of religious pluralism is relatively new to Latin America. The history of a monopolistic Church, scarce religious freedom and legal, social and cultural discrimination against minority religions has marked the region. The trend of religious pluralism has been strengthening since the first decades of the twentieth century, particularly after World War II. Figures fluctuate, of course, from one country to another. While Mexico and Argentina were the most Catholic countries in 2000 with 88 per cent of their population belonging to that Church, others had lower percentages, such as Brazil (74 per cent), Chile (70 per cent) and Cuba (47 per cent) (Hagopian 2005: Table 1). Although sources and data are not always reliable, the undeniable fact is that religious pluralism has become a reality in Latin America.

According to American scholar Frances Hagopian (2005: 1):

> Today, the [Catholic] Church faces intensifying religious competition and pluralism within these once hegemonic Catholic societies that threatens the distinctive identity of Latin America as a Catholic region. Self-identified Protestants now comprise roughly one-fifth of the population of the region, about one in ten Latin Americans identify with no religion at all, and only about 70 per cent of the population is nominally Roman Catholic.

In fact, a close look will show us that the challenges are not only for the Catholic Church, that is, for Catholic bishops and clergy, but also for traditional Protestant or reformed churches in the shape of competition coming from new Pentecostal or other Christian religious organizations or simply from 'common believers,' that is, popular religiosity.

Religious pluralism also forces us to take a new look at old phenomena such as conversions, intolerance, discrimination and social coexistence as well as at widely used and normally unquestionable concepts such as modernity and secularization. It also obliges us to adopt a different angle of observation on the role of social and individual actors, since the balance between people and communities differs from one culture to another.

Some years ago I proposed that popular religion, Catholicism and religious dissent or religious pluralism form a triangle which cannot be avoided in the analysis of the religious life of Latin America (Blancarte 2000a). More importantly, I emphasized that a conceptual framework had not yet been devised for explaining the specific forms taken by religious life in Latin America and how they relate to other similar expressions worldwide as well as to general processes, such as secularization. My main argument was that the original problem probably lay in the fact that the history and sociology of Protestantism and other forms of religious dissent or pluralism in Latin America had revolved around the paradigm of modernity, as outlined by Max Weber and Ernst Troeltsch in their writings on the relation between Protestantism and the modern world. My criticism was directed at those whose

analysis of Protestantism made the same mistake as others had done in studying Catholicism, that is, 'to suppose that there is a single model, from which all the other manifestations are only deviations.' From that 'evolutionist' perspective, Latin America would undergo a process which had occurred earlier in 'Anglo' society. By way of a 'cultural radiation' the United States of America had provided models for the 'protagonists of change' (Martin 1990: 278).

In fact, most scholars of pluralism in Latin America have explained some of the backwardness in Latin American societies in terms of a religious monopoly and the scarcity of free thinking, liberal and possibly Protestant thought. From this point of view, modern economic, social and political structures were delayed by the colonial heritage in which Catholicism was linked to the old Spanish regime. But, as I further explained, there is actually a more complex relationship between popular religion and religious pluralism in most of Latin America that is reflected in the massive expansion of evangelicalism and particularly Pentecostalism. The main idea behind this argument is that Protestantism – or what we identified as Protestantism – in Latin America does not follow the same path as Protestantism in Europe or North America. In fact, it is a form of religious dissidence that has to be explained in its own terms according to a model that does not necessarily follow the pattern of liberal economic, social and political modernization. The social model that links a form of religious evolution (Calvinism or Protestantism) to a precise socio-economic development (capitalism) and to political culture (liberalism) has to be abandoned if we are to understand what is happening in the so called Protestant world in Latin America.

According to the earlier way of thinking, for example, French sociologist Jean-Pierre Bastian (1990: 100–1) considers Protestant societies in Latin America to be societies of ideas, which means, 'privileged associative spaces for the inculcation of modern values and democratic practices.' In this way, Protestants, freemasons, liberals, spiritualists and free thinkers would allegedly have banded together in political clubs, lodges and assembly halls to combat the corporate and authoritarian society that had one of its pillars in Catholicism. Up to this point the paradigm of modernity seems to be useful as long as it follows the contours of a secularization process which translates into the strengthening of individual conscience, the weakening of ecclesiastical control and the formation of free spaces for those who do not think like conventional believers. However, Latin America does not offer a parallel to the paradigm of the European model of Protestantism in, for example, the consolidation of a class or social group that explains this dissident religious thought. In other words, there is nothing in the Latin American region to prove the existence of something similar to what Max Weber (1921) discussed, namely, a social group imbued by 'worldly asceticism' and economic development, or the emergence of a middle class influenced by religious individualism.

Departing from this position, Bastian has difficulty in explaining, for example, the geography of Protestant societies that emerged from the modern economy in the nineteenth century in Latin America. The author, one of the most insightful specialists on Protestantism and religious dissent in Latin America, claimed that 'the protestant movement was implanted and developed in Mexico, in pioneer and basically rural regions far away from power centers, with a booming agro-exporting economy' (Bastian 1994: 115–17). And concerning the social background of those Protestants, Bastian also stated that it was about social sectors who were in transition, whose dissident religious interests coincided with the vindication of regional autonomy and of a politically liberal culture, characteristics of rural environments that were on their way towards modernization and of new urban sectors.

My point here is that, rather than trying to explain the emergence of Protestantism in Latin America in terms of economic causes, it is worth analyzing the political and social reasons (external and internal) that gave rise to a distinctive geography of religious pluralism. For instance, Bastian gives other reasons for

the emergence of these societies of ideas in the nineteenth century, such as the defense of regional autonomy which, in turn, is linked to the pre-eminence of liberal groups defending a Federalist organization of Mexico. 'It was not the foreign missionaries,' he claims, 'who spread Protestantism in these rural zones, but Mexican Protestant ministers who were at the same time active liberals (most frequently freemasons).' His argument is, therefore, that 'Protestantism was essentially a way to create, in some regions, associative networks that would carry a liberal protest with both a religious and political content' (Bastian 1994: 118–19).

In other words, it is the link with liberal groups and other dissident ideological associations against the prevailing authoritarian structure that gives rise to an incipient 'Protestantism' and not economic forces or the development of emerging groups or classes. Rather than trying to produce a geography based on the effects of a modern economy, then, it is necessary to look for other sources of 'Protestantism' in Mexico and Latin America: the scope for political conflict between the newly independent nations and the Holy See; the political bonds and networks established by all kind of dissidents; and the weaknesses in Catholic ecclesiastical structure which were replaced by more effective alternatives in terms of socio-religious organization. In other words, we have to examine the places that the Catholic Church could not cover because of the historical shortage of priests and the relative advantages (in education, for example, or in the appropriation of a mutually binding identity) that flowed from membership in a different religious organization. Secondly, as a result of the links evident in other politically dissident groups, Protestantism really appears in the nineteenth century more as a beneficiary than as a generator of political liberalism. Latin American Protestantism is not, therefore, the driving force of a modern mentality but its beneficiary.

Finally, these considerations enable us to raise a question about the 'Protestant' character of the religious dissenting associations of the nineteenth century. Up to what point can it be established that these associations were religiously and culturally different from the Catholic ones? Several specialists tend to make nineteenth-century Latin American Protestantism an 'ideal' model that may never have existed in reality. Moreover, this supposedly 'classical' model of Protestantism, imbued with democratic modernity, is compared to twentieth-century modernity, which is emotional, Pentecostal and fundamentalist, and integrated into the practices and values of popular Catholic culture (Bastian 1994: 300). Nineteenth-century Protestantism is thereby transformed into a kind of 'paradise lost' in the immensity of the culture and popular religiosity of the Latin American masses. And since religious dissent is becoming more and more extensive and, as such, closer to popular religion, it tends to be disqualified because of its closeness to a corporatist and authoritarian culture.

The analysis of the different Latin American 'Protestantisms' of the nineteenth century therefore requires some additional analysis in terms of its relationship to popular religiosity. Just as Catholicism penetrated sixteenth-century pre-Hispanic American society, transforming itself into a religion similar to, but distinct from, European Catholicism, so Protestantism adapted to a corporatist and authoritarian culture in nineteenth and twentieth-century Latin America. It thereby transformed itself into something different from its European or North American origins. At the same time, the authoritarianism of contemporary Latin American Protestantism cannot be explained by endogenous factors alone. European and especially North American Protestantism has a conservative and authoritarian streak. For this reason, it is essential to avoid automatically identifying Catholicism with corporatist and authoritarian culture. Not everything Catholic is traditional and 'pre-modern.' There is in Latin America, as in Europe, an open Catholicism that is not always opposed to 'modernity.'

It is an undeniable fact that popular Protestantisms and the currently popular Pentecostalisms come from a corporatist and authoritarian culture that is present in Latin American societies, but they do not necessarily originate in popular Catholicism, which seems to be equally affected by its social context. After all, as has been noted, popular religion can also be a religion of resistance, both liberating and revolutionary. Catholicism is on occasions less corporatist and authoritarian than it is usually portrayed; and traditional Protestantism is less liberating and democratic than some would like to imagine.

The key to the interpretation of these religious phenomena may reside – as we argued above – in the elimination or at least the relativization of the modernity paradigm. It is not by contrasting or comparing the advances in Catholicism and Protestantism (or the rest of the religious groups in Mexico) with modernity that one can discover their internal characteristics, social impact and influence on the future of the Latin American region. Actually, Bastian himself has moved from a definition of 'ambiguous modernity' to a definition of 'peripheral modernity' as well as to that of 'particular modernity':

> New religious movements reconstitute the bond of the community, opposing the endogenous and exogenous forces that destroy it. They are powerful movements of affirmation of a dignity denied to the poor and the excluded. When religious demands are transformed into political demands, the way is open for a new social community actor to reach global society; and these demands insert him into a particular modernity which refuses to copy the western model of the sovereign individual because it does not want to eliminate corporatist solidarity as a fundamental basis of social action in Latin America (Bastian 1997: 214).

Another distinguished specialist, Jean-Paul Willaime (1999), differs from Bastian in claiming that Pentecostalism can legitimately be considered a form of Protestantism, though emotional and with a charismatic type of leadership, in churches that are profoundly intertwined with local culture. This argument departs from the idea that Protestantism must necessarily be associated with progressivism.

This type of reasoning is certainly relevant, in that it sets out the problem of the specificity of religious expressions in their cultural environment. Some other authors, such as David Martin (1990), touched on this problem by referring to the 'Americanization of

Latin American religion' or to the 'Latin Americanization of American religion.' However, the modernity paradigm remains at the center of this type of explanation. Willaime (1999: 24) claims, for instance: 'Pentecostalism is modern when it legitimizes the rupture with traditional customs, it is post-modern because of its capacity to manage the social and cultural fractures of modernity, it is pre-modern as it re-enchants the world.' If a religious group can be at the same time pre-modern, modern and post-modern, perhaps it is time to reconsider the concept of modernity.

This example also shows that it is relevant to decide whether Latin American Pentecostalism forms part of a Protestant tradition. But it is even more important to know when it displays distinctive traits that make it a unique movement, different from other movements, in spite of references to them. In any case, for all the above reasons, Latin American Protestantism or Pentecostalism should also be helpful in the analysis of other forms of Protestantism in the developed world by holding up a mirror to them.

In Latin America, as a consequence of the historical presence of the Catholic Church, religious pluralism has been perceived – even by some scholars – as a problem or a threat to local culture. In various cases, fuelled by Catholic propaganda, anthropologists have considered any foreign and particularly American missionary activity as part of an 'imperialist' project to subvert the cultural identity of Latin American people. In the State of Chiapas, Mexico, for example, before the 1980s, the activities of the Summer Linguistic Institute (Instituto Lingüístico de Verano), which concentrated on the translation of the Bible into various indigenous languages, were perceived as an attempt to introduce divisive American Protestant values into integrated Catholic Indian communities. Religious pluralism was seen as an external interference that would damage the integrity of the indigenous communities and as a threat to their culture, thereby ignoring not only the authoritarian aspects of that culture but also the internal tendencies towards change. The explosion of 'Protestantism' in places like Chiapas,

Guatemala, Bolivia or Ecuador, particularly among indigenous people, has led researchers to the discovery of very important internal factors that explain that growth.[4]

Moreover, some specialists now insist on the fact that 'the religious supply' is not only part of a market of faith options, but must also be understood 'in a context of power relations that mark the way in which religious discourses are interpreted,' something that runs in clear contradiction to the functional analysis that explains conversion as a restitution of lost social or individual equilibrium (Hernández Castillo 2001 quoted in Rivera Farfán 2005: 36). According to Hernández Castillo, the theoretical debate about Protestantism is caught in the same epistemological trap of general anthropological theory: that is, 'the mediation between a systemic analysis that presents individuals as victims of social forces and of historical processes and a methodological individualism that assumes a free individual, whose destiny depends on his rational options' (Hernández Castillo 1992 quoted in Rivera Farfán 2005: 42).

In any case, one of the conclusions of these works is that 'religious discourse does not lead to passive and defenseless subjects or culturally weakened or inert communities, but to a population that reinterprets the discourse and adapts it to their circumstances in historical times and specific social contexts' (Durán 1988: vii). So, as we stated in the previous section, the role of the active social subject – individual or communal – becomes essential in any explanation of the growth of religious diversity. For the same reason, religious differentiation in the case of Chiapas, according to most specialists, is basically the expression of social conflicts and a way to undermine internal communitarian authoritarianism.

Pluralism in Latin America has mainly been a phenomenon associated with conversion rather than with extension. In that sense, besides recognizing the role of the social subject, other explanations can help to make sense of the movement of millions of people to other religions. Some are related to the inadequacies of the Catholic Church's apparatus, particularly the incapacity to give a quick response to new religious needs. But there are also the organizational and doctrinal novelties of other creeds:

> ... adaptation of biblical discourse to the reality of social marginality; revalorization and practice of cultural traditions like language or music; social recognition through participation in group activities; quest for power and authority by means of the creation of new indigenous leaderships or the creation of alternative spaces for group or collective cohesion (Rivera Farfán 2005: 49).

In the end, the new religious pluralism of Latin America does not reflect an upsurge of individualism but a reaffirmation of a new communitarianism. As Bastian (1997: 214) claims, 'this neo-communitarianism belongs to the long tradition of a region where the community still precedes the individual; he does not exist without his insertion in a collective actor that allows him to define himself.'

It seems to me that this interpretation can give many clues to other religious expressions in a globalized world. Between the individual as architect of his destiny and the subject as an actor – both personal and inserted into a collectivity – Catholics, Protestants, Pentecostals and other believers find a way to articulate their identity and participation. In doing so, they reinterpret their beliefs and actions on a daily basis. But they also do it in a larger framework of power relations in which the individual conscience, the Churches or religious groups and the State, struggle to define their society and the scope of their freedoms.

SOCIAL SCIENCES BUILDING AND CULTURAL MIRRORS: THE CASE OF SECULARITY AND LAICITY

Paradigms, theories and concepts in the social sciences are conditioned in many cases by cultural and linguistic areas of influence. If Mexico and Latin America are to avoid functioning as a distorted mirror for others, it becomes important to understand the context in which a concept is produced and used in a specific cultural space. Some concepts are simply strange to certain cultures or understood differently even though they explain similar phenomena. This is the case with the concept of 'laicity' (from the French 'laïcité,' and translated into Spanish as 'laicidad'), and to a certain extent with the similar, but not identical concept, of secularization. The neologism 'laïcité,' which was unknown until recently in the English-speaking world, was used for the first time in France in 1871. From there, it made its way into other Latin countries such as Italy, Spain and of course the countries of Latin America mainly through liberal and freemasonic circles. The word 'laicity' does not exist in English. The closest term would be 'secularity.' Originally the term made reference in French administration to the secular public school ('école laïque' and 'laïcité de l'école'), which was devoid of religious instruction. Later the term became identified in Latin countries with a political system where the State and public affairs gained autonomy from religious institutions.

The term 'lay' comes from the Greek word 'laikós,' meaning 'of the people,' and it led to 'laic' in French and to 'laico' in Spanish. The term was originally used in reference to faithful Christians, making a distinction between them and the members of the clergy who control sacraments – deacons, priests and prelates or bishops. It was not until the nineteenth century that the term 'lay' made reference to a social space beyond ecclesiastical control. In other words, in Mexico and most of Latin America, 'laico' implied opposition to clerical power; and it eventually came to signify 'anticlerical' as a consequence of the civil wars between liberals and conservatives. Until the middle of that century, the word that indicated the transfer of someone or something from the religious sphere to the civil realm had been 'secularization' (secularización). For example, in many countries decrees were issued to 'secularize' cemeteries. But secularizing also meant the transfer of something or someone who was under the jurisdiction of a religious order to the secular structure of the diocese. Thus, for example, between the sixteenth and eighteenth centuries, many so-called 'doctrines' or religious organizations around convents of regular orders (Franciscans, Dominicans, and Augustinians) were 'secularized' and passed under the direct control of bishops in a parochial structure. That was part of a traditional division in the Catholic world between members of religious orders, who are not always presbyters and secular priests (that is of the *sæculum*, who live in this world). The term *sæculum* also gave rise to the Spanish word '*seglar*,' which is equivalent to 'lay' in its connotation of a member of the Church not belonging to the clergy.

In any case, it is clear that the words 'lay' and 'secular' come from the religious – and specifically Christian – world. But their meaning and application has varied according to time and circumstances. The 'lay' people are then the members of the Christian Church, the Christian people who are guided by the clerics and pastors. Nevertheless, the process of secularization has come to mean something that is no longer the transfer of things and persons from the administration of religious orders to parochial and diocesan administration. It now means a complex process of social differentiation, privatization of religion and separation between the social, political, economic and religious spheres. As a result, the 'secular' and the 'lay' are mainly understood as something different from, and even opposed to, the religious. 'Laicity' in Latin countries and the 'secular' in English-speaking cultural areas have, since the middle of the nineteenth century, applied originally to the creation of a temporal space which is independent from religious influence. The idea of preserving freedom of conscience has also led to a relative 'privatization' of religion and to its consequent marginality from the public sphere.[5] This autonomy of action of temporal power was positively associated with liberal ideas and social needs in, for example, matters of scientific development.

Certainly, differences between the terms 'lay' and 'secular' were not exclusively linguistic. In Latin countries, social reality reflected the absolute hegemony or the practical monopoly of the Catholic Church. That is why laicity's struggle to create an autonomous temporal space almost inevitably ends in fierce fighting against the dominant ecclesiastical institution. On the other hand, in English-speaking countries, religious plurality and competition – with no hegemonic ecclesiastical institutions – is more common. The 'laicity' of political institutions is not forged in the heat of battle against a single dominant Church, but is constructed in a parallel way and more or less at the same time as the secularization process of social structures.

The fact that laicity and secularization are concepts sometimes used in equivocal ways in different cultural areas – and they may not even exist in others – should not mean that scholars cannot identify the social phenomena behind them. In other words, if the word 'laicity' is not used in England or the United States of America it does not mean that those countries have not experienced certain forms of laicity. Similarly, secularization is a social phenomenon that has affected some or many aspects of all countries. In the case of Latin America, it is evident that, even if many countries display a high degree of secularization in their social structures, the process of laicization of political institutions has lagged behind because of the influence of the Catholic Church. That is why defining secularization and laicity is a prerequisite for understanding any contribution to the sociology of religion from the perspective of Mexico and Latin America.

MODERNIZATION, SECULARIZATION AND WESTERNIZATION

The theory of secularization is probably the most developed and, at the same time, the most controversial theoretical idea in the sociology of religion. One of the strongest criticisms of the paradigm of secularization is that, even if it could be applied to the social reality of economically developed countries in Western Europe and North America, it was inapplicable to the underdeveloped countries of the global South. Some critics contend that the model of secularization explains religious tendencies only in Western Europe but not in

North America because of the high level of religious influence in the social life of the USA. Of course, it all depends on definitions and on the components that we include in them: social differentiation, individualization, privatization, worldliness, etc. (see Tschannen 1991). Nevertheless, since the revision of the theory some 30 years ago, many sociologists have regarded the demise, disappearance and survival or revival of religion as the key to explaining secularization and have failed to observe not only the ups and downs of manifestations of religion in society but also the role of religion in individual and communal, private and public, life. In fact, the idea of the demise of religion was not even advanced by the founders of sociology and the sociology of religion. On the contrary, Émile Durkheim's (1985) book on the elementary forms of religion tried to prove that as long as we have society we will have collective beliefs. And although Max Weber (1921) discussed 'Entzauberung' (the end of a magical world) – a term which has been translated as 'rationalization' – he never argued that religion (not magic) was disappearing. On the contrary, he demonstrated the connection between certain forms of religiosity (Protestantism and particularly Calvinism) and modernity.

In general terms, it is also true that, until recently, most scholars have avoided the discussion of the 'theory of secularization' in the context of underdeveloped countries. Specialists in the field of religion probably work under the impression that the secularization process mainly concerns developed regions and that Southern or developing countries are the realm of magic, spirituality and religion. In doing so, once more, scholars are linking secularization to economic and social development, that is, to modernization and urbanization. To some extent, this is the case with recent works where the process of secularization is associated with 'existential security' (Norris and Inglehart 2004). Consequently, the expectation is that the countries that used to be called 'Third World' countries would have to achieve a certain degree of economic development in order to undergo at least a degree of secularization. In fact, as we will see in the case

of Mexico, secularization and what we will call the 'laicization' process can sometimes operate independently of economic factors. This means that the paradigm of modernization linked to economic development should not necessarily be tied to the process of societal secularization. In other words, the processes of secularization and of laicization can take place independently of the economic factors that undoubtedly accompanied their development in the North. This is consistent with the idea of many scholars, such as Casanova (1994) and Norris and Inglehart (2004), that there are multiple expressions of modernity and multiple forms of secularization.

This last point has consequences for the scope and ambitions of the so-called 'theory of secularization.' Indeed, either a theory has the capacity to explain the described phenomenon in the entire world, or its range of applicability is limited and questionable. If the theory of secularization can explain what happens only in Western Europe, North America and some other Western developed countries – but fails to do so in non-Western, developing or less developed countries – the pertinence and usefulness of the 'theory' are compromised. In fact, the earliest questioning of the theory came from the simple observation of what was happening in many areas of the world outside Western developed countries; and it also helped to reconsider the religious developments in Europe and North America. Thus, the redefinition of the concept of secularization and of 'laicity' or 'laicization' has emerged from a real attempt to make the theory general. As scholars have noted, there is a difference, for example, between understanding secularization as privatization and as social differentiation (see Casanova 1994). In the first case, the reappearance of religion in public life has been observed not only in the South but also in Western countries to some extent. Although the privatization of religion has clearly taken place since the sixteenth century, this has not necessarily obstructed the social role of religion. In the second case, the reappraisal of the role of religion in the public sphere does not mean that religion is still the main framework for the daily life of ordinary people in those countries. Part of the problem may be that, in the eyes of some scholars, the secularization process has been understood in relation to Churches or even individuals, instead of looking at their structural social framework of action. Nevertheless, it is the social structure that defines and frames people's behavior as much as the choices of persons and groups. Secular thinking – in developed and underdeveloped countries alike – amounts in most cases to the basic point of reference in a world where different spheres (economics, politics, culture, etc.) work largely independently of each other and where religion is only one of those spheres and is certainly not a comprehensive frame of meaning.

At the same time we need to be aware of the trajectory of the so-called 'theory of secularization' and of the political uses made of it. Indeed, from the 1930s to the 1970s, a basic misunderstanding led to the idea that one of the main causes – if not 'the' cause – of underdevelopment in many countries in, for example, the Arab world was the lack of a process of secularization similar to the one experienced in the Christian world, where freedom of conscience, separation of Church and State and the autonomy of knowledge had supposedly led to scientific and technological progress. The inevitable conclusion was that the rest of the world should either follow the same path or be condemned to underdevelopment. The reaction that led to the fall of the secular nationalist regimes in Muslim countries beginning in the 1970s was one of the facts that made scholars realize that there was something wrong with their theoretical model. Conceiving Islam more as a culture and a civilization than as a religion, in the narrow and Western secular sense, some countries and political movements began to defend a path towards modernization that would not include the classical model of secularization and its separation of spheres. The idea of a 'clash of civilizations' that Samuel Huntington developed in the early 1990s recapitulated many of the Arab and Muslim intellectual arguments and reactions to the West. And it is not yet clear how secularization, in the sense of rationalization, worldliness and social

differentiation has had an impact on their own development in, for example, Egypt, Iran or Pakistan.

What variables come into play when we define secularization? Perhaps we should make a distinction between modernization, modernity and Westernization. 'Modernization' would be the general process of economic and urban development; 'modernity' the era that we all live in following the development that occurred in Western societies after the Renaissance; and 'Westernization' the process of spreading that model to different parts of the world. That would allow us to examine more carefully the relation between modernization and secularization. Is secularization intrinsic or extrinsic to the modernization process? We could affirm that secularization is intrinsic to modernization, in the sense that secularization is the manifestation of modernity in the religious realm, although this does not mean that the secularization process should always and everywhere appear in the same manner. In fact, modernity has had a differential impact on societies because the extent and impact of Westernization has been diverse. Thus, the impact of the conquest of some regions of the American continent by Spaniards and Portuguese – although part of the Westernization process – was different from the impact of the British colonization of North America. The same can be said of how the relative Westernization of Middle Eastern and North African countries differed essentially from that of Japan or of India. The result of that process (of Westernization and, in some cases, secularization) should not be understood as more or less religion but as more or less social differentiation or more or less worldliness. The logical conclusion is that secularization theory helps us to explain what is happening everywhere, but that does not mean that secularity and modernity are expressed in a uniform way. It is precisely as a result of Westernization that certain forms of secularization were introduced into countries that had not known much economic development. The introduction of liberal thought into Latin America, for example, was not due to the rise of a social class or a social system that was pushing for reforms. Instead, for historical reasons, popular religiosity was inclined towards anticlericalism and support for the liberal measures proposed by elites close to the philosophical Enlightenment. Consequently, the relative secularization (or laicization) of political institutions was a process arising more from political considerations than from economic or social development. In fact, in many cases, it was the political process of institutional modernization that induced the process of economic development and social differentiation. In Mexico, for example, the liberal reforms that introduced freedom of belief and worship in the mid-nineteenth century, dis-entailment of Church property, separation of Church and State, secular education, the creation of a civil register, civil marriage, secularization of cemeteries, freedom of trade and speech, among other measures, created the basis for a modern lay state and economy. This surge of a so-called 'Estado Laico,' widespread in Latin countries such as Italy, France, Spain and Latin-America, is fundamental to any explanation of the distinctive development of secularization in a context where the Catholic Church was hegemonic.

Before Latin American countries gained their independence from Spain and Portugal, the Churches had established a relationship with temporal powers, as represented by 'the Crown.' The Catholic Church did not oppose these powers, as it had set up a co-operative rather than a competitive relationship with them; and once the institution called 'patronage' became customary, this relationship became one of actual subordination.[6] Functions did not distinguish between churchmen and laymen. For example, the Archbishop of Mexico City would often substitute for or replace the Viceroy of New Spain (Mexico) when he was absent; and civil authorities could intervene in the Church's internal affairs. Enlightened regalism strengthened the trend that eventually led to State interventionism. The Bourbon Reforms of Charles III (1716–1788) increased the Crown's control over the Church (and its finances) in the Americas.

Concerning the secularization and laicization process, it is important to stress that the key to understanding Mexico's type of religiosity is the weak institutional control that has been patent throughout the history of the Catholic Church in Latin America. This is partly because of the endemic scarcity of priests, a fact that also accounts for the strength of popular religion.

The Catholic Church was part of the colonial State in Mexico until the War of Independence (1810–1821), but in many Latin American countries it continued to be part of the state (more culturally than formally speaking) throughout most of the nineteenth century. The current influence and prerogatives of the Catholic Church in many countries of the region can be explained by the survival of this colonial heritage, in which the Catholic Church and religion in general legitimated political power. The attempts of Latin American States, including the Mexican State, to control Church matters by intervening in them are a direct consequence of the so-called Royal Patronage and are still prevalent in most Latin American countries. The secular State (where it emerged) was conceived as a function of necessary interventionism rather than a separation of ecclesiastical affairs and public life. In other words, the creation of a secular or lay State was not preceded by the secularization of society and did not preclude the political use of religion. In fact, in most cases, formal separation of Church and State in Latin American countries in the nineteenth and twentieth centuries did not put a stop to an informal Patronage by which the Catholic Church continued to play a social and political role.

LAICITY: HOW TO ARRIVE AT A UNIVERSAL CONCEPT

Using Latin American laicism as a mirror to the rest of the world can also help to establish a general concept of laicity which would be inclusive enough to explain the phenomenon everywhere. The problem is that until recently the concept of laicity has been closely linked to the French experience, that is, to the ideas of Republicanism and the separation of Church and State. Yet, a close observation of the phenomenon shows that, even in the case of France where the word was invented and applied in 1871 to the new public secular school (*laïcité de l'école*), the separation of Church and State was not achieved until 1905. This shows that there can be laicity even where there is no formal separation. In fact, this is true even today of most cases in Europe. In Northern European countries the dominant tradition is one where Lutheranism or Protestantism became the official or national Church, under the hegemony and protection of princes or of new States. In Eastern and Central Europe, for its part, most countries in the Orthodox tradition display a close understanding between civil and ecclesiastical powers in close association with a nationalist perspective as in Greece or Russia. Nevertheless, certain forms of laicity exist in many of these countries with Protestant or Orthodox traditions. If the existence of a Republic and the Separation of State and religion are not the most important factors explaining laicization, the question is whether laicity revolves, instead, around another factor, namely, the source of legitimization of the political institutions of the State.

I have defined 'laicity' elsewhere (Blancarte 2000b: 124) as 'a social regime whose political institutions are no longer legitimated by the sacred or religious institutions but by popular sovereignty or popular will.' The idea of a transition from legitimacy obtained through the sacred to a particular form of authority coming from the people helps us to understand that laicity – like democracy – is a process and not a fixed or definitive administrative or political form of institution. There are no societies or political regimes that are absolutely democratic or absolutely secular social and political systems. This also means that in many cases forms of sacralization of power or sanctification of political regimes persist, even in systems that are not strictly religious – such as civil religion.

One of the advantages of defining laicity as a process of transition in forms of legitimacy – from sacred to democratic or based on popular will – is that it explains more clearly the difference between laicity and the separation of Church and State. In fact, many States that are not formally lay or secular establish public policies independently from the doctrines of churches and sustain their legitimacy more by popular will than by any kind of ecclesiastical sanctification.

The criteria for the separation of Church and State are entangled with laicity because most lay States have actually adopted some measures of separation. But there are States that do not implement formal separation (like Norway or Denmark), although their government is democratic and they do not need any sacred legitimation for their political systems. On the other hand, there are formally democratic countries, like Iran, that still experience strong influence from clerics over the definition of their public policies. This distinction is essential to the understanding of most Latin American countries, since some of them are formally lay States whilst remaining under political pressure from the main churches or even under their ideological hegemony.

This broad definition of laicity also enables us to observe how, independently of the legal regime of countries, their States – that is the group of stable political institutions – depend to a greater or lesser extent on the legitimacy flowing from religious institutions. Not even countries like France, Uruguay, China, Mexico or Cuba – which pretend to be formally secular and to have lay States – dispense completely with legitimacy coming from the sacred or from religious institutions.

The Mexican or Latin American mirror has helped to revise the Franco-centric idea of laicity and to arrive at a more global agreement on the main components of the concept. This is how the *Universal Declaration on Laicity in the Twenty-First Century*, written by leading academics from different countries,[7] defined laicity as the harmonization of the three following principles among people from diverse geographical and cultural areas: (1) Respect for freedom of conscience and its individual and collective practice; (2) Autonomy of Politics and Civil Society from particular religious and philosophical norms; and (3) Non-discrimination (direct or indirect) towards human beings.

The Declaration introduced the idea of legitimacy as the key factor in understanding the transition to a new social regime as follows: 'A process of laicization emerges when the State is no longer legitimated by a religion or by a particular philosophy and when all the citizens can discuss peacefully, with equal rights and dignity, about exercising their sovereignty in the use of political will.'

In fact, the social, political and religious landscape of Mexico and Latin America has dramatically changed – especially since World War II – making it even more necessary today to establish lay States. The emergence of dissident religious groups and their growing dissemination throughout Latin America is a clear manifestation of Catholic institutional weakness, the strength of popular religion, increasing social mobility, and the subsequent growth of religious options. Therefore, a future challenge for the region lies in the management of this new diversity, in which tolerance will play a major role, even though that principle does not seem to be among the main values of the region's civil or religious history. Nevertheless, the arrival of religious diversity on a large scale, the increasing awareness of human rights and the mounting democratization of political institutions have been the driving force for a major re-definition of the roles of the Church and the State in Latin America. Thus, even if the Catholic Church has a social and political weight in the region, it cannot prevent this diversification, the secularization of society or the growing laicization of the public sphere. Civic movements for the defense of rights and liberties (for example sexual and reproductive rights) call in question the political and ecclesiastical establishment. The democratic process implies greater scrutiny, transparence and accountability of public institutions. Neither the State nor religious institutions can escape this new logic.

Finally, the Mexican and Latin American mirror poses a major challenge for the sociology of religion in the case of indigenous communities and their own path to development. It is evident that the protection of the rights of Indian communities means recognizing their cosmovision and its refusal to segregate religion into a private sphere but to live it in a communal way, thereby making it difficult to understand the separation of spheres. Unfortunately, inadequate consideration has been given to the ethnic question and its inter-action with laicity. Often what is called 'usos y costumbres' in Mexico, that is, the internal customary laws of the Indians, constitute a big obstacle to the secular vision that guarantees individual freedoms and the right to religious dissidence. This creates unresolved tensions between communities and individuals. In any case, something new is happening in Latin America – diversity, laicity and secularization are producing repercussions for the indigenous communities that live in rural or urban areas. Recent case studies reveal a very complex situation in which Indians live their popular religiosity in a communal way; but at the same time they respect the increasing differentiation of spheres, proposing their own rituals and practices, reinterpreting the doctrine that is offered to them and deciding the limits of religion in the public sphere. It is apparent that the indigenous and African-American worlds have been perceived – correctly, by the way – as having a rather holistic, religious, traditionalistic and emotional cosmovision which is distinct from the individualistic, secular, technical and rational view of the Western world. It is a mistake to think of these worlds (particularly, but not exclusively, in Latin America) as two different, homogeneous, compact, and neatly separated worlds. In fact, we could demonstrate how the Western world is less individualistic, secular, technical and rational than is commonly believed – and more holistic, religious, traditional, and emotional than is often assumed.

Therefore, even if the dividing lines between private and public, individual and communal, sacred and profane, are blurred in the indigenous world of Mexico and Latin America, there is no doubt that readily identifiable components of a process of secularization and laicity are in operation. They include increasing differentiation of spheres, religious worldliness, their own religious rationalization, growing respect for freedom of conscience and human rights in view of diversity, rising democratization, the distinction between civil and ecclesiastical affairs, and many other characteristics of the Westernization process.

The Western world is obsessed with the idea of separation, which often blurs our conception of other cultures. Nevertheless, we should keep in mind that in the West the idea of the separation of spheres (between public and private, Church and State, religion and politics) is nothing more than an 'operational distinction.' Nobody pretends that this separation is absolute – either in the Western or in the indigenous world. It is only a functional distinction that helps us to distinguish ambits of action and at the same time to regulate, more or less successfully, the peaceful coexistence of different individuals and groups within society. But an absolute separation as such does not exist. Thus, if we assume that separation is not central to laicity, we can also understand that a process of secularization and laicization can occur in non-Western societies, for example, in the Muslim world or indigenous communities. Therefore, if we distinguish the idea of separation from that of the autonomy of politics from religion – and if we remember the centrality of the new source of legitimacy of political institutions – we will be able not only to see the indigenous world in Latin America in a different light but also to adopt a new perspective on the realities of Europe, North America and the rest of the world. In this way, the system of cultural mirrors can help in the elaboration of new universal paradigms, theories and concepts for social sciences, and particularly for the sociology of religion.

NOTES

1. Mesoamérica or 'Middle-America' is a geographic region that stretches from North-Central Mexico to Honduras and El Salvador.

2. In broad terms, a cosmovision is the global conception of life and death, the Universe and the place of humankind in it. See López Austin 1989.

3. Title given to an Aztec King or Emperor.

4. Chiapas is the Federal State with the highest number of indigenous people and the lowest number of Catholics in Mexico in proportional terms. According to the Census of 2000, only 63.8 per cent were Catholics. Protestants and Evangelicals were 13.9 per cent, Jehovah's Witnesses, Mormons and Adventists added a further 8 per cent, and people with other religions or no religion amounted to 14.3 per cent. Nationwide, according to the same Census, Catholics in Mexico amounted to 88 per cent, Protestants and Evangelicals accounted for more than 7 per cent, and non-believers around 3 per cent. For more details, see Blancarte 2005: 225–99.

5. I emphasize 'relative' because privatization does not mean the end of the public role of religions, as many scholars have wrongly thought.

6. Royal Patronage (*Patronato Real*) was a medieval institution based on the fact that the Catholic Kings and Queens had discovered new lands, and in exchange for the establishment of new churches the Holy See conceded to the Crown the benefices, all revenues, protection and administration of the Church in those territories.

7. The *Declaration* was written by Jean Baubérot (France), Micheline Milot (Canada) and Roberto Blancarte (Mexico). It was presented in the French Senate on 9 December 2005, to celebrate the centenary of the constitutional Separation of Church and State in that country. The complete text can be found online at: *http://www.libertadeslaicas.org.mx* and at: *jeanbauberot-laicite. blogspirit.com/archive/2005/09/01/declaration-surla-laicite.html*

REFERENCES

Bastian, Jean-Pierre 1994. *Protestantismos y modernidad latinoamericana: historia de unas minorías religiosas activas en América Latina.* México, D. F.: Fondo de Cultura Económica.

Bastian, Jean-Pierre 1997. *La mutación religiosa en América Latina. Para una sociología del cambio en la modernidad periférica.* México, D. F.: Fondo de Cultura Económica.

Bastian, Jean-Pierre 1990. *Historia del protestantismo en América Latina.* México, D. F.: CUPSA.

Blancarte, Roberto 2000a. 'Popular religion, Catholicism and socioreligious dissent in Latin America; facing the modernity paradigm,' *International Sociology.* December 15 (4): 591–603.

Blancarte, Roberto 2000b. 'Retos y perspectivas de la laicidad mexicana,' in Roberto Blancarte (ed.), *Laicidad y valores en un Estado democrático.* México, D. F.: Secretaría de Gobernación-El Colegio de México: 117–140.

Blancarte, Roberto 2005. 'Religiosidad, creencias e Iglesias en la época de la transición democrática.' In Ilán Bizberg and Lorenzo Meyer (eds), *Una historia contemporánea de México*, tomo 2, México, D. F.: Editorial Océano: 225–99.

Casanova, José 1994. *Public Religions in the Modern World*. Chicago: Chicago University Press.

Durán, Leonel 1988. 'Presentación de la serie.' In G. Jimenez (ed.), *Sectas religiosas en el Sureste. Aspectos sociográficos y estadísticos, Religión y sociedad en el Sureste de México*, Vol. I, Cuadernos de la Casa Chata, 161, CIESAS, programa Cultural de las Fronteras, Secretaría de Educación Pública, CONAFE, México.

Durkheim, Émile 1985. *Les formes élémentaires de la vie religieuse; Le systéme totémique en Australie* 7éme édition. Paris: Presses Universitaires de France.

González Martínez, José Luis 2002. *Fuerza y sentido; El catolicismo popular al comienzo del siglo XXI*, México, D. F. Ediciones Dabar.

Hervieu-Léger, Danièle (with Françoise Champion) 1986. *Vers un nouveau christianisme ? Introduction à la sociologie du christianisme occidental*. Paris: Les Éditions du Cerf.

Hagopian, Frances 2005. 'Religious Pluralism, Democracy, and the Catholic Church in Latin America in the Twenty-first Century.' Paper prepared for the Conference 'Contemporary Catholicism, Religious Pluralism, and Democracy in Latin America: Challenges, Responses and Impact,' University of Notre Dame, Kellogg Institute.

Hernández Castillo, Rosalva Aída 1992. 'Entre la victimización y la resistencia étnica: revisión crítica de la bibliografía sobre protestantismo en Chiapas,' *Anuario 1992*, Tuxtla Gutiérrez, Chiapas, Gobierno del Estado de Chiapas: 165–86.

Hernández Castillo, Rosalva Aída 2001. *La otra frontera. Identidades múltiples en el Chiapas poscolonial*. México, D. F.: CIESAS-Miguel Ángel Porrúa Editores, quoted by Rivera Farfán [*et al.*] 2005.

Lambert, Yves 1985. *Dieu change en Bretagne; la religion à Limerzel de 1900 à nos jours*. Paris: Les Éditions du Cerf.

López Austin, Alfredo 1989 *Cuerpo humano e ideología. Las concepciones de los antiguos nahuas* (México, UNAM).

López Austin, Alfredo 1998. *Breve historia de la tradición religiosa mesoamericana*. Universidad Nacional Autónoma de México. Instituto de Investigaciones Antropológicas. Colección Textos. Serie Antropología e Historia Antigua: 2 (México, D. F.: UNAM).

Martin, David 1990. *Tongues of Fire: The Explosion of Protestantism in Latin America*. Oxford: Blackwell.

Norris, Pippa and Ronald Inglehart 2004. *Sacred or secular. Religion and Politics worldwide*. Cambridge: Cambridge University Press.

Parker, G. Cristián 2006. '"Magico-popular religion" in contemporary society: Towards a Post-Western Sociology of Religion.' In Beckford, James A. and John Wallis, (eds). *Theorising Religion. Classical and Contemporary Debates*. Aldershot, Ashgate: 60–74.

Rivera Farfán, Carolina [et al.] 2005. *Diversidad religiosa y conflicto en Chiapas; Intereses, utopías y realidades*. México, D. F.: UNAM, CIESAS, Consejo de Ciencia y Tecnología de Chiapas, Secretaría de Gobierno del Estado de Chiapas, Secretaría de Gobernación.

Spickard, James V. 1998. 'Ethnocentrism, Social Theory and Non-Western Sociologies of Religion: Toward a Confucian Alternative,' *International Sociology* 13 (2): 173–94.

Spickard, James V. 2000. 'Conformando una sociología de la religión poscolonial,' *Religiones y sociedad*, 9 (mayo-agosto): 123–40.

Spickard, James V. 2001. 'Tribes and Cities: Towards an Islamic Sociology of Religion,' *Social Compass* 48 (1): 103–16.

Tschannen, Olivier 1991. 'The secularization paradigm: a systematization,' *Journal for the Scientific Study of Religion* 30 (4): 395–415.

Weber, Max 1921. *Wirtschaft und Gesellschaft. Grundiss der verstehenden Soziologie*. Tübingen: J.C.B. Mohr.

Willaime, Jean-Paul 1999. 'Le pentecôtisme: contours et paradoxes d'un protestantisme émotionnel,' *Archives des Sciences Sociales des Religions*, 105: 5–28.

Index

Note: Each chapter concludes with a list of references. The Index includes the names of authors whose work is not only cited but discussed.